Internet Business Models

Text and Cases

Edited by Thomas R. Eisenmann
Harvard Business School

In collaboration with Roger Hallowell and Mary Tripsas
Harvard Business School

McGraw-Hill Irwin

Boston Burr Ridge, IL Dubuque, IA Madison, WI New York San Francisco St. Louis
Bangkok Bogotá Caracas Kuala Lumpur Lisbon London Madrid Mexico City
Milan Montreal New Delhi Santiago Seoul Singapore Sydney Taipei Toronto

McGraw-Hill Higher Education

A Division of The ***McGraw-Hill*** *Companies*

INTERNET BUSINESS MODELS: TEXT AND CASES

Published by McGraw-Hill, an imprint of The McGraw-Hill Companies, Inc. 1221 Avenue of the Americas, New York, NY, 10020.

This book is printed on acid-free paper.

domestic 1 2 3 4 5 6 7 8 9 0 CCW/CCW 0 9 8 7 6 5 4 3 2 1

international 1 2 3 4 5 6 7 8 9 0 CCW/CCW 0 9 8 7 6 5 4 3 2 1

ISBN 0-07-249868-4

Publisher: *John E. Biernat*
Executive editor: *Gary L. Bauer*
Developmental editor: *Nina McGuffin*
Marketing manager: *Kim Kanakes Szum*
Project manager: *Natalie J. Ruffatto*
Production supervisor: *Carol A. Bielski*
Producer, media technology: *Todd Labak*
Coordinator of freelance design: *Mary Kazak*
Supplement producer: *Erin Sauder*
Photo research coordinator: *David A. Tietz*
Cover design: *Proof Positive/Farrowlyne Associates, Inc.*
Interior design: *Proof Positive/Farrowlyne Associates, Inc.*
Typeface: *10/12 Minion*
Compositor: *Proof Positive/Farrowlyne Associates, Inc.*
Printer: *Courier Westford*

INTERNATIONAL EDITION ISBN 0-07-112363-6

www.mhhe.com

ACKNOWLEDGEMENTS

Hundreds of people contributed to this book: I wish to extend my most sincere thanks to all of them. First and foremost, on behalf of my faculty coauthors at the Harvard Business School, I wish to thank our former students. With a phenomenon as new as the Internet, teaching and learning become intertwined. Our students, bravely surfing the New Economy's big waves of change, have taught us a great deal about Internet strategy. To our classrooms they brought experience, passion for the subject, and a resolve to test our analytical frameworks. These frameworks were further battle-hardened through our work with student teams on class projects and field studies that they completed for Internet companies and for their own startups. Upon graduation, students who joined Internet companies have provided constant feedback about what they have learned and where our frameworks have worked and failed. We are especially grateful for the knowledge gleaned from former students who launched startups—we salute their hard work, determination, and willingness to take risks.

Next, on behalf of my co-authors, I wish to thank the scores of executives that supported the development of the company case studies in this book. All of our cases were researched through on-site interviews with senior managers; as a result, we believe they deliver far more insight than armchair cases based solely on published sources. Of course, the development of these cases required an investment of the scarcest resource controlled by these executives—their time. We marveled at the pace of decision making in these companies and relished the opportunity to get a first-hand look at their inner workings. We are also grateful for the confidence in the case writing process shown by our sponsors: it takes an act of trust to allow outsiders to tell your story. In doing so, we hope we have been clear, candid, and fair.

I wish to extend my personal thanks to the five other HBS faculty members who contributed cases to this book. Along with Roger Hallowell and Mary Tripsas, colleagues in the Entrepreneurial & Service Management Unit at HBS, I teach an MBA elective course on Internet business models. Roger and Mary were close collaborators on this project; their analyses of the case studies that we present in class and their feedback on my research on Internet business models have been invaluable. Likewise, I wish to thank Joanna Jacobson, a former faculty colleague and a brilliant marketing practitioner who was my partner in the classroom early in 2000, as dot com fever hit its peak. Finally, I wish to thank Jan Rivkin and Joe Bower for the cases they contributed.

On behalf of my faculty colleagues, I wish to thank the many research associates, fellows, and MBA candidates who coauthored our cases and the chapters describing Internet business models. They include Dean's Research Fellow Jon Rust; High Tech Fellows Pauline Fischer and Dan Green; Research Associates Alastair Brown, Tonica Hampton, Chris Hackett, Abby Hansen, Gillian Morris, Sanjay Pothen, and Charles Ruberto; and HBS MBA candidates Charmaine Ess, Jay Girotto, Gerrit Meier, Ann O'Hara, and Doug Rogers. Special thanks to Chris Darwall, executive director of the HBS California Research Center, who with her colleagues Liz Kind and Nicole Tempest, co-authored four of the case studies included in this book. Chris and her team have improved our work immeasurably through their connections to the Silicon Valley business community, their professionalism, and their commitment to quality.

I wish to extend special thanks to Jeffrey Rayport, founder and CEO of the Marketspace Center at Monitor & Company. During the mid-1990s, before most of us knew what the Internet was, Jeffrey and John Sviokla launched the Marketspace course that Roger Hallowell, Mary Tripsas and I now teach. Jeffrey built that course into one of the most popular electives at HBS. I am proud to have inherited that franchise and extremely grateful to Jeffrey for the insights he shared on Internet companies, the contacts he provided, and most importantly, his example as a superb instructor.

On behalf of my collaborators Roger Hallowell and Mary Tripsas, I wish to thank Professors Myra Hart and Bill Sahlman, co-heads of the Entrepreneurial & Service Management Unit at HBS, for their encouragement and steadfast support for our course and our research. My thanks as well to HBS Professors Lynda Applegate and Jay Light, who provided me with feedback on my research and course syllabus, case leads, assistance with field interviews, and support in securing research staff. Finally, on behalf of all my HBS faculty coauthors, I wish to thank Dean Kim Clark and the Division of Research for encouraging our work and generously funding our research.

Many colleagues at HBS helped with the production of the materials in this book. In particular, I wish to thank Diana Lees, Manager of Case Records, who leads the staff that secures copyright permissions and ensures that our cases are ready for distribution. The New Economy has greatly stimulated case production at HBS; Diana's staff has efficiently matched our pace, even though our work often arrives on their doorstep at the last minute. I also am grateful to Larry Bouthillier, Dave Habeeb, and their staff, who produced the Teledesic multimedia case bound into the back of this volume as a CD ROM. Finally, special thanks to my assistant, Matthew Guerrieri, for his hard work and good humor through countless deadlines.

I am extremely grateful to the team at McGraw-Hill/Irwin for their steady support, their guidance on how to best meet the needs of students and instructors, and their hard work in producing and marketing this book. On behalf of my coauthors, I wish to thank John Biernat, Publisher, Gary Bauer, Executive Editor in charge of the book, and Nina McGuffin, Development Editor. I also thank Natalie Ruffatto and Scott Becker for their support in the production process. In managing the project, I am indebted to Rafe Sagalyn, our literary agent.

Finally, I want to thank my wife, Jill Greenthal Eisenmann, for her personal and professional support. Jill is an investment banker who coheads CSFB's Media Group; in that role, she became immersed in Internet issues at the same time I began this project. Her insights on the sector have been invaluable, as have her introductions to clients and colleagues. Despite the demands of her job, she has been patient with my preoccupations. With my warmest thanks and love, I dedicate this book to Jill.

Editor's Biography

Thomas R. Eisenmann is an Assistant Professor in the Entrepreneurial & Service Management Unit and is a Class of 1961 Fellow at the Harvard Business School. His research explores Internet business models and the returns to Internet companies from accelerated growth strategies. Eisenmann teaches a course in Harvard's MBA elective curriculum on the strategic and organizational challenges facing Internet startups and established companies moving online.

Eisenmann received his B.A., M.A., and Ph.D. from Harvard University. Prior to entering the doctoral program at the Harvard Business School, Eisenmann spent eleven years as a management consultant at McKinsey & Company, where he was co-head of Media and Entertainment Practice. Eisenmann now serves on the Advisory Boards of many Internet startups and was a member of the Board of Directors of OneMain.com, one of the ten largest U.S. Internet service providers, prior to its acquistion by Earthlink.

Preface

We have five objectives for this book. First, we want to help readers understand Internet business models and enabling technologies. Second, we wish to illustrate how the Internet is restructuring industries. Third, we seek to evaluate accelerated growth strategies and explain when they are most likely to yield attractive payoffs. Fourth, we will illustrate how Internet companies weigh tradeoffs when deciding to expand their scope, for example, through product line diversification or vertical integration. Finally, we want to examine the causes and cures for the organizational inertia that inflicts many established companies as they decide whether to launch online units.

Objective 1: Understand Internet business models and enabling technologies. Our goal is to provide readers with a deeper understanding of eight Internet business models: access providers, portals, content providers, retailers, brokers, market makers, networked utility providers, and Application Service Providers (see the Introduction to each chapter for definitions of these business models). Specifically, we seek to explain these basic principles:

- *How companies that employ each business model seek to create value for customers and differentiate themselves from competitors.*
- *What the microeconomics of the business model are.* For example, do Internet companies have inherent cost advantages over their offline counterparts? Is the business model subject to network effects; that is, does the addition of new users make the service even more valuable for existing users (as with market makers such as eBay)? What drives the cost of different activities: transaction volume, numbers of new customers acquired, or headcount? How do costs "scale," given the fixed portion of total expenses? Are customer retention rates intrinsically high? What is the lifetime value of a typical customer, and what does that imply for target customer acquisition costs?
- *What major strategic issues face companies pursuing each business model.* For example, how important are alliances with offline and online companies that can drive traffic to a website? Is diversification into related businesses an attractive option? Is disintermediation a threat? Does vertical integration make sense? How important is first mover advantage? When should firms outsource business functions such as product fulfillment or customer service? When does it make sense to "hybridize" a website, combining elements of multiple business models?

In addition to describing the eight Internet business models, we seek to familiarize readers with technologies relevant to Internet companies. For example, we discuss the infrastructure required for broadband data delivery (see especially the Tele-Communications, Inc.; Teledesic; and Geocast cases), the technologies employed in customizing websites; shopping "bots" that search the Web to provide comparative price data; and technologies that facilitate the streaming or digital download of music and video content.

Objective 2: Understand how the Internet is restructuring industries. Several of the industries we profile in our case studies seem likely to be restructured in fundamental ways by the emergence of Internet distribution channels. Examples include securities brokerage (see the DLJdirect and Wit Capital cases), newspaper publishing (see the Boston.com case), music distribution (see the BMG Entertainment case), and the procurement of construction supplies (see the eBricks.com case). Our goal is to provide readers with frameworks for analyzing the potential impact on industry structure when online competitors radically alter the value proposition delivered to customers. Exploiting the Internet's capabilities, online businesses can disaggregate traditional bundles of products and services (e.g., by pulling the classified ads out of the newspaper, as Monster.com does), or by combining information and transactional services in novel ways (as CNET does by linking users directly to online retailers, after users have researched their purchase decisions using CNET's content).

Objective 3: Understand when accelerated growth strategies are likely to succeed. Managers in most Internet companies must decide whether to pursue accelerated growth strategies, that is, whether to spend aggressively on brand building and customer acquisition. Using a term popularized by Jeff Bezos, Amazon.com's founder, in this book we refer to such plans as "Get Big Fast" (GBF) strategies. While private and public capital markets are less willing to fund accelerated growth strategies now than they were prior to the April 2000 crash in Internet stock valuations, the decision whether to pursue a GBF strategy is still of great concern for companies with access to capital, as demonstrated by the case studies of Tellme Networks and Staples.com. The choice remains relevant because the structural characteristics of Internet businesses (e.g., high fixed costs, increasing returns to scale) frequently yield powerful first-mover advantages and winner-take-all dynamics. At the same time, GBF strategies are risky because they involve large, irrevocable resource commitments made in the face of high levels of environmental turbulence.

Consequently, understanding accelerated growth strategies will continue to be crucial for managers who shape the strategies of Internet companies. We hope to provide readers with frameworks that help them determine when such strategies are most likely to yield attractive payoffs and to give guidance for designing organizations that can execute GBF strategies effectively. In doing so, we will address the following issues:

- Under what conditions is an aggressive first mover vulnerable to displacement by a late arriving competitor, that is, a *second* mover? For examples of this issue, see the case studies of Teledesic; StarMedia; and Adobe.
- When two or more players simultaneously launch GBF strategies (see the case studies of Petstore.com, Tellme Networks, and DLJdirect), what are the likely consequences? When confronting what economists call "racing" behavior by competitors, what can a company do to maximize its odds of survival and success—acquire competitors? retreat to a niche? seek strategic partners who can reduce the cost of acquiring customers?
- How does the GBF payoff vary for each Internet business model? As explained in the introductions to the chapters on each model, the models vary considerably in their "stickiness" (i.e., rates of customer retention), their scalability, and the extent to which they harness network effects. These differences explain why accelerated growth strategies are much more likely to yield attractive payoffs for online market makers, portals, and networked utility providers than for Internet access providers and online retailers.
- To what extent is the payoff for accelerated growth strategies dependent on speculative excess in capital markets? If companies have access to capital and they still believe that a GBF strategy will yield an attractive payoff (in particular, because competitors are unlikely to follow suit), should they follow a contrarian approach, ignoring capital providers' current disenchantment with aggressive growth strategies? This strategy is available to established companies with strong balance sheets and has been pursued by Staples and Bertelsmann.

Objective 4: Understand the tradeoffs involved in broadening firm scope. Managers of Internet companies often face fundamental questions about their companies' scope of activities. As noted in the Introduction that follows this Preface, management has to decide whether to pursue a focused or more expansive strategy in each of four areas: the breadth of target customer segments served, product line diversity, vertical integration, and the hybridization of multiple business models within a single website. While ambitious strategies are often more appealing to investors, we aim to show readers that when young companies pursue more expansive strategies, there is a risk the newcomers will stretch their management's capabilities too thinly.

Objective 5: Understand the causes and cures for organizational inertia. Many established "brick-and-mortar" companies, such as Barnes & Noble, Toys-R-Us, and Merrill Lynch, have been slow to move online. Several explanations have been advanced for the inertia of incumbent companies, including (1) concerns about the cannibalization of their existing offline sales by online units, (2) concerns about the stock price impact of funding Internet losses, and (3) slow and often dysfunctional decision-making processes in mature organizations, in particular, the failure of traditional discounted-cash-flow analyses to support strategies that yield growth options. We leverage the examples of the *Boston Globe's* Boston.com, Black Entertainment TV's BET.com, BMG Entertainment, Staples.com, Rosenbluth International's Biztravel.com, DLJdirect, and Sothebys.com to examine the relative importance of various explanations for organizational inertia and to explore the organizational and financial structures that companies employ when they successfully avoid this inertia.

In particular, we look at the merits of what we call "hawk" versus "dove" policies (borrowing terms employed by Lincoln Millstein, CEO of Boston.com) when launching Internet units inside established companies. Hawks separate Internet units from their core businesses, staff them with outsiders, and give them an explicit mandate to cannibalize the core. Doves, by contrast, seek a high level of operational integration between Internet and core businesses in areas such as content development, advertising sales, customer service, and promotion. We also examine the advantages and drawbacks for established companies of spinning off their online units using tracking stocks, a financial innovation employed by Tele-Communications, Inc. and DLJ and under consideration in the case studies of Staples.com and Boston.com.

ORGANIZATION OF THE BOOK

We believe that to understand Internet companies' strategies, one needs a firm grasp of the generic business models that they follow. That premise guides the organization of this book: it is divided into eight sections describing different business models. Each section begins with a chapter introducing the specific business model, describing the value proposition offered by companies that pursue the model; the factors that drive their revenues, costs, and profits; and the key strategy decisions they face—for example, whether to pursue accelerated growth strategies; whether to diversify. Then we present case studies of companies that employ the business model. The following points may be relevant to the reader seeking to understand the contents of these case studies:

- The 23 cases all were researched and written by professors at the Harvard Business School, based on on-site interviews with top executives. Thus, the cases capture management's view of major strategy issues in ways that case studies based strictly on published sources cannot.

- The cases all have a general management orientation, with a special emphasis on competitive strategy and marketing issues. The cases examine the challenges of coordinating across functions (e.g., marketing, product development, customer services) and integrating strategy, operations, and organization.
- The cases also examine the interplay between product market strategy and capital market strategy, demonstrating how companies perceived as market leaders often receive higher valuations and thus have been able to raise the capital to fund continued growth in a self-perpetuating cycle.
- Ten of the cases profile online units of established companies (e.g., Staples.com, Sothebys.com, DLJdirect); the balance profile Internet startups.
- About two-thirds of the cases focus on business-to-consumer Internet companies; the balance profile business-to-business concerns.
- One-third of the cases were completed after the crash in Internet stock valuations during the Spring of 2000; the balance were written between the Fall of 1999 and the Spring of 2000.
- The cases depict companies whose success has varied widely. Many, including Yahoo!, CNET, and DLJdirect, are already profitable. Four of the companies profiled in case studies have been shut down since the cases were completed—Priceline's Webhouse Club, Geocast Network Systems, Sendwine.com, and Petstore.com. Thus, readers have an opportunity to learn from both successes and failures.
- Several cases focus on leading-edge technologies, including broadband Internet access via low-earth-orbit satellite (Teledesic), PC caching of broadband content (Geocast), and voice recognition technologies (Tellme).
- One case, on Teledesic, is in multimedia format (it is presented through a CD ROM bound into the back of the book). The case includes links to relevant Web sites and animations that show how Teledesic plans to use a constellation of 288 satellites to provide high-speed Internet access anywhere in the world. The Teledesic case also includes an interactive scenario-planning exercise that invites readers to identify key uncertainties facing Teledesic and actions the company should take to address these risks.

The reader should note that the case studies profile only companies that use the Internet to sell goods and services to end customers, not businesses that supply enabling technologies (e.g., Inktomi, Cisco) or professional services (e.g., Scient, Razorfish) to these end customer-focused Internet companies. These "arms merchants" profit from the Internet's growth, but their business models are not fundamentally new: Inktomi operates in much the same way that software suppliers have for many years, and Scient's business model closely resembles that of a traditional systems integrator.

On behalf of my co-authors, I wish the reader the very best of luck in making sense of this fast-moving and exciting arena. We hope that our book is a useful tool in that effort.

INTRODUCTION

Over the five year period beginning in 1996, Internet companies experienced a remarkable journey. During the late 1990s, as consumers and businesses rushed online to exchange information and conduct commerce, publicly traded Internet stocks surged. Three times during that period, Internet stock valuations declined by 30 percent or more, but following each dip stock prices rebounded to even higher levels. In April 2000, however, Internet stocks crashed, and they continued sliding into 2001. As investors demanded to see a path toward profitability and IPO prospects dimmed, venture capital stopped flowing freely into dot com startups. Dozens of Internet companies exhausted their funding and failed.

After trumpeting the rise of dot coms during the late 1990s, the popular press disparaged Internet companies and commenced a dot com "deathwatch." The Internet gold rush of 1999 was portrayed as an illusion fabricated by foolish speculators, greedy venture capitalists and investment bankers, and callow entrepreneurs. According to this view, the "get big fast" strategies at the center of so many dot com business plans were inherently flawed. Industry participants were getting exactly what they deserved as bankruptcies mounted and valuations plummeted.

But was the Internet simply a bubble, hype gone haywire? Without question, speculative excess fueled the rapid rise of Internet stock values, and many businesses were funded without a clear view of how and when they would earn profits. But just as overreaction marked Internet companies' rapid rise, the popular view of their precipitous decline is grossly oversimplified and too extreme. Consider the following points:

- First, despite comparisons to the frenzied bidding for seventeenth century Dutch tulips, the Internet's growth is not a frivolous, ephemeral affair. On the contrary, one might reasonably argue that the Internet will play a central role in restructuring the world economy. The new economy will be a *networked* economy, characterized by unprecedented levels of electronically-mediated communication, collaboration, and commerce.
- Second, it is true that many Internet startups have failed, but high failure rates are commonplace when launching new businesses in most sectors of the economy. About 60 percent of all startups fail in their first six years, and about one-third of the investments made by venture capitalists lose money.[1] Recent failures in the Internet sector are part of a natural Darwinian process; they do not mean that the Internet is a profitless quagmire.
- Third, while many Internet companies have failed, others have succeeded brilliantly and have done so by pursuing supposedly flawed accelerated growth strategies. AOL, Yahoo!, eBay, Monster.com, CNET, RealNetworks, and E*Trade all deliver great value for their customers and profits for their shareholders. All of these companies employ business models with structural characteristics that improve the odds of success for get-big-fast strategies.

The last point relates to a central theme of this book: *Some Internet business models are intrinsically more attractive than others.* By analyzing the structural characteristics of their business models, one can predict which Internet companies are more likely to succeed.

WHAT IS A BUSINESS MODEL?

Internet companies are not homogeneous: they can be categorized by business model, i.e., by the nature of the services they provide to customers and by the activities they perform to deliver those services. For example, Staples.com, an *online retailer* of office supplies, has a very different business model than StarMedia, a *portal* for Internet users in Latin America. Staples.com offers a wide array of merchandise along with the convenience of "24/7" (24 hours a day, 7 days a week) online ordering and home delivery. The company maintains warehouses to hold inventory, call centers to field customer inquiries, and a fleet of delivery trucks. StarMedia provides navigational assistance to Latin American Internet users and links them to relevant content and commerce sites; StarMedia also provides a wide array of communications tools to its customers, e.g., chat rooms, e-mail service.

Staples.com and StarMedia clearly differ across many dimensions. First, Staples.com focuses on a narrow customer target—small office/home office managers—whereas StarMedia targets a broad range of customer segments, including mass market consumers and business professionals. Second, Staples.com receives most of its revenue from payments for merchandise that customers have ordered; by contrast, most of StarMedia's revenue comes from advertising. Third, Staples.com's major expenses—for merchandise, delivery, and customer service—all vary with transaction volume; by contrast, StarMedia's expenses are almost entirely fixed.

Staples.com and StarMedia are typical examples of companies that employ the online retailing and portal business models, respectively. Once you understand Staples.com's economics and strategy, you will better comprehend the challenges facing other online retailers like Amazon.com. Similarly, studying StarMedia's strategy equips you to evaluate other mass market portals, like Yahoo!.

Business model is a term that is widely used but rarely defined. In science, a model is a hypothesis about cause-and-effect relationships. In architecture, a model is a stylized representation of the structure to come. A business model serves similar purposes. It is a hypothesis about how a company will make money over the long term: what the company will sell, and to whom; how the company will collect revenue; what technologies it will employ; when it will rely on partners; and, following from the last two points, how its costs will "scale" with growth. A more comprehensive definition is offered by Professors Hank Chesbrough and Richard Rosenbloom:[2]

> The functions of a business model are to (1) articulate the *value proposition*, that is, the value created for users by the offering based on the technology; (2) identify a *market segment*, that is, the users to whom the technology is useful and for what purpose; (3) define the structure of the *value chain* within the firm required to create and distribute the offering; (4) estimate the *cost structure* and *profit potential* of producing the offering, given the value proposition and value chain structure chosen; (5) describe the position of the firm within the *value network* linking suppliers and customers, including identification of potential complementors and competitors; and (6) formulate the *competitive strategy* by which the innovating firm will gain and hold advantage over rivals.

INTERNET BUSINESS MODELS: A TAXONOMY

The vast majority of companies that rely on the Internet to facilitate the delivery of information, goods, or services to end customers employ one of the following eight generic business models:

- *Internet access providers* connect consumers and businesses to the Internet through narrowband and broadband telephone lines (e.g., Earthlink); cable television systems (e.g., Tele-Communications, Inc.); and wireless technologies such as cellular phone systems, microwave transmission, or satellites (e.g., Teledesic).
- *Online portals* such as Yahoo!, StarMedia, and Tellme Networks provide navigational assistance to help users find and link to relevant third-party online content and commerce offerings. In addition to navigational aids, to encourage users to visit frequently, portals typically also provide content; community-building features such as chat and instant messaging services; shopping options such as auctions; and personal productivity applications such as free e-mail service and Web-based calendars.
- *Online content providers* such as Bertelsmann's Music Group, Boston.com (the *Boston Globe*'s website) and BET.com (the website of Black Entertainment Television) use the Internet to distribute copyrighted information and entertainment content. When content providers abandon physical media (printed books, magazines, and newspapers; videotapes; music CDs) and move online, the companies face radically different economics. In digital form, information can be stored, forwarded, and copied at nearly zero marginal cost.
- *Online retailers* of physical goods, such as Petstore.com, take title to the newly manufactured products that they sell and often rely on third party service providers (e.g., UPS, Fedex) to deliver those goods from remote warehouses. Online retailers have very different cost structures than their brick-and-mortar counterparts: real estate expenses are eliminated when retailers move online, and customer service costs may be reduced when checkout counters are replaced by online ordering.
- *Online brokers* use the Internet to help clients identify prospective trading partners and sometimes help their clients complete transactions. Examples include websites such as Microsoft Carpoint, DLJdirect, and Rosenbluth International's Biztravel. Like their offline counterparts (e.g., stock brokers, real estate agents, travel agents), online brokers represent one party in a transaction but sometimes have conflicts of interest with other parties to the deal. Managing such conflicts is a key challenge for brokers, both offline and online.
- *Online market makers,* like online brokers, are intermediaries that facilitate an information discovery process. However, while the central purpose of brokers is to represent clients in a transaction, the central purpose of market makers like Sothebys.com or eBricks.com is to organize a marketplace. In doing so, market makers provide participants with a place to trade (physical or virtual), rules to govern trading (e.g., processes for dispute resolution), and infrastructure to support trading. Some market makers are neutral intermediaries (e.g., eBay); others have strong buy-side or sell-side affiliations (e.g., the auto parts exchange Covisint, organized by the Big 3 U.S. auto manufacturers).
- *Networked utility providers,* such as Adobe Systems with its Acrobat Reader and AOL with its ICQ instant messaging service, distribute downloadable software programs that connect users with destination websites or with each other. This software allows users to complete specialized tasks that are beyond the basic capabilities of Web browsers and e-mail programs, e.g., accessing rich media or chatting in real time. Networked utility providers usually give away their "client" software in an effort to rapidly establish a

de facto technology standard, then profit from the sale of server software and ancillary services.

- *Application service providers (ASPs),* such as DoubleTwist, allow customers to use the Internet to access application software on remote servers. Through ASPs, application software is "rented," i.e., customers make regular subscription payments to ASPs, rather than buying software outright and installing it locally on their own computers. ASPs' customers thus face lower upfront costs and are relieved of some of the burden of maintaining IT infrastructure. These benefits can be appealing, especially for small and midsized companies.

DECISIONS ABOUT SCOPE

Regardless of the business model they employ, it is quite common for the managers of Internet companies to face fundamental questions about their companies' scope of activities. Internet companies are young, and so is the market they serve. Opportunities abound, and there are few fixed ideas about what a company can and cannot do. Faced with this clean slate, management has to decide whether to pursue a strategy of *focus* or *promiscuity* in each of four areas. When young companies pick promiscuous strategies, they will chase off on many adventures, often with spontaneity and perhaps some lack of discrimination. There is a risk these companies will dissipate their energies, but if they are successful, they will build a bigger business. The four decision areas include breadth of target customer segments, product line diversification, vertical integration, and the hybridization of multiple business models.

Breadth of Target Customer Segments

Most markets can be segmented according to the needs of different customer groups. An Internet company can choose to tailor its website to the needs of a single segment or can engineer value propositions that appeal to multiple segments (for case studies of companies wrestling with this decision, see "CNET 2000," "BET.com," "Sendwine.com," and "DLJdirect: Putting Our Reputation on the Line"). Focusing on a single segment improves the odds that prospects will be converted into loyal users. By contrast, the promiscuous approach pursues a larger market—an important consideration for investors. Targeting multiple segments also allows companies to employ mass media more efficiently in building their brands.

Product Line Diversification

Focused companies offer a narrow range of products or services; promiscuous companies diversify into many related lines of business (for case studies of companies debating whether to broaden their product lines, see "CNET 2000," "Staples.com," "Sendwine.com," "Priceline WebHouse Club," and "eBricks.com"). One theory behind product line diversification is one-stop shopping. Customers are offered the convenience of buying a broad array of products and services from a trusted provider, which should reduce that company's marketing and customer service costs.

Diversification tends to be easier for online companies than for their offline counterparts. Amazon.com can simply add a tab to its website when it wants to expand into a new category, say, consumer electronics. By contrast, Borders can only introduce a new product category to its brick-and-mortar stores by stealing floor space from existing merchandise lines.

Vertical Integration

The Internet value chain is comprised of four vertical levels, reflecting the basic functions that industry participants jointly perform to allow end users to retrieve information, communicate, and trade. The top level includes *destination websites,* where end users go to get something done. The second level includes *portals,* which help end users find destination websites. The third level includes *access providers,* who provide end users with connections to the Internet. The fourth level includes providers of the *hardware and software infrastructure* required by participants at the first three levels.

Most Internet companies focus their efforts at a single vertical level. Some are vertically integrated across levels. A handful, like Microsoft and AOL-Time Warner, span all four vertical levels. For example, AOL's Netscape unit provides browser and server software; America Online itself functions as both an access provider and a portal; and Time Warner owns many media properties that operate destination websites. The economic and strategic logic behind vertical integration is complex (see the case studies on Tele-Communications, Inc., Geocast, Yahoo!, StarMedia, Tellme Networks, and BET.com for examples of companies considering vertical integration strategies). Motives may be offensive (for example, foreclosing access to competitors or extending dominance at one level into an adjacent level) or defensive (avoiding foreclosure).

Business Model Hybridization

Of the eight Internet business models listed above, six are various types of destination websites. The six models include content providers, retailers, brokers, market makers, networked utility providers, and ASPs. Most Internet companies that operate destination websites remain focused in their adherence to just one business model, although some blend multiple models within a single site (for case studies of companies debating the merits of hybridizing their websites, see "CNET 2000," "Boston.com," "BET.com," "Staples.com," and "Carpoint in 1999"). Since each business model creates value for end users in a unique way, hybridizing models may allow a website to meet a broader range of users' needs. However, as we shall see, managing multiple models can stretch management's capabilities and sometimes can create conflict with a website's channel partners.

It should be clear from this discussion that remaining focused in any of these four areas is not at odds with an accelerated growth strategy. A company can put the gas pedal to the floor yet remain focused on all four fronts, that is, it can use a single business model to offer a narrow set of services to a distinct customer segment. If successful, that focused firm should Get Big Fast. Of course, a promiscuous competitor with broader ambitions may be able to Get *Even Bigger,* Fast. But as we shall see in the case studies that follow, greater potential rewards imply greater risks.

---

[1]See Amar Bhide, *The Origin and Evolution of New Businesses* (New York: Oxford University Press, 2000), p. 207 for overall startup failure rates, and p. 145 for success odds for VC-backed investments.

[2]Henry Chesbrough and Richard Rosenbloom (2000)."The Role of the Business Model in Capturing Value from Innovation: Evidence from Xerox Corporation's Technology Spinoff Companies," Harvard Business School Working Paper 01-002; see also Allan Afuah and Christopher Tucci, *Internet Business Models and Strategies: Text and Cases* (New York: McGraw Hill, 2000), p. 4 for a definition of a business model.

Contents

1

Internet Access Providers

This chapter describes the Internet access provider business model. The first section defines the model and presents different ways to categorize access providers. The second section offers a summary of the various ways that Internet access providers create value for their customers. The third and fourth sections analyze the economic models for access providers that charge a subscription fee and those that offer free service, respectively, focusing on their revenue and cost drivers. Building on that analysis, the final section examines the payoff to Internet access providers from pursuing a "Get Big Fast" strategy, i.e., investing aggressively in customer acquisition and brand building.

Internet access providers, more commonly referred to as Internet service providers (ISPs), provide residential and business customers with connections to the Internet, allowing them to receive and send online information. ISPs faced a difficult and competitive market in 2000, as they searched for sustainable business models in an environment marked by rapidly changing technology, low barriers to entry, a fickle consumer base, and volatile capital markets. Customers were able to choose among several access technologies with different performance advantages—most notably in terms of bandwidth—including "landline" and wireless phones, cable television, satellites, and microwave delivery. At the same time, in the dial-up ISP market (which provided Internet access at speeds of 56 Kbps or less to customers with PC modems linked to analog phone lines), entrepreneurs with little more than a "how-to" guide from a wholesale ISP, a small-business loan, and a bit of pluck could start their own retail ISPs. Consumers embraced these smaller ISPs as they churned away from larger access providers in search of higher quality service.

Flush with investment capital until technology stocks collapsed in the spring of 2000, entrants launched ISPs with a variety of novel business models. The industry thus defied analysts who projected consolidation, and instead fragmented into a complex

---

Assistant Professor Thomas Eisenmann and High Tech Fellow Dan Green prepared this note as the basis for class discussion.

patchwork of businesses. A few ISPs were national in their scope and accounted for most of the industry's revenues, but most remained locally focused. Some ISPs wholesaled network connectivity to retail ISPs, who served end users directly. Retail ISPs attempted to earn revenues from subscriptions, advertising sales, e-commerce transactions, Web hosting, and by selling other telecommunications services, such as paging and long-distance phone service. A few began bundling free PCs with their service, while other retail ISPs offered access itself for free, seeking to profit from advertising and transaction fees. For the ordinary consumer or business deciding how to access the Internet, the market was dazzlingly complex. It was no easier for ISPs searching for a viable business model.

If the road to profitability was not clear, the incentive to achieve it was. First, the market was large and growing, so the stakes were high. By 2000, over eight thousand ISPs in the U.S. earned aggregate annual revenues in excess of $32.5 billion annually, and the market was growing rapidly (see Exhibit 1). Second, the price for access was declining rapidly and customer churn remained high, placing pressure on the bottom line.

In fact, by the fall of 2000, little had been determined about the efficacy of the myriad of business models deployed by ISPs. The most glaring anomaly was a market structure that outwardly seemed inefficient. The number of U.S. ISPs was growing by 37 percent per year—the same pace as revenue growth—despite pundits' predictions that the industry would consolidate.[1] Fewer than 20 percent of ISPs operated nationally, and although these companies accounted for 80 percent of industry revenue, smaller, local ISPs, which focused on no-frills access, were often more profitable than national ISPs. This counterintuitive market result failed to deter the managers of national ISPs, who aggressively pursued "Get Big Fast" strategies with the belief that elusive economies of scale and scope were just ahead. Besides the likelihood of consolidation, there were other questions that remained: Would free access providers continue to drive pricing down? Would the emergence of broadband change the market dynamic so fundamentally that it would be difficult for narrowband ISPs to survive?

Exhibit 1-1 U.S. INTERNET SERVICE PROVIDER REVENUE BY MARKET SEGMENT

$ in billions	1998	2000E	2004E
Business access	$2.9	$7.5	$14.9
Consumer access	$4.7	$8.9	$11.5
Wholesale	$2.0	$4.7	$13.4
Value-added services	$3.0	$6.4	$34.2
Total	$12.6	$27.5	$73.8

Note: "Value-added services" include Web hosting, security and other services, aside from access.
Source: Adapted from "Metrics" section, "No Deposit, No Return," *The Industry Standard* (April 3, 2000): 192, citing data from IDC

WHAT IS AN INTERNET ACCESS PROVIDER?

Definition and Delimitations

An Internet access provider provides consumers or businesses with connectivity to the Internet, allowing them to receive and send online information, such as webpages, e-mails, MP3 music files, and business transaction data. Access providers are generally divided into two groups: Internet Service Providers (ISPs) and Online Service Providers (OSPs).

ISPs generally focus on the provision of Internet connectivity services; they maintain local network infrastructure—banks of modems, routers, and telecommunications lines—that facilitate the transfer of information between a subscriber's modem-equipped PC (or some other access device, such as a Web-enabled wireless phone or a TV set–top converter box) and other users of the public Internet. Although ISPs concentrate on providing access services, they typically also provide subscribers with some basic content (e.g., news headlines, stock quotes, weather) and commerce offerings (e.g., links to online travel agents or booksellers) on their "start" pages, i.e., the webpages that subscribers encounter when they log onto the Internet—unless they reprogram their browsers to open to another page.

OSPs like America Online maintain a telecommunications infrastructure separate from (but usually interconnected with) the public Internet. OSPs use that infrastructure to provide access to proprietary, off-Web content and communities (for chat and instant messaging sessions) that only their subscribers can reach.[2] In AOL's case, third-party content providers format their information using a proprietary programming language (called "Rainman"), instead of using HTML ("Hypertext Markup Language"), as they would for presenting their content on the public Internet. OSPs are sometimes called "walled gardens," because they typically lock non-subscribers "out" (i.e., they prevent access to proprietary content and communities) and sometimes even lock their own subscribers "in."[3] In the mid-1990s, for example, AOL only gradually provided its subscribers with the ability to access the public Internet (i.e., they eventually put a one-way door in the garden wall, allowing their subscribers to access the public Internet, but they still prevented non-AOL Internet users from accessing AOL's proprietary content, chat rooms, and instant messaging sessions).

In essence, OSPs are hybrids of two different business models: the *access provider* model, which focuses on providing connectivity services, and the *portal* model, which focuses on providing navigational assistance to users, along with links to third-party content and commerce offerings. The portal business model is described in detail in a separate chapter.[4] This chapter will explore some of the advantages and disadvantages that accrue to companies that vertically integrate access and portal businesses but will not discuss portals in depth.

The companies described above are *retail* access providers who directly serve end customers, both consumers and businesses. *Wholesale* access providers, the largest of which are called "Tier 1" ISPs, sell Internet connectivity to retail ISPs and OSPs. Often, wholesalers provide outsourced network management services for retail ISPs. While many retail ISPs own substantial portions of their networks, all of them lease at least some network capacity from wholesalers. Other retail access providers are "virtual" ISPs that purchase all of their network services from a wholesaler and essentially run only customer recruitment, service, and billing operations. Most commonly, wholesalers provide "backbone" connectivity from a retail ISP's modem bank to the rest of the public Internet. The leading Tier 1 ISPs in 2000 were UUNET (a division of WorldCom), PSINet, and Digex.

This chapter will primarily discuss retail access providers. In practice, retail-wholesale hybrids are common. Teledesic, for example, planned to roll out a constellation of "low Earth orbit" satellites that could allow it to wholesale network capacity, sell retail access, or both.[5] Similarly, AT&T could choose to wholesale capacity on its cable network to other ISPs, sell a retail Internet access package to its cable subscribers, or both. Many local phone companies (companies that maintain the telephone line used by residences and businesses) also are simultaneously wholesalers and retailers of Internet access. For such hybrids, managing channel conflict is an important strategic challenge.

Access Technologies

Retail ISPs and OSPs (hereafter, simply "ISPs") can sell access at a variety of bandwidth increments through several different technologies (see Exhibit 2 for a forecast of adoption rates for different access technologies). This section provides a taxonomy and brief description of these technologies. Readers interested in a more detailed explanation of how various access technology platforms work and their strengths and limitations should consult a note entitled "The Last Mile of Broadband Access" and case studies of the satellite services provider Teledesic and the cable system operator Tele-Communications, Inc.[6]

Telephone-Based Services. In the early days of the Internet, access was only available through "narrowband" services that used PC modems to "dial up" low bandwidth telephone lines. By the late 1990s, however, broadband access had taken root; in late 1999, 65 percent of the U.S. population lived in locations where broadband Internet access services were being marketed by telephone or cable television companies.[7] Narrowband dial-up services were limited to 56 Kbps due to the technical limitations of analog POTS ("plain old telephone service") over traditional "twisted-pair" copper phone lines. Dial-up services suffered from other shortcomings. They required subscribers to fully dedicate a phone line when accessing the Internet (i.e., they could not receive phone calls and surf the Web simultaneously using the same phone line), and required them to log on again for each new session (a process that could take a minute or more and that sometimes failed when the subscriber encountered network congestion, i.e., a "busy signal") or after their ISP, in an effort

Exhibit 1-2 USER BASE FOR ACCESS TECHNOLOGIES

(users in millions)	1998	2000E	2003E
ISDN	0.3	0.8	0.3
Satellite	0.1	0.4	1.6
ADSL	0.04	1.0	5.7
Cable Modem	0.5	2.8	7.7
Total	0.9	5.0	15.3

Source: Adapted from Zia Wigder, "Bandwidth and Access Strategies," Jupiter Communications, January 19, 2000, pg. 23

to avoid network congestion, terminated their connection upon detecting an extended period of user inactivity. By contrast, broadband service providers could provide much wider bandwidth (from several hundred Kbps to over 1 Mbps); connections were "persistent" (i.e., service was always "on"), so subscribers did not face the delays associated with repeatedly logging on; and services did not conflict with the ability to simultaneously deliver voice telephone traffic.

Although incumbent local exchange carriers ("ILECs") were beginning to face competition by the late 1990s from competitive local exchange carriers ("CLECs") who either "overbuilt" the existing phone plant (i.e., they constructed a second network) or resold the ILEC's capacity, ILECs in the United States tended to have a near-monopoly in providing local telephone service. Most ILECs owned their own ISP businesses (although collectively they captured less than 4 percent of subscribers), but these ILECs were also required by state and federal law to lease their "bottleneck facilities" (such as access lines and space for modem banks in their central switching offices) at regulated prices to competing ISPs.

In its simplest form, an ISP could lease ILEC capacity to offer narrowband dial-up service through existing phone lines. By the late-1990s, ILECs and independent ISPs also were using existing phone lines to offer broadband service through Digital Subscriber Line (DSL) technologies. In areas where DSL was marketed, service typically was only available to roughly one-half of all consumers and businesses who were located within 18,000 feet of a local phone company's central office (the distance limit for propagating high speed digital signals over copper phone lines).[8] Internet and voice-phone traffic could be delivered simultaneously over a single phone line using DSL technologies. Furthermore, DSL subscribers, equipped with special modems, could access the Internet at speeds of at least several hundred Kbps. Customers who required additional bandwidth could purchase (from an ILEC or a CLEC) a higher-capacity service known as a T1 line, which allowed up to 1.5 Mbps.

Cable Services. Cable television system operators were near-monopoly distributors of signals from local TV stations and national television programming networks. By the late 1990s, cable operators were using their two-way fiber, coaxial cable plant and high speed "cable modems" to deliver broadband Internet access. As with DSL, cable modem services provided an "always on" connection, one that did not interfere with the simultaneous reception of TV signals or with cable operators' ability to use their plant to deliver phone service. Cable operators could generally provide 27 Mbps of Internet access capacity to a neighborhood of between 150 to 750 homes that shared a common coaxial line.[9] The bandwidth available to each customer at any given time depended on the number of other users online. Hence, cable modem service typically was quite fast during off-peak hours but could slow during busy periods.[10]

In 2000, cable operators sold access services primarily through two affiliated Broadband Service Providers (BSPs): @Home and Road Runner. Most major cable operators held equity stakes in one or both of these BSPs. Thus, BSPs were effectively industry cooperatives that (1) installed and maintained Internet access equipment within cable operators' "headends" (facilities where cable operators modulated TV signals and voice and data traffic onto their fiber and coaxial cable plant), (2) owned or leased "backbone" network capacity to link cable operators to the public Internet, (3) managed "edge servers" that held mirror copies of frequently accessed Web pages, facilitating their rapid delivery to users, and (4) maintained marketing, customer service, billing, and other operations related to the Internet access business.

Through the 1990s, cable operators were not required by law to wholesale their Internet access services, even though they were near-monopolies like the local phone companies. By 2000, however, cable companies were facing mounting regulatory, legal, and political pressure to provide such access to competing ISPs; federal authorities had preconditioned their approval of two transformational mergers involving cable companies (the acquisitions of Time Warner and MediaOne by AOL and AT&T, respectively) on so-called "open access."

Although most cable operators sold a service that relied on a customer's personal computer for data display, by 2000 it was also possible in certain areas to access the Internet (or other online services delivered as a "walled garden") on a television set through cable lines connected to a set-top converter box.[11] Some industry observers thought that integrating TV viewing with Internet access would revolutionize the way that consumers interacted with television programming and advertising; for example, they expected viewers to access web pages or download video-mail for later viewing by clicking on "tell me more" icons that could be overlaid upon traditional advertisements, or to chat with friends online while jointly viewing a favorite TV show.

Wireless Services. Wireless networks proliferated during the late 1990s. There were five basic types of wireless access providers.

First, *satellite companies* such as Hughes Electronics, SkyBridge, and Teledesic planned to connect consumers and businesses to the Internet and other private data networks via satellite dishes. Satellite services varied widely in their bandwidth, geographic coverage, and quality of service; some promised bandwidth of up to several Mbps per customer. Among the technical factors that determined whether a service was well-suited for a given customer were the height of orbits chosen for the satellites and the latitude at which customers were located. Satellites launched into geosynchronous orbits 22,000 miles above the equator circled the Earth in exactly one day, so they remained in fixed positions relative to points below. For customers at high Northern latitudes, this implied a very low "line of sight" between a dish and the satellite's fixed position in the Southern sky—one that could be obstructed by trees, hills, or buildings. Moreover, even travelling at the speed of light, signals required one-half second to complete the round trip between a dish and a geosynchronous satellite—a frustrating delay for Internet users. This problem of high "latency" (the delay incurred in receiving and processing a signal) led some satellite companies, such as Hughes's DirecPC unit, to employ satellite/telephone hybrid technologies that "downlinked" data to users via satellite but required customers to use a dial-up ISP to send their "upstream" data requests. Other companies, such as Teledesic, proposed to minimize latency problems by launching constellations of low Earth orbit (LEO) satellites. LEO projects would incur very large capital costs: with low-orbiting satellites passing out of transmission range in as little as thirty minutes, dozens or even hundreds of satellites were required to provide uninterrupted service to any given geographic area as signals were "handed off" from one satellite to the next.

Second, *fixed wireless companies* such as Teligent and Winstar installed transmitters and receivers on rooftops in densely populated areas, and used microwaves to send and receive Internet traffic and other data. Generally, fixed wireless services targeted business customers. Service was available only to customers with a clear line of sight to a transmitter/receiver station located no more than a few miles away, but within that area could provide data-transfer speeds ranging from several hundred Kbps to several Mbps.

Third, *digital cellular telephone companies* had begun to offer limited, narrowband access to websites that had been "WAP-enabled," meaning data had been reformatted using "wireless application protocol," an industry standard for transferring data using wireless communications. Subscribers could use their digital cellular phones or Personal Data Assistants (PDAs) to check e-mail or browse a small but growing number of repurposed web sites. Wireless data delivered to cell phones suffered from many limitations in 2000: typically, the bandwidth available on a digital cellular phone was less than the bandwidth available over telephone landlines; the display on portable devices was quite small; and the limited number of buttons on a phone made it difficult to input website addresses or responses to e-mails.

Fourth, a few daring companies known as *HALOs* (for high-altitude, long-operating aircraft), such as Angel Technologies and Sky Station, planned to launch planes and dirigibles with sophisticated switching equipment into very high flight patterns over urban areas (at altitudes of 40,000 feet or more), allowing city residents with a clear line-of-sight to use the airborne platform as an airborne radio tower. It was uncertain how much bandwidth could be attained with this technique, because inclement weather could attenuate signals.

Finally, a handful of companies planned to offer *optical wireless service* between tall buildings in major metropolitan areas such as New York City. These providers, such as Terabeam, used an infrared laser at the ISP's central office to transmit signals across a city block to a customer's building, where a receiver would capture the signal, in much the same way as a satellite dish did. In theory, over very short distances (only a few thousand yards), extremely high bandwidth could be achieved, comparable to the bandwidth available on terrestrial fiber optics strands.

Fiber Optic Lines. A number of companies, often called Metro-DLECs (for Metropolitan Data Local Exchange Companies) provided Internet access and other network services through point-to-point fiber optic links. In a typical arrangement, a large corporation with high bandwidth needs would purchase or lease switches and routers and other specialized equipment and then lease access to a nearby fiber optic network. In this way, the corporation could effectively become its own node in the public Internet or in a private network. DLECs included startups, local phone companies, and in many cases, utilities companies that had piggybacked fiber optic lines on the rights-of-way they used for the distribution of electricity or natural gas.

Summary. Given the wide variety of technical options, matching access technologies to customers' needs was a complex task. Not all technologies could be economically deployed in all markets. Sparsely populated areas, for example, typically settled for low-bandwidth connections or received Internet services through satellite providers (due to the enormous expense of laying fiber or installing short-range terrestrial wireless equipment). Multinational corporations, on the other hand, often secured Internet access in their major office buildings through direct fiber-optic links. As the technologies and their underlying economics evolved, it became more practical to deliver higher bandwidth through a larger number of technologies, making the retail ISP business quite susceptible to technological change.

Many technologies were appealing only to certain customer segments; consequently, technology choices often defined an ISP's target market. Selecting a given technology would commit an ISP to serving residential versus business customers, urban versus rural customers, "newbies" (i.e., first-time Internet users) versus experienced Internet users, and high-bandwidth versus low-bandwidth users. Each type of customer was characterized by a different tendency to churn and demanded different levels of customer service. Thus, the technology choice often would define an ISP's business model.

HOW DO ACCESS PROVIDERS ADD VALUE FOR USERS?

Retail ISPs strove constantly to find ways to differentiate themselves from competition, add value, and retain customers. It was particularly important for ISPs to offer an appealing set of benefits because of the ease with which customers could change services. Monthly prices for Internet access declined throughout the late 1990s, and installation of new services was often facilitated by user-friendly CDs distributed through direct mail or by downloadable software. A user could terminate one service and jump to another in just a few minutes, and often did, resisting attempts by ISPs to sign them up for longer-term service contracts. Therefore, in an effort to outperform competition, ISPs searched feverishly for ways to differentiate themselves. As it turns out, there were ample opportunities to do so.

Technology and Network Capacity. Technology provided several potential points of differentiation for ISPs.

First, the *bandwidth* offered by ISPs proved to be important to users who ran bandwidth-intensive online applications—such as MP3 downloads or multi-player games. As a result, many dial-up ISPs began to offer tiered DSL service at successively higher price points. In fact, a common criticism of cable broadband connections was that although the connection was persistent, the amount of bandwidth available through the connection was dependent upon the time of day; peak loads could exhaust the bandwidth available on shared coaxial cable lines. Cable operators could address peak capacity constraints by deploying fiber optic lines deeper into each neighborhood, reducing the number of homes that shared a single coaxial cable feeder line. However, upgrading a cable plant in this manner could be expensive: Assuming that 25 percent of all cable subscribers eventually would acquire cable modems, it would cost about $135 per cable modem user to extend fiber to the point where 160 homes shared a common coaxial line, versus 580 homes prior to the upgrade.[12]

Second, *service availability* (also called "reliability")—the probability that a subscriber would be successfully connected to the Internet upon logging on—was a crucial driver of customer satisfaction (Exhibit 3). Because an ISP's subscribers did not all access the Internet simultaneously, the ISP did not need to maintain one modem in its facilities for every customer; in fact, user-to-modem ratios of 8:1 or 10:1 were common.[13] However, when ISPs raised this ratio too high in an effort to reduce capital expenditures, subscribers were more likely to get a "Failed to connect" message when too many users simultaneously tried to access the ISP's fixed pool of modems.

Third, certain corporate and government customers focused considerable attention on an ISP's *"quality of service,"* which reflected the likelihood that a data transmission would be received, error-free, within specified time parameters. For example, high quality of service was crucial for applications such as securities or commodities trading; authorizing credit card transactions; military operations; air traffic control; and remote medical monitoring. ISPs who rely on the public Internet—a "patchwork of networks" with no governing authority to prioritize traffic when nodes become congested—cannot guarantee such customers a high

Exhibit 1-3 INTERNET ACCESS PROVIDER PURCHASING CRITERIA

(Percent of survey respondents citing the importance of various criteria and their satisfaction with ISP performance against those criteria)

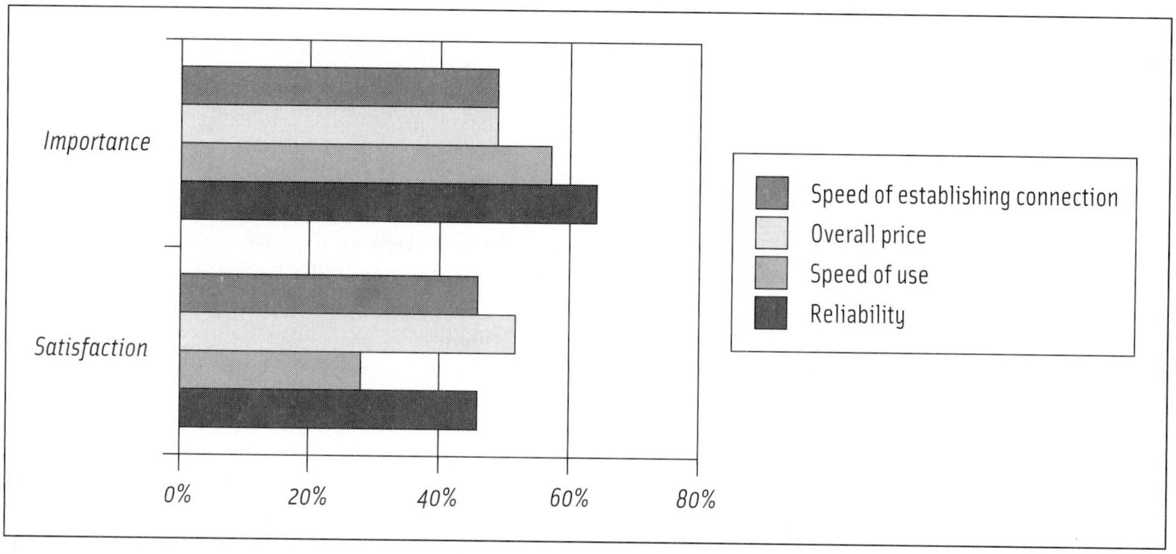

Source: Adapted from Zia Wigder, "Deriving Revenue from No-Cost Access," Jupiter Communications, November 4, 1999, pg. 8

quality of service.[14] Traffic on the public Internet typically passes through a plant owned by several Tier 1 ISPs and through dozens of routers en route to its destination. Each handoff compounds the risk of dropped packets, with associated delays as the recipient's computer requests that missing packets be re-sent. ISPs could avoid such problems and guarantee higher quality of service by building or leasing end-to-end private Internet Protocol networks—an expensive proposition.

Fourth, ISPs could differentiate themselves through the hosting services they offered their customers. Residential subscribers often maintained personal web pages, and many small businesses looked to their ISPs for help in hosting their websites. Security and reliability were important to these customers. Although meeting such demands required capital upgrades to their networks (i.e., additional servers, web server software), many ISPs began to distribute a limited amount of free-hosted file space for their residential subscribers, and some offered hosting services to small businesses at tiered prices.

Customer Service. Customer service was also a key point of differentiation between ISPs. Ease of installation, billing accuracy, and the availability and quality of technical support were major concerns for subscribers. When they signed up with an ISP, consumers valued installation software that automatically configured their browsers and e-mail software; they wanted to "drive off the lot—without getting under the hood." ISPs also had to bill customers flawlessly on a regular monthly schedule. With a plethora of promotions (e.g., "One month free if you refer a friend"), prepaid long term contracts at discounted rates (e.g., "Pay for 6 months in advance and get a $15.95 monthly rate"), and reconciliation requirements (e.g., "One day credit due for service outage this month"), this was often difficult to do. Technical support required a major commitment of resources and required ISPs to hire, train, and retain enough personnel (to avoid long wait times) who were uniquely credentialed in technical matters (addressing questions such as: "Why does my browser crash every time I launch RealPlayer?") and qualified to deal with impatient or frustrated subscribers. In short, the retail ISP business, for all its high-tech veneer, was, at its heart, a customer service-intensive business.

Content. Content was a point of differentiation for some access providers, especially OSPs that operated walled gardens. AOL, for example, made enormous investments in developing a private portal for its subscribers, complete with repurposed magazines and newspapers, shopping sites, news and weather sites, and chat rooms.

Bundling. In part due to the diversity of offerings, bundling became a common tactic for ISPs. Internet access was bundled with everything from Internet content and television programming to subsidized computers and wireless telephony. Bundling several services allowed companies to exploit differences in customers' willingness to pay without excessively discounting each service. A simple example may illustrate the nature of this opportunity. Imagine two consumers, Roger and Mary, each evaluating two services—call them "A" and "B." Roger is willing to pay a maximum of $10 for A and $8 for B. Mary will pay $8 for A and $10 for B. Assume that the cost to deliver each service is $7, and that bundling results in no cost savings (an assumption we will revisit below). If the company does not bundle and prices each service at $10, it will sell one unit of A (to Roger) and one unit of B (to Mary), and will earn profits of $6. Pricing each service at $8 would yield two sales for each service and total profits of $4. However, Mary and Roger would both purchase a bundle of the two services priced at $18, and total profits would net $8.

From a customer's perspective, there are two other ways in which bundling could be attractive, besides making a larger array of goods and services available at an attractive price. First, some customers will value the convenience of "one-stop" shopping and billing. Analysts acknowledge this advantage, but point out that some consumers who purchase bundled services may be deterred by "sticker shock"; when they are made aware of the total amount they are spending for, say, Internet access, cable TV service, and phone service together, they may be more inclined to cancel or downgrade certain services. Second, in theory, a company that has a comprehensive relationship with a customer may be able to integrate services in ways that would be more difficult for multiple independent service providers to accomplish through contractual arrangements and joint ventures. For example, because an OSP like AOL (1) knows the name and address of each of its subscribers (for billing purposes), and (2) can observe the full range of its users' online behavior, the OSP can target advertisements far more precisely than a stand-alone portal. The stand-alone portal has much less information about its users: it must rely on cookies[15] and voluntary registration data provided by users and can only observe a small portion of its users' browsing activity. More precise targeting should boost an OSP's profits and also benefit consumers, who would receive offers better tailored to their preferences.

Analysts cite potential advantages to companies from bundling, beyond these benefits shared with consumers. First, in principle, companies should realize a number of cost savings through bundling. For example, ISPs spend an average of $50 to $75 in marketing to acquire a new customer.[16] If direct mail, telemarketing, or mass media advertising costs can be leveraged across several services, acquisition costs might be reduced. Likewise, companies can economize on field service costs (e.g., installing a cable set-top converter and a cable modem during a single visit) and can save by rendering a single bill. Second, bundling with other services that have intrinsically high customer retention rates (e.g., local phone service or basic cable service) could theoretically improve retention rates for less "sticky" services (e.g., Internet access or long distance phone service). Bundling can be a risky proposition, however. A service problem for any single service might increase a customer's propensity to drop the entire bundle. Third, again in theory, bundling may allow dominant access providers to deter prospective competitors by raising the fixed cost of entry.[17] If several access providers aspire to enter a new market (say, wireless data), and one of them develops a compelling walled garden by bundling a critical mass of proprietary content, competitors are then likely to need to follow suit to stay in the game. If some drop out, bundling will have served to reduce the level of competition experienced by the firms that remain in the business.

AT&T is an example of a company that has attempted to bundle Internet access with cable television service and also with mobile and landline telephony.[18] Through a pilot "fixed wireless" phone venture called Angel, AT&T planned to offer consumers a single hardware device to manage all data, television, and voice connections. AT&T would install a wireless transmitter/receiver on the side of an Angel subscriber's house, allowing users to receive e-mail and voice-mail on their home phone, cell phone, television, or PC, as well as send messages from one device to another—all through a single connection purchased from AT&T.

AT&T also attempted to bundle Internet access, long-distance, and local phone services with its cable television offerings: protecting and expanding its core telephony franchise was the main reason the company spent over $100 billion acquiring cable systems during the late 1990s. These bundles were viewed to be a significant threat by AT&T's competitors, including AOL, which feared that AT&T would favor the Excite@Home OSP service (in which AT&T owned a majority equity stake) by blocking AOL's access to AT&T cable modem subscribers. AT&T was left awash in lawsuits, fighting town-by-town against an AOL-led movement to force AT&T to provide "open access" to its cable plant, much as local phone companies were required to provide access to their competitors. AT&T's bundling plans were likely a contributing factor to AOL's decision in 2000 to purchase the second-largest cable operator in the United States, Time Warner. AT&T's efforts at bundling were ultimately quite costly, contributing to a loss of shareholder confidence and to an announcement late in 2000 that the company would once again—for the third time in twenty years—break itself up into separate operating companies.

ACCESS PROVIDER ECONOMICS

This section examines the margin structure for access providers and describes the factors that drive their revenues and costs. For the sake of simplicity, our analysis focuses on the largest segment of access providers: retail dial-up ISPs that predominantly serve residential and small business customers and charge a monthly subscription fee. ISPs that employ other technologies or serve large corporations may have very different margin structures; some of the major differences are explained below. ISPs that provide free access services in an effort to profit from advertising and transaction revenues also have very different economics; their revenue and cost drivers are described in the next section.

Revenues. In the United States in 2000, a typical retail dial-up ISP earned about $20 per month per subscriber in revenue, with about 83 percent derived from monthly subscription fees for narrowband access services; 7 percent from web hosting and related services for business customers; 6 percent from broadband access services; and 4 percent from advertising and e-commerce transaction revenues derived from traffic on users' start pages.[19] Pricing for residential broadband access was higher: cable modem subscribers paid an average of $40 per month if they leased a modem from their cable company, and $30 if they purchased their own modem for about $250. DSL initially had been priced higher than cable modem service in most markets, but by late 2000 this pricing gap had closed.[20]

In Europe, subscribers typically paid a per-minute access charge to ISPs, although, in 2000, several U.K. ISPs introduced flat-rate pricing plans. Through these flat-rate plans, the ISPs also absorbed the per-minute phone charges that subscribers incurred for dialing into the Internet. These charges, levied by local phone companies, were previously borne by the consumer, and could amount to $23 per month for an Internet user who spent ten hours online per month.[21] In most of Europe, government regulations forced consumers to pay monopoly local phone companies per-minute charges for local calls, although such regulations were being revised in some markets in favor of flat-rate pricing, due in part to concerns that per-minute pricing of local phone calls had slowed the growth of Internet use. Flat-rate access service was offered as a loss leader by some U.K. ISPs hoping to build advertising revenue from a larger subscriber base, but as costs mounted by mid-2000, several of these companies withdrew their flat-rate offers.[22]

Variable Costs. A typical large retail dial-up ISP (with 250,000 subscribers) could plan to spend approximately $12.20 per subscriber per month in infrastructure and support costs in 1999. Most of these costs increased proportionately or in step with its subscriber base. The largest single variable cost was for maintaining network points-of-presence (POPs), facilities where traffic to and from users' modems was modulated and demodulated and was routed to and from the public Internet. POPs consisted of banks of modems, routers, and other network hardware, often located within phone company central offices. Approximately $3.66 per subscriber per month (of the $12.20 per month in total infrastructure and support costs) was spent on depreciation and leases for POP hardware and facilities.[23]

In addition to POPs, an ISP incurred charges for leasing access to telecommunications lines. Retail ISPs leased T1 lines (or wider-bandwidth lines) from the local phone company (or a CLEC) to carry users' traffic between the locations where the ISP maintained modem banks (which tended to be numerous, in order to allow users to connect through a free local call rather than a toll call) and the locations where it routed traffic to and from wholesale ISPs (which tended to be less numerous). Retail ISPs also paid wholesale ISPs to carry their subscribers' traffic over the public Internet and thereby provide subscribers with connections to other ISPs' customers. A typical retail ISP paid $1.95 per subscriber per month in network access fees to wholesale ISPs and a similar amount to local phone companies. Thus, between POP hardware and leased communications lines, a typical ISP paid $7.56 per subscriber per month in 1999, or about 38 percent of revenues.

Customer service and support (including call center operations) added another $3.17 per subscriber per month in 1999. Other costs (sometimes outsourced), such as a data center, where the ISP maintained its e-mail servers and other systems ($0.98 per month) and billing operations ($0.49 per month), rounded out the list of expenses. Again, all of these costs increased in proportion with the growth of an ISP's subscriber base.

Contribution Margin and Lifetime Value of a Customer. A typical contribution margin, therefore, was $20 in revenue per subscriber per month, less $12.20 in monthly variable operating costs, which equaled $7.80 per subscriber per month, or about $94 per year. Since a typical customer remained with an ISP for just two or three years (monthly churn for dial-up ISPs averaged 5 percent[24]), the net present value (NPV) of the contribution margin per customer (at a 10 percent discount rate) was \$155.[25] From this number, an ISP would have to fund its largest single expense—customer acquisition cost—as well as fixed administrative expenses such as those related to senior executive compensation, legal and audit fees, and human resources and finance staff.

Customer Acquisition Costs. ISPs that relied on high-growth strategies could acquire customers either through aggressive marketing programs or by acquiring other ISPs; ISPs content with slower growth could realize substantially lower acquisition costs per new customer by relying on word-of-mouth referrals from satisfied subscribers. Marketing programs included mailing installation CDs to prospects (usually offering something like one month of free service); paying bounties to computer manufacturers and retailers who secured new customers; mass media advertising (TV, radio, magazine, etc.); and, for customers willing to commit to two- or three-year contracts, rebates up to \$400 on the purchase of a new computer. By late 1999, average customer acquisition costs incurred through direct marketing campaigns had crept as high as \$200 per subscriber. However, factoring in new customers acquired through word-of-mouth referrals reduced average costs per customer acquired: in 1999, the ISP industry average was \$50 to \$75 per customer acquired.[26] MindSpring, for example, spent about \$40 per new customer, while AOL spent about \$100.[27]

It was even more expensive for ISPs to acquire customers by buying other ISPs. Through a series of acquisitions, Voyager.net (now a unit of CoreComm)purchased a large customer base in the late 1990s for approximately \$300 per customer.[28] MindSpring paid \$600 per subscriber for Netcom in early 1999.[29] In part, the willingness of ISPs to pay merger partners sums in excess of the NPV of an average subscriber's variable contribution was explained by the prevailing public market valuations of ISPs.[30] Typically measured on a per-subscriber basis, the valuations of publicly traded ISPs soared to remarkable levels in 1999. EarthLink and MindSpring, for example, two of the five largest U.S. ISPs before their merger in 2000, were both valued at about \$4,000 per subscriber in early 1999. These companies could exploit an incredible arbitrage opportunity by using their \$4,000-per-subscriber public equity to acquire ISPs for \$400 per subscriber in private market transactions. However, by early 2000—even before the broad correction in Internet stock valuations in April—the arbitrage opportunity for publicly traded, retail dial-up ISPs had closed. Dial-up ISPs' market valuations fell sharply in response to concerns about competition from free ISPs and from broadband access providers.

Profitability. With its premium pricing and strong revenue growth from e-commerce partnerships, AOL was profitable; the OSP earned a 21 percent operating margin in its fiscal year ending June 2000.[31] Yet, profits were fairly rare among other large ISPs engaged in aggressive customer acquisition efforts (see Exhibit 4 for EarthLink's profit and loss statement). Financial performance was better for many smaller ISPs. In early 1999, about 16 percent of Internet users were still served by thousands of small, community-based ISPs, up from 8 percent in 1997.[32] These "mom-and-pop" ISPs grew organically and somewhat haphazardly, relying on word-of-mouth referrals. By virtue of avoiding free trials and other expensive marketing programs and by charging installation fees (which larger ISPs tended to waive in their marketing programs), many small ISPs were profitable.[33] Some regional ISPs had established thriving businesses simply by establishing their points-of-presence outside areas where national access providers like AOL could be

Exhibit 1-4 EARTHLINK INCOME STATEMENT AND SUBSCRIBER STATISTICS

$ in millions (% of revenue)	1999		2000E		2001E	
Narrowband	$582.9	(87%)	$836.5	(84%)	$1,150.3	(76%)
Web hosting	$47.4	(7%)	$68.3	(7%)	$91.7	(6%)
Broadband	$23.5	(4%)	$57.6	(6%)	$193.0	(17%)
Advertising and e-Commerce	$16.6	(2%)	$39.3	(4%)	$75.0	(5%)
Total Revenues	**$670.4**		**$1,001.6**		**$1,509.9**	
Cost of revenues	$248.5	(37%)	$369.5	(37%)	$606.4	(40%)
Gross margin	$421.9	(63%)	$632.1	(63%)	$903.5	(60%)
Sales and marketing	$219.3	(33%)	$481.9	(48%)	$572.6	(38%)
Member support and operations	$182.1	(27%)	$301.0	(30%)	$372.9	(25%)
General and administrative	$67.9	(10%)	$103.3	(10%)	$122.8	(8%)
Operating income (before merger-related charges)	($47.4)	(-7%)	($254.1)	(-25%)	($164.8)	(-11%)
Subscriber Growth (000's)						
Narrowband	2,988		4,648		5,443	
Broadband	25		180		483	
Web hosting	109		167		229	
Total Subscribers	3,122		4,995		6,155	

Source: Adapted from "EarthLink": Goldman Sachs Equity Research, "Internet Industry Report," October 6, 2000, pg. 123

accessed through a free local phone call. One-quarter of the U.S. population resided in such communities in mid-2000.[34]

FREE ISP BUSINESS MODEL

A number of ISPs in 1999 promised to give away free access. Their business models altered the traditional economic formula for access providers in an attempt to grow their base of subscribers more quickly and thereby capture advertising revenue and leverage other economies of scale. Enthusiasm for the free ISP model peaked in September 1999, when NetZero went public with only 900,000 active users but a market capitalization of $3 billion.[35] Although the valuation of free ISPs had declined sharply by late 2000, Jupiter Communications predicted that by 2003, free ISPs would generate $901 million in ad revenue (8 percent of total online ad spending), when they would serve 13 million U.S. residential Internet users—and would represent the primary Internet connection in 9 million homes.[36]

One variant of the free ISP model—one employed by companies such as NetZero—subsidized free Internet access through ad revenue, requiring that subscribers, during their online sessions, keep open at all times a persistent advertising window. Essentially, this model availed itself of word-of-mouth and free press to slash customer acquisition costs deeply: NetZero, for example, spent less than $10 on sales and marketing per customer acquired during fiscal 2000 (see Exhibit 5 for NetZero income statement).[37] Free ISPs reasoned that their advertising opportunities would be more valuable to marketers because of their large, captive audiences: ISPs collected a great deal of demographic information about their users as a condition of service. Also, because they could observe a user's browsing behavior in real time, free ISPs could synchronize the delivery of a contextually relevant ad (e.g., they could serve an ad for the Expedia travel service when a user accessed a page from Quebec's bureau of tourism). However, as of mid-2000, free ISPs had not yet been able to exploit these advantages: NetZero's effective cost-per-thousand advertising impressions delivered (CPM) was only $2.64, lower than the $3.20 average for all ad-supported websites.[38]

Many of the ISPs that employed this model were struggling by late 2000, including Freei Networks, which filed for bankruptcy in October of that year after spending heavily on a high-profile ad campaign featuring NBA star Shaquille O'Neal. Freei lost $19 million during fiscal 1999 on revenues of less than $1 million.[39] Those ISPs that remained in business saw their valuations shrink dramatically—by November 2000, for example, NetZero's stock price had declined 96 percent from its previous 52-week high. Even though free ISPs had very low customer-acquisition costs, their customer churn rates were very high. For example, as of

Exhibit 1-5 NETZERO INCOME STATEMENT AND SUBSCRIBER STATISTICS

$ in millions (% of revenue)	1999		2000E		2001E	
Total Revenues	**$24.4**		**$84.1**		**$167.4**	
Cost of revenues	$38.6	(158%)	$82.1	(98%)	$125.5	(75%)
Gross profit	($14.2)	(-58%)	$2.0	(2%)	$41.9	(25%)
Operating Expenses						
Sales and marketing	$21.0	(12%)	$63.7	(76%)	$70.8	(42%)
Product development	$2.9	(12%)	$12.1	(14%)	$17.2	(10%)
General and administrative	$11.4	(47%)	$30.0	(36%)	$45.9	(27%)
Operating income	($49.4)	(-202%)	($103.7)	(-123%)	($91.9)	(-55%)
User Growth *(000's)*						
Year end reg. users	2,960		6,174		8,623	
Year end active users	1,450		2,716		3,793	

Source: Adapted from "NetZero": Goldman Sachs Equity Research, "Internet Industry Report," October 6, 2000, pg. 127

mid-2000 active users (who had used the service in the past month) represented only 40 percent of 5 million total registered users for NetZero.[40] Many users were concerned about their loss of privacy and were annoyed by the fact that they could not close advertising windows that monopolized a portion of their screens and flashed distracting banners. Others were disappointed with poor service availability—most free ISPs maintained high user-to-modem ratios to keep their costs down and did not have POPs in smaller communities. Users also were unhappy with the fact that technical support for free ISPs was of uneven quality and typically was available only through toll calls—again, a policy intended to keep costs low (see Exhibit 6 for a list of consumer concerns with free access providers).

While these free ISPs still held out the promise of highly targeted advertising, in mid-2000 NetZero only managed to generate about $3 in revenue per active user per month.[41] By contrast, AOL, the most successful access provider in terms of exploiting its scale, earned about $5 per subscriber per month in advertising and e-commerce revenues in late 1999.[42] Marketers remained suspicious of adverse selection problems: Was it worth advertising to customers who were too cheap to pay for high quality Internet access? At the same time, having outsourced most elements of their networks, free ISPs incurred monthly operating costs per active user in the range of $4.00.[43] This was less, to be sure, than the amount spent by full-priced dial-up ISPs (who absorbed the full cost of customer support and whose customers spent, on average, 31 hours per month online, compared to only 15 hours for active users of free ISPs[44]), but it left free ISPs with significant operating losses. NetZero, for example, had an operating loss of $90 million in fiscal 2000.[45] As capital providers grew weary of funding this experiment, several free ISPs shut down their operations.

In another common variant of the free ISP model, brick-and-mortar retailers linked with an established portal or OSP to offer services intended to (1) bring new users to the Internet, (2) capture a share of the online advertising and commerce spending, and, in the process, (3) use an Internet presence to strengthen the loyalty to their brick-and-mortar stores. In 1999 and 2000 a number of large brick-and-mortar retailers announced joint ventures to offer such services, including Kmart

Exhibit 1-6

CONSUMERS CONCERNS REGARDING FREE ISPS

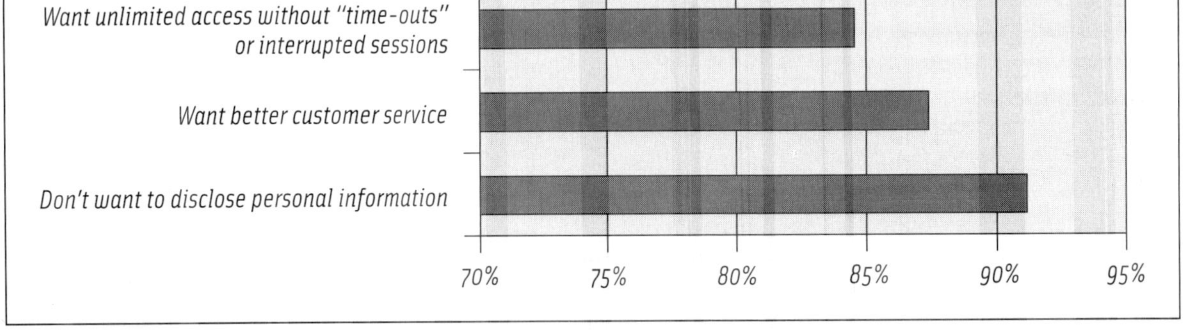

Source: Adapted from "Metrics" section, *The Industry Standard* (April 3, 2000): 193, citing International Communications Research

with Yahoo! and private label ISP Spinway; Wal-Mart, J.C. Penney, Macy's, and Sears with AOL; and Radio Shack with Microsoft's MSN.[46] Services like Kmart and Yahoo!'s BlueLight.com (named after Kmart's in-store promotional announcements, called "Bluelight Specials") maintained persistent advertising windows like the other free ISPs described above but hoped to supplement these advertising revenues with increased online shopping revenues generated at Kmart's website.

As of late 2000, the economic model for retailer-backed free ISPs had not been proven, but industry analysts were encouraged by BlueLight.com's rapid rate of customer acquisition—the service had 4.6 million subscribers in November 2000—and by the fact that investors, including Softbank Venture Capital, had provided an additional $80 million in funding to the service at a time when other free ISPs were failing due to a lack of investor support.[47] Jupiter Communications observed that other companies could benefit from closer relationships with their customers, including airlines and financial services firms, and expected such companies to follow the lead of brick-and-mortar retailers in launching free access offers.[48]

In Europe, free ISPs had proliferated because they faced competition from access providers that still employed usage-based rather than flat-rate pricing. Free ISPs like Freeserve in the United Kingdom were able to rely not only on advertising revenues but also on subsidies paid by telephone companies. Phone companies in most European countries still charged per minute of use for local phone calls; they shared a portion of this revenue with free ISPs—about $1 per online hour in the United Kingdom, but less in other countries. Such sharing was sometimes mandated by regulators, but even when it was not, phone companies often shared their revenues with free ISPs willingly, because Internet access helped them generate substantial incremental volume. Thus, the total monthly outlay in 1999 for a Freeserve subscriber who spent 10 hours online would be $23 paid to British Telecom. By contrast, an AOL UK subscriber who spent 10 hours online would pay the same $23 to BT, but also $16 to AOL.[49]

"GET BIG FAST": A STRATEGIC IMPERATIVE FOR ACCESS PROVIDERS?

Many Internet companies have pursued "Get Big Fast" (GBF) strategies, embracing "land grab" logic. According to this view, companies will find it easier to stake out wide swaths of empty territory now, rather than try to capture that territory later, after it has been settled by others. AOL pursued a very successful GBF strategy; it had acquired 22 million subscribers by October 2000 after "carpet bombing" the United States for years with diskettes and CDs containing installation software and free trials.[50] Other ISPs followed suit: By spending heavily on marketing and by acquiring MindSpring and some smaller ISPs, EarthLink grew from 1.7 million subscribers in late 1998 to 4.6 million by the end of 2000.[51] However, the stock market did not respond as favorably to EarthLink's GBF strategy as it did to AOL's: between October 1998 and October 2000, while AOL's stock price tripled, EarthLink's declined by 83 percent. Other ISPs that had pursued GBF strategies suffered similar stock price declines. This raises two questions: (1) Was AOL a special case? and (2) Is the GBF strategy fundamentally flawed for access providers?

The payoff from a GBF strategy tends to be strongest when the following conditions apply: Network effects are strong, scale economies (beyond network effects) are significant, and customer retention rates are intrinsically high. This section explores the extent to which these conditions apply for access providers.

Network Effects

Network effects occur when the adoption of a product or service by a new customer increases the value of that product or service for customers already using it because existing customers now can 'connect' with additional parties.[52] The fax machine is a good example of a product that benefits from network effects: a fax machine is worthless if you are the only one who owns one, but when many people own them they are valuable. When network effects are strong, it often makes sense for a company to invest heavily to gain first-mover advantage. As users beget users, the first mover may develop an unassailable lead.

Network effects are weak for ISPs that provide access to the public Internet. By definition, such access is open; the fact that EarthLink signs up another subscriber who may send and receive e-mail does not benefit EarthLink's existing subscribers any more than it benefits any other parties with access to the public Internet.

For access providers like AOL who operate walled gardens, however, network effects may be extremely strong, especially around communications applications like e-mail, instant messaging, and chat. Within AOL's proprietary site, chat rooms are open only to members, providing an incredibly strong incentive to join AOL and remain a member once your friends are AOL subscribers.[53] Also, notwithstanding technical and legal efforts by Microsoft, Yahoo!, and other companies to interconnect their own instant messenger applications with AOL's Instant Messenger service—against AOL's wishes—that very popular feature remains available only to AOL members and users of websites that have licensed software from AOL.[54]

Scale Economies

Companies benefit from scale economies when they can generate more revenue per user than smaller competitors and when they can spread fixed costs over a growing revenue base. With many Internet business models, costs are almost entirely fixed and operating margins increase dramatically with sales growth. Strong scale economies promote a winner-take-all dynamic: If the market leader has a superior cost structure, that company can reduce its prices or invest in superior service or features and thereby increase the company's lead.

Large ISPs are able to generate more revenue per subscriber from advertising and commerce transactions, because marketing partners are more willing to complete deals with access providers that can deliver a critical mass of potential customers. Many ISPs outsourced management of their "start page"—where such revenues originated—to a private label portal. In such arrangements, larger ISPs kept as much as 70 percent of revenues generated from the page, whereas smaller ISPs collected only 20 percent.[55] Aggressively exploiting its scale, AOL harvested about $5 per month per subscriber from advertising and e-commerce.[56] In a typical deal, a content provider paid AOL millions of dollars to have its content accessible through AOL's portal, or an online retailer paid to become the exclusive AOL vendor of a category of merchandise. In 1999, some 25 percent of AOL's gross revenue came from such placement deals and from other advertising, compared to an average of 5 percent to 6 percent for other ISPs.[57]

Having a large subscriber base also allows dial-up ISPs to configure their networks in ways that improve the odds they will attract even more customers. It is only economical for an ISP to establish a point-of-presence (POP) in a given community once it reaches a threshold subscriber penetration level, given the fixed costs associated with installing modem banks and routers. So, a large ISP will be able to afford more points-of-presence than a small one. This is a major advantage for players marketing nationally or within a large metropolitan area, because the chances are increased that any given prospect will be able to connect through a toll-free phone call. Companies that provide nationwide network coverage also can economically employ national mass media (network television, magazines), which tend to be less costly per prospect reached than local mass media (local television, radio, and newspapers). Likewise, ISPs that wish to provide "roaming" access to business travelers benefit from having a large number of POPs.[58]

While access providers benefit from scale economies, the dominant share of their cost base—including hardware costs at POPs, payments to phone companies and ISP wholesalers for network access, and customer service and billing costs—varies fairly directly with their revenues. Volume growth does yield some cost savings for access providers: It increases their negotiating leverage when purchasing equipment, telecommunications services, or outsourced services such as billing. Volume growth also allows providers to concentrate telecommunications traffic onto higher bandwidth lines, which tend to have a much lower cost per Mbps transferred,[59] and leverages the fixed cost elements of call center operations (these constitute a small share of total call center costs) and, more notably, administrative functions.

The largest source of potential scale-related cost savings for ISPs appeared to be in leasing network access; POP hardware and customer service costs, by contrast, were much less sensitive to volume. Once an ISP reached a certain scale, it could enter bilateral "peering" arrangements with other large ISPs, whereby each party agreed not to charge the other when its customers accessed sites on the other's network. Smaller retail ISPs signed "transit" agreements instead, which required them to pay for access from Tier 1 ISPs, who in turn would ensure (through their peering arrangements) that the retail ISP's traffic reached its intended destination.

It is difficult to discern the magnitude of network-related scale economies, however, from an analysis of the income statements of publicly-traded access providers. For example, AOL's network costs were skewed upwards by the fact that it operated large server "farms" to deliver content into its walled garden. When users connected to content sites through the public Internet instead of a proprietary network like AOL's, such server costs were borne by the destination sites, not by ISPs. EarthLink's network costs were skewed upward by the fact that it took time to rationalize a network after major acquisitions (e.g., to consolidate POPs and renegotiate contracts with phone companies in order to concentrate increased traffic volumes onto less expensive high bandwidth lines).

Customer Retention

The payoff for GBF strategies improves when customer retention rates are high, especially when a market is young and has many first-time users. If first-time users can be "locked in" before they sample a competitor's service, a first mover may cement its lead. Beyond the customer loyalty that can follow from solid performance against technical standards (especially availability, i.e., the probability of successfully connecting when dialing in) and in customer service and billing functions, ISPs can benefit from two other factors that improve their customer retention rates. First, as noted above, retention rates tend to be high in the face of the strong network effects engendered by an OSP's walled garden communications applications. Second, ISP customers incur several "switching costs" when they change access providers, most notably the need to provide friends, family, and professional contacts with a new e-mail address (most ISPs will not forward e-mail after a subscriber terminates service), as well as the normal hassles associated with closing a subscription account and opening a new one (e.g., contacting the current provider and installing new software).

Given the factors that promote customer retention, the industry's 5 percent average monthly churn rate for dial-up ISPs may be somewhat surprising. In fact, some ISPs that target experienced Internet users and emphasize organic growth through word-of-mouth referrals, such as Voyager.net, have achieved monthly churn rates in the 2 percent range.[60] The industry's higher average attrition rate appears to be skewed upward by players pursuing Get Big Fast strategies. GBF strategies can exacerbate churn in three ways. First, rapid growth is more likely to strain network capacity and customer support capabilities; performance shortfalls in these areas can increase attrition, as AOL discovered in the late 1990s when its customers complained bitterly about poor service from "America On Hold." Second, when access providers target first-time Internet users (known in the industry as "newbies") with free trial offers, the providers naturally sign up some customers who discover that being online simply isn't worth $20 per month for them. Furthermore, providing customer support to newbies is much more expensive, because they are much more likely than Internet veterans to call with basic questions about how to configure and maintain their computers and online connections (e.g., "What's a USB port?"). Jupiter Communications estimates that each customer service call to an ISP costs about $20 (e-mail inquiries would be less expensive), so serving a large number of inexperienced users who require a high level of support can quickly wipe out an access provider's profit margin.[61] Third, by proliferating free trial offers, access providers, like long distance phone companies, have encouraged a cohort of deal-motivated consumers to switch from ISP to ISP to exploit promotions. AOL has suffered from all of these problems; at the peak of its GBF efforts in 1996, one equity analyst estimated that AOL retained its average subscriber for only 15 months,[62] although AOL's churn had been reduced substantially by late 2000.

Summary: The GBF Payoff

In summary, it appears that the Get Big Fast strategy is most likely to yield an attractive payoff when access providers are able and willing to operate walled gardens. A walled garden approach can deny an OSP's customers the ability to communicate (through instant messaging, chat, and, in the early days of online services, even e-mail) with other access providers' customers, and thereby engenders a stronger network effect. If the people with whom you wish to communicate are network members, you must become (and remain) one, too. Of course, this strategy can backfire if an OSP fails to gain momentum, as Apple Computer discovered during the mid-1990s when it launched an online service called "eWorld," which was nicknamed "Empty World" by industry observers due to its underused chat rooms.

Whether or not to interconnect with competitors is a recurrent strategy issue that access providers face when they propagate new access technologies. We can expect this decision to be replayed in the interactive TV arena: Will cable operators allow their subscribers to chat on-screen with customers who receive similar services through satellite providers? When broadband service providers promote video telephony, will they interconnect with competing technology providers? The dilemma is vexing: on the one hand, interconnection increases the value that customers realize from a new communications technology, because they can reach more parties. On the other hand, interconnection forfeits the opportunity to exploit an even stronger network effect by keeping the technology proprietary. When denying interconnection rights does succeed in promoting a strong network effect, the strategy's very power may lead to its own reversal, as evidenced by the pressure that AOL has received from regulators to open its instant messaging service to competitors. By the time the strategy has drawn antitrust scrutiny, however, a company will have realized significant first-mover advantage. There are worse problems a company can have!

Without a walled garden, access providers have recourse to negligible network effects, and the payoff from a GBF strategy is more uncertain. ISPs do benefit from some scale economies and from switching costs that encourage customer retention, but neither advantage is strong enough to make the GBF a strategic imperative. Large ISPs have lower network costs and can profit from vertical integration into the portal business. The advantages to vertical integration between the access and portal businesses are apparent from AOL's success, which has encouraged access providers to develop or acquire portals (e.g., @Home's acquisition of Excite) and which has led portals to develop access businesses that can steer additional users (e.g., the free ISP services offered by AltaVista and by Yahoo! through its joint venture with Kmart). However, the strain of implementing a GBF strategy on network capacity and customer service capabilities can raise an ISP's operating costs and lead to customer dissatisfaction and churn.

ENDNOTES

[1]Cahner's In-Stat Group, "The U.S. ISP Industry: Growth in Revenues and Services," 2000.

[2]Through its Compuserve subsidiary, AOL also sold access to the public Internet, without providing AOL-proprietary content.

[3]A "walled garden" was defined as an online service that made it easy to access content and commerce offerings from its exclusive set of business partners, but slower and harder (or sometimes impossible) to access third party offerings. Besides AOL, Excite@Home maintained a walled garden, and many cell phone operators were developing their new wireless data services in this manner. Technically, walled gardens were maintained through selective caching, attenuated connections to the Internet at-large, and a new generation of data switches that could selectively delay data en route to and from non-preferred services. Steve McMahon, Davis Community Network, "Broadband Glossary and Bestiary," June 23, 2000, http://www.dcn.davis.ca.ns/go/steve/terms.htm; viewed September 14, 2000.

[4]For more information on the portal business model, see Thomas Eisenmann and Sanjay Pothen, "Online Portals," section 2, *Internet Business Models: Text and Cases*, or HBS Case no. 801-305, December 2000.

[5]Thomas Eisenmann, Dan Green, and Doug Rogers, "Teledesic," section 1, *Internet Business Models: Text and Cases*, or HBS Case no. 800-057, February 2000.

[6]Dan Green, Lynda Applegate, and Jay Light, "The Last Mile of Broadband Access", HBS Case no. 800-076, January 25, 2000; Thomas Eisenmann, Dan Green, and Doug Rogers, "Teledesic," section 1, *Internet Business Models: Text and Cases*, or HBS Case no. 800-057, February 2000.; Thomas Eisenmann, "Tele-Communications, Inc.: Accelerating Digital Deployment," section 1, *Internet Business Models: Text and Cases*, or HBS Case no. 899-141, August 11, 2000.

[7]Dylan Brooks, "Wireless Broadband Access," Jupiter Communications, December 29, 1999, p. 1.

[8]Ibid, p. 16.

[9]Each neighborhood, in turn, was served by a dedicated, high bandwidth, two-way fiber optic line which terminated at a node where an opto-electronic converter modulated light waves from the fiber optics lines into radio waves that could be propagated over copper (coaxial cable) lines (and vice versa). Since the bandwidth of fiber optic lines was so great, capacity constraints were encountered only in the "last mile" of the cable operator's network, where copper lines were employed. Pulling fiber to each home in order to relieve bandwidth constraints was not economically viable due to the high cost of opto-electronic converters. With hybrid fiber/coaxial cable architectures, the cost of such converters was shared by a few hundred homes linked to a common node; by contrast, with "fiber-to-the-curb" architectures, each home would need its own converter.

[10]Thomas Eisenmann, Chris Darwall, and Liz Kind, "Geocast Network Systems, Inc.," section 1, *Internet Business Models: Text and Cases*, or HBS Case no. 801-211, October 4, 2000.

[11]Other companies, such as Microsoft's WebTV unit, used existing telephone lines instead of cable plant to deliver narrowband Internet services to TV sets.

[12]Raymond Katz, "Cable Industry Overview," Bear Stearns Equity Research, April 1998, p. 24.

[13]Remember that data transfer requires modems on *both* ends of the transmission to "***mo***dulate" a signal onto the communications carrier (e.g., a phone line) then "***dem***odulate" that signal into a format that a computer can process. See Joe Keough, Kathy Olofsson, and Jeffrey Rayport, "MindSpring," HBS Case no. 899-178 for more information on dial-up ISPs' network management decisions.

[14]See Thomas Eisenmann, Dan Green, and Doug Rogers, "Teledesic," section 1, *Internet Business Models: Text and Cases*, or HBS Case no. 800-057, February 2000, for more information on the technical challenges involved in ensuring high quality of service and the types of applications that require high quality of service.

[15]A cookie is a small piece of software code downloaded into a website user's computer by the website, which allows the website to identify the user and track her whenever she logs back into the site. Cookies could be used to avoid requiring users to reenter commonly requested information, such as user names and passwords or shipping addresses.

[16]Jason Zigmont, "Free ISPs Will Work," *Boardwatch*, October 1999, p. 36.

[17]Barry Nalebuff, "Bundling," Yale School of Management working paper, November 22, 1999.

[18]Leslie Cauley, "Armstrong's Vision of AT&T Cable Empire Unravels on the Ground," *Wall Street Journal*, October 18, 2000, p. 1.

[19]Year 2000 projections for EarthLink from Goldman Sachs Equity Research, "Internet Industry Report," October 6, 2000, p. 123.

[20]Fritz McCormick, "Residential Broadband Begins to Blossom," Yankee Group, September 2000, p. 4.

[21]Bruce Kasrel, "ISPs Move From Free to Personal," Forrester Research, September 1999.

[22]Polly Sprenger, "Flat-Rate Access Goes Flatline," *Industry Standard*, July 31, 2000, p. 69.

[23]These and other economic figures, unless otherwise noted, are adapted from Zia Daniell Wigder, "The Evolution of Access: Navigating the Changing Online Landscape," Jupiter Communications, vol. 10, 1999. In a subsequent report (Dylan Brooks, "Private-Labeled ISPs," Jupiter Communications, June 2, 2000), Jupiter analysts noted that ISPs' variable costs had shifted dramatically between 1999 and 2000. Network connectivity expenses had declined rapidly—from about $0.30 in 1999 to $0.15 per hour in 2000 (with a typical residential user spending about 31 hours per month online)—due to declining equipment costs and reduced network access fees that followed from intensified competition between ILECs and CLECs and among backbone ISPs. At the same time, Jupiter estimated that customer support expenses per subscriber for national ISPs like EarthLink had nearly doubled between 1999 and 2000, at which point they represented nearly 50 percent of total costs. As noted in the section below on "Get Big Fast" strategies, this may reflect the increased cost of serving first-time Internet users that had been acquired through aggressive marketing campaigns.

[24]Zia Daniell Wigder, "The Evolution of Access: Navigating the Changing Online Landscape." Jupiter Communications, vol. 10, 1999. Other estimates of industry average monthly churn rates are higher. For example, Dean Frost, "In a Squeeze at MindSpring," *Business Week*, September 20, 1999, p. 142, estimates an 8 percent average monthly churn rate for ISPs.

[25]This calculation omits the value of word-of-mouth referrals generated by satisfied customers. At MindSpring, an ISP known for providing high quality customer service resulting in high levels of user satisfaction and low churn rates, such referrals accounted for 45 percent of all new customers (Joe Keough, Kathy Olofsson, and Jeffrey Rayport, "MindSpring," HBS Case no. 899-178, pg. 9). Examining MindSpring's rate of growth during the late 1990s, we can infer that each new customer referred approximately 0.5 additional customers (not counting any "next generation" referrals, i.e., not crediting "wave 1" customers with any "wave 3" customers acquired as a result of word-of-mouth from satisfied "wave 2" customers). In principal, the value of such referrals should be included in calculating the net present value of a customer.

[26]Jason Zigmont, "Free ISPs Will Work," *Boardwatch*, October 1999, p. 36.

[27]Ibid.

[28]Tim Weller, "Voyager.net: How to Run a Great ISP," DLJ Equity Research, August 24, 1999.

[29]Zia Daniell Wigder, "The Evolution of Access: Navigating the Changing Online Landscape," Jupiter Communications, vol. 10, 1999.

[30]We might expect the purchase price per subscriber for an acquired ISP to exceed the net present value of a subscriber for two reasons. First, as noted in note 25, acquiring a subscriber creates growth options, because that subscriber—if served well—is likely to generate word-of-mouth referrals. Second, if an acquired ISP owns portions of its network (e.g., modem banks), then the value of acquired assets should be reflected in the NPV calculation by adding depreciation back to cash flows.

[31]Company SEC filings.

[32]Seth Lubove, "Mom and POPs Thrive . . . ," *Forbes,* February 22, 1999, p. 120.

[33]Kate Delhagen, "Internet Access Winners," Forrester Research, January 1998.

[34]Dylan Brooks, "Private-Labeled ISPs," Jupiter Communications, June 2, 2000, p. 3.

[35]Tom Davey, "NetZero Zooms to $3 Billion IPO," *RedHerring.com,* September 25, 1999.

[36]Zia Daniell Wigder, "Bandwidth and Access Strategies," Jupiter Communications, January 2000, p. 26.

[37]Company SEC statements. NetZero had sales and marketing expenditures of $49 million in fiscal 2000, and acquired 5 million registered users during the year. Note that sales and marketing expense includes costs related to advertising sales commissions as well as marketing costs for customer acquisition, so the $10 figure quoted above overstates NetZero's acquisition cost per customer.

[38]Dylan Brooks, "Private-Labeled ISPs," Jupiter Communications, June 2, 2000, p. 24.

[39]Greg Johnson, "Free Online Access Gives Rise to Debate," *Los Angeles Times,* November 9, 2000, p. C–1.

[40]Company SEC filings.

[41]Ibid.

[42]Zia Daniell Wigder, "Free Access Services," Jupiter Communications, November 4, 1999, p. 14.

[43]Adam Portnoy, "Free ISP—Gimmick, or Viable Business Model?", *Boardwatch,* February 2000, p. 26. According to this article, NetZero incurs networks costs of $3.20 per user per month, and spends an additional $0.20 for outsourced e-mail services and $0.60 for advertising sales commissions.

[44]Ibid.

[45]Company SEC filings. The loss included $11 million of non-cash charges related to stock-based compensation and the amortization of intangibles.

[46]Bernhard Warner, "Sears Has AOL," *Industry Standard,* March 14, 2000; Miguel Helft, "Attention Shoppers," *Industry Standard,* December 15, 1999.

[47]"About Us" section of BlueLight.com website.

[48]Zia Daniell Wigder, "Bandwidth and Access Strategies," Jupiter Communications, January 2000.

[49]Bruce Kasrel, "ISPs Move From Free to Personal," Forrester Research, September 1999.

[50]According to Kara Swisher, *AOL.com,* (New York: Random House, 1998), p. 226, the company had distributed 250 million disks.

[51]Company SEC filings.

[52]See Carl Shapiro and Hal R. Varian, *Information Rules* (Boston, MA: Harvard Business School Press, 1999), pp. 173–225 and Philip Evans and Thomas S. Wurster, *Blown to Bits* (Boston, MA: Harvard Business School Press, 1999) pp. 112–113.

[53]According to David Card, "Chat and Instant Messaging," Jupiter Communications, September 1998, 29 percent of AOL users regularly chat online, compared to 17 percent for non-AOL users.

[54]According to David Lake, "Message in a Packet," *Industry Standard,* July 17, 2000, citing Media Metrix data, AOL's Instant Messenger service had 16.9 million unique visitors in March 2000, compared to 5.3 million visitors for Yahoo! Messenger and 4.5 million for MSN Messenger.

[55]Abhi Chaki, "ISP Revenue Strategies," Jupiter Communications, April 1998.

[56]Tim Weller, "Voyager.net: How to Run a Great ISP," DLJ Equity Research, August 24, 1999.

[57]Zia Daniell Wigder, "The Evolution of Access: Navigating the Changing Online Landscape," Jupiter, vol. 10, 1999.

[58]Lacking a widespread POP infrastructure, a smaller ISP can still provide roaming access for its subscribers by contracting with a national ISP such as AT&T's IGN unit.

[59]According to Douglas Galbi, "Growth in the 'New Economy': U.S. Bandwidth Use and Pricing Across the 1990s," FCC Common Carrier Bureau working paper, July 9, 2000, p. 9, the monthly price per Mbps for a DS–1 line (equivalent to a T–1 line, with a 1.5 Mbps data transfer rate) in 2000 was $112, versus $17 per Mbps for a DS–3 line (with a 44.7 Mbps data transfer rate).

[60]Tim Weller, "Voyager.net: How to Run a Great ISP," DLJ Equity Research, August 24, 1999.

[61]Dylan Brooks, "Private-Labeled ISPs," Jupiter Communications, June 2, 2000, p. 7.

[62]Kara Swisher, *AOL.com,* (New York: Random House, 1998), p. 159.

TELE-COMMUNICATIONS, INC.: ACCELERATING DIGITAL DEPLOYMENT

The pace of change at Tele-Communications, Inc. (TCI) had been remarkable between November 1996 and June 1998. During this period, poor financial results had prompted CEO John Malone to initiate dramatic cost reductions and transform the company's strategy. In February of 1997, Malone hired Leo Hindery as TCI's President and COO. Hindery restructured the company's cable operations to improve profit accountability, reduce debt, and capture economies of scale. While intensifying the company's operational turnaround, Malone and Hindery also were directing extraordinary changes in TCI's technology strategy. By year-end 1996, Malone had determined that the company needed to expedite the deployment of first-generation digital converters to increase channel capacity and thereby respond to a competitive threat from direct-to-home satellite broadcasters. By mid-1998, however, a growing convergence of interests between Silicon Valley and the cable industry had led TCI's top management to move beyond this defensive focus and adopt a much more ambitious technology strategy. TCI's executives were debating whether to undertake the rapid and ubiquitous deployment of second-generation digital converters, which could deliver Internet and telecommunications services, in addition to traditional video entertainment. In exchange for providing access to all of TCI's cable customers, Malone and Hindery believed that TCI could secure equity interests in emerging electronic commerce businesses, much as TCI had gained profitable stakes in cable programming ventures in the past. While the potential payoff from the proposed technology strategy seemed enormous, so did the downside risks: it would tax the company's balance sheet and its marketing and customer service capabilities.

TCI's Portfolio in 1996

With 14 million subscribers in its wholly-owned cable systems, and non-consolidated equity investments in affiliated companies serving an additional 3 million subscribers, TCI was the largest U.S. cable system operator in 1996.[1] TCI had diversified beyond its core U.S. cable system business by investing in programming, telecommunications services, direct-to-home satellite broadcasting (described below), and international cable television businesses (Exhibit 2). Through a unit called Liberty Media, TCI owned equity in a large number of programming services, including the Discovery Channel, QVC, and Black Entertainment Television. TCI also had invested in several joint ventures that employed digital technologies to deliver new telecommunications services. These ventures included *Teleport,* a "Competitive Local Exchange Carrier" (CLEC) which used fiber optic lines to bypass the incumbent telephone company and provide voice and

Professor Thomas R. Eisenmann prepared this case as a basis for class discussion rather than to illustrate either effective or ineffective handling of an administration situation.

[1]Cable system operators obtained municipal franchises to build and maintain coaxial cable plant delivering dozens of television channels to households; secured programming for these channels by negotiating for permission to retransmit signals from terrestrial television stations and from satellite-delivered programming services such as CNN, ESPN, and HBO; and marketed bundles of channels to households in their franchises. Terrestrial television stations broadcast their signals from towers. Within about 50 miles of a station's transmitter, TV sets in homes without cable could receive "over-the-air" signals using a set-top or roof-top antenna (although hilly topography and tall buildings could interfere with reception). In contrast to terrestrial TV stations, which broadcast within a single metropolitan area, the signals of satellite-delivered programming services could be received nation-wide. Their signals were broadcast by communications satellites in geosynchronous orbit (stationary over the equator) to cable systems' "headends." At cable headends, satellite transmissions were received by "earth stations" equipped with special antennas ("dishes"), then modulated (assigned channel numbers) onto the cable plant. Cable plant had a tree-and-branch architecture, with trunk lines connecting to the headend; feeder lines connecting to trunks; and drop lines connecting homes to feeders (see Exhibit 1). In a cable subscriber's home, a set-top converter was used to tune channels and to descramble authorized signals.

data transmission services for corporations; *Spectrum,* which provided Personal Communications Services (PCS), a new alternative to cellular phones; and *@Home,* which used two-way cable plant to deliver high speed Internet access to personal computers equipped with cable modems. By exploiting cable's "broadband" (*broad bandwidth*) capacity, cable modems could deliver data hundreds of times faster than conventional modems connected to ordinary "narrowband" telephone lines.

TCI's diversification had contributed substantially to its shareholders' wealth. For example, Liberty Media's equity in programming services was worth about $7 billion in late 1996, and TCI's equity in telecommunications ventures was worth over $3.5 billion. By comparison, TCI's core U.S. cable systems had a market value in excess of $22 billion (including $14 billion in debt that they supported).

The U.S. Cable Television Industry in 1996

Ninety-four million U.S. households—nearly 97% of total households—were "passed" by a cable system in 1996 (that is, cable plant had been built in their neighborhood), and 68% of these homes subscribed to cable services (Exhibit 3). By 1996, the cable industry had consolidated to the point where the 50 largest multiple system operators (MSOs) collectively served 89% of total industry customers; the ten largest served 64%.

Cable Technology Trends. In 1996, most cable operators were upgrading their plant by installing fiber optic transmission technology. By replacing coaxial copper with fiber optic lines, they could improve signal reliability and reception quality, increase channel capacity, and support the introduction of two-way services. To compensate for the gradual attenuation of signals as they were transmitted through copper lines, coaxial cable plant required amplifiers spaced at regular intervals to boost signal strength. Each amplifier introduced a small amount of distortion, which accumulated as the signal passed through successive amplifiers, eventually degrading reception quality. Amplifiers also experienced periodic failures, exposing downstream customers to service outages. By contrast, over the distances covered in typical cable systems, fiber lines required no amplifiers. Because it was expensive to rebuild an entire cable system, cable operators were replacing only a portion of their coaxial copper plant with fiber. Specifically, Hybrid Fiber/Coaxial (HFC) architectures replaced upstream copper trunk and feeder lines (the lines closer to the headend) with fiber to the point where nodes of roughly 500 homes were each served by unique fiber lines. Downstream, the existing copper feeder and drop lines were kept intact. HFC architectures thus eliminated, on average, all but four of the 20 amplifiers typically required in all-copper plant, substantially improving signal reliability and quality (Exhibit 1).

HFC architectures also allowed cable operators to more readily expand channel capacity by increasing the bandwidth of the remaining amplifiers. With long cascades of amplifiers in all-copper plant, high bandwidth amplifiers could significantly degrade reception quality, because they produced more distortion than their low bandwidth counterparts. In tandem with HFC upgrades, many cable operators were replacing the 350 and 450 megahertz (MHz) amplifiers that had limited all-copper cable plant to about 50 channels of analog television programming with 750 MHz amplifiers, which could deliver about 100 channels. Furthermore, with HFC architectures, it was easier and cheaper to install modules in the remaining amplifiers activating a reverse path, allowing customers to send signals from their set-top boxes back to the headend (e.g., pushing a "buy" button on their remote control to authorize viewing of a "pay-per-view" boxing match). The combination of upgraded amplifiers and the subdivision of the cable plant into 500 home nodes (each served by a unique set of two-way fiber lines) vastly increased potential channel capacity, allowing cable operators to introduce new services, including high-speed Internet access (through cable modems) and cable-delivered telephone service.

In 1996, cable operators also were beginning to replace analog set-top converters with digital converters, which employed compression technology to significantly increase channel capacity.[2] Combining fiber, amplifier upgrades, and compression technologies would allow cable operators to provide "video-on-demand" and a broad range of interactive multimedia services. Since each fiber line could carry a different set of at least 500 compressed channels to a node serving 500 homes, a unique channel could be dedicated to each home "on demand," using servers to provide access to a vast array of programming options. However, between 1993 and

[2]Compression involved three steps. First, a digital signal was processed using algorithms that discarded duplicated information in successive intervals of the signal. Second, the compressed digital signal was modulated onto the cable plant. Compression allowed cable operators to transmit as many as 10 or even 20 digital channels in each six megahertz block of bandwidth normally required for a single analog channel. Finally, using a set-top box with advanced processing capabilities, the digital signal was decompressed (essentially, running the algorithms in reverse) and converted to analog format for display.

1996, market trials of interactive television (e.g., Time Warner in Orlando) had been plagued by technical setbacks and cost overruns.

Cable Regulation. After a period of deregulation that began in 1986, Congress had reregulated cable rates in 1992 in response to charges that the industry had been too aggressive in exploiting its new pricing flexibility. To encourage competition from telephone companies and direct-to-home (DTH) satellite broadcasters, Congress in 1992 also required that vertically-integrated MSOs make their programming services available to competitors at fair terms (see Exhibit 4 for a list of the largest cable programming services and their owners).

During 1996, Congress reversed course and deregulated the cable industry as part of a sweeping revision of communications law. The 1996 Communications Act specified that cable rate regulation would expire in 1999, and it removed most of the legal and regulatory barriers that had prevented cable and telephone companies from entering each other's businesses. The legislation, supported by the Clinton Administration, was intended to promote competition between infrastructure companies, and thereby encourage technological innovation and the rapid deployment of the "information superhighway."

Competition to Cable. Despite these regulatory developments, by 1996, most local telephone companies ("telcos") had scaled back their previously ambitious plans to "overbuild" cable operators' plant with their own HFC networks. Three factors appeared to reduce the telcos' enthusiasm for competition. First, compared to cable operators, telcos would face a cost disadvantage in building HFC networks. Telcos would be forced to build, at great expense, new coaxial plant in the "last mile" of their networks, between fiber nodes and customers' homes. New coaxial lines would be needed to carry video signals, because the telco's existing "twisted-pair" copper lines were designed to carry narrowband voice transmissions, not broadband video signals.[3] By contrast, cable operators could simply upgrade their existing coaxial feeder lines in the last mile of their plant. Second, based on the results of market trials, telcos and cable operators increasingly were aware that head-to-head competition could lead to aggressive price cutting and escalating programming and marketing costs. Third, the Communications Act of 1996 had granted the seven Regional Bell Operating Companies (RBOCs) permission to offer long distance telephone service, relaxing a ban that these large local phone companies had faced since they were divested from AT&T in 1983. Most industry observers considered the lucrative long distance business to be a more attractive target than risky and expensive cable markets.

While the prospect of competition from telcos was fading—at least temporarily—by 1996, direct-to-home satellite broadcasting (also known as "direct broadcast satellite" service, or DBS) had emerged as a serious threat to cable. In 1994, General Motors' Hughes unit and its joint venture partners had launched DirecTV, a high-powered DTH service that used digital compression technology to deliver 180 channels directly to an 18 inch dish mounted outside a subscriber's home. By 1996, three DTH competitors—DirecTV, Primestar (owned by a consortium of cable operators, including TCI), and EchoStar, an aggressive startup that offered a low priced service—provided all of the programming services available on cable, plus dozens of channels of pay-per-view movies and sports. For example, DirecTV's NFL package, not available on cable, gave subscribers access to every NFL game, not just those games broadcast by TV stations in their local markets. Growth for DTH services had exceeded many analysts' expectations, with 4 million homes subscribing at year-end 1996. About half of these homes were passed by cable.

In February of 1997, the threat of DTH competition escalated when Rupert Murdoch's News Corp. announced plans to merge its American Sky Broadcasting, which had secured orbital slots for DTH service but had not yet launched satellites, with EchoStar. The merged entity was dubbed "Deathstar" by cable operators because it planned to use its enormous combined channel capacity to add local TV stations' signals to its programming lineup in the largest U.S. markets, neutralizing a competitive advantage that cable had over DTH. Previously, due in part to constraints on satellite transmission capacity, DTH satellites had not rebroadcast signals from the local television stations in a subscriber's community. DTH subscribers needed separate roof-top antennas to receive those stations' signals directly, and some experienced reception problems.

[3] An alternative to HFC architectures, "Digital Subscriber Line" (DSL) technology, could allow telcos to deliver digitally compressed video signals using their existing twisted-pair telephone lines. However, the lines typically had to be reconditioned before they could carry DSL signals, often at great expense. Also, due to limitations in propagating signals over twisted-pair copper phone lines, DSL was not expected to be available to the one-half of homes located more than 18,000 feet from a phone company central switching office.

Cable Industry Profitability and Stock Market Performance. Despite reregulation and the emergence of competition during the 1990s, cable system operators generated solid revenue growth and attractive and stable operating cash flow (EBITDA) margins, averaging 43% of revenue in 1996 (Exhibit 5). However, operating cash flow did not equate to free cash flow (defined by cable operators as EBITDA less interest payments, taxes, and capital expenditures). Most cable operators maintained high debt leverage to fund acquisitions and upgrades, so interest payments averaged 19% of revenue in 1996. Capital expenditures were escalating as cable operators aggressively upgraded their plant to prepare for competition; they averaged $95 per subscriber in 1996 (or 19% of revenues) and had nearly doubled since 1993. In response to concerns about capital spending and the risk of competition, MSOs' stock prices had been flat since 1994, in the midst of an exceptional bull market for equities (Exhibits 6 and 7).

TCI's History

TCI was founded in 1956 by Bob Magness, an Oklahoma cottonseed salesman and part-time rancher. Magness first heard about cable when he stopped to help two entrepreneurs who were having car trouble. He promptly sold his cattle and mortgaged his ranch to build a cable system in Memphis, Texas. Through acquisitions and franchising, TCI had become one of the largest MSOs when Magness took the company public in 1970. However, TCI's balance sheet was severely overextended by 1973, and the company was on the brink of bankruptcy when Magness hired John Malone as CEO. Malone, then the 32 year-old president of Jerrold Electronics, the leading cable equipment manufacturer, had a Ph.D. in operations research and previously had worked at Bell Labs and McKinsey & Company. Malone recalled:

> Cable stocks had been running up in response to a regulatory thaw. With debt and equity markets open, Magness went on an acquisition binge, but the financing window closed for cable companies when the new CFO at TelePrompTer, the largest MSO, blew the whistle on some flaky accounting at that company. In 1973, with interest rates rising, we had $126 million of mostly floating rate debt, revenue of just $23 million, and no cash flow to speak of. Our stock price had fallen from $37 in 1972 to less than $1. So my first job was to deal with the banks.

Cable penetration grew rapidly after HBO, a premium programming service created and owned by Time Inc., began distributing its signal via satellite in 1975; investor interest in the industry soon was revived. In 1978, TCI exploited its scale and played an important role in HBO's early success when it sold its competing premium service to HBO and granted HBO access to TCI's 700,000 subscribers. In exchange, HBO agreed to pay for the expensive earth stations that TCI required to downlink its signal and TCI received a significant discount in the subscriber fees it paid to HBO.

While TCI's balance sheet was stronger by the early 1980s, the company still lacked the capital to bid for big city franchises, and, in any case, its managers believed that the competition for such franchises had become over-heated. Instead, TCI expanded by acquiring suburban and small town cable systems, employing a range of innovative deal structures and financing techniques in the face of persistent capital constraints. For example, TCI acquired equity ownership positions ranging from 20 to 50% in 35 "affiliate" MSOs, often as an interim step to a complete merger. Negotiating on behalf of this extended family of companies, TCI increased its "footprint" and hence its leverage with programming services. Since outside investors provided much of the affiliates' equity, TCI also attained greater effective scale per dollar of TCI equity investment. Finally, TCI's affiliates provided benchmarks for managing TCI's own cable systems. Malone said, "From a day-to-day operating perspective, an entrepreneur almost always will do a better job than a hired manager in a hierarchical corporation."

When it formed joint ventures with three large media companies—Scripps Howard, Knight-Ridder, and Taft Broadcasting—TCI tapped another pool of capital as well as a source of political respectability. Corporate reputations were important for securing franchises, and TCI's had been tarnished by hard-nosed tactics like switching off the programming in its Vail, Colorado, system in the midst of stalled rate negotiations in 1973. TCI ran a blank screen with the mayor's home phone number instead! The joint ventures allowed TCI's cash-rich partners to expand in cable through off-balance sheet vehicles, avoiding earnings per share dilution. Malone recognized that concerns about the dilutive impact of cable acquisitions also might hold down TCI's stock price, and he successfully sold Wall Street analysts and institutional investors on the concept—then novel—of valuing cable companies based on operating cash flow (EBITDA), rather than book earnings.

By 1985, TCI was the largest MSO: it directly owned systems serving 3.7 million of the U.S. cable industry's 35 million basic subscribers, and through joint ventures and affiliates, it influenced management in systems serving one million additional customers. The next largest MSO, Time Inc.'s ATC, then controlled 2.5 million subscribers. During the second half of the 1980s, two factors encouraged TCI to complete a series of large acquisitions that consolidated its position as the cable industry's leader. First, liquidity increased in both debt and equity markets. As Malone recalled, "When capital structures were 'Milkenized' [a reference to Drexel's junk bond czar], we were able to help companies like Heritage [the tenth largest MSO] complete management buyouts. Also, as we grew, our own equity became more widely traded, and could be used as currency to finance deals." Second, TCI's managers realized that the company's ability to guarantee carriage in millions of homes made it an attractive equity partner for new programming services. The rapidly appreciating value of both TCI's programming investments and its cable system assets contributed to strong growth in TCI's stock price: one dollar invested in the company in 1975 was worth $800 by 1989.[4]

The early 1990s brought aggressive expansion into the United Kingdom and other international markets, along with a recognition that competition was looming in domestic markets. In 1992, the company acquired 50% of Teleport and announced plans to employ digital compression technology to deliver 500 channels of programming. In 1993, after intensive negotiations with AT&T, IBM, and Microsoft failed to yield partnerships to exploit interactive broadband technologies, TCI announced a plan to merge with Bell Atlantic, a phone company, in a stock deal valued at $33 billion. The Bell Atlantic deal was motivated by a concern that the Clinton Administration would promote competition on terms unfavorable to cable. Malone and Magness felt that TCI needed a strategic partner with capital, technology, and political clout. However, the merger fell apart after Bell Atlantic's stock price declined by over 20%, due in large part to shareholders' concerns that it would cut dividends to fund ambitious upgrade plans. Malone also was concerned that Bell Atlantic and TCI would have been forced to make unreasonable concessions to the government to secure regulatory approval for the merger.

TCI's managers had long been prolific deal makers: between 1973, when Malone joined as CEO, and 1994, the company had completed 650 acquisitions, divestitures, and joint ventures.[5] After merger plans with Bell Atlantic collapsed, the pace of deal making at TCI accelerated. The company continued to cultivate a relationship with Microsoft, announcing plans in 1994 to test Microsoft's server technology and to acquire a 20% stake in Microsoft Network. Also in 1994, TCI and three other large MSOs joined with Sprint (a large telephone company) in a joint venture called "Spectrum" that bid over $2 billion in government auctions to acquire PCS frequencies. During 1995, TCI acquired a controlling interest in @Home; entered a joint venture with Rupert Murdoch's News Corporation that challenged ESPN's dominance in sports programming; and backed Barry Diller's plans to launch a new broadcasting network. During 1994 and 1995, TCI also acquired several large MSOs in deals worth over $4 billion in cash and stock, boosting its subscriber base by 21%.

Managing Strategy at TCI

By aggressively pursuing the economies of scale and scope available to cable system operators, TCI had evolved into a large, diversified, global company (see Exhibit 8 for summary financial statements). TCI's top management had to attend to multiple markets, including cable systems, cable programming, telephony, DTH satellite broadcasting, and Internet services. Turbulence in all of those markets implied the need for constant vigilance and for the ongoing reassessment of strategies to determine whether events had rendered strategies obsolete. Turbulence also meant that new opportunities could emerge rapidly, and the capital intensive nature of many of those opportunities suggested that first movers might be able to create sustainable advantage. Finally, the breadth and capital intensive nature of opportunities available to TCI implied that the company might, at times, be able to profitably invest more capital than it could raise on reasonable terms. Consequently, the ability to establish and revise strategic priorities was critical.

Malone addressed these challenges by employing a "top-down" management style well suited to a deal-driven, turbulent environment. He had assembled a network of contacts inside and outside of TCI that kept him

[4]Ken Auletta, "John Malone: Flying Solo," *The New Yorker,* February 7, 1994, pp. 52–67.

[5]Auletta.

well informed. He relied on his deep industry experience to synthesize strategies. Secure in his position by virtue of his large personal equity stake in TCI, Malone then was willing to act decisively in the face of uncertainty. Two aspects of TCI's culture supported this top-down approach to strategic management. First, ensuring an open flow of information was a strongly ingrained cultural value at TCI. Brendan Clouston, President of TCI Communications (which held TCI's wholly-owned cable system operations) in 1996, noted, "There's an incredible honesty and lack of defensiveness or ego in our decision making. The one thing John won't tolerate is a lack of openness. When we have trouble, it's an honest autopsy. There's never any recrimination or asking, 'Who screwed this up?"' Second, TCI's managers were comfortable with conflict: they challenged each other and Malone, sharpening TCI's strategies in the process.

Processing Information. Observers inside and outside the company said that Malone had an exceptionally strong and flexible intellect.[6] Jerry Kern, a senior partner at Baker & Botts, and a TCI Board member who had served as the company's outside counsel since 1977, noted, "With John Malone, you're dealing with perhaps the best processor of information among Fortune 500 CEOs." To make sense of the heavy flow of data that reached him, Malone also relied on his 25 years of cable industry experience. For example, as a result of his involvement in structuring so many deals, Kern said, "Malone understands tax law better than most tax lawyers."

In meetings, Malone verbalized his thought processes—not just his conclusions. He described a problem from different perspectives and traced multiple, complex cause-and-effect sequences to better understand TCI's options. Through this approach, Malone constantly subjected his ideas to challenges from other members of TCI's management team. Malone said:

> I've always had a devil's advocate. Or more than one. For years it was Donne Fisher, our CFO. I would say to Donne, 'I know we're as poor as churchmice, but if I could buy Warner Cable's Pittsburgh system, we could do great things for our position there. Step over the question of how we'd pay for it. If we don't buy them now, sooner or later they'll figure out the same thing. Then we'll have to sell, because they have the high ground. And I think I can buy it now, cheap.' Donne would come back and say, 'This will push us over the edge; the rating agencies will throw us out.' So you keep bargaining. If you can turn around your devil's advocate, you probably have a deal.

Malone's tendency to "think out loud" could be difficult for less experienced managers to follow. Malone acknowledged, "I like to check my thinking, and sometimes I serve as my own devil's advocate. This can confuse my managers, so I'm very careful to only implement changes through the line organization." Senior executives at TCI explained that one role they played was translating Malone's ideas for their subordinates. Peter Barton, Liberty Media's President in 1996, said:

> A big mistake a lot of people make is thinking that when John says something, he means it. He has an amazing mind, one that works like a Rubik's cube. He thinks while he talks. He's capable of the ultimate form of sophistication in thought: holding two seemingly disparate ideas in his mind at the same time. Now, if you happen to tune in at that time, he'll tell you two different things. Or, maybe he'll only tell you one part of it. But you're a fool if you say, 'OK, John wants me to do this.' What John is doing is balancing these opposing views.

In addition to testing his ideas, Malone sometimes deliberately kept strategies fluid as they were being formulated, because he was concerned that managers might fixate on one option, then find it difficult to adapt if circumstances changed. He said:

> I often have a model in my head that's more complex and thought out than any shared perspective held by our management team. I'll keep bringing my team along, because sooner or later I'll want consensus. But I don't want consensus when I'm creating the model, I just need it when I implement. What I've found is that if you give people too much, too early, they find it hard to move to the next generation strategy. So, I try to maintain somewhat of a state of confusion, in terms of what our internal model is, until I've convinced myself that I know where I want to go. Then, I lock it up.

Willingness to Act Decisively. Facing high levels of uncertainty, TCI's managers confronted inevitable tradeoffs between investing in new opportunities early to capture

[6]For example, *Fortune* ("High Noon for John Malone," C. Loomis & A. Kupfer, January 13, 1997, p. 68) described Malone as "the man often called the smartest guy in the business," and the *Wall Street Journal* ("TCI Returns to Its Roots," Mark Robichaux, January 2, 1997) said that he "has long enjoyed a reputation as one of the most astute and influential visionaries of how new technologies are transforming the media world."

first mover advantages, and delaying commitment in order to gather more data and thereby reduce the risk of pursuing a flawed strategy. Compared with many CEOs, Malone was more secure in his position and therefore more willing to act decisively in the face of uncertainty. He owned a large block of TCI stock and controlled 40% of shareholder votes in late 1997. Malone contrasted his security to the situation confronting a CEO with a small equity position. He said, "Corporate managers are very risk averse. They know that if they make one mistake, they'll be looking for a job. For a hired manager, it's all downside."

While these factors promoted rapid strategic decision making and risk taking at TCI, aspects of Malone's management style also could slow decision making. Malone rarely gave direct orders, and as noted above, managers could struggle to decode the action implications of his multidimensional, rapidly evolving situational assessments. Clouston noted:

> I've heard managers at TCI say, the quickest ways to get in trouble here are to do *everything* John says or *nothing* he says. In fact, he never really tells you to do anything! I've never had a direct instruction from him in 15 years. Instead, I have to try to understand his point of view, then make my decisions accordingly.

Trouble in Late 1996

Malone had reason to question TCI's strategy when he learned about the company's third quarter financial results for 1996. He had been expecting double-digit growth in cash flow in the wake of a recent rate increase, but operating cash flow (before the effect of acquisitions) grew only 3%. TCI also reported an unexpected loss of 70,000 subscribers, due largely to competition from DTH services. Malone anticipated that the rating agencies, which recently had put TCI on "credit watch," would react with alarm to these developments, and that the company's stock price would continue a downward slide that had begun in 1995. He said, "The stock was telling us our strategy was flawed." Malone provided a diagnosis of the company's problems:

> Revenues came in more or less as predicted, but it all disappeared in expense growth. That got my attention! Margins in the core cable business, which had been as high as 50% as recently as 1992, were down to 38%. Half of the change was related to a deterioration in the spread between our pricing and programming costs. Programming license fees had outpaced our rate increases for years, and we had added some new services to help justify our recent rate hike. The rest of the margin erosion was from SG&A growth, mostly related to corporate projects: new call centers for customer service reps; a new billing system; staff added to develop our digital, data, and phone businesses. It was hard to say whether these expenses were one-time or recurring.
>
> At the same time, our debt was up, because our capital spending program was so aggressive. But our technology strategy was out of sync with our top priority, which was to address the threat posed by satellites' channel capacity. To do that, we needed to deploy digital video quickly, as a mass market offering. But the fact that we had positioned digital as a high-end service in our Hartford rollout [where TCI was testing new services], well, that was brain damaged! Even worse, we were getting ahead of ourselves, spending heavily on fiber upgrades so we could roll out data and voice communications, at the expense of protecting our traditional video business.
>
> The company was dysfunctional. We couldn't do anything, because we were counting on cascading miracles. We needed a massive software program before we could turn on our new call centers; we needed the call centers before we could roll out new services; and we needed to upgrade the plant before we offered the services. The probability of consecutive technological breakthroughs in an appropriate time frame was becoming zero. We needed to fundamentally rethink our capital program.

As Malone analyzed the company's problems, he also was surprised at the degree to which authority over cable system marketing and programming decisions had become centralized at headquarters. According to Malone, centralization had followed from the complex bookkeeping requirements introduced when the government reregulated cable rates, and the need to ensure that TCI met commitments it had made with programming services regarding terms of carriage:

> Good guys from middle management told me, 'We're not supposed to have anything to do with this stuff.' But how can you take responsibility for a system P&L if you have no control over programming or marketing? It was a shock to me, how far we'd centralized those functions! Other MSOs like Time Warner were *decentralizing* their operations. I guess they decided their system managers were smart enough to figure out the new rate rules and their programming deals!

Marvin Jones, a cable industry veteran who was hired in the Fall of 1996 to run a portion of TCI's cable systems, agreed with Malone's assessment and offered additional insights. He noted that the company was still wrestling with the challenge of integrating the many cable systems it had acquired. In response to the resulting confusion, headquarters management had felt the need to increase control. After decision making authority was centralized, however, no-one had clear profit accountability.

Malone acknowledged being somewhat surprised at TCI's margin erosion, the state of its capital program, and the extent to which cable system operations had become centralized. He explained that he had delegated authority to Brendan Clouston, who ran TCI's wholly-owned cable systems, allowing Malone to focus on TCI's programming and technology investments. Malone recalled, "I was catching flack from outside investors like Gordon Crawford [a money manager at Capital Research, which owned over 7% of TCI's stock] who would call and say, 'Why aren't you doing this or that?' I'd answer, 'Why don't you talk to Brendan?' I was trying to empower the guy so he could drive the business. Well, I wasn't getting the drift from my investors." Malone told *The Wall Street Journal* (1/2/97), "My ambition was to be more of an investor and director and to be less of an operating guy, and every time I look back and see poor Brendan, I see I've created quite a monster of a company here, and I had better help out from time to time." Malone explained his decision to take a 'hands-on' role in TCI's turnaround:

> A week or two after we saw the third quarter numbers, Bob Magness became seriously ill; he passed away soon afterward. That was unexpected, a bolt out of the blue. My patience was exhausted. We were lagging seriously behind the rest of the cable pack in terms of operating results [Exhibit 9]. I'd embraced the belief that the reason was the deferral of our rate increases, when other MSOs were taking them. So when that clearly wasn't the solution, I got worried. We had serious underfunded debt obligations. If Bob hadn't gotten ill, I might have said, 'It will all work out.' But that old impulse came back: I couldn't let Bob down!

Malone took three steps in the Fall of 1996 to arrest TCI's deteriorating financial performance. First, after analyzing TCI's margins, Malone set a goal of cutting SG&A costs by $100 million through a workforce reduction. He said, "We needed to show something fast to the rating agencies, without unduly disrupting customer service." In December, TCI announced that 2,500 of its 35,000 employees would be terminated. Many of these employees worked as marketers and installers. Second, Malone formulated a plan to reduce TCI's programming expenses by about $200 million by dropping certain programming services, then replacing them with new services whose owners were willing to make marketing co-op payments (reported by the trade press to be in the range of $5 to $10 per subscriber) to secure carriage and promote viewership. Third, Malone froze capital expenditures, except for spending related to bare-bones maintenance, pending a review of the company's technology strategy.

By January of 1997, Malone had concluded that TCI needed to accelerate the deployment of digital converters to respond to competition from satellite broadcasters. This represented a departure from the two-stage technology strategy previously in place at TCI. In the first stage, the company had been planning to upgrade its transmission capacity by adding fiber optic technology, replacing downstream amplifiers to boost bandwidth, and installing upstream amplifiers to activate a reverse path for two-way services. Following these transmission upgrades, in the second stage, TCI had been planning simultaneously to launch digital video, telephone, and high-speed Internet access services. Confident that existing one-way all-copper cable plant could carry digital video signals, Malone instead concluded that TCI should introduce digital converters *before* the first stage transmission capacity upgrades were completed. Malone commented on the shift in strategy:

> Most of our managers held a strong commitment to a technology strategy that had been in place for five years, with no one willing to challenge the logic. But when we converged on this rebuild architecture five years ago, digital was just on the drawing boards. The Internet was unknown. Wouldn't it be weird if the architecture we invented five years ago—the one that US WEST and other MSOs are still rolling out [Exhibit 10]—still made sense today, after so much change in technology and applications? My peers all say, 'What's John Malone doing, changing the game?' But what if we all decided that Orlando was the way to go, spending every nickel we could raise? Or if I had loved Bill Gates's first-generation servers so much I that I had decided to deploy them all over? My peers say, 'You have to have faith that the business will build after the deployment.' See, I'm just not willing to do that.

We're way ahead of the rest of the industry on digital. I'm the only guy sitting here saying, 'Wait a minute, I see an iceberg out there, called satellite.' I see this because I understand the technology of compression. I understand that Rupert Murdoch will be able to deliver local broadcast signals and serve multiple TV sets from a single receiver. It will take only two more years of microprocessor development to do this. Satellite scares me to death! It'll be price competitive, and our edge will disappear.

Malone believed that this new technology strategy would conserve capital, allowing TCI to boost free cash flow and reduce its debt. He announced these new financial objectives at a conference sponsored by Bear Stearns in October 1996, surprising investors and other cable industry executives. Malone attracted considerable attention with a promise that TCI would move from a free cash flow deficit of $750 million in 1996 to positive free cash flow (after interest payments and capital expenditures) of between $750 million and $1 billion in 1997. *Broadcasting & Cable* (11/4/96) reported one investor as saying, "The man is too smart to stand in front of that crowd and make statements that are easily measured and not deliver."[7] Less generously, *Fortune* said the projection "would amount to a miracle if it occurs."[8]

As of January 1997, Wall Street investors had responded to TCI's turnaround strategy with skepticism: TCI's stock price still languished near its five-year low of $11. *Broadcasting & Cable* quoted a securities analyst as saying, "I remain unconvinced this is the best long-term plan for shareholders. So much of the value is built on leveraging broadband across three services [video, phone, and data]. To pull back from that and put everything into digital may help the core business, but make it tough to justify the historic trading multiples [of 9 to 12 times EBITDA]. Companies that stick with a video-only strategy could be heading down into multiples in the four, five, six range."[9]

Accelerating TCI's Turnaround

When he accepted Malone's offer to join TCI, Leo Hindery ran InterMedia Partners, which controlled 1.4 million cable subscribers through a series of limited partnerships in which TCI had equity stakes ranging from 35 to 49%. Prior to building InterMedia into the ninth largest MSO in just seven years, Hindery, a 49 year-old Stanford MBA, had been CFO of Chronicle Publishing, a diversified media company; an investment banker at Paribas Becker; and an executive at Utah International, a natural resources company acquired by General Electric.

Hindery discussed the challenges he faced upon joining TCI:

We have five constituencies here, all of whom were aggrieved. Our shareholders were out of control. Our customers were leaving. Our employees were demoralized due to the RIF [reduction-in-force]. Regulators—national and local—were unhappy because we seemed to be backing away from our commitment to infrastructure spending. And the rest of the cable industry was frustrated with us. We'd long been the industry's leader, but we weren't acting like one. For example, we'd become inattentive to trade associations. So we had to attend to the concerns of all these groups, without giving preference to any one.

Hindery moved decisively to address these problems and to accelerate TCI's turnaround. His first step was to rebuild the top management team. Within a few weeks of Hindery's arrival, 25 senior executives left the company, including Clouston and Barton. Marvin Jones was tapped to head TCI's wholly-owned cable systems. Jones reflected on the challenges he encountered in his new position:

Upon visiting our systems, I found that no-one could make decisions. We had been paralyzed, with many redundant processes in place because no one wanted to hold up their hand and say, 'This is how it should be done.'

In late 1996, TCI went into crash mode to reduce expenses. The good news was that we got rid of redundant processes. The bad news was that the RIF was done in a fairly blunt-edged way. Sure, in hindsight, you would do some things differently, but we needed to get control. And sometimes to get control, you just stop doing things.

We had been doing too much promotion-driven marketing, and that was leading to expensive churn of our customer base. But when the RIF eliminated those promotions, it also wiped out much of our marketing capability. Well, this business routinely loses 25% of its customers every year, as people move or lose interest in our services, so you can't stop marketing altogether! Our actions in the Fall of 1996 worsened our subscriber losses in the following

[7] "Taking Stock of Malone's Message," Price Colman, *Broadcasting & Cable,* Nov. 4, 1996, p. 57.
[8] "High Noon for John Malone," C. Loomis & A. Kupfer, *Fortune,* January 13, 1997, p. 69.
[9] "Taking Stock of Malone's Message," Price Colman, *Broadcasting & Cable,* Nov. 4, 1996, p. 57.

months. Simultaneously, we began launching digital across the country, a major undertaking for any MSO. So we needed to quickly reassemble our field marketing teams, and we needed to build a local mindset and accountability.

TCI developed a plan for delegating more authority over marketing, programming, engineering, and government affairs to the field, and for determining the reporting requirements for managing in a more decentralized manner. Capital budgeting processes were revamped, and the field gained more control over capital spending decisions related to routine plant maintenance.

Hindery and Jones believed that TCI could strengthen field marketing capabilities by clustering its geographically scattered cable systems into a few regions. Within each region, systems could share the cost of marketing managers and promotional programs. TCI could realize other economies by clustering its systems. For example, it could dispatch field technicians more efficiently and spread the cost of equipment required for new services, such as Internet routers and telecommunications switches. Hindery moved quickly to restructure TCI's system portfolio to capture such economies. By year-end 1997, he had engineered more than 25 system exchanges and joint ventures; four million of TCI's fourteen million wholly-owned subscribers were spun into partnerships that would be managed by other MSOs, with TCI retaining equity stakes ranging from 20 to 50%. Through the partnerships, and by trading some systems with other MSOs, TCI was able to concentrate its system portfolio into six major markets where it was the dominant MSO (Chicago, Dallas, Denver, Pittsburgh, San Francisco, and Seattle) and ten other cities where it controlled a large share of cable customers. TCI also managed to reduce the ratio of debt to cash flow for its wholly-owned cable systems by shifting debt into the new partnerships.

The Team at the Top

In June of 1998, Malone reflected on the working relationship he and Hindery had developed over the past fifteen months:

> It's been working very well. The biggest fear from his point of view is that I'll undercut him, either internally or externally. The biggest fear I have is that I'll get cut off from the flow of information I need to formulate strategy. But with experience, we're gaining confidence that these problems can be managed.
>
> We perceive raw risk differently, but that's not necessarily a bad thing. He might resent the expression, but his risk aversion is more cosmetic than mine. I don't care whether debts are on- or off-balance sheet. I think if Leo can get it off-balance sheet, he thinks he's accomplished something material. My fear is that if your treasury department forgets about it, it will come back to bite you. I'd rather eat my losses up front, write them off, take the tax benefit, find some solace in taking the hit, and get it behind us. So I'm the one who usually wants to overstate problems. I don't give a damn about earnings; I'm more interested in building shareholder wealth.
>
> I'm also a little longer-sighted, more patient than Leo, more tolerant. He wants to make it all happen tomorrow. Take the example of our investment in [affiliate MSO] Lenfest. With agreements in place we can gain control of that company within several years. But Leo is impatient: he says, 'Here's an asset that's not doing us a lot of good; it could be clustered better and run better.' It just drives Leo nuts that he cannot improve the life of that asset. But I know we've got the hook set with Lenfest; we'll get there over time. I'm also more patient about losing money on startups that may be a little questionable. Leo's GE background comes through occasionally: if a startup's not successful early, he's more likely to want to kill it.
>
> Leo's been a huge hit with the Wall Street community because he delivers on his promises. Related to that, he's more focused on quarter-to-quarter results. Wall Street loves that! But to me, it's a trap, because sooner or later you have to do something stupid to keep your track record. My strategy is more eclectic, a 'screw you' attitude that says, 'If you don't see the value of my assets, then sell your stock, and I'll buy it back.' Of course, Leo's right too: we can use Wall Street's support. A strong stock is a great currency for doing deals.
>
> So, all in all, it's a great fit, because we complement each other. The partnership provides balance that each of us alone might be lacking. My only disappointment is that between us, we've stirred up enough hornets nests that I haven't been able to step back from day-to-day management like Magness did. I'm intimately involved in lots of strategy issues. What's happened is Leo's ability to implement is profoundly better than what we've had for the past ten years, so we're doing more, faster.

Investors agreed with Malone's assessment. Gordon Crawford of Capital Research, TCI's largest institutional shareholder, said, "Hiring Leo was the smartest thing John has ever done."[10]

Accelerating Digital Deployment

While TCI's operational turnaround was gathering momentum during 1997, senior management also was adjusting the company's technology strategy. Early in the year, Malone had focused the company on a defensive technology strategy that would accelerate the deployment of first-generation digital converters. By year-end, however, TCI was planning the rapid and widespread rollout of second-generation digital converters. These converters, which would function as network computers,[11] would not only harness digital compression to deliver significantly more video channels, but also would provide high-speed Internet access, integrate Web content with traditional television signals, and enable cable systems to provide telephone service. Malone explained the factors that led TCI to revise its technology strategy:

> First, we turned on the first-generation digital technology in some systems and it worked beautifully; it went from being a paper plan to a physical system. Likewise, decompression went from theory to practice. We've really got 12-to-1 compression ratios [i.e., 12 digital channels could be transmitted in the bandwidth required for a single analog channel], and the pictures are watchable. I started to look at the potential programming lineup, and it was a great proposition for the consumer.
>
> Second, microprocessor prices kept coming down. It helped when Bill Gates met with Cable Labs and told everyone we could have a $300 second-generation box. We got verification that this was not just a pipe dream. The box would cost $300, not $600; it would have a 200 MIPS [million instructions per second] processor, not 20; 16 megabytes of memory, not 2. It would have very powerful capabilities.

[10]Quoted in "Cable's Comeback Kid," Ronald Grover, *Business Week*, May 11, 1998, p. 87.

[11]With network computers, application software and files were downloaded over a network from a server into the network computer's memory for the duration of a user's session; operating system software could be similarly downloaded. Because they eliminated the need for a hard disk to permanently store application software and files, network computers would cost less than traditional personal computers. Sun Microsystems was promoting network computers that would run applications written in its Java programming language. The prospect of widespread adoption of network computers and Java posed a threat to Microsoft's hegemony: Java applications could run on any type of computer, independent of Windows or any other operating system.

Microsoft and the Open Cable Initiative

TCI's plans to deploy digital technologies gathered momentum following discussions with Microsoft in the Spring of 1997. In April, the Executive Committee (comprised of the CEOs of eight large MSOs and chaired by Malone) of Cable Labs, the industry's R&D consortium, visited Microsoft during a tour of Silicon Valley companies. In the Fall of 1996, Microsoft had acquired WebTV, which used TV sets to provide access to the World Wide Web. At the meeting in April, Bill Gates demonstrated WebTV's next generation of services, which would integrate Web content with traditional television signals. For example, WebTV could display a "click for more" icon during an advertisement, allowing a viewer to access additional information or even order the product. Bruce Ravenel, TCI's Executive Vice President—Interactive Services, recalled:

> Gates pulled off one of those classic 'blow-you-away' demos, saying, 'We can do this for you by incorporating your now proven digital technology into our WebTV box.' It was pretty cool the first time you saw it; the Executive Committee was very impressed. That triggered lots of activity at Cable Labs, including subsequent trips to Microsoft. Within about six weeks the Executive Committee received the broad outlines of a deal through which Microsoft would turnkey a system for the cable industry. At first, it sounded like a reasonable deal: Gates was willing to forego margin on the hardware in exchange for a stake in certain applications, in order to jump start the business.
>
> Around that time, in June of 1997, Microsoft signaled its commitment to cable by investing $1 billion in Comcast [the fourth largest MSO]. That got the industry's attention and Wall Street's as well: cable stocks really moved up. Shortly thereafter, in July of 1997, Gates met the Cable Labs Executive Committee in New York City to present a formal proposal for WebTV. At that meeting, Bill laid a terribly stinky egg. He basically proposed that Microsoft would control everything, crawling into half of our future revenues off the platform. It was an overreaching proposal that just fell on deaf ears; it was rejected on the spot.
>
> So, Cable Labs decided to entertain other offers. A subcommittee of industry executives that had been charged with evaluating Microsoft's business proposal developed what became the Open Cable initiative. We were clear on the model: we wanted non-proprietary, modular technology, expressly avoiding the vertical linkages between processor, operating system, and

applications that characterized the Win-Tel monopoly.[12] We sent out an RFP [request for proposal] from Cable Labs to a dozen big manufacturers. Oracle came back with their network computer; Intel was saying, 'We'll do it, we'll do it!' We drew out consumer electronics companies like Sony. Every major electronics manufacturer in the world was interested; they said they loved it in part because they saw an opportunity to put Microsoft in a box. That begged the question, what would be the right vendor strategy?

In the past, the cable industry had to scrounge around with just General Instruments and Scientific Atlanta for technology. Now, everybody in the world wanted to build advanced systems for us. And in that world of plenty John Malone was able to see an opportunity to do a deal with GI. They had just ousted their CEO and had split themselves into three companies. They were in desperate need of a future, and not unreasonably saw a huge threat to their existence. They couldn't continue with their old model of a closed proprietary system in the face of these new world-class electronics competitors. John sold them on a new future as a high volume assembler of others' technologies.

Malone negotiated a deal with GI that committed a group of large MSOs to a 15 million unit order for digital converters. In exchange, the MSOs would receive one warrant in GI stock for every converter they purchased. GI's stock surged on the news, and the value of each warrant quickly rose over $40. Ravenel said, "We had a fast moving train at that point, and it gained more momentum at Christmas-time in 1997 when TCI announced deals with Microsoft and Sun Microsystems to provide different software elements for our system. Those announcements were galvanizing events, because you saw the power of an open platform shared by Sun's Java and Microsoft. Everybody could see that'd we'd harnessed those two wild horses!"

By early 1998, the specifications for TCI's second-generation digital converter were set. The box would comply with Open Cable standards and would contain a 200 MIPS processor and sufficient memory to handle sophisticated graphics; a high speed cable modem with separate tuners for video and high speed data communications (which would allow the converter to simultaneously serve a TV in one room and a PC in another); and ports for storage devices and for "daisy-chaining" other hardware, such as PCs, printers, and digital VCRs.

[12] Win-Tel is a reference to "Microsoft **WIN**dows and In**TEL**," which had gained commanding shares of the markets for personal computer operating systems and microprocessors, respectively.

TCI's managers were still evaluating the applications they might deliver using these converters. Beyond offering a larger set of traditional television channels, the list was likely to include video-on-demand; high definition television channels; high speed Internet access; email; transactional marketing and information services that integrated Web content with traditional television signals (e.g., allowing subscribers to access statistics during a sports event); interactive games; Internet-protocol telephony; and video telephony (see Exhibits 11–15).

The Case for Ubiquitous Digital Deployment

As the courtship between Silicon Valley and the cable industry intensified, top management at TCI explored the idea of supplying second-generation digital converters to nearly all of TCI's cable subscribers, not just to customers responding to solicitations for new services. Malone said:

> Can the economics work for ubiquitous deployment? I laid this question on the world at the Western Show [a cable industry trade show] in November of 1997. Our back-of-the-envelope models showed that we were getting awfully close. You can go down the list of reasons why people would want ubiquity: AT&T would love to provide IP [Internet protocol] phone service; Madison Avenue needs broad reach. As we learned more about the cost and capability of the technology, I became intrigued with the notion of putting a digital box in *every* home. And as the market could embrace my enthusiasm, I could put my ideas forward. If I'd said this a year earlier, I'd have been a laughing stock!

Ubiquitous deployment could yield attractive deals with interactive marketers, for example, banks, travel agencies, or on-line book retailers. In exchange for preferential placement on the first screens that consumers encountered when they used TCI's digital services, TCI might receive cash payments from interactive marketers, a percentage of their transaction revenues, or possibly an equity interest in their online ventures. Ravenel said:

> For years we'd wrestled with a classic 'chicken-and-egg' problem in deploying advanced technologies. You can't deploy if you expect 25% penetration, because that's not enough volume to get box prices down. Everybody had broken their picks on the same problem for years and years. So John says, all of a

sudden, 'We're trying to solve the wrong problem. What changes if we think about *ubiquitous* deployment? 25% is not very compelling for marketers; they want to reach the whole market. Maybe some of those companies will help subsidize the box to get a preferred position on our service.

In 1998, many marketing companies were racing to build a presence on the Internet. Analysts spoke of a "land grab" in which first movers who established their brands and locked in customers would reap disproportionate rewards in the future. By providing preferential access to millions of potential customers, TCI could substantially improve an interactive marketer's competitive position. As the first MSO to provide such broad reach, TCI might be able to negotiate for equity stakes in new digital services, as it had in the past with cable programming and with technology ventures such as @Home, Teleport, and Sprint Spectrum. Malone said, "You get an opportunity to move up the food chain when you commit early."

After factoring in the value of the GI warrants and payments from parties interested in securing preferred access for their information and transactional services, TCI managers reasoned that the effective cost of second-generation digital converters could approach the $175 cost of advanced analog set-top boxes that other leading MSOs currently were deploying. So, they argued, ubiquitous digital deployment might well be affordable. Furthermore, the rapid, ubiquitous deployment of second-generation digital converters offered two other potential benefits. First, it could tap the unmet demand for interactive services in households that had not yet acquired a personal computer. Malone said, "Power users who can afford speed will want this. And those who haven't yet discovered the Net will like the TV set-top box because it will provide an easy, familiar, non-threatening way to enter. For the group that's not yet comfortable with PCs, transactional marketing on a TV set, where they've been viewing advertisements for years, will make perfect sense. I can develop a lot of services for that crowd if I can deliver scale."

Second, ubiquitous deployment would preempt competition from telephone companies seeking to deliver digital services. Malone said, "For now, we think our high speed Internet service is superior to anything the telcos can deliver. So digital deployment isn't really time-critical in that regard. But sooner or later the phone companies will figure this out, and if I can lock up a lot of share before they get in the game, that's good."

Malone, who deliberately sought devil's advocates when he formulated new strategies, said that with respect to the issue of ubiquitous digital deployment, his ideas were being tested by executives in other cable companies. Malone said, "It's Time Warner and Comcast telling me I'm nuts; it's the media. And Wall Street to some extent. But you have to run the risk of looking like a jackass in order to try out ideas like this digital strategy." Many senior managers in other MSOs believed that it would be a waste of money to install advanced digital converters in households that previously had never demonstrated interest in any services other than the basic tier of cable television programming. For example, Joe Collins, the CEO of Time Warner Cable, dismissed ubiquitous deployment: "To push these boxes out there as a field of dreams doesn't make sense."[13]

Malone acknowledged these concerns, and added one more:

> I'm increasingly convinced that this digital strategy could be a home run, but I'm worried that we might not fund it aggressively, because our free cash flow would suffer. You can't jump start this strategy without investing aggressively upfront. But if you do that, the rating agencies will eat you alive, because these days they see free cash flow [EBITDA minus interest, taxes, and capital expenditures] as a new figure of merit [in contrast to their past emphasis on EBITDA]. So, I'm exploring the idea of splitting the core cable company into two new tracking stocks.[14] Call them 'Newco' and 'Oldco.'

In the plan Malone was considering, Oldco would own TCI's existing coaxial cable plant, and would receive the revenues from analog basic and pay programming services (or the digital counterparts to those traditional services). Oldco would have minimal capital expenditures beyond routine maintenance, and thus would have

[13]Collins was quoted in "How Hot is Cable, Really?" A. Kupfer, *Fortune*, Feb. 16, 1998, p. 74. His comment about a 'field of dreams' is a reference to a film with the same title, in which the lead character ignores the protests of family and friends and constructs a baseball diamond on his farm, after hearing mystical voices that say, 'Build it, and they will come . . ..'

[14]Tracking stocks were securities that "tracked" the financial performance of a specific unit within a parent company (e.g., General Motors' "E-" and "H-" class stocks, which tracked its EDS and Hughes subsidiaries, respectively). Tracking stocks maintained separate financial statements and could pay their own dividends. However, for purposes of calculating income taxes, the tracking stock's earnings (or losses) were consolidated with those of the parent company's other operations. Also, the tracking stock's shareholders voted with the parent company's shareholders in electing a common board of directors.

strong, predictable cash flows. Newco would receive revenues from the expanded tiers of digital video channels and from new interactive and telecommunications services; it would bear the cost of upgrading TCI's plant to deliver those services, including capital expenditures on fiber and digital converters. Since the financial statements of tracking stocks remained consolidated for tax purposes, Newco's operating losses would still shelter taxes on Oldco's operating income. Malone elaborated:

> Oldco might get a valuation of 20 times free cash flow, like a radio broadcaster. And Newco would be one of these space-age companies with no cash flow, growing like crazy, with wonderful prospects. The market would value it under a completely different theory, discounting future cash flow streams. I think we might get a 30% bump in value for the combined entity.

Conclusion

TCI's operational turnaround program showed quick and impressive results. The company reported a 31% increase in operating cash flow in fiscal 1997, compared to 1996. In March 1998, Donaldson, Lufkin & Jenrette reported that TCI was on track to exceed the promises Malone had made in the Fall of 1996, when he told skeptical investors that TCI would generate $750 million to $1 billion of free cash flow in 1997. This cash flow was used to reduce TCI's debt; the company's debt-to-operating cash flow ratio declined from 5.0 at year-end 1996 to 3.8 at year-end 1997. In response, Moody's upgraded TCI's credit rating to "investment grade." Equity investors also reacted favorably to the improved financial results: TCI's stock rose from $13 in February of 1997 to $32.50 in May of 1998, a period during which other cable stocks roughly doubled in value and the S&P 500 gained 40%.

Furthermore, many investors were enthusiastic about TCI's growth prospects. With support from Silicon Valley, the costs and capabilities of digital technologies seemed certain to improve rapidly. The proliferation of the Internet would facilitate end-user interconnection and spur the development of compelling content, problems that had bedeviled past efforts to launch interactive TV technologies. Other observers, however, remained skeptical of TCI's aggressive technology strategy, noting that the company and the cable industry had failed to deliver on past promises. *Fortune* speculated that Malone's renewed enthusiasm for advanced technologies was a front, suggesting that he was "just blowing smoke, stirring his equity."[15]

TCI's top managers understood that perceptions could shape reality in the high velocity environment in which the company operated: a critical mass of optimistic partners could create a *de facto* technology standard; investor sentiment could determine whether funds were available for ambitious expansion plans; regulators and legislators could strangle industry initiatives. Tracking rapidly shifting perceptions compounded the challenges that Malone and Hindery faced as they considered whether to pursue the rapid and ubiquitous deployment of advanced digital technologies.

Unfortunately, TCI could not resolve uncertainties about the upside from ubiquitous digital deployment by testing the technology in a few markets. Some of the applications that TCI's managers envisioned were already available through the Internet, but many would need to be developed from scratch (e.g., services that integrated Web content with traditional TV advertising and programming), or would need to be revised substantially, to accommodate the lower display resolution of TV sets, compared to PC monitors. Interactive marketers and content providers were unlikely to undertake expensive application development efforts until they had some assurance they would eventually reach a mass market. Lacking a critical mass of compelling applications, market trials would be of limited value.

Since market trials were not feasible, TCI's managers faced a choice: should they deploy second-generation digital converters at the same pace as the rest of the cable industry, or commit to ubiquitous deployment on an accelerated timetable? Their decision hinged on several issues. Would first-mover advantages offset the added risk from accelerated deployment? Would TCI's newly decentralized field organization have the capability to market new services? Would TCI be able to shape deployment plans in the several million cable homes where it recently had become a minority investor? Would an 'Oldco/Newco' tracking stock arrangement increase investors' willingness to provide the capital needed for accelerated deployment?

---

[15] "How Hot is Cable, Really?" A. Kupfer, *Fortune*, Feb. 16, 1998, p. 70.

Exhibit 1

CABLE SYSTEM ARCHITECTURES

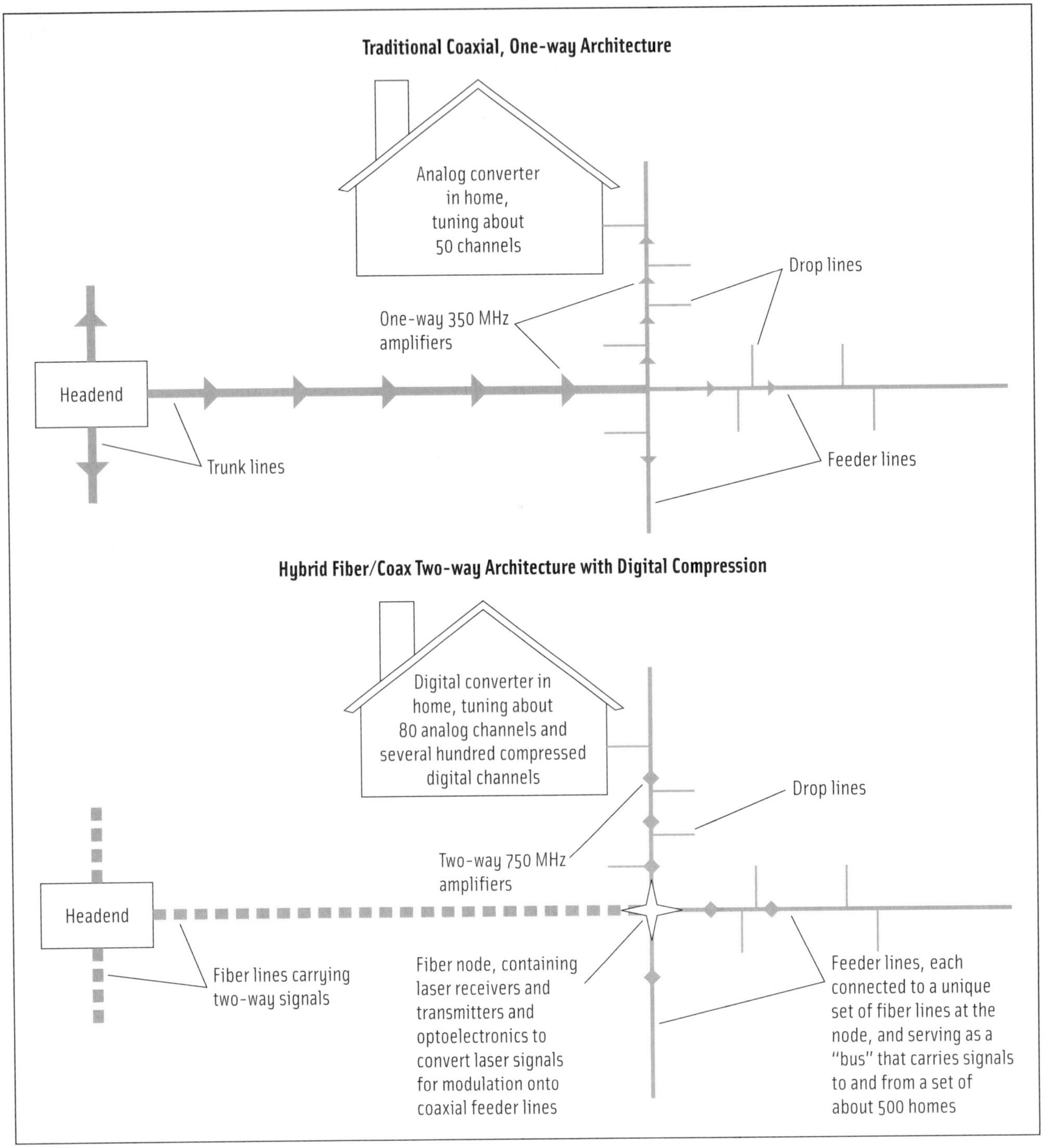

Source: TCI Engineering

Exhibit 2 MAJOR ASSETS OWNED BY TELE-COMMUNICATIONS, INC. EARLY 1997 cont.

TCI Communications
• Wholly-owned cable systems serving 14 million basic subscribers (value of equity and debt: $22 billion) • Non-consolidated investments in MSO affiliates (e.g., Lenfest Group; InterMedia Partners) serving about 3 million basic subscribers (value of TCI equity: $800 million)
TCI Technology Ventures (wholly owned by TCI Communications)
• 30% of *Sprint Spectrum* partnership (with Sprint, Comcast, and Cox) to develop Personal Communications Services (value of TCI equity: $1.4 billion) • 30% of publicly-traded *Teleport Communications Group,* (co-investors included MSOs Comcast, Cox, and MediaOne) providing telecommunications services to large business customers (value of TCI equity: $1.3 billion) • 45% of equity and 60% of voting power in *@Home* (co-investors included venture capital firm Kleiner Perkins, Comcast, and Cox) a high speed Internet access provider (value of TCI equity: $900 million) • 40% of shares and 85% of voting power in publicly-traded *United Video Satellite,* which: 1) owned Prevue, an electronic program guide; 2) distributed broadcast "superstation" signals (e.g., Chicago-based WGN) to cable headends; and 3) provided programming for the backyard earth station market (value of TCI equity: $300 million). Note that a portion of TCI's investment in United Video Satellite was held in Liberty Media. • 100% of *National Digital Television Center* ("Headend in the Sky"), providing compression, encryption, and uplinking services for satellite programmers (asset value: $150 million)
TCI International (also called TINTA; 83% owned by TCI Communications after 1995 IPO)
• 27.5% of *Telewest,* a publicly-traded UK MSO; co-investor was US WEST (value of TINTA equity: $1 billion) • 49% of UK satellite programmer *Flextech,* a public company (value of TINTA equity: $600 million) Other investments with an aggregate equity value of $1.2 billion, including: • 40% of cable system and 50% of programming ventures in Japan; co-investor was Sumitomo • 51% of *Cablevision, S.A.,* Argentina's largest MSO; interests in cable systems in France, Ireland, Israel, Chile, Malta, Dominican Republic, and Poland • 10% of Sky Latin America, a DTH business with Mexico's leading broadcaster, Grupo Televisa; Brazil's leading broadcaster, Globo; and News Corp. *Multithematique* partnership to develop digital channels with Canal Plus, France's leading premium programming service

(continued)

Exhibit 2 MAJOR ASSETS OWNED BY TELE-COMMUNICATIONS, INC. EARLY 1997 cont.

TCI Satellite (stock distributed to TCI shareholders in late 1996; value of equity and debt $900 million)

- Distributor of Primestar programming with 800,000 subscribers
- 21% equity stake in Primestar Partners, co-investors included other large MSOs
- High power satellite orbital slots and two satellites (ready for launch) available for use by Primestar or other DTH operators

Liberty Media (tracking stock distributed to TCI shareholders in 1995)

- 10% of publicly-traded equity in *Time Warner Inc.*, acquired when Time Warner merged with Turner Broadcasting (owner of CNN, TNT, Cartoon Network, WTBS, and other programming services). TCI had owned 22% of Turner's equity; other major investors included Ted Turner, Time Warner and other MSOs (value of TCI equity: $2.6 billion)
- 49% of *Discovery Communications* (Discovery Channel, The Learning Channel, and Animal Planet); co-investors included MSOs Cox and Newhouse (value of TCI equity: $1.2 billion)
- 43% of *QVC;* MSO Comcast owned the balance (value of TCI equity: $1.0 billion)
- 11% of publicly-traded *Home Shopping Network/Silver King Broadcasting;* Barry Diller was CEO and co-investor (value of TCI equity: $220 million)
- 80% of premium programming services *Encore and Starz!* (value of TCI equity: $770 million)
- 50% of *Fox Sports* (national and regional channels), co-investor was News Corp. (value of TCI equity: $900 million)
- 22% of publicly-traded *Black Entertainment Television*, major investor was entrepreneur Bob Johnson (value of TCI equity: $120 million)
- 19% of *The Family Channel;* major investor was Pat Robertson's International Family Entertainment (value of TCI equity: $270 million)
- 10% of *E! Entertainment;* largest investors were Comcast and Time Warner (value of TCI equity: $40 million)
- 33% of *Court TV;* other investors included Time Warner and Viacom (value of TCI equity: $30 million)
- Other assets with aggregate equity value of about $200 million, including Liberty's share of United Video

Sources: Company 10Ks; TCIC, Ventures, and TINTA valuations are from Morgan Stanley Research, 1/30/97; TCI Satellite and Liberty Media valuations are from Donaldson, Lufkin & Jenrette, 5/97

Exhibit 3

U.S. CABLE INDUSTRY SUBSCRIBERS, 1982–1996

Year	Homes Passed (millions)	Basic Subscribers as % of Homes Passed	Pay Units per Basic Subscriber	Monthly Revenue per Basic Subscriber
1982	49.1	55.5%	.76	$16.70
1984	60.5	56.6	.88	19.75
1986	69.4	57.2	.81	22.15
1988	77.2	59.2	.85	25.65
1990	86.0	60.2	.80	29.45
1992	89.7	61.5	.74	32.30
1994	91.6	65.2	.77	32.49
1996	93.7	67.8	.79	36.95

Note: "Basic subscribers" paid an average of $24 per month for access to a "basic" tier of cable programming, which typically included all local broadcasting stations in a community, along with satellite-delivered "basic" programming services such as ESPN and MTV. Basic services received about one third of their revenues directly from cable operators in the form of license fees, and the balance from selling spots to national advertisers. Cable customers also could pay an additional $8 per month, on average, (per service) for access to premium services such as HBO, which showed recent theatrical films without advertising interruption.
Source: Donaldson, Lufkin & Jenrette research reports citing data from Paul Kagan Associates

Exhibit 4

LARGEST BASIC AND PREMIUM PROGRAMMING SERVICES, 1996

Twenty Largest Basic Services	Subscribers (Million)	Programming Format	Largest Owners
Discovery Channel	69	Science/Nature	**TCI; Cox; Newhouse**
USA Network	68	Entertainment	**Viacom***; Universal Pictures
CNN	68	News	**Time Warner**
TBS Superstation	68	Entertainment	**Time Warner**
TNT	68	Entertainment	**Time Warner**
C-SPAN	67	Public Affairs	**MSO Consortium**
ESPN	67	Sports	Disney/ABC; Hearst
Nickelodeon	67	Childrens	**Viacom***
The Nashville Network	65	Music	Gaylord
A&E Network	65	Entertainment	Disney/ABC; GE/NBC; Hearst
The Family Channel	65	Entertainment	Int'l Family Entertainment; **TCI**
MTV	64	Music	**Viacom***
Lifetime	64	Entertainment	Disney/ABC; Hearst
American Movie Classics	62	Movies	**Cablevision Systems**; GE/NBC
CNN Headline News	60	News	**Time Warner**
The Weather Channel	60	Weather	**Landmark***
CNBC	57	Financial News	GE/NBC
QVC	56	Home Shopping	**Comcast; TCI**
VH1	55	Music	**Viacom***
The Learning Channel	51	Science/History	**TCI; Cox; Newhouse**

Largest Premium Services	Subscribers (Million)	Largest Owners
HBO	19	**Time Warner**
Cinemax	9	**Time Warner**
Showtime	8	**Viacom***
Disney Channel	6	Disney
Encore	4	**TCI**
Starz!	3	**TCI**
The Movie Channel	3	**Viacom***

Bold indicates MSO ownership
*Divested cable system assets in 1995/96
Source: *Cablevision*, Jan. 6, 1997, "Database" section

Exhibit 5 U.S. CABLE INDUSTRY FINANCIAL PERFORMANCE, 1993–1996

	1993	1994	1995	1996
Revenue ($ billion)	$22.8	$22.8	$25.1	$27.8
EBITDA as % of Revenue	44.3%	43.6%	43.8%	43.0%
EBITDA/Subscriber	$179	$170	$180	$191
Capital Expenditure/Subscriber	$52	$64	$89	$95
Debt/Subscriber	$804	$874	$903	$926

Source: Bear, Stearns research report citing data from Paul Kagan Associates

Exhibit 6 STOCK PRICE PERFORMANCE FOR MAJOR MSOs, 1993–1996

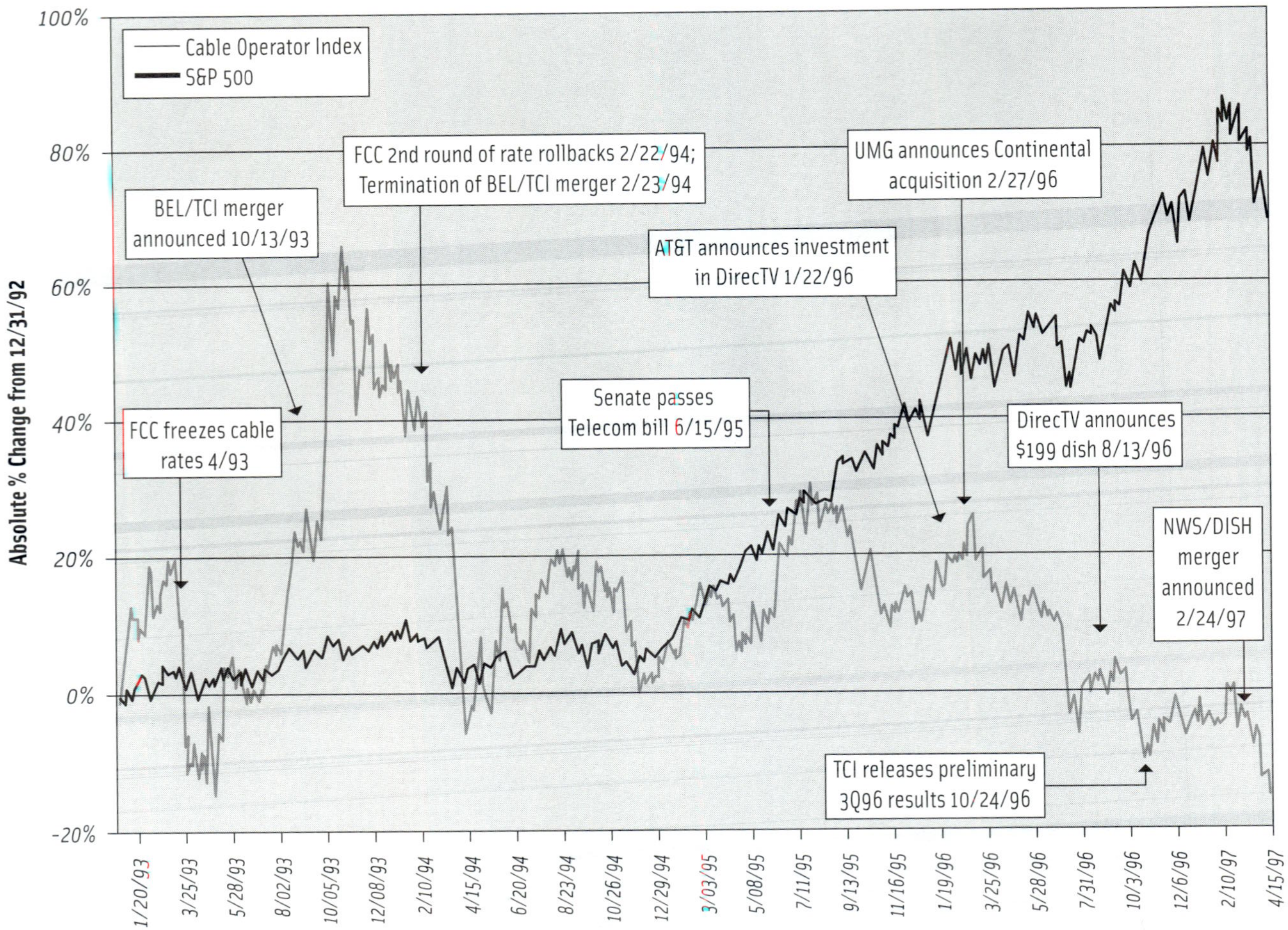

* Cable Operator Index includes: ADLAC, CMCSK, COX, CTYA, CVC, JOINA, TCAT, TCOMA, UMG. COX is averaged into Index as of 1/31/95. UMG is averaged into Index as of 10/31/95. Monthly performance shown through 04/15/97.

Source: Donaldson, Lufkin & Jenrette Research

Exhibit 7 MSOS' 1996 STOCK PRICE PERFORMANCE VERSUS DEBT LEVERAGE

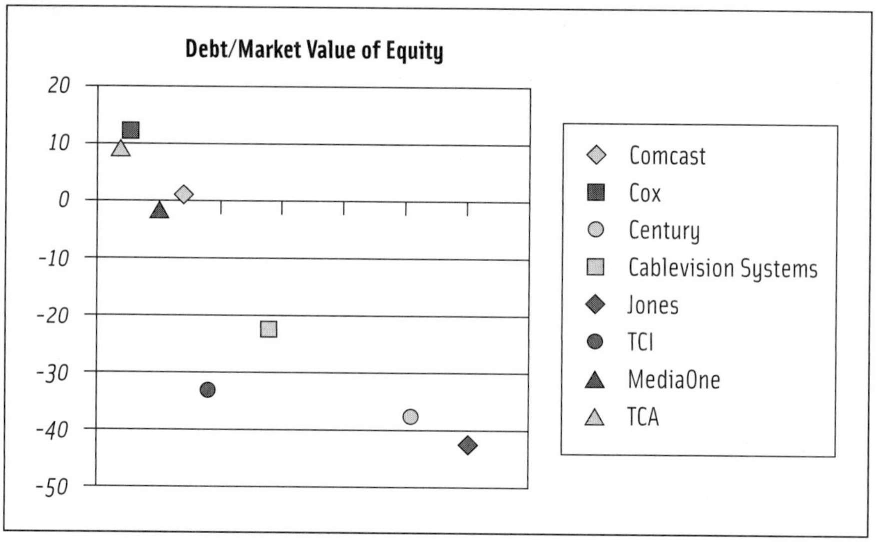

Reflects percentage change in stock price from 12/31/95 to 1/31/97; book value of debt and preferred stock divided by market value of equity as of April 1997
Source: Casewriter analysis of Donaldson, Lufkin & Jenrette Research data

Exhibit 8 TCI COMMUNICATIONS FINANCIAL PERFORMANCE, 1994–1996* ($ IN MILLIONS)

	1996	1995	1994
Basic Subscribers (million)	13.9	12.5	11.7
Revenues	$5,954	$4,878	$4,116
Operating Cash Flow (EBITDA)	2,230	2,043	1,801
Depreciation and Amortization	1,453	1,223	988
Interest Expense	1,041	962	777
Capital Expenditures	1,920	1,665	1,235
Cash Income Taxes	8	8	4
*Free Cash Flow***	(749)	(584)	(215)
Total Assets	$23,136	$20,364	$15,880
Property and Equipment (Net of Accumulated Depreciation)	7,192	6,988	5,579
*Franchise Costs (Net of Accumulated Amortization)****	14,794	11,563	9,297
Debt	14,318	12,635	10,712

*Represents financial statements for TCI's cable systems and its Technology Ventures unit, including TCI's share in operating losses of Sprint Spectrum and Teleport ($168 million and $47 million in 1996, respectively). Results for TCI International (TINTA) are consolidated, but have modest impact on the financial statements. Results for TCI Satellite ("TSAT"), which held TCI's interest in Primestar, are included through December 4, 1996, when TSAT was spun off.

Results for Liberty Media are not reflected above. In 1996, Liberty had revenues of $1.3 billion, EBITDA of $164 million, and total assets of $3.1 billion. However, since many of Liberty's investments were minority equity stakes in privately held companies, Liberty's private market value was considerably greater than the book value of its assets.

**Defined as EBITDA less Interest Expense, Capital Expenditures, and Cash Income Taxes.

***Reflects goodwill, i.e., the portion of franchise acquisition costs not assigned to Property and Equipment or other tangible assets

Source: Company 10Ks

Exhibit 9 CABLE SYSTEM FINANCIAL PERFORMANCE: TCI VERSUS OTHER LARGE MSOS, 1996

	TCI	MediaOne	Comcast	Cox
Basic Subscribers as % Homes Passed	59.1%	59.0%	61.2%	65.0%
Monthly Revenue per Basic Subscriber	$36.17	$36.88	$37.38	$35.33
Programming (% Revenue)	18.0%	20.2%	21.7%	25.5%
Plant Operations (% Revenue)	13.1	12.8	9.8	10.3
Marketing (% Revenue)	4.0	4.0	3.5	3.4
General and Administrative (% Revenue)	26.7	21.2	15.1	20.9
Operating Cash Flow (% Revenue)	38.2	41.7	49.9	39.9
Capital Expenditures per Basic Subscriber	$104	$129	$103	$129

Note: MediaOne, Comcast and Cox were the 3rd, 4th, and 5th largest U.S. MSOs, respectively.
Source: Morgan Stanley Research estimates

Exhibit 10 SYSTEM BANDWIDTH AND 2-WAY CAPABILITY: TCI VERSUS OTHER LARGE MSOS, 1998

	% of Homes Passed Less Than 550 MHz	% of Homes Passed Greater Than 750 MHz	% of Homes Passed Two-Way Activated
TCI	58%	20%	26%
Cablevision Systems	15	43	70
Comcast	17	60	60
Cox	17	56	50
MediaOne	30	45	49

Source: Bear Stearns estimates

Exhibit 11 PROJECTED ECONOMICS OF NEW SERVICES, 1998 AND 2003

Capital Costs	Hybrid Fiber/Coax Upgrade/Rebuild to 550/750 MHz, two-way plant	Digital Converter	High Speed Internet Access	Switched-Circuit Telephony ("POTS")[1]
Fixed per home passed: 1998	$250	$20	$11	$35[2]
Fixed per home passed: 2003	193	20	11	32[2]
Variable per new service subscriber: 1998	(Not Applicable)	$350	$350	$678[3]
Variable per new service subscriber: 2003	(N/A)	150	125	545[3]

Penetration Revenue & Profit	Hybrid Fiber/Coax Upgrade/Rebuild to 550/750 MHz, two-way plant	Digital Converter	High Speed Internet Access	Switched-Circuit Telephony ("POTS")[1]
Penetration of basic cable households: 1998	50%[4]	1.5%	1.3%	0.1%
Penetration of basic cable households: 2003	90%[4]	41%	24.7%	11.5%
Per subscriber monthly revenue from new service: 1998	(N/A)	$16.89	$35.69[6]	$44.52
Per subscriber monthly revenue from new service: 2003	(N/A)	17.44[5]	21.70[6]	41.48
EBITDA margin for new service: 2003	(N/A)	42%	38%	34%

[1]"*POTS*" was traditional local and long distance service delivered over a "wireline" switched-circuit network (as distinguished from *wireless services* like cellular or PCS, and from *Internet-protocol telephony*, which relied on a packet-switched network; see **Exhibit 15**)
[2]Largely reflects the cost of providing an independent source of electric power through the cable plant, so phones can continue to operate during an electric power outage (an important feature for consumers)
[3]Includes the incremental capital cost of increasing switch capacity; a "Network Interface Unit" that modulated phone signals to and from the cable plant onto phone lines in the customer's home; and capitalized installation costs
[4]Based on Bear Stearns' estimates for six large MSOs
[5]Includes $5 per month from transactional services enabled by second-generation digital converters
[6]Assumes that 25% of new customers purchase their modems in 1998 (instead of leasing from their cable company), and 100% purchase in 2003. MSOs do not incur variable capital costs when customers purchase.
Source: Donaldson, Lufkin & Jenrette Research (unless otherwise noted)

Exhibit 12

DATA ON DIGITAL VIDEO APPLICATIONS

- Donaldson, Lufkin & Jenrette projected that 1st-generation digital converters would be installed in 1 million households by the end of 1998; most of them in TCI systems. These households: 1) would receive an "extended" tier of basic programming services not otherwise available to customers with analog converters (e.g., a "suite" of niche music services from MTV), in exchange for a monthly payment of about $10; and 2) would have an opportunity to subscribe to "multiplexed" versions of premium programming services (e.g., HBO2; HBO3).
  - Early rollout experiences were encouraging: where marketed, digital converters had achieved 5 to 13% penetration within a few months.
- DLJ also projected that by 2003, households with 2nd-generation converters would generate $17.44 in incremental monthly revenue, broken down as follows: $3.53 from the monthly service fee for the extended basic tier; $3.34 from incremental premium service subscriptions (40% of homes with digital converters would pay $8.83 for such services); $4.97 from pay-per-view and video-on-demand programs; $5.00 in fees from transactional marketing services (e.g., on-line travel bookings); $0.59 from the rental of additional digital converters (31% of homes with digital converters would pay $1.89 for an extra converter).
- *Video-on-demand* ("VOD") was a promising application enabled by two-way, HFC upgrades. VOD used server technology to allow consumers to choose from a large menu of programs, viewing them at any time that suited their convenience (thus distinguishing VOD from pre-scheduled pay-per-view programs).
  - VOD would compete with the $8 billion market for videocassette rentals.
  - Rapid reduction in server costs had improved the economic prospects for VOD. According to Bear Stearns, headend servers cost $20,000 to $100,000 in 1998, down from $250,000 a few years earlier.
- *High Definition Television* ("HDTV") signals, which offered a significant improvement in picture resolution, could be processed by digital converters. The FCC had mandated that broadcasters convert their analog transmissions to HDTV by 2006. Digital cable converters could ease this transition, and also could generate incremental revenue through subscriptions to HDTV versions of basic and premium programming services. However, consumer interest in HDTV was still uncertain, and likely would be depressed by: 1) the $5,000 to $8,000 price of HDTV sets in the first few years following their introduction; and 2) by a scarcity of HDTV programming in those years.
- The development of "OpenCable" standards raised the prospect that digital converters would become a consumer electronics item sold in retail stores, rather than leased by the cable operator. Shifting ownership of the converter to the consumer would reduce MSOs' capital expenditures.

Source: Donaldson, Lufkin & Jenrette Research

Exhibit 13 DATA ON HIGH SPEED INTERNET ACCESS SERVICES

- Industry-wide, there were 111,000 cable modem subscribers at year-end 1997; TCI's systems accounted for less than 4% of those subscribers. Where marketed, cable modems had penetrated 3 to 5% of cable households after 12 months, and 6 to 8% after 24 months. Since 25% of all U.S. households used on-line services in 1998 (when 42% had home computers), these penetration rates implied that cable modems eventually could capture at least one-third of the on-line access market.
- The consumer market for on-line access was expected to grow from $6.9 billion in 1998 to $9.7 billion in 2001, with 33% of U.S. households using on-line services in 2001.
- The U.S. target market for cable modems also included 39 million small office/home office (SOHO) workers, who spent over $14 billion in 1998 on products and services related to their offices. 20% of MediaOne's cable modem customers were telecommuters.
- Cable modem advantages versus traditional telephone ("dial-up") modems:
  - With 10 to 27 Mbps (million bits per second) data transfer rates, cable modem were hundreds of times faster than 56 Kbps (thousand bits per second) dial-up modems.
  - Customers who leased cable modems typically paid a flat rate of about $40 per month; they incurred no variable usage charges, and installation fees of about $100 were often waived during promotions. The lease rate included Internet access. Users of dial-up modems purchased their modem ($100 was a typical price) and paid about $20 to an Internet Service Provider (ISP). However, dial-up modem users frequently chose to add a second phone line (at a cost of about $40), in order to leave their primary line available for voice calls. There was no such need for a second phone line with cable modem service. (Note also that cable modem use had no impact on the availability of cable signals for simultaneous TV viewing).
  - Cable modems remained constantly connected to their Internet service provider. With dial-up modems, ISPs terminated connections after a period of non-activity to manage their networks more efficiently. Reestablishing connections could be time consuming.
  - Phone companies' best near term competitive response to cable modems was ISDN (Integrated Services Digital Network), which transferred data at only 128 Kbps. In August 1998, Bell South was charging $192 for ISDN installation, a flat monthly rate of $68 (not including Internet access), and one cent per minute of use in excess of 200 hours per month.
  - Phone companies also were introducing Digital Subscriber Line ("DSL") services with data transfer rates of 1.5 Mbps or higher. However, such services would require expensive line conditioning (often costing more than $1,000 per customer), and due to limitations in propagating signals over twisted-pair copper phone lines, likely would not be available to the one-half of homes located more than 18,000 feet from a phone company central switching office. In August 1998, Bell Atlantic was offering 7 Mbps DSL for a $200 installation fee (on promotion) and a flat monthly rate of $190.
- By 1998, the cable industry had established standards for the interoperability of cable modems. This implied that consumers would soon be able to acquire and install their own cable modems, reducing their life cycle costs (and shifting a major capital item off of MSOs' balance sheets). DLJ projected that 25% of new customers would purchase their modems in 1998, and 100% would do so by 2002.

Source: Bear, Stearns Research (unless otherwise noted)

Exhibit 14 DATA ON SWITCHED-CIRCUIT CABLE TELEPHONE SERVICE

- *Plain Old Telephone Service,* or "POTS," was traditional local and long distance service delivered over a "wireline" switched-circuit network (as distinguished from *wireless services* like cellular or PCS, or from *Internet-protocol telephony,* which relied on a packet-switched network).
- According to DLJ, in the few U.S. markets where cable operators had offered POTS to residential phone customers, they had achieved 20% penetration within a few months. This was consistent with positive experiences in the UK, where cable operators had been marketing phone service for several years and had achieved 27% penetration.
- Cable operators typically marketed POTS by offering a 10% discount on the first phone line, a 50% discount on a second line, and discounts on value-added and long distance services.
- The target market for cable telephony was huge: local phone companies had revenues in excess of $100 billion from residential and business customers.
- Barriers that cable companies faced in exploiting the POTS market included:
  - *High capital costs* (see **Exhibit 11**), including expenses in the range of $25 per home passed (or $125 per phone customer if 20% of homes passed subscribed to cable phone service) to provide power to operate telephone handsets through cable lines, independent of the electric power grid. This capability would allow cable companies to market "lifeline" service in the event of an electric power outage (and hence the ability to call the local police or fire department in an emergency).
  - *Regulatory uncertainty.* Despite passage of the Communications Act of 1996, which mandated removal of the legal and regulatory barriers that had inhibited competition in local phone markets, in 1998 regulators were still negotiating the terms of interconnection agreements between competing local phone companies.

Source: Donaldson, Lufkin & Jenrette Research

Exhibit 15 DATA ON INTERNET-PROTOCOL TELEPHONE SERVICE

- *Internet-protocol ("IP") telephony* was a potential substitute for switched-circuit telephony that could significantly reduce cable companies' capital costs (e.g., by eliminating the need for switches). IP telephony broke voice traffic into data packets that were sent though data routers over the Internet, then reassembled at the receiving end. Pauses in a conversation generated little data (fewer packets) and thus required little bandwidth for transmission. Consequently, packet-switched networks were inherently more efficient in their use of bandwidth than switched-circuit networks, which held open a dedicated point-to-point circuit of fixed bandwidth through the entire duration of a phone call.
- According to Forrester Research, the U.S. market for IP telephone service was $49 million in 1998, but was projected to grow to $1.9 billion by 2003.
  - In 1998, rates for domestic long distance IP phone calls averaged 6 cents per minute, compared to 14 cents for traditional switched-circuit long distance service. Savings on international calls averaged 30 to 70%.
  - Early adopters who accessed IP phone services through their existing phone lines were inconvenienced by: 1) the need to dial additional digits to reach a local Internet gateway and to input a personal access code (cable IP telephony would avoid this inconvenience by providing a direct Internet connection); and 2) unpredictable call quality. Internet congestion could result in garbled speech and disconnected calls when packets did not reach the receiver quickly enough. Over time, Forrester Research predicted, technological advances would improve call quality.

Source: Donaldson, Lufkin & Jenrette Research

GEOCAST NETWORK SYSTEMS, INC.

In tennis, there is a move called the 'split step.' The split step occurs when, following your serve, you take three steps forward and split your feet to regain your balance. This move allows you to assess the trajectory of the service return and improve the odds of executing a volley that will close out the point. We are doing a split step now, spending three weeks or so reevaluating our strategy before we accelerate toward launch.

–Joe Horowitz, Chairman and CEO
of Geocast Network Systems, Inc.

Geocast Network Systems, Inc. (Geocast)—an early stage company based in Menlo Park, California—was funded in January 1999 by three leading venture capital firms with the goal of building and marketing a personalized broadband network and rich media delivery service. At the April 2000 annual conference of the National Association of Broadcasters, Geocast became the first company to successfully demonstrate an end-to-end solution for data broadcasting (also called datacasting) to the PC. The company's dual network and service solution combined the instant availability and high-quality video of television with the customization and interactivity features of the Web. Geocast enabled customers' PCs to receive data transmissions from terrestrial broadcasters, satellites, or cable TV. Personalized broadband information and entertainment content—including full-motion video, CD-quality audio, and software downloads—were received using the Geocast personal receiver, then cached for later retrieval. Users continued to use their Internet service provider for Web access, email, and other upstream applications. The company planned to launch its product in early 2001.

The company had seen dramatic changes in the marketplace since its funding less than two years earlier. By the summer of 2000, a number of events had led Horowitz and his team to reevaluate their strategy. Initially, they had planned to 'get big fast' by selling receivers to consumers at a price that reflected a significant subsidy and by delivering data for free; Geocast would earn revenue from advertising and fees from commerce partners. However, Nasdaq's market downturn in the spring of 2000 tightened the availability of financial capital. Private and public market investors began requiring faster routes to profitability, which called into question a strategy that assumed a large upfront investment in customer acquisition to be borne by Geocast. Geocast's original business plan also assumed that the company would first rely on terrestrial broadcasters for data transmission, followed by partnerships with satellite and cable operators. However, the Federal Communications Commission (FCC) had approved a digital television transmission standard for terrestrial broadcasters that would likely require Geocast's customers to use rooftop antennas in order to avoid the potential for reception problems, raising installation costs. Although technological developments were expected to ameliorate any potential reception problems over the next two to three years, the issue remained a real one in mid-2000.

Despite uncertainties regarding the financial markets and broadcast standards, Horowitz remained convinced that Geocast had developed a unique and compelling technology with enormous potential. He was eager to meet with his team to assess the company's strategic options. Several questions came to mind as he prepared for the "split step" exercise. Should the company change the "terrestrial, satellite, cable" launch sequence? How should Geocast's receivers be distributed—through retail outlets such as Best Buy and Circuit City, or bundled with cable, satellite, DSL (digital subscriber line) or ISP (Internet service provider) services? How should Geocast's product be priced? What additional partnerships should Geocast consider? In short, how could the company quickly gain market share, earn revenues and reach profitability?

Executive Director of the HBS California Research Center Chris Darwall and Liz Kind prepared this case at the HBS California Research Center under the supervision of Professor Tom Eisenmann as the basis for class discussion rather than to illustrate either effective or ineffective handling of an administrative situation.

Background

I joined Geocast because I wanted to work on something different. I didn't want to make the next PC cheaper or work on the latest dot-com. I wanted to be surrounded by bright people, working on something special that had a good chance of surviving over the long term. If we are successful, we will have created a new way to deliver content to the PC. That's really huge, and I want to be there first.

–Charles Marker, Director of Software Engineering, Geocast

The Geocast Concept

Several former Caltech colleagues—Castor Fu, Dag Johansen, Geoff Mulligan, Mark Peting, Tsutomu Shimomura, and Steve Waltman—originally founded Geocast in 1997. The vision of the company was then developed by Joe Horowitz, a veteran venture capitalist with extensive experience in consumer-based technology businesses. The promise of the company stemmed from its addressing two fundamental limitations of the Internet. While the Internet was considered a revolutionary innovation, it had difficulty delivering high quality audio-visual content and large file downloads to a mass audience, and that audience faced difficulty in sorting through huge amounts of information to find exactly the resources they wanted. Anita Wallgren, vice president of business affairs for Geocast, explained:

> Geocast's founders recognized that the Internet's point-to-point infrastructure was limited in terms of bandwidth. You basically had a telephone network that was designed for voice traffic, which was boosted by the addition of routers and servers to transport data and link various networks to create the Internet. That's cool, but the Internet does not handle large data files like video very efficiently, and it does not scale very well.

Marker elaborated:

> If your Website becomes twice as popular as it was yesterday, you'd better have twice as many servers to deliver that content. You'd better have twice as many DS3 lines to send it out to the network.
>
> On the Internet, there is some subset of content that everybody's interested in and then there's all the other stuff. The Internet is really good for connecting you to all the other stuff. But, if you can take that subset of content that everybody's interested in and zip it just once to everybody, it saves lots of bandwidth.

Geocast Product Architecture

The foundation of Geocast's solution was its personal receiver. (See Exhibit 1 for Geocast's network architecture diagram.) The appliance was a small desktop device that connected to the USB (universal serial bus) port on the back of PCs. It received, processed and stored—on its dedicated hard drive—personalized content for on-demand retrieval using a standard Web browser. The three components of the system were an antenna that captured the broadcast signal, a processor, and a hard drive.

Geocast enabled "intelligent caching" based on user preferences through point-to-multi-point broadcasting of data objects—video and audio clips, eBooks and other text files, software programs, data files, or Web pages—that were frequently accessed by multiple users. This approach reduced network congestion because multiple users would otherwise have repeatedly accessed those objects during peak periods. The receiver sorted incoming content according to a user's preferences. The hard drive stored only the content the user wanted to receive and refreshed it automatically; the content was then available for on-demand retrieval. Fresh content was broadcast constantly; up to 40 gigabytes of content could be captured by the Geocast receiver at any time.

Users could customize their Geocast service during installation of the personal receiver using a user-friendly interface; for example, they were able to indicate preferences for sports highlights, certain types of music, or news about various topics. The preferences could be changed at any time. Geocast had developed a "grab, bag, and tag" approach which helped solve one of the Internet user's most common problems—not being able to find what he or she wanted.

The Geocast receiver could receive DTV (digital television) signals from terrestrial broadcasters, satellite, or cable. Initially the receiver was designed to receive terrestrial datacasting, exploiting an excess of digital spectrum among terrestrial broadcasters. The FCC had mandated that all commercial broadcasters be equipped to deliver DTV by 2002; analog systems were to be phased out by

2006.[1] However, in mid-2000, less than 1% of American households had digital TVs. The two major reasons for slow adoption were lack of programming and the high cost of DTV sets—the cheapest were priced at $2,500. To spur conversion from analog to digital technologies, the FCC had granted additional spectrum to terrestrial broadcasters. This created an opportunity for broadcasters to use some of their excess bandwidth for datacasting, and Geocast had secured distribution agreements with several high quality, forward-thinking terrestrial broadcasters.

The Geocast service was fully integrated with the Web; users continued to access the Web through a standard dial-up ISP, DSL, or cable modem. When they browsed the Internet and clicked on a data object that had been cached on their personal receiver (e.g., a video clip on MSNBC.com), Geocast's software directed the browser to grab the data object from the Geocast personal receiver rather than from the Website's server.

Geocast's technology was unique. The company had developed a receiver that incorporated a true file server with a large database, but since it was used in a consumer application, it had been designed to be as reliable as a VCR (video cassette recorder). Marker elaborated on the engineering challenges Geocast had faced:

> Getting all these pieces to work together has been an incredible achievement—no one else has done it. There are companies that are fully dedicated to building servers, or building receivers, or creating a new Website. We've done all of that, from one end to the other.
>
> One of our challenges is that we've got to have software that can select what users will be interested in ahead of time, so we can cache it. We're also building this caching receiver that is very complex—it's actually a computer. It has a big disk drive with a very large database, and it has to make decisions continuously. We want it to be able to hook into home networks in the future as they become more commonplace—and it takes a real computer to do that, not a VCR. Finally, this is also a consumer device, so we want it to be flawlessly reliable. We can't allow it to crash, so we've developed self-monitoring and self-healing software. We have two versions of the operating system in every box, so one comes back up if the other fails.

Geocast was creating extensive tools that allowed content providers to identify data objects and "tag" them with descriptions. Content tagging allowed the intelligent Geocast receiver to identify and "grab" only content for which the user had expressed a preference. The software tools being developed were smart enough to ensure—for example—that a Tiger Woods video clip wouldn't be tagged for the "animals" category.

The Startup Team

> *Geocast represents a unique convergence of several industries—broadcasting, the Internet, communications, technology and consumer electronics.*
>
> –Mark Simmer, Senior Vice President, Marketing and Programming, Geocast

Geocast's founders and venture capital backers approached Joe Horowitz to develop a business model to leverage their unique technology. Horowitz held a BA from Columbia University and a Wharton MBA; his background included over 20 years of experience in early stage venture capital and in technology and consumer ventures. In the early 1990s, Horowitz had started his own company, ICON Ventures, where he became involved in the electronic television programming guide business through StarSight Telecast, which later merged with Gemstar.

Horowitz assembled a team of experienced executives including John Abel, former executive vice president of the National Association of Broadcasters; Charlie Jablonski, previously vice president of broadcast and network engineering for NBC; Mark Simmer, former vice president of online media and chief content officer at Lycos; Dave Olson, previously a principal engineer at Silicon Graphics; Jeff Weinstein, previously a principal engineer at Netscape; and Anita Wallgren, former legal advisor to FCC Commissioner Susan Ness. Geocast's software development team included founding members from Netscape, Silicon Graphics and IBM. Tom Paquin, Geocast's senior vice president of engineering was

[1]According to Digital Dictionary," http://www.nhptv.org/dtv/digdic.shtml; viewed 9-21-2000, digital television referred to a broadcast signal encoded as zeroes and ones, the digital code used by computers. DTV signals were compressed to provide four or more channels in the same bandwidth required for one channel of standard analog television. In 2000 there were three DTV product categories: standard definition television (SDTV), enhanced definition television (EDTV), and high definition television (HDTV). SDTV's display performance was roughly comparable to that of current analog broadcasts; HDTV had much greater display resolution and a wider aspect ratio (screen shape) similar to that of a movie theater screen. SDTV used the least, and HDTV the most, bandwidth.

Netscape's 7th employee and Jon Mittlehauser, also from Netscape, co-wrote the original Mosaic software. (See Exhibit 2 for Geocast management biographies.)

In January 1999 Geocast received funding from three of Silicon Valley's elite venture capital firms—Mayfield Fund, Kleiner Perkins Caufield & Byers, and Institutional Venture Partners. The three firms had backed a number of well-known technology and Internet companies including America Online, Amazon.com, BroadVision, Excite, and Netscape. Kleiner Perkins was considered by many to be the country's premier venture capital firm and was known to have a penchant for "thinking big." John Doerr, a Kleiner Perkins general partner, was named "the most influential venture capitalist of the Internet economy" by the San Francisco Business Times.[2] Will Hearst, another Kleiner Perkins partner, known for launching @Home Network, sat on Geocast's board of directors. Kevin Fong, a partner with Mayfield Fund, also served on Geocast's board; he had been profiled in a *Red Herring* article entitled: "Architects of the Digital Universe: Saluting the Eight Professionals That High Tech Couldn't Do Without."[3]

Geocast raised its second round of financing, totaling $74 million, in February 2000. Participants included Geocast's venture capital partners, as well as leading broadcasting, media and consumer electronics concerns. (See Exhibit 3 for details on Geocast's investors.) Geocast's broadcast partners—Hearst-Argyle Television, Belo Corporation and Allbritton Communications—owned or managed television stations that reached over 40% of U.S. television households. In addition to cash investments from Hearst-Argyle and Belo, Geocast's broadcast partners agreed to supply DTV spectrum and content in exchange for equity in the company and the right to participate in future revenue streams.

Geocast had also teamed with Thomson Multimedia, the nation's largest supplier of consumer electronics products, and Royal Philips Electronics, Europe's leading electronics company. Both companies invested in Geocast, and Thomson Multimedia agreed to develop, market, and manufacture an RCA-branded Geocast receiver.

The content companies that participated in Geocast's second round of financing were also high profile leaders in their industries. Liberty Media Corporation held interests in numerous globally branded television programming networks such as Discovery Channel, QVC, Black Entertainment Television, and Encore. Liberty's chairman was cable TV mogul John Malone, widely regarded as an expert in both new and old economy media. Electronic Arts, the world's leading interactive entertainment software company with 1999 revenue of $1.2 billion, was another Geocast investor.

Geocast's Initial Strategy and Business Model

Geocast's goal was to deliver an end-to-end, branded service to consumers. The company had originally planned to sell its receivers to consumers through consumer electronics retail stores for approximately $300. There would be no charge for the service itself. The box would cost about $300 to manufacture, but an additional $200 per receiver would be required to allow for marketing support and retailer margin. Geocast had planned to subsidize these costs with additional capital infusions from late round investors and potentially an IPO.

In its initial business plan, the majority of Geocast's revenues were projected to come from advertising (70%) and fees from commerce providers (30%). Advertisers would be able to deliver precisely targeted and multimedia ads, given Geocast's detailed information about user preferences and its rich media formats. Geocast would share revenues with terrestrial broadcasters in exchange for their spectrum and content. No decision had been made regarding whether Geocast or others would sell the advertising.

Geocast had been focused on getting big fast. To encourage adoption, the company took care to avoid creating a "walled garden;"[4] the objective was to offer as wide a variety of content as possible. The sequence of distribution had also been developed with rapid growth in mind. The company had planned to distribute their

[2]Levine, Daniel, "The Greatest Innovators," *San Francisco Business Times*, (January 28, 2000): p. 3.

[3]Grove, Alex and Bonnie Azab Powell, "Architects of the Digital Universe: Saluting the Eight Professionals That High Tech Couldn't Do Without," *Red Herring*, (June 25, 1999).

[4]A "walled garden" was an online service that made it easy to access content and commerce offerings from its own exclusive set of business partners, but slower and harder (or sometimes impossible) to access third party offerings. AOL and Excite@Home were common examples of "walled gardens", and many cell phone operators were developing their new wireless data services in this manner. Technically, walled gardens were maintained through selective caching, attenuated connections to the Internet at-large and a new generation of data switches that could selectively delay data en route to and from non-preferred services. Steve McMahon, Davis Community Network, "Broadband Glossary and Bestiary," June 23, 2000, http://www.dcn.davis.ca.ns/go/steve/terms.htm; viewed 9-14-2000.

product first through terrestrial broadcasters, who were eager to leverage their new datacasting capabilities and who could quickly access all U.S. homes. Allying first with terrestrial broadcasters would put pressure on satellite operators to distribute Geocast's service, which then would encourage adoption by cable operators.

In August 2000, Geocast had approximately 200 employees, with 160 of those employees in engineering, 120 in software, and 40 in hardware.[5] The company expected to ramp up quickly to 400 employees.

The Datacasting Market

In mid-2000, the datacasting market—the market for high bandwidth broadcasting of movies, music, software, and data to PCs or TVs using DTV signals—was in its infancy (see Exhibit 4 for more detail on the datacasting market); most participants had been founded in the late 1990s. Some companies, such as Geocast, planned to sell receivers that could be attached to PCs or televisions, while others were packaging spectrum for resale or were developing branded content networks. All participants planned to enter the market in either late 2000 or 2001. (See Exhibit 5 for further information on the datacasting companies discussed below, including partnerships and projected market entry dates.)

iBlast was founded by several TV station group owners as a branded network spectrum broker. iBlast planned to create an infrastructure for delivering multimedia content to stations. Programming was to be sent from the iBlast network operations center to satellite and direct fiber connections that would feed the programming to 225 local member TV stations covering 90% of U.S. households. iBlast network broadcasters would retransmit the content—using DTV signals—to DTV receiver cards that users would self-install inside their PCs. Each iBlast member contributed a portion of its digital spectrum—an average of 7Mbps of DTV bandwidth—as well as a cash investment and a guaranteed marketing commitment; in exchange, each member received equity ownership in the company, ongoing revenue sharing, and the ability to use iBlast's equipment to distribute local data content to consumers. The iBlast transmission service would be free to consumers, but some content would be available only by subscription or pay-per-view. The retail price for the DTV receiver card was expected to be $99. iBlast planned to charge content providers for the transport service and would let the content providers sell their own advertising and collect any subscription fees.[6]

The **Broadcasters' Digital Cooperative** was also a spectrum broker, but unlike iBlast did not plan to develop a data broadcasting system for delivering content. Instead, it planned to sell spectrum to third parties willing to develop applications and pay for access. Also, unlike iBlast, its agreements were not exclusive. The member station groups covered 85% of U.S. households, and each member pledged 4Mbps of DTV bandwidth to the cooperative.[7] The issue of reselling spectrum was very visible in the summer of 2000, when the House Telecommunications Subcommittee and the FCC voiced their concerns about broadcasters reselling a valuable commodity that had been granted to them free of charge to ease the transition from analog to digital television.[8] At the time, spectrum for other telecommunications applications was being auctioned by the United States government for huge fees.

iBEAM broadcast content by satellite to Internet access providers' server facilities, where the content was cached. The company's primary focus was facilitating the rapid and efficient delivery of streaming audio and video over the Internet, and as such, it had more narrowly defined goals than other players in the datacasting arena.[9]

Dotcast manufactured the Dotbox receiver, initially intended for connection to PCs, and eventually to televisions. The receiver enabled the user to receive 25GB per day of datacast content, based on user preferences. The receiver itself was to be free to subscribers of Dotcast's broadcast data service.[10]

Wavexpress was developing an end-to-end system that included content aggregation, distribution through broadcasters and satellite systems, developing an e-commerce

[5]Using Forrester's rule-of-thumb that an Internet company's burn rate—excluding marketing expenses—is equal to roughly $200,000 per employee, Geocast's annual burn rate could be estimated to be about $40 million. The rule-of-thumb does not apply to Internet companies with large numbers of employees working in customer service centers and/or warehouses.

[6]iBlast Website, http://www.iblast.com, viewed 9-25-2000; "HDTV Detour: Cable and the Broadband Revolution," Sam's Digital Television Report (Sept. 11, 2000), http://www.teleport.com/~samc/hdtv/ hdtv4.html, viewed 9-11-2000.

[7]Glen Dickson, "Getting Together over Data," *Broadcasting & Cable* (March 27, 2000).

[8]Anonymous, "TV Broadcasters Warned Against Leasing HDTV Spectrum," *The Wave Report* (Issue 2040: July 27, 2000).

[9]iBEAM Website, http://www.ibeam.com, viewed 9-25-2000.

[10]Dotcast Website, http://www.dotcast.com, viewed 9-25-2000.

infrastructure, and selling PC-compatible plug-in receiver cards. The consumer installed a DTV tuner card into his or her PC. Digital content was then cached on the user's hard drive, with the user specifying the amount of space to be used; 10MB was the minimum required. There was no monthly access fee; rather, the user either subscribed to specific content channels (e.g. movies, music) or paid per view or per purchase. Software and hardware in the tuner card handled the metering of usage and payment transactions, with the computer charging the user's credit card using a dial-up connection. Wavexpress marketed to broadcasters, satellite providers, and cable operators, suggesting that its service could bring in additional revenues to help justify DTV.[11]

Developments in Mid-2000

The runway has gotten shorter for Internet companies: profits are expected sooner than before. But I'm a big believer in the merits of assessing the need for mid-course corrections, even when the capital markets are more accommodating.

–Joe Horowitz

Three developments in the year 2000 contributed to Geocast's re-evaluation of its strategy. The first was the market crash of April 2000, which caused many young Internet companies to shut their doors, merge with other companies, or refocus on profits. Between March 10 and May 23 of 2000, the Nasdaq plunged by nearly 37%. The market crash helped highlight the reality that of the 39 key companies in the Goldman Sachs Consumer e-Commerce Index, only one company—eBay—was projected to make a profit in 2000. Although the market crash primarily influenced Internet businesses, it affected other young venture capital-backed companies as well.[12]

One aftermath of the crash was that venture capitalists were emphasizing cash flow and profitability in the second half of 2000; in addition, follow-on rounds of funding were less easy to raise than before. Venture capitalists and entrepreneurs alike referred to the "shortened runway" for startups, meaning that companies had to "lift-off" (achieve profitability) more quickly and with less fuel (capital) than in the past. Although Geocast had raised a $74 million second round in February 2000, management nonetheless believed that the company needed to fine-tune its strategy to deal with changes and uncertainties in the marketplace and to bring the company to lift-off as soon as possible.

A second factor contributing to the strategy reassessment was the debate over DTV broadcasting standards, in particular the radio frequency (RF) modulation format. Because any terrestrial TV system had to contend with signal interference that could cause reception problems, choosing the right RF modulation format for DTV was crucial.[13] Broadcasting industry participants disagreed on the best approach, with some favoring the COFDM (coded orthogonal frequency division multiplex) system in use in Europe and others supporting the 8-VSB (8-level vestigial side-band) standard. The ATSC (advanced television systems committee) had proposed the 8-VSB standard, which was adopted by the FCC. Geocast management was agnostic as to the standard as long as it allowed for good indoor reception.

One reason for the spirited debate was that neither standard had a clear advantage in all aspects of performance.[14] The ATSC-blessed 8-VSB system had several advantages, including requiring less transmitter power for equivalent coverage. The COFDM system's advantages included better performance in multipath situations.[15] Supporters said that COFDM worked well with indoor receiving antennas in many places where 8-VSB receivers could not produce a picture. While the potential for indoor reception problems caused by using the 8-VSB standard could be solved with a rooftop antenna, no one knew for certain how many homes still had such antennas—most had been disconnected since the 1980s, when cable systems proliferated. Regardless of which standard was superior, the uncertainty surrounding the

[11]Wavexpress Website, http://www.wavexpress.com, viewed 9-25-2000.

[12]Tapan Munroe, "Munroe's Column," Contra Costa Times (August 24, 2000), http://lib.harvard.edu:2096/universe/doc . . . Al&_md5=b04221da1b9ef7fcdb9498222222a9; viewed 9-13-2000.

[13]David Sparano, "What Exactly is 8-VSB Anyway?" http://www.broadcast.harris.com/8-vsb.html; viewed 9-1-2000.

[14]Bruce Franca, Alan Stillwell, Robert Bromery, Robert Eckert, and Michael Davis, "DTV Report on COFDM and 8-VSB Performance," FCC Office of Engineering and Technology (September 30, 1999).

[15]Multipath interference occurred when signals reflected off surrounding surfaces such as mountains or buildings and—having traveled further on this indirect path—arrived at an antenna with a very slight delay, compared to signals that arrived on a direct path from the broadcasting tower. Multipath was the cause of "ghosting" in analog broadcasting, but posed a more serious problem for digital broadcasting, since digital signals either worked or they did not. If the reflected signal and the direct signal were not in sync, the data was scrambled; digital TV receivers could not interpret these signals and instead displayed an ERROR message. Some industry observers felt that over time, any multipath problems in DTV could be solved with software that would filter out redundant multipath signals.

adoption of DTV standards contributed to consumers' slowness in adopting the new DTV technology.

A final—and more positive—factor contributing to strategic reassessment was the fact that hard drive price/performance was more than following Moore's Law.[16] Whereas a 20GB hard drive had cost consumers about $335 18 months before, the same hard drive cost about $115 in mid-2000.[17] In terms of storage capacity, $100 invested in a hard drive in mid-2000 allowed a consumer to store 24 to 36 hours of video programming; research indicated that by 2005, the same investment would yield 1,440 hours of content.[18] The rapid changes in hard drive economics gave Geocast more options regarding price/performance of their box, but also meant that the parameters of the box were a moving target.

These three issues—the shortened runway, the battle over DTV standards, and the rapid rate of improvement in hard drive performance—were considered when Geocast management reassessed the company's strategic options in the summer of 2000.

Options for Deployment

Geocast management believed the company faced several strategic options in deploying their breakthrough technology. Six options are outlined below: the first three focus on the company's choice of distribution partners; the balance concern product definition and pricing.

1. Accelerate Satellite Partnerships

> *Thomson did some research for us, asking consumers if they had the choice between a broadcast antenna in their window or a satellite dish on their roof, which would they choose? Surprisingly to me, they picked the satellite dish. It is a sign of prestige: 'I've got my satellite dish and I'm part of the information elite.'*
>
> –Mark Simmer

Geocast's original plan had called for terrestrial rollout to be completed first, with satellite and cable rollouts to follow. (See Exhibit 6 for selected satellite, cable, PC and DSL statistics.) One option that Geocast management was considering was accelerating their pursuit of satellite deals.

DBS (direct broadcast satellite) services, with 12.7 million U.S. subscribers in mid-2000, provided strong competition to cable TV system operators, who had 67.8 million subscribers.[19] DBS delivered hundreds of channels of digitally compressed television programming directly from satellites to small (18 to 24 inches) rooftop dishes aimed at a fixed position in the sky. With new dishes that pointed to two or even three satellite positions simultaneously, one DBS service—Echostar—had expanded its capacity to 500 channels.[20] After Congress removed a prohibition on DBS delivery of local network broadcasters' signals in 1999, Echostar used its additional channels to deliver signals from local TV stations. This removed a longstanding barrier to consumer adoption of DBS, because many DBS subscribers had required cable TV to receive these signals.[21]

There were two DBS operators in 2000: DirecTV, with its DirecTV® service and EchoStar with its DISH® service. Since EchoStar had the most satellite spectrum allocations, DISH® had a long-term channel capacity advantage over DirecTV®. In mid-2000, however, DirecTV had 8.7 million subscribers and EchoStar had 4 million subscribers.

Although consumers generally paid somewhat less for cable TV service than for DBS (especially after factoring in consumers' upfront payments for satellite dishes and installation), DBS typically offered much more programming per dollar spent.[22] Some industry experts projected that DBS would continue its high growth for a few years, but eventually level off as more cable operators deployed digital technologies, which they used to offer

[16]In 1965, Gordon Moore—co-founder of Intel—observed that the number of transistors per square inch on integrated circuits had doubled every year since the IC was invented. In subsequent years, the growth in density slowed somewhat so that data density doubled approximately every 18 months; this became the standard definition of Moore's law. Anonymous, "Moore's Law," *Internet.com Webopedia,* http://webopedia.internet.com/TERM/M/Moores_Law.html; viewed 9-1-2000.

[17]Anonymous, "Historical Notes About the Cost of Hard Drive Storage Space," The Technology Shoppe Website (latest revision 9-15-2000): p. 7, p. 9. Canadian dollars converted to U.S. dollars.

[18]Chris Forrester, "News Corp's NDS Looks to the Set Top and Beyond," *Multichannel News International Supplement* (July 2000): Vol. 6, No. 7, p. 34.

[19]Karim Zia, Dennis H. Leibowitz, Michael J. Regan, and Jeff Shelton, "Cable Industry Outlook—Spring 2000," Donaldson, Lufkin & Jenrette (June 9, 2000): p 63.

[20]Anonymous, "What is DBS?" http://www.dishesrus.com/newsrus/html/faq.html; viewed 9-7-2000.

[21]Arthur Cole, "DBS Reaches Critical Mass," *Cable TODAY* (March 2000).

[22]Anonymous, "Cable or Satellite TV—Which Service Offers Consumers the Best Value?" *Cableoptics Newsletter* (January 1, 1999—Vol. 10, No. 1): p. 13.

many more TV channels, high speed Internet access, interactive TV services, and low cost phone service. These experts argued that DBS, as a one-way broadcast medium with severe latency problems,[23] was inherently constrained in its ability to deliver the broadband, real-time interactivity that digital cable promised, and that it also lacked the channel capacity required for HDTV.[24]

Notwithstanding these constraints, the DBS industry was eager to offer interactivity to compete with digital cable, so a partnership with Geocast was likely to be appealing. Geocast management believed that distribution via satellite had several attractive aspects; the most important was satellite's "national footprint," which allowed Geocast service to be offered to anyone in the U.S. Management also believed that the expense of selling Geocast personal receivers through consumer electronics retailers would be high, and that relying on DBS operators to resell Geocast's equipment and service might be less costly. Finally, a successful satellite rollout would put pressure on cable operators to partner with Geocast.

A Geocast-DBS partnership would mean that the partner DBS operator would provide spectrum and would enlist its sales/service agents to market Geocast's service; the operator also could handle receiver distribution and installation. The DBS operator would likely charge a modest subscription premium for Geocast's service and might or might not absorb some of the cost of the box. The cost to manufacture the Geocast receiver would remain the same, with only the tuner needing to be altered. If a wire needed to be pulled from the consumer's rooftop dish to a PC in a different room than the consumer's TV, installation costs would increase—but only modestly, given that the majority of the cost was for the "truck roll" (i.e., the time that a technician spent travelling to and from the customer's home). However, if Geocast followed its original distribution plan and relied on DTV signals from terrestrial broadcasters instead of DBS, a technician still might need to snake a wire from the roof down to the PC (if a rooftop antenna was needed for high quality DTV reception). Hence, the installation cost with DBS was not necessarily an incremental expense, compared to terrestrial signal delivery.

[23]Latency refers to delays in receiving communications signals due to the time required for signal transit and processing. With their stationary (geosynchronous) orbits 22,500 miles over the earth, latency problems were severe for DBS services; even travelling at the speed of light, signals required one-half second to complete a round trip to and from a satellite. See Tom Eisenmann, Dan Green and Doug Rogers, "Teledesic," Harvard Business School (2000): competition-p. 2.

[24]Enrique Rivero, "DBS Has Height Limitations," *Video Business* (July 24, 2000): p. 4.

EchoStar was especially appealing as a potential partner for Geocast because the company had more spectrum and was about to replace all its single LNB dishes with dual and multi-position LNB dishes; replacement typically required a visit from a professional installer.[25] Although DirecTV did have more subscribers, they faced spectrum limitations and already offered Internet service.[26]

2. Proceed with Parallel Launch of Terrestrial Services

Despite the potential reception concerns with terrestrial service, there were reasons to consider launching terrestrial at the same time as satellite. A dual launch would help the company achieve scale more quickly, accelerating the development of ad-supported content. In addition, a dual launch could help preempt certain competitors such as iBlast. Launching terrestrial at the same time as satellite could also help establish the value of the DBS

[25]The LNB—which stood for low noise block down-converter—was the small electronic component that faced inward towards the center of the satellite dish. The LNB amplified the received satellite signal and converted it to a frequency useable by the satellite receiver. A single LNB dish allowed only one receiver (and thus only one TV set) to receive DBS transmissions. A dual LNB dish, like a single LNB dish, could receive programming only from a single orbital location, but viewers could connect one, two or more receivers/televisions to it, thus overcoming another adoption barrier that DBS operators faced in competition with cable TV. Consumers who wanted to receive signals from multiple satellite locations (and thus more TV channels) required the newly introduced multi-location dishes. Richard Peterson, "Satellite Television: A Consumer's Guide," Version 3 (January 1, 2000): p. 4.

[26]DirecTV had announced plans to provide two-way interactive television services via satellite/telephone hybrid technologies, through alliances with AOL and the RBOCs (the "regional Bell operating companies"). DirecTV already offered Internet service via satellite/telephone hybrid technologies through its DirecPC subsidiary, which used a satellite to downlink data, and uplinked user data requests by connecting to an ISP through a telephone modem. The service was not very popular because it offered only modest access speed improvements over standard dial-up ISP service, and because it was quite costly—it required a separate dish, and users paid separate monthly subscription fees to both DirecPC and to an ISP. DirecTV planned to offer higher speed Internet access to PCs through two-way direct links to a new generation of satellites beginning in 2002. This two-way service was expected to have high user terminal costs (it would cost about $1,000 to manufacture the two-way dish and modem) and very high space segment costs (new satellites would be launched into lower orbits to overcome latency problems and thereby provide competitive access speeds). Given these high costs, the proposed service, like the existing DirecPC offering, would be best suited for rural areas where cable modems and DSL could not be economically deployed. See Karim Zia, Dennis H. Leibowitz, Michael J. Regan, and Jeff Shelton, 'Cable Industry Outlook—Spring 2000,' Donaldson Lufkin & Jenrette Equity Research, (June 6, 2000): p. 18.

offering for consumers, as they would see similar terrestrial offers in retail stores.

Most of the reasons for delaying the terrestrial launch related to reception issues. First, deployment would be more expensive if rooftop antenna installation were required. Perhaps most importantly, a terrestrial launch would risk a quality shortfall, and management believed that it was important for clarity to be reached regarding transmission issues. A third reason for delay was the political climate surrounding the sale of DTV spectrum, which created some uncertainty about how spectrum could be used.

Horowitz described his concerns about a terrestrial launch:

> One of the reasons that we've shifted our thinking away from being so aggressive in rolling out terrestrial service is that we don't want to risk the first consumer experience being a negative one. If there is any uncertainty or lack of predictability of spectrum reception, I don't want to launch our business through terrestrial channels until that uncertainty is resolved.

3. Accelerate Negotiations with Cable Systems Operators

The U.S. cable television industry had come under competitive pressure beginning in the late 1990s from DBS operators, digital subscriber line (DSL) providers,[27] and cable overbuilders.[28] A majority of *new* multichannel subscribers had opted for DBS since 1998 (see Exhibit 6); DSL providers were adding new households at a rapid rate; and overbuilders—whose economics had been unattractive for several years—were suddenly being funded due to the viability of new revenue streams from digital video, telephone, and data services. Cable operators were aggressively pursuing these same new revenue streams in response to increased competitive pressures.

Cable operators were moving rapidly into the **digital video** arena, pushed by the success of DBS, which used digital compression technology to offer more programming channels than analog cable systems. Almost every major cable operator had launched a digital video product beginning in 1999. The move to offer digital set-top converters accelerated as prices dropped from $400 when first introduced in 1997 to around $250 to $300 for the second-generation product. Besides increasing channel capacity through digital compression, the new boxes offered increased memory and processing power, allowing advanced applications such as interactive advertising/e-commerce, Internet over television, e-mail, and video-on-demand. Although trials were underway, most cable operators were still following a "wait-and-see" policy with regard to the wide deployment of interactive TV and other advanced applications. However, industry analysts were optimistic about their potential: incremental revenue per digital subscriber was projected to average $13 to $25 per month. With incremental cash flow projected at $10 to $15 per month, the payback period for cable operators' investments in digital converters was expected to be around two years.[29]

Cable operators also had begun marketing **cable modems** more aggressively in 1999, pushed by the popularity of DSL, which was growing at a rapid rate and was projected by some industry observers to pass cable modem sales in the near future.[30] Cable modems connected a PC to the Internet via cable TV lines and provided a high-speed alternative to regular dial-up modems. Although a cable modem subscriber could experience access speeds from 1.5 to 3.0 Mbps, performance often was much slower due to general congestion on the Internet, and also because cable modems relied on a shared access platform (like an Ethernet LAN in an office). Performance could suffer when many customers who were connected to the same coaxial cable "branch" were using their cable modems at the same time. One option cable operators had when this occurred was to allocate additional 6 MHz (megahertz) video channels for high-speed data; another was to deploy high capacity fiber lines deeper into their networks, so fewer subscribers shared each coaxial cable branch line. Upgrading plant in this manner was expensive: assuming that 25% of all cable subscribers eventually acquired cable

[27]DSL employed existing twisted-pair copper telephone lines to deliver Internet traffic at speeds up to 1.5 Mbps (megabits per second)—comparable to cable modem speeds. DSL, priced in many markets between $50 and $100 per month, provided (like cable modems) an "always on" connection to the Internet, and allowed users to make phone calls over the same line while they accessed the Internet. Due to technical limitations, DSL signals typically could not be received by customers who were more than 12,000 to 18,000 feet from a phone company central office switch—a constraint which affected almost half of U.S. consumers.

[28]A cable overbuilder was a company that installed new fiber and coaxial cabling along the same rights-of-way as an incumbent cable franchisee.

[29]Karim Zia, Dennis H. Leibowitz, Michael J. Regan, and Jeff Shelton, "Cable Industry Outlook—Spring 2000," Donaldson, Lufkin & Jenrette Equity Research (June 9, 2000): p. 44.

[30]Bob Metcalfe, "The Fall Lineup, Part 2," *Infoworld* (September 11, 2000): p. 112.

modems, it would cost about $135 per cable modem user to extend fiber to the point where 160 homes shared a common coaxial line, versus 580 homes prior to the upgrade.[31]

There were two reasons why cable operators might want to consider expanding their broadband delivery capacity through a partnership with Geocast. First, deploying Geocast's service could help relieve the network congestion problems confronting cable modem users. Second, freeing cable network bandwidth by leveraging Geocast's caching solutions also could help cable operators respond to: 1) competition from well-funded overbuilders, who offered very high capacity and an "open access" architecture; and 2) regulatory pressures that might require them to provide open access to their plant. Telephone operators were considered "common carriers" and as such were required to provide access to all companies—including ISPs—wishing to use their networks. In the summer of 2000, as the proposed merger of AOL and Time Warner (the second largest cable system operator) raised concerns among ISPs and other Internet companies about whether they might be denied access to the merged entity's cable customers, a regulatory debate had ensued over whether cable modem providers should be required to offer the same open access to the Internet that already existed through phone lines.[32]

One challenge Geocast faced if it pursued distribution through cable systems was helping cable operators position a partnership with the outside world. Promoting Geocast as a superior broadband solution would be tricky for cable operators, as it would force them to acknowledge the limitations of their own cable modems. If Geocast were to license the Geocast technology to @Home or RoadRunner—the main providers of cable modem service for AT&T and Time Warner, respectively—the problem might be avoided if Geocast's technology were bundled with these services. Alternatively, if open access quickly became a reality, Geocast could license its technology to other ISPs. Under that scenario, Geocast might operate as an unbranded technology provider. A final option for Geocast under the open access scenario was offering a Geocast-branded service in direct competition with existing cable modem services and other ISPs.

A second challenge for Geocast would be reaching an acceptable deal with powerful cable companies. In mid-2000, AT&T Broadband and Time Warner accounted for a combined 41% of cable subscribers. The next four largest cable operators accounted for another 40% of the market. Notwithstanding the recent emergence of competition, cable operators tended to view the world through the lenses of entrenched monopolists, and negotiated with prospective partners accordingly.

4. Reposition the Personal Receiver as a Personal Server

> *Every technology revolution has started with a device that had to overcome hurdles to get it into consumers' homes. Knowing that can lead you to think of your device as a problem rather than an opportunity. At first, we called our product a 'receiver'. We also called it 'a box' and 'a brick.' But we began to see that we really had an incredible unexploited asset, 'the personal server.'*
>
> –Mark Simmer

With increased interest in home information networks—as well as growing momentum for digital downloads of music, e-books, games and software—another alternative available to Geocast was repositioning its box as a unique server that could "unleash the PC's true potential." This strategy would put the box front-and-center, highlighting its unique capabilities rather than apologizing for it.

In the summer of 2000, a growing number of people used PCs as personal servers to self-publish Websites, manage their own e-mail accounts, share files, and perform other server-related tasks. The biggest driver behind the growth in personal Web servers was the exponential increase in downloading music files.[33] With the average MP3 song using 4 MB of space, storage and transfer were not feasible for most consumers until the year 2000, when—for the first time—$150 bought a 30 GB (gigabyte) hard drive capable of holding 614 CDs in MP3 format. This was all the more impressive given that the average music owner owned 30 CDs and the average

[31] Raymond Katz, 'Cable Industry Overview,' Bear Stearns Equity Research (April 1998): p. 24.

[32] The FCC was willing to approve the pending AOL–Time Warner merger only if AOL–Time Warner accepted restrictions similar to those proposed by the FTC: allowing rival Internet services to have control of the all-important "first screen" and allowing the competitor to bill the customer. John R. Wilke "Both Sides Get Touch as Crunch Time Nears on AOL–Time Warner," *The Wall Street Journal* (September 25, 2000): pp. A1, A21.

[33] Julio Ojeda-Zapata, "Personal Web Servers Becoming More Common," *ITSpace.com* (July 29, 2000), http://www.itspace.com/Itsp . . . Ipha/News/mainfeatures/feat000729_04.asp; viewed 9-6-2000.

music enthusiast owned only 200.[34] In addition to music downloads, software downloads were increasing as well. During the summer of 2000, CNET announced that downloads of ICQ's ("I Seek You") instant messaging software had surpassed the 100 million mark,[35] and thousands of consumers downloaded new software and software updates from companies such as Microsoft as well. Increased availability of high-speed DSL lines and cable modems had also made Web servers more practical.

One additional indicator that increased downloads and home networking were on the horizon was Microsoft's recently announced ".Net" (pronounced 'dot-net') initiative. The initiative—announced in June 2000—was intended to develop a new Internet-based operating system that would provide seamless connectivity and information sharing across all consumer electronic devices from smart phones to PCs to PDAs to DTV receivers.[36] Microsoft also intended to use the initiative to move into new markets such as interactive TV.[37]

Repositioning the Geocast receiver as a personal server implied the ability to interconnect multiple PCs and potentially other devices—including television set-top boxes, eBook readers, and audio equipment—via a local area network (LAN). Geocast was compatible with wireless LAN technology, which would minimize the labor needed to connect the various devices. In addition, repositioning the box as a personal server implied a stronger focus on commerce—especially related to the sale or rental of downloaded software and content. Such a focus might allow for higher revenues early in the technology's life.

If Geocast pursued this strategy, it would have to compete with several other startups and established companies that had expressed an interest in developing server-based home information systems. These systems provided centralized storage and distribution of data and applications such as address books, family calendars, and music.[38] For example, Sony's President had announced that Sony expected to reposition its home PCs as personal servers.[39] Other companies, such as Compaq, also planned to move into the home networking market in response to continued strong growth in online households and multi-PC households.

TiVo, a company that provided "personal television services" in a TV set-top box, also had the opportunity to move into the personal server market. In mid-2000, TiVo was the leader in the digital video recorder (DVR) market—also called the personal video recorder (PVR) market—with 51,000 subscribers. DVRs solved the television programmers' dilemma: broadcasters had sophisticated data showing them what their audiences wanted to watch, but they were constrained by a linear programming schedule. If the scheduling constraint could be removed by installing a home-based storage device, programmers could potentially provide much more content to viewers.

To use TiVo's service, a consumer first paid $299 for a receiver manufactured by Philips or Sony, and then a $199 one-time fee for lifelong service.[40] The TiVo receiver had a 27.2GB hard drive and stored 30 hours of programming. The receiver needed to be plugged into a phone jack to receive nightly programming schedule updates; however, TiVo did not need a dedicated phone line. TiVo's software—Linux on an embedded chip—captured consumer preferences, both stated and observed, which were stored in the receiver unit. TiVo users could skip over television commercials when watching stored programs.

In mid-1999, both TiVo and its major competitor—Replay TV, which offered a similar DVR service—announced investments from content providers; AOL invested in TiVo, receiving in return a hardware platform over which to offer its services, while Time Warner, NBC, and others invested in Replay.

5. Create a Targeted Offering for Online Retailers

Slow Web connections were a major contributor to abandoned shopping carts for online retailers; in addition, rich graphics and video could be effective in selling

[34]Bill Gurley, "Music, Morality and Moore's Law," *Above the Crowd*—a monthly online column also featured in *Fortune* magazine (September 18, 2000).

[35]Anonymous, "CNET Announces 100 million Downloads for #1 Product on Download.com," CNET Networks, Inc. Press Release (June 16, 2000).

[36]Barry McCall, "Microsoft Unveils .Net Web Initiative," *ElectricNews.Net* (June 23, 2000), http://www.electricnews.net/tm209a2084b962424000c965102400.html; viewed 9-1-2000.

[37]Bob Trott and Tom Sullivan, "Microsoft's Ongoing Success Hinges on Adopting Standards," *Infoworld* (September 11, 1000): p. 20.

[38]Anonymous, "Linux-Based Home Network Startup Gets Seed Capital," *Client Server News* (April 24, 2000).

[39]Kunitake Ando, "Strategy in the Broadband Era," Sony Corporation's Investor Meeting (December 13, 1999), http://www.world.sony.com/R/Meeting/Challenges/2000/opening.html; reviewed 9-17-2000.

[40]Consumers could opt to pay $9.95 per month in lieu of the $199 up-front fee. TiVo Website, http://www.tivo.com/what/faq_sub.html; viewed 9-18-2000.

certain products. Geocast had the option of creating a service offering that could address these needs for online retailers. A technical challenge presented by that option was that most online retailers offered thousands of SKUs (stock keeping units) displayed on hundreds of Web pages, with each page generating only a small portion of overall sales. Downloading a large number of online catalogs, each with a large volume of rich media content, could exhaust the capacity of Geocast's servers. One potential solution was to download the online catalog only for the heaviest customers of a given online retailer and/or only for those customers targeted to receive a rich media e-mail promotion from the retailer.

6. Revise Pricing and Revenue Sharing Agreements

At the same time that Geocast was reviewing the strategic options described above, management was also considering various pricing and revenue sharing alternatives.

Consumer Pricing. Geocast had originally planned to offer the Geocast service to consumers for free, charging them around $300 for the Geocast box, then subsidizing the additional $200 or so required for marketing support and retailer margin through equity capital infusions. An industry analyst had projected that numerous devices with built-in hard disk drives would be introduced to compete with DVRs; he projected that prices would vary depending on disk drive capacity, but that $200 would be the takeoff point for mass consumer adoption.[41] Since Geocast could no longer count on over-heated capital markets to subsidize equipment costs, could it meet this price target? Consumer electronics manufacturers might consider absorbing some of the cost in exchange for a share of Geocast's ongoing revenue. Moving into services and away from the hyper-competitive, low-margin hardware business had great appeal for many manufacturers. The 1997 Thomson-Gemstar deal provided an example of this type of partnership. Gemstar, the leading provider of electronic programming guide (EPG) services had entered into a joint venture with Thomson whereby Gemstar's EPG was deployed in Thomson's TVs and VCRs, and the two companies explored ways to pursue advertising opportunities for the EPG. The biggest issue for Geocast with such an arrangement was trading away a portion of the company's future upside.

Changing capital market conditions, in particular the "shortened runway" confronting Internet startups, also raised the issue of whether the company should consider charging subscription fees on an annual or a monthly basis. There were two issues associated with subscription fees. The first was identifying the premium that Geocast's service could support. Geocast executives knew that cable modems had a $10 per month premium over dial-up ISP service when the consumer supplied the modem (which cost approximately $250), and a $20 premium when the modem was bundled with the service. One pricing approach that Geocast management was considering was introducing additional subscription services, e.g. a music subscription zone that would allow a subscriber to gain access to MP3 files and games for an additional $10 per month.

The second issue was determining the extent to which receiver sales might be inhibited by charging a subscription fee—a serious concern, because advertisers valued scale. Simmer commented:

> Advertising-based business models depend entirely on critical mass. Even though advertisers say that they want to do one-to-one marketing, the reality is that they want to do one-to-one marketing with a base of 20 million people.

Content Provider Pricing and Revenue Sharing. Geocast originally had planned to share ad revenue with content providers. Management expected its service to generate healthy ad revenues per subscriber, because market research indicated that more than 21% of broadband users had incomes over $100,000, and the average high-speed Internet surfer was twice as likely to shop online as a dialup user. However, the market for rich media advertising over broadband Internet services was still very young: the majority of revenue for broadband providers such as Excite@Home still came from access fees, with advertising income averaging only around $2 per subscriber per month.[42]

Given the evolving state of the rich media ad market and the need to manage for near term profits, Geocast

[41]Richard Shim, "Digital Devices to Kill VCRs?," *ZDNet News* (May 18, 2000), http://www.zdnet.com/filters/printer/friendly/0,6061,2571471-2,00.html; viewed 9-18-2000.

[42]Alexei Oreskovic, "Broadband or Bust," *The Industry Standard* (June 19, 2000): p. 216.

management was considering whether to charge its content partners up-front "slotting fees."[43] Such fees would be based on Geocast's economic value-added from two sources: reduced network delivery costs (partners would spend less on hosting and bandwidth), and increased user retention/page views due to the high quality broadband experience. Akamai Technologies (Akamai) had proven that there was value to moving content rapidly. Akamai—founded with the goal of making Websites respond more quickly—installed servers close to its Website partners' users and mapped congestion patterns around those servers to optimize content movement. The company charged its partners fees based on megabytes of data handled.[44]

Geocast management hoped to avoid a "walled garden" feel and planned to offer a wide variety of content, which implied partnerships with multiple content providers in a given category. However, management expected that some content players would push for exclusivity during partnership discussions. One item on the strategy discussion agenda was which types of exclusivity arrangements might work without hampering long-term growth. Of course, if Geocast did enter into some exclusive arrangements, partners would be expected to pay a substantial premium. But as Geocast management tried to lock in revenues during its launch phase, should they risk bargaining hard with key accounts, who would, after all, be taking a risk with a new service? The possibility of entering into some exclusive partnerships also raised the issue of control with respect to the "look and feel" of the Geocast service—and how much control Geocast should exercise to provide a coherent navigational experience and a consistent brand image. Content providers were likely to want to brand their Geocast offering and preserve their own look and feel.

Conclusion

Horowitz knew that the issues Geocast faced were challenging ones; nonetheless, he was extremely optimistic about Geocast's future. He was confident of the power of Geocast's technology and proud that the company had been able to assemble a management team with great depth and breadth. Further, Geocast had world-class investors and an impressive array of business partners. As he headed from his office to the company's conference room for the management team's strategy session, Horowitz looked forward to a lively discussion of the company's options.

[43] "Slotting fees" referred to fees paid by a producer of consumer goods to a retailer in exchange for shelf space. In this situation, it referred to charging fees to content providers in exchange for carrying their content.

[44] Max Smetannikov, "Frontier Picks Akamai for Cisco Connection," *Interactive Week* (September 22, 1999), hhtp://www.zdnet.com/intweek/stories/news/0,4164,2339242,00.html; viewed 9-5-2000.

Exhibit 1 GEOCAST NETWORK ARCHITECTURE

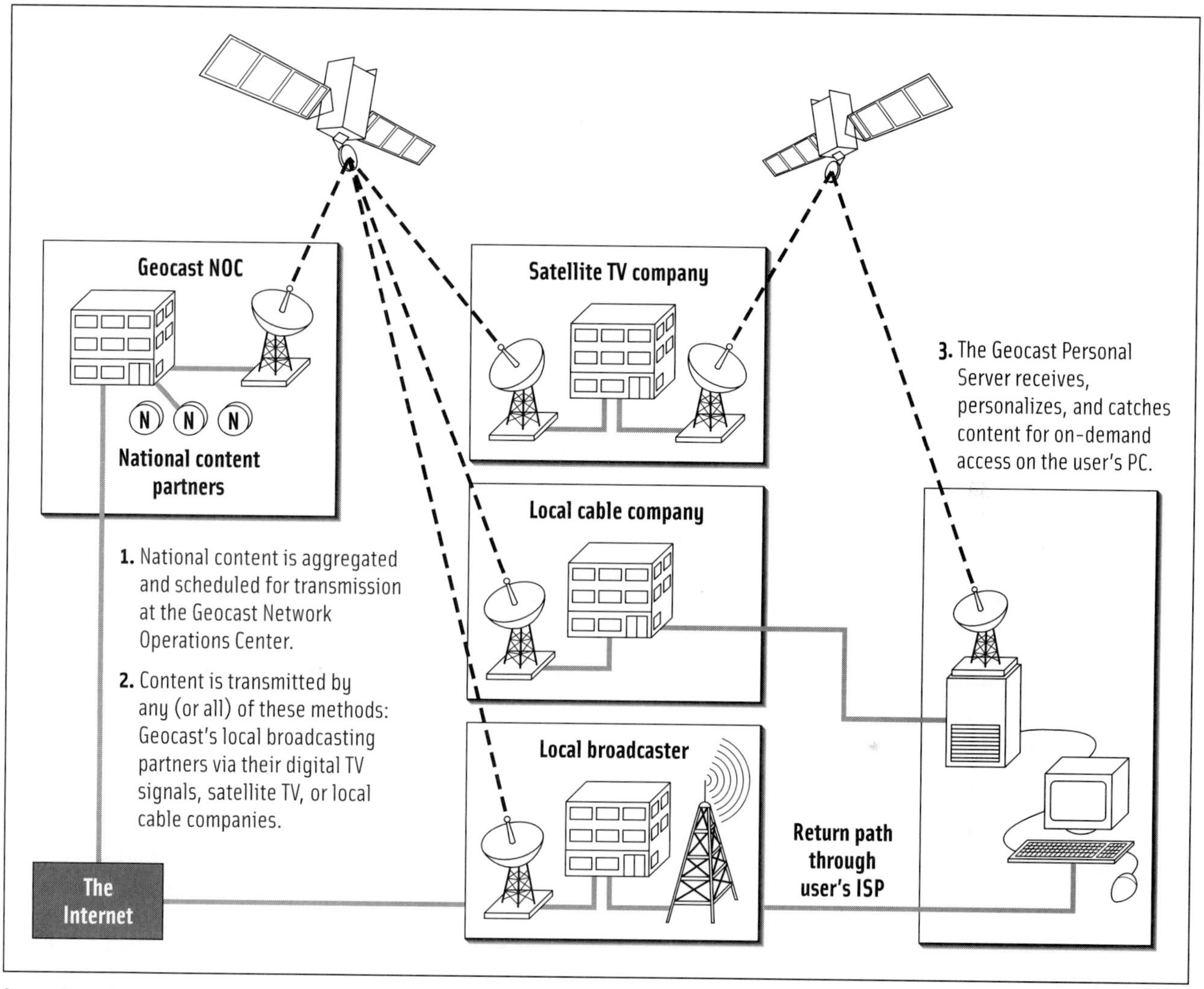

Source: Geocast

Exhibit 2

GEOCAST MANAGEMENT TEAM

H. Joseph Horowitz
Chairman and CEO
Horowitz was a veteran venture capitalist with more than 20 years of experience in forming and guiding technology and consumer start-up companies. During 10 years at U.S. Venture Partners, the firm invested in companies as diverse as Sun Microsystems, StrataCom, Ross Stores, and Avia. As founder of ICON Venture Advisors, Horowitz had been an advisor to or a director of Pacific Microsonics (sold to Microsoft), Telecruz, Microtune, Imedia (sold to Terayon), Classroom Connect, Encompass (sold to Yahoo!), Stream Machine, eAlity, Visto, 3 Day Blinds, Netsys (sold to Cisco), and Evans Rents (sold to Cort). His experience in television and media dated back to 1991 when he became involved with StarSight Telecast, a company he was instrumental in building and merging into Gemstar International, whose market value in mid-2000 was over $12 billion. Horowitz graduated from Columbia University where he studied engineering and economics, and had an M.B.A. from the Wharton School of Finance.

Charles Jablonski
Senior Vice President of Network Engineering and Operationsr
Jablonski joined Geocast after serving as vice president of broadcast and network engineering for NBC for six years. During that time he oversaw all of NBC's technology and engineering functions for the network, stations, and development activities. During his 16-year tenure with NBC, Jablonski received numerous industry accolades, including three Emmy Awards, one for NBC's Olympic Games coverage. He was president of the Society of Motion Picture and Television Engineers and served on the board of directors of the National Association of North American Broadcasters. He was also chairman of the NATAS (Emmy) Awards Committee for science and technology.

Tom Paquin
Senior Vice President of Engineering
Paquin formerly managed the client and server engineering team at Netscape, where he was the company's seventh employee. He also managed client-side software, with an emphasis on Java and JavaScript, and was named a Netscape fellow. Before joining Netscape, Paquin worked on graphics hardware at Silicon Graphics and IBM Research. He had a B.S. in applied mathematics from the University of Colorado.

Mark Simmer
Senior Vice President of Marketing and Programming
Simmer joined Geocast from Lycos, Inc., where he served as both vice president of online media and chief content officer. Simmer joined Lycos before its 1996 IPO and led its design, content, and production teams as the company grew to become the world's fourth-largest web destination and a NASDAQ 100 company. Before joining Lycos, Simmer was editor in chief at Point Communications, one of the first Web directories and one of the first websites to sell banner advertising, acquired by Lycos in 1995. Prior to that, Simmer spent 10 years in local television with Seattle-based King Broadcasting at its Spokane and Portland affiliates, moving up from reporter and producer to managing editor and assistant news director at KGW-TV in Portland.

John Abel
Vice President of Broadcasting Development
A former executive vice president of the National Association of Broadcasters, Abel was instrumental in the broadcasting industry's development of digital television. He was a founding board member of the Advanced Television Test Center, and served as vice chairman of the systems subcommittee of the FCC's industry committee on advanced television service. Abel also was president and CEO of Datacast LLC, a partnership of broadcasters working to advance digital broadcasting. Prior to that, he was chairman of the department of telecommunications at Michigan State University, and served as a consultant to the FCC. He had both a master's and a doctoral degree from Indiana University.

Jerry Agresti

Vice President of Broadcast Engineering

Agresti joined Geocast after serving as director of engineering and operations at WRC-TV in Washington, where he managed the engineering and operations departments. While there, he implemented WRC's conversion to 601 digital and DTV in support of the engineering efforts of the NBC Washington news bureau. Prior to that, Agresti was director of engineering at WCPX, (now WKMG) in Orlando, Florida and at KCRA, in Sacramento. He had also worked as a technical director and EIC for many news, sports and entertainment programs. Agresti had certification as a broadcast engineer by the Society of Broadcast Engineers and served as chairperson of the Sacramento chapter. He was also a member of SMPTE and served as manager of the Sacramento chapter.

Jessica Algazi

Vice President of Content Partnerships

Algazi joined Geocast from Discovery Communications, Inc., where she served as vice president, business affairs. At Discovery she was responsible for negotiating programming content agreements for all of the Discovery television networks worldwide, including Discovery Channel, TLC, Animal Planet, Travel Channel, Discovery Health, and numerous Discovery digital networks. Prior to joining Discovery Communications, Algazi served as vice president of business affairs with Metro-Goldwyn-Mayer Studios, Inc., where she negotiated domestic and international distribution licenses related to the film libraries of MGM, United Artists, Cannon, and Metromedia.

Edward Casaccia

Vice President of Content Operations and Planning

Casaccia joined Geocast from Sony Electronics Broadcast and Professional group where he served as the newsroom marketing manager. Prior to joining Sony Electronics, Casaccia was the news director for the Orange County NewsChannel for five years. Prior to that, Casaccia was the executive producer at KGO-TV news in San Francisco. He had a B.A. from California State University, Fresno.

Reese Faucette

Vice President of Technology

Faucette joined Geocast from The Kernel Group where he held the position of chief technology officer for two years and then became the CEO. As CEO of The Kernel Group, Faucette helped increase the company's revenue by $11 million in under two years. He had a computer science degree from Caltech.

Hilary Goodall

Vice President of Programming

Goodall joined Geocast from Cox Interactive Media, a subsidiary of Cox Enterprises, Inc., where she served as vice president of content programming. A member of the founding group at Cox Interactive Media, Goodall helped build a network of locally focused city Web sites across the country designed to serve residents and advertisers in local communities. Prior to that, Goodall was managing editor with @Home Network, where she developed an innovative content service for the broadband network's launch. Goodall also held senior level editorial and content development positions with Apple Internet Services and Taft Broadcasting, and was part of the BBC CEEFAX team that developed the world's first electronic news and information service. Goodall had a B.A. with honors in history from the University of Kent at Canterbury. She earned a post-graduate research scholarship and held a teaching faculty position in interactive publishing at Miami University (Ohio).

Michael Gustafson

Vice President of Network Operations

Gustafson came to Geocast from CellNet Data Systems where he served as the director of engineering, overseeing the development of a 900 MHz wireless network communications system. Prior to CellNet, Gustafson was director of product engineering at Digital Microwave Corp. where he and his team were responsible for developing new microwave radio systems. He had an engineering degree from the University of Arizona.

Allison Hopkins
Vice President of Human Resources
Hopkins was the founder and CEO of Core Elements, a human resources consulting firm for technology and service organizations. She consulted for companies such as Bay Networks, Netscape, NetObjects, Lucent Technologies, Marimba, CrossWorlds Software, Stream Machine, Gymboree, and others. She had also served as vice president of human resources for Cunningham Communications and director of human resources for Syntex.

Jim Jackson
Vice President of Hardware Engineering
Jackson was a specialist in computer architecture, VLSI design, and high-speed networks, and had held senior management positions at PMC-Sierra, Pyramid Technologies, and Convex Computer. He held an M.S. degree in electrical engineering and a B.S. in computer engineering from the University of Illinois.

Brian L. Klosterman
Vice President of Channel Distribution and Services
Before joining Geocast, Klosterman was president of StarSight Telecast, Inc., a subsidiary of Gemstar. Before the company's May 1996 acquisition by Gemstar, he was president and COO of StarSight, responsible for both the company's direction and operation. Prior to that, as vice president of Sony's consumer Television Products Co., Kosterman managed all key elements of U.S. television operations, including product strategy and development, marketing and program development, pricing strategy, national advertising, and public relations. He also held sales, marketing, and product development positions with Thomson Consumer Electronics (RCA), and had broad experience in retail and wholesale electronics distribution.

Naresh Makhijani
Vice President of Program Management
Makhijani came to Geocast from CyberStar, where he held several key positions, most recently that of vice president of product engineering. While there, he established a customer solutions group and led the development and integration of various satellite-based multicast applications, including video streaming, multicast file delivery, video kiosk, and broadband Internet access. Makhijani also led the program management function and managed the CyberStar data network operation center. Before CyberStar, he was an executive director at Space Systems Loral, where he led the design, development, integration, and testing of communications systems for several European accounts.

Charles Marker
Vice President of Engineering
Marker began his career at Honeywell Information Systems on the MULTICS development team, moving from there to the Special Projects group at Lawrence Livermore National Laboratory where he worked on super computer operating system development. Marker held various development and senior management positions, first at MIPS Computer Systems and later at SGI. At SGI, he was responsible for software development for desktop systems and most recently was responsible for the SGI Linux strategy. Marker held a B.S. in electrical engineering from the Massachusetts Institute of Technology.

Jim Omura
Chief Scientist
A former UCLA professor of electrical engineering and founder of two Silicon Valley companies, Omura had extensive experience bringing technical products and services to market. He founded and served as chairman, CTO, and acting CEO of Cylink, a network security and wireless products company that had a successful IPO in 1996. He also co-authored textbooks on spread-spectrum communications and digital communications. Omura was a fellow of the IEEE and a member of the National Academy of Engineering.

Jim Plant
Vice President of Marketing Communications
Plant joined Geocast from ReplayTV, Inc., where he served as the director of marketing and director of corporate communications for the pioneering personal television service company. At ReplayTV he wrote the company's first marketing and public relations plans and oversaw the public relations launch at the 1999 Consumer Electronics Show, where ReplayTV won 'Best of Show' honors in the video category. Before joining ReplayTV, Plant was the founder and chief executive officer of AMG Media until its sale to Miller Freeman in 1996. At AMG Media he was the founding editor-in-chief of Avid, The Amiga-Video Journal and Video Toaster User Magazine. He also oversaw the development of Alpha Visual FX Magazine and Lightwave Pro. Prior to starting AMG Media, Plant was the director of corporate and educational sales at HT Electronics focusing on 3D visual effects and desktop video production.

Anita Wallgren
Vice President of Business Affairs
Before joining Geocast, Wallgren was the legal advisor to Federal Communications Commissioner Susan Ness. She also served as vice president of legal and business affairs at Sony Worldwide Networks; vice president and associate general counsel for Citicasters, a radio and TV station holding company; communications policy specialist at the National Telecommunications and Information Administration; and manager of governmental affairs at Taft Broadcasting. Wallgren had a B.A. and a law degree from the University of Michigan.

Source: Geocast.

Exhibit 3

GEOCAST INVESTORS

Television Broadcasters

Hearst-Argyle Television, Inc.

Hearst-Argyle Television, Inc. owned and/or managed 26 network-affiliated television stations, and owned and/or managed seven radio stations in geographically diverse U.S. markets. The company's television stations reached about 17.5% of U.S. television households, making it one of the two largest non-network-owned television station groups in the U.S. and one of the seven largest television groups overall, as measured by audience delivered.

Belo Corporation

Belo Corporation was one of the nation's largest media companies, with a diversified group of assets in television broadcasting, newspaper publishing, cable news, and electronic media. In 2000, the company's television group reached 13.6% of U.S. television households, including three stations in the top 12 television markets: WFAA-TV (ABC) in Dallas/Fort Worth, KHOU-TV (CBS) in Houston, and KING-TV (NBC) in Seattle/Tacoma. Belo had six stations in the top 30 markets and 11 stations in the top 50 markets. The company owned four ABC network affiliates, six CBS affiliates, five NBC affiliates, and two FOX affiliates. In addition, the company managed four television stations through local marketing agreements and owned four local or regional cable news channels.

Allbritton Communications

Based in Washington, D.C., Allbritton Communications owned or operated ABC-affiliated television stations in seven markets: Washington, D.C.; Birmingham, Alabama; Little Rock, Arkansas; Tulsa, Oklahoma; Harrisburg, Pennsylvania; Charleston, South Carolina; and Lynchburg, Virginia. An Allbritton affiliate also owned News Channel 8, the 24-hour cable news channel serving the Washington, D.C. area.

Consumer Electronics Firms

Thomson Multimedia

With 1999 sales over $6 billion and approximately 55,000 employees in more than 30 countries, Thomson Multimedia (NYSE: TMS) was the fourth-largest global supplier of consumer electronics products. The group had four main divisions: displays and components, consumer products, new media services, and patents and licensing. Within these areas, Thomson Multimedia developed, manufactured, and sold television displays and components, and consumer products such as televisions, VCRs, camcorders, audio and communications products, digital decoders, DVD players, and professional video equipment. Thomson Multimedia was the parent company of the U.S.-based Thomson Consumer Electronics, Inc.

Royal Philips Electronics

Royal Philips Electronics was one of the world's largest electronics companies and the largest in Europe, with sales of EUR 31.5 billion in 1999. The company was a global leader in color television sets, lighting, electric shavers, color picture tubes for televisions and monitors, and one-chip TV products. Its 226,900 employees in more than 60 countries were active in lighting, consumer electronics, domestic appliances, components, semiconductors, medical systems, and IT services.

Media Firms

Liberty Media Corporation

Liberty Media Corporation held interests in a broad range of video programming, communications, technology, and Internet businesses in the U.S., Europe, South America, and Asia. Liberty's interest in video programming included numerous globally branded entertainment networks, such as Discovery Channel, TV Guide, QVC, STARZ, and Encore. Liberty's assets also included interests in international video distribution businesses, international telephony and domestic wireless telephony, plant and equipment manufacturing, and other businesses related to broadband services.

Electronic Arts

Headquartered in Redwood City, California, Electronic Arts was the world's leading interactive entertainment software company. Founded in 1982, the company posted revenues of more than $1.2 billion for fiscal 1999. The company developed, published, and distributed software worldwide for personal computers and video game systems such as PlayStation and the Nintendo 64. Electronic Arts marketed its products under eight brand names: Electronic Arts, EA SPORTS, Maxis, ORIGIN, Bullfrog Productions, Westwood Studios, and Jane's Combat Simulations. The company had international subsidiaries or distribution in more than 75 countries and 13 major development operations in locations throughout the world: Redwood City, Carlsbad, Irvine, and Walnut Creek, Calif.; Baltimore, Maryland; Austin, Texas; Maitland, Florida; Seattle, Washington; Las Vegas, Nevada; Vancouver, British Columbia; the Gold Coast, Australia; the United Kingdom; and Japan.

Venture Capital Firms

Mayfield Fund

In 2000, the Mayfield Fund had $1 billion in capital under management and had invested in more than 300 information technology and healthcare companies, whose total market value exceeded $100 billion. The Mayfield Fund's investments included SGI, Redback Networks, The Motley Fool, BroadVision, Inc., Skystream, and Omneon Video Networks. Kevin Fong served on Geocast's Board of Directors.

Kleiner Perkins Caufield & Byers

Kleiner Perkins was one of the nation's leading venture capital firms. It had been instrumental in creating the personal computer and Internet industries, and had a strong position in biotechnology. Its long list of investments included Amazon.com, Netscape, @Home, Sun Microsystems, America Online, Excite, Intuit, Marimba, Healtheon, Sportsline, and Genentech. Will Hearst served on Geocast's Board of Directors.

Institutional Venture Partners

Institutional Venture Partners was a leading venture capital firm specializing in growing technology markets such as e-commerce, digital TV, Web infrastructure, and medical devices. Among the 200 companies IVP funded were Ask Jeeves, Bay Networks, Mpath, Excite, TiVo, Juniper Networks, MMC Networks, and Foundry Networks. Geoff Yang served on Geocast's Advisory Board.

Source: Geocast Web site.

Exhibit 4 BACKGROUND ON THE DATACASTING MARKET

Datacasting[45] was in its infancy in the year 2000. Datacasters assembled content, generally sold advertising at the local and national level, managed a delivery network, and provided customer service for the hardware and subscriptions sold. The datacasting opportunity arose as a result of the government mandate that broadcasters convert from analog to digital by 2002, discontinuing analog broadcasts by 2006. TV stations were eager for additional revenue streams to support the conversion, and stations were able to free between 2 to 10 Mbps for datacasting depending on whether they broadcast SDTV or HDTV.

Because the datacasting industry was very young, and many competitors had yet to launch their products, little market data existed. In mid-2000, data on streaming[46] media usage was just becoming available, and provided some insight into the datacasting market. (See **Table A** below.) Approximately 11% of Websites offered some type of broadband experience in the form of video, Internet radio or other streaming media, and 89% of Websites were projected to offer streaming media by 2002.[47] However, only 10% of U.S. households had broadband access. Analysts projected that that number would grow to between 23% and 32% of households within two years.[48]

Table A Streaming Media Users (millions)

	January 2000	July 2000
High Speed Users (>56Kbps)	2.5	4.8
Narrowband Users (< or = 56Kbps)	22.2	28.2
Total Streaming Media Users	24.7	33.0

Source: David Lake, "Tracking the Net's Media Stream," *The Industry Standard* (October 2, 2000): p. 176. Data from RealPlayer, Quicktime, and Windows Media Player usage only.

Although the move to broadband content and access seemed inexorable, the profitability of delivering broadband remained an issue. The revenues that Websites earned from selling advertising space was estimated to range from $12.50 to $23.50 for a thousand views, while the cost ranged from $14.10 per thousand for FM-quality Internet radio to $75 per thousand for VHS-quality video. (See **Table B** below.) Only very low quality video and FM-quality radio streams covered the gap between content delivery costs and ad revenues.

Table B Broadband Content Delivery Costs

Streaming Content Delivered	Type	Length (seconds)	Speed (Kbps)	Size (MB)	Cost per 1,000 Users
VHS-quality video	3 min.+ 20 second ad	200	0.300	7.5	$75.00
Low-quality video	3 min.+ 20 second ad	200	0.100	2.5	$25.00
Internet radio-CD quality	2.5 songs+ 20 second ad	470	0.080	4.7	$47.00
Internet radio–FM quality	2.5 songs+ 20 second ad	470	0.024	1.4	$14.00

Source: Mark Mowrey, "Streaming Media Bleeds Cash," *The Industry Standard* (October 2, 2000): p. 173.

[45]Datacasting was defined as a form of telecommunication allowing for simultaneous transmission of electronic/digital data from one point to many points within the service area of a specific network (terrestrial or cable) or footprint (satellite).

[46]Streaming was a technique for transferring data such that it could be processed as a steady continuous stream. Streaming technologies became important with the growth of the Internet because most users did not have fast enough access to download large multimedia files quickly. With streaming, the client browser could start displaying the data before the entire file had been transmitted. If data didn't come through quickly enough, the presentation of data was not smooth.

[47]Mark Mowrey, "Streaming Media Bleeds Cash," *The Industry Standard* (October 2, 2000): p. 173.

[48]Ibid.

Exhibit 5

DATACASTING COMPANIES

Company (Location)	Year Founded	Product	Selected Partners & Investors	Projected Market Entry
Geocast (Menlo Park, CA)	1997	Datacast receiver	Hearst-Argyle Television, Belo Corporation, Allbritton Communication, Thomson Multimedia, Royal Philips Electronics, Liberty Media, Electronic Arts	2001
iBlast (Beverly Hills, CA)	2000	Branded network spectrum broker	Cox Enterprises, McGraw-Hill, Media General, the New York Times Company, the Washington Post Company, Gray Communications, the Tribune Company, Gannett	2001
Dotcast (Palo Alto, CA)	1999	Linux-based receiver (NTSC & DTV)	Intel, Softnet Systems, PBS National Datacast, the Tribune Company	2001
Wavexpress (New York, NY)	1999	Datacast receiver	Sarnoff, Wave Systems, Compaq, Panasonic, Sinclair Broadcasting, Capitol Broadcasting, TeraLogic	2001
Broadcasters Digital Cooperative (led by Granite Broadcasting Corp., NY, NY)	2000	Spectrum broker	Granite Broadcasting, Paxton, Capitol Broadcasting, Gray Communications	2001
IBEAM Broadcasting (Sunnyvale, CA)	1998	Satellite data-casting	Intel, Covad, Microsoft, Sony, RealNetworks, Williams Communications, Liberty Media, Network Appliance	2001

Sources: "HDTV Detour: Cable and the Broadband Revolution," Sam's Digital Television Report, *http://www.teleport.com/~samc/hdtv/hdtv4.html;* viewed 9-11-2000. Glen Dickson, "Getting Together Over Data," Broadcasting and Cable (March 27, 2000). Anonymous, "TV Broadcasters Warned Against Leasing HDTV Spectrum," Wave Report (Issue 2040, July 27, 2000). Company websites: *www.iblast.com, www.dotcast.com, www.wavexpress.com, www.ibeam.com;* all websites viewed 9-25-2000.

Exhibit 6 SELECTED SATELLITE, CABLE, PC AND DSL STATISTICS

(Households and Subscribers in Thousands)							
	1998A	1999A	2000E	2001E	2002E	2003E	2004E
U.S. Households(HH)	102,448	103,738	104,966	106,054	107,093	108,231	109,484
Television HH	99,600	100,802	102,045	103,154	104,217	105,376	106,649
Basic Cable Subs	66,100	67,300	68,175	68,788	69,201	69,478	69,617
Digital Video Subs	1,252	3,723	8,357	14,357	21,357	28,857	35,857
Satellite (DBS) Subs	8,694	11,468	14,959	18,159	21,059	23,759	26,259
Other MultiChannel	4,071	4,348	3,598	3,198	2,896	2,673	2,527
Total Multichannel	78,865	83,116	86,732	90,145	93,156	95,910	98,403
PC HH	53,000	57,700	61,900	64,700	67,500	69,500	71,500
Online HH	37,600	44,900	51,500	57,200	62,200	66,700	70,200
DSL-Ready Homes	3,000	29,100	45,000	53,027	64,256	67,644	71,165
DSL Subscribers	30	396	2,289	5,289	8,789	12,539	16,539
Cable Telephony-Ready Homes	1,257	4,116	11,032	24,014	34,061	41,937	46,569
Cable Telephony Subs	49	198	868	2,401	4,769	7,549	9,780
Cable Modem-Ready Homes	19,833	37,340	62,844	69,639	72,988	76,474	80,119
Cable Modem Subs	389	1,331	3,627	6,627	9,877	13,377	17,127

Source: Karim Zia, Dennis H. Leibowitz, Michael J. Regan, and Jeff Shelton, 'Cable Industry Outlook-Spring 2000,' Donaldson, Lufkin & Jenrette (June 9, 2000), pp. 52, 63.
Note: Digital Video Subscribers are a subset of Basic Cable Subscribers.

2

Online Portals

Por·tal *n* A doorway, gate, or entrance, especially a large and imposing one

—*Webster's New World Dictionary*

Through the late 1990s, the Internet continued to evolve at a frenetic pace. From a little-known channel for data exchange between academic researchers, by late 2000 it had been transformed into a global network connecting over 100 million host computers containing 2.7 billion webpages.1 With a profusion of websites, it was only natural that portals emerged to help guide Internet users through all the clutter. Portals quickly became the most heavily trafficked Internet destinations against all metrics: unique audience, reach, and visits per person (see Exhibits 1 and 2). By 2000, they had become central hubs for online content, communication, community, and commerce. At the same time, however, some industry observers questioned the future of portals. As Internet users became more comfortable navigating the World Wide Web, would the value proposition of portals remain compelling?

This chapter describes the online portal business model. The first section defines the model, offers a summary of the various ways that online portals create value for their customers, and presents different ways to categorize portals. The second section analyzes the business model for portals, focusing on the tactics they can use to acquire new users, turn new users into repeat visitors, and monetize user traffic. The third section examines portal economics, describing their revenue and cost drivers. Building on that analysis, the fourth section examines the payoff to Internet portals from pursuing a "Get Big Fast" strategy, i.e., investing aggressively in customer acquisition and brand building. The final section explores the challenges facing companies that aspire to develop portals for new online access technologies, such as wireless data and interactive television.

Assistant Professor Thomas Eisenmann and Research Associate Sanjay T. Pothen prepared this note as the basis for class discussion.

Exhibit 2-1 TOP CATEGORIES BY AUDIENCE REACH

Category Name	Monthly Unique Audience	Reach (%)	Visits Per Person
Search engines/portals	74.4	88.8	5.5
Telecom/internet services	51.3	61.2	3.0
Entertainment	49.0	58.5	2.1
News and information	41.2	49.1	2.2
Shopping	40.5	48.3	2.1
Electronics and software	39.6	47.2	2.1
Online communities	36.9	44.0	2.4
Directories/classifieds	28.6	34.1	1.6
Family and lifestyles	26.3	31.4	1.7
Finance/insurance/invest	24.9	29.7	2.8
Corporate information	23.8	28.4	1.5
Sweepstakes/coupons	21.8	26.1	3.3
Travel	20.4	24.3	1.4
Adult	20.1	23.9	1.6
Education	18.6	22.2	1.5
Government/nonprofit	15.9	18.9	1.8
Sports	12.5	14.9	2.7
Automotive	10.1	12.0	1.4

Notes: Unique Audience = the number of different individuals that visit a given type of website over the course of the month
Reach = the percentage of online individuals that accessed a given type of website over the course of the month
Source: Adapted from *Nielsen//NetRatings,* June 30, 2000

WHAT ARE PORTALS, AND HOW DO THEY ADD VALUE FOR USERS?

The only place anyone has to go to find something, connect with someone, or buy anything.

—Yahoo! mission statement[2]

As Internet use accelerated beginning in 1994, the number of websites also proliferated. This self-reinforcing phenomenon led to a need for help with navigation. To that end, two types of sites, directories and search engines, came into being.

Exhibit 2-2 TOP 10 WEBSITES BY AUDIENCE

Property	Unique Audience	Reach (%)
AOL websites	48.1	57.3
Yahoo!	44.8	53.5
MSN	33.2	39.6
Microsoft	30.1	35.9
Lycos Network	22.8	27.2
Excite@Home	20.6	24.6
Go Network	18.1	21.6
AltaVista	12.8	15.3
Time Warner	12.7	15.1
NBC Internet	12.1	14.5

Notes: Unique Audience = the number of different individuals that visit a website over a specific period of time
Reach = the percentage of online individuals that accessed a specific website over a specific period of time
Source: Adapted from *Nielsen//NetRatings*, June 30, 2000

Directories were guides to the Web compiled by human editors and organized by category (e.g., arts, business, news, health). Users followed a hierarchy of headings and subheadings (e.g., arts>awards>music>genres>country) to locate sought-after information. The end result was usually a link to a specific webpage that contained the information needed. Critical success factors for directories included comprehensiveness and clear, coherent organization of the hierarchies. Examples of directories included Yahoo!, LookSmart, Snap!, and Northern Light. Search engines, on the other hand, compiled key words from webpages into databases that users could query. These search engines continually "crawled" the Web capturing, storing, and indexing the latest site information. The critical success factor for search engines was the number of webpages indexed. The larger the index, the more likely it was that the search engine maintained a comprehensive record of the Web. Yet, with large indexes new organizational challenges emerged, most notably, how do we give the user *just* what they want? Examples of search engines included AltaVista, Excite, Infoseek, and Lycos.

Due to the need for navigational services, directories and search engines quickly grew to be among the most heavily trafficked sites on the Web, and prospered with a business model that monetized this traffic by selling advertising. Since ad revenue increased in direct proportion to the number of "eyeballs" delivered, these sites gradually shifted their strategies away from quickly linking users to destination sites; they began encouraging users to linger. With that goal, directories and search engines sought to build user loyalty by adding content and "sticky" features such as e-mail and user chat rooms. In the process, the directories and search engines began to more closely resemble each other: Directories like Yahoo! added search engine capabilities by licensing technology from vendors such as Inktomi, and search engine sites organized their new content into directory-like "channels." Eventually, strategies to boost the frequency and duration of user visits caused searches to become a smaller percentage of total page views. At that point, industry observers began to refer to the original search and directory sites as "portals," a term coined in 1997 by Halsey Minor, then CEO of CNET.[3]

In the spirit of the Internet, the definition of a portal kept changing. At its simplest, as the name implied, a portal was a doorway to the Web, a launching pad that a user could employ as a homepage before heading to other destinations. As explained by David Marshak, a vice president at Patricia Seybold Group Inc., "Portals diminish the amount of flailing people have to do online."[4] At the same time, portals were evolving into sites that a user continually returned to throughout the day in order to manage a multitude of daily online activities, for example, checking news headlines and stock quotes, sending e-mail and instant messages, and joining chat groups.

Thus, portals performed many different functions, yet, their essence was comprised of five core elements: search, content, community building, commerce, and personal-productivity applications:

- *Search services* included search engines, directories, Yellow Pages services for locating local businesses, "people finder" services for tracking down phone numbers and/or e-mail addresses, MP3 finders for locating downloadable music files, and "shopping bots" for locating merchandise and comparing the prices offered by different online retailers.
- *Content* comprised topical information such as news headlines, stock quotes, sports scores, weather forecasts, and local event listings; reference information such as maps and dictionaries; entertainment options including games and links to Internet radio stations; and third-party produced content in special interest areas, (e.g., information about automobiles, travel destinations, or personal health).
- *Community-building features* included chat rooms, message boards, instant-messaging services, online greeting cards, applications for exchanging digital photos, personal classifieds (e.g., "Single Male, 35, seeks . . ."), and free personal homepages.
- *Commerce offerings* included classified advertisements for jobs, cars, and homes; auctions; shopping malls aggregating small online retailers' websites; and links to external shopping sites nested within relevant content categories.
- *Personal productivity applications* included Web-based e-mail, address books, calendars, file storage, and bill payment services.

Portal users spent about one-third of their time conducting searches, one-third sending messages and participating in chat groups, and one-third accessing other content.[5]

None of the features described above were unique to portals. For example, for search services, Yahoo! partnered with Google, the acknowledged search engine leader in terms of webpages indexed. Also, for the most part, portals did not create the content they presented but rather obtained it through a variety of partnerships with online content providers. For instance, Yahoo! and Snap! offered the same mapping feature, which was licensed from Vicinity. Likewise, while portals offered access to online shopping, they themselves were not retailers: Portals did not make merchandising decisions, nor did they take title to goods or arrange for their shipment. Thus, a user could turn to stand-alone sites for most of the services offered by portals. The unique value proposition for portals was the convenience they offered users by aggregating and organizing a vast array of content, commerce, and applications developed by others.

The discussion above, along with much of the analysis that follows, focuses on portals that help users navigate the World Wide Web. However, portals have emerged to fill similar convenience needs with respect to other new online technologies, including wireless data delivered to cell phones and Personal Data Assistants (PDAs), interactive television services, and voice recognition services (e.g., Tellme, BeVocal) that deliver pre-recorded or speech-synthesized information in response to requests spoken into a landline or mobile phone. Whenever new technologies have emerged, three sets of players have tended to vie to fill the portal role: startups, existing Internet portals (such as Yahoo! and AOL); and the infrastructure companies who deploy the enabling technologies and who have direct relationships with customers who use it. The strategy issues facing competitors who aspire to create portals to serve users of new online technologies are discussed in the final section of this chapter.

Portal Taxonomy

As the industry evolved, two types of portals emerged, delineated by the breadth of content and commerce offerings they aggregated. *Horizontal portals* (also referred to as mass-market or general-purpose portals) directed users to a broad range of content and commerce destinations; they tried to be "all things to all people." Examples of horizontal portals included AOL, AltaVista, Excite@Home, Go Network, Lycos, Yahoo!, and MSN. *Vertical portals,* on the other hand, directed users to content and commerce offerings within a single thematic area such as personal finance, music, or sports. Examples of vertical portals included CNET, iVillage, MarketWatch.com, and SportsLine.com.

Horizontal Portals. Horizontal portals could be further divided into three categories: "The Big Three," "Also Rans," and "Portals with a Wrinkle." The Big Three were AOL, Yahoo!, and MSN. Also Rans included AltaVista, Excite@Home, Disney's Go Network, NBCi (which included Snap!) and Lycos. Lastly, Portals with a Wrinkle—labeled as such because they differentiated themselves by providing navigational assistance in a unique manner—included Ask Jeeves, Google, and GoTo.com, among others. These sites focused on their search and directory services; they typically did not provide all of the other core elements of a portal cited above, i.e., content, community building, commerce, and personal productivity applications. Their search and directory "wrinkles," which attempted to tackle some of the limitations that Internet users encountered when they relied on more traditional directories and search engines, were as follows:

- *Ask Jeeves* employed a user-friendly interface built around its British butler-like "Jeeves" character, with a natural language search engine that delivered search results more likely to be relevant to the user. For example, asking Jeeves, "Who really discovered America?" yields several sites that directly address the question. Entering *discovery of America* into Yahoo!'s search engine without putting parentheses around the phrase (a search convention that many Internet users do not understand) yielded 67 site matches as of November 2000, only a handful of which were relevant. The first three results listed included links to a television show about witchcraft trials on the

Discovery Channel, a tour operator that specialized in journeys of self-*discovery,* and a company that specialized in forensic data *discovery* for corporate *America.*

- *Google* employed a page-ranking system to improve search results. The value of a given page was determined by the number of links to that page from other websites. Links were interpreted as votes of confidence in the page, and links that came from pages that had themselves been linked to many times were weighted more heavily. By contrast, most other search engines simply used the incidence of keywords on a given page to determine the priority of listing. With this traditional approach, search engines tended to unearth many obscure and often irrelevant pages that happened to repeat a search term frequently.
- *GoTo.com* enabled marketers to bid in an ongoing auction for priority placement in the company's search results; marketers were listed in descending order of bid price. Each marketer paid GoTo.com the amount of its bid (which was plainly visible to consumers as part of the search results) whenever a consumer clicked-through on its listing. For example, in November 2000, iGo.com, which provided "solutions for people on the go," paid GoTo $0.04 for each click-through following searches on the term "laptop adapters."[6] Some observers looked askance at a process that allowed marketers to openly "bribe" a search engine. GoTo argued that its process served consumers well, because marketers would only pay for placement when they had products or services that met consumers' needs.

The logic of this delineation was evident upon comparison of the portals' operating statistics (see Exhibit 3). As of June 30, 2000, it was clear that AOL, Yahoo!, and MSN had broken away from the pack in terms of unique visitors and, consequently, overall reach (i.e., the percentage of Internet users that visited a site during a period of time). AOL , Yahoo!, and MSN were drawing 48 million, 45 million, and 43 million unique monthly visitors, respectively, which translated into a reach of approximately 57, 54, and 40 percent. These statistics were in sharp contrast to the performance of the other horizontal portals. For example, the Also Rans only drew between 13 and 23 million unique visitors per month, representing a reach of 15 to 27 percent. Portals with a Wrinkle only garnered between 3 million and 8 million unique users per month, equating to a reach of 4 to 10 percent.

The three-level split also bore itself out in "stickiness" (i.e., the amount of time the average user spent on a portal) and "page view" metrics. Against these measures, Yahoo! reigned supreme as the only portal with a time-per-person-per-month of over one hour and with monthly page views per user in excess of 120. MSN was a close second, while other portals dropped off dramatically. GoTo.com's users, for example, spent only four minutes per month on the site. Yet, GoTo's management maintained that this result was consistent with its business model: By asking marketers to bid for placement in search results, users could quickly retrieve what they needed; they did not have to wade through page after page of irrelevant search results or through a multi-level directory hierarchy. GoTo argued that its competitors' inefficient search processes sacrificed users' needs in order to generate more page views and advertising impressions.[7]

Vertical Portals. Vertical portals revolved around users' interests; thus, they came in many varieties. Affinity portals were designed to appeal to an audience's self-identity, based on factors such as gender, race, age, religion, and sexual preference. Examples

Exhibit 2-3 HORIZONTAL PORTALS COMPARISON: OPERATING STATISTICS

Property	Unique Audience	Reach (%)	Page Views	Visits per Person	Pages per Person	Time per Person
Big Three						
AOL websites	48.1	57.3	2,197.4	7.0	46	0:29:23
Yahoo!	44.8	53.5	5,575.6	8.3	124	1:07:04
MSN	33.2	39.6	2,853.2	8.4	86	0:48:23
Also Ran						
Lycos Network	22.8	27.2	998.1	3.3	44	0:16:40
Excite@Home	20.6	24.6	943.1	4.4	46	0:27:29
Go Network	18.1	21.6	669.8	3.7	37	0:22:58
AltaVista	12.8	15.3	420.8	3.6	33	0:14:58
Portals with a Wrinkle						
Ask Jeeves	8.4	10.0	162.5	2.5	19	0:11:05
GoTo.com	5.8	6.9	49.7	2.1	9	0:04:35
Google	3.1	3.8	78.6	3.2	25	0:08:22

Notes: Unique Audience = the number of different individuals that visit a website over a specific period of time
Reach = the percentage of online individuals that accessed a specific website over a specific period of time
Page Views = the number of times a webpage is requested over a specific period of time
Source: Adapted from *Nielsen//NetRatings,* June 30, 2000

included iVillage for women, BET.com for African-Americans, iTurf for teens, and PlanetOut for gays and lesbians. Avocational portals provided content and commerce opportunities around users' hobbies and entertainment interests. Examples were SportsLine.com, Epicurious (for cooks), and LAUNCH.com (for rock music fans). Still other vertical portals served users' professional interests, e.g., SolidWaste.com.

These vertical portals, like their horizontal counterparts, tended to include most or all of the core elements cited earlier as essential to a portal: search and navigational services, content, community building services, commerce offerings, and personal productivity applications. Notwithstanding this point, the distinction between vertical portals and other Internet business models can easily be blurred. For example, several of the examples cited in the previous paragraphs (e.g., CNET, Epicurious) produced a majority of their content in-house (although they also licensed a significant portion of their content from third parties). In that regard, they were more properly defined as online content providers than vertical portals. Likewise, online brokers such as Microsoft CarPoint provided links to a wealth of third-party information to enable consumers to research purchase decisions, but the site's purpose in doing so was to help facilitate a transaction—not to help users navigate the Web. Since most vertical portals had another Internet business model at their core—and in order to avoid confusion in explaining the central characteristics of the portal business model—the balance of this chapter will focus exclusively on horizontal portals.[8]

Horizontal Versus Vertical Portals. By 1999, vertical portals were gaining share at the expense of horizontal portals. While the total time spent on the Web per user grew by 6.3 percent in 1999, the total time per user spent visiting horizontal portals actually declined by 4.7 percent. In contrast, the time spent per user visiting a group of vertical portals nearly doubled over the same time period.[9] Industry observers were not surprised by these trends; they expected that as Internet users became more familiar with the Web, they would bookmark specialized sites that met their needs, and would bypass general-interest portals.[10] By 2000, there was even more evidence that consumers were behaving in this manner. Between February 1999 and August 2000, the average number of unique sites visited in a month had declined from 15 to 10.[11] Consistent with this finding, Jupiter Communications reported survey results that indicated that consumers, when seeking online destinations, were less likely to use a search engine (35 percent of consumers said they were likely to do so in 2000, down from 41 percent in 1999) or visit a portal's shopping channel (2 percent in 2000, down from 6 percent in 1999).[12]

This shift in user preferences had implications for portals' revenue growth prospects. Through the late 1990s, by virtue of their status as largest aggregators of online users, horizontal portals had received a disproportionately large share of ad revenue compared to their share of total page views generated by ad-supported websites. Advertisers have historically been willing to pay a premium for media properties that generate superior reach, because advertisers often value the ability to simultaneously expose a large number of unduplicated prospects to their messages. *People* and *TV Guide,* for example, which were two of the largest consumer print magazines, commanded advertising rates per impression that averaged 22 percent more than rates charged by other magazines that were ranked among the top 130; top-rated network television shows commanded a similar premium.[13] But the premium accorded to horizontal portals was much greater: According to Forrester Research, in 1999 the seven largest horizontal portals generated 20 percent of the page views for ad-supported sites but captured 65 percent of total Internet advertising revenue.[14] Based on the magnitude of this premium, it seemed possible that advertising on a well-established, mass-market portal like Yahoo! was seen by many marketing executives as a safe way to venture online—in the same way that buying a mainframe from IBM was once seen as a low-risk way to introduce information technology to a corporation.

In 1999, vertical portals (defined by Forrester as the other 93 sites among the 100 most heavily-trafficked, ad-supported websites) accounted for 20 percent of page views—the same amount as the seven largest horizontal portals—but vertical portals earned only 24 percent of total online ad revenue.[15] Forrester predicted that the reach premium commanded by horizontal portals would decline over time. Forrester projected that by 2004 horizontal portals would receive 40 percent of total online advertising (down from 45 percent in 1999), compared to 32 percent for vertical portals (up from 24 percent in 1999) (see Exhibit 4). This migration of ad dollars to vertical portals was seen to be largely at the expense of four Also Ran portals (Lycos, Excite, AltaVista, and Go Network), which Forrester projected would capture only 3 percent of ad dollars by 2004 (down from 20 percent in 1999). In other words, portal delineation was expected to continue: The Big Three were seen as coexisting with a multitude of smaller vertical portals, while the horizontal midtier portals would be forced to adjust their business models. By late 2000, this adjustment was underway: AltaVista had laid off 25 percent of its workforce after announcing plans to refocus around its core search capabilities,[16] Disney's Go Network had relaunched as an entertainment and leisure portal, and Excite was

Exhibit 2-4 PERCENTAGE OF TOTAL TRAFFIC AND AD REVENUE FOR CATEGORIES OF AD-SUPPORTED SITES

Companies	Traffic		Ad Revenue	
	1999	2004E	1999	2004E
AOL/Yahoo!/MSN	15%	20%	45%	40%
Other broad-based portals	5%	1%	20%	3%
Vertical portals	20%	24%	24%	32%
Rest of Web	59%	55%	11%	25%

Notes: "Other broad-based portals" include AltaVista, Snap, Excite, Go, and Lycos.
Source: Adapted from Charlene Li, "The Parting of the Portal Seas," Forrester Research, December, 1999

repositioning itself as a broadband content portal, leveraging the fact that it was owned by the cable modem service provider @Home.[17]

PORTAL BUSINESS MODEL

Portals followed a three-step business model: (1) acquiring new users, (2) turning new users into repeat visitors, and (3) monetizing user traffic. This section describes the strategies and tactics available to portals as they sought competitive advantage at each step.

Acquiring New Users

As noted above, search and directory services, the initial raison d'être for portals, still accounted for about one-third of horizontal portal traffic in 1999. Portals acquired a large share of their new users by providing such navigational services, which were particularly important for newcomers to the Web. Of course, to encourage new users to try their search and directory services, portals had to build awareness of their brands through online and offline advertising and word-of-mouth referrals. In addition, portals had four other avenues for acquiring new users: "Utility" services, Internet access enablers, vertical integration with destination sites, and offline promotion through affiliated media properties.

Utility Services. Portals could acquire new users by providing utility services for communication or for improving personal productivity. These took many forms, including free e-mail, online greeting cards, instant messaging, free Web-based file storage, calendars and address books, and bill payment applications. Portals often acquired these services as free-standing companies and then integrated them into their homepages; in the process, the acquired service's existing users might be converted into new users of the broader portal. For example, in January 1998, Microsoft paid around $400 million for the free Web-based e-mail service Hotmail and acquired 9.5 million Hotmail users.[18] Lycos acquired the personal homepage and community building site Tripod for $81 million in 1998, along with the site's one million registered users.[19] Other examples include the acquisitions of the greeting-card site Blue Mountain Arts by Excite and Web-based instant messenger ICQ by AOL. By mid-1999, ICQ had 34 million registered users, only 7 percent of whom overlapped with AOL's subscriber base.[20]

Internet Access Enablers. In order to use the Internet or other online services, consumers dealt with a series of hardware, software, and service providers. For example, to access the World Wide Web on a PC, a user interacted with a modem-equipped personal computer, the computer's operating system and Web browser, and with an Internet service provider (ISP) or an online service provider (OSP).[21] Each of these points of contact provided an opportunity for portals to acquire new customers—especially when dealing with first-time Internet users.

Distribution Deals with PC Manufacturers. To supplement their low margin hardware sales with service revenues, some PC makers offered Internet connectivity with their equipment. Portals were able to partner with PC makers to provide a co-branded start page for such Internet access services. One example of this strategy was a deal between Dell Computer and Excite to create a custom version of the portal for Dell's ISP customers.

Vertically Integrated Browsers. In 2000 the Web browser market was dominated by Microsoft and Netscape (a unit of AOL), with 65 percent and 35 percent of users employing Microsoft's Internet Explorer and Netscape's Navigator, respectively.[22] Both firms could program their browsers to default to their own portal sites—MSN.com for Microsoft and Netscape.com for Netscape—unless specifically directed by the user (or an ISP) to another homepage. According to a Netscape executive, 50 percent of its browser users defaulted to the Netscape homepage.[23] As one observer remarked, "Great power lies in such default settings—power built on the seemingly inexhaustible well of human laziness."[24]

ISP Partnerships. Portals often partnered with ISPs to provide their subscribers with a start page. This was done by preprogramming the portal's homepage to launch whenever a subscriber installed the ISP's software. The portal and ISP then split the ad and e-commerce revenues generated through the homepage, with larger ISPs typically retaining 60 to 70 percent of revenues as of 1998.[25] One example of this strategy was Yahoo!'s partnership with MCI to develop a co-branded access service. Yahoo! Online, offered at $14.95 per month, included Yahoo!'s various content channels and its search and directory services. As part of the deal, Yahoo! received a bounty for new customers it steered to MCI's ISP and to other MCI services (e.g., long distance and cellular phone services).

Vertically Integrated ISPs/OSPs. Portals themselves could move a step beyond ISP partnerships and seek to acquire new users by entering the access business, in one of three ways. First, companies could own both an ISP and a portal, managing them in an integrated manner. The acquisition of the portal Excite by the broadband service provider @Home was an example of such joint ownership. Microsoft provided another example of this approach: It operated an ISP called MSN, with 3.5 million subscribers as of November 2000.[26] The start page for MSN subscribers defaulted to a portal with the same name. However, the MSN portal was freely accessible to Web users who relied on other ISPs, and MSN ISP customers who wished to reprogram their browser to open to another portal could do so.

A second approach involved portals outsourcing their branded ISP operations to another company. AltaVista, which relied on 1stUp.com to manage its free ISP service, was an example. Similarly, Yahoo! relied on Spinway to manage the infrastructure and customer service operations for the BlueLight.com free ISP service that Yahoo! offered through a joint venture with the retail giant Kmart.

Online service providers (OSPs), like AOL, were a third type of vertical integration. OSPs maintained a telecommunications infrastructure separate from (but typically interconnected with) the public Internet. OSPs used that infrastructure to provide access to "walled gardens" that contained proprietary, off-Web content and communities for chat and instant messaging sessions.[27] Only the OSP's subscribers had access to the walled garden, which was organized as a portal. In addition to such proprietary content, OSPs such as AOL also provided its subscribers with access to the World Wide Web, but AOL users spent only a modest portion of their online time accessing websites: They spent an average of 40 percent of their total online time accessing the company's proprietary content and commerce offerings, 23 percent on e-mail, 20 percent on chat, and just 17 percent accessing Internet sites.[28]

Vertical Integration with Destination Sites. In addition to backward integration into access, portals could integrate forward and become the owners of content and commerce destination websites. Portals that owned popular destination websites were able to use those sites to drive new users back to the portal. Disney's Go Network was an example of this strategy. The Go.com portal benefited from traffic received from Disney.com, ESPN.com, ABCNews.com, and other Disney-owned Web properties. Similarly, MSN acquired traffic through Microsoft's stable of destination websites, including the car-buying service CarPoint, the online travel agency Expedia, and the news service MSNBC.com. Expedia, for example, received 54 percent of its visitors from MSN in late 1998.[29] Perhaps the most telling example of the benefits of integrating portal and destination websites, however, was the $166 billion acquisition by AOL of Time Warner, the world's largest media and entertainment company, announced in January of 2000.

Offline Promotion through Affiliated Media Properties. Lastly, companies that owned both Internet portals and offline media companies could run promotional ads on those offline media properties to drive new users to their portals. Examples of horizontal portals that benefited in this manner included Disney's GO.com, NBC's NBCi, and AOL through its link to Time Warner's businesses. Other media companies used similar promotional strategies to drive traffic to vertical portals that they owned, including Black Entertainment Television, which owned BET.com, and Discovery Communications, which owned Discovery.com, a vertical portal devoted to science and nature news and information.

Retaining Traffic

Step two of the portal business model entailed retaining the new users acquired in step one. The more frequently a user visited a portal and the more time he or she spent during each visit, the greater the opportunity for the portal to profit by collecting personal information, displaying ads, and selling goods. Portals attempted to retain users in several ways (some of which overlapped with acquisition tactics mentioned above). First, they sought to offer comprehensive and high quality directory/search services and content. Sometimes this meant securing proprietary access to content, to promote differentiation vis-à-vis other portals. Second, portals developed community-building features, including chat and instant messenger services. A portal could boost its traffic substantially when users with common interests interacted regularly in its chat rooms. AOL and Yahoo! went to great lengths to promote community building. For example, Yahoo! spent roughly $4 billion in February 1999[30] to acquire GeoCities, a service that provided users with the ability to create their own webpages and that aggregated these pages into communities of common interest. Third, portals offered a wide range of personal productivity applications that, along with attracting new users, encouraged users to return regularly, e.g., free Web-based e-mail, bill payment services, online calendars and address books, and free Web-based file storage. Finally, most major portals provided users the ability to customize their homepage to deliver news and information tailored to users' personal interests, e.g., home-town sports scores and weather, stock portfolio tracking, and horoscopes. Users who customized homepages in this manner tended to be more loyal. For example, My Yahoo! users spent about 30 percent of their total online time at Yahoo!, compared to an average of 10 percent for other Yahoo! visitors (see Exhibit 5).

Many of the features that portals offered to boost retention required user registration, i.e., users were asked to provide, at a minimum, an e-mail address and often additional personal information. For example, Yahoo!, which had 166 million unique monthly visitors in September 2000, had registered 185 million users by 3rd Quarter 2000. About 55 million of Yahoo!'s registered users had been site visitors within the prior 30 days, and these "active" registered users accounted for 55 percent of Yahoo!'s total page views.[31] Registration data was very valuable for portals in their marketing efforts: Having a user's e-mail address allowed the portal to "push" special offers to that user. Furthermore, acquiring additional personal information through registration could be helpful in serving targeted advertisements, which portals sold at higher rates.

Portals' efforts to promote user retention led to feature proliferation: When one portal introduced a feature, others typically followed suit very quickly. The net

Exhibit 2-5 COMPARISON OF REGISTERED VS. NON-REGISTERED VISITORS

	My Netscape	Netscape	My Yahoo!	Yahoo!
Breakdown				
Unique audience (millions)	1.4	9.1	2.4	20.6
Pages/person at portal	77	19	238	58
Hours/person at portal	1.7	0.4	3.8	0.8
Total hours online per person	12.6	9.2	12.6	7.9
Percent of Total Online Time Spent				
At portal listed above	13.7%	4.4%	30.4%	9.6%
At MSN	0.7%	1.5%	1.7%	2.0%
At Go Network	1.1%	2.6%	1.4%	2.0%

Source: Adapted from "Metrics" section, *The Industry Standard* (June 14, 1999): 102

result was that portals had become increasingly homogenous in terms of content, search technology, and even site structure and layout. Furthermore, despite the expensive proliferation of features intended to increase stickiness, many portal users remained "promiscuous"—they were likely to frequent several different portals in any given month. For example, in June 2000, 46 and 45 percent of Yahoo!'s users were also visitors to AOL.com (i.e., AOL's site on the public Internet, not its walled garden) and MSN.com, respectively; a similar share of the latter two websites' users frequented the other leading mass market portals (see Exhibit 6). Consistent with this data, Microsoft research showed that only one-third of portal users demonstrated "portal behavior," defined as using at least three services within the same portal site.[32]

Monetizing User Traffic

Step three of the portal business model involved monetizing the traffic that the portal generated. Foremost, advertising comprised approximately over 90 percent of portal revenue in 2000.[33] Most of the balance was earned from fees related to commerce offerings, e.g., auctions and hosting small retailers' websites in portal shopping channels. In the future, fees from commerce offerings were expected to account for a growing share of portal revenues, as were direct payments from users for premium services. For example, in late 2000, Microsoft charged $10 per month for access to its popular multi-player game, Asheron's Call, and AOL had announced plans to charge a $5 subscription payment for access to information and communications services delivered by phone through voice recognition services.

Advertising on portals took a variety of forms, including banner ads linked to certain directory entries or search keywords (e.g., Hewlett-Packard might buy banners adjacent to search listings for a query on laptops) and sponsorships of contextually relevant content (e.g., Autoweb.com might sponsor Yahoo!'s content on new cars). Ad revenue was primarily generated on the basis of "impressions," although marketers were increasingly demanding deals whereby they would only "pay for performance," i.e., for click-throughs on their banners or for new customers acquired. One impression equaled one set of eyeballs passing over an ad one time. In 1999, online marketers paid for typical banner ads at an average CPM rate of

Exhibit 2-6 PORTAL USER (DIS)LOYALTY—JUNE 2000 (% OF PRIMARY SITE'S USERS THAT ALSO VISITED A SECONDARY SITE)

	Secondary Site				
Primary Site	**AOL.com**	**Yahoo.com**	**MSN.com**	**Lycos.com**	**Excite.com**
AOL.com	100.0	50.9	33.9	18.2	13.0
Yahoo.com	46.2	100.0	45.4	21.8	16.6
MSN.com	40.4	59.5	100.0	21.7	16.5
Lycos.com	54.0	71.2	54.0	100.0	26.7
Excite.com	47.4	66.7	50.7	32.9	100.0

Notes: For example, 59.5% of those people who visited MSN.com during June 2000 also visited Yahoo.com.
Source: Adapted from *Nielsen//NetRatings*, June 30, 2000

$34.22, where CPM ("M" for the Roman numeral 1,000) meant the cost per thousand impressions delivered.[34] CPMs could vary widely depending on how likely the users exposed to a given impression were to respond to that ad, which in turn was related to where the ad appeared on a portal (see Exhibit 7). For example, a cruise line sponsoring a portal's travel channel might pay a CPM ranging from $30 to $100. By contrast, "run of site" banner ads had CPMs of $5 to $25. Such ads could appear anywhere on the portal (at the portal's discretion), for example, adjacent to chat sessions or online games, where ads were unlikely to be contextually relevant to users and were unlikely to garner much in the way of user response.

One could calculate the monthly ad revenue generated by a portal by multiplying (1) the site's number of unique monthly visitors, (2) the average number of visits per user per month, (3) average page views per visit, (4) the average CPM divided by 1,000, (5) the sellout ratio, i.e., the percentage of pages viewed for which the site has received any payment from advertisers, and (6) the average number of impressions on pages that generate any ad payments. By definition, the last figure would equal or exceed one, because websites sometimes sold more than one banner ad per page. Sellout ratios would, by definition, be equal to or less than 100 percent, because most websites failed to sell their entire advertising inventory and because some pages intentionally carried no ads (e.g., the page explaining a site's privacy policies). According to projections by ABN AMRO, the typical portal could be expected to sell 25 to 30 percent of its inventory at a CPM of $20 to $30, with each page carrying 2.0 to 2.5 ads.[35]

"Tenancy deals" with online marketers contributed a significant share of advertising revenues for horizontal portals; such deals were distinguished from ordinary ad campaigns by their scale and by their duration—they often involved multi-year commitments. The ubiquity of tenancy deals was evident in survey findings, which indicated that approximately two-thirds of online retailers had a portal deal in place in 1999; of those that did not, one-half planned to develop some type of portal relationship in the future.[36] Furthermore, Jupiter Communications estimated that 18 percent of online shopping transactions in 1999 resulted from portal deals.[37]

In late 1999, a typical tenancy deal ran for 20 months and had a total value of $4.5 million; some, however, were substantially more expensive (see Exhibit 8). Deals were quite diverse in terms of other contractual provisions, e.g., the degree of exclusivity required by each party and whether the portal would be paid for raw impressions delivered, click-throughs to the partner's site, or new customers actually acquired by the partner. Most deals provided guarantees from the portal in terms of how many impressions it would deliver to its partner and where banners and sponsorships would be exhibited.

Exhibit 2-7 PERFORMANCE OF PORTAL BANNER ADS

	Cost (CPM)	Click-Through	Sell-Through
Run of site banner	$5–$25	0.1%–1.0%	2%–5%
Keyword banner	$20–$50	1%–5%	2%–10%
Sponsorship/co-branded pages	$30–$100	3%–20%	2%–10%

Source: Adapted from ABN AMRO, "Internet Portals," June 2000, pg. 58

Exhibit 2-8

TERMS OF SELECTED PORTAL DEALS

Company	Portal	Date	Price	Term
CDNOW	Yahoo!	8/97	$3.9 million	1+ years
CBS SportsLine	AOL	10/98	$23 million	3 years
CNET	AOL	2/99	$14.5 million	2.5 years
eBay	AOL	3/99	$75 million	4 years
drkoop.com	AOL	7/99	$89 million	4 years
1-800-Flowers.com	AOL	9/99	$37 million	4 years

Source: Adapted from Michele Slack, "Portal Tenancy Deals," Jupiter Communications, July 25, 2000, p. 4

In addition to such deals with online retailers, portals secured revenues—and a significant portion of their content—through tenancy deals with online content providers. Again, these deals were highly diverse in their structures. Some content providers paid the portal to place content within a channel, but then kept all of the ad revenue generated through portal page views. Others provided their content to the portal free of charge, then split ad revenues. Content providers viewed their portal distribution deals as important vehicles for customer acquisition; thus, they were eager to ensure that their brand was prominently displayed and that links were provided back to their site for consumers seeking deeper information.[38]

In light of the high cost of tenancy arrangements, it was not surprising that by 2000 these deals had suffered a predictable backlash from marketers and content providers. In a December 1999 Forrester Research survey, only 57 percent of retailers said portals deals were worth the price they paid, and only 69 percent of them planned to renew their deals.[39] The director of marketing for Petstore.com, for example, complained that his company's acquisition cost per new customer had been $200 through a Yahoo! portal deal, compared to a $20 target.[40] Other marketers reported that the price of portal deals had declined by as much as 75 percent, in response to concerns about efficiency and a winnowing out of online marketers (of the four leading pet supply sites, for example, Petstore.com and Pets.com had failed by late 2000, and Petopia had laid off most of its workforce and eventually was sold to Petco).[41] It was difficult to determine how much of this reflected self-serving posturing versus a true shift in bargaining dynamics between portals and advertisers. Yahoo!'s renewal rates for its advertising deals, for example, had slipped in late 2000 but still remained quite high: 85 percent of its 200 largest clients had renewed their deals in 3rd quarter 2000, down from renewal rates in the high 90 percent range in previous quarters.[42]

PORTAL ECONOMICS

The economic model for online portals is, at its core, fairly simple. Portals incur mostly fixed costs to aggregate content, community-building features, and personal productivity applications; the variable costs associated with service delivery are minimal. Portals then invest in marketing activities to drive users to their site and generate page views. Finally, portals hire a direct sales force to sell these page views to advertisers. Ad spending varies directly with the number of users; the number of users varies directly with marketing spending—provided the company has spent enough to develop an appealing product. If the portal does not need to continue to spend heavily on marketing to retain customers—a crucial assumption—then profits should grow rapidly once the portal's customer base generates enough ad revenue to cover the portal's fixed costs mentioned above.

The balance of this section explains the economic model of portals in greater detail. First, the section looks at portals' operating costs and their costs related to customer acquisition. Next are an examination of the question of profitability and a comparison of the cost of acquiring customers to the discounted present value of the contribution margin those customers bring to the portal. After all, if you pay more to attract customers than they are worth, economic success will be elusive!

Operating Costs. Operating costs for a horizontal portal fell into four categories: (1) cost of revenues, (2) ad sales costs, (3) product development costs, and (4) general and administrative (G&A) expenses. The first three categories are examined below; G&A expenses included typical overhead items such as salaries for legal, human resources, and finance staff and payments for professional services and are not discussed further.

Cost of Revenues. Cost of revenues included license fees paid to third-party content providers and search-engine technology providers and payments to firms providing hosting and telecommunications services. Although larger portals benefited from greater purchasing clout, such costs tended to vary fairly directly with revenues. For Yahoo!, cost of revenues was projected to be 14 percent of 2000 revenues. For Lycos, which was about one-third of Yahoo!'s size, cost of revenues was projected to be 17 percent of 2000 revenues.[43]

Ad Sales Costs. Portals maintained large direct sales forces comprised of reps selling on commission. Portals did not disclose how much they spent on their ad sales operations; such costs were combined with marketing expenses in portals' financial statements. Yahoo!, for example, spent $215 million (37 percent of revenue) in 1999 on "Sales and Marketing"; of this amount, $80 million was spent on advertising for customer acquisition and brand building, and a portion was spent securing distribution (e.g., deals to provide links to Yahoo! services on the desktops of new PCs sold by computer manufacturers such as Hewlett-Packard). Hence, we can infer that Yahoo! spent approximately 10 percent of its revenue on ad sales operations in its 14 U.S. sales offices and 16 international locations.[44]

Since ad sales reps are paid on commission, expenses associated with ad sales operations do vary to some extent with site traffic and sales volume. However, if revenues triple over a three-year period, it is not likely that ad sales expenses will also triple: Sales reps typically are assigned a certain number of accounts, and their sales targets for earning commissions from any given account tend to be adjusted upward each year. However, if revenue growth stems from signing new accounts, then the company is likely to need to add sales reps; thus its ad sales cost will increase in absolute terms. Yahoo!, for example, had benefited both from growth in the number of advertisers it served and from increased spending per advertiser. In the 2nd quarter of 2000, 3,600 companies placed ads on Yahoo!, a four-fold increase since mid-1997. These advertisers each spent an average of $67,000, also a four-fold increase since 1997.

Product Development Costs. Portals spent heavily on system development staff and the professional services they contracted to enhance and maintain their sites. Product development expenses—which included the cost of staff engaged in organizing directory listings—were projected to be $97 million in 2000 (9 percent of revenue) for Yahoo! and $55 million (16 percent of revenue) for Lycos. Even though such costs were almost completely fixed, they had not declined much as a percentage of revenue (Yahoo! spent 13 percent of 1998 revenue on product development) because portals continued to invest heavily in site improvements, in new technologies such as broadband and wireless delivery, and in international expansion.

Customer Acquisition Costs. As noted in the previous section, most customers were acquired as a result of online and offline brand building efforts. In 1999, Yahoo! spent $80 million (14 percent of revenue) on such advertising; for the fiscal year ended July 31, 2000, Lycos spent $23 million (8 percent of revenue). Dividing advertising costs by the increase in unique visitors during that period provides an indication of a portal's acquisition cost per new customer. Against this metric, Yahoo! clearly benefited from its strong brand recognition and from the scale economies available in mass media advertising: Yahoo! spent about $3 in advertising per new user in mid-2000, whereas Lycos spent about $7.[45]

Profitability. Once a portal expanded revenues beyond the point where it covered its fixed costs, profit growth could be very strong. This was clearly evident upon review of Yahoo!'s financial performance, compared to Lycos's (see Exhibit 9). Yahoo!'s revenues had grown from $21 million to $589 million between 1996 and 1999 and were projected to nearly double in 2000 to over $1 billion. In 2000, Yahoo! was projected to earn $412 million in operating profit—a 38 percent margin on revenues. Lycos, with less scale, had only recently reached the breakeven point: The company was projected to earn a 10 percent operating margin in calendar year 2000, compared to −7 percent the prior year.

Analysts saw the potential for further margin expansion. Bear Stearn's equity analyst, for example, predicted that Yahoo! could eventually earn a 62 percent operating margin as it reduced advertising expenses to the 7 percent range more typical for leading-brand marketers like Coca-Cola and McDonald's, and as it continued to leverage fixed costs in product development and administrative functions (see Exhibit 10).

Lifetime Value of a Customer. A company creates value when it spends less to acquire a new customer than the discounted present value of the variable contribution margin that customer will generate. To calculate the lifetime value of a portal customer, we need to estimate the average duration of a customer relationship. ABN AMRO speculates that such relationships might last 10 years on average.[46] Although little data is available to estimate this critical parameter, 10 years seems excessive, since (1) competition between portals is strong, (2) the Internet continues to evolve rapidly and new companies may emerge to better meet customer needs, especially related to new technologies, and (3) few offline media businesses manage to achieve average customer-relationship life spans in excess of three to four years. Assuming (1) a relationship of five years duration, (2) $6 in annual revenue per visitor (Yahoo! generated about $8 in 2000; Lycos realized about half that amount), (3) an 85 percent variable contribution margin, and (4) a 10 percent discount rate, then the present value of the variable contribution margin from a customer is about $19. This compares favorably with the customer acquisition costs

Exhibit 9

LYCOS AND YAHOO!: PROFIT AND LOSS STATEMENTS ($IN MILLIONS, % OF REVENUE)

	1999		2000E		2001E	
Lycos						
Revenues	$198.2		$349.2		$525.7	
Cost of revenues	37.5	(18.9%)	59.5	(17.0%)	87.9	(16.7%)
Gross profit	160.6	(81.0%)	289.7	(83.0%)	437.8	(83.3%)
Operating expenses	173.9	(87.7%)	255.7	(73.2%)	362.7	(69.0%)
Sales and marketing	110.0	(55.5%)	170.0	(48.7%)	235.1	(44.7%)
Product development	38.7	(19.5%)	54.7	(15.7%)	80.6	(15.3%)
General and administrative	25.1	(12.7%)	31.0	(8.9%)	46.9	(8.9%)
Operating income (loss)	(13.3)	(-6.7%)	34.0	(9.7%)	75.1	(14.3%)
Yahoo!						
Revenues	$588.6		$1,084.7		$1,490.0	
Cost of revenues	92.3	(15.7%)	154.6	(14.3%)	217.4	(14.6%)
Gross profit	496.3	(84.3%)	930.1	(85.7%)	1,272.6	(85.4%)
Operating expenses	308.4	(52.4%)	518.2	(47.8%)	696.9	(46.8%)
Sales and marketing	209.0	(35.5%)	366.7	(33.8%)	500.0	(33.6%)
Product development	64.1	(10.9%)	96.8	(8.9%)	129.1	(8.7%)
General and administrative	35.3	(6.0%)	54.7	(5.0%)	67.8	(4.6%)
Operating income (loss)	187.9	(31.9%)	411.9	(38.0%)	575.8	(38.6%)

Note: Years refer to calendar year-ends.
Source: Adapted from Jeffrey Fieler and Manuel A. Hernandez, "Lycos, Inc.," Bear Stearns, October 17, 2000, p. 84; Jeffrey Fieler and Manuel A. Hernandez, "Yahoo!, Inc.," Bear Stearns, September 29, 2000, p. 83

cited above in the range of $3 and $7 for Yahoo! and Lycos, respectively. Given these economics, we might expect Yahoo! and Lycos to continue to invest aggressively in marketing, i.e., to pursue a Get Big Fast strategy.

GET BIG FAST: A STRATEGIC IMPERATIVE FOR ONLINE CONTENT PROVIDERS?

Many Internet companies have pursued Get Big Fast (GBF) strategies, involving massive upfront investment in customer acquisition and brand building. The premise of such strategies is that the early days of the Internet are a "land grab": According to this view, companies will find it easier to stake out wide swaths of empty territory now, rather than try to capture that territory later, after it has been settled by others. The payoff from the GBF strategy tends to be strongest when the following conditions apply: Network effects are strong, scale economies (beyond network effects) are significant, and customer-retention rates are intrinsically high. This section explores the extent to which these conditions apply for portals.

Network Effects. Network effects occur when the adoption of a product or service by a new customer increases the value of that product or service for customers already using it. This occurs because existing customers now can connect with more parties.[47] The concept of connectivity applies to any network that facilitates point-to-point transactions, e.g., a postal system, a telephone network, or a rail-

Exhibit 2-10 YAHOO!'S FINANCIAL TARGETS

	Current Guidance (1)	Bear Stearns Long-Term (2)
Gross margin	85%	86%
Sales and marketing as % of sales	35%	14%
Product development as % of sales	10%	6%
General and administrative as % of sales	5%	4%
Operating margin	**35%**	**62%**
Tax rate	38%	38%

Notes: (1) = Management's guidance to Wall Street on likely economics for the next 12-18 months
(2) = Expected performance to be achieved between 2010 and 2025
Source: Adapted from Jeffrey Fieler and Manuel A. Hernandez, "Yahoo!, Inc.," Bear Stearns, September 29, 2000

road. To use the classic example, the value of each existing fax machine increases very slightly for its owner upon the sale of every new fax machine, because each party in the network can reach additional users. Or, to use an online example, nothing is lonelier than an empty chat room! In fact, according to what has become known as Metcalfe's law (after Bob Metcalfe, inventor of Ethernet), the value of a network is equal to the number of its users squared; hence, there is an exponential benefit from a linear increase in the size of a network.

Two of the portals' core services—search/directory services and the aggregation of content—were not subject to network effects. However, portals were able to exploit strong network effects in several other areas, including chat, instant messaging, auctions, multi-player games, Web-based photo albums, classified ads, personals, communities of interest comprised of users' personal webpages, and hosting websites for small online retailers (hosting more retailers attracts more shoppers, which attracts more retailers, etc.). Given the broad range of applications that are subject to network effects, portals can realize fairly strong first-mover advantages: Early movers like AOL and Yahoo! found it relatively easy to maintain momentum, whereas late-comers like Disney's Go Network and NBCi found it difficult to engage prospects. They instead gravitated toward established portals that already serve their friends, family members, and co-workers.

Scale Economies. As should be evident from the analysis of costs in the previous section, portals are subject to extremely strong economies of scale. Variable costs are only about 15 percent of revenues, so a significant portion of any revenue growth translates directly into either (1) increased profits or (2) the ability to reinvest in website improvements. Thus, a first mover that gains momentum can sustain that momentum by exploiting its superior margin structure to outspend its rivals.

Retention Rates. If a site has a high retention rate, then GBF investments in customer acquisition are likely to have a higher payoff. If retention rates are low, then a website becomes a "leaky bucket": New customers are acquired, but they leak away and need to be replaced, incurring additional acquisition costs.

Retention rates tend to be high in the presence of network effects. As noted above, portals benefit from network effects in a number of key applications—most notably chat and instant messaging—so we would expect their rates of user retention to be reasonably high. Even in the absence of strong network effects, websites may still have intrinsically high retention rates if there is a solid basis for competitive differentiation in the business (beyond network effects) or if they benefit from some type of switching cost. For example, in the case of online brokerage firms, the hassle associated with terminating a funded account creates a strong switching cost.

Online portals have relatively few meaningful opportunities for competitive differentiation, compared to some other Internet business models, such as online content providers (where distinct journalistic styles may appeal to diverse user tastes). Because portals aggregate content and applications that have for the most part been created by third parties, any point of differentiation introduced by a portal is usually copied quickly by its competitors. Exceptions to this rule tend to involve Portals with a Wrinkle—companies like Ask Jeeves or GoTo.com—which build an entire site around a novel search methodology.

With respect to switching costs, portals benefit from personal productivity features that require users to invest in data entry, e.g., customized home pages, Web-based calendars, address books, and bill payment services. Although only about 20 percent of users customized a portal homepage,[48] users that did so, as mentioned earlier, demonstrated substantial greater stickiness (see Exhibit 5). Also, to the extent that portal users relied on free e-mail service, portals benefited from the fact that changing one's e-mail address is a hassle: It requires the user to notify friends, family, and co-workers, because most services will not forward e-mail to a new address. OSPs (like AOL) that provided a user's principal e-mail account were especially strong beneficiaries of this switching cost.

Summary. With moderately high network effects, extremely powerful scale economies, and moderately high intrinsic user retention rates, portals are subject to strong first mover advantages and thus to "winner-take-all" dynamics. The short history of the portal business bears this out: AOL, Yahoo!, and MSN have steadily pulled away from the pack of portal contenders, and late-comers like Disney's GO.com and NBCi have never gained much traction.

But why AOL, Yahoo! and MSN? Each story is unique. AOL organized as a vertically integrated OSP. It developed an easy-to-use, consumer-oriented walled garden rich with content and with opportunities for users to interact. AOL then "carpet bombed" the United States with a quarter of a billion disks offering free trial service. Users attracted more users as a strong network effect emerged around AOL's chat and instant messaging applications.

Why AOL and not Prodigy, a joint venture between IBM and Sears, which had a substantial market share lead over AOL in the OSP business during the early 1990s? Some observers believe that Prodigy (which was acquired by Prodigy executives and International Wireless in 1996) failed to match AOL's success because Prodigy never engendered a strong network effect around chat: Its conservative owners wanted to keep the service family-oriented. They were nervous about the sexual content of many chat room conversations and put censorship measures in place that alienated users.[49]

In contrast to AOL, MSN failed to gain momentum in its first incarnation as an OSP with proprietary news and entertainment content offerings.[50] However, Microsoft adjusted its strategy, relaunching MSN as an Internet portal rather than an OSP (although Microsoft also continued to offer ISP service) and scaling back its investment in content sites in favor of transaction-oriented sites like Expedia, CarPoint, and HomeAdvisor. Microsoft was able to drive traffic to the MSN portal through its control of the Windows desktop and the Internet Explorer browser, and by providing links between the portal and its very strong transaction destination sites.

Why MSN and not Netscape, which had a commanding lead during the early phase of the browser wars and was able, like Microsoft, to benefit from browser users that defaulted to its start page (a portal called Netcenter)? It is beyond the scope of this chapter to explain Netscape's defeat in the browser wars, but it seems clear that Netscape squandered an opportunity to develop a leading portal because its senior managers viewed the company, at its core, as a *software* business that made money by giving away browsers and charging companies for server applications. Having "mooned the giant," in the words of researchers Yoffie and Cusumano, Netscape was consumed by its competition with Microsoft: Most of its energy went into its browser and server software development and marketing efforts.[51]

Finally, Yahoo!'s remarkable success is more difficult to explain: The company lacked the intrinsic advantages of an OSP like AOL or a browser provider like Microsoft. Still, Yahoo! did execute brilliantly in terms of both site design and brand marketing: Users appreciated Yahoo!'s fast-loading pages and the clear comprehensive organization of its directories. They also identified strongly with the company's friendly but slightly irreverent brand image.

Why Yahoo! and not other early movers in the search and directory business, such as Excite, Lycos, AltaVista, and the failed Magellan? Again, each story is idiosyncratic. As should be apparent from the analysis in the previous section, Lycos has fared reasonably well: We might simply speculate that the company executed its Get Big Fast strategy successfully but not quite as well as Yahoo! AltaVista, by contrast, stalled in part due to resource constraints at its parent company, the struggling minicomputer manufacturer DEC. Excite, after it merged with cable modem service provider @Home, suffered from the fact that AT&T (@Home's largest investor and the largest owner of U.S. cable systems) had made a public commitment to avoid developing Web-content businesses. AT&T had made this commitment in order to secure regulatory approval for its cable acquisitions; AT&T's mergers had faced a flurry of challenges from companies like AOL and Disney, who feared that AT&T would deny them access to its broadband infrastructure.

From this analysis, we might conclude that GBF was a smart strategy for Web portals, but that the question is now moot, because the portal wars are over. Perhaps this is true: It seems unlikely that a full-frontal assault on the leading general interest portals—like the attack launched by Disney—would be able to dislodge AOL, Yahoo!, or MSN from their commanding positions. However, the GBF strategy is still quite relevant for companies aspiring to develop portals for new access technologies, as explained in the next section. Furthermore, some Portals with a Wrinkle have been following GBF strategies and have been able to gain Web users at remarkable rates during 2000. For example, CBS-backed iWon, which runs cash give-away sweepstakes for users who click through iWon's content and commerce offerings, grew rapidly following its October 1999 launch and had become the twenty-first most heavily trafficked U.S. website, with 10 million unique visitors in October 2000. Likewise, Google, which received its first venture capital funding in June 1999, exploited its superior search technology to grow rapidly: It had 6.5 million unique visitors in October 2000 (making it the forty-fifth largest U.S. website) and had licensed its technology to Yahoo! and other websites.[52] Google was projected to reach profitability by the second quarter of 2001.[53]

DEVELOPING PORTALS FOR NEW ONLINE ACCESS TECHNOLOGIES

I think we're now quite early in the building of the Evernet, this always-on, high-speed, ubiquitous, multiformat Web. There are really six Webs, and only one of them is deployed now—that's the PC Web. And last I checked there were only 180 million users of it out of six billion people on the planet. Then there's the voice Web, and I mean literally voice, as in Tellme. There's the hand Web for handheld devices like Handspring or Palm. There's this broadband Web, where by the end of the year seven million U.S. homes will be getting ten megabits of two-way Internet access for $30 or $40 a month. There's also the video Web, which you can see in the video servers from TiVo, Replay, and Geocast. And finally there's the eWeb, which is machine-to-machine communication. So I think there will be just as much innovation in the next ten years as there has been over the past few.

—John Doerr, venture capitalist, Kleiner, Perkins, Caufield & Byers[54]

As John Doerr's comments indicate, the Web portal wars are likely to be replayed as several new online access technologies are deployed over the next several years. In each case, new technology will broaden the availability and capability of existing content, commerce, and communications offerings and will make many new offerings available. Hence, consumers will need assistance finding relevant offerings: They will need portals. These new technologies include:[55]

- *Broadband Internet Access to PCs,* provided through cable modems, digital subscriber lines (DSL), satellite and terrestrial broadcasting, and microwave technologies. The dial-up modems that most consumers use to access the Internet today are poorly suited for the delivery of broadband content—e.g., video, music, and large software and data files—for two reasons. First, their speed is limited to 56 Kbps. Second, the Internet's point-to-point architecture is inherently inefficient for the delivery of information that is consumed by multiple parties: A separate, identical data stream has to be dedicated to each recipient. Cable modems, DSL, and certain wireless technologies relax the first constraint by providing "fatter pipes" in the "last mile to the home." Datacasters such as Geocast address the second constraint by using over-the-air technologies to broadcast broadband information to many users simultaneously, using hard disk drives to cache the information at the user's PC for later retrieval.
- *Interactive TV,* available through cable and satellite system operators, will provide consumers with (1) greater control over TV viewing choices, e.g., the ability to request programs on demand, smart agents that automatically record (again, onto a local hard disk drive) programs likely to be of interest, and (2) access to the full array of content, commerce, and communications services available over the Internet. Marketers are especially interested in the ability to integrate interactivity into traditional TV advertisements. For example, a "Tell Me More" icon might appear during a TV ad for a new car. Clicking on that icon would allow the viewer to immediately access additional information on the car (and perhaps book a test drive) or store such information in a video mailbox for later retrieval.
- *Wireless data delivery* is now available to cell phones and personal digital assistants (PDAs). Such services rely on screen displays to deliver e-mail and an

array of time- and location-sensitive information and commerce offerings, such as airplane-departure updates, news headlines, and stock trading.

- *Voice-recognition services* provide the same type of information as wireless data providers but do so over regular telephones through a voice interface instead of relying on keyed input and screen output.

Across all of these technologies, two strategic issues consistently confront companies that aspire to build portals. First, are the dominant portals likely to be developed by *incumbent Web portals* (e.g., Yahoo! or AOL), *communications carriers* (e.g., cellular-telephone service providers, cable system operators), *hardware/software providers* (e.g., PDA or video-game console manufacturers or "middleware" software developers), or *pure play startups?* Second, should companies develop portals as open platforms or as walled gardens, with a limited selection of proprietary content and restricted abilities to interconnect with users served by competing portals?

Likely Winners

New access technologies vary in the extent to which they allow consumers to choose a portal. In some cases, consumers may have a limited range of choices, because portal services are inextricably bundled with access hardware or communications services. For example, a mobile-telephone service provider may program a wireless data start page into the phones it provides to its subscribers, and may not allow subscribers to reprogram a different start page. In that event, the only way to use a different portal is to switch mobile-phone service providers. In other cases, consumers may have unrestricted choice with respect to the portal they use. For example, voice-recognition services rely on ubiquitous telephone equipment and "plain old telephone service" (POTS), so switching portals is simply a matter of dialing a different telephone number.

Although consumers may have restricted choice in the examples above, there is still an issue as to who will provide them with portal services, because communication carriers and equipment providers can outsource this function (often to the highest bidder) rather than develop their own portals. The advantages and disadvantages of companies that might develop dominant portals for new access technologies are described below.

Web Portals. The leading Web portals all have embraced "anytime, anywhere" strategies; they believe it is their manifest destiny to meet their users' information needs, in any location, through a wide array of electronic media. Users seem likely to value the ability to access their e-mail, calendars, and time-sensitive information (e.g., stock portfolio quotes, favorite sports teams' scores) from a single source through a range of devices. Such an approach would minimize redundant data entry and would allow for "follow me" services, such as cell-phone alerts notifying the user of a flight cancellation after the user had booked a trip through a Web travel service. With their central position on the Web, horizontal portals such as Yahoo!, AOL, and MSN seem well positioned to deliver on this anytime, anywhere promise. They have strong relationships with tens of millions of users, as well as relationships with the dozens of content and commerce partners whose offerings populate their portals.

The leading Web portals have taken steps to extend their franchises to each of the new technologies mentioned above. For example, MSN has announced plans to offer DSL service bundled with a broadband version of its portal and browser, with special features exploiting broadband's "always on" capabilities. AOL acquired Time Warner in part to secure access to its cable systems and plans to use this vertical linkage to develop interactive TV services. Yahoo! and AOL have dueled over prime position on the list of wireless data services that Sprint offers to its mobile-phone subscribers. Yahoo! and AOL also have launched voice-recognition services that make their communications and content applications available to users through regular telephones.

Carriers. Communications carriers often market online access services directly to users and thus have a more direct relationship with prospective users than Web portals. Specifically, cable companies market cable-modem service and interactive TV service, local phone companies offer DSL service and voice portal services, and mobile-phone service providers offer wireless data service and voice portals. Carriers have several incentives to develop portals: (1) They can earn incremental revenue from advertising and transaction fees, and, in the case of mobile-phone carriers, from selling incremental airtime, (2) by providing value-added services, they differentiate themselves from competing carriers, and (3) by providing sticky portal applications that require data entry and customization, they lock in customers and thereby reduce churn for their core communications services.

However, carriers face certain disadvantages in developing portals. First, they lack skills in programming, interface design, and advertising sales. Second, they lack relationships with content and commerce partners. Finally, some carriers—for example, cable system operators and local telephone companies—are not national in their scope of geographic coverage, whereas many portal applications are subject to network effects. Unless geographically focused carriers negotiate interconnection agreements with their neighbors, they may fail to exploit such network effects.

Equipment Manufacturers. Access-equipment providers are sometimes positioned to build portals. This is not usually the case when a communications carrier bundles access hardware into its subscription service, as with cable modems, cable TV set-top converter boxes, or cell phones in the United States. In such circumstances, the carrier determines the choice of access hardware and the equipment manufacturer has, at best, a limited relationship with the end user. In other cases, however, access-equipment manufacturers market their products bundled with unbranded communications services or rely on POTS for online access. Examples of this approach include Research in Motion's BlackBerry PDA and TiVo's personal video recorder, which relies on a phone link to update the recorder's electronic program guide.

Startups. Pure play startups, while lacking the resources and relationships of Web portals, carriers, and hardware makers, have the advantage of being focused and flexible. In certain circumstances, startups also benefit from their neutrality. The managers of Tellme Networks, for example, believe that marketers will want a neutral intermediary (in the words of one executive, a "Switzerland") to aggregate their voice-recognition services. Thus, eBay will want its voice-enabled auctions to be available through a voice portal but will not be comfortable if that voice portal is run by Yahoo! or MSN, each of which offer competing Web auctions.

Walled Gardens or Open Platforms?

Regardless of who emerges as the dominant provider of portals for new access technologies, companies that develop such portals will need to decide whether to build walled gardens or more open platforms. There are strategic, economic, and ergonomic arguments for and against walled gardens.

Strategic Arguments. Strategically, if a company can deny users the ability to interconnect with users of competing portals, the company may engender a stronger network effect that yields competitive advantage. For example, imagine that consumers come to value the ability to instant message their friends as they watch the same TV show. Cable operators might decide to block instant messages from subscribers to direct-to-home satellite broadcasting services (which compete directly with cable in its core television-programming business) to encourage households to subscribe to cable. Of course, this tactic can backfire if (1) it alienates consumers, (2) it fragments usage over several technologies, so none of them offers a compelling network to consumers, and as a result all the technologies stall, or (3) a competing technology follows suit in refusing to interconnect and gains stronger momentum.

Strategic benefits may also accrue to technology providers who employ walled gardens to advance a proprietary standard. The network effects previously described in this chapter have all been *connectivity-based.* A second category of network effects are *software supply-related;* such effects often are present when standards govern the creation of new hardware and/or software. When software supply-related network effects are strong, the propagation of a standard leads to the creation of more software that employs the standard, which in turn leads to the further propagation of the standard, and so forth. Sony PlayStation would be an example: Rapid growth in the sale of PlayStation consoles encourages game developers to write for that platform (because the platform requires the development of specialized code that cannot be readily "ported" to another gaming hardware platform), which in turn supports additional console sales, and so on.

In the same way, companies offering interactive TV applications may benefit from software supply-related network effects. Creating such applications is likely to be expensive: Companies cannot simply repurpose their text-rich websites for display on televisions, because the display resolution of TV monitors (designed to be viewed from across the room) is much lower than the resolution of PC monitors. Content providers and marketers will only undertake the expensive task of developing new applications for interactive TV portals that they expect to achieve broad reach. Given that constraint, companies who wish to develop the dominant interactive TV portals might seek to do so by attempting to create a widely used proprietary standard for content creation and delivery.

While as yet there is no common industry standard for interactive TV applications, some of the other new access technologies described above rely on open standards. For example, industry participants have negotiated a standard called Wireless Application Protocol (WAP) for the transmission of wireless data and another called Voice Extensible Markup Language (VXML) for formatting and delivering voice-recognition services. In such cases, the option of relying on a walled garden to propagate a proprietary standard obviously is not available. When the option is available, limiting access to a platform in order to win a standards battle is a high-stakes game—and one where players with national scope (such as leading Web portals or technology providers able to negotiate agreements with multiple access providers) have a clear advantage over regionally focused players (such as cable or local phone companies, who would need to stitch together consortia to offer national reach).[56]

Economic Arguments. Economically, if "real estate" on a portal is scarce, then a portal may maximize its revenue by auctioning tenancy to the highest bidder. The counter argument is that consumers value choice and may be disinclined to adopt a portal that deliberately restricts its range of content and commerce offerings.

Ergonomic Arguments. Finally, walled gardens seem better suited to certain new technologies on ergonomic grounds. For example, users who rely on cell phones to receive wireless data face serious input and output constraints. The screen on a cell phone often displays no more than nine lines of data, and the twelve small keys are poorly suited for entering the equivalent of website URLs. Thus, wireless data providers may actually improve the user experience by offering a limited selection of services. Since wireless data services are most likely to be used to retrieve a narrow range of time- and location-sensitive information, it should not be too difficult to populate a walled garden either. Furthermore, much of the required information is of a commodity nature (e.g., stock quotes, news headlines), so restricting consumer choice in terms of providers should not be problematic.

ENDNOTES

[1]Matrix.net November 1, 2000 press release for number of host computers; Laura Carr, "100 Numbers You Need to Know," *Industry Standard*, November 20, 2000, p. 291 (citing NEC research) for number of webpages.

[2]Michael Parekh, "Yahoo! Inc." Goldman Sachs Equity Research, October 27, 2000, p. 6.

[3]Kara Swisher, " 'Portal' Industry Looks for New Name," *Wall Street Journal Europe*, 21 September 1998.

[4]Andrea Petersen, "What Is a Portal—and Why Are There So Many of Them?", *Wall Street Journal*, December 10, 1998.

[5]Jan Rivkin and Jay Girotto, HBS Case: 9-700-013, "Yahoo!: Business on Internet Time," January 6, 2000, p. 3.

[6]According to Jamie Kiggen, "GoTo.com," DLJ Equity Research, August 13, 1999, 69 different advertisers were willing to pay GoTo for listings in the insurance category. The $3.50 per click-through payment by the highest bidder in that category amounted to a $3,500 CPM—a very high rate by Web standards.

[7]According to Jamie Kiggen, "GoTo.com," DLJ Equity Research, August 13, 1999, GoTo generated 850 referrals per thousand page views, compared to only 81 referrals per thousand page views for Yahoo! With its transaction-based model, GoTo did not require "stickiness" to earn a comparable profit per user.

[8]For more information on the online content provider business model, see Thomas Eisenmann and Alastair Brown, "Online Content Providers," section 3, *Internet Business Models: Text and Cases*, or HBS Case no. 801-261.

[9]Arthur Newman, "Internet Portals: Evolution or Extinction," Schroeder & Co., September 7, 1999.

[10]Aram Sinnreich, "Portal Evolution—Building Share Market by Market," Jupiter Communications, April 26, 2000.

[11]Jeffrey Fieler and Manuel Hernandez, "Yahoo! Inc.," Bear Stearns Equity Research, September 29, 2000, p. 46, citing Nielsen/NetRatings data.

[12]Michele Slack, "Portal Tenancy Deals," Jupiter Communications, July 25, 2000, p. 10.

[13]Chris Charron, "The Great Portal Shakeout," Forrester Research, March 1998.

[14]Charlene Li, "The Parting of the Portal Seas," Forrester Research, December 1999.

[15]According to Forrester, "The Rest of the Web," i.e., ad-supported websites ranked below the top 100, generated the remaining 60 percent of page views accruing to ad-supported sites but received only 11 percent of total online ad revenues.

[16]Tom Geck, "AltaVista Is Still Searching," *Red Herring*, November 13, 2000, p. 51.

[17]Richard Greenfield, "Walt Disney Internet Group," Goldman Sachs Equity Research, August 10, 2000.

[18]David Wilson, "Microsoft Buys E-mail Provider," *The Toronto Star* (January 2, 1998): B9.

[19]Jeffrey Fieler and Manuel Hernandez, "Lycos, Inc.," Bear Stearns Equity Research, October 17, 2000, p. 17.

[20]Jamie Kiggen, "Internet Observer: Where Seek Is Find," DLJ Equity Research, May 18, 1999.

[21]ISPs generally focus on the provision of Internet connectivity services; they maintain local network infrastructure—banks of modems, routers, and telecommunications lines—that facilitate the transfer of information between a subscriber's modem-equipped PC (or some other access device, such as a Web-enabled wireless phone or a TV set-top converter box) and other users of the public Internet. OSPs like America Online maintain a telecommunications infrastructure separate from (but usually interconnected with) the public Internet. OSPs use that infrastructure to provide access to proprietary, off-Web content and communities (for chat and instant messaging sessions) that only their subscribers can reach.

[22]Browser Study–1999, conducted by Zona Research, 300 IT experts were asked "which browser do you use most at work?"; for more info see: http://www.zonaresearch.com/browserstudy/1999/nov99/index.htm

[23]Michael Parekh, "Internet Portals," February 5, 1999, Goldman Sachs Equity Research, citing Mike Homer, Netscape EVP.

[24]Scott Rosenberg, "Any Portal in a Storm," *Salon* (June 22, 1998).

[25]Abhi Chaki, "ISP Revenue Strategies," Jupiter Communications, April 1998.

[26]Alec Klein, "AOL seeks cable pact with MSN," *Washington Post* (November 18, 2000): E01.

[27]A "walled garden" is an online service that makes it easy to access content and commerce offerings from its own exclusive set of business partners, but slower and harder (or sometimes impossible) to access third party offerings. AOL and Excite@Home are common examples of "walled gardens," and many cell phone operators are developing their new wireless data services in this manner. Technically, walled gardens were maintained through selective caching, attenuated connections to the Internet at-large and a new generation of data switches that can selectively delay data en route to and from non-preferred services. Steve McMahon, Davis Community Network, "Broadband Glossary and Bestiary," June 23, 2000.

[28]Patrick Keane, "Portal Deals," Jupiter Communications, July 1999.

[29]Saul Hansell, "Where Does Microsoft Want You to Go Today?", *New York Times,* November 16, 1998.

[30]Simon Tuck, "GeoCities Turns Freebies into Billions . . .", *The Globe* (February 25, 1999): T2.

[31]Michael Parekh, "Yahoo! Inc.", Goldman Sachs Equity Research, October 27, 2000, p. 6.

[32]Saul Hansell, "Where Does Microsoft Want You to Go Today?", *New York Times,* November 16, 1998.

[33]Arthur Newman, "Internet Portals," ABN AMRO Equity Research, June 2000, p. 48.

[34]For current and historical CPM rates see Adknowledge.com.

[35]Arthur Newman, "Internet Portals," ABN AMRO Equity Research, June 2000, p. 37.

[36]Fiona S. Swerdlow, "Portal Deals: Forecasts and Metrics for Acquiring Customers Through AOL, Yahoo! and Other Portals," Jupiter Communications, 1999.

[37]Patrick Keane, "Portal Deals," Jupiter Communications, July 1999, p. 1.

[38]For more information on content syndication deals, see Thomas Eisenmann and Alastair Brown, "Online Content Providers," section 3, *Internet Business Models: Text and Cases*, or HBS Case no. 801-261.

[39]Charlene Li, "The Parting of the Portal Seas," Forrester Research, December 1999.

[40]Suein Hwang, "Yahoo!'s Grand Vision for Web Advertising Takes Some Hard Hits," *Wall Street Journal,* September 1, 2000, p. A6. In 1999, online retailers spent, on average, $82 to acquire a new customer, according to Boston Consulting Group/shop.org, "The State of Online Retailing 3.0," April 1999; Charlene Li, "The Parting of the Portal Seas," Forrester Research, December 1999, quotes an online retailer affiliated with a bricks-and-mortar chain as saying that its customer acquisition costs through portals had averaged $55, compared to $12 through nonportal websites.

[41]Suein Hwang, "Yahoo!'s Grand Vision for Web Advertising Takes Some Hard Hits," *Wall Street Journal,* September 1, 2000, p. A6 cites interactive ad agency executive Anna Collins as saying that whereas Yahoo! once charged her clients $20 million for a three-year deal, clients now could sign one-year deals for $1-2 million. Bob Tedeschi, "Advertising Grows Easier on Portals," *New York Times,* November 13, 2000, reports a 75 percent decline in costs over the prior 18 months, quoting Al Noyes, head of marketing for online retailer SmarterKids.com. Finally, David Smith, head of media buying firm Mediasmith, reported the CPM for portal ad buys had declined from $18–20 in 1999 to less than $5 by the end of 2000 (Leslie Kaufman, "Testing the Retailing Net," *New York Times,* November 21, 2000).

[42]Michael Parekh, "Yahoo! Inc." Goldman Sachs Equity Research, October 27, 2000, p. 4.

[43]All Yahoo! data in the "Portal Economics" section not specifically referenced in an exhibit are from Jeffrey Fieler and Manuel Hernandez, "Yahoo!, Inc.," Bear Stearns Equity Research, September 29, 2000. Likewise all Lycos data are from Jeffrey Fieler and Manuel Hernandez, "Lycos, Inc.," Bear Stearns Equity Research, October 17, 2000.

[44]Lycos, in its SEC filings, disclosed that 419 of its 902 U.S. employees as of mid-2000 were engaged in sales and marketing operations. Another 359 were employed in product development functions. The remaining 124 were involved in finance and administrative activities.

[45]Jeffrey Fieler and Manuel Hernandez, "Yahoo! Inc.," Bear Stearns Equity Research, September 29, 2000, p. 62.

[46]Arthur Newman, "Internet Portals," ABN AMRO Equity Research, June 2000, p. 37.

[47]See Carl Shapiro and Hal R. Varian, *Information Rules* (Boston, MA: Harvard Business School Press, 1999), pp. 173–225 and Philip Evans and Thomas S. Wurster, *Blown to Bits* (Boston, MA: Harvard Business School Press, 1999), pp. 112–113.

[48]Daniel Frank, "Now the Browser Gets Interesting," *Business2.0,* August 22, 2000, p. 204.

[49]Kara Swisher, *AOL.com* (New York: Random House, 1998), p. 226.

[50]David B. Yoffie, "Microsoft Goes Online: MSN 1996," HBS Case no. 798-019, November 1997; David B. Yoffie, "Microsoft Goes Online: MSN 1997," HBS Case no. 798-035, January 1998; David B. Yoffie, "Microsoft Goes Online: MSN 1998," HBS Case no. 798-035, May 1998; David B. Yoffie, Michael G. Rukstad and Carl Johnston, "Microsoft—2000," HBS Case no. 700-071, April 2000.

[51]Michael A. Cusumano and David B. Yoffie, *Competing on Internet Time: Lessons from Netscape and Its Battle with Microsoft* (New York: FreePress, 2000).

[52]Traffic data for iWon and Google from MediaMetrix.com; launch dates and background information from company websites.

[53]"Tech Is Still the Growth Industry," *Fortune,* November 27, 2000, p. 95.

[54]Ibid.

[55]For cases pertaining to these new technologies see Thomas Eisenmann, Chris Darwall, and Liz Kind, "Geocast Network Systems, Inc.," section 1, *Internet Business Models: Text and Cases*, or HBS Case no. 801-211, October 4, 2000; Thomas Eisenmann, Dan Green, and Doug Rogers, "Teledesic," section 1, *Internet Business Models: Text and Cases*, or HBS Case no. 800-057, February 2000; Dan Green, Lynda Applegate, and Jay Light, "The Last Mile of Broadband Access," HBS Case no. 800-076, January 25, 2000; and Thomas Eisenmann, "Tele-Communications, Inc.: Accelerating Digital Deployment," section 1, *Internet Business Models: Text and Cases*, or HBS Case no. 899-141, August 11, 2000.

[56]See Thomas Eisenmann and Alastair Brown, "Networked Utilities," section 7, *Internet Business Models: Text and Cases*, or HBS Case no. 801-309, January 2000 for more on standard battles.

YAHOO!: BUSINESS ON INTERNET TIME

The word "portal" . . . is now the second-most-meaningless word in Netspeak. (The most meaningless word is "strategy," which appears to mean something along the lines of "blind, headlong, mindless pursuit of the latest analyst-endorsed Internet fad.")[1]

Tim Koogle, CEO of Yahoo!, leaned back in his bright yellow chair. Huddled around the purple table with him were Jerry Yang, co-founder of the company and Chief Yahoo, and President Jeff Mallett. The trio debated the recent flurry of competitive moves and puzzled over their options.

Several days earlier, on January 19, 1999, @Home had announced its plan to acquire Excite, Yahoo!'s arch rival. Like Yahoo!, Excite sought to provide consumers a point of entry into the World Wide Web. @Home offered high-speed access to the Internet via networks owned by cable television companies. The Excite/@Home deal came only two months after America Online, the online service provider with the largest number of subscribers, acquired Netscape. Netscape not only manufactured the browser software that many people used to navigate the web, but its Netcenter web site was one of the most popular portals on the web. Months earlier, Disney had taken a large stake in the portal Infoseek, and NBC had allied with Snap. Rumors swirled that Lycos, a portal with an array of online "channels," was also in the midst of merger talks.

Koogle, Yang, and Mallett had grown used to rapid change and adjustment in their three years together at Yahoo!. Even by Internet standards, however, January of 1999 was an unusually hectic month. Soon, Yahoo! might be the only portal without a major partner. Independence and a simple vision had served Yahoo! well so far. The company aimed to be "the one place in the world that anyone would need to go to find anything, locate anybody, or buy anything."[2] Through its web pages, Yahoo! sought to tailor the vast information available on the Internet to suit individual web users. It then "delivered" those users to companies that hoped to sell products to the users. Payments from the companies, not from the individual users, made up Yahoo!'s revenue. Though its service had evolved over the years (Exhibit 1), its basic approach had remained the same.

Investors had bet heavily that Yahoo! would make this approach profitable. The company's market value stood at $30 billion, up 2,600% since its IPO in April, 1996. Yahoo! booked revenue of $203 million in 1998, and analysts projected growth to as much as $362 million in 1999 (Exhibits 2 and 3). While most of its direct rivals were losing money, Yahoo! had recorded over a year and a half of increasing profits.

Koogle and his team now debated whether, and how, the company should adjust its approach in light of recent events. Publicly, the team had been silent on its options. Rumors circulated, however, that major media companies, telecom providers, banks, online retailers, and other portals were interested in deeper relationships with Yahoo!. In addition, with its lofty stock price, Yahoo! had the financial muscle to acquire any of an array of other Internet companies.

Jay Girotto, MBA 1999, and Professor Jan W. Rivkin prepared this case as the basis for class discussion rather than to illustrate either effective or ineffective handling of an administrative situation.

Evolution of the World Wide Web

The Internet. The Internet emerged from an infrastructure initiative undertaken by the Department of Defense in the 1960s. To ensure that the military communications system could survive a nuclear strike, the Department developed a new kind of network that had no central authority and could function even if most of the system were in tatters. Two principles guided the development of the network: networked computers had equal status, and each sent and received messages. If one node

[1] Fred Moody, "Doin' the Portal Rag," ABCNEWS.com, 12 October 1998.

[2] Interview with Grant Winfrey, Yahoo! Senior Brand Manager, 29 January 1999.

were destroyed, the others could continue to communicate. All of the messages were sent in packets going from one node to another. The routing of information packets along many paths remained a distinguishing characteristic of Internet technology in 1999.[3]

Until the end of the 1970s, use of the nascent Internet was confined to the military and to defense contractors. In 1986, the modern Internet was born when the National Science Foundation used five supercomputers to link scientific researchers from around the country. Researchers used the Internet chiefly to exchange electronic mail and to transfer files. Between 1986 and 1991, the Internet remained a tool used in a limited fashion by the military and by academic researchers.

The World Wide Web. In 1991, Tim Berners-Lee, a researcher at the European Laboratory for Particle Physics, wrote the basic parameters of a new language for describing computer documents. The language, known as hypertext mark-up language or HTML, could describe text, data, graphics, video, or audio. By clicking on certain pieces of text or images called hypertext links, a computer user could transfer automatically from one HTML document to another. As individual computer users wrote documents in HTML and placed them on the host computers that constituted the Internet, the World Wide Web emerged.[4]

In 1994, a small team at the U.S. Center for Supercomputer Applications created a "browser," a piece of software that permitted computer users to view HTML documents easily. Marc Andreesen, the mastermind of this effort, left the Center and, with James Clark, founded Netscape Communications to commercialize the product for the mass market. Netscape gave users copies of the reworked browser for free.

As the software required for the web proliferated, so did the hardware. Personal computers (PCs) penetrated homes and offices rapidly during the 1990s as PC prices fell and performance improved at a dramatic clip. From 1990 to 1997, worldwide shipments of personal computers grew at a rate of 24% per year. By 1999, an estimated 367 million PCs were installed around the globe. Modems, which permitted PCs to communicate with computer networks over telephone lines, were standard equipment on new machines. (See Exhibit 4.)

In January, 1999, more than 100 million individuals used the World Wide Web. It was estimated that the web added 42,000 new users a day, or one new user every two seconds (Exhibit 5).[5] The number of "host computers," storing HTML documents for public access, rose from approximately 2.2 million in January, 1994, to 43 million in January, 1999.[6] Though first popular in the United States, the World Wide Web was growing rapidly around the globe. In 1998, major U.S. sites reported that between 10% and 30% of traffic came from users outside of the U.S. Of international visitors to U.S. sites, 39% came from Europe, 28% from Asia, and 26% from Canada. In addition, sites based outside of the U.S. were prospering and drawing international visitors. The sites of the Japanese newspaper *Asahi Shimbun* and the British *Daily Telegraph*, for instance, drew more than 40% of their users from outside their home countries.[7]

Portals

Both capitalizing on and catalyzing the early growth of the World Wide Web was a small group of web sites that helped users navigate the web. Before these sites arose, users learned about interesting web pages either by following hypertext links from one page to another or by receiving a lengthy web address (or universal resource locator, URL) from a friend. Starting in 1994, with a web page entitled "Jerry's Guide to the World Wide Web" (later renamed Yahoo!), navigational sites began to catalog individual sites on the web. Some navigational sites, such as Yahoo!, classified web destinations under general headings in a manner similar to the way the Library of Congress categorized books. Users followed a hierarchy of headings and subheadings to find relevant web pages. Other navigational sites, such as Lycos and Infoseek, compiled keywords from web pages into databases which users could query. These "search engines" typically used software called "spider technology" that continuously combed the web to capture, store, and index the latest site information. (See Exhibit 6.)

Navigational sites grew to be among the most viewed sites on the World Wide Web, capturing 15% of all online traffic in 1998. (By comparison, the six major television networks captured 67% of the total viewing audience in prime time.) Early on, Infoseek and Lycos

[3]"The Worldwide Web and Internet Technology," HBS case 198-020.
[4]*Ibid.*
[5]"The Web in Perspective," Media Metrix/ IPRO, 1998.
[6]Internet Domain Survey, Network Wizards, July 1998.
[7]Media's Global Future," *The Forrester Report: Media & Technology Strategies*, August 1998.

focused on search technology. Lycos was awarded several patents for its spider technology, while Infoseek began to charge 10¢ per search. Over time, various search technologies emerged, and several of the navigational sites decided to outsource the search function to third party providers. Companies such as Alta Vista developed search technologies and licensed them to a number of different navigational sites.

In early 1997, two of the prominent navigational sites—Yahoo! and Excite—began to add content and features to their sites at a quickened pace. Other companies soon followed. The first additions provided users with information: news headlines, sports scores, stock prices, and so forth. By late 1997 and into 1998, the sites added more sophisticated features. Navigational sites gave users e-mail boxes and provided them space to create personal homepages. Auctions, shopping, and financial services allowed users to buy and sell items online. Chat rooms and online gaming brought users together in a community. A timeline in Exhibit 7 shows, for example, the sequence of moves by which the major companies added online games to their sites.

Increasingly, industry executives and observers referred to the sites—no longer just navigational tools—as "portals," a term coined by Halsey Minor, the CEO of CNET, in 1997.[8] Exhibit 8 ranks some of the major portals along a number of dimensions that were closely followed in the Internet community.

Customers. Portals had two distinct sets of customers: the non-paying web users who came to a portal's web site to use its services, and the paying companies that were trying to market products or services to the users.

Individual users turned to the World Wide Web in order to look for information, to communicate with others, and to buy and sell items. Users counted on portals to guide them efficiently to the information, people, and products they sought. Users spent approximately one-quarter of their online time conducting searches and using reference directories; one-third sending messages and chatting with other users; and one-third exploring other web-page content.[9] The demographic profile of portal users mirrored that of web users as a whole. In 1998, men aged 18 or above accounted for 48% of web users, women aged 18 or above accounted for 34%, and children between the ages of 2 and 17 constituted the remaining 18%. Among households with web users, most had an income greater than $60,000, and 79% had a household member with at least some college education. A typical visit to a portal lasted over 8 minutes and consisted of viewing 6 separate pages.[10]

Web users selected among portals based on quality of information, ease of interface use, and brand recognition. Sheer habit also played a role. When launched, web-browsing software went automatically to a particular web site, the user's start page. The software maker designated this page initially. A knowledgeable user could change the start page easily, but many users never bothered to do so.

All of the major portals made their basic services freely available to the public. Portals earned revenue not by charging individual users, but by charging companies which hoped to sell products and services to users. For such companies, the portals displayed advertisements and guided users to the companies' own web sites, where they might buy goods. In return, the portals earned advertising revenue and, in some cases, a referral fee if a user went to an advertiser's site and bought a product.

Advertisers structured their payments to portals in a number of ways. Under the most common arrangement, the advertiser paid the portal a fee per 1,000 users exposed to the advertisement (cost per thousand, or CPM). Advertisers paid more for "targeted placements" of ads. For example, an advertisement for Charles Schwab placed on a portal's finance page or on a page generated by a finance-related search would achieve more "click-throughs" to the Schwab site than would a similar ad placed on the portal's main page. Accordingly, Schwab would pay more for the former than for the latter. Typical CPMs ranged from $5 for a placement on a main page to as much as $200 for a targeted placement. For comparison, Exhibit 9 shows CPMs for other media.

Total expenditures for web-based advertising increased from essentially $0 in 1994 to an estimated $2 billion in 1998. Expenditures were expected to rise in line with the number of web users. Projections of expenditures in 2002 ranged from $8 billion to $15 billion. Forrester, an information technology research company, estimated that portals claimed 52% of total expenditures on web-based advertising in 1998. By comparison, the top six television networks captured 84% of the

[8]Kara Swisher, "'Portal' Industry Looks for New Name," *Wall Street Journal Europe*, 21 September 1998.

[9]"Analyzing the Aggregators," CIBC Oppenheimer, 1998.

[10]"The Web in Perspective," Media Metrix/ IPRO, 1998.

TV-based prime-time advertising in 1998.[11] (See Exhibit 10.)

Portals also earned referral fees from electronic commerce providers, that is, companies selling goods via the web. For instance, if a web user on Yahoo! clicked on an Amazon.com ad and bought a book, Amazon might pay Yahoo! a percentage of the revenue generated by the purchase. Such percentages ranged from 2% to 30% depending on the type of transaction, the prominence of partner placement, and the volume of transactions. Total electronic commerce expenditures by consumers were estimated to be $8 billion in 1998 and were projected to reach as much as $52 billion by 2002. Portals usually preferred to be paid per click-through rather than as a portion of revenue since the former was more easily audited.

Marketing executives of many companies expressed mixed feelings about online advertising and commerce. On one hand, the web allowed a consumer to purchase an advertised good almost immediately after seeing the ad. It also permitted advertisers to target consumers more precisely than did traditional mass media. On the other hand, most marketing executives were unsure about how to create and place online advertisements. In response to this uncertainty, a host of new companies arose to help marketers create online ads, place them on appropriate web sites, and monitor their performance.

Suppliers. Information content, advertising media, labor, and technology were the major inputs employed by portals. As the number of portals rose, portals increasingly tried to provide unique information in order to attract users and extend the length of their site visits. Portals purchased information content from traditional media companies such as the Cable News Network, Dow Jones, and Walt Disney. Excite, for instance, obtained most of its sports-related content from CBS's Sportsline site and relied on Intuit to design and provide information for its finance pages. When Infoseek sold a minority stake to Disney, it gained access to content such as ABCNEWS.com and ESPN SportsZone.

Portals struck a variety of deals with information providers. For unique content like real-time news with a recognized brand name, portals paid the provider a fee which might approach $50,000 per month. For specialized content less crucial to the portal, monthly fees in the $2,500 to $20,000 range were typical. Smaller content sites seeking exposure might receive no payment at all up front; indeed, they might give a portal exclusive rights to their content in exchange for placement. Advertising revenue associated with such deals was often split between the portal and the information provider. The content provider might retain 60% of the advertising revenue in addition to or instead of a flat fee. The precise terms of deals between information providers and portals varied substantially, with more popular portals striking much more favorable deals than less popular ones.

Portals spent approximately half of their composite revenue on sales and marketing in 1998. The cost of building a recognizable brand name on the Internet was estimated to be $60 million–80 million per year in 1998 and had risen substantially recently. Most of a portal's marketing dollars were spent on spot television advertising. Several portals had just made the move to national advertising with the 1999 Super Bowl. Much of the print and consumer marketing was done through barter agreements. The most powerful marketing for portals often involved online/offline consumer promotions. For example, for the 1998–99 season, Yahoo! was the official online site to vote for the NHL all-star team. In exchange for NHL coverage on Yahoo! Sports, Yahoo! received announcements and advertising at ice hockey arenas.

Portals competed intensely for labor, especially because most of the portals were headquartered in Silicon Valley, where skilled programmers and engineers were currently in great demand. As portal stock prices rose, it became difficult to attract top talent with the prospect of stock option appreciation. It was estimated that the annual cost of supporting a full-time worker in Silicon Valley was $200,000; a typical estimate elsewhere was $100,000. Turnover added to the high cost of labor. It was easy and common for sought-after computer programmers to "job-hop" when the perceived value of their options faltered.

Portals performed much of their computer programming in-house, but also turned to technology partners to add some forms of functionality to their sites. Common partners included companies that offered secure financial transactions, communication tools such as e-mail and instant messaging, and software tools for creating homepages. For many technology partners, adoption of a technology by a leading portal was a major event that marked the "arrival" of the partner.

Complements. To gain access to the World Wide Web, an individual needed a computer with a modem, browser

[11] "The Great Portal Shakeout," *The Forrester Report: Media & Technology Strategies,* March 1998.

software, and a telecommunications connection to the Internet. A wide variety of companies sold computers in a hotly competitive market. Two products dominated the market for browsers: Netscape's Navigator and Microsoft's Internet Explorer. Microsoft's browser was bundled with its operating systems and distributed with most PCs. Many users of Navigator obtained it by downloading the software over the web.

Telephone companies, cable television providers, online services companies, and specialized Internet Service Providers (ISPs) vied to sell access to the Internet.[12] Most home users got access to the Internet over conventional copper telephone lines, which tended to provide relatively slow connections at 28.8 or 56 kilobits per second. In contrast, new "broadband" technologies could transmit signals at rates from 1.5 megabits per second (mbps) to as high as 50 mbps. In 1999, companies were pursuing a range of broadband technologies. Many local telephone companies hoped to use "digital subscriber line" technology, which utilized existing copper telephone lines more efficiently. Other companies were trying to use the cable television infrastructure that passed 70% of U.S. homes.

Many users had high-speed access to the Internet at work, and with 750,000 subscribers at the end of 1998, broadband had established a small beachhead in the home ISP market. Industry experts were divided over how quickly home users would migrate to high-speed access. One observer quipped that "broadband technology has been 3–5 years off for 3–5 years." Others felt that the technology verged on a commercial breakthrough. The new technologies required infrastructure investments that ranged from a few hundred dollars per subscriber to more than $1,000. These costs were likely to decline over time.

To permit the rapid loading of web pages at slow transmission rates, many web sites were currently designed to include little but text and simple graphics. High-speed access might open the web to a host of new services, including movies delivered on demand, videoconferencing, interactive shopping, and games with multiple players and rich graphics.

Yahoo!

History. Yahoo! began as a hobby of David Filo and Jerry Yang. Ph.D. candidates in Stanford's Electrical Engineering Department, Filo and Yang started the first guide to the web in April, 1994, as a way to keep track of the addresses of interesting web sites being sent to them by friends. As the guide made the transition to a web site, it was given the name Yahoo!, short, some claimed, for "Yet Another Hierarchical Officious Oracle." The first homepage resided on Yang's student workstation, "akebono," while the underlying database was lodged on Filo's computer, "konishiki."[13] (The machines were named after legendary Hawaiian sumo wrestlers.)

During 1994, Filo and Yang converted Yahoo! into a customized database designed to serve the needs of thousands of users, and the service began to be used throughout the close-knit web community. Filo and Yang spent less and less time working on their Ph.D. studies and incorporated Yahoo! as a business on March 5, 1995. Soon after that, Yahoo! hired its sixth employee and new CEO Tim Koogle.[14] Koogle, then 44, served as Yahoo!'s "designated adult," trying to channel the energy of a bunch of Net enthusiasts toward creating a profitable business.

A number of principles guided the early development of the company. Koogle and his team saw Yahoo! not as a search engine, but as a modern media company, comparable to a television network or film studio. Accordingly, they shaped the organization with "producers" developing online "properties." By August, 1995, Yahoo!'s managers were measuring themselves against media companies, not just Internet firms. At the same time, they developed a team of engineers building backend databases, a distributed sales force attacking the important media markets, and a small group of corporate marketers establishing the Yahoo! brand name. Koogle commented on building the organization:

> This has been a real joy. One of the cool things is that we got to start with a clean slate. . . . In hiring, we follow the "No Bozos Rule." Don't hire bozos. Hire really smart people. Get clear on what you're going to execute. Then push decisions out, and get out of the way. But stay accessible. . . . If you're uncompromising in hiring, you get an organization that clones itself. We talk a lot about having a scalable organization.[15]

During 1996 and especially 1997, Yahoo! added content, commerce, communication, and community

[12]This section draws on Mary Kwak, "The Broadband Race: Industry Note," Harvard Business School Case 799-106.

[13]Yahoo! Annual Report, 1997.

[14]"Yahoo! The Company, the Strategy, the Stock," *Business Week*, 7 September 1998.

[15]Interview with Tim Koogle, 28 January 1999.

offerings aggressively, branching out to be more than a guide to the web. For users who registered with Yahoo!, the company provided My Yahoo!, a personalized service delivering tailored content to them from classifieds, chat rooms, and news wires. The company purchased Four11, a provider of directory services and free e-mail, and it entered into a partnership with Visa to bring consumers together with hundreds of on-line and off-line merchants in popular shopping categories.[16] Yahoo! also began to build country-specific and city-specific sites.[17]

Yahoo!'s site traffic grew from approximately 23 million page views per day in December, 1996, to over 167 million page views per day in December, 1998.[18] At the same time, Yahoo! increased its roll of registered users to more than 35 million, and the number of distinct individuals visiting its site rose to 50 million. Yahoo!'s advertising revenue also grew, with the number of companies buying ads rising from 550 during the fourth quarter of 1996 to 2,225 during the final quarter of 1998.[19]

Yahoo!'s Properties. Yahoo!'s primary services, called "properties," fell into several categories.

- *Navigation properties* helped consumers find relevant information more easily. The company made a distinction between so-called "search-and-browse" areas and properties that Yahoo! programmed itself. A line extended across Yahoo!'s main homepage, roughly one-third of the way down the page (Exhibit 1). Below the line were search-and-browse areas: essentially a set of categories (e.g., entertainment or science) that led in a hierarchical fashion to finer categories and, eventually, to others' web pages. Above the line were properties programmed by Yahoo!. Yahoo! News, for instance, used sources ranging from the Associated Press to the Hollywood Reporter and covered a wide variety of topics, from technology to human interest. Yahoo! Finance provided stock price quotes, graphs, analysts' ratings, company information, and other financial information.
- *Community properties* helped consumers connect and communicate. Yahoo! Address Book, for instance, enabled users to use a personal address book from any Internet-connected computer. Yahoo! Mail offered free e-mail accounts. Users could turn to Yahoo! Chat to join chat groups about a wide variety of topics and Yahoo! Message Boards to post and request information.
- *Personalization properties* could be customized by a consumer to satisfy his or her personal interests. A user might, for instance, pick his or her favorite topics from stocks to weather in order to create a customized site.
- *Electronic commerce properties,* including shopping, travel, and real estate properties, were organized and coordinated by Yahoo!, but partners actually carried out the sales. The shopping property, for instance, guided a user through a hierarchy to items sold by a host of online merchants. Travel bookings carried the Yahoo! brand, but were arranged through American Airlines' Sabre travel service.
- *International properties* in Australia/New Zealand, Canada, Denmark, France, Germany, Hong Kong, Japan, Korea, Norway, Singapore, Spain, Sweden, Taiwan, and UK/Ireland targeted local users and advertisers. Yahoo!'s team in each country catalogued tens of thousands of local web sites, created guides in the local language, and tailored content to local needs.

Yahoo!'s many properties shared a very similar "look and feel." A user familiar with one property would quickly feel comfortable with another. In addition, properties were linked to one another. When searching Yahoo!'s Yellow Pages for pizza in Boston, for instance, one would see links to online maps, restaurant reviews, regional directories, and shopping services. In developing new properties, Yahoo! preferred "quiet launches." Koogle explained, "We don't want to be too far out in front of our properties. We set it up, prove it, *then* tell people about it."[20]

Operations. Yahoo! ran its operations from two buildings in a rather nondescript office park typical of Silicon Valley. A visitor's first hint that this office park housed an unusual company, however, came in the parking lot, where employee's purple cars were emblazoned with the yellow slogan, "Do You Yahoo?" The color scheme continued inside. Employees sat at close quarters in purple cubicles which showed no sign of hierarchy. "The tight space helps us communicate," Koogle said. "Besides, we're cheap."

[16]"Yahoo! and Visa Together Again," *Business Week,* 11 August 1997.
[17]Yahoo! Annual Report, 1997.
[18]Yahoo! Annual Report, 1998.
[19]*Ibid.*

[20]Interview with Tim Koogle, 28 January 1999.

The layout of headquarters reflected the company's organizational chart, with each functional group sitting together. Operations were divided into three groups: property development, marketing and sales, and international (Exhibit 11). Property development, in turn, consisted of the production, engineering, and surfing functions. "Producers" were responsible for Yahoo!'s properties. The producer of Yahoo! Weather, for instance, designed Yahoo!'s weather services, wrote the basic HTML involved in the weather pages, and tracked competing weather-related sites on the web. Engineers performed the heavy-duty technical tasks, building data feeds and servers to deliver the content of the properties. Members of the surfing department constantly combed through new web sites and updated the directories in Yahoo! Search. Surfers not only classified new sites, but they also alerted producers when they spotted a relevant site.

Marketing and sales encompassed three functions: corporate marketing, sales, and business development. The corporate marketing staff was responsible for developing the Yahoo! brand name among the web-surfing public. Spot television advertisements accounted for most of the marketing budget, but Yahoo! also employed radio, print, consumer promotions, and, recently, national television. Ads were focused especially on "near surfers," consumers who were likely to surf the web for the first time soon. Many of Yahoo!'s corporate marketers came not from Internet-related backgrounds, but from traditional consumer packaged-goods companies such as Procter and Gamble.

Sales people sold the advertising inventory on Yahoo!'s 167 million page views per month. The company used both inside and outside sales people to take orders as small as $1,000.

A business development staff, a recent innovation, arranged Yahoo!'s numerous partnerships with other firms. When a producer identified a need for a partner, the business development staff determined the most suitable partner and negotiated the deal. Yahoo! had a reputation for tough negotiation. The business development staff also fielded the hundreds of unsolicited partnership proposals that flooded into Yahoo! each month. "You try not to be distracted by all the proposals that come in," said Elizabeth Collet, senior manager of business development and planning. "And a lot come in."[21]

In negotiating partnerships, the business development team operated by a handful of principles. Ellen Siminoff, vice president of business development and planning, outlined the top precepts:

> Integration across the Yahoo! properties is key. Put the product first. Do a deal only if it enhances the customer experience. And enter no joint venture that limits Yahoo!'s evolvability.[22]

A substantial portion of Yahoo!'s employees belonged to the international group. International personnel were responsible for all aspects of business in the 18 countries in which Yahoo! operated, including production, engineering, surfing, sales, marketing, and business development.

Formal mechanisms linking the functions were rare. Grant Winfrey, a senior brand manager explained:

> There's a huge respect for expertise here. You don't see a lot of cross-functional teams. We just check in with each other, and we don't get into each other's business. Everyone here knows that you shouldn't be a maverick, going off into someone else's business without checking in.[23]

Siminoff noted that she and Tim Brady, vice president of production, tried never to be in same meeting. "After all, we look after each other's interests."[24] Further down in the organization, however, business development and production personnel jointly attended meetings with potential business partners. "The redundancy is necessary for decentralization," Collet explained. "If my counterpart on the production side and I agree that something is good for Yahoo!, the odds are good that we're right. There's a system of checks and balances in place."[25]

Partnerships. Yahoo! had so-called "distribution deals" with a number of computer makers. Under these arrangements, users of new computers going onto the web for the first time would automatically connect to a Yahoo! web site. Certain Compaq and Gateway computers, for instance, came equipped with a customized version of Microsoft's Internet Explorer which led users first to Yahoo!. Similar agreements were in place for Hewlett-Packard's Pavilion PCs and IBM's Aptiva PCs.

Yahoo! had struck similar deals with certain Internet service providers. AT&T Yahoo! Online, a partnership with the largest long distance carrier in the U.S., combined Yahoo!'s services with Internet access provided by

[21]Interview with Elizabeth Collet, 29 January 1999.

[22]Interview with Ellen Siminoff, 29 January 1999.

[23]Interview with Grant Winfrey, 29 January 1999.

[24]Interview with Ellen Siminoff, 29 January 1999.

[25]Telephone interview with Elizabeth Collet, 8 April 1999.

AT&T WorldNet. With British Telecom (BT), Yahoo! launched Yahoo! Click, which combined Internet access from BT with the services of Yahoo! UK & Ireland.

Yahoo! also sought partners to develop information and services for its users. These relationships were especially prominent in the area of electronic commerce. ONSALE, Inc., a leading electronic retailer in interactive online auctions, offered Yahoo! Auctions, an online, person-to-person auction service. In the Yahoo! Finance section, E*TRADE, DATEK, DLJ Direct, Ameritrade, Quick & Reilly, and WebStreet provided links to online trading. Ticketmaster gave Yahoo! users information about entertainment events and the ability to purchase tickets online. A relationship with National Public Radio added audio content to Yahoo! News. Yahoo! Sports and Fox Sports Online teamed up to offer comprehensive coverage of the 1998 World Series through a site hosted on Yahoo!.

Yahoo! received much of its information content for free. In exchange, information providers received links back to their sites. Providers might also receive a share of the advertising revenue generated by the information. A share of 7.5%–15% was typical.

Planning, Control, and Compensation. Yahoo! consisted primarily of enthusiastic Stanford graduates under the age of 30. Koogle, Mallett, Yang, and their senior team tried to direct the energy of the company without dampening it. The short-run controls that Koogle helped to develop reflected both his experience in manufacturing and his love of automobile racing:

> Early on, we put an infrastructure in place to measure how we generate a non-paying audience of customers and sell that inventory to paying customers. We have a weekly document called the Flash Report that functions like the dashboard on a race car. It measures all of our crucial metrics from user base growth to advertising bookings. . . . We distribute it pretty widely to the employees.[26]

While the Flash Report reflected weekly conditions, the basic strategy of the company had remained virtually unchanged since Yang, Filo, and Brady wrote Yahoo!'s first business plan in the spring of 1995. Yang discussed the strategy:

> Our long-run success depends on our ability to reach the user and the level of trust we develop with that user. Yahoo! has always been about building an online environment where the technology is transparent to the user. Ultimately, it will be about the brand, the users, and being global.[27]

Between the Flash Report and the fundamental strategy was a one-year operating plan which detailed the financial goals and defined the top priorities, typically five or fewer in number. The revenue forecast was an aggressive goal while the expense plan was conservative. Individual functional areas had similar medium-term plans. Corporate marketing, for instance, plotted out its use of television six months in advance, but used radio spots to adjust its marketing efforts with as little as three weeks' notice. "You don't spend too much time on detailed marketing plans because they don't last very long," said Grant Winfrey, a senior brand manager. "The point is to stay ahead of the competition in 60-day windows."

Like most of its Silicon Valley counterparts, Yahoo! offered its employees stock options as well as a base salary. The company's soaring stock price had made many of its managers well-off. Yahoo!'s success made it popular among job seekers, but the lofty stock price had made it harder to attract new recruits.

Competition

Yahoo!'s competitors fell into categories that were widely recognized in the industry: companies combining Internet access and content; portals allied with traditional media companies; portals that, like Yahoo!, were independent; and specialized, "vertical" sites. See Exhibits 12–14 for a comparison of services offered and audience reached.

Access and Content Providers

America Online/Netscape. America Online (AOL) was one of the few online contenders that predated the World Wide Web. Starting in 1985, AOL tried to provide information, communication, and electronic commerce services within a self-contained, proprietary community of subscribers. From its early days, AOL distinguished itself from online rivals by its user friendliness and its aggressive direct marketing to home computer users. With the advent of the World Wide Web, many analysts

[26]Interview with Tim Koogle, 28 January 1999.

[27]Interview with Jerry Yang, Chief Yahoo!, 8 February 1999.

predicted the demise of AOL; the web offered much of what AOL did but with a much wider community and no subscription fee. AOL defied these predictions by marketing itself vigorously to the wave of new online users. Flat-rate pricing for unlimited access, a user-friendly interface, and wide distribution of free software brought AOL more subscribers than its infrastructure could initially handle.

In January, 1999, AOL offered both a subscription service and a web site, AOL.com, that was open to the public. With 14 million subscribers, AOL had by far the largest captive audience in cyberspace. Subscribers had access to services such as private chat rooms and free personal homepages that were not available to the general public. They also could use AOL to gain access to the wider World Wide Web. A subscription bundled the full range of online services, a browser, online access, and an electronic mailbox into one seamless package.

AOL.com was available to all Internet users, not just AOL members. AOL.com's range of content, features, and tools was comparable to those available from other portals.

In November, 1998, AOL announced its plan to acquire Netscape Communications for stock then valued at $4.2 billion. By developing the first widely commercialized Internet browser, Netscape had catalyzed the growth of the World Wide Web. Netscape's Communicator continued to hold 45%–50% of the browser market, and the company had extensive contacts in the corporate sector, where AOL was weak. A bruising battle with Microsoft's Internet Explorer, however, had pushed Netscape's stock price from the high 80s in 1995 to the mid-teens in early 1998.

AOL's acquisition of Netscape not only gave it control of a leading browser, but also added Netscape's Netcenter portal to AOL's arsenal. Netscape had entered the portal arena gradually. Its first search and directory page, launched in March of 1996, simply sent browser users to one of five established portals (Excite, Infoseek, Lycos, Magellan, or Yahoo!). After a brief portal partnership with Yahoo!, Netscape launched its own portal, Netcenter, in September, 1997. Netscape configured its browsers to go to Netcenter unless instructed otherwise by a user. By January, 1999, Netcenter had more than 9 million registered users. Daily traffic had increased by 50% over the previous six months, but "reach," or the portion of web users visiting the site each month—a closely followed statistic throughout the Internet community—had hit a plateau.

Steve Case, CEO of AOL, commented on the company's acquisition of Netscape:

> The acquisition of Netscape is a big step forward for America Online that will greatly accelerate our business momentum. Netscape has played a key role in helping consumers benefit from the enormous power of the Internet, and we share the same mission. With Netscape, we will broaden our global audience at home and at work, and add world-class technology to support an expanded range of America Online interactive products and services.[28]

Microsoft Network (MSN). Software giant Microsoft largely ignored the World Wide Web in the web's early days. By mid-1995, however, Microsoft recognized the importance of the web. In an internal memo dated May, 1995, CEO Bill Gates gave the Internet "the *highest* level of importance. The Internet is the most important single development to come along since the IBM PC was introduced in 1981. . . . The Internet is a tidal wave. It changes the rules."[29] Accordingly, Microsoft launched a number of web-related efforts. Its browser software, Internet Explorer, became a major rival to Netscape's product by late 1996. Microsoft's Advanced Technology and Research Group invested more than $400 million in web-based R&D in 1997.[30]

In addition to developing software related to the Internet, Microsoft launched or acquired a set of online services. The centerpiece, MSN, was originally intended to resemble AOL's subscription service: a proprietary community in which subscribers paid for a bundle of access, browser software, and online services. Software for MSN came bundled on new computers with the Windows95 operating system. At launch, MSN was the only online service bundled with Windows95. In March, 1996, however, Bill Gates reached a major deal with Steve Case of AOL. Microsoft agreed to include on the Windows95 desktop a folder containing AOL and other online services. In exchange, AOL agreed that Microsoft's Internet Explorer would be the default browser distributed to its subscribers.[31] The deal bolstered Internet Explorer in its battle against Netscape's

---

[28]"America Online, Inc. to Acquire Netscape Communications in Stock Transaction Valued at $4.2 Billion," AOL-Netscape press release, 24 November 1998.

[29]Quoted in David B. Yoffie and Michael A. Cusumano, "Judo Strategy: The Competitive Dynamics of Internet Time," *Harvard Business Review*, January-February 1999, p. 76.

[30]Microsoft Annual Report, 1997.

[31]David B. Yoffie and Michael A. Cusumano, "Judo Strategy: The Competitive Dynamics of Internet Time," *Harvard Business Review*, January-February 1999.

Communicator, but weakened MSN relative to AOL. In October, 1996, MSN shifted from being a proprietary community to being a freely accessible, web-based portal like Yahoo!. Unlike Yahoo!, however, Microsoft operated as an ISP, selling Internet access to customers. By late 1998, Microsoft connected 2 million subscribers to the Internet.

Microsoft also invested heavily in developing web content and commerce. In December, 1997, it acquired the popular e-mail service Hotmail. Other ventures included CarPoint, a car-buying service; Expedia, a travel booking service; and Sidewalk.com, a guide to cities and to buying. MSNBC, a joint venture with broadcast network NBC, provided online news. In recent efforts, Microsoft appeared to be shifting away from online entertainment toward electronic commerce. Microsoft was also integrating its web properties more tightly.[32] Increasingly, MSN relied on content and commerce providers that were owned by Microsoft. MSN licensed its search technology from AltaVista, Lycos, Infoseek, and Snap on a rotating basis.[33]

In September, 1998, Gates commented that a few of Microsoft's content properties were beginning to break even.[34] Observers noted that Microsoft, with $14 billion in cash, could afford to sustain losses in its Internet businesses. Gates intended the company's web-related businesses eventually to become its fourth major business group, alongside PC operating systems like Windows, PC applications like Word and Excel, and server software.[35] The combined reach of the Microsoft homepage and MSN eclipsed Yahoo! in December, 1998.

@Home/Excite. On January 19, 1999, @Home announced its plan to acquire the portal Excite for $6.7 billion. @Home was an Internet service provider. Through 2002, it had exclusive rights to deliver high-speed Internet access over the networks of 19 cable-television providers. These cable networks had the potential to serve 60 million homes worldwide. With 330,000 subscribers in 1998, @Home generated revenue of $48 million. @Home's major investor, the cable company TCI, was itself being acquired by AT&T.

Prior to the acquisition, Excite developed two flagship brands on the web. The main brand, Excite itself, was a full-service portal aiming to provide the "20% of the content and tools that 80% of the people want."[36] Excite was known for the ease with which users could personalize its services to meet their needs. Early Excite ads asked listeners whether they were "still with that same old Yahoo." Excite's second brand, Webcrawler, acquired from AOL in 1996, offered a no-frills approach to searching with a focus on speed and simplicity.[37] In 1998, the company as a whole lost $28 million on revenue of $154 million.

Plans for the merged company were far from clear. Industry observers speculated that Excite would be an important advertising channel for @Home, encouraging web users to migrate to broadband access. Excite might also lead the way in developing web content that made full use of broadband technology. Tom Jermoluk, CEO of @Home, commented that "probably the hidden gem of the whole deal is how we'll be able to implement their targeting and database technology to deliver advertising to the individual user."[38]

Before @Home made its winning offer for Excite, a number of companies, including Yahoo! and Microsoft, were rumored to be interested in bidding for the company.[39]

Portals with Traditional Media Partners

Disney/Infoseek. In June, 1998, Infoseek became the first leading portal to ally with a major media partner, Disney. Under the agreement, Infoseek received $70 million in cash and Disney's ownership position in Starwave, a producer of Internet-based sports, news, and entertainment services (e.g., ESPN SportsZone and ABCNEWS.com). In return, Disney acquired 43% of Infoseek, a minority position on the Infoseek board, and options to increase its ownership in the future.[40]

Following the merger, Infoseek went on a six-month hiatus to develop the GO Network, a new portal combining all Infoseek and Disney properties. Michael Eisner, CEO of Disney, was personally involved in much of the

[32]Eric Nee, "Welcome to My Store," *Forbes,* 19 October 1998, pp. 140–144.

[33]"MSN.com Does Search Deals," *CNET News.com,* 21 September 1998.

[34]"Internet: Big Guns Close in on Portals, Search Engines," *Network Briefing,* 9 September 1998.

[35]Eric Nee, "Welcome to My Store," *Forbes,* 19 October 1998, pp. 140–144.

[36]"The Great Portal Shakeout," *The Forrester Report: Media & Technology Strategies,* March 1998.

[37]Excite Annual Report, 1997.

[38]Amy Harmon, "Excite and At Home Confirm $6.7 Billion Merger," *New York Times,* 20 January 1999.

[39]John Markoff, "Internet Service Is Planning $6 Billion Deal to Buy Excite," *New York Times,* 19 January 1999.

[40]"Disney and Infoseek Combine Forces on the Internet," Infoseek press release, 18 June 1998.

GO initiative right down to selecting its traffic light logo. Launched on January 1, 1999, GO looked similar to other portals, but clicking on a link to "news" or "sports" or "kids" led directly to Disney-generated content. Every other Disney web site linked back to GO, to form what Disney hoped would become a largely self-contained set of services.[41] Prior to the launch of GO in December, 1998, Infoseek was the 9th most trafficked site on the web with a reach of 22.1% while the Disney Online properties were the 8th most popular site with a reach of 23.9%.[42] As a stand-alone company, Infoseek lost $9 million in 1998 on revenue of $63 million.[43]

NBC/Snap. NBC, one of the major television networks in the U.S., announced in June, 1998, that it would purchase a 5% equity stake in CNET, a company devoted primarily to providing technology news and information over the web. Together, NBC and CNET would operate Snap, CNET's full-service portal site. NBC also acquired an unspecified minority stake in Snap, reported by *Fortune* to be 19% with options to increase its holdings to 60% in the future.[44] Snap continued to be promoted as a separate brand without the NBC label.

On January 19, 1999, Snap announced its Cyclone project, a new portal designed specifically for users with broadband access to the Internet. Cyclone would, for instance, allow broadband users to watch certain NBC television broadcasts on their computers. Halsey Minor, CEO of CNET, explained, "Internet portal users who have access to higher-speed Internet connections are looking for a rich, full experience, not just text-based lists of web sites. With our groundbreaking Snap 'Cyclone' service, we will become the first Internet portal company to offer these users the ability to move beyond text to a world of video, audio, animation and more."[45]

NBC's overall web strategy targeted a broader audience than that of the fledgling Snap site. MSNBC, its joint venture with Microsoft, attempted to draw people interested in general news. CNBC attracted people interested in finance and business while NBC.com drew consumers interested in entertainment. NBC Interactive gave affiliate stations a set of local web gateways with regional classifieds, headlines, and weather reports.[46]

Independent Portals

Lycos Network. Lycos billed itself not as a unified portal but as a network of separate services. The flagship member of the network, also named Lycos, was a full-service portal comparable to other portals. A new design for the site, unveiled in October, 1998, had a less complicated interface than did earlier versions. It pointed users toward electronic commerce services and made elaborate searches easier. Indeed, the company had long touted itself as providing the best search technology on the web. Lycos commercials featured a Sherpa and later a guide dog.

Other members of the Lycos Network included HotBot, a particularly sophisticated search engine; Tripod.com, which provided tools for building web pages and promoted online communities known as "pods"; Whowhere, a directory service; and Wired.com, a leading source of technology news. Lycos linked the elements of its network only in a limited way and tended to promote and develop the elements separately. For instance, an extensive advertising campaign for HotBot did not mention Lycos.

Partly because it acquired sites with widely different audiences, the Lycos Network more than doubled its reach during 1998, taking it close to Yahoo!'s reach (Exhibit 14). Lycos lost $8 million on revenue of $89 million in 1998.

AltaVista. AltaVista originated in Digital Equipment Corporation's research lab as a highly technical search engine. Initially marketed as an engine that could be embedded into other services, AltaVista gradually became a portal in its own right. Following its 1998 acquisition of Digital, computer maker Compaq announced plans to spin-off AltaVista in January, 1999. "By establishing AltaVista as a separate company, it can better focus on providing the best user experience on the Internet, from search, to commerce, to communication and community," said Eckhard Pfeiffer, Compaq president and CEO. "We see this as a significant opportunity for Compaq to expand its share of the rapidly growing Internet market for content and services and also enables

[41]"With GO Network, Disney Steps into the Portal Wars," *The New York Times,* 13 December 1999.

[42]Media Metrix, December 1998.

[43]"Internet & New Media Update," Warburg Dillon Read, 16 November 1998.

[44]"The Latest, Hottest Internet Stocks," *Fortune Investor,* 20 July 1998.

[45]"NBC and CNET's Snap Announces Next Generation Internet Portal for High-Speed Users," Snap press release, 19 January 1999.

[46]"Go Ahead, Kill Your Television. NBC Is Ready," *Wired,* December 1998.

us to unlock the tremendous value of AltaVista for our shareholders."[47] Compaq hoped that AltaVista would become the leading destination site for information and e-commerce on the World Wide Web.

The AltaVista site traditionally lacked many of the features offered by major portals. In recent months, the company had announced a series of partnerships including an agreement with Microsoft's MSN. Under that agreement, AltaVista offered users free e-mail with an AltaVista-branded version of Microsoft's Hotmail service. AltaVista gained rights to Microsoft's instant messaging technology in the future, and the companies agreed to work together on a range of other web-based communications and community-building services.

Vertical Sites

A growing number of "vertical" sites featured in-depth information and electronic commerce tailored to special interests. CNET and ZDNet covered technology news, for instance, while Motley Fool gave advice to stock market day-traders, ESPN SportsZone provided sports news, iVillage featured women's topics, and Quicken.com focused on personal finance. Such sites offered depth in individual interest areas that portals such as Yahoo! did not match. Some vertical sites were becoming familiar enough to users that users went directly to them, without using a portal. The most popular vertical sites relied less and less on referrals from portals, and increasingly, they could strike favorable deals with portals.

Taking the Next Step

With the flurry of recent mergers and partnerships, competitors had placed very large—and very different—bets on the future. Now the Yahoo! team had to decide whether and how to adjust their own wager. Tim Brady, who helped write Yahoo!'s original business plan, emphasized that the company balanced adjustment and continuity:

> It's tough to ferret out strategy from tactics because the industry moves so fast. If you make the wrong tactical move, you can't follow the strategy. But the strategy has been the same since day one. Yahoo! is a social engineering project. We bring people together. We never wanted to create a cool technology.[48]

Rumors circulated that a number of suitors were interested in a partnership, perhaps even a merger, with Yahoo!. Some large, traditional media companies such as Time-Warner and News Corporation had not yet established significant operations on the web. Several financial institutions seemed eager to play a larger role in online commerce and investing. Telecommunication companies such as MCI/Worldcom and AT&T, who were already major providers of Internet access, appeared interested in providing web content. Content requiring broadband access might be especially appealing to such companies.

Closer to the web, the Lycos Network was widely rumored to be for sale. Industry observers speculated that portals might build stronger ties with leaders in electronic commerce, such as Amazon.com. Moreover, Yahoo! was already in acquisition discussions with the management of GeoCities, in which it held a minority stake. GeoCities provided software tools and server space that allowed individuals to build their own web pages, which were then organized in communities of interests, or neighborhoods, on the GeoCities' site. Neighborhoods ranged from Nashville, for those interested in country music, to Area 51, for science fiction aficionados. In terms of reach, GeoCities trailed only AOL, Microsoft, Yahoo!, and the Lycos Network.

Despite the many changes and opportunities in their business, Yahoo!'s senior managers remained focused on a handful of priorities. Koogle remarked:

> As a company, we're heavily externally focused. We maintain a level of paranoia about the environment that is pretty healthy, and we seldom actually get surprised. If anything tectonic is going on, Jerry, Jeff, or I get word of it before it occurs. When that happens, we come back to fairly basic fundamentals. Are we still doing the right things?[49]

[47]"Compaq Creates the AltaVista Company Extending Its Internet Leadership Position," Compaq press release, 26 January 1999.

[48]Interview with Tim Brady, 29 January 1998.

[49]Interview with Tim Koogle, 28 January 1998.

Exhibit 1

EVOLUTION OF YAHOO!'S HOMEPAGE

1st Homepage

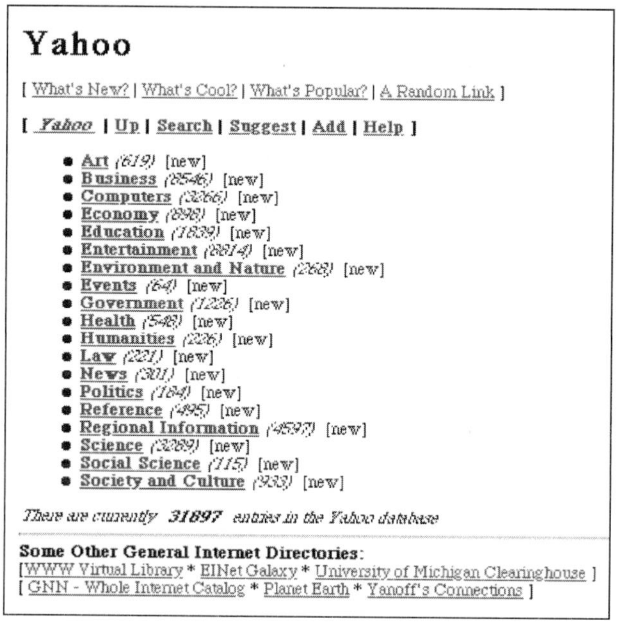

1995

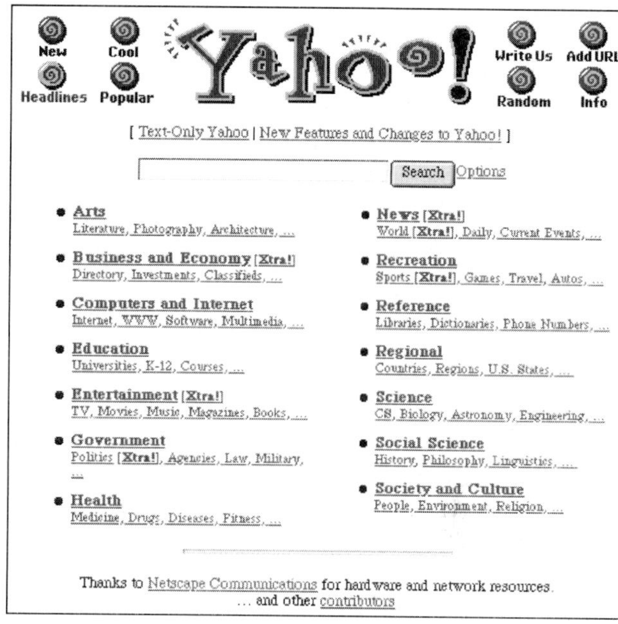

1997

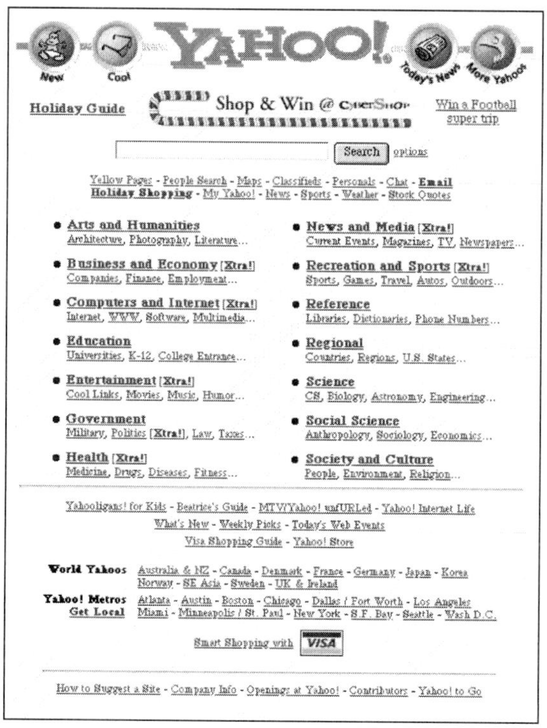

1999

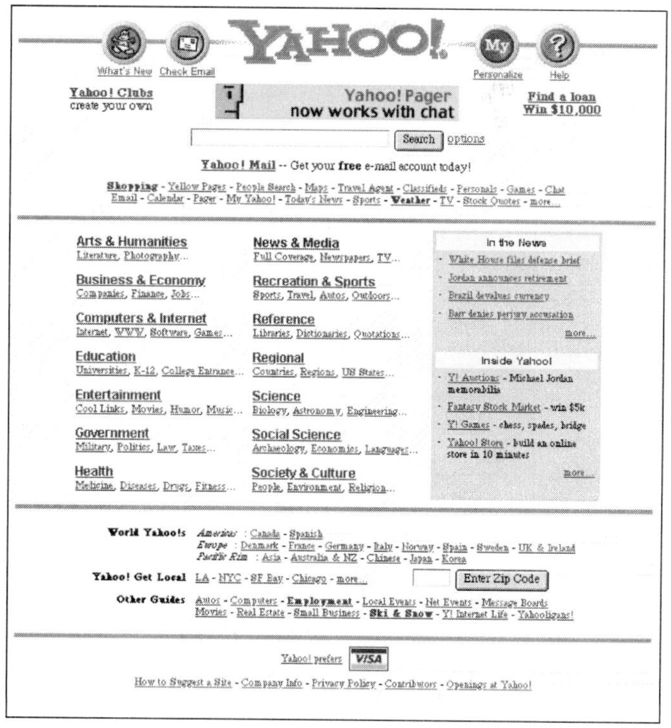

Exhibit 2 YAHOO! FINANCIAL RESULTS AND PROJECTIONS (MILLIONS OF U.S. DOLLARS)

	1996	1997	1998	1999E	2000E	2001E	2002E	2003E
Total revenue	21.5	70.5	203.3	361.6	511.3	719.8	1,007.7	1,410.7
Cost of revenue	4.7	10.9	26.7	42.8	56.5	77.4	100.8	141.1
Gross margin	16.8	59.6	176.5	318.8	454.8	642.4	906.9	1,269.7
Operating expenses								
Sales and marketing	16.2	45.8	92.4	148.8	201.7	284.0	392.2	536.1
Product development	5.7	12.1	22.7	37.6	49.1	68.4	94.4	127.0
General and administrative	5.8	7.4	11.2	16.3	23.0	32.4	45.3	62.0
Non-recurring and other	-	25.1	21.4	4.1	4.1	4.1	4.1	4.1
Total	27.7	90.3	147.8	207.0	278.0	388.9	536.0	729.2
Operating income (loss)	(10.9)	(30.8)	28.8	111.8	176.8	253.5	370.9	540.5
Net income (loss) before non-recurring	(6.4)	(0.4)	49.9	93.0	127.8	169.4	239.0	340.3
Current assets	99.7	108.5	467.2					
Total assets	113.0	143.5	621.9					
Current liabilities	8.3	24.4	80.0					
Long-term liabilities	0.5	0.7	5.7					
Total stockholders' equity	104.2	118.4	536.2					
Net cash provided by (used in) operations	(2.4)	0.5	110.3					
Net cash provided by (used in) investments	(76.2)	19.6	(329.9)					
Net cash provided by (used in) financing	107.2	9.6	281.3					
Net change in cash	28.5	29.3	61.9					

Source: Actual figures from company data. Projections from Warburg Dillon Read, January 25, 1999

Exhibit 3 YAHOO! OPERATING STATISTICS

	1996	1Q97	2Q97	3Q97	4Q97	1Q98	2Q98	3Q98	4Q98
Millions of pages viewed per day at end of quarter	21	30	38	53	65	95	115	144	167
Millions of registered users	-	-	-	-	-	12	18	25	35
Revenue/daily page delivered	$0.94	$0.37	$0.41	$0.38	$0.43	$0.32	$0.36	$0.38	$0.46
Portion of advertising "inventory" sold		18%	20%	17%	16%	16%	17%		20%
Average CPM	$21	$20	$23	$24	$24	$25	$25		$20
Number of advertisers	550	700	900	1,200	1,700	1,600	1,800	1,950	2,225
Revenue/advertiser	$35,813	$14,379	$15,674	$15,112	$17,768	$17,998	$23,160	$27,989	$34,312

Source: Company data, case writer calculations

Exhibit 4 TECHNOLOGY PENETRATION

	84	85	86	87	88	89	90	91	92	93	94	95	96	97	98	99E	00E
Millions of PCs shipped	9	9	10	12	14	16	19	24	31	41	50	60	71	84	98	114	130
Millions of PCs in use[a]	23	28	35	40	45	52	61	73	90	115	146	182	222	265	313	367	426
Portion of PC users with second PC[b]	2%	2%	3%	5%	6%	7%	8%	10%	15%	20%	22%	23%	25%	28%	30%	33%	37%
Millions of e-mail users[c]	1	1	2	3	4	5	6	8	12	18	25	35	60	80	130	180	200
Millions of Internet/ web users	<1	<1	<1	<1	<1	<1	<1	<1	1	1	3	9	28	46	82	134	157
Millions of households online	-	-	-	-	-	-	-	-	-	-	-	6	17	25	35	48	61
Millions of Internet host computers	<0.1	<0.1	<0.1	<0.1	<0.1	0.1	0.2	0.4	0.7	1.3	2.2	5.8	14.4	21.8	29.7	43.0	–

[a]Assumes that PCs have an average useful life of four years
[b]Estimated number of PC users that use second PCs: home, office, and portables
[c]Estimate of all e-mail accounts
Sources: Morgan Stanley Dean Witter Research Estimates, Network Wizards (www.nw.com)

Exhibit 5 ADOPTION CURVES FOR MEDIA TECHNOLOGY IN THE UNITED STATES

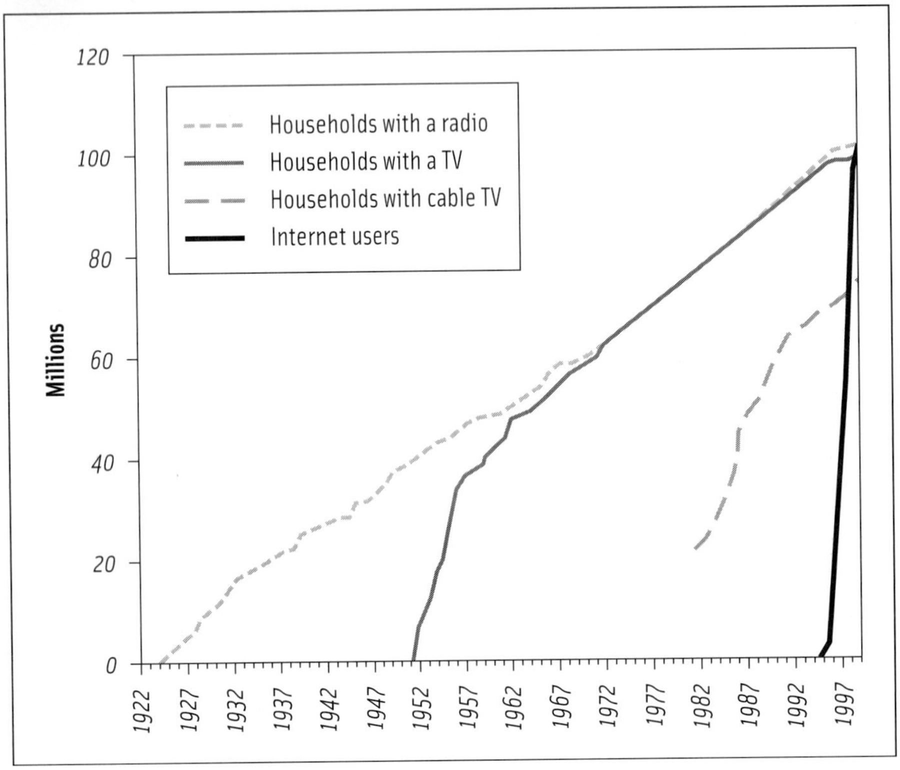

Source: Morgan Stanley Dean Witter Technology Research

Exhibit 6

PORTALS AND THE WORLD WIDE WEB

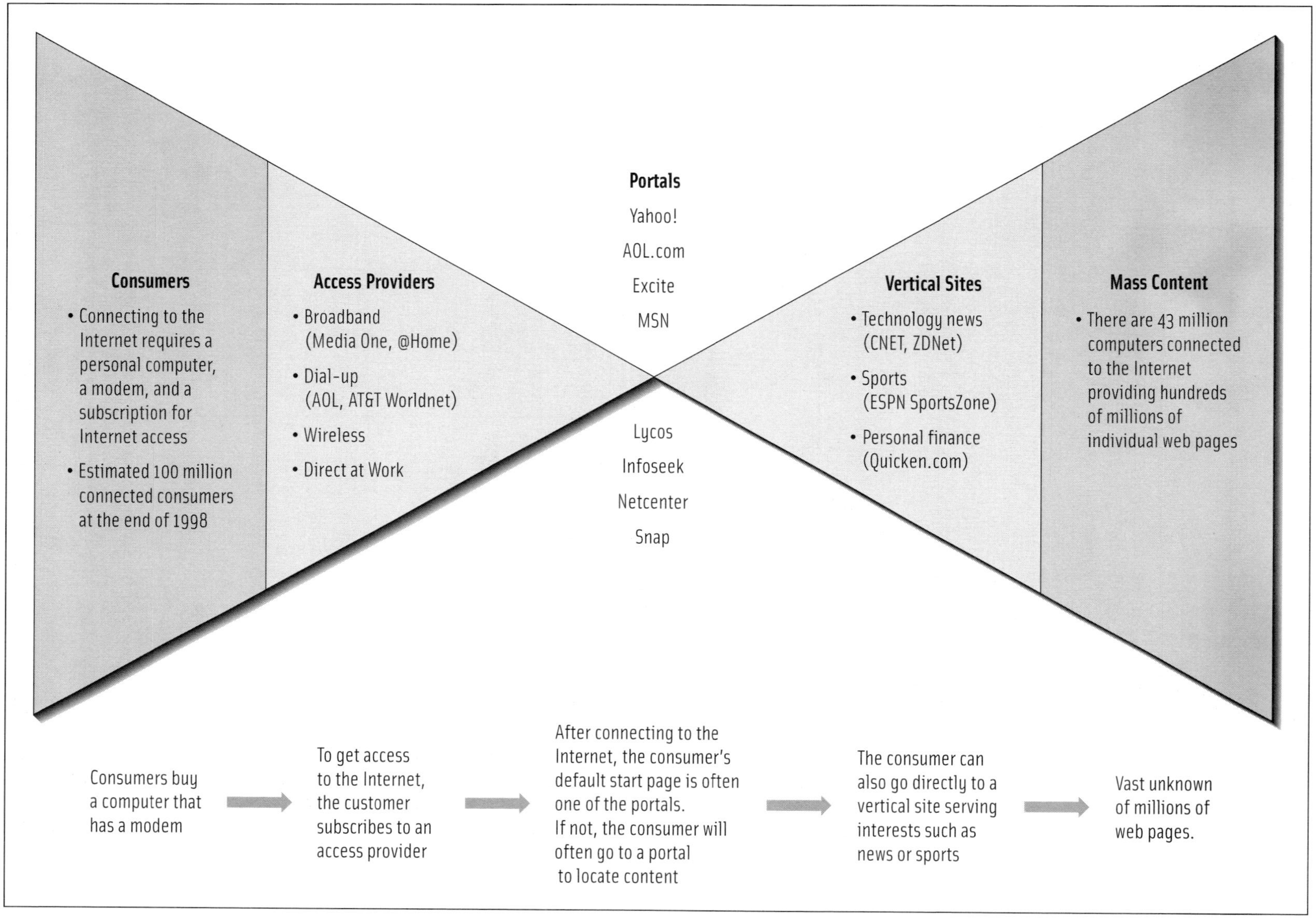

Exhibit 7 ADOPTION OF ONLINE GAMING

Portal	Date	On-Line Offering
Yahoo!	31-Mar-98	New site offers free, real-time, multi-player access to classic games within comprehensive card and board game environment. Board games: backgammon, checkers, chess, go, reversi. Card Games: bridge, cribbage, euchre, gin, hearts, poker, and spades.
Lycos	12-May-98	Head-to-head Lycos online gaming action. Lycos Games features comprehensive classic card and board games from checkers and chess to hearts and spades. The technology for Lycos Games is provided by veteran gaming and technology company, go2net, Inc.
Excite	27-May-98	Excite and Total Entertainment Network invite web users to cut the deck with classic card games. The new Excite game area lets Internet users play classic card games including euchre, hearts and spades at no cost and with virtually no download or installation delays.
Infoseek	27-May-98	Infoseek and Total Entertainment Network partner to bring interactive gaming to Infoseek users. Infoseek users initially will have unlimited access to seven classic board and card games free of charge and without downloads straight from TEN's premier gaming site.

Source: Company press releases

Exhibit 8 PORTAL COMPARISONS, 1998

	Yahoo!	AOL*	Lycos	Infoseek	Excite
Financial statistics ($ mm)					
Revenue	203.3	2,599.5*	89.5	63.2	154.1
Gross margin	176.5	921.2	69.8	53.5	125.1
Operating income	28.8	222.1	(13.4)	(11.6)	(4.7)
Earnings (without charges)	49.9	91.8	(8.4)	(9.4)	(27.8)
End-of-year cash	433.5	631.0	135.2	54.5	61.6
Market capitalization ($ bn)	30.3	75.0	3.8	2.3	5.5
Operating statistics					
Millions of pages viewed per day	167	N/A	50	33	70
Number of advertisers	2,225	N/A	850	673	1,500
Average CPM	$20	N/A	$23	$20	$23
Millions of registered users	35	14**	15	8	20
Portion of advertising "inventory" sold	20%	N/A	32%	26%	22%
Employees	900	8,500	600	750	800
Brand-name recognition					
Among Internet users	44%	60%	7%	8%	11%
Among non-users	2%	17%	-%	-%	-%

* AOL revenue consists of $2,161 mm for online service and $439 mm from advertising, commerce, and other sources. Excludes Netscape and Netcenter

** Number of paying subscribers

Source: Company data, research reports, Intelliquest First-Quarter Worldwide Internet Tracking Services Study

Exhibit 9 TYPICAL CPM RATES FOR TRADITIONAL MEDIA

	1995	1996	1997	1998
Network television, nighttime	$8.79	$10.20	$11.18	$12.59
Spot television, nighttime	$13.36	$17.22	$17.30	$18.08
Magazine, black & white page	$27.05	$30.28	$34.23	
Daily newspaper	$46.67	$53.60	$52.77	
Sunday newspaper	$40.49	$43.56	$46.51	

Source: Television Bureau of Advertising, *www.tvb.org/tvfacts/index.html*

Exhibit 10 ONLINE ADVERTISING AND COMMERCE PROJECTIONS

	1995	1996	1997	1998E	1999E	2000E	2001E	2002E
Total expenditures on all media advertising ($ bn)	117	127	137	149	161	178	190	206
Expenditures on online advertising ($ mm)	55	301	850	2,060	3,350	6,685	9,755	14,865
Expenditures on electronic commerce by consumers ($ mm)	49	706	3,007	8,010	13,620	22,135	34,750	52,125
Portal share of all Internet traffic		15%	15%	15%	16%	17%	18%	20%
Portal share of all online advertising expenditures		61%	59%	52%	48%	40%	35%	30%
Total portal advertising revenues		184	502	1,071	1,608	2,674	3,414	4,460

Source: Forrester Research, Jupiter Communications, CIBC Oppenheimer & Co., case writer estimates

Exhibit 11 YAHOO! ORGANIZATION CHART

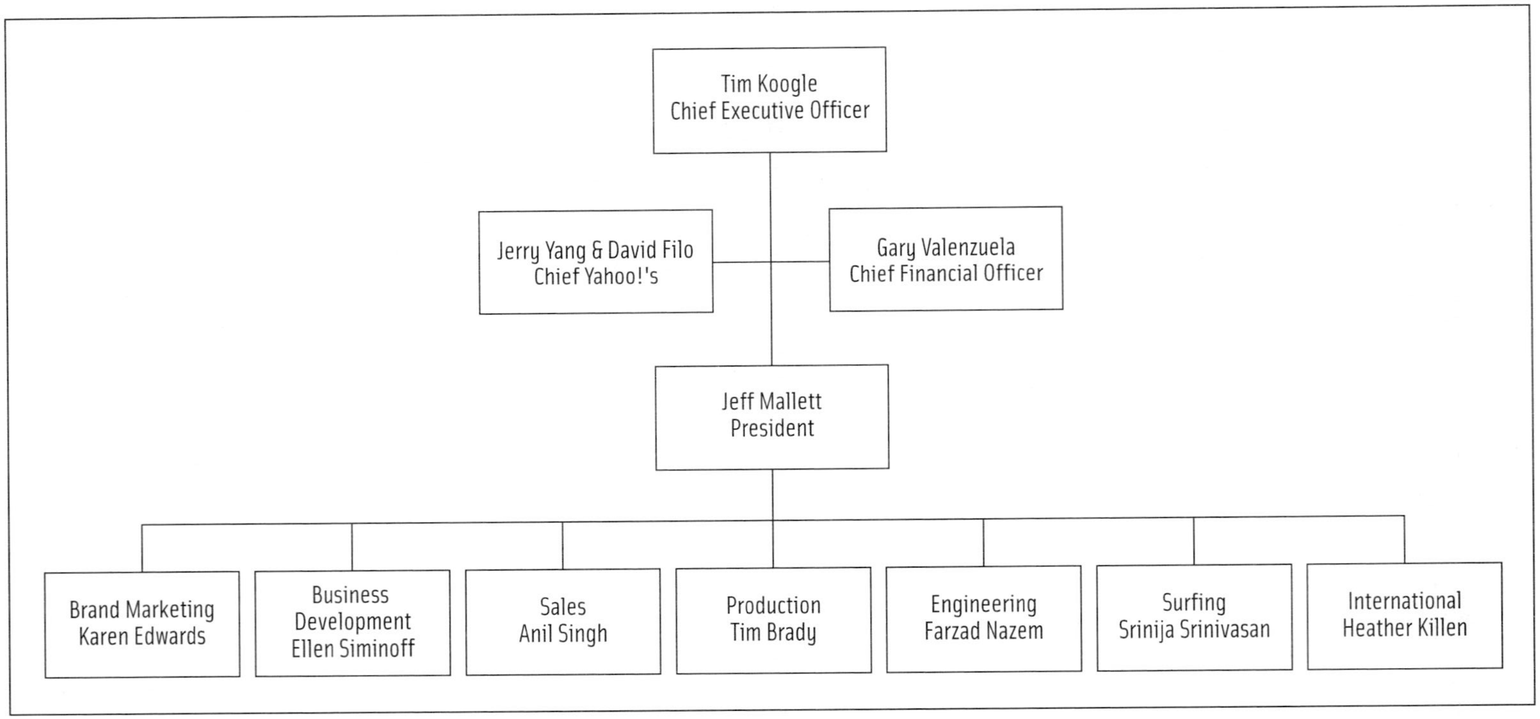

Exhibit 12 HOMEPAGES OF OTHER PORTALS

Excite[1]

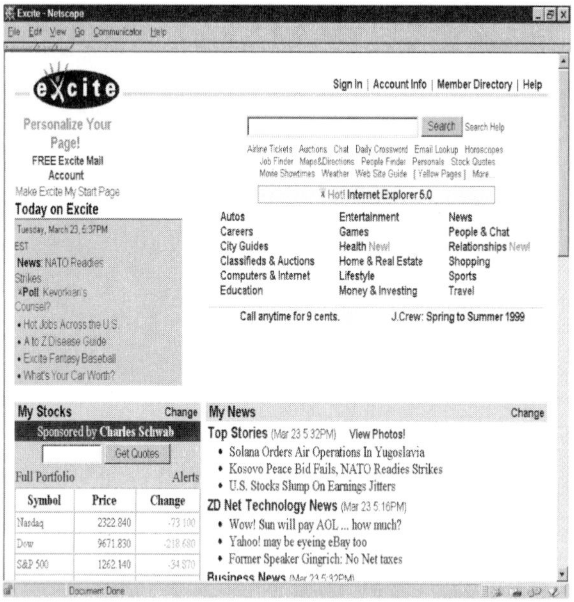

Lycos[2]

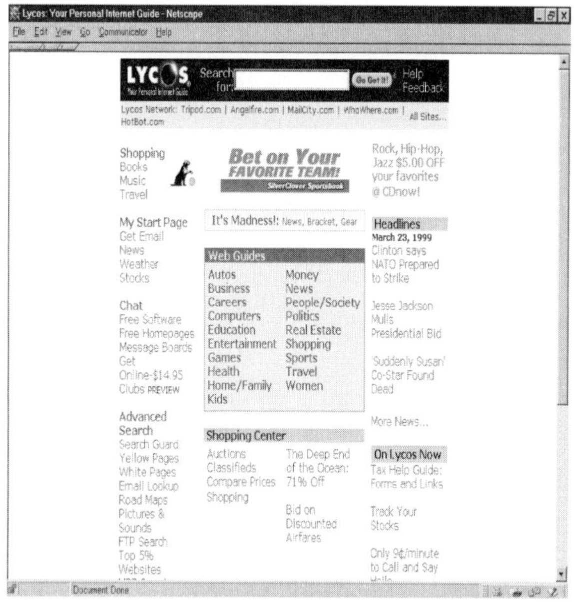

Infoseek[3]

Netcenter[4]

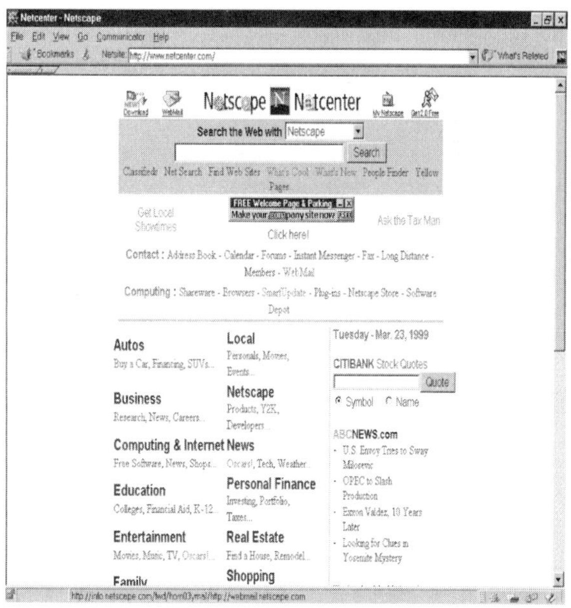

Exhibit 13

PORTAL FEATURE COMPARISON, 4Q1998

	Excite	Lycos	Infoseek	Yahoo!
International Sites	Australia, France, Germany, Japan, the Netherlands, Sweden, UK	Germany, Italy, Japan, UK, Spain, the Netherlands	Brazil, Denmark, Holland, France, Germany, Italy, Sweden, UK, Spanish version	Australia/New Zealand, Canada, Denmark, France, Germany, Japan, Korea, Norway, Singapore, Spain, Sweden, UK/Ireland
Recent Acquisitions	8/96: The McKinley Group, creator of Magellan Online Guide	2/98: Tripod, a provider of personal web pages	6/98: Disney took a 43% stake in Infoseek. Infoseek received $70M cash and ownership position in Starwave, a producer of Internet-based sports and news	10/97: Four11, a privately held online communications and Internet directory
	2/97: NetBot, advanced search technology	5/98: WiseWire, directory-building & enhanced searching	8/98: Quando, creates and licenses constantly updated, customized directories and guides	12/97: Less than 20 percent equity position in AudioNet, a provider of Internet broadcasting services
	3/97: WebCrawler, search and directory technology	6/98: Guestworld, an online guest book provider		12/97: Less than 20 percent equity position in GeoCities, a provider of free personal web pages
	2/98: MatchLogic, management and optimization of Internet advertising campaigns	8/98: Whowhere, offered free homepages, e-mail, and directory services		6/98: Viaweb, an Internet commerce firm that rents its server-based software and web storefronts to merchants
	6/98: Classifieds 2000, provider of online classifieds	10/98: Wired Digital, provided several web services (HotBot, HotWired, and Wired News)		10/98: Yoyodyne, an Internet-based interactive direct marketer
Partners & Sponsors	Amazon.com, BarnesandNoble.com, Preview Travel, N2K, CDNOW, Netscape, AOL, Prodigy Services, Pointcast, Dell, Apple Computer, Sega Enterprises, WebTV, Intuit	Juno Online Services, Fragrances Online; Test Drive, AT&T Worldnet Service, CDNOW, Preview Travel, AutoConnect, E-Loan, Homesshark, BarnesandNoble.com	Bell Atlantic Electronic Commerce Services, Southwestern Bell, Sprint, CNET, Auto-by-Tel, CarPoint, CMP Media, Borders Online, Microsoft Investor, DLJ Direct, Datek, Ameritrade	Amazon.com, CDNOW, Reel.com, Videoserve, Autoweb, Microsoft, CarPoint, E-Loan, DLJ Direct, E*Trade, Ameritrade, Datek, AT&T Worldnet, HP, Gateway, Compaq

Exhibit 13

PORTAL FEATURE COMPARISON, 4Q1998 cont.

	Excite	Lycos	Infoseek	Yahoo!
Content Providers	Reuters New Media, UPI, Charles Schwab, ESPN Sportsticker, The National Enquirer, The Tribune Company, GTE New Media	Reuters New Media, Wired News, Suck.com, Careerpath.com, iVillage	Reuters New Media, Business Wire, Hoover's, Inc, PR Newswire, USENET News Groups	Reuters New Media, Zacks, CDA/Wiesenberger, Motley Fool, ESPN Sportsticker, The Sporting News, Weathernews, E! Online, MTV
Channels	Autos, Careers, City Guides, Classifieds & Auctions, Computers & Internet, Education, Entertainment, Games, Health, Home & Real Estate, Lifestyle, Money & Investing, News, People & Chat, Relationships, Shopping, Sports, Travel	Autos, Business, Careers, Computers, Education, Entertainment, Games, Health, Home/Family, Kids, Money, News, People/Society, Politics, Real Estate, Shopping, Sports, Travel, Women	Automotive, Family, News, Business, The Good Life, Real Estate, Careers, Health, Shopping, Communications, Internet, Sports, Computer, Kids, Travel, Entertainment, Money, Women's	Arts & Humanities, Business & Economy, Computers & Internet, Education, Entertainment, Government, Health, News & Media, Recreation & Sports, Reference, Regional, Science, Social Science, Society & Culture
Web Sites Under Network	City.net, classifieds2000.com, hoopmadness.com, jango.com, webcrawler.com	Tripod.com, Mailcity.com, Whowhere.com, HotBot.com, Angelfire.com, Wirednews.com, Hotwired.com, Suck.com, Webmonkey.com	ABC.com, ABCNews.com, Disney.com, ESPN.com, Family.com, Showbiz.com	Yahoo.com
Other Features	Instant messaging, chat, free e-mail, personal homepage publishing, personalized start page, community web site development, calendar, games, shopping	SafetyNet, personal homepage publishing, personalized start page, games, free e-mail, shopping	Chat, free e-mail, personal homepage publishing, personalized start page, community web site development, calendar, games, shopping	Shopping, yellow pages, people search, maps, classifieds, personals, games, chat, free e-mail, calendar, instant messaging, personalized start page, personal homepage publishing

Source: Company Press Releases and Web Sites; K. A. Porter and S. P. Bradley, "Excite, Inc. (1998)," HBS Case N9-799-044

Exhibit 14 PORTAL REACH AND DURATION OF VISIT

	Reach of Top 10 Consolidated Networks from Home (%)						
	Nov-97	**Jan-98**	**Mar-98**	**May-98**	**Jul-98**	**Sep-98**	**Nov-98**
AOL Sites	47.4	47.7	48.3	45.4	46.0	47.3	49.2
Yahoo! Sites	42.6	41.8	44.4	44.4	41.8	40.7	43.7
Microsoft Sites	30.3	33.1	35.4	36.9	36.7	38.4	43.1
Lycos	15.9	14.1	24.9	23.8	24.5	31.0	39.1
GeoCities.com	22.8	23.9	23.9	26.9	25.9	24.2	27.9
Netscape.com	27.6	27.5	27.7	25.6	25.4	24.6	25.0
Excite Network	24.1	23.8	26.2	28.5	27.6	24.7	24.8
Walt Disney Online	15.0	14.0	14.6	14.1	17.7	20.1	21.0
Infoseek Sites	17.0	19.2	18.3	18.5	17.2	14.3	15.8
Time Warner Online	13.8	13.4	13.8	14.0	14.0	15.2	14.5
	Reach of Top 10 Consolidated Networks from Work (%)						
	Nov-97	**Jan-98**	**Mar-98**	**May-98**	**Jul-98**	**Sep-98**	**Nov-98**
Yahoo! Sites	46.6	52.7	54.8	54.1	50.5	49.8	49.6
Microsoft Sites	37.7	38.5	43.0	42.6	43.2	49.2	48.7
Lycos	16.8	21.6	26.1	30.3	28.2	33.9	39.3
AOL Sites	35.0	35.4	39.4	39.3	34.1	36.9	36.3
Netscape.com	41.8	44.7	41.1	37.4	40.0	42.5	36.0
Excite Network	27.4	32.4	31.3	34.8	34.3	31.9	27.5
GeoCities.com	16.7	19.7	21.2	22.8	22.1	22.7	24.2
Walt Disney Online	12.2	13.9	15.0	15.0	20.0	22.9	23.8
Infoseek Sites	21.8	26.8	25.7	27.0	23.6	21.2	20.4
Time Warner Online	16.8	17.6	19.4	20.7	17.0	24.1	19.5
	Estimated Total Minutes of Use per Month per User for the Top 10 Consolidated Networks						
	Nov-97	**Jan-98**	**Mar-98**	**May-98**	**Jul-98**	**Sep-98**	**Nov-98**
eBay	0	71	69	117	105	120	132
Hotmail.com	17	16	17	15	18	57	76
Microsoft Sites	21	35	34	33	36	39	59
Yahoo! Sites	32	37	39	36	46	45	57
ESPN Internet Group	12	12	13	18	20	36	37
New York Times	17	20	23	17	18	34	30
Onsale.com	0	11	11	30	18	26	28
Excite Network	16	16	22	25	29	26	28
Walt Disney Online	38	29	34	33	27	27	26
Egghead.com	22	22	21	19	24	25	20

Source: Media Metrix
("Reach" is the percentage of individuals that visit a specific site in a given month out of the total number of individuals using the web)

STARMEDIA: LAUNCHING A LATIN AMERICAN REVOLUTION

In Latin America, we represent a shift. You know, "the media is the message." Well, we are the message. The message is that this is a new generation, that the Internet enables people to redefine their relationship to capital, their relationship to business, and that the big leveraging that goes on is ideas—not access, not friends, not connections. This is the new reality, and what's happening—to quote Mao—is that "a thousand flowers are blooming."

—Fernando Espuelas,
StarMedia CEO and co-founder[1]

By the fall of 1999, StarMedia had sprinted to a sizeable lead in the race to acquire Latin American Internet users. Its pan-regional, horizontal portal was the first to target Spanish- and Portuguese-language speakers on the Internet, registering 1.2 billion page views in the third quarter of 1999. Thirty-three-year-old StarMedia co-founder Fernando Espuelas was the toast of Silicon Alley[2] and a recognized hero throughout Latin America. A picture of him on the cover of *Internet World* magazine—ripping his shirt open to show the StarMedia logo, like Superman, summed up the spirit of the company. But each day brought an announcement of a new initiative by a heavyweight Lex Luthor.[3] To maintain its lead, StarMedia raised and spent money at a frenetic pace, promoting its brand, acquiring companies, and launching new web initiatives. Losses for 1999 were projected to be $90 million on revenues of $19 million, a burn rate made sustainable by private and public financing rounds that had netted the company half a billion dollars since its 1996 inception. By December 1999, StarMedia had evolved from a pure web company to an integrated media company that stretched into the ISP, mobile phone and broadband production businesses. Co-founder Jack Chen explained:

> Websites develop in Latin America much faster because you can take a look at what's worked in the United States and immediately apply it into the region. So the demand for quality is different at our stage of development than at a comparable stage of development in the United States. In the United States the web developed over a period of time in a sequential way, but we must attack opportunities in parallel. We decided to be a whole bunch of companies at the same time—whether it's Yahoo!, Doubleclick, or ABC News.

Dean's Research Fellow Jon K. Rust prepared this case under the supervision of Professor Thomas Eisenmann as the basis for class discussion rather than to illustrate either effective or ineffective handling of an administrative situation.

---

[1]Claudi Juehl and Anna Maria Virzi, "StarMedia's Serenade of Latin America," *Internet World*, November 1, 1999.

[2]Silicon Alley was the name for an area in Manhattan marked by a concentration of Internet company offices.

[3]Lex Luthor, a brilliant inventor, was the sworn enemy of Superman.

At the end of 1999, StarMedia employed more than 700 people in 12 countries with offices in Barcelona, Bogota, Buenos Aires, Caracas, Madrid, Mexico City, Miami, Montevideo, Rio de Janeiro, San Francisco, San Juan, Santiago, and São Paulo (see Exhibit 1).

The major question facing StarMedia's executive team as the new millennium dawned was how to best leverage this infrastructure to maintain and extend its traffic leadership—and to monetize its audience—in an environment that was becoming both more competitive and more sophisticated. For nearly two years, StarMedia had been alone in targeting the pan-regional Latin American market. But 1999 saw Telmex, the telephone monopoly in Mexico, announce a $100 million partnership with Microsoft to establish a regional Spanish-language portal that would leverage its ISP properties. AOL joined with Latin American media powerhouse Cisneros Group to launch its own site, while Terra, the Internet division of Spanish telecom behemoth Telefonica, began acquiring Latin American Internet properties like some people collect postage stamps. In addition, Yahoo! enjoined the battle for Latin America with an additional $100 million investment in its Yahoo! en Español, while start-ups QuePasa, Yupi, and El Sitio sought to gain their own traction, and national ISPs like UOL in Brazil aspired to become pan-regional players.

In effect, StarMedia was being squeezed from three directions at the same time: by local access providers, regional media conglomerates, and U.S. Internet portals. In the face of such ferocious competition, Fernando and Jack were surprisingly calm. In their minds, they were the leader; as long as they kept innovating, no one could catch them. Still, some questions remained. If another company offered ubiquitous access to the Internet—via dial-up, wireless and cable—and could leverage that access to drive traffic to its portal, was StarMedia vulnerable? Should StarMedia seek to mitigate that potential vulnerability by more aggressively entering the dial-up ISP, wireless, or cable businesses?

Second, StarMedia had originally chosen not to partner with any of the traditional Latin American media companies, in part because such partnerships would have meant giving up too much control. Instead, StarMedia formed strategic alliances with U.S. content companies and sought to acquire local, Latin-American Internet start-ups. But as the Latin American Internet population quadrupled over the next three years, would the "newbies" gravitate to familiar, national media—now energized by the Web—thus allowing the media companies to trump StarMedia's penetration country by country, if not pan-regionally? Now that it was more established, should StarMedia revisit its media-partner strategy, especially as Latin American start-ups gained more suitors, thus driving up their prices?

Finally, StarMedia was exploring the development of its own vertical channels. A sports-related site and a women-related site were under discussion. Until now, however, StarMedia had remained largely neutral in providing content to its users, preferring the flexibility of being able to do the best deals with the best content providers, thus ensuring users the best experience. StarMedia's new competitors—and their deep pockets—made this strategy more difficult, however, and the company sought to create its own verticals. But where should it start? With so much of the Latin American Internet market wide open, how should StarMedia executives decide where to plant new flags? And what risks did they face with current partners if they began to compete with them directly?

Background on StarMedia

The underlying idea for StarMedia is community. When I first spoke about the idea of the Internet being that historical moment that would allow us to reconnect the people of Latin America, to give them a bridge to communicate, people literally thought I was out of my mind. Because for the last 200 years, since the wars of independence, the ruling classes of Latin America have told us that we were all foreigners to each other—that across the border were alien beings. I never meant that the borders would disappear necessarily. What I meant was that the mental borders would disappear, that people given the opportunity to share ideas and connect and debate each other and do commerce with each other would jump at the chance.

—Fernando Espuelas[4]

Until he was nine years old, Fernando Espuelas, the son of an affluent real estate entrepreneur, led a charmed life in his native Uruguay. After a difficult divorce, however, his mother was left destitute, and she and Fernando

[4]Juehl and Virzi, op. cit.

moved to live with her brother in Connecticut, where she did menial jobs. Fernando entered the public school system and quickly befriended Jack Chen, whose father had moved his family to the States from China. Their international heritage and common struggle with English helped them form an early bond, and together they displayed a zeal for entrepreneurship. As seventh graders, Fernando and Jack founded an insurance company to replace lost pencils and organized a class government and student newspaper. In high school they won the state debate championships as a two-man team. Although the two went to different colleges, they remained close friends. Jack graduated from Harvard with high honors in computer science. Fernando graduated with distinction from Connecticut College with a degree in history. When Fernando married his college sweetheart, Jack served as best man.

After college, Jack worked as an investment banker at Goldman Sachs before earning his MBA at Harvard Business School. From 1994 to 1995, he was a securities analyst at CS First Boston. Fernando went to work in the advertising industry, gaining experience with several firms. From 1991 to 1994 he lived in Argentina, where he opened a direct marketing office for Ogilvy & Mather and became Regional Account Director for Latin America. O&M was the world's fourth-largest advertising agency; its slogan at the time was "To be the Agency Most Valued by Those Who Most Value Brands." But Fernando sought to have more direct impact on his native Latin America. He was excited by the economic ferment he witnessed: "Argentina was basically being reborn," he said. "It was throwing off 40 years of tumult and social strife and economic chaos."[5] He left O&M and joined AT&T, quickly rising to Managing Director of Marketing Communications for the Americas. Despite his success, Fernando grew frustrated with AT&T's bureaucracy. He had joined the company with the hope of gaining "big budgets to put ideas to work,"[6] but found that internal politics often trumped good ideas.

Soon after his promotion to be AT&T's youngest managing director, Fernando took a month off and traveled with his wife to India and Nepal. Trekking in the Himalayan Mountains, Fernando received the inspiration for an Internet "town square" that would connect all of Latin America. He also experienced an epiphany about the ability of individuals to effect change: "I realized that we in the western world are really pathetic, lame complainers and do not understand how much power we have in this society to do whatever we want."[7] He forgot his aching legs and began racing up a mountainside, leaving his wife and sherpa far behind. By the time they caught up, the idea for StarMedia had been born. He called his friend Jack from the first phone he could find.

When AT&T would not fund his plan, Fernando decided to pursue the opportunity as an entrepreneur. He opened as many personal credit card accounts as he could, anticipating a need for start-up capital. Jack took a second mortgage on his home. Then both quit their jobs, pooled their savings—around $300,000—and in September 1996 opened an office in a run-down house in Riverside, Connecticut owned by Jack's father. For two weeks they researched the situation in Latin America, where a lack of technological infrastructure and unfavorable telecommunications regulation had raised access costs and limited Internet penetration. However, the top 20% of the population was highly desirable to multinational marketers, and this affluent group, which controlled 65% of the region's wealth, was already gravitating to the Internet. Fernando and Jack believed that if they could build an Internet site based on the model of Yahoo! that appealed to these wealthy Latin Americans, as the Latin American infrastructure developed and computers and Internet access became more affordable, they could attract less affluent consumers as they migrated online. Additionally, they would position themselves to serve the U.S. Hispanic market.

For Fernando, the effort presented an opportunity to change the history of his native geography. He explained:

> There's a huge demographic bubble in Latin America. Something like 70% of all people are under the age of 35. In Mexico, roughly 50% of the population is under the age of 20. The Internet, by being such a pervasive, powerful medium that is controlled by people as opposed to institutions, would give this new generation an opportunity to reinvent our concept of each other, the concept of countries, our relationships between society and each other, society and the world. And that process, which would by definition be deeply democratic, would lead not to tumult but to the opposite: to optimism, to prosperity, to progress. And I wanted to play a significant role in doing that.[8]

[5]Ibid.

[6]CNN interview of Fernando Espuelas, "Movers with Jan Hopkins."

[7]Ibid.

[8]Juehl and Virzi, op. cit.

After hearing rumors that America Online would enter Latin America within the year, Fernando and Jack realized speed was critical. They hired a bare-bones staff, and by December 1996, the site—which included chat, some content and classified ads—was up. "I felt I was working around the clock, "said Fernando. "I literally was getting three hours of sleep. If the site went down, I'd get calls in the middle of the night." "We got it up," agreed Jack, "but when we looked at the plan we devised and compared it to where we should have been, we were still behind."[9] They were also running out of money. For the next several months the co-founders presented their company to potential investors, but were repeatedly rejected. Venture capitalists were concerned about the lack of infrastructure in Latin America, the boom-and-bust nature of the region's economies, currency fluctuations, high inflation, political instability, and the overall attractiveness of the market. They also questioned the ability of a start-up to compete with AOL and Yahoo!, and with telephone and media companies in the region. Finally, Fernando and Jack were dismissed for not having the local, insider connections that had been historically necessary for conducting business in Latin America.

With hope and money about to run out, the two entrepreneurs convinced Flatiron Partners, an East Coast venture capital firm specializing in Internet start-ups, to fund their vision. A few weeks later, in July 1997, Chase Capital Partners, a $4 billion private equity subsidiary of Chase Manhattan Bank, signed on. The two firms invested $3.5 million and gave Fernando and Jack expert advice and instant credibility.

The Internet in Latin America

Projections for the size of the online universe in Latin America mark it as the fastest growing major region worldwide, outpacing not only the United States but also Europe and Asia in sheer growth. In fact, the compound annual growth rate of 48% over the next four years—resulting in a total online population of 38 million individuals across the region in 2003—will actually exceed U.S. online user growth during the Internet boom of the last four years.

—Jupiter Communications, November 1999[10]

In aggregate, Latin America represented a population of approximately 500 million people—nearly double the population of the United States (see Exhibit 2). While the region encompassed 23 countries, citizens shared similar cultural affinities—including religion, music and sports—and spoke either Portuguese or Spanish. Dialects could vary dramatically around the region, however, and national rivalries could be fierce. Educational levels were highly disparate within countries. For example, in Brazil 20% of the population was considered illiterate and only about two-thirds had four years of education or more. Only 10% of primary students continued on to the secondary level, which for the majority comprised short-term vocational training. Income disparities were pronounced throughout the region: the top 20% of the Latin American population had a per-capita GDP comparable to that of Germany and the United Kingdom. Many of the affluent were accustomed to traveling abroad to make purchases.

While the most affluent Latin Americans had enough disposable income to go online, their efforts to do so were hampered by a lack of Internet infrastructure in the region. In 1999, fewer than 13% of households had a fixed-line telephone.[11,12] Overall, the region suffered from a legacy of protectionist government policies that had retarded technology development. For decades, laws throughout the region—particularly in Brazil—had mandated that if a technology was manufactured locally, foreign imports were disallowed. The goal of such policies was to incubate a local industry; frequently, the result was to create family-owned monopolies that produced shoddy knock-offs of products developed elsewhere. Similar regulations, as well as cozy political and personal relationships, created monopolies in other sectors, too, including media. In Mexico, for example, 80% of the broadcast and cable television industry was owned by one company, Televisa.[13] In Brazil, Globocabo dominated cable TV with a 70% share. Also dampening the economic vitality of the region was a Byzantine maze of tariffs between countries that precluded common-market trading and reinforced the ascension of locality over quality for those who could not afford to travel abroad to make purchases.

[9]Harold Goldberg, "Porta Rica," *The Industry Standard,* March 8, 1999.
[10]Lucas Graves, "Online Growth Spells Opportunity in Latin America, But No Mass Market," Jupiter Communications, November 23, 1999.

[11]World Bank.
[12]According to Audits & Surveys Worldwide, household telephone penetration rates in Latin America's major economies ranged from 40%–70%.
[13]Goldman Sachs. Latin America Equity Research.

Privatization and the loosening of trade restrictions in the 1990s began changing Latin American business. Mercosur and NAFTA created some barrier-free markets.[14] And in terms of technology, a noteworthy precedent was established; instead of following the course of technology development in the United States, many Latin American markets began to leapfrog it. The adoption of wireless telephony was a case in point. For decades, governments owned and controlled telecom services throughout Latin America. In the mid-1990s, however, several governments opened their country's cellular markets to foreign competition. The result was an explosion in wireless phone adoption, fueled by two factors. First, the government-owned phone monopolies did a poor job of extending and servicing basic telephone services, so wireless service was more reliable. Second, because the government phone companies did not offer unlimited local telephone calls for a monthly fee but instead charged by the minute, Latin Americans—in contrast to most U.S. consumers—were already accustomed to paying metered-fees for local usage.

In most countries, the opening of cellular competition was initiated in tandem with privatization of government phone monopolies. Brazil, Argentina and Chile auctioned their telecom properties to the highest bidder with Spain's Telefonica gaining majority control. In exchange for a period of private monopoly (in Brazil, a duopoly), the purchasing companies committed to improving and extending telecom services under strict guidelines. This privatization and the new wireless competition accelerated the number of Latin Americans with access to phones. Low PC penetration—due to the high relative cost of computers—and high metered costs for Internet access, however, still prevented most Latin Americans from subscribing to Internet services (see Exhibit 3). For the four percent of the Latin American population that was online at the end of 1999, online commerce was constrained by low credit card penetration throughout the region and by unreliable delivery services.

Nevertheless, Internet usage was expected to grow faster in Latin America than in any other region in the world, albeit from a lower starting point (see Exhibit 4). Annual compound growth rates between 40% and 75% were projected for the next several years compared to 13% and dropping in the United States. By 2002, between 25 and 40 million Latin Americans were expected to be online. From 1998 to 2003, online advertising spending was expected to grow to $949 million from $20 million,[15] and e-commerce was projected to jump from $240 million to $84 billion.[16]

StarMedia Strategy and Operations

> *There is no such thing in this business as going too fast. You can think of it as a wide-open field where you can see your goal in the distance. The idea is to run as fast as possible, cover as much ground as possible, claiming the land for yourself. You may go off in the wrong direction every so often, but because it's so wide open it's much more important to keep moving forward and shifting your direction. Making mistakes and correcting them is more important than getting everything right but moving more slowly.*
>
> —Jack Chen, co-founder

The rumor about AOL's impending entry into Latin America in 1997 turned out to be wrong, and for two years StarMedia was the only pan-regional portal in Latin America. During this time, the StarMedia management team expanded the network's functionality, initiated numerous strategic partnerships, and—inspired by Fernando's drive to make the name StarMedia synonymous with "the Internet" in Latin America—promoted the brand in bold new ways. The team also raised money from strategic investors, developed local operations throughout Latin America, and moved its headquarters to New York City's Silicon Alley (see Exhibit 6). In the process, what had been a staff of six at the beginning of 1997 grew to 200 in 1998 and more than 700 in 1999, demanding at times a creative ability for finding workspace that recalled the movie "Being John Malkovich."[17]

[14]Mercosur (Southern Cone Common Market) was a free-trade agreement among Argentina, Brazil, Paraguay and Uruguay, signed in 1995, which had led to a soaring of trade between the four countries. The agreement dissolved roughly 90% of tariffs between the countries and instituted a common tariff for trade with organizations outside the group. NAFTA (North American Free Trade Agreement), signed in 1992, created a free-trade bloc on products and services passing between Mexico, Canada, and the United States. Ongoing negotiations sought to expand both Mercosur and NAFTA.

[15]Forrester Research, "Interent Advertising Skyrockets," August 1999.

[16]The eGlobal Report, published by eMarketer, July 1999.

[17]In the comedy "Being John Malkovich," a company creates new office space by constructing a "half-floor" between two normal floors, where the workers are forced to stoop the entire day because the ceiling is only four feet high. StarMedia's headquarters were not quite so cramped, but conference rooms were reserved on five-minute intervals, and Fernando and Jack were often forced to take their work to other desks to allow department meetings in their offices.

On May 26, 1999, StarMedia went public, raising more than $120 million and earning its founders—at least on paper—as much as $400 million each.

The Interface

The site represented the "best of breed" of U.S. portals' functionality, and was organized around interest-specific channels. When a new concept was developed by a leading edge U.S. Internet company, StarMedia quickly adapted the idea for its network. Thus, by 1999 there were 19 channels within StarMedia grouped into Community services, and Content and Commerce services (see Exhibit 7). Initially, the StarMedia staff created little original content; instead, the company partnered with leading media companies in the United States and translated their content into local languages as appropriate. A key to the portal's organization was the welcome page, which upon first visit asked the user to indicate what country they were from and whether they preferred to receive content in Spanish or Portuguese. A cookie,[18] subsequently downloaded, enabled StarMedia to use this information to target both content and advertising by subject matter and language. Another key organizational element was the site's layout, which allowed users to navigate directly from any channel on the network to any other channel.

At traditional media companies, content responsibilities typically fell under editorial or creative departments that were organized as cost centers. At StarMedia, however, Fernando and Jack placed content under the control of the business development function with the expectation that content would generate revenue. A result of this organization was that StarMedia's content was developed almost exclusively according to market demand and not editors' prerogatives. An important mechanism for achieving this market orientation was the "Lo Quiero"[19] feedback button located throughout the site, which allowed users to request additional features. In addition, StarMedia tracked the movement of its users closely, and conducted extensive marketing surveys about their likes and dislikes. Betsy Scolnik, senior vice president of Business Development, explained:

> We discovered a science for going pan-local. We launch in a new market with a small advertising campaign, and we use broad, general interest content to attract users and to start building community. We interact with these users to determine how they differ from users in other countries. Then we begin either buying or building compelling local content. Once we build what we believe is a powerful local experience, we go out and do a massive advertising campaign to drive traffic to the site in that country.

Strategic Partnerships

StarMedia gained quick credibility among users—and investors—by negotiating dozens of strategic partnerships to provide high quality content and cutting edge functionality within each of its channels. These partnerships also helped StarMedia promote its brand. The company's relationship with Netscape illustrated how StarMedia leveraged strategic alliances. In May 1998, the two companies developed and launched *Netscape Guide by StarMedia* in both Spanish and Portuguese. The guide became one of the core services available as part of Netscape's Latin American Spanish and Portuguese browsers. Bookmarks on the browser linked users directly to StarMedia's network, and the news ticker on the browser linked directly to StarMedia's general news area.

Similarly, a partnership with RealNetworks, the leading provider of software to enable streaming audio and video over the Internet, established StarMedia as the only in-language Internet company featured as a default channel on both the Spanish and Portuguese versions of RealNetworks' RealPlayer G2. By the end of 1999, StarMedia also had ongoing alliances with Ziff-Davis, Fox Sports Latin America, Disney, CDNOW, Reuters, eBay, NBC, Hearst Communications, Cyberian Outpost, Latin Grocer, Fininvest, Barnes & Noble, Mpath, Viajo.com, FAO Schwartz and others. Many of these relationships provided StarMedia with exclusive rights to exploit the partners' content or product features in Spanish- and Portuguese-language markets. Content partnerships typically were structured as advertising revenue sharing agreements, while commerce partners usually paid a sponsorship fee and a percentage of transaction revenues.

In addition to these alliances with content and commerce websites, StarMedia teamed with partners to accelerate the construction of the e-commerce infra-

[18]A cookie was a small piece of software code downloaded into a website user's computer by the website, which allowed the website to identify the user and track her traffic whenever she logged back onto the site. Cookies could be used to avoid requiring users to reenter commonly requested information, such as user names and passwords or shipping addresses.

[19]"I want it."

structure in Latin America. A May 1999 deal with logistics specialist SkyBox laid the foundation for an e-commerce delivery system that would handle customs forms, inventory warehousing and shipping. Previously, an online order might take six weeks or longer for fulfillment and still get stopped at a country's border if the customs form was not filled out properly. StarMedia solved these problems and at a lower cost. Meanwhile, the company launched a partnership with Hewlett Packard that offered medium-sized Latin American businesses an e-commerce "virtual store" solution, and signed a deal with Visa International to promote credit card use. It partnered with Dell to provide direct-to-market computer sales.

In mid-1999, StarMedia announced a partnership with AT&T to offer dial-up Internet access, starting in Brazil in September 1999 (see Exhibit 5). According to StarMedia executives, this entry into the ISP business was "more tactical than strategic." It didn't matter how Internet users got to StarMedia, just that they did. Jack explained:

> We're agnostic whether users access us through our ISPs, someone else's ISPs or a whole other form. But we partnered with AT&T because the ISP infrastructure in Latin America wasn't reliable. If you don't have quality from beginning to end, it degrades the consumer experience. We want to provide a world-class product as good if not better than what is available in the United States.

Revenues from the new division, StarMedia Acesso,[20] were downplayed, and StarMedia's push into the business could hardly be termed aggressive; Jack and Fernando did not see the ISP business a core focus for the company. "We don't see the paid model as the best place to be," said Fernando. "We watch the rest of the world and understand the free ISP movement. Wherever there are per-minute local charges, a free-ISP market is likely to emerge.[21] We look to foment the free ISP movement in Latin America, because the more people on line, the better it is for us. And a free ISP market is a threat to our competitors. We win either way."[22]

Promotion

When Fernando and Jack received the $3.5 million initial investment from Flatiron Partners and Chase Capital Partners, they dedicated $2 million of it to advertising and promotion (see Exhibits 8 and 9). In addition, they negotiated a barter deal with Fox LatinAmerica where StarMedia received commercial spots on Fox TV in exchange for online banners and Fox news and sports content on some of their channels. Thus, StarMedia became the first Internet company anywhere in the world to market itself heavily using broadcast television. Later, it would negotiate similar deals with other broadcast companies, including CBS Telenoticias, MTV Latin America, and the USA Network.

The reliance on TV for promotion was premised on the low penetration of the Internet in Latin America. Commercials were developed around different StarMedia channels, seeking to introduce consumers to the benefits of the Internet. The ads were highly visual with a single narrator so they could be localized to each market with the proper accent and city references. But the underlying message of each spot was community-oriented and pan-regional: "They are far. They are near. They are communicating through StarMedia."[23]

The second theme of the advertising strategy was to appeal to potential advertisers and investors by branding StarMedia as being synonymous with Spanish- and Portuguese-language Internet services. In Latin America, the target audiences overlapped; the top 20% of the consumer population contained all of the local advertising trade buyers. In the United States, the promotional targeting was even more deliberate. StarMedia ran trade advertising in *The Wall Street Journal, The New York Times, The Los Angeles Times,* and *The Miami Herald.* Patricio Carmody, vice president of Marketing, said:

> In New York City, where there is a large Hispanic market, we started with advertising on the subways. Many Hispanics go on the subway, and so do many Wall Street investors. Likewise, in Miami, our target is both consumers and media buyers, since many

[20]"Acesso" was the name used in Brazil; in Spanish-speaking countries, the Spanish "Acceso" was employed. For purposes of this case, we will use only one of the titles for StarMedia companies that have both Spanish and Portuguese names.

[21]Free ISPs emerged in Europe when ISP companies there struck deals with local phone companies to provide Web access free to customers in exchange for a cut of the local, metered telephone revenue incurred while ISP customers were online. Because European telephone companies profited greatly from the long hours ISP customers spent online, it was to their advantage to increase the number of Web users. Thus, the arrangement was mutually beneficial, although it did shift power from the ISPs to the phone companies.

[22]Presentation by Fernando Espuelas to financial analysts at the Bay Club, Boston, Massachusetts, sponsored by Goldman, Sachs, & Company, October 13, 1999.

[23]Tagline for StarMedia's "People" television commercials in a $21 million 1998 media campaign.

multinationals base their Latin American advertising divisions there.

StarMedia also spent lavishly throughout Latin America on billboards, cinema and star-studded launch parties. After investing $2.1 million on sales and promotion in 1997—5 times revenues—the promotional budget skyrocketed to $29 million in 1998 and double that amount in 1999. Fernando also became a fixture throughout Latin America—and in the States—in TV, magazine, and newspaper interviews. His visibility and "dynamic vision" led one Latin American magazine to dub him the "Bill Gates of Latin America" while *Time* magazine named him one of the "Leaders of the New Millennium." Brazil's *O Exame* magazine selected him "Man of the Year" in 1999, the first time a non-Brazilian had been awarded that distinction in the publication's venerable history.

Finance

By late 1998, StarMedia would set an $80 million record for the largest single private equity transaction by a new media company, surpassing Yahoo!'s previous high. Investors included BancBoston Robertson Stephens, Intel, David Rockefeller, Warburg Pincus, GE Equity Capital Group, KKR, and Morgan Stanley Dean Witter. In a final private equity offering in the spring of 1999, StarMedia raised an additional $41 million, this time from strategic investors in media and technology fields, including eBay, Critical Path, Hearst Communications, NBC and Reuters. Steve Heller, chief financial officer at StarMedia, explained StarMedia's appeal:

> In terms of our business model, we are not unlike an iVillage or CNET. The difference, though, is that our opportunity is so much broader. In some ways we have a schizophrenic investor base. On one side are firms who invest in Latin American companies. On the other are investors in Internet and technology companies. Communicating our vision to the technology side hasn't been difficult. Technology investors look at us as the next huge opportunity. They think, "I know this story. It's the horizontal portal story. I didn't invest in Yahoo! when it was at $5 a share, but I can invest in StarMedia at that price. I know this business model works. Do I know Latin America? Maybe not. But I can find out if they are the leader. And I can figure out whether the market dynamics should be any different from the United States. And I understand the portal business model better than some of the emerging Internet plays in the United States." It's easy for us to tell our story, because it is one of the first times that a leader in the marketplace has been able to go around and tell a story that people understand. Most importantly, these technology investors understand the advantage that capital affords an Internet company.
>
> On the Latin American side, investors are unfamiliar with high Internet valuations based on revenue opportunity. They're more used to buying companies at 5-times cash flow, not 50 times projected revenues. That is a tough sell for many of them. They question why we have so much unspent capital on our books, why we invest so much in marketing ahead of revenues. It's interesting, because sometimes we'll get into a room with investors and we don't even have to say anything while the technology side lectures the Latin American side.

On May 26, 1999, StarMedia raised $120 million in an IPO that valued the company at $2.5 billion. Four and a half months later, in a follow-on secondary equity offering,[24] the company raised an additional $200 million. On January 1, 2000, StarMedia had more than $300 million in cash on its balance sheet (see Exhibits 10 and 11).

Acquisitions

According to the company's IPO filing with the SEC, a publicly traded stock would allow StarMedia to continue to aggressively "pursue strategic acquisitions." In the first two quarters of 1999, StarMedia acquired several leading local Internet brands, including OpenChile, the most popular online destination in that country, and Cadê? and Zeek!, the two most popular search engines in Brazil. After the IPO, it purchased Barcelona-based LatinRed, a Spanish-language community site that provided a suite of free community services targeting Argentina, Mexico, Colombia, Spain, and U.S. Hispanics. In most cases, StarMedia left the acquisitions to operate as before; consolidating some technology and back-office support and maintaining separate brands, but encouraging continued

[24]A "follow-on" offering is different from a traditional "secondary offering" in that no (or very little) existing stock is sold by insiders. Instead, the round consists of new shares issued by the company.

innovation. Indeed, one of the goals of the deals was to acquire the management of each firm and spur them to faster growth with promotional expertise and financial investment.

In the third quarter of 1999, StarMedia expanded its scope by acquiring PageCell International Holdings, a provider of advanced mobile communications services; and Webcast Solutions, a streaming media company focused on the global delivery of audio, video and other Internet-based interactive media. In these cases, the acquisitions were folded into new brands—StarMedia Mobile and StarMedia Broadband—marking StarMedia's transition from a pure Internet company to a full-fledged media company.

In contrast to the ISP business where StarMedia saw modest value in owning the distribution platform, the opportunity to be the leader in mobile Internet services excited Fernando and Jack. As Betsy Scolnik pointed out: "More people in Latin America are purchasing mobile communication devices than hardwire telephones. Handheld mobile devices will likely be the first way many people experience the Internet." The technology also presented a potential obstacle to StarMedia's goal of ubiquitous availability if the company did not enter into the space. Accordingly, Fernando and Jack believed that being a first mover in mobile Internet delivery services was critical. Within a month of acquiring PageCell, StarMedia Mobile signed a partnership with Telemig, one of the largest cellular phone companies in Brazil, to provide wireless Internet e-mail, stock, sports, weather, lottery, and horoscope connections to its 600,000 subscribers.

StarMedia saw a similar opportunity to be the first-mover in Spanish- and Portuguese-language broadband production. After experimenting for several months with Webcast Solutions on a number of advertising projects in Puerto Rico, including "Bud House," an MTV-type "Beach House" sponsored by Budweiser, StarMedia acquired the Silicon Valley-based streaming-media company. To Fernando, the acquisition positioned StarMedia for the convergence of TV, radio, and the Internet in Latin America. He envisioned setting up studios throughout Latin America not only to produce content for the Internet, but to be a new resource for servicing advertising clients. In addition, Webcast had already begun building an international clientele for its broadband services; StarMedia executives believed there was an opportunity to extend that business model more aggressively. Tracy Leeds, a 1992 graduate of Harvard Business School and StarMedia COO in 1999, explained: "Webcast developed a webcast studio in a box. They can send you a studio overnight as a permanent facility or as a temporary one. This capability allows us to really cover the region."

In conjunction with these acquisitions, StarMedia launched an internal division to develop content—narrowband and broadband—and was considering the launch of a venture capital arm to make investments in Latin American start-ups that would likely include vertical plays in content and commerce.

Multiple Brands

When Fernando and Jack studied the evolution of the U.S. Internet market they noticed that over time a shakeout occurred in most categories, with one brand dominating and only two or three other brands surviving behind it. Certainly that was the case with horizontal portals, where Yahoo! dominated and the others struggled to maintain traction, often being forced to merge so as not to stagnate. This observation sparked an idea at a StarMedia NILOT[25] meeting, where Fernando had gathered his top executives. Leeds said:

> No matter how you define the pie, any market niche in the United States is really dominated by three players, who tend to occupy 50% of the traffic. The top 10 sites garner 75% of the web advertising spending. As we looked at our market and how it was heating up, we asked, "Why should we let slots 1, 2, or 3 be occupied by a competitor? Why shouldn't we occupy those other slots ourselves?"

The meeting accelerated StarMedia's transition from a single brand to a multi-brand company with all the accompanying complexity. A plan to carve out specific niches for its various brands was hatched, with StarMedia being the community- and entertainment-oriented *über*-brand; LatinRed an alternative destination for home-page building and chat; and local search engines—like Cadê?—the individual nation brands. StarMedia also decided it should develop a more serious, customizable portal more akin to Yahoo!'s MyYahoo than StarMedia's more AOL-like community channels. It launched Periscopio on

[25]NILOT stands for "No Issues Left on the Table." Weekly, Fernando would gather his top executives into his office—or by phone if necessary—to hash out whatever problems or new ideas were on their minds. Oftentimes, he used the group as a sounding board for his ideas about new strategy. The meeting did not end until a decision had been made on each issue aired.

September 16, touting its "advanced proprietary search and personalization tools."[26]

Pan-regionalization, Localization, Globalization

StarMedia's corporate headquarters were located in New York City's "Silicon Alley," where its executives had access to financial and international marketing networks and local technical expertise. But to be successful—and to legitimize their claim to be a local Latin American company—Fernando and Jack knew early on that significant presence in individual Latin America countries was needed. Their initial challenge was to find anyone with Internet experience to staff offices there. Adriana Kampfner, one of the first employees at StarMedia and a former analyst at Chase Securities, opened the first local sales office in Mexico in 1997 at age 25. Mexican traffic and advertising revenue quickly grew to a third of the overall site. By 1999, Kampfner had become senior vice president of Global Sales and Strategy. She said:

> At an execution level, Latin America is not a single region, it is nine markets—or 10, if you include the U.S. Hispanic market. If you take advertising, which is the basis of our business model, the money spent in Latin America by U.S. multinationals totals something in the hundreds of millions. Meanwhile, advertising by local companies, aggregated country-by-country, totals over $30 billion. That's a huge difference. But now consider the complexity in capturing that opportunity compared to Yahoo!'s early execution challenge in a largely homogeneous, single market. Take a look at how media industries really work in Latin America. There is a huge emphasis on relationships. A huge emphasis on brands. The media-buying decision is localized 90% of the time. That led us to understand that we had to have a local sales presence. We opened offices in Brazil and Mexico at about the same time. Next, Colombia, Argentina, Chile, then later followed by Puerto Rico, our U.S. Hispanic sales operation, and Venezuela. Madrid is our latest.
>
> We realized there was a tremendous first-mover advantage not only on the user side, but on the advertiser side as well. Our whole premise from the very beginning on the user side was that the first brand to market was going to be by far the most powerful brand. And we had that space entirely to ourselves for quite a long time, probably two years. So although we spent a lot of money, building user traffic was relatively low cost because our share of mind was 100%. We were the first Internet company to advertise in mass media and television. Nowadays, there are so many people trying to do what we do that for somebody new to achieve the same impact would be unbelievably expensive.
>
> On the advertiser side it's the same scenario. The first company to come in and establish itself with the local advertising community as a brand, as Yahoo! did in the United States, would also, as long as you have the user base, achieve some sort of disproportionate share. So we hired local general managers and local ad sales teams. In Argentina they're Argentinian, in Colombia they're Colombian—and all are people who had some prior experience with advertising media. Now the challenge here is that you're dealing with local teams that have absolutely no experience with *Internet* advertising sales, led by a GM with absolutely no experience in interactive media, trying to lead a market that has absolutely no idea what interactive media is. So our strategy was to invest in the education and training. And we didn't just train our teams. We trained the market. We invested a lot in presentations and conferences. We had open door policies where agencies could come over and learn. We did a lot of work for our clients.
>
> The other area where we really had to invest was in client service. Traditional media is a more straightforward transaction when it comes to placement of media. For example, when you want to run a 30-second television spot, you just give someone a videotape. Interactive media is not that way. In fact, the real work starts when the campaign goes live because clients can get real-time feedback on the results of their campaigns; they can track click-throughs, where people are going on their site, how people are responding to their message. There's an opportunity to change the message or placement of the ads mid-campaign until you achieve the results you wanted to achieve. That's the opportunity of the Internet. And it is the responsibility of StarMedia to help our clients realize that opportunity.
>
> Players in the U.S. market have an easier time, because their clients use interactive media agencies, and the agencies do much of the thinking. So they

[26]Press release: "StarMedia Network Announces New Subsidiary Periscopio Inc. and Unveils Powerful Spanish-Language Portal: Periscopio.com," September 16, 1999.

take the numbers—the results are automatically generated by our software—then they do all the analysis and just give us new creative and say put it up here. In our local markets, our client services team must do the thinking, make the suggestions, actually do the creative in most cases. Delivering this service required another huge investment.

At the end of 1999, Wall Street estimates had StarMedia commanding one-third of Internet advertising revenues in Latin America.[27] It was able to charge a significant CPM premium to the rest of the market—five times the rate of mass horizontal portals in the United States—because of its coveted user base and dominant traffic figures (see Exhibits 12, 13, 14 and 15).

Competition

If StarMedia can tenderize this market, that's great. We think that although the user base is growing, there aren't enough users to justify spending a lot of money. We're patient, and we can afford to get the timing right.

—Heather Killen, vice president,
Yahoo! International, February 1999[28]

Competitors to StarMedia fell into three main categories: Spanish and Portuguese versions of U.S.-based portals; national sites often affiliated with ISPs, media, or telecom companies; and competing pan-regional start-ups.

Yahoo! Yahoo! was the first to follow StarMedia into Latin America with a pan-regional concept, launching Yahoo! en Español in June 1998. Initially, the site had little localized content and Yahoo! did not invest in a local sales strategy; the site failed to gain traction. Starting in Spain in late 1998, however, Yahoo! began launching country-specific sites. In June 1999, it launched Yahoo! Brazil, followed by Yahoo! Mexico. Meanwhile, Yahoo! initiated country-specific news for the five next largest Latin American countries under the Yahoo! en Español umbrella. Yahoo! was a formidable global player with more than 20 international properties, including the leading portals in the United Kingdom, Japan, Germany, France, Italy, and Korea. In September 1999, it boasted 105 million unique users (38 million in the United States) and strong global brand recognition. Yahoo!'s model was to remain a pure aggregator of third-party content that appealed to the largest potential audience. As of year-end 1999, it still had virtually no local operations within Latin America.

America Online. America Online entered Latin America through a 50-50 partnership with Venezuela-based, pan-regional media conglomerate Cisneros Group. Together, they launched a Portuguese-language site in November 1999. At the time, AOL president Robert Pittman acknowledged that Brazil's Internet market was already among the world's most sophisticated but countered, "The game has barely begun here."[29] Customized sites for Mexico and Spain were scheduled for 2000. By partnering with Cisneros—whose media holdings included several television and radio networks—AOL gained needed brand recognition in the region, as well as local sales and content development staffs. Each company pledged to invest $100 million in the effort, and Gustavos Cisneros, chairman of Cisneros Group promised, "We will spend what is needed to be the market leader."[30] A public offering in 2000 was expected.[31]

AOL—like Yahoo!—was one of the few Internet companies making a profit; 1999 earnings were estimated at $400 million. In contrast to Yahoo!, however, AOL relied heavily on ISP access fees for revenues. In part because of this reliance, attempts to extend its operations internationally had been disappointing. When ISPs in Europe began partnering with telephone companies to provide consumers free Internet access in exchange for a portion of the local telephone fee, AOL resisted the trend, and saw its first-mover advantage collapse within weeks. Nevertheless, AOL remained a deep-pocketed, industry standard-bearer with 52 million unique users and extensive experience in content development.

[27]For comparison, Yahoo! commanded an 8% share of the U.S. market in 1996 at a similar point in Internet development there.

[28]Robert McGarvey, "A Star is Born," *Upside Magazine,* March 1999.

[29]Peter Fritsch, "AOL Takes Major Step in Latin America," *The Wall Street Journal,* November 16, 1999.

[30]Ibid.

[31]AOL's official launch in Brazil was shaky. On December 7, 1999, Dow Jones Business News reported "The launch party for America Online's Brazilian service allegedly cost $1 million and was covered profusely in Brazil's society pages, but it couldn't save AOL from the public relations backlash coming just three weeks after going live." According to the report, CDs which AOL had flooded the market with in November altered the hard-drive configurations of user's computers against consumer wishes. The resulting negative press led to the "mutually-agreed" departure of AOL's Brazilian subsidiary president.

Telefonica/Terra. By 1999, Telefonica was the largest telecommunications provider to the Spanish and Portuguese world—controlling one of every three phone lines in Latin America and nearly all in Spain (see Exhibit 16).[32] It pursued a roll-up strategy in Latin America's Internet space that was marked by an aggressive business attitude some critics described as "conquistador capitalism."[33] Its modus operandi in acquiring telecommunications assets helped establish the reputation: bid high, cut costs, expand fast, and use heavy-handed political pressure as necessary. Furthermore, many of its Latin American assets were consolidated into umbrella companies run out of Madrid, often to the detriment of Latin American minority shareholders. Telefonica's chairman Juan Villalonga called this strategy a quest for scale and efficiency, and it was rewarded by financial analysts.[34] Such tactics, however—compounded with poor public relations—alienated many Latin Americans. In October 1999, Telefonica moved its European and Latin American Internet access and content properties into a new entity called Terra, which was spun off several weeks later at an initial public valuation more than $9 billion, raising $818 million for the subsidiary.

Among Terra's holdings was Olé, Spain's most popular portal, which Telefonica had purchased several months prior[35] and then extended with local content into Argentina, Chile, Colombia, Peru, Uruguay, and Venezuela. Terra filled these Latin American Olé sites' content channels—and drew traffic—almost exclusively by purchasing competitors; for example, it acquired two of Argentina's leading local portals and folded them into its Argentine Olé in November 1999. Terra also built traffic through ISP acquisitions, purchasing ZAZ in Brazil and Infosel in Mexico, those two countries' second biggest ISPs. In September 1999, ZAZ had 280,000 subscribers, roughly 13.3% of Brazil's Internet market share. Terra's total ISP customer base was 860,000 across Brazil, Mexico, Peru, Chile, Guatemala, Spain and Argentina. According to the company, its portals generated in aggregate more than 290 million page views and more than 22 million visitors in the month of September.

In addition to Terra's Internet acquisition strategy, Telefonica invested heavily in infrastructure. It signed a multimillion dollar contract with Lucent Technologies to build a 15-country broadband IP-based data network, and partnered with Cisco to jointly explore market opportunities for Internet/intranet services, xDSL and broadband access technologies, online services, and IP and ATM transport.[36] In 1999 alone, it invested $1.9 billion in Brazil, with the majority of the funds used to expand its telecom network in São Paulo. The company's philosophy was that access gateways such as ISPs and mobile digital phones would ultimately decide the portal winners (see Exhibit 17).

Telmex/Prodigy/Microsoft. Telefonos de Mexico SA (Telmex) was the dominant telephone company and largest ISP in Mexico with 311,000 Internet subscribers and growing fast. To improve its ISP capabilities, Telmex partnered with U.S.-based Prodigy, which had 2 million Internet subscribers in the United States, including the Southwest, where 60% of U.S. Hispanics lived. In July 1999, Telmex launched a sales campaign with Acer, Compaq, and Apple that bundled a new computer with Internet access. More than 1,000 new customers a day began signing up for the service. In October, the company announced a $100 million venture with Microsoft to develop a portal aimed at Spanish speakers throughout the Western Hemisphere that would be localized by country. Telmex was late to the pan-regional game and lacked significant Latin American alliances outside of Mexico, but it had strong presence in Mexico and deep pockets. One area where Telmex was unlikely to enter directly was Brazil, where Microsoft was already involved in a joint venture with the dominant cable TV operator Globocabo.

Universo Online. Universo Online was Brazil's largest ISP with half-a-million paid subscribers in November 1999 and a growth rate of 12% a month. The company contested StarMedia's claims to being the world's largest non-English website, claiming that 80% of Brazilian net surfers visited its site daily.[37] UOL was controlled by Brazil's second and third largest media groups, Abril SA and Grupo Folha de São Paulo SA, which helped it stock its 28 channels with content from the country's leading newspapers, magazines and news services. Other channel offerings included e-commerce, video streaming and community sites. Because of its media parentage, UOL

[32]Revenues for Telefonica were projected to exceed $11 billion in 1999, with Latin American revenues representing roughly 35%.

[33]Matt Moffett and Craig Torres, "'Conquistador': Spain's Telefonica Jolts Latin America With Tough Tactics," *The Wall Street Journal*, November 18, 1999.

[34]Ibid.

[35]It is interesting to note that more than two dozen Olé employees quit when the announcement of Telefonica's purchase was made.

[36]The Yankee Group, "The Telefonica Report," November 1999.

[37]Fritsch, op. cit.

had universal name recognition in Brazil. Outside the country, however, it was little known. UOL signed a partnership with a leading Argentine publishing group, Perfil, in the second half of 1999 and announced plans to enter other Latin American countries in 2000. UOL raised $100 million in a private round in September that included investor Morgan Stanley Dean Witter.

Also taking aim at StarMedia were Internet start-ups El Sitio, QuePasa and Yupi. El Sitio, based in Argentina, and Yupi, in Miami Beach, targeted the pan-regional Latin American market. Both were in the process of developing more local content by country. El Sitio's strategy also included acquiring ISPs in the region, and at the end of 1999, it had about 80,000 subscribers in Argentina, Brazil, and Colombia. Chicago Cubs home-run hitter and Dominican Republic native Sammy Sosa was signed as company spokesman for 2000 and 2001. In December 1999, El Sitio went public, raising $131 million. Yupi had yet to go public, although it received a $67 million cash infusion in late 1999 from strategic investors including Sony, News Corp., and IFX Corporation. One of its differentiation points was its Ciudad Futura site, which empowered users to design the site themselves. QuePasa, based in Phoenix, Arizona, focused exclusively on the U.S. Hispanic market with plans to enter Latin American and Spain only after establishing dominance in the United States. It had hired Latin singing sensation Gloria Estefan as its spokesperson. QuePasa, whose investors included Spanish-language TV giant Telemundo, raised $42 million in an initial public offering in mid-1999. In December 1999, it announced a partnership with ISP startup NetZero to market free ISP service to U.S. Hispanics with QuePasa providing the homepage.

Strategic Challenges 2000

When StarMedia began 1999, it was a mass horizontal portal that gained its content primarily from third-party providers and through strategic alliances. As it entered the new millennium it had become an integrated media company involved in Internet access, mobile technology, and broadband services. It helped merchants build virtual stores in less than 24 hours. And it was gearing to provide its customers with financial tools like online-wallets, escrow financing, and online purchase insurance. It was doing all these things while managing more than a half-dozen brands across three continents in three different languages. Tracy Leeds described the strategy as being "opportunistic in the best sense of the word." She said: "We're developing a company that can get into these businesses very quickly and can stay as flexible as possible. That way, we can transform those businesses into what they need to be to get to our ultimate goal. The goal is delivering the very best user experience."

Perhaps the biggest challenge in front of StarMedia's management team was that almost anything seemed possible. Consequently, establishing strategic boundaries was important. But where should they draw those lines? Also looming were concerns about the ISP business. Fernando and Jack both were confident that StarMedia had already proven itself with consumers who had chosen their site without being forced through a StarMedia-controlled ISP gateway. Nothing indicated to them that the future would be any different, as long as they kept improving their offerings. Consequently, they saw no need to accelerate StarMedia's modestly scaled participation in this area. The mobile gateway was more sensitive, because mobile phone companies had more control over the interface. But with the purchase of PageCell Holdings, Fernando and Jack believed themselves to be the first movers in this new platform and, thus, in the position of power. How to develop new, vertical channels—and manage their many brands—was a more uncertain challenge. But if one plan didn't work, they could always adapt. Their team was used to doing that. Indeed, adapting quickly to change was StarMedia's most prized capability. Angel Parada, country manager in Spain, recalled his first days at StarMedia:

> My first feeling with StarMedia was that it had a big brain in New York with short legs in the different countries. I remember telling Fernando that if we wanted to really run and not just walk, we needed longer legs; we needed to work in a different way. But with the Internet, I've realized that distance is not the key point here. If I need to speak with Adriana, I speak with Adriana. If I need to speak with Fernando, I speak with Fernando. If I have a technical question, I speak to the appropriate technical people. We're like a big family, where everyone trusts and respects each other, which is the best situation possible. We have this big brain in New York that is always transmitting new ideas, and we have to run to keep up. Sometimes we create and recreate the company daily, sometimes weekly. But we all have responsibility for making it successful. I've worked with a lot of people in my life, but Fernando is the star. He has an absolutely clear and clever vision.

Angel's words were curiously reminiscent of one of StarMedia's biggest television campaigns: "They are near. They are far. They are communicating through StarMedia." They also hearkened Fernando's revolutionary words about creating a new society in Latin America: "The Internet represents a historic opportunity to reunify Latin America, to allow people to come together, to share ideas, to do commerce with each other." The difference was that Angel was talking about StarMedia itself. Perhaps in the midst of revolutionizing Latin America through Internet technology, Fernando and Jack were also revolutionizing the traditional business model. It was the kind of effort even Lex Luthor might admire—but still seek to crush. . . .

Exhibit 1

STARMEDIA'S OFFICES

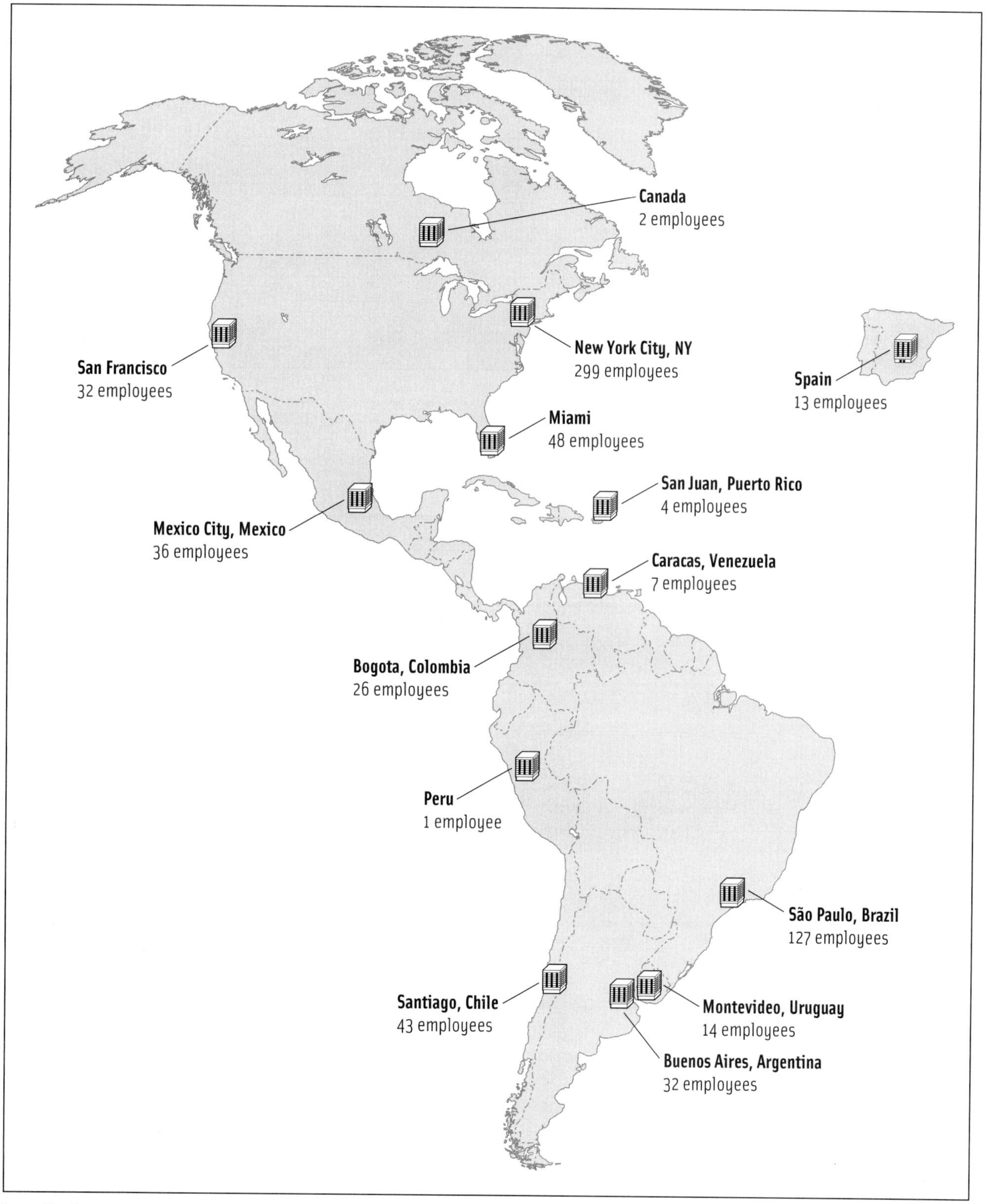

Source: The Company

Exhibit 2

STARMEDIA'S ADDRESSABLE MARKETS

	Population (millions)	% of Latin American Population	Population Growth	GDP ($ billion)	Annual Real GDP Growth	GDP per Capita	Population Below Poverty Line	Inflation Rate (1998 est.)	Income Share of Top 20% of Population[a]	(Per 1,000 People) TV Sets[a]	PCs[a]	Tele-density[d]
Argentina	36.7	7.5%	1.3%	$374.0	4.3%	$10,300	25.5%	1.0%	n/a	347	39	23.7%
Belize	0.2	0.0	2.4	0.7	0.5	3,000	n/a	−0.5	n/a	n/a	28	13.7[a]
Bolivia	8.0	1.6	2.0	23.4	4.7	3,000	66.0	4.4	48.2%	202	n/a	8.8
Brazil	171.9	35.3	1.2	1,035.2	0.5	6,100	17.4	2.0	64.2	289	26	11.7
Chile	15.0	3.1	1.2	184.6	3.5	12,500	20.5	4.7	61.0	280	54	21.8
Colombia	39.3	8.1	1.9	254.7	0.2	6,600	17.7	16.7	61.5	188	33	18.8
Costa Rica	3.7	0.8	1.9	24.0	5.5	6,700	n/a	12.0	51.8	220	n/a	17.7
Dominican Republic	8.1	1.7	1.6	39.8	7.0	5,000	20.6	6.0	55.7	84	n/a	9.1
Ecuador	12.6	2.6	1.8	58.7	1.0	4,800	35.0	43.0	52.6	148	13	6.8
El Salvador	5.8	1.2	1.5	17.5	3.7	3,000	48.3	2.6	54.4	250	n/a	5.9
Falkland Islands	0.003	0.0	2.4	n/a	n/a	n/a	n/a	n/a	n/a	n/a	n/a	n/a
French Guiana	0.2	0.0	3.2	1.0	n/a	6,000	n/a	2.5	n/a	n/a	n/a	29.9[a]
Guyana	0.7	0.1	−0.3	1.8	−1.8	2,500	n/a	4.1	n/a	n/a	n/a	6[a]
Guatemala	12.3	2.5	2.7	45.7	5.0	3,800	n/a	6.4	63.0	122	3	3.3
Honduras	6	1.2	2.2	14.4	3.0	2,400	50.0	14.5	58.0	80	n/a	3.7
Mexico	100.3	20.6	1.7	815.3	4.8	8,300	27.0	18.6	55.3	193	37	9.5
Nicaragua	4.7	1.0	2.8	11.6	4.0	2,500	50.3	16.0	55.2	170	n/a	3.1
Panama	2.8	0.6	1.5	19.9	2.7	7,300	n/a	1.4	60.1	229	n/a	12.0
Paraguay	5.4	1.1	2.7	19.8	−0.5	3,700	21.8	14.6	62.4	144	n/a	3.9
Peru	26.6	5.5	1.9	111.8	1.8	4,300	54.0	6.7	50.4	142	12	8.0
Suriname	0.4	0.1	0.7	1.5	2.0	3,500	n/a	20.0	n/a	n/a	n/a	14.6[a]
Uruguay	3.3	0.7	0.7	28.4	3.0	8,600	n/a	8.6	n/a	305	22	26.0
Venezuela	23.2	4.8	1.7	194.5	−0.9	8,500	31.3	29.9	51.8	180	37	17.0
Latin America Totals/Averages[b]	487.2	100.0	1.5	3,278.3	2.4	6,729	n/a	n/a	54.0	232	27	12.5
Portugal	9.9		−0.1	144.8	4.2	14,600	n/a	2.8	n/a	367	74	40.2[a]
Spain	39.2		0.1	645.6	3.5	16,500	n/a	2.0	40.3	509	122	40.3[a]
Cuba	11.1		0.4	17.3	1.2	1,560	n/a	n/a	n/a	n/a	n/a	3.4
Puerto Rico	3.9		0.6	34.7	3.1	9,000	n/a	5.7	n/a	n/a	n/a	43.0
US Hispanic[a]	30.7		3.0	n/a	n/a	n/a	n/a	n/a	n/a	n/a	n/a	n/a
Addressable Market[b,c]	582.0		1.5	4,120.7	2.6	7,481	n/a	n/a	47.7	235	33	13[a]
United States	272.6		0.9	8,511.0	3.9	31,500	13.0	1.6	45.2	806	407	64[a]

Source: Except where noted, *Central Intelligence Agency World Fact Book 1999*

Notes: Population figures are July 1999; GDP are 1998 estimated; GDP is determined by "purchasing price parity."

[a]World Bank 1997
[b]Latin America and Addressable Market are weighted averages.
[c]Addressable market does not include U.S. Hispanic, except for population figures.
[d]Preliminary Latin American Telecom Services Forecast, August 2, 1999.

Exhibit 3

MONTHLY WEB ACCESS COST BY REGION/COUNTRY[a]

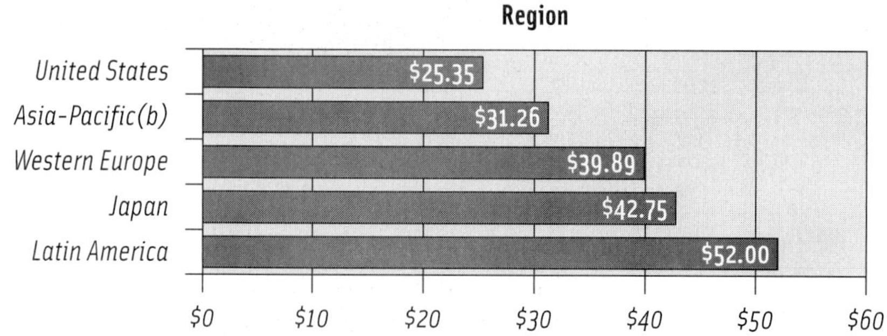

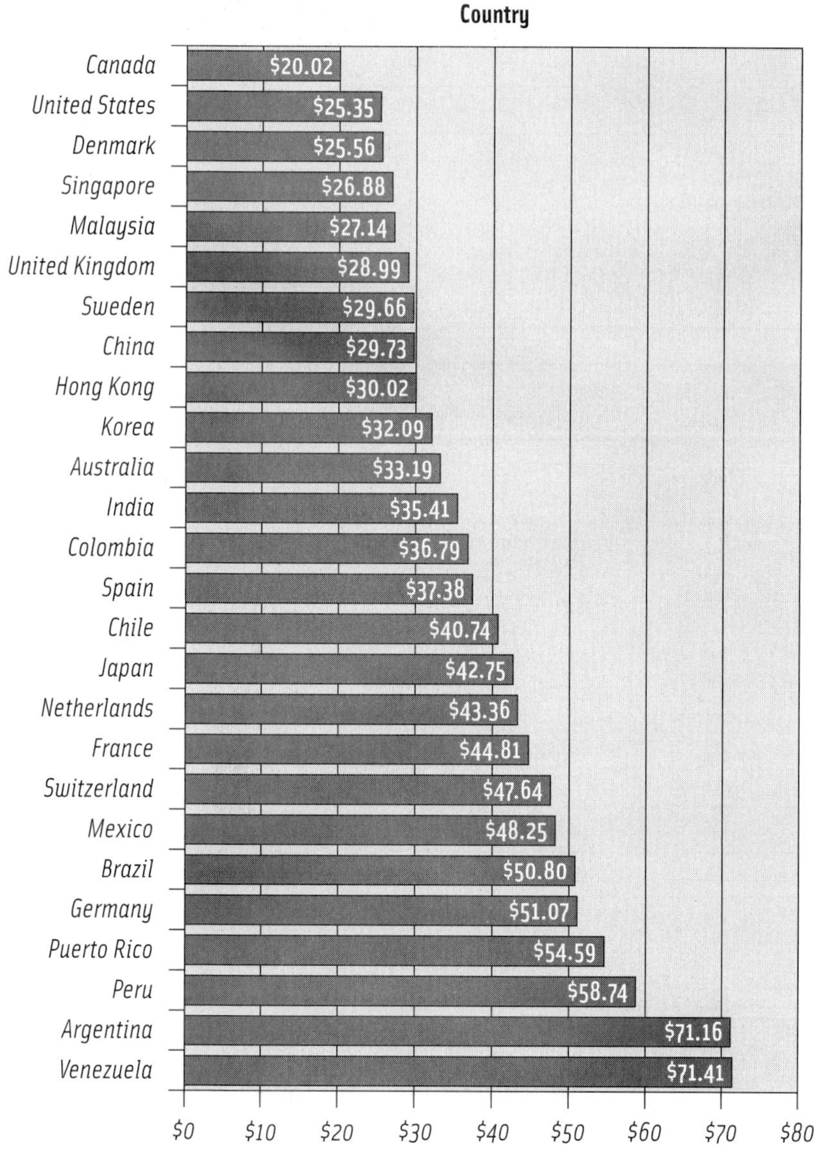

Source: *www.thestandard.com*
(a) Respondents estimated total monthly household expenditures for ISP, telephone, and phone line fees. Responses converted to U.S. dollars. (b) Excluding Japan, from an online survey of nearly 29,000 respondents who were recruited via responses to banner ads on 16 portals in 13 languages in 28 countries. IDC estimates the results are more indicative of advanced Internet users rather than Internet users overall in these countries. Source: International Data Corp.

Exhibit 4 LATIN AMERICA VS. THE REST OF THE WORLD (MILLIONS OF INTERNET USERS)

	1998	1999	2000	2001	2002	CAGR
Latin America	1.6	4.1	8.7	16.3	26.6	75%
Brazil	0.98	2.22	n/a	n/a	n/a	n/a
Mexico	0.35	0.77	n/a	n/a	n/a	n/a
United States	48.0	59.0	66.0	78.0	88.0	13%
Canada	5.9	6.8	7.8	9.2	10.1	11%
Europe	24.6	38.2	48.8	64.2	84.3	28%
Asia/Pacific Rim	14.1	21.6	38.4	48.4	60.7	34%
Rest of World	1.2	1.9	2.3	6.9	12.3	59%

Source: eMarketer

Exhibit 5 BRAZILIAN ISPS AND ESTIMATED PAYING ACCOUNTS

Company	Estimated Accounts (September 1999)	Market Share (percent)	Ownership/Affiliation
UOL	470,000	22.4	Folha de São Paulo, Editora Abril
ZAZ/Telefonica[a]	280,000	13.3	Nutec Informática S.A., 51% owned by Telefonica and the remaining 49% by RBS group and others
PSINet	126,800[a]	6.0	PSINet
BR Home Shopping	100,000	4.7	Banco Rural
Mandic	92,000	4.4	El Sitio
Matrix[a]	45,000	2.1	Grupo Amauri
Originet	23,500	1.1	Origin Brazil Ltda.
Dialdata	15,000[b]	0.7	Via Net.Works and others
Others	945,700	45.3	
Total	**2.1 million**	**100.0**	

Source: ISPs, ABRANET, and the Yankee Group
[a]Numbers include franchise ISPs.
[b]Numbers estimated by the Yankee Group.

STARMEDIA PRESS RELEASES

Date	Announcement
12/22/1999	StarMedia Network Acquires All Rights to Chat Software Technology of Magma Communications, Ltd.
12/21/1999	BigStar and StarMedia Bring Videos and DVD's to Hispanics Across the U.S. and Puerto Rico
12/20/1999	Periscopio.com Selects E-Lingo for New Translation Services for Spanish Services
12/16/1999	Softnet's ISP Channel and StarMedia Network Join Forces
12/15/1999	AT&T Unveils Spanish-Language Internet Service
12/07/1999	StarMedia and Dell Announce e-Commerce and Marketing Agreement
12/06/1999	Leading Hispanic Organizations Join Forces to Promote the Latino Vote in Elections 2000 Through Online Education Campaign
12/06/1999	Financialweb.Com to Deliver Innovative Financial Information
12/01/1999	StarMedia Opens Corporate Headquarters in Uruguay
12/01/1999	StarMedia Is the Official Sponsor of "StarMedia Senior Cup"
12/01/1999	StarMedia Presents a Redesigned Arts and Entertainment Channel
11/29/1999	StarMedia and Fao Schwarz Bring Hottest Toys to Latin American Consumers
11/08/1999	StarMedia and Visa International Announce E-Commerce Alliance
10/27/1999	Celia Cruz Visits StarMedia for Her First Online Chat and Webcast Ever!
10/26/1999	StarMedia Announces Third Quarter 1999 Financial Results
10/25/1999	Chat with Latin Star "La India" on StarMedia
10/11/1999	StarMedia and Telemig Launch First Mobile Internet Service in Brazil
10/19/1999	The Y2K Millennium Bug
10/18/1999	Chat with Humberto Rogue Villanueva, Presidential Precandidate of Mexico
10/13/1999	StarMedia and eOffprice Announce E-Commerce Partnership
10/07/1999	Chat with Vicente Fox
10/05/1999	Chat Conversation with Artist Fernando Botero
09/30/1999	Get in Shape with StarMedia Fitness!
09/29/1999	StarMedia Network Expands Management Team
09/28/1999	Live Chat and Webcast with Carlos Ponce
09/21/1999	StarMedia Network Announces the Creation of StarMedia Mobile
09/16/1999	StarMedia Network Announces New Subsidiary Periscopio Inc.
09/15/1999	StarMedia Network Announces Creation of New Division: StarMedia Broadband
09/15/1999	StarMedia Brings New Spanish-Language Internet Games Service
09/15/1999	StarMedia and Mpath Announce Strategic Partnership to Bring Internet Games Service
09/09/1999	Hewlett-Packard and StarMedia to Form Strategic E-Commerce Alliance for Latin America
09/01/1999	StarMedia Network Launches Premium Internet Access Service in Latin America
08/19/1999	StarMedia and LatinGrocer Announce an E-Commerce Partnership
07/28/1999	StarMedia Announces Second Quarter 1999 Financial Results
07/21/1999	StarMedia Acquires LatinRed
07/13/1999	StarMedia Announces the Acquisition of OpenChile and Panoramas.Cl
06/24/1999	StarMedia Brings the First Total E-Commerce Solution
06/10/1999	StarMedia Network Launches Operations in Puerto Rico
05/26/1999	StarMedia Network Announces Initial Public Offering
04/20/1999	Billboard Online Partners with StarMedia Network
03/18/1999	StarMedia Network, Inc. Files Registration Statement for Initial Public Offering
03/17/1999	StarMedia Network Unveils Research Results
03/08/1999	StarMedia Emphasizes the Power of Pan-Local Community
02/20/1999	Key Appointments Further Bolster StarMedia Network's Executive Team
02/19/1999	StarMedia Exports Executive to Occupy the Vice-Presidency
01/22/1999	StarMedia Is Carnival 99 Address in the Internet
12/21/1998	StarMedia Launches Latin America's First Spanish Language Instant Messaging on the Internet
11/23/1998	StarMedia's Burgeoning Operations Call for Creation of COO Post
11/09/1998	StarMedia Network Launches Entry into U.S. Hispanic Market

Exhibit 6 STARMEDIA PRESS RELEASES cont.

Date	Announcement
11/01/1998	StarMedia Network, Inc. Builds Global Sales Team
10/14/1998	The Second Annual Fortune Americas Internet Strategy Conference
10/12/1998	StarMedia Network Secures $80 Million Private Financing
08/10/1998	Cyberian Outpost Announces Initiative for Latin America
07/27/1998	Teleglobe and StarMedia Take Strategic Electronic Mail Initiative
07/22/1998	StarMedia Opens Miami Sales Office
07/20/1998	StarMedia Network Launches StarMedia Orbita
07/14/1998	StarMedia to License WeatherLabs Content
06/03/1998	StarMedia Partners with Netscape
06/01/1998	StarMedia Covers WorldCup '98 in Spanish and Portuguese
05/18/1998	StarMedia Network Launches Multi-Million Dollar Advertising
05/18/1998	StarMedia Names Key Latin America Posts
03/09/1998	StarMedia Closes $12 Million in Second Round Financing
12/15/1997	Excite and StarMedia Enter Exclusive Partnership
12/15/1997	StarMedia and ZDNet to Bring Content to South America
12/15/1997	StarMedia and USA Latin America in New Marketing Partnership
11/11/1997	StarMedia to Benefit from New Technology Investment Fund
11/04/1997	ANS Communications, Inc. Provides Web Hosting and Virtual Private Network Connections for StarMedia
07/28/1997	StarMedia Network Receives Backing from Chase Capital Partners

Source: *www.starmedia.com*

Exhibit 7 CHANNEL DESCRIPTIONS

COMMUNITY SERVICES

StarMedia Bate-papo/Charlas® (chat)

StarMedia Bate-papo/Charlas is our chat community and the foundation of our Network. Bate-papo/Charlas creates "virtual communities" where participants can interact in real-time groups or one-on-one discussions in both Spanish and Portuguese. These communities include broad interest areas like sports, romance and current events. Our users can host their own scheduled chats, create their own interest-specific rooms or participate in moderated celebrity events.

StarMedia® Mail (email)

StarMedia Mail is our free Web-based email service and is offered in both Spanish and Portuguese. We have over 1,600,000 registered email users. StarMedia Mail allows users to access electronic mail from any computer with Web browser. We believe that providing this service increases user loyalty and therefore, increases traffic on our Network. We have also developed a series of "postales," which are interactive greeting cards that users can send to friends and family members.

StarMedia® Fórum/Pizarras (bulletin boards)

Our bulletin board area—Fórum/Pizarras—further enhances user interaction. From politics and religion to music and travel, this user-generated content augments each channel and maintains a record of ongoing communication about a particular topic on our Network.

Homepages StarMedia Órbita/Orbita® (personal homepages)

Homepages StarMedia Órbita/Orbita enables users to create personalized Web pages on the StarMedia Network. Using a variety of proprietary publishing tools in Spanish and Portuguese, users are able to quickly and easily create fully personalized homepages. Individual homepages reside in designated communities of interest like family, business and technology. We believe that users will be more attracted to our Network when they can publish content and share experiences with others through their personalized homepages.

StarMedia® Express (instant messenger)

This instant messaging service enables users to know whether their friends and other users with similar interests are online and to send messages directly to them. Our partnership with PeopleLink enables us to subscribe to specific interest groups and communicate with people from around the world who share similar interests.

Namoro Personet℠/Romance Personet℠ (personals)

Namoro Personet/Romance Personet is an interactive meeting place for visitors in search of new friends and relationships. Personet connects people from a wide range of interests, backgrounds and origins. On Personet, people meet in a variety of ways, including through personal ad postings and in discussion forums.

StarMedia® Classificados/Clasificados (classifieds)

StarMedia Classificados/Clasificados is our classifieds marketplace, spanning numerous product and service areas from electronics to real estate. Buyers and sellers from across Latin America can trade timely information on goods and services.

StarMedia® Horóscopo (Horoscope)

StarMedia Horóscopo features your daily astrological reading and also allows you to find out what is in store for your favorite stars as well as family, friends and that special someone! On the horoscope page, you can also find out how compatible they are with your present or potential love interest! This feature in addition to receiving one's lucky numbers, special word of the day and a rating of work, fortune and love by the stars has made the horoscope section a favorite destination by our users.

CONTENT AND COMMERCE SERVICES

StarMedia BuscaWeb® (search and guide)

StarMedia BuscaWeb is our Internet search engine with in-language functionality. It utilizes Inktomi's sophisticated search capabilities, which have been customized to support country-specific, regional and worldwide searches in both Spanish and Portuguese.

StarMedia® Notícias/Noticias (news)
StarMedia Notícias/Noticias delivers a comprehensive selection of international, regional and local news. Content for news and all information services is provided by top syndicated wire services, local partnerships and by our team of editors, producers and writers throughout Latin America. Users can react to the latest headlines through chats, debates and polls. Our partners include Reuters, Agencia EFE and Agence France Presse.

StarMedia® Esportes/Deportes (sports)
Through the StarMedia Esportes/Deportes channel, we provide comprehensive local, regional and global sports news and information. Users can access headlines, results, commentary, analysis and daily polls. They can also purchase merchandise and win prizes through our interactive games. In addition, we are the exclusive webcaster of Fútbol de Primera, the world's most popular syndicated radio talk show about soccer, hosted by Andrés Cantor.

StarMedia® Money (finance)
StarMedia Money provides online financial news and information. In addition, users can obtain research about top Latin American companies, access information on personal banking products and services, and track their individual investment portfolios in Spanish and Portuguese. Information is provided by a host of leading financial information publishers, including Avance Económico, Enfoque, El Economista, El Universal and Quote.com.

StarMedia® Digital (technology)
StarMedia Digital offers the latest in technology news, product reviews and free downloads from ZDNet. The information provided by ZDNet helps users make informed buying decisions about technology products, which they can purchase through StarMedia's relationship with vendors like Outpost.com.

StarMedia® Saúde/Fitness (Health and Fitness)
StarMedia Saúde/Fitness allows users to find the latest highlights about health and wellness today. With headline news, tips, quizzes, search functions and community interactivity, this channel entertains and informs users who wish be healthy.

StarMedia® Shopping (electronic commerce)
StarMedia Shopping acts as a virtual central plaza for online Latin American consumers. Users are able to purchase a variety of merchandise, including computers, books and CDs, from a host of global and local retailers like bn.com (Barnes & Noble), CDNOW, Inc, CIM and Outpost.com. Products from the StarMedia Shopping channel are also merchandised within appropriate channels. For example, there are direct links that allow a literary chat group to easily purchase books of interest from barnesandnoble.com.

StarMedia® Arte e Espetáculos/Arte y Especáculos (entertainment)
Entertainment and music are united in the StarMedia Arte e Espetáculos/Arte y Especáculos channel. Our partnerships with USA Network, Fox Latin America, eDrive, Retila, Successo CD and CDNOW provide content that creates a bridge between online and traditional programming. (V)Pulse® offers a popular selection of easily playable music videos. StarMedia TV and StarMedia Radios provide Internet broadcasts of popular television and radio stations from Latin America and around the world.

StarMedia® Viagens/Viajes (travel)
StarMedia Viagens/Viajes offers travel guides and news through an exclusive relationship with Lonely Planet, as well as advice about preparing for a trip, links to travel resources on the Web and a forum for exchanging travel stories and tips.

StarMedia® Tempo/Tiempo (weather)
StarMedia Tempo/Tiempo provides up-to-the-minute weather conditions and extended forecasts for 3,000 cities around the globe.

StarMedia® Jogos/Juegos (games)
The Newest StarMedia channel, StarMedia Jogos/Juegos, offers a compilation of interactive games in which our users can participate and compete for prizes. These games include fantasy sport games such as Béisbol Virtual and Olé, as well as a variety of trivia games. In addition, StarMedia Jogos/Juegos offers a host of free, downloadable games, which are updated several times per week. This channel also includes a guide to our editors' picks of the best in Spanish and Portuguese online game sites.

Source: The Company

Exhibit 8

"NEW WORLD" TELEVISION COMMERCIAL

Source: The Company

Exhibit 9 STARMEDIA PRINT ADS TARGETING CONSUMERS

Source: The Company

Exhibit 10 CONDENSED CONSOLIDATED STATEMENTS OF OPERATIONS (UNAUDITED)

	Three Months Ended		Nine Months Ended	
	Sept. 30, 1999	**Sept. 30, 1998**	**Sept. 30, 1999**	**Sept. 30, 1998**
Revenues	$5,618,000	$1,646,000	$11,092,00	$2,496,000
Operating Expenses				
Product and technology development	9,987,000	1,761,000	20,006,000	4,939,000
Sales and marketing	14,274,000	7,735,000	37,200,000	13,750,000
General and administration	3,902,000	956,000	9,544,000	1,989,000
Nonrecurring charges	590,000	–	1,613,000	
Depreciation and amortization	1,684,000	211,000	3,328,000	459,000
Stock-based compensation expense	1,848,000	666,000	4,860,000	3,916,000
Total Operating Expenses	32,285,000	11,329,000	76,551,000	25,053,000
Loss from operations	(26,667,000)	(9,683,000)	(64,459,000)	(22,557,000)
Interest income	1,785,000	44,000	3,189,000	163,000
Interest expense	(238,000)	25,000	(507,000)	(4,000)
Net loss before provision for income taxes	(25,120,000)	(9,614,000)	(62,777,000)	(22,398,000)
Provision for income taxes	(116,000)	–	(116,000)	–
Net loss	(25,236,000)	(9,614,000)	(62,893,000)	(22,398,000)
Preferred stock dividends and accretion	–	(1,908,000)	(4,266,000)	(2,628,000)
Net loss available to common shareholders	$(25,236,000)	$(11,522,000)	$(67,159,000)	$(25,026,000)
Historical basic and diluted net loss per common share	$ (0.43)	$ (0.96)	$ (1.97)	$ (2.31)
Historical number of shares used in computing basic and diluted net loss per share	58,142,334	12,041,161	34,131,502	10,834,299
As a % of Revenue				
Product and technology	178%	107%	180%	198%
Sales and marketing	254%	470%	335%	551%
General and administrative	69%	58%	86%	80%
Operating margin	-432%	-577%	-516%	-749%

StarMedia's Long-term Margin Goals	
	Target
Production and content	34%–36%
Sales and marketing	24%–26%
General and administrative	6%–8%
Operating margin	28%–30%

Source: Company documents

Exhibit 11

DISCOUNTED CASH FLOW MODEL ($ MILLIONS)

Projections	For Year Ending				
	12/31/00	12/31/01	12/31/02	12/31/03	12/31/04
Latin American Internet Advertising	121	259	517	949	1647
StarMedia Share	30%	28%	24%	24%	24%
Other revenue (ISP, e-commerce)	2	16	35	50	100
Revenues	39	88	160	275	500
Expenses	125	193	225	250	325
Operating income	(86)	(105)	(65)	25	175
+ Depreciation & amortization	11	20	22	24	26
= EBITDA	(75)	(85)	(43)	49	201
– Taxes	–	–	–	–	–
– Working capital needs	3	5	8	14	25
– Capital expenditures	5	5	5	5	6
Unlevered free cash flow	(84)	(95)	(56)	30	170

Present Value of Free Cash Flow	
Discount Rate	**PV of FCF**
10%	(70)
12%	(74)
14%	(77)
16%	(80)
18%	(83)
20%	(85)

	Present Value of Terminal Value				
2004 EBITDA	201.2	201.2	201.2	201.2	201.2
Terminal Value Multiple (Fwd)	20.0x	25.0x	30.0x	35.0x	40.0x
2003 Terminal Value	**4,025**	**5,031**	**6,037**	**7,043**	**8,049**
Discount Rate: **10%**	2,499	3,124	3,749	4,373	4,998
12%	2,284	2,855	3,426	3,996	4,567
14%	2,090	2,613	3,135	3,658	4,181
16%	1,916	2,395	2,874	3,353	3,832
18%	1,759	2,199	2,639	3,079	3,518
20%	1,617	2,022	2,426	2,830	3,235

Exhibit 11 DISCOUNTED CASH FLOW MODEL ($ MILLIONS) cont.

Net Debt 12/31/99	
Debt	–
Preferred	–
Cash	294
Options Pr	20
Net Debt	(314)

Fully diluted shares:	71.6

	Present Value of Enterprise				
Terminal Value Multiple	20.0x	25.0x	30.0x	35.0x	40.0x
Discount Rate: **10%**	2,429	3,054	3,679	4,304	4,928
12%	2,210	2,781	3,352	3,923	4,494
14%	2,013	2,536	3,058	3,581	4,103
16%	1,836	2,315	2,794	3,273	3,752
18%	1,677	2,116	2,556	2,996	3,436
20%	1,533	1,937	2,342	2,746	3,150
	Present Value of Equity				
Terminal Value Multiple	20.0x	25.0x	30.0x	35.0x	40.0x
Discount Rate: **10%**	2,744	3,368	3,993	4,618	5,243
12%	2,524	3,095	3,666	4,237	4,808
14%	2,327	2,850	3,372	3,895	4,418
16%	2,150	2,629	3,108	3,587	4,066
18%	1,991	2,431	2,870	3,310	3,750
20%	1,847	2,252	2,656	3,060	3,465
	Present Value of Equity Per Share				
Terminal Value Multiple	20.0x	25.0x	30.0x	35.0x	40.0x
Discount Rate: **10%**	38.33	47.06	55.78	64.51	73.24
12%	35.26	43.24	51.21	59.19	67.16
14%	32.51	39.81	47.11	54.41	61.71
16%	30.04	36.73	43.42	50.11	56.81
18%	27.81	33.96	40.10	46.24	52.39
20%	25.80	31.45	37.10	42.75	48.40

Source: Thomas Weisel Partners

Exhibit 12 SUMMARY REVENUE AND USER STATISTICS

	Q1:98	Q2:98	Q3:98	Q4:98	Q1:99	Q2:99	Q3:99
Revenue (in millions)	$0.3	$0.6	$1.6	$3.3	$1.6	$3.9	$5.6
Active e-mail accounts ('000)	56	108	177	293	425	1,204	1,557
Quarterly Pageviews (in millions)	46	111	150	164	133	686	1,168
Barter revenue						37%	26%
Total advertisers	3	16	25	44	45	160	259
% Top 5 customers						31%	27%
Personal homepages					91,000	151,000	211,400

Source: The Company

	1998A	1999E	2000E	2001E
Average CPM	$117	$78	$53	$45
Sell-through rate[a]	9.70%	7.60%	11.10%	14.00%

Source: Thomas Weisel Partners

[a]Sell-through is a ratio determined by total ads sold divided by total ad inventory; page views × inventory sell through (%) × CPM = advertising revenue example: 10,000,000 × 50% × $5.00 = $25 million

Exhibit 13 INTERNET COMPANIES' REVENUE PER THOUSAND PAGES[a]

Company	Revenue (1,000 pages)	As of:
StarMedia	**$20.12**	**4Q98**
CINet	19.38	3Q98
Excite	10.89	4Q98
Infoseek	9.75	3Q98
Lycos	8.98	3Q98
SportsLine USA	8.80	3Q98
Broadcast.com	5.43	3Q98
Yahoo!	5.06	4Q98
TMP Worldwide	3.13	3Q98
TheGlobe.com	2.09	3Q98
GeoCities	1.54	3Q98

Source: Company reports and Salomon Smith Barney

[a]Revenue per Thousand Pages is not the same as a CPM ad rate. CPM indicates the ad rate that an advertiser is charged for 1,000 pageviews. Revenue per Thousand Pages measures revenue per thousand pages of content, which is impacted by the number of ads on a page and the sellout ratio, i.e., the portion of possible ad impressions that are actually sold to advertisers. In short, a strong Revenue per Thousand Pages figure suggests that the Website is making productive use of ad inventory and the revenue opportunity presented by its traffic.

Exhibit 14 LATIN AMERICAN INTERNET ACCOUNTS AND STARMEDIA'S USER DISTRIBUTION

Latin American Internet Accounts

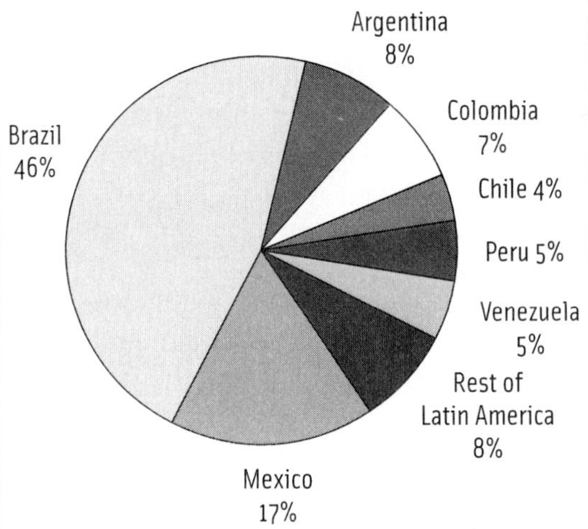

Source: International Data Corporation

StarMedia's User Distribution in Latin America Only

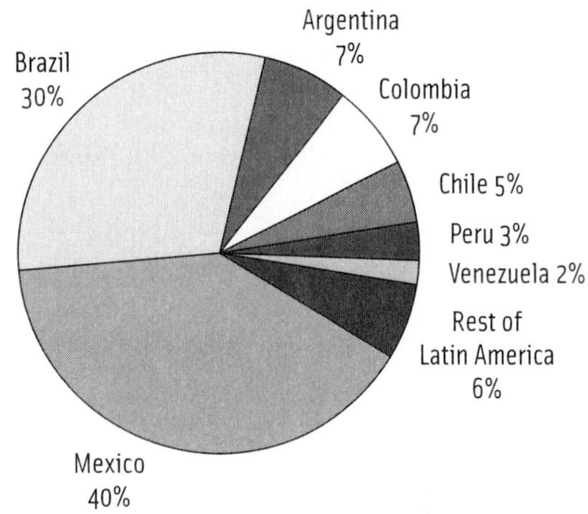

StarMedia's User Distribution in United States, Latin America, Iberia

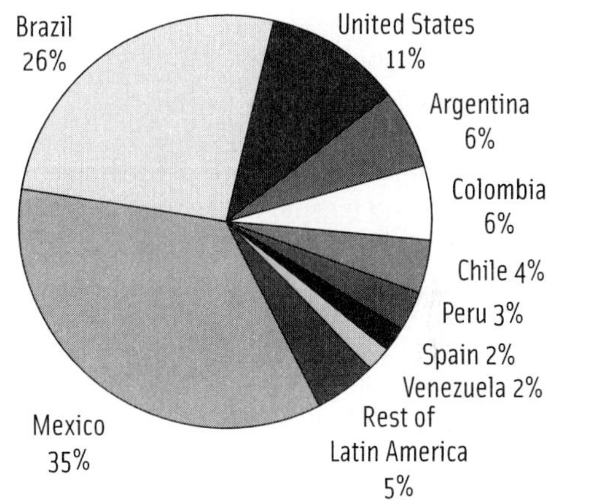

Source: The Company

Exhibit 15 STARMEDIA USER PROFILE

DEMOGRAPHICS

GENDER		EMPLOYMENT STATUS	
Female	22%	Employed	63%
Male	78%	College Student	24%
		High School Student	10%
AGE		**EDUCATION**	
Under 17 Years	11%	High School or Less	22%
18 to 24 Years	34%	Some College	40%
25 to 35 Years	33%	College Graduate	27%
35 to 44 Years	15%	Postgraduate	11%
45 Years and Older	7%		

USER BEHAVIOR

INTERNET USAGE

- StarMedia users are experienced on the Internet as 78% have been using the Web on a regular basis for over six months
- Users spend an average of 8.2 hours per week online
- 47% spend less time reading newspapers and magazines and 46% spend less time watching TV or cable as a result of Internet usage
- StarMedia users spend an average of 5.1 hours in front of a computer per day which is greater than the total amount of time spent reading newspapers and magazines, watching TV or cable and talking on the telephone combined
- 76% have Internet access in their homes, 61% have a connection at work and 38% can go online at school

ONLINE ACTIVITIES

- Most frequent online activities of users include sending/receiving email, chatting, surfing or browsing, finding product or service information, meeting new people and reading national/international news

ONLINE SHOPPING

- 29% of StarMedia users have already made a purchase over the Internet
- 59% are likely to make a purchase over the Web and 61% have credit cards
- The average household size of StarMedia users is 3 persons, 1 of which is under the age of 18 years

ONLINE ADVERTISING

- 83% of StarMedia users click on Web advertisements about products or services in which they are interested
- A majority (60%) click on Web ads that feature a contest or incentive
- Web advertisers are considered progressive or forward thinking by 63% of users

Source: StarMedia user survey, December 1998; conducted by The Laredo Group; data compiled from 12,253 responses

Exhibit 16 TELEFONICA IN SPAIN AND LATIN AMERICA

	Subscribers (in thousands)			
	YE97	YE98	1Q99	2Q99
Fixed Line	28,348	35,979	36,856	37,490
– Spain	16,737	17,406	17,749	17,928
– Latin America	11,611	18,573	19,107	19,562
Cellular	5,224	10,808	12,328	14,429
– Spain	3,187	4,894	5,717	6,540
– Latin America	2,037	5,914	6,611	7,889
Pay TV	2,059	2,377	2,336	2,351
– Spain	77	289	286	313
– Latin America	1,982	2,088	2,050	2,038

Source: Telefonica and the Yankee Group

Exhibit 17 TELEFONICA IN LATIN AMERICA

	Basic	Domestic Long-Distance (DLD)	Int'l Long-Distance (ILD)	Cellular	PCS	Cable TV	ISP	Data	Portal
Argentina	√	√	√	√	√	√	√	√	√
Brazil	√	√	√	√			√	√	√
Bolivia									
Chile	√	√	√	√		√	√	√	√
Colombia							√	√	√
Ecuador									
El Salvador		√	√	√					
Guatemala		√	√		√		√		√
Honduras									
Mexico							√		√
Nicaragua									
Panama									√
Paraguay									√
Peru	√	√	√	√		√	√	√	√
Puerto Rico		√	√	√	√				
Uruguay							√		√
Venezuela	√	√	√	√			√	√	√

Source: The Yankee Group, 1999

TELLME NETWORKS, INC.

On August 31, 2000, just prior to boarding his flight back to San Francisco, Mike McCue, co-founder and CEO of Tellme Networks, Inc. (Tellme)—a leader in the voice services market—learned that America Online (AOL) had just agreed to acquire Quack.com (Quack), one of Tellme's competitors. McCue, who was returning from meetings with investors in an effort to raise $125 million in a Series D round, spent most of the flight home mapping out alternative strategies for Tellme, given the changing competitive environment.

Tellme offered both *voice directory services* for consumers (through its branded 1-800-555-TELL service, and by helping its business partners set up their own 800 numbers) and *network services,* which allowed companies to outsource the development and operation of voice-enabled applications. Tellme's strategy was to serve as an "aggregator," allowing consumers to use its directory to access voice-enabled content, commerce, and communication services that ran on Tellme's network. Tellme's directory was aimed at fundamentally changing the way that people placed phone calls, and its network was aimed at fundamentally changing the way that businesses answered these calls.

With news of the Quack/AOL deal, it was clear that competition in the voice directory market was intensifying. By the fall of 2000, approximately half a dozen start-ups had launched full-fledged voice directory services, and industry observers expected the major Internet portals to enter the market soon. Competition on the network side was also increasing as speech recognition software providers (e.g., SpeechWorks International) and pure-play application service providers (e.g., NetbyTel) stepped up their efforts to build voice-enabled applications for businesses. As a result, Tellme had to determine whether to pursue a "get big fast" strategy (i.e., spending aggressively on brand building and customer acquisition) in its directory business, network business, or both.

On the directory side, pursuing a get big fast strategy would help Tellme secure its market leadership position among the independent voice directory services. It might also give Tellme significant first mover advantages relative to the Internet portals, making it more difficult for the portals to capture users once they were ready to launch their own voice services. On the network services side, the market was in such a nascent stage of development that no clear market leader had emerged, suggesting that it was an important time to invest in building a leadership position. Moreover, to date, Tellme had generated most of its revenue from the network side of the business, and the network business appeared to offer greater margins than the directory business, although the synergy between the two businesses made it difficult to disaggregate their respective contributions to overall profit growth. Given public and private investors' renewed interest in profitability following the technology stock market downturn in March 2000, Tellme's managers felt even more compelled to focus on its more profitable lines of business.

Having raised $238 million (including the Series D round) in just 14 months, Tellme had the financial resources to pursue a get big fast strategy. However, Tellme's management had to decide whether pursuing a get big fast strategy and being a first mover would help Tellme build a sustainable competitive advantage. Or, would aggressively pursuing a wide range of directory and network services deals exhaust Tellme's resources, dilute its focus, and diminish its perceived expertise in both markets? Was it important to pursue a get big fast strategy on both the directory and network services side simultaneously? How would investors react to a get big fast strategy? How would a get big fast strategy affect Tellme's organization? McCue had seen the effects of pursuing a get big fast strategy at Netscape, and was cautious. However, with the competitive landscape changing rapidly, he knew that he and his colleagues needed to decide whether and how to pursue an aggressive growth strategy.

Nicole Tempest prepared this case at the HBS California Research Center under the supervision of Professor Thomas Eisenmann as the basis for class discussion rather than to illustrate either effective or ineffective handling of an administrative situation.

Company Background

The concept behind Tellme's directory service was to offer audio-based directory access to the benefits of the Internet to anyone owning a fixed-line or wireless phone. Instead of using a computer, cell phone, or modem-equipped Personal Digital Assistant (PDA) to access Internet text and/or graphics by typing in commands, Tellme users dialed a toll free number from any phone (wireless callers incurred per minute usage charges from their carrier, but no long distance charges), then spoke commands to navigate within the voice directory, which delivered the requested information as pre-recorded or computer-synthesized voice output. As McCue described Tellme's directory service, "It's an online service for every phone."[1] Users of Tellme's branded directory service (1-800-555-TELL) could obtain information from a variety of categories, including weather, sports scores, traffic reports, news, and stock quotes (see Exhibit 1 for a list of Tellme's categories as of October 2000). Tellme also enabled users to connect free of charge to a host of outside services, including taxi companies and airlines. In addition, Tellme offered users a free two-minute phone call to anyone in the United States through its Tellme Phone Booth service.

Tellme's goal was to take advantage of the ubiquity and simplicity of the telephone to bring consumers the content and transactional capabilities of the Internet. As McCue explained, "I wanted to build something that my mom would use and understand. The everyday normal consumer who is fed up with technology angst and the complexity that's come about from the rise of the Internet can still use the Internet."[2] In 2000, there were approximately 1.7 billion telephone lines worldwide,[3] compared to only 150 million people with Internet access through personal computers and just 5 million with cell phones or PDAs equipped to receive wireless application protocol (WAP) Internet text. While many investors were excited about the potential for WAP-based mobile Internet services, many consumers—especially automobile drivers—balked at the prospect of having to view Internet text on tiny screens and having to type in commands using small keys. Given the ubiquitous availability of wireless and land-based telephones, the potential market opportunity for voice-enabled directories seemed enormous. The Kelsey Group estimated that 45 million Americans would be registered with what they described as "voice portals" by 2005.[4]

As a network service provider, Tellme helped companies build their voice applications, and then leveraged AT&T's network infrastructure to act as a "host" for operating those services. Tellme charged these customers a professional services fee for developing the voice application and a per-minute fee for hosting the service. Given the technical complexity of developing a robust speech recognition system and the high capital costs of the hardware and software required to operate a voice-enabled phone application, Tellme positioned itself as a cost-effective "one-stop-shopping" alternative to in-house development.

Management

Tellme's senior management team came from opposing sides of the Internet browser wars (see Exhibit 2 for the backgrounds of Tellme's senior managers). Tellme's founder, CEO, and chairman, Mike McCue, came from Netscape where he had served as vice president of technology, heading up the Netscape Communicator team. Prior to joining Netscape, McCue had been the founder and CEO of Paper Software, Inc.—a 3D Internet software manufacturer—that was acquired by Netscape in 1996. Both of Tellme's other co-founders, Angus Davis and John Giannandrea, also hailed from Netscape. Davis—known in the industry for his technical wizardry—started with Netscape when he was just 18 years old, making him Netscape's youngest employee for many years. Giannandrea served as Netscape's chief technologist for its browser group and was involved in releases 1.0 to 4.5 of the Navigator product. After AOL acquired Netscape, McCue, Davis, and Giannandrea began to develop their idea for a voice directory and network. As they worked on the plan, they turned to a longtime rival, Hadi Partovi, for help. Partovi, who was heading up Microsoft's Internet Explorer team, had been instrumental in helping Microsoft steal market share away from Netscape. While Partovi and McCue had been fierce competitors, they also had developed a

[1]"Calling the Web—Voice Portals Let You Use the Phone to Access the Net," *San Diego Union Tribune,* June 20, 2000, p. 127.

[2]Charles Piller, "Innovation at Last. An Internet Device That Really Is Simple to Use." *Los Angeles Times.* May 22, 2000, p. C1.

[3]"Portal in a Storm: Look No Hands! Now You Can Get the Latest Web Reports Over the Phone, Writes Lucy Atkins," *The Guardian,* August 24, 2000.

[4]May Wong, "Tellme Rolls Out Nationwide Service Offering Web-access from Phones," Associated Press Newswires, July 24, 2000.

deep respect for each other. As a result, Partovi signed on as Tellme's vice president of production in early 1999.

Funding

When Tellme's founders sought seed capital in 1999, they turned again to former rivals. Jim Barksdale, formerly CEO of Netscape, and Brad Silverberg, formerly a senior executive at Microsoft, joined forces in July 1999 to commit $6 million in seed stage financing to Tellme. Silverberg joined Tellme's board along with Peter Currie—a partner with Barksdale's venture capital firm, and formerly the CFO of Netscape.

Tellme raised its second round of financing in December 1999, attracting $47 million from Benchmark Capital and Kleiner Perkins Caufield & Byers, along with a follow-on investment from Barksdale and Silverberg. In May 2000, shortly after Tellme began testing its service, AT&T invested $60 million in the company. While specific terms of the deal remained confidential, AT&T would provide network access, call routing features, and marketing support for Tellme. The AT&T deal was a major achievement for Tellme's management team, since they had made an early decision to operate their own 1-800 number, rather than "sitting within" a major carrier and, therefore, being dependent on that carrier for distribution and marketing. Tellme's managers had seen other speech recognition services (e.g., Wildfire) struggle under that structure and vowed not to face that same situation. As McCue explained:

> The decision we made to not be dependent upon carriers was very important for the history of the company. We wanted to go direct to the consumer with an 800 number, which took a lot of guts. Now, it seems commonplace, but back then it was not at all obvious, because an 800 number is very expensive to run. However, once we had made the commitment and generated positive results from our trials, we were able to go to a company like AT&T in a position of strength and say, "Look, we've connected well with consumers and we have strong interest from prospective partners. How can you help us accelerate this?" AT&T's CEO, Mike Armstrong, and his staff were very excited about what we'd done, because we'd built a whole new use for their existing 800 network, which has become a mature business. They were willing to work out a very significant deal with us.

Milestones

Tellme began beta-testing 1-800-555-TELL in May 2000; three months later, in late July, the company officially launched the service. While Tellme had received considerable attention from the press, the company did not begin advertising until the official launch date. Even then, the company opted for a relatively limited media campaign, consisting primarily of billboards, busboards, and some radio ads in New York, Los Angeles, and San Francisco. Nevertheless, in its first month of operation, Tellme reported receiving one million calls and expected the number to grow to four million calls per month by year-end. Early usage patterns showed that users averaged five calls per month and call duration averaged four minutes per call.

Technology

Tellme's architecture combined elements of the "plain old telephone system" (POTS), the Internet, and speech recognition software. Calls to Tellme's platform were received through the traditional phone network on a toll free line. When the calls reached Tellme's platform, Tellme leveraged speech recognition software licensed from Nuance Communications Inc. (Nuance) to translate the caller's request into an Internet command, and then mapped it to a destination server. The server then retrieved the requested information from a select group of predetermined Internet sites. The information retrieved was formatted using VXML (Voice eXtensible Markup Language)—an emerging industry standard for creating voice-enabled Internet content and services accessible by phone. Lucent, IBM, AT&T, and Motorola—along with other companies in the speech, Internet, and communications markets—had worked together to develop the open VXML specification. As Maria Martinez, vice president and general manager of the Internet and Connectivity Solutions Division of Motorola explained: "Just as standardization of HTML [Hypertext Markup Language] drove the adoption of traditional Web applications, standardization of VXML will drive the adoption of voice-enabled applications."[5]

Tellme could only retrieve data from sites that supported VXML. Once Tellme had retrieved the VXML

[5]"AT&T, Lucent Technologies and Motorola Create VXML Forum; Companies Seek Open Standard to Promote Voice Access to Web Services." VoiceXML Forum Press Release. March 2, 1999.

data, its platform converted the data into spoken words, and delivered it back to the caller through the standard phone network. (See Exhibit 3 for a diagram showing Tellme's architecture.)

Speech recognition software, like that developed by Nuance Communications, had made significant advances during the late 1990s due to improvements in speech-recognition algorithms and in the price/performance of computers. Speech recognition was inherently complex due to enormous variability in speech patterns, including differences based on gender, age, race, accent, speed, and clarity of speech. As a result, speech recognition technology required computers to have high levels of both processing power and memory. Processing power was required to enable the computer to keep "real-time" pace with the speed of normal speech, while computer memory was required to hold the large database of linguistic data required to translate speech.

Based on these advances, by 2000, speech recognition accuracy rates were estimated to have reached 95%—the minimum required to render voice-enabled applications useful to consumers. As a result, the market for voice-enabled services had emerged. However, some serious limitations persisted, including the impact of background noise, which could drive accuracy rates below 70%. In addition, high pitched voices, children's voices, speech impediments, and accents reduced accuracy. Furthermore, accurately interpreting the *context* of language proved a challenge, although Lernout & Hauspie's Natural Language Understanding (NLU) software had made significant advances on that front. Industry pundits had mixed views on the potential for speech recognition. Professor Ken Stevens of the MIT Speech Research Lab believed that the technology had reached a plateau and required more work in the area of NLU.[6] Others, including Jupiter Communications, offered a more positive view: "After much tinkering, speech recognition technology is ready for prime time. Users may encounter some snafus, but their frustration will likely be mitigated by the fact the call [to a voice directory] is free."[7] While Tellme was proud of its overall speech recognition accuracy rates, the company still planned to utilize live operators to enter shipping information for its commerce applications, due to difficulties in accurately translating non-standard information such as users' names and addresses.

Speech synthesis involved a different set of technologies than speech recognition. Tellme had made a considerable investment in pre-recording as many words and messages as possible to avoid the use of computer-generated speech, which often sounded like a "drunken robot." In fact, to develop its database of pre-recorded information, Tellme had hired dozens of human readers to capture the millions of words necessary.

Consumer Directory

Content. As of October 2000, Tellme's 1-800-555-TELL service offered consumers 16 categories of content. By registering on Tellme's Web site, users could establish preferences for their favorite content (e.g., which stock quotes or horoscopes they wanted to hear) and for the delivery sequence of that content. If users did not register, Tellme as yet made no effort to deliver them personalized information or ads, even though many non-registered users called Tellme repeatedly from the same phone number.

Tellme could use the first few digits of the calling party's phone number to identify the neighborhood of a fixed-line caller and the home market of a cell phone user; Tellme used that information to provide locally tailored information (e.g., movie times, traffic, weather, restaurant recommendations.) However, Tellme was not yet planning to take "location-aware" services to the next level by exploiting the extremely precise location data available from global positioning system (GPS) equipped cell phones. As Partovi explained, "That doesn't mean we won't ever do that, but when something requires fancy new phones [i.e., with GPS chips], we prefer to wait until there are enough of them out there."

Over time, Tellme planned to add additional content categories to its directory service. To determine which categories to offer, Tellme took into account the proposed category's reach, its potential to drive call frequency, and its business model. Since voice directories incurred a per-minute charge associated with operating a 1-800 number, it was best if content categories generated enough revenue to cover the variable cost of the call. While Tellme planned to let consumer feedback dictate which categories to add, the ideal content was context sensitive (i.e., specific to time and/or place) and simple, with terse menu choices, since most people could hold

[6] Rony Douek, Jessica Kutash, Stefan Reyniak, "Speech Recognition on the Wireless Web," research paper submitted to Tom Eisenmann, April 28, 2000, p. 11.

[7] Seamus McAteer, *Speech Portals: The Next Mass Market Interactive Platform?* Jupiter Communications, p. 2.

only 5 to 9 menu items in their short-term memories and only had the patience to listen to 20 to 25 seconds of output (see Exhibit 4 for suitability rankings for voice directories).

One application that appeared to have strong consumer appeal was driving directions, which Tellme planned to beta-test in Q3 2000 with plans for a Q4 launch date. While Tellme expected that driving directions would generate high consumer reach and frequency, the standalone business model for them was questionable, since it would be difficult to generate enough revenue from promotions and sponsorships alone to cover the telecommunications costs associated with a long phone call.

Commerce. Tellme also planned to introduce commerce applications in Q2 2001. These applications would allow consumers to be connected to retailers in order to place verbal orders, with Tellme retaining a percentage of the transaction value. The Kelsey Group estimated that by 2005, 18 million "speech shoppers" would purchase $30 billion of goods and services, resulting in $2.8 billion in fees to voice directory services.[8] Industry analysts expected that consumers were most likely to use voice-activated commerce applications for replenishment items (e.g., groceries, health, beauty products) and for simple predetermined purchases (e.g., books, music, stocks); they were not expected to be well suited for purchases which required more in-depth research. While some industry analysts expressed concerns regarding consumers' willingness to provide credit card and personal identification numbers over the phone in public places, the voice-equivalent of a one-touch "wallet"—whereby a user provided all the pertinent information once, and thereafter simply directed retailers to use their wallet by saying a password—was expected to help address this problem.

Communications. In addition to content and commerce, Tellme also planned to offer consumers a series of communication applications. As of September 2000, Tellme's main communication application was its "phone booth" service, which offered users a free two-minute phone call to anywhere in the United States. The user simply dialed a number, was connected to that number for two minutes, and then returned to the Tellme service at the end of the call. The fact that Tellme brought the caller back to its service at the end of the call reflected a high degree of "call control." The Kelsey Group explained the concept and importance of call control:

> Users never "leave" the portal until they hang up. This implies an underlying element of call control—the portal can hang back while specific messages, tasks, or even calls to external public switched network numbers are made, then reappear to perform the next mission. This is the essence of stickiness and persistence, but the price is a call-supervision architecture that can recapture the caller after a discrete task is accomplished.[9]

Tellme also planned to add "voice dialing" during Q2 2001, which would enable users to upload their address books and make calls through Tellme simply by saying the person's name (e.g., "call mom"). While Tellme management had considered adding a "read my e-mail" feature due to the strong demand for such a service, they decided against it, at least over the near term, due to: (1) concerns about the business model for the application, specifically, whether it would generate sufficient revenue to cover variable costs; (2) complex challenges with synchronization[10] and with accessing e-mail servers through corporate firewalls; and (3) inherent problems with converting e-mail text into speech. As Partovi explained: "The speech synthesis software that converts text-based e-mail into spoken voice is really bad. The average consumer just can't understand what the computer is saying, or at a minimum, it's really choppy. Plus, if there are acronyms or misspellings—which occur frequently in e-mails—the software can't translate them."

Tellme was considering offering some of its more advanced communication and personalization options as fee-based ("subscription") services—similar to premium services in the cable business. However, Tellme management did not plan to offer subscription services until 2001 for two reasons. First, they wanted to position Tellme as a free service to boost adoption rates

[8]Mark Plakias, *Foundations of Speech Portals,* The Kelsey Group, February 2000, p. 17.

[9]Ibid, February 2000, p. 2.

[10]For each mode of e-mail retrieval—office desktop, home desktop, laptop, PDA, voice directory—users had to specify whether messages should be left on the e-mail server or removed upon receipt. Removal eliminated the need to review the same messages in multiple locations, but meant that past messages might not be available at a given location when needed. Users who accessed e-mail from multiple locations also had trouble: (1) keeping track of which e-mails they had responded to; and (2) maintaining a complete record of their responses at all locations. Users could solve these problems by copying themselves on all messages, but this increased message volume and thus meant more review time.

during the launch phase. Second, structuring billing arrangements was expected to be a complex task.

Tellme's Strategy

Tellme positioned itself as an "aggregator" that brought together consumers and businesses over the phone through its voice-activated directory and network. As McCue explained:

> You cannot separate Tellme into two separate businesses. Think of us as climbing a mountain. We're not going to stop at "camp 1" [directory services] or "camp 2" [network services]. Our goal is to reach the summit. We want to connect consumers and businesses in a whole new way, using voice recognition and the Internet. We monetize that connection by allowing businesses to build a presence on our network, then we provide a directory that allows consumers to access those businesses. Businesses pay us for professional services, per-minute usage fees, and for placement and promotion within 1-800-555-TELL.
>
> Don't think of us as a portal—a portal doesn't have a platform; it doesn't offer network services. They don't do any hosting. It's more accurate to think of us as providing the next generation of dial tone services that will allow businesses and consumers to connect more effectively than ever before.

The Kelsey Group estimated that the market for speech applications would reach $12.3 billion by the year 2005 (Exhibit 5), with $5.7 billion coming from the directory side (advertising, subscription fees, and commerce) and $6.6 billion coming from the network services side (hardware, software, and carrier fees.)

Since Tellme launched its consumer directory service ahead of its network services, Tellme had developed a reputation within the general public as a directory service. However, Tellme management explained that from the beginning, the concept behind Tellme had been to offer an integrated directory and network service that helped companies *build, run,* and *promote* their voice-enabled services. When the company was first developing its directory service, the engineering team realized how complex the technical integration issues were and how valuable Tellme's bundled "solution" would be to other companies. The complexity stemmed from the fact that none of the components required to voice-enable a site—telephone service, the Internet, and voice recognition technology—had been designed to work together, resulting in a daunting integration challenge. As Charles Moldow, Tellme's senior vice president of business development and sales, explained:

> This is a massive integration challenge. To build a voice-enabled phone presence, a company needs the right voice application software, extensive telecommunications infrastructure, experts in speech recognition and speech synthesis on staff—and the list goes on. But we've effectively built a bundled one-stop-shopping solution. It works like an operating system underneath our user interface. No one else has built anything nearly as extensive. So a company has the choice of cobbling together a voice-enabled service, working with multiple vendors, or having Tellme provide a complete solution. (See Exhibit 6 for services Tellme offered as part of its one-stop-shopping solution.)

Tellme executives pointed to examples of other companies which had successfully pursued "aggregator" strategies, including Broadcast.com (which had been acquired by Yahoo!) and Sony Playstation. In the case of Broadcast.com, the company offered consumers a destination Web site where they could hear live broadcasts from radio stations throughout the United States. At the same time, the company helped radio stations manage their Web broadcasting servers. The more radio stations Broadcast.com Web-enabled, the more consumers would visit Broadcast.com's site, and vice versa.

For Tellme, Zagat Survey (Zagat) provided a tangible example of how the aggregator strategy worked. Zagat surveyed thousands of frequent diners and compiled their restaurant reviews and ratings in paperback guides for over two dozen U.S. cities. In 1998, one of Zagat's competitors, Foodline, introduced a voice-activated information line for Boston residents which allowed callers to search for a restaurant, hear a review, and then be transferred to the restaurant to make a reservation. Foodline rapidly rolled out its service to other cities in 1999. Threatened by Foodline's aggressive strategy, Zagat decided that it needed to both further promote its brand and build its own easy-to-use phone-based information and reservation service. However, instead of developing the service in-house—which would have taken an estimated six months—Zagat turned to Tellme for development. In this "win-win" partnership, Tellme benefited from having a familiar and trusted brand on its voice directory, and from Zagat's promotion of 1-800-555-TELL on the back cover of its restaurant guides; Zagat benefited from Tellme's system integration and operations expertise, and from having Tellme promote its brand through 1-800-555-TELL.

Other large Internet companies, such as eBay and Amazon, also were considering options for developing their own voice-enabled phone services. While these companies believed that the phone represented an important channel for commerce, many were hesitant to tackle the complex technical integration issues in-house. Furthermore, if every Web company developed its own phone service, consumers would need to remember multiple phone numbers. As a result, Tellme executives believed there was a need for a "neutral" aggregator. As Moldow explained:

> There's a need for a Switzerland in this space. Amazon, Priceline, Sportsline, and eBay all are going to want to voice-enable their services. They can each have their own 800 number or they can live inside some aggregated service's phone number or both. But eBay won't want its voice-enabled auctions residing within Yahoo!, which offers competing auctions.

Over the long term, Tellme's vision was to become "dial-tone 2.0," meaning that callers would pick up the phone, automatically connect to Tellme, speak a name into the phone, and Tellme would connect the caller to that person. The goal was for Tellme to become as natural a part of using the phone as typing http://www was to using the Internet.

Tellme's Customers

Consumer Directory

Tellme's consumer voice directory was targeted at the "average American"—not the technically savvy person who was an early adopter of the latest technologies, nor the technically illiterate. As Partovi explained, "We're going after the average users. Tellme is not targeting the top 5% of connected elite, nor the unconnected bottom 15%."

By positioning itself squarely in the middle, Tellme aimed to tap into the large mass market for its service. While it was tempting for Tellme's engineering team to develop state-of-the-art applications, the company was careful to keep its focus on its target customer. Partovi noted, "It takes discipline to say that we don't want to target the Palm VII or WAP phone users. We're targeting soccer mom-types."

Network Services

On the network services side, Tellme helped companies build and (leveraging AT&T's infrastructure) operate their voice applications. Companies from a wide variety of industries looked to Tellme to voice-enable their front-end sales channel and/or their back-end customer service operations. As the Aberdeen Group explained:

> Telephone-based natural language speech-recognition applications solve the real problems large service businesses face every minute of every day. Whether it is a call to get information, to order a product, to pay a bill, to get support, or simply to reach someone in an organization, often the first impression customers have of an organization when they do business by telephone is the way their calls are handled by the interactive voice response (IVR) system [with IVR, the caller used touch-tone phone keys to enter a menu option and the service responded verbally with synthesized speech] or auto-attendant. For many organizations this first impression tends not to be a good one. Customers with touch-tone telephones must plod through slow, frustrating IVR menus, press the right buttons, and then they are usually put on hold. Or they "zero out" to a live attendant, who usually also puts them on hold. As everyone knows, all of this amounts to a serious quality-of-service problem. . . . Most people in the business community do not yet know that state-of-the-art telephone-based speech recognition applications are in fact now able to solve problems such as these, and more.[11]

Tellme's services ranged from developing voice-enabled applications and providing hosting services on a stand-alone basis, to offering a fully integrated solution whereby Tellme developed the service, hosted it, *and* included it on Tellme's consumer directory. (See Exhibit 7 for Tellme's terms of exchange with partners.) Due to the technical complexity associated with developing a voice-enabled channel, some industry analysts recommended that companies outsource both development and ongoing operations. To illustrate the level of investment required, Forrester Research noted: "Enterprise level speech systems will have to handle

[11]"Nuance Communications," The Aberdeen Group, 1999, p. 1.

thousands of calls simultaneously and scale to peak usage. Firms will have to add additional T1 lines and network hardware, coordinate Web team and telecom team efforts, and assign employees to manage the system."[12]

Given the push toward outsourcing, demand for Tellme's services outstripped its resources, making it important for the company to prioritize its efforts. McCue described Tellme's prioritization criteria:

> We apply three criteria when we evaluate potential business partnerships. First, does the partnership add value to the overall consumer experience? Boeing would love to give their employees access to their calendars, but we aren't going to execute on that opportunity ourselves because it doesn't add value to 555-TELL. Instead, we would probably have a certified third party partner build that sort of application for Boeing. On the other hand, our deal with Zagat to provide restaurant reviews does add lots of value to 555-TELL, so we would probably execute on that type of opportunity ourselves.
>
> Second, we take into account whether the deal is going to work for our business partner. For example, even though companies are willing to pay us to build e-mail applications, we've learned that listening to your e-mail over the phone just doesn't work yet for a whole variety of reasons. The same is true for doing a Web search over the phone. It doesn't make sense for us to put a lot of energy against applications that aren't ready for the marketplace.
>
> Third, we consider how much revenue the deal is going to generate for Tellme. Some companies are very focused on extracting revenue. They think they have this huge halo effect and Tellme should be paying them, instead of the other way around. But we're not interested in "loss leader" deals; we want long-term, predictable, sustainable revenues.

Structuring agreements with business partners helped Tellme refine its prioritization criteria. As Moldow explained: "These are big decisions, and our negotiations are helping us refine our strategy. We'd love to be able to sit in a room with a whiteboard and say, <this is exactly what we are.> But our business is moving too fast for that, so we're defining ourselves as we go, especially with respect to our partnership deals."

[12]"The Web's Speech Impediment," Forrester Research, April 2000.

Tellme's Business Model

Tellme generated revenues from four sources: professional service fees for designing a company's voice application, per-minute charges for hosting that company's voice application, sponsorship fees for promoting the company on Tellme's directory, and promotion fees from non-network partners who wanted to advertise on Tellme's directory service. As of fall 2000, most of Tellme's revenue came from professional service fees. However, as Tellme finished its development work, it would begin to receive hosting revenues, which were expected to run around $0.15 per minute—although the company expected competition to eventually put downward pressure on prices. Tellme estimated that it would cost a company between $.30–$.50 per minute to develop and operate a voice-enabled service itself. By way of comparison, an IVR call averaged $.35[13] and an operator-handled call ranged from $1.95 to $5.00 per call.[14]

In terms of promotion revenues, Tellme's goal was to monetize the eardrums that accessed its directory much in the same way that Internet portals tried to monetize the eyeballs that visited their sites. Tellme charged companies for promotion and sponsorship spots on Tellme's directory service. Sponsorship tended to be short—five seconds or less in length—(e.g., "Tellme News sponsored by E-Offering—the future of investment banking"), whereas promotions often enabled consumers to drill down to "hear more" or connect through to a merchant. Given an average call time of approximately four minutes, Tellme was able to deliver between two to three promotions or sponsorships per call. By way of comparison, companies were paying around $30 per thousand page views for banner ads on Web sites. Tellme expected its rates to increase over time as the service's reach expanded. However, over the near term, Tellme executives did not anticipate that the promotion and sponsorship revenue associated with commodity information (e.g., news headlines, sports scores) would cover variable costs. McCue explained, "Delivering commodity information is not at the core of our business model; it's a necessity, a convenience we provide to get people to call. We justify that as a cost of customer acquisition." Over time, Tellme also expected to generate revenue from

[13]Tony Floyd, "Creating a New Customer Experience," Bank Systems and Technology, January 2000, PR13.

[14]Nuance Communications, Amended SEC Form S-1.

transactions (where users purchased a good or service via the directory, and a percentage of the transaction value was retained by Tellme) and subscription services (premium services paid for by users.)

On the cost side, the per minute price charged by long distance telephone companies for 800 number service ranged from around \$.04 per minute for very high volume customers to \$.10 per minute for small-to-average volume customers. However, over time, these costs were expected to decline due to the ongoing deregulation of the telephone industry and the use of Internet Protocol (IP) telephony.[15] Tellme also incurred semi-variable costs associated with its "ports"—the hardware and software required to receive and process inbound and outbound calls. Each port handled one call at a time and cost approximately \$5,000, which was depreciated over two years.[16] Because users did not all call at the same time, one port could support between 200 to 1,000 users, depending on average call length and the share of users calling at peak times. In terms of fixed costs, Tellme employed 150 people as of September 2000. For Internet companies that did not employ large numbers of employees in call centers or warehouses, industry analysts typically estimated a company's total overhead (including salaries, rent, and outsourced professional services, but excluding marketing spending for customer acquisition) to be around \$200,000 per employee.

Competitors

Tellme faced competition from a wide variety of industry segments, including voice portals, voice ASPs (application service providers), software providers, WAP services, telecommunication carriers, and mass market Internet portals.

On the voice portal side, at least a dozen players were expected to launch their services by the end of 2000, making it a hotly contested marketplace, similar to the Web portal wars in the late 1990s. (See Exhibit 8 for background on voice directory competitors.) Tellme's competitors included a host of start-ups—BeVocal, Quack.com, TelSurf Networks, Audiopoint, and Talk2. All of these services were free to callers and offered much of the same core information, e.g., weather, stock quotes, traffic. The services tried to differentiate themselves on the breadth of content offered, ease of navigation, and the sophistication of their voice recognition systems. For example, on the content side, BeVocal offered callers local driving directions within California and TelSurf offered users the ability to read or send e-mails. Prior to its acquisition by AOL, Quack had teamed up with Lycos to enable callers to have audio access to their personalized portal home page. Many voice portals offered the ability to create personalized accounts, which allowed callers to specify the information they wanted and the delivery sequence they preferred.

While competition promised to be intense, Randy Corke, Quack's vice president of marketing explained, "The market is plenty big for several of us. There are billions of people with phones in this world."[17] On the other hand, many industry analysts were skeptical that all of the players could successfully differentiate themselves. As a result, they believed that an industry shakeout was likely, with Tellme emerging as a winner, given its strong early foothold in the market.

Tellme also faced competition from "pure-play" voice ASPs, including UCallNet and NetbyTel. Voice ASPs fell into at least seven categories based on their focus (Exhibit 9). For example, some ASPs focused on voice-enabling transaction-oriented businesses, while others focused on developing speech applications for wireless and wireline carriers. The Kelsey Group estimated that there were between 75–140 different players across the seven categories.

Providers of speech recognition software represented a potential competitive threat to Tellme. For example, Nuance, one of the leaders in speech recognition software—which developed the software used by Tellme—offered a complete speech recognition platform, including its Nuance 6 "engine," a set of development tools, and its Nuance Voyager speech browser. SpeechWorks International and Lernout & Hauspie offered similar products. While executives at Tellme acknowledged a compet-

[15]Deregulation would help reduce long distance rates as: (1) the Regional Bell Operating Companies (RBOCs) were granted permission to enter the long distance business; and (2) the RBOCs, facing competition from cable TV system operators offering local phone service and from other competitive local exchange carriers (CLECs), were pressured to decrease the access fees they charged long-distance carriers. IP telephony was inherently more cost efficient than the traditional circuit-switched phone network: IP telephony relied on packet switched technology, which broke a phone conversation into packets, co-mingled packets from many simultaneous conversations onto a single phone line, routed the appropriate packets to their respective destinations, and then reassembled them at the receiving end. By contrast, circuit-switched networks dedicated a line to a single call for its full duration.

[16]Port costs were expected to decline to \$2,000 per port over time as semi-conductor price-performance improvements reduced the cost of information processing and storage, according to Mark Plakias, *Foundations of Speech Portals,* The Kelsey Group, February 2000, Appendix B.

[17]Joshua Kwan, "Calling the Web. Voice Portals Let You Use the Phone to Access the Net," *The San Diego Union Tribune,* June 20, 2000, p. 6.

itive threat from this group, they were not overly concerned about it. According to Moldow:

> While outsiders might view Nuance as a competitor, we view them as a partner. Each time we sign up a network services customer, we buy another license from Nuance. So, in effect, we end up reselling their product, which is good for both of us. There are strong synergies between our two businesses.

WAP services represented a less direct competitive threat to Tellme. WAP (wireless application protocol) was an international open technology standard developed by Phone.com, Motorola, Ericsson, and Nokia, among others, that enabled wireless subscribers to access the Internet using wireless mobile devices. WAP essentially "translated" regular HTML text into a special stripped down version known as wireless markup language (WML) that was suited for display on the small screens of WAP-enabled phones and PDAs. WAP phones were introduced in the United States in 2000 and were priced from $50 on up, depending on the level of promotional support from wireless carriers. WAP service ranged from being free to costing $20 per month. Industry analysts were mixed on the market opportunity for WAP phones. Arguments against them included the fact that only a small percentage of Web sites had been WAP-enabled; they weren't able to display graphics; and a user couldn't browse the Web and receive a phone call at the same time. In short, WAP phones were best suited for the delivery of simple text-based information such as short message services (SMS), news headlines, sports scores, stock quotes, and weather forecasts. Jane Zweig, executive vice president for Herschel Shosteck Associates, Ltd—a telecommunications research firm—commented, "This content may never be interesting to people. It's text-based and very limited, and people will want more."[18]

Other analysts believed that WAP phones represented a complement (rather than a substitute) to the personal computer—one which offered users real-time information from the road. The Yankee Group estimated that by the end of 2000 there would be 15 million WAP phones in the United States out of a total of approximately 105 million wireless phones. While the jury remained out as to whether WAP phones would become a big success in the United States, wireless data services had already proven themselves in Japan, where in just 16 months, 8.4 million people had subscribed to I-Mode—the cell phone-based data service from Japan's telecom giant, Nippon Telegraph & Telephone. At that pace, I-Mode subscribers would exceed the number of modem-equipped PCs in Japan within two years.

Telecommunication (telecom) carriers (e.g., MCI, BellSouth) also represented a competitive threat to Tellme. In fact, Tellme management believed that in the end, telecom carriers might represent the greatest source of competition to Tellme, given their focus on network *and* directory services. On the one hand, offering a voice-enabled service was a natural fit for carriers since the major long distance carriers and RBOCs (regional bell operating companies) had an estimated 120,000 ports of excess capacity for handling voice recognition services.[19] On the other hand, developing a consumer directory and offering network services required a different skill set, making some analysts skeptical of the phone companies' chances for success. As Jupiter Communications noted, "Carriers lack the focus, media savvy, deal-making skills, ad sales force and entrepreneurial gusto to aggressively roll out a compelling service. Carriers are better advised to partner than to own a service."[20]

There were a number of ways that a carrier could partner with Tellme. For example, wireless carriers could bundle Tellme minutes into a rate plan or offer a voice directory "powered by Tellme." However, to date, most carriers had not taken any steps to enter the voice directory or network services markets. Some were taking a "wait-and-see" approach, while others simply had not yet focused on the markets. Moldow explained:

> Over the last few years, carriers have made big investments in WAP, since they viewed it as a way to use excess network capacity, tighten customer relationships, and tap into transaction revenues. But WAP adoption has been slower than expected since consumers have to purchase a new phone, subscribe to a new service, and then when it's up and running, consumers find out it's slow and has a clumsy user interface. Yet carriers have been so focused on WAP that they haven't spent much time thinking about voice-enabled services. Now that they've realized the magnitude of the voice opportunity, they've taken a 180-degree turn and they are very excited about the market. That said, if and when the WAP opportunity

[18]"The Next Thing or The Next BIG Thing," *Star Tribune Newspaper of the Twin Cities Minneapolis-St. Paul,* July 31, 2000, p. 1D.

[19]Mark Plakias, "Voice & Wireless Commerce," The Kelsey Group, June 2000, p. 7.

[20]"Wild Card: Tellme Becomes the Telco" from "Speech Portals: The Next Mass-Market Interactive Platform?" Jupiter Communications, May 3, 2000.

grows large enough to be attractive, we will be prepared with a service that integrates voice and data. This type of service will be well suited for applications like driving directions where the combination of voice and graphics can be very powerful.

Emerging Strategic Issues

By the fall of 2000, Tellme was making significant progress against its business plan. The company had launched its consumer directory service in July, had hired 150 people, and was weeks away from closing on a $125 million Series D round of financing. However, the competitive landscape was rapidly changing—as demonstrated by the AOL/Quack announcement—and Tellme had to quickly determine whether to step up its investment in marketing and promotion in order to pursue a "get big fast" (GBF) strategy in its directory business, network business, or both.

Over the past year, a half dozen start-ups had launched full-fledged voice directory services. Most of these services had attracted venture capital funding and had secured partnerships with established content providers, including some of the major Internet portals. The entrance of so many players in such a short period of time suggested that industry insiders believed that consumer demand for voice directory services would be strong. On the other hand, rapid growth in the number of players entering the market suggested that entry barriers were relatively low, especially since voice directory services could license one of the most complex technology components—speech recognition software. As a result, most industry pundits believed a shakeout would eventually occur, with Tellme emerging a winner among independent voice directories given its greater share of industry "buzz," the strength of its management team and investors, and its access to capital.

Another potential competitive threat in the directory business came from the major Internet portals who many industry analysts believed would eventually introduce voice-enabled services to fulfill their "anytime, anywhere" promises. Since the Internet portals already had large established user groups for which they already had collected a host of personal and preference data, many believed that once the portals launched a voice service, they would rapidly gain market share. In addition, given their established base of business partners, the Internet portals had the opportunity to quickly develop a host of content, commerce, and communication applications for their users, which could drive traffic to their voice services. Nonetheless, Tellme executives did not view Internet portals as a serious competitive threat. As McCue explained: "We don't compete with AOL or Yahoo—we have a fundamentally different business. AOL isn't going to spend time helping a company like eToys build its voice service, but we will, because it will enhance our directory service." Furthermore, executives at Tellme believed that most of the portals viewed voice services as more of a parity feature for their existing users than as a stand-alone growth opportunity. As Moldow explained:

> If you talk to AOL, they'll say they feel that this is a required service, something that their customers will demand as a result of the launch of standalone voice directories like Tellme; it's not something that AOL actually wants to do. It would cost them $50–$60 million to build their own platform and then they would face significant telecommunications costs to get things moving, and AOL is terrified of runaway telecommunication costs. So they are unlikely to push voice services aggressively—but they might offer them as a premium service. Our fundamental proposition is to create an *industry* around voice services, whether it be content, commerce, call center integration, or voice dialing. There are a lot of things that we want to do with our platform that I just don't see AOL doing.

Most analysts believed that the portals would focus first and foremost on voice-enabling their core messaging services, rather than on content or commerce applications. Ironically, messaging applications were some of the most technically difficult to develop and most challenging to monetize. McCue acknowledged that Internet portals were likely to deploy messaging applications, but felt this displayed a lack of understanding of user needs. Even if the Internet portals did attempt to enter the voice directory space, Tellme executives estimated that it would take them at least 6 to 12 months to develop a competitive service (6 months if they acquired one of Tellme's competitors, 12 months if they tried to do it themselves), allowing Tellme to maintain its significant first mover advantage.

Tellme's executives also did not believe that the Internet portals would aggressively pursue the network services business, given that it was too far afield from the portals' core business and would require too great an investment in technology and infrastructure. For example, Quack's service was built with proprietary software on a Windows NT platform, making it challenging to scale. In order to compete in the network services marketplace, Tellme executives believed that AOL would have to invest heavily in rebuilding Quack's platform.

Despite these arguments against the competitive threat posed by Internet portals, Forrester Research projected that the Internet portals would eventually emerge as winners in the voice services market, because consumers wanted information to be aggregated into a *single* location, especially their address and calendar information—which many consumers had already entered into an Internet portal's database.

As competition from independent voice directory services and Internet portals intensified, Tellme had to decide whether to invest heavily in marketing and sales to promote its directory service as part of a GBF strategy. GBF strategies tended to work for businesses characterized by strong network effects (i.e., users attracted more users), significant scale economies, and intrinsically high customer retention rates. Tellme's business matched these criteria. First, attracting more users to Tellme's consumer directory service helped the company build its network services business, which in turn helped the company build its consumer directory service (since businesses wanted to go where consumers were, and vice versa). In addition, as Tellme attracted more users, its reach would increase, enabling Tellme to raise its promotion and sponsorship rates. Finally, by integrating a broad range of content, commerce, and communications applications into Tellme's directory, the service had a good chance of becoming "sticky," meaning that consumers who had invested the time and energy into learning Tellme's interface and entering their personal data (e.g., "favorites," "wallet" information) would be less inclined to later migrate to a competitive service.

The fact that Tellme already had a significant lead in the directory marketplace argued both in favor of and against pursuing a GBF strategy. On the one hand, it was important for Tellme to protect its leadership position; on the other, with competitors ceding the market to Tellme, significant investment might not be necessary. Moldow summarized some of the arguments in favor of a GBF strategy:

> There's definitely an argument that says, "blow it out," spend $80 million on a 1999-style consumer branding campaign. We've got the cash. We've got partnerships on the cost side that will prevent us from "killing ourselves with success." And, we've got first mover advantage; the market really likes first movers, so we need to make sure we don't cede that position.

Pursuing a GBF strategy on the directory side also could help give Tellme an insurmountable first mover advantage relative to the Internet portals. As Moldow explained:

> A lot of the portals, like AOL, Yahoo!, and Microsoft's MSN, think that they can afford to wait and see whether companies like ours ever get traction before they do anything. The challenge for them is that we think we are sitting on a really good opportunity and we are building a solid first mover advantage.
>
> There's an analogy to eBay here. These companies all had the opportunity to acquire eBay early on, but they all passed because they couldn't justify its valuation. But eBay was growing like a weed and its valuation was going up with it. Eventually Yahoo! launched its own auction service, but there's no way they will ever catch the first mover in that market. So, at some point, they might have to double back and say, "Okay, I've got a $70 billion franchise. How important are auctions to the franchise? Should we keep investing in our own auctions, or just absorb eBay for $17 billion?

One way to pursue a GBF strategy was to partner with one or more of the major Internet portals. Not only could Tellme help voice-enable the portal itself, but it could also voice-enable the portal's business partners, giving consumers access to a host of services through the front-end portal. Portals would pay Tellme a professional services fee for developing their voice applications and then pay a per-minute fee to Tellme for hosting their voice-enabled service on Tellme's carrier-grade infrastructure. Given the per-minute fee structure, the more traffic the directory generated, the more revenue Tellme would earn—an attractive proposition for Tellme. While partnering with a major Internet portal would certainly help Tellme get big fast, executives at Tellme still had to decide whether helping an Internet portal voice-enable its services might pose a short-term competitive threat to Tellme's own branded directory service.

Tellme managers also had to decide how important pursuing a GBF strategy in its directory business was to its network services business, and vice versa. The network services business offered plenty of opportunities to get big fast since companies from a wide range of industries were interested in building voice channels. Pursuing a GBF strategy on the network side could help Tellme establish itself as one of the leading players in the market. By investing heavily in an enterprise sales force, Tellme could aggressively pursue large customers who were actively searching for a voice solution to their business needs. By attracting a handful of high profile customers, Tellme could rapidly build its credibility in the network services business. Furthermore, since the margins in the network services business were attractive, pursuing a GBF strategy could shorten Tellme's path to profitability—an important issue for investors in late 2000.

However, pursuing a GBF strategy on the network side required growing the organization, since each customer required a customized solution. McCue discussed his experience with this at Netscape:

> The reason Netscape failed was they got too big, too fast. I'm determined to make sure this doesn't happen at Tellme. I would much rather be in a position where we prioritize and turn down opportunities than try to grow too fast to absorb all our opportunity. I'd rather have fewer employees who are really, really great than some whom are great, some of whom are mediocre. The DNA for this company is all about great people.

Pursuing both a GBF strategy on the directory side *and* the network services side had even greater implications for the size and growth of Tellme's organization. However, given Tellme's role as an aggregator, the company might have little choice *but* to pursue both markets aggressively if they adopted a GBF strategy. It was a complicated issue, as Moldow explained:

> Does getting big fast and being a first mover help you win in the network services business? In the directory business? By moving aggressively in both directory and network services, do we risk becoming a jack-of-all-trades, master of none?

Tellme executives knew that pursuing a GBF strategy posed a fair amount of risk for a start-up company in an emerging market. Changes in the market and competitive landscape could occur quickly, and it was important for Tellme to remain nimble in order to respond rapidly and effectively. On the other hand, *not* putting a stake in the ground and moving forcefully to shape the market and establish a leadership position also posed its own significant threats.

The Future

Industry pundits held widely opposing viewpoints on the future of voice-enabled services. On the bullish side, the Kelsey Group offered this perspective:

> The Kelsey Group anticipates increased velocity from DTMF (touch-tone) interfaces to speech recognition. Indeed, by 2005, touch-tone user interfaces will be a curious relic—much as it is highly unusual to get a busy signal today in an environment of highly penetrated voice mail.[21]
>
> Several generations of Americans have been trained to "call now, it's free" using 800 networks. The Voice ASP model is based on solid foundations of phone commerce—the original e-commerce platform. Voice ASPs are not just speech-enabling the Web—they are writing the newest chapter in the long history of phone-based commerce.[22]

Jupiter Communications offered an even more bullish outlook:

> As speech technology evolves, dial pads will disappear from cellular phones by 2008. Callers will say the name of the person they want to speak with or look up the name in a speech-driven directory and be connected automatically. In place of a dial pad, phones will incorporate a color screen that is used to graphically display data requested by a caller from a content provider.[23]

On the other hand, Forrester Research painted a dimmer view:

> Although voice technology vendors are bullish about speech-enabled content and commerce, today's applications face serious technical and human factor limitations. The range of commercially-viable applications will be confined to a small subset of Web content, affecting only a handful of providers. Despite the hype, few firms need a short-term voice strategy.[24]

As the market leader on the consumer directory side and a credible—although relatively unproven—force in the network services market, Tellme had the potential to shape the market's evolution. With the company receiving positive press and raising a sizable war chest, many analysts believed that in the end, it was Tellme's game to lose—at least in the directory business. While McCue and his team were excited about the opportunity they faced, McCue also knew from his Netscape experience how quickly opportunity could slip away due to poor strategic decisions. As a result, he knew it was critical to carefully assess whether to pursue a get big fast strategy. In light of the recent AOL/Quack announcement, McCue felt an even more urgent need to develop a shared perspective on this issue with his management team.

---

[21]Plakias, Mark. *Foundations of Speech Portals.* The Kelsey Group, February 2000, p. 15.

[22]Plakias, Mark. *Voice ASPs: Teleservicing the New Economy.* The Kelsey Group, June 2000, p. 15.

[23]"Wild Card: Tellme Becomes the Telco" from "Speech Portals: The Next Mass-Market Interactive Platform?" Jupiter Communications, May 3, 2000

[24]"The Web's Speech Impediment," Forrester Research, April 2000.

Exhibit 1

TELLME CATEGORIES AS OF OCTOBER 10, 2000

Blackjack:	Enabled callers to play a game of blackjack against a Tellme dealer.
Election:	Enabled callers to take a quick poll on the 2000 presidential election.
Horoscopes:	Offered callers today's, yesterday's, and tomorrow's horoscope by sign.
Lottery:	Allowed callers to receive the results of statewide lottery games for all 50 states.
News:	Offered callers headline news from CNN and *The Wall Street Journal.*
Movies:	Allowed callers to search for movie locations and times at any theater in the United States.
Phone Booth:	Enabled callers to make a free two-minute call to anywhere in the United States.
Restaurants:	Helped callers locate restaurants by city or type of food. Enabled callers to access Zagat restaurant reviews and connect directly to a particular restaurant to get directions or make a reservation.
Soap Operas:	Enabled callers to receive the latest update (and the previous day's update) on 10 of the most popular soap operas.
Sports:	Offered callers scores, game times, and updates for teams in the NBA, NFL, NHL, and Major League Baseball, among others.
Stock quotes:	Offered callers stock quotes (20 minutes delayed) on any publicly traded company or on one of four major market indices. Also offered callers Market Updates from *The Wall Street Journal Radio,* stock fundamentals (e.g., stock highs/lows, P/E ratios), and headline news on companies.
Taxi:	Enabled callers to be connected to a local taxi company. Tellme offered listings for approximately 8,000 taxi companies in the United States.
Time:	Offered callers the exact time from anywhere in the United States.
Traffic:	Offered callers up-to-the-minute traffic reports for many metropolitan areas.
Travel:	Allowed callers to be connected to major airlines, hotels, and rental car agencies. Tellme offered listings for over 150 domestic and international airlines, 50 major hotel chains, and 11 national rental car agencies.
Weather:	Offered callers the latest information (and extended forecasts) on weather for over 35,000 cities in the United States.

Source: *www.Tellme.com*

Exhibit 2 TELLME MANAGEMENT

Mike McCue: Chief Executive Officer, Chairman, and Founder

Prior to joining Tellme, McCue served as vice president of technology at Netscape, where he played a leading role in establishing product, technology, and business strategy for the company's client, portal, and server businesses. Prior to Netscape, McCue was the founder and CEO of Paper Software, Inc., a leading provider of 3D Internet software. Paper Software was acquired by Netscape in 1996.

Angus Davis: Director of Production, Co-founder

Prior to co-founding Tellme, Davis was with Netscape since 1996. Davis served as product manager for Netscape's Communicator product, and later oversaw Netscape's next generation browser technology, code-named "Gecko." Davis also worked in Netscape's technology group where he prototyped next-generation products and services, oversaw due diligence on potential acquisition targets, and contributed to the company's legal strategy.

John Giannandrea: Vice President Platform Development, CTO, and Board Member

Prior to joining Tellme, Giannandrea served as chief technologist and principal engineer in the browser group at Netscape/AOL where he was involved in releases 1.0 to 4.5 of the Navigator product. At Netscape, Giannandrea also led the development of many Web browser technologies and contributed to many Web standards and protocols. Prior to joining Netscape, Giannandrea worked on the Telescript and MagicCap technologies at General Magic.

Hadi Partovi: Vice President Service Production and Board Member

Prior to joining Tellme, Partovi served as group program manager for Microsoft's Internet Explorer team, where he was responsible for product strategy, design, and project management. Partovi oversaw four major releases of the Explorer product.

Charles Moldow: Senior Vice President Business Development and Sales

Prior to joining Tellme, Moldow was general manager of MatchLogic—a digital marketing technology and solutions company from *Excite@Home.* Before @Home's merger with Excite, Moldow served as vice president of @Media sales and marketing, where he forged relationships with over 150 content providers. He also oversaw @Home's Interactive Advertising Group and previously served as vice president of business development for @Home Network. Prior to joining @Home, Moldow worked at TCI where he was part of the founding team for @Home. Prior to TCI, Moldow worked at Merrill Lynch.

Andrew Volkmann: Vice President Finance and Administration

Prior to joining Tellme, Volkmann was the senior director of finance at Netscape where he was responsible for financial planning and analysis for Netscape's Netcenter division. Prior to that, Volkmann served as the director of finance for the research, development, and marketing groups within Netscape's enterprise software division. Prior to Netscape, Volkmann served as a product line finance manager at National Semiconductor and as worldwide planning manager at Hitachi.

David Weiden: Vice President Marketing and Business Solutions

Weiden joined Tellme from AOL where he was vice president for Community, Communications and Instant Messaging products and drove registered users to over 50 million. Prior to AOL, David was vice president and general manager of Netscape's directory and security business. Weiden worked at Morgan Stanley and McCaw Cellular prior to Netscape.

Exhibit 3 TELLME'S ARCHITECTURE

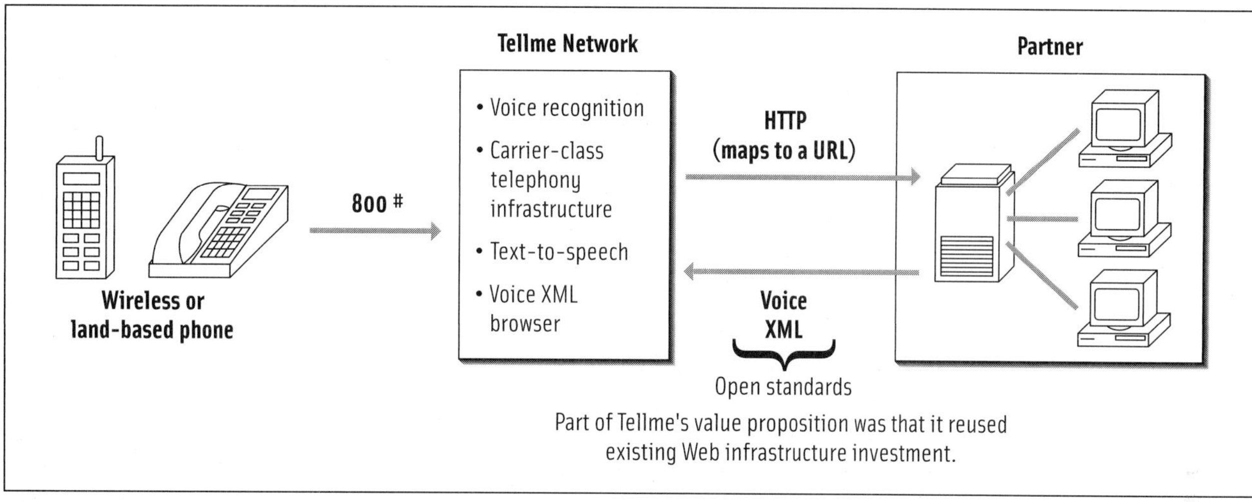

Source: Company interviews

Exhibit 4 VOICE DIRECTORY SUITABILITY RANKINGS

Applications	Brief	Personalized	Recorded
Horoscope	Yes	Yes	Yes
Shopping, replenishment[a]	Yes	Yes	Yes
Sports stories	Yes	Yes	Yes
Weather	Yes	Yes	Yes
Personal calendar	Yes	Yes	Partially
Stock prices	Yes	Yes	Partially
Traffic	Partially	Yes	Yes
News	No	Yes	Yes
Shopping, considered[b]	No	Partially	No
Email	No	Partially	No
Directions	No	No	No

Legend: ● Yes; ◐ Partially; ○ No

Source: Adapted from Forrester Research, Inc.
Note: The greater the number of yes's, the better the fit with a voice directory service.
[a]E.g., groceries, pharmaceuticals.
[b]E.g., clothing, books, furniture, automobiles.

Exhibit 5 PROJECTED MARKET SIZE FOR VOICE SERVICES, 2005 ($ BILLIONS)

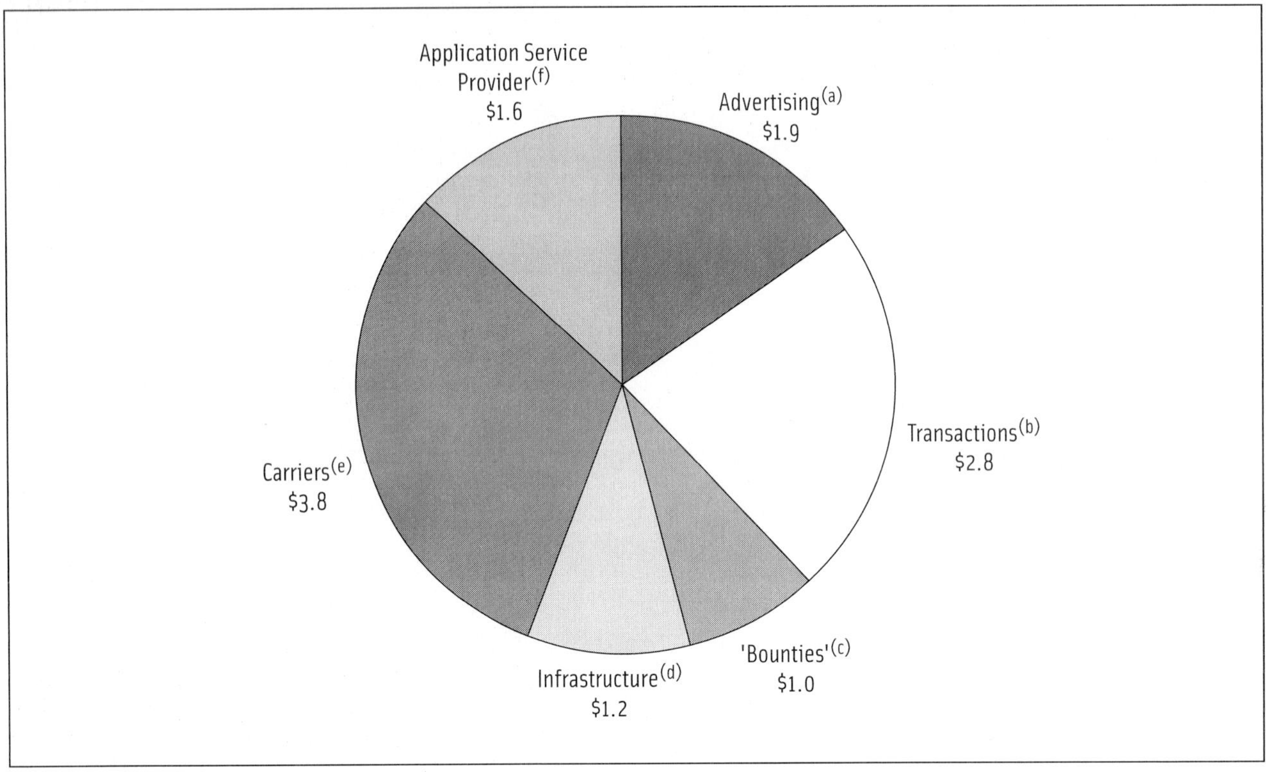

Source: Adapted from Mark Plakias, *Foundations of Speech Portals,* The Kelsey Group, February 2000, p. 17

Notes: (a) Revenue portal receives from impression-based advertising and sponsorships. Advertising can range from short branding announcements to "clickable" audio banner ads that allow callers to drill down to hear more. Sponsorships enable "anchor tenants" to pay for the right to be the first/default provider of specific voice-commerce or information categories.

(b) Revenue portal receives from purchases of goods and services made through its service. Portals retain a percentage of the transaction value.

(c) Revenue portal receives from wireless network operators and other service providers who sell subscriptions to users for an ad-free service.

(d) Includes revenue derived from software integration, user interface design, and speech object development associated with developing speech applications. Also includes licensing fees charged by the suppliers of automated speech recognition (ASR) technology.

(e) Revenue generated by wireline or wireless networks as a result of incremental traffic across their networks.

(f) Per-minute charges levied by application service providers for hosting speech portal applications and services.

Exhibit 6 SERVICES TELLME OFFERED AS PART OF ITS "COMPLETE" SOLUTION

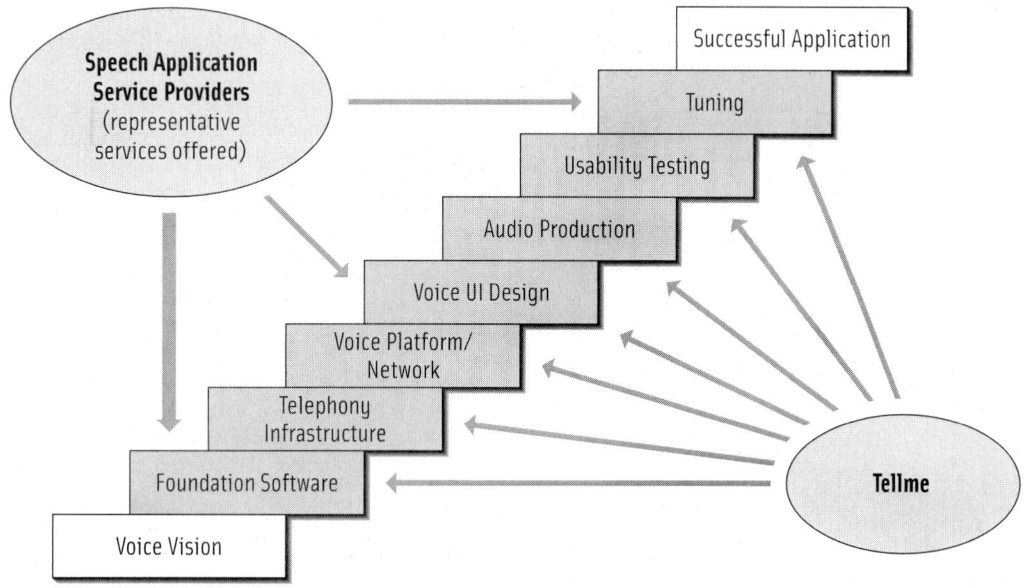

Source: Tellme marketing materials

Exhibit 7 TELLME'S TERMS OF EXCHANGE WITH BUSINESS PARTNERS

Tellme Provides:	Partner Provides:
Platform services	Money (through per-minute and one-time setup fees)
Hosting	Brand association and promotion of 1-800-555-TELL (if they get a Tellme keyword)
Telecommunications minutes	Traffic to 1-800-555-TELL
A separate 800 number (for some partners)	
A Tellme keyword (for some partners)	
Promotion within the Tellme portal (for some partners)	
Professional services; e.g., how to improve service performance (for some partners)	

Source: Company interviews

Exhibit 8 VOICE PORTALS (AS OF MID-OCTOBER 2000)

Voice Portal	Phone	URL	Date Founded	Date Launched	Key Investors	Key Points of Differentiation
Audiopoint	888-38AUDIO (888-382-8346)	*www.myaudiopoint.com*	June 1999	December 1999	NextGenCapital, LLC	–Billed itself as "first" voice portal –Offered more in-depth business news –Allowed for advanced customization options
BeVocal	800-4BVOCAL (800-426-6225)	*www.bevocal.com*	March 1999	June 2000	Mayfield Fund, US Venture Partners, Technology Crossover Ventures, Trans-Cosmos USA, Angels	–Emphasized location-relevant content such as turn-by-turn driving directions and the address of the nearest FedEx drop-off box
HeyAnita	800-444-ANITA (800-442-6484)	*www.heyanita.com*	August 1999	October 2000	SOFTBANK Capital	–Callers could have their Yahoo! e-mails read to them over the phone; other e-mail services to be added in the future –Had a well-developed international strategy, including a joint partnership with Korea Telecom
Quack.com	800-73QUACK (800-737-8225)	*www.quack.com*	November 1998	April 2000	Acquired by AOL in September 2000. Prior to AOL, investors included Jefferson Partners, Bid.com, and ELab Technology Ventures	–Offered callers many opportunities to personalize the service
Talk2	N/A	*www.talk2.com*	October 1998	Not launched yet; expects to have signed up at least one wireless carrier by early 2000	Hewlett-Packard, Smart Technology Ventures, NewMedia Venture Partners, SunAmerica Investments, Thomas Weisel Partners, Oracle Corporation, BlueVector	–Focused on the enterprise market, offering secure voice access to corporate e-mail, enterprise applications, and m-commerce. Positioned itself as an add-on service for wireless telecommunications companies' business customers
TelSurf	800-TEL-SURF (800-835-7873)	*www.888telsurf.com*	January 1999	February 2000 in select markets	Angel-backed	–Callers could have their Yahoo! e-mails (and any POP3 e-mail) read to them over the phone – Partnership with Yahoo! also enabled callers to have news items from their MyYahoo! page read to them – Offered an audio calendar which enabled callers to dictate appointments and have them read back later on

Source: Literature search, company Web sites

Exhibit 9 SEGMENTATION OF VOICE ASPS

Type	Estimated Number of Players	Estimated Number of Ports (today)	Examples
Transactional ASP[a]	5–10	<20,000	NetBy Tel, UcallNet, Voci, ShopTalk
Contact-Centric ASP[b]	10–15	<30,000	Tellme, BeVocal, HeyAnita
Incumbent/Contact[c] *Centric*	25–50	150,000	BFD, Call Interactive, Nextlink Interactive, PriceInteractive, USAN, West Teleservices
Carrier/VRU[d]	6–12	120,000–150,000	AT&T InfoWorx, MCI, Sprint PROMO, Pacific Bell Info Services
Carrier ASPs[e]	5–10	<10,000	Parigon, Talk2, Quack, Voice Access, Wildfire
Multi-Modal/Incumbent[f]	20–35	50,000–75,000	Xpedyte, Hanover
Multi-Modal/ASP[g]	3–5	<10,000	Inzigo, Conita, BeVocal

Source: Adapted from Mark Plakias, *Voice ASPs: Teleservicing the New Economy,* The Kelsey Group, June 2000, pp. 10–11

Notes: (a) Transactional Application Service Provider (ASP): This category consists of ASPs focused on order capture and speech-enabled commerce. Typically, the ASP allows phone access to existing online shopping sites.

(b) Contact-centric ASP: This category is a more general-purpose ASP using speech to allow access to a broad range of applications, usually through a portal infrastructure that provides callers with easy navigation to multiple sources and speech sites.

(c) Incumbent/Contact-centric: This category covers existing players offering touch-tone-based (DTMF) access to customer service applications.

(d) Carrier/Voice Response Unit (VRU): This is the domain of the three major long-distance carriers' toll-free-based voice response platforms. These are used for both pre-call routing and playing voice information and/or additional enhanced applications such as promotional contests, order capture, and screening.

(e) Carrier ASP: This covers ASPs that are specifically focused on providing private-label speech applications for wireless (and wireline) carriers.

(f) Multi-model/Incumbent: This category covers existing players who provide multiple media types to clients on both an inbound and outbound basis. Examples include fax broadcast, reverse 911, voicemail broadcast, and playing outbound pre-recorded messages.

(g) Multi-model/ASP: This is an emerging area of specialization that combines speech-enabled inputs with data (i.e., e-mail, WAP) or fax output.

3

Online Content Providers

This chapter describes online content providers, companies that use the Internet to distribute copyrighted content, including news, music, games, books, movies, and many other types of information. This content is usually produced in-house by the online content provider itself, but sometimes it is licensed from another party. Often, the content has been "repurposed" for the Web (like most of the content on *The New York Times* website), having originally been created for an offline medium. Sometimes, however, the content has been uniquely developed for Internet consumption (like the online magazines Salon.com and Slate.com).

The first section of the chapter defines the online content provider business model, explains the differences between that model and the business models employed by some other Internet companies (such as portals, online retailers, and online brokers), and describes different ways to categorize the content available on the Web. The second section presents a summary of the various ways that online content providers create value for their customers. The third section analyzes the economic model for online content providers, focusing on their revenue and cost drivers. Building on that analysis, the fourth section examines the payoff to online content providers from pursuing a "Get Big Fast" strategy, i.e., investing aggressively in customer acquisition and brand building. The final section explores a series of management and strategy issues relevant to online content providers, including (1) When does it make sense to pursue a hybrid strategy, combining the online content provider model with another Internet business model, such as retailing? (2) What unique challenges do offline content companies face when they move their business online? (3) What opportunities and challenges does the emergence of broadband infrastructure pose for online content providers? and (4) What are the tradeoffs for an online content provider considering whether to "syndicate," i.e., license its content for redistribution by other websites?

Assistant Professor Thomas Eisenmann and Research Associate Alastair Brown prepared this note as the basis for class discussion.

WHAT ARE ONLINE CONTENT PROVIDERS?

Definition

In our everyday lives we run across many different forms of content, or "something expressed through some medium, such as speech, writing, or a work of art."[1] We consume offline content through a range of media, including printed books, magazines, and newspapers; broadcast television and radio programs; and music CDs. Online content, however, can be consumed over a network, using desktop and laptop computers, cell phones, personal digital assistants, TV set-top converter boxes, or other digital devices.

Online content providers are defined here as companies that are engaged principally in the delivery to consumer and business users of professionally-produced, copyrighted content. The stuff being delivered, be it a song, video game, or news article, was created by people who make their living as content producers. Somebody owns a copyright to their work—i.e., the legal right to exploit the content commercially. The content's *producers* may themselves be employed by the online content *provider*, or they may work for a third party. In other words, content providers may be vertically integrated into both content production and distribution, or they may serve strictly as distributors of content created by others, having licensed the exclusive right to exploit that content on the Web, specifically, the right to determine who may or may not exhibit or resell the material online.

A key distinction in the definition of content providers is between professionally produced and "user-generated" content. Many websites enable users to communicate with each other through chat rooms and bulletin boards. Such messages may be a very rich form of content and may create considerable user traffic and "stickiness," i.e., long sessions by individual users. However, because such content is provided by users free of charge, websites (such as GeoCities, Tripod, and theglobe.com) that generate most of their page views from user-generated content have a very different business model than sites that deliver professionally-produced content. That model—referred to as "online community builder"—is not discussed in this chapter.

Distinctions Between Internet Business Models

The distinction between online content providers and other Internet business models can easily be blurred, as demonstrated by the following examples. First, consider the difference between online content providers and portals. Portals provide navigational assistance to users; they aggregate and organize links to third-party destination sites into useful categories (channels), then point users to sites where they will find relevant content or commerce offerings.[2] A portal may *re*distribute some content that has been syndicated by an existing online content provider (see the discussion of syndication in the final section). However, most of a portal's page views will come from search results and from linking users to its partners' content or commerce offerings.

Second, is bn.com (Barnes & Noble's website) acting as an online content provider when it sells Robert Ludlum's *The Hades Factor* in "eBook" format, i.e., as a digital file that can be downloaded to a customer's PC? No, bn.com is an online retailer in this case. It has not licensed online distribution rights, and thus does not control who can and cannot sell the eBook online. Those rights are held by St. Martin's Press, the book's publisher.[3]

Third, online content providers may be confused with online brokers, which help clients find other parties with whom the client might do business, and which sometimes negotiate transactions on behalf of their clients.[4] Brokers usually collect and process a great deal of information that is professionally-produced and frequently is copyrighted. So, are brokers really content providers? By our definitions, they are not. A broker's central purpose is to represent one party in a transaction; the content they distribute is a means to an end—a successful transaction. By contrast, for online content providers, transmitting information is an end in itself—their central purpose.[5]

CNET, a self-described "information intermediary" which focuses on technology products and services, illustrates how a company can simultaneously play the roles of content provider, portal, and broker.[6] CNET has a staff of several hundred editors who write reviews of computer products and news articles about technology trends—it clearly operates as a *content provider* in this regard. However, to provide users with comprehensive and convenient access to all the resources they may need in researching and purchasing technology products, CNET also provides links to (1) third-party content sites, including articles published by its direct competitors (a *portal* role), and (2) offers comparative pricing data for a full range of online retailers, then provides links to those retailers, so users can purchase computer goods after they have completed their research (a *broker* role).

Content Categories

Having defined the online content provider business model and delineated it from other Internet business models, we next examine different ways to categorize online content. One way is to ask how and why the content will be used, which draws a distinction between (1) news (e.g., CNN.com, MSNBC.com), (2) information (e.g., CNET, MapQuest.com), and (3) entertainment (e.g., QuokkaSports, MP3.com). Although most websites tend to specialize, a single website may provide all three content types. For example, on ESPN.com, one can access sports scores (news), participate in fantasy baseball leagues (entertainment), and, in its "Training Room" section, find information on exercise and nutrition programs (information).

A second categorization approach asks how long content will be relevant after it is produced. By definition, most news (including sports scores, weather forecasts, and stock quotes) is quickly obsolete. By contrast, although sporting events tend to be carried live, most other entertainment content (e.g., books, music CDs, movies, and video games) tends to have a much longer "shelf life." The Internet offers advantages in delivering both short- and long-lived content: Users can access short-lived news on a "24/7" basis, and they can retrieve long-lived content from archives that have virtually unlimited storage capacity. However, live events pose a problem on the Internet due to its point-to-point architecture. Using such an architecture to serve the same content to many simultaneous users (e.g., a Victoria's Secret fashion show) is an inherently inefficient way to use limited bandwidth. Point-to-multipoint technologies (e.g., TV or radio broadcasting) are much more effective for transmitting ("streaming") live events.[7]

A third way to categorize online content is by how one pays to receive it: (1) indirectly, i.e., by viewing advertising, (2) upon each use, e.g., based on time spent on the site, (3) through outright purchase, e.g., through digital download of an eBook, and (4) by subscription. Although a large number of online content providers rely on advertising for the dominant share of their revenue, some sites employ multiple payment methods, e.g., WSJ.com—the website of the *Wall Street Journal*—charges a subscription payment to its users, carries advertising, and charges for each article accessed from its archives.

Fourth, online content may be categorized by the bandwidth required for its delivery. At one extreme, text requires only modest bandwidth; at the other extreme, delivering high quality, full-motion video requires a high-bandwidth connection—unless the content can be cached in advance on the user's hard disk for later retrieval.

HOW DO ONLINE CONTENT PROVIDERS CREATE VALUE FOR USERS?

Information wants to be free.

— Hackers' dictum, attributed to Stewart Brand[8]

Online content providers create value for consumers in many ways. They do so first and foremost by following their fundamental economic imperative: Produce once, then distribute widely. Compared to most goods and services, which incur a variable cost in their production and delivery, information content has unusual economics: Information is often expensive to *produce* initially, but inexpensive to *reproduce* subsequently. For the same reason that a printed newspaper costs just 50 cents, CNN.com can be accessed for free. Scale economies in content production and distribution are amplified on the Internet, because the physical carrier of the content (e.g., the printed paper, the CD) can be eliminated. Information stored in digital form can be copied and distributed over a network almost for free.

Second, online content providers create value because they are available at any time of the day from any place with network access. If an earthquake were to strike California at five in the morning, an online newspaper would carry the story immediately, whereas readers of its print sibling could not receive this news until the following day, because the newspaper's hundred-million–dollar printing presses and hundreds of delivery vehicles cannot be put instantly into motion. The immediate availability of information is vital for certain applications, such as day trading.

Third, the sheer amount of information that can be accessed online dwarfs the capacity of any offline medium, such as a book. In the same way that indices, references, and footnotes serve to integrate a book into a larger body of knowledge, the interactive nature of the Web allows users to instantly explore links to a vast array of related sources—without requiring a return trip to the library. In this way, an online classified ad can be much richer than an ad displayed in a newspaper. A "help wanted" ad, for example, can provide more information about the position and a link to the prospective employer's website. And because online job seekers can conduct keyword and parametric searches of classified ad databases, they can access relevant job listings more easily.

Fourth, a website can "remember" a user's preferences and thereby tailor an experience to his or her personal needs. For example, many content sites ask consumers whether they would like to receive e-mails containing news or information about specific topics. Furthermore, technology advances, such as the cookie[9], allow companies to monitor page views and behavior on a website. For example, BET.com, a portal targeted to African-Americans, planned to use such technologies to dynamically serve relevant content to its users. Someone who accessed a story on the incidence of heart disease among blacks might subsequently see a story about healthy foods and might be served an advertisement for a home blood pressure monitor.[10]

Fifth, online content providers can create value for the user by unbundling different types of content that historically had been aggregated into a single offline media product, in order to exploit scale economies in production and distribution processes.[11] Newspapers provide a classic example of this unbundling phenomenon. Offline, many different content elements are bundled into a printed newspaper—e.g., headlines, classified ads, stock quotes, comics, "circulars" for grocery stores, and sports scores. Many readers have little interest in certain elements, but they might welcome even more content of a given type. However, all readers receive the same product: Printing technologies cannot affordably handle the "mass customization" of hundreds of thousands of newspapers, and even if they could, dropping a unique product onto each subscriber's driveway every morning would be an enormous logistical challenge. To accommodate scale economies in newspaper production and distribution, "one size fits all." Every day, retirees get the help wanted ads and families who own no individual equities get the stock tables.

Sixth, consumers can benefit from the networking capabilities of online content providers. For example, a "role-playing" adventure game entitled Ultima Online allows 25,000 players to be logged in at the same time, interacting in the same virtual world. Remarking on the rich experience that such multi-player games provide, *Computer Gaming World's* editor in chief, Johnny Wilson said "role-playing games will be the true religion of the twenty-first century."[12] While this may be an overstatement, wouldn't a gamer rather be in the middle of a war with thousands of troops running in each direction, requiring collaboration, planning, and execution, than fighting a static computer generated enemy?

Seventh, online content providers can create value for consumers—albeit illegally—from the costless copying of copyrighted materials. As content is digitized, it becomes easier to copy. In this way, computer programs, music, movies, and books that are traditionally protected by copyright laws are at risk of piracy. Content providers have tried many approaches for preventing piracy, including elaborate encryption and registration, yet most approaches have been, at best, only moderately successful. Determined hackers can break most encryption codes, and rigorous registration schemes tend to inconvenience consumers (e.g., when they replace their PC, then try to reinstall software authorized for use on a single machine).[13]

Napster, a website that facilitates the sharing of MP3s that users have "ripped" from music CDs and stored on their PCs, is a recent example of this phenomenon.[14] Using Napster and a high speed Internet connection—available in most college dormitories—it is possible to find almost any song ever recorded and to download an entire CD within five minutes. Fueled by these benefits and by strong network effects (i.e., new users increase the value of a networked service, thereby attracting more new users), Napster grew at an exponential rate during 1999 and 2000. Record companies have accused Napster of piracy; Napster has countered that it simply facilitates the exchange of files between its users, and cannot control their actions. Legal challenges to Napster were unresolved at the time of this writing.[15] Still, Napster and similar "peer-to-peer" file-sharing systems demonstrate that copying and transferring digital content has become much easier and will likely increase in the future.

ONLINE CONTENT PROVIDER ECONOMICS

The economic model for online content providers is, at its core, fairly simple. Still, this model can be quite powerful: A producer typically makes a one-time, upfront investment to create content, and then a distributor—often the same entity as the producer—exploits that content as widely as possible, because the variable costs associated with delivering the content to incremental users are minimal. More precisely, the distributor maximizes revenue by optimizing the rates charged to users and/or advertisers who want access to those users. Since payments by advertisers tend to be proportional to the size of the audience for their messages, online content providers often conclude that they can maximize revenue by maximizing their user base—which means charging users nothing for the content.

So, in general, revenues tend to vary with the size of an online content provider's user base. Most costs for a content provider—e.g., ad sales, site development, and administrative overhead—are largely fixed. If the content provider has an in-house editorial staff, the costs of content production also are fixed. If the content provider is a distributor of content produced by another company, payment for that content may take the form of a fixed fee, a fee that varies with user traffic, a share of revenue, or some combination of these payment methods.

One cost category that does not scale well for content providers is marketing. Given the economic imperative to "produce once, then distribute widely," online content providers often engage in intensive online and offline customer acquisition campaigns, and measure the productivity of these marketing campaigns in terms of cost per new customer acquired. When a content provider's business model is working well, these new customers will become loyal users, and only modest marketing expenditures should be necessary to sustain their traffic. Once a large share of its customers are repeat visitors, assuming an online content provider has acquired enough total customers to cover its largely fixed costs, then it will be profitable.

From that point forward, profits may increase steadily due to the structural characteristics of ad-supported businesses. Advertising tends to grow at the same pace as the overall economy; put another way, in aggregate, companies reinvest a more or less constant percentage of their revenues into marketing. So, as long as an ad-supported content provider maintains its share of total ad spending, its revenues should grow at the same rate as the gross national product (GNP). But, as noted above, the content provider's costs are mostly fixed—once the business matures, these costs should grow at about the rate of inflation. Since GNP growth tends to be two or three percentage points above the rate of inflation (reflecting real growth in the economy), ad-supported businesses can be profit machines: Their revenues and costs are basically decoupled, and the underlying growth rate for their revenues is *faster* than the rate of growth for their costs! Of course, market forces will try to pull the machine back to earth. New competitors will be attracted by excessive profits, and rates of compensation to individuals engaged in creating content (e.g., writers, actors, game developers) will be bid up.

Ad-supported online businesses share these characteristics, and benefit further from an interesting multiplier effect. In the previous paragraph, content providers were seen as benefiting if they simply maintained their share of total advertising spending. But Internet companies, in aggregate, have been sharply increasing their share of total ad spending as the Internet grows and as marketers learn the value of this new medium (see Exhibit 1). If online content providers can maintain their share of Internet ad spending—a reasonable goal—they will rapidly increase their share of total advertising spending.

The balance of this section offers additional background on revenue and cost drivers for online content providers.

Exhibit 3-1 AD SPENDING ONLINE AND ITS SHARE OF THE OVERALL AD MARKET

	1999	2000	2001	2002	2003	2004	2005
Spending ($ billions)	$3.5	$5.3	$7.3	$9.5	$11.9	$14.3	$16.5
% of total ad market	2%	3%	4%	5%	6%	7%	8%

Source: Adapted from "Online Advertising Through 2005," Jupiter Communications, Sept. 2000

Revenue Streams

Online content providers can collect revenue in three different ways: (1) by selling advertisements, (2) by charging users directly for content, either on a "per use" or subscription basis, or (3) by licensing (i.e., syndicating) their content to other websites, then either charging those websites a fee or sharing ad revenue from the page views generated.

Ad Revenue

Despite efforts to date to diversify their revenue streams, ad revenue remains the dominant source of revenue for most online content providers, and it appears it will remain that way in the foreseeable future (see Exhibit 2). While this source of revenue is growing at a tremendous rate (see Exhibit 1), some industry observers

Exhibit 3-2 ONLINE CONTENT PROVIDERS' REVENUE MIX, 1999 AND 2002

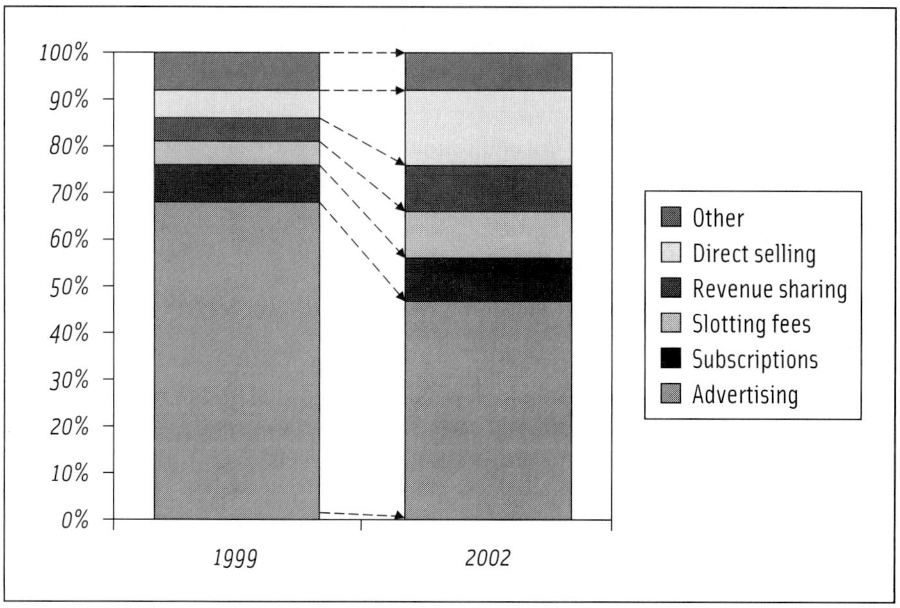

Source: Adapted from "The Content-Commerce Collision," Forrester Research, 1999

believe that excessive reliance on ad revenue is misguided, and, for this reason, contend that the future for online content providers is uncertain. These analysts point to the failure of a number of online content sites during 2000 (e.g., APBnews.com, Pseudo.com, Pop.com) and layoffs at other sites (e.g., Salon.com, NBCi) as evidence to support their view.

Ad revenue is primarily generated on the basis of "impressions." One impression equals one set of eyeballs passing over an ad one time. In 1999, marketers paid for typical banner ads at an average CPM rate of $34.22, where CPM ("M" for the Roman numeral 1,000) means the cost per thousand impressions delivered (see Exhibit 3). CPMs can vary widely depending on how likely the users exposed to a given impression are to respond to that ad, as well as the intrinsic profitability of the goods and services being marketed. For example, a credit card company soliciting new customers on the homepage of the news site MSNBC.com will pay a much lower CPM than an online computer retailer advertising laptops adjacent to a CNET review of the latest laptop models. Thus, CPMs for automotive sites averaged $39.15 during the first half of 2000, whereas CPMs for game sites averaged only $23.35.[16]

Charging per impression is the simplest form of advertising payment, but increasingly, marketers have demanded payment structures that shift performance risk back to the content provider (i.e., they have sought to "pay for performance"). Some advertisers prefer to pay at a rate proportional to the number of times users "click-through" their banner ads (see Exhibit 3); others focus on conversion rates, i.e., the number of users who actually complete a purchase.

One can calculate the monthly ad revenue generated by a website by multiplying (1) the site's number of unique monthly visitors, (2) the average number of visits per user per month, (3) average page views per visit, (4) the average CPM divided by 1,000, (5) the sellout ratio, i.e., the percentage of pages viewed for which the site has received any payment from advertisers, and (6) the average number of impressions on pages that generate any ad payments. By definition, the last figure will equal or exceed one, because websites sometimes sell more than one banner ad per page. Sellout ratios will, by definition, be equal to or less than 100 percent, because most websites fail to sell their entire advertising inventory, and because some pages intentionally carry no ads (e.g., the page explaining a site's privacy policies).

The first three figures in this calculation are typically available from traffic measurement services such as Media Metrix and often are published in companies' SEC filings and/or Wall Street research reports. The last three figures are less readily available from public sources, but multiplied together, they equal revenue per page view, which can be calculated from publicly-available sources (see Exhibit 4). Given an average revenue per thousand page views of $23 for the content sites profiled in Exhibit 4, and if we assume that these sites sell their ads at the industry average cost

Exhibit 3-3 AVERAGE CPM RATES AND CLICK-THROUGH RATES

	1998	1999	2000 (Qs 1, 2 and 3)
CPM (dollars)	$36.60	$34.23	$33.71
Click-through rates	roughly 4%	NA	roughly 0.4%

Sources: Adknowledge.com for CPM rates and First Union, "Internet/New Media," June, 2000, pg.19

Exhibit 3-4

ADVERTISING REVENUE STATISTICS, 1999

	Revenue/avg. user	Revenue/1,000 page views	Click-through rates at home	Click-through rates at work
CNET	$12.92	$26.53	0.14%	0.53%
iVillage	$9.88	$32.03	0.25%	0.43%
MarketWatch.com	$10.28	$16.01	0.02%	0.08%
SportsLine.com	$14.25	$18.05	0.08%	0.23%
Women.com	$7.16	$18.85	0.14%	0.53%
ZDNet	$12.08	$28.82	0.10%	0.04%
Averages	$11.10	$23.38	0.12%	0.31%

Source: Adapted from First Union, "Internet/New Media," June, 2000

per thousand impressions of $34, and that they deliver, on average, one impression on each page that carries an ad, then we can infer that these successful, publicly-traded content sites have an average sellout ratio of 69 percent.[17]

Average CPMs have declined over time (see Exhibit 3) for at least two reasons. First, marketers have shifted their advertising mix to the Web more slowly than users have increased their Web usage; inevitably, this means less ad revenue per page viewed. Second, marketers are concerned that click-through rates have declined over time (see Exhibit 3), perhaps due to user fatigue, which implies a reduced return on their investment in banner ads. Two trends may reverse the downward trend in CPMs: The use of "rich media" ads and improved targeting. Rich media ads use animation and audio—which have become more accessible to users through the spread of broadband connections and browser "plug-ins"—to promote deeper user engagement. Click-through rates for broadband ads can average twice the rates for traditional banners.[18]

Advertisers often will pay a substantial premium if they can target their ads to specific demographic groups, e.g., based on sex, age, income, and/or geographic location. To enable such targeting, websites must be able to identify their visitors. However, despite the Web's promise of one-to-one marketing, most online content providers know surprisingly little about individual users. As noted above, few content sites charge users directly, so they lack basic data that would be available for subscribers to an offline magazine or newspaper, such as a user's name and address. Furthermore, to avoid creating barriers to usage so they can maximize traffic, most content sites have elected not to require upfront registration, i.e., they do not ask first-time users to provide data, such as their names, e-mail addresses, or zip codes, before they can access content. Many content sites do use cookies to track a user's page views, but unless the cookie is used to capture registration data, it is of limited value in determining a user's demographic profile.

Whether to require registration in order to obtain information is a difficult decision for an online content provider. On the one hand, registration can lead to far fewer people visiting one's site—it requires extra work and many users avoid providing data to protect their privacy. In fact, 94 percent of Web users surveyed said they have refused to provide information to a website and 40 percent say they have lied when giving the information.[19] On the other hand, when sites require registration, the traffic that *does* visit will clearly be more valuable. One executive from an online newspaper stated in class that he believed that requiring upfront registration (and password entry prior to subsequent visits) might cause traffic to be cut in half, but impressions could be sold at twice the CPM, making the strategy revenue neutral.[20] Generally only those sites with highly differentiated offerings and well established reputations—like *The New York Times* on the Web—can benefit from upfront registration. Other sites can seek to collect registration data more gradually, e.g., by asking users for data when they respond to promotions, sign up for e-mail reminders, or request access to special sections such as news archives.

Paid Content

Content providers may charge end-use customers for their proprietary content (see Exhibit 5). An example is WSJ.com, which charges a $59 annual subscription fee for access to a digital copy of the *Wall Street Journal.*[21] Some sites employ a pay-per-use model, such as Boston.com, which charges $2.95 per article for access to its archives. Other content sites charge once for the digital download of eBooks or MP3s, in effect an outright purchase. For example, when Stephen King released his novella, *The Plant,* as an eBook in July 2000, he charged $1 per chapter, on an honor system. King told readers that he would only post additional chapters if he was paid by at least 75 percent of those who downloaded the previous chapter.[22]

Still other sites offer a mix of free and premium content, similar to the strategy commonly employed in the software industry, where many applications have basic and professional versions. For example, ESPN.com offers access to most of its site for free, but charges for participation in its fantasy sports leagues. Players pay about $30 to assemble a team by drafting and trading professional athletes throughout the season, then track their fantasy team's results based on the players' real-world performance. Likewise, Sony Online Entertainment offers most of its games for free, but charges for several of its popular multiplayer games, e.g., the role-playing game Everquest, for which 325,000 subscribers pay a $10 monthly fee.[23]

These examples are exceptions: Only 6 percent of the top-100 most trafficked sites charge for content.[24] Furthermore, in a recent survey, 46 percent of respondents indicated that they would never pay for online content.[25]

Licensing

Some content providers earn revenues by licensing their proprietary content to other websites (see Exhibit 6). For example, according to its 10K filing, ZDNet, a provider of technology news and product information, "has strategic alliances with

Exhibit 3-5 REVENUE FROM PAID ONLINE CONTENT

$ in millions	1998	2000	2003
Subscriptions	$275	$555	$1,208
Pay-per-view	$25	$51	$179
Paid content households	2.7	6.1	18.7

Source: Adapted from "Consumer Content Strategies," Jupiter Communications, Dec. 1999

Exhibit 3-6 LICENSING REVENUE FROM ONLINE CONTENT

$ in millions	1998	2000	2004
Total licensing revenue	$126	$343	$1,481
Revenue per content provider	$3.6	$4.4	$5.1

Source: Adapted from "Consumer Content Strategies," Jupiter Communications, Dec. 1999

many of the Web's leading sites, including Yahoo!, AltaVista, GO.com, Lycos, and iVillage pursuant to which selected ZDNet-branded content is displayed on their sites in exchange for traffic, brand recognition, content, or a percentage of the revenue generated from those sites." ZDNet's competitor CNET (which acquired ZDNet in July 2000) has generally been less willing to syndicate its content to mass-market portals, in part due to concern about weakening the CNET brand if consumers are trained to turn to mass-market portals for technology news and product information.[26] The potential benefits and risks associated with content syndication are discussed in more detail below in "Other Strategic Issues," the final section of this chapter.

Cost Categories

Online content providers' expenses can be divided into two main types: costs related to ongoing operations and costs related to customer acquisition.

Operational Costs

Operational costs may be further divided into four categories: content development/licensing, website development, ad sales (for ad-supported sites), and general and administrative expenses (see Exhibit 7 for profit-and-loss statements for a sample of content companies). With a few exceptions noted below, these operational costs are largely fixed.

Content Development/Licensing. For three publicly-traded Internet companies that rely largely on original content that they produce in-house: CNET, MarketWatch.com, and iVillage, cost of sales—which is comprised largely of content production costs—is projected to average $44 million per site in 2000 (see Exhibit 7). These costs are largely fixed—they are related mostly to compensation for creative staff, such as reporters, editors, and producers. Such costs do tend to increase over time as companies steadily increase the quantity and quality of content they provide. For the sample companies, content production costs were projected to increase about four-fold between 1998 and 2002. However, revenues have increased more rapidly, therefore, measured as a percentage of revenue, content-production costs have declined sharply over time from 57 percent of revenues in 1997 to 36 percent in 2000, and are expected to reach 25 percent of revenue in 2002.

Websites that largely offer content repurposed from another medium, such as ZDNet (which licenses content from a number of Ziff Davis magazines, including *PC Magazine* and *Computer Shopper*) and Boston.com (the online affiliate of the *Boston Globe* newspaper) have very different content development costs. Many such

Exhibit 3-7 PROFIT AND LOSS STATEMENTS FOR A SAMPLE OF CONTENT PROVIDERS

$ in millions (% of revenue)	1998		2000E		2002E	
CNET						
Revenue	$56.8		$217.2		$445.0	
Cost of revenue	$30.1	(53%)	$95.1	(44%)	$187.2	(42%)
Gross profit	$26.7	(47%)	$145.9	(67%)	$353.4	(79%)
Sales and marketing	$14.6	(26%)	$89.6	(41%)	$133.5	(30%)
Product development	$3.4	(6%)	$17.1	(8%)	$37.8	(8%)
General and administrative	$6.8	(12%)	$27.5	(13%)	$42.3	(10%)
EBITA	$1.9	(3%)	$11.7	(5%)	$139.8	(31%)
MarketWatch.com						
Revenue	$7.0		$53.7		$110.6	
Cost of revenue	$2.0	(29%)	$18.4	(34%)	$27.6	(25%)
Gross profit	$5.1	(73%)	$35.3	(66%)	$82.9	(75%)
Sales and marketing	$4.7	(67%)	$29.5	(55%)	$33.2	(30%)
Product development	$1.4	(20%)	$10.3	(19%)	$13.8	(12%)
General and administrative	$3.4	(49%)	$13.5	(25%)	$19.9	(18%)
EBITA	($4.4)	(-63%)	($18.0)	(-34%)	$16.0	(14%)
iVillage						
Revenue	$15.0		$96.0		$247.0	
Cost of revenue	$12.4	(83%)	$40.9	(43%)	$78.8	(32%)
Gross profit	$2.6	(17%)	$55.1	(57%)	$168.2	(68%)
Sales and marketing	$28.5	(190%)	$54.2	(56%)	$74.1	(30%)
Product development	$2.1	(14%)	$7.8	(8%)	$12.4	(5%)
General and administrative	$7.4	(49%)	$29.1	(30%)	$37.1	(15%)
EBITA	($35.4)	(-236%)	($36.0)	(-38%)	$44.6	(18%)

Source: Adapted from First Union, "Internet/New Media," June, 2000

sites pay a license fee or royalty to their offline siblings—equal to 3 to 5 percent of revenue for ZDNet and roughly 5 to 10 percent for Boston.com[27]—and also hire staff to: (1) reformat the offline content for Web display (e.g., adding hypertext links to archival material and relevant third-party information sources), and (2) create additional content to augment the offline material. At Boston.com, for example, fifteen out of eighty total employees in mid-1999 were engaged in updating and reformatting stories from the print newspaper.[28]

Website Development. Website development costs for online content providers vary widely, depending on the extent to which they customize their site features instead of relying on off-the-shelf software templates. Most sites spend heavily to build their sites initially, often relying on outsourced system development staff. After launch, most online content providers invest continuously in upgrading their site features. Out of a total staff of 253, for example, TheStreet.com, an established provider of stock market news and commentary, employs fifty-one employees in technology development and twenty-five employees who provide technical support for users.[29] Consequently, although website development expenses are basically fixed, they have tended to increase at nearly the same pace as online content providers' revenues: Such expenses averaged 13 percent of revenues for sample companies in 1998 and are projected to average 8 percent of revenues in 2002 (see Exhibit 7).

Ad Sales. Smaller online content providers tend to outsource their ad sales to companies like DoubleClick, which manage networks of sites where advertisers can place banners. Such companies tend to retain about 30 to 50 percent of the revenues they generate for content providers.[30]

Larger companies have their own in-house ad-sales forces who call on advertising agencies and call directly on marketers. For example, Boston.com employed about thirty of its eighty employees in the ad sales function in July 1999. Assuming that compensation, benefits, and travel and entertainment expenses per employee were in the range of $100,000, Boston.com spent about 30 percent of its 1999 revenue on ad sales operations.[31] ZDNet, with eighty-six ad sales personnel in 1999, spent about 10 percent of revenue on ad sales operations, based on the same assumptions.[32] Since ad sales reps tend to be paid on commission, these compensation expenses do vary to some extent with site traffic and sales volume. However, if revenues triple over a three-year period, it is not likely to be the case that ad sales expense will also triple: Sales reps typically are assigned a certain number of accounts, and their sales targets for earning commissions from any given account will tend to be adjusted upward each year as site traffic grows (i.e., the rep covering E*Trade will not typically be paid three times as much commission for her E*Trade sales in 2003, even if E*Trade spends three times as much in 2003 as it did in 2000). However, if revenue growth stems from signing new accounts, the company is likely to need to add sales reps and its ad sales cost will increase in absolute terms.

Customer Acquisition Costs

Online content providers acquire new customers through many channels, including offline advertising (TV, radio, and print) and through online partnerships with portals.

Customer acquisition costs for online content providers are typically lower than for other Internet business models (see Exhibit 8). While from quarter one 1999 to quarter one 2000 it cost an ISP (Internet service provider) between $201 and $350 to acquire a new customer, it cost iVillage, a content site for women, only $8 to $19. To illustrate how a content site might incur a cost of this magnitude, imagine that the site negotiates a "keyword" deal with a mass-market portal at a $40 CPM, i.e., a banner ad for the content site appears adjacent to search results when a portal user conducts a search involving any of a number of pre-specified terms likely to be relevant to the content site's users (e.g., "football" for ESPN.com). Assuming that the click-through rate for such banners is 0.5% (about the average for all banner ads)

Exhibit 3-8 ACQUISITION COST PER CUSTOMER FOR VARIOUS INTERNET BUSINESS MODELS

In dollars	ISP	Financial	Health	Retail	Content
1Q 1999	$201	$195	$150	N/A	$8
1Q 2000	$350	$237	$198	$240	$19
Examples used:	EarthLink	E*Trade	PlanetRx.com	Pets.com	iVillage

Source: Adapted from "Online Advertising Through 2005," Jupiter Communications, Sept. 2000

and that no current users click-through the banners, the content site will receive five new users for every 1,000 impressions, and will have paid $8 per new user acquired via the portal deal.

How valuable are the new customers that content sites attract? This answer can be ascertained by calculating the lifetime value of a customer. Continuing with the example of iVillage.com, to simplify, assume that (1) each new iVillage user generates about $10 in revenue per year, (2) marginal costs (for hosting, ad sales commissions, etc.) are 15 percent of revenues, and (3) new customers remain loyal for three years, on average (a fairly typical figure for offline content businesses such as newspapers, magazines, and cable TV). If these assumptions are accurate, then the discounted lifetime value of a customer (at a 10 percent discount rate) would be $21, before the $8 to $19 acquisition expense. Therefore, iVillage's acquisition efforts appear to be profitable, but not by a very comfortable margin.

GET BIG FAST: A STRATEGIC IMPERATIVE FOR ONLINE CONTENT PROVIDERS?

Many Internet companies have pursued Get Big Fast (GBF) strategies, involving massive upfront investment in customer acquisition and brand building. The premise of such strategies is that the early days of the Internet are a "land grab": according to this view, companies will find it easier to stake out wide swaths of empty territory now, rather than try to capture that territory later, after it has been settled by others. The payoff from the GBF strategy tends to be strongest when the following conditions apply: Network effects are strong, scale economies (beyond network effects) are significant, and customer retention rates are intrinsically high. This section explores the extent to which these conditions apply for online content providers.

Network Effects

Connectivity-related network effects occur when the adoption of a new product or service by a new customer increases the value of the product or service for customers already using it, because existing customers now can connect with more parties.[33] The concept of connectivity applies for any network which facilitates point-to-point transactions, e.g., a postal system, a telephone network, a railroad. To use the classic example, the value of each existing fax machine increases very slightly for its owner upon the sale of every new fax machine, because each party in the network can reach additional users. Or, to use an online example, nothing is lonelier than an empty chat room! In fact, according what has become known as Metcalfe's law (after Bob Metcalfe, inventor of Ethernet), the value of a network is equal to the number of its users squared; hence, there is an exponential benefit from a linear increase in the size of a network.

Unfortunately, with some important exceptions—for example, multi-user games—connectivity-related network effects tend to be fairly weak for online content providers. Remember that a content provider is defined by its professionally-produced copyrighted content. Value does not increase for existing user A when new user B consumes a content provider's information. Many sites enable online chat between users—an application which is subject to very strong connectivity effects—but such user-generated content tends to be a byproduct of the delivery of copyrighted content.

Connectivity effects should be distinguished from *software supply-related network effects,* which often are present for standards that govern the creation of new hardware and/or software. When software supply-related network effects are strong, the propagation of a standard leads to the creation of more software that employs the standard, which in turn leads to the further propagation of the standard, and so forth. Sony PlayStation would be an example: Rapid growth in the sale of PlayStation consoles encourages game developers to write for that platform (because the platform requires the development of specialized code that cannot be readily "ported" to another gaming hardware platform), which in turn supports additional console sales, etc. At a macro level, the growth of the Internet is a powerful example of software supply-related network effects: once HTML was invented and Web browsers became available, companies created websites, which encouraged the adoption of more browsers, and so forth.

Beyond that very important macro dynamic, software supply-related network effects tend not to be very important for most online content providers. Because Internet Protocol standards have now been universally adopted, content providers cannot harness new standards to expand their potential market any faster than the growth in the base of Internet users at large. One important exception to this observation involves content that requires software plug-ins that extend browser capabilities, such as Shockmachine, a "media jukebox" used to access, play, and store a wide range of animation and music content. Shockwave.com had registered 15 million users of Shockmachine by March 2000.[34] Many online content providers, including the creators of the popular animated television series "South Park," were engaged in the creation of entertainment programming that ran exclusively with Shockwave software.

Finally, one might argue that some people derive pleasure from consuming content that they know is popular. Many content businesses—movies, music, TV programs, and books—are hit driven: A small share of titles generates a large share of total industry sales. This "tipping" phenomenon goes beyond the usage simulation that follows from positive word-of-mouth: If everyone at the office is talking about the TV show, "Survivor," then I am more likely to watch the show.[35] By watching the show, the value of watercooler gab sessions increases for everyone else who saw the show: a connectivity effect of sorts. While this network effect is common in other content businesses, the Internet has not yet produced the equivalent of what the television network NBC (in advertising its popular Thursday-night program lineup) describes as "Must See TV." Perhaps as broadband technologies proliferate and online content providers can offer a richer multimedia experience, Internet companies will be able to move beyond simply fueling the network effect (by facilitating chat) for offline blockbusters such as *Titanic,* Pokemon, and Britney Spears, and will become a medium that can actually launch its own hits.

Scale Economies

As explained in the previous section, a large share of online content providers' costs are fixed, hence, they benefit from very significant scale economies. In addition to these cost-related benefits, ad-supported content sites will tend to accrue a premium from advertisers for generating high levels of unduplicated reach. As they seek to balance reach and frequency objectives for their ad campaigns,[36] advertisers typically are willing to pay a higher CPM for ads that reach a large audience in a single exposure. Put another way, advertisers will tend to pay more for a single banner ad that reaches one hundred thousand unique users one time, than they will for ten banner ads that each reach ten thousand unique users ten times. Offline, two of the largest consumer print magazines, *People* and *TV Guide,* commanded advertising rates (measured in terms of dollars per impression delivered) that averaged 22 percent more than other magazines that ranked among the 130 largest; network television broadcasters commanded a comparable premium for superior reach.[37] Online content providers were expected to benefit from similar scale advantages.

Customer Retention

The stickiness of a customer refers to the likelihood of a customer returning to a site over and over again. If a site has a high retention rate, then GBF investments in customer acquisition are likely to have a higher payoff. If retention rates are low, then a website becomes a "leaky bucket:" Customers are acquired at a high cost, but they leak away and need to be replaced, incurring additional acquisition costs. In the absence of strong network effects, websites may still have intrinsically high retention rates if there is a solid basis for competitive differentiation in the business (beyond network effects and pure price discounting) or if it benefits from some type of switching cost. For example, in the cases of ISPs and online brokerage firms, the hassles associated with changing one's e-mail address or terminating a funded account, respectively, create strong switching costs.

Compared to some other Internet business models, online content providers have meaningful opportunities for competitive differentiation: Users' tastes vary widely, and they often develop strong emotional attachments to their favorite authors, columnists, radio talk-show hosts, TV shows, and musicians. It stands to reason that users will, over time, develop online counterparts to these offline attachments. Just as a loyal reader of *Time* magazine probably can explain why he or she strongly prefers it to *Newsweek;* a loyal reader of the Slate.com is likely to have clearly articulated preferences for that online magazine, compared to Salon.com.

Notwithstanding such preferences, *Time* magazine benefits from the fact that most of its readers receive the magazine on a subscription basis: Its weekly arrival in the mail provides a stimulus for consumption. By contrast, content websites must rely on proactive decisions by their users to visit their site; content is not pushed to users (unless they elect to receive e-mails), so if they are not deeply engaged, they may simply never return to the website.

In an effort to increase retention rates, online content providers can employ several measures. For example, they may offer communication features such as bulletin boards and chat groups which can increase a user's emotional engagement with a site, or productivity tools such as event calendars which add value to the user and encourage the user to make a sticky investment in data entry. Content also can be pushed to users who sign up for e-mail services.

All of these measures have the added benefit of requiring some type of user registration. As noted above, absent the data gleaned through registration, online content providers know very little about their users; they lack even basic information about user identity, and cannot reliably track whether users return to a site. Planting cookies may provide some information about the usage patterns of non-registered visitors, but the use of cookies for tracking retention rates is problematic for three reasons: (1) Cookies are specific to a machine, so an individual who visits a site from different computers at home and work would be tracked as two distinct users, (2) cookies have limited life spans—they may be rendered obsolete when a user buys a new machine, upgrades or switches browser software, or reformats a disk drive, and (3) some users, concerned about privacy, instruct their browsers to prevent the receipt of cookies.[38]

In the experience of the authors, online content providers tend not to know much about their retention rates: In our conversations with a couple of dozen sites, we have yet to find one that systematically tracks its retention performance. One analyst has speculated that at iVillage, about 30 percent of registered users are heavy, repeat visitors; registered users, in turn, represent only 35 percent of total unique visitors to the site.[39] As the Internet matures, we would expect that online content providers will shift their focus from acquiring customers to increasing user loyalty. In the meantime, our hypothesis is that on average, online content providers, benefiting from their ability to achieve competitive differentiation, will have moderately high retention rates—similar to those for an offline newspaper, magazine, or premium cable services (such as HBO).[40] In these offline content businesses, about one third of customers tend to churn every year.

Summary: The GBF Payoff

In summary, online content providers experience weak network effects (with some exceptions, such as multi-player game providers and developers of content for browser plug-ins), they benefit from very strong scale economies; and they have moderately high intrinsic customer retention rates. Given these characteristics, pursuing a Get Big Fast strategy might be an economically reasonable option for an online content provider, but a positive payoff is by no means guaranteed. In the absence of network effects, which tend to ensure that the new customers drawn to a service will have a strong need for that service, a massive promotional effort is likely to attract some new users whose needs are very well met by the content site, and some for whom the fit is marginal. Retention rates for this latter group are likely to be low, reducing the average lifetime value of customers acquired through GBF promotions. Furthermore, in the absence of strong network effects, acquisition costs per new user are not likely to decline over time with a GBF strategy; in fact, they may increase after the market for the most attractive prospects becomes saturated and incremental growth increasingly comes from prospects whose needs are not met as well by the site's content.

As an alternative to the GBF strategy, promoting a content site at a more measured pace has several advantages. First, promotions can be more surgically targeted, avoiding the practice of "casting a wide net" that will catch prospects who are unlikely to become loyal users. Second, it takes time for users to develop an emotional attachment to a content provider, but once they do, they are more likely to become "apostles" who can help the site attract like-minded prospects through word-of-mouth—the least expensive channel for customer acquisition. Finally, a strategy of steady growth allows a site's creative staff to fine tune their content, improving it in response to user feedback—this could be called a "Get It Right First" rather than a Get Big Fast strategy. With a GBF strategy, if a site changes its positioning in this manner, it must alter its advertising message. Shifting a site's brand promise in this manner can be very confusing to prospects who were exposed to earlier promotions: They might ask, "Should I bother to spend time with these guys, if they can't make up their mind about who they are?"

Michael Kinsley, the editor of the online magazine Slate.com, analyzed the situation as follows:[41]

> *One miracle of the Web is that serving two million visitors costs barely more than serving two dozen—and serving four million costs barely more than that. But you can squander this advantage easily enough, and there are plenty of Web-is-special theories to help you justify doing so. Among these are the importance of establishing a brand, the value of being the first mover, the pointlessness of ending up No. 2 or (God forbid!) No. 3 in a category. Take your pick. But the basic idea—spend big and early to make a splash and create unstoppable momentum—is not new. It is familiar to anyone from the world of traditional paper magazines. Also to anyone familiar with the fable of the tortoise and the hare.*
>
> *Sometimes the hare does win. More often, the money runs out and all that remains is the memory of a lavish launch party . . . After watching this mistake made again and again, I strongly suspect that the best thing a new magazine can do is buy time. Time to experiment, to make mistakes and still to have another chance. Time to develop a real publication, instead of trying to market a still-imaginary one. Time to find new talents instead of whoring after old ones. Time to acquire a flavor, a reputation, a following, instead of trying to buy these off the shelf. . . ..*
>
> *Maybe the Internet does change everything, but it seems to me that tortoise-and-hare reasoning ought to be even more true online. Online you are developing not just a new product but a new medium. Figuring out what works and finding an audience for it should take even longer.*

In addition to the factors discussed above, whether an online content provider should Get Big Fast or pursue a strategy of steady growth (i.e., Get It Right First) also should hinge on whether (1) the company faces head-to-head competition from sites targeting a very similar user base; and (2) whether those competitors seem likely to implement GBF strategies. Companies that can avoid what economists call "racing behavior" may all grow steadily toward profitability, seeking ways to differentiate themselves and profitably divide the market—as CNET and ZDNet managed to do for many years.[42] But if a competitor launches a GBF strategy, an online content provider has only two options: Lose share, hoping that the competitor will ultimately damage itself by exhausting its financial reserves, or match the competitor's spending, which runs the risk of accelerating an arms race.

OTHER STRATEGIC ISSUES

Should Online Content Providers Leverage Other Internet Business Models?

As discussed in the first section of this chapter, the distinctions between an online content provider and other types of Internet business models can be subtle. Other business models have different revenue streams that are often attractive to online content providers, who tend to be highly dependent on advertising. Therefore, it is not surprising that online content providers often feel internal or external pressure to become hybrids with other types of business models.

Vertical Portals. Vertical portals establish links to third-party content and commerce offerings and provide navigational assistance around an interest area such as sports or antique collecting; such portals do not themselves produce much original content and the majority of their sites' page views come from content licensed from others or from search results that help link users to destination sites. Content sites often feel pressure to add links to other websites and thereby evolve into a hybrid between an online content provider and a vertical portal, in order to better serve users by aggregating a more comprehensive body of relevant content. For example, CNET management undertook an initiative to make their site an exhaustive source of information on technology products and services. If CNET's large editorial staff did not produce information in a certain area, in an effort to be complete, they would provide links to a site that did—even if that site was one of CNET's direct competitors. The objective was to ensure that no user who came to CNET looking for information would leave unsatisfied, because such users might be inclined to never come back.[43]

Still, becoming a vertical portal and linking to third-party content has its risks. First, the quality of the third party's information might not meet the online content provider's quality standards, putting the content provider's brand reputation at risk. Second, depending on the relative bargaining strengths of the two sites, it might be costly to negotiate links to other sites. Rather than sharing ad revenue from traffic sent to another site, an online content provider may prefer to omit the link and hope that the user will stay, even though that user cannot find all the information they are seeking. Third, when one diverts a user elsewhere, one not only sacrifices page views and revenues, but one may introduce them to a place where "the grass is greener": What if that customer goes directly to the third party next time and forgets about your site?

Horizontal Portals. Horizontal portals (e.g., Yahoo!, Lycos) provide search engine and navigational assistance across a broad range of interest areas. Many offline media companies also are horizontally focused either due to their conglomerate structure (e.g., Time Warner with its vast collection of media properties, including CNN, *Sports Illustrated,* Time-Life books, Warner Music Group, *Time* magazine, the WB television network, etc.; Viacom with MTV, Paramount Pictures, Nickelodeon, Simon & Schuster Books, CBS Television, etc.), or due to the broad topic areas covered by their individual properties (e.g., NBC with its news, entertainment, and sports programming; *The New York Times* with deep coverage in national and international news, business, sports, travel, and the arts). As they consider their online strategies, these horizontally-focused offline content providers have had to consider whether to launch horizontal portals.

Disney (which also owns ABC and ESPN) is an example of a media conglomerate that has launched sites for its individual offline properties (e.g., ABCNews.com) as well as a horizontal portal called GO.com, which was designed to compete directly with Yahoo! and AOL. GO.com prominently displays links to Disney's individual content sites, which themselves feature links back to GO.com. The result is a synergistic transfer of traffic between Disney's Web properties. Disney spent nearly $2 billion acquiring and developing the properties that became GO.com, but the media behemoth has had limited success with its strategy. Despite heavy promotion, the monthly reach of Disney's Go Network never exceeded 35 percent of U.S.

Internet users, whereas America Online and Yahoo! get over 60 percent.[44] Pressured by ongoing losses, Disney repositioned GO.com during the summer of 2000 to focus more on entertainment content, reducing the breadth of its horizontal focus.

Disney's lack of success with the horizontal portal/online content provider hybrid strategy—and the poor results realized by Time Warner, News Corp., and NBC with similar strategies—do not necessarily imply that the strategy of linking a horizontal portal with individual destination sites is intrinsically flawed.[45] Microsoft, for example, has achieved strong cross promotion between its MSN portal and its destination sites, including MSNBC, HomeAdvisor, Expedia, CarPoint, and Investor.

Companies pursuing this strategy must confront the consequences of "weak links": Is ABCNews.com compromised in its ability to secure attractive distribution deals with portals such as Yahoo! or AOL by virtue of its association with GO.com? It probably is. Conversely, if ABCNews.com lags its online competitors, would GO.com—restricted in its ability to source news from outside parties—suffer due to weakness in a key content category? Again, it probably would.

Online Retailers of Physical Goods. Online content providers also face pressure to diversify their revenue streams by becoming online retailers of physical goods. In fact, 59 percent of content providers admit to feeling strong or extreme pressure to integrate commerce into their sites.[46] For example, why shouldn't ESPN.com sell hats and T-shirts for professional sports teams? ESPN.com's thought process might go as follows: Since we generate strong traffic and we know a lot about our users' interests, why shouldn't we sell them stuff directly? We'd keep all of the margin, instead of simply linking users to an established online retailer from whom we now earn only a modest affiliate fee equal to 5 to 10 percent of the purchase price.

There are two principal reasons why content providers might choose to avoid online retailing. The first relates to the reactions of users and advertisers who might be confused or alienated by such efforts. The second is related to the intrinsic difficulty of managing retail operations.

Content sites realize that it takes time to build a community. Yet most have commercialization in their long-term plans, despite the risk of alienating users who want truly independent content and retailer advertisers who would have to compete directly with the content provider. Content sites expect a growth in commerce fees from 16 percent in 1999 to 36 percent of their total site revenue by 2002.[47] In one executive's words: "Commercializing our content is not a negative. Commerce offers placed next to related content is a service, not a hard sell. Our site helps people get things done, and commerce is a part of our overall service offering."[48] Users might see things differently: If CNET actually sold PDAs, could it be trusted to give objective advice if it got a higher margin on some models than others?

Adding commerce capabilities also can pose operational challenges for online content providers. As a result, a number of content sites (e.g., ESPN.com, Salon.com, Women.com, iVillage.com) that had developed in-house retailing units have abandoned those efforts in favor of affiliation arrangements with outside partners, after realizing that running a retailing business requires an entirely different set of skills.[49] Commenting on this trend, Sean Kallor, of e-Commerce at Nielsen, said, "The clear message to content companies [in the past] was have commerce, community, and content. But grow up and focus! Outsource the commerce if you're a content company or outsource the content if you're a commerce company."[50]

Overall it seems as though CNET executive Shelby Bonnie might have had it right when he said, "In a technology marketplace a media company has a far better place in the food chain then a retailer." Being an information intermediary requires none of the tremendous overhead of a retailer. Nevertheless, "without people selling products there is no advertising, and without a vehicle to advertise there's no way to sell products."[51] In other words, content providers are a vital part of a symbiotic relationship. According to this view, rather than struggling to become a hybrid they should concentrate on their core capability of creating and distributing quality content, thereby benefiting from a symbiosis with manufacturers and retailers who wish to present promotional messages to an audience drawn to that content.

Online Brokers. Finally, some online content providers feel pressure to develop hybrid business plans that also position them as online brokers. For example, *Consumer Reports* magazine offers terrific information that consumers can use in buying a new car, e.g., dealers' prices, model reliability data. Could *Consumer Reports* leverage this content and create a site that helps users identify a dealer and negotiate a fair price for a new vehicle? Perhaps, but it is important to note that the leading online car buying sites—Autobytel.com and CarPoint—put users in touch with just a single affiliated dealer (which means that the user does not receive competing bids that might result in a superior price). Autobytel.com and CarPoint receive most of their revenue in the form of referral fees from those dealers. Clearly, it would be difficult for *Consumer Reports* to accept referral payments from dealers in this manner, yet still position itself as a credible consumer advocate. It would have to find an alternative revenue model that secured payment directly from its consumer clients—a tricky proposition on the Web, when so many other high quality services are available for free.

CNET has moved in this direction, however, positioning itself as an online broker by allowing its users, after they research their computer hardware and software purchase decisions, to identify which online retailers carry the goods (and at what price), then link to a selected retailer to complete the transaction. This service is free for users; retailers pay CNET (1) for placement on CNET's lists of retailers (retailers who make such payments can display their logos, and they are moved to the top of lists that also include retailers who do not pay placement fees; users can re-sort these lists by price), and (2) lead generation fees for prospective customers referred by CNET. This business is very lucrative for CNET, but the company must be very careful: If retailers who are not CNET advertisers are seen by consumers as being unfairly excluded from the referral process, then CNET's credibility with consumers could be undermined.[52]

Challenges Facing Offline Incumbents, Part I: Editorial Values

Offline media companies have many powerful advantages when they move their content online: They already have incurred a large share of the cost of creating the content, and they have established brands and relationships with prospective users. Notwithstanding these advantages, offline companies have not been especially successful in moving their franchises online: Only four of the top 50 most heavily trafficked websites were operated by offline media companies in April 2000 (Time Warner, Viacom, The Weather Channel, and News Corp.), and only 27 of the 100 largest magazines had websites ranked on Media Metrix's list of the 3,000 most heavily trafficked sites.[53]

One reason for this lack of success is the cultural barriers with which offline companies must contend when they seek to repurpose their editorial content for online consumption. The first impulse for an offline media company tends to be to worry about self-cannibalization. Then, after its executives realize that they can either cannibalize themselves or see online competitors erode their offline franchise, they tend to respond aggressively. Their initial efforts often involve simply "shoveling" their existing offline content onto a website, but this approach rarely meets the unique requirements of online users.[54] Three cultural issues are especially salient as offline content providers seek to create editorial that is better suited to online users' needs: (1) concerns about linking to third-party content and accommodating user-generated content, (2) concerns about a lack of clear separation between editorial and business priorities within online units, and (3) difficulty in adapting offline presentation styles to the requirements of the online medium.

Third Party/User-Generated Content. Many editors and producers with offline experience have a natural aversion to linking to third-party content, i.e., to embracing a hybrid online content provider/portal role. As committed professionals, editors and producers want to control their product, maintain high quality standards, and ensure factual integrity. When linking to third-party sites, these requirements must necessarily be relaxed.

Along with third-party content, editors and producers with old media backgrounds sometimes fear facilitating user interaction, even though the ability to interact with other users is a key element of the online experience. What if a disgruntled visitor starts ranting in a chat room about how bad the site is, or posting defamatory remarks? Should user-generated content be closely monitored, and, if necessary, censored?

"Church-State" Separation. Like their offline counterparts, online content providers are in the business of creating a community, and a community must be based on trust. If that trust is broken in some way, then "no amount of heroic reporting, graceful writing, or bold photography will ever win them over."[55] Yet, as content companies search feverishly for new ways to monetize their traffic, the distinction between journalism and advertising has become blurred.

The Internet is full of examples of advertiser-provided editorial content, e.g., Microsoft-supplied "advertorials" run by Forbes.com that are easily mistaken for content written by the site's editorial staff.[56] Conventional journalists have been trained to insist on what they call a strict separation of "church and state," i.e., editorial decisions that are free from interference by ad sales executives who worry about the impact of a good or bad article on a key advertiser. It remains to be seen whether online businesses that preserve these offline values will have an advantage over "born on the Web" businesses in which the online creative staff has a more relaxed attitude about a blurred relationship between content and advertising.

Creative Style. The editorial style of online content is often vastly different from its offline counterparts. First, people are less willing to read online due to the glare of a screen and the need for constant scrolling. Consequently, online writing tends to be shorter and more to the point. Rather than delivering a tease in the opening paragraph to build the reader's interest, then following with the main message, an online journalist will tend to share the key points of an article within the first few sentences. The article then presents links that allow the reader to click for more detailed information. Offline content providers that fail to tailor their articles in this manner often find that online users ignore it.[57]

Online journalists also confront deadlines that are much more stringent than those facing their offline counterparts. For example, whereas offline newspapers are published daily, providing time for journalists to carefully mold a piece, online newspapers are updated throughout the day. Online journalists must constantly make difficult decisions about whether to post a fresh version of the story, or take more time to verify sources and polish their prose.[58]

Challenges Facing Offline Incumbents, Part II: Disintermediation of Publishers/Labels/Studios

> *Your increasingly obsolete information industries would perpetuate themselves by proposing laws, in America and elsewhere, that claim to own speech itself throughout the world. These laws would declare ideas to be another industrial product, no more noble than pig iron. In our world, whatever the human mind may create can be reproduced and distributed infinitely at no cost. The global conveyance of thought no longer requires your factories to accomplish.*[59]
>
> —John Perry Barlow,
> *A Declaration of Independence of Cyberspace*, February 8, 1996

Content providers who distribute individual creative works that are sold to consumers through offline retail channels—books, music CDs, movies, and video games—face serious challenges when those works can be digitally downloaded from the Internet. Understanding these challenges requires a digression to explain the offline economics of these businesses. Content distributors serve as intermediaries between creative talent and offline retailers. In books and video games, this role is filled by publishers; in music, by labels; and in movies, by studios. In all cases, there is a profusion of unsigned new talent eager to showcase their work; distributors scan the landscape and sign up promising creative talent, then promote their work—often through expensive grassroots marketing programs (e.g., author book signings or shipping sample CDs to college radio stations)—in an effort to build sales.

In all of these businesses, however, only a small share of releases by new artists become profitable: For example, in the case of music, only about 20 percent of recordings recover their costs.[60] To recover their investment in the many new works that fail to reach an audience, distributors typically ask all unsigned artists or authors for the rights to release a number of their future titles; in music, for example, contracts with new acts usually grant the distribution rights for their next six to seven records. Since most unsigned artists have limited bargaining power—they are grateful to have become the "needle in the aspiring artist haystack"—they readily sign such contracts. With multi-title contracts in place, the distributor is protected from "hold up" by the small fraction of new artists whose works do become hits. Having signed multi-title contracts, those artists have limited ability to bargain for increased advances or royalties for their follow-on work. Consequently, distributors can earn healthy margins on those titles, assuming that the artists continue to build an audience.

Over time, some of these breakthrough artists become established stars. After they fulfill their original multi-title contracts, these stars have considerable bargaining power with distributors. Given the fixed cost characteristics of content businesses described above, the blockbusters that these stars often release can be enormously profitable. Stars can capture a large share of that profit by auctioning their work to the highest bidding distributor. However, the incumbent has an advantage in such auctions, having typically retained the distribution rights for the artist's backlist titles, i.e., their earlier works.[61] Backlist titles are usually very profitable, because they typically can be sold at full price to fans eager to build a complete collection of the artist's work. When an artist releases a new title, a distributor often will simultaneously promote backlist titles; such promotions are harder to arrange if the artist has switched distributors.

How might the digital downloading of creative works change the structure of these industries? At both ends of the "artist life cycle," i.e., unsigned artists and established stars, talent appears ready to embrace new online distribution channels, threatening to disintermediate incumbent publishers, labels, and studios. Stars with well established brands may choose to self-distribute their new work to capture an even larger share of the economic rent it generates. As noted above, Stephen King has already done so in books; in music, David Bowie, Prince, and the Beastie Boys have marketed titles directly to their fans.[62]

Unsigned artists—with little to lose and much to gain if they gain exposure for their titles—have flocked to a new set of "aggregators" that have emerged to facilitate the digital distribution of creative works, e.g., in books, Fatbrain.com and iUniverse.com; in music, MP3.com and LAUNCH.com; in film, AtomFilms and IFILM.com. Established distributors have had a difficult time determining whether they should view this development as a threat or an opportunity.[63] On the one hand, the new aggregators serve as a filter to identify and promote new talent. Promising artists will still need offline distribution, so one strategy is to ally with the new aggregators to secure offline distribution rights for their pre-screened talent. In fact, as noted in the next section, the economic model for filmed or animated programming produced originally for the Web often is predicated on such offline licensing arrangements. On the other hand, there is a risk that the new aggregators will themselves enter the offline distribution business, as MP3.com has done by contracting with new artists to release their CDs, granting them a 50 percent royalty—much higher than the music industry standard of 12 to 14 percent.[64]

Thus, for offline distributors, the strategic issue is whether to ally with or acquire new online aggregators, or perhaps try to build one themselves. In all cases, they must contend with channel conflict: Any effort to stimulate online sales will meet with resistance from their offline retail partners. In-house development of an online aggregation business by an offline distributor is hampered by the fact that consumers: (1) are attracted to an artist's brand, and with rare exceptions (e.g., Disney) pay little attention to the distributor's brand, and (2) expect online aggregators to offer a critical mass of the work release by all distributors within a given content category. Since any distributor only controls the rights for a fraction of the relevant titles, they would need to form a joint venture with other distributors (as Bertelsmann Music Group did with Universal) to launch a new online aggregator. If they acquire an existing online aggregator (as Bertelsmann subsequently did with CDNOW), then they must contend with the risk that other distributors will be reluctant to supply a service owned by a competitor.

Broadband Challenges

Broadband technologies will allow online content providers to deliver a richer experience to users and advertisers. Broadband will greatly reduce the delays and quality problems that are commonplace with narrowband Internet access technologies, which transmit data using dial-up modems connected to analog phone lines at a maximum speed of 56 Kbps. Currently, broadband users account for only 4.6 percent of U.S. online households, but in those homes, content sites generate about 30 to 40 percent more page views per user.[65] Given this small target market, should content providers add broadband content to their sites and risk alienating the much larger population of narrowband users? Should they set up alternate sites to service broadband users? The answer is mixed: on the one hand broadband users are projected to grow from 1.7 million in 1999 to 18.2 million in 2003. On the other hand, the 2003 figure still only represents 28 percent of the projected total number of U.S. online households.[66] While broadband technologies may eventually be pervasive, adoption seems likely to come slowly.

Quokka.com, a sports enthusiast's site, is an example of an online content provider that harnesses the potential of broadband technologies to deliver what they describe as "Total Sports Immersion."[67] This involves, in the words of CEO Al Ramadan, "Looking at an event through the eyes, mind, and heart of the competitor, instead of from the outside looking in." For example, in a recent sailing race, Quokka allowed users to view the sailboat's positions on a map, get current weather conditions in the sea, check sailors' vitals, watch video through a camera located on the deck, and read daily accounts of the voyage. Quokka has learned that many of its users access the site from work, where broadband connections are prevalent. Despite Quokka's success, Ramadan has expressed concern that reliance on broadband content may limit Quokka to a niche position.[68]

Other broadband content providers have not fared as well. By the Fall of 2000, several companies specializing in the delivery of broadband entertainment content produced originally for the Web had shut down, including Pop.com, Digital Entertainment Network, and Pseudo.com. Analysts cited two main reasons for their failures. First, even when relying on nonunion labor and low-cost digital cameras and editing equipment, original video content is much more expensive to produce than content based on text and photographs. *Red Herring Magazine* estimated that a three minute "webisode" would cost $22,000 to produce, and might earn $3,500 in ad revenue and sponsorship fees, based on a total viewership of 550,000 at a destination site and through syndication to other websites.[69] Under these assumptions, the webisode only would be profitable if it was subsequently licensed for use in other media, such as movie theaters, video cassettes, or cable television.

Second, bandwidth is not free, and broadband content is expensive to deliver: Transmission costs for broadband sites in 2000 ranged from $14.10 per thousand users for streaming about eight minutes of FM-quality Internet radio to $75 per thousand users for a VHS-quality video stream of about half that length (see Exhibit 9). By contrast, the advertising rates that websites could earn from these content streams were estimated to range from $12.50 to $23.50 per thousand views. Depending on the number of ads that could be sold with a given content stream, it appeared that only very-low–quality video and FM-quality radio streams covered the gap between content delivery costs and ad revenues.[70]

Exhibit 3-9 BROADBAND CONTENT DELIVERY COSTS

Streaming Content Delivered	Type	Length (seconds)	Speed (Kbps)	Size (MB)	Cost per 1,000 Users
VHS-quality video	3 min. + 20 second ad	200	0.300	7.5	$75.00
Low-quality video	3 min. + 20 second ad	200	0.100	2.5	$25.00
Internet radio-CD quality	2.5 songs + 20 second ad	470	0.080	4.7	$47.00
Internet radio–FM quality	2.5 songs + 20 second ad	470	0.024	1.4	$14.10

Source: Adapted from Mark Mowrey, "Streaming Media Bleeds Cash," *The Industry Standard* (October 2, 2000): p. 173

Syndication Opportunities

Syndication involves licensing content for redistribution by other companies. The online magazine Salon.com, for example, earned about 10 percent of its revenue during the second quarter of 2000 from syndication.[71] Online content providers face tradeoffs in deciding whether to syndicate their content. On the one hand, syndication can provide (1) cash license fees and/or a share of ad revenue generated by the partner's site, (2) brand exposure, if a co-branding arrangement is negotiated, and (3) traffic that flows back to the online content provider's site, if a link is provided for users seeking more detail. On the other hand, when a company syndicates content it risks losing users that otherwise might have visited its own site. At the extreme, those users may come to view the syndicator's partner as the key destination for relevant content. Once the partner has built those loyal user relationships, the partner might then be inclined to position itself as a direct competitor to the syndicator, producing content in-house, instead of licensing it.

One way to judge whether syndication is a good idea or not is to think about the depth of a site. If a site's comparative advantage is that it provides in-depth information, when others are more shallow in their offerings, then perhaps syndication makes more sense. The syndicator's partners could provide broad exposure, helping to steer more enthusiasts to the deep content available on the syndicator's site. However, if the syndicator's content is relatively shallow, then making this information available to partners might eliminate the need for users to visit the content provider's site at all. Under those circumstances, the company might strictly limit itself to the role of syndicator (like the news service Reuters) and avoid investment in a destination website. Alternatively, a company with shallow content might choose to avoid syndication altogether, presenting its content exclusively on its own site.

ENDNOTES

[1]*Webster's College Dictionary,* (Random House 1992): 265.

[2]For more information on the portal business model, see Thomas Eisenmann and Sanjay Pothen, "Online Portals," section 2, *Internet Business Models: Text and Cases*, or HBS Case no. 801-305, December 2000.

[3]For more information on the online retailer business model, see Thomas Eisenmann and Alastair Brown, "Online Retailers," section 4, *Internet Business Models: Text and Cases*, or HBS Case no. 801-306, December 2000.

[4]For more information on the online broker business model, see Thomas Eisenmann and Alastair Brown, "Online Brokers," section 5, *Internet Business Models: Text and Cases*, or HBS Case no. 801-307, January 2000.

[5]Similar logic applies in distinguishing online content providers from online market makers, who—unlike brokers—represent *both* parties to a transaction, and who create and manage the infrastructure (technical; legal; etc.) required for these parties to do business online. As with brokers, market makers collect, process, and deliver a great deal of information to facilitate matches between prospective parties to a transaction. But again, their central purpose is to make a market, not deliver information. For more information on the online market maker business model, see Thomas Eisenmann and Chris Hackett, "Online Market Makers," section 6, *Internet Business Models: Text and Cases*, or HBS Case no. 801-308, December 2000.

[6]Thomas Eisenmann and Pauline Fischer, "CNET 2000," section 3, *Internet Business Models: Text and Cases*, or HBS Case no. 800-264, July 19, 2000.

[7]Thomas Eisenmann, Chris Darwall, and Liz Kind, "Geocast Network Systems, Inc.," section 1, *Internet Business Models: Text and Cases*, or HBS Case no. 801-211, October 4, 2000.

[8]For a discussion of this quote's lineage see (http://www.anu.edu.au/people/Roger.Clarke/II/IWtbF.html).

[9]A cookie is a small piece of software code downloaded into a website user's computer by the website, which allows the website to identify the user and track her whenever she logs back into the site.

Cookies could be used to avoid requiring users to reenter commonly requested information, such as user names and passwords or shipping addresses.

[10]Thomas Eisenmann and Pauline Fischer, "BET.com," section 3, *Internet Business Models: Text and Cases*, or HBS Case no. 800-283, February 2, 2000.

[11]Philip Evans and Thomas S. Wurster, *Blown to Bits* (Boston, MA: Harvard Business School Press, 1999), pp. 39–44.

[12]Amy Jo Kim, "Killers Have More Fun," *Wired* (May 1998).

[13]For background on efforts to combat the piracy of copyrighted materials, see Brian Dipert, "Media Security thwarts temptation, permits prosecution," *EDN Magazine* (June 22, 2000): 101.

[14]MP3 is a standard for compressing music into digital files, which facilitates their transmission over the Internet.

[15]Spencer E. Ante, "Inside Napster," *Business Week* (Aug. 14, 2000): 112.

[16]"Metrics" section, "Net Ads Keep Ticking," *Industry Standard* (September 11, 2000): 177.

[17]Sellout ratios vary widely, depending on both a site's performance and the sheer number of page views it has to offer. For example, CNET's sellout ratio was estimated to be 95 percent by Carolyn Trubuco of First Union Securities Equity Research ("Internet/New Media," June 13, 2000). Forrester Research estimated the average sellout ratio for online content providers to be 67 percent ("Valuing Online Audiences," November 1997). At the other extreme, a McKinsey study of magazine publishers' online sites indicates that their sellout ratios averaged only 6 percent (David Lieberman, "Study Says Magazines Shouldn't Rush to the Web," *USA Today*, October 23, 2000).

[18]Alexei Oreskovic, "Broadband or Bust," *Industry Standard* (June 9, 2000).

[19]Carl Shapiro and Hal R. Varian, *Information Rules* (Boston, MA: Harvard Business School Press, 1999), p. 35.

[20]Comments by Lincoln Millstein, CEO of Boston.com, in a Harvard Business School class in February 1999.

[21]The charge is $29 for subscribers to the print newspaper.

[22]Satisfied with the response from his readers, King was planning to release the novella's fourth installment on October 23, 2000.

[23]67,000 players were logged on to Everquest one evening in October 2000.

[24]Anya Sacharow, "Consumer Content Strategies," Jupiter Strategic Planning Services (December, 1999).

[25]Survey of 1,611 people by Jupiter Research (August 1999).

[26]See Thomas Eisenmann and Pauline Fischer, "CNET 2000," section 3, *Internet Business Models: Text and Cases*, or HBS Case no. 800-264, July 19, 2000 for more information.

[27]Royalty rates are from parent company SEC filings.

[28]Thomas Eisenmann and Jon Rust, section 3, *Internet Business Models: Text and Cases*, or HBS Case no. 800-165, "Boston.com," February 23, 2000.

[29]Jennifer Greenstein, "The Web Content Conundrum," *Industry Standard* (July 3, 2000): 65.

[30]Loren Fox, "DoubleClick Climbs to the Top of the Ad World," *Upside* (February 2000).

[31]Thomas Eisenmann and Jon Rust, "Boston.com," section 3, *Internet Business Models: Text and Cases*, or HBS Case no. 800-165, February 23, 2000.

[32]Jamie Kiggen, "ZDNet," DLJ Equity Research (May 1999).

[33]See Carl Shapiro and Hal R. Varian, *Information Rules* (Boston, MA: Harvard Business School Press, 1999), pp. 173-225 and Philip Evans and Thomas S. Wurster, *Blown to Bits* (Boston, MA: Harvard Business School Press, 1999) pp. 112–113.

[34]Macromedia SEC filings. For more information on the business model of companies that distribute browser plug-in media players, see Thomas Eisenmann and Alastair Brown, "Networked Utility Providers," section 7, *Internet Business Models: Text and Cases*, or HBS Case no. 801-309, January 2000. For another example of such a company, see Mary Tripsas, "Adobe Network Systems, Incorporated," section 7, *Internet Business Models: Text and Cases*, or HBS Case no. 801-199, September 25, 2000.

[35]See Winslow Farrell, *How Hits Happen* (New York, NY: HarpersBusiness, 1997) and Malcolm Gladwell's, *The Tipping Point: How little things can make a big difference* (Little Brown & Company, Feb. 2000).

[36]Reach is the share of their target market that sees any ad during the campaign, and frequency is the average number of ads seen by those who are exposed to the message.

[37]Chris Charron, "The Great Portal Shakeout," Forrester Research (March 1998).

[38]Joe Nickell, "Cookie Dough," *Business2.0*, p. 120 cites the tenth Annual GUV World Wide Web User Survey, which indicates that 95 percent of expert Web users have changed their browser settings to restrict cookie reception.

[39]Henry Blodget, "iVillage," Merrill Lynch Equity Research (November 11, 1999).

[40]This hypothesis may overstate the retention performance of online content providers: in November 1997, Forrester Research estimated that a typical online content provider retained only 40 percent of its user base from year to year ("Valuing Online Audiences").

[41]Michael Kinsley, "Tortoises Will Win the Dot-Com Race," *The Wall Street Journal* (August 29, 2000).

[42]Thomas Eisenmann and Pauline Fischer, "CNET 2000," section 3, *Internet Business Models: Text and Cases*, or HBS Case no. 800-264, July 19, 2000.

[43]Ibid.

[44]Data from Media Metrix: (http://www.mediametrix.com/landing.jsp).

[45]For an account of media conglomerates' difficulties in the portal business, see Saul Hansell, "The Medium Gets the Message," *The New York Times* (August 14, 2000).

[46]Survey with 48 respondents from "The Content-Commerce Collision" by Chris Charron, The Forrester Report, (Cambridge, MA: March 1999).

[47]Online retailing revenue growth statistic and growth in commerce fees as a percentage of total site revenue from "The Content-Commerce Collision" by Chris Charron, The Forrester Report, (Cambridge, MA: March 1999).

[48]Quote from an unnamed executive in "The Content-Commerce Collision" by Chris Charron, The Forrester Report, (Cambridge, MA: March 1999).

[49]Jennifer Couzin, "Women's Sites Shop for Profits," *Industry Standard* (July 31, 2000): 85.

[50]"Outsourcing the Store," *Business2.0* (October 10, 2000): 48.

[51]Quotes from Shelby Bonnie, a CNET executive, from Thomas Eisenmann and Pauline Fischer, "CNET 2000," section 3, *Internet Business Models: Text and Cases*, or HBS Case no. 800-264, July 19, 2000.

[52]Thomas Eisenmann and Pauline Fischer, "CNET 2000," section 3, *Internet Business Models: Text and Cases*, or HBS Case no. 800-264, July 19, 2000.

[53]Carolyn Trubuco of First Union Securities Equity Research ("Internet/New Media," June 13, 2000) citing Media Metrix data for the top 50 sites as of April 2000; David Lieberman, "Study Says Magazines Shouldn't Rush to the Web," *USA Today,* October 23, 2000 for magazine industry data.

[54]See Thomas Eisenmann and Pauline Fischer, "CNET 2000," section 3, *Internet Business Models: Text and Cases*, or HBS Case no. 800-264, July 19, 2000, for an example of this dynamic.

[55]Comments by Mike France, "Journalism's Online Credibility Gap," *Business Week* (Oct.11, 1999).

[56]Mike France, "Journalism's Online Credibility Gap," *Business Week* (October 19, 1999): 122.

[57]See Thomas Eisenmann and Pauline Fischer, "CNET 2000," section 3, *Internet Business Models: Text and Cases*, or HBS Case no. 800-264, July 19, 2000, p. 8 for further discussion of the unique requirements of online journalism.

[58]Thomas Eisenmann and Jon Rust, "Boston.com," section 3, *Internet Business Models: Text and Cases*, or HBS Case no. 800-165, February 23, 2000, p.11.

[59]John Perry Barlow, co-founder of the Electronic Frontier Foundation: (http://www.eff.org/pub/Publications /John_Perry_Barlow/barlow_0296.declaration).

[60]Jeffrey Rayport, Cate Reavis and Carin-Isabel Knoop, "RCA Records: The Digital Revolution," HBS Case no. 800-014, October 25, 1999 and Harold Vogel's, *Entertainment Industry Economics* (Cambridge, MA: Cambridge University Press, 1998).

[61]Backlist is the term of trade for books; in music, the equivalent term is catalog, and in movies, library.

[62]See 1) Steve Jones, "The Artist Ready to Reconcile . . . ," *USA Today* (April 13, 1999), 2) "New Musical Express," *Retail Week* (Oct. 15, 1999), 3) "Beasties Rap to the *Direct* Tune," *Precision Marketing* (Feb. 8, 1999)

[63]For an example, see Jan Rivkin and Gerrit Meier, "BMG Entertainment," section 3, *Internet Business Models: Text and Cases*, or HBS Case no. 701-003, July 3, 2000.

[64]Jeffrey Rayport, Cate Reavis and Carin-Isabel Knoop, "RCA Records: The Digital Revolution," HBS Case: 800-014, October 25, 1999.

[65]Carolyn Trubuco of First Union Securities Equity Research ("Internet/New Media," June 13, 2000) citing Nielsen//NetRatings data.

[66]Statistics in these two paragraphs are from Alexei Oreskovic's "Broadband or Bust," *The Industry Standard*, June 19, 2000.

[67]Evantheia Schibsted, "A Fresh Tack," *Business2.0* (January 1999): 81.

[68]Steve Bradley and Thomas Eisenmann, "Quokka Sports," HBS Case: 701-011, September 25, 2000.

[69]Robert La Franco, *Red Herring Magazine,* "Hollywood's Funk," November 13, 2000.

[70]Thomas Eisenmann, Chris Darwall, and Liz Kind, "Geocast Network Systems, Inc.," section 1, *Internet Business Models: Text and Cases*, or HBS Case no. 801-211, October 4, 2000: Exhibit 4.

[71]Company SEC filings.

BOSTON.COM

The newspaper industry has been battered and given up for dead for several years now. But something funny is happening on the way to the graveyard.

—Lincoln Millstein, CEO, Boston.com[1]

Lincoln Millstein, chief executive officer of Boston.com, peered out the jet window at Boston's hazy skyline. Only two nights before, on July 16, 1999, similar conditions had contributed to the tragic crash of John F. Kennedy, Jr., who had been piloting his private plane to nearby Martha's Vineyard. Kennedy's untimely death was felt heavily throughout the region, and nearly a million people had logged onto Boston.com to follow the event, establishing new records for traffic at the site. This was part of the macabre nature of the news business, thought Millstein. But the tragedy also indicated how strongly the online affiliate of *The Boston Globe,* Boston.com, dominated online news coverage in New England (see Exhibits 1A and 1B).

Millstein was on his way home from Chicago, where he had chaired Connections '99, the largest industry conference for online newspaper executives. Boston.com's traffic over the weekend reaffirmed his opening remarks there:

> If I may crib from William Drewry of Donaldson, Lufkin, Jenrette, the latest data from Media Metrix shows that in all of the country's major markets, the local newspaper is either number one or two in online news penetration. For example, Boston.com is currently running at 16.3% audience penetration in the Boston market. By comparison, the top national general news site, cnn.com, is at a 7.7% penetration. What this means is that newspaper websites are gaining traction in becoming the dominant local providers of news and information in the digital realm, as they already are in the paper and ink world. So far, in 18 out of 38 different markets measured, the top-rated local newspaper site has a bigger audience than any national competitor.

For the past six months, after making a commitment to providing "viral content" on its site, Millstein had overseen a constant increase in traffic at Boston.com. The unveiling of its new auction marketplace less than a month before had boosted traffic by half a million page views (see Exhibit 2). Other non-newspaper-related content like interactive features on Major League Baseball's All-Star Game and golf's Ryder Cup, both to be held in Boston during 1999, also helped attract a larger audience.

Notwithstanding this growth in traffic, serious questions remained, not the least being that Boston.com still required investment capital from its corporate parent, the New York Times Company. For decades, newspapers were accustomed to 20%-30% profit margins. Newspapers' online sites not only failed to achieve such margins—if they were profitable at all—but some members of the print old guard grumbled that the online sites cannibalized the core print business. For example, since Boston.com began providing the *Globe* online at no charge in late-1995, circulation at the *Globe* had dropped 10% on Sundays and 8% Monday through Friday (see Exhibit 3). Classified Help Wanted advertising, which represented more than 35% of total advertising revenues in the print product, had dropped more than 6% in the past 12 months. While Millstein and others contested whether Boston.com was the cause of such declines, the trends had contributed to the recent replacement of the publisher of *The Boston Globe,* Ben Taylor.

As the jet touched down, Millstein could not help but wonder how the management changes at the *Globe* would affect his operation. Would Boston.com be pressed by its corporate owners to temper its aggressive push online? Or would it be given more free rein, as he wanted, to define a new business model for the entire

Dean's Research Fellow Jon K. Rust prepared this case under the supervision of Professor Thomas Eisenmann as the basis for class discussion rather than to illustrate either effective or ineffective handling of an administrative situation.

[1]Speech by Lincoln Millstein, "Welcoming Remarks," Newspaper Association of America Connections '99 Conference, Chicago, Illinois, July 15, 1999.

company, even if that meant attacking the core franchise? Specifically, how would the changes affect Boston.com's new auction site, which could be seen as a direct threat to the print advertising franchise? Would Boston.com be forced to scale back its plans to provide local retailers with e-commerce store fronts? And how would the organizational structure of Boston.com be impacted? Only a month before, Boston.com had been moved into New York Times Digital along with *The New York Times on the Web* and several other New York Times Company websites. An IPO or a tracking stock was being considered, but was that a good thing? Should Boston.com be more closely integrated with the *Globe*? With the New York Times Company and its other properties?

History of *The Boston Globe* and Boston.com

The Boston Globe was founded in 1872 by six Boston businessmen, led by Eben Jordan, founder of the Jordan Marsh Co. The paper soon ran into financial difficulty, however, and Jordan hired Charles H. Taylor to restore profitability. Taylor stabilized the paper, and as a result of his loyalty and success, became a partner with Jordan—the only original investor still supporting the paper.[2] For the next 127 years a Taylor family member would serve as publisher of the *Globe*. During that period *The Boston Globe* won 15 Pulitzer Prizes for editorial excellence and established a track record of innovation. It was the first newspaper to use bylines to tell readers who wrote the story, the first to receive a news story by telephone, and the first to introduce color Sunday supplements, which included magazines and "free-standing inserts" from department stores and other retail advertisers. Such innovation had been rewarded in the marketplace: by 1999, the *Globe* was read daily by 1.4 million people (averaging almost three readers per copy and 472,000 copies sold) and on Sundays by more than 2.2 million people (751,000 circulation). It employed more than 450 people in news and editorial and 230 in advertising sales and support.

Until 1973 when it became a subsidiary of Affiliated Publications, formed that year and controlled by the Taylor family, the *Globe* was a private company. On October 1, 1993, Affiliated merged with the New York Times Company in a transaction valued at more than $1.1 billion. The deal included a "non-intervention" clause that precluded the new owner from changing *Globe* upper management for a period of five years. In July 1999, eight months after the clause's expiration, and one year after two prominent *Globe* news columnists were forced to resign upon admitting to plagiarism and story fabrication, the New York Times Company replaced the fifth-generation Taylor family publisher with one of its own executives, Richard Gilman, whose only tie to Boston was a 1983 MBA from Harvard Business School. The move sent shock waves throughout Boston's media community as journalists and media observers wondered whether the newspaper would be able to maintain a voice distinct from that of its corporate flagship, *The New York Times*. Corporate pronouncements indicated that improving profit performance and stanching declining circulation were among the parent company's top priorities.

[2]"History: 125 years of service," Boston.com.

Boston Globe Electronic Publishing (BGEP)

> *When we started the enterprise, it was a midnight strike. We knew we wanted to start a website, but what did we want to put on that website? My original answer was that we were going to put the newspaper on the website. The question then came back, "Why can't we charge for it?" But in 1994 no one was charging for content. The publisher responded, "All right, I'll go along with that, because there is no audience anyway." Thus, our publisher really entered into the enterprise without a clear vision of why we were putting the news online. Within a matter of years, however, our audience got to be fairly significant. Then the question became quite profound: Are we in essence destroying our business model? We're charging people for this product on paper, but on the web we're giving it away for free. What's the endgame?*
>
> —Lincoln Millstein, CEO, Boston.com

When the New York Times purchased the *Globe*, it also acquired the *Globe*'s separate electronic news subsidiary, Boston Globe Electronic Publishing (BGEP), which was founded early in 1993. At the time Millstein was a seasoned veteran news editor of the *Globe*. He said:

> I'm really the accidental CEO of Boston.com. I came to my job because back in 1993 only a handful of people at *The Boston Globe* knew what I was talking about. A few of us were already attuned to the warning signs that a significant revolution was about to occur in the publishing industry.

Millstein was aided by the fact that Stephen Taylor, a senior *Globe* executive and a member of the ownership family, was a champion for entering the online arena, having risen through the Management Information Systems (MIS) ranks. A Stanford MBA, David Margulius, was hired to write a business plan for an online version of the *Globe.*[3] Margulius's analysis suggested that a growing newspaper online site would ultimately cannibalize both print subscription and advertising revenues. Despite this conclusion, the *Globe*'s management approved the plan after Taylor and Millstein argued that the paper could cannibalize itself or be cannibalized by others. The two then circumvented the normal New York Times capital budgeting process and took the idea directly to several executives on the parent company's board. These Times executives were designing their own Web initiative and intuitively understood the self-cannibalization argument.

Wholly Owned Subsidiary. Millstein and Taylor were convinced that the new enterprise needed to be agile and experimental, and thus decided to incorporate BGEP as a separate, wholly owned subsidiary. Other advantages to this strategy were discovered once Millstein and Margulius began building the online entity. For example, nonexempt employees of a subsidiary would be free of union membership rules, so the website would not have to sign inflexible collective-bargaining agreements. Also, if online ads were not sold by a separate sales force, Millstein worried, key clients might never view the Web as having intrinsic value as an advertising medium. He feared that a joint sales force would focus on more lucrative print sales and toss online ads into bundles for large print clients as free incentives.

In addition, Millstein believed that the website should have its own brand so the *Globe* wouldn't be thought of as an "online newspaper." This designation might limit its ability to experiment with new advertising and editorial forms (e.g., partnerships with local broadcasters), and might be a liability with web users who were younger, on average, and much less likely to be loyal readers of print newspapers. In 1995, Boston.com was established at offices a mile and a half from the newspaper's main location in Dorchester. The site debuted on October 30, 1995, heralding its partnership with 23 Boston-area media and cultural organizations, including the city's three main TV stations, several radio stations, *Boston Magazine,* and the Museum of Fine Arts.

Leveraging *Globe* Resources. While Millstein, Margulius, and Taylor were defining the shape of BGEP and its partnerships outside the *Globe,* they also considered how the new organization should leverage *Globe* resources. Chief among these was the newspaper's extensive news coverage: the *Globe* had more journalists employed in the greater Boston area than all other newspapers and TV stations combined. Boston.com, it was decided, should have full access to the *Globe*'s news content. It was also decided that print and online classified ads sales efforts would be coordinated, allowing advertisers to place ads in the paper and on the website simultaneously. Phone orders would be fielded by *Globe* sales reps, and Internet orders by Boston.com staff.

In practice, however, coordination between the two entities was often bumpy. Some *Globe* managers were reluctant to allow an autonomous subsidiary to offer the *Globe*'s news content for free to non-subscribers. Hence, Boston.com was prohibited from "scooping" the *Globe* on major news articles and was not allowed to hire its own reporters or columnists.[4] In addition, Boston.com personnel were not invited to *Globe* daily news meetings, where news gathering priorities were established. Meanwhile, little cross-selling of advertising between the print and online businesses took place, and classified advertising coordination was limited by technology constraints: classified ads could be uplinked to the website only after being retyped and reformatted for HTML.

Notwithstanding these issues, Boston.com received significant financial and technological support from the *Globe.* Millstein and Taylor convinced *Globe* executives that it would take time to find a successful model for online news, so experimentation was critical. The *Globe*'s senior executives agreed, freeing Boston.com of the obligation to be profitable within any specific timetable. *Globe* management also waived the requirement to precisely track shared overhead costs and absorbed without a transfer charge the cost of providing news and support in the areas of MIS, human resources, legal, and

[3]Portions of this section are paraphrased from a paper on Boston.com by Daniel J. Green, HBS MBA '99, prepared for Professor Joseph Bower's Strategic Management class at Harvard Business School.

[4]A prohibition on "scooping" meant that Boston.com could not publish a major story until it had appeared in the pages of the newspaper. Through mid-1999, the one exception to this followed the merger of BankBoston and Fleet Bank, the two largest regional banks. Even here, pointed out Teresa Hanafin, online news editor for Boston.com, the impetus for breaking the story online was fear of preemption by *The Wall Street Journal* (which also had received early news of the merger), rather than a desire to get the information to Boston-area consumers as rapidly as possible.

corporate control. Finally, Boston.com had carte blanche to run ads in the *Globe* at no charge. In total, the first-year investment in Boston.com was about $3.5 million, slightly less than 1% of the *Globe*'s operating budget.

In addition to providing resources, the relationship with the *Globe* shaped Boston.com's cultural values. Millstein observed that Boston.com's heritage prevented it from sacrificing editorial integrity in the interest of commercial gain, as Internet city guides sometimes had done. Like the *Globe,* Boston.com would never blur the line between content and commerce. Boston.com would not, for example, allow payment for preferential placement of stories or deliberately publish stories favorable to large advertisers.

The Newspaper Industry

The revenue mix of a typical major metropolitan newspaper comprised two key sources: advertising, which accounted for 78% of revenue; and circulation (i.e., direct payments by consumers), which represented the balance.[5] At the *Globe* approximately 70% of circulation revenue was derived from sales of home delivery subscriptions; the balance was from single copy sales through newsstands or vending machines (see Exhibit 4). Advertising revenue was broken into three categories: retail display, free-standing inserts (or preprints), and classifieds. Retail display advertising was predominantly sold to local accounts, such as department stores and supermarkets. National accounts, such as airlines, represented a smaller percentage of display advertising. Preprinted inserts were distributed along with the editorial sections of the newspaper and were "free standing," in contrast to display advertising, which was printed alongside articles within the editorial pages themselves. Classified advertising was composed largely of help wanted, which represented roughly 65% of classified revenues at the *Boston Globe*; and automotive and real estate advertising, which split the balance (see Exhibit 5).

Due to increased competition from other forms of advertising—including broadcast and cable television and direct mail (see Exhibit 10 for data on the reach of different media)—newspapers' share of total advertising revenue had been falling for years, dropping from 24.4% to 21.5% between 1993 and 1998 (see Exhibit 6). The shift in advertising dollars to other media had placed pressure on newspaper managers to increase circulation revenue. Increased circulation revenue could yield powerful profit leverage, because the newspaper business conformed to the economic model typical in many information industries: once the first newspaper was produced, reproductions had a modest incremental cost—for the most part, just extra paper and ink. The costs of news gathering, distribution systems, and printing presses were fixed.

Online Threat. As newspapers lost advertising share to other media, newspaper executives saw profit margins decline from 40% in the 1970s to the low teens by the mid-1990s. Many feared that margins could erode further if classified advertising shifted from print to online city guides such as America Online's Digital Cities or Microsoft's Sidewalk, which provided local news, weather, sports, event information, and traffic reports (see Exhibit 7).

With the explosive growth of the World Wide Web, the threat to newspapers became unmistakable. First, news was being distributed free over the Internet, threatening circulation revenues. Second, classifieds, a $15 billion market in 1997, was becoming commoditized. Classified ads that cost more than $100 per day in major market newspapers often could be placed online for free until an item was sold. Shaken, large newspaper companies cautiously began to counterattack. By 1998, each of the top 100 newspapers had a website. And they had begun to join hands in areas like online job advertising, car classifieds and auctions. Nevertheless, they had lost considerable ground to upstarts like Monster.com, CarPoint, and eBay. (See Exhibits 8 and 9 for a list of online competitors and cooperative ventures between newspaper companies.)

Boston.com Strategic Initiatives, 1997-1998

For its first three years, Boston.com maintained clear brand distinction from the *Globe,* even though the newspaper's content was its main draw. The early plan to offer the best of all local media—except for the competing *Boston Herald* newspaper—fizzled due to lack of online commitment by most of its partners. "The partnerships with TV stations didn't deliver tremendous value," said Lisa DeSisto, Boston.com's vice president and general manager. "Except for New England Cable News, which

[5]Statistics for major metropolitan newspapers are derived from the 1998 Inland Press Cost and Revenue Study for newspapers the size of the *Boston Globe.* The Inland Press figures are recognized as industry norms.

was providing us with news video, they were just links to our partners' homepages." Now, less concerned about frightening away potential content partners, Boston.com began incorporating the *Globe* name into its site. This co-branding helped increase traffic by positively differentiating Boston.com from Microsoft's Boston.sidewalk.com and from other competing brands that were foreign to Boston consumers.

Classified Advertising. Boston.com had moved aggressively to develop online classified advertising. Explained Keith Yocum, director of classifieds for Boston.com: "The classified business is huge for newspapers because it's highly profitable. For example, the cost—just paper and ink, not labor or overhead—for a classified page with Sunday distribution in *The Boston Globe* is around $3,200. And for that page the newspaper gets $72,000[6] in revenue." To protect this franchise from online encroachment by others—not just pure Internet start-ups, but also radio and TV competitors who had enviously eyed newspapers' classifieds for decades—*The Boston Globe* and other large newspapers uplinked all their print classifieds for free, seeking to become a one-stop buy for both media and to destroy the profit potential for pure-play Internet classifieds providers. Yocum said that Boston.com had gone a step further:

> Two years ago, we quietly put together an online order form that allowed recruiters to put up help wanted ads for 28 days for $95 *without* running in the newspaper. It was a standalone feature with no promotion, but it immediately began to be used. No other newspaper in America would even think about putting up such a form. "Aren't you competing against your own classifieds?" we were asked. Meanwhile, *Globe* executives wanted to know who was using this form and how did they find it without promotion. There were *Globe* declines in classifieds in '97, and they wanted specific data to determine if Boston.com was impacting their print. But we couldn't find any patterns regarding Internet usage. Today, we generate between $36,000 to $55,000 per month just from this form. Our total classified budget this year is $1.7 million, and because of this form we will have more [online] classified revenue than almost any other newspaper in the country.

[6]Yocum cites the cost of a classified section-front, full-color, full-page ad. An inside, full-page, black-and-white recruitment ad was $58,000.

Online Yellow Pages. After promoting the *Globe* news content and creating the online classified form, Boston.com's next big push was to create the area's most complete directory listing, i.e., an online "yellow pages" listing local merchants and service providers. It partnered with Zip2, an Internet start-up specializing in local directory software, and dedicated 12 sales people to the effort in late 1997. Along with listing each merchant's business and contact information in the directory—including interactive maps—Boston.com helped build microsites for its clients and hosted them on its servers. After some initial success, sales stalled and the dedicated sales force was reduced through a combination of transfers and attrition. Nevertheless, the directories' effort became a rich learning experience, yielding improvements in customer support systems; lessons about the importance of following up with accounts to promote retention; and lessons about customer targeting—dry cleaners just didn't have a pressing need for a website!

Rejecting Auctions. During this period, Boston.com also considered offering e-commerce and auctions on its site. It launched what DeSisto described as "the longest e-commerce beta in history," with a local software company that "imploded" when the firm was acquired and subsequently lost interest in the beta test. Abandoning the test sent Boston.com back to square one in offering e-commerce solutions to its clients. Auctions, meanwhile, weren't initially considered an attractive offering. DeSisto explained:

> We don't really have a business development function here. The vendors who are successful in working with us are the ones that are most persistent and who get our attention. I actually think it is a fault of ours that we are not more proactive; we're actually reactive. Auctions are one example.
>
> I remember these guys from FairMarket, who were peddling software for auction sites, calling me before eBay was big. I told them I really didn't see the need for auctions on our site. We also thought it posed a conflict with classifieds—imagine someone selling their car through an auction instead of a classified listing —and we didn't want to further cannibalize the newspaper. Then, the eBay explosion came in late 1998 and we got nervous because we saw they could disintermediate the newspaper classifieds here. We also recognized we could own a local niche, especially for big items that you didn't want to ship, like furniture, or for selling local services like restaurant

reservations or timeshares and housecleaning. So we changed course and decided to get into that space. Not long after, eBay announced that they were going to offer local auctions in Los Angeles, so we knew we had to scramble. Thirty days after we signed our contract with FairMarket, we launched.

Strategic Initiatives, 1999

There's some confusion now. You see that these companies are spinning out pieces of their existing business. But the question now is do you take it public? Do you create an entirely separate company? Do you move it a mile down the road and give it carte blanche to run over the existing business or do you try to take the long view and keep it more integrated? It's a huge crisis that is today still unanswerable.

—William Drewry, DLJ equity analyst[7]

In mid-1998 Millstein read and then recommended to his management team the book, *Unleashing the Killer App.*[8] The book's message was that if you weren't destroying your own business model and establishing something new, someone else would. That idea bolstered Millstein's plans to shift Boston.com toward more community-initiated content in 1999. At Connections '99, he explained the concept and challenged online newspapers to exploit their print legacies while not being dragged down by them:

> There are people in our industry who say that we can't compete with the pure play Internet companies, because they have Internet currency that we don't have to fund brand build-up and acquisitions. These pure play Internet companies move at lightning speed; therefore, we must create new entities to compete. New entities cannot move fast if they are tightly integrated with their print newspaper parents. I would characterize people who espouse this view as the new media hawks. To me the doves are the people who would say, wait a minute, we have a tremendous asset here at the print newspaper. We have a tremendous brand, tremendous legacy, and it would be foolish not to leverage that.
>
> I go back and forth between being a hawk and a dove. As the CEO of a small company, I spend a lot of my energy recruiting and retaining people. If my parent company can buy me an army with Internet currency so that I can retain these programmers and salespeople, I'm really in favor of that. So on that score, I tend to be a hawk. I see the traditional media as being really handicapped by our current compensation systems.
>
> The other area where I'm a hawk is content. Frankly, 1998 was a year of some struggle for us. Boston.com launched in 1995; 1996 and 1997 were years of strong growth. But in 1998 our traffic growth started to slow, and it really worried us. We didn't know what was going on. So starting in 1999 we embarked on a strategy to build traffic with content that wasn't from our parent newspaper. We wanted viral content, produced by users of Boston.com. Along these lines, the most significant thing that we did in 1999 was to launch Boston.com Auctions. In our four-year history, that led to our single largest growth in traffic. As we look ahead, we're thinking more and more along these lines: user-created content. I don't know if our newspaper content has hit a wall or not. But I'm thinking like a hawk.
>
> I have a dove side. We couldn't have built Boston.com without *The Boston Globe* behind it. Every time we launched something, if we hadn't done an ad campaign in the *Globe,* I don't think that we'd have been very successful. And we get shared services from the *Globe* that really help us at Boston.com.
>
> So, I'm not religious one way or another. It's very difficult for us to walk this tight rope. But walk it we must.

Boston.com Operations in 1999

In July 1999, 80 full-time employees worked at Boston.com, supplemented by 15 interns. Stephen Taylor was president, Millstein was CEO, and DeSisto was vice-president and general manager. Reporting to DeSisto were six department heads, overseeing technology development, editorial, classifieds, operations, finance, and sales (see Exhibit 11).

Major and Local Account Advertising Sales. In the summer of 1999 the sales department consisted of two areas: major and local accounts. Major accounts included businesses like Bank Boston, Staples, Filene's, and Dunkin

[7]Comments by William Drewry, "Power of the Package: Print and Online Panel," Newspaper Association of America Connections '99 Conference, Chicago, Illinois, July 15, 1999.

8Larry Downes, Chunka Mui, Nicholas Negroponte, *Unleashing the Killer App: Digital Strategies for Market Dominance* (Boston: Harvard Business School Press), May 1998.

Donuts, who were targeted to buy section sponsorships and banners. Major account representatives were organized by category, e.g., one rep called on all financial clients and another on retail department stores. The major accounts staff included five sales people, a manager, and support person. Budgeted revenue for 1999 was $4.2 million. The local accounts unit—which included seven representatives, one manager, and one support person—sold ads primarily in the yellow pages directory. Local accounts were organized by geography and represented $1.8 million of budgeted revenue in 1999 (see Exhibit 12).

Initially, there had been little coordination between Boston.com and *Globe* sales reps. Then in 1997, a plan was approved to pay commissions to print reps whenever their accounts advertised on Boston.com, whether the print reps helped sell the online ads or not. In addition to this "double commission" plan, advertising dollars spent online would count towards fulfillment of print sales contracts, allowing *Globe* advertisers to receive volume discounts. Around that time, the online sales force began successfully targeting advertisers who weren't active in print. A notable example was Dunkin Donuts, which represented more than $113,000 in 1998 revenue online but spent virtually nothing in the *Globe.* These developments led *Globe* sale reps to be more open to working with their online counterparts. Said Donna Rice, sales director at Boston.com: "We do a lot more of what we call 'four-legged' sales calls with the *Globe* now, but we don't allow them to slow us down. If they aren't going to work really hard to get us through the door of some account, we go off on our own."

Classified Advertising. The classified department included 10 sales and support staff and one manager. Six worked in recruitment advertising—or "Help Wanted"—with the remainder divided between real estate, automotive and classified support. Classified revenue totaled $747,000 in 1998 and was on pace to surpass $1.7 million in 1999. The budgeted 1999 revenue distribution was help wanted, 60%; autos, 18%; and real estate, 16% with "other" the remainder. In addition, .5% of *Globe* classified advertising revenues were allocated to Boston.com., representing $800,000 in 1998 and a budgeted figure of $720,000 in 1999 (see Exhibit 13). Pricing for online classifieds depended on the category and format—with all *Globe* classifieds in their original form uplinked at no additional charge. All recruitment classified listings on the Boston.com site were subsequently uplinked free of charge to CareerPath.com, which was the national job recruiting site owned by several newspaper companies, including the New York Times. Internal market research by Boston.com indicated that jobseekers used Boston.com as often as rivals Monster.com and JobFind, but human resource managers nevertheless believed that Monster.com was more popular with candidates (see Exhibit 14).

In auto classifieds, Boston.com had lagged Internet "pure plays" CarPoint, Autoweb, and Autobytel in introducing new and used car inventory packages. When a dealer contracted for such a package, an online site would manage the dealer's recordkeeping (e.g., state legal forms), and automatically update online lists of cars for sale by the dealer. As with recruitment ads, all Boston.com car classified ads were uplinked to a national online site owned in part by the New York Times Company, cars.com.

Boston.com was finding it difficult to penetrate the real estate classified ad market. While some newspaper websites had been able to negotiate online listings agreements with their area's multiple-listing services (which were created and maintained by consortia of local realtors), providing them with complete data on every house for sale in the market by a broker, Boston.com had yet to reach such an agreement. It also had failed to convince the area's largest brokers to put all their listings on the site, in part because the hot Boston real estate market had reduced the need for realtors to advertise aggressively. Boston.com also was hampered by its partnership with the national online real estate sites managed by Classified Ventures, another newspaper joint venture. Classified Venture's Apts.com was aimed at large complexes, which were uncommon in the Boston market, and its "New Homes" site did not draw many visitors from New England, where new-home construction was uncommon.

Classified Computer Systems. Having to work within the constraints of the *Globe*'s computer systems was often frustrating for personnel at Boston.com. According to Monica Hubert, director of operations and design at Boston.com:

> The *Globe* has these old systems. A classified ad is typed in as a continuous chunk of text: "Two bedrooms, two baths, quiet street." The data is bad because it's not fielded. So as much as we can, we try to parse these ads with a computer program so that the data can be searched more efficiently online, but it still produces bad data. I tried to press the idea of a web-to-print model at a *Globe* long-term strategy meeting a few weeks ago. Shifting to a data-based

input model has been on the table for years but hasn't gotten anywhere. The computer system. Union. Culture. Everything. But if we want to be successful and have a good arts and entertainment product and have good classified data, then we're going to need to do this.

Keith Yocum expressed similar frustration about working with several of the national newspaper classified sites owned in part by the New York Times Company.

> If I have a criticism of cars.com, it is that newspaper people run it, and newspaper people don't always stay up to speed. They've done okay because they've been publishing lists. But in the future the higher value added will be around connectivity issues and more sophisticated usage of technology (see Exhibit 15). CareerPath, for example, represents a classic, newspaper-centric view of the web as a simple list. But they're coming around—slowly. It's kind of like the Titanic trying to turn. There's all these weird sounds, clanking and grinding. We need one database. We need a whole new model, in which all the partners input ads using a common set of fields.

At Boston.com, Yocum's model was to build "the largest listing of things." He explained:

> Our mission is to grab share. It's to build relationships. Too many newspapers have modest goals, because they don't want to compete against themselves. They can meet these modest goals without too much disruption. But they lose the market. Eventually, their solutions become ludicrous, like trying to buy out the competition that never should have been given a toe hold. *The Boston Globe* is number one in our market in print classifieds. But we are number three in this marketplace for online classified revenue, behind Monster and Jobfind. I don't know how to get number one unless you put the sales people out there. I'm not sure how many sales people Monster has in this market. Twenty? The Top 100 *Globe* accounts, originally, were hands off for Boston.com. Thankfully, that dropped by the wayside pretty quickly.

Online News. The news organization of Boston.com was divided into features and news, both reporting to Teresa Hanafin, editorial director. Features was staffed by six full-time employees and three interns and was located at Boston.com's offices. They built and enhanced sections like Health, Technology and Going Out, as well as special features like the Ryder Cup. Some of the staff's time was spent developing the "look and feel" of the site, creating links to non-*Globe* information and implementing partnerships with content providers like MIT's *Technology Review* and *Boston Magazine* (see Exhibit 16). The content staff generated little original copy.

The news arm comprised 10 staff members and 3 interns and was responsible for breaking news, i.e., for keeping stories on current events fresh throughout the day. It resided within the newsroom of the *Globe* in Dorchester in what was called "The Pod." The Pod, manned 24-hours a day, did not originate news; staffers rewrote wire stories[9] or transcribed events from WBZ-AM radio, local TV stations, CNN, Fox News, or MSNBC.

There were two different areas for *Boston Globe* news within Boston.com (see Exhibit 17). The first area was called *The Boston Globe* Online, which was like a site within a site where the full edition of the newspaper was uplinked at midnight after the newspaper had gone to press—so as not to "scoop" the print product—and preserved without changes during the day. The *Globe* Online precisely replicated the layout of the print newspaper. In contrast, the news in the rest of Boston.com was constantly updated and supplemented with non-*Globe* content, and the layout decisions were made by Hanafin and her staff. "Our audience is different from the *Globe*'s, so we make different choices than the *Globe* editors," said Hanafin.

Hanafin believed that constantly refreshing the site was critical. "We change the look and feel of the Boston.com news pages as often as we can," she said. "There is an entire menu of stories from the *Globe* we can draw upon. We check the wires. Generally, there is something new there. What we do on the Boston.com homepage is gradually push the original *Globe* stories lower and lower over the course of the day and put the breaking news on top" (see Exhibit 18).

According to everyone else at Boston.com, Hanafin, who had joined the online operation in May, was a major asset. She had risen through the ranks at the *Globe* and was a former Metro editor there, a position that often represented the heart and soul of a metropolitan newspaper. Her camaraderie with the *Globe* news staff and her understanding of how the paper operated enabled her to get things done. "For three years we had been trying to set up online chats with popular *Globe* columnists," said

[9]A wire service is an agency, like Associated Press, Reuters or Dow Jones, that sends out syndicated news copy to subscribing news media by wire, satellite transmissions or the Internet.

DeSisto. "And Teresa set it up with a yell across the news room."

Hanafin was nevertheless circumspect about the relationship between the newspaper and website. Integration, she said, was one of the major challenges facing both operations. She tried to imagine *Globe* reporters filing stories onto the website throughout the day:

> It would be a big adjustment because print reporters are accustomed to having 8-10 hours to fully and thoroughly report a story before they have to let it go to be edited. They're uncomfortable releasing some of the information after only one or two hours. But they have to understand that people aren't sitting around twiddling their thumbs waiting for the *Globe* to be put on their doorstep at six in the morning. People are getting information all day long from a variety of sources and if we don't give it to them, they're just going to go someplace else. By putting our own stories out there with the *Globe* by-line rather than stories off the AP it carries a certain caché. I've heard concerns about doing this, one being that reporters ask "Why should I scoop myself?" And I respond, Don't kid yourself. You're being scooped all day long by radio and TV.

Strategic Challenges, 2000

> *In a world defined merely by the quality of information, what should the New York Times be scared of? We have the best information in the world, with our commitment to quality journalism, our commitment to honest reporting, and our commitment to provide reporting that people read to make their lives successful. In an era defined as the information age, that has to have some value. Our business is information—quality value-added information. What defines us—and what is to me the core of newspapering—is taking the information and making it valuable . . . putting it in context . . . making it accessible to your audience. If you accept that, then everything else is just means of distribution.*
>
> —Arthur Sulzberger, Jr., chairman, New York Times Company[10]

There were several key issues facing Boston.com in mid-1999. One had already been decided. Until recently, Boston.com had chosen not to require its users to register before accessing the site. For a few weeks after its launch in 1995 it had done so, but hundreds of e-mails from users denounced the requirement. At the time, Millstein knew that the audience for Boston.com had more options for similar content than did the audience for its big sister *The New York Times on the Web,* which had successfully implemented registration requirements. Nevertheless, Millstein also realized that having specific information on site users and being able to identify and serve them specially targeted advertising was valuable. To secure such information now, Boston.com was implementing voluntary "universal registration," where users would be asked to give basic information to gain access to certain areas of the website. For example, receiving a weekly e-mail about new movies in town, accessing the story archives, or entering contests would require registration. Viewing the auction site did not require registration, although participating did. Eventually, the plan was that the same registration i.d.—or, if the user okayed it, a cookie[11]—would be used to gain access to all portions of the website needing authorization, allowing Boston.com to build a database on its users.

Auctions. The mission statement of Boston.com was "To support, defend and extend the franchise of *The Boston Globe.*" However, in the case of Boston.com auctions, there was little doubt that the online site could undermine the newspaper's classified advertising. Classified advertising in the newspaper, after all, was basically an auction in slow motion with interested buyers phoning sellers who ran ads in the paper to negotiate a deal. As a case in point, cars for sale by their owners (which had an average value of $5,000) were one of the most popular auction items on Boston.com. In the paper, a typical private car ad would bring in a minimum of $70. In its deal with FairMarket, Boston.com retained all revenues from banner advertising sold in the auction section of the website, and auction transaction fees would be split equally. Because he believed it would help build the user base, Millstein had convinced FairMarket to join him in waiving the fee for at least the first two months of the service. But when and how high should listing and/or transaction fees be set? (See Exhibit 19 for comparative pricing for eBay.)

---

[10]Speech by Arthur O. Sulzberger, Jr., "Jefferson or Barnum: The Values of Our Information Age," Tufts University, April 9, 1996. Quoted in "*The New York Times* Electronic Media Company," HBS Case No. 897-051.

[11]A cookie was a small piece of software code downloaded into a website user's computer by the website, which allowed the website to identify the user and track her traffic whenever she logged back into the site. Cookies could be used to avoid requiring users to reenter commonly requested information, such as user names and passwords or shipping addresses.

Some Boston.com staffers were also pushing Millstein to expand auction services to local businesses in a formal relationship. Already, businesses could list auction products on their own. One new idea was to create "merchant kiosks" on the site, a sort of virtual store. In addition to helping stores liquidate overstocked items through auctions, Boston.com could set up an e-mail service where losing bidders of private item auctions would be sent invitations to find similar merchandise at the appropriate kiosks.

Finally, one reason Boston.com had decided to work with FairMarket was that it was already providing auction services to websites elsewhere in the United States, e.g., Lycos and ZDNet. FairMarket pooled all of its customers' listings and allowed each customer to offer the entire pool under its own brand. So when Boston.com launched its auction area, there were already more than 60,000 items waiting for bids. Unlike AuctionUniverse, which was the national newspaper auction site started by Classified Ventures, FairMarket's network arrangement allowed for "private labeling." Items placed on Lycos's auction site, for example, would also appear on the Boston.com site without any indication as to where the item had been originally listed. Given this access to a rapidly growing nationwide list of goods and services, Boston.com was debating whether to push its auctions as a competitor to eBay, Amazon, and others on the national level. Should it also seek a partnership with AuctionUniverse, which was quickly adding other newspapers? Or should it try to reduce the out-of-area listings already on the site and simply seek to carve its niche as the dominant New England auction place?

To Integrate or Not. Another quandary facing Millstein and his team in mid-1999 was the appropriate degree of separation between the Boston.com and *Globe* sales forces. Millstein recognized that an important sales message might be missing because of lack of coordination. At the Connections conference, he confessed:

> I don't think any of us have exploited the power of the print-online package. *The Boston Globe* newspaper in our market has an impressive reach, with 2 million some-odd readers, and then you layer on that the reach of Boston.com, much of which is non-duplicative, and it's tremendous coverage. But we haven't been operating our entities to exploit that. We haven't tried to sell that total package.

The reverse position was that the two sales forces should be separated even more, allowing the online entity to take full, unobstructed aim at the newspaper. Keith Yocum was one proponent of this route:

> It's the third rail[12] of the newspaper industry right now: How should newspaper companies organize their sales forces to work with their online units? You can tell a lot about a company by how it organizes the sales force. It's kind of a Rorschach test.[13] But when there is a structural change in an industry, that's when you need the courage to compete against yourself—no holds barred. Otherwise, you end up as a buggy whip manufacturer in the age of cars.

Yocum argued that classified advertising should be separated from the newspaper. Or, at a minimum, it should be "upsold," meaning that *Globe* classifieds should be uplinked to Boston.com only if the advertiser agreed to pay an additional fee. While stopping the free uplink would diminish the number of listings found at Boston.com, Yocum believed the gains would offset any drawbacks:

> Currently, some people who place classified ads don't know their ad is also being listed online. Others don't understand they're getting it for free, they think it's already part of the classified rate. We not only fail to generate any revenue, but the advertiser isn't even assigning any value to what we're doing for free. And if they don't understand the value, they can't make good judgments. There's no wonder the consumer is valuing the online companies' classifieds more highly than ours, they're out in front of them *selling* it to them while we're not.
>
> Even we don't understand the value of our offerings. We were sitting around in a room talking about raising the rates of the recruitment form from $95 to $119, and I'm agonizing over the increase like a *Globe* manager would. Then I call one of my online classified sales people and ask, How many people have complained about the rate being $95? "Complained?" he asked. "Complained?" And then he understood what I was getting at: "No one! They say they can't believe it is so low." So we knew we could raise the rate. Last Friday, we changed it to $149. That is still less than Monsterboard.

[12]The "third rail" is a metal rail through which electric current is led to the motors of electric vehicles like subway cars. Touching one can be deadly.

[13]Rorschach personality and intelligence tests asked subjects to interpret ink blot designs in terms that revealed intellectual and emotional factors ("I see dragons chasing paperboys . . ."). They were designed by Swiss psychiatrist Hermann Rorschach in the first half of the twentieth century.

Upselling classifieds from the *Globe* harbored other challenges, however. Operations Director Hubert knew the computer systems were not optimal since they lacked data base capabilities. Trying to add upsell charges and then new routing for specific ads would create more system headaches. Moreover, she outlined a cultural challenge:

> *Globe* classified sales people have been there, most of them, for a long time. It's a group that is somewhat archaic. They just redesigned the whole department about a year ago, which is a great thing, because it was dark and there were no windows and it's just a lot of people yelling, "Pick up the phone, pick up the phone." It's a hard job, and they need to know so much about the different products already. I'm not sure how much specific training that they have and some of them are intimidated by technology. If someone says the word "Internet," they transfer the call over to us. They don't even try to answer the question. That's not everybody. But they just don't have time to learn. The last thing you would ever see is somebody in classified surfing the web, because they're constantly under pressure.

Millstein understood the cultural challenges of working with the *Globe.* More than once he had confronted charges that the newspaper's declining classifieds and circulation were his fault. But he believed these managers missed the point; there was a change in lifestyle taking place. Boston's fastest-growing demographic was the young professional moving into the metro center. The print newspaper was struggling to reach that demographic. He explained:

> All the studies I have seen have yet to find any evidence of significant cannibalization of the newspaper by the website. Of course, I hear anecdotally: "Yeah it's great, now I can get the *Globe* online and I canceled my subscription to the paper." And lots of people at the *Globe,* in the circulation department and in the news side, come and tell us that. But on the other hand, Boston.com is a tremendous channel that has allowed the *Globe*'s circulation department to sell as many as 10,000 new subscriptions in the first half of 1999 just from our online subscription area. So every time I hear anecdotally that someone is canceling the paper, I can say, "Last week we started 170 papers online."

Tracking Stock. The final issue facing Millstein was what his priorities should be in light of the New York Times Company's consideration of a tracking stock for New York Times Digital. Already, shifting BGEP out from under the *Globe* newspaper and into New York Times Digital earlier in the year had created new tensions between his operation and the *Globe.* Some of his managers had recently returned from long-term strategy sessions at the *Globe* offices having found that Boston.com was nowhere on the agenda. Some *Globe* staffers claimed they no longer knew where Boston.com managers' allegiances were.

The same kinds of questions were being asked throughout the New York Times empire. After the chairman of the company, Arthur O. Sulzburger, Jr., emphasized the importance of the Internet operations in his annual State of the Times speech at the company's shareholder meeting, the *New Yorker* magazine reported that folks at the flagship newspaper were heard saying, "What are we? Chopped liver? It's all digital, digital, digital."[14]

The *New York Times,* while a powerful brand, was no financial juggernaut. In fact, in 1999 America Online had a greater market capitalization than all of the newspaper companies traded publicly on the New York Stock Exchange combined. Hence, NYT executives were enamored with the idea of a tracking stock. By selling a piece of New York Times Digital, the hope was that enough cash would be generated to buy interests in other Internet enterprises or to invest in the software and personnel needed to establish New York Times Digital as a major Internet player. Revenues for Time Company Digital were expected to reach $29 million in 1999 with Boston.com representing about one-third of that (see Exhibit 20).

If a tracking stock was issued, one challenge would be determining how costs and assets should be transferred between the print and online entities. And what about stock options? Should *Globe* personnel be given options in Boston.com? These questions were on Millstein's mind as he closed his comments to the newspaper executives at Connections '99:

> I think we're all learning. We all put a stake in the ground, and the first thing that we did was publish the newspaper online, and we all went through a cycle where we got good results from that. But now we're seeing that this has its limits, and the question is at this point: If we've hit the wall there, where do we go now? We're all trying different strategies to get to that next curve. But it's the big question; which ones are right? And is local success enough—or even sustainable—in this new economy?

---

[14]Susan Tifft and Alex Jones, "Scion of the Times: How Arthur Sulzburger, Jr., has struggled to keep the family newspaper what it was—and what it must become," *New Yorker,* July 26, 1999.

Exhibit 1A

PERCENTAGE PENETRATION OF TOP DOMAINS IN BOSTON AREA

Q3'99 Rank	Domain	Apr-99	May-99	Jun-99	Q2 Avg.	Jul-99	Aug-99	Sep-99	Q3 Avg.
1	Yahoo.com	48.2	43.7	48.5	46.8	52.1	55.0	54.2	53.8
2	AOL.com	48.4	48.2	39.3	45.3	47.5	51.1	45.2	47.9
3	MSN.com	38.1	35.5	30.9	34.8	42.6	48.0	42.8	44.5
4	Netscape.com	37.9	33.0	33.0	34.6	28.5	38.5	32.4	33.1
5	Microsoft.com	28.8	29.6	25.3	27.9	25.5	32.2	32.1	29.9
6	GO.com	32.6	32.6	30.1	31.8	27.5	31.8	27.6	29.0
7	GeoCities.com	31.3	26.4	29.1	28.9	31.6	28.5	26.3	28.8
8	Lycos.com	27.7	27.8	23.5	26.3	26.5	24.0	23.2	24.6
9	Amazon.com	19.4	19.4	18.5	19.1	24.1	24.3	22.6	23.7
10	AltaVista.com	24.9	21.5	18.5	21.6	16.9	23.6	26.5	22.3
11	Excite.com	22.7	20.1	23.7	22.2	21.1	21.8	22.7	21.9
12	**Boston.com**	18.2	16.4	17.7	17.4	20.5	21.8	20.0	20.8
13	Angelfire.com	14.2	19.4	17.3	17.0	21.3	15.5	19.2	18.7
14	BlueMountainArts.com	22.9	20.3	20.2	21.1	19.3	15.4	17.3	17.3
15	Tripod.com	16.9	16.1	14.5	15.8	15.5	14.6	17.7	15.9
16	eBay.com	14.8	14.4	15.2	14.8	14.2	16.3	17.0	15.8
17	Passport.com					15.3	16.4	14.2	15.3
18	Hotmail.com	14.3	15.5	13.9	14.6	14.2	15.0	15.6	14.9
19	Real.com	12.2	12.3	14.2	12.9	14.0	12.1	18.4	14.8
20	**About.com**	9.5	8.8	11.0	9.8	9.9	13.1	18.8	13.9
21	LookSmart.com	5.8	11.5	6.8	8.0	13.3	14.5	12.8	13.5
22	HotBot.com	15.1	17.3	8.0	13.5	8.9	13.8	13.6	12.1
23	**DigitalCity.com**	9.7	11.7	8.7	10.0	14.6	11.3	9.0	11.6
24	Snap.com	16.0	13.9	11.2	13.7	9.5	10.1	15.0	11.5
25	**ZDNet**	10.6	10.8	7.7	9.7	9.3	12.7	11.8	11.3
26	**Weather.com**	7.0	7.0	5.7	6.6	9.1	9.4	14.7	11.1
27	**MSNBC.com**	8.1	11.2	5.7	8.3	12.7	9.2	10.5	10.8
28	BankBoston.com	8.5	8.2	7.6	8.1	11.1	11.3	9.8	10.7
29	Infospace.com	13.0	10.9	11.6	11.8	11.2	11.8	7.3	10.1
30	Xoom.com	12.6	13.7	10.0	12.1	9.4	9.0	11.6	10.0
Other News/Information/Entertainment/Classified Sites									
31	**Pathfinder.com**	13.0	10.9	11.6	11.8	11.8	9.7	8.2	9.9
34	**Disney.com**	6.6	10.3	7.4	8.1	10.3	9.8	8.9	9.7
37	**Sidewalk.com**	8.8	10.0	9.6	9.5	11.2	11.0	5.9	9.4
41	**SportsLine USA**	8.0	5.7	6.5	6.7	9.5	6.4	8.8	8.2
49	**Monster.com**	4.1	6.2	5.7	5.3	7.2	6.6	5.6	6.8
50	**ESPN**	6.1	6.1	6.0	6.1	6.1	6.5	7.2	6.6
51	**CNN.com**	7.7	7.1	6.6	7.1	10.2	6.2	3.4	6.6
57	**Sony Online**	6.3	4.4	5.8	5.5	4.4	8.1	5.9	6.1
58	**ABCNews**	6.3	5.5	3.0	4.9	7.0	5.5	5.8	6.1

Source: Adapted from Media Metrix

Domains in bold indicate news/information/entertainment/classified sites.

Exhibit 1B TOP 10 BOSTON.COM TRAFFIC DAYS THROUGH OCTOBER 1999

Rank	Date	Page Views	News Event
1	7/21	1,963,545	JFK, Jr., crash—bodies found
2	9/16	1,846,201	Hurricane Floyd
3	4/19	1,809,733	103rd Boston Marathon
4	7/19	1,798,766	Search for bodies from JFK, Jr., crash
5	10/12	1,723,648	Heroics of Martinez, O'Leary win Game 5 for Sox
6	10/18	1,709,902	Final Game of the Red Sox-Yankees series
7	7/20	1,579,857	JFK, Jr., crash coverage continues
8	10/4	1,505,832	Red Sox secure wild card spot
9	10/19	1,503,942	Red Sox defeated by Yankees in playoffs
10	9/13	1,494,612	Hurricane Floyd continues

Source: Adapted from Media Metrix

Exhibit 2 MONTHLY PAGE VIEWS

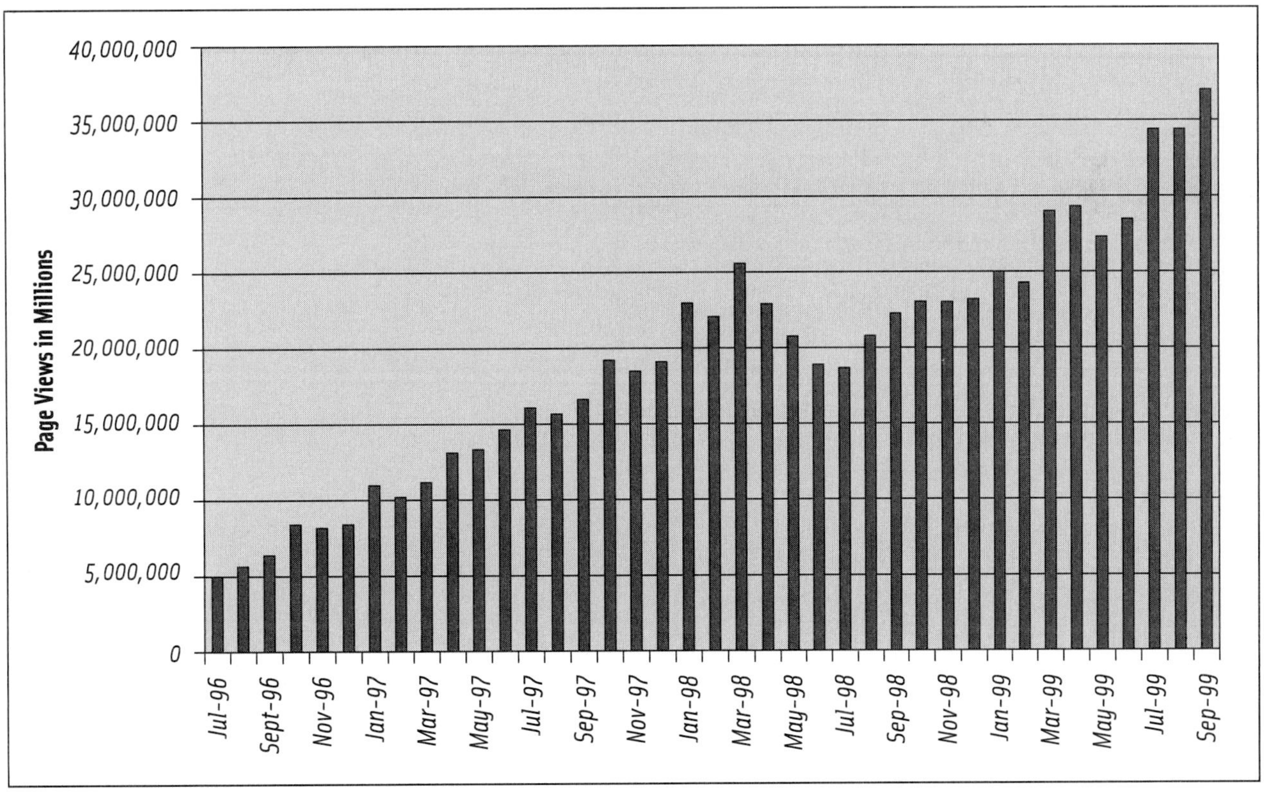

Source: Adapted from Media Metrix

Exhibit 3 BOSTON GLOBE CIRCULATION, 1989–1999

	1989	1990	1991	1992	1993	1994	1995	1996	1997	1998	1999
Daily	509.6	523.0	517.0	505.7	504.9	500.3	500.6	486.4	466.3	472.7	469.3
Sunday	787.4	787.9	798.3	808.3	811.4	815.3	785.9	777.9	751.4	748.7	730.4

Source: *The Boston Globe*

Exhibit 4 BOSTON GLOBE CIRCULATION REVENUE, 1989–1998 ('000)

	1989	1990	1991	1992	1993	1994	1995	1996	1997	1998
Home Delivery	52,021	62,677	72,108	77,568	72,035	74,543	81,858	88,146	90,994	92,822
Single copy	34,871	31,902	31,447	29,247	34,936	35,868	39,526	44,249	41,017	37,907
Total Revenue	86,892	94,579	103,355	106,815	106,971	110,411	121,384	132,395	132,011	130,729
% single-copy sales	40%	34%	30%	27%	33%	32%	33%	33%	31%	29%

Source: *The Boston Globe*

Exhibit 5 AD REVENUES FOR A TYPICAL MAJOR MARKET NEWSPAPER THE SIZE OF *THE BOSTON GLOBE*

Local Display	National Display	Classified	Free-Standing Inserts	Total Advertising
$104 million	$22 million	$172 million	$59 million	$357 million
29%	6%	48%	17%	100%

Source: Adapted from Inland Press Association, "Cost and Revenue Study for Daily Newspapers, 1998"

Exhibit 6 THE U.S. ONLINE ADVERTISING MARKET

	1999	2000	2001	2002	2003	2004
U.S. Online Ad spending (millions)	$2,805	$5,358	$8,680	$12,587	$17,244	$22,244
- Annual growth rate	119%	91%	62%	45%	37%	29%
- Percent of traditional advertising	1.3%	2.4%	3.7%	5.1%	6.6%	8.1%
- Performance-based spending (millions)	$421	$1,393	$3,038	$5,412	$8,622	$11,790
- Revenue per thousand page views	$7	$9	$10	$12	$13	$15
- Barter-type effects (millions)	$561	$857	$1,128	$1,259	$1,207	$1,112
- US online households (millions)	39	44	51	56	60	63
U.S. Online Retail Spending (millions)	$18,152	$33,029	$52,244	$76,269	$108,031	N/A
- Annual growth rate	132%	82%	58%	46%	42%	N/A
- Percent of traditional commerce	1%	1%	2%	2%	6%	N/A
- Online advertising/online commerce	15%	16%	17%	17%	16%	N/A
- Traditional advertising/traditional commerce	8%	8%	8%	8%	8%	N/A
U.S. per Capita Ad Spending						
- Online	$40	$67	$94	$124	$160	$195
- Magazine	$56	$58	$60	$62	$65	$67
- Radio	$89	$92	$96	$100	$103	$108
- Newspaper	$335	$348	$362	$376	$391	$406
- Television	$258	$268	$279	$290	$301	$313

Source: Adapted from Forrester Research, "Internet Advertising Skyrockets" (August 1999)

Exhibit 7

IMPACT ON NEWSPAPER CLASSIFIED REVENUE DUE TO ONLINE COMPETITION

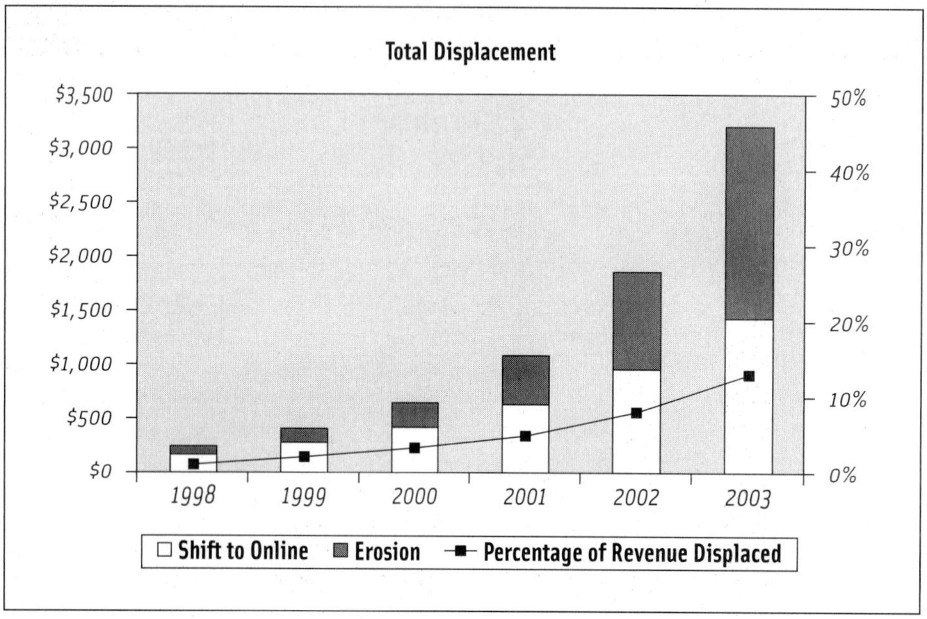

Source: Compiled from Jupiter Communications, "Classifieds: Online Projections" (July 1999)

Note: Read bars of graph to left figures; percentage line to right.

Explanation: "Shift to Online" is the amount of print classified advertising revenue projected by Jupiter to move to online classified players. In 2003, $1.4 billion is projected to shift from potential newspaper print classified to online.

"Erosion" is the impact on the off-line classifieds market caused by free and discounted classifieds necessitated by the new competitive landscape. In 2003, Jupiter projects that $1.8 billion in potential classified revenue will be lost to newspapers due to such discounting.

"Percentage of Revenue Displaced" is the percentage of revenues lost by newspapers if there were no online classifieds. It is determined by adding the effects of erosion to the revenues of online classified players. In 2003, Jupiter projects newspapers to lose $3.2 billion in traditional classified revenues, or 13% of what the market would be without online classifieds.

Exhibit 8 CLASSIFIEDS ONLINE LANDSCAPE

Aggregators						Classified Competitive Landscape Analysis
Company	**Value-Added Services**	**Distribution Partners**	**Revenue Model**	**Owners/ Investors**	**Traffic (in 000s)[a]**	**Analysis**
Classifieds2000 Excite *www.classifieds2000.com*	Aggregates classifieds into categories: auto, employment, real estate, rentals, personals, services, and auctions; an e-mail feature called Cool Notify. Tag Line: The Internet classifieds.	Excite, Infoseek, WebCrawler, LookSmart, Netscape, Snap, ZDNet, iVillage, Bigfoot, GeoCities, InfoBeat, Quote.com, NetGuide	Excite Careers Network charges for job listings; other classifieds are free of charge. Banner and sponsorship revenue from Excite Network.	A division of Excite Inc. acquired April 1998	1,081	By allowing person-to-person bids on certain categories, such as computers, Classifieds2000 is taking classifieds to the next level. However, this is a tough space to compete in, given eBay's dominance of person-to-person auctions. Don't expect Classifieds2000 to topple eBay anytime soon.
Classified Warehouse AdOne Classified Network *www.classifiedwarehouse.com*	Listings include employment, automotive, real estate, franchises, and other person-to-person trade and services.	Lycos, theglobe.com	Revenue sharing from newspaper affiliates, banner, and sponsorship revenue.	AdOne Classified Network, acquired by a consortium, including MediaNews Group, Hearst, the E. W. Scripps Co., Advance Publications, and Donrey Media Group. Also acquired Franchise Solutions November 1999.	2,300	Because the site culls ads from local newspaper affiliates, it is easy for users to place an ad both online and in print; the site features a handy clipping service to save particular ads. However, Classifieds Warehouse serves as further proof that newspapers just don't understand the Internet. Its ads are brief, abbreviated, and aggregate everything from vacation rentals to cars to pets for adoption; without targeting a specific vertical market, the site will have trouble succeeding.
InfoSpace *www.infospace.com*	Aggregates classifieds and directory listings plus related content, maps, and commodity data. Tag Line: The Ultimate Directory.	Syndication and distribution through partners, including AOL, Netscape, Lycos, MSN, Dow Jones, MetaCrawler, NBC, Snap, Playboy, and Dow Jones	Aggregates content from third-party sources, integrating it with value-added content and syndicating it for affiliates. Majority of revenues gained from advertising and sponsorships, plus ad revenue sharing from affiliate sites.	Public company	5,306	Classifieds aggregated from other online databases are only one of the various types of listings available on the site. Because users can only search one database at a time, it is difficult to see why they would use InfoSpace rather than going directly to a vertical classified provider.

Exhibit 8 CLASSIFIEDS ONLINE LANDSCAPE cont.

Automobiles							Classified Competitive Landscape Analysis
Company	**Value-Added Services**	**Distribution Partners**	**Rate Card/ Revenue Model**	**Owners/ Investors**	**Number of Dealers and Listings**	**Traffic (in 000s)[a]**	**Analysis**
MSN CarPoint Microsoft Corporation *carpoint.msn.com*	Kelley Blue Book, finance and insurance section, news, ratings, reviews, calculator, interest rates	Yahoo! Excite, Infoseek, HotBot, WebCrawler	Dealers pay for generation of leads and can list their used car inventory for a monthly fee. Carpoint also hosts dealer showcase websites for initial setup and maintenance charges.Additional banner and sponsorship revenue.	Microsoft; Ford Motor Company, launched July 1996	2,000 dealers	1,991	Microsoft understands the auto classifieds market. The company provides services not only for the car buyer, but also for the car owner, and attracts repeat visits by offering personal information on tune-ups, recalls, and repairs. Ford's investment in MSN CarPoint allows the car manufacturer to see customer shopping patterns and help them build-to-order vehicles using MS technology.
Autobytel.com *www.autobytel.com*	Leasing, financing application, pricing, reviews, articles, credit reports, warranties, mechanical breakdown, a rewards program, and insurance available. Tag Line: We're changing the way America buys cars.	Excite, Infoseek, Netscape, Lycos	Receives a commission and/or fees from dealer referrals, insurance, financing, and leasing. Dealers pay initial subscription fee plus a monthly fee of $600.	IPO filed; financed by GE Capital services, AIG, Media One Interactive Services; launched 1995	2,560 dealers, as of March 1999	740	Autobytel.com has added much deeper content of the car buyer, indicating that the company understands what it takes to succeed in the automotive classifieds market. Additionally, it recently launched a personalized car care service, extending the consumer relationship beyond the buying process.
Cars.com Classified Ventures *www.cars.com*	Reports, reviews, news, loan calculator, rates	AOL, Excite, Alta Vista	Car dealers form relationships with Cars.com's affiliate newspapers, and list their vehicles in print and online. Internet marketing package offered to dealers can include generation of leads, customized websites, and/or full inventory posting on a fee basis.	Classified Ventures (An online classifieds service owned by a newspaper consortium of The New York Times, Washington Post, Chicago Tribune, McClatchy Co., Knight Ridder, Gannett and CNI.)	340 dealers 125,000 listings, as of January 1999	995	Cars.com is rich in content and ancillary services. The site also includes advice from Car Talk radio show hosts Tom and Ray Magliozzi. The search results interface is one of the sleekest and easiest to navigate. The company also has developed (somewhat complicated) discount deals for its users.

Exhibit 8

CLASSIFIEDS ONLINE LANDSCAPE cont.

Real Estate							Classified Competitive Landscape Analysis
Company	**Value-Added Services**	**Distribution Partners**	**Rate Card/ Revenue Model**	**Owners/ Investors**	**Number of Dealers and Listings**	**Traffic (in 000s)[a]**	**Analysis**
Realtor.com *www.realtor.com*	Neighborhood information and school reports for fee Tag Line: Your next home is here.	Provides listings on AOL's Real Estate Center, Classifieds, and Digital Cities (co-branded), Excite, WebCrawler, Classifieds2000, Netscape Netcenter, Infoseek, Lycos	Free basic listings can be upgraded, list as a Feature Home or include a virtual house tour for an additional fees	HomeStore.com, public company formed by merger of Real Select and Spring Street	1.3 million listings	1,602	The site caters as much to realtors as to home buyers, and it does an excellent job of walking home buyers through the many steps of a complicated process. Realtor.com has some interesting marketing partnerships, such as Home Depot and Kmart, but they are buried deep within the site.
MSN Home Advisor Microsoft *homeadvisor.msn.com*	Mortgage tools and neighborhood and school information crime reports	Provides listings on GeoCities, Yahoo!, Infoseek, Switchboard, Pathfinder, Tripod, mortgage service to InfoSpace	Free of charge to brokers and agents. Generates revenue by matching qualified home buyers with leading institutions, also obtains advertising revenue	Microsoft	500,000 listings	788	The site has very strong content offerings for everyone from neophytes to experienced home hunters, with an easy-to-use interface and navigation. Microsoft has made some aggressive moves in attracting buyers: It offers a free PC when customers close a loan. The site is also cutting smart advertising deals, such as its strategic alliance with Sears.
Homes.com *www.homes.com*	Mortgage center, property reports, school information, demographics, community data. The most comprehensive Web site available for real estate.	Yahoo!, Classified2000, Virtual Relocation, iOwn.com	Real estate brokers and agents can list their properties through Preferred Pages Web sites, $2,000 to $9,000 plus monthly fees, or through the print magazine.	Listings from Homes and Land magazine	300,000	262	A recent redesign has added deeper content for home seekers, yet the site still relies heavily on content from its print magazine. Too much extraneous content, such as information on owning a franchise of its magazine, detracts from the home-buying process. Homes.com has also added deeper content for realtors and brokers.

Exhibit 8 CLASSIFIEDS ONLINE LANDSCAPE cont.

Real Estate (continued)							Classified Competitive Landscape Analysis
Company	**Value-Added Services**	**Distribution Partners**	**Rate Card/ Revenue Model**	**Owners/ Investors**	**Number of Dealers and Listings**	**Traffic (in 000s)[a]**	**Analysis**
HomeHunter.com *www.homehunter.com*	Locally based content, services, information, finance guide Tag Line: Your online guide to buying and selling a home	Partners with Real Cities; distribution on AOL, Excite, Infoseek, PointCast, Yahoo!	Revenue sharing from affiliated newspapers, Real Cities sites, realtors' listings, banners, and sponsorships	Classified Ventures	N/A	N/A	HomeHunter.com is currently under redesign (again) and doesn't provide users with any upcoming information other than a list of newspaper partners. The site is missing an opportunity to gather potential homebuyer information to inform them of the relaunch.
NewHomeNetwork *www.newhomenetwork.com*	Floor plans, maps, school and community information, mortgage and affordability calculators, photos, save search results	AOL, Excite, Infoseek, PointCast, Yahoo!	Paid model, builder, and community showcases, advertising and sponsorships	Classified Ventures	N/A	N/A	An excellent resource for new home buyers, with professional advice, well-written columns, and useful tools. Probably the best of the Classified Ventures real estate sites.
Apartments.com *www.apartments.com*	Moving center relocation resources, credit reports, calculators	Infoseek, AOL, Yahoo!, Snap, Excite, Netscape, WebCrawler, InfoSpace, PointCast, USA Today	Property managers pay to list their rentals; packages available range from basic to Platinum; incremental banner and sponsorship revenue.	Formerly Apartments Plus, acquired by Classified Ventures	800,000 rentals	298	Apartments.com packs a great deal of information into individual listings, providing a useful guide for consumers looking into apartment rental market. Additionally, the site contains relocation tools most of its competitors lack.
HomeStore.com *www.homestore.com*	Provide real estate-related information, products, and services through Realtor.com, Remodel.com, HomeBuilder.com, SpringStreet.com, HomeFair.com, Commercial Source.com	Excite@Home, Digitial City, AOL, @Home Network, Netscape, MediaOne, CompuServ, NBC, WebCrawler, PointCast	N/A	Kleiner Perkins, Witney Equity Partners, national Association of Realtors	8 million	2,285	Its niche focus distinguishes HomeStore.com from its competitors and the site provides a deeper home-searching experience. HomeStore.com acts as the entry way for its niche sites.

Exhibit 8

CLASSIFIEDS ONLINE LANDSCAPE cont.

Recruiting							Classified Competitive Landscape Analysis
Company	**Value-Added Services**	**Distribution Partners**	**Rate Card/ Revenue Model**	**Owners/ Investors**	**Number of Dealers and Listings**	**Traffic (in 000s)[a]**	**Analysis**
Monster.com TMP Worldwide *www.monster.com*	My Monster, résumés and cover letter management, company profiles, e-mail search agent, Careers Network, chat, message boards	Alliances with Advertising Age, AOL, College Town USA, Future Pages, Excite, iVillage, Neoforma, Netscape, PlanetIT, Yahoo!, USAToday.com	$225 per single ad, posted for 60 days. Membership packages, company profiles, résumés database access, banners, buttons, and sponsorships available	TMP Worldwide	195,000 listings	2,582	Monster.com's push at off-line branding has created a significant lead over competitors. True to its name, Monster.com is probably the most well-recognized career site. The company has taken a broad strategy, amassing a significant database of résumés and listings, and should remain a leader for general job listings for some time. In addition, facing competition from smaller and niche recruiting sites, Monster.com has begun to develop industry-specific sub-sites—a smart move.
CareerPath.com *www.careerpath.com*	Save job search results, submit online résumés, company profiles, news, content offerings, virtual job fairs Tag Line: You can go anywhere from here.	The Boston Globe, The Chicago Tribune, The Los Angeles Times, The New York Times, The San Jose Mercury News, The Washington Post, The Austin American-Statesman, The Fort Worth Star-Telegram, The San Antonio Express-News, The Bellingham Herald, The Herald Dispatch, The Kansas City Star, The Jackson Sun, and the News and Observer; 90 affiliates in total supply listings and direct readers to CareerPath site	Affiliate relationship with newspapers provides local or network advertising. Subscriptions to résumé database available for three months for $1,000 or one year for $3,000. Provides company profiles, and corporate job listing uploading is available for a fee. Banner and sponsorship revenue.	Financially backed by Knight Ridder, The New York Times Co., The Tribune Co., The Washington Post Co., Cox Interactive Media, Gannett, and Hearst	380,000 listings	1,004	While bolstered by content from newspaper affiliates, CareerPath.com has an enormous number of job listings. However, most listings are from print newspapers and the search results often offer very limited information. Site does not truly exploit the Internet as a recruitment tool, because listings are basically reprints from print publications. Navigational and user interface difficulty make CareerPath.com a very weak player.

Exhibit 8

CLASSIFIEDS ONLINE LANDSCAPE cont.

Recruiting							Classified Competitive Landscape Analysis
Company	**Value-Added Services**	**Distribution Partners**	**Rate Card/ Revenue Model**	**Owners/ Investors**	**Number of Dealers and Listings**	**Traffic (in 000s)[a]**	**Analysis**
BrassRing Inc. *www.brassring.com*	Virtual career fairs/ online recruiting through Terra-Star and thepavement. Skills assessment through Kaplan and hiring management through HireSystems are all under one roof.	Terra-Star.com, thepavement, kaplancareeerfairs.com, HireSystems	N/A; site launch in spring 2000	Kaplan, Washington Post, Tribune, and Accel Partners	N/A; site launch in spring 2000	N/A; site launch in spring 2000	As CareerPath.com falters, two of its lead investors try again. Because BrassRing is very late to market, it will have to spend aggressively to have any chance to catch up to its competitors. It is essential that it use the resources of the Washington Post and the Tribune can provide.
Headhunter.Net *www.headhunter.net*	Confidential résumé posting Tag Line: This is the way to work.	Supplies listings to Yahoo! and Alta Vista; affiliate program with GeoCities; sponsor of Tripod's Jobs and Careers section.	Free for basic listings, upgrades available for \$25 to \$75 per month.	Financed by ITC Holdings Company	260,000 listings	687	This site's interesting model allows employers to upgrade their job listings–and job seekers to upgrade their résumés for higher visibility (for a fee)–but it is doubtful that users will take advantage of the service when there are so many free competitors
HotJobs.com *www.hotjobs.com*	Users can block résumés from companies (privacy and control), résumé statistics (e.g., number of times résumé has been viewed, number of jobs applied for), company profiles, personal search agent, free e-mail, message boards, no headhunter listings Tag Line: The experienced professional's job board.	Yahoo!Classified, theglobe.com, AltaVista, usenetgroup, America's Job Bank	\$150 per ad, per month. Membership includes 20 postings for \$600 per month. Banners, buttons, sponsorships, and marketing partnerships available	Privately funded by founders	Over 130 member companies; 17,000 listings (as of March 1999)	584	HotJobs.com offers job seekers deep company information and a streamlined application process. The company's privacy features are a competitive advantage that many other recruitment sites lack.

Source: Adapted from Jupiter Communications, "Classifieds: Online Landscape," Marissa Gluck, December 1999
[a]Media Metrix, September 1999

Exhibit 9 RECRUITMENT, REAL ESTATE, AUTOMOTIVE SITES AUDIENCE REACH

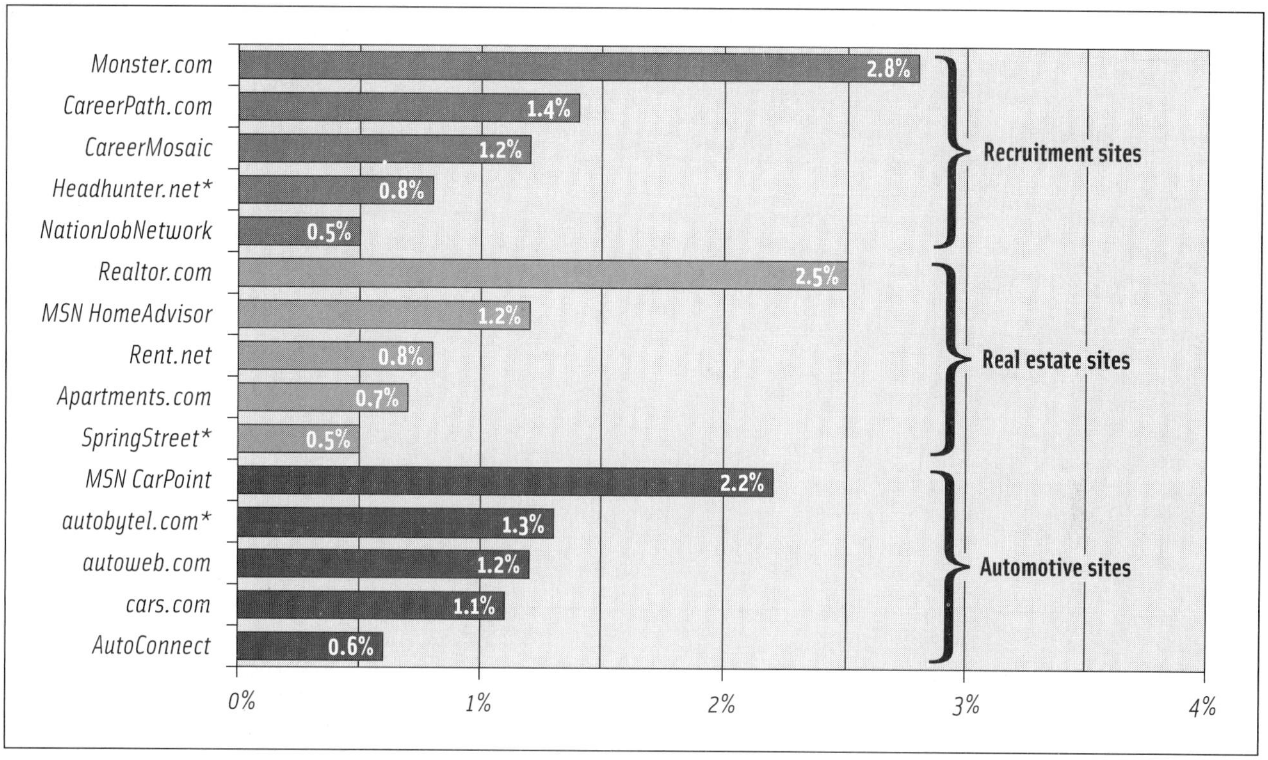

Source: © 1999 Jupiter Communications
*Based on network aggression

Exhibit 10 COMPETITIVE MEDIA INDEX: % OF ADULTS REACHED BY VARIOUS MEDIA

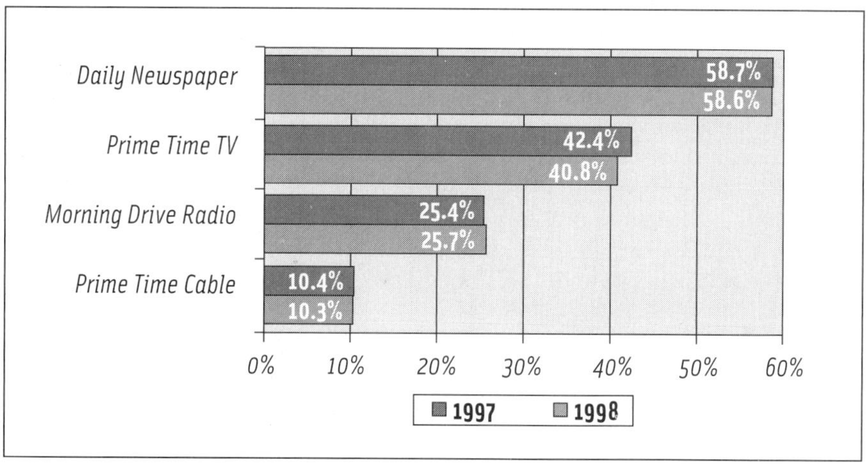

Source: Scarborough Research–"Top 50 DMA Market Report," 1996–1998

Exhibit 11

BOSTON.COM ORGANIZATION CHART JULY 1999

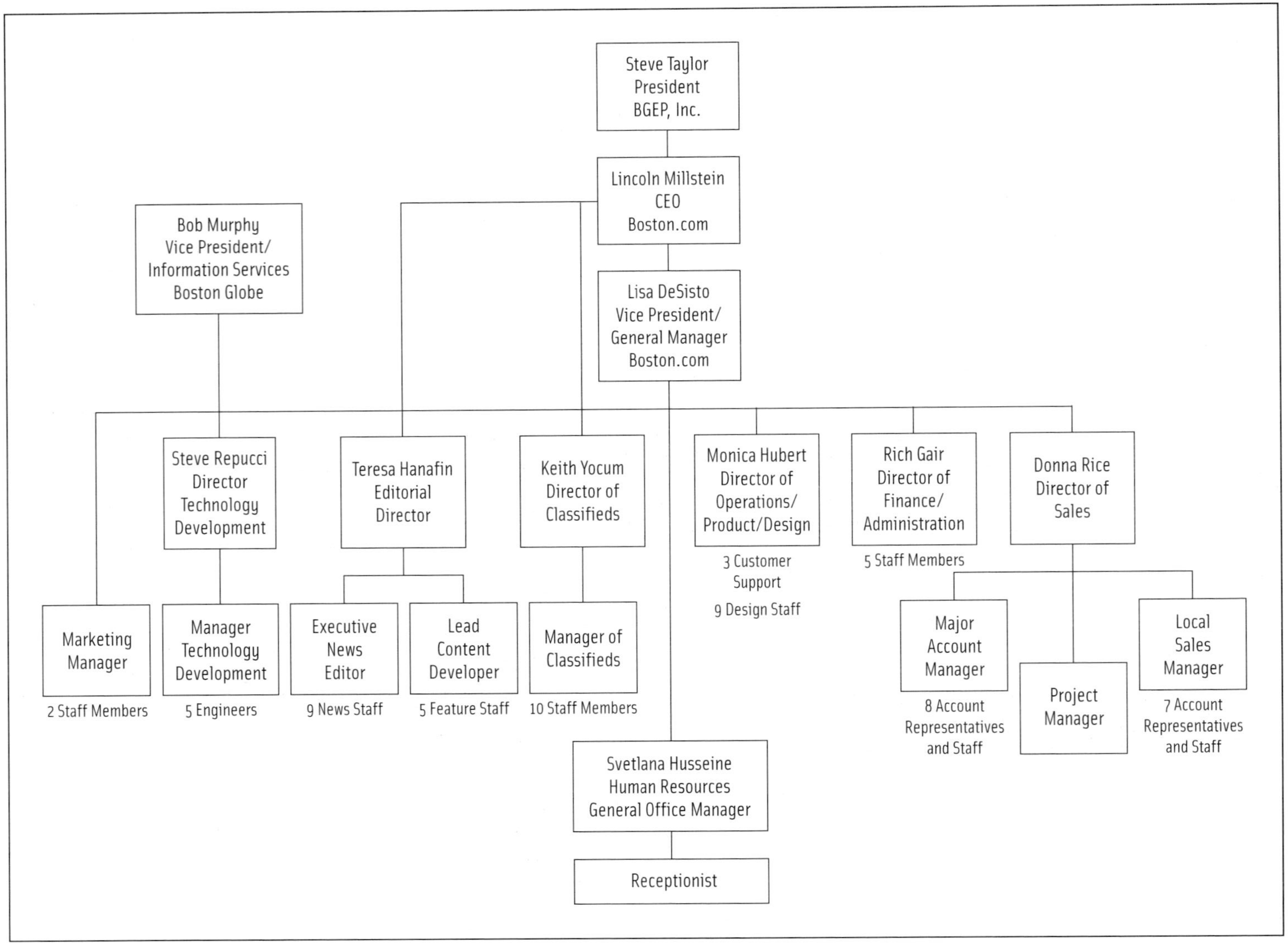

Source: The Company

Exhibit 12

BOSTON.COM ADVERTISING REVENUE

	1995	1996	1997	1998	Actual 1999-Q1	Budget 1999-Q1	% to Budget-Q1	Budget 1999
Classified	–	20,443	230,012	747,349	367,137	252,794	145%	1,420,355
Class/Allocation	–	–	–	800,000	180,000	180,000	100	720,000
Classified–Total	–	20,443	230,012	1,547,349	547,137	432,794	126	2,140,355
Majors	5,200	464,970	1,207,411	2,084,092	533,950	700,000	76	4,150,000
Local	–	–	–	477,420	245,422	373,851	66	1,844,331
Archives	–	31,602	357,233	1,035,754	342,803	224,003	153	896,000
Other	–	112,010	50,237	278,347	74,333	73,260	101	443,180
Totals	5,200	629,025	1,844,893	5,422,962	1,743,645	1,803,908	97	9,473,866

Source: Company documents

Exhibit 13

BOSTON.COM CLASSIFIED ADVERTISING REVENUE BY CATEGORY

	1995	1996	1997	1998	1999 - Q1	1999 Budget
Real Estate	–	–	–	42,750	46,245	227,305
Autos	–	–	12,600	95,500	36,720	256,655
Help Wanted	–	200	125,208	523,617	269,180	848,195
Other	–	20,243	92,204	85,482	14,992	88,200
Total Classified	–	20,443	230,012	747,349	367,137	1,420,355
Allocation[a]	–	–	–	800,000	180,000	720,000
Total	–	20,443	230,012	1,547,349	547,137	2,140,355

Source: Company documents

[a]Allocation from *Globe* is based on .5% of newspaper classified ad categories that are sent to Boston.com for listing

Exhibit 14 HELP WANTED ADVERTISING RATES FOR BOSTON.COM AND MONSTER.COM

Type of Product	Boston.com price[a]	Monster.com price[b]
Sponsorships, banners, tiles	$3,500 per month and up	N/A
Wraps	$750–$1,900 per month	Customized
Employer profiles	$417 per month	$270–$570 per month[c]
Bulk job listings	$59–$89 per listing	$65–$224 per listing
Individual job listings	$149 per listing	$275 per listing
Other services provided	Resume searches, virtual job fairs	Auctionplace for independent pros

[a]Company document
[b]Monster.com rate sheet
[c]Annual contract rate

Exhibit 15 EVOLUTION OF CLASSIFIED ADVERTISING

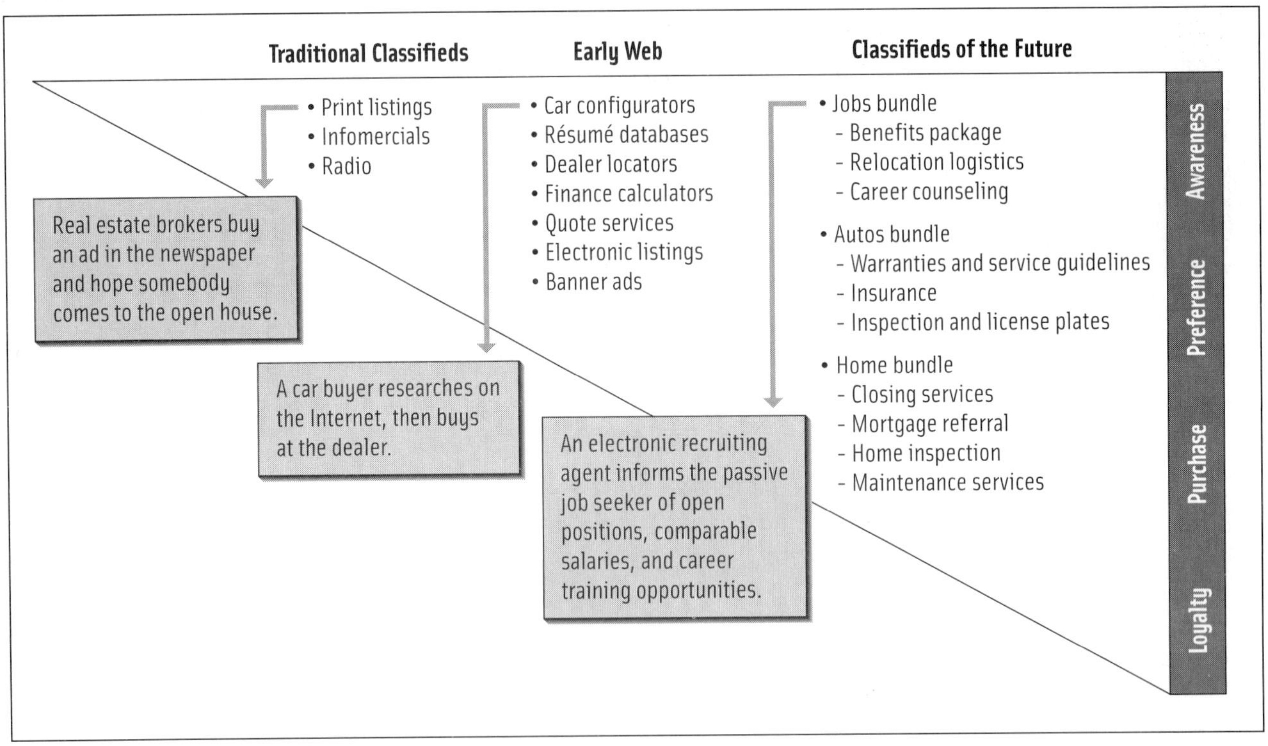

Source: Forrester Research, Inc.

Exhibit 16 BOSTON.COM SITE INDEX AND MEDIA PARTNERS

MEDIA PARTNERS
Boston Globe
Banker & Tradesman
Boston Magazine
Mass High Tech
On Call Magazine
Panorama Boston Guide
Portland Press
Yankee Mag.
Homes Mag.

RADIO STATIONS
KISS108
MIX 98.5
STAR 93.7
WBCN-FM
WBOS-FM
WBUR
WBZ-AM
WCRB
WRKO AM680
WXRV The River 92.5
WZLX-FM

TELEVISION
WBZ Ch. 4
WCVB Ch. 5
WGBH Ch. 2
WHDH Ch. 7
NECN
NESN

ARTS & MUSEUMS
American Repertory Theatre
ARTS/Boston
Boston Ballet
Boston Symphony
Computer Museum
DeCordova Museum
Emerson Majestic
Garden in Woods
Gardner Museum
Handel & Haydn
Huntington Theatre
Mass. Horticultural
Museum of Afro American History
Museum of Fine arts
Museum of Science
N.E. Aquarium
NEXT Ticketing
Revels
USS Constitution
The Wang Center
Wine Today

COMMUNITY
Irish Famine Mem.
Boston Public Lib.
Jimmy Fund
Mass Audubon Society
March of Dimes
United Way
Virtually Wired

MORE
Appalachian Mountain
Better Business Bureau
BusinessWire
CarTalk.com
Cybersmith
Ford Hall Forum
PR Newswire
Nordby International
SmarTraveler Traffic
Weather Service

Site index

Auctions
Books, Movies, and Music, Collectibles and Memorabilia, Computers, Entertainment, Gifts & Travel, General Merchandise, Sports & Recreation, Travel and Vacations, Vehicles

Autos
In partnership with cars.com
Used cars, Dealers, Antiques, trucks, motorcycles, more, Sell your car,
Loan rates, Loan calculator, Buyer resources, Model reports, Advice, Car Talk, Driver resources

Business
News, Stock quotes, Emerging Business, Reliability reports, Banking, Events, License search, Banking resources, Latest banking news, Credit cards and student loans, Office equipment search

Careers
Search, Employer profiles, Place ads, Links, Events, Post a resume

Chat
Commoners, Internet Stocks, Peter Hotton, Red Sox, Patriots, Celtics,
Bruins, Revolution, Ryder Cup, SportsTalk

Education Resources
Preschool, Kindergarten, Middle School, High School, College, Adult education, Special education, Teacher certification

Going Out/Arts
Movies, Books, Music, Television, Museums, Performance, Partners, A & E news wire, Horoscopes, Personals, MovieMail, Dining, Other listings

Health
News, Physician Profiles, Calendar, Studies and volunteers, Drugs and medications, Links, Fact sheets, Emergency numbers

Music (MP3)
Getting Started, Upload Center, Download Center

Personal Finance
Calculators, College, Financial News, Home Buying, Loan Rates, Quote Center, Retirement, Your Portfolio

Real Estate
Homes, Apartments, Office space, Cape Cod, Commercial space, Links Open houses, Out of state, Recent sales, Sell your home on-line, Mortgage rates, Mortgage calculator, Vacation rentals, Place print ad, Place online ad

More
What's new & hot on Boston.com
Contests & giveaways
Marketbasket
Online personals
This day in history

Sports/Outdoors
News, Bruins, Red Sox, Patriots, Revolution, Golf, Scoreboard, Activities, TV/Radio

Technology
Techie corner, Downloads, Discussions, Conferences, Mass high tech listings, Software library, Computer news, On computers, Cybernotes, Local ISPs

Traffic
Current traffic conditions, Boston and Cambridge roads, Logan airport conditions, Get a map, Get directions, Current Commuter Rail conditions, Related links

Travel
Features, Airfares, Daytrips, Destinations, Boston, Cape and Islands, New England, US & World, Camp Guide Consumer reports, Taking the kids

Weather
Five-day Boston forecast, New England, United States, Europe, Asia, Marine, Radar imagery, Satellite imagery

Weddings
Your Wedding, Articles, Free Enrollment, Enrolled Couples, Guests, Gift Registry & Shopping Local Services

Yellow Pages
Auto, Community, Going Out, Health, Hotels & Travel, Money & Law Real Estate, Shops/Services, Sports

Your Town
Find Your Town, City Weekly, North Weekly, Northwest Weekly, South Weekly, West Weekly

New on Boston.com

Is This You?
Identify yourself in one of these photos taken around Boston and you could win $100.

Abuzz
Real people, real answers. Sign up for Abuzz and join Boston's circle.

MovieMail
Sign up for Boston.com's MovieMail, a free weekly e-mail providing you with upcoming film highlights, openings, schedules, and more.

MP3
We've got hundreds of local bands and their songs for you to download. Check out the Spotlight section for a weekly band feature and a calendar of shows by our bands.

Source: Adapted from Boston.com

Exhibit 17 HOME PAGE IMAGES: THE BOSTON GLOBE ONLINE AND BOSTON.COM, OCT. 1, 1999 (10:52 A.M.)

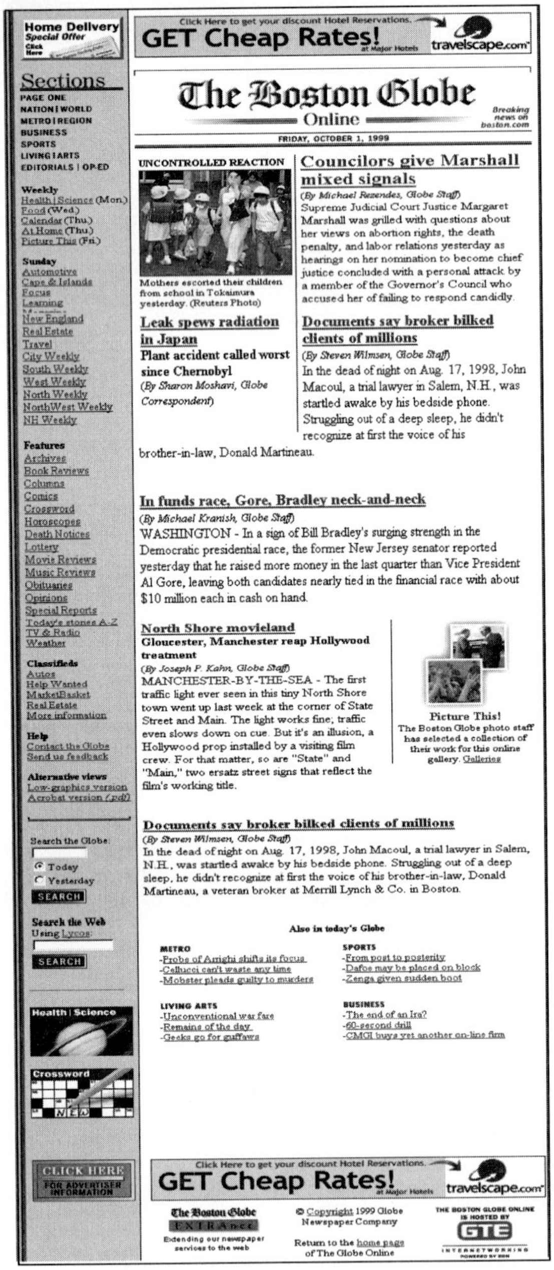
Home Delivery Special Offer Click Here

Click Here to get your discount Hotel Reservations. GET Cheap Rates! at Major Hotels travelscape.com

The Boston Globe Online

Breaking news on boston.com

FRIDAY, OCTOBER 1, 1999

Sections

PAGE ONE
NATION | WORLD
METRO | REGION
BUSINESS
SPORTS
LIVING | ARTS
EDITORIALS | OP-ED

Weekly
Health | Science (Mon.)
Food (Wed.)
Calendar (Thu.)
At Home (Thu.)
Picture This (Fri.)

Sunday
Automotive
Cape & Islands
Focus
Learning
New England
Real Estate
Travel
City Weekly
South Weekly
West Weekly
North Weekly
NorthWest Weekly
NH Weekly

Features
Archives
Book Reviews
Columns
Comics
Crossword
Horoscopes
Death Notices
Lottery
Movie Reviews
Music Reviews
Obituaries
Opinions
Special Reports
Today's stories A-Z
TV & Radio
Weather

Classifieds
Autos
Help Wanted
MarketBasket
Real Estate
More information

Help
Contact the Globe
Send us feedback

Alternative views
Low-graphics version
Acrobat version (.pdf)

Search the Globe:
Today
Yesterday
SEARCH

Search the Web
Using Lycos:
SEARCH

Health | Science

Crossword

CLICK HERE FOR ADVERTISER INFORMATION

UNCONTROLLED REACTION

Mothers escorted their children from school in Tokaimura yesterday. (Reuters Photo)

Leak spews radiation in Japan

Plant accident called worst since Chernobyl

(By Sharon Moshavi, Globe Correspondent)

Councilors give Marshall mixed signals

(By Michael Rezendes, Globe Staff)

Supreme Judicial Court Justice Margaret Marshall was grilled with questions about her views on abortion rights, the death penalty, and labor relations yesterday as hearings on her nomination to become chief justice concluded with a personal attack by a member of the Governor's Council who accused her of failing to respond candidly.

Documents say broker bilked clients of millions

(By Steven Wilmsen, Globe Staff)

In the dead of night on Aug. 17, 1998, John Macoul, a trial lawyer in Salem, N.H., was startled awake by his bedside phone. Struggling out of a deep sleep, he didn't recognize at first the voice of his brother-in-law, Donald Martineau.

In funds race, Gore, Bradley neck-and-neck

(By Michael Kranish, Globe Staff)

WASHINGTON - In a sign of Bill Bradley's surging strength in the Democratic presidential race, the former New Jersey senator reported yesterday that he raised more money in the last quarter than Vice President Al Gore, leaving both candidates nearly tied in the financial race with about $10 million each in cash on hand.

North Shore movieland

Gloucester, Manchester reap Hollywood treatment

(By Joseph P. Kahn, Globe Staff)

MANCHESTER-BY-THE-SEA - The first traffic light ever seen in this tiny North Shore town went up last week at the corner of State Street and Main. The light works fine; traffic even slows down on cue. But it's an illusion, a Hollywood prop installed by a visiting film crew. For that matter, so are "State" and "Main," two ersatz street signs that reflect the film's working title.

Picture This!
The Boston Globe photo staff has selected a collection of their work for this online gallery. Galleries

Documents say broker bilked clients of millions

(By Steven Wilmsen, Globe Staff)

In the dead of night on Aug. 17, 1998, John Macoul, a trial lawyer in Salem, N.H., was startled awake by his bedside phone. Struggling out of a deep sleep, he didn't recognize at first the voice of his brother-in-law, Donald Martineau, a veteran broker at Merrill Lynch & Co. in Boston.

Also in today's Globe

METRO
-Probe of Arrighi shifts its focus
-Cellucci can't waste any time
-Mobster pleads guilty to murders

SPORTS
-From post to posterity
-Dafoe may be placed on block
-Zenga given sudden boot

LIVING ARTS
-Unconventional war fare
-Remains of the day
-Geeks go for guffaws

BUSINESS
-The end of an Ira?
-60-second drill
-CMGI buys yet another on-line firm

Click Here to get your discount Hotel Reservations. GET Cheap Rates! at Major Hotels travelscape.com

The Boston Globe EXTRAnet
Extending our newspaper services to the web

© Copyright 1999 Globe Newspaper Company
Return to the home page of The Globe Online

THE BOSTON GLOBE ONLINE IS HOSTED BY GTE INTERNETWORKING

63, Sunny at Logan Airport [More weather]
Boston.com was last updated at 10:51 AM

SEAPORT HOTEL Boston's newest waterfront hotel. Click Here

The Boston Globe's boston.com

Welcome home!
PULL DOWN FOR OTHER SECTIONS

CLICK HERE FOR The Boston Globe ONLINE

FRIDAY, OCTOBER 1, 1999

SEARCH:
Keyword
Boston.com
Web LYCOS

Auctions
Careers
Cars
Classifieds
Real Estate
Shopping
Weddings
Yellow Pages
Business
Chat
Going Out/Arts
Health
MP3 Music
Personal Finance
Sports
Technology
Traffic
Travel
Weather
Your Town

Specials

All Souls
A four part series of excerpts reprinted from "All Souls: A Family Story from Southie"

Pet Contest
A snapshot of why we love our pets

Spotlight team
The Globe Spotlight series on corruption and favoritism in Massachusetts communities.

BOSTON.COM
Advertising info
Help
Contests
Site index
What's new

BOSTON GLOBE
Newspaper services
Home delivery
Globe advertising

BOSTON.COM IS HOSTED BY GTE INTERNETWORKING

GEEKS GO FOR GUFFAWS

Jay Stevens (left) and John Hargrave film "Computer Stew", their daily show, in the Cambridge offices of on-line publisher ZDNet.
• Check out the story
• Computer Stew

State OK's $16b bank merger

State officials gave a final nod yesterday to Fleet Financial Group Inc.'s proposed acquisition of BankBoston Corp., eliminating the last regulatory hurdle to a deal that creates New England's dominant bank.

RELATED MATERIAL
• VIDEO: Region's largest bank is born

BUSINESS/TECHNOLOGY

60 second drill

Entrepreneurs show off their 'elevator pitches'

Jay Wilkins and Marc Lind each had just 60 seconds - the time it takes to ride an elevator down a dozen floors in an office building - to describe their Internet start-up companies, the market opportunities for them, and why they will prosper.

RELATED MATERIAL
• Ebay will expand regional service

TGIF - ALEX BEAM

Remains of the day haunt a billionaire

For Internet billionaire David Wetherell, a funny thing happened on the way to building his personal high-tech Xanadu. Well, maybe not so funny from Wetherell's point of view.

Councilors give Marshall mixed reviews

Supreme Judicial Court Justice Margaret Marshall was grilled with questions about her views yesterday as hearings on her nomination to become chief justice concluded with a personal attack by a member of the Governor's Council who accused her of failing to respond candidly.

RELATED MATERIAL
• Two law professors criticize Marshall for her 1992 letter
• McGrory: Cellucci can't waste any time

Picture This!
A collection of photographs from local and world-wide events viewed through the lenses of the Boston Globe's photography staff [Galleries]

Health / Science

Exotic twist to perils of life in NYC: mosquitoes

The area around Powell's Cove Park in northern Queens is a tidy, upper-middle-class neighborhood. It hardly seems like the breeding ground for a disease more commonly found in the Third World.

Scientists eye possible weakness in the AIDS virus

US researchers believe they may have found a chink in the armor of the AIDS virus, which could lead to a new generation of drugs designed to disable the virus before healthy cells are infected.

An artists rendering of the new Pizza Hut logo as it will look on a Russian rocket in November. (AP Photo) [Story] [A closer look]

Home Delivery Special Offer

boston.com Auctions Bid now!
Sharp 13" TV/VCR Combo

Market Watch
DOW 10,240.30 (-96.8)
NASDAQ 2,718.24 (-27.92)
Stock Quotes | Local Indexes

Sports News [Section]

Latest Sox worry: Nomar's wrist [Story]

CELTICS
Hall of Fame Day for McHale [Coverage]

FANTASY FOOTBALL
Sign up all season [Here]

Ryder99.com ONLINE GOLF GUIDE

New on the site

beehive
Help us test Beehive. Ask questions, get answers. Learn more

Read local high school journalists on Highwired.net

Other top stories

MASS | NEW ENGLAND
-Motorist who Stephen King indicted

TECHNOLOGY
-Celebrating 25 years of humble bar code
-1999's Ig Nobel awards announced

BUSINESS
-Searching for the worst boss

CONTINUOUS WIRE REPORTS
Sports

New England Cable News Click here for video clips of current news

— Friday, October 1 —

MOS movie
"Mysteries of Egypt" opens today at the Museum of Science's Mugar Omni Theater.

The music scene:
Linda Ronstadt and Emmylou Harris appear at the Orpheum, Gov't Mule visits Avalon, and more.

IN TODAY'S GLOBE
The FleetCenter, reports Names & Faces, still needs a headliner for New Year's Eve.

Is This You?
See if you show up on Boston.com.

All makes, models, modems
Cruise through our cars section.

Save on tickets
Find out what's on sale today from Arts/Boston.

Advertise on boston.com
or
Use Boston.com to do business with the Boston Globe: advertise, subscribe, contact the news room, and more.

Click here for assistance.
Please read our user agreement and user information privacy policy.

© Copyright 1999 Boston Globe Electronic Publishing, Inc.

Source: The Company

Exhibit 18 THE POD SCHEDULE

Time	Function
12 a.m.	Embargo on *Boston Globe* news stories lifted. Next morning's full newspaper content uploaded to *The Boston Globe* Online within Boston.com.
6 a.m.	Homepage editor begins building Boston.com front page based on *Globe* news articles.
7 a.m.	Deadline for having Boston.com homepage up and active. Editors review site from home.
7-9 a.m.	Few changes to homepage unless major story breaks. The Pod selects wire story updates.
9 a.m. to midnight	Layout of homepage is changed at least every 60 minutes by rotating different *Globe* stories onto the front or by superceding with breaking wire stories, either re-written by The Pod or run unedited.

Source: Company interviews

Exhibit 19 AUCTION FEES FOR eBAY

Insertion Fees

When you list your item for sale at eBay, you pay a non-refundable Insertion Fee. Insertion Fees **vary by the type of auction** you choose:

- ***Regular Listings***
  The Insertion Fee is based on the opening value or minimum bid for your item. However, Insertion Fees for Non-Binding Bid Categories and Vehicles are on a fixed schedule.
- ***Reserve Price Listings***
  The Insertion Fee is based upon the reserve price of the item you list for sale. Insertion Fees are non-refundable.
  When you list a Reserve Price Auction, you will also be charged a Reserve Price Auction Fee, which is based upon the reserve price. Reserve Price Auction Fees are fully refundable. At the end of the auction, **if** your item sells, the Reserve Price Auction Fee is refunded to your account. This also applies to Real Estate and Vehicles.
- ***Dutch Listings***
  The Insertion Fee is based upon the opening value or minimum bid of the item you list for sale multiplied by the quantity of items you offer. The maximum insertion fee for any Dutch auction is $2.00.

Opening Value or Reserve Price	Insertion Fee
$0.01–$9.99	$0.25
$10.00–$24.99	$0.50
$25.00–$49.00	$1.00
$50.00 and up	$2.00

Exhibit 19

AUCTION FEES FOR eBAY cont.

Insertion fees for items covered by the Non-Binding Bid policy and items in the Vehicle categories:

Item Category	Insertion Fee
General Vehicles: Cars *General Vehicles: Trucks* *General Vehicles: RVs* *Collector Vehicles: Collector Cars*	$25.00
Miscellaneous: Real Estate	$50.00

Additional Reserve Price Auction fee (**fully refunded if item sells**):

Reserve Price	Reserve Price Auction Fee
$0.01–$24.99	$0.50
$25.00 and up	$1.00

Fees for Additional Listing Options
When you list your item for sale, you can choose several listing options to promote your listing. Make it stand out and get more bids! These options also have non-refundable fees.

Additional Options	Insertion Fee
Bold	$2.00
Category Featured Auction	$14.95
Featured Auction	$99.95
Gift Icon	$1.00
Gallery	$0.25
Featured Gallery	$19.95

Final Value Fees
At the end of an auction, you will be charged a Final Value Fee based on the final sale price (final value) of your item:

- **Regular and Reserve Auctions** (when the reserve has been met) The final value is the closing bid. Remember, there is no Final Value Fee charged if the reserve is not met.
- **Dutch Auctions** The final value is the lowest successful bid, multiplied by the quantity of items you sold.

Then **here's how you calculate** your Final Value Fee (if you sold real estate or vehicles, see below):

1. Take the first $25 of your final value, and calculate 5% of that. If your item sold for $25 or less, this is your Final Value Fee.
2. If your final value was more than $25, take the additional amount, from $25.01 to $1,000, and calculate 2.5% of that.
3. If your final value was more than $1,000, take that additional amount and calculate 1.25% of the remaining amount.
4. Add these amounts together and you have your Final Value Fee!

Source: Adapted from information on eBay.com

Exhibit 20 THE NEW YORK TIMES COMPANY AND NEW YORK TIMES DIGITAL (JUNE 1999)

The New York Times Company

The New York Times Company (NYSE: NYT) is a diversified media company including newspapers, magazines, television and radio stations, and electronic information and publishing. The Company's core purpose is to enhance society by creating, collecting, and distributing high-quality news, information, and entertainment.

The Company, which had 1998 revenues of $2.9 billion, publishes *The New York Times, The Boston Globe* and 21 regional newspapers; publishes three magazines, including *Golf Digest*; and operates eight network-affiliated television stations and two New York City radio stations.

The Company operates nearly 50 websites, including nytimes.com, boston.com, and winetoday.com as part of its New York Times Digital business unit. It also operates news, photo, and graphic services as well as news and feature syndicates. The Company holds interests in one newsprint mill, one supercalendered paper mill, and the International Herald Tribune S.A.S.

New York Times Digital
(Figures as of June 1999)

National Sites

The New York Times on the Web
www.nytimes.com
The New York Times on the Web has over 7.8 million unique registered users. It recorded more than 85 million page views for the month of June and attracted more than 384,000 new registered users in that month alone (source NYT registration database). Users spent an average of 42.6 minutes per month with The New York Times on the Web, more than any other comparable news site and in the top five across all sites on the Internet (source: Media Metrix, June 1999).

The New York Times Learning Network
www.nytimes.com/learning
From The New York Times on the Web, the The New York Times Learning Network serves as an online resource for educators, parents, and students in grades 6 through 12. It provides daily lesson plans based on the content of the newspaper, online news quizzes, crossword puzzles, and other activities for students, and links to valuable online education resources for parents. In addition, vocabulary from *The New York Times* articles links to definitions from *Merriam-Webster's Collegiate Dictionary,* and country names to maps through *Microsoft Encarta* concise encyclopedia.

Wine Today
www.winetoday.com
This unique vertical site features comprehensive and timely news on the California Wine Country, averaging more than 130,000 unique visitors and 700,000 per month.

Golf Digest
www.golfdigest.com
Golf Digest is a vertical site currently under development based on content from *Golf Digest* magazine, the largest-circulating golf publication in the world. The website is designed to be a leading provider of quality content and e-commerce.

Source: Adapted from New York Times Company documents

Exhibit 20

THE NEW YORK TIMES COMPANY AND NEW YORK TIMES DIGITAL (JUNE 1999) cont

Regional Sites

Boston.com

www.boston.com

Boston.com is the country's largest regional gateway serving all of New England with more than 28.5 million page views in June.

New York Today

www.nytoday.com

New York Today is New York's leading online source of local lifestyle and entertainment news and information. It recorded 3.8 million page views in June.

Regional Newspaper Group

New York Times Digital also encompasses the websites for 18 daily and 3 nondaily award-winning newspapers located in Florida (9), Alabama (3), Louisiana (3), North Carolina (3), California (2), and South Carolina (1). Total print circulation for the regional newspaper group is, dailies: 736,800—weekday; 787,600—Sunday. Nondailies: 32,600—weekday; 14,500—Sunday.

Source: Adapted from New York Times Company documents

Exhibit 21 DLJ NEWSPAPERS.COM

DLJ
Media
Research
Feb. 15, 2000

NEWSPAPERS.COM

The DLJ Monthly Fast-Fax V.2, No.1

Monthly Commentary- William B. Drewry US (404) 897-2838

Monthly Commentary: Let the Games Begin

On January 28th, the New York Times Company announced that it had filed a registration statement to issue a tracking stock for New York Times Digital, the arm of NYT that houses all of its Internet operations. The stock responded on the following Monday by trading down by 1.35%. The biggest Internet-related announcement probably ever in the newspaper industry and the market said "so what?" Not an incredibly encouraging start to the Internet era for newspaper stocks. But then again, it wasn't an unexpected move. Perhaps it was a prime example of "buy on the rumor and sell on the news." But at NYT's current stock multiple, we doubt that. The stock has actually outperformed the overall market (S&P 500) year to date, mostly on the basis of a blowout Q4 earnings report. NYT's Internet revenues were up for the quarter by 145%, though we wonder if anyone even noticed. So, the near term takeaway seems to be that Internet tracking stocks are not important. We can't disagree for the near term, but beyond that period, we certainly do not concur.

The issue for newspaper stocks and Internet spinouts has always been two-fold: what is the implication for the new security and what is the ultimate implication back to the parent company? We continue to believe that the long-term effect of putting newspaper Internet operations into a separate company or security should be a major positive back to the parent company. For New York Times Company (or Knight Ridder (KRI – Buy) or Gannett (GCI – Buy) for that matter), a separate Internet security serves to make the Internet operations as transparent to investors as they possibly can be. This is important in a sector where investor perception has been negatively biased towards the newspaper's ability to succeed in a digital world. To date, it has been difficult to ascertain where the companies were in terms of progress and transparency takes care of that. NYT is using ultimate transparency with a separate tracking stock and hence a completely separate P&L. Other companies like Tribune (TRB – Buy), Knight Ridder and eventually Times Mirror (TMC – Buy) are taking a bridge approach by putting their online operations into a separate line item in segment reporting. Less detail than the NYT approach but better than before.

As this information works its way into the market, the attention turns back to the core company operations. We believe that the potential effect on the stocks has been underestimated by the market. When evaluating NYT for example, we believe that investors will potentially see three sets of numbers, similar to the approach that Ziff Davis (ZD+) took when it issued a tracking stock for ZD Net last year. There should be NYT consolidated, NYT "core operations" and NYTD "core operations". We believe, if prior investor form holds true, that NYT will be valued on the "core operations" numbers and some add back of value from NYTD. The parent stock may not get full credit for the value of the NYTD security on a day to day basis but to us, that is not the most important issue. The important issue would be the fact that the NYT core operations numbers will look even better than they already do once the NYTD losses, which have been building steadily for the last five years, are stripped out. It makes a cheap stock look even more cheap. It also makes the EBITDA growth margins even higher than before. Higher margins generally equate to higher returns.

The bottom line is that the bear case on newspaper stocks and Internet cannibalization has been falling apart over the last six months. The isolation of Internet operations from the core business only bolsters the bull case (our long held position) for newspapers as it shows the core operations to be healthy and growing. Advertising revenues are growing at a steady and improving clip, costs are under control and margins have been consistently increasing. With help wanted advertising volume in a recovery mode after a cyclical (and perhaps a bit of secular) downturn in 1998/99, the outlook is better today than it was even twelve months ago.

On the question of tracking stock versus spinout, the jury is still out. Many pundits in the market "pooh pooh" tracking stocks, saying they don't mean much and there is no takeout premium to be had since the parent company owns all of the assets. Well, maybe, maybe not. However, we would point out that there has not been a lot of tracking stocks in this sector and this could be somewhat of uncharted territory. We mentioned Ziff Davis, which is not a good analogy for the newspaper stocks, for obvious reasons. We would point to the tracking stocks that TCI used to great effect and investors did very well with Liberty Media and TSATA. Meanwhile, the parent stock zoomed up the charts during 1997 and 1998 pre-take out and was eventually sold for a major premium. Maybe not a great analogy either for potential newspaper company tracking stocks but as we said, there are not a huge number of pure media comparisons to use for the near term to chart the course.

Finally, we continue to believe that newspaper stocks still have a negative Internet bias priced into them and the stocks are suffering as of late from rate hike worries and newsprint price hike concerns. The short term cyclical factors should dissipate as investors get better visibility on what should be strong earnings in Q1, a situation similar to what we saw happen back in 1997, which was the last rising newsprint price environment (by the way, the stocks outperformed every quarter). However, on the Internet side, we believe that a potentially successful New York Times Digital offering could spur other companies to come to the market this year (like Dow Jones (DJ – Market Performance), Knight Ridder, Tribune and Gannett). And as the market digests what this actually means, that there is a new fast growing business but also a healthy base business, we believe that the stocks will respond positively.

Exhibit 21 DLJ NEWSPAPERS.COM cont.

Internet side, we believe that a potentially successful New York Times Digital offering could spur other companies to come to the market this year (like Dow Jones (DJ – Market Performance), Knight Ridder, Tribune and Gannett). And as the market digests what this actually means, that there is a new fast growing business but also a healthy base business, we believe that the stocks will respond positively.

Potential Implications for Other Newspaper Companies

The table below is an analysis of the estimated equity value that each of our large cap newspaper companies could potentially extract from their Internet operations, based on the latest revenue trading multiples for edit-driven content companies such as ZDNet, MarketWatch.com, CNET, Inc., and others (see valuation comparison). Applying a median multiple for the comparable group of 12.5x EV/Revenues in 2000 and a 7.4x multiple in 2001, we conservatively determine that the large cap newspaper companies could extract more than $4 billion of value by spinning off these assets or by creating a tracking stock. We say conservative, because looking at the live example of NYTD, we estimate that the market could reasonably attribute a 20x 2000 multiple, or an equity value of $1.05 billion to the stock, when NYTD comes to market. On an operating cash flow basis, the companies benefit from monetizing these assets, because they can strip out Internet losses from the core business to boost core operating cash flow – and therefore, market value. On top of this, the newspaper companies' stock prices also benefit from the equity value of the Internet business shares that they own. This is a simplified analysis, of course, but it supports the thesis that we have been building for quite some time now that newspaper companies are real players on the Internet and can extract the hidden value of their successful Internet operations to build on the value that we've argued has been present all along in the core business.

Internet Forecast and Preliminary Valuation Analysis for the Newspaper Group

Company	Internet Revenues			% YoY Change		Target EV/Rev Multiple		Estimated Enterprise Value		Estimated Per Share Value		80% Est. Per Share Value	
	1999	2000E	2001E	2000E	2001E	2000E	2001E	2000E	2001E	2000E	2001E	2000E	2001E
Gannett (GCI)	$40	$70	$119	75%	70%	12.5x	7.4x	$875	$881	$3.11	$3.13	$2.49	$2.50
Knight Ridder (KRI)	$32	$55	$94	72%	70%	12.5x	7.4x	$688	$692	$7.06	$7.10	$5.65	$5.68
New York Times (NYT)	$31	$53	$92	73%	74%	12.5x	7.4x	$661	$681	$3.68	$3.79	$2.95	$3.03
Dow Jones (DJ)	$43	$55	$72	28%	30%	12.5x	7.4x	$688	$529	$7.53	$5.80	$6.02	$4.64
Washington Post (WPO)	$17	$43	$72	150%	70%	12.5x	7.4x	$531	$535	$52.60	$52.94	$42.08	$42.35
Times Mirror (TMC)	$20	$35	$60	75%	70%	12.5x	7.4x	$438	$440	$5.79	$5.83	$4.64	$4.67
Tribune (TRB)	$20	$30	$45	50%	50%	12.5x	7.4x	$375	$333	$1.58	$1.40	$1.26	$1.12
						Large Cap Total		***$4,255***	***$4,090***				
Large Cap Median	***$31***	***$53***	***$72***					***$661***	***$535***				

Source: Company Reports. DLJ.

Note: All estimates are general ranges and are subject to change. DJ's estimates only include wsj.com and dowjones.com and excludes Factiva, which in Internet-related, and the company's 50% interest in smartmoney.com. Including these, total online revenues are currently at a run rate of more than $150 million.

Valuation Comparison

Company	Ticker	YTD Perform	Stock Price 2/14/00	Market Cap	Enterprise Value	EV/Revenues 1999	EV/Revenues 2000	EV/Revenues 2001	P/E 1999	P/E 2000	P/E 2001
Edit-driven Content											
About.com, Inc.	BOUT	-15.0%	$76 1/4	$1,121	$1,061	39.3x	12.0x	6.4x	NM	NM	NM
CNET, Inc.	CNET	-8.3%	52 1/16	3,801	3,627	34.5x	23.2x	N/A	NM	NM	NM
iVillage Inc.	IVIL	-5.2%	19 3/16	524	439	10.9x	5.3x	3.0x	NM	NM	NM
MarketWatch.com, Inc.	MKTW	17.1%	42 3/4	594	574	24.8x	13.1x	7.7x	NM	NM	NM
theglobe.com, inc.	TGLO	-23.9%	6 3/8	187	121	5.8x	2.5x	N/A	NM	NM	NM
TheStreet.com, Inc.	TSCM	-17.9%	15 3/4	422	295	9.6x	4.7x	N/A	NM	NM	NM
Ticketmaster Online - CitySearch, Inc.	TMCS	1.3%	38 15/16	3,232	3,145	31.5x	19.0x	11.2x	NM	NM	NM
ZDNet	ZDZ	52.4%	32	2,589	2,551	26.2x	18.5x	13.8x	NM	NM	NM
Ask Jeeves	ASKJ	-25.7%	83 7/8	2,280	2,228	116.6x	35.8x	N/A	NM	NM	NM
Median		***-8.3%***		***$1,121***	***$1,061***	***26.2x***	***13.1x***	***7.7x***	***NM***	***NM***	***NM***
			Total	**= $14,749**							
Newspaper Publishing Companies											
Dow Jones & Company	DJ	-8.4%	62 5/16	5,644	5,691	2.8x	2.8x	2.6x	25.8x	29.9x	26.5x
Gannett Inc.	GCI	-17.7%	67 1/8	18,633	19,802	3.6x	3.3x	3.2x	20.7x	17.9x	16.2x
New York Times Company	NYT	-3.2%	47 9/16	8,417	8,387	2.7x	2.5x	2.3x	27.5x	23.8x	20.7x
Times Mirror Company	TMC	-16.0%	56 1/4	4,206	6,607	2.1x	2.1x	2.0x	17.3x	14.4x	12.8x
Tribune Co.	TRB	-27.7%	39 13/16	9,459	9,543	3.0x	2.7x	2.5x	25.9x	22.3x	19.9x
Washington Post Company	WPO	-9.1%	505 1/2	4,763	5,432	2.5x	2.3x	2.1x	21.9x	24.4x	20.1x
Median		***-12.6%***		***$7,031***	***$7,497***	***2.7x***	***2.6x***	***2.4x***	***23.9x***	***23.0x***	***20.0x***
			Total	**= $51,121**							

$ in millions.

Source: Company Reports. DLJ Estimates. Wall Street research reports.

CNET 2000

Our mission is to be the most important company to the most important industry in the world—the IT industry. Now, I understand that Bill Gates believes Microsoft is the most important company in the IT industry. So we know who our competition is: all we have to do is displace Microsoft! But kidding aside, if you become the leading information intermediary, you have great power.

—Shelby Bonnie, CNET co-founder and Vice Chairman

In June of 1999, San Francisco-based CNET was considered by most industry observers to be a true Internet success story. Relying on advertising and "lead generated" revenue, derived when CNET referred prospective customers to its e-commerce partners, CNET had successfully positioned itself as a leading market maker for technology-savvy individuals looking to outfit themselves or their companies with technology products (see Exhibit 1 for data on CNET traffic). The company had posted revenue gains and quarterly profits in each of the five preceding quarters; this strong financial performance was reflected in a tenfold increase in CNET's share price between April 1998 and April 1999 (Exhibit 2). On the heels of this success, CNET announced that the company would undertake an aggressive $100 million marketing campaign aimed at increasing brand awareness. Immediately following the July 1999 announcement, CNET's stock price declined by 10%. This decline puzzled some analysts: over the past two years, the capital markets typically had rewarded Internet companies pursuing 'Get Big Fast' strategies. Did the reaction to CNET's announcement signal a sea-change in investors' preferences—perhaps a growing impatience with the deferral of earnings by Web startups?

In December of 1999, the casewriters met with Shelby Bonnie, CNET's co-founder and vice-chairman, and other members of the company's senior management team, to talk about CNET's strategy and the decision to invest heavily in brand building. Bonnie and his colleagues described 'CNET 2000', a year-long planning process completed during 1999. Bonnie and CNET co-founder and CEO Halsey Minor organized a team that spent about six months in highly interactive, small group sessions that involved each of the company's 600 employees. In these sessions, the groups discussed CNET's strengths and weaknesses and the threats and opportunities facing the company. The team also undertook extensive consumer research. After synthesizing their conclusions and formulating a new strategy for CNET, the team then conducted a series of workshops over several months during which they presented their findings to every CNET employee, to secure their feedback and buy-in. CNET 2000 had three important outcomes.

First, it clarified the markets and customer segments that CNET would address. Specifically, the planning process led CNET's management to conclude that they had defined the technology market too narrowly, and faced an enormous untapped opportunity in their core business. Thus, they decided to avoid diversifying beyond technology into other vertical markets, such as car buying or personal financial services, and resolved to extend their coverage of technology beyond PC computing and the Internet into huge new segments such as enterprise computing, consumer electronics, and telecommunications equipment. They also resolved to expand CNET's reach beyond computer hobbyists and corporate IT professionals to encompass managers in large companies who were technology 'novices', but who were increasingly influencing IT purchasing decisions.

Second, CNET 2000 led to a rearticulation of the company's business model. Prior to CNET 2000, many employees had perceived CNET to be a traditional content provider: a company that attracted an audience by creating high quality editorial content, then sold that audience to advertisers. The CNET 2000 team saw an opportunity to create greater value for end users,

---

High Tech Fellow Pauline Fischer prepared this case under the supervision of Assistant Professor Thomas Eisenmann as the basis for class discussion rather than to illustrate either effective or ineffective handling of an administrative situation.

marketers, and shareholders as an 'information intermediary.' As an information intermediary, CNET would serve end users' needs as they researched technology products and services by aggregating a more complete body of original and third party information, and also by providing links to a large set of resellers who could complete the sale. In addition to providing advertising opportunities and generating leads, CNET would serve manufacturers and resellers as an information intermediary by creating a common data architecture for describing the myriad features and the cross-compatibility of technology products, and by channeling information on shifting end user preferences. By helping resellers improve their marketing effectiveness, CNET would profit from increased advertising and lead generation revenues. The CNET 2000 team's decision to focus on the information intermediary business model reinforced a past judgement that the company should avoid moving directly into electronic retailing.

Third, having clarified the company's target market and its business model, the CNET 2000 team addressed the question, 'How do we win?' Doing so led them to widen their view of the competition beyond traditional technology information providers such as Ziff Davis, IDG and CMP to include information 'aggregators' such as Yahoo! and transaction 'executors' such as Amazon. With this new view of their competition, CNET's managers then recognized ways to improve their websites and thereby better meet end users' need for information that was complete, convenient to use, and credible. Likewise, the team identified additional opportunities to help manufacturers and resellers build awareness and sell their products and services.

Realizing these opportunities would necessitate organizational change and would require employees in several key functions—editorial, ad sales, product development—to reconceive their roles. For example, after analyzing end-user needs, CNET's managers agreed they should update their editorial content more frequently and provide more links to third party information sources. For editorial employees with traditional journalism backgrounds these were significant policy shifts. Such employees were accustomed to the rhythms of print periodicals, where updates might occur on a quarterly or even annual schedule, and to exercising a high level of quality control that ensured that CNET's award-winning content reflected a deep level of insight and expertise—control they would cede when linking to third party content sources. Similarly, to succeed as an information intermediary, CNET's ad sales staff would have to build new skills. Beyond their traditional role of selling banner ads to help accounts build awareness, the sales staff would now help accounts increase their sales by: 1) creating sponsorship opportunities to generate sales leads; and 2) leveraging CNET's data on market trends and user preferences to help resellers improve their merchandising practices.

Finally, after formulating the new strategy and mobilizing the organization for its implementation, the CNET 2000 team saw the need to market the new strategy. Research indicated that CNET's brand awareness was low within the customer segments the company planned to target, which led to the decision to embark on an aggressive marketing campaign.

Target Markets

The CNET 2000 team evaluated the size and attractiveness of the technology market in order to determine whether the company should seek to diversify into other vertical markets. Ultimately, they decided to remain focused on information technology. Bonnie explained:

> Wall Street analysts would say, 'Technology's going great, but why don't you do autos? Why don't you do finance?' The advantage that Amazon had, from a market valuation standpoint, was that people could project more tabs on them. First there was books, then music and videos. People thought, 'Gosh, they're just going to keep adding tabs,' and you could imagine Amazon being a $200 billion company. The problem we always had in our category was that there was nothing like that for us. People looked and said, 'They're a single tab, what else is there?' So we went through the CNET 2000 exercise to determine how big is big.
>
> We learned that the IT business, as we defined it in the US, was a $511 billion business in terms of annual end-user spending. Abroad it is another $500 billion. We realized that we were barely scratching the surface of that huge market. Up to that point, we had mostly focused on people buying personal computer products for small- and medium-sized businesses [see Exhibit 3 for Jupiter forecast of U.S. online spending on personal computer products]. We realized that we were missing whole categories of service businesses, like systems integrators. We were missing the enterprise software category. We were also missing consumer electronics, telecommunica-

tions products, lots of stuff. And you looked out and said, 'Three years from now are people going to spend more money on technology products and services?' The answer is yes, even factoring in price declines. Looking at that $1 trillion business, the portion spent on advertising and marketing is in the range of 5 to 12%. And a growing share of that total marketing budget is spent online.

Business Model

CNET's original business plan aimed to deliver an integrated mix of television and online programming about technology products. After their first cable television programs aired in April of 1995, CNET management observed that their website generated much more traffic than they expected, so they steadily increased their emphasis on Internet activities. By 1999, while still producing several syndicated cable television programs,[1] the company had expanded to a network of over 11 websites, including News.com, which provided news about technology products and businesses; Download.com, which helped consumers identify, evaluate and download thousands of software titles; Computers.com, which provided reviews, specifications, and other relevant information for consumers seeking to purchase PCs and peripherals; and Shopper.com, which provided tools to facilitate price comparisons across products and retailers, as well as links to retailers to complete a purchase (see Exhibit 4 for website screen shots). Across these websites, CNET aggregated traffic from consumers interested in learning more about technology products, then monetized that traffic by selling advertisements or by collecting lead generation fees after linking prospective product buyers with appropriate sellers. In doing so, CNET functioned as an 'information intermediary.'

Bonnie explained how CNET, as an information intermediary, served the needs of consumers evaluating technology products and services:

> Technology products are considered purchases. They are expensive, they are complicated, and they change often, so anyone who makes product decisions tends to do research. Contrast that with something like purchasing a book—most people have more comfort going directly to a retailer and picking up a book than they do walking directly into a computer retailer and picking up a computer. You do research. Our role is to provide that research. We do so by providing information that is complete, convenient to use, and credible. As an information intermediary, we go a step further: once they make a purchase decision, we make it easy for the end user to find the right reseller who can complete the transaction.

Industry analysts sometimes challenged CNET's decision to avoid the direct retailing of technology products. Bonnie explained why CNET's top management team preferred to remain a market maker connecting consumers and retailers:

> We have always believed firmly that in the technology marketplace, a media company has a far better place in the food chain than a retailer. Look at CompUSA or any other hardware or software reseller. They have to employ hundreds or thousands of people earning minimum wage, answering phones and stuff like that. They struggle to break even in cutthroat competition. Compare that to our business or to Ziff Davis's. You could roll together all the retailers in our category, and together they probably don't earn as much profit as Bill Ziff's properties. Even Amazon is questioning whether pure retailing is where you want to be in the food chain; they are adding elements of what a media company does. For example, auctions puts them in the classifieds business, and their Z-Shops is a lot like an online Yellow Pages. Those are media models.
>
> At the same time, it's an interrelationship. Without people selling products, there's no advertising, and without a vehicle to advertise, there's no way to sell products. Early on, we realized our business model was dependent on there being good online resellers. When they get better, our model works better, but we've got a long way to go on that score. Just a few months ago we showed one of the leading software retailers that they didn't carry 40% of the top 1,000 titles. And no reseller has ever come close to doing for this category what Amazon did in books—putting up fair and neutral reviews, deep information, a complete product database. Resellers have asked us to license our reviews and articles, but so far we haven't done it.

Bonnie explained how CNET could serve manufacturers and resellers as an information intermediary:

[1]CNET produced such shows as *CNET Central,* a half-hour series featuring news and feature stories about computers; *The Web,* a series focused on new web sites and technology; *The New Edge,* a magazine show covering technological developments from elite laboratories and garages; and *Cool Tech,* a series focused on consumer technology.

Think about the difference between Egghead online and the bricks-and-mortar retailing experience. You go into a local store to buy a Palm V after they advertise an aggressive price. When you buy it, the sales rep says, 'Hey, you'll need a hard cover for that, because otherwise you'll turn the thing on by mistake and run the battery down. And you'd better get an extra cradle for work. And here are a couple of great software applications. And maybe you want an extended warranty.' You walk in to get a great deal on a Palm Pilot, and you walk out with 5 other things, and the store probably makes more money on those items than they do on the first.

That doesn't happen online. Name me a time when you've ever bought a product and an electronic retailer has done a good job of cross selling to you. Amazon is the only example I can think of. No one gives you good specification data; Egghead might not even have a picture of the product. As an information intermediary, we can create this data and help retailers do a better job of merchandising their goods. And we can provide them information about what's selling, to guide their buying and inventory management. We can show them demand curves, help them understand the value of their brand—what happens if you are 10% or 30% higher than the lowest available price. Likewise, we can tell manufacturers which other products consumers are evaluating next to theirs. They can't get that data from a magazine, and no-one is systematically watching in a bricks-and-mortar store.

Bonnie described how the information intermediary could play an important role in defining the data architecture that manufacturers and resellers used to describe technology products:

What we see emerging is a kind of information distributor which owns the underlying information infrastructure both in terms of how the market is educated and how it trades. As the information distributor, you are in the place where people transact, so you understand trends in demand. You are in the place where supply is aggregated, so you understand trends in supply. If you pull that off, you are incredibly valuable. We believe that there is a real opportunity for us to become a 'central data vault.' To this end, we've recently purchased GDT, a Swiss company. GDT, renamed CNET Data Services, creates underlying product information which we use and also resell to retailers and distributors. GDT provides every specification you'd ever want to know about for each and every product. They identify any accessories associated with the product, and they have complete data on whether any given product is compatible with another. GDT gives us the ability to create the underlying data definition for our industry. It's an unbelievable business, maybe the most important deal we've ever done.

The information distributor can create value for users, too. This fall, we bought a company that scans your hard drive. They analyze your software and hardware and make recommendations. They might say, 'Turns out the Real Player you have is two versions old, do you want to download the latest? Turns out you only have 32 megs of RAM, but you seem to be a gamer, want to buy some more?' Of course, we can then link them to Download.com or to another CNET site that allows them to get what they need.

Competition

Prior to CNET 2000, most CNET employees, including senior management, considered Ziff Davis, IDG, and CMP—technology-focused publishing companies that had extended their print franchises online—to be their main competition (see Exhibit 5 for data on competitor traffic and Exhibit 6 for information on Ziff Davis's online unit, ZDNET). However, they realized that other well-known Internet properties were moving into their marketplace. Matthew Barzun, Senior Vice President of CNET Online, explained:

In the few years since 1995, other Internet companies had started entering our market, trying to sit between technology users and advertisers. When we evaluated the competitive landscape we saw 'the old guys' like Ziff, IDG and CMP, but we also saw people we would never have thought of as competitors like Microsoft, Yahoo! and Amazon. If you define anyone sitting between buyers and sellers of technology products as competition, then all of them were in some way competitors and competing with each of them is very different.

We view the market as being three-tiered. On top sit what we called 'Aggregators,' they include companies like Yahoo!, AOL and Excite—search engine-type companies that help you find information on the Internet. The next tier is what we call the 'Provider' tier. These companies include Ziff, IDG, CMP, and CNET—for the sake of argument we'll include ourselves there. Then on the bottom tier you have the 'Closers' or 'Executors', like Egghead or Amazon. These are the companies that actually sell things.

From the top tier, the thing that Yahoo! can do well is *aggregate* all content providers so that users can get multiple viewpoints, find lots of information that's relevant to their needs. Theoretically, they can then link you up with someone who'll sell you the goods. In addition, they can offer advertisers good targeting, broad reach, and low CPMs, and in that way they can try to cut CNET right out of the loop. However, their service is not as well integrated as ours because they have to aggregate content from so many disparate third party sources. In principal, we should be a better aggregator than Yahoo! because we have 600 people with expertise in what Yahoo! thinks of as a single category, whereas they have just three or four employees working on their 'Computers & Internet' channel. We should be able to find all the information that's out there and also tell you whether a given article is a good one to point to.

The challenge from below is very different. What Amazon can do very well is *integrate* information: they can put product reviews just where you'd like to see them, create tools that let you compare products, present product specifications in a consistent manner across all their offerings. In addition, they can offer great targeting to marketers, saying, 'Hey, we can provide eyeballs when they are most valuable—right before consumers make a purchase decision.' The downside with Amazon, however, is that they are just one vendor. As a consumer dealing with a single retailer, you can't be completely sure you've found the best product or the best price available in the marketplace. And, you might be suspicious about whether the information they provide is complete and objective.

We've figured that we have to out-aggregate Yahoo! and out-integrate Amazon to dominate this vertical—and while doing so maintain our lead as the most trusted provider of high quality, original editorial content. The way we do that is to offer users and advertisers what they want and aggressively market ourselves.

Meeting the Needs of Users and Advertisers

Barzun explained how this new view of CNET's competition translated into an action plan for improving CNET's ability to meet users' and advertisers' needs:

> Our goal became to serve all the technology-related needs of our users; pure and simple. But we had to answer the question, 'What do they want?' The problem is our users want different things. When we tracked what information our users most often accessed we learned that the single most popular thing researched represented only 0.3% of all searches. There's no 80/20 rule here. So what we believe our users really want is for us to be useful. That means being *complete* and being *helpful.*
>
> Completeness means, along the technology information spectrum, being as wide and as deep as everyone else. To help us visualize this, we used the image of a dark room. We said, 'What we've been doing over the past three or four years is shining flashlights onto a few major technology categories. But we want to light up the whole room.' Once each category had a bright light shining on it, it would be complete. However, being complete is only half the problem because we knew we also had to be helpful. The requirements for 'being helpful' depend on whether you are helping people stay up-to-date, which is about 30% of what people do on our sites, versus helping them get something done, which is the remaining 70%. Staying up-to-date is easy—it's about scanning, browsing, rechecking. We're great at that.
>
> If users are trying to get something done, being helpful means providing them the ability *to explore, evaluate* and *execute.* Exploring means searching and drilling down; seeing all your options. Evaluating happens once you've narrowed down the field of potential purchases. This requires us to have an opinion on the products you've selected, so that you can compare and contrast them. Executing could mean buying or it could mean downloading free software.
>
> In our internal presentations, we referred to categories in which we believed we already had the capabilities required to effectively serve our customers as 'Red.'[2] That is where we believed we had 'expert' coverage and could shine a bright flashlight. This would include editorial produced in-house that was in-depth and opinionated in addition to providing links to other areas of interest. For example, we are dark red in providing tech news for IT professionals and with software downloads. Areas in which we didn't quite have the in-house capabilities required to be the absolute authority, say, our coverage of Linux, we called 'Pink.' This means that the category has links to everything useful done by third-party information providers, is an authority in a few areas, and points to

[2]Note: CNET's logo is red and their company colors are red and yellow.

others where they don't have the answer. Selective but still complete. In 'White' categories, we didn't offer anything beyond a list of links to third party data sources. And unfortunately, in some categories, we offer almost nothing for our users. Examples would be providing advice on building a website for beginners or general news for investors interested in technology companies.

Implementing this strategy meant linking to our competitors. We got emails from our competitors laughing at us for sending more traffic, say, to a CMP news story than they could generate on their own. But we got emails from users saying they loved it; they had stopped checking our competitors' sites because they knew we'd point to anything worthwhile that our competitors had to offer. In a way, this is unique to the Internet, which at its best is a weird mix of integrator and aggregator. On TV, you'll never see CNN telling people to tune in to MSNBC, because they have better coverage of a plane crash.

To bring the idea of red, pink, and white categories to life, the CNET 2000 team implemented a point system whereby the editors would score the content on CNET's sites. For instance, if someone were to visit a site and they got exactly what they wanted, the content would receive 10 points. If someone visited the site and received some basic objective information produced by CNET, but no recommendation from CNET as to whether to buy the product, the content would receive 5 points. Finally, a simple list of links to third-party data about the product—a 'White' category—would receive a single point. If, however, someone were to visit a CNET site and find *nothing* of relevance, the content would receive negative ten points. Barzun explained:

> From our point of view, the point system really spelled out our completeness goal. We were able to show that it was much better to receive some ones and fives until you could get to tens than it was to get negative tens. Our employees really understood that, but this requires a big shift in attitude for journalists who are accustomed to being true experts on a topic. Pink or white is hard for perfectionists, and most great journalists are perfectionists.

Besides linking to third party sources, CNET 2000 led to other product changes. The goal of being complete implied a need to constantly update features. Previously, many of CNET's features had been updated on the same infrequent schedule as a print periodical. Barzun said:

> Due to space constraints in a magazine, they might do their big 'printer roundup' every November, reviewing 200 products. But what if you want to buy a printer in October? Online, people don't want to wait six months to read the next roundup. If a new printer is introduced, they want to find out about it right away.

Also, CNET's editorial employees came to realize that the nature of the Web required a different style of writing than print periodicals. Bonnie explained:

> In print, you start with a thesis, then build an argument, then end with a conclusion. Well, people aren't willing to read as much when they are online. Knowing it's unlikely most people will get past the first paragraph, you need to start with a one to ten rating of the product and a paragraph that provides the conclusion, along with a link to the rest of the review. Then you give bullet points about the important factors, and a snapshot of the product specs, with a link to a page of complete specifications. Also links to other reviews of similar products. Some people will like to go really deep, but most won't, so you need to aggregate all of the useful information in a way that accommodates their preferences. This isn't how they teach you to write at the Columbia Journalism School.

After the CNET 2000 team redefined their competition and their product strategy, they turned to the task of integrating the company's websites. Bonnie explained:

> Before CNET 2000, we had these great services, but they were like islands, almost like separate magazines. Download wouldn't point to Gamecenter, and Gamecenter wouldn't point to Download. We wanted to present a network to users, and position cnet.com as the keystone of the network. That required integrating the look and feel of the sites, building the appropriate links, and implementing universal registration. Behind the scenes, it involved a huge amount of work building a common infrastructure so you could easily share data and move users around. Previously, we had nine different servers, nine different databases. Now everything runs on a single machine.
>
> By God, I'd hate to be running a company which has grown primarily through the acquisition of sites built on different platforms by different people in different places. It was incredibly hard for us to achieve integration, and we built all these sites ourselves.

Organizing for Success

CNET 2000 was designed to create institutional momentum behind a new strategy. Bonnie recalled:

> People have asked us why we felt the need to do 'change stuff' when we were so young, but we had a lot of employees and we realized our biggest challenge was getting everyone going in the same direction.
>
> Content is a piece of our strategy but it is not the end. We do something that is more powerful. Providing data about product decisions is valuable, helping people figure out what products to buy, whether they're in stock or not and what they cost is valuable. What ended up happening internally, however, was that we had factions that felt differently about our mission. The journalists, for instance, had one set of views and our product people had another. CNET 2000 provided a clearer definition of our purpose for everyone.

Bonnie explained that CNET 2000 required employees in nearly every function to change their attitudes about the roles that a media company could play on the Internet. For example, the ad sales staff would need to move beyond their traditional role of selling branding packages to helping accounts actually sell their products. Product managers would need to think differently about how to aggregate third party content. Bonnie explained that CNET 2000 would lead the editorial staff to change their behavior in many ways:

> For example, it was a struggle to persuade some editorial people to point to a listing of products and prices. They would say, 'That's like sacrilege,' because journalists are trained to be vigilant about advertisers compromising their objectivity. Now, we will *always* insist on absolute neutrality when we review products in Computers.com. Our credibility depends on that. But remember, in addition to being credible, we must be complete and convenient. Convenience means making it easy for our audience to purchase a product that they have researched.

In addition to attitudinal change, CNET 2000 required employees in most functions to develop a new set of skills. Hence, the CNET 2000 planning process included a broad management training program to help managers understand the skill sets that CNET employees required and to help improve their recruiting and employee development practices.

Bonnie reflected on some of the organizational challenges of managing a network of websites in a rapidly changing environment:

> We've struggled endlessly with whether to run CNET as a centralized versus a decentralized organization. We started out highly decentralized; we had teams feeling like they were running their own businesses, which was very entrepreneurial but got a little chaotic. If you're too decentralized, you can spin out of control, and it can be hard to set priorities. With a decentralized structure, if we were to say, 'Let's go after a new area like enterprise computing in a big way,' it would be very hard to reallocate resources. Then we became highly centralized in areas like design and sales, which was more efficient, but we wasted lots of energy with people complaining about who controlled what. Now we're a hybrid mix of centralized and decentralized functions, but we are still searching for the right balance.

Marketing Campaign

As part of CNET 2000, the company commissioned a study which revealed that their brand achieved only 4% unaided brand awareness among their target user segments. Bonnie explained:

> Learning that we only had a 4% unaided brand awareness was depressing. We knew we had built the best product out there. But if users didn't know how to find us, chances are that they'd get their product information from retailers, despite the fact that that is not the best way for them to make purchasing decisions. Our competition really wasn't another Internet company—it was ignorance.
>
> We recognized a huge customer need for the type of information we provide. We knew if we could just let people know we existed that once they showed up, they'd love us. Unlike other Internet start-ups, we had spent years getting the kinks out of the system and perfecting our product before driving traffic to our site.

Bonnie explained the economics behind CNET's decision to increase ad spending (see Exhibit 7 for a projected income statement for CNET and Exhibit 8 for an equity analyst's discounted cash flow valuation):

> The numbers are straightforward. Right now, we generate about $12 in revenue per year from each unique

visitor. Our marginal cost related to servers and bandwidth and sales commissions is about 15%. So, if you can bring in someone who generates $10 per year for you, is it a good deal to spend $40 acquiring them? It probably is, assuming you hang on to them for a few years.

It's interesting to compare our economics to *PC Magazine's*. They have 3.3 million readers, and they do about $100 per year in advertising per reader. Given all the ways we add value to users and advertisers, shouldn't we do more revenue per user than *PC Magazine?* We think so. Part of the problem goes back to resellers not doing a great job of selling products on the Web. When they do better, we'll do better. With that in mind, our marketing investment will look even better if we can grow our current $12 per year in revenue to $40 per year or more.

Not only did the CNET 2000 team realize that their brand was not well known, but they also realized that they were chasing an ever-changing target market. Annie Williams, Senior Vice President of Marketing, explained:

> Our research indicated that our consumer base had drastically expanded since 1995. Technology decision-making is broadening. For instance, now the vice president of sales will actually decide which laptop to buy for her salesforce. No longer is it the lone IT guy in headquarters making the purchasing decisions. As a marketer of technology products, it used to be that you only had to find the IT managers and make them aware of what you had to offer. You could do this by advertising in *PC Week* or *PC Magazine* or getting a big booth at Comdex, the industry's trade show. Well, guess what, technology has become so critical to an organization's success that it is not unusual for the CEO, CFO or that vice president of sales to get involved with these decisions.
>
> We call this new person buying technology products, the 'technology influencer.' They're not just geeks anymore, and you have to go to non-traditional places to reach them. That is why you now see so many technology advertisements in the *Wall Street Journal, Business Week* and *Fortune*.

In response to their research results, CNET's Board decided to embark on an unprecedented $100 million nationwide marketing campaign that would include print, television, radio and outdoor advertising. The $100 million amount dwarfed their marketing budget of less than $1 million for the entire year 1998 and for the first time in over a year would leave the company with net losses. Bonnie explained the rationale behind the decision:

> We made a couple of calculated decisions regarding our marketing expenditures. We had five quarters of profitability prior to our marketing announcement. One of the risks we were taking was that we would have to go back and change the Street's expectations. People had begun to make a big deal about us being a profitable Internet company—we were on a short list that included AOL, Yahoo!, and eBay—and that created an awkward tension. We knew such a large marketing expenditure would put us in a loss position, but what do you do? Part of the decision we made was that if we were going to be a bear, we were going to be a grizzly bear. Once you go into the red, it doesn't make a big difference whether you lose $5 million or $25 million.
>
> Having sold equity interests in Vignette and Snap, two companies we had built, we had a very strong balance sheet—we had over $500 million of cash in the bank—so we didn't need to worry about the impact of the announcement on our stock price, at least as it related to our ability to fund the marketing campaign. We've had a very good record as an investor and we concluded that one of the best investments we could make was against our own brand.

CNET planned to spend $65 million of the $100 million marketing budget during the last two quarters of 1999, with the balance to be spent during the first half of 2000. Immediately following this announcement in early July, CNET's stock dropped by about 10%. Williams analyzed the press reaction to the announcement:

> There was some confusion in the press as to whether we were broadening our focus to include novices. We were, but that didn't mean grandmothers going online for the first time, it meant targeting business decision-makers—technology influencers—who are 'novice-like.' We still serve IT professionals and technology-savvy hobbyists but we felt it necessary to increase our reach to this growing segment.
>
> Our research uncovered three major needs in the market. First, IT professionals need to stay on top of masses of new information in order to get their job done well. Second, business decision makers need a sort of 'cheat sheet' so that they can look smart to their IT department or their board members. And third, tech enthusiasts who are early adopters need to

know about the latest thing. We were able to segment our message for these three audiences in print, but in our broadcast and outdoor advertisements, which cut across everything, we had simplified the message and that caused some observers to wonder whether we had changed our target market.

Bonnie further explained:

Our bet was we'd do better if we really doubled down in terms of ad spending during this period instead of dragging it out and spending smaller sums of money over a lot of quarters. Instead, we said we were going to endure the negative operating income for three quarters and spend some of our cash. Then, our numbers for 2000 should look more or less the same as they would have without the marketing campaign, and we should enjoy big benefits in 2001 and beyond. Given this picture, you might have expected our stock price to go up. But people don't like change, so we recognized it was likely that our stock would go down.

Conclusion

Bonnie reflected on the challenges and opportunities facing CNET and on the outcome of the CNET 2000 process:

> Change has been hard, even in a young company. I would hate to be doing this inside a big company with lots of history in terms of reporting structures and all that baggage. But we've learned a lot. We've been willing to experiment, and we'll continue to rethink our strategy over and over again.

Exhibit 4a

CNET WEBSITE: HOME PAGE

Exhibit 4b

CNET WEBSITE: INDIVIDUAL PRODUCT PRICE LISTING

CNET - Shopping - Latest Prices - Palm Vx - Netscape

File Edit View Go Communicator Help

Back Forward Reload Home Search Netscape Print Security Shop Stop

Bookmarks Location: //cnet.com/shopping/resellers/0-7085-311-1432994-0.html?tag=st.sh.1257.pop.7085-311-1432994 What's Related

TSS FRCC Lab Reservation Facility Reques OSS Work Reques OSS Supply Requ Baker Online Ca

CNET | News | Hardware | Downloads | Builder | Games | Jobs | Auctions | Prices | Tech Help Free Email

CNET Shopper Search Go! Advanced · Tips In Shopping

Visor is the handheld for people... handspring Click Here!

CNET Shopping Handhelds Systems Latest Prices

Palm Vx More product info

Manufacturer:	3Com Corp.
Part Number:	3C80401U
List Price:	$399.00
Lowest Price:	**$396.00**

ADVERTISEMENT buy.com Jornada 690 Color, Win CE $778.95

Pricing and availability are updated twice daily. To view latest information click on the prices below.

	Merchant	bizrate.com Merchant Ratings	Price	State	CLICK NUMBER TO CALL	Shipping	In Stock	Last Updated
Buy Info	Computers 4 Sure.com CNET Certified Merchant *Value, Selection, Satisfaction* More company info	★★★★★	$399.00	CT	800-585-4080	$8.60	No	7/21/2000
Buy Info	ONVIA.com Work. Wisely. CNET Certified Merchant *#1 small-biz emarketplace* More company info	★★★★★	$399.00	WA	800-331-2822	Free	No	7/21/2000
Buy Info	PC Zone CNET Certified Merchant *In Business Since 1986* More company info	★★★★	$399.98	WA	888-246-3306	$5.49	No	7/20/2000
Buy Info	buy.com CNET Certified Merchant *The Internet Superstore* More company info	★★★★★	$399.00	CA	888-880-1030	Free Shipping	No	7/21/2000
Buy Info	The New Egghead.com CNET Certified Merchant *Leading computer retailer* More company info	★★★★★	$399.00	WA	800-EGGHEAD	$6.95	No	7/21/2000
Buy Info	Solutions4SURE.com CNET Certified Merchant More company info	★★★★★	$399.00	CT	800-595-9333	$8.60	No	7/21/2000
Buy Info	firstsource.com CNET Certified Merchant More company info	★★★★	$399.00	CA	800-858-9866	9.95+	see site	7/21/2000
Buy Info	Compu America CNET Certified Merchant More company info	No rating	$439.00	CA	800-533-9005	7	IN STOCK AGAIN	7/21/2000
Buy Info	goVoom.com CNET Certified Merchant More company info	No rating	$410.95	CA	949-753-7056	FREE	No	7/20/2000
Buy Info	Infinity Micro CNET Certified Merchant More company info	No rating	$449.00	CA	800-589-1234	7+	NO	7/21/2000
Buy Info	eLinux.com CNET Certified Merchant More company info	No rating	$399.99	CA	877-39-LINUX	Starts at $5.00	No	7/21/2000
Buy Info	LA Computer Center CNET Certified Merchant More company info	★★★★	$439.00	CA	800-400-5886	12+	YES	7/20/2000
Buy Info	Multiwave Direct More company info	★★★★★	$399.00	CA	800-234-3358	see site	NO	7/21/2000
Buy Info	RCSeShop More company info	No rating	$399.00	NY	877-746-7727	$6.99+	YES	7/20/2000
Buy Info	shoppingplanet.com More company info	No rating	$435.30	CA	800-572-7894	see site	yes	7/20/2000
Buy Info	AllBusiness.com CNET Certified Merchant More company info	No rating	$399.00	CA	800-467-9866	9.95+	see site	7/21/2000
Buy Info	Harmony Computers CNET Certified Merchant More company info	No rating	$419.00	NY	800-898-7275	$19.99	YES	7/20/2000
Buy Info	California Computer Center More company info	No rating	$399.00	CA	800-727-2522	20+	see site	7/20/2000

Re-sort By Price / Sponsor

who love being organized... handspring Click Here!

CNET Services: Auctions · Check Latest Prices · Downloads · Enterprise Business · Find a Web Host · Find an ISP · Free Newsletters · Gadgets · Games · Hardware · Help & How-Tos · Latest PCs · News · Publish Your Opinion · Search · Stock Quotes · Tech Jobs · Web Building

CNET Jobs | Corrections | How to advertise | Join CNET's Affiliate Program | Support About CNET

Back to Top Join CNET, we're hiring

All the vendors pay to be included in our product database; Premier and Preferred vendors pay extra for premium positioning in our listings.

CNET disclaims any responsibility for product information and products described on this site. Some product information may be confusing without additional explanation. All product information, including prices, features, and availability, is subject to change without notice.

Copyright ©1995-2000 CNET Networks, Inc. All rights reserved. Privacy policy.

Exhibit 4c

CNET WEBSITE: INDIVIDUAL PRODUCT REVIEW PAGE

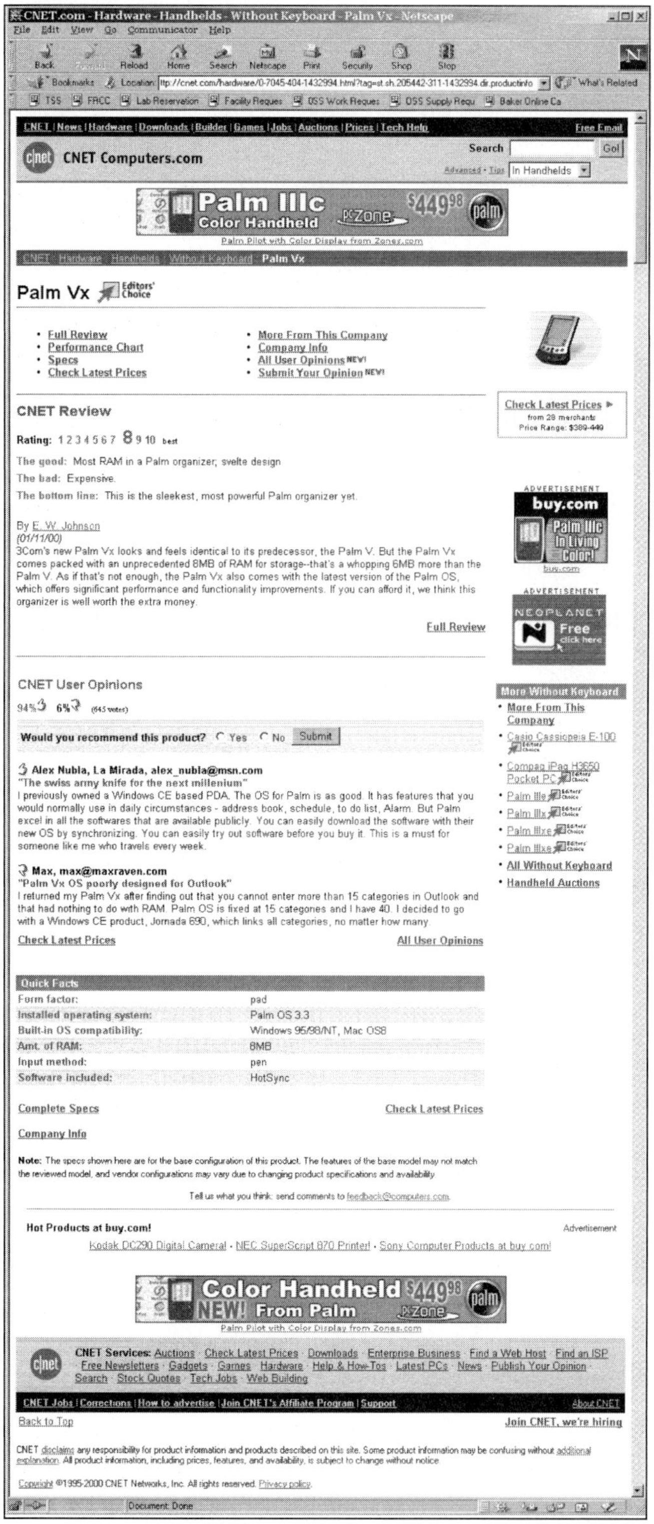

Exhibit 5 TECHNOLOGY SITE TRAFFIC, AUGUST 1999

	CNET	ZDNET	IDGNet	CMPNet
- Total Reach (% of Internet users accessing site)	13.5%	13.5%	5.6%	2.6%
–Home	10.6%	10.3%	3.5%	1.6%
–Work	13.5%	15.8%	7.9%	3.6%
- Avg. time spent per session (minutes)	11.2	24.5	8.1	6.8
- Avg. days viewed per visitor per month	2.2	3.4	2.2	1.6

Source: Media Metrix data cited in Mandana Hormozi, "CNET: From E-Content to E-Commerce," Lazard Frères & Co. equity research report, Nov. 1, 1999

Exhibit 6 ZDNET PROFILE

- ZDNET, CNET's closest competitor, is a tracking stock 84% owned by Ziff Davis, Inc., which provides content from its stable of 75 print periodicals (including *PC Magazine, PC Week,* and *Computer Shopper*) that have a combined worldwide circulation of 7 million
- ZDNET has a staff of 149 editors who integrate this content from Ziff Davis magazines and create original content for the website
- Ziff Davis also owns units which run computer industry trade shows (e.g., Comdex), as well as a 24-hour cable programming service, ZDTV
- ZDNET trades content for distribution from portals, including Yahoo!, Lycos, Excite@Home, and MSN; ZDNET obtains about 5-10% of its revenue from syndicating content to such providers

Source: Jamie Kiggen, "ZDNET," DLJ Equity Research, May 1999

Exhibit 7 HISTORICAL AND PROJECTED CNET INCOME STATEMENT, 1996–2002

($ in 000s)	1996	1997	1998	1999E	2000E	2001E	2002E
Revenue							
Internet	10,134	26,717	49,374	100,520	154,072	210,597	263,180
Television	4,697	6,922	7,058	6,641	6,674	6,708	6,741
Total revenue	14,830	33,640	56,432	107,161	160,747	217,304	269,922
Year over year growth	*NA*	*126.8%*	*67.8%*	*89.9%*	*50.0%*	*35.2%*	*24.2%*
Cost of revenue							
Internet	9,121	19,813	23,292	33,724	45,234	59,000	70,067
Gross margin	*10.0%*	*25.8%*	*52.8%*	*66.5%*	*70.6%*	*72.0%*	*73.2%*
Television	6,213	6,904	6,741	7,303	6,508	6,540	6,573
Gross margin	−32.3%	0.3%	4.5%	−10.0%	2.5%	2.5%	2.5%
Total cost of revenue	15,334	26,717	30,034	41,028	51,742	65,541	77,180
Gross Profit	(503)	6,922	26,398	66,133	109,005	151,764	192,741
Gross margin	*NA*	*20.6%*	*46.8%*	*61.7%*	*67.8%*	*69.8%*	*71.4%*
Operating expenses							
Sales & marketing	7,821	11,603	14,530	93,104	65,407	71,465	81,359
Development	3,438	13,609	3,454	6,956	6,221	6,843	7,356
General & administrative	3,772	6,849	6,807	12,828	15,246	16,771	18,029
Total operating expense	15,032	32,060	24,792	112,889	86,874	95,079	106,743
Total % of sales	101.4%	95.3%	43.9%	105.3%	54.0%	43.8%	39.5%
EBITA	(15,535)	(25,138)	1,607	(46,755)	22,131	56,684	85,998
EBITA margin	NM	NM	2.8%	NM	13.8%	26.1%	31.9%
Amortization of intangibles	0	0	0	11,963	27,176	27,176	15,205
EBIT	(15,535)	(25,138)	1,607	(58,718)	(5,045)	29,508	70,793
EBIT margin	NM	NM	2.8%	NM	NM	13.6%	26.2%

Source: Adapted from Mandana Hormozi, "CNET: From E-Content to E-Commerce," Lazard Frères & Co. equity research report, Nov. 1, 1999

Exhibit 8

CNET VALUATION BASED ON DISCOUNTED CASH FLOW PROJECTION

($ in 000s)	1999E	2000E	2001E	2002E	2003E	2004E	2005E	2006E	2007E	2008E	2009E
EBIT	(58,718)	(5,045)	29,508	70,793	116,808	186,893	270,995	372,618	484,404	581,284	668,477
x(1-t)	(35,231)	(3,027)	17,705	42,476	70,085	112,136	162,597	223,571	290,642	348,771	401,086
Depreciation & Amortization	11,963	27,176	27,176	15,205	15,965	16,764	17,602	18,482	19,406	20,376	19,357
Cash Flow From Operations	(23,268)	24,149	44,881	57,681	86,050	128,899	180,199	242,053	310,048	369,147	420,443
Capital Expenditures	(12,000)	(12,000)	(7,000)	(7,000)	(7,000)	(7,000)	(7,000)	(7,000)	(7,000)	(7,000)	(7,000)
Working Capital	8,037	13,663	16,298	16,195	17,815	19,240	20,394	21,414	22,485	23,159	23,854
Unlevered Free Cash Flow	(43,305)	(1,514)	21,583	34,485	61,235	102,659	152,804	213,638	280,563	338,987	389,589
Year		1	2	3	4	5	6	7	8	9	10
WACC		12.4%	12.4%	12.4%	12.4%	12.4%	12.4%	12.4%	12.4%	12.4%	12.4%
Factor		1.12	1.26	1.42	1.59	1.79	2.01	2.26	2.54	2.86	3.21
PV of FCF		(1,348)	17,090	24,298	38,392	57,273	75,858	94,375	110,285	118,572	121,260
Cumulative PV of FCF		(1,348)	15,742	40,040	78,433	135,706	211,564	305,939	416,224	534,796	656,056

WACC Calculation	1999	Valuation			
Debt, Net of Cash & Value of Public Equities	0	PV of FCF	656,056		
Weighted Average Cost of Debt	0.0%	PV of Terminal Value	5,774,226	g	10.0%
Tax Rate	40.0%	Corporate Value	6,430,282	r	12.4%
(1−t)	60.0%	Debt, net	(704,801)	cf	389,589
Rf: 30-Year Bonds	6.00%	Private Equity Value	7,135,083	v	16,508,022
Rm-Rf:	5.80%	Public Market Discount	20.0%	mult	24.0
Beta	1.1	Public Equity Value	5,708,066		
Cost of Equity (CAPM)	12.38%	Shares o/s (f.d.)	95,000		
		Target Price	$60		
Shares Outstanding	95.0				
Share Price	$47.00				
Market Value	4,465				
Market Capitalization	4,465				
%Debt	0.0%				
%Equity	100.0%				
$r_d(1-t)D/V + r_e(E/V) = WACC$	12.4%				

Source: Mandana Hormozi, "CNET: From E-Content to E-Commerce," Lazard Frères & Co. equity research report, Nov. 1, 1999

BET.COM

Scott Mills, Executive Vice President and Chief Operating Officer of BET.com, sat in his office on the BET Holdings campus in Washington D.C. contemplating the work that would need to be done to successfully meet the February 2000 launch date of the company's new website. Seven months earlier, Mills and Robert Johnson, founder, Chairman and CEO of BET Holdings, the parent company of the Black Entertainment Television cable network among other media and entertainment related properties, had discussed the idea of creating a portal targeting African-American consumers. After Johnson green-lighted the project, Johnson recruited several strategic partners, including Microsoft; John Malone's Liberty Media, a unit of AT&T; Rupert Murdoch's Fox Broadcasting; and Barry Diller's USA Networks. The group together contributed $35 million toward the launch of BET.com.

Mills knew that BET.com's $35 million war chest far surpassed any previous investment in a website targeting the African-American market. He also knew that simply having a lot of resources would not ensure success. In fact, BET Holdings, in partnership with Microsoft, had been only moderately successful in its first attempt at creating an online presence, MSBET, and BET had learned a lot from that experience. With the launch date rapidly approaching, Mills was still in the midst of pulling his management team together and finalizing agreements with web site developers, advertising agencies, and potential content providers and sponsors. Mills was also still dealing with fundamental decisions about the site's strategic direction. Johnson and Mills had decided to principally target the African-American market. However, Mills was concerned that such a focus would allow online competitors to capture the "urban market" that was also attracted to BET Holding's cable network.[1] In addition, Mills was concerned that BET.com's primary emphasis on the African-American market could create branding problems because urban-oriented music was slated to become a very important component of the BET.com website.[2]

Could BET.com serve both the African-American and urban markets from a single portal? The answer to this question, just weeks before their announced launch date, was still not crystal clear to Mills. Nor was it clear whether BET.com should attempt to provide additional products and services to their target market including BET branded internet access. What was clear was the need to move quickly to launch the site: since BET.com had announced its plans, several online competitors had attracted significant investments.

BET's History

BET was founded in 1979 by Robert Johnson, then a lobbyist working for the National Cable TV Association. In 1979, there were only a handful of cable networks—CNN and MTV, for example, had not yet been launched. Johnson saw an opportunity to provide cable programming to the underserved African-American market. After borrowing (with permission) the business plan for a cable network targeting elderly viewers, Johnson substituted the word "black" for "elderly" and presented the plan to John Malone, then CEO of TCI, the largest U.S cable system operator. Over time, Malone would become Johnson's close friend and ally. Within 45 minutes, the two had inked a deal that would provide Johnson with $500,000 in seed capital to launch BET.

One year later, BET was airing music videos, black college sports, and public affairs programming every

High Tech Fellow Pauline Fischer prepared this case under the supervision of Professor Thomas Eisenmann as the basis for class discussion rather than to illustrate either effective or ineffective handling of an administrative situation.

[1]The urban audience, more fully described later in the case, was young, cross-racial and had distinctive tastes in music, clothing, and periodicals.

[2]Music was only one of many areas in which there was some overlap between the African-American and urban markets. However, according to Mills, there were some important distinctions between the two demographics, including the fact that 70% of urban merchandise was purchased by non African-Americans.

Friday and Saturday night into 2 million households. Over the next several years, the network expanded its daily programming schedule to 24 hours and grew steadily as Johnson was able to secure additional investments and carriage commitments from other major media companies, including Time Inc., the second largest cable system operator.

BET's business model was simple and its programming was inexpensive. Music videos were provided free of charge by record labels hoping to obtain exposure for their artists. Since no other network was airing black college sports at the time, their broadcasting rights were not costly. Consequently, BET's operating margin was close to 50% through most of the 1980s and 1990s, compared with 35% for other mainstream cable networks.[3] By 1999, BET's programming lineup was still dominated by music videos which accounted for roughly 65% of programming hours. BET also aired original movies and syndicated entertainment (Exhibit 1).

In 1991, BET went public, becoming the first black-owned and controlled company on the New York Stock Exchange. That same year the company began an aggressive diversification program that led to the acquisition of *Emerge*, a magazine focused on public affairs of concern to African-Americans; the in-house launch of *YSB* (Young Sisters and Brothers), a lifestyle magazine, and United Image Entertainment, which produced movies by black film-makers; and the creation of BET Direct, a direct marketer of cosmetics, apparel, and other products targeted to African-Americans.

In the mid-1990s, BET had a bright future with Johnson at the helm. By then, BET was available to nearly all African-American cable subscribers, and the BET brand was recognized by over 95% of black Americans according to company research. Johnson's aggressive acquisition strategy and new business development was founded on his belief that he could transform BET's logo "into the pre-eminent brand name for African-Americans by stamping it on everything from restaurants to credit cards, apparel and magazines."[4] The company continued its diversification by launching BET Jazz, a cable network which aired jazz music; creating BET International to distribute its programming overseas; forming joint ventures to increase its production of movies for home video, cable and pay-per-view markets; and opening a music-themed restaurant chain. BET also opened the BET Soundstage Club at Disney World, launched a skin care products line and a credit card (with Chevy Chase Bank), and acquired Arabesque, a publisher of romance novels.[5]

However, as BET accelerated its diversification, the company's stock began to take a beating in the market (Exhibit 2). While other cable programming companies were trading at 18 to 20 times earnings, BET was trading at only 12 times earnings. Some analysts complained that the corporation was making investments that were well outside of its core competencies, and many institutional investors wanted to see the huge profits created by the cable network paid out as dividends, rather than reinvested in new ventures. Other analysts and investors complained that Johnson lacked a "road map" for where the company was headed. They feared that BET was stretching its brand too far.

Despite pressure from Wall Street, Johnson stood firm in his belief that BET could and would become an African-American household name and brand akin to Disney's. In 1998, in a move that surprised Wall Street, Johnson and equity partner Liberty Media (the company that held TCI's programming investments) offered to repurchase the 6 million shares of BET Holdings that they did not own for $63 dollars per share. BET Holdings again became a private corporation owned 64% by Johnson himself, 34% by Liberty and 2% by Debra Lee, president and chief operating officer of BET Holdings. The company employed 500 people in 1999 and had an estimated market value of $1.5 billion.[6] (See Exhibit 3 for the most recent publicly available financial statements for BET Holdings; Exhibit 4 for a list of properties owned by BET.)

BET on the Internet

BET.com would not be the company's first foray onto the Internet. In 1996, BET and Microsoft Corp. announced a joint venture called MSBET to create a website which would provide information and entertainment content targeting African-American consumers. By then, it was clear to Johnson that BET should be on the web "in a big way." After a meeting in which AOL-backed startup NetNoir.com (described below under 'Competition')

[3]Adam Zagorin, "BET's too hot a property," *Time*, 20 October 1997.

[4]Adam Zagorin, "BET's too hot a property," *Time*, 20 October 1997.

[5]David Whitford, "Taking BET back from the Street," *Fortune*, 9 November 1998.

[6]Donna DeMarco, "Internet-Site Partnership is BET Holdings' Latest Move to Extend Reach," *Washington Times*, 27 September 1999.

declined Johnson's offer to acquire the company, Johnson called on John Malone for guidance. Malone introduced Johnson to Peter Neupert at Microsoft (now CEO of Drugstore.com) and the two signed an agreement. At the time, Microsoft was investing heavily in proprietary entertainment and information content to differentiate its online service, Microsoft Network, from AOL and other competitors.[7]

The MSBET joint-venture announcement had created high hopes for all involved. The venture, however, encountered problems almost from the start. Microsoft had dramatically changed its Internet strategy, reducing its emphasis on information and entertainment content and instead investing more heavily in its transactional services such as Expedia (an online travel agency) and Microsoft CarPoint (a car-buying service). As Johnson explained:

> Our strategy for MSBET underwent substantial changes between conception and execution. The initial execution of MSBET was very much the traditional media company version 1.0 website [meaning the site consisted largely of reconstituted content from BET's offline media properties, a schedule of on-air programming and a single news feed from a 3rd party provider]. Despite the scaleback, MSBET was one of the leading African-American sites and provided BET with some valuable insights into African-Americans' utilization of the Internet.

As the Internet took off in 1998, it became clear to BET management that the company could not rest on its laurels. In January of 1999, when Johnson and Mills reviewed the business plan for a new African-American portal, Johnson knew that BET had to make a decision. Johnson said:

> I was becoming more aware of the power and potential of the Internet by going to conferences and talking to people. I knew there was a larger opportunity for BET on the Internet and the African-American portal strategy was the right path for us.

In May of 1999, BET's management decided to reinvigorate its Internet strategy. Johnson tapped Mills to head the new Internet division. Mills had joined BET's Business Development group in 1997 from the Investment Banking Division of Lehman Brothers. Having worked in finance-related functions since graduating from the University of Pennsylvania in 1990, Mills had no prior operating experience. However, this did not deter Johnson. He explained:

> I am pretty comfortable with people who I know can get things done. I had seen Scott in action at Lehman Brothers during an attempt to build an arena in DC, and then observed him in BET's launch of our restaurants and other deals. I was impressed by his analysis and ability to critique businesses. Scott was always on point.

While Mills developed the BET.com business plan, Johnson contacted friends, colleagues and former media and technology partners. The two men pitched their portal concept to prospective partners. BET secured cash investments from Microsoft, USA Networks, News Corp, and Liberty Digital. The terms of the joint venture agreement allowed BET Holdings to own 50.1% of BET.com with the remaining 49.9% divided among the various partners. The partners committed a total of $35 million to the joint venture. In negotiating the BET.com partnership, Johnson and Mills avoided in-kind investments (e.g., contributions of content and/or on-air promotion) both because of the difficulty in valuing such in-kind contributions and because one key investor, Liberty Media, had a more limited ability to make such contributions.[8] Johnson explained:

> I can call up Barry Diller and get $10 million for just about anything because he knows me and knows I'll invest the money wisely. It's not a whole lot of money for him. But, if I were to say 'Barry, not only do I want $10 million but I also need content or marketing support;' then he's got to pass my request along to managers within his organization. They might say 'Well Barry, that's a little more than I think this BET thing is worth.' So, my approach is to first prove the BET.com model by leveraging BET content and marketing. Once we've proved the payoff we can either ask our partners for in-kind marketing or buy it from them at favorable in-house rates.

[7]For example, Microsoft had launched Slate, an online magazine, and Sidewalk, which provided city-specific news and event listings. Microsoft also had entered a joint venture with NBC to develop the cable programming service MSNBC and its companion website. See David B. Yoffie "Microsoft Goes Online: MSN—1996," HBS No. 9-798-019 (Boston: Harvard Business School, 1997), "Microsoft Goes Online: MSN—1997," HBS No. 9-798-035 (Boston: Harvard Business School, 1998), and "Microsoft Goes Online: MSN—1998," HBS No. 9-798-108 (Boston: Harvard Business School, 1998) for a history of Microsoft Network.

[8]Liberty owned minority equity stakes in a large number of cable programming services, including the Discovery Channel and QVC. However, as a minority investor, Liberty was not likely to be able to require that these services share content with BET.com or provide on-air promotion.

African-Americans on the Web

BET's Board believed that the market conditions were ripe for a portal targeting African-Americans. Forrester Research had recently reported that there were approximately 3.8 million African-American households online; other studies had reported as many as 6.6 million African-American Internet users in 1998.[9] While that represented only 23% of African-American households, compared with Internet penetration of 43% for white Americans, 36% for Hispanics, and 64% for Asian-Americans, African-Americans were the fastest growing online segment.[10] Forrester estimated that by the year 2000, online usage within the black community would grow to over 40% of households.[11] (See Exhibit 5.)

The initial lag in Internet usage by the African-American community had been attributed to everything from high PC prices to lack of perceived relevance of Internet content.[12] Johnson remarked:

> African-Americans aren't going to sit by and let their kids not participate. I think as computer prices fall, we'll participate. What BET has to do is provide compelling content.

Mills believed that the "four Cs" of a traditional portal (content, communications, community and commerce) were well suited to an African-American portal. For example, regarding content, Mills noted that African-Americans have demonstrated an affinity for culturally-oriented content in all other media platforms (television, print, radio, movies, theater, etc.). Furthermore, he felt the Internet provided real opportunities to target compelling information to African-Americans. Compared with other demographic groups, African-Americans relied disproportionately on television as their primary source of information. Mills asserted:

> Television is actually a poor medium for serving certain information needs of this community. African-Americans have unique issues, and therefore unique information needs in certain areas, such as health, investing and education. It is difficult to effectively address these needs in the format of a TV show.
>
> For example, there are specific health issues facing the African-American community. We suffer disproportionate incidences of certain diseases and higher genetic dispositions to others. BET.com's producers can create content that is relevant to our target market and create interactive forums that allow people with related experiences to share their issues, insights and solutions.

Competition

The idea of providing rich information to the black community was not a new one. In October 1999, there were several websites targeting African-Americans; a few had been in the market for as long as 5 years. Mills believed, however, that BET.com would become "the leading provider of interactive services that educate, enrich, empower and entertain African-Americans." He explained that:

> It's going to require a tremendous amount of money and massive marketing and distribution to compete. We really see capital as the primary barrier to entry in this space. Without marketing, no one will show up. In fact, our focus groups support this notion: among blacks using the Internet more than 7 hours per week, unaided recall for our strongest competitors was extremely low. Among that population, very few had ever actually visited one of our competitor's sites. At best, a small fraction were regular visitors.

These low awareness and traffic figures, according to Mills, signaled underpenetration by BET.com's competitors. Mills said:

> Each site claims to have at least 500,000 unique visitors per month. If we believe that there are roughly 5 million African-Americans online today and if Net Noir, Black Voices and all the others each really have 500,000 visitors, that means that these African-Americans sites each have only captured 10% of the total black population online. Let's juxtapose that penetration with a site like Yahoo!. Yahoo! is believed to reach 56% of the total online audience. There is massive underpenetration in this market.

---

[9] Ekaterina O. Walsh et al, "The Digital Melting Pot," Forrester, March 3, 1999. Available from http://www.forrester.com/ER/Research/Brief/0,1317,5703,FF.html; accessed 23 November 1999 and the Scarborough Study in the BET.com "Media Kit."

[10] Ibid.

[11] Ibid.

[12] Professors Donna L. Hoffman & Thomas P. Novak, "The Evolution of the Digital Divide: Examining the Relationship of Race to Internet Access and Usage Over Time," Owen Graduate School of Management, Vanderbilt University Draft Working Paper, 1999, 18.

NetNoir.com (www.netnoir.com)

NetNoir.com was founded in 1995 as the first website targeting content for African-Americans. The site offered a mix of entertainment-related news and information relevant to African-American consumers. In the spring of 1995, NetNoir became a partner of the AOL Greenhouse and AOL eventually became a 20% stakeholder in the venture. Since BET.com's announced launch in October 1999, NetNoir was reported to have received a $14 million additional capital infusion from various venture investors.

NetNoir.com was relaunched in late 1999 as "NetNoir—The Black Network, the premier black online service." The site offered personalization, e-mail, an online store, and chat functions through a variety of branded "microcommunities." The official launch of NetNoir companion sites such as blacknetwork.com, blackshopping.com and netnoirdollar.com was set for early December 1999. In addition, CEO David Ellington had hinted at the imminent announcement of significant strategic partnerships and international expansion.

Blackvoices.com (www.blackvoices.com)

Blackvoices.com was launched in April 1997 by the Tribune Company, owner of the Chicago Tribune newspaper and other holdings in television and radio broadcasting, publishing and education. Blackvoices.com was an "African-American community" that attempted to bring together job seekers and employers. The site also offers news and entertainment as well as e-commerce opportunities in the form of auctions and online affiliate programs.

Blackvoices considered itself the premiere destination site for "highly-skilled, career oriented African-Americans on the web."[13] Nielson/I-Pro estimated that the site received roughly 850,000 unique visitors and over 10 million page views per month.[14]

Blackfamilies.com (www.blackfamilies.com)

Blackfamilies.com was created through a partnership between Cox Enterprise, Inc. and Equitable Life Assurance Society. Cox Enterprises, Inc. was one of the largest privately-held media companies in the U.S., owning Cox Newspapers, Inc. (including the flagship Atlanta Constitution Journal and other daily and weekly newspapers, books and direct mail), Cox Broadcasting, Inc. (including television and radio stations), Cox Communications (offering cable television service, telephone service, direct to home satellite television and high speed internet access), and Manheim Auctions (automobile auctions). The site was launched in January 1999 targeting for African-American adults who wanted family-oriented content, services, and resources. The site provided information about family finance, relationships, and parenting as well as opportunities to chat with other visitors and links to other useful African-American oriented sites.

Time Warner's Volume.com

As of October 1999, the competitive landscape was evolving rapidly. In addition to incumbent players, Mills had heard what he believed were reliable rumors that Time Warner was creating a portal targeting the African-American and urban markets, to be called Volume.com. Time Warner, the world's largest media company, had significant resources and content relevant to African-Americans. For example, they owned the television station WB, one of the only television stations in the 1999-2000 season to offer television programming depicting African-Americans in leading roles and centered around African-American characters. Time Warner also owned the premium cable network HBO (Home Box Office) which frequently provided original programming, sporting events, and comedy shows featuring African-Americans. HBO, in fact, was calling itself "the hippest voice in black entertainment."

Although no formal announcement had been made about Time Warner's site, Mills had heard that the site would have a $16 million startup budget. In addition to utilizing Time Warner's video content, Mills had heard that Volume.com hoped to incorporate content from other Time Warner properties, for example, the Warner Music Group, *Sports Illustrated,* CNN, and the Road Runner high speed Internet access network.

Prior to the emergence of well-funded competitors, BET.com saw its superior funding as a significant element of its competitive advantage. However, as additional competitors became known and the company's operating strategy evolved, Mills recognized that his immediate competitive advantages were the programming and

[13]See website.

[14]See website.

marketing support of the BET Cable Network and the strong BET brand.

BET.com Strategy and Operations

Mills and Johnson saw an opportunity for BET.com to become the dominant website serving both the African-American market and the urban music market. Deciding on the target market for BET.com was difficult because BET's brand had become increasingly attractive to mainstream America and to what had come to be called the "urban" audience. The urban market was defined as a young (14-25), cross-racial demographic with an affinity for recording artists like Dr. Dre, Master P and Wu Tang Clan; for clothing made by designers like FUBU and Tommy Hilfiger; and for magazines like *Vibe, Blaze, The Source* and *XXL.* (Exhibit 6)

The urban market had grown rapidly in the last few years and the audience was being served by both online and offline media properties like MTV, The Source, and Peeps.com. Mills explained:

> From a pure marketing perspective the urban market has tremendous attraction. It's hot. It's catchy. It's a big market, and there are many marketers focused on that space. Because of this there has been tremendous competition between media companies to capture that marketing spending.

Mills explained the decision to principally target African-Americans instead of focusing entirely on the urban market:

> When a lot of people pitch ideas to BET.com they keep saying 'stop thinking of yourselves as black, picture yourselves as urban.' Well, it's really trendy to do that but our brand clearly says 'black.' Of course, most of our music programming is very crossover; urban and black. It can appeal to both markets. But, for example, an issue-oriented show like BET Tonight or Lead Story is not really the urban experience—it's about a black experience. The same is true for a music program like the Gospel Hour or for a magazine like *Emerge.* We do believe that there are also places where there is clear overlap between urban and black, but there are clearly places that are primarily black.
>
> Our view is that BET has major assets that enable us to compete in both the African-American and urban online market segments, and we believe that both of these segments are very attractive market opportunities. As a result, we developed a strategy that we believe will allow us to successfully pursue both segments.
>
> Our primary objective is to establish ourselves as the leading African-American portal. We believe that we have superior competitive assets here, it's a lucrative market and there are fewer powerful competitors. However, we believe that we can leverage BET's urban music assets to allow us to capture a major share of the urban segment as well. Thus, our secondary objective is to be the leading online urban music destination. By focusing on urban music instead of urban lifestyle trends [e.g., fashion, events, celebrities], we believe we can carve out our segment of the urban music market while still serving our primary market.

Roughly two-thirds of the programming on BET's cable network featured music videos. This fact, coupled with its pre-existing relationships with record labels and BET's ability to provide national promotion and exposure to new artists, gave BET.com a competitive advantage relative to other African-American and urban-oriented sites. "Right now," Mills said, "there is no dominant site for an urban music audience. BET.com could become that site and enjoy a tremendous advantage over pure Internet companies in securing content." In fact, record labels had been charging Internet sites fees for distributing audio and video clips of their artists (in contrast to their policy of providing music videos for free to cable TV networks) and had been asking for equity positions in the websites in exchange for non-exclusive rights to stream their videos. Given BET Holdings' important role in promoting artists, Mills expected that BET.com would be able to negotiate better deals with labels than pure-play websites and avoid giving up equity stakes. Mills explained:

> Currently, the labels see the Web as primarily a promotion, not distribution, vehicle. BET.com can offer the labels substantially superior promotional opportunities by leveraging the BET Cable Network. We will aggressively promote our URL during cable programs, and we will coordinate the content on our website with what's happening on TV. When an artist premieres a new video, a user will be able to access our music page and find interviews with the artist drawn from our deep video archives. We'll also offer an online showcase for unsigned artists. We'll be very attractive to new artists because of the exposure we can offer across TV and the Internet. Showcasing these new artists will differentiate our website in a

powerful way, because hard core urban music fans are very much concerned with staying on top of what's coming next.

Although there were tremendous advantages in serving both the African-American and urban audiences, Johnson and Mills acknowledged that there were risks associated with targeting both groups. For instance, Mills wondered whether both the 39 year old mother of three and the 15 year old hip-hopper could be well-served by a single site. At the same time, however, Mills was concerned that if BET.com did not incorporate urban content into the site he would forfeit that audience, which was significantly African-American.

Content and Communications

BET.com would offer the services and products of a mainstream portal like Yahoo! (including e-mail, personal web pages, chat, search and calendars and address books), general interest information like news, entertainment (including music), personals, event listings, job boards, and horoscopes; and specific features that would appeal to African-American consumers. These features would include "channels" with in-depth information on fitness and health, personal finance, lifestyles, food/recipes, romance and careers. (See Exhibit 7 for details.) The site would offer what Retha Hill, Vice President of Content, described as "the black perspective." She explained:

> The value of our site will be aggregating both general market news and information of particular interest to African-Americans. On our site, for example, users will be able to find out how the stock market is doing on any given day, but for those blacks who are not in the market, they will also get information on why we as a people have not been as well represented in the market as have other groups and how the users, as individuals, can get into investing and save more. Similarly, there will be information about raising black children as well as parenting tips in general; there will be news about black entertainers, film producers, authors and artists as well as general entertainment information.

Mills added:

> Our objective is to be the home page for a significant portion of the African-American online population, not simply a destination African-Americans visit when they want niche content. Consequently, we have to provide both general market and black content because that is how African-Americans use the Internet. When we looked at the African-American online user, we found that they do not surf the Web first as African-Americans; instead they surf as *Web surfers* and then secondarily or tertiarily as *African-Americans* seeking ethnically oriented content or community.
>
> So the issue becomes, what do people surfing the web really like? People like the absence of boundaries and borders. If you start talking to people about creating closed environments, about limiting their options, you get really negative feedback—especially in the Internet space. The unique value proposition we offer with our 'News Channel,' for example, is that we will provide, through our partnerships, not only general market news but also news that is germane to the black community. For instance, if some terrible thing happens in Alabama that the African-American community should know about we can provide breaking news on the subject via our news partners and have our internal content staff develop additional in-depth coverage that would reflect an African-American perspective. There are many news items on which African-Americans have either different or additional perspectives that simply do not get presented by the general press. Everything from the recent rash of high school shootings to African-American males' longstanding difficulties in hailing taxicabs in New York City. In light of these differences, and the tremendous frustrations they can often create, we believe that African-Americans will value our content.

Both Mills and Hill acknowledged that it would be challenging to fully integrate both general and specific content on the site. However, Hill also believed that the site's content would be one of its competitive advantages.

> I think that one difference between BET.com and some of the existing African-American sites in terms of content is that we can go out and do deals with multiple major content providers. These content providers are expensive, but we have the money to license their content. In addition to our own content development staff, we also have great content that we can draw on from the BET properties.

BET.com not only planned to provide vast amounts of pertinent information but to also allow users to customize and personalize their experience. Chief Technology Officer, Craig Maccubbin said:

> Our goal is to dynamically serve content that is of interest to users without them having to ask for it explicitly. If users are looking for information on heart disease, for example, we'll present other content like a news wire on the issue or an article on the prevalence of heart disease within the black community. We'll also display banner ads for relevant products to them, say, a blood pressure monitor. Our technology will allow us to infer from a user's past searches and page visits what the user is interested in learning more about.

Early on, the majority of BET.com's content would be produced by the BET.com content staff and sourced from third parties. Eventually, however, Hill hoped to add content from all of BET Holding's properties onto the site including the cable network shows and print magazines. In obtaining this BET content, Hill stated:

> Original content will be a major part of our content value proposition. As we create this content, we scour the BET Cable Network's rich video archives of events, interviews and performances over the past twenty years to create online multi-media experiences. BET's Publishing Group has wonderful feature content that I would like to use. However, like many magazine groups, they are evaluating how to deploy this content online in a way that is not detrimental to their core business. We're working closely with them to develop an arrangement that will allow BET.com to use their feature content. We can't have this rich source of African-American news and information sitting here and not utilize it online. Our competitors don't have access to that type of information and we need to use it to our advantage.

Community and Commerce

Initially, while Mills believed BET.com's content would draw communities around each channel within the site, little immediate focus was planned on chat and communities at launch. However, upon reexamination of the potential opportunities for drawing incremental African-Americans online, Johnson and Mills expanded BET.com's community offerings to include personalized web pages and a free and paid personals database. The company believed putting these community features in place and leveraging them through cable network exposure would help to capture a large share of the African-American market.

Mills expected the communities to spur commerce. Although BET.com would launch without an online mall, Mills planned to roll out the e-commerce initiative by the summer of 2000, in time for the back-to-school rush. The initial product categories would include urban apparel (activewear, outerwear, sportswear and footwear), books by African-American authors, music, beauty supplies, financial services, arts and gifts, and travel. Mills believed that these retail products were culturally distinct, had high demand among African-American and urban consumers, were well suited for online retailing, and were consistent with BET's brand image.

One of the issues Mills wrestled with was whether BET should be the direct seller of the goods offered for sale on the site, versus an affiliate providing links to other online retailers. Mills said, "The place where we'll likely leverage a third party are things like flowers, travel and online brokerage where there are big infrastructure costs associated with getting up and running." Products such as books, music, and gifts could be sourced from distributors, thereby avoiding inventory holding costs and inventory obsolescence—a big risk for fad-driven music. Mills hoped that many apparel and beauty supplies could be sourced directly from manufacturers. By working with manufacturers directly, BET would limit inventory risk and receive a greater margin on those items.

Some distributors and manufacturers were not equipped to ship directly to consumers. For these vendors, BET.com would need to manage fulfillment. Through their strategic partnership with USA Networks, BET.com would have the ability to contract with Home Shopping Network (HSN) for fulfillment and customer service.

Marketing

"I'm confident we'll do everything possible to make BET.com successful," said Debra Lee, "but I still have some fear that we'll build this thing and they won't come." To avoid this, BET.com was planning an aggressive marketing campaign to drive traffic and establish market dominance; a $8 to $9 million campaign Mills believed would be one of the largest ever for any African-American product or service (with the exception of a few movies). The marketing strategy involved promoting BET.com across all BET media (print and cable), integrating site marketing and promotion into BET programming and editorial content, advertising in other African-American and urban-targeted offline media, securing online distribution, and advertising online across multiple websites.

Given that the majority of African-Americans were not yet online, most of BET.com's marketing campaign would be spent offline. Mills had hired Stacie Turner (HBS alum '96), a former product manager at Sprint who was trained in product marketing at Procter and Gamble, to lead the marketing effort. In October 1999, Turner had just begun to determine how her marketing budget would be spent. She said:

> There is no significant precedent for marketing a website to African-Americans. None of our competitors has done broad scale marketing offline or online. As a result, we will develop a campaign that focuses on the offline media habits of African-American Internet users and seeks to achieve a high reach and frequency against this audience.
>
> One of our challenges is producing a single marketing campaign that speaks to both the general African American audience and the urban music audience. To address this challenge, we developed a marketing plan with a unifying message that supports multiple creative executions oriented towards specific demographic groups.
>
> While our budgeted media spend is modest relative to many Internet companies, we benefit from the fact that most African-American media is substantially less expensive than general market media. As a result, our advertising dollars go further against our target audience. I expect that about 95% of our budget will be spent offline. We're looking to do a combination of TV, print, radio and outdoor marketing plus billboards, street level promotion and other grass roots tactics like e-mail announcements to reach our demo.

Traffic and Headcount

Mills and Turner anticipated that BET.com's marketing efforts would attract 1.5 to 2.0 million unique visitors to the site each month by year-end. Furthermore, Mills expected that each of these visitors would make 8-10 page views during a given month. (See Exhibit 8 for comparables from other content-oriented websites.) To develop and support such traffic, Mills expected to hire 35 people over the next several months thereby raising his total headcount to 60 by year-end 2000. The majority of the hires would be into the content, technology, ad sales and commerce departments.

Organization

When BET.com was announced, the Internet venture created some organizational challenges for Mills and for managers in the parent company, BET Holdings. As Debra Lee explained, she worked hard to balance Mills' excitement and enthusiasm for the new venture with the expectations of senior members of BET Holdings management.

> I've tried to build a team that will work together and understand that one important way to increase the value of BET Holdings is to pay down its debt—we took on $600 million in debt during our 'going private' transaction. The way to pay down that debt is to drive our core business—the BET cable network—which is our cash cow. To do that, we'll have to improve programming, improve ratings and increase advertising revenue. So that's what I've been drilling into people. Now along comes the dot.com business and it's apparent we could take the dot.com business public relatively quickly. This could, of course, increase the value of Holdings. We don't have another venture that has that potential. So, what I have to do is convince BET Holdings' management team that the dot.com business is very important to everyone. We're going to all have to pay attention to it and cooperate. Cooperation requires that the programming people support it, the advertising people help it, and the magazines freely give up their content.
>
> I've told Scott that he can't think of the dot.com business as a separate business—that will never work. BET.com needs the services of BET. It needs the cooperation of BET Holdings' senior management and it needs BET's content. Consequently, Scott needs to be sensitive to his colleagues perceptions.

One organizational issue debated extensively was whether to extend BET.com stock options to BET Holdings' employees. Johnson and Lee decided that the only BET Holdings' staff to receive options would be the television network's advertising staff, which would be called upon to cross-sell Internet ads to existing clients. In addition, BET.com would employ a separate ad salesforce that would call on Internet-only accounts and assist the Holding's salesforce with their cross-selling efforts. This incentive was viewed as important in ensuring that BET.com would receive the full attention of the sales force because initially, Internet ad revenues would be dwarfed by the TV network's ad revenues. Under the plan, if the ad sales staff hit their sales targets, they would receive BET.com's options. Lee noted:

> This is a big issue. We've had some failures when we've started businesses that don't relate back to TV ad sales. These guys have strong relationships with their accounts—they drive $100 million in revenue to BET every year.
>
> But relying exclusively on the TV ad sales force poses problems, too. Our top TV sales guy says, 'I can sell the Internet ads. Let my staff do it.' But we have partners in BET.com who may worry that the TV sales team is not paying full attention to dot.com because TV is an easier sell that yields bigger commissions.

Unresolved Issues, Late 1999

As of December 1999, Mills still had some pressing issues that had to be addressed. In particular, Mills had to decide whether to move forward with a branded ISP strategy and how music should be incorporated into the BET.com site.

BET-Branded ISP

In late 1999, Mills struggled to decide whether BET.com should become a virtual Internet Service Provider. There seemed to be a natural opportunity for BET to couple access with the BET.com portal. Mills explained the potential benefits from providing BET branded access:

> There are three good reasons for BET to get into the ISP business. The first is the need to get more African-Americans online. The second is the ability to vertically integrate and drive traffic to our site. The third is to capitalize on incremental revenue opportunities.

A primary barrier to offering access was the fact that a significant portion of BET.com's target customers did not already own computers. With PCs being given away in exchange for long-term access contracts (and vice versa), many access contracts were being consummated before consumers left the store where they purchased their first PC. Mills thought that it would be difficult to compete under these circumstances unless BET.com could enter into a partnership with a PC manufacturer. After unsuccessful negotiations with a few leading PC manufacturers, Mills decided to put the ISP issue on hold. He explained:

> The ISP market and business model are in a real state of flux. The price for access has dropped, and in many instances access has become free, so the economics for ISPs have become less attractive. The economic model for free access providers like NetZero may not work for a niche play, because the models require significant scale to be effective. A free ISP model still has to cover $10-15 per subscriber per month of pre-marketing variable costs related to network access and customer service. We've considered partnerships with ISPs that would charge us $6.50 per subscriber for network access and customer service but collect 20% of all access and portal revenue. This type of deal would be better for us than a traditional virtual ISP arrangement [under which BET would pay the full $10-15 per subscriber monthly cost of leasing network access and customer service capabilities from third party providers] if our monthly revenues per subscriber were less than $21-22—which seems likely given the current competitive environment. We believe that we can step into the ISP market at a later date and retain our ability to compete. There are more timely and promising opportunities, like music and communities, that require our immediate focus and attention.

Online Music Initiative

While Mills recognized the tremendous value of offering music online given BET's strong position within the music industry, he struggled to determine the how music should best be integrated into the BET.com site. Mills explained:

> Music labels like the idea of BET getting into the online music market. However, for us it's a branding issue. We are uniquely challenged in this respect because of our target audience. Do we really want urban music fans wading through 'high brow' information on personal finance and health issues on their way to their music? You may jeopardize the coherence of the site and the brand if you try and integrate too many disparate activities.

Mills had learned a few weeks earlier that the company owning the popular, urban market-oriented *Vibe, Blaze,* and *Spin* magazines was being shopped for a price likely to exceed $200 million. Mills believed that this might present an opportunity for BET Holdings to purchase *Vibe* and use its strong brand name to launch an online music site. An entirely different site, separately branded from BET.com, might entice hot urban music companies to partner with BET, because they might secure a more substantial equity stake in the business than would be available with the larger BET.com. Conversely running two sites would raise marketing costs, dilute cross-marketing opportunities and would not fully exploit BET's strong brand equity with music fans.

Conclusion

The launch of BET.com had been postponed from the originally announced December 1999 date to February 2000. This breathing room would allow Mills to more fully consider the questions before him, stretch his marketing budget further by avoiding the crush of pre-Christmas dot.com advertising that had inflated fourth quarter CPMs, and allow BET.com to capitalize on Black History Month in February. The postponement would not, however, buy Mills more time to make critical decisions about the music site. Mills had a meeting planned for the following day in New York City with Russell Simmons, a prominent producer of urban market music. He then would leave for Los Angeles to meet with other music labels. MP3 was still looking for a partner and it was clear to Mills that the time was right to seriously consider additional strategic partnerships.

In addition, the competition was heating up. Since BET.com's announcement, websites targeting the African-American and urban audience were attracting additional funding from investors. For example, UBO.com, an urban oriented site under development, was said to have completed a second round $40 million raise and have nearly 200 employees on board, and Blackvoices.com announced that the company was hoping to close a $25 million round of financing by year-end 1999. The company also hoped to IPO in the following 18 months and eventually become a multimedia company that would "extend beyond the Internet into broadcasting and print."[15]

As Mills packed his briefcase for the evening he pondered the timing for BET.com's own IPO. He and Bob Johnson had met with investment bankers who had assured them that the public equity markets would embrace BET.com's plans and that June 2000 would be the perfect time for an IPO. Was that right? What were the risks in going public so soon after the site's launch?

---

[15]"Cooper Cultivates Community," Advertising Age Interactive Special Reporting Supplement, 1 November 1999 [journal online]; available from OneSource; accessed 23 November 1999.

Exhibit 1

SAMPLE BET CABLE NETWORK PROGRAMMING

Show	Description
Morning Moves	Start your day with an adrenaline booster that gives you the best sounds and the latest visual concepts. No VJ, just the music and more hot videos, morning to midday.
BET Videolink	Each half-hour of videos has a different thread running through it. What's the link? Figure it out in this visually cutting-edge show.
JamZone	Join Cita, the new cyberhost of Jam Zone—you never quite know what's going to fall out of her computer-generated mouth. She's programmed to play great videos—but can she help it if she's got a point of view?
All	The topics are hot and so is the music. Join host Liza Michelle for the day's most provocative topics and best music.
Rap City: Tha Bassment	Tigger goes to New York to hang with the one and only Q-Tip.
Hits from the Street	He's irreverent. He's in your face. He makes you mad. He plays the giant videos. His name is Hits, and if you're not careful, he'll be on your street next.
Sparks	What happens when a bright, beautiful female attorney joins an inner-city LA law firm run by a patriarch and his bickering sons? Sparks!
Amen	A small Philadelphia church hires a new reverend to increase attendance—and watch the fun when you see what he does. Sherman Hemsley stars as Reverend Reuben Gregory.
ComicView	It's hilarious, wild and wacky. It's the new season of ComicView, blazing into the new millennium.
Live from LA	It's bold, edgy and topical. Join Michael Colyar and Rachel along with the Live from LA band, high profile celebrities, live musical performances, sketch comedy and a live studio audience.
BET Tonight	BET Tonight features the top news stories of the day along with enlightened and provocative conversation live with high profile celebrities, politicians and newsmakers.
Midnight Love	Smooth, sultry sounds by superstar balladeers. Slip into the night and cuddle up with Bob on Midnight Love.
Jazz Discovery	Who's going to be the latest sensation in the world of jazz? Discovery gives unknown or unsigned artists a chance to show their stuff. See them today—because they could be superstars tomorrow.

Source: MSBET.com

Exhibit 2 BET HOLDINGS STOCK PERFORMANCE FROM 1992–1998 (FORMER TICKER: BTV)

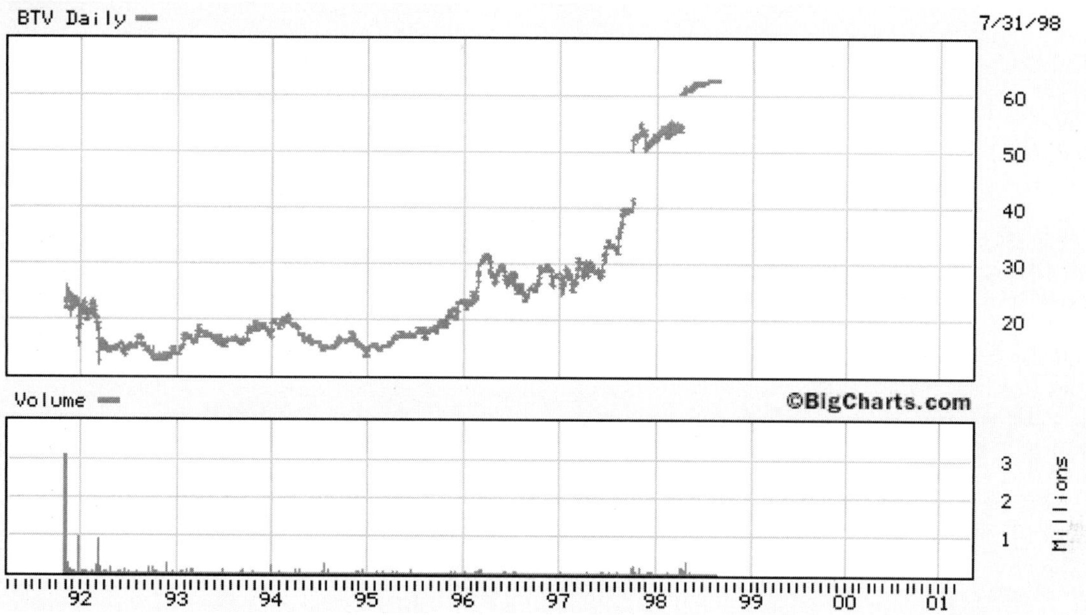

Exhibit 3 BET HOLDINGS FINANCIAL PERFORMANCE ($MILLIONS)

	1994	1995	1996	1997	1998*
Operating Revenue	97.5	115.2	132.3	154.2	129.5
Operating Income	26.4	37.5	42.8	53.8	46.4

Fiscal Year Ended July 31st.
*Unaudited, 9 months ended April, 30th.
Source: Forms 10-K and 8-K filed with SEC

Exhibit 4

BET HOLDINGS PRODUCTS AND SERVICES

- Action Pay-Per-View (subscription movies)
- BET Arabesque (made-for-TV movie production)
- BET Cable Network
- BET Gospel Channel
- BET International (sales)
- BET Movies/Starz!3 (joint venture with Encore Media)
- BET on Jazz
- Clothing (BET Design Studio)
- Financial Services (credit cards, joint venture with Chevy Chase Bank)
- Online services (MSBET, joint venture with Microsoft)
- Publishing
  - Arabesque (African-American romance novel publisher)
  - "BET Weekend" (monthly Sunday newspaper supplement)
  - "Emerge" (monthly news publication)
  - "Heart & Soul" (semi-monthly beauty & fitness publication)
- Restaurants
  - BET on Jazz Restaurant (upscale restaurant)
  - BET SoundStage (theme restaurant)
  - BET SoundStage Club (theme club)
  - Tres Jazz (theme restaurant inside Park Place Entertainment's Paris Las Vegas casino/hotel)

Source: OneSource

Exhibit 5-A ETHNIC BACKGROUND AND ONLINE ADOPTION

	% of US Households*	% of Households online**	% of Households online in 2000
Caucasian American	85%	34%	44%
African American	12%	23%	40%
Asian American	3%	64%	68%
Hispanic American	8%	36%	43%
Total Population		33%	44%

*Percentages in this column do not add to 100% because Hispanic American is not independent of other categories
**The total population percentage in this column is not the average of the five ethnic groups due to possible overlap
Source: Adapted from Forrester Research

Exhibit 5-B TOP FACTORS THAT INFLUENCE TECHNOLOGY ADOPTION FOR INDIVIDUALS LIKELY TO GO ONLINE IN 1999

1. *Income*
2. *Technology Optimism*
3. *Age*
4. *Education*
5. *Entertainment Motivation*

Source: Adapted from Forrester Research

Exhibit 5-C

CHARACTERISTICS OF ONLINE ADOPTERS AND HOUSEHOLDS LIKELY TO GO ONLINE IN 1999[16]

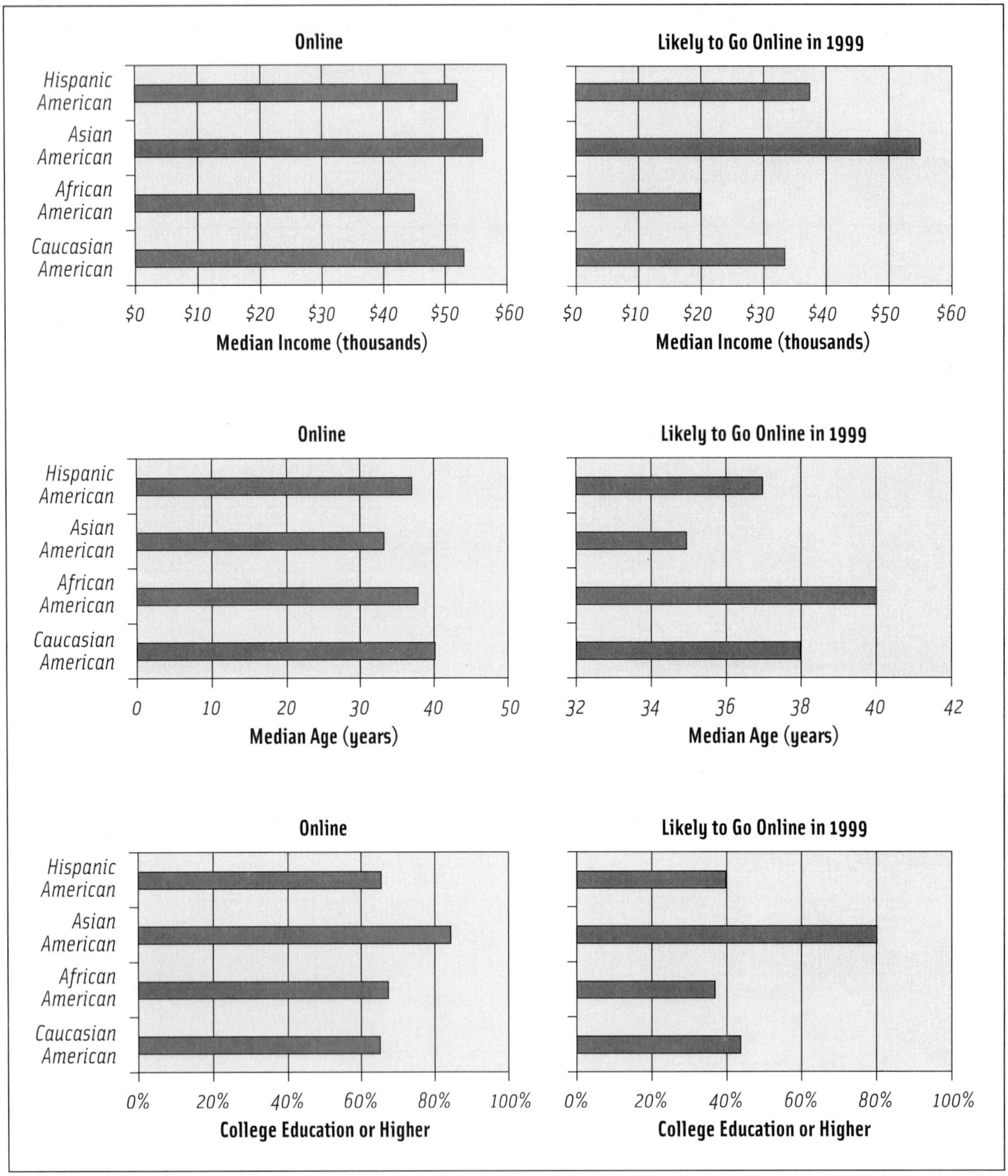

[16]Source: Adapted from Forrester Research

Exhibit 5-O EXPERIENCE AND ONLINE ACTIVITIES BY ETHNIC GROUP

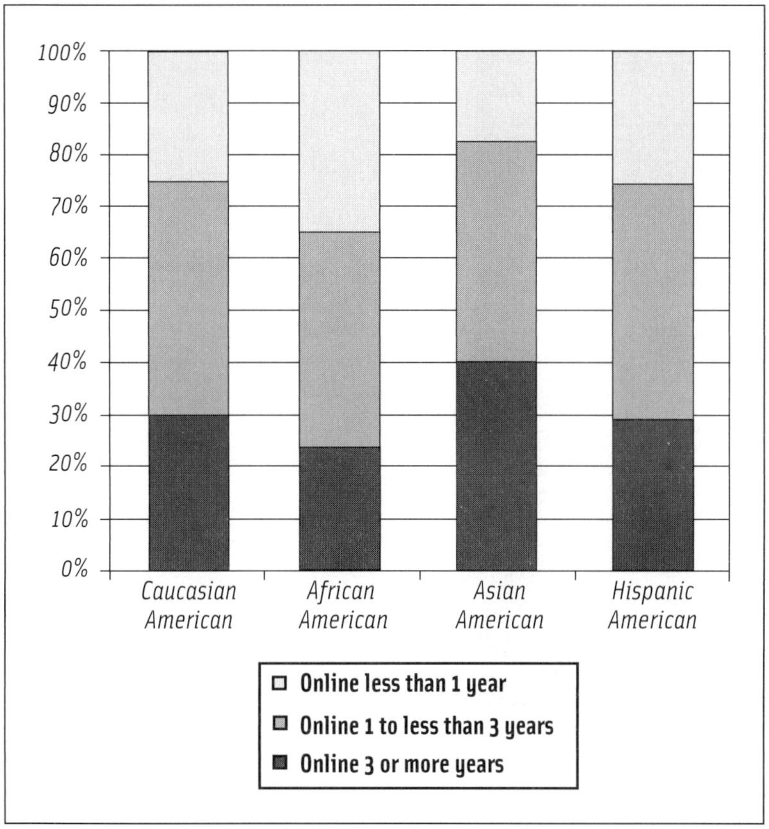

Source: Adapted from Forrester Research

Exhibit 6

SAMPLE MAGAZINE COVERS AND ADVERTISEMENTS TARGETED TO THE URBAN AUDIENCE

– a. *The Source*

– b. *XXL*

Exhibit 7

SAMPLE BET.COM CHANNEL CONTENT[17]

Channel	Description	Potential Providers	Content
News	Top news and information of interest to African Americans, moderated chat with newsmakers	Reuters, Lexis/Nexis, BET Properties, BET.com Producers	General market and African-American news, African-American news from African-American media, BET Tonight, Lead Story, Emerge, Feature Content
Entertainment	Movie, music, and other entertainment previews, urban entertainment report, the latest news and gossip from Hollywood to Harlem, comedy, games, and local A&E calendars	Reuters, CitySearch.com, Urban Content Partner, BET Properties, BET.com	Breaking Entertainment News, Local news and events, Urban Entertainment News & Gossip, African-American News, Feature Content
Music	Streaming music videos and related artist content, urban "indie" music uploads and downloads, Internet radio, celebrity chats and top news	Internet Radio, "Indie" Music Center, Streaming Music Videos	Multiple BET Branded Urban Online Radio Channels (R&B, Hip-Hop, Jazz, etc.), Free music uploads and downloads of independent artists' music, Network promotion of top "indie" artists
Personal Finance	Top financial market news, investment tools, stock quotes, portfolio manager, investment guide, retirement planner, and financial health assessment tools. Moderated chat with financial and investment experts	Reuters, Big Charts, Sponsor Content, BET.com Producers	Business and financial news; Stock quotes, portfolio tracking, financial indexes; Investment content, functionality, and discussions; Feature content
Health	Top health news, coverage of health issues affecting African-Americans, diagnostic health tools, symptoms and drug data bases, doctor search, support communities, Q&A with health providers	Reuters, Health Scout, GWU Medical Center, BET Proper ties, BET.com Producers	Top health news; Health news and major medical database; Columns, FAQs and chats hosted by GWU African American Physicians; Heart & Soul and Emerge; Feature content
Sports	Top sports news, game scores, profiles of key players, coverage of HBCUs, fantasy leagues, and chats with sports superstars	Sports Ticker, BET Properties, Freelancer, BET.com	Comprehensive sports news content, sports scores, features and fantasy sports
Career	Jobs database, career advice, resume, interviewing and salary negotiation tips, hot jobs guide	Monster.com, Freelancers, BET.com	Massive job search application, career guides, career search materials; Career features, columns and related information; Feature content
Food	Exciting recipes, urban restaurant guide, recipe contents, interactive meal planner, healthy meals guide, cookbook reviews, chats with celebrity chefs, style setters and cookbook authors	Content sponsor, Heart & Soul, BET.com producers	Interactive food features, sweepstakes, contest; Recipes; Urban restaurant guide, recipes, healthy meal guide, cookbook reviews, chats with celebrity chefs, style setters and cookbook authors original features and additional content

[17]Source: BET.com

Exhibit 7 SAMPLE BET.COM SITE USAGE[18]

	"Adrienne"
	19-year-old junior at Hampton University, loves hip hop and art
9:05 a.m.	Checks out news and current events
11:30 a.m.	Researches places around the area to get hair braided
4:16 p.m.	Checks out BET internship opportunities to pass on at business club meeting
6:25 p.m.	Chats with Maxwell, falls in love and joins fan club
8:00 p.m.	Checks out new art exhibit at the Hip Hop Hall of Fame in Cleveland
	"Malik"
	22 years old, single, new job in corporate America, avid jazz fan
8:15 a.m.	Checks out stock quotes over coffee
10:25 a.m.	Gets salary negotiation tips and grad school information
1:00 p.m.	Works on defensive strategy of Fantasy Football team
4:33 p.m.	Investigates stock performance
7:45 p.m.	Downloads Billie Holiday vintage performance and calls it a night
	"Monica & Kevin"
	Married 4 years with 2 kids and a dog. She loves R&B. He loves Reggae. They share the same interests in travelling, history, reading and even share a computer.
5:30 a.m.	Both read about the latest on African American newsmakers
6:20 a.m.	Kevin checks out stats and scores
6:28 p.m.	Monica emails cousin with latest gossip on Taye Diggs
4:30 p.m.	Gets tips on making dinnertime fun for the kids
6:55 p.m.	Participate in chat with financial expert on home buying
9:20 p.m.	Kevin downloads mortgage calculator to start planning to buy new house
	"Stephanie"
	32 years old, single, looking for a career change and loves gospel music
8:15 a.m.	Browses through jobs database for interesting leads
9:20 a.m.	Researches doctors in her area
1:40 p.m.	Uses online calorie counter to assess the damage lunch did
4:10 p.m.	Finds new recipe to try on dinner "work" date
6:42 p.m.	Downloads "Joe Sample" for background music as the doorbell rings . . .
11:17 p.m.	Emails girlfriend the "scoop" on tonight's date
	"Alvin"
	42 year old divorcee, entrepreneur, heavy investor
7:45 a.m.	Surfs the Business channel
8:05 a.m.	Checks out health site for nutritionist in his area
12:09 p.m.	Sends email to business associate confirming 7:00 dinner meeting
4:10 p.m.	Utilizes investment guide for next business moves
9:45 p.m.	Downloads Method Man's latest cut in attempt to better understand teenage son
10:23 p.m.	Checks the entertainment channel for a schedule of jazz shows in the city

[17]Source: BET.com

Exhibit 8 TRAFFIC AND REVENUE COMPARABLES

	Reach*	Avg. Daily Page Views	1998 Annual Revenue Per Monthly Visitor
C/Net	11.4%	8 million	$9
Sportsline	4.5%	6 million	$12
Marketwatch	N/A	N/A	$8

4th Quarter 1998.
Source: Lanny Baker, Salomon Smith Barney, "The Online Media Rule Book: Volume 1," 13 September 1999

BMG ENTERTAINMENT

Forty floors above Times Square, Strauss Zelnick and Kevin Conroy met in Zelnick's corner office. As President and CEO of BMG Entertainment, one of the world's leading record companies, Zelnick faced a tough set of decisions about how to organize and operate the company. He knew he could count on Conroy, Senior Vice President of Worldwide Marketing and New Technology, for a clear opinion.

The discussion came in August, 1999, as the global music industry faced a period of potentially tumultuous change. Two of the six companies that dominated the industry had merged a year earlier, and at least one other was rumored to be looking for a buyer. Customer tastes and buying habits were in flux. The Internet brought the promise—or specter—that consumers would buy much of their music online rather than purchase it from storefront retailers. Soon, customers might download music rather than buy prerecorded compact discs or cassette tapes. With this change, the traditional chain linking artists through record companies and retailers to consumers might take on an entirely new form. Certain industry analysts and participants even predicted—some gleefully—that the new technology would spell the end of the major record companies. Chuck D of the rap group Public Enemy took an extreme position:[1]

> Soon you'll see a marketplace with 500,000 independent labels—the majors can co-opt all they want, but it's not going to stop the average person from getting into the game. Today a major label makes a CD for as little as 80 cents, then sells it wholesale for $10.50 so retailers can charge $14—that's highway robbery. . . . The true revenge will come when the major labels start dropping their prices. I can see the public saying, "OK, I could go to the store and pick up the album I want for $5, but I can get it on the Net for . . . $3."

Among major music companies, BMG had been one of the most eager to embrace the new technology, despite the threats it might pose. Conroy and Zelnick had steered BMG toward online opportunities as early as 1995. BMG was the first major record company to create a set of branded web sites tailored to particular genres of music in order to attract music fans. It was also the first to use downloading technology to promote the sale of conventional, prerecorded CDs and cassettes.[2] Via an innovative agreement with America Online, consumers who played the CDs of certain BMG artists on their computers were linked automatically to relevant web sites.

Changing technology created a new set of "digital customers" for BMG: online retailers such as CDNow, which shipped CDs and tapes to consumers; storefront retailers such as Tower Records that were establishing online operations; web sites that enabled consumers to download music directly from the web; and individual consumers who were visiting BMG's music web sites. Zelnick now had to decide how to organize BMG to serve its digital customers. One option was to give the existing distribution organization responsibility for the new class of customers. Alternatively, BMG could set up a separate division to handle digital distribution. The mandate of the digital organization was also at stake. How loyal would BMG remain to its traditional customers, storefront retailers? How eagerly would it pursue other retailers or consumers themselves? Regardless of its structure and mandate, the digital organization would soon face difficult choices about technology. A number of companies such as Microsoft, Liquid Audio, and IBM were developing technologies to support the downloading of music over the Internet. Should BMG continue to forge non-exclusive partnerships with a wide range of technology vendors, or

---

Gerrit Meier, MBA 2000, prepared this case under the supervision of Professor Jan W. Rivkin as the basis for class discussion rather than to illustrate either effective or ineffective handling of an administrative situation.

[1]J. Freund, "Listen Up," *Wired*, March 1999.

[2]Personal communication from Kevin Conroy, Senior Vice President, Worldwide Marketing and New Technology, February 14, 2000. "BMG Entertainment's Award-winning Genre-based Web Sites to Feature Liquid Audio Technology," BMG Entertainment press release, November 3, 1997.

was it time to focus on a smaller number of exclusive relationships? Zelnick and Conroy knew that others in the industry would watch BMG's moves carefully.

Development of the Global Music Industry[3]

Before the advent of the phonograph, music was disseminated by means of printed sheet music. Sheet music was published much like books: publishing companies bought the works of composers and lyricists, printed the works, and sold them through retail concession stands and licensed agents. Composers and lyricists often tried to bypass publishing companies and go directly to the consumers by playing their music in piano bars and public places, or if they were able to afford it, having their music sung by professional singers in evening dance halls and restaurants. As publishing companies forged relationships with retail outlets and developed mail-order lists, however, composers and lyricists increasingly relied on publishers. By the late 19th century, the music-publishing business was centralized in New York City, particularly in an area of lower Manhattan called Tin Pan Alley. The first popular song to sell one million copies, "After the Ball" (1892), sparked rapid growth in the industry. Composers and lyricists were hired to turn out simple, memorable, emotionally appealing songs for a mass market.

Sound recording devices were invented in 1877 by Thomas Edison in the United States and Charles Cros in France. Edison's cylinder-based talking machine was first sold to the public in 1889. Edison soon faced competition from Alexander Graham Bell's American Graphophone Company and Columbia, a maker of coin-operated music cylinders. In 1901, the Victor Talking Machine Company launched disc recordings. Victor's discs, invented by Emil Berliner, quickly displaced cylinders. Edison continued to produce his fragile, lower capacity cylinders until 1913 when he introduced his very own "Edison Diamond Discs." Edison discs required a different player, used different material, and ran at a different speed than Berliner discs. Although Edison discs provided better sound quality than Berliner discs, consumers and most popular artists had already switched to Berliner discs and remained with them.

The Early Oligopoly. Protected by patents, Edison, Columbia, and Victor maintained an oligopoly in the recording market for many years. Through alliances and partnerships with smaller companies, the trio extended their reach around the globe. For instance, the newly established Gramophone Company became Victor's European representative. Edison, Columbia, and Victor initially produced and distributed records in order to convince consumers to buy phonograph machines. By the 1920s, however, the companies focused on records, not machines, as their primary products. Sheet music shrank to account for about fifteen percent of music publishing revenues, and recording royalties became the major revenue stream of the music business. The music publishers of Tin Pan Alley continued to manage the copyrights of composers and lyricists. Record companies took on the job of finding talented performers to make records as well as the tasks of manufacturing, marketing, and distributing recordings.

The U.S. music industry saw significant growth until 1923, when broadcast radio, a new technology, posed a serious threat. As consumers purchased radios, record sales declined dramatically for a couple of years. Columbia, for instance, came perilously close to bankruptcy. The electric microphone and amplifier, new technologies developed alongside the radio, made it possible to record music with much greater fidelity. Record companies initially refused to promote electrical recording because their warehouses were full of old acoustic discs. Soon, however, they adopted the new technology. The higher quality associated with electrical recordings and a widespread economic boom brought strong growth to the industry during the late 1920s.

In 1929, the Depression hit the recording industry at its peak, sparking consolidation. Edison went out of business, and the Radio Corporation of America (RCA), which had prospered as a result of radio's popularity, acquired Victor. In 1931, rivals Columbia, Parlophone and the Gramophone Company merged to become Electric and Musical Industries (EMI), based in England. The American operations of EMI passed into the hands of CBS, another radio network. The companies that emerged from the consolidation—RCA/Victor, EMI, and CBS Records—led the music industry in the following decades. Indeed, they

[3]This section draws heavily on the following sources: P. Gronow and I. Saunio, *An International History of the Recording Industry,* London: Cassell, 1998; G.P. Hull, *The Recording Industry,* Boston: Allyn & Bacon, 1997; C.A. Waterman, "Popular Music," Microsoft Encarta Online Encyclopedia, 1999; S. Shemel and M.W. Krasilovsky, *This Business of Music* (6th edition), New York: Billboard Books, 1990; and M. Fink, *Inside the Music Industry* (2nd edition), New York: Schirmer Books, 1996.

formed the core of three of the five major music companies that dominated the industry in 1999.

Industry leaders continued to experiment with new formats for distributing music. In 1948, CBS Records introduced a long-playing (LP), 33-rpm disc pressed from vinyl and an affordable phonograph that could also play older, 78-rpm shellac discs. One year later, RCA/Victor launched the 45-rpm single and a longer, extended play (EP) disc. Confused by the competing formats, customers bought neither. In a compromise, the two companies agreed to sell players for the 33-rpm and 45-rpm discs, and they discontinued the EP.

A few new, significant record companies—including Decca, Mercury, and Capitol—joined RCA/Victor, EMI, and CBS Records during the 1930s and 1940s. Despite the arrival of new competitors, the production, marketing, and distribution of music remained concentrated among a handful of firms. Between 1946 and 1952, the six largest companies produced 158 of the 163 records which achieved "gold record" status, and RCA/Victor and Decca represented 67 percent of *Billboard*'s Top Pop Records chart.

The Impact of Rock and Roll. The 1950s brought a host of new styles of music targeted at the newly affluent teenage market—most famously, rock and roll. Hundreds of record companies were founded within a few years. With an endless supply of young musical talent, any startup record company that specialized in the right genre at the right moment and kept overhead and production costs low could make a profit on a single release that sold only a few thousand copies. Many of the new companies proved short-lived, but a handful enjoyed lasting success. For example, the sons of the Turkish ambassador to the United States used a $10,000 loan from their dentist to found Atlantic Records. Older record companies such as RCA/Victor and CBS Records long ignored the opportunities posed by the teenage market and rock and roll. These new genres originated far from Tin Pan Alley, with which the established record companies had longstanding relationships. Moreover, some record company executives felt that, by selling to teenagers, they would risk the goodwill they had built up over the years with parents.

In 1955, RCA's country section paid $35,000 for the contract of a little-known rock-and-roll artist from Sun Records, a small company established in 1952. RCA's strong marketing organization placed the artist, Elvis Presley, in prominent venues such as the Ed Sullivan Show in 1956. Elvis earned his first gold records the same year. RCA's signing of Elvis along with Decca's contracts with Bill Haley and Buddy Holly signaled the full entry of the major record companies into the rock-and-roll market. Still, between 1955 and 1959, small independent record companies accounted for 101 of the 147 records that made it into the U.S. Top Ten chart. In 1962, the records of 42 different labels appeared on the *Billboard* album charts, and the six largest corporations accounted for less than half of the *Billboard* albums.

With the advent of rock and roll and FM stereo broadcasting, radio and disc jockeys (DJs) became the paramount tools for record companies to promote their products. Especially during the 1950s and 1960s, the number of new songs released each year grew to be far more than radio stations could feature. Record companies actively encouraged DJs to play their records, and rumors of "payola"—bribery—spread widely. Senior managers of record companies became, and indeed remained, concerned that they had no direct control over their most important promotional medium.

The distribution system linking record companies to consumers became more elaborate during the 1950s and 1960s. Earlier, record companies had signed exclusive deals with distributors to deliver records to retailers. With the advent of rock and roll, the introduction of jukeboxes, and growth in retail outlets, a layer of subdistributors who carried products from all record companies developed. Rack jobbers began to buy records from distributors and manage shelves, or racks, in leased locations or departments. The largest retail chains built warehouses of their own. In 1955, CBS Records' Columbia division launched the first record club, allowing consumers to purchase records directly from the record company by mail.

Re-consolidation. With developments in the distribution network and promotional channels, small, independent record companies increasingly sold out to major companies or reached agreements under which major companies distributed records on their behalf. It became common during the 1960s for music corporations to operate multiple "labels"—separate divisions with distinct operations and images, sharing certain overhead, manufacturing, and distribution activities. Labels within a corporation were managed largely as separate organizations in order to preserve creative talents and distinct images. By 1972, although the top five *labels* accounted for only 31.4% of the charts, the top five *corporations* distributed 58.2% of industry output. The distinctive musical styles of the 1970s—disco, glam rock, punk rock, new wave, reggae, and funk—were pioneered by independent labels and musicians far from the mainstream, but were quickly adopted by the major music corporations.

Industry revenue declined in the late 1970s and early 1980s, but revived in the mid-1980s. The debut of Music Television (MTV) in 1981 and the introduction of the digitally recorded compact disc (CD) in 1983 sparked a surge of consumer interest in music. The CD had an especially large impact on industry revenue, as owners of LPs and tapes replaced their entire collections with the new format.

Mergers and acquisitions, which had played a role in the music industry since the Depression, accelerated during the 1980s and 1990s. By 1999, nearly 85% of the global market for recorded music rested in the hands of five corporations—the "majors": BMG Entertainment, EMI, Sony Music Entertainment, Warner Music Group, and Universal Music Group. Exhibit 1 describes each of the majors.

Organization of the Music Industry in 1999

"Businessmen, they drink my wine."

—*Bob Dylan,* All Along the Watchtower, *1968*

In 1999, the major record companies stood at the center of a complicated industry. Composers, lyricists, and performing artists provided the raw artistic input for the business. Music publishing companies mediated between composers and lyricists on one hand and record companies on the other. Retailers and distributors delivered products from record companies to consumers. Radio and music television stations provided the primary promotional channels for record companies. Rights agencies saw to it that royalties were distributed properly. (See Figure 1.) Exhibit 2 shows the size and geographic distribution of the global industry over time.

Composers and Lyricists. Composers created the score for a piece of music while lyricists wrote the words for a composition. If not the same person, the composer and lyricist of a song shared the copyright. During the time of sheet music distribution, composers and lyricists were often contractors hired by publishing houses, writing songs on demand. Over the years, they became more independent. Composers and lyricists were compensated through advances or one-time fees from music publishers, from royalty payments that accrued when their music was sold downstream, or by both means.

Performing Artists. Artists either performed their own compositions, in which case they were also composers and lyricists, or used repertoire created by others. A countless number of unknown artists performed live gigs and made demo recordings in hopes of being signed—that is, taken under contract—by a record company. Artists typically signed for five or more albums at a time. As a result, artists tended to stay with a single company for some time.

Once signed, an artist enjoyed a degree of creative and economic freedom that depended largely on his or her popularity. Record companies could largely dictate the creative moves of newcomers like Britney Spears. Super-

Figure 1-1 MUSIC INDUSTRY ROLES

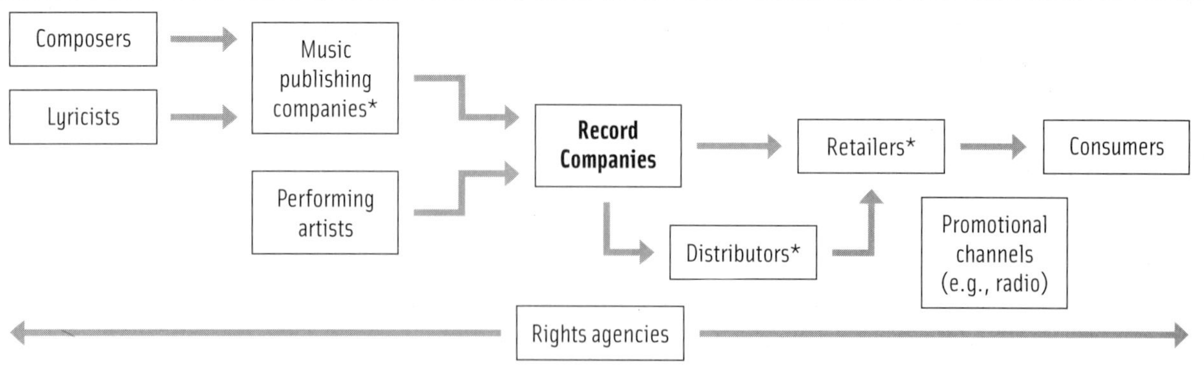

* Major record companies owned their own music publishing and distribution operations. Some majors also had retail interests, as described in the text.

stars like Whitney Houston, in contrast, had extensive creative freedom. When contracts lapsed, established artists sometimes switched record companies in search of better contractual arrangements or more creative latitude.

Artists earned income primarily from royalty fees paid by record companies for the sale of their recordings. Concerts and merchandise provided additional income. A cadre of personal and business managers, assistants, agents, and lawyers typically accompanied a successful artist. The artist paid this entourage out of his or her royalty income. Artists differed dramatically in how successful they were and how long their successes endured.

Music Publishers. Music publishers purchased the partial or total rights to pieces of music from composers and lyricists. The publishing houses then promoted the music vigorously through a variety of channels. Key to success was striking the proper balance between selling the same piece through multiple channels and regulating content tightly so as not to cheapen the content. This balance often raised tensions between the artists and the business people who ran the publishing houses. Over time, each of the majors had acquired or created a publishing arm to be part of its operations.

Record Companies. Record companies were widely considered the central players in the music industry. In addition to the five majors, "Indies," or independents, played this pivotal role. Each record company took performing artists under contract, purchased musical rights from publishing houses, managed the recording process, manufactured CDs and cassettes, distributed CDs and cassettes to retailers and other channels, and promoted its products aggressively. During this process, the company paid for all costs associated with launching new music. In return, it received the wholesale price of the CD or cassette, less the royalty fees paid to the artists and the publisher and other costs associated with each sale.

"Breaking" new artists—that is, bringing them to commercial success—and managing their life cycles were keys to a record company's profitability. Having prominent artists under contract not only brought greater sales directly, but also helped a record company gain precious retail shelf space for lesser known acts. Promising new artists tended to be attracted to record companies which had the best artists under contract and showed a strong history of successful management. Sometimes the demands of premier artists could undermine the profitability of a record company for that specific act. Consequently, product managers had to balance the benefits of an artist's big name with the cost of holding the artist under contract. In an effort to escape his contract with Warner Music, the well-known artist Prince tried various tactics, including changing his name to [symbol], an unpronounceable symbol, and claiming that his old contract did not apply to The Artist Formerly Known as Prince. During subsequent disputes, he appeared in public with the word "slave" inscribed on his cheek to reflect his relationship with Warner Music. Warner released him from his contract in 1995. The Artist's next albums were distributed by his own label and promoted primarily via the Internet. Though sales volumes were low, The Artist claimed that his net proceeds were higher than they had been with Warner. In 1999, he returned to a major record company, signing with BMG's Arista label.

The major record companies shared a basic organizational structure (Exhibit 3). With the exception of EMI, each was part of a larger diversified corporation. Within the record company itself was a central manufacturing division that made and packaged cassette tapes, a central distribution system that delivered CDs and cassettes to retail outlets and independent distributors, a music publishing operation that managed copyrights, and a number of distinct "labels." Several of the majors also had retail interests. BMG, Time Warner, and Sony operated record clubs. All three had interests in online retailers, as did Universal. EMI had only recently divested itself of retailer HMV.

Historically, the majors had carried out manufacturing locally in order to reduce transportation costs and avoid duties and taxes during export and import. With the development of economic free trade zones, the record companies consolidated their production plants. Sony, for instance, manufactured products for the European market in the Netherlands, while Warner produced in Germany. Worldwide, a major record company such as BMG might maintain ten or more production facilities.

Each of a record company's labels operated largely autonomously, with a separate president, P&L responsibility, and brand identity based around genre and artist roster. Usually, there were four functions under each label: artist & repertoire (A&R), marketing, business affairs, and accounting. A&R was responsible for finding new artists and developing new repertoire. It also found songs for artists who did not write their own. Marketing, usually the largest function of a label, handled sales, promotion, advertising, publicity, and artist relations. Business affairs dealt with legal issues such as artist negotiations, producer agreements, and licensing arrangements. This function also finalized foreign licensing and distribution deals.[4] Accounting played a crucial role because of the numbers of parties involved in each recording project. The accounting department handled the order-to-cash cycle, financial and managerial reporting, and the payment of royalties. Historically, most labels were split between U.S. and international operations, with the four functions sometimes duplicated in the two regions or even in specific countries.

Independent Distributors. Although major record companies often distributed their product directly to large retailers using their own trucks and resources, a handful of distribution companies remained independent of the majors in 1999. For example, Koch International distributed Indies' products to retailers. Indies, however, increasingly struck distribution agreements with the distribution arms of the major record companies. BMG, for instance, distributed on behalf of the independent labels Beyond, Logic, Milan, Razor & Tie, Restless, V2, Wind-Up, and Jive. Although independent distributors were often regional, some distributors had national reach, supported mainly through cross-regional alliances and mergers.[5]

Retail Channels. In 1999, music was sold to consumers through brick-and-mortar storefronts, record clubs, mail order, and increasingly, online retailers. Exhibit 4 shows the breakdown of sales in the United States by type of retail outlet. International chains like Tower Records, HMV, and Blockbuster and national chains such as WOM in Germany and fnac in France played leading roles in the distribution of music. The number of small independent retailers had declined rapidly during the 1980s and 1990s as investments in stores and retail technology grew. The largest eight chains in the United States accounted for 17.5% of all retail sales in 1982 and 57.8% in 1992. Over the same period, total retail sales increased by 55% while the number of store locations declined by 15%.[6] The number of products offered at retail had grown even more rapidly than the size of the average store, leading to a shortage of retail shelf space.

Under "cooperative advertising" arrangements, record companies paid for part of the advertising efforts of retailers. In return, retailers agreed not to advertise prices below certain levels. Antitrust authorities were currently reviewing these arrangements. Despite such practices, retail price wars were common in the mid-1990s.[7]

Consumers. The activities of all of these businesses and artists were directed at individual consumers. Consumers had widely different tastes in music, and the range of genres had broadened over the years. Genres from classical music to hard-core rap enjoyed loyal audiences. Exhibits 5 and 6 show the popularity of genres and shifts in buyer demographics during the 1990s.

Promotion. Consumers were likely to buy music they heard on the radio or saw on music television stations. In a typical week, record companies released 135 singles and 96 albums, each averaging 10 tracks, while most popular radio stations added only three to four new songs to their playlists.[8] Consequently, record companies aggressively lobbied radio and music television stations to get their new releases aired. Tales of illegal incentives were legendary. Allegedly, record companies had paid for DJs' vacation rentals and listed DJs as royalty-receiving co-composers of songs, for instance.[9]

Rights Agencies. Many composers, lyricists, performing artists, and music publishing houses were paid in the form of royalties: payments tied to the actual use of music. Accordingly, a set of rights agencies arose around the world to monitor the use of music. Performing rights agencies surveyed radio stations, television broadcasts, live concerts, and many other venues in order to keep tabs on the performance of copyrighted music. Mechanical rights agencies supervised the use of music in the production of CDs, cassette tapes, and other mechanical formats. These agencies delivered reports and payments to member composers, lyricists, artists, and publishers. With few exceptions, one performing rights and one mechanical rights agency operated in each country, either separately or together. Examples included ASCAP/BMI and the Harry Fox Agency in the United States, GEMA in Germany, and PRS/MCPS in the United Kingdom.

---

[4]G.P. Hull, *The Recording Industry,* Boston: Allyn & Bacon, 1997.

[5]G.P. Hull, *The Recording Industry,* Boston: Allyn & Bacon, 1997.

[6]United States Department of Commerce, Bureau of the Census, *Census of Retail Trade,* 1982 and 1992.

[7]D. Lawsky, "Major Record Companies in Deal with U.S.," *Reuters,* May 10, 2000. "Is Biz Poised for Renewed Price Wars?" *Billboard,* January 8, 2000.

[8]R. Burnett, *The Global Jukebox,* London: Routledge, 1996.

[9]P. Gronow and I. Saunio, *An International History of the Recording Industry,* London: Cassell, 1998.

Industry Economics. The flow of money within the music industry was as complicated as the set of actors. Exhibit 7 lays out the way in which revenue from an average CD was divided among various players. The average figures, however, mask important variation from one album to another. Some recordings were far more successful than others. A hit album could sell more than 10 million copies while a flop might sell only a few thousand. It was extremely difficult for music industry executives to predict which albums would be hits before investing heavily in development and promotion. This was especially true of albums by new artists. Accordingly, making a recording was a risky venture. Many labels stated that less than 20% of the recordings they released recouped their costs.

A system of "recoupable costs" affected who bore the costs of an album's failure and who enjoyed the fruits of success. During the production and marketing of a record, some of the costs incurred by the record companies were classified as recoupable from the artist's royalties. These costs were deducted before any payments were made to the artist. For a typical recording, a record company might spend $300,000 up front in production and marketing costs. Of this, $200,000 might be classified as recoupable. If the artist's royalty rate were $2 per unit sold, then the artist would receive nothing until 100,000 units had been sold. Thereafter, he or she would earn $2 per unit. This arrangement put the burden of a failed recording on the record company, but also made it possible for the company to earn a profit before the artist received any payment.

BMG Entertainment

BMG Entertainment was a subsidiary of Bertelsmann AG, a German media conglomerate. The world's fourth-largest media company, Bertelsmann had interests in book publishing and clubs; music labels and record clubs; professional information; magazines and newspapers; television, film, and radio; print and media services; and online services and multimedia. The corporation was privately owned by the Bertelsmann Foundation, the Mohn family, and the Zeit Foundation. Exhibit 8 shows the composition of Bertelsmann's 1998-99 revenue of DM26 billion.

BMG Entertainment was managed autonomously from its headquarters in New York City. In 1999, it was a $4.6 billion music and entertainment company with more than 200 record labels and operations in 53 countries. Its revenue was derived from North America (51%), Europe (32%), Latin America (9%), and Asia-Pacific (8%).[10] Among its worldwide superstars were Christina Aguilera, Carlos Santana, Whitney Houston, Sarah McLachlan, Puff Daddy, Dave Matthews, and a long list of other gold and platinum artists. BMG distributed five of 1999's ten best-selling albums.

Strauss Zelnick took the helm of BMG in July, 1998, after leading BMG's North American operations for three and a half years. Prior to joining BMG, Zelnick had worked in a series of film, television, video, and multimedia companies including 20th Century Fox and Columbia Pictures. When he arrived at BMG North America in 1995, he found a division that had diversified, largely unsuccessfully, into businesses such as video distribution and apparel licensing. All but three of 25 units within the division were losing money. Zelnick rapidly withdrew from loss-making positions, cut the costs of operations, and refocused the division on music. BMG's North American music market share soon began to grow.[11] In the eyes of many observers, Zelnick typified a new type of music executive. Traditionally, individuals had risen in record companies based on their creative talents and track record of breaking new artists. In contrast, Zelnick was best known for his strong business background and his focus on efficiency and profitability. Zelnick held MBA and law degrees from Harvard.

Much of BMG's business activity took place within its more than 200 labels, which included Arista Records, Ariola, RCA Records, the Windham Hill Group, Buddha Records, and BMG Classics. Manufacturing, distribution, music publishing, and some sales and marketing activities were centralized and coordinated across the labels.

Manufacturing. Led by CEO Uwe Swientek, the Storage Media division of BMG manufactured compact discs, cassettes, and related packaging. Facilities in Argentina, Brazil, Germany, Hong Kong, Ireland, Mexico, South Africa, Spain, and the United States produced more than 2.5 million CDs each day. A technology group within the division, established in 1994, tracked the development of new media products and served as a contact point within BMG for technology questions.

Distribution. BMG Distribution, led by Pete Jones, lay at the center of the music marketing process, linking

[10]Figures relate to fiscal 1998/99.

[11]Interviews with Strauss Zelnick, President and CEO, and Kevin Conroy, Senior Vice President, Worldwide Marketing and New Technology, February 14, 2000.

BMG's labels to brick-and-mortar retailers. Distribution personnel called on major retailers, promoted BMG's latest products, negotiated prices and terms, took orders, oversaw shipments, visited retail sites to assist with product placement, and handled credit and collection. The division not only served BMG's own labels, but also distributed on behalf of a number of independent labels.

Music Publishing. BMG's music publishing division, under Nick Firth, controlled the copyrights to more than 700,000 songs. Through some 150 acquisitions, it had accumulated the catalogs of diverse artists such as the Beach Boys, B.B. King, Barry Manilow, and Santana. The division's primary role was to acquire rights to songs and administer those rights. It also sought to generate royalties from its copyrights by placing its songs in films (e.g., *The Runaway Bride* and *The Matrix*), television (e.g., *Friends* and *Buffy the Vampire Slayer*), and advertising campaigns (e.g., Cadbury and Mercedes).

Sales. Millions of consumers enrolled in one of BMG's music clubs, the largest collection of music clubs in the world. Club members ordered a set of introductory CDs or cassettes at a very low price. Subsequently, they received a selected album each month, which they could decline to purchase, as well as a catalog of other available albums. BMG Special Products developed specialty albums to assist companies such as Avon, Coca Cola, AT&T, and Shell Oil in their marketing efforts.

Marketing. At BMG and other major record companies, marketing had traditionally been managed entirely within individual labels. BMG's labels continued to be responsible for day-to-day marketing activities and the promotion of individual artists. Recently, however, BMG had placed Kevin Conroy in charge of corporate marketing. In this new role, Conroy coordinated the marketing activities of separate labels and established strategic alliances and partnerships with other companies (e.g., Visa, AT&T). As the Internet became a promotional tool that spanned label boundaries, Conroy increasingly led BMG's approach to digital distribution, e-commerce, new music formats, and other emerging technologies. BMG's approach to the Internet is described in greater detail below.

The Other Majors

The five major record companies represented different artists and operated under diverse labels (Exhibit 1). In many ways, however, they resembled one another closely. All were organized in the same fashion. All operated around the globe and were large enough to do so effectively. All had labels that covered the full spectrum of musical genres. All performed the same basic functions, though with different degrees of efficiency. Artists chose among the majors largely on the basis of characteristics of particular *labels,* not corporations. Personal relationships between label managers and artists were especially important in attracting and retaining artists.

Universal Music Group, the world's largest music company, emerged from Seagram's acquisition of Universal Studios in 1995 and Seagram's purchase of PolyGram in 1998. Industry observers believed that the merger had been difficult. Beyond music, Seagram participated in the production and distribution of spirits and wine, film and television production, the operation of theme parks, and specialty mall retailing.

Sony Music Entertainment was part of Sony, the Japanese entertainment and electronics giant. Sony produced not only music, but also hardware to play music, such as the Walkman. Other divisions made video games, films, television programs, computers, wireless telephones, semiconductors, and magnetic media. The corporation prided itself on its cutting-edge technology.

Warner Music Group was a member of Time Warner, a U.S. media conglomerate. The corporate parent operated a set of cable channels including CNN and HBO, published magazines and books, produced feature films and television programs, and provided cable television connections to more than 12 million homes. With its cable system, one of the most technologically advanced in the United States, Time Warner was providing high-speed Internet access to roughly 300,000 households and was experimenting with services such as video on demand, high-definition television, and interactive television.

Among the majors, only the U.K.-based EMI was not part of a diversified corporation. EMI's current lineup of artists was arguably weaker than that of its rivals; the company had fewer current global superstars than other labels. Nonetheless, EMI had a strong history with bands like the Beatles, and EMI's music publishing division was the largest music publisher in the world. Its catalog included some of the industry's most valuable copyrights, including songs by the Beatles, the Rolling Stones, Pink Floyd, and Frank Sinatra. In 1999, many observers felt that EMI was looking for a buyer.

The financial results and market shares of the five major record companies are shown in Exhibits 9 and 10, respectively.

The Internet

Music was one of the categories of merchandise most affected by skyrocketing use of the Internet in the late 1990s. The Internet accounted for 0.3% of all music sales in 1997 and 1.1% in 1998, and it was forecast to account for 10% by 2005.[12] Music was marketed and sold over the Internet in several ways. Through sites such as CDNow and Amazon.com, consumers could purchase conventional, physical CDs and cassettes and have them shipped to their homes. Downloaded music was a more radical departure from convention: new technology allowed surfers to transfer files containing music directly over the Internet to their computers. Thousands of sites posted illegal, pirated copies of songs. Supported by new software and hardware, a growing number of sites offered legal digital downloads.

Online Sale of Physical Products

A number of Internet retailers offered consumers a comprehensive selection of prerecorded CDs and cassettes. CDNow was typical of this new type of retailer.[13] In late 1999, CDNow boasted a selection of 390,000 CDs, cassettes, and related items. Visitors to its site could browse the selection by genre, search for favorite artists, albums, or songs, listen to music samples, and read countless articles related to music. Once shipping charges were included, CD and cassette prices at CDNow were comparable to those posted by storefront retailers. Shipping charges were typically $2.95 for one CD and $3.95 for two or three CDs.

CDNow held virtually no inventory and relied on Valley Media, a music distributor, to ship products to customers. Valley Media also handled the 1-2% of merchandise that customers returned to CDNow. A third-party credit card processor managed CDNow's billing operations. The company focused its own internal efforts on the development of its web site and aggressive marketing to consumers. Its 1999 marketing expenses were anticipated to approach $90 million. Analysts expected CDNow to lose more than $110 million in 1999 on sales of $150 million.

[12]National Association of Recording Merchandisers, 1998 Annual Survey. NewsEdge Corporation, January 28, 2000, AFX, File: f0126013.900.

[13]Information on CDNow comes especially from the company's Form 10-K, December 31, 1999.

Downloaded Music

Technology of Downloading. Thousands of web sites gave surfers the opportunity to download copies of songs or albums directly over the Internet. The downloading of music involved software and hardware beyond a computer, an Internet browser, and an Internet connection. The first element of additional software was a compression protocol—basically, a standard for reducing the computer file that contained a song to a size that could be downloaded quickly. MP3 was the most common protocol. A typical MP3 file containing a three-minute song could be downloaded by a computer with a 56K modem in 7 minutes or by a computer with a cable modem in less than one minute.

A second element of software, a player, opened the compressed file and played the downloaded song. Internet users could download the most popular players—including RealJukebox, Winamp, Liquid Player, and Microsoft's Media Player—to their computers for free.

To play a downloaded song someplace other than on one's computer, a user needed additional hardware. Computers were increasingly equipped with CD drives that could write files to a compact disc, not simply read from a disc. For about $200, Diamond Media offered a Walkman-sized gadget that could store up to one hour of downloaded music, typically in a MP3 format. Sony's Memory Stick stored up to two hours of music on a device smaller than a stick of chewing gum. One could plug the stick into a computer, download music, then move the stick to a portable player. The Memory Stick and associated player retailed for roughly $500. Empeg's Empeg Player, an MP3 player for cars that could store up to 70 hours of music, retailed for about $200.[14]

Because MP3 files could be copied repeatedly, many record companies associated MP3 with illegal music piracy. "MP3" was the term most commonly submitted to Internet search engines, and most of the 150,000 MP3-formatted songs on the Internet circulated without any compensation to the artist or copyright holder.[15] Forrester Research estimated at the beginning of 1999

[14]C. Reavis, C. Knoop, and J. Rayport, "RCA Records: The Digital Revolution," HBS Case 800-014.

[15]C. Reavis, C. Knoop, and J. Rayport, "RCA Records: The Digital Revolution," HBS Case 800-014, pp. 4–5.

that over 3 million infringing MP3 files were being downloaded every day.[16]

A number of companies vied to provide software that would make downloading easy and piracy difficult. Liquid Audio, for instance, marketed a complete system to companies that wanted to sell downloadable songs. Consumers who registered with Liquid Audio received a free "passport" in exchange for personal contact information and credit card details. Passport holders could then go to any site using Liquid Audio's system, purchase a song, download it (in MP3 format or an alternative), and play it on their computers. Liquid Audio managed the billing of the customer. Songs downloaded via the Liquid Audio system were re-mastered using proprietary technology. Such "Liquid tracks" could be copied only once digitally to a CD. Copies carried a "digital watermark" that would allow authorities to trace any illegal copy back to the original purchaser. Competing systems, or components of such systems, were offered by technology giants such as IBM and Microsoft and new ventures such as Intertrust and Reciprocal.

Industry groups were also working to enable downloading without piracy. Most prominently, the leading music trade associations, record companies, and technology companies launched the Secure Digital Music Initiative (SDMI) in December, 1998. Involving dozens of companies, SDMI aimed to set open technology standards that would ease digital distribution while protecting copyrights. The organization intended to have a full set of standards in place by March 31, 2000.[17]

Downloading Entrepreneurs. A host of new ventures sought to tap the opportunities posed by music downloads. *MP3.com,* perhaps the best known of the start-ups, aimed to create a meeting ground for consumers and musicians.[18] The company helped artists set up web pages on its site at no charge. Each page included free, downloadable samples of music posted by the artist. If a consumer liked the samples, he or she could use a credit card to purchase the artist's entire album. Once an order was placed, MP3.com arranged for an outside contractor to manufacture a CD and ship it to the customer. Artists set their own album prices within a range of $5.99 and $14.99. MP3.com and the artist shared the proceeds of each sale, net of manufacturing costs, 50/50.

MP3.com provided artists a set of computer tools that made it very easy for them to set up web pages and load samples. The company also gave artists daily information on the numbers of visitors to their pages, numbers of downloads, and rankings within genre. The web site guided consumers to artists by genre and by online popularity. As of late 1999, MP3.com's site contained more than 180,000 songs from more than 31,000 artists. The most popular musicians, however, were absent from the site, in part because the major music companies did not allow participation.

MP3.com was founded in March, 1998, by Michael Robertson, formerly the CEO of a company involving digital photography. In 1999, MP3.com was projected to lose more than $40 million on sales of approximate $20 million. More than 90% of its revenue came from advertisements placed on its site. CD sales accounted for the rest of its revenue. In the first few months after its July 1999 IPO, its market capitalization fluctuated between $1.5 and $7 billion.

As of late 1999, *EMusic.com,* a second start-up, had secured exclusive rights to sell digital downloads from 140 independent record labels.[19] These Indie labels represented 1,500 artists with over 300,000 songs, of which 27,000 were already available for downloading from EMusic.com's site. Consumers paid $0.99 to download a song or $8.99 for an entire album. Half of the proceeds, net of administrative costs, was paid to the label. The labels currently under contract represented 12–15% of the Indie market. EMusic.com's management team hoped to increase this share to 40%. The company had recently inked agreements to offer its downloadable music library through Yahoo! and America Online. It had also acquired the Internet Underground Music Archive, which hosted the home pages of 5,000 artists.

EMusic.com was founded in June, 1998, by Robert Kohn, an entertainment attorney, and Gene Hoffman, a developer of privacy software. In the year ended June 30, 1999, EMusic.com lost $18 million on revenues of $92,300. In late 1999, its market capitalization was roughly $500 million.

[16]Web site of the International Federation of the Phonographic Industry (www.ifpi.org), citing Forrester Research.

[17]SDMI Press Release, "Worldwide Recording Industry and Technology Companies Kick Off Work of Secure Digital Music Initiative," February 26, 1999.

[18]Information on MP3.com comes especially from P. Leigh and P. Benyola, "MP3.com," Raymond James and Associates Equity Research, November 15, 1999, and MP3.com's Form 10-K, December 31, 1999.

[19]Information on EMusic.com comes especially from V.A.G. Vickers and J.C. Ignalls, "EMusic.com," ING Barings, October 11, 1999, and EMusic.com's Form 10-K, June 30, 1999.

Listen.com aimed to be the comprehensive directory of legal, downloadable music.[20] Although Listen.com did not sell music itself, its online directory classified music into 600 genres and sub-genres and led Internet users to hundreds of sites that did sell music. The company directed users only to sites which it believed to be selling music legally. Its team of editors wrote independent reviews of artists' work and pointed users to favored artists. Its site also featured guides that helped users learn how to download music.

Founded in December, 1998, by Rob Reid, a former venture capitalist, and launched on the web in June, 1999, Listen.com soon struck a wide array of alliances. In June, 1999, it announced partnerships with leading online music-selling sites such as EMusic.com to get their artists into Listen.com's directory as soon as possible. Soon afterwards, seven leading independent labels agreed to work with Listen.com to increase their artists' Internet exposure. By then, Listen.com had signed deals to syndicate its music directory through the portals of Excite@Home, Snap, and HotBot. The company was allegedly in investment discussions with all five of the major record companies.

Napster, founded by 19-year-old Shawn Fanning, enabled Internet users to tap one another's music collections. Each user of Napster's free software indicated which of the MP3 files on his or her computer hard drive were available to others. Napster maintained a list of the users currently online and the titles those users were making available. A user could search the list for a song, then download the desired file directly from another user's hard drive. Copyright holders received no payments for such downloads.

Retailer Reaction

Traditional brick-and-mortar retailers saw both the online sale of prerecorded music and the downloading of music over the Internet as serious threats. By the end of 1998, 70% of the members of the National Association of Recording Merchandisers (NARM), the trade association of U.S. music retailers, had established some web presence. Another 15% expected to do so in 1999. Retailers used their sites primarily to promote music and provide customers with information. Many sold prerecorded CDs and cassettes through their sites. Of those that did, most allowed customers to return unwanted CDs and cassettes purchased online to traditional storefronts. One-third offered some ability to download music, and another quarter expected to add downloading capabilities during 1999.[21]

The web sites of major retail chains such as Virgin, HMV, and Tower Records were similar in character. Tower, for instance, went online in 1996, but relaunched its site in the middle of 1999 with new features that matched those of CDNow and Amazon.com. Through its site, Tower sold new, used, and out-of-print CDs. It offered music reviews, columns, and a function that let shoppers know what other customers were buying. The site also included a catalog of downloadable Liquid Audio songs.[22] Many industry experts were skeptical of Tower's online prospects. Analysts pointed to the lower margins associated with Tower's online sales and the hefty expenses it was incurring related to e-commerce.[23]

While developing their own web sites, traditional retailers asked the major record companies for assurances that the majors would continue to support storefront retailing. At the same time, retailers were considering a full range of options. Simon Wright, managing director of Virgin's retailing group, commented, "At the moment, the view in Virgin is that the terms being offered by the record companies would not justify further investment in music. Ultimately we could pull out of music altogether."[24] Pamela Horovitz, president of NARM, took a more combative stance: "If the record companies want to start marginalizing the retailers, then retailers will start looking to become labels themselves and signing up bands themselves."[25]

The Majors' Actions

As entrepreneurs pursued the opportunities posed by the Internet and traditional retailers coped with the technology's potential threats, the major record companies responded with a flurry of initiatives, deals, and alliances that reached a fever pitch in 1999.

BMG Entertainment. BMG launched its first online efforts in 1995, soon after Zelnick's arrival. Though Zelnick was focused at the time on stemming losses in numerous

[20]Information on Listen.com comes primarily from press releases available on the company's web site.

[21]National Association of Recording Merchandisers, "Annual Survey Results, 1998," p. 11.

[22]InfoWorld, Jan. 10, 2000, p. 46.

[23]Reuters, March 22, 2000.

[24]NewsEdge Corporation, January 28, 2000, AFX, File: f0126013.900.

[25]M. Richtel, "Internet Strains the Ties of Record Companies and Stores," *New York Times,* February 29, 2000.

units, Kevin Conroy convinced him to invest $1 million per year in the nascent World Wide Web. With the funds, BMG set up a series of web sites dedicated to particular genres of music: Peeps.com for hip-hop and rhythm and blues, Bugjuice.com for alternative, TwangThis.com for country, Connect2music.com for adult contemporary, Rockuniverse.com for rock, and so on. The sites linked fans to exclusive information about BMG artists, interviews with the artists, live broadcasts, chat rooms, and promotional downloads. By placing the sites' web addresses on albums and other media, BMG attracted hundreds of thousands of unique visitors to the sites without a distinct advertising campaign.[26]

Initially, the sites were not designed to sell music to consumers. Rather, they focused on promotion. Peeps, for instance, began to publicize pop sensation Britney Spears eight months before her first album was released. The site gathered the names of 100,000 potential fans, 80% of whom later bought the album.[27] The CDs of certain BMG artists included the software of America Online (AOL), the online service provider. When played in a computer, the CDs would enable consumers to sign up for AOL service. Customers who signed up would then be directed to BMG's websites.[28] BMG hoped to develop the genre sites as distinct brands that could stand on their own. The goal, Conroy explained, was both to "create a digital connection between our artists and their fans" and to "test the conventional wisdom that consumer branding isn't relevant in the music business."[29]

Universal Music artists were added to the sites in April 1999, after BMG and Universal announced a new venture, Getmusic.com. Getmusic not only served as an umbrella for the genre sites, but also included an online store comparable to CDNow or Amazon.com. The store's selection included albums by all the major labels, but BMG and Universal artists were featured most prominently. Links on the genre sites directed surfers who wanted to buy an album to the Getmusic store. Prices in the store were often 20% higher than at CDNow or Amazon.com.[30]

BMG had experimented with downloaded music since November, 1997, when it became the first of the majors to use downloads for promotional purposes.[31] It did not sell downloaded music routinely, however. In June, 1999, BMG announced that it would begin selling music directly over the Internet by late in the year. It did not make public which artists and works it would sell, what technology it would use, or what prices it would charge.[32] At the same time, along with the other majors, it began a trial in San Diego to sell music over the Internet using Time-Warner's cable service and IBM technology.[33]

BMG took an active role in industry initiatives such as SDMI. Through a large number of relatively small arrangements and partnerships with companies such as Microsoft, Liquid Audio, Real Networks, AT&T, and IBM, it maintained relationships with all of the players involved in setting the technological standards for downloadable music. Senior executives tried to stay very much in the center of the industry's "deal flow" related to the Internet. As a result, they had hundreds of due diligence files on potential deals. Zelnick explained some of the rules he used in sorting through opportunities:[34]

> Don't sell your copyrights or license them exclusively. Don't make long-term deals that you can't change. Once you've followed those rules, be willing to take risks and try things out. If God forbid you're wrong, you still own your copyrights.

Sony Music Entertainment. Like BMG, Sony Music Entertainment was among the first and most eager of the majors to embrace new technology for music distribution. Its Columbia House subsidiary, jointly owned with Warner Music, launched Total E, an online store selling conventional CDs and cassettes, in mid-1998. In July, 1999, Sony and Warner announced plans to acquire CDNow and merge it into Columbia House.[35]

The company also pursued digital downloads. In May 1999, Sony publicized plans to sell singles directly over the Internet using compression and copyright protection

[26]Interview with Kevin Conroy, Senior Vice President, Worldwide Marketing and New Technology, February 14, 2000.

[27]S. Hansell, "Key to Music Deal is E-promotion Direct," *New York Times* April 8, 1999.

[28]"BMG Entertainment North America Announces Partnership with America Online to Provide Online and Internet Access on CDs," BMG Entertainment Press Release, April 21, 1997.

[29]Interview with Kevin Conroy, Senior Vice President, Worldwide Marketing and New Technology, February 14, 2000.

[30]S. Hansell, "Key to Music Deal is E-promotion Direct," New York Times April 8, 1999.

[31]"BMG Entertainment's Award-winning Genre-based Web Sites to Feature Liquid Audio Technology," BMG Entertainment press release, November 3, 1997.

[32]M. Richtel, "Questions Abound on Downloading Digital Music," *New York Times,* June 30, 1999.

[33]M. Richtel, "Questions Abound on Downloading Digital Music," *New York Times,* June 30, 1999. J. Pareles, "Leading Recording Companies to Test Online Digital Sales," *New York Times,* February 9, 1999.

[34]Interview with Strauss Zelnick, President and CEO, February 14, 2000.

[35]S. Hansell, "Sony and Time Warner Make Music Deal," New York Times, July 14, 1999.

technology from Microsoft. Fred Ehrlich, Sony's general manager for new technology and business development, said that download prices would be comparable to those of singles purchased in retail stores.[36]

At nearly the same time, the company announced that it would help a start-up firm install "digital kiosks" in retail stores. At the kiosks, shoppers could select among 4,000 albums, roughly half of Sony's catalog. The kiosk would then download the album via a proprietary computer system, imprint the album on a CD, and print liner notes and packaging within 10-15 minutes. The kiosk, said Danny Yarbrough, chairman of Sony Music Distribution, "offers the retailer the ability to offer titles they wouldn't be able to physically carry. . . ."[37] An initial test of the kiosk was expected in the fall of 1999.

Sony Music's corporate parent had broader interests in new music technology. Its consumer electronics division hoped to establish its Memory Stick as the leading portable device for downloaded music. The music division's initial hesitation to make its music available for downloading—because it feared piracy—had allegedly created a serious rift in the corporation. Sony Corporation was the first to propose specific copyright protection methods for approval by SDMI.[38]

Universal Music Group. Through Getmusic, its venture with BMG, Universal sold conventional CDs and cassettes and promoted its artists online. Universal also took part in SDMI. In early May 1999, however, while SDMI was still hashing out standards for digital downloads, Universal announced that it would soon distribute music online using technology developed in conjunction with a Silicon Valley start-up. In doing so, it became the first of the majors to commit itself to digital downloads. Industry observers felt that Universal had "broken ranks" with the other majors. Larry Kenswil, head of electronic commerce at Universal, offered a different interpretation. Universal's efforts, he said, would "run in parallel" with SDMI and be flexible enough to comply with the standards that eventually emerged.[39] Soon afterwards, Sony and BMG announced similar plans for music downloads.

Warner Music Group. Through its stake in Columbia House, Warner Music participated in Total E and the pending merger with CDNow. It also took part in industry forums such as SDMI and the San Diego downloading trial. In 1999, the company offered promotional digital downloads featuring some two dozen artists, and it was conducting market research to assess the impact of the promotions.

Overall, however, Warner's migration toward the Internet had been slow, in part due to its corporate parent Time Warner. Since 1994, Time Warner had championed a corporate-wide Internet initiative dubbed "Pathfinder." An ambitious effort to combine all of Time Warner's publishing, film, cable, and music interests in one portal, Pathfinder collapsed under the weight of corporate bureaucracy and conflicts of interest. By 1999, Time Warner was scrambling to catch up in the online arena.[40]

EMI. Among the majors, EMI had been the last to announce plans for online activity. In June, 1999, it reached an agreement with musicmaker.com, a start-up company that made customized CDs and sold songs over the Internet. For five years, only musicmaker.com would be allowed to use EMI songs in customized CDs.[41] In return, EMI received a 50% stake in the venture. Soon afterwards, EMI announced that it would use Liquid Audio's technology to encode its songs for future digital delivery.[42]

Organizing for Digital Distribution

Amidst the moves of competitors, customers, and entrepreneurs, Zelnick and Conroy considered how to organize BMG to serve the emerging set of "digital customers." Such customers would want to purchase bytes from BMG, but might not buy a physical product like a CD or a cassette. It was unclear who these customers would be. They might be online merchants, traditional retailers, consumers, or altogether new intermediaries, for instance.

One option was to set up a separate division within BMG to serve the new customers exclusively. According

[36]M. Richtel, "Sony, Following Universal, to Sell Digital Music Online," *New York Times,* May 12, 1999.

[37]L. Napoli, "Sony Music Plans to Test Use of In-store Digital Kiosks," *New York Times,* June 10, 1999. An initial test of the kiosk was expected in the fall of 1999.

[38]J. Markoff, "Sony to Propose a Method for Protecting Digital Music," *New York Times,* February 25, 1999.

[39]M. Richtel, "Record Label Will Distribute Music Online," *New York Times,* May 5, 1999.

[40]A. Harmon, "How Blind Alleys Led Old Media to New," New York Times, January 16, 2000.

[41]"EMI Takes Major Equity Position in musicmaker.com," EMI press release, June 10, 1999.

[42]"EMI Recorded Music Selects Liquid Audio to Encode Music Library for Digital Delivery," EMI press release, June 21, 1999.

to recent rumors, Universal was pursuing this path: a distinct organization would dedicate itself to making music available through computers, kiosks, TV set-top boxes, and portable devices.[43] Skeptics felt that Universal was doing this primarily to create a division that it could later spin off in an IPO.

Another option was to give BMG's current distribution organization responsibility for digital customers. For years, the distribution division had successfully managed accounts, generated orders, overseen collections, reported sales, and delivered physical products. Pete Jones, the head of the organization, had little experience with digital technology, but then no one in the company had such experience. By all accounts, Jones was one of the few people in a contentious industry who was uniformly trusted and liked by retailers and artists.

However it was structured, the digital organization would soon need to choose a posture toward technology partners. To date, BMG had maintained relationships with the full array of companies—such as Liquid Audio, Microsoft, and IBM—who were involved in setting the standards and clearinghouse mechanisms for downloaded music. It was unclear whether BMG should continue to play the field in this manner or place a firm bet by backing one partner.

Zelnick and Conroy knew that their decisions would be highly visible in the close-knit music community. Competitors and customers alike would view the choices as signals of BMG's longer-term intentions. As Zelnick spoke, Conroy glanced at a painting across the office. In big bold letters, the painting carried a slogan: "A Man of Vision."

[43] "Universal Music Group Strengthens Commitment to E-commerce Activities With Formation of New Division," Universal Music press release, January 18, 2000.

Exhibit 1 THE MAJORS

Record Company	Parent	Origins	Major Labels	Selected Major Acts
BMG Entertainment	Bertelsmann, a German media conglomerate	• Built on Bertelsmann's 1986 purchase of RCA	• Arista, Ariola, RCA, BMG Records, Red Seal, Windham Hill Group	• Christina Aguilera, Dave Matthews Band, Grateful Dead, Kenny G, Barry Manilow, Notorious B.I.G., Puff Daddy, Santana, Sarah McLachlan, Whitney Houston, ZZ Top
EMI	None	• Formed from Depression-era merger of Columbia, Parlophone, and the Gramophone Company	• Chrysalis, Capitol, Virgin, Parlophone, Blue Note, Priority, EMI Classics	• Beastie Boys, Blur, Garth Brooks, Snoop Dogg, Lenny Kravitz, Smashing Pumpkins, Spice Girls, Robbie Williams, Hikaru Utada
Sony Music Entertainment	Sony, a Japanese entertainment conglomerate	• Built on Sony's 1988 purchase of CBS Records	• Sony Records, Columbia, Epic	• Aerosmith, Mariah Carey, Miles Davis, Celine Dion, Plácido Domingo, Gloria Estefan, Aretha Franklin, Lauryn Hill, Billy Joel, Yo-Yo Ma, Wynton Marsalis, Pearl Jam, Bruce Springsteen
Universal Music Group	Seagram, a Canadian distiller	• Formed from Seagram's 1995 purchase of Universal Studios from Matsushita and 1998 purchase of Polygram from Philips. Universal descended from MCA, Decca, others	• A&M, Geffen, MCA, Universal, Interscope, Mercury, Island, Polydor, Motown, Def Jam, Decca, Philips, Deutsche Grammophon	• Bryan Adams, Beck, George Benson, Boyz II Men, Melissa Etheridge, Elton John, Limp Bizkit, LL Cool J, Marilyn Manson, Luciano Pavarotti, Sting, Shania Twain, U2
Warner Music Group	Time Warner, a U.S. media conglomerate	• Formed primarily from independent labels acquired in the 1960s and 1970s	• Reprise, Atlantic, Elektra, Asylum, Rhino, EastWest, Warner Brothers Records	• Barenaked Ladies, Eric Clapton, Phil Collins, Goo Goo Dolls, Madonna, matchbox20, Natalie Merchant, Alanis Morissette, R.E.M., Third Eye Blind

Source: Company annual reports and web sites. P. Gronow and I. Saunio, International History of the Recording Industry

Exhibit 2 SIZE AND GEOGRAPHIC DISTRIBUTION OF THE GLOBAL MUSIC INDUSTRY

	1991	1992	1993	1994	1995	1996	1997	1998	1999
Retail value of sales (US$ bn)	27.8	29.5	31.2	36.1	39.7	39.8	38.6	38.7	38.5
Units sold (bn)	2.8	2.9	3.0	3.3	3.4	3.6	3.6	3.6	3.6
Percent of retail value of sales									
North America	30.4	32.6	34.0	35.2	32.9	33.1	33.4	36.6	39.4
Europe	39.7	37.8	35.0	33.3	34.8	34.5	33.3	33.6	33.8
Asia	20.4	21.8	22.6	23.3	24.5	22.9	22.6	20.3	19.2
Latin America	4.2	4.2	4.7	4.8	4.3	5.4	6.6	6.1	5.8
Rest of world	5.3	3.7	3.6	3.4	3.6	4.1	4.0	3.4	1.9

Source: International Federation of the Phonographic Industry, *The Recording Industry in Numbers*
Note: Units include CDs, cassettes, and LPs

Exhibit 3 ORGANIZATIONAL STRUCTURE OF A MAJOR RECORD COMPANY

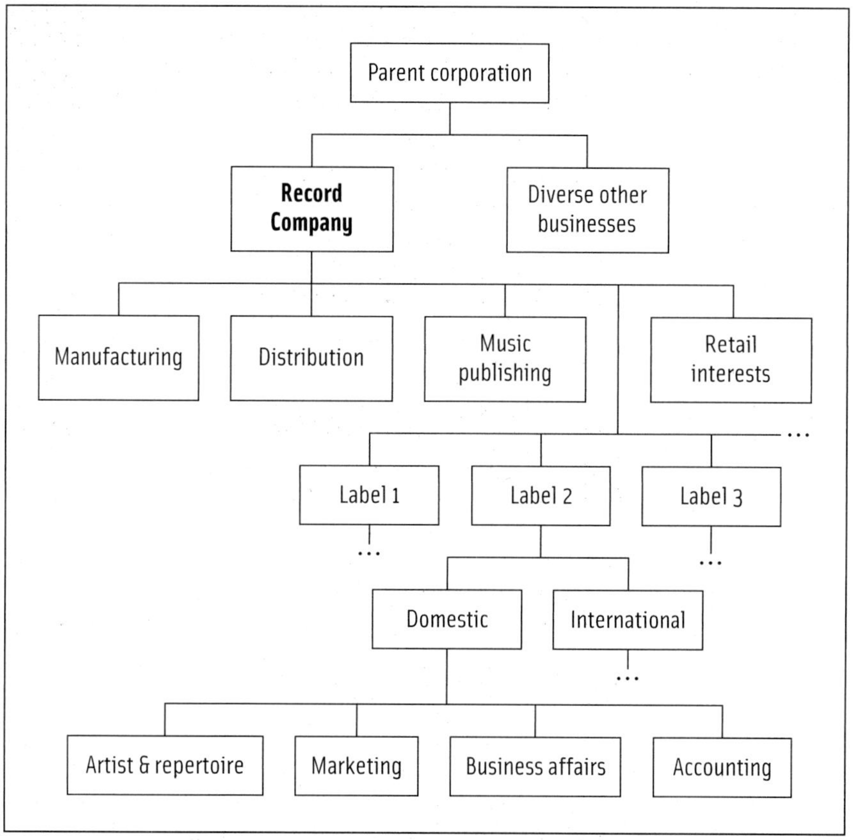

Exhibit 4 MUSIC SALES BY TYPE OF OUTLET IN THE UNITED STATES (%)

	1990	1991	1992	1993	1994	1995	1996	1997	1998
Record store	69.8	62.1	60.0	56.2	53.3	52.0	49.9	51.8	50.8
Other store	18.5	23.4	24.9	26.1	26.7	28.2	31.5	31.9	34.4
Total stores	88.3	85.5	84.9	82.3	80.0	80.2	81.4	83.7	85.2
Tape/record club	8.9	11.1	11.4	12.9	15.1	14.3	14.3	11.6	9.0
Mail order	2.5	3.0	3.2	3.8	3.4	4.0	2.9	2.7	2.9
Internet	N/A	N/A	N/A	N/A	N/A	N/A	N/A	0.3	1.1

Source: National Association of Recording Merchandisers–1998/1994 Annual Survey
Note: Totals may not add up to 100% due to 'don't know/no answer' responses. Percentages reflect dollar sales, not units sold

Exhibit 5 MUSIC SALES BY GENRE IN THE UNITED STATES (%)

	1990	1991	1992	1993	1994	1995	1996	1997	1998
Rock	36.1	34.8	31.6	30.2	35.1	33.5	32.6	32.5	25.7
Country	9.6	12.8	17.4	18.7	16.3	16.7	14.7	14.4	14.1
R&B	11.6	9.9	9.8	10.6	9.6	11.3	12.1	11.2	12.8
Pop	13.7	12.1	11.5	11.9	10.3	10.1	9.3	9.4	10.0
Rap/Hip Hop	8.5	10.0	8.6	9.2	7.9	6.7	8.9	10.1	9.7
Gospel	2.5	3.8	2.8	3.2	3.3	3.1	4.3	4.5	6.3
Classical	3.1	3.2	3.7	3.3	3.7	2.9	3.4	2.8	3.3
Jazz	4.8	4.0	3.8	3.1	3.0	3.0	3.3	2.8	1.9
Soundtracks	0.8	0.7	0.7	0.7	1.0	0.9	0.8	1.2	1.7
Oldies	–	–	–	–	0.8	1.0	0.8	0.8	0.7
New age	–	–	–	–	1.0	0.7	0.7	0.8	0.6
Children	0.5	0.3	0.5	0.4	0.4	0.5	0.7	0.9	0.4
Other	7.5	6.5	7.4	6.6	5.3	7.0	5.2	5.7	7.9

Source: National Association of Recording Merchandisers–1998/1994 Annual Survey
Note: Totals may not add up to 100% due to 'don't know/no answer' responses. Percentages reflect dollar sales, not units sold

Exhibit 6 DEMOGRAPHICS OF MUSIC PURCHASERS IN THE UNITED STATES (% OF PURCHASES)

	1990	1991	1992	1993	1994	1995	1996	1997	1998
– **Gender**									
– Female	45.6	45.9	47.4	49.3	47.3	47.0	49.1	51.4	51.3
– Male	54.4	54.1	52.6	50.7	52.7	53.0	50.9	48.6	48.7
– **Age**									
– 10–14	7.6	8.2	8.6	8.6	7.9	8.0	7.9	8.9	9.1
– 15–19	18.3	18.1	18.2	16.7	16.8	17.1	17.2	16.8	15.8
– 20–24	16.5	17.9	16.1	15.1	15.4	15.3	15.0	13.8	12.2
– 25–29	14.6	14.5	13.8	13.2	12.6	12.3	12.5	11.7	11.4
– 30–34	13.2	12.5	12.2	11.9	11.8	12.1	11.4	11.0	11.4
– 35–39	10.2	9.8	10.9	11.1	11.5	10.8	11.1	11.6	12.6
– 40–44	7.8	6.7	7.4	8.5	7.9	7.5	9.1	8.8	8.3
– 45+	11.8	12.5	12.9	14.8	15.4	16.1	15.1	16.5	18.1

Source: National Association of Recording Merchandisers–1998/1994 Annual Survey
Note: Totals may not add up to 100% due to 'don't know/no answer' responses. Percentages reflect dollar sales, not units sold

Exhibit 7

AVERAGE REVENUE AND COST OF A COMPACT DISC SOLD AT A RETAIL OUTLET

		Notes
- **Retailer economics**		
- Retail price	$16.98	
- Wholesale price (COGS)	10.75	
- Gross margin	6.23	
- Staff cost	1.36	
- Distribution cost	1.36	
- Rent (in a shopping mall)	2.55	As low as $1.53 for a free-standing store
- Operating profit	0.97	
- **Record company economics**		
- Wholesale price	$10.75	
- Cooperative advertising	0.86	
- Manufacturing of CD	0.60	
- Manufacturing of CD booklet	0.15	
- Distribution and sales	1.40	As high as $2.15 for independents
- Marketing and promotion	2.15	Advertising, video clips, PR, tour promotion, etc.
- Artist and repertoire	1.08	Includes production studio costs
- Royalty payment to performing artist	1.29	15% of wholesale price minus 3% recoupment
- Royalty payment to composer and lyricist	0.70	7¢ per song x ten songs
- Overhead and mailing	1.94	
- Operating profit	0.59	

Source: "Is Biz Poised for Renewed Price Wars?" *Billboard,* January 8, 2000

Exhibit 8 COMPOSITION OF BERTELSMANN REVENUE, 1998–99

By business segment		By geographic segment	
Books	30.8%	*United States*	34.7%
BMG Entertainment	30.1%	*Germany*	28.1%
Print and media	14.0%	*Rest of Europe*	29.6%
Magazines and newspapers	19.9%	*Rest of world*	7.6%
Professional information	3.4%		
Multimedia	1.8%		

Source: Bertelsmann public documents

Exhibit 9 FINANCIAL RESULTS OF MAJOR RECORD COMPANIES, FY 1999

	BMG Entertainment	EMI	Sony Music Entertainment	Universal Music Group	Warner Music Group
Revenue ($ mm)	4,306	3,596	6,336	3,751	3,834
Assets ($ mm)	N/A	2,950	6,298	16,392	7,483
Operating income ($ mm)	177	367	320	-439	179
Return on sales	4.1%	10.2%	5.1%	-11.7%	4.7%
Return on assets	N/A	12.4%	5.1%	-2.7%	2.4%

Source: Company annual reports, casewriter calculations
Notes: For BMG, Sony, Universal, and Warner, results are for music business segment only. Because corporations differ in how they classify revenue, revenue totals shown here are not reliable for calculating market shares; see Exhibit 10 for market share information. BMG revenue figure differs slightly from figure given in text because fiscal year is different from calendar year. Universal asset figure is inflated by recent purchases. Universal operating income figure includes $313 mm restructuring charge

Exhibit 10 MUSIC INDUSTRY MARKET SHARES (%, U.S. ONLY)

	1991	1992	1993	1994	1995	1996	1997	1998	1999
- Total albums*									
- BMG	9.2	10.7	12.0	12.9	12.4	13.5	14.5	14.2	17.3
- EMI	13.4	11.6	11.8	11.2	9.8	7.9	11.9	12.3	9.3
- Sony	16.5	17.2	17.3	15.3	13.9	14.3	12.8	16.6	16.9
- Universal**	25.0	24.8	22.8	23.6	23.2	23.9	25.4	24.3	25.5
- Warner	26.5	24.0	21.7	21.1	21.6	20.8	19.3	18.2	15.8
- Others	9.5	11.7	14.6	15.9	19.1	19.6	16.1	14.3	15.3
- Current albums*									
- BMG	–	–	–	–	13.5	16.5	17.6	16.8	20.8
- EMI	–	–	–	–	9.8	7.2	12.3	12.5	8.2
- Sony	–	–	–	–	13.4	14.5	11.9	17.3	17.8
- Universal**	–	–	–	–	22.6	23.3	25.6	23.9	25.5
- Warner	–	–	–	–	22.0	20.6	18.6	17.5	14.0
- Others	–	–	–	–	18.7	17.9	13.9	11.9	13.7

Source: SoundScan, BMG

*"Current" albums exclude sales of old albums from a company's catalog. "Total" albums include both current albums and catalog sales

**Universal figures incorporate Polygram sales prior to purchase of Polygram

4

Online Retailers

This chapter describes online retailers of physical goods—companies that use the Internet to sell a variety of products ranging from dog food to jewelry. The first section of the chapter defines online retailers and describes different ways to categorize them. The second section summarizes the various ways that online retailers create value for their customers. The third section analyzes the economic model for online retailers, focusing on their revenue and cost drivers, and how this model compares to the experience of offline retailers. Building on that analysis, the fourth section examines the payoff to online retailers from pursuing a "Get Big Fast" strategy, i.e., investing aggressively in customer acquisition and brand building. The fifth section briefly describes a set of "best practices" that online retailers should employ to improve their odds of success. The sixth section discusses the unique challenges that offline retailing companies face when they move their businesses online. The final section explores a series of management and strategy issues relevant to online retailers, including (1) the implications of shopping "bots," software programs that consumers use to identify Internet retailers with attractive prices for a given product, (2) the threat of disintermediation that online retailers face from manufacturers of the products they sell, and (3) the arguments for and against pursuing a hybrid strategy, e.g., combining the online retailing model with another Internet business model, such as online content provider or Internet access provider.

Assistant Professor Thomas Eisenmann and Research Associate Alastair Brown prepared this note as the basis for class discussion.

WHAT ARE ONLINE RETAILERS?

Definition and Delimitations

Online retailers are companies that (1) use a website to merchandise newly manufactured physical goods for which they take title, and then (2) rely on third-party service providers (e.g., the U.S. Postal Service, UPS) to deliver those goods from remote warehouses. Three delimitations of this definition are important. First, the chapter is not concerned with online auction sites that create a market for second-hand (used) goods, such as eBay. While eBay may determine how the goods are presented, it does not merchandise its site, because sellers determine the selection of goods available for sale. Furthermore, eBay does not take title to the goods traded on its site and does not arrange for their shipment; delivery arrangements are negotiated directly between the buyer and seller.

Second, the chapter does not describe the business model for online retailers with their own infrastructure for local delivery, e.g., Webvan or Kozmo.com. Compared to companies that rely on third-party shippers, firms that maintain local delivery capabilities face very different strategic issues—most notably the need to achieve high density of sales within a given geographic area to increase the utilization of delivery personnel.

Finally, the chapter does not discuss companies that use the Internet to sell services (e.g., American Airlines) or information goods (e.g., companies that offer the digital download of software or music). Such companies have cost structures unlike those of retailers of physical goods and thus face different challenges for competitive success. Specifically, scale economies are often very high for companies that sell services and information goods online, because the cost structures of such businesses tend to be dominated by fixed elements. Scale economies, along with high operating leverage, provide an especially strong incentive for such companies to pursue aggressive growth strategies. In contrast, for physical goods retailers, variable expenses for merchandise, delivery, and customer service tend to represent a large share of total costs.

Taxonomies

Online retailers can be categorized in two ways: First, we can divide them by their merchandising emphasis. Some retailers are horizontal in their focus (i.e., they sell across many product categories), whereas others are vertical, selling in one distinct area. In the offline arena, mass market discounters like Wal-Mart and department stores like Macy's would be considered horizontal retailers, while Toys "R" Us and Home Depot would be considered vertically focused. Online, Amazon.com would clearly be a horizontal retailer because it sells an increasingly broad range of products, including books, music, consumer electronics, kitchen appliances, power tools, health and beauty products, and patio furniture. In contrast, Garden.com, eToys, and Pets.com would be considered vertically focused because they concentrate on a single category of merchandise.

Second, online retailers may be categorized by the pricing format they employ. The most common format, both on or off the Web, is fixed pricing. Yet, some sites employ other models. For example, Egghead.com sells computer hardware and software products (for which it holds title) through auctions. "Group buying" (also known as "demand aggregation") sites, such as

Mercata.com and MobShop.com, employ a pricing scheme whereby increased purchasing prior to a deadline reduces the price of that product (based on a "demand curve" prenegotiated with the product's supplier) for all shoppers who previously had made a purchase commitment. Finally, some online retailers, such as buy.com, have experimented (unsuccessfully) with a "deep discount" model. Buy.com once sold products at cost, hoping to profit by assembling a database of consumer preferences and then selling manufacturers access to those consumers for advertising and marketing programs. After this experiment yielded poor results, buy.com raised its prices.

HOW DO ONLINE RETAILERS CREATE VALUE FOR CUSTOMERS?

The total U.S. retailing market, worth roughly $1.6 trillion in 1999,[1] is currently split between three selling formats. Internet retailing now makes up about 1 percent of the total, while traditional printed catalogs account for 7 to 8 percent, and "brick-and-mortar" store operations control the remaining 90 percent. When it fully matures, however, online retailing is expected to grow to roughly 15 to 20 percent of total U.S. retail spending, or two to three times the existing market share for printed catalog retailers.[2]

Catalog and Web purchases are similar in two important ways: in neither case can consumers directly inspect the goods prior to purchase, nor can they access the goods immediately after purchase—unlike customers of brick-and-mortar stores, catalog and Web shoppers must wait until delivery for inspection. Given these similarities, the prediction that sales for online retailers will eventually be two to three times greater than catalog marketers' revenues is noteworthy: It suggests that Web retailing adds significant value for consumers, beyond what printed catalogs can deliver. This value added will be manifested in three ways: (1) an increase in online households (expected to grow from 37.3 percent of households in 1998 to 63.4 percent in 2003), (2) an increase in the percentage of people online who are purchasing (expected to grow from 23 percent in 1998 to 54 percent in 2003), and (3) increased spending online per buyer (expected to more than double from $412 in 1998 to $919 in 2003) (see Exhibit 1).

Exhibit 4-1 ONLINE SHOPPING STATISTICS

	1998	1999	2000	2001	2002	2003
Total U.S. online shopping (billions)	$7.8	$14.9	$23.1	$34.6	$53.0	$78.0
Percentage of U.S. households online	37.3%	44.0%	49.9%	54.8%	59.4%	63.4%
Percentage of people online who purchase annually	23%	29%	34%	40%	47%	54%
Spending per online buyer	$412	$518	$589	$668	$788	$919

Source: Adapted from Jupiter Communications, "Online Shopping Report," 2000

Attributes of Product Categories Well Suited for Web Retailing

While Internet retailers are expected to account for 15 to 20 percent of overall U.S retail spending, the share they capture will vary greatly by product category. For example, analysts predict that over 40 percent of PCs will be bought on the Internet by 2003 but only about 2 percent of footwear (see Exhibit 2). Many factors determine whether a category will be well suited for Internet retailing, including the following attributes.

- *Information-Rich Products.* Websites can offer graphics and detailed text information (e.g., objective third-party reviews) to help prospective buyers better understand a product's features and benefits. Streaming video can demonstrate a product in use. Comparison shopping and collaborative filtering[3] tools can guide consumers to products that best fit their preferences. Whereas the quality and availability of sales help often is uneven in brick-and-mortar stores, websites can consistently deliver a clear, compelling sales pitch. Such benefits are most salient for products that are feature-rich and differentiated along multiple dimensions.
- *Large Selection.* Internet retailers can offer a nearly unlimited product selection, which is especially important for categories such as books, whereas brick-and-mortar and catalog retailers face space constraints that prevent them from offering a full range of products.
- *Little Need for Hands-on Service or Product Trial.* Products such as apparel often are sold only after product trial and thorough examination—buying leather pants over the Web is a risky proposition. Likewise, some goods are

Exhibit 4-2 U.S. E-COMMERCE FORECAST BY CATEGORY

	1998 (online % of total category)	2000 Online Sales	2000 (online % of total category)	2003 Online Sales	2003 (online % of total category)
Software	8.6	$1.3	20.7	$3.5	48.9
PCs	11.1	$5.2	24.3	$10.2	40.4
Air travel	2.6	$7.8	10.3	$13.6	15.4
Books	2.5	$1.9	6.3	$4.9	14.3
Music	1.1	$0.6	3.8	$2.6	14.0
Videos	0.4	$0.3	3.0	$1.1	10.3
Toys	0.3	$0.5	1.9	$1.6	5.6
Flowers	0.8	$0.3	1.9	$0.8	5.0
Footwear	0.1	$0.2	0.3	$1.2	2.1
Furniture	0.0	$0.1	0.1	$1.4	2.1

Source: Adapted from "Metrics" section of *The Industry Standard*, August 7, 2000, citing Forrester Research Data

bundled with extensive customer service that lends itself to face-to-face encounters between the shopper and the sales representative. For example, if you are building a patio, you might prefer to go to a Home Depot brick-and-mortar store and have one sales associate answer all your questions, rather than be stuck chatting electronically or by phone with someone from a Web outlet.

- *High Value-to-Weight Ratio.* Internet retailers either ask consumers to bear shipping costs or absorb such costs themselves through "free shipping" promotions. Consequently, heavy or bulky goods, such as dog food, which have a low ratio of product value to shipping cost, can be difficult to sell online at a profit. By contrast, music CDs are well suited for online retailing because they can be shipped easily, and their value-to-weight ratio is quite high.
- *Easily Customizable Products.* Complex, multi-featured products that lend themselves to customization are well suited to the Web. For example, Dell, a leading PC manufacturer, generates about half of its sales online, allowing customers to custom-order a PC by selecting its processor speed, amount of memory, hard-drive size, and so forth.[4]
- *Rapid Changes in Stock Availability, Demand, and/or Price.* Consumers can use websites to check the availability of hard-to-find items (e.g., a PlayStation 2 console in October 2000), information that can be frustrating and time-consuming to obtain by phoning or visiting brick-and-mortar retailers. Likewise, when demand for a product emerges rapidly (e.g., for the lipstick that Monica Lewinsky wore during her interview with Barbara Walters), selling through the Web avoids the delays endemic in shipping goods through distributors to thousands of brick-and-mortar outlets.
- *Replenishment Driven.* Internet technology can be employed to automate the frequent reordering of groceries, pet supplies, pantyhose, and similar items used daily. Internet retailers who can lock customers into a "sticky" replenishment cycle then have an opportunity to cross-sell additional products and services to these consumers.
- *Unpleasant Brick-and-Mortar Retailing Environments.* Most consumers dislike grocery shopping, finding it time-consuming and repetitive. Parents often dislike shopping for toys with their children because in a toy store children tend to become very excitable. Car buyers often find car salesmen manipulative, pushy, and dishonest. The Internet helps consumers avoid these unpleasant brick-and-mortar retailing environments.

Besides these category-specific attributes, which determine where Web retailers will find success, online retailing has several generic advantages over other shopping formats. First, like printed catalogs but unlike most brick-and-mortar stores, online retailers can offer "24/7" service, i.e., consumers can shop 24 hours a day, 7 days a week. Second, because the Web can be accessed anywhere, online retailers (like catalogs) can reach consumers who might live too far away to shop at their brick-and-mortar stores. Third, like catalogs but unlike brick-and-mortar stores, many online retailers in the United States currently can offer consumers the opportunity to shop without paying sales taxes, due to a federal government moratorium on Internet taxes.[5] One University of Chicago economist, Austan Goolsbee, has predicted that if this tax moratorium ends, online spending will drop 30 percent.[6]

Barriers to Online Shopping

Although prices offered by online retailers have been estimated to be 6 to 10 percent below the prices offered by their brick-and-mortar competitors (after factoring in shipping costs and sales taxes),[7] there are still many reasons why consumers might not shop via the Web, e.g., the inability to handle the product before purchasing it or confusing website navigation (see Exhibit 3). The principal barrier to online shopping, however, continues to be consumer concern about sending credit card information over the Web. This fear has spawned a number of initiatives to boost online shoppers' confidence, e.g., the development of secure "electronic wallets"—software programs that store consumers' personal data and make it unnecessary for them to reenter this information when ordering.[8]

Consumers' lack of familiarity with the brands of some pure-play companies (i.e., companies that were "born on the Web" and lack a brick-and-mortar or print catalog heritage) can compound consumers' concerns about credit card theft. Consumers with limited Internet shopping experience worry that "fly-by-night" outfits will take the money but never ship the merchandise. Thus, building consumers' trust is an especially important task for young websites.[9]

Another difficulty with online shopping is that customers must be willing to wait for home delivery. The inability to provide instant gratification is a more serious shortcoming for some types of products than others, however; in particular, consumers tend to be less concerned about delayed delivery when they are purchasing gifts for a special occasion. Likewise, when consumers purchase a custom-ordered product, (e.g., a Dell computer), they expect to wait a few days for delivery.

Still, even if consumers are willing to defer gratification, home delivery is difficult to manage. Seventy percent of the population is not home during the day.[10] Theft and fraud issues may arise if a package is simply left on a doorstep, and many consumers do not have access to package delivery services at their workplace.[11] A solution to this problem could be for a consumer to install a lock box that is accessible only to package delivery services. One online grocery delivery service, Streamline.com, has even extended this idea by installing refrigerators inside its customers' garages.

Exhibit 4-3 REASONS FOR NOT PURCHASING ONLINE

Reason	Online Households That Did Not Purchase (%)
Uncomfortable sending credit card data via the Net	50
Prefer to see the product first	41
No credit card	37
Not enough product information to make a decision	22
Not confident with online merchants	20
Can't talk to salesperson	17

Source: Adapted from Ernst & Young, "Global Online Retailing," January, 2000, p. 20

Different Types of Shoppers

Of course, different consumers will have different reactions to the advantages and disadvantages associated with Internet retailing. A website must often tailor its pricing, merchandising approaches, and customer service to the needs of distinct customer segments. According to the ebates.com Dot-Shopper Survey, conducted by Harris Interactive, online shoppers might be classified into the following groups:[12]

- *E-Bivalent Newbies.* Newest to the Internet, this population is somewhat older, likes online shopping the least among the six types, and spends the least amount of time online.
- *Time-Sensitive Materialists.* This group is most interested in saving time and maximizing convenience and is less likely to read product reviews, compare prices, or use coupons.
- *Clicks and Mortar.* These individuals tend to shop online but prefer to buy offline, are more likely to be female homemakers, have privacy and security concerns about buying online, and visit brick-and-mortar shopping malls most frequently.
- *Hooked, Online, and Single.* Members of this group are more likely to be young single males with high incomes, have been on the Internet the longest, play games, download software, bank, invest, and shop online the most often.
- *Hunter-Gatherers.* More likely to be married, this group is typically age 30 to 49 with two children and most often goes to sites that provide analyses and comparisons of products and prices.
- *Brand Loyalists.* These people are the most likely to go directly to the site address of a merchant they know, are the most satisfied with shopping online, and spend the most online.

ONLINE RETAILER ECONOMICS

Economics for Online versus Offline Retailers

A central debate surrounding the burgeoning online retail market is whether online retailers, when they reach maturity, will truly have margin structures that are superior to those of their offline counterparts. Initially, there was great excitement on Wall Street about e-commerce, but enthusiasm—and dot-com stock prices—faded between the spring and fall of 2000. This begs the question, why were investors so excited during 1999? *Do* online retailers have intrinsic economic advantages over brick-and-mortar stores?

Operating Costs. One possible intrinsic advantage is tremendous operating cost reductions that may be obtained—at least in theory—by online retailers, once they reach scale. In fact, a Banc of America Securities analysis of the economic models for a brick-and-mortar book retailer and an online book retailer at maturity (see Exhibit 4) suggests that the online retailer will have an operating margin 4 percent lower than the margin for a traditional superstore, derived as follows:

- Brick-and-mortar stores spend 10 percent of revenue on rent and 14 percent on in-store labor for checkout, stocking shelves, etc. By contrast, a mature online bookseller is projected to spend only 3 percent of its revenue developing and maintaining its website and 12 percent of revenue on its warehouses, customer service, and other operating expenses.

- Lacking a physical location to attract customers, the online retailer is expected to spend more on advertising—4 percent of revenue, net of co-op ad reimbursements from publishers—compared to 2 percent for the brick-and-mortar chain.
- Finally, the online retailer is expected to have lower general and administrative expenses than its offline counterpart (1 percent of revenue versus 3 percent), presumably due to the latter's need for a regional management infrastructure to coordinate the activities of several hundred stores.

Although this operating cost advantage is impressive, it is not large enough to offset the effects of pervasive discounting by online merchants and the fact that larger offline players command volume discounts that reduce their cost of goods sold. Reflecting these differences, Banc of America projects a 28 percent product margin for a mature Internet bookseller, compared to a 40 percent product margin for a superstore chain. As a percentage of revenue, the online retailer also is expected to pay higher inbound freight charges (due to its lower sales volume, it earns more modest discounts) and higher credit card processing fees,[13] but it can offset a portion of these higher costs by earning a modest profit on shipping—a common practice among printed catalog retailers.[14] After accounting for these cost elements, the gross margin for an online bookseller is estimated to be 25 percent, versus 38 percent for a brick-and-mortar chain. Subtracting operating costs equal

Exhibit 4-4 COST STRUCTURES FOR AN ONLINE BOOKSELLER AT MATURITY VS. A BRICK-AND-MORTAR BOOK RETAILING CHAIN

	XYZ.com	XYZ Superstore
Product margin	28.0%	40.0%
Freight in	-2.0%	-1.0%
Credit card charges	-2.5%	-1.0%
Shipping revenue, net	1.5%	0.0%
Gross margin	**25.0%**	**38.0%**
Store occupancy costs		10.0%
Store operating expense		14.0%
Distribution and customer service	12.0%	
Research and development/tech costs	3.0%	
Gross advertising	7.0%	4.0%
Co-op reimbursement/ad sales	-3.0%	-2.0%
General and administrative	1.0%	3.0%
Total operating costs	**20.0%**	**29.0%**
Operating margin	**5.0%**	**9.0%**

Source: Adapted from Banc of America, "Thinking Outside The Big 'Box,' " August, 1999

to 20 percent and 29 percent of revenue for the online and offline players, respectively, yields an operating margin of 5 percent for the Internet company versus 9 percent for the brick-and-mortar retailer.

Working Capital. With a lower projected operating margin than offline players, why were online retailers so attractive to investors in 1999? To understand the appeal of online retailers, we must examine the second economic advantage of Internet retailers: Again, at least in theory, they utilize working capital in an extremely efficient manner. Online retailers, as with most businesses, pay their suppliers after sixty days or so. Consumers pay by credit card, so accounts receivable are minimal. Online inventory also turns very quickly, especially when retailers rely on distributors to hold inventory and manage fulfillment.

- Inventory turns at least ten times per year for many Internet retailers, versus three to five times for their offline counterparts.
- Even when online retailers carry their own inventory, they can hold much less stock concentrated in far few warehouses than brick-and-mortar retailers must hold at hundreds of stores.[15]
- Online retailers also have an inventory carrying cost advantage over printed catalog marketers (who otherwise share the advantage of only needing to maintain inventory at a limited number of warehouse locations). If a catalog marketer runs out of inventory, it cannot remove an item from its catalogs once they have been printed and mailed; consequently, it must maintain inventory at levels that are sufficiently high to minimize stockouts that could lead to customer dissatisfaction. An online retailer, by contrast, can simply take a product off its website if it runs out of stock.

With minimal receivables, modest inventories, and two months to pay suppliers, many online retailers have negative working capital. In 1998, for example, Amazon's working capital was −14 percent of revenue; the company actually generated cash as it grew![16]

Fixed Capital. The third economic advantage that online retailers have over their offline counterparts stems from the fact that Internet companies do not need to invest capital in stores. Property, Plant, and Equipment (PP&E) expenses for online retailers tend to be much lower as a percentage of sales, compared to brick-and-mortar chains. For example, in 1998, before Amazon invested in its own warehouses, its PP&E was only 5 percent of sales, compared to 19 percent for Borders, a major brick-and-mortar chain.[17] So, with negative working capital and very low investment in fixed assets, investors in 1999 believed that online retailers could earn lower operating margins and still earn substantially higher rates of return on invested capital than their offline counterparts.

Current Margin Structure for Online Retailers

The analysis above projects the margin structure for an online retailer that has reached maturity. How far are Internet retailers from achieving these long-range targets? Exhibit 5, which presents historical and projected income statements for a sample of three publicly-traded online retailers (Amazon.com, eToys, and PlanetRx.com), suggests that as of 2000, the sample companies are far from earning a 5 percent operating margin!

Exhibit 4-5

PROFIT AND LOSS STATEMENTS FOR A SAMPLE OF ONLINE RETAILERS

	1998		1999		2000E		2001E	
	($ in millions)	(% of revenue)	($ in millions)	(% of revenue)	($ in millions)	(% of revenue)	($ in millions)	(% of revenue)
Amazon								
Revenue			1,639.8		2,756.8		4,200.0	
Cost of revenue			1,349.2	82.3	2,125.4	77.1	3,203.7	76.3
Gross margin			290.6	17.7	631.3	22.9	995.4	23.7
Sales and marketing			412.6	25.2	583.9	21.2	664.0	15.8
Product development			160.0	9.8	268.4	9.7	267.7	6.4
General and administrative			70.4	4.3	111.0	4.0	118.5	2.8
Operating income			−352.4	−21.5	−331.9	−12.0	53.9	1.3
eToys								
Revenue	30.0		151.0		353.3			
Cost of revenue	24.2	80.1	122.0	80.8	275.4	78.0		
Gross margin	5.7	19.1	29.1	19.2	78.1	22.1		
Sales and marketing	20.7	69.3	120.4	79.7	150.6	42.6		
Product development	3.6	12.0	43.4	28.7	64.5	18.3		
General and administrative	4.6	15.3	16.9	11.2	32.4	9.2		
Operating income	−23.2	−75.6	−151.6	−98.1	−169.4	−47.9		
PlanetRx								
Revenue			9.0		41.8		60.0	
Cost of revenue			7.6	84.4	35.6	85.2	51.0	85.0
Gross margin			1.4	15.7	6.2	14.8	9.0	15.0
Sales and marketing			55.2	613.2	75	179.4	65.0	108.3
Product development			12.5	143.9	25.4	60.8	31.0	51.7
General and administrative			6.5	71.8	10.5	25.1	12.0	20.0
Operating income			−73.2	−813.2	104.7	−250.5	−99.0	−165.0

Source: Adapted from Goldman Sachs Global Equity Research, "Internet Industry Report," October 6, 2000

Gross Margin. Gross margin for online retailers typically is calculated as revenue from product sales and shipping fees paid by the customer (less the cost of goods sold), shipping expenses paid to third-party courier services, and credit card processing fees. Gross margin is determined by retailers' pricing policies, their purchasing clout, and their distribution strategies.

With respect to pricing, as noted earlier, most online retailers price at a discount to their offline counterparts. Yet, during the year 2000, investors expressed increasing concern about the sustainability of Internet companies' business models, which caused many online retailers to raise their prices and thus improve their gross margins. For example, Buy.com recently raised prices of their DVD players from $1,499 to $1,749, while Beauty.com and Bluefly.com raised shipping charges.[18]

Gross margins also tend to improve as retailers grow and exert more purchasing leverage over manufacturers and distributors. At a threshold scale that varies by product category, it is economical for online retailers to build their own warehouses and purchase directly from manufacturers, rather than relying on distributors for fulfillment. Ernst & Young reported in early 2000 that among a sample of 38 online retailers, 53 percent operated their own warehouses, 26 percent outsourced fulfillment, and 11 percent shipped directly from their suppliers (the balance relied on a mix of methods).[19] Amazon invested aggressively in in-house fulfillment operations in 1999, building warehouses that allow the company to directly ship fast-moving items. Slower moving backlist book titles are still inventoried and shipped by Amazon's distributors.

According to analysts at ABN AMRO, purchasing economies that follow from volume growth should allow online retailers over time to improve their gross margins by 300 to 500 basis points. Furthermore, Goldman Sachs suggests that several gross margin improvement opportunities are available as online retailers increase their sales volume. First, by sourcing directly from manufacturers, online retailers can increase gross margin by 3 percent to 10 percent. Second, volume discounts can add an additional 0.5 to 1.0 percent. Third, co-op marketing funds that become available when a retailer buys directly from manufacturers can contribute 4 to 6 percent of sales in some product categories, thereby reinforcing the first two effects.[20]

The gross margins for the sample companies in Exhibit 5 are projected to average 19.9 percent in 2000. This compares favorably to the 12.0 percent gross margin earned in 1999 by a larger sample of 27 publicly-traded Internet retailers,[21] but lags the 25 percent target gross margin (27.5 percent before credit card charges) for a mature online bookseller presented in Exhibit 4. However, Amazon appears to have reached that target. For the quarter ending September 30, 2000, the company reported a gross margin of 27.2 percent (before credit card charges, which Amazon records as Sales and Marketing expenses) in its core U.S. book, music, and video unit.[22]

Distribution and Customer Service Expenses. Online retailers incur significant variable costs associated with picking and packing merchandise in their warehouses (or in outsourcing this function) and answering customer inquiries (by e-mail and phone) about orders. A BCG survey indicated that customers of pure-play online retailers (i.e., companies with no brick-and-mortar stores or printed catalog operations) generate 1.1 service contacts per order versus 0.4 contacts for orders placed to online units of retailers with brick-and-mortar and/or print catalog operations (i.e., "multichannel" retailers). If each contact took just five minutes to process, then customer service costs for a pure-play online retailer would account for nearly 8 percent of the value of an average order.[23]

Both distribution and customer service call centers are subject to some economies of scale, but the dominant share of costs in both functions are labor-related, and the per transaction savings realized as volume grows beyond a threshold level are modest.[24]

For these categories, the long range cost target for an online bookseller (see Exhibit 4) is 10 percent of revenue. For the quarter ending September 30, 2000, Amazon reports that the portion of its sales and marketing expenses related to fulfillment (which includes warehouse depreciation, labor costs related to receiving goods and picking and packing shipments, customer service costs, and credit card processing fees) were 15.1 percent of revenue—reasonably close to the long range target, after backing out credit card fees that are estimated to be 2.5 percent for a mature online bookseller (see Exhibit 4).

Website Development. Online retailers incur ongoing costs to add features to their websites, e.g., personalization options, broadband content, customer relations management (CRM) systems that give call center personnel an integrated view of a customer's purchase history, and collaborative filtering that delivers recommendations to shoppers based on the user's browsing patterns as compared to those of other customers. These technology development costs are fixed; it should not cost much more for a large site to add such features than a small site. Consequently, website development expenditures should decline as a percentage of revenue as sales volume grows, which has been the case for the companies profiled in Exhibit 5. For example, Amazon is projected to spend $267.7 million (6.4 percent of revenue) in 2001 on product development, compared to $160 million (9.8 percent) in 1999. By comparison, the target spending on R&D and technology for a mature online bookseller is 3.0 percent (see Exhibit 4).

Sales and Marketing. Pure-play online retailers have spent very heavily on sales and marketing to build their brands and acquire customers. PlanetRx.com, for example, is projected to spend $75 million on sales and marketing in 2000, or 179 percent of revenue, compared to 43 percent and 21 percent for eToys and Amazon, respectively. These figures must be interpreted carefully, however. For eToys and Amazon, the figures include fulfillment costs related to distribution, customer service, and credit card processing (PlanetRx.com is less specific about its accounting policies, so it is unclear how such fulfillment costs are booked). When fulfillment costs are subtracted from sales and marketing expenses, Amazon spent 6.6 percent of its revenue on advertising, promotion, and the salaries of marketing personnel in the quarter ending September 30, 2000. This compares favorably to a long range target of 4 percent of revenue for a mature online bookseller (see Exhibit 4).

General and Administrative. The administrative overheads incurred by an online retailer—such things as senior management compensation and costs for legal, finance, and human resource functions—tend to be semifixed, i.e., such overheads will increase, but not in direct proportion to sales growth. As a company grows, it will need more human resources personnel to recruit employees, will process more accounts payable transactions, will pay larger fees as its auditors check more complex books, and so forth. Projected 2000 spending on general and administrative (G&A) expenses is $11 million (25 percent of revenue) for PlanetRx.com, $32 million (9 percent) for eToys, and $111 million (4 percent) for Amazon (see Exhibit 5). These figures suggest that online retailers must grow substantially before they reach the 1 percent target for G&A spending for a mature online bookseller (see Exhibit 4).

Will pure-play online retailers ever be profitable? As of late 2000, many investors have grown skeptical of these companies' mounting losses. At the time of this writing, only one pure-play, publicly-traded online retailer—FragranceNet.com, which sells discounted perfumes—has earned a profit, although data from BCG indicates that about one-quarter of all pure-play online retailers (including privately-held companies) are already profitable.[25] Furthermore, based on the earlier analysis, it appeared that Amazon was tracking toward operating profitability. Goldman Sachs projected that the company would earn a positive operating margin in 2001. Even as Amazon has diversified into additional product categories, it has made steady progress at improving its gross margins, reducing its distribution and customer service expenses and its advertising and promotion costs as a percentage of revenue, and leveraging fixed and semifixed website development and administrative costs over a growing sales base.

Skeptics may fairly note that Amazon is a special case. With an 18-month head start over its brick-and-mortar competitors, it has dominated its core category to a degree that most other online retailers will never be able to match. Offline players in other product categories, such as office supplies, pet supplies, and health and beauty aids, have witnessed the consequences to Barnes & Noble and Borders of being "Amazoned" and have mounted vigorous efforts to avoid preemption by pure-play Internet retailers. So, again, can pure-play online retailers in these and other categories ever reach profitability? The answer is a qualified "yes". It should be clear that profit margins in online retailing are sensitive to scale, which in turn implies that companies must steadily acquire customers. However, in doing so, they must balance the cost of customer acquisition against the lifetime value of these new customers. This raises the question then, should online retailers pursue a Get Big Fast (GBF) strategy, i.e., should they invest aggressively in customer acquisition and brand building?

GET BIG FAST: A STRATEGIC IMPERATIVE FOR ONLINE RETAILERS?

Many Internet retailers have pursued GBF strategies, embracing "land grab" logic. According to this view, companies will find it easier to stake out wide swaths of empty territory now, rather than trying to capture that territory later, after it has been settled by others. Getting Big Fast through a single website is a lot easier than it would be offline, where rapid growth requires store-by-store expansion. For example, in the case of retailers, Amazon.com reached $1 billion in sales in three years, whereas it took six to ten years for the brick-and-mortar chains Home Depot, Wal-Mart, and Staples to reach that level of sales (at which point these chains had 60, 229, and 174 physical stores, respectively).[26] The payoff from a GBF strategy tends to be strongest when the following conditions apply: Network effects are strong, scale economies (beyond network effects) are significant, and customer retention rates are intrinsically high. This section explores the extent to which these conditions apply for online retailers.

Network Effects

Network effects occur when the adoption of a product or service by a new customer increases the value of that product or service for customers already using it, due to the fact that existing customers now can connect with additional parties.[27] The fax machine is a good example of a product that benefits from network effects. A fax machine is worthless if you are the only one who owns one, but when many people own them, they are valuable. When network effects are strong, it often makes sense for a company to invest heavily to gain first-mover advantage. As users beget users, the first mover may develop an unassailable lead.

Network effects are minimal for online retailers because Internet shoppers typically do not communicate with each other. My shopping session at Pets.com is in no way enhanced by the fact that you may have just shopped at that website. Chat groups and customer recommendations are among the few features of retailing websites that benefit from increased usage (and then only to a certain extent, e.g., chat rooms can become crowded), and these features tend to be of secondary importance in consumers' decisions about where to shop online.

Scale Economies

Companies benefit from scale economies when they can spread fixed costs over a growing revenue base. With some Internet business models—for example, portals—costs are almost entirely fixed, and operating margins increase dramatically with sales growth. Strong scale economies promote a winner-take-all dynamic: If the market leader has a superior cost structure, that company can reduce its prices or invest in superior service or features and thereby increase its lead.

While online retailers benefit from scale economies, a large share of their cost base—including the cost of goods sold and a significant portion of distribution and customer service costs—varies directly with revenues. Unlike content providers, who may costlessly reproduce their product, retailers must pick, pack, and ship each order. Volume growth does yield economic benefits for online retailers: It increases their purchasing clout and allows them to purchase directly from manufacturers and thereby internalize the margin earned by third-party distributors. Volume growth also leverages the fixed cost elements in warehouse and call center operations and more notably in website development and administrative functions.

The magnitude of scale benefits varies by product category. McKinsey & Company estimates that a pure-play online apparel retailer can improve its operating margin by only 2 percentage points (from 6 to 8 percent) by increasing its sales from $100 million to $1 billion. For an online computer retailer, the same revenue change is estimated to yield a 12-percentage–point margin improvement, from −3 to 9 percent.[28] McKinsey then calculates the breakeven point for pure-play competitors in different online retailing categories, and compares that sales level to 2003's total projected online spending in the category. In both the bookselling and drugstore categories, the breakeven sales point for a pure-play online retailer is $1.2 billion. However, McKinsey projects total revenues in 2003 of $4.9 billion for all online booksellers—implying room for four players to operate at the breakeven point—versus $2.5 billion for all online drugstores—implying room for just two players.[29] Based on this analysis, online drugstore companies have an economic incentive to consider a GBF strategy. However, if several competitors embrace this logic, the results can be ruinous, as noted below in the discussion of the online pet supply category.

Retention Rates

The payoff for GBF strategies improves when customer retention rates are high. If customers can be "locked in" before they sample a competitor's service, a first mover may cement its lead. Retention rates tend to be high in the face of strong network effects—once an auction marketplace aggregates a dominant share of the buyers and sellers of a given product, participants are reluctant to do business elsewhere. Other factors can also promote customer retention, most notably "switching costs," such as the hassles that customers incur when they switch Internet service providers and must obtain a new e-mail address, or when they switch online brokers and must transfer funds between accounts.

Online retailers have only a few attributes that promote customer retention. First, users may develop loyalties to a site based on its customer service performance or simply by gaining familiarity with the site's layout, but such loyalties do not tend to provide a significant switching barrier. Second, sites like Amazon.com that deliver personalized recommendations based on an analysis of past purchases can provide better advice if users concentrate the bulk of their category purchases at the site. Personalization technology is still not widely deployed, however, and recommendations may be confounded when users purchase gifts instead of buying goods for themselves.[30] Third, sites like Staples.com, which support replenishment ordering, create a switching cost related to users' time invested in entering past orders; subsequent order entry for replenishment items takes less time (the same is true for sites like Amazon that allow consumers to store their shipping and credit card information to complete "one-click ordering"). Finally, retailers that introduce loyalty programs encourage customer retention, but such programs have not been especially effective to date due to the difficulty of paying rewards large enough to change consumers' behavior. Rewards are constrained by the typical consumers' limited online spending in any given category, and by the thin variable contribution margins for most products (in contrast to airline travel, where rewards can be granted in the form of seats that otherwise would fly empty).[31]

Why the GBF Strategy Fails

It should be clear from the analysis above that the structural characteristics of online retailing typically prohibit an attractive payoff for companies embracing a GBF strategy. First, online retailers do not benefit from a network effect, where new customers beget more new customers, so their acquisition costs per customer are unlikely to decline during a period of concentrated marketing spending. Second, online retailers do not benefit from significant scale economies, at least compared to other Internet business models. As an Internet retailer's volume increases, it does not gain a dramatic cost advantage over rivals. Third, online retailers do not benefit from intrinsically high customer retention rates. Having spent heavily to acquire new customers, it may be difficult for them to encourage repeat purchases by those customers.

So, if the payoff from the GBF strategy is questionable, why did companies in category after category—e.g., toys, pet supplies, furniture, health and beauty, and apparel—pursue GBF strategies during 1999? In hindsight, the explanation seems to be that Amazon.com's incredible success spawned a wave of imitation. Scrutiny of the list of attributes of product categories well suited for online retailing suggests that Jeff Bezos found the "sweetest spot" in the market. Amazon's team then executed a GBF strategy brilliantly. Notwithstanding the lack of network effects and switching costs in their business, Amazon drove traffic to its site through portal deals and mass media advertising, built a brand that resonated with early Internet users, and delivered excellent customer service, thereby engendering strong customer loyalty and word-of-mouth recommendations. It took Barnes & Noble and Borders eighteen months to mount a response, and by then, Amazon had raised huge amounts of capital to comfortably fund the trench warfare that ensued.[32]

Scores of entrepreneurs and venture capitalists looked at Amazon's huge valuation—$4 billion in September 1998—and developed plans to become the "Amazon of the XYZ category." In most categories, however, dozens of startups vied to fill that role, and incumbents vowed not to be Amazoned. Competitors engaged in what economists call "racing behavior": Their belief was that the capital markets would disproportionately reward the market leader. The leader then would use its access to "free capital" to vanquish its rival. To this end, managing investors' perceptions was seen as crucial. Companies signed portal deals and aired expensive TV ads in part to drive traffic to their sites, and in part as a way to signal investors that they were still in contention for the leadership position. The race was on! Who would be the first in a category to go public?

As demonstrated by the experience of online pet supply retailers, winning that race could be a Pyrrhic victory.[33] In the pet supply category, by early 1999, a couple of dozen aspirants had been winnowed down to four well-funded players, all pursuing similar GBF strategies: Pets.com, which had Amazon.com as an investor; Petstore.com, which sold a majority equity position to the cable programming company Discovery Communications; PETsMART.com, owned by the largest brick-and-mortar retail chain of the same name; and Petopia, which had Petco, the second largest brick-and-mortar chain as an investor. All four firms embarked on aggressive programs of customer acquisition: They bid up the cost of portal deals and deluged prospective customers with half-off and free-shipping offers. Pets.com turned its sock puppet "spokesanimal" into a celebrity with a Macy's Thanksgiving Day Parade float and a multi-million dollar Super Bowl ad.

Savvy investors backed these companies, and it seems likely that the investors knew that they were speculating—betting that the "horse they backed" would either emerge as the winner in the GBF race and be rewarded handsomely through an IPO or that, in the worse case, investors would sell out to the winner and receive valuable equity. As long as valuations for e-commerce companies held up, the risks seemed acceptable. Even if you thought dot-com valuations were excessive, the right question to ask was: Will you get your money back before valuations tumble?

However, the very logic that led several investor groups to separately conclude that it was reasonable to place speculative bets on online pet supply retailers ultimately led in aggregate, to a bloodbath in the category. In the year following their launches in early 1999, the four pet supply retailing sites lost, in total, about $400 million. Truly savvy investors might have foreseen that when four well-funded startups simultaneously launched GBF strategies, the startups were bound to get locked in an expensive war of attrition. Investors also might have reached three other conclusions about the intrinsic attractiveness of the online retailing of pet supplies:

First, like most other online retailers, pet supply sites do not exhibit the characteristics associated with a positive payoff for a GBF strategy. In particular, online pet supply sites experienced a high level of customer churn, reinforced by the sites' willingness to offer promotional discounts. One magazine article quoted a "promiscuous" consumer as saying, "They all e-mail me specials. I order from whoever has the special. Sometimes, it's even free."[34]

Second, like most other online retailers, it was difficult for pet supply sites to achieve differentiation. By purchasing through offline distributors, pet supply sites had few opportunities to distinguish themselves from competitors through the breadth or depth of their product offerings. Also, after Amazon had demonstrated the value of developing an information-rich site, most e-tailers took that aspect of website design as a given. Finally, e-tailers could seek to differentiate themselves through the quality of their fulfillment operations and customer service—a realization that eventually led Amazon to invest hundreds of millions of dollars in building its own warehouses. However, it takes time to build the capabilities that yield superior service, and time is the enemy of a startup pursuing a GBF strategy.

Third, building on the previous point, online retailing is executionally-intensive: It does not scale as readily as some other Internet business models, because e-tailers have to receive goods, pick and pack the right items, deliver them to consumers when and where expected, and quickly and accurately answer customers' questions about merchandise and the status of their transactions. A retailing order can go astray at many points—a challenge that Yahoo! does not face in serving its users. The challenge of executing orders smoothly was compounded for online pet supply retailers in two ways: (1) Their executives were so tightly focused on driving traffic to their sites and raising more capital that they often lacked time to focus on the quality of their logistics, fulfillment operations, and customer service, and (2) their websites and information systems were new and were built in a hurry. As many e-tailers discovered in the rush to fill orders during the 1999 Christmas season, a cascading chain of events can lead to deteriorating customer service performance and escalating costs.[35]

- When their suppliers run out of stock, e-tailers cannot fill orders. In the case of online pet supplies, all of the top sites were located in California, and tended to rely on distributors within that state. When customers took advantage of deep discounts, the resulting surge of orders could exhaust distributors' stocks.
- Unless there are strong communications links between the managers of the e-tailer's website and the managers in the company's fulfillment operations—a rarity in the chaotic rush to launch and grow an online company, especially when fulfillment is outsourced, as was the case for most of the competitors in the pet supply category—there can be a lag between the emergence of an out-of-stock condition and the removal of that item for sale on the website. Items may be ordered by consumers even though they cannot be immediately shipped.
- If the consumer receives, without explanation, an order that is only partially complete, he or she is likely to call the e-tailer to ask about the status of the order. If call center personnel, operating in outsourced facilities (as was the case for the most of the pet supply competitors), lack clear visibility into warehouse inventory management systems, they may have to manually track the order status and may be unable to answer the customer's inquiry on the spot. Links between call centers and warehouse databases require system integration; in their zeal to get big fast, startups may decide to launch before such integration efforts are completed.

By the fall of 2000, Petstore.com and Pets.com had failed, and Petopia had laid off a large share of its staff. In category after category, results for online retailers were similar. Valuations plummeted as investors fled from the sector; companies that had burned through their private equity funding were unable to raise additional capital. By the fall of 2000, a number of online retailers that had pursued GBF strategies—including CompUSA-backed Cozone.com, apparel retailer boo.com, Disney-backed ToySmart.com, sporting goods retailer Fogdog, and Garden.com—had failed, and many others (e.g., jewelry retailer Blue Nile, PlanetRx.com) had laid off workers.

So, is the GBF strategy *always* a bad idea for online retailers? Not necessarily; Staples.com has been executing a GBF strategy with results that have been impressive, albeit not yet rewarded by investors.[36] The situation facing Staples.com was well suited for a GBF strategy in three ways. First, the channel structure in office supplies retailing does not easily accommodate entry by pure-play online retailers: buying from wholesalers, the cost of goods sold for pure-plays would be more than 15 percent higher than COGS/revenue for "big box" retailers like Staples (which leverages sales in excess of $7 billion in buying directly from manufacturers).[37]

Second, *offline* competition in office supplies retailing is relatively fragmented. Together, the three leading superstore chains—Office Depot, Staples, and OfficeMax—only account for 10 percent of category sales. Consequently, Staples.com could pursue the large base of small office/home office buyers who were not yet offline customers of any "big box" retailer. With ample opportunities for increasing offline and online sales to this large prospect base, Office Depot and OfficeMax did not feel obliged to escalate their own online marketing efforts in response to aggressive moves by Staples.com.

Finally, office supplies retailing involves replenishment ordering. The ability to automate reorders to avoid reentering data, and the ability for office managers to set and monitor spending limits leads to a fairly sticky customer relationship. With restrained competition, Staples.com has been able to maintain an acquisition cost per new customer in the range of $100, even with aggressive marketing programs. Annual spending per customer is expected to be in the range of $1,000, with a variable contribution margin of about 10 percent.

Lifetime Value of a Customer

The Staples.com example points to a broader rule: GBF-style investments in customer acquisition make sense for online retailers only when the lifetime value of new customers acquired exceeds the cost of acquiring those customers. As shown in the pet supply category, overheated competition will tend to drive up acquisition costs and drive down retention rates—and also lifetime value—while in other cases higher intrinsic retention rates may make aggressive customer acquisition worth it.

It is instructive to turn again to Amazon to determine how it measures against this rule. Amazon had average sales per customer of $97 in 1999 (see Exhibit 6). If the company reaches the long-range margin targets suggested for a mature online book-

Exhibit 4-6 CUSTOMER ACQUISITION COSTS, SALES PER CUSTOMER

	1999	2000 (2Q)
Customer Acquisition Costs		
Amazon	$19	$17
Ashford	$309	$253
bn.com	$29	$25
eToys	$55	$72
Sales per Customer		
Amazon	$97	$26
Ashford	$463	$108
bn.com	$49	$12
eToys	$79	$12

Note: "Sales per Customer" for 1999 reflects spending over a full year, so it is not directly comparable to spending in the second quarter of 2000.
Source: Adapted from Goldman Sachs, "Path to Profitability Monitor," October 25, 2000

seller presented in Exhibit 4, Amazon will have a variable contribution margin of 13 percent (gross margin less distribution and customer service expenses). Assuming that the average duration of Amazon's customer relationships is three to four years (a typical figure employed by industry analysts when evaluating online retailers, although little data is publicly available on actual customer retention rates[38]), then the present value of the variable contribution generated by each new customer would be $30. Since Amazon spent $19 to acquire each new customer in 1999 (see Exhibit 6), we may conclude that its marketing efforts are economically justified. The same is not likely to be true for eToys, which had lower sales per customer than Amazon in 1999 ($79 versus $97), a comparable gross margin (19 percent versus 18 percent), and much higher acquisition costs per new customer ($55 versus $19).

TACTICS FOR SUCCESS

Given the description above of the economic challenges facing online retailers—especially pure-plays—the obvious question might be: What tactics should they use to achieve success? Many "best practices" revolve around the competitive advantages outlined above in the section titled "How Do Online Retailers Create Value for Consumers?" To succeed, online retailers must leverage the Web's advantages, rather than simply moving a physical store-front or printed catalog online.

Customer Service. A first tactic is to offer very high quality customer service. Some analysts believe that online retailers will achieve parity on selection and price, so service will be the biggest differentiator.[39] Four key aspects of high quality online service are stock availability, site design, reliable delivery, and responsiveness to customer inquiries. To date, most online retailers have fallen woefully short on all four dimensions of service. For example, Andersen Consulting (now Accenture) reported that 40 percent of online shoppers encountered problems during the 1999 holiday season (see Exhibit 7) and 35 percent of these consumers said they left a site when they experienced trouble and shopped elsewhere. While this performance is somewhat alarming, it should be seen in light of consumers' overall lack of satisfaction with their retailing experience—both online and offline. In fact, 73 percent of the consumers surveyed by Andersen Consulting reported that they were satisfied with online shopping, compared to 60 percent for brick-and-mortar stores and only 56 percent for catalog shopping.[40]

The most frequent problem cited in the Andersen Consulting survey was stock shortages, mentioned by 64 percent of consumers. Managing stockouts is tricky for online retailers: Should they bear the cost of increased inventories to avoid disappointing consumers? Amazon followed this approach in the toy category during the 1999 holiday season and ended up writing off $39 million of excess inventory.[41] Again, to avoid disappointments, should retailers remove an item from their website when it is out of stock, forfeiting sales from consumers who might be willing to wait for the item to be shipped? Furthermore, if consumers are allowed to order out-of-stock items, what is the impact on service costs, as customers call or e-mail to check on the status of their order?

With respect to site design, the website should load quickly, be easy to navigate, and provide simple and straightforward ordering procedures. In a survey of consumers' satisfaction with online shopping, 18 percent cited slow site performance as a problem and 6 percent said they could not easily search for products.[42] Poorly designed sites have a high rate of abandoned shopping baskets (purchase orders

Exhibit 4-7 PROBLEMS EXPERIENCED BY ONLINE SHOPPERS DURING 1999 HOLIDAY SEASON

Problem	% of Shoppers Affected
Product was out of stock	64
Product was not delivered on time	40
Shipping cost was too high	38
Difficulty in connecting to or downloading from website	36
No confirmation or status report on purchase	28
Selections were limited	27
Website was too difficult to navigate	26
Website didn't provide info needed to make purchase	25
Prices were not competitive	22
Website did not offer enough gift ideas	16

Note: The people surveyed were those who had encountered at least one problem.
Source: Adapted from John Sterlicchi and Barbara Gengler, "E-Tailers' Costly Lessons," *Upside* (June 2000), citing a survey by Andersen Consulting

that are not completed after products have been chosen due to frustration with ordering processes or other reasons, e.g., the customer's reaction after shipping charges are calculated); the overall rate of failed purchase attempts for online retailers has been estimated at 28 percent.[43]

Online retailers also have performed poorly in terms of on-time delivery. Forty percent of the consumers in Andersen Consulting's survey cited this issue (Exhibit 7). Much of the problem may be attributed to "growing pains," i.e., the difficulty of maintaining process control in the face of annual growth rates often in excess of 100 percent. Another cause is reliance on manufacturers and distributors for fulfillment. Outsourcing fulfillment compounds an online retailer's coordination challenges, especially when the items in a single order are shipped from multiple locations. Bringing fulfillment in-house can improve on-time delivery performance, although the required investment in inventory and warehouses raises the asset intensity of the business.

Finally, the ease with which customers can communicate using e-mail and their ability to track order status on some websites (e.g., Dell's) have raised expectations regarding online merchants' responsiveness to order inquiries. Nonetheless, most online retailers have performed poorly in these aspects of customer service (see Exhibit 8). During the 1999 holiday shopping season, for example, 10 percent of online shoppers reported problems with slow e-mail responses and 5 percent complained that they could not speak directly to a customer service representative.[44]

Community. Second, retailers should utilize the networking abilities of the Web. In many categories, customers may form communities around the buying activity. For example, Garden.com, a site which sold garden supplies, had organized forums and chat groups about gardening. Its customers could interact with each other and with experts who could recommend specific products and explain how to use them.

Exhibit 4-8 ONLINE PURCHASE PERFORMANCE STATISTICS

Tracking Area	% of Survey Respondents
Order Confirmations	
Incorrect/contained misinformation	1
No order confirmation was received	12
Sent, but didn't include all necessary information	28
Included extra beneficial information	14
Met standards	45
Shipping Confirmations	
Incorrect/contained misinformation	4
No shipping confirmation was received	39
Sent, but didn't include all necessary information	17
Included extra beneficial information	9
Met standards	31
Not Able to Access Order Info Via Telephone	
More than 24 hours after checkout	2
Immediately after checkout	60
Order Confirmations	
1–24 hours after checkout	11
E-mail Queries Regarding Purchases	
No response	18
Response within an hour	7
Response in 1–6 hours	21

Source: Adapted from Electron Economy, "Order Disorder," *Business2.0*, October 10, 2000

Personalization. Third, online retailers should personalize their offerings to increase affinity for the site and thereby improve customer retention rates. Retailers should be able to e-mail a customer about new products similar to items the customer has already purchased. Retailers also should be able to give advice on what to purchase given a customer's shopping history. By "upselling" additional goods related to an initial purchase, sites can increase their average order size.

One form of personalization involves manipulating price to the site's advantage. For example, many first-time shoppers purchase small items from a website to measure how well the site performs; if satisfied, these new customers are more likely to return to buy larger items. In fact, first-sale revenue is generally between 10 and 30 percent of fourth sale revenue.[45] Ashford.com, an online jewelry retailer, reports that its repeat buyers spend twice as much per order as first time buyers.[46] When a site has an indication that it is dealing with a first-time visitor (because the visitor's PC has never before received the site's "cookie"[47]), the site can dynamically serve on its homepage a promotional offer that may appeal to the prospect.

ISSUES FACING OFFLINE INCUMBENTS

This section examines some of the strategic and organizational challenges confronting brick-and-mortar retailers as they extend their businesses online. It reviews the advantages and disadvantages that incumbents face as they compete with pure-play Internet retailers, then speculates as to how the competition between incumbents and pure-plays may evolve.

Incumbents' Advantages

Among online retailers, only one publicly-traded pure-play (FragranceNet.com) had reported profits as of late 2000, whereas there were many examples of offline incumbents whose online units were already profitable, including iQVC and Eddie Bauer.[48] In fact, a BCG/Shop.org study of a sample of 412 privately-held and publicly-traded online retailers in late 1999 found that 72 percent of catalog companies that had moved online were profitable, compared to just 24 percent of the pure-plays (see Exhibit 9). This difference in profit performance may be explained by the considerable advantages that offline retailers bring to the Internet.

Branding and Customer Relationships. First, incumbents have a brand name that is firmly established and have relationships with offline customers who may be encouraged to buy online. For example, the Gap.com site is quite successful amidst a glut of online apparel retailers because its parent company has already built a strong reputation for quality and service.[49] A strong brand and existing customer relationships translate into lower marketing costs for incumbents compared to pure-plays, which must build a brand from scratch. BCG reports that in 1999 the acquisition cost per new customer for multichannel online retailers was only $12 (down from $22 in 1998), versus $82 for pure-plays (up from $42 in 1998).[50] Incumbents may exploit their brand strength and access to offline customers through cross promotions, driving traffic to their website by offering coupons and displaying dot-com signage on shopping bags and throughout their stores. An increasingly common tactic for incumbents is to locate computer kiosks in high traffic brick-and-mortar retail stores, thereby exposing offline shoppers to their websites; 67 percent of such brick-and-mortar incumbents planned to introduce such kiosks by year-end 2000.[51] Incumbents may also cross-promote in the other

Exhibit 4-9 PROFITABILITY OF ONLINE RETAILERS

	Catalog-Based, Multichannel	Store-Based, Multichannel	Pure-Plays
Overall e-commerce sites	72%	38%	24%
Retailers online for more than one year	79%	50%	38%

Source: Adapted from "Metrics" section, "Catalogers Wise To The Net," *The Industry Standard*, May 29, 2000, citing data from Boston Consulting Group/Shop.org study

direction: exploiting their website to encourage online shoppers to visit their brick-and-mortar outlets.

Supplier Relationships. Second, existing supplier relationships allow incumbents to build their online business at a lower cost. As noted above, larger retailers enjoy scale economies in procurement through volume discounts, by purchasing directly from manufacturers and by securing co-op marketing funds from their suppliers. Offline retailers like Toys "R" Us have advantages in procuring scarce merchandise for their online units—a critical capability in the hit-driven toy business—due to their clout with suppliers.[52]

Fulfillment and Customer Service Operations. Third, offline incumbents with catalog operations have existing warehouse and call center operations geared toward servicing individual customers. While brick-and-mortar retailers often have warehouses, these facilities generally ship full pallet quantities to stores, not small shipments to individual households. The assets held by catalog retailers and their access to seasoned managers who can leverage these assets can translate into cost and performance advantages over other online retailers. BCG reports that in 1999, the average fulfillment cost per order for catalog retailers' online units was $10.30, versus $12.50 and $18.10 for pure-plays and the online units of brick-and-mortar retailers, respectively. Furthermore, the online units of catalog retailers shipped a higher percentage of orders on time, compared to other types of online retailers, and delivered orders to consumers more quickly (see Exhibit 10).

Cross-Channel Delivery and Returns. Lastly, incumbents can offer consumers the convenience of picking up merchandise ordered online from a brick-and-mortar store or returning unsatisfactory merchandise purchased online to a brick-and-mortar store. Extending this advantage, Barnes & Noble has experimented with using its brick-and-mortar stores as a base for same-day delivery of merchandise ordered online.[53]

Incumbents' Disadvantages

Incumbents face certain barriers as they move online (see Exhibit 11). First and foremost, incumbents worry about the threat of cannibalization of their offline business. Is this a legitimate concern? Yes, assuming there is fixed cost leverage in their existing offline channel, then a shift in sales from the offline channel to the

Exhibit 4-10 FULFILLMENT COSTS

	Fulfillment Cost per Order	Order Fulfillment Time	Orders Fulfilled on Time
All	$11.80	1.7 days	88%
Pure-play	$12.50	1.8 days	86%
Multichannel (catalog-based)	$10.30	1.5 days	91%
Multichannel (store-based)	$18.10	1.9 days	86%

Source: Adapted from April 1999 Boston Consulting Group/Shop.org "The State of Online Retailing 3.0"

Exhibit 4-11 REASONS FOR BRICK-AND-MORTAR RETAILERS NOT SELLING ONLINE TO CONSUMERS

Reason	Percentage of Firms Surveyed
Conflicts with our investments in physical stores	67
Lack necessary technology infrastructure	67
Lack necessary distribution network	50
Don't believe investment is worth the expected return	33
Product not appropriate for online sales	17
Don't believe consumers will buy our products online	17
Legal/regulatory reasons	9
Other	9

Note: Those surveyed do not sell through the Web and do not plan to.
Source: Adapted from Ernst & Young, "Internet Shopping Study," 1999, p. 20

online unit will result in an overall reduction in profits, even if the online unit earns the same margins as the offline channel did before the shift in sales volume occurred. According to one analyst, a 15 percent reduction in volume for a typical brick-and-mortar retailer will reduce its operating margin by 5 percentage points (from 5 to 0 percent).[54]

One response to cannibalization is to simply embrace its inevitability. If other Internet retailers are going to capture your business anyway, wouldn't you rather self-cannibalize than fuel a competitor's growth? A second response is to ask Is it possible to capture enough *upside* from new customers or increased sales from existing customers to compensate for the *downside* impact of cannibalization? Given the value added by online retailing, category expansion seems plausible, which might lead to more revenue. Also, as noted above, multichannel retailers can use their websites to support their stores, and vice versa. For example, a recent survey by the National Retailing Federation indicates that people who surf a store's Internet site before going to the physical store spend 33 percent more than those that do not.[55]

In fact, there is ample evidence that customers who shop in multiple channels spend much more heavily than those who shop in a single channel. For example, Eddie Bauer reports that its customers who shop through all three of its channels (stores, catalog, and website) spend, in total, five times more than its "catalog-only" customers.[56] Staples reports similar results: Its customers who shop in three channels spend five times as much as customers who shop only in Staples stores.[57] One might suppose that these are simply the retailer's most loyal customers, who might have spent the same amount even if multiple channels were not available. The experience of The Gap suggests otherwise. Tracking longitudinal data for individual customers, The Gap reports that 50 percent of its multichannel shoppers spend more now than they did when they shopped only in The Gap's brick-and-mortar stores; the rest spend about the same amount as they did before.[58]

In addition to selling more goods to existing customers, offline retailers like Staples have targeted new customers through their Internet channel. In doing so, multichannel retailers must operate more like pure-plays; they often invest heavily to build prospects' interest and encourage trial. To date, this strategy has been successful for Staples. The company reports that 70 percent of the sales by its online unit represent incremental volume that the company would not have realized prior to the launch of its online business.[59]

A second barrier confronting incumbents as they move online involves the very considerable challenge of coordinating offline and online activities. Legacy information systems and online systems must work in tandem; a consumer who uses L.L. Bean's website expects to be able to call a catalog customer service rep to check what size "Bean boots" she ordered two years ago. Also, coordinating pricing policies can be difficult. Some customers expect Internet retailers to charge lower prices, while others may demand that a company's brick-and-mortar store match the lower price offered on the company's website.

Who Wins?

Pure-plays claim to be more focused and flexible than incumbents, who often have been conflicted in their online strategies—worried about cannibalizing their core businesses or depressing their earnings and stock prices by investing too aggressively. Yet, pure-plays are now constrained by less accommodating capital markets, and as noted above, incumbents have considerable advantages as they move online. A review of the twenty most heavily trafficked retailing websites in August 1999 (see Exhibit 12) quickly indicates that incumbents are well represented among online leaders: The list includes Sears, Barnes & Noble, J.C. Penney, Staples, Best Buy, J.Crew, Old Navy and others. In fact, according to a BCG/Shop.org study in late 1998, 59 percent of online shopping came from incumbent's sites.[60]

Not surprisingly, many startups and established retailers have begun linking up in order to leverage each other's expertise. Pure-plays want access to the purchasing leverage, brand and customer relationships, and distribution and customer service capabilities of offline retailers. Established companies, on the other hand, seek to jump-start their efforts in an arena where they lack expertise. Examples include CVS's June 1999 purchase of Soma.com, Hollywood Video's purchase of Reel.com, and PETsMART's merger of its online operations with those of pure-play Petjungle.

OTHER STRATEGIC ISSUES

Shopping Bots

Shopping bots such as mySimon.com and DealTime are websites that employ software "spiders" to "crawl" across the Web, collecting information from multiple online retailers on their product pricing, features, and availability.[61] Shopping bots allow users to compare goods along several dimensions but most frequently are employed to discover the cheapest price for a given product. Some industry observers believe that bots are revolutionary and will cause price wars between online retailers.[62]

Other industry analysts note that despite the ease of gathering pricing information online and the fact that 40 percent of consumers say they comparison shop before they buy online,[63] pricing dispersion (i.e., the difference between the highest and lowest prices offered for a given item by different retailers) is actually *greater* on the Web than it is offline.[64] Furthermore, Amazon, while offering substantial discounts compared to brick-and-mortar booksellers, has never had the lowest online prices, yet it has captured an 80 percent online market share. This suggests that

Exhibit 4-12 TOP 20 RETAILERS AMONG U.S. HOME USERS, AUGUST 2000

Rank	Website	Unique visitors (000's)	Overall reach (%)	Projected buyers (000's)	Buy rate (%)
1	Amazon.com	18,998	22.4	1,607	8.5
2	ticketmaster.com	5,396	6.4	595	11.0
3	buy.com	3,568	4.2	466	13.1
4	CDNOW.com	7,297	8.6	441	6.0
5	Sears.com	4,075	4.8	359	8.8
6	bn.com	6,322	7.5	358	5.7
7	JCPenney.com	4,293	5.1	351	8.2
8	Real.com	13,457	15.9	305	2.3
9	drugstore.com	1,674	2.0	240	14.4
10	Pets.com	2,048	2.4	213	10.4
11	PlanetRx.com	2,834	3.3	208	7.3
12	More.com	1,319	1.6	146	11.1
13	Half.com	6,770	8.0	146	2.2
14	Staples.com	1,825	2.2	140	7.7
15	eToys.com	1,224	1.4	138	11.3
16	BestBuy.com	3,393	4.0	135	4.0
17	Office.com	926	1.1	130	14.1
18	jcrew.com	1,131	1.3	128	11.3
19	Gateway.com	2,689	3.2	124	4.6
20	oldnavy.com	2,451	2.9	119	4.9

Source: Adapted from PC Data Online survey data cited in September 13, 2000 press release (*http://www.pcdataonline.com/press/pcdo091300.asp*)

online shoppers—like their offline counterparts—are willing to pay a premium for high quality customer service and for the security of dealing with a reputable retailer that will stand behind its brand.

Given these disparate views, online retailers face a difficult choice in deciding whether to cooperate with shopping bot sites. At one extreme, some bots allow retailers to pay for superior placement on lists that they generated in response to users' inquiries. At the other extreme, it is technically possible for a website to block access to a bot's spiders. By doing so, a site reduces its exposure to comparison shopping but also eliminates a potential source of sales referrals.

Disintermediation

Disintermediation occurs when manufacturers sell directly to consumers rather than through retailers. Disintermediation was expected to be the "biggest, baddest" impact of the Internet retailing revolution. To date, however, its impact has fallen short. Most manufacturers fear alienating their retailers by selling directly on the Web. In fact, more than 90 percent of manufacturers do not sell online.[65]

One example of failed disintermediation involves the online activities of blue-jeans manufacturer Levi Strauss. Levi's pulled the plug on its online retailing operations in 1999, just one year after it announced ambitious plans to sell directly to consumers. The reason was that powerful retailers such as JC Penney's and Macy's had complained loudly and publicly. Alienating retailers and being preoccupied by its failed Internet strategy has apparently taken a toll on Levi's: The company has lost roughly 25 percent of the market share they once enjoyed.[66]

Another example of a retailer deterring its suppliers from selling online involves Home Depot. The home building supplies and hardware chain has reportedly threatened its vendors that it will refuse to purchase from them if they launch e-commerce initiatives.[67]

Hybrid Business Models

Hybrid business models include combinations of online retailing with other Internet business models. For example, Garden.com might be considered a hybrid between a retailer and a content provider. The site included an online magazine with a rich array of articles of interest to gardeners. In theory, access to such information should have attracted visitors to Garden.com's site, who should have been inclined to spend more as they immersed themselves in their hobby. In practice, Garden.com, like many other online retailers, struggled to reach profitability. Facing difficulty raising funds to sustain its GBF strategy, the company closed its consumer operations in December of 2000.

Retailing/content provider hybrids like Garden.com can be difficult to manage for at least two reasons. First, they require mastery of diverse skills. The risk is that in trying to be both a retailer and a content site, a company will be great at neither. Second, sourcing content can be expensive, and a retailer like Garden.com that operates an online magazine is almost certain to forfeit advertising from competing retailers—typically a major source of revenue for a content provider.

Another hybrid approach combines online retailing with the Internet access provider business model. For example, Kmart, in partnership with Yahoo!, provides free Internet access service under the brand name 'BlueLight.com' (the name used in Kmart stores to announce special promotions). By managing the "start page" for 4 million BlueLight.com subscribers, Kmart can strengthen its relationship with these customers and encourage them to shop online.[68] Other large retailers have launched similar ventures, including Radio Shack, which inked a deal with Microsoft, and Circuit City, which formed a partnership with America Online.[69] These companies reason that if they can run their ISP businesses at or near breakeven, they will accrue significant strategic benefit from establishing closer relationships with their online customers.

ENDNOTES

[1]Goldman Sachs, "Internet Retailing," June 1999, p. 2.

[2]Ibid.

[3]Collaborative filtering involves software that analyzes a user's page-views and/or purchases, and based on their behavior concludes that he or she is most "like" a set of other users who have been observed to purchase certain other goods. Based on these inferences, a site can give recommendations or highlight special items that should be appealing to the user.

[4]Stephanie Stoughton, "The Next Economy Virtual Businesses and Bricks-and-Mortar Companies try to Blend the Best of Both Worlds," *The Boston Globe,* October 10, 2000: F5.

[5]Like printed catalog marketers, online retailers are only required to charge sales tax if they have a "nexus" of operations in the state (e.g., brick-and-mortar stores or a warehouse) where an order is placed. This favorable tax treatment was extended by the U.S. government in October 1998 to encourage the growth of the Internet when Congress declared a three-year tax moratorium. As of October 2000, legislators were still debating whether to level the playing field between brick-and-mortar and online retailers by introducing an Internet sales tax.

[6]Mike France, "A Web Sales Tax: Not If, but When," *BusinessWeek*, June 6, 1999: 104.

[7]Erik Brynjolfsson and Michael D. Smith , "Frictionless Commerce?," *Management Science* (April 2000): 563–585; others posit a 14–21% discount (excluding taxes and shipping) for electronics, food and other categories: "Faster! Better! Cheaper?", *Business2.0*, April 2000: 376–378.

[8]Nancy Imperiale Wellons, "E-Wallet's Potential Is Unfolding," *Orlando Sentinel*, November 15, 2000: D26.

[9]Cheskin Research and Sapient, "eCommerce Trust Study," January 1999.

[10]Denise Caruso, "Technology: Digital Commerce," *New York Times*, March 30, 1998: D5.

[11]Jupiter Communications, " Pricing Strategies," July 1998.

[12]All shopper types are from the ebates.com Dot-Shopper Survey, conducted by Harris Interactive with 3,042 respondents who have made at least one purchase online.

[13]According to the *Wall Street Journal* (Jason Sapsford, "Survey Says Online Fraud Increasing," November 3, 2000), online use accounts for 5 percent of all credit card transactions but 50 percent of fraudulent transactions. Online retailers are responsible for the cost of most fraudulent credit card claims, because their transactions fall into a category called "card not present."

[14]In the quarter ending September 30, 2000, Amazon's net profit on shipping was equal to 2.4 percent of its revenue, according to SEC filings.

[15]To maintain a given level of stock-outs, inventory must increase exponentially with a linear increase in the number of locations.

[16]Even after Amazon built its own warehouses in 1999 to handle high turnover merchandise—thereby boosting its inventories—it maintained negative working capital in excess of 14 percent of revenue.

[17]Amazon's PP&E as a percentage of sales rose to 19 percent in 1999 after it spent $300 million to build five warehouses: Robert D. Hof and Heather Green, "Suddenly, Amazon's Books Look Better," *BusinessWeek*, February 21, 2000: 80. This percentage was expected to decline over time, because Amazon built capacity ahead of demand and only utilized 40 percent of its warehouse capacity in 2000: "Internet Industry Report," Goldman Sachs Global Equity Research, October 6, 2000, p. 208.

[18]Rebecca Quick, "Shoppers Find Blowout Sale On Net Is Over," *Wall Street Journal*, June 26, 2000: B1.

[19]Ernst & Young, "Global Online Retailing," January, 2000, p. 51.

[20]Goldman Sachs, "Path to Profitability," October 25, 2000, pp. 6–7.

[21]ABN AMRO, "You've Got Mail!: Direct Marketing Moves Online," July 2000, p. 21.

[22]Company SEC filings.

[23]Boston Consulting Group, "The State of Online Retailing," 1998; Note that average order size used is $26.65. Furthermore, we assume the fully-loaded cost of a representative is $50K/year and the representative works 2,000 hours per year.

[24]For example, according to Roger Hallowell, "Everdream," section 8, *Internet Business Models: Text and Cases*, or HBS Case no. 800-251 (June 20, 2000), most operating costs for a call center (e.g., labor, telecommunications, rent) vary directly with transaction volumes. Capital costs are an exception—capital spending for a 33-seat facility is about 50 percent of spending for a 100-seat facility. However, the depreciation of capital costs accounts for only a modest portion of total call center expenses. Hence, total operating cost per seat for a 100-seat facility is only about 4 percent lower than the cost per seat for a 33-seat facility.

[25]Jennifer Couzin, "Net Retailers Aren't All Losers," *The Industry Standard*, November 6, 2000: 63 cites FragranceNet profitability; for BCG study, see Exhibit 9.

[26]BancBoston Robertson Stephens, "E-tailing Update," 1999, p. 11.

[27]See Carl Shapiro and Hal R. Varian, *Information Rules* (Boston, MA: Harvard Business School Press, 1999), pp. 173–225 and Philip Evans and Thomas S. Wurster, *Blown to Bits* (Boston, MA: Harvard Business School Press, 1999) pp. 112–113.

[28]McKinsey Quarterly, "From Retailing to E-tailing," Number 1, 2000: 144.

[29]Goldman Sachs, "Internet Retailing," (June 1999): 23; Goldman also sees a 50 percent market share as a natural ceiling in many online retailing categories, whereas they contend that the comparable offline ceiling is 25 percent. See also "Pure-Play: A Losing Model?," *The Industry Standard*, June 26, 2000: 192.

[30]Seamus McAteer, "Proactive Personalization," Jupiter Communications, August 19, 1999.

[31]For a survey of loyalty programs' developments see Grahame R. Dowling and Mark Uncles, "Do Customer Loyalty Programs Really Work," *Sloan Management Review*, Summer 1997.

[32]Robert Spector, *Amazon.com: Get Big Fast* (New York: HarpersCollins Press, 2000); Jeffrey F. Rayport and Dickson L. Louie, "Amazon.com," HBS Case no. 897-128; Jeffrey F. Rayport, Dickson L. Louie, Carrie L. Ardito and Holly S. Cameron, "Amazon.com," HBS Case no. 898-084; Lynda M. Applegate and Meredith Collura, "Amazon.com: Exploiting the Value of a Digital Business Infrastructure," HBS Case no. 800-330.

[33]Thomas Eisenmann, "Petstore.com," section 4, *Internet Business Models: Text and Cases*, or HBS Case no. 801-044.

[34]*BusinessWeek,* "For Online Pet Stores, It's Dog-Eat-Dog," March 6, 2000.

[35]For an in-depth analysis of these dynamics, see R. Hallowell, "Service in E-Commerce: Findings from Exploratory Research," HBS case no. 800-418 and "Service and Value in E-Commerce," HBS case no. 800-384.

[36]See Joanna Jacobson, Thomas Eisenmann, and Gillian Morris, "Staples.com," section 4, *Internet Business Models: Text and Cases*, or HBS Case no. 800-305 for more information.

[37]Figures in the preceding paragraph are taken from: Danielle Turnof Fox, "Company Update: Staples," *JP Morgan*, December 29, 1999.

[38]Banc of America, "Thinking Outside the Big 'Box' Superstore," 1999 and "Pure-Play: A Losing Model?," *The Industry Standard*, June 26, 2000: p.192, citing McKinsey data both adhere to three-year rule. Furthermore, according to Mike May, "Commerce Site Metrics," Jupiter Communications, August 1, 2000, only 74 percent of retailing sites even track data on repeat visitors.

[39]Goldman Sachs, "Internet Retailing," 1999.

[40]Numbers in the preceding paragraph are from John Sterlicchi and Barbara Genegler, "E-tailers' Costly Lessons," *Upside*, June 2000: 195, 200, citing Andersen Consulting.

[41]Robert D. Hof and Heather Green, "Suddenly, Amazon's Books Look Better," *BusinessWeek*, February 21, 2000: 78.

[42]Alan T. Saracevic, "Hope for the Holidays," *Business2.0*, October 10, 2000: 150, citing Jupiter Communications.

[43]Boston Consulting Group, in association with the e-commerce trade organization Shop.org as reported in "Shopping Trips," *Business2.0*, May, 2000: 451.

[44]Alan T. Saracevic, "Hope for the Holidays," *Business2.0*, October 10, 2000: 150, citing Jupiter Communications.

[45]Forrester Research, "Retail Revs Up," October 1997.

[46]Dennis K. Berman and Heather Green, "Cliff-hanger Christmas," *BusinessWeek*, October 23, 2000: 31–37.

[47]A cookie is a small piece of software code downloaded into a website user's computer by the website, which allows the website to identify the user and track her whenever she logs back into the site. Cookies could be used to avoid requiring users to reenter commonly requested information, such as user names and passwords or shipping addresses.

[48]David E. Bell, "Eddie Bauer," HBS Case no. 500-034 and Jeffrey F. Rayport, Dickson L. Louie, and Michelle Toth, "iQVC," HBS Case no. 897-123, April 13, 1998.

[49]Louise Lee, "Clicks and Mortar' at Gap.com," *BusinessWeek*, October 18, 1999: 150–152, citing Forrester Research.

[50]BCG/Shop.org data found in "The Detail On E-Retail," *The Industry Standard*, May 8, 2000: 207.

[51]Seema Williams, "Mixing Bricks With Clicks," Jupiter Communications, June 2000.

[52]Bernhard Warner, "How Culture Clash Sank the Toys "R" Us Deal," *Industry Standard,* August 30, 1999, p. 28.

[53]Jeanette Brown, "Barnes & Noble Joins the Dot-Com Speedy Delivery Stakes," *BusinessWeek Online,* June 9, 2000.

[54]Michael De Kare, *e-Shock* (New York: Amacom, 1999): 11.

[55]Nora Macaluso, "E-Shopping Key to Retail Health," *Commerce Times*, 2000; Furthermore, according to Evie Black Dykema, "Online Retail's Ripple Effect," *Forrester Research*, September 2000, 55 percent of surveyed e-tailers said they did not know the percentage of their online sales that is incremental to offline volume, 15 percent said less than 20 percent of online sales are incremental, 14 percent said 20–50 percent, and 17 percent said more than 50 percent of their online sales were incremental.

[56]K. Berman, "Cliff-hanger Christmas," *BusinessWeek*, October 23, 2000: 30.

[57]Gary Putka, "E-Commerce: Roundtable...," *Wall Street Journal*, July 17, 2000: R52.

[58]Louise Lee, "Clicks and Mortar' at Gap.com," *BusinessWeek*, October 18, 1999: 150–152; QVC reports similar results; its TV buyers spent, on average, 25 percent more after they move online according to Dennis K. Berman and Heather Green, "Cliff-hanger Christmas," *BusinessWeek*, October 23, 2000: 31–38.

[59]Danielle Turnof Fox, "Company Update: Staples," *JP Morgan*, December 29, 1999: 8.

[60]Boston Consulting Group, "The State of Online Retailing," 1998.

[61]Ken Cassar, "Shopping Bots," Jupiter Communications, May, 1998; Michael May, "As Bots Reach Adolescence . . . ," Jupiter Communications, September 7, 1999; for a beginners explanation see (*http://www.zdnet. com/zdhelp/stories/main/0,5594,903492,00.html*).

[62]Jeffrey Kephart and Amy Greenwald, "When Bots Collide," *Harvard Business Review*, March–April 2000.

[63]Stacy Lawrence, "Window-Shopping," *The Industry Standard,* May 15, 2000.

[64]Erik Brynjolfsson and Michael D. Smith , "Frictionless Commerce?", *Management Science*, April 2000: 563–585; "Faster! Better! Cheaper?", *Business2.0*, April 2000: 376–378.

[65]Neil Weinberg, "Not.coms," *Forbes*, April 17, 2000: 424.

[66]"Levi's Internet Blues Keep Keepin On," *The Industry Standard*, November 15, 1999: 80.

[67]Katrina Brooker, "Awfully Nervous," *Fortune*, August 16, 1999: 28.

[68]Evie Black Dykema, "Online Retail's Ripple Effect," *Forrester Research*, September 2000.

[69]"March of the Marts," *Industry Standard,* December 16, 1999.

STAPLES.COM

As she walked up to the main entrance of Staples Inc.'s headquarters in Framingham, Massachusetts, Kelly Mahoney thought that the building—where, to her surprise, Staples' dotcom division was located—looked even more imposing than she had imagined. As the chief marketing officer at Arnold Direct, Mahoney was a skilled direct marketing strategist and was looking to parlay her experience into a new opportunity on the Internet (see Exhibit 1 for Kelly Mahoney's resume). She was weighing several opportunities, including an offer from Staples.com, the online division of the office products giant.

From her due diligence and from past project work with Staples Inc., Kelly was familiar with Staples' reputation for excellent customer service, an innovative and entrepreneurial culture, and a commitment to serving the needs of small-business owners. However, Kelly wanted to learn more about the online division's strategy. Did Staples.com have a plan to claim the number one industry position? Would this job offer her the best personal and financial rewards?

Staples Inc.

When Tom Stemberg and Leo Kahn opened the first office-products superstore in 1986, they launched an entire industry. Winning over skeptics who believed there was no market for a 'big box' office products retail chain, Staples targeted the burgeoning, yet under-served, small-business market.[1] In 1989, Staples launched Staples Direct, its catalog division, and created its online site in 1998. That year, the company achieved $7 billion in sales. In 1999, it had a workforce of 46,000 employees and 1,100 stores in six countries.

Kelly was familiar with Staples' strong brand. She knew that the company's management team was skilled at utilizing customer feedback and leveraging that information into a competitive advantage. With low-cost, high-impact direct marketing tactics, Staples had acquired a remarkably loyal customer base of over six million small-business owners and office managers. (See Exhibits 2 and 3 for financial forecasts for Staples.Com and Staples, Inc.)

Competitive Landscape

The office supplies industry had tremendous growth potential, due to strong rates of small business creation, an increase in the number of home offices, and technological advances that made office products more affordable. Staples was one of three major contenders for the dominant position in this fast-growing industry. Staples, Office Depot, and Office Max together controlled about 10% of the $250 billion office supplies market; their low collective market share reflected a highly fragmented competitive environment, which included local drugstores, supermarkets, small, independent stationers, and general merchandise discounters like Wal-Mart.

As the industry's revenue leader with 1999 sales of $10 billion, Office Depot was foremost on the minds of Staples' senior management. Office Depot had a sizable share of contract sales to larger companies, and its direct mail division, Viking, was highly profitable and well regarded by industry analysts. Like Staples, Office Depot had a multi-channel sales strategy spanning the retail, catalog, contracts, and online channels.

Despite online competition from Office Depot and other bricks-and-mortar players, Staples senior management believed that prospects for extending their reach through Internet sales were promising. Forrester Research estimated that the U.S. online office supplies industry was

Research Associate Gillian Morris prepared this case under the supervision of Senior Lecturer Joanna Jacobson and Professor Tom Eisenmann as the basis for class discussion rather than to illustrate either effective or ineffective handling of an administrative situation.

[1]See www.staples.com/about/media/corporate_history.asp for further details (accessed 2/7/00).

a $1.3 billion business in 1999; online sales were expected to reach $65 billion by 2003, when the combined online/offline marketspace was projected to reach $500 billion.[2]

Staples.com Strategy

Staples.com's goal was to earn $1 billion in revenue and acquire 1 million customers by 2003. To do so, Staples.com would leverage the Staples brand and other benefits of a "clicks-and-mortar" business model, most notably the parent company's competitive advantage in execution, fulfillment, and service. An aggressive customer acquisition strategy targeted toward untapped market segments was planned to drive awareness and traffic. For example, Kelly learned that Staples.com was in negotiations with Yahoo!'s Small Business channel to become the featured office-supplies merchant. Once in command of the core office supplies sector, Staples.com would stretch its brand into business services. Diversifying into services would likely confront Staples.com with a new set of online competi-tors. Companies like American Express, AT&T, and Intuit were also expected to develop portals providing a range of information content, products, and services for small businesses.

Target Markets

Jeanne Lewis, president and CEO of Staples.com, had a clear model of how the dotcom division fit into its industry. She divided the customer base into Fortune 1000 companies, medium-sized firms comprising of 100-500 employees, and small businesses with less than 100 employees (see Exhibit 4 for Lewis's industry diagram). Small businesses (the "small-office, home-office," or SOHO, market) were the principal target customers for Staples' retail stores, its catalog business, and Staples.com.[3] To capture this market, Staples.com offered over 100,000 SKUs as opposed to the 8,000 stocked in the retail stores, it featured order tracking and real-time inventory visibility, and it provided time-saving features geared specifically toward the needs of small businesses.

As Staples.com achieved its goal of becoming the leading online retailer of office supplies to small businesses, Lewis planned to simultaneously broaden the dotcom's line of offerings to include a range of services required by small businesses. Staples.com would pursue alliances with companies providing intranet, telecommunications, payroll, accounting, and other services. Through such alliances, Staples.com could become a one-stop product and service destination for small businesses. Lewis felt that the Internet channel was well-suited for describing and selling complex services.

In planning this move into services, Lewis planned to exploit Staples' database of over six million customers. By tailoring web page views to particular customers based upon their database profile, Lewis hoped to gradually build a small-business community around Staples.com. By leveraging information that customers provided the company, such as product reviews and service feedback, Staples.com would take another step toward the parent company's mission of "cutting the cost and hassle of running your office."

Lewis knew that Staples.com would need to stretch the Staples brand to encompass a broader product and service vision. She said, "Our challenge now is to attach additional attributes to our existing great brand. In a recent focus group, customers could connect the idea of selling services to the Staples brand, but we weren't on their short list. Our brand opportunity is to extend our value proposition from helping small businesses save time and money on office products to service." The key attributes that Lewis sought to attach to the Staples.com brand were expertise, guidance, information, and helpfulness.

Kelly Mahoney knew that adapting the Staples brand personality to better suit the dotcom's strategy would be one of her tasks if she joined the company. Jeanne Lewis explained to her, "Our advertising right now has high likeability measures and high recall; people say, 'I love those ads, they make me laugh.' Associating that personality with office products is low risk, but if we're offering services and expertise, we need to infuse the brand with credibility and expertise." Kelly wondered if the parent company's marketing team was working in conjunction with the dotcom marketing strategy. Did the two teams share the same objectives, or were they working at odds with each other?

Marketing Commitment

To a large extent, Lewis's background as the senior corporate marketing executive for Staples Inc.—the position she held before accepting the top job at Staples.com—provided Kelly the answer to her question. Lewis had an integrated vision for how the web division would market itself in concert with the company as a whole. She

[2]From www.staples.com/about/media/website_ecomm.asp (accessed 2/7/00)

[3]Other Staples divisions served the mid- and large-scale business customers: Quill and Quill.com offered high-quality services and products to medium-sized businesses, while StaplesLink and StaplesLink.com served as the company's contract division for large firms.

planned a campaign using a variety of media to link the website to the parent company's well-known brand. Lewis said, "Unlike some of these new 'dotcoms,' we know how to plan a cohesive marketing campaign and how to target it selectively to different segments of office managers and small businesses. Since our target customers consume multiple media as they move through their day, we've taken a multichannel approach." In September 1999, Staples and Staples.com co-launched "Your Online Office Manager," a cross-channel campaign using billboards, appointment television spots, and other traditional offline media. In a decision contrary to other web players fighting for mindshare, Lewis chose not to advertise heavily online. She remarked, "Online marketing is still surgery with a blunt instrument."

The pace of the marketing efforts also differed from the usual start-up approach. Lewis' primary concern was creating great content and ensuring strong performance for the web site; expanding advertising came second. She expected to spend the first six months of 2000 perfecting the site, explaining, "I'm looking at the second half of the year as the time to begin to really get the message out about the new services that we'll offer online." Lewis planned a similarly prudent approach to spending her marketing budget: "Though we're going to be very aggressive in marketing ourselves, there's no need for us to spend \$100 million or \$200 million like a CNET all on one medium like broadcast. We have very effective—and cost-efficient—direct-marketing strategies that have proven themselves repeatedly in Staples' other businesses."

Customer Acquisition Goals

As Kelly continued her day of interviewing, she realized that to achieve aggressive customer and revenue goals, the web division's strategy for customer acquisition and pricing would be key. Staples management was of one mind: the web site would be the latest channel in their multichannel approach to acquiring customers and encouraging them to spend more dollars with Staples. John Mahoney (no relation to Kelly), Staples' chief administrative officer, recalled when the company had added its catalog operation to the retail store base: "We found that customers didn't cannibalize the store in favor of the catalog. In fact, the opposite was true—customers who shopped more than one channel were our best customers, spending two or three times as much as they did before." The management expected the online channel to yield similar results. To Kelly, John stressed the importance of "share of wallet." He said, "If we can maximize our opportunities to interact with our customers, we can get a bigger share of each customer's total office supplies budget. We need to take share of wallet away from the other channels that nip away at our heels—like discounters and mass merchants."

However, Kelly learned from Jeanne Lewis that increasing market share, not wallet share, was the principal concern of the dotcom's marketing team as they developed plans to reach their 1 million customer goal by 2003. By capturing more of the as-yet untapped market—the 90% not owned by the top three superstores—Lewis believed Staples.com could reach its targets. She said, "Gaining new customers is how we'll meet our growth targets and extend our brand into new arenas." Pursuing both existing and new customers certainly seemed vital to Kelly, yet she wondered if targeting both groups would stretch the dotcom's marketing resources too thinly.

With such a high level of interrelationship between all of Staples' sales channels, Kelly also was curious about the growth expectations for Staples' other divisions. She learned from John Mahoney and Lewis that the company expected the retail and catalog divisions to expand their customer base in 2000 with double-digit increases. If the traditional channels had their own aggressive targets to meet, how much energy and resources could they devote to helping the dotcom division meet its high growth objectives?

Organizational Issues

Retail, as a business, is going to change radically over the next several years, and I think that our dotcom business is going to facilitate our ability to understand what's going on. I expect online will transform our entire business, but it won't make the bricks-and-mortar retail environment obsolete. One scenario is that five years from now, when our stores and our Internet business are inextricably linked and working well together, we might put them back together again.

—John Mahoney

One month after its November 1998 launch, Staples.com became an independent SBU with its own growth targets, infrastructure, and a complex set of relationships to the company's corporate staff units and its other divisions. In most functional areas, the online division remained closely integrated with Staples' core operations. Staples.com relied on the parent organization for inventory purchasing support and fulfillment. For example, the next-day delivery service offered by both the catalog and the web channels operated from the same warehouses. With such close coordination across business units, Kelly wondered if all the procedural questions had been ironed out.

Lewis noted, "If we were a pure play—if we were, say, OfficeSupplies.com—then we wouldn't be entering the online space with a wonderful brand and a team of experienced veterans." Kelly realized that such an established infrastructure could enable the dotcom division to quickly ramp up its operations. However, being somewhat familiar with the methodical, highly analytical internal processes at Staples, she wondered if such a degree of integration came with risks in the fast-paced world of Internet retailing.

Creating a Dotcom Culture

As she walked between John Mahoney's and Lewis's offices, Kelly noted that Staples.com was unlike other dotcom offices that she had seen. Staples' expansive corporate offices reflected the success of the parent company and provided the space and logistical support for the Internet unit. Because the web business was so closely linked to the company's core business for merchandising, inventories, delivery, and back office support, Lewis felt it was critical for the dotcom to be in close proximity to these operations and resisted the impulse to move Staples.com off-site. She said, "I need to make sure that we are firmly planted in the midst of this large, multibillion dollar company. We needed to be in the hearts and minds of those we need to be on our side." With this unique relationship, though, came challenges in creating a culture that reflected the entrepreneurial spirit, energy, and creativity of a more typical Internet start-up. For Lewis, the challenge was twofold:

> How do we create a subculture that is meaningful to the type of talent that we want to attract from the outside world? We want to insulate this team in a way that enables a distinct Staples.com culture to grow, but at the same time, we don't want to isolate ourselves from the rest of the organization and not be able to tap into the expertise, the resources, and the knowledge that is the obvious benefit of being part of the larger Staples organization.

Lewis decided to distinguish the Staples.com entity from the parent through the design of its office space. While the imposing façade of the company headquarters was impossible to change, Lewis hoped to inscribe the dotcom's offices with a unique architectural feel. In January 2000, she hired a design team familiar with Internet spaces to create the feeling of an Internet start-up; the team planned a new color scheme, screens on which hourly sales figures could be projected, and perks like free coffee and candy and a game room complete with pool and ping-pong tables. She noted, "It's not just about trying to look like an Internet company, but for us it makes a statement that we're a little different from the rest of the company."

When she considered this distinction that Lewis was trying to create between the dotcom and the other SBUs, Kelly wondered if there might be negative repercussions. Senior management had great expectations for the dotcom division and had committed considerable resources toward establishing its infrastructure. She speculated that the other divisions might view the web division as a "favored child, with access to more money and resources."

Indeed, when forming her management team, Lewis leveraged Staples.com's unique positioning by blending internal and external hires. At its heart, Staples had always been an entrepreneurial company. The new web division provided another new outlet for this energy, and many managers clamored to be a part of it. John Mahoney wryly noted, "Jeanne's had to fight people off more than she's had to lure them into the dotcom. People here have been yearning for those thrilling days of yesteryear." Indeed, all nine direct reports to Jeanne Lewis were experienced Staples managers, although the split between Staples insiders and outside hires became roughly 25/75 at the director and manager levels right below these nine direct reports. Both Lewis and John Mahoney thought it critical that external hires, particularly in the fields of technology and marketing, be brought in to counterbalance the more conservative tendencies of some long-time Staples managers. As John explained,

> We need to have two kinds of people. First, we want people that aren't willing to put up with infrastructure and discipline and just want to get things out on the Web and get things happening. But we also need people who, traditionally, are oriented in favor of bulletproof systems and organization.

Kelly realized, however, that if she signed on with Staples.com, she would be the only external hire directly reporting to Lewis. She knew that Staples Inc., compared with other large corporations, was remarkably innovative and fast-paced; nevertheless, she wondered if the team could adjust to moving at Internet speed. The knowledge that Lewis planned more external hires did much to assuage Kelly's concerns. Such a blend of internal expertise and external technology and marketing expertise would seem to capitalize upon Staples.com's close relationship to its parent and its status as a separate business unit—provided the division could attract scarce Internet talent from outside.

Tracking Stock

On September 15, 1999, the Staples board of directors announced plans to issue a tracking stock for Staples.com, in part to help lure qualified managers and to raise capital to fund marketing plans and potential acquisitions.[4] John Mahoney explained, "Staples is not capital constrained, but we wanted to create a currency that would allow us to attract people who can help us build a successful web business. People are the scarcest resource that we have."

Not only did Staples management have to attract new talent to its web division, it also had to mobilize employees and managers within its core catalog and retail businesses and align their interests with those of the dotcom division. With these units liable to view the dotcom division as a competitor despite the company's integrated approach, management had to ensure cooperation across the SBUs. To Kelly, John explained that the allocation of Staples.com stock options was carefully planned to address this potential concern. He said, "The Staples catalog business may be most immediately cannibalized by Staples.com. So, in their current stock option package, we granted them 60% Staples.com stock, 40% Staples Inc. stock. Everyone that receives stock options will be getting some dotcom shares, though in varying proportions." Store managers that received options annually in Staples stock would also receive some shares in dotcom stock. Though top management had hoped to extend dotcom shares in a higher ratio throughout the company, this raised the risk of over-diluting the dotcom stock. John noted, "We couldn't make the shares go down as far in the organization as you'd like to go with a pure allocation of 75/25. At lower levels, say below the VP level, our goal was to still make it a meaningful and incremental award of dotcom stock options."

In November 1999, as an effort to gain exposure for the tracking stock and to secure advice from knowledgeable outsiders, the company issued a 5% equity stake in Staples.com to five venture capital and private investment firms, including General Atlantic, Highland Capital Partners, and other leading East Coast investment firms. Like many other companies, Staples planned to issue a public offering of the tracking stock sometime during 2000 to take advantage of Wall Street's generous valuations for web companies. Such an offering would accomplish a second critical goal: that of creating a separate set of metrics against which the web division could be evaluated.

By separating the web business from Staples' core business, senior management hoped to create value for their existing shareholders by attracting new investors with different risk preferences—investors who would assign a higher valuation to the prospective cash flows of the Internet operation. They also realized the tracking stock would require additional investment coverage. John Mahoney noted that one of Staples' requirements in selecting a lead investment bank was coverage from a separate Internet analyst. To date, however, signals from the capital markets as to how investors would value the Staples.com stock were unclear. After the announcement of the tracking stock on September 15, Staples' stock price had gone from 21 1/8 to 20 4/5 on December 15, 1999. If she signed on with Staples.com, Kelly would be offered both Staples, Inc. and Staples.com stock options. Would investors and analysts come to understand the reasoning behind the tracking stock? Would the Staples, Inc. stock reflect the firm's opportunities in Internet retailing? If it did not, Kelly was aware that she ran the risk of lower financial remuneration than she might earn if she signed on with a pure-play Internet start-up.

To Join?

Many factors weighed on Kelly's mind as she left Staples headquarters that afternoon. The opportunities seemed enormous for Staples.com, with the high value of their brand, industry experience, and ample capital. In addition, she felt that everyone she had met at Staples was truly committed to making Staples.com an unqualified success. The choice of Jeanne Lewis as president and

[4]Tracking stocks were securities that "tracked" the financial performance of a specific unit within a parent company (e.g., General Motors' "E-" and "H-" class stocks, which tracked its EDS and Hughes subsidiaries, respectively). Tracking stocks maintained separate financial statements and could pay their own dividends. However, from a legal and tax perspective, they were not fully independent. Consequently: (1) for purposes of calculating income taxes, the tracking stock's earnings (or losses) were consolidated with those of the parent company's other operations; and (2) the tracking stock shareholders either had no voting rights or voted with the parent company's shareholders in electing a common board of directors.

CEO of the division increased Kelly's confidence: Lewis was a strong leader with an accomplished track record inside Staples, a formidable work ethic, and the energy to quickly scale up operations.[5] Still, Kelly still had a number of concerns.

With so many close links to its parent, Staples.com did not resemble most other Internet start-ups in 2000. The "clicks-and-mortar" model was largely untested, and Kelly wondered if the division would move fast enough and spend enough money to become a frontrunner in its industry. Would the high level of divisional integration be a help or a hindrance to Staples.com's efforts to get big fast? Could the other divisions, accustomed to rigorous, fact-based analysis and to consensus-based decision processes, adapt to Internet time?

Kelly also had some concerns with the web division's strategy. Their business model was reliant on high-quality service. Could Staples.com continue to deliver such quality service in high growth mode? With so many new customers and new service offerings, could they maintain standards without being directly in control of customer service? In addition, would their customer acquisition and pricing strategies maximize the possibilities of Internet commerce? Was this a bricks-and-mortar company fighting a losing battle—or was this the future of Internet business?

[5]For additional information on Jeanne Lewis, see HBS Cases N9-499-041, *Jeanne Lewis at Staples, Inc. (A)* and *(B)*.

Exhibit 1 KELLY MAHONEY'S RESUME (ABRIDGED)

KELLY A. MAHONEY

Education

1982-1983 **BABSON BUSINESS SCHOOL**

1976-1980 **UNIVERSITY OF MICHIGAN**

Awarded B.A. in General Studies, June 1980.

Experience

1996-1999 **ARNOLD DIRECT COMMUNICATIONS**

(one of the top 15 advertising and communications agencies in the United States, with annual billings in excess of $1 billion)

Chief Marketing Officer:

• Developed marketing strategies for brands including Bell Atlantic, IBM, McDonald's and Volkswagen. Created brand and marketing strategies for pre-IPO businesses, including JuniorNet and Wall Street Journal.com

• Provided clients with B2B and B2C customer optimization programs, leveraging all forms of direct media, including television, print, mail, telephone, and interactive communications

• Spearheaded Arnold Direct new business efforts; increased agency fees by 50% in 1997, exceeding all profitability targets; increased client base by 60% in 1998

1991-1996 **BRONNER SLOSBERG HUMPHREY**

(the third largest direct marketing/customer base management agency in the United States)

Senior Vice President

• Established Teleservices Division, which grew to 50 professionals in three years, with annual billings in excess of $40 million

• Created Business Process Redesign group, focusing on infrastructure development and interactive strategies

• Developed e-commerce strategies for clients including IBM, FedEx, Kraft.com, and AT&T

Exhibit 2 J.P. MORGAN FORECAST FOR STAPLES.COM 1998–2003E($ IN MILLIONS)

	1998	1999E	2000E	2001E	2002E	2003E
Total Revenues	**16.89**	**83.65**	**217.21**	**401.52**	**674.08**	**1,017.26**
Cost of goods sold and occupancy	12.72	64.73	170.98	310.73	508.17	761.80
Gross profit	4.17	18.92	46.24	90.80	165.91	255.47
Operating and selling	2.49	26.74	87.48	103.42	116.33	145.03
General and administrative	2.44	17.06	33.18	44.25	40.59	40.91
Operating Profit	(0.76)	(24.88)	(74.42)	(56.88)	8.99	69.52
Profitability						
Cost of goods sold and occupancy/sales	75.3%	77.4%	78.7%	77.4%	75.4%	74.9%
Gross margin	24.7%	22.6%	21.3%	22.6%	24.6%	25.1%
Operating and selling expense/sales	14.7%	32.0%	40.3%	25.8%	17.3%	14.3%
General and administrative/sales	14.4%	20.4%	15.3%	11.0%	6.0%	4.0%
Operating margin	-4.5%	-29.7%	-34.3%	-14.2%	1.3%	6.8%

Source: Adapted from Danielle Turnof Fox, JP Morgan Equity Research, Dec. 29, 1999

Exhibit 3 J.P. MORGAN FORECAST FOR STAPLES, INC., 1998–2001E ($ IN MILLIONS)

	1998	1999E	2000E	2001E
Revenues				
Retail and Delivery Revenues	7,106	8,824	10,633	12,291
Staples.com Revenues	17	84	217	402
Total Revenues	**7,123**	**8,907**	**10,850**	**12,693**
Retail and Delivery Gross Profit	1,722	2,195	2,663	3,103
Staples.com Gross Profit	4	19	46	91
Total Gross Profit	**1,726**	**2,214**	**2,709**	**3,194**
Retail and Delivery Gross Margin	24.2%	24.9%	25.0%	25.2%
Staples.com Gross Margin	24.7%	22.6%	21.3%	22.6%
Total Gross Margin	**24.2%**	**24.9%**	**25.0%**	**25.2%**
Retail and Delivery Op. Profit	415	555	738	928
Staples.com Op. Profit	(1)	(25)	(74)	(57)
Total Operating Profit	**414**	**530**	**664**	**871**
Retail and Delivery Op. margin	5.8%	6.3%	6.9%	7.6%
Staples.com Op. Margin	-4.5%	-29.7%	-34.3%	-14.2%
Total Operating Margin	**5.8%**	**6.0%**	**6.1%**	**6.9%**

Source: Adapted from Danielle Turnof Fox, JP Morgan Equity Research, Dec. 29, 1999

Exhibit 4

JEANNE LEWIS' INDUSTRY DIAGRAM

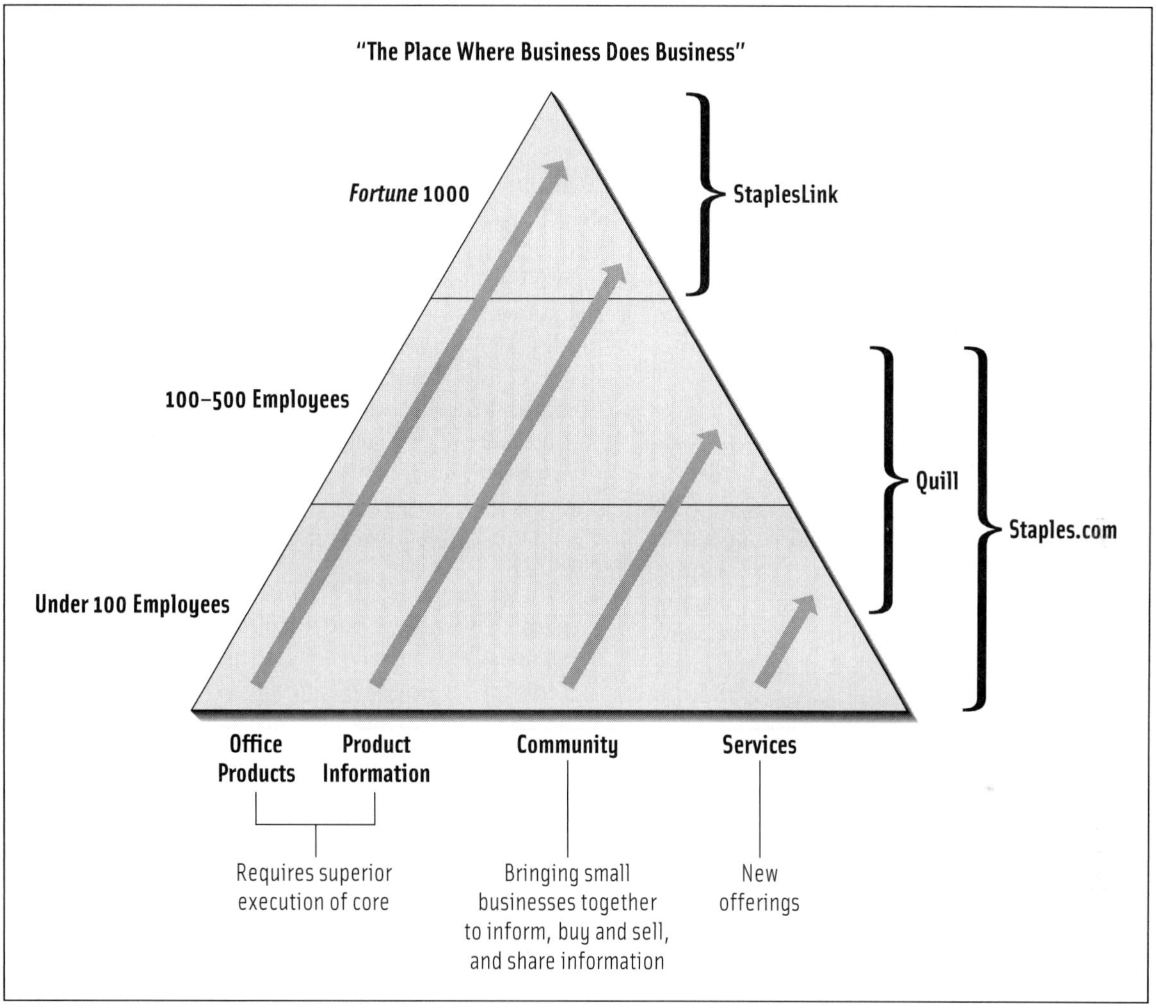

PETSTORE.COM

Dogs drink at the river Nile running along, so that they may not be seized by the crocodiles.

—Phaedrus, 8 A.D., *Fables*

In the fall of 1999, the senior management team of Petstore.com sat in a conference room with their investment bankers, high above Manhattan. The group was debating whether to raise $40 million to fund an aggressive customer acquisition campaign. Just then, a biplane passed close by their conference room window, towing a banner that read, "PETS.COM—SAVE 50% ON DOG FOOD". That fly-by ended any debate over the need for a bigger marketing budget.

Petstore.com was one of the four leading contenders in the hyper-competitive online pet supplies business; the others were Pets.com, PETsMART.com, and Petopia.com (see Exhibit 1 for background on online pet competitors and Exhibits 2, 3 and 4 for excerpts from a Lehman Brothers private placement offering describing Petstore.com's strategy and the pet supply industry). The startups were engaged in a fierce battle for strategic partners, for customers, and for credibility with prospective investors.

Decisions About Strategic Investors

Of freedom and life he only is deserving
Who every day must conquer them anew.

—Johann Wolfgang von Goethe, *Faust*

Petstore.com's strongest competitors all found strategic partners during the spring and summer of 1999. Pets.com received an investment of over $55 million from the venture capital firm Hummer, Winblad and Amazon.com, with Amazon acquiring about 50% of the startup's equity. By promoting Pets.com to its 16 million customers through emails, brochures included with deliveries, and perhaps eventually a tab on its website, Amazon could help Pets.com acquire customers. Next, PETsMART, the leading bricks-and-mortar pet supply retailer, merged its online business with PetJungle.com, a startup backed by Bill Gross's idealab! Finally, Petopia.com, originally funded by Technology Crossover Ventures, received a major equity investment from Petco, the number two bricks-and-mortar chain.

In the face of these moves by competitors, Petstore.com's management team recognized the need to secure strategic partners who could help drive traffic to their website. Josh Newman, CEO and co-founder of Petstore.com, reflected:

> When everybody else started selling half of their company, it was hard not to follow suit, both for good business reasons and to manage capital market perceptions, so we could continue to raise money. There's a laser-like focus on our category; prospective investors are watching to see whether anyone is pulling ahead of the pack or falling behind. The metric used to gauge success has shifted rapidly: in the spring you had to have portal deals to stay in the running; in the summer, it was strategic partners. Now, in the fall, you have to have a big television ad campaign to be seen as viable.
>
> Offline advertising requires at least $5 million: you have to reach a threshold scale to afford that, which is why we all started with online campaigns costing just a few hundred thousand dollars. But in other ways, online advertising is expensive: our acquisition costs with banner ads have averaged in the range of $150 to $200 per new customer, which is what you get with 1% click-through rates and 1% conversion rates. Contrast that to customers acquired at a $20 cost through our partnerships with veterinarians or animal shelters. Frankly, it's too soon to say whether our TV ads will work better, in terms of driving traffic at affordable costs. But even if offline marketing doesn't move the needle in terms of customer acquisition, you could argue that it is perfectly logical as a signal that you are still a strong contender in this race.

Professor Thomas Eisenmann prepared this case as the basis for class discussion rather than to illustrate either effective or ineffective handling of an administrative situation.

> When you make these marketing decisions—whether to advertise or cut prices or offer free shipping, you have to consider the balance sheet value of new customers in addition to their income statement value. In the current market, you could reasonably argue that every additional $1 of revenue this quarter might increase your market capitalization by $300 next quarter.

After discussions with several potential strategic partners, Petstore.com's team narrowed their list of candidates. Their first option was an investment by Discovery Communications, which owned several television programming networks, including its flagship Discovery Channel, which delivered science and nature programming to 76 million U.S. households (see Exhibit 5 for background information on Discovery Communications). Their second option was an investment by a consortium of three companies: another television programming network, a large grocery chain, and a European conglomerate that had assembled a venture capital portfolio.

The deal with Discovery seemed attractive. With a market capitalization estimated at $12 billion,[1] the company had enormous resources. In 1996, Discovery Communications had successfully launched a television programming network focused on pets and wild animals, called Animal Planet, which reached over 50 million U.S. households in 1999. Discovery proposed to invest $92 million in exchange for just over 50% of Petstore.com's equity. Discovery's investment would consist of cash, on-air and online promotion, and a multi-year license of the Animal Planet trademark and the rights to exploit the television network's programming content online. With assistance from managers at Discovery Communications, the Petstore.com team would develop the Animal Planet website into a portal focused on pets and wild animals, with rich content, community and commerce capabilities (Exhibit 6). While the site's branding strategy was not yet settled, it seemed likely that Petstore.com would be preserved as a unique destination site, nested within the Animal Planet site.

The deal with the consortium also seemed attractive: Petstore.com would receive $10 million in cash at a $50 million pre-money valuation, with options for the consortium to expand their investment at a $75 million pre-money valuation by contributing another $8 million in cash plus $26 million worth of promotion by the television network and the grocery chain (which had a "frequent shopper" program with millions of members). After exercising the options, the consortium would own a minority equity stake in Petstore.com.

The choice between these deals was difficult: the Petstore.com management team was split down the middle. Those in favor of the deal with the consortium argued that that Petstore.com would maintain its independence, and that the presence of a financial investor (the European conglomerate) would bring more "rationality" to their Board's deliberations over strategy. In other words, the financial investor would argue for policies that maximized Petstore.com's value, whereas the other strategic partners might favor decisions that met strategic objectives in their core businesses, possibly at the expense of Petstore.com's valuation. The principal downside of the consortium deal was that it would take longer to close than the Discovery investment. According to Furqan Nazeeri, VP-Business Development, "It wasn't a done deal, and negotiating with three partners takes more time. We were acutely aware of the need to close a deal rapidly to maintain our competitive position."

With support from their outside Board members, Petstore.com's management team decided to pursue the deal with Discovery. Newman commented:

> When Pets.com was funded by Amazon, we knew we needed a gorilla. It came down to a choice between three 200 pound gorillas who all brought something different and important to our company, and one 800 pound gorilla, who brought tremendous brand equity and a powerful ability to drive traffic to our site. But at the core, this wasn't a business decision, this was a "Who do we want to be?" decision. In some ways, it became a Faustian bargain: we'll get amazing support from Discovery—they won't let us fail, at least not due to a lack of resources.[2] But this is a big corporation: will they move fast and flexibly enough to let us win this race?

Decisions About Branding

Like a dog, he hunts in dreams.

—Alfred, Lord Tennyson, *Locksley Hall*

After Discovery Communications invested in Petstore.com, the two companies confronted the challenge of integrating their respective online brands. Petstore.com would

[1]Laura Martin, "Discovery Communications, Inc." Credit Suisse Equity Research, September 15, 1999.

[2]Faust sold his soul to the Devil in exchange for a lifetime of fame, fortune and power.

be incorporated into a relaunched Animal Planet website, which would be positioned as a portal for "All Things Animal." Reflecting the television network's programming, the website would focus on pets, wild animals, and wildlife conservation. AnimalPlanet.com would supplement the television network's programming, delving more deeply into topics by providing both original content and links to other Internet sites. Community features such as chats with experts would connect people with a common interest in animals. Finally, the AnimalPlanet.com site would encourage shopping. Pet supplies would be offered, along with animal-themed apparel, travel (e.g., safaris; scuba tours), and toys.

Petstore.com management faced some fundamental decisions in integrating their brand with Animal Planet's. Should they maintain two URLs? Animal Planet already had strong brand equity, whereas Petstore.com had not yet been established as a mass consumer brand. So, did it make economic sense to build and support two separate brands? As an alternative to employing a single URL and brand, Petstore.com might be maintained as a separate pet supplies retailing destination within AnimalPlanet.com, with links to AnimalPlanet.com's pet-related content and community features. Under this approach, Discovery and Petstore.com management would have to decide: 1) whether to redesign the Petstore.com site to closely mirror the "look-and-feel" of the AnimalPlanet.com site; and 2) whether to aggressively promote the Petstore.com site independently of AnimalPlanet.com.

The Animal Planet website, in turn, would be nested within the Discovery Online umbrella site, which would provide tabs leading to other vertical destination sites related to the various properties owned by Discovery Communications, including the Discovery Channel, The Travel Channel, and Discovery Health. Petstore.com management anticipated that the AnimalPlanet.com site would receive considerable traffic from the other Discovery Online vertical sites, but also saw some potential for overlap between the sites. Specifically, the animal-themed travel packages and the advice from veterinarians that AnimalPlanet.com planned to offer might overlap with commerce and content offered by sites related to the Travel Channel and Discovery Health, respectively. Newman was concerned that consumer confusion about the various sites' product offerings would be exacerbated by the ubiquitous presence of a Discovery Online "top hat", a one-half inch strip of tabs to other Discovery Online vertical sites that ran across the top of every page within each site. Would pet owners looking for veterinary advice click on the 'Health' tab by mistake? Would potential Petstore.com customers be confused by the top-hat's 'Shopping' tab, which linked to an online retailing site for the products offered by Discovery's 120 bricks-and-mortar retail stores (including its mall-based Nature Company stores)? Newman noted that other companies that managed networks of multiple websites, e.g., Disney and Microsoft, did not brand their umbrella networks so strongly, nor did they give such prominence to navigational aides that linked their sites to each other. Jeff Luhnow, the Petstore.com executive in charge of the AnimalPlanet.com site, said, "The Discovery Online tag line is, 'Adventures for Everyday Living.' Should that message be front-and-center on every page of a site that sells dog food?"

Andy Sharpless, SVP of Discovery Interactive and one of four Discovery representatives on the seven-member Petstore.com Board of Directors, acknowledged these concerns, but said:

> If users are confused by the top hat, they'll learn after their first mistake. Maybe they'll even find something else of interest to them. The fact is, the verticals will have a lot of freedom within our network framework. They'll control the entire left side of each page—that's the most important real estate, where consumers look for navigational aides. Each of our verticals has concerns about leakage, but leakage works in two directions—that's really the point of the umbrella site! Verticals like Petstore.com will benefit greatly from being part of our network, from the loyalty of Discovery Channel's core audience, and from the fact that there will be a Discovery-endorsed pet supply site.

Sharpless raised another branding issue:

> Our Board has made a commitment to a big on-air campaign promoting our Internet properties across all of our television networks. We've got to decide whether to promote only the Discovery Online brand, or whether to also promote our individual vertical sites. Do you drive people to the umbrella site first, then let them discover what's there? Or do you drive them to the vertical that's most relevant for them, then hope they'll link to the rest of our sites? The latter approach may make sense for the commerce sites like Petstore, where on-air promotion can be a call-to-action, leading directly to sales.

Conclusion

The pet category is an embarrassment to humanity. Keep an eye out for crash and burns. They will come in the B-to-C market in the next six to twelve months. There is just too much trash in this sector.

—Geoffrey Moore, Venture Partner, Mohr, Davidow Ventures[3]

On December 9, 1999, Pets.com filed an S-1 with the Securities and Exchange Commission, the first step toward a Merrill Lynch-led IPO that was likely to occur during the first quarter of 2000. Pets.com's filing increased the pressure on Petstore.com's management team: perceptions could shape reality in the hyper-competitive online pet supply business, and as the first publicly-traded competitor, Pets.com might be perceived as the emerging category leader. As he and his colleagues debated a range of marketing decisions, Josh Newman reflected on the online pet supply category and on the opportunities facing Petstore.com:

> Sure, this is a demanding category. Look at the execution challenges: in just a year, we've had to figure a thousand things out. How do you do gift wrapping? Is it really important to give consumers the choice of using FedEx versus UPS versus USPS? When one item out of seven is backordered, do you ship the rest? And look at the competition. We understand that when Pets.com tried to build support for an IPO earlier in 1999, investment bankers were skeptical. They said, 'Added together, the top two bricks-and-mortar chains in this category have a market cap of less than $750 million, but the four online startups are planning IPOs that will yield a projected $4 billion in total market value.' If you have a "glass half empty" view of this business, that can't work.
>
> But we have a "glass half full" view. The pet supply category is bigger than books or toys or music and videos. And it has higher gross margins than those businesses. With a strong need for replenishment, we're already seeing very high reorder rates. The logistics are tough to work out: it's expensive to ship forty-pound bags of pet food. But this can be a terrific, profitable business if you reach a scale where you can lower your shipping costs by having five or six distribution facilities nationwide and if you can maintain gross margins at or above 30%.

[3]Carol Picketing, "Choking on Cash," *Business 2.0*, January 2000,page 64.

Exhibit 1

EXCERPT FROM PETSTORE.COM INVESTOR PRESENTATION

How Will We Beat the Competition?

Criteria	AnimalPlanet.com: Animal Planet	AnimalPlanet.com: Petstore.com	Pets.com (Amazon)	PETsMART.com (PETsMART)	Petopia.com (Petco)	Ranking
Brand	Strongest all-animal media brand available 60% of programming is pet related URL piggy-backs on brand	No Brand yet Positioning (Expertise) is the strongest URL is the strongest	No Brand yet (not piggy-backing on Amazon) "Convenience" message is not distinctive URL confuses some	Has Brand Equity Superstore positioning, with low expertise URL is good	No Brand Yet "Internet Pet Paradise" URL is difficult to spell & remember	**#1: Animal Planet / Petstore** **#2: PETsMART.com**
Customer Acquisition	53 million subscribers 100 retail stores Discovery.com 1.8MM uniques / month	30 million Safeway frequent buyers 21 million AAHA customers $43 million of Discovery media	12 million Amazon customers	~ 6 million PETsMART frequent buyers	~ 4 million Petco frequent buyers	**Next 6 Months: #1: Pets.com** **Next 6-18 Months: #1: Animal Planet / Petstore**
The Site	Current Site is placeholder USWeb doing 1.x launch for 2/28 2.0 Relaunch in June Deep content from broadcast assets Media personalities are strongest	Most skus (pet supplies + fish + APL Licensed Products) Easiest Shopping (<4 to buy) Best Aesthetics 20 Experts Branded AAHA content	Good Skus Up to 10 clicks to buy Mediocre look and feel 2 experts Unbranded content	Good Skus (except no 40# dog food) Good shopping engine Mediocre look and feel Minimal experts Unbranded content	Good Skus Ok shopping engine Nice Cartoon Look Some Experts Good Content	**#1: Petstore** **#2: Petopia**
Current Metrics	One page within Discovery.com site that receives 1.8 million uniques / month	Probably #1 or #2 in revenue (because of Flying Fish) # 1 in product margin #4 in unique visitors (advertising just started)	Probably #3 is revenue Low product margin from heavy discounting #2 in unique visitors	Probably #1 in revenues Low product margin from heavy discounting #1 in unique visitors	Probably #4 in revenue Low product margin from heavy discounting # 3 in unique visitors	**#1: PETsMART** **#2: Petstore or Pets**
Fulfillment	Existing catolog operation 3 DC's for 100 retail stores (check data!)	Cost + 0% Supply Agreement from S&S Supplies 130,000 sq. ft. DC Yantra WHS supports 5 DC's and 200 drop-ship vendors	180,000 sq. ft. DC	~$2 Billion purchasing power 5 DC's support 500 retail stores Existing catalog operation	Currently using midwest distributor Probably switching to Petco	**# 1: PETsMART**
Customer Service	n/a	40 Seat internal call center	Outsourced	Outsourced	Outsourced	**#1: Petstore**
Overall Ranking						**#1: Animal Planet / Petstore** **#2: Pets.com (Amazon)**

PETSTORE.COM CONFIDENTIAL
5/16/00 5:13 PM

Page 10

Petstore.com

Exhibit 2 EXECUTIVE SUMMARY OF AUGUST 1999 PETSTORE.COM PRIVATE PLACEMENT MEMORANDUM

Overview

Petstore.com is a leading online retailer of pet food, supplies and related products. The Company was the first major online retailer to sell a full line of pet food and supplies and has continued to demonstrate leadership through the addition of pet related gift and novelty products and the largest range of tropical fish in the United States. The Company has an exclusive strategic relationship with the American Animal Hospital Association (AAHA), an umbrella organization of 6,510 veterinarian clinics serving 21 million customers across the United States. The Company is working with AAHA veterinarians to drive traffic to Petstore.com. The Company's version 2.0 web site is due to be launched in October 1999 and the development timetable is on track. The Company believes that its version 2.0 web site will be the most functional of the online pet retailing sites, integrating content and commerce in a way that will redefine the online consumer experience. In recent survey by Gomez Advisors (www.Gomez.com), Petstore.com ranked first of all online pet retailers for relationship services, and ranked third overall.

The online pet food, supplies and related gift and novelty market is extremely attractive with an estimated size of $3 million–$6 billion in 2002 and average gross product margins in the 37%–43% range. To date, no competitor has captured broad public awareness, creating an opportunity for Petstore.com to translate its operational leadership into brand and category dominance.

Petstore.com's approach to the market is highly differentiated. The Company offers a high quality product selection, which is broader than that available at traditional and online pet superstores. The Company's product merchandising approach avoids displaying thousands of products in long catalog lists which would overwhelm consumers. Rather, consumers are offered complete solutions to their pet care needs. This is accomplished by first identifying the major problems that pet owners face and then providing authoritative content that explains the most appropriate solution, and most importantly, featuring a product bundle for convenient one-click purchasing. The Company avoids the impersonal feel of a superstore by humanizing its website with online expert personalities. Currently the Company has six veterinary and animal experts that answer e-mail questions, and will soon add more experts such as animal behavior specialists from leading animal shelters, product specialists and health specialists. The version 2.0 website will further personalize the shopping experience through a "My Petstore" feature, which will allow customers to tailor the product and content offerings based on their pet type and interests.

In addition to its exclusive relationship with AAHA, the Company has, and is continuing to establish, exclusive relationships with other "influencer" groups such as animal rescue shelters and breeders. The Company's online marketing campaign began in May 1999 and has continued with a focus on high traffic, strategic portal sites with exclusive or semi-exclusive agreements. The Company has also established permission marketing and public relations campaigns, and has planned a comprehensive offline campaign to be launched in October 1999. The Company's affiliate program has proved to be very successful to date, with close to 5,000 affiliates.

The Company was founded by a deeply committed and talented management team with strong industry and functional area experience including one co-founder who previously founded and ran the dominant chain of pet retail stores in the City of San Francisco.

The Company has a turnkey operation in a 17,000-square-foot facility near Oakland, California, with a staff of 95 people. The operation includes all engineering, marketing, web operations, executive and administrative functions. It also houses a 10-seat, 7-day customer service call center, and a semi-automated distribution center where 5,000 current products are inventoried and picked, packed and shipped. Having all operations under one roof helps the Company create the highest quality customer experience and to move extremely rapidly on projects that require cross-functional coordination.

The Company is backed by Battery Ventures and Advanced Technology Ventures, who contributed $9 million during a Series A Preferred Stock financing in April 1999.

Progress to Date

The Company's e-commerce store (http://www.petstore.com) has achieved substantial financial progress since its launch in May 1999, just weeks after receiving venture funding. Revenues to date in August 1999 show an annual run-rate of approximately $3 million with a gross margin of 52%.

The business is growing at a high rate, with orders increasing from 178 in May to 1,590 in July, and projected orders in August of 2,647. Average order size in July was over $32, and projected average order size in August is approximately $57 (including an average order size of $196 for Flying Fish Express). Further, the website has generated tremendous traffic growth over its first three months of operations, rising from 64,032 site visitors in May 1999 to a projected 488,000 visitors in August 1999.

In addition to this rapid growth, customer response has been extremely positive. In follow-up calls to customers who have received orders, 99% of customers said they were satisfied with the experience, 92% reported that their order arrived when they expected it; 98% indicated that their order was correct; and 99% reported that their order arrived in good condition. This customer satisfaction is already translating into customer loyalty. Twenty-five percent of August's orders are projected to be from repeat buyers, up from 12% in July.

The Company has a track record of leading the market with key innovations. Of the major pet supply competitors, Petstore.com was the first to offer dog and cat food online, the first to offer subscription food service, the first to build a complete store with in-house fulfillment, the first to deploy a customer newsletter, the first to deploy a customer loyalty program, and with the recent acquisition of Flying Fish Express, the first to offer aquatic livestock online. Moreover, the Company was the first to launch a robust affiliates program, and cogently has close to 5,000 affiliates generating some 5% to 10% of daily order volume.

With the scheduled October 1999 launch of its version 2.0 website, Petstore.com intends to establish a leadership position through several innovations. This site will feature a completely new look and feel and a user interface developed by the same team that designed the Levi.com and Apple.com websites. The 2.0 site will be the first to offer consumers solution based product bundles and will continue to humanize the online shopping experience through a broad array of experts and be the first to offer high margin extended category stores including, for example, a travel store, a shelter store, and partner stores.

Exhibit 2 EXECUTIVE SUMMARY OF AUGUST 1999 PETSTORE.COM PRIVATE PLACEMENT MEMORANDUM cont.

The 2.0 website will also have innovative back-end systems that support "best in breed" features. From the customers' perspective, the new site will feature one-click to buy, cross-sell and up-sell product suggestions, product comparison engines, user reviews, loyalty and rewards programs and special promotions. From the back-end perspective, the site will have a state-of-the-art warehouse management system that supports electronic interchange with up to 200 drop-ship vendors and real-time decision-algorithms for fulfillment out of multiple stocking distribution centers.

The Company has also secured a number of key strategic relationships. The Company has an exclusive partnership with the AAHA that includes exclusive use of the AAHA brand, authoritative pet care content, and off-line customer acquisition through AAHA clinics. Petstore.com also has an exclusive relationship with two large animal shelters and is currently negotiating with several other large animal shelters and national clubs. For online customer acquisition, the Company has exclusive or semi-exclusive deals with Yahoo!, Lycos, AOL.com, Women.com, Looksmart and SpringStreet.

Petstore.com considers its vendors as key strategic partners. On the supply side, the owner of S&S Supplies, a distributor of 14,000 nonfood pet products, made an equity investment in the Company and S&S Supplies sells all goods to the Company at fully-burdened cost. For off-line advertising, the Company works with Black Rocket, which is the lead creative agency for Yahoo!, Discover Brokerage, and Buy.com. Petstore.com also recently acquired Flying Fish Express, an online retailer of tropical fish with over 2,000 SKUs and 1998 revenues of more than $750,000. Petstore.com will soon offer Flying Fish merchandise on its website.

The Company has all the ingredients necessary to dominate the important holiday selling period. It has a proven economic model of acquiring high-margin and loyal customers, a version 2.0 website with leapfrog innovations, a national advertising campaign ready to launch, and the infrastructure to handle growth.

Market Opportunity

According to the American Pet Products Manufacturers Association (APPMA), 61% of U.S. households own at least one pet. The pet food, pet supplies, equine products and gift/novelty market, fueled by growth in the pet population and the trend towards better pet care, is expected to generate $27.4 billion in U.S. sales in 1999, made up by a $12.1 billion pet food market, a $4.5 billion pet supplies market, a $8.3 billion equine products market and a $2.5 billion pet-related gift and novelty market. The pet market offers attractive product margins, with blended margins of pet food and supplies retailers in the 37%–43% range.

The Company estimates the total value of online pet food and supplies retailing to be in the $3–$6 billion range, representing approximately 10% to 20% of the total pet food and supplies market in five years. The pet food and supplies market size appears to compare favorably with other e-commerce categories that have been successful e-tailing concepts, including software, books, music CDs and flowers (see Figure 13). Forrester Research projects online sales in these categories to gain significant market share, representing up to 25% of their respective markets by 2003.

Strategy

The Company's goal is to become the dominant provider of pet products and services over the Internet. To accomplish this goal, the Company has adopted the following strategic objectives:

- *Offer Complete Pet Care Solutions to Customer Needs.* Petstore.com's commerce strategy is to offer value-added content and merchandising that will help customers solve specific pet care problems, by pre-screening products, offering an editorial perspective on its products and developing an extensive set of custom product bundles to address specific needs, such as starter and adoption kits. The Company also has a proprietary on-line comparison feature that will allow customers to compare products across brands and key criteria (e.g., nutritional content or price). Finally, the Company is building out its offering of related categories such as aquatic livestock, gift/novelty, equine products, books, videos and toys.
- *Provide a Superior Customer Experience.* The Company strives to provide a superior customer experience through the ease of use of its website design, layout, navigation and order processing; high level of customer service; innovative technology and personalized service.
- *Build Strong Brand Recognition.* Petstore.com's strategy is to increase its brand equity and visibility through a superior customer experience and a variety of advertising and promotional activities, including: (i) online marketing efforts through exclusive or semi-exclusive relationships with major portals such as Yahoo! and Lycos, as well as with more targeted websites such as Women.com and SpringStreet; (ii) close to 5,000 affiliate program websites; (iii) communicating with current customers through opt-in e-mail; (iv) its planned Fall off-line advertising launch in the top 20 Internet-penetrated markets; (v) an ongoing public relations campaign; and (vi) strategic alliances, such as its relationship with the AAHA.
- *Strengthen and Expand Strategic Partnerships.* One of the Company's top priorities is to align with the key "influencers" of the pet food and product spending decision, including veterinarians, animal shelters, breeders, groomers and umbrella organizations such as the ASPCA. Recognizing that rapid expansion can be accomplished by acquiring companies that have already built a comprehensive inventory as well as a devoted customer base, the Company is continually examining additional strategic acquisitions and relationships with complementary businesses.
- *Build a Sustainable Business Model.* The Company is focused not only on acquiring customers, but on managing those customers to profitability by migrating customers from lower margin (food) products to higher margin supplies and gift and novelty items though one-to-one marketing techniques afforded by the Internet.

Exhibit 2 EXECUTIVE SUMMARY OF AUGUST 1999 PETSTORE.COM PRIVATE PLACEMENT MEMORANDUM cont.

- *Maintain Technical Leadership.* With the upcoming release of version 2.0 of the Company's website, Petstore.com will implement a robust e-commerce back end supported by Fort Point (front-end architecture), Yantra (fulfillment) and Great Plains (accounting). Beyond the initial release of version 2.0, the Company will make continuous improvements to the look and feel and functionality of the on-line store and the efficiency of its fulfillment services.

Online Store

Petstore.com's online store is a single place where pet owners can come to get expert care, authoritative advice, and assistance in selecting the right products for the animals they love. The Company currently offers over 5,000 pet food and supplies SKUs with plans to offer over 8,000 by mid-fall. Petstore.com stocks a wide variety of dog and cat foods in all size packages at competitive prices, emphasizing premium brands that are generally not available to customers in supermarkets or mass merchandisers due to manufacturers' restrictions. The Company also sells dozens of specialty pet foods for all other companion animals at competitive prices. In addition, Petstore.com offers a complete selection of pet supplies including collars/leashes, dishes/feeders, grooming tools, flea & tick control, litter, toys, carriers/crates and chews. Through its recent acquisition of Flying Fish Express, Petstore.com has become the largest online retailer of tropical saltwater fish in the United States, carrying more than 2,000 SKUs of aquatic livestock. In the future, gift and novelty items will account for a growing proportion of the Company's products.

The Company's emphasis on commerce has resulted in an easily navigable website, where a customer can purchase a product within a few clicks. Alternatively, Petstore.com's subscription service allows pet owners to automatically receive a set amount of food, litter and other supplies at their home on a regular basis as they determine. The Company ships all orders via UPS. Currently 80% of orders are shipped same day or next day. All orders under 50 pounds cost just $4.95 for delivery, with an additional $4.95 charge for each additional 25 pounds.

Petstore.com also provides a variety of pet-related content to enrich the customer's shopping experience, including: *Experts on Call,* featured articles, care guides, and seasonal/promotional topics such as a flea and tick or travel section. The Company's version 2.0 website will include additional content such as a pet selector, pet training modules, starter guides, common problem solution guides, a guide to adopting pets and a *Just for Kids* section.

The Company's community plan includes creating discussion forums on a variety of topics, publishing customer stories and photos of their pets, creating pictures and messages that visitors can send to friends, and hosting live discussions with animal health experts, behaviorists and writers.

Management Team

Petstore.com has a talented and experienced management team, which has relevant experience across all functional areas of the Company's operations. Management's background includes 25 years of collective experience in pet food and supplies retailing and significant start-up seasoning, with the four co-founders having started more than 10 companies among them. Further, the team has meaningful experience in Internet marketing, brand management, customer service, Web operations, fulfillment and IT. Selected management team profiles are as follows:

Mr. Joshua Newman–President and CEO	Former CEO and Managing Director of Amerigon, Inc. and VP of Sales and Marketing at Delta Three, Inc. Harvard MBA.
Mr. Chris Luhnow–SVP, Corporate Development	Former President and CEO of Flightways Manufacturing, Inc. Wharton MBA.
Mr. Brian Sherman–Vice President, Merchandising	A founder of Sammy's Pet World, the largest petstore chain in San Francisco. Stanford MBA.
Mr. Mark Reilly–Vice President, Inventory Management	Former VP of Inventory Control and Merchandising Planning at Petco, Inc. Stanford MBA.

Source: Petstore.com

Exhibit 3

ADDENDUM TO PETSTORE.COM PRIVATE PLACEMENT MEMORANDUM

PETSTORE.COM
ADDENDUM TO THE AUGUST 1999 PRIVATE PLACEMENT MEMORANDUM
NOVEMBER 29, 1999

Executive Summary

Petstore.com (the "Company") is the leading provider of pet products and supplies on-line. Since August 1999, the Company has made substantial progress including: completing two transformational strategic partnerships, launching its second generation website in conjunction with a national brand building campaign, and building the infrastructure necessary to support its rapid growth. Today, Petstore.com is not only positioned at the forefront of the "pet wars," but will also be the first to launch a world class animal theme destination site.

In October 1999, the Company entered into a major strategic partnership with Discovery Communications Inc. ("DCI"), the global media company and creator of the Animal Planet cable channel. Animal Planet is the leading, branded "all animal" 24-hour cable channel, with 53 million subscribers in the U.S., and proprietary rights to *Lassie, The Crocodile Hunter, Emergency Vets, Judge Wopner's Animal Court* and other pet-centric shows. Animal Planet is the #1 animal related brand with a wide variety of compelling programming for people interested in animals, including pet related shows, personality driven adventure programming, real life drama, sports and comedy. As part of the partnership arrangement, DCI contributed $92 million in cash, promotion and a long-term license to the online Animal Planet brand (including the URL "animalplanet.com," animal planet content and customer data).

This partnership between Petstore.com and Discovery provides an opportunity for the Company to create a new but related business that has unlimited potential: to build a world class animal theme destination on the World Wide Web for animal lovers and enthusiasts. The destination site will integrate shopping and entertainment around a common theme of "all things animal." The site will feature a robust animal related shopping component including pet e-commerce, adventure travel, toys, books and more. The total estimated market size for these categories is in excess of $39 billion in the US and an order of magnitude larger internationally.

Operationally, Petstore.com will manage the Animalplanet.com site design and implementation utilizing internal resources, external vendors and a 7-person dedicated team at DCI. In November the Company retained USWeb/CKS and initiated development work on the site with a scheduled re-launch in March 2000. The initial re-launch will integrate the look-and-feel of the current Petstore.com site with the broader vision of animal related content, community and commerce.

The Company has also formed a strategic marketing alliance with Safeway Inc., one of the nations largest grocery and drug retail chains. With over 1,650 retail stores, 30 million Safeway Club Card members and over $25 billion in annual sales, Safeway brings marketing, purchasing and fulfillment expertise unparalleled in the online pet category. As part of the alliance, Safeway will provide $11 million in cash and promotion and a commitment to deliver 500,000 new customers to Petstore.com within 24 months through promotion in its bricks-and-mortar stores, direct mail, print, radio, TV and online advertising. Safeway and the Company are also in the process of negotiating additional alliances and relationships in the areas of purchasing, distribution and fulfillment.

In early November 1999, the Company launched a redesigned website after a six month, multi-million dollar development effort. The new site integrates over 1000 pages of relevant content with expert advice from more than 20 animal behaviorists, veterinarians and product experts. The merchandise is presented in a way that makes it easy to navigate through the 7,000 plus product assortment. There are a number of theme mini-stores, over twenty "solution bundles" intended to address specific customer needs, and shopping features, including a sort capability, that make it easy to find desired products quickly. The site is designed to be intuitive for first time visitors and familiar and efficient for repeat customers. All of this results in a shopping experience that is differentiated from the competition and clearly communicates the company's brand identity while placing Petstore.com in an elite group of world class e-commerce companies. Extensive user testing and feedback to date has been extremely positive.

To support the launch of the redesigned site, the company launched a $15 million national TV, radio, and print advertising campaign. The television campaign, currently airing in New York, San Francisco, and eight other wired markets, features a collection of six ads, all shot in black and white, which feature people and pets in familiar, sometimes funny, situations. The tag line, "Hey, we know" communicates the brand message that Petstore.com understands the depth of the relationship between people and their pets.

Finally, to support existing and expected growth, the Company continues to invest heavily in infrastructure. Petstore.com recently opened a 130,000 square foot warehouse and fulfillment center in San Leandro, CA that currently stocks over 7,000 products and is capable of shipping in excess of 5,000 customer orders per day. The Company also opened a new 40-seat call center which is housed in a 5,000 square foot facility in Emeryville, CA. Finally, the Company re-located its "Flying Fish Operations" into a new 5,000 square foot facility in Inglewood, CA.

From inception through October, the Company has booked $1,050,621 in cumulative revenue with $361,109 and $452,009 in September and October respectively, while gross product margin remained steady at approximately 41%. In addition, Flying Fish Express revenues (from sales of live tropical fish) are up over 25% since its purchase in August. In October, the website generated almost 1 million site sessions and a conversion rate of approximately 1% with 40% of orders from repeat customers. At the end of October, the Company employed approximately 150 full-time equivalent employees.

Source: Petstore.com

Exhibit 4

INDUSTRY OVERVIEW

The Pet Food Segment

Retail pet food constitutes a $12.1 billion market in the U.S. in 1999. Of this, dog food represents approximately 52% and cat food 40%. Premium pet foods constitute approximately 30% of the total food market as follows:

U.S. Pet Food Market 1999 ($ billions)

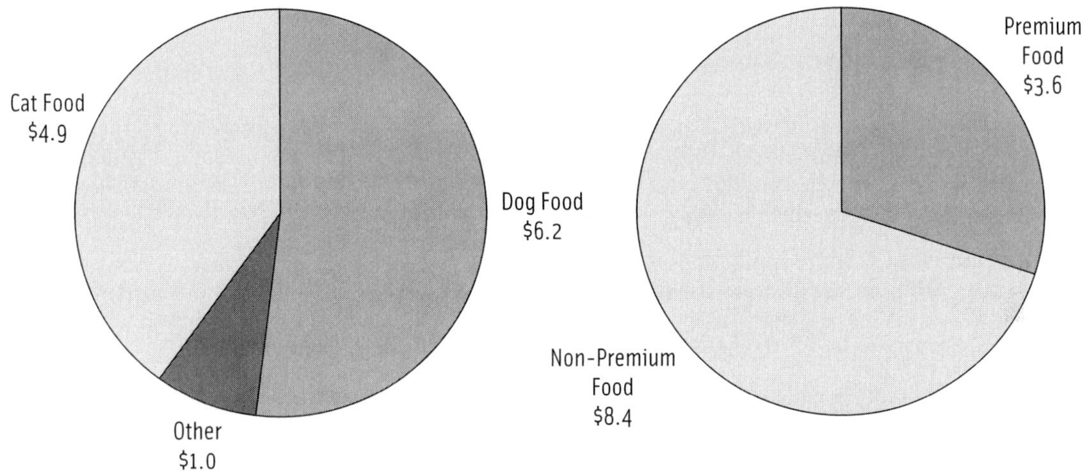

Source: Adapted by Petstore.com from Wall Street Research, Business Trends Analysts

While the overall pet food market is projected to grow at approximately 4.6% per annum through 2002, the premium pet food market is predicted to continue growing at a faster rate (approximately 15%) as consumers become increasingly aware of the benefits that diet can play in the health of pets. Premium pet foods carry higher margins (approximately 20%–25%) than non-premium foods (approximately 15%–20%).

There are three primary channels through which pet food is sold in the U.S.: pet specialty stores, supermarkets and mass merchandisers, and veterinarians. Pet specialty stores sell the vast majority of premium foods due to channel restrictions imposed by manufacturers, which require superior service levels and a knowledgeable staff who can educate customers as to the benefits of premium food. Supermarkets and mass merchandisers carry a limited range of non-premium food. The third pet food channel is veterinary clinics. Veterinarians can prescribe therapeutic foods and supplements that are not available through pet specialty stores or mass merchandisers. Generally, veterinary clinics offer pet food as a convenience for their customers and have a limited product offering. Moreover, they typically lose money through these sales.

The Pet Supplies Segment

The U.S. pet supplies market is estimated at $4.5 billion in 1999. This market consists of thousands of products that are often categorized in terms of the pets that they serve. The major categories of companion pets are dogs, cats, fish, birds, small animals and reptiles/amphibians. The major products are cat litter, dog/cat supplies, non dog/cat pet supplies and rawhide chews. Pricing is generally not as competitive for supplies as it is for pet food, since purchases tend to be impulse buys by customers making their regular purchases of consumables. As a result, supplies carry margins in the 50% range. The channels of distribution for pet supplies are highly fragmented with products sold by many types of retailers, including specialty pet stores, supermarkets, mass merchandisers, direct mail houses and veterinarians.

Exhibit 4 INDUSTRY OVERVIEW cont.

Major Retail Players

Traditional pet stores. The retail pet food and supplies market has historically been dominated by small family-run businesses. Pet owners in need of pet care and feeding advice, often relied on personalized advice and service offered by the staff of small pet stores which spent years building relationships with their customers and had consequently flourished. Over the past ten years, however, the position of these independent pet stores has been challenged by the emergence of pet "superstores" that offer more competitive pricing and a larger product selection. More recently, the independents have begun to see a return of their customer base due to the disappointing experience in most pet superstores.

Pet superstores. These large chain stores include market leaders PETsMART and Petco, which hold approximately 7% and 3% market shares, respectively, with respective LTM revenues of $2.1 billion and $840 million. These market shares, while large, do not translate into domination of the category, which remains highly fragmented. These retailers typically derive a considerable portion of their revenues from premium food products (approximately 20% - 25% of sales at PETsMART). Research by the APPMA suggests that the consumer experience at chain stores is considerably less pleasing than at the traditional independent pet retailers. The Company believes that these results are due to the lack of well-trained and knowledgeable staff, the lack of real customer relationships and the large crowds found at these stores.

Supermarket and mass merchandisers. Supermarket and mass merchandisers such as Wal-Mart and Kmart carry a limited range of non-premium food and supplies. While these outlets have historically captured the greatest share of dog and cat food sales, that market leadership is currently being eroded as consumers increasingly turn to premium pet food products.

Other. Other players include catalog companies, drug stores and hardware/garden stores.

1998 Retail Sales of Pet Food and Supplies by Channel

Sales of pet food and supplies by retail channel during 1998 were as follows:

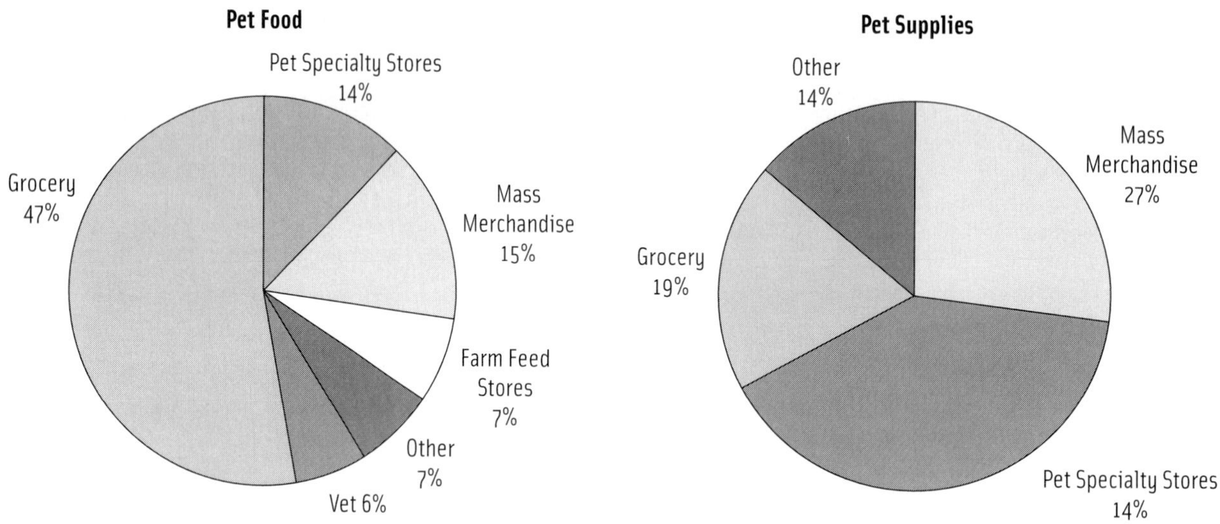

Source: Adapted by Petstore.com from Maxwell Report, 1988 and Kalorama Information, LLC.

Exhibit 4 INDUSTRY OVERVIEW cont.

Retail Margins

Substantial Margins. The blended gross product margin for pet food and supplies retailers ranges from 37%–43%. On the low-margin end are bulk food and litter products which typically carry margins in the 15%–20% range and account for approximately one-third of total revenue. Premium foods have a higher margin of approximately 20%–25%. Pet supplies and accessories carry higher margins at 40%–60%. The highest margin products are in the gift and novelty area, as well as aquatic livestock with gross margins as high as 70%.

Price Sensitivity. The Company believes that consumer price sensitivity varies by product category as follows:

- Key items–Approximately 100 items with respect to which customers are highly price sensitive and which shape the retailer's price image in the eyes of the consumer. Examples include large size dry dog and cat food and all sizes of canned dog and cat food.
- Highly shopped items–Approximately 700 items with respect to which customers are somewhat price sensitive and might engage in comparison shopping. Products include smaller size dry foods, other consumable items and high retail ticket items.
- "Blind items"–All other items. These items are generally priced based on a target margin for the relevant category and are not comparison shopped. Products include leashes, toys and other low-ticket items that are typically impulse purchases.

The higher volume, low-margin products tend to be distributed through the supermarkets and mass merchandisers, whereas the high-margin, lower-volume products tend to be distributed through the veterinarians and pet specialty stores (see Figure 14 below). Product margins also correlate positively with the level of involvement required to make a purchase. On the one hand, dog food and cat litter are easy purchases to make, whereas veterinary prescribed therapeutic diets are a very high involvement purchase that requires expert consultation and a special trip prior to making a decision.

Product Comparison by Gross Margin and Retail Distribution Channel

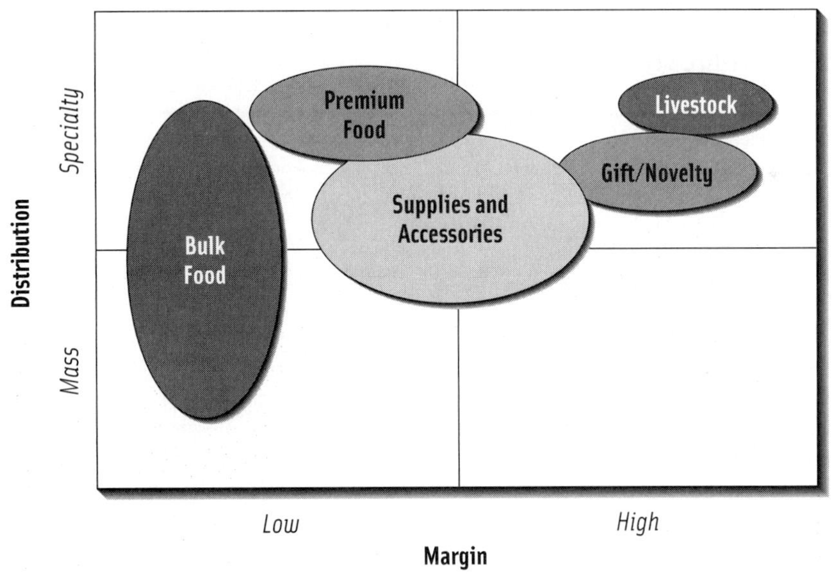

Note: Size of bubble indicates relative category revenue.
Source: Company estimates.

Distributors

Distribution in the pet food and supplies industry is fragmented, consisting of one national pet food and supplies distributor, Central Garden & Pet Company, six super-regional distributors, and many smaller distributors concentrated in local geographic regions. Premium foods are often distributed directly by the manufacturer (e.g., IAMS, Hills/Science Diet). The major distributors of other food and non-food supplies in Northern California are Central Garden and Pet, Western Farm Center, and S&S Supplies.

Manufacturers

U.S. pet food manufacturing is dominated by the "big four" companies Ralston Purina, Nestle, Heinz and Mars. Together, these four companies comprise almost 50% of the overall market, with 17%, 12%, 11% and 9% market shares, respectively. The five largest premium food manufacturers are Hills (Science Diet), Iams, Nutro, Ralston Purina (Pro Plan), and Heinz (Nature's Recipe). Hills and Iams have the largest share and have roughly equal shares of this market (Iams was recently acquired by Proctor & Gamble). Nutro and Ralston Purina have approximately equal shares which are less than one half of Hills/Iams market shares. Heinz is the next largest with a substantially lower market share. There are also many niche brands in this market segment.

The Hartz Mountain Corporation has the largest market share of non-food pet supplies overall and a major share in most individual product categories. There are over 2,000 companies competing in the highly fragmented pet supplies and accessories market. Market leaders in individual categories are: Ralston Purina in cat litter, Doskocil in dog and cat shelters, Warner Lambert in fish supplies and Harper Leather Goods in rawhide chews.

The Equine Products Industry

The equine industry is a mature industry with limited growth opportunity. However, it is a sizable, affluent market that has four main categories of consumers that include Performance (racing/trotters), Show, Working/Ranch, and Pleasure. The Company believes the U.S. horse population has remained relatively constant over the last decade. The largest distributor of equine products in the U.S. is Bradley Caldwell, which distributes to 22 States. The largest retailer of equine products in the U.S. is State Line Tack, a catalog operation owned by PETsMART.

The Pet Related Gift & Novelty Industry

The Company believes that pet owners are heavy consumers of gift and novelty items related to their pets. The Company further believes that consumers desire additional opportunities to purchase pet related gift and novelty items. The gift and novelty industry is extremely fragmented. The Company plans to offer items in two main categories. The first and largest component will be pet related items for use by people rather than by pets. This category includes items such as pet motif clothing, photo frames, coffee mugs, animal figurines, etc. The second category of items will be very high-end items for pets such as jeweled collars, precious metal pet ID tags and high-end pet furniture.

Source: Petstore.com

Exhibit 5 EXCERPTS FROM CREDIT SUISSE/FIRST BOSTON REPORT ON DISCOVERY COMMUNICATIONS

CREDIT SUISSE FIRST BOSTON

CREDIT SUISSE FIRST BOSTON CORPORATION

Equity Research

Americas | U.S./Cable/Entertainment | September 15, 1999

Discovery Communications, Inc.

Focus on Value Series: Rapid Cash Flow and Valuation Growth Continue

Laura Martin, CFA
1 626 395 5100
laura.martin@csfb.com

Patrick Wang
1 626 395 5105
patrick.wang@csfb.com

- **Discovery Communications, Inc. (DCI) is one of the highest-quality television programming franchises in the world.**
- **With its strong, high-quality brands and U.S. and international expansion opportunities, DCI should be one of the finest high-growth businesses in the United States for the next decade.**
- **We estimate that DCI is worth approximately $12 billion; about $10.6 billion (after subtracting debt) is net equity value.**
- **Since DCI is not a separately traded company, investors must purchase either Liberty Media (49.3% owner) or Cox Communications (24.65% owner) to participate in DCI s dramatic growth.**

Exhibit 5 EXCERPTS FROM CREDIT SUISSE/FIRST BOSTON REPORT ON DISCOVERY COMMUNICATIONS cont.

Introduction and Overview

DCI is organized into four business units: Discovery Networks-U.S.; Discovery Networks International; Discovery Enterprises Worldwide; and Discovery Retail.

- *Discovery Networks U.S.* includes the Discovery Channel, The Learning Channel (TLC), Animal Planet, the Travel Channel, and the six digital networks.
- *Discovery Networks International* consists primarily of Discovery Latin America, Discovery Europe, Discovery Asia, and Discovery India.
- *Discovery Enterprises Worldwide* comprises DCI's brand extension businesses in on-line services, video, publishing, catalogs, licensing, and education.
- *Discovery Retail* is made up of more than 120 retail stores, including 52 Nature Company stores, 67 Discovery Channel Stores, and two Discovery Channel Destination flagship stores.

Table 1 includes an overview of Discovery's major assets and includes our estimates of value for each.

Table 1

Discovery Communications Valuation Overview

$ in millions

	Private Market Value	Percent of Value
Discovery Networks		
The Discovery Channel	$6,300	60%
The Learning Channel	2,835	27
Animal Planet	750	7
The Travel Channel	465	4
Digital Networks	150	1
Subtotal Discovery Networks	$10,500	99%
Discovery Networks International		
Discovery Latin America	$378	4%
Discovery Europe	340	3
Discovery Asia	230	2
Discovery India	138	1
Other International Channels	100	1
Subtotal Discovery Networks International	$1,186	11%
Discovery Enterprise Worldwide (DEW)		
Home video	20	0%
Other Enterprises[1]	80	1
Subtotal DEW	$100	1%
Retail (including Nature Co.)	250	2%
Non-consolidated Assets	50	0
Less: Estimated debt	(1,500)	(14)
Total	$10,586	100%

[1]Includes Interactive, Education, Publishing, Travel, Catalog and Licensing.
Source: Credit Suisse First Boston estimates.

Exhibit 5 EXCERPTS FROM CREDIT SUISSE/FIRST BOSTON REPORT ON DISCOVERY COMMUNICATIONS cont.

Strategy

Management has several strategic objectives designed to enhance long-term cash flow growth:

- *New channels.* In June 1996, Discovery launched Animal Planet, its third analog channel. In 1997, Discovery launched four digital services: Discovery Kids Channel, Discovery Science Channel, Discovery Home and Leisure Channel, and Discovery Civilization Channel. In 1998, DCI added two additional services: Discovery Wings and Discovery Health. In the first quarter of 1999, Discovery acquired the remaining 30% of the Travel Channel for $55 million. Discovery Health is currently being converted to an analog service, and management expects it to become DCI's fifth largest distributed network.
- *Build library value.* Discovery's strategy is to steadily build a children's library, a science library, and a history library in order to provide programming for the new digital services. The Discovery Channel and The Learning Channel each have an active inventory of programming that exceeds 2,000 hours, with an overall average cost (purchased and original programming) of $20,000-30,000 per episode per hour per year. On average, it costs approximately $90,000-100,000 per hour for purchased programming for the Discovery Channel and The Learning Channel, and DCI has the right to air this programming three to four times over the term of the contract.
- *Brand image.* Management's global strategy is to enhance Discovery's brand image by pursuing line extensions and subbrands in the consumer products, home video, publishing, school, multimedia, and on-line markets.
- *Global alliance.* In March 1998, Discovery formed a $600 million global strategic alliance with the British Broadcasting Corporation (BBC). Together, DCI and the BBC will develop new programming and launch new channels in the United States and abroad. DCI will handle the distribution of all BBC and Discovery product in the Americas. DCI's minimum initial financial commitment is for $560 million over the next five years. This is made up of $175 million for BBC produced programming, $100 million to launch BBC America (which had 10 million subscribers at June 30, 1999), and $285 million to develop new cable networks.
- *Retail stores.* At June 30, 1999, DCI had a total of 121 retail stores made up of 52 Nature Company stores, 67 Discovery Channel Stores, and two Discovery Channel Destination flagship stores. The U.S. retail stores are used for cross-promotion of all DCI's programming services. Management uses the retail stores to enhance consumer awareness of its channels and to generate incremental demand for its services.
- *Internet.* While we expect DCI's Internet strategy will be an important contributor to value, no announcements have been made to date and, therefore, we await details before adding this asset to our valuation model.

THE DISCOVERY CHANNEL U.S.

The largest asset of DCI is the Discovery Channel in the United States. We estimate that the Discovery Channel represents approximately 60% of DCI's total value.

Programming

The Discovery Channel airs nonfiction documentaries during prime time, and home improvement, cooking, and how-to programs during the daytime. Table 2 includes selected examples of the Discovery Channel's programming.

Exhibit 5 EXCERPTS FROM CREDIT SUISSE/FIRST BOSTON REPORT ON DISCOVERY COMMUNICATIONS cont.

Table 2

Sample Discovery Channel Programming

Time	Monday–Friday
9:00 am	***Interior Motives:*** Friend or Faux
9:30 am	***Start to Finish:*** Gardening; Kids' Clothes; Ornaments
10:00 am	***Home Matters:*** G. Bugialli/Veggie, Garden/Paris Apartment
11:00 am	***Lynette Jennings Design:*** Texas 50s Ranch; Bungalow Reno
12:00 noon	***Interior Motives:*** California Dreamin'
1:00 pm	***Home Matters:*** Perfect Flowers/Vases; Plaster Repair
2:00 pm	***Lynette Jennings Design:*** New Orleans Veaux Cerri
3:00 pm	***Interior Motives:*** Dynamic Designers
4:00 pm	***Great Chefs:*** Tuna Parfait; Roast Chicken; Tart
4:30 pm	***Great Chefs of the World:*** Pheasant in Phyllo; Noblemen's Dessert Box
5:00 pm	***Gimme Shelter:*** A New Outlook
6:00 pm	***Your New House with Michael Holigan:*** Replacing Sliding Glass Doors; French Drains
6:30 pm	***Fix-It Line:*** Mantle; Screen Door; Refinishing Tips; Staining and Sealing
7:00 pm	***Wild Discovery:*** Born to Run–Impalas
8:00pm	***On the Inside:*** Non-Lethal Weapons
9:00 pm	***The New Detectives: Case Studies in Forensic Science***–Women Who Kill
10:00 pm	***The FBI Files:*** World Trade Center Bombing
11:00 pm	***On the Inside:*** Non-Lethal Weapons
12:00 am	***The New Detectives: Case Studies in Forensic Science***–Women Who Kill
1:00 am	***The FBI Files:*** World Trade Center Bombing
2:00 am	***Wild Discovery:*** Born to Run–Impalas

Source: Discovery Communications Inc.

Exhibit 5

EXCERPTS FROM CREDIT SUISSE/FIRST BOSTON REPORT ON DISCOVERY COMMUNICATIONS cont.

Distribution

The Discovery Channel is available to approximately 98% of all U.S. cable households. Over the past four years, subscribers have grown 4% annually; about half came from cable subscribers and the balance from direct-to-home satellite. Viewership ratings are stable for the Discovery Channel. Looking ahead, we expect subscribers to increase approximately 3-4% per annum.

Brand Strength

Discovery's brand strength is significant. Discovery Channel ranked fifth in overall quality when measured against 270 other consumer brands by Equitrend in the fourth quarter of 1998.

Table 3 includes a summary of the 1998 Equitrend survey ranking the top consumer brands.

Table 3

1998 Equitrend Survey of Top Five Brands	
	Quality Score
Kodak Photographic Film	82.7
Craftsman Tools	82.3
Hallmark Greeting Cards	81.3
Chiquita Bananas	81.3
Discovery Channel	**81.2**

Source: Discovery Communications Inc.

In the first quarter of 1999, Equitrend published its 1999 list of quality media brands. Discovery Channel ranked number one on Equitrend's 1999 list of quality media brands, marking the third year in a row at the top slot.

Table 4 includes the results of Equitrend's 1999 quality media brand survey and highlights DCI's highest-ranking quality brands.

Table 4

1999 Equitrend Survey of Top Media Brands

1999 Rank	DCI Channel Name	Quality Score
1	Discovery Channel	81.2
3	The Learning Channel	78.0
5	Discovery Kids	74.4
19	Animal Planet	71.1

Source: Discovery Communications Inc.

The strength of DCI's brands attracts noncable subscribers. In addition, the high quality of DCI's brands facilitates greater pricing power with advertisers.

Fundamentals

The cable programming business is predominantly a fixed-cost business. Therefore, revenue growth drives rapid cash flow expansion. The Discovery Channel continues to report strong revenue growth.

Affiliate Revenue On average, we estimate that the Discovery Channel received $0.25 per subscriber per month from cable operators in 1998, representing about 40% of the Discovery Channel's total reported revenue.

Advertising Revenue In 1998, advertising represented approximately 55% of the Discovery Channel's revenue. We estimate that the Discovery Channel receives a cost per thousand (CPM) of $5.15, representing an aggregate of $4,600 per 30-second spot in prime time, based on an average prime-time rating of 1.19 (75.5 million subscribers at December 31, 1998, times 1.19 rating times $5.15 CPM).

Discovery Channel ratings have grown steadily since 1991, reaching a total-day rating of 0.65 and a prime-time rating of 1.17 for 1998. At June 30, 1999, the Discovery Channel's total-day rating reached 0.66 in prime time and 1.18 for the full day. Chart 1 plots the Discovery Channel's ratings from December 31, 1991, to June 30, 1999.

Chart 1
Discovery Channel Ratings Trends-2

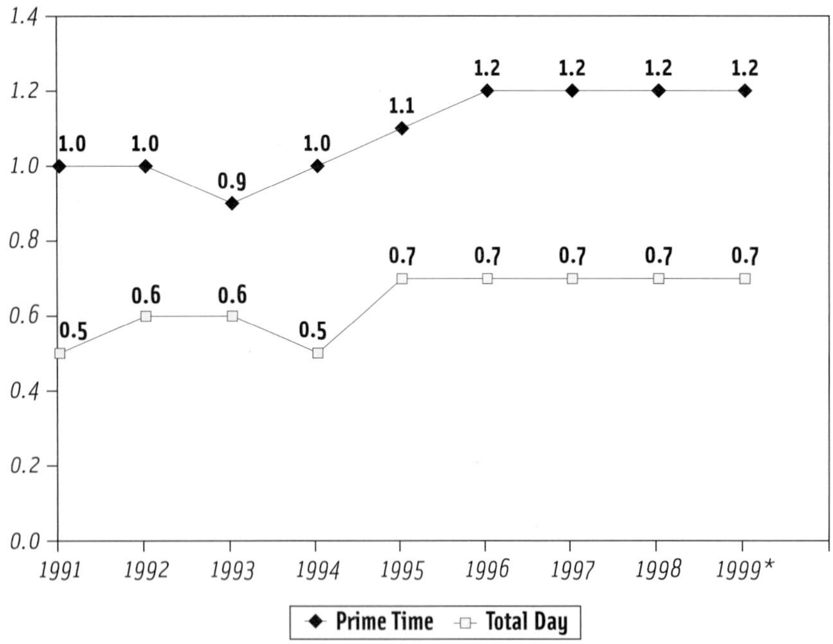

Through June 30, 1999.
Source: Discovery Communications Inc.

As for advertising revenue, it is difficult for the Discovery Channel to increase distribution faster than new household penetration because of ubiquitous reach. Therefore, advertising revenue growth must be driven by higher CPMs, or higher ratings. Advertising prices are largely determined in the upfront advertising market in July and August of each year.

We estimate that the Discovery Channel received 10-12% average annual CPM increases in the 1999-2000 upfront market and that sell-out was 50% of total advertising inventory. These price increases, combined with 3-5% annual subscriber growth and higher ratings, should result in strong revenue growth at the Discovery Channel in 1999 and 2000.

Exhibit 5

EXCERPTS FROM CREDIT SUISSE/FIRST BOSTON REPORT ON DISCOVERY COMMUNICATIONS cont.

Valuation

We estimate that the Discovery Channel will generate approximately $300 million of EBITDA in 1999.

We value the Discovery Channel at a private market multiple of 21 times 1999 cash flow and a public market multiple of 16 times, based on the strong brand name, high-quality consumer franchise, line extension opportunities, favorable cost structure, and strong management. Table 5 includes our valuation analysis for the Discovery Channel.

Table 5

Discovery Channel Valuation $ in millions

	Public Value	Private Value
1999E EBITDA	$300	$300
Multiple	16	21
Aggregate value	$4,800	$6,300

Source: Credit Suisse First Boston estimates

Animal Planet

In October 1996, Discovery launched Animal Planet to two million subscribers. At June 30, 1999, Animal Planet, one of the fastest-growing cable networks in the United States, reached 50 million subscribers, driven by demand and significant affiliate sales. Chart 4 includes subscriber data for Animal Planet from 1996 to June 30, 1999.

Chart 4
Animal Planet Subscriber Data, 1996–99

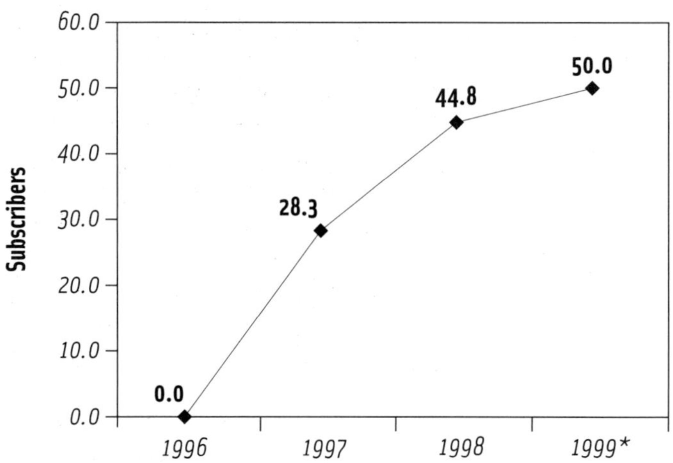

* = As of June 30, 1999.
Source: Discovery Communications Inc.

Exhibit 5 EXCERPTS FROM CREDIT SUISSE/FIRST BOSTON REPORT ON DISCOVERY COMMUNICATIONS cont.

Animal Planet is a prototype for content-specific and genre-neutral cable programming. Animal Planet provides 24 hours per day of programming about animals and the environments in which they live, people and their pets, animals just for kids, and exploring the majesty of the animal kingdom. Animal Planet uses programming from the Discovery Library plus animal documentaries from the BBC, TV New Zealand, and others. Animal Planet is available for both digital and analog distribution.

Animal Planet's most popular shows include *Crocodile Hunter, Emergency Vets, Zoo Venture, Petline,* and *All Bird TV.*

Animal Planet pays $5.00 upfront to cable operators for launch support. Each MSO then pays Animal Planet $0.08 per month per subscriber, escalating annually. We estimate that it takes Animal Planet approximately four years to recoup its launch support costs. Typically, affiliate contracts are five to ten years.

Table 8 includes sample programming for Animal Planet.

Valuation

Animal Planet generated operating losses of $30 million in calendar 1997, $16 million in 1998, and $10 million in 1999. We expect Animal Planet to break even in 2000.

We define Animal Planet as a developing channel because of the inability to value it on a cash flow basis. We believe that Animal Planet will break even in 2000; therefore, using a multiple of cash flow to determine value understates its value. Instead, we value Animal Planet based on its 50 million current subscribers at $15 per subscriber, which results in a value of $750 million.

Table 8

Sample Animal Planet Programming	
Time	**Monday–Friday**
6:00 am	***Madison's Adventures—Growing Up Wild:*** Penguins on Parade
6:30 am	***Mother Nature:*** Grebes
7:00 am	***Acorn the Nature Nut:*** Woodsy Home Movies
7:30 am	***Jim Henderson's Animal Show:*** Fish
8:00 am	***Mother Nature:*** Grebes
8:30 am	***Acorn the Nature Nut:*** Woodsy Home Movies
9:00 am	***All Bird TV:*** Follow the Food—Montana
9:30 am	***PetLine:*** Sign Language, Bird, Hedgehog, Puppy Training
10:00 am	***Petsburgh:*** USA: Saltwater Fish
10:30 am	***Amazing Tails:*** Body by Shatzie; Sabrina; Canine Companions for Independence I & II
11:00 am	***Animal Doctor:*** Leopard Fertility; Dog Rescue; Cat Rescue, Wombat, Rhino
11:30 am	***Judge Wapner's Animal Court:*** No Cat Naps
12:00 noon	***All Bird TV:*** Follow the Food - Montana
12:30 pm	***PetLine:*** Sign Language, Bird, Hedgehog, Puppy Training
1:00 pm	***Petsburgh USA:*** Saltwater Fish

Exhibit 5 EXCERPTS FROM CREDIT SUISSE/FIRST BOSTON REPORT ON DISCOVERY COMMUNICATIONS cont.

Table 8 *(continued)*

Sample Animal Planet Programming

Time	Monday–Friday
1:30 pm	***Amazing Tails:*** Body by Shatzie; Sabrina; Canine Companions for Independence I & II
2:00 pm	***Animal Doctor:*** Leopard Fertility; Dog Rescue; Cat Rescue, Wombat, Rhino
2:30 pm	***Judge Wapner's Animal Court:*** No Cat Naps
3:00 pm	***Jaws & Claws:*** Our Best Friends
3:30 pm	***Animal Planet Zoo Adventure:*** Philip, Brittany, Kent, Andrea
4:00 pm	***Lassie(New):*** Poster Pup
4:30 pm	***The Crocodile Hunter's Corc Files:*** Pig in the Outback
5:00 pm	***Celebrity Crusaders:*** In the Land of the Grizzlies (World of Audubon)
6:00 pm	***Petsburgh USA:*** To Spay or Not To Spay
6:30 pm	***Amazing Tails:*** Doo Dah Day, Sheepdog Trials, Sheep, Hedgehog
7:00 pm	***Judge Wapner's Animal Court:*** No Cat Naps
7:30 pm	***Animal Doctor:*** Beak Trim; Dog Abuse; Snake Microchip; Pig Sunburn; Cat Cyst
8:00 pm	***Planet Safari:*** Wild Heart of Africa
9:00 pm	***The Great African Wildlife Rescue:*** Oxpecker–Size Doesn't Matter
9:30 pm	***Wildlife Emergency:*** Condition Critical!
10:00 pm	***Emergency Vets:*** Two Hip to Ignore
10:30 pm	***Wild Rescues:*** El Nino Horse, Papillon Saves Girl, Hidden Harbor Turtle
11:00 pm	***Planet Safari:*** Wild Heart of Africa
12:00 am	***The Great African Wildlife Rescue:*** Oxpecker- Size Doesn't Matter
12:30 am	***Wildlife Emergency:*** Condition Critical!
1:00 am	***Emergency Vets:*** Two Hip to Ignore
1:30 am	***Wild Rescues:*** El Nino Horse, Papillon Saves Girl, Hidden Harbor Turtle
2:00 am	***Celebrity Crusaders:*** In the Land of the Grizzlies (World of Audubon)
3:00 am	***Lassie (Classic):*** Here Comes Glory #1
3:30 am	***Timmy & Lassie:*** Heat Wave
4:00 am	***Jeff Collie:*** Happy
4:30 am	***Skippy:*** Episode 42
5:00 am	***Lassie (Classic):*** Here Comes Glory #1
5:30 am	***Lassie (New):*** Poster Pup

Source: Discovery Communications Inc.

Exhibit 5 EXCERPTS FROM CREDIT SUISSE/FIRST BOSTON REPORT ON DISCOVERY COMMUNICATIONS cont.

Other Businesses

Retail Expansion

At June 30, 1999, DCI had 120 stores made up of 52 Nature Company stores, 67 Discovery Channel Stores, and two Discovery Channel Destination flagship stores.

Discovery is in the third year of a five-year plan to convert Nature Company Stores to Discovery Channel stores. Management expects that once converted, each store will generate revenue of approximately $1.2 million. Operating income is about $200,000 per store. Stores that have been converted generally have higher customer traffic, higher margins, and positive same-store comparables.

In March 1998, DCI launched its first Discovery Destination flagship store in Washington, D.C. In the first quarter of 1999, DCI opened its second store in San Francisco. Management plans to open a total 40 stores over the next five years.

Home Video

Launched in 1989, Discovery's home video business is growing rapidly. With more than 2,000 hours of programming, DCI owns one of the finest documentary and special interest video libraries in the world. Two of the most popular videos in 1998 were *Titanic: The Complete Story* and *God Speed: John Glenn.*

This is a high-margin business because it represents a repackaging of Discovery's programming with very little incremental cost. On the high side, Discovery can sell 50,000 units at an average contribution of $10 per unit, representing $500,000 of incremental revenue. On average, Discovery sells 20,000 home video units at $19.95 per unit (although some titles sell only 5,000 units). The average contribution is $10.00 per unit, so the average profit per title is $200,000 from home video. Management is expanding this business, and we expect cash flow from this source to grow rapidly.

On-Line

Discovery has launched several on-line services and several CD-ROM titles as well. With Discovery On-line (www.discovery.com) users can explore a full range of narrative stories brought to life by video, sound, digitalization, and real-time discussions. On-line advertising revenue is projected to be $10 million in 1999, and e-commerce revenue is growing rapidly.

We estimate that DCI will invest $15 million in these new businesses in 1999. We value DCI's on-line assets at $35 million based on their after-tax losses to date.

Discovery Channel Pictures

In the spring of 1998 in U.S. IMAX theaters, DCI introduced its large-format film entitled *Africa's Elephant Kingdom* shot in Kenya's Amboseli National Park. A second film, *Wildfire,* was released in the first quarter of 1999.

We value Discovery Channel Pictures at $30 million based on its after-tax losses to date.

Cash Sources and Uses; Ownership

In 1999, we estimate that DCI will generate an after-tax cash deficit of $400 million. The Discovery Channel represents virtually all of DCI's cash flow. Launch support costs for Animal Planet and Travel Channel represent the primary use of cash as well as acquisition spending for Eye on People, Knowledge TV, and the remaining 30% of the Travel Channel.

We estimate that DCI's debt will be approximately $1.5 billion at December 31, 1999.

Exhibit 5 EXCERPTS FROM CREDIT SUISSE/FIRST BOSTON REPORT ON DISCOVERY COMMUNICATIONS cont.

Table 17 includes a summary of cash sources and uses for 1999.

Table 17	
After-Tax Free Cash Flow $ in millions	
	1999 Estimate
Net income after-tax	$(80)
D&A	115
Net film spending	(65)
Capital expenditures and launch support spending	(200)
Acquisition Expenditures	(170)
Free cash flow	$(400)

Source: Credit Suisse First Boston estimates

Budget expenditures do not require board approval, although the entire budget does require approval annually.

DCI has a simple ownership structure, with Liberty owning a 49% interest and Newhouse (a private company) and Cox each owning 24.6%. CEO John Hendricks owns 1.4% of DCI's common stock, representing $148 million in value. However, the "put" values for the Hendricks' shares, Hendricks' incentives, and manager incentives under agreement with the company are determined by a formula that is likely to differ from our simple valuation. Hendricks, along with the top 40 managers, participates in a phantom equity plan that is designed to create a long-term commitment to the company. We estimate that the current value of Hendricks' phantom equity is equal to the Hendricks' common stock value, producing a total value of Hendricks' stock and incentives of approximately $300 million.

To date, Cox and Newhouse have each invested $35 million for approximately 25% of DCI. Liberty Media (through Tele-Communications Inc.) invested $35 million for its original stake and subsequently purchased United Artists' 25% ownership stake. Today, we estimate that Cox and Newhouse each own approximately $2.6 billion and Liberty Media owns $5.2 billion worth of DCI.

Table 18 includes the common stock ownership of each of the principal shareholders of DCI, our estimate of their investment to date, and the current value of their shareholdings.

Table 18			
Discovery Ownership Structure $ in millions			
	Ownership Common Stock	**Equity Invested**	**Estimated Private Value**
Liberty Media	49.30%	$70	$5,216
Cox Communications	24.65	35	2,608
Newhouse	24.65	35	2,608
John Hendricks	1.40	0	148
Total	100.0%	$140	$10,580

Source: Credit Suisse First Boston estimates. Source: Credit Suisse First Boston

Exhibit 6 EXCERPTS FROM PETSTORE.COM/ANIMAL PLANET PRESENTATION

Conceptual View of AnimalPlanet.com

PETSTORE.
5/16/00 4:55 PM

AnimalPlanet.com Vision: "All Things Animal"

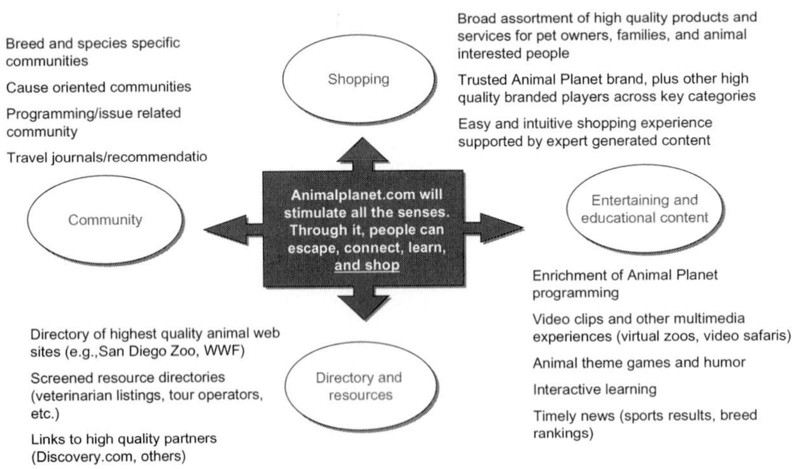

PETSTORE.COM CONFIDENTIAL
5/16/00 4:56 PM

Page 11

Exhibit 6 EXCERPTS FROM PETSTORE.COM/ANIMAL PLANET PRESENTATION cont.

Why Is an "All-Things-Animal" Destination Site a Good Idea?

- Animal interested people represent a significant (>75%) portion of the US population
- These groups spend large amounts on goods and services related to animals
- Nobody has successfully claimed the space
  - Over 1 million animal related web sites but nobody aggregating eyeballs or monetizing effectively
  - Non-profits and zoos have the best content
  - Nothing yet from National Geographic, Disney, or Warner
- A natural for on-line
  - Aggregation play for animal related products and services
  - Entertainment and education possibilities with broadband coming are tremendous
  - Animal interested community opportunities abound

PETSTORE.COM CONFIDENTIAL Page 3

Destination Site Will Attract Viewers Through Several Paths

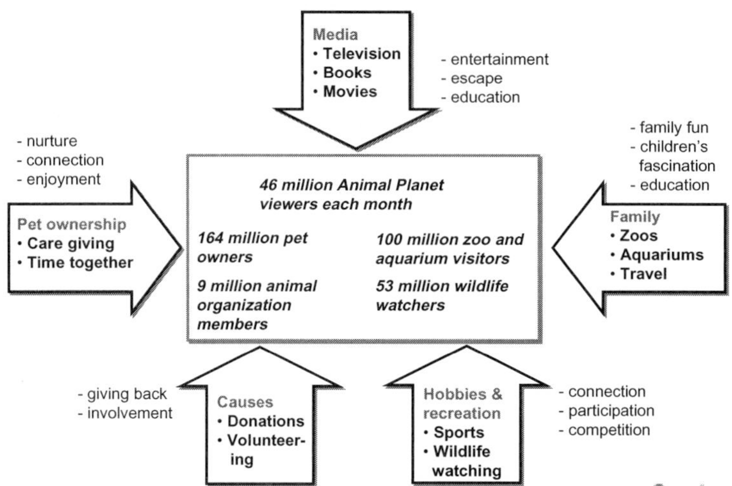

PETSTORE.COM CONFIDENTIAL Page 4

Exhibit 6

EXCERPTS FROM PETSTORE.COM/ANIMAL PLANET PRESENTATION cont.

How Large Are the Markets?

- Market for pet related products is $28 billion - coming on line quickly
- $6.4 billion in animal toys (estimate)
- $2 billion in ticketing for zoos and aquariums
- $0.5 billion in books, videos, and gifts (estimate)
- Over $3 billion in travel related opportunities (estimate)
- Other categories include:
  - Apparel
  - Educational tools and distance learning
  - Art and collectibles
  - Auctions
  - Charitable giving

PETSTORE.COM CONFIDENTIAL
5/18/00 4:56 PM

Page 5

Petstore.com

SENDWINE.COM

Lack of focus has killed a lot of companies, but in a consumer e-commerce startup, focus can actually kill you. Sometimes it feels like racing a sailboat through a raging storm. If we focus on surviving the storm, we lose the race. If we focus on winning the race, we could lose the ship. We are in a constant state of change. In fact, change is the only thing we can focus on.

—Sendwine.com founder and CEO Mike Lannon

At the end of 1998, Mike Lannon, President and Founder of Massachusetts-based Sendwine.com, was able to celebrate both a successful holiday season and raising $10 million in the startup company's first round of financing. He said, "Successful Christmas sales fueled venture capital interest. It sealed the deal for us."[1]

What started as a hobby had turned into the "Wine Line" business via phone, and now into a ".com" business with customers in 17 different countries and a network of wine merchants covering over 80 percent of the US population. Through these merchants, Sendwine. com provided a gift-giving service that allowed consumers to send elegantly packaged individual bottles of fine wine.

With the recent windfall of venture capital funding, Lannon had the opportunity to accelerate Sendwine. com's growth. The $10 million question was: "How should I spend my VC money?" The two major alternatives seemed to be to either invest more heavily in the current Sendwine model or to aggressively fund a "beyond wine" diversification strategy, offering new gift categories that would be marketed under an umbrella brand called "Send.com."

Sendwine.com's History

It took me 8 months to raise $500,000, 4 months to raise $10 million, and the next round of financing for $20 to $30 million will take 30 days. Once you raise $10 million from top tier investors, you enter a completely different category. We are now one phone call away from all the key players in the industry. The big challenge once money is in the bank, is how to make that money attract even more money, at a much higher valuation.

—Mike Lannon

With 20 years of business experience but no technology background, Sendwine.com founder Michael Lannon was not your average e-commerce entrepreneur. Raised in Boston, Lannon attended St. Michael's College in Vermont. After graduation, he pursued a career in advertising. At age 24, he started his own advertising agency and spent six years building a profitable business. In 1990, he sold his company to his partner and accepted a job as VP of Marketing with his former client Leasecomm, a Boston-based financial services company.

In the summer of 1995, Lannon, then age 36, left his job at Leasecomm, was engaged to Mary Obana, and made plans to follow her to her new job with Coca-Cola in Atlanta. That summer was full of uncertainty and surprise for Lannon. In the midst of the many changes in his life, it was the simple act of trying to send a gift of wine from Boston to his fiancée that would have the most profound impact on his future. Hoping to surprise her on her first day at her new job with a bottle of her favorite Champagne, Lannon's good intentions were thwarted by state laws that made it impossible for him to ship alcohol across state borders. Given his immediate need, Lannon's only gift option was flowers, an uninspiring choice that left him frustrated but intrigued. Why couldn't he send wine as easily as flowers?

Having run his own business in the past and eager to do so again, Lannon sensed a business opportunity. His self-imposed unemployment afforded him the time to explore his idea. Lannon's next step was to create a

---

Charmaine Ess (MBA '99), Ann O'Hara (MBA '99) and Professor Thomas Eisenmann prepared this case as the basis for class discussion rather than to illustrate either effective or ineffective handling of an administrative situation.

[1]Raik-Allen, Georgie. "No Crime to Buy Wine Online", *Red Herring Online,* March 23, 1999. Unless otherwise noted, casewriter interviews are the source for other quotes in this case.

business plan, which he drafted during his honeymoon in the Caribbean. Upon his return, Lannon joined his wife in Atlanta and conducted market research which he disguised as wine tastings. He spent six months learning how, why and when people bought wine. Based on this knowledge, Lannon refined his business plan. "Everyone I spoke to had either given or received wine as a gift, but virtually no one had ever *sent* wine as a gift," said Lannon. The fieldwork validated his instincts, and his business mission became clear: to make sending a gift of wine as fast and as easy as sending flowers.

As Lannon had discovered accidentally, modern day convenience was irreconcilable with laws that dated back to the days of Prohibition. Every state had different regulations for shipping alcohol, and nearly all states prohibited the direct shipment of wine to consumers across state borders: liquor could only be sold to consumers by licensed retailers, who in turn were required to buy through licensed wholesalers. The only legal solution was to create an FTD-like network of fine wine merchants throughout the country.[2] This would be extremely time consuming, but as Lannon said, "Given the fact that our business is extremely customer service intensive, I wanted to meet each merchant to ensure that they were as customer service-oriented as I was and that their products were of the highest quality."

With a fledgling distribution network in place, Lannon approached potential investors, but with no success. Undeterred, Lannon poured his life savings of $150,000 into the business and in December 1997 launched what was to become Sendwine.com. The initial company was called The Wine Line. Like FTD, The Wine Line primarily took orders by phone. Off-duty waiters fielded many of the toll free calls. Orders were then directed to and delivered by a network of wine and liquor stores located in most major states.

Using a "build-your-own-website" kit to explore e-commerce in early 1998, Lannon saw that the Internet would enable easy ordering and high quality graphics that could display The Wine Line's gift packaging. He sold a group of angel investors on a plan to convert the Wine Line into Sendwine.com, raising $500,000 to fund website development and marketing. The Sendwine.com web site was launched during the Fall of 1998. Soon afterward, Lannon purchased the URL "Send.com" for $20,000 to give Sendwine the option to expand into a broader array of gift categories. By Christmas 1998, Sendwine.com was a full-fledged Internet company with eight employees.

Launching Sendwine's website before the 1998 holiday season was crucial. Existing customers were sent fliers describing how they could use the Internet to send gifts of wine. A radio ad campaign costing $150,000 was launched in the New York City, Boston and San Francisco areas. Financing was tight but Lannon's bet on the Internet paid off: sales quadrupled over the 1998 holiday season, compared to the prior year. For all of 1998, Sendwine.com had revenues just under $1 million. More importantly, Lannon had developed and proved a profitable revenue model for his business—something many other "dot coms" had not done.

Lannon decided to approach venture capitalists during the successful 1998 Christmas season. Initially, he only was seeking to raise about $1 million dollars from one or two VC firms. Lannon said that seemed like a lot of money at the time: "It took me a while to get used to saying 'I need one million dollars'." To his surprise, the VCs kept pushing him to raise more money, telling him that $1 million was "merely a drop in the bucket." By March, Sendwine.com had secured financing totaling $10 million dollars from four top-tier VC firms: Greylock Management Corp., Highland Capital Partners, Charles River Ventures, and Benchmark Capital. The VCs bought into Lannon's successful wine gift service, as well as the potential to expand into new gift categories via Send.com. Lannon, at the age of 40, thus found himself at the center of an e-commerce revolution—his new goal was to redefine what it meant to give gifts over the Internet.

Sendwine.com's Business Model

How often have you been too busy or forgotten to buy someone a gift for a special occasion? Suddenly, the gift needs to be there yesterday! But it needs to be a *beautiful* gift, not just a cheap card or boring flowers. You want to make sure the recipient feels special, and sees that you put thought into a gift just for them. Perhaps you also want to make sure that you look good by sending a gift that communicates thoughtfulness and quality.

Sendwine.com catered to just this situation. The company delivered elegantly packaged bottles of fine wine, Port or Champagne within two business days, and in many cases, on the same day. Each bottle was individually polished, wrapped in crisp white linen, and crowned

[2]Florists' Transworld Delivery is a centralized order processing company that routes consumer orders for floral gifts to be delivered by "affiliate" florists within the gift recipient's local community.

with an embossed copper seal. Along with the gift came a personal message on a handwritten card, as well as a stylishly illustrated booklet on storing and serving wine (see Exhibit 1 for web pages).

The Target Customer: Busy people with good intentions but no time

Sendwine identified four customer segments: the busy professional, the frequent gift-giver, the mass-market consumer, and the wine expert. Sendwine mainly targeted busy professionals and frequent gift-givers. Mass-market consumers and wine experts also used the service, but to a lesser extent due to concerns they had about pricing and product selection issues, as described below.

The busy professional was generally male (although a recent Jupiter Communications study indicated that executive women increasingly were purchasing online)[3]. It was important that the professional's gift was sent quickly and made the sender look good. The details of packaging or the exact wine were not especially important as long as the impression made was a good one. Orders were in the $150 range and served to reinforce either personal or business relationships.

The frequent gift-giver was generally female. She or he was thoughtful and sent gifts to friends who liked wine. It was important that the sender not feel ignorant in selecting the gift. Packaging also was crucial to the frequent gift-giver and needed to look as good as, if not better than, something that sender could have been done on their own. Prices tended to be in the $50–75 range.

Operations

Sendwine's operations were designed to work in compliance with state and federal laws related to shipping alcohol. The company maintained a network of approximately 100 established retail stores (who in turn purchased from licensed wholesalers) covering over 80 percent of the US population. After a customer placed an order at the Sendwine.com website (or through the company's toll free telephone number), Sendwine faxed the order to a retailer in the same state as the gift recipient,[4] and purchased wine from this retailer on the customer's behalf. The retailer then selected and packaged the gift (handwriting a card based on instructions from the sender) and hired a courier service to deliver the gift.

Retailers received packaging kits from Sendwine. After they completed a delivery, they received reimbursement from Sendwine for: 1) courier charges; 2) the retail price of the wine, less a modest discount (which recognized Sendwine's status as a large customer); and 3) taxes incurred.

Product Selection and Pricing

By partnering with local bricks-and-mortar retail stores, Sendwine avoided storage and distribution costs and could guarantee speedy delivery. The downside of not holding its own inventory, however, was that Sendwine could not guarantee its customers the delivery of specific bottles of wine: Sendwine lacked real-time data on each retailer's inventory, and lacked the leverage to insist that retailers maintain specific bottles in stock. On its retail web site, Sendwine offered approximately 40 different gift packages (e.g. Transatlantic Challenge, Sparkling Tribute, Down Under Discover Set, Red and White Dinner Celebration). None of these packages allowed the customer to specify exact bottles and vintages; instead, each package listed several possible bottles and vintages that were representative of the type of wine that might be sent. Retailers selected bottles from their stock that were consistent with the theme of the package.

Sendwine packages ranged in price between $39 and $750; all prices included shipping. Sendwine's gifts were priced well above liquor store retail prices but a little below the prices that restaurants would charge for the same bottles (restaurant prices, excluding tips, tended to be about twice the level of liquor store prices). Thus, in contrast to the pricing policies of most Internet retailers, who discounted more deeply than their bricks-and-mortar competitors, Sendwine commanded a price premium over liquor stores. According to Jupiter Communications analyst Ken Cassar, "In a lot of other product categories I would say they were crazy, but online shoppers are much less price sensitive when buying gifts."[5]

Retailers

In recruiting retail partners, Sendwine avoided big liquor stores, preferring to do business with mid-sized wine stores operated by their owner. Lannon said that small

[3] Swerdlow, Fiona. "Analyst Note", Jupiter Communications, October 26, 1998

[4] In August 1999, Sendwine introduced "MerchantLink" service, which would send orders electronically to retailers over an extranet; provide tools to help the retailer generate order labels and interface with shippers; and allow the retailer to submit confirmation of delivery electronically.

[5] Raik-Allen, Georgie. "No Crime to Buy Wine Online", *Red Herring Online*, March 23, 1999

stores lacked the inventory to fulfill Sendwine's orders and said, "For the big-volume store, we're just one more thing for them to do, but we can say to the [mid-sized] boutique: 'We have the potential to be your best customer.'"[6]

Marketing/PR

As of mid-1999, marketing had been mainly through radio advertising in the New York, Boston and San Francisco areas and a Father's Day ad campaign in the *Wall Street Journal.* Sendwine.com's management realized, however, that building the brand was key. With $10 million in VC funding, Sendwine now could approach major PR and advertising firms about taking its marketing program to the next level.

Staffing

As of July 1999, Sendwine had 46 employees. Eight employees were involved in marketing; ten worked in the call center (although Sendwine had repositioned itself as a web retailer, about 20 percent of customer orders still were placed via toll free telephone calls); 15 to 20 employees worked in Technology and Operations on web site development, order processing, and other logistics on behalf of retailer partners (e.g., shipping packaging materials). The balance of Sendwine's staff was engaged in administrative functions such as accounting and human resources.

Online Gift Retailing

The web was well suited for gift purchasing: compared to shopping in retail stores, the Web was fast and convenient. The classic problem facing online retailers—their inability to provide immediate gratification—was less often an issue, since the purchaser did not personally use the goods that were acquired, and typically deferred a gift's delivery until some special occasion. Gift giving also was an attractive market for Web retailers because gift purchasers tended to be less price sensitive than Internet shoppers acquiring goods for their own use.

Among online buyers, 59 percent reported that less than 10 percent of their online purchases were gift-related.[7] (See Exhibit 2, Figure A.) However, the robust growth of online retailing during the 1998 holiday season—46 percent of total 1998 online retail sales were generated during the Christmas holidays—suggested that online shoppers might be increasing their propensity to use the web for gift buying.

As the online gift business exploded during the holidays, so did the competition for this market. Among incumbent online retailers, 29 percent had developed the ability for offer gifts. The number of websites solely focused on gift giving also increased during the fourth quarter of 1998 (Exhibit 3). Along with increases in the number of gift retail competitors, the quality of their services improved. Website functionality frequently included recommendations, gift certificates, and registries. Typical services included next day shipping, guaranteed shipping, personalized cards, gift wrapping, and handling returns. (see Exhibit 2, Figure B).

Notwithstanding competition and the challenge of developing features, the gift market was quite promising. Overall online retail sales were projected to reach $29 billion by 2002, up from $5 billion in 1998. Online specialty gift sales (including flowers, wines, chocolates, gourmet foods and greeting cards) were expected to account for $1.4 billion of the year 2002 total (up from $179 million in 1998). If Sendwine could capture just 5% of the online specialty gift giving market, they would be a $70 million dollar business in 2002.

Competitive and Regulatory Environment

Sendwine believed that their main competition was the inertia of busy people. Too often, a person had the need to send a beautiful gift quickly, but ultimately did nothing and let the gift giving opportunity slide by. Their inertia stemmed from a lack of time and from the hassles involved in gift giving—including figuring out what to send and how to send it. Sendwine was designed to overcome this inertia.

Online Gift Retailers

Sendwine's second main source of competition was other online gift retailers. These companies sold a variety of items from flowers to gourmet food. Sites such as Harry & David's, 911gift and eGift overlapped considerably with Sendwine in terms of target customer segments and price ranges. (See Exhibit 3 for a list of gift site URLs.)

A related threat came from the recent move by portals into online shopping. In early 1999, Yahoo! spent $49 million on Viaweb and thereby acquired the ability to

[6]Reidy, Chris. "Wine Seller for the 90s," Boston Globe, Nov. 27, 1998.
[7]Jupiter Communications, "Online Gift Buying," October 1998, which is the source for data in the rest of this section.

host small and medium sized retailers moving online, providing them with software templates to create websites. Lycos acquired similar turnkey capabilities through a revenue sharing deal with ecommerce software provider Open Market. While portals did not yet offer wine gifts, they did host sites selling food and wine accessories and retailers focused on gift giving. Merchants that signed up with the portals benefited from the portals' huge traffic and from the trust that customers placed in the portals' brands.[8]

Amazon.com. An additional threat came from the renowned online retailer, Amazon.com.[9] Amazon launched its original book-selling website in July 1995, and steadily increased sales through new related offerings (e.g., videos and CDs) and acquisitions. Amazon.com introduced a gift service in November 1998. Items included books, videos, CDs, personal electronics, and toys. Amazon also offered advanced features such as Gift-Click (which allowed gift-givers to enter only the recipient's e-mail address, relying on Amazon to track down the recipient's physical address) and Gift Matcher (a recommendation service that suggested gifts based on the recipient's interests).

The Amazon.com gift site doubled in size in the six months following its launch. The site had expanded to include not only Amazon.com gifts, but also gifts from partners with offerings more closely related to Sendwine's, such as FragranceNet.com, Garden.com, and GourmetMarket.com. The threat from Amazon escalated in September 1999 when the company launched zSHOPS, which would host e-commerce sites for thousands of small and medium sized retailers.

Virtual Vineyards. Virtual Vineyards was the best recognized of the many sites selling wine online (see Exhibit 4 for partial results of a April 1999 Yahoo! search for "wine"). Founded in 1995, Virtual Vineyards sourced quality wines from small and medium sized vineyards that lacked the scale to secure nationwide distribution in retail stores. Virtual Vineyard's site described its selection of about 500 hard-to-find wines in a compelling manner, and provided a wealth of information about collecting and enjoying fine wine.

When asked about this competitive threat, Lannon maintained that Virtual Vineyards was a *wine-retailing* site, targeting consumers who bought wine by the case for their own consumption, whereas Sendwine was a *gift-retailing* site that sold wine by the bottle. Although one-third of Virtual Vineyard's revenues were reportedly derived from gifts,[10] these gifts were not packaged with the same elegance as Sendwine's. Moreover, with continued tightening in the regulatory environment Virtual Vineyards could no longer deliver product in a timely fashion: order fulfillment often required 8–10 days or more.

Regulatory Issues

By selling through its network of local retailers, Sendwine.com avoided legal problems related to the interstate shipment of wine. That was not the case for other online wine retailers. Virtual Vineyards, other online marketers, and some wineries had been shipping directly to wine lovers via UPS or Federal Express across state borders for years, while state authorities mostly looked the other way.[11] Some sites sought to avoid responsibility for potential legal problems following from interstate delivery. For example, K&L Wine Merchants' site carried the disclaimer, "Every sale we make is made within California, and non-California residents are responsible for determining whether they may lawfully import alcoholic beverages into their state. We make no representation relative to your right to import wines or spirits into your state."

Publicity about the Internet's sales potential—along with state governments' concerns about lost tax revenues from online sales that bypassed retail stores[12]—eventually precipitated a crackdown. Between 1996 and 1999, six states passed laws making direct wine shipment a felony, while other states explicitly targeted the Internet (e.g., in 1997, Minnesota passed a law prohibiting wine orders over the Web). Also, in 1997, Maine rescinded a law making it one of 13 "reciprocal" states (the group included wine producers California and Oregon among others). Reciprocal states had agreed to allow small shipments of wine for personal consumption from other reciprocal states.[13] In 1998, Federal Express and wholesalers in Massachusetts sued Virtual Vineyards. The state attorney sided with the wholesalers, forcing Virtual

[8]Troug, David. Forrester 1999

[9]Information regarding Amazon.com are taken from Amazon.com press releases available on their website.

[10]Reidy, Chris. "Wine Seller for the 90's," The Boston Globe, Nov. 27, 1998

[11]The U.S. Postal Service classifies wine as a hazardous substance and refuses to ship it according to: Associated Press. "Shipping Rules Sour Wine Business", December 19, 1998.

[12]In 1998, Congress passed a three-year Internet sales tax moratorium to encourage the growth of web commerce.

[13]Emert, Carol. "Wine-Selling Woes; Prohibition-era Rules Impede Direct Shipping Out of State", The San Francisco Chronicle, December 19, 1998.

Vineyards to comply with laws that forced liquor retailers to source from licensed wholesalers, rather than shipping directly from their own warehouses. Finally, in August 1999, following the Senate's lead, the US House of Representatives reinforced these trends by voting overwhelmingly in favor of a bill curtailing the online sale of alcohol for interstate delivery directly to consumers.

These actions had chilling effects on the direct shipment of wine. Kendall-Jackson of Santa Rosa stopped all direct shipments in 1997 after being fined $35,000 in 1997 by the state of Maryland. Alghren Vineyards, a small family winery in the Santa Cruz mountains, halted shipments to nonreciprocal states in 1996 after the felony laws emerged. In 1998, Virtual Vineyards had to completely revamp its business model: instead of shipping wine directly to end-consumers via UPS from its warehouse, it partnered with a Chicago-based distributor, Lionstone International, to distribute through a network of local distributors and wholesalers.[14]

Online Wine Retailers Gird for Battle

Concern over regulatory issues had prevented Virtual Vineyards from launching an IPO and funding a "get big fast" strategy. As Robert Olson, the company's founder said, "You can't break the law and go public."[15] Consequently, Virtual Vineyards, one of the first commercial websites, had, according to the Dow Jones News Service, "fallen into near obscurity" when compared to Amazon.com and other e-commerce startups.[16]

With a new distribution channel that solved its regulatory problems, Virtual Vineyards was able to reinvigorate its strategy in mid-1999. The company raised $30 million in a new venture capital round, hired a new CEO, and prepared an aggressive marketing campaign to relaunch its site as wine.com.

Virtual Vineyards would face strong new competition. A startup called WineShopper.com recently had raised $46 million from Kleiner Perkins and other venture capital firms. Like Virtual Vineyards, WineShopper planned to employ a network of local wholesalers to avoid regulatory problems. WineShopper aspired to offer depth of selection and information in wine retailing that was equivalent to what Amazon.com offered in books: eventually, the company planned to offer 20,000 different wines. A Kleiner Perkins partner acknowledged that "it was very possible that WineShopper will enter into formal marketing agreements with several of his firm's portfolio companies, including Amazon.com."[17]

Lannon had respect for these competitors and their backers, but believed that their business models were flawed. His research found that the average bottle of wine in the U.S. sold for less than $10 and more than 90% of the wine was consumed within 24 hours of purchase. He said:

> The vast majority of wine drinkers in the U.S. don't think much about wine until they need it to drink at dinner or to bring over to someone's house. Most people don't stock up on wine by the case, they prefer to buy it by the bottle as they need it. That puts the local retailer in the best position to serve customers. That's a big reason why we focused on gifts rather than being an on-line wine store like Virtual Vineyards. We create more value for customers as a service that makes sending wine as a gift fast and easy rather than as a way to buy 'mail-order' wine by the case for yourself. Plus, gifts are a bigger, less competitive category for us. The online wine retail business is incredibly crowded with thousands of sites shipping wine illegally and legally over the Internet.

In Lannon's view, WineShopper also was unlikely to be able to source fine wines that wine collectors would like to buy in case quantities, despite its relationships with regional wholesalers. He said, "'Amazoning' a category requires deep discounts and deep selection, but for the top names in fine wine, wholesalers can sell every case they can get their hands on through retailers at full retail price. Why would they go through WineShopper?" An alternative strategy for WineShopper would focus on high volume, lower priced wines (e.g., Gallo), but Lannon maintained that consumers would not buy such wine by the case, since it was widely available through retail outlets and shipping costs would be very high as a percentage of the total purchase price. Nevertheless, Lannon was concerned about competition from WineShopper.com. He said:

> We track competition relative to its impact on our ability to raise money. If they are smart, other guys will try to scare the best capital away from me. And let

[14]Ibid.

[15]Wingfield, Nick. "Heard on the Net: Virtual Vineyards to Boost Marketing Effort," Dow Jones News Service, June 18, 1999.

[16]Ibid.

[17]Spirrison, Bradley. "Venture Firms Toast Online Wine Industry," Venture Capital Journal, July 1, 1999

me tell you, the guys at Kleiner and Amazon are the pros at this. It's a well developed model now. They launch a company, and announce they've raised $46 million, when they've maybe only got $7 million actually in the bank and loose commitments for the rest. They say they're going to 'Amazon' the category with deep discounts, deep selection, deep information. And they say Amazon itself is going to lend its marketing muscle. All this is designed as a scare tactic to deter other startups, and let me tell you, very often it works!

Building Trust Online

Repeat business—that will be our lifeblood. For us, that's the promised land.

—Mike Lannon[18]

With a track record spanning less than one year, Sendwine's management lacked a clear understanding of what share of its new customers were likely to be converted into repeat users. Preliminary data suggested that to date, about 20 percent of new customers had used the service again. These repeat buyers turned out to be very heavy users, spending an average of $800 per year on the service. Of course, it was not yet clear if these patterns would hold as Sendwine scaled up its acquisition efforts, but this preliminary data suggested that the lifetime value of a loyal Sendwine customer might be very high. Lannon knew he needed to manage his marketing programs accordingly.

Through a Spring 1999 market research study conducted by an HBS field study team, Sendwine explored an inherent e-commerce hurdle: building trust online. Consumers had to trust online merchants in different ways than physical merchants because online customers didn't get to handle the product prior to purchase or carry it away immediately upon purchase. This issue was compounded for Sendwine since its gift senders rarely saw the product at all: it was shipped directly to the recipient. The field study team interviewed 25 customers, posing open-ended questions about their shopping experience then asking, "Why did you trust Sendwine?" Some of the specific results of the survey can be found in Exhibit 5, which includes data such as "Where They Came From"; "Top Three Reasons to Use Sendwine"; "Top Three Reasons to NOT Use Sendwine"; "Why did You Trust Sendwine?"; and "Why did You Hesitate?".

The field study team's conclusions were twofold. First, about one-third of the customers surveyed completed their purchase on their very first visit to the Sendwine.com website: they needed to find a gift quickly. The balance had previously discovered and explored Sendwine, but only made a purchase after two to four visits. Building trust with these two groups posed different challenges in terms of website design and marketing.

Second, in overcoming the trust hurdle, Sendwine had to address issues related to *credibility* and *quality. Credibility* (e.g., "they won't misuse my credit card") was critical to making the initial purchase and could be enhanced through the presentation of a secure and professional-looking web site; a professional-sounding radio ad; the listing rank on a Yahoo search; and even overhearing other people placing orders in the background when you called the toll-free phone number. *Quality* was relevant at the time of purchase and afterward; it was critical to repeat purchasing. Quality was enhanced through the elegant look of the web site and through the photos of product packaging both on the web and in print ads.

In considering how to enhance consumer trust and build the Sendwine brand, Sendwine.com's management team faced decisions in three areas: website design, content development, and marketing strategy.

Website Design

The field study survey provided customer feedback about a lack of simplicity and flexibility in site navigation (see Exhibit 5J, "Did They Like the Navigation"). In response, Lannon noted that upon its launch in November 1998 the site's design was very linear: "You saw the gift options, you chose the gift, entered the information and then left. There was no option to move around the site freely or browse." Since then, Lannon had hired a Director of Web Design, Paul Griffiths, and charged him with redesigning the site. The next version of the web page was under development. Knowing that online shopping lacked one important feature—touch and feel—could Paul and his development team create a convincing shopping experience with the functionality and flexibility which the first site had lacked?

[18]Reidy, Chris. "Wine Seller for the 90's," The Boston Globe, Nov. 27, 1998

Content Development

Another point of concern was whether to add content to the web site on choosing and serving wines. At The Wine Line, waiters had offered wine selections and descriptions, but what information should be offered to online customers? Survey results suggested that less than half of Sendwine's customers were interested in additional content (see Exhibit 5C, "Did They Want More Information on Wine?"). Also, the information needs of the "just browsing" consumer were clearly different from those of the "goal-oriented" consumer who wanted to make a quick purchase. Could the Web site cater to both types of customers while maintaining its elegance and simplicity? And if Sendwine added more content, where would it come from?

Marketing Strategy

Marketing budgets for growing online businesses had shifted during 1999, from an emphasis on banner ads and portal deals to heavier spending on traditional media (TV, radio, print and billboard ads). In one of the most radical moves by a start-up company, Monster.com had spent about $5 million in January 1999 to advertise on the Super Bowl, a sporting event which consistently drew one of America's largest television audiences. Radio campaigns and print media had seemed to be effective for Sendwine in the Boston, New York and San Francisco areas during the 1998 Christmas season. Also, Sendwine's 1999 Father's Day ads in the *Wall Street Journal* (Exhibit 6) had drawn a solid response. What media would be most appropriate for Sendwine's next wave of brand building efforts? TV was very expensive, but would provide a great way to show Sendwine's packaging and to communicate the emotions associated with gift giving. Also, what emotional chords should Sendwine's ads touch: should they 'press the fear button' (i.e., 'we'll protect you from embarrassment') or emphasize more positive aspects of gift giving ('you'll look clever!')? And most importantly, how much should the company spend on advertising in 1999? Debating these issues, Lannon said:

> The stakes are going up every month. Startups are coming into markets with huge marketing budgets trying to buy first mover advantage. The Internet is both causing this and enabling this. It used to take years to build well-known brands. Now it can happen in a matter of months. Very few people ever heard of Priceline or eToys or eBay a year ago. Now they are well-known brands. This presents a huge opportunity for companies like mine, but also a huge risk. On the positive side, we have the ability to create the market leader brand in our category essentially overnight.
>
> On the flipside, the risk is threefold. First, we would have to dedicate an incredible amount of money to the strategy, and spend it in a very short timeframe, so there is no margin of error. Second, if we can build a brand that fast, so can someone else with a lot of money—and by beating us to the punch, they could kill our ability to raise money ourselves. And third, driving traffic to our website before we can really handle the business is expensive and tremendously inefficient, and we could end up disappointing a lot of customers. And they are the audience who will ultimately determine whether we succeed or fail.

In addition to relying on advertising, Sendwine drove traffic to its website through an affiliate program that offered commissions ranging from 8 to 15 percent of the revenue generated (Exhibit 7). To accelerate customer acquisition efforts, Lannon and his team wanted to find high potential partners and offer them targeted deals. Given that the current affiliate program was generous, could Sendwine afford to offer more? Also, should Sendwine pursue affiliations with websites focused on providing information about wine, including Wine Spectator, Wine 101, Epicurious and/or Food & Wine? Or did his potential customers not research their wine gifts using these content sites?

Send.com

Given the present customer base and the potential of the www.send.com name, Lannon was considering other gift categories that might fit with the company's image and operations. He said, "I know my customers need to buy other gifts. When I have more products to offer, I'll really be able to lock them up." New products would have to be attractive to busy executives and frequent gift givers, and easily described on the web. Hard-to-find gifts were appealing because they could help Send.com maintain the price premium that Sendwine had achieved with wine. Some candidate categories included cigars, gourmet food, and other liquor or beer. Lannon was especially interested in gifts that were consumed by the recipient as part of a larger group:

> Gift giving is a social experience: you have a sender and a receiver. Giving fine wine as a gift is even *more* social, because the gift tends to be displayed for a long time like a trophy, then it is often consumed by a larger group, on a special occasion. There's a powerful viral marketing element to our wine gifts, because so many people are exposed to them. We'd like to duplicate this social dynamic with other Send.com gift offerings. For example, we've thought about things like golf lessons and gift certificates for fine restaurants and health spas.

Given the rapid development of the company, Lannon wondered not only which categories were appropriate, but also how long it would take to launch. How quickly could a new website be developed? How long would it take to line up sources of supply and fulfillment operations? He thought he might be able to launch Send.com in the fourth quarter of 1999. Was that too soon? Was he spreading his management team too thinly before they really had an opportunity to solidify the core Sendwine.com business?

There were no clear market leaders in most of the premium gift categories that Send.com might enter. So, fear of competitive preemption was not motivating the early implementation of a diversification strategy. However, the prospect of increased competition in the online wine category was encouraging Lannon to consider accelerating Send.com's launch. He said:

> I cannot afford to compete head-to-head against WineShopper.com, Kleiner Perkins and Amazon in a game that goes, 'We're wine, you're wine.' They'll suck all of the oxygen out of that room. So I'll give them wine. We're not in the *wine* business anyway.

Organizational Issues

Money was no longer a major concern now that Sendwine.com was on the VCs' radar screen, but Lannon knew he would face major challenges recruiting new talent, maintaining Sendwine's culture, and managing his own and his team's time.

Recruiting

Recruiting talented people for technical, strategic, and operational roles was a very high priority. Lannon said, "We're somewhat unusual for an Internet startup, in that we're trying to build for the long term. That requires building a great culture and a great workforce. Given the workload, we could easily have 80 employees now if I just stuffed cubicles. But there's a precious shortage of *good* people, and we've checked our staff growth somewhat to ensure we get people that meet our tough screening criteria." Lannon added:

> There aren't many people out there with ".com" experience, so we ask, 'Is this person smart? Do they have the right constitution for our business?' Just today one of my managers came in crying; she said she couldn't take it anymore. We don't run a sweatshop here, but in an Internet startup, you face huge change daily. For people that need structure and precision—and let me tell you, this woman is a perfectionist—this environment can be a killer.

The top management positions at Sendwine were still filled by members of the original startup team. Lannon said, "The team members have accepted any new role thrown at them. That's remarkable given the pace and magnitude of change here. To date, we've been able to grow organically. Look, I'd like to remain the CEO of this company, but along with my investors I constantly have to ask whether I'm the right guy. If we become a public company, we'll face an entirely new set of challenges that will require new management skills."

In recruiting, it was difficult managing expectations regarding compensation. Lannon said, "Money creates problems. There are a bunch of 23 year olds here making $100,000 who could leave tomorrow for $150,000. But you can't win by trying to pay up to the market. You keep them by creating a great culture, and by providing challenge and opportunity. And through stock options." He noted that all of Sendwine's managers at the director level and above had stock options, but said that below that level, few employees held options. He said:

> Everyone I interview knows someone with options. No one knows how to value them, they just know that they need them, and that more are better. So I spend a lot of time educating recruits. You know, you won't find senior executives in Internet startups making $300,000. It pretty much tops out at $125,000, then people take their upside in options. So when someone complains that they're taking a $40,000 pay cut to work here, I ask them, 'Would you invest $40,000 in lost wages for the chance to make $1 million?'

While Sendwine's managers focused considerable energy on recruiting, they did not expend much effort on employee retention. Lannon explained, "Ten percent of our people will leave, and I've learned that there's not much I can do about it. We don't lose them to other Web startups—one guy just left for an administrative job at a high school. They leave for lifestyle reasons."

Culture

Lannon was concerned about maintaining the scrappy accountability and thriftiness of a small start-up. This would be difficult, because Sendwine was hiring new members of management at a remarkable pace. Rapid headcount growth meant that members of the original startup team were greatly outnumbered by employees who hadn't witnessed the company's early trials and successes. Lannon noted that new managers went through a predictable cycle upon joining:

> Every time I hire a bright, energetic, successful employee, they come with all their preconceived notions. I have to say, 'Thank you for your ideas, but just wait 30 days before you implement them, and let the business come to you.' And we find that a light bulb goes off after about 30 days, and they realize, 'Wow, everything I thought was so obvious has to be questioned.' We're in virgin territory here; we're the first to build an online premium gift service, so we don't have metrics and common wisdom about best practices. We just don't know whether a typical customer wants to visit our site four times before they buy on the fifth visit.

Could the tenured minority imprint the right cultural values on these recent arrivals, and prevent them from importing solutions that were inappropriate for Sendwine's business? And, as rapid growth made it impossible for Lannon to maintain day-to-day contact with all of his managers, how could Lannon best shape the company's culture and its strategy? Lannon said:

> The growth process here is like cell division. As people's jobs get bigger, we split the job. With so many new managers, we have a real issue with communications. People ask, 'Who's the new guy in marketing, and what's he up to? I used to call his boss to give or receive a certain piece of information. Should I call the new guy instead?'
>
> I've made myself the focal point for a lot of communication, integrating information to develop our strategy, and feeding information back to people who need it. That takes a lot of my time. But the alternative would be to have my managers in meetings with each other all day long, and we don't have time for that either.

Conclusion

Having raised capital, time and focus became Sendwine's scarce resources: Lannon and his colleagues scrambled to exploit growth opportunities at Internet speed. Lannon said, "There is no excuse now to say 'I can't do that.' The money is available, we just need to manage our time." This crunch for time was best expressed by Sendwine's Director of Web Design, Paul Griffiths: "I'm trying to determine which one of my number one priorities is my number one priority!"

Lannon knew that Sendwine was in a race against time to become the market leader in the premium online gift giving category: only leaders prospered in Internet businesses. So far, Sendwine was winning the race. Lannon said, "If there were other clear leaders, we wouldn't have been funded to the extent we were and by the caliber of VCs involved." So his $10 million question resurfaced: "How should I spend my VC money?" Given the competitive environment and constraints on his management team's time, should he focus on improving Sendwine.com's operations and increasing the marketing push behind its wine gift service? Or should he accelerate the move into new gift categories under the Send.com umbrella brand? Could he do *both*?

Exhibit 1 SENDWINE SITE

Exhibit 2 ONLINE GIFT RETAILING—JUPITER REPORT[19]

Figure A: Online Shoppers' Percent of Total Online Spending on Gifts

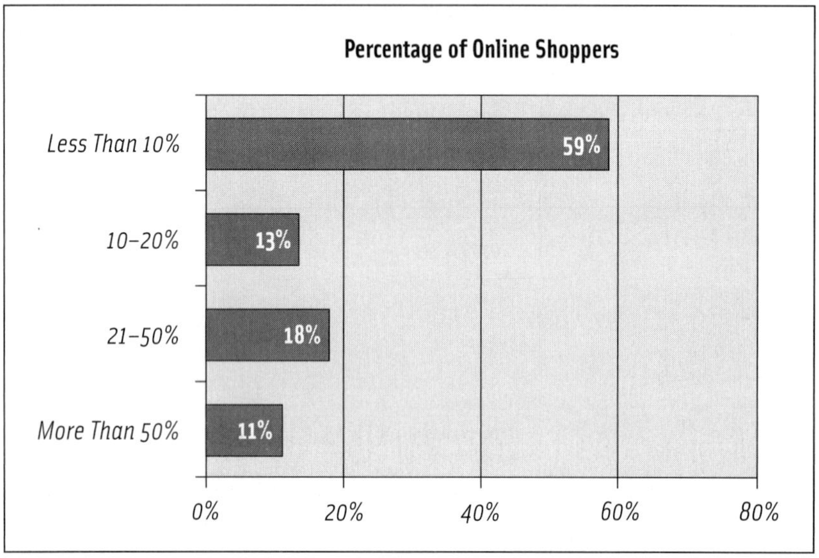

Figure B: Percentage of merchants that plan in 4Q 1998 to offer Gift Functionality

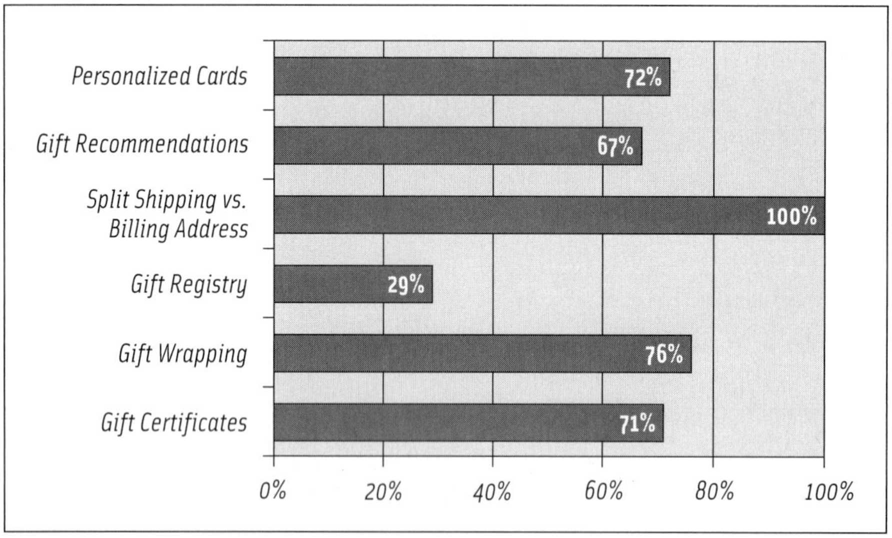

[19]http://www.jup.com/sps/shopping/briefs/9810/dcs11/index.html

Exhibit 3

SAMPLE OF ONLINE GIFT COMPETITOR URLS

Portal Sites Selling Gifts or Recommending Gift Sites	YAHOO!: *http://search.shopping.yahoo.com/search?cp=gift&P=all* ATT (and Market Square): *http://www.worldnet.att.net/shop/gifts.html* EXCITE: *http://www.excite.com/shopping/gifts_and_collectibles/* HOTBOT: *http://www.hotbot.com/shop/gifts/*
Sites specifically for Gifts	*http://www.thegift.com/* *http://www.911gift.com/* *http://www.1giftbasket.com/* *http://justflowers.com/jgb/* *http://www.giftbasketexpress.com/*
Online Sites selling Gifts	AMAZON: *http://www.amazon.com/exec/obidos/subst/gifts/gift-services/gift-services.html/* CD-NOW: *http://www.cdnow.com/cgi-bin/mserver/SID=1771719413/pagename=/RP/GC/main.giftcenter.html* Other: *http://cybershop.com/*
Retailers selling Gifts online	*http://www.harryanddavid.com/* *http://www.jcrew.com/cgi-bin/index.cgi* *http://www.brookstone.com/* *http://www.ftd.com/*
Wine Sites offering Gifts	Virtual Vineyards: *http://www.virtualvin.com/exec/query?page=home&shop=giftshop* Others: *http://www.amivin.com/GiftWizard/* *http://tahoewines.com/* *http://www.jersey.net/~leali/*

Exhibit 4

PARTIAL RESULTS OF YAHOO! SEARCH ON "WINE"

- *Pop's Wine & Spirits* - seller of fine & rare wines. Includes catalog and online ordering.
- *Premium Italian Wines and Spirits*
- *Prime Wine*
- *Provin* - top quality Slovenian wines.
- *QuanXing Distillery* - produces wine.
- *Rare Wine Cellar* - vintage wine and gifts.
- *Robert Wright & Associates* - shipping and export services including private brands and custom labels for California and Washington wineries.
- *Rushworth & Woof*
- *Sainsbury's Wine Direct* - Mail order your wine from Sainsbury's. This service allows you to browse a selection of wines sold in our stores and have them delivered to your door.
- *SendWine.com* - send gifts of fine wine, port or champagne nationwide.
- *Signature Wine Cellars* - offering custom-designed labels and wines for special events and gifts.
- *Silver Spirits* - Fine Wine and Spirits. Newsletter published monthly by owner Barry Silver. It captures the essence of what's best in new releases, current releases, and rarities in the world of fine wines.
- *Simeon Wines@*
- *St. George Spirits* - distillers of eaux de vie (fruit brandies), grappas, marcs and pure fruit dessert wines.
- *Tarkington's* - offering wine, beer, gift baskets and specialty foods.
- *TasteTour* - series of guides for anyone who enjoys wine or is in a profession where wine expertise is considered a personal or business asset.
- *Tinamou Wine Company* - premium French wines and vintage ports; price list included.
- *Tincknell & Tincknell* - provides services and consultation to wineries, wine industry business partners, and other luxury products companies.
- *Transylvania Imports* - presents the Vampire Vineyards line of fine spirits imported directly from the Transylvanian Alps of Romania.
- *United Grand International Ltd.* - We offer the opportunity to invest in fine wines. We import and distribute wine in China and deal mainly with French and Portuguese wines.
- *Vergina Inc.* - specializing in Greek wine.
- *Victoria Wine* - home delivery and gift services.
- *Vignerons de Buzet, Les* - cooperative cellar includes information about grape variety, production, les châteaux and more. (In French and English)
- *Vinexpert* - Vintners reserve selection, Chai Maison and Barons.
- *Vinexport* - exporter and marketer of Romanian wines.
- *Vineyard Collection* - includes much information regarding the French wine producers and growers; (in French and English).
- *Vintime* - offers rare wines, shipped worldwide.
- *Virtual Vineyards* - sells wines and specialty foods. Buy wine by the bottle or case. Also has a wine-of-the-month membership club.
- *Virtual Wine from Hitchins Marketing* - personalized wine labeling; delivered anywhere in the world.
- *Warre's Port* - founded in 1670, with vineyards in Portugal's Douro valley.
- *Washington Tasting Society* - hosts regular wine, beer, food tasting events.
- *What's The Big Occasion?* - wine and champagne overnight delivery service with custom labeling.
- *Whitley On Wine* - subscription-based newsletter by syndicated wine columnist.
- *Wigglesworth Wine Company* - stock holders of fine & rare wines.
- *Wine - The Interactive Gourmet* - Over 900 fine wines of France, Italy, the US and more. wine search database. ask Daniel Johnnes. Restaurant listings.
- *Wine Authority, The* - information and buying service to provide an intelligent and economical wine buying decision.
- *Wine Broker, The*
- *wine country connection* - travel, lodging, gourmet food and wine - a selection of the best from Northern California wine country.
- *Wine Country of Missouri* - wines, wineries, special events, B&Bs, restaurants, shops, varietals, wine history, wine and health.
- *Wine Etc.* - selling gift baskets, personalized wine labels, glass etching, plus Californian and imported wines.
- *Wine Hunter NYC* - wine consultation, tips and more.
- *Wine Messenger, The* - direct order wine service.
- *Wine of Australia* - official Internet venue of the Australian wine industry. Provides information on the wineries and wine regions of Australia.
- *Wine Society of the World* - buy from a selection of rare, fine, allocated and hard-to-find wines, ports and other fine beverages.
- *Wine Specialist, The* - offers a range of single malt scotches and fine wines.
- *Wine Time* - order fine wines and gourmet foods online. Offers worldwide shipping.
- *Wine.com*
- *WineLink UK Ltd.* - specialist Internet marketing service for growers, shippers, wholesalers and merchants of wine.
- *Wineport* - provides mail order service from a selection of wines from Portugal's Douro demarcated region where the authentic Port Wine comes from.
- *Wines on the Internet* - listing of wine events, resources and information to learn about wines, virtual tasting room and virtual wineries.
- *WineStore, A* - offers hard to find wines, normally distributed only at the winery.
- *Winetel Italy* - dedicated to Italian wine; contains list of DOC wines, producers, and the Italian wine news.
- *WineWeb* - a worldwide showcase of wines and wineries with extensive search capabilities. Online ordering provided for member wineries.
- *World Wide Wine Network* - learn about Australian and New Zealand wines and then buy them online.

Exhibit 5 SOME RESULTS OF THE SPRING 1999 HBS FIELD STUDY RESEARCH[20]

A) Where Did They Come From?

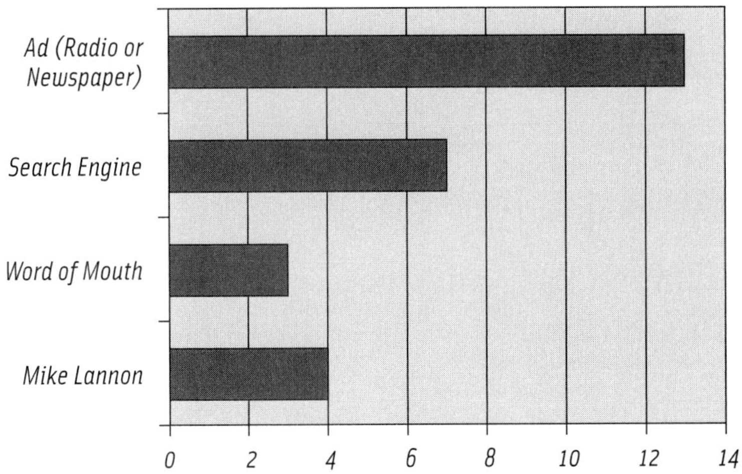

B) Did They Shop Around?

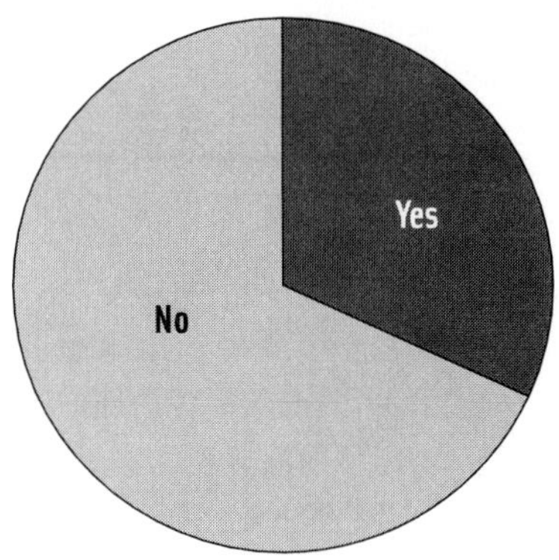

C) Did They Want More Information on Wine?

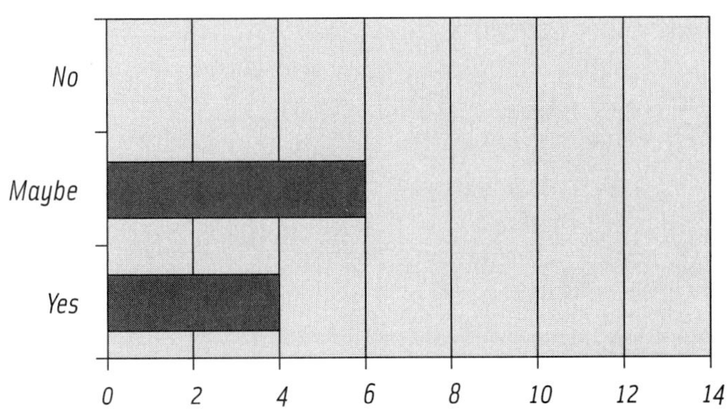

[20]"Sendwine.com & Trust"—a Harvard Business School Field Study completed by Charmaine Ess and Ann O'Hara, May 1999.

D) Who Was the Recipient?

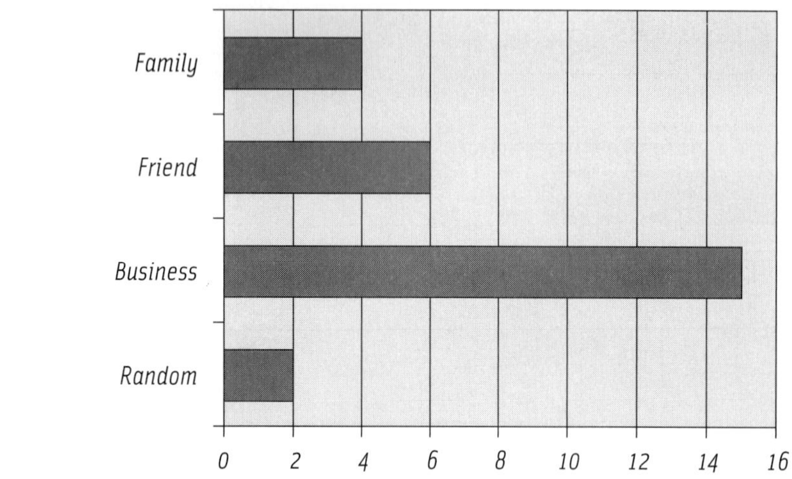

E) What Was the Occasion?

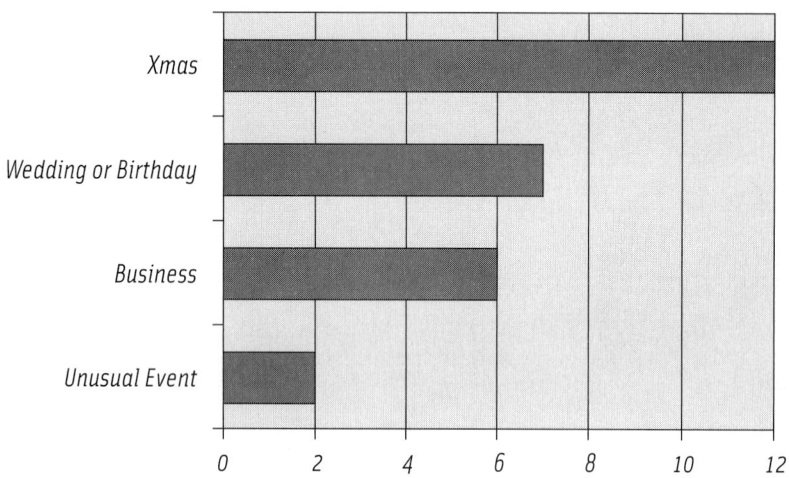

F) How Quickly Did the Gift Need To Be Delivered?

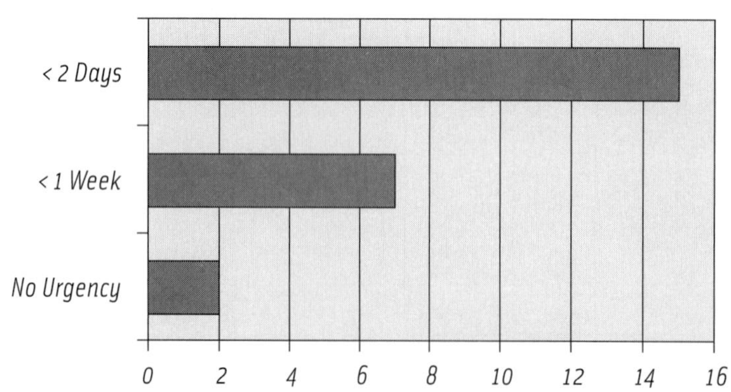

G) Top Three Reasons to Use Sendwine[21]

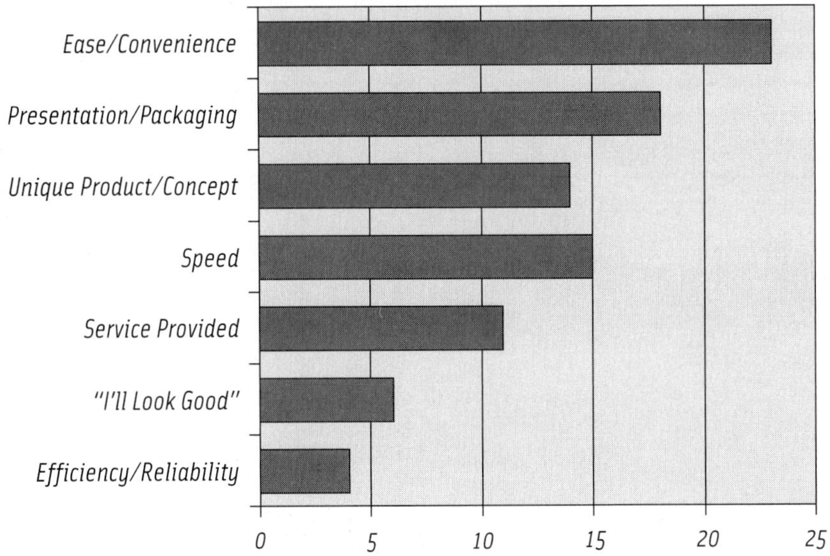

H) Top Three Reasons to Not Use Sendwine

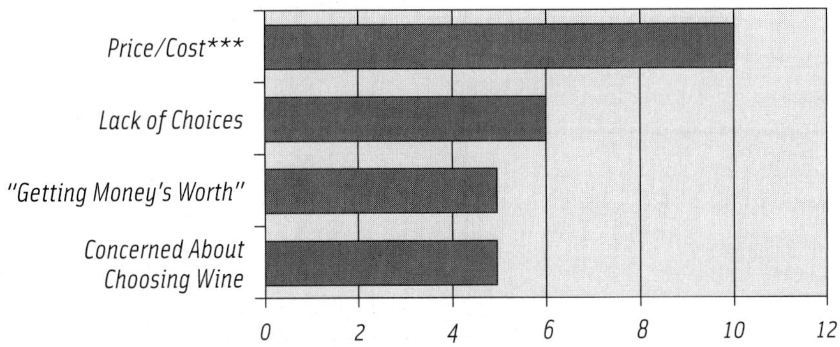

***While customers listed this reason, it was often named as "perhaps it is too expensive for most people" or "too expensive for the occasion."

[21]Note: Multiple Responses were recorded

I) Why They Trusted Sendwine

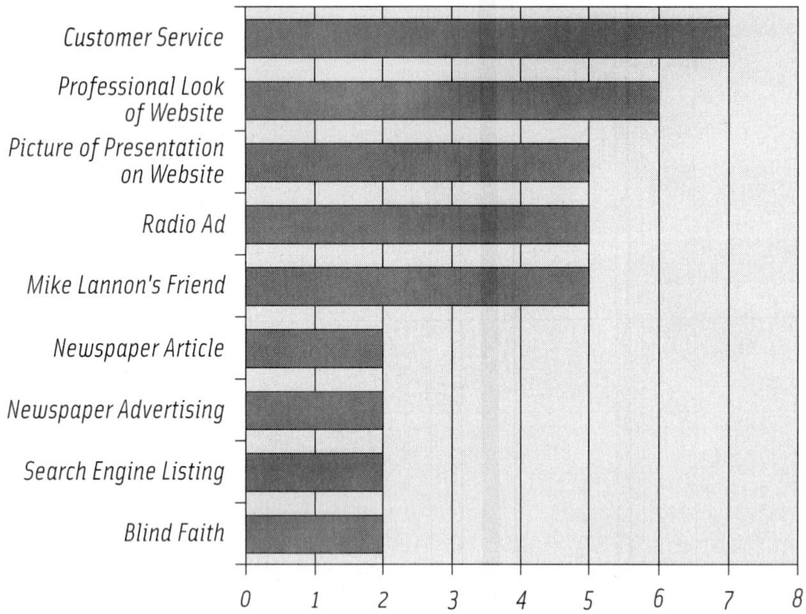

J) Did They Like the Navigation?

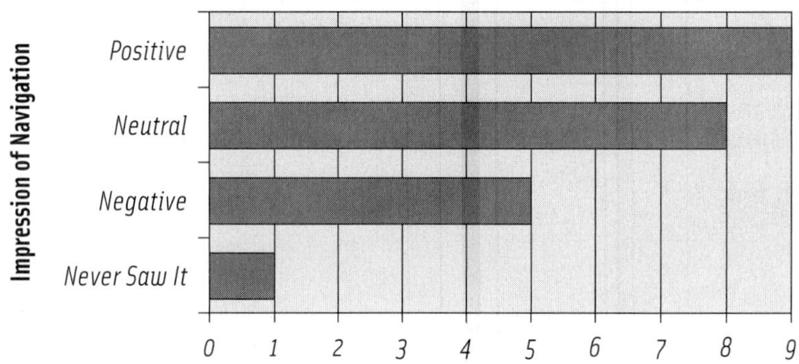

Exhibit 6 SENDWINE 1999 FATHER'S DAY AD IN WALL STREET JOURNAL

Exhibit 7 SOME FOOD AND WINE AFFILIATE PROGRAMS

CandyNation.com. The CandyNation affiliate program offers to pay 15% commissions on all sales of candy from your web site. Checks are issued quarterly, once commissions have reached $100. A variety of graphics are made available. Rating: $$

Great American Spice Company. The Great American Spice Company (GASC) is one of the few that offers affiliates commissions on sales after the initial referral. For one year after you initially send a customer to GASC you will be entitled to receive commissions, even if the visitor never visits your site again. Commissions are 10% on all products, and online commission tracking is made available. Sales are tracked through unique affiliate ID numbers. Another great aspect of this program is that checks are issued on a monthly basis, with no monthly minimum check sizes. Rating: $$$1/2

Indian River Fruit. Indian River affiliate program pays 10% commissions on all sales referred from your site for these items. Additionally, IRF pays follow-up commissions on all additional purchases customers you refer make for a whole year, even if they don't link from your web site again. Rating: $$$$

Seattle's Finest Gourmet Coffee. Seattle's Finest offers a new affiliate program that pays 20% commissions on all sales referred by your site. Products range in price $9 to $29 per pound, with most varieties available in 1 and 5 pound bags. Sales are tracked through a unique URL and cookies, and are monitored by Yahoo! Store (formerly Viaweb). Online commission tracking is available and updated daily. Rating: $$$1/2

Sendwine.com. Sendwine.com offers an affiliate program through the respected Be Free third-party affiliate service. You will be able to earn commissions up to 15% on all sales referred from your site. Their commission schedule is somewhat complicated however (Standard and Vintage membership?) and which type of affiliate membership your site is given is up to the sole discretion of Sendwine.com. Commissions are dependent on this status, and on the dollar volume of sales you refer in a quarterly period. The Sendwine.com web site does proclaim that their gift prices range from $39 to $750 per sale, resulting in some potentially hefty commissions. Average sale has been quoted at $89 or so. Some may also see their exclusivity condition as overly strict, but being one of the first wine-related affiliate programs, this shouldn't represent a problem for most. Rating: $$$

Virtual Vineyards. Virtual Vineyard allows you to partner with one of the best established brands on the Internet, insuring customer trust in their purchases. As an affiliate, you are able to earn 8% commissions on all sales that are referred from your site. The program is administered though the LinkShare network, which handles all sales tracking. Online commission reporting is also made available from the LinkShare site. Virtual Vineyards provides a variety of text copy, buttons and banners for affiliate use, and you are allowed to link to any page on their site, be it the home page, or a specific product. Checks are issued each month, once commissions reach $50. Rating: $$$

Source: Quickclick.com

5

Online Brokers

This chapter describes online brokers, companies that use the Internet to help clients identify prospective trading partners and sometimes help clients negotiate terms of sale. Online brokers have emerged in most of the businesses where brokers play important roles in the offline economy, e.g., real estate, securities trading, and travel reservations. As is often the case with offline brokers, online brokers may be retained to represent one party to a potential transaction (e.g., the buyer) yet may still maintain business relationships with parties on the other side of that transaction (e.g., the seller). These relationships can lead to conflicts of interest. Online and offline, a central challenge for brokers is managing such conflicts.

The first section of the chapter defines the online broker business model, demonstrates different ways to categorize brokers, and explains the differences between that model and the business models employed by other Internet companies, most notably online market makers. The second section presents a brief summary of the various ways that online brokers create value for their clients. The third section analyzes the economic model for online brokers, focusing on their revenue and cost drivers. Building on that analysis, the fourth section examines the payoff to online brokers from pursuing a "Get Big Fast" strategy, i.e., investing aggressively in customer acquisition and brand building. The fifth section asks, When does it make sense to position a business as an online broker versus an online retailer or an online market maker? The final section explores some of the challenges that offline brokers and their clients face when brokers move their businesses online.

Assistant Professor Thomas Eisenmann and Research Associate Alastair Brown prepared this note as the basis for class discussion.

WHAT ARE ONLINE BROKERS?

Definition

A broker is defined as "a person hired to act as an agent or intermediary in making contracts or sales."[1] Brokers play important roles in many offline businesses: Real estate agents, independent insurance agents, stock brokers, travel agents, talent agents, headhunters, independent manufacturers' sales representatives, and personal shoppers all play a brokerage role. Brokers are retained by *clients;* brokers help their clients identify potential transaction partners and sometimes help negotiate the transaction itself. Online brokers undertake these same functions, exploiting the Internet's ability to facilitate searches and communications.

Categorization and Conflicts of Interest

Brokers might be categorized in several different ways: for example, those who deal with businesses versus consumers, those who maintain an ongoing relationship with clients (e.g., stock brokers) versus assisting with a single transaction (e.g., real estate agents), and those with buyers versus sellers as clients. The last of these distinctions can become fuzzy: Who is the client for a travel agent? Apparently, the client is the consumer or business seeking help with travel plans. While travel agents must meet the needs of these buyers to attract and retain business, they are actually paid by the airlines, i.e., by the sellers. Airlines sometimes offer travel agents special bonuses (called "overrides") to push tickets for specific routes. This creates an incentive for the travel agent to suggest travel plans that may not be ideal for a client in terms of cost and/or convenience. Of course, a travel agency is likely to lose business if it repeatedly abuses its clients' trust and puts its own interests ahead of clients' needs. But due to information asymmetry there is a lot of "wiggle room" in such a relationship: Until the advent of online travel agencies, clients did not have access to data from computer reservation systems (CRSs), so they were unlikely to be aware of options that their travel agent had rejected.

Conflicts of this sort are pervasive in brokerage relationships, both online and offline. For example, "flesh-and-blood" stock brokers are expected to help a client pick investment vehicles that are consistent with the client's risk and liquidity preferences. However, stock brokers are regularly instructed to push securities underwritten by their employers. Likewise, residential real estate brokers who represent a buyer often split the 6 percent commission—paid by the seller—with the seller's broker. Does that arrangement give the buyer's broker an appropriate incentive to find the property that best meets the buyer's needs or negotiate the best possible price? Of course not!

Distinctions Between Internet Business Models

The distinction between online brokers and other Internet business models can easily be blurred, as demonstrated by the following examples. First, consider the differences between online content providers and online brokers. Online content providers are defined as companies that use the Internet to deliver professionally produced, copyrighted information.[2] Online brokers often offer such information as well. For example, brokers might maintain comprehensive and up-to-date lists of sellers (or buyers), which help them attract and serve clients. So, is REALTOR.com, which publishes lists (professionally produced and copyrighted) of homes for sale, an online content provider? Not by our definitions: A broker's central purpose is to represent one party in a transaction. The content they distribute is a means to an end—a successful transaction. By contrast, for online content providers, transmitting information is an end in itself—their central purpose.

CNET, a self-described "information intermediary" that focuses on technology products and services, illustrates how a company can simultaneously play the roles of content provider, portal, and broker.[3] CNET has a staff of several hundred editors who write reviews of computer products and news articles about technology trends—and clearly operates as a *content provider* in this regard. However, to provide users with comprehensive and convenient access to all the resources they may need in researching and purchasing technology products, CNET also (1) provides links to third-party content sites, including articles published by its direct competitors (a *portal* role) and (2) offers comparative pricing data for a full range of online retailers, then provides links to those retailers, so users can purchase computer goods after they have completed their research (a *broker* role).

Second, what is the difference between an online market maker and an online broker? A broker's central purpose is to represent a client in a transaction. By contrast, a market maker's central purpose is to organize and manage a marketplace. In doing so, market makers provide, on behalf of multiple buyers and sellers, three sets of services: (1) a place to trade (physical or virtual), (2) a set of rules that govern exchanges between marketplace participants (e.g., the types of goods that may be traded, payment terms, and processes for dispute resolution), and (3) infrastructure needed to ensure that transactions can be completed smoothly (e.g., legal codes, information systems that facilitate the matching of buyers and sellers).[4] While many market makers are neutral intermediaries (with no clients), some *are* strongly affiliated with buyers or sellers; in those instances, market makers have clients in the same sense as brokers.

Therefore, *some market makers play a brokerage role, but many do not.* Similarly, *some brokers play a market maker role, although many do not,* because they organize and maintain a marketplace. When the two roles overlap, the question of whether to classify a firm as a market maker or a broker must hinge on the admittedly vague concept of purpose: Does the firm see its central purpose to be client representation or marketplace organization?

Based on these definitions, it should be clear that Priceline.com, which allows consumers to "name their own price" for airline tickets and other goods and services, is an example of an online market maker rather than an online broker.[5] Priceline does not have a clear-cut buy- or sell-side affiliation: It creates value for both consumers, who benefit from deep discounts, and airlines, who use the service to liquidate excess inventory. Furthermore, Priceline provides (1) a place to trade (its website), (2) rules for market governance (e.g., consumers cannot specify a preferred airline), and (3) infrastructure needed to complete the transaction (e.g., software that determines whether Priceline will meet a consumer's bid).

By contrast, offline and online travel agents (e.g., Travelocity) better fit the description of brokers.[6] Unlike Priceline, travel agents do not establish rules that govern exchange—those rules tend to be set by the airlines themselves. Nor do travel agents provide market participants with a place to trade or infrastructure to complete transactions; those functions are fulfilled by market makers who operate computerized reservation systems (such as Sabre) that knit together airlines and travel agencies.

We can further "stress test" our definitions by asking whether Microsoft CarPoint, an online car-buying service, is a broker or a market maker.[7] This is a more difficult call. CarPoint allows consumers to avoid face-to-face haggling with auto dealers. When a consumer's request for a price quote for a specific vehicle is referred to a CarPoint-affiliated dealer, that dealer is expected to respond with a non-negotiable offer. Beyond haggle-free buying, CarPoint offers consumers a wide array of information that is useful as they research their purchases, e.g., detailed vehicle specification data and dealer invoice prices. Notwithstanding these considerable benefits to consumers, CarPoint's RFQ (request for quotation) process is structured to the advantage of its affiliated dealers, because CarPoint grants its dealers territorial exclusivity. A consumer's request for a quote on a Camry will be forwarded only to the closest CarPoint-affiliated Toyota dealer; by contrast, some of CarPoint's competitors with stronger buy-side affiliations (e.g., OpenAuto.com) organize reverse auctions between multiple dealers. Consistent with CarPoint's sell-side affiliation, most of CarPoint's revenue is derived from subscription fees paid by affiliated dealers.

So, CarPoint meets a key test for being a broker: It has clients, namely, its dealers. But does CarPoint also meet the tests for being a market maker? Yes, it provides a place to trade, although the information exchanged between buyers and sellers in CarPoint's marketplace is fairly limited. CarPoint also establishes rules governing exchange (i.e., no haggling allowed). Finally, CarPoint provides the information infrastructure needed to manage the RFQ process. So, CarPoint looks like both a broker and a market maker. Hence, we need to invoke the test of purpose: CarPoint appears to view its central objective to be generating leads for dealers—a brokerage function. To the extent that CarPoint also fulfills market maker functions, it does so to advance that objective.

HOW DO ONLINE BROKERS CREATE VALUE FOR CLIENTS?

Although online brokers create value in many ways for clients and for their trading partners (collectively referred to as website users), the most important way is reducing search costs. Users can quickly and conveniently search vast online databases, accessible 24 hours a day, from any location with Internet access. By publishing such databases online instead of in printed form, brokers reduce their production and distribution costs and can offer users more comprehensive and up-to-date information. The immediate availability of information is vital for users who track changing market conditions, such as day traders—individuals who buy and sell stocks based on minute-by-minute price fluctuations.

Online brokers also create value by relying on software to "remember" a user's preferences, then tailoring an online experience to the user's personal needs. For example, online stock brokers allow their clients to program alerts to be sent when a stock trades above or below a certain price. Of course, flesh-and-blood brokers can provide the same service, but at a much higher cost.

Finally, online brokers exploit the ubiquitous connectivity afforded by the Internet to facilitate communication between clients and their prospective trading partners. Frequently, facilitation takes the form of forwarding leads. For example, the shopping "bot" (short for "robot") mySimon.com uses software "spiders" that constantly "crawl" across the Web, searching online retailers' sites for their current prices for a wide range of products. Consumers searching for a given product receive a list of retailers and their prices; then consumers can click on a retailer's name to be linked directly to the retailer's webpage that features that item.

These benefits offered by online brokers suggest the attributes of industries where online brokers are likely to be most successful:

- *Information-Rich, Complex Products and Services Suited for Parametric Searches.* Examples include the purchases of homes, cars, PCs, insurance, and airline tickets. In each case, buyers have to choose between many product varieties with different features, most of which are specifiable in ways that allow parametric searches.
- *Inventory Is Perishable; Supply and Demand Conditions Are Highly Dynamic.* The Internet's ability to continuously update inventory and price information provides a great advantage for online brokers in businesses like stock trading or air travel, where prices change by the minute.
- *High Search Costs.* Search costs rise as the number of potential trading partners increases. Consider, for example, the time saved in using mySimon.com to search for pricing information for a Palm V from several dozen websites. In addition, search costs are dependent on the two attributes already listed: When products are complex and their prices change rapidly, it will take longer to research alternatives.

In some businesses, online brokers make available information that previously has never been directly accessible to consumers. For example, REALTOR.com allows prospective home buyers to access data from the multiple listing services maintained by a consortium of local real estate agents. Likewise, online travel agents give consumers direct access to data from computer reservation systems.

Although the analysis above suggests that online brokers can add considerable value by reducing search costs, online brokers typically cannot match their flesh-and-blood counterparts in helping clients negotiate a transaction. Home-buying sites may deliver qualified leads and may automate the labor intensive exchange of legal documents, but it will be many years before software agents can replace human brokers in guiding buyers and sellers through the complex and often emotionally wrenching process of negotiating purchase terms.

ONLINE BROKER ECONOMICS

This section describes the revenue and cost drivers for a sample of five leading online brokers: Autobytel.com (a car-buying service similar to CarPoint); Homestore.com (a portfolio of real-estate–related websites, including REALTOR.com), E*Trade (an online stock broker that has diversified into online banking and other financial services), Travelocity (an online travel agency), and InsWeb (a website that helps consumers secure quotes for insurance policies). Because these online brokers operate in such different businesses, it is difficult to generalize about their economic models. However, the brokers have one thing in common: With the exception of E*Trade, which earned a $34 million operating profit (before the amortization of goodwill and merger-related charges), each broker lost between $29 million and $35 million (before merger-related amortization and stock compensation charges) during the first three calendar quarters of 2000 (see Exhibit 1).[8]

Exhibit 5-1 SAMPLE ONLINE BROKERS' P&LS FOR FIRST THREE QUARTERS OF 2000

	Autobytel	Homestore	InsWeb	Travelocity	E*Trade
$ in Millions					
Revenue	$49.7	$151.0	$18.8	$127.2	$1,122.3
Cost of revenue	0	40.0	0	51.5	408.5
Gross profit	49.7	110.9	18.8	75.7	713.8
Sales and marketing	50.4	90.4	31.0	80.8	402.0
Product development	18.1	9.8	7.2	13.8	106.6
General and administrative	10.0	39.5	15.8	12.4	171.0
Operating income	(28.8)	(28.8)	(35.2)	(31.3)	34.2
% of Revenue					
Cost of revenue	0%	26.5%	0%	40.5%	36.4%
Gross profit	100	73.4	100	59.5	63.6
Sales and marketing	101.4	59.9	164.9	63.5	35.8
Product development	36.4	6.5	38.3	10.8	9.5
General and administrative	20.1	26.2	84.0	9.7	15.2
Operating income	−57.9	−19.1	−187.2	−24.6	3.0

Source: Adapted from company SEC filings, retrieved via EDGAR.

Revenue Streams

Online brokers collect revenue in many different ways, including:

- *Commissions and Other Transaction-Related Fees.* Commissions and transaction fees were the largest source of revenues for Travelocity, E*Trade, and InsWeb. Commissions on travel bookings accounted for 75 percent of Travelocity's revenue (most of the balance came from advertising); such commissions, paid by airlines, hotels, and rental car companies, represented 5.6 percent of the value of gross bookings made through Travelocity. Likewise, transaction fees (earned when consumers clicked-through listings on InsWeb to secure a quote from an insurance company) accounted for 84 percent of InsWeb's revenue (the balance came from system integration fees).
- *Subscription Fees.* Subscription fees, which do not vary directly with transaction volume, were the dominant source of revenue for Autobytel and provided 53 percent of revenue for Homestore (the balance came from advertising). Autobytel charged its 5,200 affiliated dealers monthly fees to receive leads. Homestore charged subscription fees for hosting personalized webpages for its 131,000 affiliated real estate agents and for providing them with lead management tools.

- *Advertising.* Online brokers typically generated heavy traffic from consumers researching a purchase—a very attractive audience for advertisers. Among the sample companies, Homestore and Travelocity have been the most successful at exploiting this opportunity, earning 47 percent and 23 percent of their revenues from advertising, respectively.
- *System Integration Fees.* To facilitate the real time management of leads, online brokers frequently had to integrate their information systems with those of their clients. Some online brokers were able to charge for this effort. For example, InsWeb earned 16 percent of its revenue from system integration fees.

With the exception of E*Trade, none of the sample companies earned appreciable revenue by charging consumers directly. As was the case with online content providers, consumers seemingly had come to expect online brokers to deliver their services free of charge.

Of course, the questions "Who pays you?" and "Where does your revenue come from?" inevitably beg the question "Where do your loyalties lie?" For example, even at E*Trade, where direct payments from consumers comprised over 90 percent of revenues, critics charged that the company sometimes pursued policies that increased revenue at its customers' expense.[9] Specifically, E*Trade earned 6 percent of its revenue from order-flow rebates, paid by other broker-dealers who executed E*Trade customers' trades. These broker-dealers profited from the spread between the bid price and ask price for a security. The practice of accepting order-flow rebates was commonplace in the securities industry, and broker-dealers were subject to regulatory scrutiny intended to ensure that customers received the best possible prices. Nevertheless, many day traders believed that directing trades to third-party broker-dealers led to sub-par price realization because a stock's price might move during the time it took an online broker to hand off a trade, and because a broker-dealer would still seek to maximize its spread within the constraints posed by regulators. For this reason, day traders often preferred to trade through firms that provided "Level II quotes," which gave day traders direct access to current bid-ask information across the entire market, and allowed them to specify the parties with whom they wished to trade.

Cost Categories

Online brokers' expenses can be divided into four main categories: cost of revenues, product development costs, sales and marketing costs, and general and administrative (G&A) expense. The first three categories are examined below. G&A expense includes typical overhead items such as salaries for legal, human resources, and finance staff, along with payments for professional services; it will not be discussed further.

Cost of Revenue. Two of the sample companies that were engaged principally in lead generation—Autobytel and InsWeb—did not even present an accounting category called "cost of revenue"; this made sense, because few of the operating costs varied directly with transaction volume. By contrast, cost of revenue was quite high as a percentage of revenue for the two sample companies that helped consumers complete transactions: 36 percent and 41 percent for E*Trade and Travelocity, respectively. For both firms, costs that varied with transaction volume included (1) website hosting and telecommunications and (2) the very substantial costs associated with maintaining call centers to field customers' phone and e-mail inquiries. By way of comparison, in April 1999, 288 of online stock broker DLJdirect's total staff of 466 were employed in customer service functions.[10] E*Trade also booked expenses for third-party content (e.g., stock quotes, research reports, news services) under cost of revenue, along with expenses incurred in clearing and settling trades. While E*Trade did not report the latter expense category separately, "Brokerage, Clearing, and Exchange Fees" amounted to 15 percent of revenue for competitor DLJdirect.

Product Development. Website development costs for online brokers varied widely in both absolute terms and as a percentage of revenue, depending on the nature and scale of the transactions that brokers processed. There was a significant fixed-cost component in building and maintaining a website; hence, the three largest firms—E*Trade, Homestore, and Travelocity—spent substantially less on product development as a percentage of revenue (10 percent, 7 percent, and 11 percent respectively) than the two smallest companies, Autobytel and InsWeb, which spent 36 percent and 38 percent, respectively.

Sales and Marketing. Online brokers spent heavily on online and offline advertising and on distribution partnerships designed to drive consumers to their websites. Through distribution partnerships with portals and online content providers, online brokers often paid a share of revenues generated by any new users that these distribution partners directed to brokers' sites. In addition, some online brokers maintained direct sales forces, e.g., Autobytel, which needed a sizable direct-selling staff to recruit and train the 5,200 dealers in its network.

Advertising and distribution expenses had both fixed and variable components. In particular, a threshold spending level was required to employ offline mass media effectively (e.g., TV, radio, magazines). Below that threshold level, ad campaigns failed to generate enough impressions to break through background advertising clutter and encourage consumer trial. Given this fixed element in marketing budgets, larger online brokers tended to spend less on marketing as a percentage of revenue than smaller online brokers—although spending by online brokers was still extremely high when compared to offline brokerage firms. The three largest companies in the sample, E*Trade, Homestore, and Travelocity, spent 36 percent, 60 percent, and 64 percent of their revenues on sales and marketing, respectively, whereas the two smallest companies, Autobytel and InsWeb, spent 101 percent and 165 percent, respectively.

Lifetime Value of a Customer

As noted above, online brokers spent heavily to acquire new customers. But were brokers' marketing efforts economically justified? This can best be determined by calculating the lifetime value of a customer, which equals the discounted present value of the variable contribution generated by a customer, less the cost of acquiring that customer. E*Trade, for example, reported in SEC filings that it spent an average of $263 in fiscal 2000 to acquire each new account. Based on industry averages for online stock brokers, we might expect E*Trade's customers to generate about $600 in revenue per year.[11] Variable costs for online stock brokers averaged about 50 percent of revenue, and customer retention rates were quite high, averaging about 90 percent per year. High retention rates were explained in part by high levels of customer satisfaction, and in part by the hassles involved with closing a securities brokerage account and transferring stocks and fund balances elsewhere. Discounting $300 of annual variable contribution at 10 percent over the ten-year average life of a customer relationship[12] yields a present value of $1,843 per customer—comfortably in excess of the cost of acquiring a customer. We can surmise that E*Trade's aggressive marketing efforts were yielding a positive economic payoff, consistent with the observation that E*Trade was the only firm in our sample that earned a positive operating margin in 2000.

The lifetime value of a customer calculation yielded a negative value for some of the other online brokers in the sample. As noted above, Autobytel spent 101 percent of its revenue on sales and marketing through the first three quarters of 2000. This figure was alarming for two reasons. First, if Autobytel was in launch mode, such heavy spending might be understandable, but that was not the case. Autobytel was a well-established Internet brand—the first mover and still the leader in its category, with a 50 percent share of all online transactions.[13] Second, whereas online stock brokers benefited from high customer retention rates, online brokers that assisted customers with infrequent purchases (e.g., cars, homes, or insurance policies) found it much more difficult to encourage repeat traffic. So, Autobytel was spending 101 percent of revenue to attract consumers who might not have a reason to visit the site for another three to five years. Could loyalty be sustained under those circumstances? It seems questionable whether Autobytel's economic model was sustainable in the face of aggressive competition, which could rapidly depreciate Autobytel's investments in building brand equity. InsWeb, which spent 165 percent of revenue on sales and marketing, faced a similar dilemma. Not surprisingly, InsWeb had laid off one-half of its staff during mid-2000.[14]

GET BIG FAST: A STRATEGIC IMPERATIVE FOR ONLINE BROKERS?

Many Internet companies have pursued Get Big Fast (GBF) strategies, involving massive upfront investment in customer acquisition and brand building. The premise of such strategies is that the early days of the Internet are a "land grab": According to this view, companies will find it easier to stake out wide swaths of empty territory now rather than try to capture that territory later, after it has been settled by others. The payoff from the GBF strategy tends to be strongest when the following conditions apply: Network effects are strong, scale economies (beyond network effects) are significant, and customer retention rates are intrinsically high. This section explores the extent to which these conditions apply for online brokers.

Network Effects

Network effects occur when the adoption of a product or service by a new customer increases the value of that product or service for customers already using it, because existing customers now can connect with additional parties.[15] The fax machine is a good example of a product that benefits from network effects: A fax machine is worthless if you are the only one who owns one but when many people own the machines, they are valuable. When network effects are strong, it often makes sense for a company to invest heavily to gain first-mover advantage. As users beget users, the first mover may develop an unassailable lead.

By their nature, many online brokers are subject to strong network effects: They attract more clients (typically sellers of complex, information-rich products or services) by aggregating large numbers of prospective trading partners (typically consumers who need assistance researching their purchasing decisions). Continuing the cycle, brokers attract more prospective trading partners as they attract more clients, and so forth. The same relationship holds true if the buyer is the client and the trading partner is the seller. Either way, the strength of this network effect depends on two key factors:

- *Buyer and Seller Heterogeneity.* Home buyers and sellers are both likely to value additional marketplace liquidity because each home is unique and because buyers have idiosyncratic preferences. By contrast, it is unclear whether or not InsWeb can increase its appeal to prospective insurance policy buyers in the same way. While insurance policies are complex, they are not as idiosyncratic as homes. Once InsWeb presents data from a reasonable number of carriers, further increasing its selection is unlikely to yield significant price or performance benefits.
- *Client Exclusivity.* An online broker will experience much stronger network effects if it is the sole representative for an important class of clients. For example, Homestore's REALTOR.com has achieved this status: By virtue of the National Association of Realtors' strategic equity investment in Homestore, REALTOR.com has secured the exclusive online rights to publish data from 750 of the 800 U.S. multiple listing services, covering more than 90 percent of existing homes for sale.[16] Autobytel, by contrast, tried to further its early lead in the online car-buying category by forcing dealers into exclusive relationships, but its affiliated dealers successfully resisted this effort and now tend to maintain relationships with several online services.

For online stock brokers and online travel agencies that focus on helping consumers execute transactions, network effects are not especially strong. In both cases, online brokers were able to immediately access the full range of trading partners (hence there were no exclusive arrangements) on behalf of their clients. Online brokers did so by tapping into well-organized, electronic marketplaces organized by long-standing market makers (e.g., New York Stock Exchange, NASDAQ, Sabre).

Scale Economies

As explained in the previous section, a reasonably large portion of online brokers' costs are fixed—especially for firms engaged in generating leads for clients rather than completing transactions on behalf of consumers. Hence, online brokers tend to benefit from strong scale economies. This, in turn, promotes a "winner-take-all" dynamic: If the market leader has a superior cost structure, that company can reduce its prices or invest in superior service or features, thereby increasing its lead.

Customer Retention

The "stickiness" of a customer refers to the likelihood of a customer returning to a site over and over again. If a site has a high retention rate, then GBF investments in customer acquisition are likely to have a higher payoff. If retention rates are low, a website then becomes a "leaky bucket": Customers are acquired at a high cost, but they leak away and need to be replaced, forcing the site to incur additional acquisition costs.

Strong network effects promote user retention: Once an online broker has aggregated a critical mass of prospective trading partners, users are less likely to defect.

Even in the absence of strong network effects, websites may still have intrinsically high retention rates if (1) there is a solid basis for competitive differentiation in the business (beyond network effects and pure price discounting) and/or (2) a website benefits from some type of switching cost.

To a greater extent than many other Internet businesses, online brokers by necessity are able to differentiate themselves through their website design and features. This follows from the fact that brokers help users research complex products: Users value comprehensive, objective data from third-party content providers, clear navigation paths, intuitive and reliable search tools, "configurators" that allow users to search for trading partners by specifying their needs across multiple dimensions, and speedy page downloads. For example, Microsoft CarPoint has earned praise for its use of 3D technology, which allows users to spin an image of a vehicle to view it from different angles.[17] DLJdirect has promoted the fact that its software executes trades more quickly than its competitors'—an attribute highly valued by experienced online traders. Finally, online brokers that complete transactions on behalf of consumers can differentiate themselves through the quality of their customer service operations. Online and offline, it remains difficult to manage a call center that responds quickly, courteously, and competently to customer inquiries.[18]

Switching costs also are reasonably high for the clients of many online brokers. For example, as mentioned above, the hassles associated with terminating a funded account create strong switching costs for online stock brokers. Switching costs also follow from clients' investments in integrating their information systems with those of a broker (e.g., to check inventory availability or manage leads on a real time basis). Autobytel and its competitors are achieving such integration with their affiliated dealers, and InsWeb has linked its systems with those of its insurance-carrier clients. Finally, users' investments in data entry create switching costs. Online travel agencies like Travelocity benefit in this manner when customers enter their flight preference profiles, frequent flyer numbers, and contact information.

Summary: The GBF Payoff

So, does the GBF strategy make sense for online brokers? The answer is "It depends." Homestore, for example, benefits from strong scale economies and from very strong network effects related to the heterogeneity of real estate buyers and sellers and to REALTOR.com's exclusive access to listings. Notwithstanding the fact that consumers will only visit the site every few years (which is likely to keep branding costs high), renewal rates for real estate professionals should be very high. With these advantages, it probably makes sense for Homestore to seek to accelerate its growth.

Other online brokers are subject to weaker network effects. In the case of E*Trade and Travelocity, for example, existing electronic intermediaries allow the two websites to access a full range of prospective trading partners on behalf of their clients; therefore there is no client exclusivity, and network effects are low. In the cases of InsWeb and Autobytel, recruiting additional clients with fairly homogeneous product offerings seems likely to yield diminishing returns to consumers who are planning a purchase. With weaker network effects for these four firms, the payoff for a GBF strategy hinges on retention rates. Against that test, E*Trade and Travelocity do benefit from high switching costs, so a GBF strategy is more likely to yield an attractive return. By contrast, it is less clear whether InsWeb and Autobytel will be able to retain their clients (auto dealers and insurance carriers, respectively). Like Homestore, InsWeb and Autobytel suffer from the fact that they must market to consumers who only have a reason to visit the brokers' sites once every few years.

REFERRAL, RETAILING, AND REVERSE AUCTIONS

If you're a marketplace, it's almost like you're too neutral. With that model, you have to keep banks and consumers happy. In fact, all you really have to do is keep consumers happy.

— Chris Larsen, CEO of E-LOAN, explaining the superiority of retailing over referral models for selling mortgages online[19]

[Homestore] is not about cutting out the middleman, it's about giving customers what they want, and they want a Realtor when they are making the biggest purchase of their life. It's completely unrealistic to think we are going to get rid of the people who make this industry work.

— Stuart Wolff, CEO, Homestore[20]

In many commerce categories, online brokers face competitors pursuing alternative business models, including *online retailers* who sell products and services directly to consumers (avoiding intermediaries) and *online market makers* who organize reverse auctions on behalf of buyers. In online car buying, for example, referral sites like Autobytel and CarPoint compete with direct online buying services such as CarsDirect.com.[21] CarsDirect promises consumers a no-haggle, binding quote within the lowest 10 percent of the market's pricing range. CarPoint then buys and resells the vehicle from an existing dealer, frequently absorbing losses when it has to pay more to a dealer than it receives from the consumer. Online auto referral services also face competition from firms organizing reverse auctions, including Priceline and OpenAuto. OpenAuto sends a consumer's request for quotation to a number of local dealers, then collects a $150 fee from the dealer that makes the sale.

Similarly, alternative business models coexist in the online mortgage category. Microsoft's HomeAdvisor serves strictly as a referral agent. E-LOAN and Quicken brand and fund their own loans, in addition to generating leads for other lenders. Finally, LendingTree runs a reverse auction process.

Three factors determine the relative attractiveness for consumers of the referral, retail, and reverse auction models:

- *Expected Price Realization.* A well-organized reverse auction should yield the best price for consumers (although if poorly informed consumers use Priceline's "name your own price" car-buying service, they may be "taken for a ride"). Whether or not referral services deliver the best possible price depends in part on the strength of their sell-side affiliation. As noted above, the online auto-referral services forward a consumer's request for quotation to a single dealer, so that dealer experiences no direct competitive pressure. InsWeb, on the other hand, allows users to comparison shop for quotations from multiple insurance carriers. In contrast to referral and reverse auction sites, online retailers typically do not provide comparative pricing information. Consequently, unless consumers have conducted research elsewhere, they have no assurance of being offered an attractive price. Recognizing that this is a barrier to closing a sale, some online retailers do provide information on competitors' prices. Progressive Insurance, for example, offers quotes for comparable policies from three competitors.[22] United Airlines goes a step further on its website: It steers users to competitors' cheaper fares and will actually sell its competitors' tickets. Fifteen percent of the tickets sold on UAL.com in 1999 were for competing carriers.[23]

- *Convenience.* Referral services and reverse auctions are two-step buying processes. A consumer visits one website where she is matched to a prospective seller, then must contact that seller—offline or online—to close the transaction. By contrast, online retailers offer the ability for consumers to "click and close" in a single transaction—a valued convenience.
- *Need for Consultative Selling.* Finally, as indicated in the quote above from the CEO of Homestore, some transactions are so complex that consumers benefit from a face-to-face exchange with a flesh-and-blood sales representative. In those situations, referral models should dominate because websites alone cannot address the full range of buyers' concerns. Not surprisingly, there is disagreement about which products are too complex to be sold online. For example, some offline incumbents insist that a "human touch" is necessary to close auto or insurance sales; online retailers in these categories disagree.

For companies deciding whether to serve as online referral agents or online retailers, three factors are important beyond consumers' acceptance of the respective models. First, referral agents must assess the risk to their reputations should they hand off leads to clients who handle those leads in a haphazard or inept manner or fail to respond at all. Online auto-referral services such as Autobytel and CarPoint invest heavily in monitoring their affiliated dealers' compliance with no-haggle rules and guidelines for speed of response to consumers' requests for price quotes.[24]

Second, referral agents must assess the risk of channel conflict if they pursue the direct sale of ancillary products and services to prospects. In the auto business, such ancillary sales are very lucrative: Dealers make a significant share of their profits from selling car loans and insurance policies. Unlike some of its online referral competitors, CarPoint has deliberately avoided such ancillary sales, which has helped the site rapidly expand its dealer network.[25] Online retailers, on the other hand, face no such channel conflict when they sell ancillary products and services.

Third, companies deciding whether to position themselves as referral agents should ask, "Who will own the customer relationship?" For example, in contrast to competitors such as QuickenInsurance that can close policies online, InsWeb refers leads to offline agents, who then close the sale.[26] Agents receiving referrals from InsWeb are first paid by an insurance carrier for the initial sale and then again whenever the policy is renewed. However, InsWeb receives no revenue upon renewal because it has ceded control over the customer relationship.

CHALLENGES FACING INCUMBENTS

In deciding whether to move aggressively online, offline brokers (i.e., incumbents) have to weigh their upside opportunities from the Web against the potential costs of self-cannibalization. The clients of offline brokers also have opportunities to move online and have to weigh the gains from disintermediating their offline brokers against the costs of channel conflict.

Self-Cannibalization by Offline Brokers

For transactions traditionally handled by human brokers, online processing frequently affords substantial cost savings, which sometimes are passed through to clients by online brokers in the form of reduced fees. Stock trading provides a typical example: A trade placed by a human broker might incur a $250 commission, whereas a discount online broker like Ameritrade would charge $8 for the same trade.[27] Understandably, offline incumbents like Merrill Lynch, with thousands of human brokers, are conflicted when trying to decide whether to move online (cannibalizing a profitable business). Merrill Lynch finally embraced the Internet in mid-1999.[28] Would profits from new clients attracted by online offerings offset the cost of shifting existing customers to lower priced products? To date, Merrill Lynch's experience has been encouraging: As of mid-2000, 38 percent of the assets in its Unlimited Advantage online accounts were from clients that had not previously been Merrill Lynch customers.[29]

Real estate brokerage provides another interesting example. Moving multiple listing services online reduces brokerage costs by allowing prospective buyers to prescreen properties online. Internet buyers visit only half as many homes as buyers who rely only on offline brokers for information. This means that buyers' brokers spend less time chauffeuring buyers to properties that are of little interest.[30] But if offline brokers add less value and incur lower costs when listings are available online, will their 6 percent fee come under pressure?

Notwithstanding predictions that "the Internet would change everything," to date, offline brokers have protected their margin structure.[31] Despite the industry's fragmented structure and the fact that many offline brokers lack computer skills, the National Association of Realtors (NAR) has coordinated an effective response to online threats and opportunities. The NAR was a founding investor in Homestore, receiving a 15 percent equity stake and ongoing royalties (equal to 15 percent of REALTOR.com's revenues) for licensing the "Realtor" trademark to REALTOR.com.[32] At the same time, despite aggressive competition from Microsoft's HomeAdvisor and other competitors, REALTOR.com managed to obtain the exclusive rights to publish property listings from multiple listing services (MLSs)—which were controlled by a consortium of local real estate agents—covering over 90 percent of U.S. existing homes for sale.[33] REALTOR.com typically paid MLSs 10 to 12 percent of its ad revenue in exchange for these rights.[34]

NAR's gains from its investment in Homestore have been substantial. Rather than redistribute these gains to its members, NAR has decided to co-invest with outside capital providers in a plan to spend $200 million on a technology platform that will automate the extremely labor intensive process of exchanging legal documents between parties to a real estate transaction.[35] Some industry observers believe that the NAR's control of such a valuable asset will cement their gatekeeper role in the real estate business.

Disintermediation by Clients

Offline brokers and their clients frequently spar over how to divide the value they jointly create. The emergence of the Internet changes this bargaining dynamic, and encourages some clients to ask, "If the Internet can supplant offline brokers by greatly reducing search costs and transaction processing costs, why do we need an intermediary? Why can't we commandeer this promising new channel and capture the value it will create?" Of course, these clients realize that if they aggressively pursue a strategy of online disintermediation, they also will escalate channel conflict with their offline partners.

The leading U.S. airlines, including American, United, Delta, Continental, and Northwest, have embraced such a disintermediation strategy[36] and have formed a joint venture to launch an online travel agency called Orbitz.[37] The airlines have long sold tickets directly to consumers, so this move does not represent a new threat to offline travel agencies. However, Orbitz represents a significant challenge to the online travel agencies Travelocity and Expedia. Orbitz has drawn scrutiny from antitrust authorities, due to concerns that its airline partners may use the joint venture to share data, coordinate capacity and pricing, and favor the venture by withholding their deepest discounts from competitors.

ENDNOTES

[1]*Webster's New World Dictionary,* (The World Publishing Company, 1970): 180.

[2]For more information on the online content provider business model, see Thomas Eisenmann and Alastair Brown, "Online Content Providers," section 3, *Internet Business Models: Text and Cases*, or HBS Case no. 801-261.

[3]Thomas Eisenmann and Pauline Fischer, "CNET 2000," section 3, *Internet Business Models: Text and Cases*, or HBS Case no. 800-264, July 19, 2000.

[4]Thomas Eisenmann and Chris Hackett, "Online Market Makers," section 6, *Internet Business Models: Text and Cases*, or HBS Case no. 801-308, December, 2000.

[5]Ibid.

[6]William A. Sahlman and Nicole Tempest, "Preview Travel," HBS Case no. 899-085, October 19, 1998.

[7]Thomas Eisenmann and Gillian Morris, "CarPoint in 1999," section 5, *Internet Business Models: Text and Cases*, or HBS Case no. 800-328, October 6, 2000.

[8]Unless otherwise noted, all financial results reported in this section are based on data for the first three quarters of calendar 2000, as presented in Exhibit 1.

[9]See, for example, Anjali Arora, "Online Trading: More Power to the Investor," *Industry Standard,* September 4, 2000.

[10]Gillian Morris and Thomas Eisenmann, "DLJ*direct*: 'Putting Our Reputation Online,'" section 5, *Internet Business Models: Text and Cases*, or HBS Case no. 800-164, November 2, 1999.

[11]The online stock brokerage industry averages cited in this paragraph are from Gillian Morris and Thomas Eisenmann, "DLJ*direct*: 'Putting Our Reputation Online,'" section 5, *Internet Business Models: Text and Cases*, or HBS Case no. 800-164, November 2, 1999.

[12]The formula for determining the average life of a customer relationship is $1/(1–x)$, where x equals the average annual retention rate.

[13]Jeetil Patel, "Autobytel.com," Deutsche Banc Alex Brown, August 2, 2000, p. 5.

[14]Company SEC filings.

[15]See Carl Shapiro and Hal R. Varian, *Information Rules* (Boston, MA: Harvard Business School Press, 1999), pp. 173–225 and Philip Evans and Thomas S. Wurster, *Blown to Bits* (Boston, MA: Harvard Business School Press, 1999) pp. 112–113.

[16]Tim Albright, "Homestore.com," Salomon Smith Barney, November 24, 2000.

[17]Thomas Eisenmann and Gillian Morris, "CarPoint in 1999," section 5, *Internet Business Models: Text and Cases*, or HBS Case no. 800-328, October 6, 2000.

[18]See Roger Hallowell, "Rosenbluth International and Biztravel.com," section 5, *Internet Business Models: Text and Cases*, or HBS Case no. 800-416, June 19, 2000 for a case study of a company that has achieved exceptional levels of customer service in its online operations.

[19]Megan Barnett, "Mortgaging the Future," *Industry Standard,* May 17, 1999: 64.

[20]John Wilke, "Homestore Uses Its Lock on Listings to Widen Realtor Net," *Wall Street Journal,* August 6, 1999: A1.

[21]Thomas Eisenmann and Gillian Morris, "CarPoint in 1999," section 5, *Internet Business Models: Text and Cases*, or HBS Case no. 800-328, October 6, 2000.

[22]Bob Tedeschi, "E-Commerce Report," *New York Times,* March 20, 2000: C12.

[23]Todd Woody, "A Fast Takeoff for Airline Sites," *Industry Standard,* June 14, 1999: 52.

[24]Thomas Eisenmann and Gillian Morris, "CarPoint in 1999," section 5, *Internet Business Models: Text and Cases*, or HBS Case no. 800-328, October 6, 2000.

[25]Ibid.

[26]Lynda Applegate, "QuickenInsurance: The Race to Click and Close," HBS Case no. 800-295, February 16, 2000. InsWeb is licensed to close car insurance policies in California and was moving to secure approval in other states.

[27]Gillian Morris and Thomas Eisenmann, "DLJ*direct*: 'Putting Our Reputation Online,'" section 5, *Internet Business Models: Text and Cases*, or HBS Case no. 800-164, November 2, 1999.

[28]V. Kasturi Rangan and Marie Bell, "Merrill Lynch: Integrated Choice," HBS Case no. 500-090, May 18, 2000.

[29]Anjali Arora, "Online Trading: More Power to the Investor," *Industry Standard*, September 4, 2000.

[30]Jayson Blair, "Real Estate Commissions Endure a Web Assault," *New York Times*, August 20, 2000.

[31]Michelle Raffa, "Open House," *Industry Standard*, June 21, 1999: 34.

[32]Tim Albright, "Homestore.com," Salomon Smith Barney, November 24, 2000, p. 10. By late 2000, NAR's equity stake had been reduced to 5 percent.

[33]John Wilke, "Homestore Uses Its Lock on Listings to Widen Realtor Net," *Wall Street Journal*, August 6, 1999: A1.

[34]Tim Albright, "Homestore.com," Salomon Smith Barney, November 24, 2000, p. 10.

[35]Patrick Barta, "Realtors Invest in Job Security on the Internet," *Wall Street Journal*, November 6, 2000: B1.

[36]More precisely, the airlines plan to disintermediate *their trading partners'* brokers. We previously have defined *consumers* (not airlines) to be the clients of travel agencies.

[37]See Jennifer Barrett, "Airlines Delay Online Travel Agency," *New York Times*, September 25, 2000: C4.

DLJ*direct*: "PUTTING OUR REPUTATION ONLINE"

The clock on his office wall slowly ticked away the seconds before midnight on September 8, 1999. Blake Darcy, CEO of DLJ*direct,* watched as midnight came and went, then switched on his computer with trepidation. All systems were normal; the first hurdle associated with Y2K, that of the 9/9/99 rollover problem, had been surmounted. Darcy could relax for a moment before he set his mind to the many other challenges facing DLJ*direct* in the highly competitive online brokerage business.

Two challenges were especially important: deciding whether to broaden DLJ*direct*'s target customer base and determining the firm's marketing budget. The dominant competitors in the online brokerage industry, Schwab and E*Trade, had been spending heavily on marketing and customer acquisition. As a result, they had built strong brands that were highly regarded by mainstream consumers, and controlled over 40% of the market between them. The May 1999 tracking stock spin-off of DLJ*direct* from its parent Donaldson, Lufkin & Jenrette, Inc. had yielded DLJ*direct* enough cash to compete in the online brokerage advertising wars for the first time. DLJ*direct* planned to spend $65 million on marketing in 1999—a 250% increase over 1998—in order to maintain or increase its 4% share of online brokerage trades. But with some competitors planning to spend as much as $300 million on marketing in the coming year, was $65 million the right spending level for DLJ*direct*? The firm's goal was to attract affluent, self-directed investors who would value access to DLJ's equity research and to IPOs underwritten by the parent company's investment bank. Such customers were highly profitable, yet Darcy wondered if this target market was too narrow. Was the company forfeiting opportunity by not aggressively pursuing day traders and/or less affluent mainstream investors?

Donaldson, Lufkin & Jenrette, Inc.

Enough! I'm tired of hearing this "little-big-firm" talk. We are a BIG firm, and let's never forget that.

—Joe Roby, DLJ's President, responding in 1995 to internal debate about whether DLJ was a "big little firm" or a "little big firm"[1]

Donaldson, Lufkin & Jenrette, Inc., founded in 1959, was a young firm by Wall Street standards. Initially a boutique investment bank known for its outstanding institutional equity research, during the 1970s and 1980s DLJ excelled at raising capital for young, less-established companies. A public company since 1995, at year-end 1998 DLJ was 72% owned by The Equitable Companies, which was in turn 60% owned by French insurance giant AXA (see Exhibit 1 for description of DLJ's lines of business). Backed by its parent companies, DLJ pursued an aggressive strategy to break into the "bulge bracket" of leading Wall Street firms during the 1990s. For example, when the high-yield debt market collapsed and junk bond powerhouse Drexel Burnham Lambert failed in 1990, DLJ expanded its franchise by hiring 150 former Drexel traders and investment bankers—a contrarian move that eventually yielded huge returns. DLJ also accelerated the expansion of its investment banking and trading operations into international markets. During the second half of the 1990s, DLJ's Banking Group continued to serve smaller companies in need of high-margin equity and debt financing and merger advice, but gradually broadened its client base to include larger corporations. High profile deals led by DLJ included Fleet's $16 billion acquisition of BankBoston, Olivetti's $65 billion hostile takeover of Telecom Italia, and TCI's $69 billion merger with AT&T.

Research Associate Gillian Morris prepared this case under the supervision of Professor Tom Eisenmann as the basis for class discussion rather than to illustrate either effective or ineffective handling of an administrative situation.

[1]*Crain's New York Business,* "DLJ Chief Builds Investment Bank for a New Age," April 20, 1998.

DLJ's dynamic strategy resulted in significant growth in revenues, profitability, and shareholder value (Exhibit 2). For fiscal 1998, the company's net revenues were $4.0 billion and net profits were $370 million. By mid-1999, the market value of the firm's equity was worth nearly $9 billion, up from $1.5 billion in mid-1995. As of June 1999, DLJ was ranked the #1 underwriter of U.S. high-yield debt issues, the #4 underwriter of U.S. equity offerings, and had moved into the top ten in terms of worldwide M&A transactions.

Pershing Division

"The money is in the money."

—Gates Hawn, Pershing CEO

In 1977, DLJ, Inc. diversified into the securities clearing business through the acquisition of Pershing & Co. Working mostly on behalf of smaller brokerage firms (larger brokers tended to "self-clear"), clearing agents like Pershing provided a range of trading and "back office" processing services that allowed their clients (called "correspondents") to complete customers' transactions. Clearing agents executed correspondents' trades; they maintained records and sent confirmation statements and tax reporting forms to correspondents' customers; and they held the correspondent customers' assets on their own balance sheets. In this last role, clearing agents could extend margin loans to their correspondents' customers, and in doing so were obliged to reserve sufficient capital to comply with regulatory requirements. Margin lending was extremely lucrative; for many large, self-clearing brokers, net interest from margin lending exceeded 100% of pre-tax profit.

By year-end 1998, Pershing served over 550 correspondents with a total of 2.5 million customers and account balances of $279 billion; its 11% share of NYSE trades narrowly trailed that of leading clearing agent Bear Stearns. With 3,000 employees in 1999, Pershing had been growing rapidly and was a significant profit generator for DLJ. DLJ's Financial Services Group, which included Pershing and two smaller units, provided retail brokerage services and investment management products to very high net worth individuals and a range of products to investment management firms. The group had nearly $1.2 billion in revenue in 1998, and accounted for almost one-quarter of DLJ, Inc.'s operating profit.

Entering the Online Brokerage Business

For the first couple of years, we'd sit around in a room and wait for orders. We could tell when we got one, because we'd hear the dot-matrix printer cranking up, eeeeeeeYUP! We'd tear the order off the printer and place the trade. If we did a dozen trades a day, we'd be on top of the world. My friends thought I was nuts.

—Blake Darcy, CEO DLJ*direct*[2]

Prodigy was a mass market online service created during the mid-1980s by a joint venture between IBM and Sears. Predating the World Wide Web, Prodigy employed a proprietary dial-in network (like AOL's), rather than an Internet protocol network. Prodigy's managers decided to offer an exclusive online discount brokerage service and approached established brokerage companies for help in creating the service. Most were not interested. Full service brokerages, including Sears's own Dean Witter unit, were not willing to cannibalize their business by launching a discount operation. Firms serving institutional investors, such as Lehman Brothers, Goldman Sachs, and Morgan Stanley, lacked the processing capabilities to serve retail customers and in any case had little interest in that market. Discount broker Charles Schwab already had a thriving business and passed on the opportunity. However, DLJ's Pershing division submitted a bid to Prodigy. This was consistent with Pershing's entrepreneurial corporate culture; every year the division launched a few new businesses to serve the rapidly evolving needs of its correspondents, many of whom were themselves startups. In this case, however, the new Pershing unit would compete directly with many of Pershing's customers. Dick Pechter, Pershing's CEO during the mid-1980s and the Chairman of DLJ's Financial Services Group, decided to proceed: Pershing had successfully confronted such channel conflicts before, since DLJ owned a retail brokerage business that served very high net worth individuals. Furthermore, he reasoned, trading volumes from the highly speculative online venture were likely to be too small to attract much attention from Pershing's customers.

Pershing won the bid, and launched its service in 1988. To help alleviate the concerns of Pershing's customers, the new venture was named PC Financial Net-

[2]Andy Serwer, "A nation of traders," *Fortune,* October 11, 1999, pp. 116–120.

work, avoiding an obvious brand affiliation with either Pershing or DLJ. From the beginning, DLJ corporate management took a hands-off approach to the small online business, allowing Pechter and Blake Darcy, who headed PCFN, to experiment with business strategy. Pechter recalled that building the business was "ridiculously easy, like shooting fish in a barrel. About 10% of Prodigy subscribers became our customers. We were one of the few Prodigy services that people could actually do something with." PCFN offered trades at $60, a significant discount from standard commission rates of $150–200 per trade charged by full service, bricks-and-mortar brokers. As Prodigy's customer base grew to two million in 1994, PCFN grew in tandem, with annual revenues of $35–40 million. Since it had minimal marketing and customer acquisition costs—PCFN relied on e-mails to existing Prodigy customers—the online broker was very profitable from the start.

Despite PCFN's success, the new unit struggled inside Pershing to secure resources to build the data processing systems required to support its growth. During the second half of the 1980s, the core clearing business also was expanding rapidly, straining its information systems staff. Gates Hawn, Pershing's COO during the mid-1980s and its CEO as of mid-1999, noted, "A lot of Pershing managers wondered, 'What are we doing? We're futzing around with this idea that even IBM and Sears wouldn't get involved with, when we can't spare the resources.' So to keep the parent from killing PCFN, we set it up as a separate company in a separate location, with its own information systems staff."

Despite its early lead in developing the mass market for online services, by the mid-1990s Prodigy was incurring huge losses and its growth had stalled. Pechter said:

> Prodigy's executives lacked the patience and perspective to take advantage of their market position. Even though they invented it, they never saw the power of chat, and thus they never saw AOL as a real threat. They were too concerned about making money for their parents in the near term to invest aggressively in customer acquisition, the way AOL did. As AOL grew, we had to decide if we should give up our exclusive contract with Prodigy to pursue a relationship with AOL—who wouldn't guarantee exclusivity.

Management decided to abandon the Prodigy exclusivity model and pursue a multiple-channel distribution strategy instead, entering a non-exclusive partnership with AOL and offering access to non-AOL customers through an Internet website. By the mid-1990s, competitors pursuing similar distribution strategies were challenging PCFN's early lead in the online brokerage industry, posing a threat to PCFN's revenues and profits.

PCFN Becomes DLJ*direct*

> *The more money that an Internet company loses, sometimes the more the market values it, because investors believe that share growth can yield big payoffs in the future. When DLJdirect was wholly-owned by Pershing and DLJ, we were trying to create earnings for our parent companies—which was really unfair. It made it impossible to compete. So the question was, how could we unlock the value of our company?*
>
> —Gates Hawn, Pershing CEO

With their aggressive marketing campaigns and deeply-discounted trades, online brokerages like E*Trade, Ameritrade, Datek, and Charles Schwab quickly became high-profile competitors. While most of these competitors had dropped their commission rates to $30 or lower by 1997, PCFN held to a $60 price point, and lost share despite its superior graphic interfaces and cutting-edge technology. Pechter said:

> We weren't a start-up—we were an established business with profits. When you have real revenues, it's a lot harder to make a decision to cut your prices in half—especially when you have a strong culture that values profitability. The problem was that we were still doing well enough to avoid that painful decision.

Another source of pressure on PCFN's management came from its parent company. DLJ had gone public in 1995 and thus was under close scrutiny from Wall Street analysts, who based their valuations on earnings and were unforgiving of unprofitable Internet divisions.

In mid-1997, Darcy and his colleagues decided to rework their business strategy. At that time, PCFN had few links to DLJ that were visible to consumers. Darcy proposed to DLJ corporate management that PCFN be renamed DLJ*direct* and be given access to the parent company's research and to IPOs underwritten by its investment bank. DLJ's corporate management anticipated some resistance to these changes within the firm's Capital Markets Group: if the firm's research was freely available to retail investors, institutional investors might complain that they had lost a trading edge. Also, during the late 1990s, shares in Internet IPOs were in very heavy demand, because they frequently surged on the first day of trading, and investors typically could earn a quick profit by "flipping" shares. Reserving a portion of an IPO for retail investors would reduce the number of shares available for institutional investors, who expected to be allocated IPO shares in view of the volume of other trades they placed through DLJ. Nevertheless, DLJ corporate management was fully supportive of the proposals, and promised to remove any barriers to their implementation. They saw the soaring stock market valuations of other online brokerage firms and they hoped that with increased visibility, the value of their online unit might be more fully reflected in DLJ, Inc.'s stock price. Also, building awareness of DLJ's online business could benefit DLJ investment banking teams, who were increasingly being asked by prospective clients whether the firm had Internet distribution capabilities.

Coupled with these changes that linked the online unit more closely to DLJ, Inc., DLJ*direct*'s management decided to lower its commission rates to $20 a trade. Darcy said, "With our focus on the high end of the market, we'd have preferred to match Schwab's $30 price point, but we knew we didn't have the brand name to support that. Moving down to $10 was out of the question, because we were still worried about earning profits for our parent company." While the price cut resulted in a temporary revenue slippage in 1997, by 1998, DLJ*direct*'s commission revenues had increased by 55% over 1997, active accounts had grown by 46%, and total transaction volumes had risen by 84%.[3]

The next challenge DLJ*direct* management faced was how to respond to its competitors' marketing campaigns. As Hawn noted, "DLJ*direct* is not about sizzle—we're about substance. Many of our competitors' ads are irresponsible, naïve, and downright dangerous." However, the witty, ironic marketing campaigns of E*Trade, Ameritrade and other online brokers appealed to the American public and captured the do-it-yourself spirit of on-line trading. While Darcy was uncomfortable matching the tone and message of those ads, he felt that DLJ*direct* had to increase its commitment to marketing and customer acquisition efforts in order to prevent further market share erosion. His competitors' huge marketing budgets were funded by the skyrocketing valuations of pure-play Internet companies during the late 1990s. Locked within the valuation framework of the traditional financial services industry, DLJ*direct* was unable to harness this "Internet currency" and thus lacked its competitors' spending power.

There were several options available to address this problem. DLJ could simply sell its online brokerage business, and let someone else fund its growth; the parent company had received many unsolicited offers to acquire the online business. Alternatively, DLJ*direct* could be separated completely from the parent company through a spin-off. Finally, the parent could retain management control and partial equity ownership of the online brokerage through a separately valued tracking stock.[4] According to Pechter, Hawn, Darcy and other DLJ*direct* executives, achieving complete independence from the parent company had little appeal for DLJ*direct*'s executives and Pershing senior management. Nearly all of them had worked for DLJ for the bulk of their careers, and valued the support they received as part of the DLJ family. As Hawn said, "There are no stars here—Blake might justifiably be viewed as a star at another company, but he's never asked for and never received that kind of special treatment. Here, it's always been team effort."

On the other hand, a tracking stock had drawbacks. Establishing a new publicly traded company would force Pershing management to formalize decision making processes that previously had a somewhat casual quality. Hawn explained:

> In the past, Blake would say, "I think we should do this." And we'd say, "Sure, let's do it." If we needed to spend $50 million on something, we just told DLJ Corporate that's what we were going to do. Pershing was very profitable, so DLJ's CEO pretty much left us alone. We spent maybe 30 seconds on PCFN in our annual budget reviews with Corporate. It was nice not to have to worry about separate balance sheets and overhead allocations, but governance issues become very important when you're a publicly-owned company.

[3]James Marks, John Conley, and Kristin Rolfes, "DLJ*direct*," Deutsche Banc Alex. Brown research report, June 8, 1999.

[4]Tracking stocks were securities that "tracked" the financial performance of a specific unit within a parent company (e.g., General Motors' "E-" and "H-" class stocks, which tracked its EDS and Hughes subsidiaries, respectively). Tracking stocks maintained separate financial statements and could pay their own dividends. However, from a legal and tax perspective, they were not fully independent. Consequently: 1) for purposes of calculating income taxes, the tracking stock's earnings (or losses) were consolidated with those of the parent company's other operations; and 2) the tracking stock shareholders either had no voting rights, or voted with the parent company's shareholders in electing a common board of directors.

DLJ management also was aware that some prospective investors might be uncomfortable with the fact that tracking stock shareholders had little say over their company's governance. Cautionary language in the tracking stock IPO red herring (e.g., "The [DLJ] board of directors may make decisions that favor DLJ at the expense of DLJ*direct*"; "There can be no assurance that DLJ will not expand its operations to compete with DLJ*direct*") reinforced the fact that DLJ*direct* would remain in many ways at the mercy of its parent. Furthermore, since transfer prices for both clearing services rendered by Pershing and for overheads provided by DLJ, Inc. were based on internal negotiations, investors had no guarantees that such agreements would match the market rates that a truly independent unit could negotiate from third parties. After weighing these concerns, DLJ management decided to proceed with a tracking stock IPO, with DLJ, Inc. retaining 84% of DLJ*direct*'s equity. The DLJ*direct* tracking stock was issued in May 1999 at $20, valuing the online unit at $2 billion. After reaching a high of $46, the tracking stock had drifted down to $15 by October 1999, following the pattern of stock price declines for its online brokerage peer group (see Exhibit 3 for stock price histories for DLJ, DLJ*direct*, and other online brokers).

Online Brokerage Industry in 1999

In 1994, there were few online investors, and there was little basis for predicting the phenomenal rise of online brokerage. However, due to a variety of converging factors, the second half of the 1990s saw a tremendous growth in the online brokerage business. Key factors included falling computer prices and the development of faster modems that made timely online trading possible. Also, the growing acceptance of the Internet as a legitimate channel for retail purchases convinced many consumers of the security and ease of online trading. Financial services were well suited for the Internet, because consumers did not need to see or touch the offerings to know their value. Finally, the unparalleled bull market of the 1990s, coupled with the growing popularity of equity investments, convinced many investors that they could successfully manage their own portfolios. These factors, along with lower commissions, the wealth of information available on the Web, and extensive media coverage, created an entire industry seemingly overnight.

Initially comprised largely of technologically-savvy, aggressive investors, the consumer base for online investing soon expanded to the mainstream. Many investors held multiple accounts with different brokerages; thus, the total number of online investors was difficult to determine. However, Forrester research predicted there would be 5.4 million unique accounts by year end 1999, held by over 100 online brokerages. Assets managed by online brokerages were $415 billion in 1998; this figure was expected to grow to over $3 trillion by 2003. (Exhibits 4 and 5) By early 1999, about 16% of all equity trades were completed through online brokerages.[5] Thus, by the late 1990s, online brokers posed a significant threat to traditional bricks-and-mortar brokerage houses.

Online Brokerage Economic Model

> *The top 5 online firms have increased their market share from 67.5% to 71.3% since Q1 98. At the root of this widening gap is the all-encompassing importance of scale. From a financial perspective, scale enables firms to invest large amounts of money in their business from an absolute perspective, but low amounts from a relative perspective. For example, Schwab's marketing spending is the second lowest in the industry in terms of percentage of revenues, but the second highest in terms of absolute dollars. While Schwab could simply take the "savings" from scale and push it into net income, instead it uses the savings to increase investment in other areas of its business such as technology, service and product development.*
>
> —Bill Burnham, Credit Suisse First Boston analyst, June 1999[6]

By early 1999, a sample of five publicly traded online brokers showed average annual revenues per active account (i.e., accounts that had completed a transaction during the past 12 months) of about $600 (Exhibit 6). Trading commissions provided the largest share of online brokers' revenues—about 70% of total revenue, on average. Active accounts completed an average of 15 to 20 trades per year. Commission rates had fallen substantially throughout the 1990s, from an industry average of $53 in early 1996 to $16 by the end of 1997, when rates had leveled (Exhibit 7). Schwab, Fidelity, and DLJ*direct* maintained higher commission

[5] Bill Burnham, "Online Trading Quarterly: 1st Quarter 1999," Credit Suisse First Boston research, June 1999.

[6] Ibid.

price-points and relied upon fewer, larger trades from their clients, while Datek and others with a $10 price point in 1999 relied upon more frequent, small trades. Jupiter projected a gradual decline in the average commission rate to $13.50 by 2003, suggesting that alternative revenue streams were needed.[7] As mainstream investors moved online, joining online "day traders" who rapidly churned their portfolios, the average number of trades per online account also was expected to decline. Fewer trades per account, coupled with declining commission rates, implied that firms with higher assets per account might be better positioned—provided they could link their revenues to these assets, perhaps in the form of "wrap" fees levied as a percentage of account assets. Assets per account averaged about $50,000 for online brokers, but varied widely: Schwab had $92,000 in assets per account, whereas E*Trade had only $23,000.

Order flow rebates, mutual fund distribution fees, and net interest income comprised the balance of revenues for most online brokers. Order flow rebates averaging about $2–3 per trade were paid by market makers that executed online brokers' trades; market makers in turn profited from the spread between the bid and ask price for the stocks they traded. Distribution fees paid by mutual funds and money-market funds were linked to an account's ongoing balance in the fund. Net interest income included the yield on margin debt. Margin loans averaged about 7% of account assets for publicly-traded online brokers.

Online brokers' operating margins, prior to marketing expenses, averaged 33%. Costs related to technology and customer service were substantial. In the wake of several highly publicized systems failures for E*Trade and other online brokers in early 1999, online brokers faced increasing infrastructure costs as they installed higher-bandwidth servers, staffed new customer service centers, and developed redundant system capability (see Exhibit 8 for estimates of the profit consequences of site outages). In addition, preparing for the Y2K problem required heavy spending during 1998 and 1999. At the same time technology and customer service costs were rising, marketing costs had started to climb as the playing field grew more crowded. Marketing costs per new account averaged $165 in early 1999. As a percentage of revenue, marketing expenses averaged 18%, but varied widely by firm, from 6% for Schwab to nearly 50% for E*Trade.

Wall Street analysts were divided about the prospects for the online brokerage industry. Despite increasing costs, some analysts remained sanguine about long-term profit prospects, citing the "stickiness" of the average customer and the "scalability" of online brokers' business models. Investors tended to maintain their existing brokerage accounts because it was a hassle to transfer money and securities between accounts. With year-to-year retention rates in the range of 95%, online investors were among the most loyal customers in any Internet segment. Due to these high retention rates, the present value of an average online brokerage account, net of acquisition costs, was high. Other analysts were more pessimistic about long term prospects for online brokers. For example, shortly after American Express entered the online fray in October 1999 with an offer of free trades for customers who maintained at least $100,000 in their accounts, Morgan Stanley's analyst projected escalating losses due to advertising wars and commission rate cuts. He called the situation facing online brokers "dire," and downgraded the entire sector.

Customer Segmentation[8]

According to Forrester Research, four customer segments had emerged for online brokerage services, which differed according to their net worth, risk tolerance, frequency of trading, and site feature requirements. The segments included:

Retirement by the Book (RBB). These mass-market investors with a moderate risk tolerance were looking to invest for a comfortable retirement. RBBs were interested in reliable trade execution, user-friendly interfaces, and variety of financial offerings. RBBs were appealing to many online brokers because of their healthy asset balances (around $50,000 per online account, on average) and long-term stability.

Portfolio Cruise Control (PCC). With average total assets of over $350,000, PCCs were by far the most wealthy and oldest customer segment, and were typically more at ease with offline, traditional brokers than with online trading. The most important feature to this segment was advice and quality information. Since they traded

[7]Robert Sterling, Robert Leathern, Marc Johnson, "Financial Services: Online Projections," Jupiter Communications, July 1999.

[8]This section is based on Forrester's customer segmentation model in "Investors Grade eBrokers," February 1999.

infrequently, these individuals would not yield significant online trading commissions, but could provide significant management fees linked to high account asset balances.

Aggressively Affluent (AA). The most common segment among Internet investors in the late 1990s, AAs were high-net worth individuals who traded more than 10 times a year. AAs sought timely execution and low trading commission fees, and typically were willing to pay a modest premium for consistent high-quality service. With average total assets of $300,000, AAs were highly desirable clients who could provide both consistent commissions and high account fees.

Get Rich Fast (GRF). Also referred to as "day traders," GRFs were the most visible clients of online brokers. Often young individuals with modest net worth, GRFs made frequent, small trades in the hopes of accumulating gains related to minute-by-minute fluctuations in stock prices. The segment most averse to commission fees, GRFs were also most concerned with the speed of transaction execution, since even small delays could wipe out their trading profits. Finally, GRFs tended to avoid online brokers that executed trades through their own market making units, believing that such trades were slower and less likely to yield the best possible price. Instead, they favored online brokers like Datek that executed trades through leading ECNs.[9]

In 1999, AAs and GRFs comprised the majority of Internet investors; however, most forecasters believed that as online investing developed into a more mainstream industry, online brokers would have to rework their product offerings and revenue models, and aggressively market their brands in mainstream channels (see Exhibits 9 and 10).

[9]According to *Industry Standard,* October 5, 1998, "when a customer asks a broker to buy stock on NASDAQ, the broker typically buys it from a market maker. The market maker will sell the shares to the broker for slightly more than he or she paid for them and pocket the difference, known as the spread." Instead of routing equity trades to human market makers, who usually required at least three minutes to complete a trade, Electronic Communications Networks, or ECNs, relied on computer algorithms to complete transactions much more rapidly and often at a reduced spread—provided there was sufficiently liquidity in the stock to complete the trade "within the black box" (i.e., within the set of bid and ask prices visible to the ECN's algorithms). According to Credit Suisse First Boston research (June 1999), about 20–25% of NASDAQ volume was traded through ECNs. Unlike most of its competitors, Datek, an online broker that specialized in serving day traders, relied heavily on ECNs, and had invested in Island, the leading ECN. Datek promised to reduce its commissions if it could not execute a trade within 60 seconds.

The Competition

Several different types of companies had entered the online brokerage industry (see Exhibit 11 for market share data). Bricks-and-mortar discount brokers, such as Charles Schwab, had successfully managed the transition to Internet trading. Pure-play Internet brokers, like E*Trade, capitalized upon high Wall Street market valuations to compete against established players. Traditional full service retail brokers, like Merrill Lynch, were late in moving to the Internet, yet were still expected to be formidable rivals. Finally, other financial service companies, such as mutual fund behemoth Fidelity and credit card issuer American Express, were aggressively pursuing online brokerage business.

Charles Schwab

Schwab had pioneered the discount brokerage model after the 1975 deregulation of the industry. By offering discounted trades to well-informed, technologically-savvy customers through multiple distribution channels (including bricks-and mortar offices and phone-based service), the company built a reputation for low cost, high-quality service. Ahead of most of its established brokerage competitors, Schwab ventured onto the Internet in 1996 with eSchwab. In 1998, Schwab made the risky decision to extend to Internet traders the free customer service options that previously had only been available to customers paying much higher commissions to place trades through a "live" broker.[10] When this policy was initiated in January of 1998, Schwab's stock fell and revenues slipped. However, customer assets and accounts grew rapidly and Schwab soon came to dominate the online brokerage industry. By 1999, Schwab managed $433 billion in customer assets and carried over 2 million active web accounts; its 30 percent share of online trading volume was the largest by far of any brokerage firm.

Strategically, Schwab sought to maintain its market position by continuing to cater to a stable base of "Retirement by the Book" and "Portfolio Cruise Control" customers. The company claimed to have no plans

[10]Previously, Schwab had charged an average commission of $80 for trades placed through a live broker. Internet trades were priced at $29.95, but prior to the introduction of Schwab's new pricing policy, Internet traders were allowed only one free customer service call per month. See Harvard Business School case No. 300-024, "Charles Schwab Corporation (A)"

to match the $10 trading commission rates offered by Datek and other online brokers. As Credit Suisse First Boston analyst Bill Burnham observed, "It is ironic in an industry [where] everyone talks about prices . . . the number one player has the highest price."[11] Instead, Schwab relied upon its brand reputation, mutual fund supermarket, and accessible web site to draw and retain its customer base. Toward the end of the 1999, however, Schwab sought to broaden its market position by launching a new website, (www.activetrader.com) better tailored to the needs of aggressive investors and by upgrading its Pinnacle and Platinum services for high-end customers.

Fidelity

Fidelity Investments, the world's largest mutual fund provider with $458 billion in retail assets under management and over 10.8 million retail customers, was the second largest Internet brokerage in terms of number of accounts. Fidelity's strong reputation allowed it to attract mainstream investors without spending heavily on marketing.

Like Schwab, Fidelity was expanding its online offerings to meet the special needs of more active traders. Specifically, in September 1999, the company launched a new brand, Powerstreet, accessible from fidelity.com. Through an alliance with Internet portal Lycos, the Powerstreet site offered investors financial planning, research and account information on personalized web pages. Along with viewing weather, sport scores, and news, customers could trade stocks and maintain their portfolios on an all-in-one page. At the same time, in another move designed to attract technologically-savvy customers, Fidelity partnered with Palm Pilot to create an Instant-Broker service for the Palm VII model which offered wireless Internet access. As one spokesman said, the new technology meant that an active investor could literally "trade from the hip."[12]

E*Trade

The dynamic CEO of E*Trade, Christos Cotsakos, had made his firm a dominant force in the industry, with a $9.5 billion market capitalization and 14% of online trades in 1999, second only to Schwab. E*Trade had employed a "Get Big Fast" strategy; making E*Trade a "digital financial media company" was Costakos's ultimate goal.[13] E*Trade in 1999 catered to customers who wanted the clarity, organization, and information of a complete financial portal. With that market position in mind, E*Trade had acquired online retail bank Telebanc in autumn of 1999 for $1.8 billion; 18% of Archipelago, an ECN; and 2% of online mortgage broker E-Loan. E*Trade also had acquired 28% of online investment bank E*Offering, which allowed E*Trade to provide access to IPOs for its retail clients. E*Offering had proposed eliminating the traditional IPO road show, splitting IPO shares equally between institutional and retail clients, and dropping its IPO underwriting fees to 4–5%, rather than the standard 7% Wall Street fee.

With an aggressive and controversial advertising campaign, E*Trade emphasized its differences from traditional Wall Street brokerages and promoted its brand as the site for knowledgeable, hands-on investors. It funneled an enormous amount of money into its marketing and customer acquisition budget—a projected $300 million in 1999—by leveraging its high stock market valuation. E*Trade's $19.95 per trade commission and user-friendly website marked it as a mid-tier online brokerage catering to the "Aggressive Affluent" and "Retirement by the Book" market segments. However, due to a series of highly visible systems failures in February 1999, E*Trade's perceived reliability and security had suffered. Some analysts questioned its mainstream marketing position as "everyman's financial portal" stating that: "only a niche group of people is going to be willing to live in an Internet-only environment."[14]

Merrill Lynch

Like most other full service bricks-and-mortar retail brokerages including PaineWebber, Dean Witter, and Smith Barney, Merrill Lynch was slow to recognize how the online trading would affect its business. When the threat became clear, Merrill then feared that offering an Internet service would cannibalize the profitable business conducted by its 15,000 retail brokers, endangering their livelihood. As late as early 1999, CEO Launny Stef-

[11] "Schwab treats the web like any other channel," *FutureBanker*, April 1999, p. 335.

[12] "Fidelity-Palm Pilot pair up to trade from the hip," *Reuters News Service*, September 9, 1999.

[13] Daniel Roth, "E*Trade's Plan for World Domination," *Fortune*, August 2, 1999, pp. 95–98.

[14] Ibid.

fens had declared that Internet-based banking and trading, by encouraging reckless trading, represented "a serious threat to Americans' financial lives."[15]

In June 1999, however, Merrill announced plans to establish a discount online brokerage arm, to the surprise of many analysts. Some analysts were skeptical as to whether Merrill's plans would position the company as a competitive online player. "Do-it-yourself" online trades of $29.95 would be available, but Merrill was expected to emphasize a second program through which customers could make an unlimited number of commission-free Internet trades and still have full access to their existing human broker for a fee of 1% of total assets (or a $1,500 minimum fee).

Despite Merrill's restraint in introducing online trading, channel conflict continued to plague the firm. *The Wall Street Journal* reported in September 1999 that many of Merrill's brokers were jumping ship for other firms—and taking their customers with them.[16] Other analysts, however, saw Merrill Lynch as a strong contender for industry leadership, given its enormous asset base, well-recognized brand, and the tangible benefits of human advice. According to these analysts, if the bull market turned bearish, the benefits of an established, full service bricks-and-mortar brokerage—including superior execution of trades, error protection, and advice—would become more apparent. See (Exhibit 12) for a summary of the pros and cons of trading online versus through a human broker.

Datek

By 1999, Datek was the clear leader among deep-discount online brokerages. These firms, including Ameritrade and Waterhouse Securities, catered to the burgeoning ranks of young day traders, offered trades under $10 on basic, no-frills websites. Datek often topped Ameritrade and Waterhouse Securities for speed of execution (guaranteed within 60 seconds) and quality of service. With an average of 12 trades a day per account, Datek maintained 180,000 accounts with $3.8 billion in total assets as of year-end 1998.

By providing information such as real-time, streaming quotes accessible through almost any corporation's firewall, Datek provided a low-cost service well-targeted to the needs of "Get Rich Fast" investors. However, as commission-based revenue structures were pressured, Datek had to reconsider its customer target. By appealing to a broader audience and by trying to increase its asset base, Datek might compete against E*Trade and other financial portals. In 1999, Datek seemed well placed to do so when it received $300 million—one of the single largest venture capital investments ever made—from TA Ventures, Microsoft co-founder Paul Allen's Vulcan Ventures, and the European e-commerce VC arm of Group Arnault, the parent company of Louis Vuitton Moet Hennessy.

DLJ*direct*'s Operations

Catering to people who are basically gambling isn't what we do. Day traders do not make money for the most part. They do not make money in bull markets, so they're clearly not going to make money in bear markets. My view is that most of those people will blow themselves up .

—Blake Darcy[17]

Customer Focus

DLJ*direct* sought to gain an edge on its extensive competition by focussing its customer acquisition efforts. According to its prospectus, "DLJ*direct*'s broad range of investment services is targeted at self-directed, sophisticated online investors, who on average have higher account balances than other online investors." Unlike E*Trade, Schwab, and Fidelity, which attempted to attract all customer segments, DLJ*direct* specifically sought customers in the "Aggressively Affluent" segment: knowledgeable investors who had high net worth and a moderate to high level of trading activity. DLJ*direct* decided to focus on customers with net worth in excess of $100,000 because high-end accounts were 7 times more profitable than lower-end customers, on average.[18] DLJ*direct*'s target customers were more likely to buy large blocks of stock, trade on margin, and own a diverse

[15]Megan Barnett and Bernhard Warner, "Merrill Lynch Faces a 'Schwabized' Market," *The Industry Standard,* June 14, 1999.

[16]Charles Gasparino and Rebecca Buckman, "Some Top Brokers at Merrill Are Jumping Ship as Company Prepares to Enter Online Waters," *The Wall Street Journal,* September 15, 1999.

[17]In September 1999, the North American Securities Administrators Association issued a report on the trading patterns of full-time day traders, who made 100 or more trades per day and accounted for 36% of all online trades. According to the report, 70% of this group would eventually "lose everything" they had invested. See Dallas Morning News, October 4, 1999, "Self Sabotage: All Investors Can Learn from Day Traders' Mistakes."

[18]Merrill Lynch research report, June 21, 1999.

array of financial investments, so they produced higher commissions per trade, higher interest income, and higher account maintenance fees. In 1998, DLJ*direct*'s average commission was $27 per trade, as compared with E*Trade's average of $23 and Ameritrade's $17.

Many of DLJ*direct*'s target customers were customers of discount brokers like Schwab or Fidelity, and were seeking to migrate to a higher end online broker. Others—about one-half of DLJ*direct*'s new accounts, according to Goldman Sachs research—were customers of full service brokers such as Merrill Lynch. Richard Brueckner, Pershing's COO, explained:

> A lot of these customers will set aside 10% of their $1 million in assets to invest themselves. They're tapping into the entertainment value of trading: they want to see how well they can do on their own. But they want to do business with a quality online broker and have access to first class information. They don't want to make these trades within their core brokerage account, then have their broker call up afterward to ask, "What did you do that for?"

Two other factors contributed to DLJ*direct*'s decision to target these customer segments. First, a focus on high net worth individuals leveraged DLJ, Inc.'s elite brand reputation; likewise, building up DLJ*direct*'s "mind-share" produced greater brand recognition—and more investment banking business—for DLJ, Inc., which previously had never advertised to consumers. Second, high-end customers yielded greater stability for the firm. If DLJ*direct* aggressively pursued day traders, the company's financial performance would be closely linked to the ups and downs of the stock market.

Web Site and Client Offerings

> *Even though it was barely mentioned in the* DLJ*direct* *IPO prospectus, because we didn't want to distract investors, our software development unit iNautix probably could go public itself, given its size and the market's current enthusiasm for this type of company. You might reasonably expect iNautix to have a valuation of one half billion dollars! But in the great DLJ "Russian Doll" tradition, we've put the iNautix doll inside the* DLJ*direct* *doll, which was inside the Pershing doll, which is inside the DLJ doll, which is inside the Equitable doll, which is inside the AXA doll. And we keep asking, is this the best way to maximize iNautix's value?*
>
> —Richard Brueckner, Pershing COO

DLJ*direct*'s web site contained the full range of information and transactional services that online investors had come to expect from the industry. In addition to equities, customers could trade options (7% of total orders), mutual funds (1% of orders), and fixed income securities, and they could acquire insurance or apply for a mortgage. The site also offered free access to news feeds and stock quotes and portfolio tracking services that provided alerts when share prices moved outside of a specified range (see Exhibit 13 for an image of DLJ*direct*'s home page).

DLJ*direct*'s service was differentiated in several ways. First, DLJ*direct* was the only online brokerage firm to offer new customers the ability to apply online and begin trading immediately without forwarding cash to cover their initial investment. After passing an online credit reference check, DLJ*direct* allowed new customers to buy up to $15,000 of securities as a first transaction. Second, DLJ*direct*'s customers who maintained asset balances in excess of $100,000 had access to DLJ research. These customers were offered a more comprehensive and higher quality selection of reports than customers of other leading online brokers; in addition, DLJ*direct*'s customers faced much shorter delays between the release of these research reports to institutional investors and their availability on the website. Third, DLJ*direct* provided tiered service levels for accounts with high asset balances. For customers with asset balances in excess of $100,000, in addition to proprietary DLJ research, DLJ*direct* provided greater access to DLJ-managed IPOs. For clients with $1 million or more in assets, DLJ*direct* also reduced certain commission and account fees, provided a personal service team, offered after-hours trading opportunities, and included mutual funds in determining the amount of margin debt available to a customer. Fourth, DLJ*direct* was ranked near the top of the industry in terms of speed of execution (Exhibit 14). Its performance edge increased in 1997, when DLJ*direct* introduced its MarketSpeed proprietary software, a Windows product that customers downloaded on their desktops. The software installed graphics, streaming quotes, and other interfaces that were continually updated through a direct Internet connection. Because these interfaces were pre-installed, MarketSpeed was roughly five times faster than other online brokerage services for information retrieval and trade execution.

MarketSpeed had been developed by iNautix, the software development group controlled by DLJ*direct*. iNautix, which had about 200 employees in September 1999, had created most of DLJ*direct*'s information systems, and also developed software for Pershing and other DLJ units. In addition, iNautix sold software through Pershing correspondents to many of DLJ*direct*'s online brokerage competitors (although DLJ*direct* typically allowed itself a modest head start in deploying new technologies), and had helped create one-third of all on-line financial services sites. The iNautix group contributed fees of $13.4 million in 1998—11% of DLJ*direct*'s revenue, and was an invaluable source of leading edge technology.

Marketing Strategy

DLJ*direct* had pursued high end customers with a variety of marketing slogans in the early 1990s, such as "If you think people with more money have better information, you're right" and "A higher form of intelligence for serious online investors." In 1997, the firm spent $13 million, or 19% of total revenue, on marketing. In late 1997, to reinforce the firm's name change, DLJ*direct*'s management decided to increase the 1998 marketing budget to $25 million. The new advertising slogan, "Putting our reputation online," reflected the close relationship between DLJ, Inc. and DLJ*direct*.

In 1999, DLJ*direct* planned to spend $65 million on marketing, although Darcy still debated whether to further increase fourth quarter spending. About 30 percent of the budget was spent online, including $12.5 million per year for a two year distribution deal with AOL that featured DLJ*direct* as one of four online brokers within AOL's proprietary service. The balance of the advertising budget was spent on traditional media, concentrated in high-end business publications such as *Forbes*, *Barron's*, and *The Wall Street Journal*, and in radio and television programs (e.g., CNBC; golf matches) likely to appeal to wealthy prospects (Exhibit 15).

Clearing and Customer Service Operations

> *On occasion, some of* DLJ*direct's senior managers will complain that if they were self-clearing, they'd pay $4 per trade like E*Trade. We say, "Maybe, but if you were self-clearing, you wouldn't be in this building, sitting in my cafeteria, or using my legal department." You can't just take the miscellaneous data point that says how much does it cost on the margin, negotiated at arms-length.*
>
> —Gates Hawn, Pershing CEO

Pershing had cleared trades for its online brokerage since its inception as PC Financial Network. At the time of DLJ*direct*'s IPO, Pershing and DLJ*direct* managers negotiated a ten year contract for the services that Pershing supplied, which provided for successive 5% reductions in per trade clearing fees when DLJ*direct*'s annual trading volume reached 4 million and 6 million.[19] The relationship with Pershing was beneficial for DLJ*direct* in that it reduced the need to invest in technical support, personnel, and infrastructure. In addition, DLJ*direct* benefited from order flow rebates from Pershing. During the late 1990s, however, this profitable source of revenue for online brokers was under pressure due to the narrowing of trading spreads, which in turn was related to the rise of ECNs and a move toward trading in decimal rather than fractional units.[20] Because of its long term contract with Pershing, DLJ*direct* appeared to be better situated than many of its competitors. Whereas the average per trade rebate earned by online brokers had declined 45–60% between 1997 and 1998 to the $2.20–$2.90 range, DLJ*direct*'s rebates only decreased 14% to $3.07.[21]

On the other hand, the relationship with Pershing was also potentially costly for the online brokerage firm. In 1999, DLJ*direct* was the only major online brokerage that did not clear its own trades; thus, its competitors gained an edge by retaining the profits from their own, in-house clearing activities.[22] Although DLJ*direct* shared net interest income with Pershing as part of its clearing contract, DLJ*direct* earned less in net interest income than its self-clearing competitors. According to analysts at Deutsche Bank, DLJ*direct*'s close relationship with Pershing risked blinding its managers to future changes in relative costs. Furthermore, according to these analysts, due to DLJ*direct*'s ownership structure, the company might forfeit leverage in future negotiations with Pershing over clearing fees that an independent buyer would otherwise realize due to its volume growth. However, concerns that

[19]Trading volume was 2.9 million in 1998. Through mid-1999, trading volumes were running about twice the level for the comparable period during 1998.

[20]Decimalization, which would be introduced during the year 2000, involved trading stocks in one cent units, rather than fractions of a dollar. Since the smallest fractional unit traded was one-sixteenth of a dollar, using decimals would reduce trading spreads between the bid and ask price for NASDAQ securities with high trading volumes. Market makers, who profited from trading spreads, were thus expected to experience profit erosion in the wake of decimalization.

[21]Goldman Sachs research report, August 20, 1999.

[22]Pershing cleared trades for one of DLJ*direct*'s medium-sized competitors, National Discount Brokers.

DLJ*direct* might be disadvantaged in terms of trade processing costs due to its captive relationship with Pershing were lessened in July 1999 when Pershing, DLJ, and DLJ*direct* announced plans to join Schwab, Fidelity, and market maker Speer, Leeds & Kellogg in forming an ECN.

Customer service was critical to DLJ*direct*'s high end customers. Telephone support was provided 24 hours a day, 7 days a week, free of charge. Rapid growth had challenged DLJ*direct*'s ability to maintain high service levels: in April 1999, of the firm's 466 employees, 288 worked as customer service representatives, a figure that was projected to grow to 800 by year-end 1999.

What Next?

Mercedes doesn't necessarily spend as much as Chevrolet, but Mercedes does just fine.

—Blake Darcy[23]

It was getting late. Blake Darcy hoped to get home before the markets opened in London, where DLJ*direct* had been "soft launching" its service for a few months to ensure that systems met customers' expectations. He answered e-mail from his management team in Tokyo, where DLJ*direct* had entered a 50/50 joint venture with financial services giant Sumitomo to offer online brokerage services. In both markets, DLJ*direct* was an early mover; among U.S. online brokers, only Schwab and E*Trade had matched its pace in developing international operations. Darcy tapped his pen against the desk as he pondered two of the challenges facing his company. Should DLJ*direct* join the growing battle for day traders' business? And how much should the firm spend on marketing in the coming year?

Competition for Day Traders

In late 1999, online brokerage firms were competing aggressively for day traders' business. Firms such as TradeCast, which provided software to "direct access" brokers operating bricks-and-mortar offices frequented by full-time day traders, were beginning to offer their specialized software to investors trading online from their homes. This software allowed investors to: 1) view NASDAQ "Level II" quotes, which meant investors could see the bid and ask quotes of individual market makers; and 2) link directly to ECNs and to NASDAQ's SelectNet system, which let investors send orders to the market makers of their choice. TradeCast, which had received a $40 million equity investment from the Bass Brothers of Texas, began offering its services to home traders with a base commission of $19.95. Meanwhile, E*Trade, Schwab, Fidelity and other mainstream online brokerages were offering new products to attract active investors. Fidelity, for example, offered $14.95 commissions to accounts trading at least 12 times per year, and Level II data to accounts trading at least 36 times per year (which represented 4% of Fidelity's customer base). Schwab's chief strategist said that the company "wants very much to be there for the active trader," because the "very, very small population" of accounts that made 100 or more trades per year accounted for 60% of the company's retail trades. Bill Burnham, who had been the top-ranked equity analyst following online brokers prior to joining Softbank as a venture capitalist, described the very high profits generated by day traders as the industry's "dirty little secret."[24]

Darcy reflected on the opportunity for DLJ*direct* to pursue day traders more actively:

> If we snapped our fingers and said our price point will be $9.95 tomorrow, I'm sure we could double our volume over some short period of time. We debate this back and forth, all the time. We could offer the day traders a better mousetrap—better information, faster execution—at a price that matches the lowest rates out there. And we'd probably increase our stock price, at least over the short term. But it's less clear to me we'd be building a foundation for long term profitability. Look at the discounted cash flow of day traders, compared to high end customers. You need to assign a higher discount rate to the day trader's volatile cash flows, because they swing with the health of the stock market. And you need to ask whether you can assign any terminal value for day traders, because they tend to go broke due to trading losses over some period of time. Finally, there's probably less opportunity to cross-sell other services to day traders, because they are less affluent.

[23]Jennifer Kingson Bloom, "DLJdirect's Chief Seeks Richest Net Users," *American Banker,* January 27, 1999, p. 16.

[24]Rebecca Buckman, "Online Brokers, Day-Trade Firms Start to Encroach on Each Other's Cyberturf," *Wall Street Journal,* October 6, 1999. This article is the source for Burnham's quote and other information in this paragraph.

The Marketing Lever

> *We know the problem of growing too fast. It's hard to find and train people qualified to answer the phone. You end up disappointing your higher end customers who are paying more. You have to put that into the equation when you consider whether to aggressively step up your ad spending. And regulators hover all over this, especially as we approach Y2K. They want to know, "What are your capacity plans, your people plans? Do you have redundant facilities?"*
>
> —Blake Darcy

The battle between online brokers for customers was highly visible on television, billboards, radio, and print, as marketing expenses grew at a rapid rate. In October 1999, *The New York Times* reported that the top ten online brokerages had budgeted about $1.5 billion in advertising and marketing for the coming year. E*Trade, Ameritrade and other pure-play online brokers planned to spend over half of their projected revenues on blitzkrieg marketing campaigns that included spots during the World Series and the Superbowl. The firms were lining up celebrity spokespersons: actresses Geena Davis and Anna Nicole Smith for T. D. Waterhouse and E*Trade, respectively, and Russian teen tennis star Anna Kournikova for Schwab. E*Trade, eager to remain the industry's top advertiser, was expected to spend about $300 million on advertising and other marketing programs, including promotional giveaways such as free long-distance minutes, frequent flier miles, and coupons for free trades. In response, Ameritrade announced plans to spend $200 million. Executives at Charles Schwab also were prepared to challenge E*Trade's advertising supremacy. Len Short, Schwab's EVP-Advertising estimated that it took $300 million per year in ad spending to build and sustain a mass consumer brand, and said, "We are not going to be the leader if we underspend the competition."[25]

Due to these aggressive marketing plans, the cost to acquire a new customer was rising rapidly. Whereas online brokers had spent $100–200 to acquire a new customer as recently as 1998, Ameritrade had warned analysts in the fall of 1999 that it would be spending $500 for each new customer. E*Trade and National Discount Brokers also said that their acquisition costs had doubled to $400–500 per new account. Bill Burnham remarked, "It's a war of attrition. If they go over $500, the stock trading business stops making sense."

Darcy and the management team at DLJ*direct* felt prepared to enter the fray (see Exhibits 16 and 17 for data on DLJ*direct*'s financial performance). They knew they had a strong message to sell: many third party rating services, like Gomez Advisors, had placed DLJ*direct* at the top, or near the top, of online brokerages in terms of quality of service and reliability. Most visible was their #1 ranking in *Barron's* 1999 survey of online brokerages. In other rankings by *Time, Worth,* and J.D. Powers, DLJ*direct* was first. And with the tracking stock IPO, DLJ*direct* could fund a bigger marketing budget. But given competitor's aggressive plans, was $65 million in marketing for 1999 enough to maintain DLJ*direct*'s market share and continue to attract self-directed, high net-worth customers? And how much should the company spend on marketing during the year 2000?

---

[25]Joseph Kahn, "The On-Line Brokerage Battle," *The New York Times,* October 4, 1999, p. C1. This article is the source for the quotes and other information contained in this paragraph and the paragraph following.

Exhibit 1 DLJ, INC.'S PRINCIPAL OPERATING SEGMENTS 1998

	Revenues (millions)	Description
Banking Group • Investment Banking • Merchant Banking • Sprout Group	$1,486.8	• Equity and debt underwriting; merger advice • Leveraged private equity investments • Venture capital investments
Capital Markets Group • Equities Division • Fixed Income Division	$1,273.3	• Research, sales, and trading in U.S. & foreign equities • Research, sales, and trading in U.S. & foreign fixed income securities
Financial Services Group • Pershing • DLJ*direct* • Asset Management Group • Investment Services Group	$1,248.4	• Correspondent brokerage services • Online discount trading • Advisory and trust services for high-net worth clients • Advisory and trust services for high-net worth clients; cash management services for institutional clients

Source: Adapted from DLJ, Inc. 10-K

Exhibit 2 DLJ, INC.'S FINANCIAL PERFORMANCE 1994–1998 (IN MILLIONS)

	1994	1995	1996	1997	1998
Net Revenues	$1,504.9	2,078.0	2,757.5	3,487.3	3,951.2
Net Income	$123.0	179.1	291.3	408.3	370.8
Total Assets	$33,261.6	44,576.5	55,503.7	70,505.8	72,282.2

Exhibit 3 PRICE HISTORY FOR DLJ, INC., DLJ*direct*, AND COMPETING ONLINE BROKERS

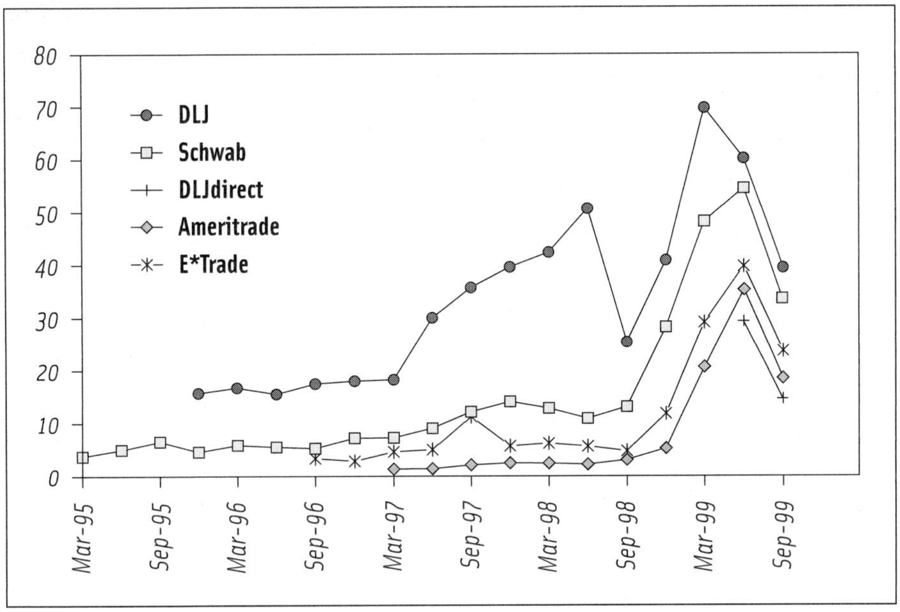

Source: Adapted from Bloomberg Information Services

Exhibit 4 ASSET UNDER MANAGEMENT IN ONLINE BROKERAGE (IN BILLIONS)

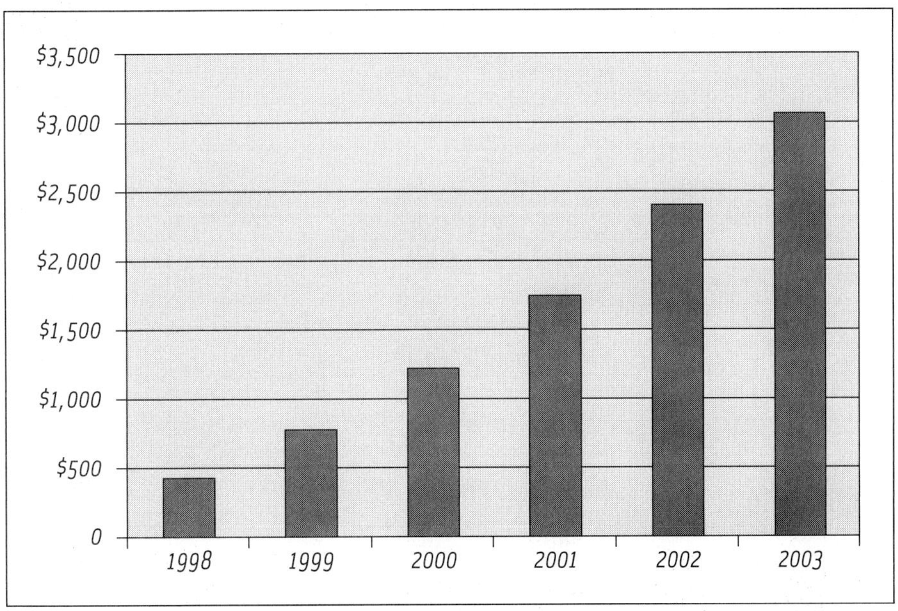

Source: Adapted from Jupiter Communications, "Financial Services Online Projects," July 1999

Exhibit 5 PROJECTED ONLINE BROKERAGE ACCOUNT GROWTH (MILLIONS)

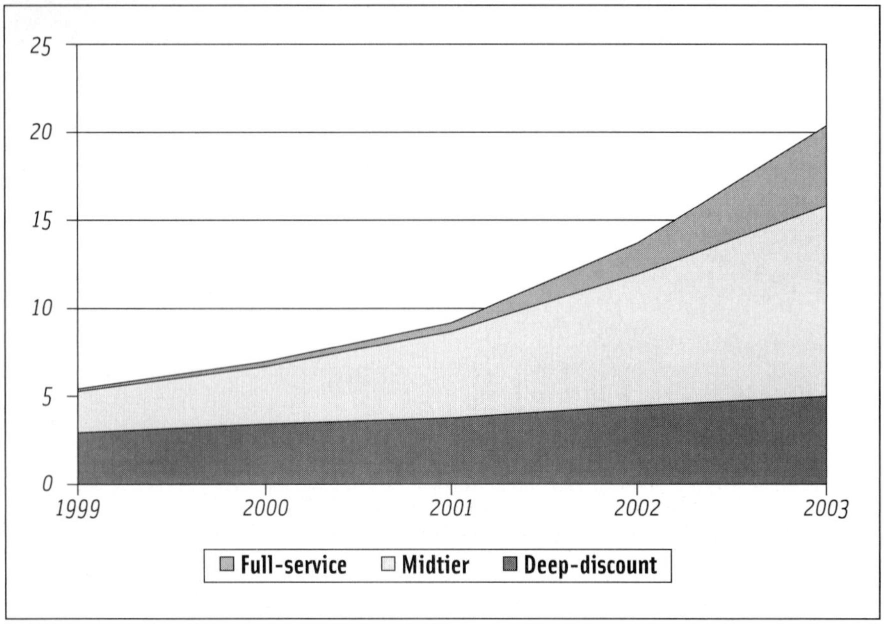

Source: Adapted from Forrester Research, "Net Investing Goes Mainstream," March 1999

Exhibit 6 ONLINE BROKERS' OPERATING AND FINANCIAL STATISTICS Q1 99

Key Operating Metrics	Ameritrade	DLJ*direct*	E*Trade	Schwab	Waterhouse
Active OnlineAccounts	569,000	243,000	909,000	2,500,000	780,000
Average Daily Online Trades	41,774	18,148	64,400	137,400	69,451
Commissions/Trade	$13.68	26.06	18.83	47.72	21.54
Order Flow Rebates/Trade	$1.79	2.60	2.31	NA	NA
Net Revenue/Trade	$20.66	38.38	29.66	73.34	34.60
Average trades/ account/quarter	4.3	4.4	4.2	3.2	5.3
Revenue/account/year	$448	777	557	581	529
Assets/account	$34,271	46,091	23,212	86,400	NA
Net new accounts added in Q1 (000)	84.0	33.0	233.0	388.0	148.0
Marketing cost/net new account	$156	184	257	135	84
Marketing as % of revenues	20.7%	12.9%	47.3%	5.5%	5.0%
Pre-Marketing Operating Margin	40.5%	36.8%	29.2%	30.3%	30.8%
Operating Margin	19.8%	23.9%	-18.1%	24.8%	25.8%

Source: Adapted from Credit Suisse First Boston research report, June 1999

Exhibit 7 AVERAGE COMMISSION CHARGED BY TOP 10 ONLINE BROKERAGES

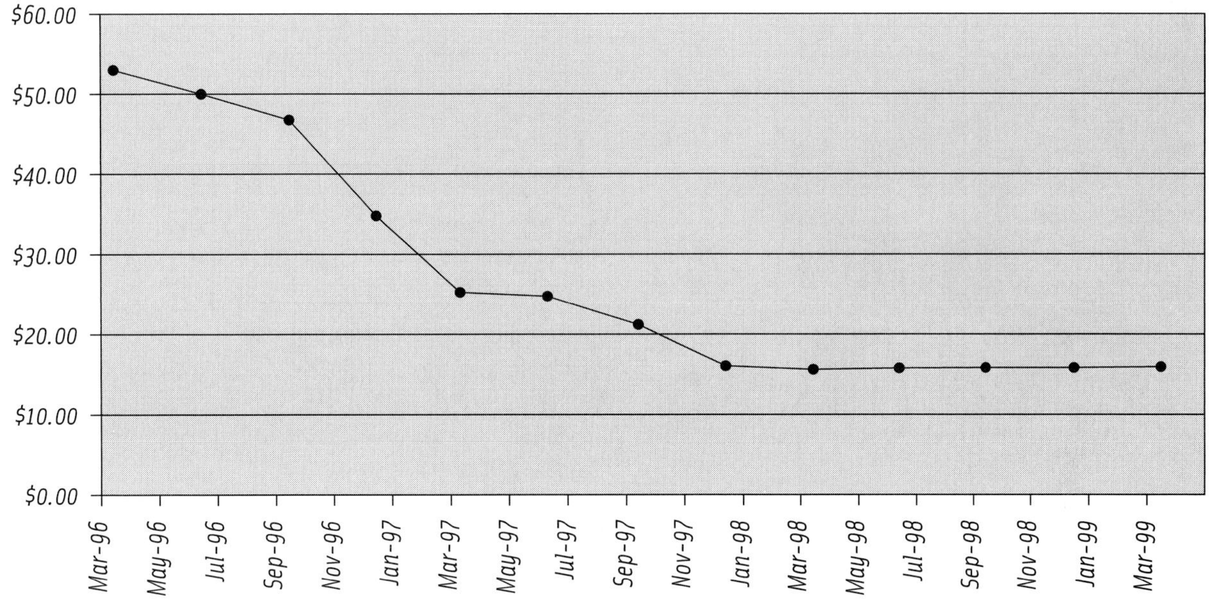

Source: Adapted from Credit Suisse First Boston research report, June 1999

Exhibit 8 ESTIMATED FINANCIAL LOSS DUE TO A SITE OUTAGE

	Average Brokerage Site
– *Direct Revenues Loss*	$204,000
– *Compensatory Loss*	$0
– *Lost Future Revenues*	$4,810,320
– *Worker Downtime Loss*	$141,729
– *Other Costs*	$64,110
– **Total Financial Impact**	$5,220,159

Source: Adapted from *The Industry Standard,* 10/4/1999, citing data from InterMedia Advertising Sources and Competitive Media Reporting; assumes an eight-hour brokerage site outage during a typical trading day.

Exhibit 9 CUSTOMER BEHAVIOR BY SEGMENTATION

	Retirement by the Book	Get Rich Quick	Portfolio Cruise Control	Aggressive Affluent
Average Age	37	38	47	42
Average # of Trades per year	1	9	3	10
Average income	$43,000	$37,000	$75,000	$77,000
Average net worth	$49,000	$38,000	$362,000	$323,000
Risk Tolerance	Moderate	High	Low	High
Features sought	Advice, account information, ease of use	Low fees, transaction confidence, site performance	Advice, account information, site performance	Transaction confidence, low fees

Source: Adapted from Forrester Research, "Investors Grade eBrokers," February 1999

Exhibit 10 MARKET SEGMENTATION OVER TIME

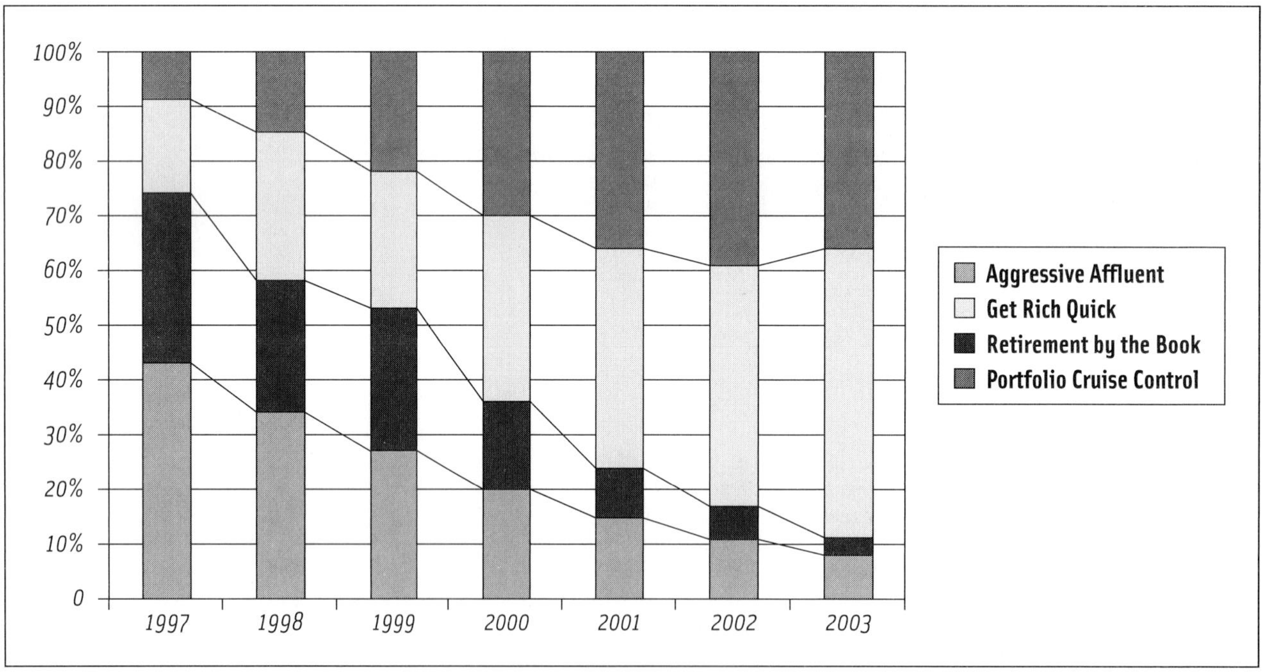

Source: Adapted from Forrester Research, "Net Investing Goes Mainstream," March 1999

Exhibit 11 ONLINE BROKERS' SHARE OF ONLINE TRADES Q1 1999

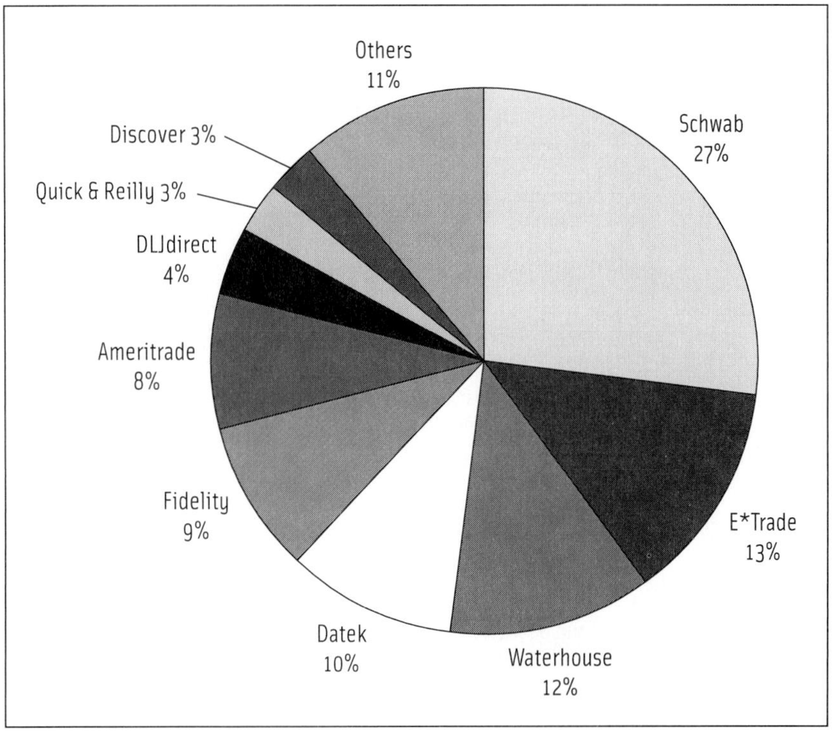

Source: Adapted from Credit Suisse First Boston research report, "Online Trading Quarterly" 1st Quarter 1999, June 1999

Exhibit 12

PROS AND CONS OF ONLINE AND OFFLINE BROKERS

Ten Reasons to Use an Online Broker	Ten Reasons to Use a Full-Service Broker
1. Cheaper to Trade—How much cheaper? "We're way less than the full-service firms," says John Miller, co-owner of Wilshire Capital Management, a small New York discount brokerage firm that is geared towards active online traders. "It could be one-tenth the cost. There's a reason. We don't render advice."	**1. Trade Less**—Trading through a full-service broker may cost more. But customers of full-service brokerage firms also seem to trade far less. "If we let our customers trade the way they do online, the regulators would be all over us," says Robert Yevich, president of Tucker Anthony, a Boston-based full-service brokerage firm.
2. No Pressure—"I'd rather have a warm computer than a cold call," quips Don Montanaro, president of Suretrade Inc., an online broker based in Lincoln, R.I. "There's no pressure. You're making your own decisions in your own time."	**2. No Procrastination**—"As full-service brokers, we help investors remove emotions from the process," says Gregory Hurlbrink, a broker with Legg Mason, Inc., a Baltimore full-service brokerage firm. That can mean encouraging spendthrift investors to save more or pushing nervous investors to put at least some money in the stock market.
3. Who Needs Advice?—Full-service brokers aren't the only source of investment information. Suretrade, for instance, provides access to consensus earnings estimates, stock charts, real-time quotes and stock research. "Even if your broker has access to good stock-market research—which is debatable—do you have access to him?" Mr. Montanaro asks. "Where are you on his list of people to call?"	**3. Receive Advice**—This is a full-service broker's biggest selling point. "Our clients are people who value advice," Mr. Hurlbrink says. "A lot of this growth in online trading is a function of the bull market. People think it's a lot easier than it is. The market has prevented people from making huge mistakes. When the market turns, the mistakes will be magnified."
4. Faster Execution—With an online computer, completing a trade is just a few mouse clicks away. "If you trade online, we're talking seconds," says Mr. Miller of Wilshire. "If you have to call somebody, it could take minutes. Chances are you're not calling the order room."	**4. Better Execution**—Full-service brokerage firms play up their efforts to get the best stock prices for customers. The implication: Online brokers aren't so scrupulous, a charge the online brokers vehemently deny.
5. More Fun Than an Index Fund—Investing isn't just about making money. It's also fun. And what could be more fun than buying and selling stocks using your computer? It sure beats sticking your money in an index fund and merely matching the performance of a market average.	**5. More Comforting Than an Index Fund**—True, most investors would get better results by putting their money in a market-tracking index fund. But have you seen all the doggy stocks in those funds? It's so much more comforting to have a broker looking out for you.
6. Old People Use Brokers—"A full-service broker will tell you that the value that he provides is a relationship," Mr. Montanaro says. "To us, that's just chitchat. You can get chitchat in a chat room on the Internet and you don't have to pay for it."	**6. We All Grow Up, Eventually**—"It seems to me that there is a certain entertainment aspect to trading on the Internet," Mr. Yevich says. "I can see 60-year-olds with $1 million keeping $20,000 at E*Trade to play with. That's their Atlantic City money. But with their serious money, they're investing with the help of a professional."
7. I Already Have a Monkey—Let's face it, how good at picking stocks are all those brokers and the analysts they draw on? Brokers are primarily trained to be salespeople, while analysts rarely issue a sell recommendation on a stock. Much of the time, a monkey could do just as well by flinging darts at the newspaper stock tables.	**7. Stock-Picking Ideas**—Mr. Yevich concedes that "there's a lot of information online," he says. "It's not getting the information that's the problem. It's interpreting it. What you get with a full-service broker is somebody who's trained to separate the good stuff from the noise."
8. What's a Bear Market?—"Yes, when the bear market comes, you'll want some handholding," Mr. Miller agrees. "But you'll also want those low commissions and faster trades even more. Whether it's a bull market or a bear market, you will still want to jump on the winners and the losers," and you will want to do so as quickly and cheaply as possible.	**8. Hand-Holding in Bear Markets**—When stocks finally tumble, full-service brokerage customers can turn to their brokers for advice. But online investors will be on their own. "This online boom has started in a bull market, when stocks go up every day," Mr. Yevich says. "When the market goes down, you'll see a huge drop in the trading in online accounts because they won't be making money and they'll freeze."

Exhibit 12 PROS AND CONS OF ONLINE AND OFFLINE BROKERS cont.

Ten Reasons to Use an Online Broker	Ten Reasons to Use a Full-Service Broker
9. Nobody Calls—Ever get those irritating cold calls from brokers in the middle of dinner? They don't come from online brokerage firms. "If somebody has a question, we'll answer it," Mr. Miller says. "But we're not in the business of rendering opinions. We won't be calling you with the stock of the week."	**9. Somebody to Call**—Who's calling whom? "My clients call me during dinner," Mr. Hurlbrink says. "They have life-changing events going on and they want advice. They want it whenever they want it, and my job is to give it. If it's during my dinner, so be it."
10. No Crooked Brokers—Sure, the vast majority of brokers are straight arrows. But what if you end up in the hands of a slick-talking salesman who pushes high-commission funds and prods you to trade stocks way too much, just so he can earn fat commissions?	**10. No Crummy Computers**—When you have to buy or sell a stock, which would you rather rely on, getting your order through by computer or getting through by telephone? Telephone companies may not be America's most admired corporations. But when you think about all those computer crashes, they start to look awfully good.

Source: Adapted from *The Wall Street Journal*, June 14, 1999, p. R21

Exhibit 13 DLJ*direct* WEB PAGE

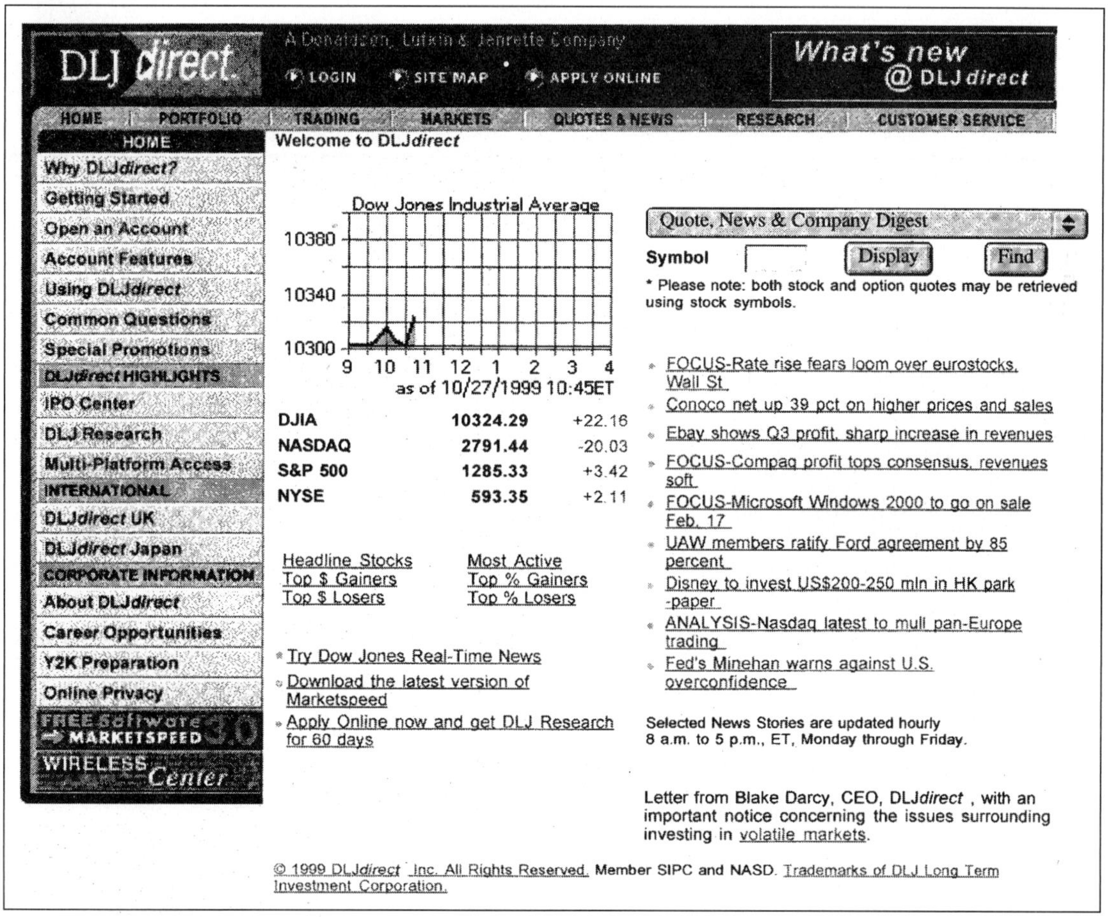

Exhibit 14 RATING BROKERS BY SPEED OF EXECUTION AND AVAILABILITY

Broker	Response Time (seconds)[a]	Availability[b]
DLJdirect	4.32	99.4%
Waterhouse	4.63	99.2%
Ameritrade	5.22	96.2%
*E*Trade*	7.44	97.3%
Datek	10.03	98.1%
Discover	10.58	97.6%
Quick & Reilly	12.71	98.7%
Fidelity	12.73	95.3%
Charles Schwab	17.97	98.4%
Suretrade	20.38	79.3%

Source: Adapted from *The Industry Standard,* February 15, 1999, citing data from Keynote Systems
[a]Time required for accessing and downloading the home page of each brokerage web site during business hours
[b]Availability of each brokerage's home page during business hours

Exhibit 15 EXAMPLE OF DLJ*direct* AD

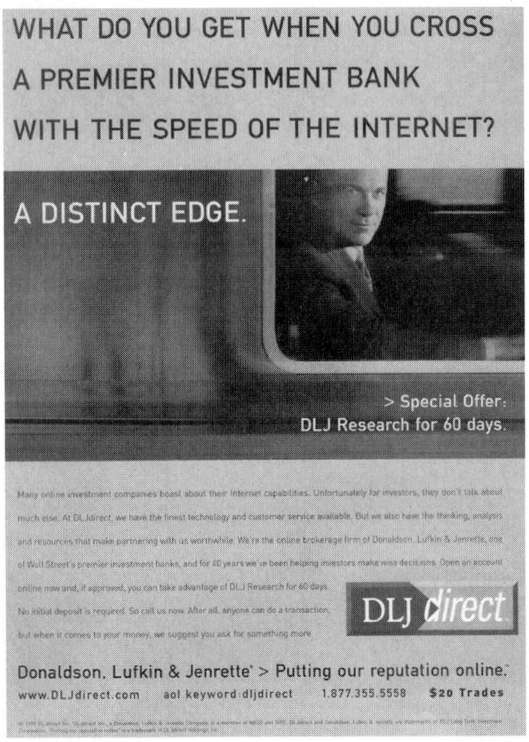

Exhibit 16

DLJ*direct* INCOME STATEMENT (IN MILLIONS)

	Years Ended December 31,					Nine Months Ended September 30,	
	1994	1995	1996	1997	1998	1998	1999
Revenues							
Commissions	$28.5	$40.4	$54.2	$51.0	$78.7	$54.3	$98.4
Fees	3.8	5.1	6.4	12.1	25.5	18.4	38.3
Interest	1.9	1.9	2.6	4.2	12.7	9.8	25.0
Total revenues	**34.1**	**47.3**	**63.2**	**67.2**	**117.9**	**82.5**	**161.8**
Costs and expenses							
Compensation and benefits	5.4	7.4	11.2	17.2	28.3	20.3	41.4
Brokerage, clearing, exchange, and other fees	9.6	11.7	15.4	20.9	28.3	19.7	26.9
Advertising	2.0	4.2	9.1	13.1	25.1	19.9	37.5
Occupancy and equipment	1.2	1.4	1.9	3.4	5.0	3.7	6.0
Communications	.7	1.0	1.5	2.8	5.6	3.9	8.1
Technology costs	4.4	5.4	5.2	5.1	4.1	3.1	2.6
Other operating expenses	3.2	4.5	5.6	10.8	18.9	12.5	20.5
Total costs and expenses	**26.5**	**35.7**	**49.9**	**73.3**	**115.5**	**83.1**	**143.0**
Income (loss) before income tax provision (benefit)	**$7.7**	**11.6**	**13.3**	**(6.1)**	**2.5**	**(.5)**	**18.7**

Source: DLJ*direct* prospectus

Exhibit 17

DLJ*direct*'s KEY FINANCIAL AND OPERATING PERFORMANCE ($ IN MILLIONS)

	1994	1995	1996	1997	1998	1999E	2000E
Total Trades	475,000	660,000	929,000	1,535,000	2,875,000	4,900,000	7,559,500
Average Daily Trades	1,900	2,600	3,700	6,100	11,400	19,368	29,900
Total Customer Assets	$1,300	1,900	2,500	4,600	8,900	16,800	28,330
Total Accounts	153,000	207,000	280,000	390,000	529,000	768,000	1,120,000
Total Active Accounts[a]	NA	NA	113,000	144,000	210,000	326,400	487,200
Trades/Average Active Account	NA	NA	NA	11.9	16.2	18.3	18.6

Source: Adapted from Merrill Lynch analyst report, "DLJ*direct*," June 21, 1999
[a]Active accounts defined as accounts with trading activity during previous 12 month period or positive account balances.

CARPOINT IN 1999

The senior managers of CarPoint were in a conference room, 48 hours before they would unveil an alliance between CarPoint and Ford Motor Company. They had made plans to contact other strategic partners immediately after they made the announcement, but it was hard to predict how these partners would react. The alliance would mark a major shift in strategy for CarPoint.

The online auto industry and CarPoint's market position had changed significantly since CarPoint was launched in 1996. In addition to long-standing competitors like Autobytel and AutoWeb, CarPoint now faced new competition from dealers, manufacturers, and from start-ups with new business models like StoneAge, OpenAuto, and CarsDirect. However, despite these competitive challenges, CarPoint had moved from the number three position among online auto buying services in terms of website traffic to the head of the pack. At the end of 1999, the company's site was highly ranked for responsiveness and software quality, and boasted 140,000 referrals a month, resulting in over $600 million in monthly sales by affiliated dealers.

Now, in mid-September 1999, CarPoint's management faced a new set of challenges. After several months of negotiations, the company was poised to partner with Ford. An alliance between CarPoint and the automotive behemoth would allow customers to custom-order vehicles and thereby streamline Ford's manufacturing and logistics processes. But would the alliance with Ford alienate other auto manufacturers and their dealers? Would CarPoint's category become polarized, with different manufacturers each pursuing an exclusive relationship with one of the online referral services? While debating these questions, CarPoint's management had to consider the fact that new competitors pursuing a direct sales model were growing rapidly. Was CarPoint allocating enough resources to developing its response to such challengers?

Research Associate Gillian Morris prepared this case under the supervision of Professor Tom Eisenmann as the basis for class discussion rather than to illustrate either effective or ineffective handling of an administrative situation.

The Auto Industry in 1999[1]

Buoyed by consumer optimism, the automotive industry—the largest retail sector in the U.S. economy—had a banner year in 1999: 17 million new vehicles were sold at an average price of $20,534, up from 16 million in 1998. The used car market also expanded slightly, with 41 million vehicles sold at an average price of $8,828.[2] In total, Americans spent about $1 trillion buying and financing cars in 1999.[3]

Dealers and the Buying Process

Dealerships were the main distribution channel for the auto industry. Nationwide, there were 22,400 new car dealers franchised by auto manufacturers in 1999, responsible for virtually all new car sales and about 40% of used car sales. The balance of used car sales were completed by independent (i.e., non-affiliated) dealers or by private parties. State governments, reliant upon vehicle sales tax revenues, had protected dealers' status as middlemen with legislation that prevented auto manufacturers from selling directly to consumers. Despite this protection, the dealership business was highly competitive and margins were thin: according to NADA, the dealers' trade association, the average dealership earned a gross margin in 1999 of just 12.6% and a 1.8% pretax profit margin.

Dealers served as intermediaries between the consumer and the manufacturer, and often succeeded in frustrating both parties. Customers were met at the dealership by experienced and sometimes unscrupulous salespeople who could gauge and exploit a customer's lack of product and financial acumen, and who, paid on commission, had

[1]The following two sections update portions of "Microsoft CarPoint," written by Harvard MBA candidates Avnish Bajaj, Steffan Haithbox and Michael Kadyan under the supervision of Professor Jeffrey Rayport, Harvard Business School case no. 898-280, June 23, 1998.

[2]"Automotive Retail: Quarterly Review," Morgan Stanley Dean Witter analyst report, August 17, 2000.

[3]David Reidel and L. Keith Mullins, "AutoNation," Salomon Smith Barney analyst report, April 13, 2000.

an incentive to make quick sales. Motivated consumers could try to even the scales by obtaining the dealer's invoice price and by researching cars in consumer magazines. However, dealers could obfuscate the total price for a new car by negotiating the terms of financing, extended warranties, trade-in prices, and dealer-installed options. Consumers often drove away from dealerships feeling that they had lost time, money, and their sanity.

The negative reputation of their dealers hurt auto manufacturers. Manufacturers had limited direct contact with the customer, making it difficult to win back their loyalty. To address this problem, General Motors, in launching its Saturn brand during the 1980s, had designed a stress-free buying experience with a no-haggle-pricing policy. During the 1990s, Ford had attempted to buy some dealerships and consolidate them into a "haggle-free network." However, Ford backed away from this initiative when it was resisted by dealers and challenged by state legislatures.

Online Referral Services

Online services promised to revolutionize the much-reviled car buying process. The large amounts of information relevant to the process could easily be organized and accessed via the Internet, as evidenced by the fact that 40% of new car buyers used the Internet to research their purchases in 1999, up from 25% in 1998.[4] Online automotive services were soon expected to offer built-to-order vehicles, much like Dell Computer's strategy.

A typical online buying experience began when a prospective customer went to the website of a online referral service, such as CarPoint, Autobytel, or Autoweb. These services provided links to independent sources of data on new car features, performance ratings, and pricing (e.g., Kelley's Blue Book, Edmunds). After completing their research, a prospect could submit a request to buy a specific model. The online referral service forwarded the prospect's contact information to a single affiliated dealer, based on geographic proximity. The dealer was then supposed to promptly contact the customer to offer a non-negotiable price. Some online car buying services also offered insurance and financing packages and thus provided "everything except a way to kick the tires."[5]

2.7% of new car sales were completed through online buying services in 1999.[6] Academic research indicated that these online sales resulted in both savings for consumers and increased profits for dealerships.[7] According to this research, controlling for the type of car purchased, consumers who used an online service saved $379, on average.[8] Although consumers paid less, online sales were not necessarily less profitable for dealers (even after factoring in payments to online referral services, which were about $100–200 per car sold), for two reasons: 1) online selling did not rely upon mass media advertising (which averaged about $400 per new vehicle sold via traditional methods) to drive prospects to the dealership (Exhibit 1); and 2) compensation payments to dealer sales reps per online transaction were much lower than for traditional offline transactions. The $150–200 commission typically paid to dealer reps handling online sales was about half the amount paid for an offline sale, and an online sales rep, often dealing with a well-educated buyer, could complete far more transactions every month.[9] Analyzing detailed accounting data for one dealership, the researchers concluded that the average cost to complete an online transaction was $600 less than for an offline sale.[10] Furthermore, the dealership reported that 60% of its online transactions represented incremental sales, suggesting that dealerships affiliated with online referral services could boost profits by leveraging their fixed costs.

---

[4]Brian Akre, "More new-vehicle buyers using the Internet to shop," AP Newswire, July 12, 1999.

[5]*Business Week,* "Downloading Their Dream Cars," March 3, 1998.

[6]Internet.com, "Online Auto Shopping Keeps Rising," September 26, 2000.

[7]The data cited in this paragraph are from a September 2000 working paper titled "Internet Car Retailing," by Fiona Scott Morton (Yale School of Management), Florian Zettelmeyer (Haas School of Business), and Jorge Silva Risso (J.D. Power and Associates). The researchers analyzed 195,772 transactions completed in 1999 and early 2000, combining data provided by J.D. Power and Autobytel.

[8]A portion of the savings may be attributed to the fact that Autobytel-affiliated dealers tended to offer lower prices for all transactions than non-affiliated dealers—both online and offline. After controlling for this effect, consumers using Autobytel to complete their purchase still saved $284, on average.

[9]Dealers only earned about half as much profit per online transaction from ancillary services (e.g., financing; extended service contracts), compared to offline sales. Only 64% of online buyers financed their cars through dealers, compared to 76% of offline buyers, and only 18% of online buyers purchased insurance or repair contracts from their dealers, versus 29% for offline buyers. Since online buyers were more affluent, it is difficult to determine whether their lower purchase rates for dealer-provided ancillary services could be directly attributed to their use of online referral services (which did market such services in competition with the dealer): even if they had not used Autobytel, it seems possible that many of these sophisticated, affluent consumers would have self-financed their vehicles or shopped elsewhere for better deals on ancillary services.

[10]Other analysts had estimated even greater savings. Scott Morton and her colleagues cite Lehman Brothers equity research that reports a $1,000 cost savings per transaction for sales through Autobytel.

CarPoint's Services and Strategy

CarPoint was introduced in July 1996 as an information product, working with Autobytel, the first online referral service. In May 1997, however, CarPoint entered the referral business directly, negotiating a contract with Reynolds and Reynolds (R&R), a company that provided information systems for 90% of U.S. auto dealers.[11] R&R's several hundred sales representatives signed up dealers for CarPoint. In return, R&R received a commission based on sales fees. This arrangement allowed CarPoint to enlist dealers rapidly and enhanced their ability to electronically tie into dealers' information systems. For example, CarPoint used R&R's inventory management systems to directly upload car availability information to their website, whereas some other online referral services asked dealers to manually input or fax inventory information.

Features. CarPoint's website provided information and tools similar to those available at other leading online referral sites. For consumers considering a new car purchase, CarPoint offered independent research services like the Kelley Blue Book, crash test ratings, car reviews, and links to manufacturer and dealer Web pages. CarPoint also offered a dual-car comparison feature. In 1999, CarPoint launched a "Personal Auto Page" feature. This tool—which encouraged repeat visits from consumers who might otherwise visit the site only every few years, when they were in the market for a new car—allowed car owners to maintain their automotive records online, receiving e-mail reminders and information on maintenance and recall notices.

CarPoint offered customers access to financing and insurance services, both potentially lucrative profit streams. However, unlike some competitors, CarPoint did not offer these services directly; instead, it referred interested consumers to websites such as InsWeb and E-LOAN. CarPoint's decision to restrict its role in marketing these services served to reduce conflict with dealers, who earned a considerable share of their total profits from such ancillary services (Exhibit 2).

Finally, CarPoint also had compelling features for consumers interested in used cars, including up to date listings, enhanced information provided directly from the dealer (e.g., that a car had only one owner or never had been smoked in), and information to designate certified vehicles. In its popular Surround Video Gallery, CarPoint offered 360 degree views of some used cars, with exterior and interior images so detailed they revealed the carpet condition and wear and tear on door handles.

Business Model. Like the other online referral services, CarPoint earned most of its revenue from subscription fees paid by affiliated dealers,[12] who each paid about $1,000 per month on average. CarPoint also earned revenue by referring users to insurance and financing services, and by displaying other advertising on its website, principally from auto manufacturers. Advertising by auto manufacturers was a huge market, with $3.7 billion in 1995 spent across all U.S. media, or about $250 per new vehicle sold.

Marketing. A distinct edge that CarPoint held over its competitors was its relationship to Microsoft, and its status as a part of the MSN portal. The second most heavily trafficked website in the U.S. after Yahoo.com, MSN.com attracted over 30 million unique visitors per month in October 1999. CarPoint's prominent and exclusive placement in the network assured it a steady stream of visitors. Even with this visibility, CarPoint advertised elsewhere on the web. The majority of its advertising budget was slated for search engines (e.g., Yahoo!, Excite, and HotBot) and other automotive sites (e.g., Kelley Blue Book). CarPoint had invested little in traditional mass media advertising (e.g. print, radio, and TV).

Dealer Relationships. In addition to the benefits of brand association with Microsoft, CarPoint leveraged the software company's superior technology. Microsoft produced proprietary technology for the referral service that gave it an edge over its competitors. One such tool was DealerPoint, a critical factor in CarPoint's relations with its dealer network. This proprietary tool would enable dealers to use CarPoint to market more effectively, e.g., by using templates to fine-tune banner ads and marketing specific used cars with pop-up ads, more detailed descriptions, and images. DealerPoint would also enable dealers to receive and act on new car buying leads electronically.

With new competitors emerging, it was important for CarPoint to continue to strengthen its relations with

[11]R&R sales brochure.

[12]According to SEC filings, Autobytel.com earned about 11% of its 1999 revenue from: 1) selling advertising on its site; 2) marketing insurance and financing services; and 3) international licensing of its business model.

dealers. According to Mary Dolan, Product Manager—New Car Buying Service, CarPoint's partnership with Reynolds & Reynolds continued to be highly effective, particularly after R&R shifted responsibility to a new 12 person unit (including 8 field reps) dedicated exclusively to selling and servicing CarPoint dealers. Previously, each of R&R's more than 300 reps had spent a small portion of their time on CarPoint business.

Dolan explained that CarPoint had undertaken a number of actions to improve dealer performance. First, CarPoint introduced a performance element to its pricing structure for dealers; under a new tiered pricing program, dealers' payments were based on the average volume of leads they received. Second, CarPoint management constantly evaluated dealer productivity, analyzing consumer activity to determine whether to renew dealers or seek to attract new ones in a given geographic area. Finally, CarPoint managers had learned that conversion rates (sales per lead) were maximized when consumers received a dealer response within one day; Steve Fox, manager of CarPoint's dealer channel, explained, "Now, it's a reply within an hour or two that really moves the needle." Accordingly, the CarPoint team had accelerated its deployment of DealerPoint software. The team also intensified dealer training efforts, focusing on providing dealers with guidance on the types of skills to look for when recruiting Internet sales specialists and how to compensate their specialists.

Direct Competitors[13]

Although CarPoint had more user traffic by late 1999, Autobytel still led the industry in terms of its number of new car dealers and car sales. Launched in March 1995, Autobytel operated its own field sales force of 25–30 reps to recruit dealers. Leveraging its early lead, Autobytel was the only online service that had required its dealers to sign exclusive agreements, although competitive pressures eventually forced it to relax exclusivity requirements.

By the fall of 1999, Autobytel generated 200,000 referrals a month for its 3,000 registered dealers, who converted 28% of these leads into sales; Autobytel accounted for 12% of total sales in these dealerships.[14] To solidify its strong brand awareness, Autobytel spent $15 million on advertising in the third quarter of 1999. This brand-building came at a price: Autobytel was not profitable and was not expected to earn a profit over the near term (see Exhibit 3 for income statements of publicly traded online car buying services).[15]

Other online referral services, such as Autoweb and Autovantage, also followed the strategy of referring customers to local dealers in exchange for fees. To retain their dealer network in the face of increased competition, Autoweb changed its pricing structure from a flat monthly fee to charging dealers $30 per sales lead. In an effort to develop a vertical portal of auto enthusiasts, Autoweb also offered community features, e.g., bulletin boards with commuting horror stories and online chats with mechanics.

A new referral service, StoneAge.com, had entered the market in 1996 with a slightly different strategy. Focusing on customer satisfaction and an easy-to-use website, StoneAge.com emphasized both new- and used-car sales. Used car sellers could list their car for $20—a one-time fee good until a final sale. With over 3 million visitors a month, the site was directly responsible for helping sell 108,000 cars, representing over $2 billion in sales revenue, in 1998. Unlike its competitors with heavier marketing expenditures, StoneAge.com, which relied on word-of-mouth referrals from satisfied customers, was profitable in 1998.

In September 1999, yet another new referral service was poised to enter the fray: OpenAuto.com. By tweaking the familiar business model, OpenAuto hoped to quickly make itself known. Instead of building an exclusive relationship with a small dealer network, OpenAuto sought to simulate a more typical car-buying experience by offering a customer's bid to all local dealers. A customer would then comparison shop between all bidding dealers. The site's revenue model was based solely upon a $150 sales fee from the dealer, with no monthly network fees. Starting with 17 employees and 1,400 participating dealerships, OpenAuto was primarily designed for customers seeking popular vehicles who were willing to compromise total control over the buying process in exchange for a more competitive price.

[13]The information contained within this section and the next section ("Competing Car Buying Models") was based upon a range of public sources, including the companies' 10-Ks, websites, and news articles. The following press articles were most significant: Robert McGarvey, "In the Driver's Seat," *Upside*, 4/1999, 68–70; Robert McGarvey, "Car Chase," *Upside*, 12/99, 156–164; Susan Moran, "Tire Clickers," *Business 2.0*, 9/99, 159–164; and Scott Woolley, "A Car Dealer by Any Other Name," Forbes, 11/29/99, 113–116.

[14]The Wall Street Transcript, November 2, 1999.

[15]Information contained within this paragraph was compiled from the Auto-by-Tel 10-K, the company's website, and public news articles, especially: "In the Driver's Seat," Robert McGarvey, *Upside* 4/99, 66–70.

Competing Car Buying Models

Once the referral system exposed its strengths and weaknesses, other firms launched competing online initiatives. Some, like newspapers, traditional dealers, and manufacturers, were extending familiar propositions to the Internet. Others, like Priceline and direct sales companies, were exploring entirely new distribution and sales models (see Exhibit 4 for a summary of the value propositions for leading services).

Classifieds Services

In late 1999, the two largest classified sites advertising new and used cars were Cars.com and Yahoo!'s automobile section. Cars.com was funded by Classified Ventures, which was itself founded by eight newspaper companies. Cars.com became a much more visible site after it committed $26 million to advertising and marketing in 1999. Over 1,000 dealers signed on as clients for a monthly fee ranging from $500–$1,000. As opposed to traditional print classifieds, dealers could list their entire inventory, and in more detail than newspapers allowed. The site generated 15,000 leads a week for these dealers. Yahoo.com had offered free auto classifieds since its inception, but had expanded its scope in 1999 with the explosion of the online automotive industry in general. On its exclusive auto shopping section, Yahoo! offered over 700,000 free classified ads personalized by location and customer preference; it also had expanded its loan and car financing listings and offered troubleshooting and repair advice.

A recent entrant into the classified sector of the market was AutoTrader.com. The site was launched in May 1998 by Cox Enterprises, a media conglomerate that owned Manheim Auctions, one of the leading used car auction companies. By working with Automated Data Processing (ADP), Cox gained access to dealer inventories of used cars and started its AutoTrader site with over 5,000 dealerships. By year-end 1999, AutoTrader offered listings for 1.25 million vehicles, the largest inventory of used car classifieds ever compiled. With 99% of the listings less than three weeks old, AutoTrader had become the complete source for used car classifieds. Initially, AutoTrader relied on banner advertising on its site to bring in revenue; as dealer enthusiasm grew, though, it moved towards a "Yellow Pages" model. Dealers had a standard listing for free, but could pay for "attention-grabbing extras such as bigger, bolder listings and Web site links."[16] Like most of its competitors, AutoTrader sacrificed near-term profitability to achieve market mindshare and to lock in dealers for its network.

Priceline

The well-known consumer-to-business company Priceline brought its "name your own price" model to new car sales in July 1998, starting in the New York metropolitan region.[17] Guided by dealer invoice prices available on Priceline's site, customers made offers on particular car models complete with their desired options and the range of counties to which they were willing to travel to close the haggle-free deal. Priceline faxed the offer to all relevant dealers; the first dealer to notify the company received the sale. On completed deals, buyers paid the site $25 and dealers paid $75; if the customer failed to respond to a dealer's offer, $200 was deducted from their credit cards by Priceline, with the proceeds equally divided between the responding dealer and the web site. A critical distinction between Priceline and car referral services like CarPoint was that Priceline kept the customer's name anonymous until a dealer accepted the offer. In addition, with no up-front dealer fees, Priceline's arrangements suited both small dealerships and large dealerships seeking to liquidate inventory.

When Priceline launched its IPO in April 1999, it received a market valuation of $12.9 billion. Much of this valuation was based on projected expansion beyond its core airline ticket business into additional vertical markets, such as automotive sales. In July of that year, Priceline teamed with AutoNation, which owned the largest chain of car dealers in the U.S.; their agreement was that Priceline would send customer bids to AutoNation retailers first. If no AutoNation dealers responded, Priceline then would extend the offer to other dealers in the area. The partnership gave Priceline instant national scale and garnered attractive leads for AutoNation's dealers. In the fall of 1999, Priceline also teamed with Ford. Visitors to Ford's website would be directed to Priceline if they wished to buy vehicles. Users would thus have access to dealer invoice prices through Priceline (unavailable on Ford's site). Priceline announced that it was in the midst of other negotiations with other automotive manufacturers to create similar links.

[16] David Freedman, "Would you buy a used car from this site?" *Forbes ASAP,* 11/29/99, 56.

[17] By year-end 1999, Priceline was the second-most recognized Web brand among adults in the United States.

Dealers

Originally introduced to the Internet through referral services like CarPoint and Autobytel, both individual and group dealerships began to see the possibilities of web sales. Because of their legally-protected position as final sellers, dealers could, in theory, post their own websites and compete with referral services. By the end of 1999, 74% of dealers had their own Internet site, up from 61% the year before. Sid DeBoer, CEO of Lithia Automotive Group, stated, "The middle person won't thrive in the future. We can take Web-based service and do it ourselves."[18]

The country's largest group dealer, Republic Industries, launched Autonationusa.com in 1999. CEO Mike Jackson focussed the company's efforts on re-branding their 400 dealerships with a common identity, instituting one-price, no-haggle sales, and focussing on margin share, not market share. The company dedicated a 900 person sales force to managing Internet leads, and cut its response time down to 1.9 hours—a noticeable cut above its competition. By July 1999, the site had sold 15,000 vehicles worth over $350 million, and was expected to sell more than $1 billion by the end of 1999, and $1.5 billion in 2000. As two industry analysts noted:

> AutoNation is unique among e-tailers in that it can actually participate in all parts of [the process] and actually complete the transaction. Other participants simply sell the name, contact information and car preference of a customer to a dealership near the customer where they take delivery. This prevents the development of any relationship between the dealership and the customer to tap into other more lucrative lines of business, especially service and parts.[19]

Manufacturers

Like dealers, Detroit manufacturers were initially slow to recognize the potential of Internet sales; however, some industry heavyweights, particularly General Motors, began to pursue more aggressive strategies in 1999. In March, GM launched GM BuyPower in an effort to reduce its dealers' reliance upon third-party services like CarPoint and Autobytel. Like the other referral models, BuyPower sought to match customers with dealers; however, the service was free to GM dealers. For the customers, the site offered information unavailable on other online sources. According to one Internet sales director, GM "can offer proprietary information such as what our incentives are on cars and actual inventory at a dealer. Online services won't have access to that, and we won't give them that kind of information."[20] Notwithstanding these information benefits for the consumer and the elimination of referral fees, many GM dealers were skeptical of BuyPower and initially were slow to sign on.

The next development in GM's Internet strategy was to consolidate all of its e-commerce sites, including BuyPower, into one subdivision: e-GM. The major goals for this project were to integrate web technology into every aspect of the company's bricks-and-mortar business; GM sought to reduce design time, to link customers with dealers and suppliers, and to create a "web car" that customers could "test drive" online. Ultimately, GM wanted the capability to build a car to order, much like Dell Computer's successful strategy of building personal computers for individual customers. Such a revolution could create large-scale efficiencies in automotive production.

Similarly, Ford Motor Co. had been making aggressive moves into the retail market with its Ford Retail Network, launched in 1997. In an effort to trim distribution costs, retain brand control, and reconnect with increasingly disaffected consumers, the company made minority equity investments in dealerships, then consolidated them into networks in Tulsa, Oklahoma City, San Diego, and Rochester, N.Y. With salesmen operating on salary, not commissions, the Ford Retail Network dealers offered fixed-pricing, no-haggle transactions. In response, Ford dealers in neighboring counties chose to undercut Ford Retail Network dealers' prices; consequently, Network dealers were unable to attract enough consumers to their showrooms. When Ford attempted to introduce its new business model to the highly competitive Texas market, dealers were outraged and sought legislation in 1999 to prevent manufacturers from owning equity stakes in dealerships. Following suit, legislatures in a dozen other states were considering new franchise laws that would prohibit manufacturers from owning any dealership within 45 miles of

[18]Alex Lash, "Car dealers grapple with online sales," *The Industry Standard,* 2/22–3/1/99, 28.

[19]David Reidel and Ryan Johnston, "AutoNation," Salomon Smith Barney analyst report, 12/29/99.

[20]"Car race in cyberspace," *The Wall Street Journal,* 2/18/99.

an existing dealer.[21] Though Ford officials insisted that dealers in the Retail Network would not receive preferential treatment (such as access to popular models and easy financing for consumers), most of its dealers remained unconvinced. By the fall of 1999, Ford had scaled back plans to invest in additional dealerships.

Direct Sales

In 1999, three companies with distinctly different business models entered the online car buying market. CarsDirect.com, founded by Scott Painter and Bill Gross (from idealab!) and backed by Michael Dell (CEO of Dell Computer), Goldman Sachs, Primedia, and other investors, was prominently launched in May 1999. The inefficiencies of the referral services were the basis for CarsDirect.com's direct sales model. With referrals, dealers could not be strictly bound to their original quotes; they sometimes haggled with customers over their bids despite the best efforts of the referral sites to prevent such behavior. Furthermore, the referral process relied upon the dealer contacting the customer, an unreliable system. Like its competitors, CarsDirect offered research and financial and insurance information. However, CarsDirect sought to remove contact with the dealer from the customer's experience. By buying cars from dealers and essentially reselling them to interested buyers, the company offered convenience and a hassle-free buying experience to its customers. It promised a firm quote in the lowest 10% of the price bracket, backed by its own willingness to "eat the loss" if they could not find an interested dealer. This policy was expensive to implement; by the end of 1999, the company was losing $200 on average for each vehicle sold.

CEO Painter professed not to be unduly concerned about losses, and in fact expected to spend $80 million on brand building in 2000 and 2001. Painter said CarsDirect could cut the typical dealer's customer acquisition costs to $50 from $500; Painter claimed, ". . . we can create other efficiencies in the process. There's money to be made selling cars."[22] With over 30% of a new car's cost incurred beyond the factory gate—in shipping cars to dealers, manufacturers' branding investments, and dealers' operating expenses—eliminating inefficiencies in the process could yield profits. By also selling insurance and financing, CarsDirect hoped to lock in profitable transactions with consumers and build lifetime loyalty.

CarOrder.com was launched soon after CarsDirect, though it garnered less attention. Backed by Trilogy Software, CarOrder pursued the same direct sales model but claimed to have lower prices. Like CarsDirect, the company faced the problem of state regulations limiting car sales to bricks-and-mortar dealerships. It cut through this regulatory tangle by acquiring low-rent dealerships on the outskirts of major cities and turning them into online distribution centers staffed not by salesmen, but by Internet specialists.

In September 1999, DriveOff.com became the third online dealer to pursue the direct sales model. DriveOff promised both dealers and shoppers an improved car buying experience. Like other direct sales sites, the company offered research, firm price quotes, and delivery. The only contact the customer would have with a dealer would be to sign the papers. However, unlike other business models, the dealer was encouraged to build a relationship with the customer after the final sale to capitalize on high-margin activities like maintenance and service. A Navidec CyberShopper survey showed that nine out of ten car buyers wanted a relationship with a local dealer after the sale.[23]

Partnership with Ford

In such a noisy and competitive arena, the proposed venture with Ford posed significant questions about the future of CarPoint and, indeed, the online car buying industry as a whole. The terms of the venture stated that Ford would acquire a significant minority stake in CarPoint, and would be the first partner in Microsoft's new Build-to-Order system. CarPoint CEO Lindsay Sparks explained, "This software will link customer-specific vehicle and feature requests with Ford's supply-chain operations, and positioned CarPoint to lead the next revolution in online car sales. By offering our site visitors the opportunity to custom-order vehicles, much as they can with Dell computers, CarPoint will be changing its business strategy. In addition to referring customers to dealers, we will be serving as the conduit for a new, efficient automotive marketing process."

The proposed joint venture was not exclusive for either side. Ford would be free to pursue relationships

[21]Earl Elridge, "Car sellers, automakers haggle over dealerships," *USA Today*, 11/15/99, B10.

[22]Robert McGarvey, "Car Chase," *Upside*, 12/99, 160.

[23]Lisa Everitt, "Dealers OK launching online 'lot'," *Chicago Sun-Times*, 10/11/99, N2.

with other Internet partners; Microsoft would be free to pursue arrangements with other manufacturers. Microsoft and Ford also had a clear understanding that Ford would receive no preferential placement nor any other special treatment on the CarPoint site. In particular, Ford would not have any control over CarPoint's editorial product. If CarPoint posted a review saying a new Ford model was a brick with wheels, Ford had no ability to pull the review.

For Ford, the advantages of an alliance with CarPoint were abundant. Much like its rival GM, Ford welcomed the direct access to its customers that it would gain through the online car buying process. With new knowledge about consumer preferences and buying patterns, Ford planned to streamline inventories and tailor packaged-options more accurately. CEO Jacques Nasser stated, "The term lean manufacturing is about to take new meaning."[24] The alliance with CarPoint was another important step in Ford's wide-ranging effort to integrate the Internet and web technology into every step of their business.

Similarly, the deal could be a boon to Microsoft, CarPoint's parent. While Ford had long been a customer of Microsoft, the CarPoint alliance could cement their relationship and could set the stage for additional software sales. For CarPoint itself, the alliance would be a vote of confidence in its market position, a unique point of differentiation valued by customers, and a sign of the company's willingness to change its business strategy in a rapidly evolving competitive arena.

In spite of these benefits, however, CarPoint's management team had some concerns about the joint venture. First, a public alliance with one major manufacturer might alienate other manufacturers and their dealers. Though the Microsoft technology developed with Ford for custom-ordering vehicles was theoretically available to other dealers, CarPoint's managers worried that the industry would become polarized, with each auto manufacturer aligning with a different Internet car buying service. Industry trends suggested that polarization was a distinct possibility. When informed of the planned deal with Ford, Toyota had announced that it had no interest in developing such a relationship with CarPoint.

Second, with Ford signing on as a minority stakeholder in CarPoint, CarPoint's relationship to its parent, Microsoft, would become more complex. The joint venture between Ford and CarPoint clearly aligned Ford and Microsoft more closely, which could yield considerable business benefits for Microsoft as software sales evolved into service relationships. But Microsoft sold software to other large auto manufacturers: would these sales be jeopardized in any way by a CarPoint/Ford joint venture? Finally, for CarPoint, having two shareholders with different agendas could complicate the strategic direction-setting process in an fast-paced industry where decision-making delays could be enormously expensive.

Adding to the complexity was the possibility that Microsoft would spin out CarPoint in an IPO. Microsoft was rumored to be weighing this option in the fall of 1999. As Internet companies continued to realize enormous Wall Street valuations, spinning off Microsoft's Internet divisions was one way to generate the cash needed to build their brands and acquire customers. Already, Microsoft had registered its Expedia travel service for an IPO. Industry observers speculated that an Expedia IPO would be "one way to give Microsoft a better indication of how other units it might spin off would be valued if a split-up of its major business units actually happened" in the wake of the Justice Department's antitrust case.[25] For CarPoint, an IPO could raise the capital needed to be a frontrunner in the online car sales industry. However, management was aware that the time-consuming IPO process could distract the team when a rapidly evolving competitive environment demanded their focused attention.

Indeed, the CarPoint management team's time and resources were already stretched across a wide range of priorities. Gwen Weld, the director of international business development, was planning significant expansion of CarPoint's services into Canada, Europe and Japan. Other executives continued to improve CarPoint's technology and consumer interfaces (see Exhibit 5 for a screenshot of CarPoint's home page). However, CarPoint's major strategic initiative in 1999 was the proposed Ford alliance. Betsy Frost, CarPoint's Group Product Manager, noted:

> While the CarPoint team was putting lots of time and effort into the Ford negotiations, our competition was building steam. With a small team focused on a big project, there's always a risk that you'll find a competitor plowing past you.

Members of the CarPoint team had a lot to consider as they stared at the phone on the conference room table. At a tactical level, they had to decide whether to

[24]"Net to revolutionize business," *The Times of India,* 11/24/99.

[25]*Dow Jones Business News,* 11/10/99.

announce the Ford deal now or in the future, when they might have news about more joint ventures with other manufacturers. According to Liza Thomas, Director of Business Development, who led the negotiations with Ford, deferring the news until CarPoint had multiple manufacturer partners might temper dealers' concerns that CarPoint would unduly favor Ford. On the other hand, perceptions shaped reality in a powerful way for Internet businesses: if a competitor were to preempt CarPoint with an announcement about their own alliance with a manufacturer, then CarPoint would lose the benefits from being perceived as an industry leader in this area.

At a strategic level, the team continued to wrestle with broader concerns about the Ford joint venture. Would CarPoint lose credibility with other manufacturers' dealers? Or were alliances like these the future of the industry? Some critics of referral services had charged that introducing a new set of online intermediaries to a fundamentally flawed consumer buying process had been like "putting lipstick on a pig." In this view, rather than add new players (the referral services) to the auto industry's value chain, the right answer was for auto manufacturers to simply buy out their dealers then offer fixed prices, doing away with the haggling that customers hated, and thereby eliminating a major reason that referral services had emerged in the first place. Ford had made aggressive moves in this direction earlier in the year, but had been rebuffed by its dealers. Now Ford had embraced the new online intermediary, and Microsoft CarPoint was its preferred partner. But did the benefits for CarPoint outweigh the risks?

Exhibit 1 FRANCHISE DEALER STATISTICS IN 1999

	New Cars	Used Cars
Average Price/Vehicle	$24,321	$13,205
Average Gross Profit	$1,557	$1,426
Average Gross Profit Margin	6.4%	10.8%
Average Marketing Expenditure per Car Sold	$410	$200[b]

Note: Franchise dealers are affiliated with specific auto manufacturers; non-affiliated dealers are referred to as "Independents."
Source: Adapted from "Auto Dealership Update," Robertson Stephens analyst report, April 20, 2000

Exhibit 2 DISTRIBUTION OF DEALERSHIP PROFITS BY SOURCE, 1999

New vehicle sales	39%
Used vehicle sales	19%
Service and parts sales; financing and other	42%

Source: Adapted from "Auto Dealership Update," Robertson Stephens analyst report, April 20, 2000

Exhibit 3 1999 INCOME STATEMENTS FOR AUTOBYTEL, AUTOWEB, AND CARSDIRECT ($ IN MILLIONS)

	Year Ended December 31		
	Autobytel	**Autoweb**	**CarsDirect**
Revenues	$40.3	$29.5	$15.2
Operating Expenses:			
Sales and Marketing	44.2	33.2	33.4
Product Development	14.3	5.1	2.1
General and Administrative	8.6	7.2	19.9
Other			14.2
Total Operating Expenses	67.0	49.7	72.3
Income (loss) before provision for taxes	(23.3)	(18.2)	(72.3)
Employees	255	218	70

Source: Company SEC filings

Exhibit 4

VALUE PROPOSITIONS AND COMPARATIVE DATA FOR ONLINE CAR BUYING SECTOR (YE 1999)

	Value-Added Services	Revenue Model	Owners/Investors	Size of Dealer Network	Unique Monthly Visitors(000)
Autobytel	Online leasing, financing, and insurance available; warranty and credit reports; members' rewards program with personalized features	Dealers pay subscription fees; also earns fees from insurance, financing, and leasing services	Public company; investors included GE Capital Services, AIG, MediaOne Interactive Services	3,300 dealers	567
Autoweb	Kelley Blue Book, online financing and insurance, credit reports, reviews; provides links to accessory merchandise	Dealers pay on per-lead basis; advertising and revenue-sharing from third-party services	Public company	4,700 dealers	1,010
CarPoint	Kelley Blue Book, finance and insurance section, ratings, reviews, 3/D graphics, interest rate calculator. "My Personal AutoPage" offers recall information and repair and tune-up reminders	Sells customer leads to dealers in network; sells used car classified space to dealers; banner and sponsorship revenue	Microsoft, Ford Motor Co.	2,300 dealers	1,441
Cars.com	Automotive reports, reviews, loan calculators, largest selection of used-car classifieds. Advice from NPR's *Car Talk* hosts.	Affiliate newspapers link to dealers, who can post ads both off- and online. Allows dealers to post full inventories and aids in customizing dealer websites	Classified Ventures, owned by a consortium of newspaper publishers	Not relevant	891
CarsDirect	Offers direct online purchase capability with research, pricing information, design and financing available	Direct purchase model (consumer fee to initiate process, later deductible from purchase), with additional revenues from financing and insurance	BankOne, ideaLab!, Dell, Foundation Capital, Morgan Stanley Dean Witter, Hambrecht & Quist, Oracle, Goldman Sachs, et al.	Not relevant	554

Source: Adapted from Jupiter Communications, "Classifieds Market Competitive Landscape," December 1999; SEC filings

Exhibit 5

CARPOINT HOME PAGE

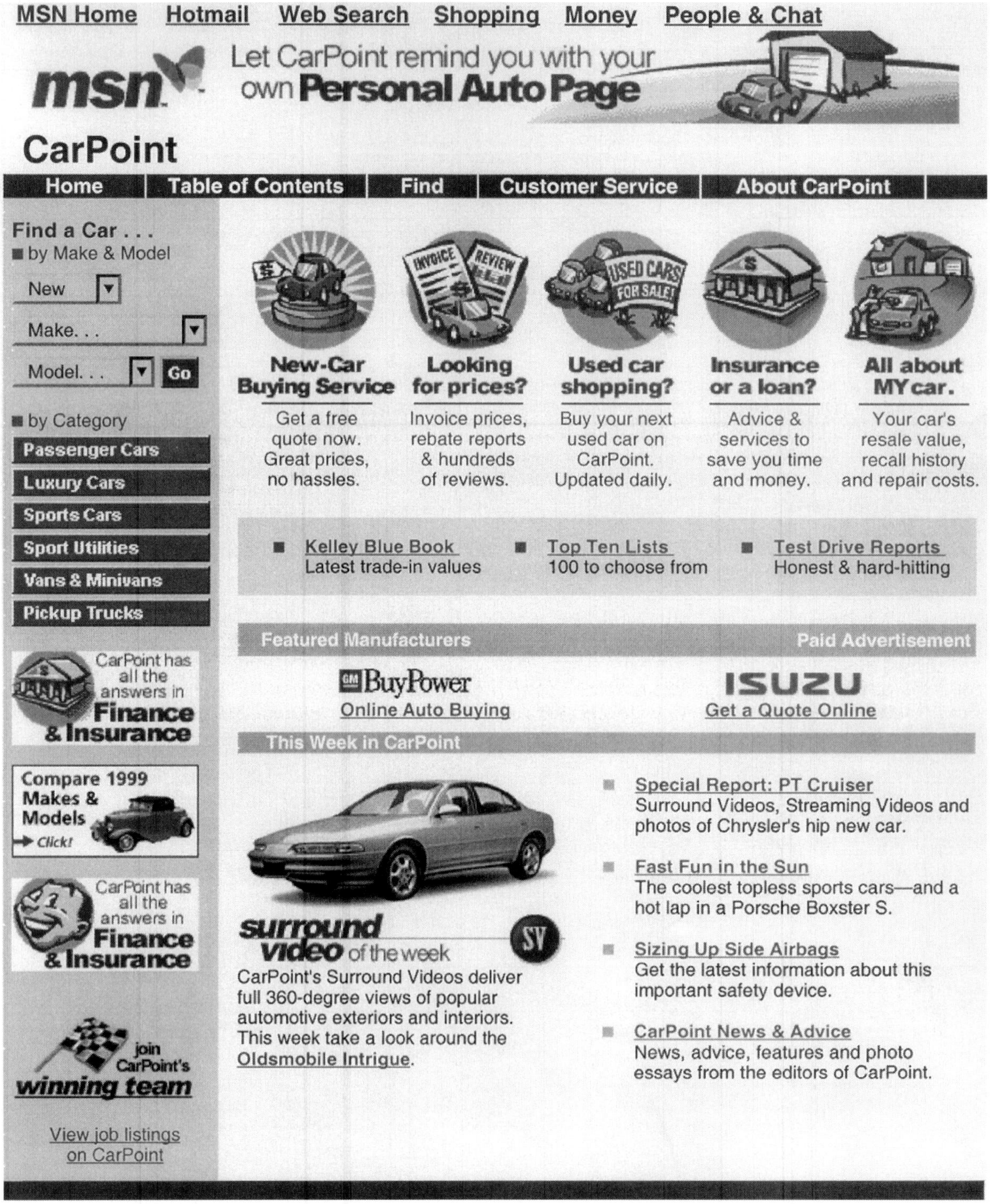

ROSENBLUTH INTERNATIONAL AND BIZTRAVEL.COM

Introduction

Neal Bibeau could smell the freshly baked cookies he'd grown accustomed to eating each Friday afternoon since joining Rosenbluth International (the third largest travel agency in the U.S.) as the president of its Internet subsidiary. A graduate of The Tuck School at Dartmouth, Bibeau believed that the Internet presented Rosenbluth with a great opportunity. However, he wondered whether he was exploiting it correctly.

The conventional (and to-date successful) service model most Internet companies adopted was to reduce customer interactions with live representatives to a bare minimum. Bibeau believed that all of his competitors had adopted this model. He noted, "One of my competitors makes it so difficult to speak with a live person customers have to punch in a confirmed reservation number before they can get into the 'phone queue." These Internet companies believed that they could only achieve what venture capitalists referred to as "infinite scalability" by reducing human intervention in sales and service to near zero.

Infinite scalability was important to some Internet companies because it justified the investment of large sums in organizations that were not profitable and had no prospect of profitability in the near-to-intermediate future. These companies often had a willingness to grow at almost any cost because they believed that once their fixed costs were covered, their very low variable costs would deliver high margins on incremental volume.

In contrast to its competitors, Biztravel placed its toll-free telephone number prominently on its website, made e-mail and on-line chat easy and all but immediate, and prided itself on high service standards—including hold times that were short or nonexistent, and well-trained, capable employees who could answer questions and solve problems.

While Bibeau's strategy sounded good from a customer service perspective, it flew in the face of the economics of infinite scalability. He wondered if all those other executives, and the venture capitalists and consultants behind them, knew something he didn't.

Professor Roger Hallowell prepared this case with the assistance of Research Associate Tonica Hampton as the basis for class discussion rather than to illustrate either effective or ineffective handling of an administrative situation.

Part I—Rosenbluth International

The Traditional Travel Agency Industry

Traditional bricks-and-mortar travel agencies served business and leisure travelers. Business travelers used travel agencies as one-stop shops for air, rental car, and hotel arrangements. Leisure travelers used travel agents for additional advice on where to vacation and how to get there. Travel agencies built relationships with both constituencies and served as an intermediary between suppliers (airlines, car rental agencies, hotels, etc.) and customers. Airlines used travel agencies as their primary distribution channel, directing business travel to them, and stimulating leisure travel. Commissions to travel agents were the airline's third largest operating expense.[1]

With airline deregulation in the late 1970s, airline ticket fares for leisure travelers decreased. As a result, the airlines no longer needed travel agents to stimulate leisure demand. By the late 1980s, many travel agents spent much of their time finding the lowest fares for their leisure customers, the most convenient itineraries for their business customers, and creating and delivering tickets. Until the mid-1990s, the primary source of revenue for travel agencies was a ten-percent-of-ticket-price commission paid by the airlines to the agencies. Hotels, car rental agencies, cruise ships, and tour operators also paid commissions of varying amounts.

[1]Clemons, Eric. K., and Hann, Il-Horn, "Rosenbluth International: Strategic Transformation of a Successful Enterprise," *Journal of Management Information Systems,* Fall 1999, Vol. 16, No. 2.

Rosenbluth Travel

In 1892, Hungarian emigrant Marcus Rosenbluth founded a steamship ticket agency in Philadelphia. While his initial concept was to provide a way to help Europeans emigrate, the business later evolved into a typical travel agency serving predominantly leisure travelers. In the mid-1960s, Rosenbluth began to serve corporations, focusing almost entirely on corporate travelers by the 1980s. In 1985, Hal Rosenbluth, who had spent most of his career at the company, was named President. Two years later, he became CEO. Hal Rosenbluth was known in the industry as a progressive leader and an astute competitor.

From Travel Agents to Corporate Travel Managers

In 1984, DuPont examined its travel needs and determined that they could best be met by a single agency, as opposed to the multiple local agencies it (and other large companies) were using at the time. Rosenbluth was selected to consolidate DuPont's travel in the United States. Rosenbluth's corporate travel service grew rapidly as a number of companies followed DuPont's lead. In the process, Rosenbluth transformed itself from a traditional travel agency to what managers called "a travel *management* company" that used its resources to lower costs for its clients.

Rosenbluth accomplished this transformation by developing two important skills. First, the firm became expert in collecting and analyzing data on client travel patterns, and using this data to negotiate travel discounts with airlines and later, hotels and car rental agencies. Second, the company gained the ability to manage call centers efficiently and effectively, delivering high quality service at relatively low cost. This contributed to Rosenbluth's ability to refund 40 percent of its 10 percent commission to its clients, helping to reduce their travel costs further. Rosenbluth's expertise also resulted in two new sources of revenue for Rosenbluth and other large corporate travel managers, some of which was shared with clients. The first of these new sources of revenue was "overrides."[2] An airline paid an override to a travel agency if that agency was able to change the airlines' market share on a specific route. For example, if an agency could issue enough tickets on the Boston to Chicago route to increase United Airlines' market share on that route, United might pay the agency 3 percent of the value of those tickets.

Very large agencies also began to receive payments from the Computerized Reservation Systems (CRSs) the agencies used to book tickets. The CRSs, such as SABRE and Apollo, had data from the individual airlines on schedules, seat availability, and prices. CRSs charged the airlines a fee per ticket booked through them. The CRS payments to very large travel agencies were generally one dollar for each ticket booked.

By the late 1980s, the travel services industry had divided into two sectors: unmanaged leisure and small business, and managed corporate. Rosenbluth's major competitors in the managed corporate sector were American Express and Carlson Wagonlit Travel (which unlike Rosenbluth also served numerous leisure travelers). 53 percent of the individual airline discounts negotiated by agencies in the managed-travel segment of the industry reduced the price of tickets on the specified carrier between six and 15 percent.[3] Discounts, however, were only part of the value provided to corporate clients, many of which also demanded service. Thirty percent (the largest category) of respondents to a survey of corporate travel clients who had changed agencies reported that they did so because of poor service from their old agency.[4]

Rosenbluth's Recent History

In 1981, Rosenbluth opened the travel industry's first centralized reservation center in Philadelphia. This enabled Travel Service Associates (Rosenbluth's title for agents) in one centralized location to handle calls from travelers in several geographic regions. This centralization through technology was increased in 1988, when Rosenbluth's management saw that simply offering locations around the world was no longer sufficient to meet the global needs of business travelers. The firm became the first travel management company to link its offices through a central computer system that enabled Rosenbluth to provide travelers personalized service worldwide. This system gave the majority of Rosenbluth Travel Service Associates world-wide access to any traveler's itinerary, personal travel preferences, and company travel policy.

[2]Ibid.

[3]See Runzheimer International 1998 Survey and Analysis of Business Travel Policies and costs—9th Edition.

[4]Ibid.

In 1994, Rosenbluth opened its first "IntelliCenter," a centralized reservation facility in Fargo, North Dakota. In contrast to the industry's typical reservation centers, which were small offices located near individual clients, an IntelliCenter could be half a continent in distance from the multiple clients it served, and often employed 200 to 300 associates.

The firm positioned its IntelliCenters in areas with low cost real estate, and, according to several managers, "Highly productive, service-oriented employees." IntelliCenter Travel Service Associates were assigned to a particular client company, but were cross-trained to serve other clients in order to meet peaks in demand. Individual travelers did not have a single agent assigned to them. A manager explained:

> Our travelers want to get their reservations made correctly, as quickly as possible. We lose some intimacy by not assigning travelers to specific associates, but we are more efficient as a result. We don't suffer from quality problems because our associates do the job right—we know because we monitor them closely.

Associate to coach (supervisor) spans of control were approximately 14 to 1 at IntelliCenters. Coaches spent 80 percent of their time working with associates and 20 percent on the phone with clients. Management estimated that the cost to issue and support an airline ticket was one-third lower through an IntelliCenter than through a traditional, smaller Rosenbluth office.

Soon after opening the Fargo IntelliCenter, Rosenbluth launched a new data analysis tool called "DACODA" (Discount Analysis Containing Optimal Decision Algorithms). DACODA helped clients to identify optimal airline-ticket purchasing strategies based on their historical travel patterns. Managers believed that it was the only information analysis and management system of its kind in the industry. A manager commented, "While an airline's objective is to maximize revenue per seat, DACODA harnesses the power of yield management to maximize a client's value per seat." DACODA enabled clients to decipher complex airline pricing, optimize their travel spending, negotiate favorable airline contracts, and thus create a holistic cost-saving travel strategy. A client with a market cost for travel of $5.8 million might save 6.3 percent on standard Rosenbluth negotiated rates and another 6.1 percent as a result of DACODA.

In 1994, Rosenbluth also opened its Network Operations Center, described by a manager as the industry's first "nerve center," designed to monitor world news and weather. Rosenbluth's travel associates used information from the Network Operations Center to reroute customers during emergencies. For example, when Taiwan experienced an earthquake in 1999, a fax was sent to all travel associates to reroute passengers on trips to, or through, Taiwan. Calls to Rosenbluth associates in Taiwan were rerouted to other Rosenbluth offices. The Network Operations Center also monitored call volume in real time for 20 of Rosenbluth's domestic reservation centers (including the IntelliCenters), having alerts that warned when telephone service levels fell below acceptable levels, directing managers to reroute calls to centers with excess capacity.

Rosenbluth's smaller reservation centers weren't monitored by the Network Operations Center. For these locations, Rosenbluth depended on its local account management to alert the Network Operations Center staff when calls needed to be rerouted. Routing options varied based on client preferences. Some clients used an "intelligent call router" system that looked at the real-time data and decided where the call would be answered fastest. Other clients routed their calls to different locations by time of day, day of week, area code of caller, prompter (press 1 for domestic travel, 2 for international, etc.). Some clients preferred automatic call bouncing: if calls in location A were not answered within 20 seconds, they were automatically routed to location B.

Rosenbluth also used the Network Operations Center to monitor Travel Service Associates (each associate was monitored twice a quarter) and passenger records (randomly selected records were monitored four times a quarter). The latter involved checking records for a variety of important elements: errors, lowest applicable fare, seating preference achieved, frequent flier number entered, and so forth.

The following were typical Rosenbluth call center service standards:

- 90 percent of calls answered within 20 seconds
- <2 percent of calls abandoned
- <5 percent of calls taken as callbacks (an agent answering, but promising to call back when free)
- average callback time 30 minutes

A manager stated:

> We define quality as doing things that make the customer happy without making mistakes the airlines charge us for. How do we do it? Get the right people, train them, give them the tools they need, and

measure and reward performance. We also work to streamline our processes. We ask, "what's fluff—what do we do to cover our rear ends, and what's necessary—what adds value?" We try to eliminate everything but the latter.

In April of 1999, Rosenbluth launched an on-line travel management application called "@Rosenbluth." @Rosenbluth allowed corporate travelers to book reservations on an @Rosenbluth site located on their company's intranet. In addition, @Rosenbluth was customized to that client's needs. This enabled the client's employees to book tickets within its travel policies. Employees could disregard policies (for example choosing to fly a non-preferred airline), but doing so triggered the generation of an exception report delivered to the client company's travel manager (a similar policy applied to tickets booked through Travel Service Associates). Clients using @Rosenbluth incurred lower costs for Rosenbluth and were charged lower fees.

Organization Structure

Prior to 1996, Rosenbluth's regional operations were segmented into three areas: operations (Travel Service Associates), account management, and sales. Although this organization structure matched the industry standard, it led to some problems. A manager explained:

> The problem was that if a reservation agent in operations was not making a client happy, the account management group would not find out about it until it was too late, particularly if that agent was well liked in the operations group. On top of that, the operations and account management (relationship) people were in different vertical silos—so accountability and communications were limited

As a result, Rosenbluth combined its operations and account management groups. Exhibits 1 and 2 illustrate the change in structure.

Corporate Culture and Human Resources

Rosenbluth managers believed that what they called the firm's "feeling" stemmed from its leadership. As a result, managers were selected very carefully. One manager noted that "It's not that complex, we're looking for nice, capable people." Cecily Carel, Vice President of Human Resources described ways the firm had developed to determine if a potential hire was nice:

> One of the best ways is to see how the person treats associates at all levels. We often speak with Josie, our receptionist, about how the applicant treated her when he or she came in for the interview. Typically, Josie calls us proactively if someone is less than polite and respectful. We also try to put the person into a relaxing situation to see how they conduct themselves when they're at ease—it's the reverse of a stress interview and we have found it to be much more effective. On certain occasions, we invite candidates to our ranch in North Dakota and see how they do there. Hal will often take a drive with someone—we're trying to listen between the lines, to pick up on their body language, to observe decision making patterns and styles, and driving etiquette.

Hal Rosenbluth believed that all employees were crucially important to the firm's success:

> Quality work stems from quality people. We strive to create an environment that promotes our associates' satisfaction, which we believe results in ultimate client satisfaction. All our growth is client driven, so all our success hinges on people.

Cecily Carel commented on front-line recruiting, "This needs to be taken very seriously—when someone decides to leave his or her job to join our company, we have a big responsibility." New Travel Service Associates were usually from outside the travel industry. Each prospective hire generally had three interviews on at least two different occasions and spent an hour (preferably more) observing what the day-to-day life of a Rosenbluth Travel Service Associate was like before being hired. Rosenbluth also used what one manager called "behavioral event interviewing," asking potential employees to tell them what they had done in a specific situation. Because the prospective employee was given no time to think about his or her response, seasoned interviewers believed they could tell if the response was sincere. A typical question was, "Tell me about a mistake you've made and how you dealt with it." According to Carel, "Even the finest associates have made mistakes—the issue is, do they admit it immediately, accept responsibility for it, fix it, and learn from it?"

Rosenbluth managers also stressed the importance of training, which they called "Learning and Development." Managers believed that most learning was done on-the-job. Thus after a new Travel Service Associate's nine weeks of classroom-based skills training and customer service orientation, he or she was assigned a coach who focused on helping two or three associates manage the transition from the classroom into the office. This assistance lasted for one to three months. During this period the number of phone calls each new associate was expected to take was limited. Ongoing training for approximately three days per month lasted indefinitely. Training also included relationship-building skills (to enhance relationships with both colleagues and personal friends), and behavioral testing to establish an associate's learning style. This enabled trainers to tailor training appropriately to the degree possible.

During classroom training, hard skills taught involved how to find itineraries and book tickets. Soft skills included specific language to use with travelers (see Exhibit 3), and how to guide customers through the booking process. Each associate's computer contained scripts to follow for basic interactions with travelers. These helped to insure that all necessary information was conveyed in both directions, and helped to keep call time down. When travelers strayed from the script, associates were trained to gently bring them back to it, for example, "One moment ma'am, I need to get your name."

The Dickinson, ND IntelliCenter provided a good example of the Rosenbluth environment. Located off a gravel road, the building was sheathed in beige metal siding. Inside, ceilings were eleven feet high. State-of-the-art indirect lighting reduced computer screen glare, as did coatings on the windows recently applied to enable the blinds to remain open during the day. Travel Service Associates were seated around the outside of the building, near the windows, with management offices and "thought centers" (meeting rooms) in the center of the immaculately clean facility. Only two of the 220 individuals employed at Dickinson had offices, all other associates and managers worked "on the floor." Five of the 220 were full-time trainers.

Interior walls had numerous bulletin boards with information on jobs available throughout the company, confidential hotlines to councilors for employees feeling stressed, recent praise from travelers, information about special events such as semi-weekly massages, and volume and productivity numbers for specific clients. One section was decorated for Valentine's Day with numerous hearts hanging from the ceiling. Each computer screen was capped with a four-by-twelve–inch name card. Cards were color coded to indicate Travel Service Associates that had recently finished introductory training.

Each section of the building (called a pod) was dedicated to a particular account. Each account had a large "television" monitor illustrating the number of associates on calls, doing after call clean up work, not available, and available for calls. The monitor also showed the duration of each ongoing call. Each associate's phone had a blinking light when there was a queue (traveler waiting to speak with an associate) and showed how long the travelers with longest wait had been holding. Associates had the option of turning off the blinking light and queue information if they chose.

The Dickinson, ND IntelliCenter was located in an area known for its heavy snowstorms. During storms, employees living nearby received transportation to and from work in company supplied four-wheel-drive vehicles. Employees living a distance from the office could opt to stay in local hotels at Rosenbluth's expense. Employees working during snow emergencies earned extra vacation days. The Center had a generator with a one week's supply of diesel fuel.

Travel Service Associates received monthly bonuses based on 1) client satisfaction, and 2) productivity. A client satisfaction rating of 4.5 on a one to five scale was required for associates to receive any bonus. Productivity measures included the number of airline tickets sold per associate per day, (fourteen being the standard, star associates averaging 25). Bonuses began to accrue (subject to the 4.5 out of 5 quality standard) at six tickets per day. On average, approximately one-third of an associate's cash compensation came from bonuses. A manager noted: "We like to increase bonuses, but work hard not to decrease them. If an associate's bonus falls, we'll pay at the higher bonus that month and develop an action plan with him or her to get performance back up. It almost always works." Associates were expected to answer 40 calls per day. The average call took between five and six minutes, plus some time for "clean up work" after some of the calls. A ticket sale typically required three calls, one each for information, booking, and a change. An additional fraction of a call per ticket was also required for en-route rebooking.

Rosenbluth's managers believed that the company's competitive positioning, culture, operations, and human resource practices had contributed to its success. They defined success using several criteria, including: a recent employee turnover rate that was 43 percent lower than the industry's mean, numerous awards for excellent service (listed in Exhibit 4); and a 1998 client retention rate of 97.5 percent. As a privately held firm, Rosenbluth did not make any financial data publicly available. Industry sources stated that Rosenbluth International had 1998 revenues of approximately $3.7 billion, positioning it behind American Express and Carlson Wagonlit Travel.[5] Rosenbluth employed over 5,000 people in the 24 countries in which it had offices.

Changes in Airline Commissions

By 1999, U.S. airline commissions had declined to 5 percent and were capped at $50 per domestic round-trip ticket (prior to 1995, there had been no caps). A Rosenbluth manager commented, "We anticipated these changes and restructured our revenue sources." Rosenbluth began to charge its clients management fees while rebating all commissions and overrides received from airlines to the client. By 2000, Rosenbluth's management fee was generally a negotiated percentage of the client's travel cost plus an additional charge to cover Rosenbluth's cost to issue tickets. In a few cases, Rosenbluth charged a fixed fee per ticket issued. This averaged approximately $50, however, the amount varied widely. Rosenbluth's company-wide average total cost (including fixed charges) to issue and support an airline ticket was $45, although this varied dramatically based on each client's service requirements. The average price of a ticket issued was $600. A manager commented on the management fee structure, "It's really better for everyone. There is no longer any question of a conflict of interest as we have no incentive to book a more expensive ticket than is absolutely necessary." Many travel management companies restructured their fees in similar ways during the late 1990s.

Part II–Biztravel.com

The On-Line Travel Industry

Total on-line travel bookings constituted 3 percent of the U.S. travel market in 1999, but estimates suggested that total on-line travel bookings would grow from $4.2 billion in 1999 to just over $16.6 billion by 2003.[6] Approximately one-half of on-line travel bookings were made through on-line travel agencies.[7] Exhibit 5 illustrates on-line travel bookings by agency. Exhibits 6 and 7 illustrate the on-line travel market by distribution channel and service segment (air, hotel, etc.).

On-Line Business Travelers

Internet research firms identified four classes of on-line business travelers (see Exhibits 8 and 9), including "Heavy Bookers," "Light Bookers," "Lookers," and "Sideliners."[8] On-line agencies struggled to improve "Book to Look" ratios (book referring to booking a ticket, and look referring to viewing a website), which usually ranged from three to seven percent. Seventy percent of people who looked and didn't book went on to buy that trip elsewhere (usually from an offline travel agency).[9] Exhibit 10 illustrates reasons for looking and not booking.

On-Line Agency Sources of Revenue[10]

On-line travel agencies generally had five sources of revenue: commissions, advertising/sponsorships, wholesale mark-ups, licensing, and merchandising.

- Commission: most airlines paid a flat $10 commission to on-line travel agencies, arguing that on-line agencies shouldn't receive the standard fee in light of their offering few services. Car rental companies and hotels paid a commission of five to ten percent, and cruise lines and vacation tour package suppliers paid between ten and fifteen percent. Overrides were not paid to on-line travel agencies as they did not manage their clients to change airlines' market share. On-line agencies were not powerful enough to negotiate fees from the CRSs.

[5]"Travel Weekly's Top 50 Travel Agencies," *Travel Weekly FOCUS,* Volume 58, Number 51, page F6, June 1999, Section 2.

[6]Cohen, Evan, and Swerdlow, Fiona S. "Travel On-line Projections," May 1999, *http://www.jup.com/sps/research/report.jsp.*

[7]Swerdlow, Fiona, and Vanderbilt, Nicole. "Disintermediation—Brand and Affinity Position Suppliers to Circumvent Agencies," August 1998, *www.jup.com/sps/research.report/jsp* (January 3, 2000).

[8]Forrester Brief—"Business Travelers' Net Benefit: Convenience," 12/7/99, *http://www.forrester.com/ER/Research/Brief/0,1317,7679,FF.html.*

[9]Sileo, Lorraine and Courtmanche, John. "Chapter 7—Obstacles and Opportunities," *The PhoCusWright Yearbook 1999, Analysis, Assumptions and Assessments for the On-line Travel Marketplace,* Sherman, CT, October 1999, p. 92.

[10]Much of the information in this section was gathered from: Sileo, Lorraine, and Courtmanche, John. "Chapter 3—On-line Travel Agencies," *The PhoCusWright Yearbook 1999, Analysis, Assumptions and Assessments for the On-line Travel Marketplace,* Sherman, CT, October 1999, pp. 38–39.

- Advertising/Sponsorships: sales of advertisements, preferred "product" placement, and links to other sites.
- Wholesale Mark-up: several on-line agencies purchased discounted airline tickets in bulk and resold them to travelers.
- Licensing: booking-engine technology was often licensed to third parties that built their own travel services around the licensed booking engine.
- Merchandising: some agencies sold travel-related products such as luggage, travel insurance, clothing, or travel guidebooks.

Major On-line Travel Agencies are described in Exhibit 11.

Rosenbluth's Opportunity and Biztravel.com

In 1998, SOHO (small office, home office) business travelers accounted for an estimated 16 percent of the total U.S. travel market (see Exhibit 12). Rosenbluth hadn't targeted the SOHO travel segment as management believed the company couldn't cost-effectively serve it. However, management believed the Internet provided a way to serve the SOHO market.

In 1999, Rosenbluth purchased a majority stake in Biztravel.com, an on-line travel agency that targeted the SOHO market. Other investors included: Accel Partners, British Airways, Comcast Corporation, Continental Airlines, Excite@Home, Hummer Winblad Venture Partners, Marriot International, and Sun Microsystems. A manager commented on the other investors:

> British Airways, Continental Airlines, and Marriott provided access to inventory, had multiple frequent flier programs, and were highly respected companies in the travel industry. Our relationship with Sun Microsystems will make Biztravel the "Marquee" Sun website.

Biztravel had approximately one million members, some of whom were purchasing customers. Many of those were repeat customers.

The following describes how managers believed that Rosenbluth and Biztravel would compliment each other in several ways:

- *Live agent support 24 hours per day, seven days per week including world-wide en-route assistance (not offered by other agencies).* Biztravel outsourced its customer service to Rosenbluth. 17 Travel Service Associates were dedicated to Biztravel in Rosenbluth's Dickinson, ND IntelliCenter. A Rosenbluth manager stated: "Because of the complexity of dealing with customers through telephone, e-mail, or on-line chat, we've put our most experienced associates in Biztravel." Biztravel associates received an additional week of training spent getting to know the Internet and the Biztravel website, during which they "shadowed" a more experienced agent and role-played customer/agent interactions. Knowledge developed on the job was shared via emails, memos, and meetings that served as on-going training.
- *Rosenbluth Service Levels.* A Rosenbluth manager commented on the service levels before and after the acquisition:

> Customers had 10 to 15 minute hold times, associates weren't well trained, emails were responded to after a day or more, and associates weren't proactive in contacting customers if their flight schedules changed. There was no service-level tracking. In some cases, logistical issues such as credits and exchanges were just ignored. We found a drawer full of items needing attention that were months old when we took over.
> Now, 85 percent of the phone calls are answered within 30 seconds [see Exhibit 13]. Eighty percent of emails receive a response within six hours. On-line chats occur almost instantaneously.

Biztravel customer service received an average of 150 telephone calls, 100 emails, and 50 on-line chats per day, including 10 on-line requests for a telephone call from Biztravel. (Exhibit 14 provides data on on-line shoppers' service preferences.) The number of interactions with customers had not changed since Rosenbluth acquired Biztravel. However, the volume of tickets issued had increased by about one-third, and the nature of the issues underlying many of the interactions had changed. Prior to the acquisition, more than half of all interactions were complaint-related (as opposed to questions), sometimes complaints being logged a second or third time. Improvement was suggested by the numerous after-acquisition testimonials Biztravel received from travelers (see Exhibit 15), and an 80 percent reduction in debit memos, or credits issued at Biztravel's expense because the site, or an agent, had made an error. This occurred despite a reduction in operating costs (costs had declined by one-half, despite employing the same number of Travel Service Associates).

- *Rosenbluth negotiated fares.* All Biztravel customers received up to 50 percent discounts on some fares for certain routes flown by Air New Zealand, America West, British Airways, Continental Airlines, TWA, and US Airways. Typical discounts were lower, but still substantial.
- *Innovation.* Biztravel used existing Rosenbluth technology to develop its "Fare Guard" feature. This feature continued to search for the lowest fare after a ticket was purchased, up until the day of departure. If a lower fare was found, and a customer would save money after any ticket change penalties, he or she was contacted. Biztravel also used Rosenbluth expertise to develop its "My Company" feature, designed to compete with Trip.com's "CompanyTrip," although at no charge to the user. "My Company" was designed to serve clients spending between $20,000 and $1 million a year on travel. Finally, Rosenbluth managers were developing technology to link personal digital assistants with Biztravel's booking engine. For example, if a customer entered "meeting on January 17 in Philadelphia, at 10 AM" into his or her Palm Pilot, Biztravel could search for appropriate itineraries based on the traveler's preferences.

Exhibit 16 lists other Biztravel.com service features.

When a customer became a member of Biztravel.com, he or she was invited to fill out a personal profile and tell Biztravel all of his or her travel preferences. Each time the customer booked a trip, Biztravel used those preferences (which could be easily changed) to design a flight, rental car, and or hotel itinerary based upon his or her needs.

A Biztravel manager commented on the site:

> Biztravel.com is a much friendlier site. For example, I believe the biggest drawback to Travelocity is that it tends to show its roots as a sophisticated Customer Reservation System (CRS), sometimes using cryptic codes and acronyms in the product descriptions.

In June of 1999, Biztravel received the Yahoo! Internet Life Gold Star Sites Award for Best Travel Hub and Best Place to Book a Business Trip. A Yahoo manager stated, "We rated this Best Travel Hub for its all-around excellence, but there's a reason it's called Biztravel.com: all the bells and whistles a jet-set exec could want can be found here."[11] Another Internet award-issuing company listed Biztravel in its list of Top 25 Web Sites, noting:

> Perhaps better than any other travel site, Biztravel enables customers to create personalized travel itineraries . . . customers can select from a variety of options to make airline, hotel and car reservations. In addition to the impressive personalization features, the site enables customers to receive important travel information via alerts.[12]

Sources of Revenue and Costs

Biztravel's primary sources of revenue were commissions and sponsorship (approximately 67 percent of total revenues), and advertising. Sponsorship revenue was received primarily from airlines. Sponsor airlines paid Biztravel for "preferred placement": the first screen given to customers after they told Biztravel their specified destination and travel dates suggested one or two (preferred) airlines. Virtually all possible flight combinations were given if a customer clicked "more options." Biztravel also charged airlines a fee for sending emails on their behalf to Biztravel customers. For example, if Biztravel sent an email on special fares from Boston to Chicago, each airline listed as offering a special fare paid a fee.

Ads appeared on Biztravel's website and its newsletter. Biztravel charged approximately $35 per one thousand viewers (called "cost per thousand impressions," or CPM). This meant that a company advertising on Biztravel.com would pay $35 for every 1000 pages viewed. The on-line travel industry standard was $7 to $15 CPM.

Biztravel's on-line competitors received a fixed ten-dollar-per-ticket commission from the airlines. Biztravel's commission was different. According to a manager this was due to "Rosenbluth's relationships with the airlines and its ability to change market share."

The site had a look-to-book ratio of 50 percent. The average price of an airline ticket sold by Biztravel was $415 (on-line competitors' average ticket price was $300). The company typically received $25 in revenues (commissions and other non-advertising sources) from the sale of a ticket. A typical customer took five to six business trips per year. Biztravel's variable cost per ticket,

[11]Source: http://misc.biztravel.com/misc/awards.htm (January 12, 2000).

[12]Ibid.

including the cost of customer support, was $10.00 (80 percent of tickets issued were etickets). The cost to maintain the website was approximately $9 million per year. Biztravel estimated its loyal customers would use the service for ten to fifteen years.

Offline vs. On-Line Service

> *When we bought Biztravel, they saw themselves as an Internet site that provided travel. We see ourselves as Travel Associates who serve our customers via the Internet.*
>
> —A Biztravel manager

Hal Rosenbluth commented on the expectations of business travelers:

> The business traveler has always looked at this industry as one that is very simple: simple to provide a ticket, a car rental, or a hotel. And yet it's very complex, and to be able to do it error free takes an awful lot of studying, resource planning, and deployment. I think the traveler also has high expectations that everything will go right. People spend an awful lot of money on traveling, and if you really break it down, there are hundreds of opportunities to err with a reservation. It's our responsibility to have the right people and processes in place so that the process doesn't break down.[13]

A manager commented on how traditional customer service changed with the advent of on-line business travel agencies:

> Traditionally, the travel agent was our safety net. He or she had all the information for the customer. But our Biztravel customers' definition of good service is different. First, it focuses on the web-site interface and the information provided. We have to provide the *right* information *so well* that the customer is not forced to interact with a travel agent. Our on-line customers expect a website that's easy to navigate, quick, personalized, and contains enough content to meet their travel needs. Of course, they also want the option to receive assistance from a live person via the telephone, email, or live chat.

[13]"How to Get a Good Night's Sleep, An Interview with Hal Rosenbluth," *LEADERS Magazine,* April, May, June 1998, Volume 21, Number 2.

Delivering on-line travel services was also different. A Travel Service Associate working for Biztravel noted:

> It's more fun to be at Biztravel because it's not call after call after call. Some days you do calls, other days it's on-line chat and emails. And we rotate the jobs like returns and exchanges.

Because Rosenbluth's telephone technology was developed prior to the popularization of email and on-line chat, these were not integrated into Biztravel's voice communication system. As a result, Travel Service Associates were rotated to either respond to on-line chats and email (including requests for an associate to call a customer) or incoming telephone calls. Because each associate had the ability and technology to handle both types of service, if demand peaked on either, associates could switch themselves from one to the other.

Although most tickets booked never required Travel Service Associate intervention, a number of issues had to be handled manually, including: upgrade requests, invalid frequent flier numbers, fares the booking engine delivered to a customer but could not be confirmed, fare-guard induced reductions, exchanges, and lost tickets. In addition, requests came for help in getting specific routings (i.e., Boston to Venice *via* Zurich rather than Milan) and other travel-related issues. Over 50 percent of total client interactions involved questions on the use of the Internet and the web site rather than travel. In contrast, only 29 percent of questions asked *via* email and on-line chat were technology-related. The ratio of tickets booked to client interactions (telephone, email, or on-line chat) was one-to-one (plus a fraction of a call for en-route rebooking). Interaction volume increased when site traffic was high and site response speed slowed.

Because of the uncertainty with the new operation, Rosenbluth Associates assigned to Biztravel had higher base pay, but no incentives. This situation was described as temporary.

A manager noted one of the challenges Travel Service Associates faced:

> We sometimes get customers contacting us with questions they wouldn't ask their local travel agent—they don't want to bother someone they know personally unless they're sure they want to take the trip. We also sometimes get e-mail requests like, "What are the best fares to Italy this weekend?" Clients should be able to get that through the web site. We respond with the information they want, and sometimes add information on how they could

get it themselves. I wonder if we should just ask them to go to the web site?

The average telephone call lasted three minutes, however, variance was high. On-line chat required between five and fifteen minutes, although a single associate could chat with multiple customers simultaneously (the Biztravel "record" was four at once). Emails required very little time to answer unless the response required research. Customers sending questions by email identified the type of inquiry they had *via* a pull-down menu (for example, air travel, car, or hotel). This enabled associates to choose inquiries they wanted to answer and rapidly identify potential template responses that might help speed their answer. According to both managers and associates, most answers had to be completely customized. Prior to the acquisition, Biztravel had used numerous completely automated responses to respond to a variety of queries. Most of these had been discontinued.

Some email and on-line chat interactions were described as "frustrating" by associates. They attributed the problem to customers not giving them the right information; according to an associate, "There are so many technical issues, it's hard to know what to ask—and it's so much harder when you can't hear the person's actual voice—you're just that much further removed."

Biztravel's email and on-line chat software was a package purchased by the company and customized. It included an automated spelling and grammar check. A team leader noted, "Because we're using our most experienced people, we really don't need the check, but it's nice to know it's there."

The need for en-route traveler support was as significant for Biztravel as for Rosenbluth International. During a January snowstorm that covered much of the East Coast of the United States, 70 percent of calls to Biztravel were from travelers requesting en-route re-routing. On a typical day, that figure was closer to 10 percent. An associate commented:

> During a crisis you just strap yourself in—you might not take lunch, you plan to work overtime. It takes half as long as a typical call to do a re-routing, so it's not that bad. Still, we put aside anything that can wait, like credits and exchanges, and focus on those travelers.

Industry observers noted other elements of service important to on-line travel customers:

> Winning that target customer requires developing and maintaining a site where pages load quickly and cleanly; where email is answered promptly, fully, and correctly; where minimum keystrokes and clicks get the user right to a fare quote within seconds of loading the home page; and where a confirmation and itinerary are immediately emailed to the user for follow-up.[14]

In order to assure ease of navigation throughout its website, Biztravel site developers worked with customer focus groups that were exposed to numerous mock websites. Developers worked to reduce the number of clicks per booking and the wait times for itineraries and downloads. They also worked to optimize the number of pages on the site and the positioning of the information customers wanted. Biztravel site developers also read customer emails that suggested ways to improve the website. A slightly revised version of the website was released approximately every six weeks. A manager commented:

> We've found that when we provide better information and make it easier for customers to get around the web site, we have fewer related interactions. For example, we've increased the information on the site about ticket exchanges, and we've simplified the process of exchanging a ticket by creating specific fields customers fill in. Now we get fewer calls about exchanges. But this is complicated. It doesn't work to just increase the Frequently Asked Questions (FAQs)—people don't like FAQs—I know I won't use them.
>
> Our strategy has been to keep our existing customers by focusing on fixing customer support and logistics first. By doing that we've learned a lot about how to improve the site. Now we're beginning to think about major changes to the web site in terms of how it looks and feels—and, of course, its speed.

Conclusion

Hal Rosenbluth wanted his Internet strategy to succeed. As a result, Bibeau knew he had to get the Biztravel model right, right away. Biztravel was projected to issue 400,000 tickets in 2000, which Bibeau believed he could double or triple in the near future. A tripling of ticket volume would require an increase in fixed costs of only

[14]Swerdlow, Fiona S., and Vanderbilt, Nicole. "Disintermediation-Brand and Affinity Position Suppliers to Circumvent Agencies," August 1998, *www.jup.com/sps/research/report.jsp* (January 3, 2000).

$2 million due to excess capacity in the current system. Marketing costs would vary based on the method chosen. Highly targeted electronic direct marketing could be conducted via e-mail or advertising placed on other websites. For either, the cost was $40 CPM with an expected conversion-to-buyer rate of 7.5 percent when a $50 discount on a ticket was offered as an incentive. Traditional mass media advertising via radio or print resulted in a $200 to $400 cost to acquire a customer. Another option involved developing a sales force for the MyCompany service: managers believed they could target companies with 50 to 100 travelers at a total cost to acquire a customer of about $25 (including the cost of the two month training period each new sales person required). Early results suggested these small-business customers generated an average ticket price of $800.

Bibeau was also considering acquiring existing small travel agencies (or pieces of large agencies) serving the SOHO market making their customers Biztravel users. The cost to acquire a customer under this scenario was expected to fall approximately half-way between the cost using targeted electronic direct marketing and the cost using the MyCompany sales force.

Using one or a combination of these methods, Bibeau believed he could "blow out" Biztravel, dramatically increasing its volume.

But was this high-service model the right model to blow out? In addition, Rosenbluth was in the process of opening a leisure travel site called Travelution.com, targeting the personal and leisure needs of its business travel customers. This site would offer assistance and advice on where to go as well as how to get there. Should it follow the Biztravel high-service model?

Also, although Rosenbluth was a privately held company, there were rumors of a possible dot-com spin-off IPO. Would service affect a valuation, and if so, how?

Finally, any major initiatives Bibeau proposed would have to be approved by Hal Rosenbluth. How would he respond to these ideas?

Exhibit 1 ROSENBLUTH INTERNATIONAL'S ORGANIZATION STRUCTURE PRIOR TO 1996

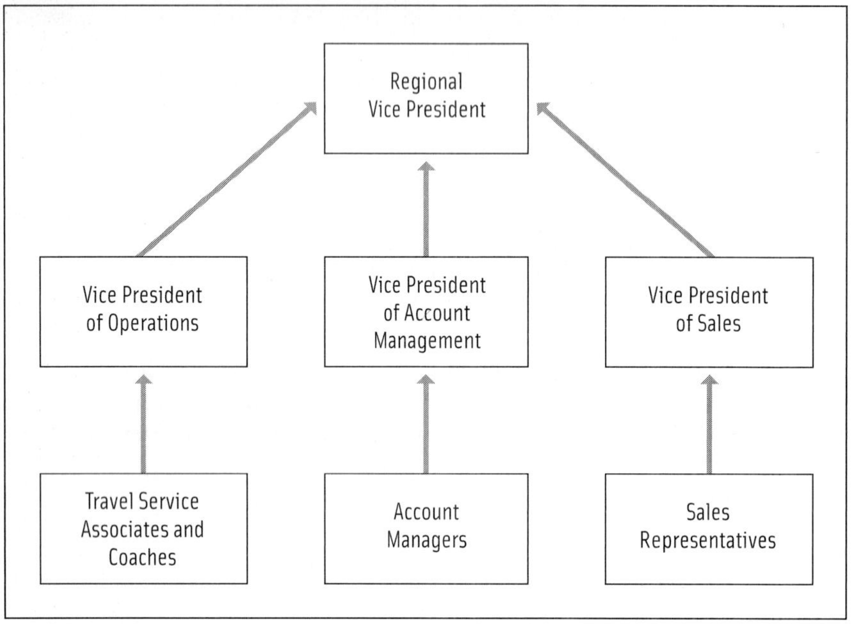

Source: Company interviews

Exhibit 2 ROSENBLUTH INTERNATIONAL'S ORGANIZATION STRUCTURE AFTER 1996

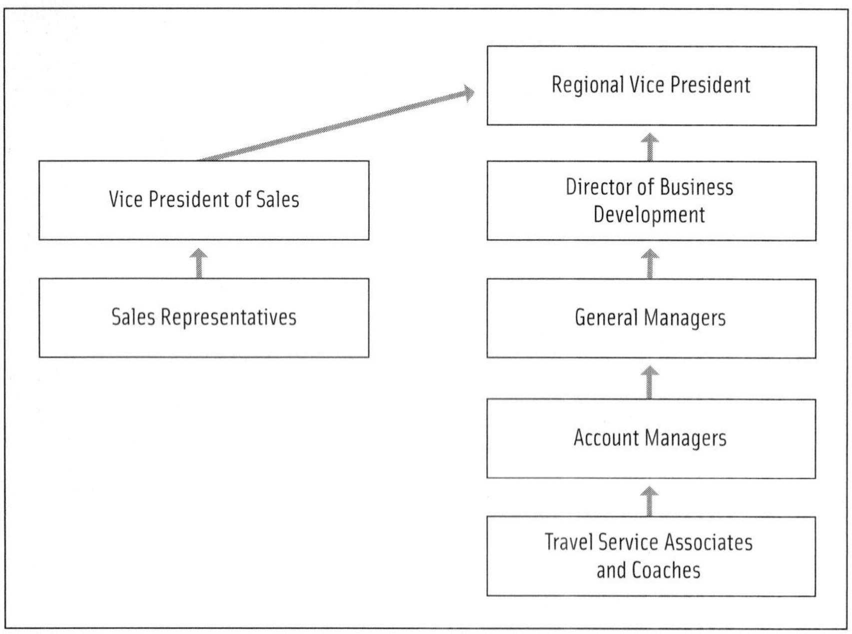

Source: Company interviews

Exhibit 3 SPECIFIC LANGUAGE FOR USE WITH TRAVELERS

"Live the Spirit" Elegant Phrasing
Welcome to Rosenbluth International. This is ______. How may I help you?
Good morning. Good afternoon. It would be my pleasure.
May I please place you on hold?
Would you prefer to be on hold while I research that information or shall I call you back?
Thank you for your patience.
Susan is out of the office at the moment. May I be of assistance to you?
Susan is out of the office at the moment. It would be my pleasure to take a message for her.
Thank you for calling Rosenbluth International. It's been my pleasure to assist you.
We appreciate your call. Good-bye.

Source: Rosenbluth Documents

Exhibit 4 ROSENBLUTH INTERNATIONAL AWARDS

- *Fortune* "100 Best Companies to Work for in America" (January 1998)
- WebMaster "50/50" (May 1997)[a]
- Philips Consumer Electronics "Supplier of the Year" (1996)
- Intel "Preferred Quality Supplier" (1996 and 1995)
- "Top Ten Companies to Work for in America" (February 1993)
- *"CIO"* 100 for Outstanding "Service" (August 1999 and 1993)
- "Service Company and Pioneer of the Year" awarded by Tom Peters (1989)

Source: Rosenbluth International
[a]Award received for recognized excellence in execution, innovative uses of technology, and demonstrated benefit of 50 exemplary Internet sites and 50 Intranet sites.

Exhibit 5 ON-LINE TRAVEL AGENCY GROSS BOOKINGS PROJECTED FOR 1999 (IN MILLIONS)

Service (Owner)	1999 Estimated
Travelocity.com (Sabre)[a]	$725.0
Expedia.com (Microsoft)	750.0
Preview Travel	435.0
ITN.net (GetThere.com)	260.0
TravelWeb.com (Pegasus)	110.0
Priceline.com	300.0
Hotel Reservations Network (USA Network)	130.0
Trip.com	70.0
Cheap Tickets	100.0
1travel.com	80.0
Biztravel.com (Rosenbluth)	40.0
Lowestfare.com	105.0
Travelscape.com	35.0

Source: Adapted from Sileo, Lorraine, and Courtmanche, John. "Chapter 3—On-line Travel Agencies," *The PhoCusWright Yearbook 1999, Analysis, Assumptions and Assessments for the On-line Travel Marketplace,* Sherman, CT, October 1999, p. 37. Gross bookings are the retail value of travel sold over the Internet (air, car rental, hotel, vacations/tours/cruises).

[a]Travelocity.com and Preview Travel announced plans to merge in first quarter 2000.

Exhibit 6 1999 ESTIMATED DISTRIBUTION CHANNELS FOR ON-LINE TRAVEL

Travel Agency Websites	52%
Airline Websites	33%
Hotel Websites	9%
Car Rental Websites	5%
Other	1%

Source: Adapted from Sileo, Lorraine, and Courtmanche, John. "Chapter 2—Market Size and Forecasts," *The PhoCusWright Yearbook 1999, Analysis, Assumptions and Assessments for the On-line Travel Marketplace,* Sherman, CT, October 1999, p. 21.

Exhibit 7 1999 ESTIMATED TRAVEL SERVICES SOLD ON-LINE

Air	73%
Hotel	16%
Car Rental	9%
Other	2%

Source: Adapted from Sileo, Lorraine, and Courtmanche, John. "Chapter 2—Market Size and Forecasts," *The PhoCusWright Yearbook 1999, Analysis, Assumptions and Assessments for the On-line Travel Marketplace,* Sherman, CT, October 1999, p. 18.

Exhibit 8 ON-LINE BUSINESS TRAVELERS

- **"Heavy bookers"** were primarily business travelers taking more than 20 business trips a year. Heavy bookers researched 70 percent of their business trips on the Web and booked 81 percent of the trips they researched. They constituted four percent of U.S. business travelers.
- **"Light bookers"** researched and booked fewer of their business trips on-line, and traveled less for leisure. These individuals were 9 percent of U.S. business travelers.
- **"Lookers"** researched on-line but wouldn't click the "book now" button. They took more than seven business trips a year and researched more than half of them on-line. Lookers constituted 37 percent of U.S. business travelers.
- **"Sideliners"** didn't look or book. Sideliners constituted approximately half of U.S. business travelers and traveled about seven times a year for business.

Source: Adapted from Forrester Brief—"Business Travelers' Net Benefit: Convenience," 12/7/99, *http://www.forrester.com/ER/Research/Brief/0,1317,7679,FF.html*

Exhibit 9 CHARACTERISTICS OF ON-LINE BUSINESS TRAVELERS

	Sideliners	Lookers	Light Bookers	Heavy Bookers
Demographics				
Occupation: professional/manager	49	60	68	73
On-line access from work	39	48	58	69
Business Travel				
Use an offline agent for business travel	25	49	47	54
Number of business trips taken per year	7.1	7.4	3.8	20.8
Business trips researched on-line per year	NA	4.2	2.4	14.5
Number of business trips booked on-line per year	NA	NA	1.6	11.7

Source: Adapted from "Forrester Brief—Business Traveler's Net Benefit Convenience." *http://www.forrester.com/ER/Reseasrch/Brief/0,1371,7679,FF,html*, December 7, 1999

Exhibit 10 WHY LOOK AND NOT BOOK?

Reasons for Not Booking	All
Required to use employer's corporate travel agency	19%
Wanted to compare traditional travel agent's price to on-line price	33
Wanted to compare airline's price to on-line price	36
Uncertain about when to travel	46
Credit card security	48
Uncertainty about the trip	51

Source: Adapted from Sileo, Lorraine, and Courtmanche, John. "Chapter 7—Obstacles and Opportunities," *The PhoCusWright Yearbook 1999, Analysis, Assumptions and Assessments for the On-line Travel Marketplace*, Sherman, CT, October 1999, p. 94. Note: Survey data based on a PhoCusWright national random sample of 513 Americans who use the World Wide Web on a monthly basis and travel by air at least once a year.

Exhibit 11 INFORMATION ON SELECTED INTERNET TRAVEL AGENCIES

Cheap Tickets, Inc. Cheap Tickets was established in 1986 as a discount airfare provider. The company launched its website in 1997 as an additional distribution channel. Cheap Tickets purchased large volumes of tickets at discounted fares which were then marked up and sold to travelers at prices that were often lower than published fares. Customer support was provided via email.

Expedia.com Expedia.com was launched in 1996 as a part of the Microsoft Network. Expedia had 7.5 million registered members (individuals who had looked and registered) in 1999, and was designed to appeal to the general traveling public. Customer support was provided *via* telephone and email.

Preview Travel Launched in 1996, Preview Travels' strategy was to diversify its revenue streams by 1) selling higher margin travel products (e.g., cruise and tour products), 2) expanding on-line advertising revenues, and 3) augmenting travel bookings with complementary products (e.g., travel apparel and gear, and travel insurance). Preview had more than 8.1 million registered members and more than 3.3 million purchasers (individuals who made at least one purchase) in 1999.

Preview announced the following statistics in early 1999: Its cost to acquire a new registered member was just under $6 and its cost to acquire a new purchaser was $51. Rosenbluth managers estimated that Preview received the standard $10 in revenue for booking an airline ticket, and that its variable cost to issue and support a ticket was $8.10. Advertising revenue per ticket was $5.62, and the average ticket price was $318. The percentage of members making a purchase by the end of their first year of "membership" was approximately eight. Customer support was provided *via* email.

Priceline.com Priceline.com was launched in April 1998 and initially focused on selling "distressed" airline seats (seats airlines could not sell through conventional channels). Priceline.com instituted a reverse-auction model, asking a potential customer how much he or she would pay and then matching that offer with a willing seller. Users could not specify their request beyond city pair and day of travel—(they could not specify an airline, a routing, or time of travel), and were required to pay for any bid an airline accepted.

Travelocity In 1996, Sabre[a] launched Travelocity.com, which was designed to appeal to the general travel market. By 1999, Travelocity had over seven million registered members.[b] Customer support was provided *via* telephone and email.

Travelocity focused on facilitating the booking (and thus purchasing) process by reducing the number of clicks required to book. In addition to airfares from traditional travel suppliers, Travelocity offered consolidator fares (highly discounted) through a partner. Travelocity and Preview Travel planned to merge in 2000.

[a]Sabre was the original reservation system for American Airlines in 1963. As Sabre became widespread, additional airlines joined the network, paying AMR a segment fee for each booking. In 1996, parent company AMR Corporation spun off Sabre Inc. while retaining 83 percent ownership of the company.
[b]Source: *www.travelocity.com/affiliates/facts.html* (January 10, 2000)

TRIP.com TRIP.com was an on-line travel service that targeted the mobile professional market. TRIP.com had interactive technology products including FlightTRACKER and intelliTRIP. FlightTRACKER allowed users to track commercial flights en-route to their destination anywhere in the U.S. IntelliTRIP was a search technology that allowed users to identify the lowest airline, hotel, and rental car fares in less than 90 seconds (excluding downloading).

TRIP.com also offered travel management services to small and medium-sized companies. Through its travel management tool, companyTRIP, the firm assisted in the creation of travel policies and then helped employees adhere to them. TRIP.com used companyTRIP to create customized travel sites for clients designed to: a) Integrate rates the company had negotiated with the airline (corporate rates) into the website. b) Generate detailed reporting on travel expenditures. c) Create and manage travel policies. d) Enable a client's travel coordinator to plan and purchase travel on behalf of others.

TRIP.com charged for companyTRIP based on usage.[c]

TRIP.com's audience of independent business travelers included: employees of small companies, self-employed workers, and employees of large companies working in remote locations.

[c]Source: Adapted from "TheTrip.com Monitoring Business Travel," *Inc.*, page 52, March 16, 1999

An Excerpt from PC Magazine Regarding Trip.com TRIP.com makes an easy task of booking a flight quickly, and you don't have to register or create a user profile to get going. Of course, there's the drawback of having to enter your preferences each time you book a flight. If making flight arrangements leaves you scratching your head in confusion, you'll appreciate the Further Assistance section, which offers advice on how to secure the lowest fare . . . The Historical Airfare section is also worth noting, as it provides data on the average fares over the past year for over 1,000 destinations . . . And if you're looking for great deals, you can be notified of them (up to ten destinations) via e-mail with the Deals-2-U service . . . In general, TRIP.com is well above average if you want to make travel plans on an infrequent basis. If you're a frequent flier, you'd do better with some of the other sites, which track mileage and save your preferences and itineraries.

Source: Adapted from "TheTrip.com," *PCMagazine*, page 258, April 6, 1999. *http://globalbb.onesource.com/SharedScripts/Articles* (January 10, 2000)

Individual Profile:
- 25–52 years old
- Average household income: $77,000 per year
- 62 percent male
- 72 percent married

Other characteristics:
- Frequent travelers: six or more trips per year
- Members of multiple frequent user/traveler programs
- Doing for themselves out of necessity and economy, not choice
- Believers in automation to increase productivity
- Appreciate convenience, helpful services
- Fly coach

Work Profile:
- Average company size: 10–500 employees
- Largest industry group: health/legal/educational services (20 percent)
- Next largest group: manufacturing (18.3 percent)

Source: Adapted from *www.trip.com*

Exhibit 12 SEGMENTS OF THE U.S. TRAVEL MARKET

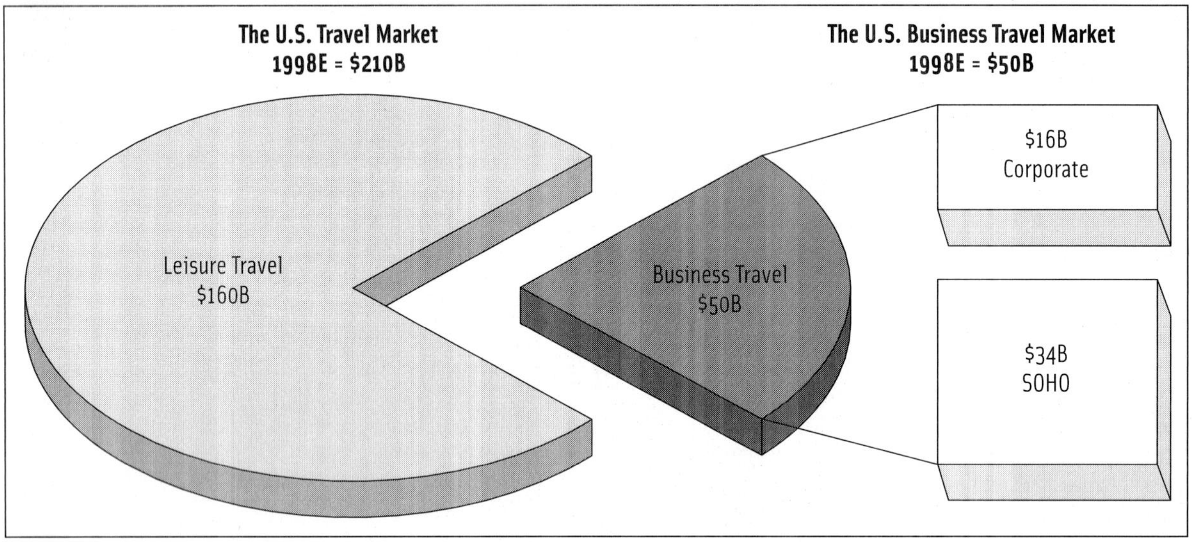

Source: Adapted from Warburg Dillion Reed, Analyst Report, January 15, 1999

Exhibit 13 BIZTRAVEL SERVICE STATISTICS FOR TELEPHONE INTERACTIONS WITH CLIENTS

Month	Calls from Clients	% Abandoned	Avg. Speed of Answer (sec)	Answered w/in Goal [1]	Comments
Dec-98	1,972	12	48	not measured	
Jan-99	6,271	28	242	not measured	
Feb-99	6,213	33	325	not measured	
Mar-99	6,757	27	252	not measured	
Apr-99	4,513	23	195	not measured	
May-99	3,848	15	140	not measured	
Jun-99	3,917	14	99	not measured	
Jul-99	3,243	7	45	not measured	
Aug-99	3,343	9	44	not measured	Rosenbluth acquires Biztravel.com
Sep-99	3,731	10	54	not measured	
Oct.99	Incomplete Statistics, call center moved to North Dakota				
Nov-99	3,689	0	55	78%	incorporate chat/call-back center
Dec-99	3,056	0	15	87%	
Jan-00	3,782	0	13	88%	
Feb-00	3,321	0	15	85%	

[1] Goal: Calls answered within 30 seconds.
Source: Rosenbluth International

Exhibit 14 ON-LINE SHOPPERS' DESIRE FOR LIVE SERVICE

Product Category	% Wanting Live Customer Service
Airline tickets	47
Loans	39
Investing	32
PC hardware	28
PC software	22
Clothes	20
Consumer electronics	17
Books and music	8

Source: Rosenbluth International, adapted from an August 1998 Jupiter Communications Study of 2,136 On-line Users

Exhibit 15 BIZTRAVEL CUSTOMER TESTIMONIALS

"In the past week or so, I have used Biztravel.com to make 3 different reservations . . . I am amazed at how easy this is to navigate through. I don't imagine the travel agencies are real happy that you exist, but I certainly am. I have told a few people already about this site and I'm sure I'll tell a few more."

"I think you offer a great service . . . I had to call and speak with one of your representatives recently as I was temporarily without computer access and needed to complete a transaction for airline tickets. I spoke with Jan. She was simply wonderful. She was very hospitable and truly went the distance to help me complete my booking . . ."

". . . I recently planned a trip to Santa Monica via LAX. Though the task was simple the consistent changes to the schedule made things difficult. Today the plans changed again. Fortunately, Wendy was there to save the day. She worked with the reservations, retrieved my tickets (before they left the office) and had them changed. It is refreshing to find someone who is willing to help. Her quick response and recommendations saved me time and money, which are oftentimes wasted. Wendy is a credit to your organization and truly is a jewel . . ."

"I have used many travel agencies, as well as American Express Platinum to book business and personal travel for the past twenty years. Your service, by far, is the best travel service I have ever used."

"The site is very useful, easy to use, and fast. Most impressively, you've combined some very simple graphics and basic web design to create one of the most professional-looking sites I've seen so far in several years of intense web surfing . . ."

"Glad you are doing this stuff . . . .HORRAH . . . much better than Expedia . . . I have converted!!!"

"Having the ability to take control of my own travel arrangements, from the comfort of my home office makes my line of work a little lighter."

Source: Rosenbluth International

Exhibit 16

BIZTRAVEL.COM'S ADDITIONAL WEBSITE FEATURES

- **Biz Reservations**—kept track of a customer's frequent flyer account activity each time a trip was booked at Biztravel.com. Managers stated that Biztravel.com was the only website that searched different combinations of airline, hotel, and rental car itineraries to find the one that earned the most miles for a customer's preferred frequent flyer programs.
- **Automated Upgrades**—When a customer indicated his or her desire for an upgrade on the website, Biztravel sent a request to the airline on the customer's behalf, and kept trying until an upgrade was available.
- **Pager Alert**—This service paged a customer one hour before his or her scheduled departure to indicate flight status, gate number, and weather in the destination city. Pager Alert was also provided for connecting flights and automatically rerouted passengers if he or she was going to miss his or her next flight.
- **Flight tracker**—If a customer knew the airline and flight number for a flight about to depart or currently en route to its destination, Biztravel gave its expected time of arrival. A map of the aircraft's current location was made available to the customer.

Source: Adapted from *www.biztravel.coms*

WIT CAPITAL: EVOLUTION OF THE ONLINE INVESTMENT BANK

Ron Readmond considered the whirlwind events that had transpired in the year since he became the co-chief executive officer and president of Wit Capital, an online investment bank headquartered in New York City. Readmond and his colleague, Bob Lessin, chairman and co-chief executive officer, had put together a capable team of investment bankers. Wit Capital had established key alliances with other Internet companies, started co-managing initial public offerings (IPOs), and increased its allocation of IPO shares. The firm had also begun producing research on leading Internet and technology companies, a capability managers believed would enhance Wit Capital's credibility among prospective clients and investors. In addition, Goldman Sachs and venture capital firm Capital Z each invested $25 million in Wit Capital. Finally, in June, 1999, Wit Capital went public, its stock price increasing from $9 to $38 per share over a period of two weeks.[1]

Despite the accomplishments of 1998 and early 1999, Readmond knew that the firm could not afford to rest on its laurels. Competition was emerging from both established and new quarters. Two online investment banks, E*Offering and W.R. Hambrecht, had begun distributing IPOs over the Internet, and traditional investment bank brokerage houses such as Merrill Lynch were enabling their clients to trade securities at a low-cost on the web. Readmond was confident, but like many forward-thinking executives, he wondered if the ability to sustain a competitive advantage was different because of the technology-intermediated nature of his service, and if so, how?

Readmond commented on Wit Capital, "We are a true Internet company. We couldn't exist without the World Wide Web."

Research Associate, Tonicia Hampton prepared this case under the supervision of Professor Roger Hallowell, drawing in part on initial research conducted by Will Beamer (MBA '99) and Ted Jackson (MBA '99), as the basis for class discussion rather than to illustrate either effective or ineffective handling of an administrative situation.

[1]As of September 24, 1999, Wit's stock price was approximately $20 per share.

The Market for Initial Public Offerings

The IPO

When a company decided to "go public" and raise capital on the open market, it searched for an investment bank to shepherd it through the initial public offering (IPO) experience. The process began by interviewing and selecting a bank to be lead manager and several others to be co-managers.

Banks chosen to manage the offering began the underwriting process by completing "due diligence" on the company and writing a prospectus. This document stated the company's business strategy and why it was trying to raise money. In the prospectus, the investment bank began the process of valuing the company, although the actual price of the securities was often not set until just prior to their sale.

The investment banks then took the senior officers of the company on a "road" or "dog and pony" show, giving executives of the company an opportunity to tell their story to potential investors. It was not unheard of for a company to go to fifteen cities in ten days and speak to 50 audiences. During the road show, the lead manager maintained a "book" that tracked the interest and preliminary commitments of potential buyers of the IPO shares. Audiences were typically analysts and investment managers who bought shares for their mutual funds or institutional clients.

Public companies wanted institutional investors and mutual funds to hold their shares for two reasons. First, institutional investors held large numbers of shares and traded in large volumes creating liquidity. Second, analysts had a tendency to follow stocks of companies with large institutional holdings, thus information and analysis (including buy and sell recommendations) were available on these companies. Many companies believed that this combination of liquidity and information resulted in a more accurate valuation of their equity.

Just before the offering, the investment banks priced the shares and bought all of them. The banks then offered to sell the shares to their clients. Traditionally banks sold the shares of high-demand IPOs to their best clients (those generating the most revenue for the investment bank).

Investment banks often underpriced IPOs by 10 to 20 percent to encourage investors to purchase IPO shares. As a result, the stock price of an IPO often "popped" during the first day of trading, rising 10 to 20 percent or more.

Usually more than one investment bank participated in an IPO. Issuers chose multiple co-managers because different banks had expertise and credibility in different markets. The lead manager underwrote the deal, taking on more of the risk and performing most of the work. As a result, the lead manager was allocated more shares to distribute to its best customers. The lead manager received a fee of approximately seven percent of the total amount of capital raised, with co-managers earning approximately four percent.

The lead and co-managers occasionally offered some of the IPO shares to other investment banks for distribution among their best customers. This type of exchange took place primarily to enhance relationships among banks for future business transactions. Banks sometimes accepted less popular IPO shares in order to get better IPO shares in the future.

The Internet Frenzy and IPOs

High tech Internet firms were engaged in numerous activities ranging from providing access to the Internet, to directing traffic, to being a destination, to selling goods and services. There were also a number of high tech companies that helped to build the Internet and networking infrastructure. Some of these companies had been extremely successful; investors in Dell's 1988 IPO saw their stock appreciate 300-fold; an investment in America Online's IPO in 1992 multiplied 100 times.

Because of these successes, some investors tried to predict which of the new high-tech companies going public would be the next AOL or Dell. These were generally firms doing business related to the Internet, if not actually being what had become known as a ".com." Some retail investors (ordinary individuals) had become particularly interested in these companies, despite their high stock prices. Internet stocks tended to be overvalued according to traditional valuation methods such as price earnings ratios or discounted cash flow analyses. Amazon.com, which as of September 1999 had never made a profit, had a market capitalization of over $20 billion. Investors justified the high prices they paid for high-tech, Internet-related firms by considering the potential they had to revolutionize markets and thus deliver outstanding results in the future.

Internet IPOs sometimes had "blockbuster" first days. Theglobe.com priced its IPO at $9 per share and on the first day of trading the stock rose to over $90 per share before closing at $63 per share. VerticalNet rose three times its offering price on the first day, and Healtheon closed at almost four times its opening price. The success of these IPOs created a frenzy for shares of any new company with a ".com" after its name. In contrast, IPOs of some nonhigh-tech, Internet-related companies, such as Ravenswood Vineyard and Pepsi Bottling had lackluster first days as public companies.

Retail investors making their own investment decisions often traded through discount brokerage houses. Several of the competitors in this industry were E*Trade, Charles Schwab, Fidelity Investments' Discount Brokerage, Ameritrade, National Discount Brokers, Waterhouse Securities, Datek, Suretrade, and Discover Brokerage. Each of these companies allowed individuals to trade stocks at a much lower cost than traditional brokerage firms—$7.95-$29.95 compared to over $100 per trade. Through "chat rooms" on the Internet, retail investors, often day traders,[2] could create enough interest in a tech stock that its price might increase over 10 percent on a day when the company itself made no announcements. Few retail investors could get access to IPOs of any type through discount or traditional stock brokers.[3]

Wit Capital

Early History

Wit Capital had its origins in Spring Street Brewing Company, a small beer company formed in 1993 by Andrew Klein, a Manhattan securities attorney. In February 1995, needing more capital to sell the firm's *witbier,* Klein and his friend Tim Kelm came up with the idea of raising money over the Internet. After putting together a prospectus and creating a website, they man-

[2]Day traders bought and sold stock in the same day, sometimes buying and selling the same stock several times in one day.

[3]Some brokerages offered access to some IPOs to retail investors with high balances, for example over $100,000. Instituional clients, however, always received first priority in the distribution of their shares.

aged to raise $1.6 million in roughly ten months, selling 860,000 shares to 3,500 new investors.

Seeing an opportunity to raise capital in a new way, Klein formed Wit Capital, which began operations in 1997. Klein's objective for his new company was to offer retail investors access to IPOs, creating truly "democratic" financial markets.

Enter Ron Readmond and Bob Lessin

In February 1997, Readmond became an equity investor in Wit Capital as well as nonexecutive chairman (his title later changed). In April, 1998, Bob Lessin joined the firm becoming chairman and co-chief executive officer. Readmond had been vice chairman of Charles Schwab, a managing director at Alex Brown and Sons, and chairman of the board of the National Securities Clearing Corporation. Lessin, a graduate of a prominent northeastern business school, had over 20 years of experience on Wall Street. Prior to joining Wit Capital, he had been vice chairman of Salomon Smith Barney. Prior to joining Salomon Smith Barney, Lessin was with Morgan Stanley serving as vice chairman of the investment banking operating committee and chairman of the strategic planning committee.

Readmond and Lessin recruited a number of bankers and executives from investment banks and brokerage houses. As of September 1999, Wit Capital had approximately 208 employees and offices in New York and San Francisco. The firm's primary businesses were investment banking and brokerage.

Investment Banking

Wit Capital's investment banking operations produced three "products": IPOs, mergers and acquisitions, and investment research.

- *IPOs*—Investment bankers and analysts called on potential clients in an effort to solicit their involvement in IPO transactions. Wit Capital participated in the underwriting process (prospectus drafting, road show preparation, valuation, due diligence, and selling shares) as "E-Manager," a specialized co-manager. The E-Manager concept, pioneered by Wit Capital, signified the firm's ability to serve as a conduit between the IPO issuer and online retail investors. Wit Capital typically secured ten to fifteen percent of the offering shares for online investors. The firm sometimes received smaller allocations of shares (as part of a "syndicate") of IPOs for which it was not "on the front page" as an active co-manager. See Exhibit 4 for a list of selected IPO clients.
- *Mergers and Acquisitions*—Wit Capital's M&A practice was unusual for an investment bank. Lessin commented, "We don't have a traditional M&A model. If you tell me you want help buying billboards, I'll tell you to go to Goldman Sachs. However, if you want help with your Internet strategy—especially deciding what to buy in the virtual world, I'm there." Wit Capital was often given the opportunity to co-invest in these transactions.
- *Research*—Wit Capital's analysts produced regularly updated reports on a number of firms it had taken public. Lessin believed that analyst coverage of Wit Capital clients enhanced the firm's credibility and provided more value to retail customers, who did not have access to similar reports from traditional investment banks. Lessin commented:

> Because we are known for our research on Internet companies, retail investors know that they can come to us for timely and free research. Issuers like our research coverage because it allays their fear that their stock will get lost in the crowd. Our research coverage encourages issuers to allocate shares to Wit Capital.

Brokerage

Retail customers gained access to Wit Capital's IPOs through its retail online brokerage operation. The brokerage also enabled them to trade other stocks, bonds or other financial instruments, just like any discount brokerage house. Wit Capital charged a discounted commission, $14.95 per online trade or $50 per trade if an order was placed over the telephone. Eighty percent of trades were made over the Internet. The firm's customer base grew from 5,000 in June of 1998 to approximately 100,000 in September of 1999. Sixty-seven percent of accounts were active.

Unlike other brokerage firms, Wit Capital did not rely on intensive marketing for customer acquisition. Instead, the firm relied on word-of-mouth referral. Lessin commented:

> We have a customer acquisition cost of zero. Other online brokerages pay between $400 and $500 per customer. By making appealing IPOs available to retail investors, customers find their way to us. Everyone wants access to IPOs. If you want Wit Capital IPOs, you have to come to Wit Capital.

In order to open a brokerage account with Wit Capital, a customer needed to deposit $2,000. The Securities and Exchange Commission required that brokerage firms qualify customers prior to selling them IPO shares (dubbed "speculative investments"). The officers of Wit Capital's account services group used their judgement in combination with the following criteria to qualify customers for IPO shares:

- Securities to be purchased could not exceed 10 percent of income or net worth.
- Account balance should be at least $2,000 cash or equivalent securities.
- Customer should have at least one or two years of experience investing in stocks.
- Customer should have over $50,000 of annual income or assets.

Customers were instructed to hold their shares for 60 days before selling them. If a customer "flipped" (sold his or her shares within this holding period), he or she would not be given access to other oversubscribed IPOs until 60 days after the "flip."

E-syndicate

Wit Capital also made its IPO shares available to 25 other online brokerage firms. These "e-dealers" were members of Wit Capital's "E-syndicate." By creating these "E-syndicates" with other online brokerages, Wit Capital offered its client companies access to over one million Internet investors. In the aggregate, Wit Capital managers believed that these firms handled approximately 29 percent of the total number of online brokerage trades in the fourth quarter of 1998. Lessin commented on the E-syndicate, "It doesn't really matter if retail investors go to a syndicate member versus us. I'd rather have access to one third of the online brokerage community versus a bigger piece of a smaller pie." Wit Capital shared its selling commissions with E-syndicate members.

IPO Share Distribution

The distribution process began with an IPO "alert." Approximately 200,000 emails were sent to Wit Capital's retail account customers, registered website visitors,[4] and E-syndicate members. This email contained a hyperlink to an issuer's prospectus and information on possible pricing and timing of the offering. Wit Capital customers went to its website to place their orders. Customers of E-syndicate brokerages went to their firm's website to place orders. All orders (Wit Capital and E-syndicate customers) received the same priority in a random drawing to determine which customers would receive shares in the typically oversubscribed offerings. One in four customers typically received about 100 IPO shares.

Wit Capital did not limit the number of IPO offerings it would manage over a specified period of time. A manager commented:

> The most IPOs we have handled in one day is three and in one week, eight. We never let our capacity to handle new issues constrain us. On one deal we were expecting 7,000 email responses, instead we received 27,000 over only 12 days. We opened about 13,000 accounts from that deal.

Future Services

Lessin envisioned future revenue being derived from capital raising (50 percent), brokerage (25 percent), and strategic advisory services (25 percent). By the end of fourth quarter 1999, Wit Capital planned to implement its "digital trading facility" (DTF), a virtual trading floor, or what some managers called "an eBay for stocks." The DTF was expected to offer clients the opportunity to trade publicly held stocks on Wit Capital's website directly with one another. The DTF would be available for use 24 hours a day, seven days a week. Wit Capital planned to eliminate broker spreads on stock trades, in theory giving investors more competitive execution prices. It remained to be seen whether the DTF would focus on a core group of Internet and technology stocks, or if it would encompass all major market stocks. Other companies, such as Instinet and Island ECN, were using similar models, but targeted institutional as well as retail investors.

The firm was also considering offering private placement services. Wit Capital would help small private companies find willing investors online. This type of offering under the Securities and Exchange Commission's Regulation D allowed the issuing company to avoid registration requirements and save underwriting fees by offering shares directly to institutional and accredited investors.

[4]Wit Capital allowed individuals without accounts who had registered on its website, to review information on pending IPOs.

Readmond commented on the firm's international plans and private equity offerings:

> We see global opportunities for our specialty products—research and IPO offerings. Prior to October 1, 1999, it took seven years for a company to go public in Japan. The laws have now been reformed enabling investment banks to act more quickly. Our model will allow us to do that very inexpensively. We just entered into a joint venture with Mitsubishi creating Wit Capital Japan.
>
> We also see significant growth coming from our private equity activities. We've just closed a $35.5 million private equity fund named Arista designed to make venture-capital types of investments. We're already working on a fund that will be twice as large.

Value Proposition

> *Most conventional financial service products have become commodities. We're focusing on specialty financial products—research and IPO offerings.*
>
> —Ron Readmond

Value for IPO Issuers

Wit Capital managers stated that the company offered IPO issuers: (1) benefits from an ongoing relationship as well as (2) credibility, and (3) objectivity.

- *Relationships*—Wit Capital not only gave an issuer access to its retail brokerage customers, but also to approximately one million investors from its E-syndicate. Not only were retail investors potential (or existing) buyers of stock, they were also potential customers for the issuer. Wit Capital's customers were generally familiar with the Internet and purchased goods and services via the web. Also, because Wit Capital had a database of shareholder email addresses, it could place the company in virtually instant contact with a sizeable fraction of its shareholders. Lessin believed that there was an additional benefit to the issuer:

> An issuer is less likely to feel the effect of a sale by a retail investor than an institutional investor. The volatility of the stock is reduced if someone sells 100 shares versus 10,000 shares. We also have rules against flipping.

- *Credibility*—Wit Capital's investment bankers and executive staff had reputations in finance and brought extensive experience to the company.
- *Objectivity*—Wit Capital bankers noted that their clients relied on them to provide advice on which investment bank would be the best candidate for lead manager. Because of its stand-alone position as E-manager, Wit Capital's bankers believed the firm served as a trusted consultant to Internet companies preparing to go public.

Value for Retail Investors

- *Nonpreferential access to IPOs*—Wit Capital's value proposition for individual investors was rooted in the notion of democratic, nonpreferential access to financial products and information. Managers believed that the cornerstone of this philosophy was giving retail customers access to what was once the holy grail of institutional privilege: the IPO offering. Managers believed that Wit Capital's use of a random number generator to issue requested shares illustrated its democratic attitude.
- *Free research* was another aspect of Wit Capital's value proposition for retail investors. Any visitor to Wit Capital's website could view its proprietary company research, a degree of access which was still largely taboo among bulge-bracket Wall Street firms. Eventually, Wit Capital hoped to give all its retail investors access to companies' road show presentations (pre-IPO) and conference calls (post-IPO) via the web.
- *Discounted trades*—Wit Capital's online brokerage offered retail investors a commission structure that was competitive with many other online brokerages.

Value for M&A Clients

Wit Capital advisors met weekly with M&A clients. A manager commented:

> Many *very, very* large companies are desperate to understand how the Internet will affect them or how they can take advantage of it. Bob Lessin's reputation gives them confidence in our advice. We're one of the only firms capable of giving advice to large companies about how their Internet strategy, or their acquisition of Internet-related companies, will affect their stock price.

Selected Competitors and Complementors

E*Offering

Announced in January 1999, E*Offering was a joint venture between E*Trade (an online brokerage with over one million clients) and Sandy Robertson, founder and former CEO of Robertson Stephens (a well-known brokerage house). E*Offering was positioned as "the investment bank of E*Trade," and its stated goal was to provide E*Trade's customers with access to IPO stocks. E*Offering stated on its website that it would distribute "up to 50%" of every IPO it underwrote to online retail investors. As of September 1999, E*Offering primarily had played the role of co-manager in 22 IPOs and six follow-on offerings, and had been the lead underwriter in one of its IPOs, First Sierra Financial.[5]

W.R. Hambrecht

Founded by Bill Hambrecht (co-founder of the investment bank Hambrecht & Quist), this firm introduced the Dutch auction model to IPO stock distribution. In the Dutch auction model, retail customers indicated both the number of shares they wished to buy and the price-per-share they were willing to pay. Once all bids were received, W.R. Hambrecht calculated the price of the offering (the lowest price at which all shares would sell). Any customer who bid at or above that price received shares (paying the lowest price) while those who underbid the price did not.

Hambrecht hoped to attract issuers by charging companies reduced fees for underwriting and managing an offering. Observers believed that Hambrecht's IPO process was less demanding, since the market, not the investment bank, determined the price of the offering.

Discover Brokerage

Morgan Stanley announced in late-April 1999 that it planned to distribute allocations of certain Morgan Stanley-led IPOs to its online subsidiary, Discover Brokerage. However, only customers with $100,000 or more in their accounts could apply for shares. Also, Morgan Stanley provided no indication of the quantity of IPOs, or the percent of their shares, it would make available to Discover Brokerage customers.

Lead Managers

Lessin commented on the firm's relationship with lead managers:

> We complement one another. Wit Capital is not looking to spoil the party for the big guys. We don't want to be lead manager. We have a give and take relationship. A lot of Internet start-up CEOs see us as their advocate and we refer them to the best lead managers. In turn, the big guys enhance our credibility by partnering with us on deals. However, we are pushing for an increase in the retail investor allocation of IPO shares. Eventually, I'd like it to be as high as 50 percent. Currently, in the deals we co-manage, retail investors receive about 10 percent of the IPO shares (largely from us) and institutional investors receive the other 90 percent.

Operational Issues

As an online brokerage, Wit Capital interacted with customers continuously. Customers communicated with the firm via telephone or email. Given Wit Capital's growth, it continually encountered capacity constraints involving people and office space.

Customer Service via the Telephone

The chief information officer commented on customer service via the telephone:

> When I joined Wit Capital in January of 1999, there were days when the phones would ring off the hook. Our electronic systems couldn't keep up. Our phone systems certainly couldn't handle all the requests. We received about 50,000 calls on our worst days. Now we partially outsource our telephone-based customer service function. We feel that the cost of outsourcing is lower than not outsourcing, and infinitely lower than losing a customer.

Wit Capital currently had two telephone numbers for customers to call for assistance. One number reached Wit Capital's in-office call center and the other number went to a contracted (outsourced) call center that received calls on behalf of Wit Capital. Customers were given both numbers but did not have information on where they were calling. As of September 1999, the in-office and contracted call centers each received approximately 500 calls per day, with demand spiking to over 1000 calls per day

[5]Source: E*Offering's website, www.eoffering.com/offerings/offering.shtml.

per call center. Telephone volume had decreased during 1999 as retail customers encountered fewer problems with their accounts, became more comfortable communicating by email, found the answers to commonly asked questions on the website, and new account volume slowed. Phone calls were received from 8:30 AM to 12 midnight. By the first quarter of 2000, Wit Capital planned to have more office space and phone lines allowing it to have a single telephone number, although a back up contractor would still be used for regularly occurring over flow.

A manager commented on how Wit Capital selected a vendor for its outsourced call center:

> We used several criteria to evaluate and select our call center including:
>
> - *Reputation*—A firm's reputation and experience in the brokerage industry is essential.
> - *Capacity*—The call center has to be equipped to handle spikes in call volume. We consider the number of staff that are "on call" if needed. Flexibility is very important.
> - *Location*—It's great if we can find a contractor near a university. College students are a "wide open job market" –they have a variety of skills, are seeking work, and are very upbeat.
> - *Quality of service*—Employee language skills are very important. Prior to selecting a call center, we make test calls to the center. Our quality assessment team continues to monitor language skills at our internal call center and our outsourced contractor by listening to about three customer calls a week at each location, and making ten to fifteen test calls per week.

Customer Service via Email

The chief information officer commented on customer service via email:

> In the electronic world, customers' expectations of access have gone from "sporadic and painful" to "virtually instantaneous with high ease." The level of service interaction between a customer and an online company has changed from "just being able get information on the company from its website" to "doing business with the company on its website." Customers tell us, "When I type, I expect someone to be on the other side." They want a quick and timely response. A lack of fast response is death. Customers will call if they don't get an email response quickly—and that has huge implications for our costs.

Wit Capital used its internal call center employees to respond to emails when they were not working on the telephone. The firm received between 300 and 4,000 emails per day, varying based on the level of IPO activity. Employees were expected to respond to emails within 24 hours. Wit Capital's employees worked two shifts: 40 employees worked from 8:30 AM to 6:00 PM. Twenty employees worked from 6:00 PM to 2:00 AM. The night shift was given the responsibility of responding to the majority of emails, as telephone volume typically was lighter at night.

Emails were monitored monthly by Wit Capital's quality assessment team, a sample of ten to 20 emails per employee were examined. Employees were evaluated on promptness of response, quality of response, and the number of responses made. Quarterly bonuses were given based on these criteria, but no information was available on their weighting.

Email Technology

Wit Capital's email software prompted employees with suggested standardized responses called "templates." The firm had a database of standard responses. The system filtered emails into 30 to 40 different pools; e.g., general, complaints, urgent, etc. Certain pools had priority over others, and emails were also sorted by date. This software helped employees handle the numerous complex tasks customer service in brokerage entailed.

The New Hire Process

A manager commented:

> When we interview potential call/email center employees, they meet with human resources and departmental supervisors. We don't perform prehire testing. Prospective hires are required to have Series 7 and 63 licenses.[6] Although we didn't plan to, we have a tendency to attract young, college educated people with two to three years of brokerage experience. We also look for good references.

New hires received one to two months of on-the-job training in the form of supervision by a more experienced employee and a departmental supervisor. The first five to ten days were spent with a supervisor. New hires

[6]Series 7 and 63 licenses authorized individuals to act as brokers under different circumstances.

began responding to emails independently after their first ten days. After a month they were put on phone duty as well.

Future Customer-Service Initiatives

Managers hoped to move more customer inquiries from telephone to email in the future. As of September 1999, 50 percent of customer inquiries were made via email. The firm planned to reduce the total number of inquiries by making more information available on the Internet. A formal cost analysis had yet to be conducted on the cost of communicating with customers via phone versus email. However, managers believed that due to the use of templates on the email system, two to three emails could be responded to in the same amount of time taken by one telephone conversation with a customer.

In general, the firm believed that service was related to delivering the latest technology. The chief information officer commented:

> We're trying to stay one step ahead of the technology curve and always be on the cutting edge. For example, our newest systems will support customers who gain access to the web over their cable line—they get great graphics, ease of movement through the site, and plenty of speed. Of course, customers still accessing the web via their telephone line will have to wait a bit for each page to download.

Contemplating the Future

Wit Capital managers had announced that they planned to build experience in areas other than Internet related companies including consumer goods, education, and health care, as a bulwark against a possible downturn in the Internet IPO market. However, they had been so busy serving their existing niche that no one was sure when they would have time to develop new specialties. Readmond and his colleagues wondered how they would sustain their preeminent position in the electronic investment banking world? How could they continue to add more value for issuers and M&A clients? What role would service to retail customers play, and how should that service be delivered? Would more front-line service providers at Wit Capital be needed, or could much of customer service be outsourced as it currently was? Could all contact with customers be conducted via email, or would a hybrid strategy, as was currently in place, be necessary? How would this affect Wit Capital's pricing and total value proposition vis a' vis that of its competitors?

Sources

AuWerter, Stephanie. "ASK SMARTMONEY: Getting In On An IPO." *Dow Jones Newswires,* March 24, 1999. Found at *http://interactive.wsj.com/archive/retrieve.cgi?id=BT-CO-19990324-005832.djml.*

Batstone, David. "Just Say No to IPO." *Business 2.0,* March 1999.

Branstein, Lisa, and Nick Wingfield. "Hambrecht Serves Little Guy, Tweaks the Big Guy, Online." *Wall Street Journal Interactive Edition,* February 8, 1999. Found at *http://interactive.wsj.com.*

Buckman, Rebecca. "Morgan Stanley's Online Unit to Get Piece of IPO Pie." *Wall Street Journal,* April 28, 1999, p. C24.

Chang, Yi Hsin. "The ABCs of IPOs," "How to Get in on an IPO," and "Unconventional IPOs," *Motley Fool* website, March 16 1999. Found at *http://www.fool.com.*

Corrigan, Louis. "Why Stock Offerings Should Make You Nervous." *Motley Fool* website, April 11, 1997. Found at *http://www.fool.com.*

Dorsey, David. "The Many Lives of a Wall Street Angel." *Fast Company,* Nov 1998 (Vol. 19), p. 230. Found at *www.fastcompany.com/online/l9/angel.html.*

E*Trade website, *http://www.etrade.com.*

"E*Trade Morphs into a Bank." *Wired News* (Reuters story), January 12, 1999. Found at *http://www.wired.com/news.* Fraser, Andrew. "Chunk of Duds in '98 Online IPOs Serve as Warning for Individuals." *Wall Street Journal Interactive Edition,* February 1, 1999. Found at *http://interactive.wsj.com.*

Gasparino, Charles, and Rebecca Buckman. "Goldman Sachs to Acquire 22% Stake in Internet Brokerage Firm Wit Capital." *Wall Street Journal Interactive Edition,* March 30, 1999. Found at *http://interactive.wsj.com/archive/retrieve.cgi?id=SB922749759901005733.djm.*

Gazala, Michael E., and Liz Valentine. "Net Investment Banks Stir The IPO Industry." *Forrester Brief,* March 1, 1999. Found at *www.forrester.com.*

Gimein, Mark. "Why the IPO Business Only Works for Some." *Industry Standard,* February 12, 1999. Found at *http://www.industrystandard.net.*

Gompers, Paul. Associate Professor, Harvard Business School. Interviewed by Beamer and Jackson in Boston, MA, April 28, 1999.

Gompers, Paul and Brav, Alon. "Myth or Reality? The Long Run Underperformance of Initial Public Offerings: Evidence from Venture and Nonventure Capital Backed Companies." *The Journal of Finance,* Vol. LII, No. 5. December 1997.

Grady, Barbara, and Austin Bunn. "Part 3: Cutting Corners to an IPO." *Wired News,* September 17, 1997. Found at *http://www.wired.com/news.*

Humer, Caroline. "Online Invest Bank Wit Capital Receives $25M From Capital Z." *Dow Jones Newswires,* March 1, 1999. Found on *Wall Street Journal Interactive Edition* website: *http://interactive.wsj.com.*

Ibbotson, Roger G., and Jay R. Ritter. "Initial Public Offerings." *NorthHolland Handbooks of Operations Research and Management Science: Finance,* April 5, 1993.

Ip, Greg. "IPO Profusion: Bull Market Has Sired A Lot of New Stocks, But Few Become Stars." *Wall Street Journal,* September 15, 1998, p. A1.

Kaplan, Michael. "Wit Capital Formation." Wired, September 1998 (Vol. 6.09). Found at *www.wired.com/wired/archive/6.09/updata pr.html.*

Klein, Andrew. "WallStreet.com." Wired, February 1998 (6.02). Found at *www.wired.com/wired/archive/6.02/wallstreet pr.html.*

Lipschultz, David B. "IPOs for the People." *Smart Money,* April 1998. Found at *http://interactive.wsj.com/archive/retrieve.cgi?id=BT-CO-19990318001496.djml.*

"Making Hay From the Chaos Of Internet Trading: Do something now to protect naive online traders from their mistakes." *CNNfn,* April 1, 1999. Found at *http://www.cnnfn.com.*

Mittner, Greta. "IPOs for Everyone!" *Red Herring Online,* January 13, 1999. Found at *http://www.redherring.com/insider/1999/0 l l 3/invetrade.html.*

Phillips, Jason. Vice President, Wit Capital. Interviewed by Beamer and Jackson in Boston, MA, April 7, 1999.

Simon, Ruth. "Advisers Warn Investors to Tread Softly in IPOs." *Wall Street Journal Interactive Edition*, Feb 24 1999. Found at *http://interactive.wsj.com.*

Tully, Shawn. "Can the Net Revolutionize IPOs?" *Fortune,* March 15 1999, pp. 35–36.

Wit Capital, S-1 Filing with Securities and Exchange Commission, March 18 1999. Found at *http://www.sec.gov/Archives/edgar/data/1071620/0000940180-99-000295.txt*
Wit Capital website, *http://www.witcapital.com.*

"Wit Capital/IPO-2: Plans to Expand Investment Banking Staff." *Dow Jones Newswires,* March 18, 1999. Found at *http://interactive.wsj.com/archive/retrieve.cgi?id=BT-CO-19990318002174.diml*

W. R Hambrecht website, *http://www.wrhambrecht.com.*

Exhibit 1

WIT CAPITAL GROUP, INC. AND SUBSIDIARIES CONSOLIDATED STATEMENTS OF FINANCIAL CONDITION DECEMBER 31, 1998 AND 1997

Balance Sheet (1997–1998)		
	1998	**1997**
Assets		
Cash and cash equivalents	$18,110,146	$ 1,110,787
Receivable from clearinghouse	119,312	136,364
Securities owned, at market or fair value	758,293	540,504
Prepaid expenses	95,671	1,582,657
Investment banking fees receivable	512,952	–
Furniture, equipment and leasehold improvements, net of accumulated depreciation and amortization of $243,527and $98,757 at December 31, 1998 and 1997 respectively	615,181	335,044
Computer software, net of accumulated amortization of $560,277 and $127,050 at December 31, 1998 and 1997, respectively	1,614,735	1,926,420
Other assets	421,351	204,870
Total assets	$22,296,406	$5,836,646
Liabilities and Stockholders' Equity		
Liabilities:		
Accounts payable and accrued expenses	$1,032,463	$875,871
Deferred advisory fees	595,486	–
Other liabilities	60,203	101,500
Total liabilities	1,688,152	977,371
Commitments:		
Stockholders' Equity:		
Series A Preferred Stock, $.01 par value, 10,000,000 shares authorized; 8,997,952 and 7,720,002 shares issued and outstanding at December 31, 1998 and 1997, respectively	89,980	77,200
Series B Preferred Stock, $.01 par value, 3,000,000 shares authorized; 2,304,982 shares issued and outstanding at December 31, 1998	23,050	–
Series C Preferred Stock, $.01 par value, 6,500,000 shares authorized; 5,902,750 shares issued and outstanding at December 31, 1998	59,028	–
Series D Preferred Stock, $.01 par value, 10,000,000 shares authorized;9,993,334 shares issued and outstanding at December 31, 1998	99,333	–
Common stock, $.01 par value, 60,000,000 and 25,000,000 shares authorized; 11,264,600 and 7,056,095 shares issued and outstanding at December 31, 1998 and 1997, respectively	112,647	70,561
Additional paid-in capital	39,534,657	9,786,065
Note receivable from stockholder	(5,750,000)	–
Series A Preferred Stock subscriptions receivable	–	(308,000)
Accumulated deficit	(13,560,441)	(4,766,551)
Total stockholders' equity	20,608,254	4,859,275
Total liabilities and stockholders' equity	$22,296,406	$ 5,836,646

Source: Wit Capital S-1 filing with Securities and Exchange Commission, June 3, 1999.

Exhibit 2

WIT CAPITAL GROUP, INC. AND SUBSIDIARIES CONSOLIDATED STATEMENTS OF OPERATIONS FOR THE YEARS ENDED DECEMBER 31, 1998 AND 1997 AND FOR PERIOD FROM MARCH 27, 1996 (INCEPTION) TO DECEMBER 31, 1996

Wit Capital Income Statement (1996–1998)			
	1998	**1997**	**1996**
Revenues			
Investment banking	$ 1,515,105	$ 42,567	$ –
Brokerage	294,454	10,403	–
Interest	182,880	53,821	31,172
Other	45,370	138,750	10,000
Total revenues	2,037,809	245,541	41,172
Expenses			
Compensation and benefits	4,444,271	1,549,958	378,337
Technology development	1,155,959	511,076	532,265
Marketing[a]	899,899	503,379	326,114
Depreciation and amortization	896,652	229,209	9,438
Professional services	877,822	329,334	282,806
Data processing and communications	625,231	237,608	49,599
Occupancy	237,334	200,673	41,889
Brokerage and clearance	186,322	5,563	1,750
Other	1,474,128	(351,729)	177,444
Total expenses	10,797,618	3,215,071	1,799,642
Loss before income tax provision	(8,759,809)	(2,969,530)	(1,758,470)
Income tax provision	34,081	23,051	15,500
Net loss	$(8,793,890)	$(2,992,581)	$(1,773,970)
Net Loss Per Share			
Basic	$ (1.23)	$ (.41)	$ (.33)
Diluted	(1.23)	(.41)	(.33)
Weighted average shares used in the computation of net loss per share:			
Basic	7,140,123	7,303,013	5,378,167
Diluted	7,140,123	7,303,013	5,378,167

Source: Wit Capital S-1 filing with Securities and Exchange Commission, June 3, 1999.

[a]Wit Capital's marketing expenses were associated with promoting its investment banking business and acquiring new brokerage customers. The increase in marketing expense during 1997 and 1998 reflected its increasing efforts to develop name brand recognition.

Exhibit 3

WIT CAPITAL GROUP, INC. AND SUBSIDIARIES CONSOLIDATED STATEMENTS OF CASH FLOWS FOR THE YEARS ENDED DECEMBER 31, 1998 AND 1997 AND FOR PERIOD FROM MARCH 27, 1996 (INCEPTION) TO DECEMBER 31, 1996 cont.

	1998	1997	1996
Cash Flows form Operating Activities			
Net loss	$(8,793,890)	$(2,992,581)	$(1,773,970)
Adjustments to reconcile net loss to net cash used in operating activities–			
Noncash expenses	1,522,901	–	–
Noncash expense reimbursement	–	(750,000)	–
Depreciation and amortization	896,652	229,209	9,438
(Increase) decrease in operating assets–			
Receivable from clearing broker	17,052	(35,753)	(100,611)
Securities owned	(217,789)	(540,504)	–
Prepaid expenses	(139,584)	(132,659)	–
Investment banking fees receivable	(512,952)	–	–
Other assets	(265,246)	45,848	(185,127)
Increase (decrease) in operating liabilities–			
Accounts payable and accrued expenses	132,709	231,328	659,996
Deferred advisory fees	595,486	–	–
Long-term portion of capital lease obligation	–	30,666	–
Other liabilities	(8,600)	(5,400)	15,500
Net cash used in operating activities	(6,773,261)	(3,919,846)	(1,374,774)
Cash Flows From Investing Activities			
Computer software purchased	(121,542)	(588,470)	–
Payments for purchases of furniture, equipment and leasehold improvements	(436,243)	(239568)	(194,233)
Cash used in investing activities	(557,785)	(828,038)	(194,233)
Cash Flows From Financing Activities			
Proceeds from issuance of common stock	60,301	–	1,818,875
Proceeds from issuance of preferred stock	24,278,918	5,071,952	500,000
Proceeds from long-term debt	–	36,851	–
Payments on long-term debt	(8,814)	–	–
Net cash provided by financing activities	24,330,405	5,108,803	2,318,875
Net increase in cash and cash equivalents	16,999,359	360,919	749,868
Cash and cash equivalents, beginning of period	1,110,787	749,868	–
Cash and cash equivalents, end of period	$18,110,146	$1,110,787	$749,868
Supplemental Disclosure of cash Flow Information			
Cash paid during the period for–			
Interest	$ 7,211	$ 4,362	$ –
Taxes	43,181	19,337	–
Noncash Transactions			
Issuance of Common and Preferred Stock For computer software	$ –	$ 400,000	$1,125,000
Issuance for Common Stock for website development	203,650	–	–
Issuance of Common and Preferred Stock for advertising credits	–	1,150,000	300,000
Series A Preferred Stock subscriptions receivable	–	308,000	–
Issuance of Common Stock to stockholder for note receivable	5,750,000	–	–
Repurchase of Common Stock	–	250,000	500,000
Conversion of Common Stock to Preferred Stock	–	5,000	–

Source: Wit Capital S-1 filing with Securities and Exchange Commission, June 3, 1999.

Exhibit 4 SELECTED WIT CAPITAL IPOS

Issuer	Lead Underwriter
1-800-FLOWERS.COM, Inc.	Goldman, Sachs & Co.
24/7 Media, Inc.	Merrill Lynch & Co.
Autobytel.com, Inc.	BT Alex, Brown
Barnesandnoble.com, Inc.	Goldman, Sachs & Co.
Blockbuster Inc.	Salomon Smith Barney/Lehman Brothers
Cleveland Indians Baseball Company, Inc.	McDonald & Company Securities, Inc.
Convergent Communications, Inc.	Goldman, Sachs & Co.
Corinthian Colleges, Inc.	Salomon Smith Barney
DoubleClick, Inc.	Goldman, Sachs & Co.
Drkoop.com, Inc.	Bear, Stearns & Co. Inc.
Engage Technologies, Inc.	Goldman, Sachs & Co.
EToys Inc.	Goldman, Sachs & Co.
Garden.com	Hambrecht & Quist
Hoover's, Inc.	J.P. Morgan & Co.
Internet Capital Group, Inc.	Merrill Lynch & Co.
IVillage Inc.	Goldman, Sachs & Co.
Juniper Networks, Inc.	Goldman, Sachs & Co.
Juniper Networks, Inc.	Goldman, Sachs & Co.
Liquid Audio, Inc.	Lehman Brothers
LookSmart, Ltd.	Goldman, Sachs & Co.
Mail.com, Inc.	Salomon Smith Barney
NationsRent, Inc.	Bear, Stearns & Co. Inc.
NetZero, Inc.	Goldman, Sachs & Co.
OneMain.com, Inc.	BT Alex, Brown
PlanetRx.com	Goldman, Sachs & Co.
Prodigy Communications Corporation	Bear, Stearns & Co. Inc.
Rubio's Restaurant's, Inc.	Thomas Weisel Partners LLC
Stamps.com Inc.	BancBoston Robertson Stephens
The Goldman Sachs Group, Inc.	Goldman, Sachs & Co.
theglobe.com, Inc.	Bear, Stearns & Co. Inc.
TicketMaster Online-CitySearch, Inc.	NationsBanc Montgomery Securities LLC
Tweeter Home Entertainment Group, Inc.	BT Alex, Brown
uBid, Inc.	Merrill Lynch & Co.
US SEARCH.com Inc.	Bear, Stearns & Co. Inc.
Wit Capital Group, Inc.	Bear, Stearns & Co. Inc.
Ziff-Davis Inc.–ZDNet	Goldman Sachs & Co.

Source: http://www.witcapital.com/stok/home.html.

Exhibit 5

BROKERAGE ACCOUNT DATA FROM SELECTED FIRMS

Firm	Charles Schwab (Brokerage)	E*Trade	Fidelity (Brokerage)	Wit Capital
Number of active brokerage retail accounts	6,200,000	1,241,000	2,692,500	67,000
Number of active online brokerage accounts	2,800,000	1,241,000	2,227,500	67,000
Percentage of all equity trades made online	67%	N/A[a]	79%	80%
Average daily number of trades made online	136,781	80,600	44,102	1,377

[a]This information was not available from E*Trade. However, trades could be made online or over the telephone with a person or a voice response unit.
Sources: Charles Schwab corporate communications data as of June 1999; "E*trade Sets Industry Record for Account Growth Adding 332,000 Accounts, Customer assets at $26 Billion, up 130 Percent," July 19, 1999; http://www.etrade.com; Fidelity Brokerage Bulletin, August 1999; Wit Capital 10Q report, June 30, 1999.

WIT CAPITAL: EVOLUTION OF THE ONLINE INVESTMENT BANK (B)

Founded in 1996, Wit Capital Group, Inc. rapidly evolved into an online investment bank, serving as co-underwriter and consultant to Internet companies and as an online retail securities brokerage. In 2000, Wit revised its mission and value proposition for both companies accessing the capital markets and individual investors.

In January 2000, Wit merged with SoundView Technology Group, a boutique investment bank specializing in technology stocks. SoundView primarily served institutional clients.[1]

In October 2000, Wit acquired competitor E*Offering, the investment-banking unit of E*Trade Group Inc., a leading online retail brokerage. At the same time, Wit sold E*Trade its approximately 100,000 retail brokerage accounts, each of which held approximately $10,000 in assets. In addition, Wit acquired the right to be the exclusive provider (for up to five years) of IPOs, secondary offerings, and other investment-banking products to E*Trade's approximately 3 million investors. E*Offering had experienced losses, plagued by both a lack of deal flow and heavy management and analyst turnover.[2] Wit's brokerage unit had generated 15% of the firm's revenue and was expected to lose $20 million in 2000.[3]

According to Thomson Financial Securities Data, as of September 21, 2000, Wit had co-managed 40 year 2000 deals that raised a total of $4.4 billion, earning Wit a 25th place ranking in IPO underwriting. Over the same period, Morgan Stanley Dean Witter & Co., the fourth-largest IPO underwriter, participated in 59 deals, raising $33.8 billion. Also in the same period, investment banks considered technology specialists, such as SG Cowen and Thomas Weisel Partners, raised $7.3 billion through 42 IPOs and $12.4 billion through 39 IPOs, respectively.[4]

In a recent *Wall Street Journal* interview, Wit's Chairman and CEO Robert Lessin said "'we are always looking to move to the left,' referring to the place lead underwriters are mentioned on a prospectus."[5] According to the *Wall Street Journal,* "Wit is evolving into a traditional investment bank that seeks to underwrite stocks and bonds, advise on mergers, and provide research to institutional investors such as mutual and pension funds. It has beefed up its investment-banking capabilities."[6]

The *Wall Street Journal* also noted that:

> . . . like the handful of other fledgling online investment banks, analysts say Wit faces some tough challenges amid an IPO market that seems to be waning. It has to convince its skeptics that it can compete effectively in the clubby world of stock and bond underwriting where a steady flow of deals depends on establishing and maintaining strong relationships with issuers.[7]

Industry observers voiced similar concerns. Stephen Franco, an analyst who follows online securities firms for U.S. Bancorp Piper Jaffray commented, "They have not gained much attraction in the investment-banking business—and the IPO market has dried up. They have no economic clout and they do not have a proven track record."[8]

Research Associate Charles G. Ruberto prepared this under the supervision of Professor Roger Hallowell from published sources as the basis for class discussion rather than to illustrate either effective or ineffective handling of an administrative situation.

---

[1]Aaron Elstein, "Despite Calculated Moves, Wit Struggles to Boost Stock," *Wall Street Journal Interactive Edition* (New York: *http://www.wsj.com,* October 12, 2000).

[2]Avital Louria Hahn, "Wit's Hat Trick: first beer online, then IPOs for the masses; now the thrust is institutions," *Investment Dealer's Digest.* (New York: Securities Data Publishing, June 19, 2000).

[3]Avital L. Hahn, "Wit's Hat Trick," *Investment Dealer's Digest.* (New York: Securities Data Publishing, June 19, 2000).

[4]Aaron Elstein, "Despite Calculated Moves," WSJ.COM, October 12, 2000.

[5]Aaron Elstein, "Despite Calculated Moves," WSJ.COM, October 12, 2000.

[6]Ibid.

[7]Ibid.

[8]Ibid.

Exhibit 1

WIT SOUNDVIEW GROUP INC. SHARE PRICE, NOVEMBER 1999–NOVEMBER 2000

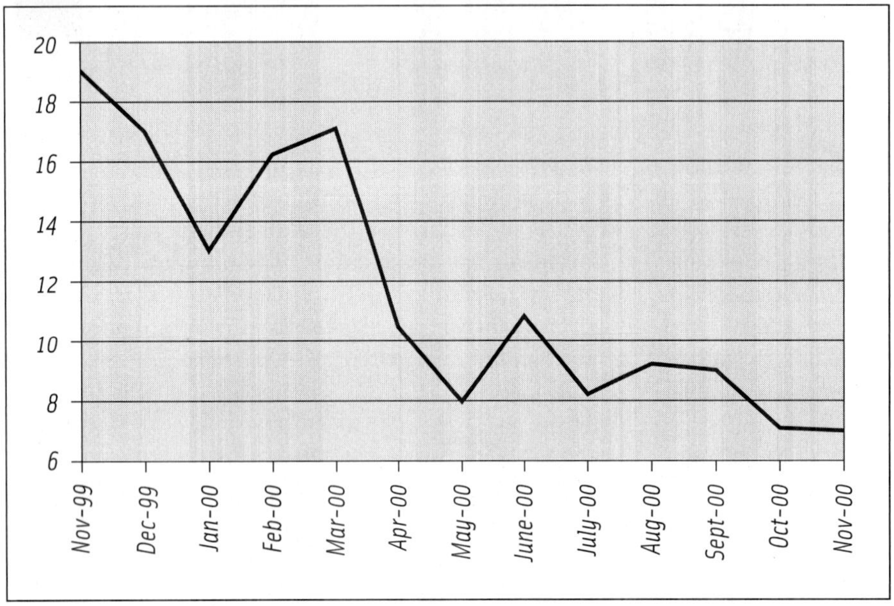

Source: Adapted from data from Bigcharts.com

Exhibit 2

WIT SOUNDVIEW GROUP, INC. AND SUBSIDIARIES—CONDENSED CONSOLIDATED STATEMENTS OF FINANCIAL CONDITION, JUNE 30, 2000 AND DECEMBER 31, 1999

Balance Sheet	June 30, 2000 (Unaudited)	December 31, 1999
Assets		
Cash and cash equivalents	$101,683,112	$12,447,885
Receivable from clearing broker	64,617,088	681,807
Securities owned, at market or fair value	40,631,449	114,468,173
Investment banking fees receivable	24,013,602	3,570,176
Investments	62,350,382	–
Investments in affliates	21,280,463	17,511,403
Intangible assets, net of accumulated amortization of $6,873,500 at June 30, 2000		
Goodwill	196,183,278	–
Institutional client relationships	63,502,087	–
Other	9,298,605	–
Furniture, equipment and leasehold improvements, net of accumulated depreciation and amortization of $5,830,514 and $1,110,369 at June 30, 2000 and December 31, 1999, respectively	14,225,481	6,312,242
Computer software, net of accumulated amortization of $1,147,005 and $1,212,907 at June 30, 2000 and December 31, 1999, respectively	3,742,266	3,706,112
Prepaid expenses	2,542,941	1,610,628
Other assets	37,130,523	3,309,750
Total assets	$641,300,277	$163,618,176
Liabilities and stockholders' equity		
Liabilities:		
Securities sold but not yet purchased, at market value	$1,066,814	$39,234
Accounts payable and accrued expenses	10,093,831	5,130,675
Accrued compensation	103,194,374	13,506,087
Deferred tax liabilities	31,304,300	–
Other liabilities	4,246,914	540,647
Total liabilities	$149,906,233	$19,216,643
Stockholders' equity		
Preferred Stock, $.001 par value, 30,000,000 shares authorized, no shares outstanding at June 30, 2000 and December 31, 1999	–	–
Common Stock, $.01 par value, 500,000,000 shares authorized, 78,797,470 and 61,629,828 shares issued and outstanding at June 30, 2000 and December 31, 1999, respectively	787,974	616,298
Common Stock, Class B, $.01 par value, 75,000,000 shares authorized, 11,666,666 shares issued and outstanding	116,667	116,667
Common Stock, Class C, $.01 par value, 159,000,000 shares authorized, no shares issued and outstanding at June 30, 2000 and December 31, 1999	–	–
Additional paid-in capital	558,034,349	196,777,759
Notes receivable from stockholders	(22,886,640)	(15,333,070)
Deferred compensation	(19,976,993)	(3,311,765)
Accumulated deficit	(24,681,313)	(34,464,356)
Total stockholders' equity	$491,394,044	$144,401,533
Total liabilities and stockholders' equity	$641,300,277	$163,618,176

Source: Wit SoundView Group, Inc. 10-Q Filing with Securities and Exchange Commission, August 14, 2000.

Exhibit 3

WIT SOUNDVIEW GROUP, INC. AND SUBSIDIARIES—CONDENSED CONSOLIDATED STATEMENTS OF OPERATIONS FOR THE THREE AND SIX MONTHS ENDED JUNE 30, 2000 AND 1999

	Three Months Ended June 30 (Unaudited)		Six Months Ended June 30 (Unaudited)	
Income Statement	**2000**	**1999**	**2000**	**1999**
Revenues				
Investment banking	$ 54,157,901	$ 8,246,614	$114,506,995	$ 11,369,034
Brokerage	38,902,164	1,567,584	75,427,117	2,001,791
Asset management fees	(185,171)	–	7,647,863	–
Interest and investment income	2,828,299	1,176,599	4,647,512	1,368,269
Unrealized gains on investments	585,437	289,507	647,317	444,331
Other income	(155,140)	–	(155,140)	–
Total revenues	$96,133,490	$11,280,304	$202,721,664	$415,183,425
Expenses				
Compensation and benefits	$55,704,769	$8,588,459	$ 120,647,125	$ 15,146,585
Brokerage and clearance	6,561,750	1,303,597	12,758,456	1,564,225
Marketing and business development	4,574,604	844,747	7,621,634	1,057,086
Amortization of intangible assets and goodwill	4,124,100	–	6,873,500	–
Professional services	2,201,238	1,085,302	4,478,359	1,76,811
Data processing and communications	2,568,757	884,043	4,341,020	1,183,654
Write-off of computer software and equipment	–	–	1,339,772	–
Depreciation and amortization	1,501,702	278,558	2,777,536	499,053
Technology development	1,547,400	526,088	2,590,201	861,883
Occupancy	1,077,455	213,496	1,869,570	303,503
Other	2,824,842	353,881	4,159,134	498,658
Total expenses	$82,686,617	$ 14,078,171	$169,456,307	$ 22,881,458
Net income (loss) before provision for income taxes and equity in net loss of affiliates	$13,446,873	$ (2,797,867)	$ 33,265,357	$ (7,698,033)
Provision for income taxes	6,683,389	–	17,291,555	–
Net income (loss) before equity in net loss of affiliates	$ 6,763,484	$ (2,797,867)	$ 15,973,802	$ (7,698,033)
Equity in net loss of affiliates	(4,481,070)	–	(6,190,759)	–
Net income (loss)	$ 2,282,414	$ (2,797,867)	$ 9,783,043	$ (7,698,033)
Net income (loss) per share:				
Basic	$ 0.03	$ (0.11)	$ 0.13	$ (0.48)
Diluted	$ 0.02	$ (0.11)	$ 0.10	$ (0.48)
Weighted average shares used in the computation of net income (loss) per share:				
Basic	79,410,828	24,486,238	76,204,016	15,923,484
Diluted	98,800,933	24,486,238	98,443,344	15,923,484

Source: Wit SoundView Group, Inc. 10-Q Filing with Securities and Exchange Commission, August 14, 2000.

6

Online Market Makers

Market makers are intermediaries that aggregate three services for market participants: a place to trade, rules to govern trading, and infrastructure to support trading. *Online* market makers provide these services for parties conducting transactions over electronic networks. By late 2000, online market markers were exploiting the low-cost connectivity provided by the Internet to re-engineer many different markets. The impact of Internet technologies in some markets has been remarkable. For example, a CD-ROM containing all U.S. phone directories fetched a price of $10,000 when it was introduced by NYNEX in 1986; today, the same information is freely available over the Internet.[1] In 2000, five record companies controlled a $40 billion market in music CD sales. Enter Napster, an online market maker that facilitates the exchange of MP3[2] music files. Napster, launched in May of 1999, had spent less than $20 million through late 2000, yet it had the potential to re-engineer the worldwide market for recorded music, and topple the "big five."

Two observations may help put the emergence of online market makers into historical perspective. First, market making was not invented with the Internet; indeed, it has been around since merchants first gathered to trade in Bronze Age cities. The New York Stock Exchange, currently the largest market maker, with 1999 transactions worth $8.9 trillion, traces its origins to the Buttonwood Agreement signed in 1792.[3] Second, the Internet is by no means the first instance of a new technology with the capacity to disrupt business models and re-engineer markets. The growth of railroads and telegraph lines during the Victorian Age led to dramatic changes in trading patterns. In 1841, the trip from London to Exeter (175 miles) took 21 hours by stagecoach. Six years later, an express train made the journey in six and one-half hours, at less cost.[4]

This chapter describes the online market-maker business model. The first section of the chapter proposes a definition of market making and presents different ways to categorize online market makers. The second section describes how online market makers create

---

Assistant Professor Thomas Eisenmann and Research Associate Chris Hackett prepared this note as the basis for class discussion.

value for market participants. The third section examines the economics of market making, focusing on revenue and cost drivers, using both online and offline examples. Building on that analysis, the final section examines the risks and potential payoffs to online market makers from pursuing a "Get Big Fast" strategy, i.e., investing aggressively in customer acquisition.

WHAT ARE ONLINE MARKET MAKERS?

Definition

At its core, market making is an information discovery process. Before completing transactions, market participants come to a market to share information about products and services including their features, pricing, and availability.[5] There are three sets of services that characterize market makers and distinguish them from brokers, retailers, distributors, and other market participants. Market makers are intermediaries whose central purpose is to organize a marketplace by providing, on behalf of multiple buyers and sellers, a place to trade, market governance, and infrastructure to enable transactions.

- *A Place (Physical or Virtual) for Participants to Meet and Trade.*[6] Traditionally, market makers furnished a physical location for participants to meet and trade. Examples stretch from the markets of ancient Babylon to the New York Stock Exchange. The advent of computer networks allows markets to be built in cyberspace. For instance, Nasdaq does not maintain a physical presence, it simply provides access to electronic networks that link broker dealers who make markets in Nasdaq securities.[7]
- *Market Governance.* Market makers develop and enforce the rules for membership and engagement for market participants. Typically, market makers define the types of goods and services sold, specify a list of permitted transactions, provide for dispute resolution and payment terms, and set ground rules as to data ownership. For instance, eBay supports two types of auctions (English, with or without a reserve, and Dutch) and offers anonymous bidding. Also, eBay requires market participants to register and accept a detailed agreement defining their relationships with eBay and each other. In addition, eBay reserves the right to ban participants for rule violations and publishes the results of a rating system through which parties to transactions grade their trading partners' performance.
- *Infrastructure to Enable and Enhance Transactions.* Market makers supplement publicly-available infrastructure in order to create a smoothly functioning market. Infrastructure falls into two categories: commercial and technical. Publicly-available commercial infrastructure includes money and the legal system's commercial code. Examples of commercial infrastructure privately provided by market makers include vetting and provenance services, payment settlement, and logistical support. Online market makers also must provide technical infrastructure to facilitate information exchange and trading. Publicly-available technical infrastructure includes the public Internet itself, including the network of telecommunications lines, routers, and host computers as well as the software, protocols, and programming languages used to transfer information (e.g., browsers, TCP/IP, HTML, XML, Java, etc.). Additionally, some Internet market makers need to supply a software integra-

tion platform that provides links to market participants' legacy information systems, for example, the participants' existing enterprise system software. As of late 2000, companies including Ariba, Commerce One, SAP, and i2 Technologies were racing to build software tools that would bridge the gap between existing Internet infrastructure and proprietary information systems.

Four features of this definition are important. First, *the central purpose of market makers is to organize a marketplace.* In this regard, market makers are distinguished from brokers (e.g., real estate agents, stock brokers), whose central purpose is to provide matching services on behalf of clients and who sometimes help their clients negotiate transactions. While many market makers are neutral intermediaries, some are strongly affiliated with buyers or sellers; in those instances, market makers have clients in the same sense as brokers. These market makers with a strong buy- or sell-side affiliation fulfill brokerage functions but, by definition, neutral market makers do not, because they do not have clients. Thus, *some market makers play a brokerage role but many do not.* Similarly, brokers sometimes provide their clients and their clients' trading partners with a place to trade and infrastructure to support trading. Thus, *some brokers play a market-maker role, other brokers do not organize and maintain a marketplace.* When the two roles overlap, the question of whether to classify a firm as a market maker or a broker must hinge on the admittedly vague concept of purpose: Does the firm see its central purpose to be a client representative or a marketplace organization?

Second, market makers are defined as *intermediaries* who provide services to both buyers and sellers. This excludes retailers and distributors—who are sellers themselves—from our definition of market makers. In some cases, the market maker may briefly take title to the products being exchanged and may even profit from a "spread," reselling them to the buyer for a higher price than the market maker paid to the seller. But market makers only act as resellers in the context of specific transactions; in this regard market makers differ from retailers and distributors, who hold permanent inventory as principals (not as agents or intermediaries), speculating that they will be able to sell goods at a profit over the purchase price.

Third, defining market makers as intermediaries who serve *multiple* participants on both sides of a transaction also excludes single corporations who have Web-enabled their internal procurement processes. In doing so, companies may provide their suppliers with a place to trade, rules of engagement, and enabling infrastructure, but the companies do so strictly as *principals* (in this case, as buyers), not as intermediaries. Some market makers are organized by consortia of buy- or sell-side participants (e.g., Covisint, a company that facilitates auto-part trading, established by the leading auto manufacturers). Such consortia are not *neutral* intermediaries: These principals, as joint owners of the intermediary Covisint, have an opportunity to tilt the terms of engagement to their collective advantage and may exclude certain competitors (e.g., the principals may define themselves as an industry co-op with limited membership). However, consortia-backed online market makers still fit our definition because they involve multiple participants on both sides of a transaction.

Fourth, while market-making activities are often associated with business-to-business (B2B) transactions, it should be clear from the definition above that market makers may also facilitate business-to-consumer (B2C) and consumer-to-consumer transactions. As explained below, Priceline.com and Monster.com are examples of B2C market makers; eBay is a consumer-to-consumer market maker.

We can further "stress test" this definition with several examples. First, is a company that provides an online directory listing contact information and qualifications for patent lawyers a market maker? Clearly it is not: While the information available on the site may facilitate matching, the online directory does not maintain a marketplace where specific transactions are completed. Such an online directory is more properly defined as an online content provider.

Second, is Monster.com, a site where job seekers can review "help wanted" ads and can post a resume that may be evaluated by prospective employers, a market maker? Yes, it is, but this is a more difficult call. On the one hand, Monster.com is focused on matching candidates to specific positions (unlike a directory site, which simply lists market participants and describes their qualifications). Furthermore, Monster.com establishes marketplace rules (e.g., provisions for protecting confidentiality, so that a job hunter's status is not revealed to her current employer) and provides infrastructure (e.g., templates for publishing resumes, procedures for forwarding online resumes to prospective employers). On the other hand, recruiters and candidates do not actually complete their transaction online; Monster.com simply facilitates the first step of the hiring process. But requiring a company to handle an entire transaction from start to finish to be defined as a market maker is too restrictive: Purchasing transactions, for example, are not complete until goods have been shipped and payment has been settled. Some market makers assist market participants with shipping logistics and payment processing, but many do not.

Third, is Priceline.com a market maker when it allows consumers to "name their own price" for airline tickets? Yes, Priceline does connect multiple participants on each side of a transaction, providing them with a place to trade, clear (and unique) rules of conduct, and proprietary infrastructure. Whereas many market makers add value by increasing transparency in a market (i.e., they increase the odds that buyers will find sellers who offer the right goods and services at the right price), Priceline, by contrast, profits as an intermediary in a double blind pricing process. Priceline knows, but does not publish (a) the lowest prices that airlines will accept for specific routes, and (b) the prices that consumers have named for these routes. By avoiding transparency, Priceline earns a profit when the spread between (b) and (a) is positive.

Taxonomy

Market makers can be categorized along three dimensions: (1) product focus: customized vs. standardized; horizontal vs. vertical; and direct purchases vs. indirect purchases; (2) transaction type: catalog, auction, and exchange; and (3) affiliation: buyer, seller, or neutral. Choices along these dimensions tend to be driven by the purchasing behavior of targeted buyers, the nature of the underlying product being traded, and the realities of building market liquidity. As explained below, such choices are neither mutually exclusive nor static.

Product Focus: Customized vs. Standardized, Horizontal vs. Vertical, Direct vs. Indirect Purchases

Customized vs. Standardized. Supplying customized products requires a higher level of communication and collaboration between buyers and suppliers. Suppliers must be able to ask questions about product specifications, the acceptability of design modifications, and material substitutions that might lower cost or improve product performance. Buyers need assurance that suppliers can actually meet quality and delivery standards—buyers will have a strong preference for dealing with suppliers who have served them reliably in the past. By contrast, for standardized products, less communication and collaboration is required; buyers tend to be more focused on price.

Horizontal vs. Vertical. Customers from a diverse range of industries purchase the goods and services traded in horizontal markets. Typical items include office supplies, accounting services, steel, electricity, legal services, and personal computers. Examples of horizontal market makers include Ariba and Mondus.

Goods and services sold only to customers within a single industry are traded in vertical markets. Examples of such items include ink used for offset printing, aircraft parts, paper-making machinery, agricultural equipment, sports legal services, and hops used as an ingredient in beer. Covisint, PlasticsNet.com, and MyAircraft.com are typical vertical market makers.

Direct vs. Indirect. Business-to-business markets can also be described as focusing on either direct purchases or indirect purchases. Direct purchases are items incorporated into a product, e.g., paper in book publishing, memory chips in a PC. Indirect purchases are items consumed in the process of designing or manufacturing a product, e.g., janitorial services, electricity for air-conditioning a factory, and test instruments used by engineers. One important category of indirect purchases includes "Maintenance, Repair, and Operating" (MRO) supplies, e.g., spare parts for machines, hand tools used by workers, and lubricants for equipment.

Consider, for example, a motor manufacturer that buys ball bearings under long-term contracts for use as parts in its motors—these are a direct purchases. The motor manufacturer undoubtedly also purchases replacement ball bearings for machinery used in its production processes—these are indirect purchases. The following chart summarizes the distinctions between direct and indirect purchases.

Chart 6-1 ATTRIBUTES OF DIRECT VS. INDIRECT PURCHASES

	Direct Purchases	Indirect Purchases
Purchase predictability	Volatile, driven by external market demand	Internally-driven, typically against budgets
Purchasing approach	Usually large, long-term contracts, some spot buying	Varies: some ongoing contracts, some ad hoc RFQs
Order size	Large lots, sized to production runs	Often small
Collaboration with suppliers	Varies: usually high, but low for commodity inputs	Varies: low for MRO supplies, high for equipment and professional services
% of total $ spent	80%	20%
% of total number of purchase orders	20%	80%
End customer	External customer	Internal employees, often at department level

Sources: Morgan Stanley Dean Witter, *The Internet B2B Report*, April 2000; Bill Cafiero, *Electronic Commerce Boot-Camp Seminar*, GEIS, October 21, 1999

While direct purchases represent the bulk of industrial purchases by dollar volume, to date, most purchases made through online market makers have been indirect because online market makers have been better able to reduce transaction costs for such indirect purchases. This is because transaction costs (incurred in searching for items and processing orders) have historically represented a larger share of total spending for indirect goods and services. For direct purchases, which tend to involve a smaller number of very large orders, companies often have been able to reduce transaction costs by relying on electronic data interchange (EDI) technologies.[8] EDI automates the ordering process through dedicated, point-to-point telecommunications links between buyers and their suppliers. Dating back to the 1970s, EDI was the original e-commerce technology, but its point-to-point architecture is fairly expensive. Hence, EDI typically has been used by large corporations to automate high volume direct purchase orders rather than indirect purchasing.

Transaction Type: Catalog, Auction, Exchange

Market making mechanisms may be divided into three categories, ranging from static pricing models (catalogs), to dynamic pricing models (auctions), to exchanges (which are essentially continuous auctions).

Catalogs. Multivendor catalogs are listings of standardized goods (or services) from multiple manufacturers (or service providers) compiled by a publisher or a market maker. Offline examples include the Official Airline Guide, the Thomas Register, and W.W. Grainger. These offline catalogs are printed and are not transaction-enabled; customers have to contact a manufacturer or distributor by mail, phone, or fax to place their orders. When market makers publish catalogs online, those catalogs tend to be transaction-enabled. Online examples include Napster, OrderZone, and Ventro, which has launched online market makers in several vertical markets, including its Chemdex service; it provided a multivendor catalog for laboratory chemicals prior to being shut down in December 2000.

Catalogs present fixed prices; they are most likely to be used when (1) the transaction costs that would be incurred with a dynamic price discovery mechanism (i.e., the time that would be spent by purchasing agents and sales reps on price negotiations) would be large in relation to the value of merchandise ordered, and (2) supply and demand are fairly stable or predictable, so prices are not too volatile. Even with fixed prices, however, online catalogs may still facilitate price discovery, assuming they include multiple suppliers and provide buyers with the capability to search based on price.

Online catalogs also are helpful for matching supply with demand when they allow a buyer to look into a supplier's inventory to check on stock availability. However, this capability requires the integration of a market maker's databases with sellers' inventory management systems—a complex and usually expensive project.

Auctions. In the popular imagination, auctions are initiated by sellers (e.g., eBay, Sotheby's), but buyers also can initiate auctions—these are known as reverse auctions. In B2B markets, reverse auctions often take the form of "request for quotation" (RFQ) processes, which are often used by buyers procuring goods that require customization. FreeMarkets and Mondus are examples of companies that organize online markets around RFQs. Auctions can be very effective mechanisms for price discovery; auctions are most useful for maximizing the price realized by sellers (or minimizing the price paid by buyers in reverse auctions) for one-of-a-kind items or perishable products and services.[9] In both of these instances, there is no published price for the merchandise, and marketplace participants may have very different assessments of value. A well-run seller-initiated auction should net the seller an amount equal to the "willingness-to-pay" of the bidder with the second highest assessment of value.

Efficient methods of price discovery often lead to price volatility. Unlike exchanges (see below), the price volatility resulting from auctions usually cannot be hedged because there are not enough transactions of a like item or service to develop forward contracts.

Exchanges. Exchanges are continuous auctions for standardized products and services (e.g., gold, electric power, trucking capacity from point A to point B) that face changing supply and demand conditions, leading to price fluctuations. Prices are determined by the relationship between bid and ask prices posted on the exchange. Price volatility results from efficient price discovery but can usually be mitigated by forward contracts. Examples of exchanges include Altra Energy, Enron's Bandwidth Exchange, and the New York Stock Exchange.

Market makers often use a mix of transaction types. For example, PaperExchange.com offers a real-time trading exchange for members to buy and sell paper. In addition, PaperExchange offers an online catalog, through which members can buy and sell new and used equipment such as forklift trucks and paper-making machinery, and a job listing service.

Affiliation: Buyer, Seller, Neutral

Market-maker affiliations range from sell-side to neutral to buy-side. Affiliation dictates who sets the terms of exchange and thus can determine whether a market maker biases those terms to the advantage of either buyers or sellers. Sell-side market makers tend to predominate in industries with fragmented buyers but concentrated suppliers, e.g., VerticalNet's SolidWaste.com. Neutral market makers tend to exist in industries with fragmented buyers and suppliers, e.g., Citadon in construction supplies and the New York Stock Exchange. Buy-side market makers tend to succeed in industries with concentrated buyers but fragmented suppliers, e.g., Covisint, the buying exchange being built by GM, Ford, DaimlerChrysler, Commerce One, and Oracle.[10]

Affiliation is a critical consideration when developing a market. Consider the example of Industry Net, one of the pioneer market makers in the Internet B2B space. Headed by Jim Manzi, former president of Lotus, Industry Net burned through $25 million of venture funding before declaring bankruptcy in 1997. One of the most oft-cited criticisms of Industry Net was their strong buy-side affiliation; so strong in fact that Industry Net could not attract a critical mass of sellers to their market.[11]

Affiliations are not necessarily static; for instance, a market maker may assume a sell-side affiliation to build volume, then move to a neutral affiliation. As Mark Walsh, president of VerticalNet is fond of saying, "Don't get out of the Trojan horse until you are in the city."[12]

HOW DO ONLINE MARKET MAKERS CREATE VALUE FOR MARKET PARTICIPANTS?

Online market makers can generate several different types of benefits for marketplace participants, including increased liquidity, transaction-processing cost savings, improved integration of supply chain partners' business processes, and benefits related to anonymity. As market makers design their sites and seek to recruit users, it is important for online market makers to have a clear sense of which source of value they plan to emphasize.

Liquidity Benefits

Transaction costs accrue at each of the three stages of the buying process: *Search costs* are incurred to identify prospective trading partners, *negotiating costs* are incurred as trading partners seek agreement on the terms of a transaction, and *transaction processing costs* are incurred after an order is placed. Trading partners realize liquidity benefits when they experience cost reductions in the first two stages, i.e., search and negotiation. Liquidity benefits follow from increased transparency in a market with respect to price, product availability, and/or product selection. When search and negotiation costs are high, liquidity tends to be low. Buyers and sellers may not find it economical to trade with additional partners; thus, buyers may forfeit opportunities to find products that better meet their needs, to find a better price for the goods they want, or to locate items that are out of stock. Similarly, sellers may miss opportunities for additional sales to customers who would value the merchandise sellers offer or the level of service they can deliver. Online market makers can dramatically lower search costs by eliminating the need for costly and clumsy catalogs and for labor-intensive phone calls to explore product availability. Market makers also can reduce negotiation costs for customized products by moving the RFQ process online, replacing faxes and phone calls with webpages and e-mails.

Aggregating suppliers online reduces search costs by bringing together information from a large collection of suppliers into a searchable format. Traditional printed directories (e.g., the Thomas Register) aggregate information in this manner but face two limiting factors: (1) Directories are not transaction-enabled and (2) because of printing and distribution costs, directories are expensive to keep current. Because it is expensive to add pages and to update the directory, there is a trade-off between the accuracy and *richness* (i.e., the depth of information on any given product) on the one hand and the distribution *reach* of the directory on the other hand.[13] The Internet eliminates the physical carrier of information (i.e., the printed directory) and thereby greatly reduces the marginal costs associated with adding information to a directory, updating that information, and distributing it.

Who benefits most from increased marketplace liquidity? When a buy-side–affiliated market maker brings more sellers to an RFQ-style auction, the impact on pricing is straightforward: One buyer plus more sellers equals better prices for the buyer. For example, FreeMarkets, which organizes and hosts online reverse auctions on behalf of large companies, claims to deliver average cost savings of 10 to 15 percent for large, multimillion-dollar purchases.[14]

However, *both* buyers and sellers may benefit when they can leverage an online marketplace to identify additional trading partners. For example, before eBay was launched, a Peoria, Illinois, musician wanting to buy a second-hand, high-end guitar was limited to what she could find in local music stores and through classified ads in the local newspaper. Peoria being a small city, the selection was limited. A seller of a high-end guitar located in Davenport, Iowa, would have little chance of finding her. Davenport, also being a small city, has few musicians interested in expensive used guitars. Without the expanded geographic reach available through eBay, the seller ends up taking less for his guitar than he could get if he had a larger audience, and our buyer in Peoria ends up purchasing a guitar that is not exactly what she wants.

Assuming that the reduction of search costs adds buyers and sellers to a marketplace in roughly equal proportions, increased liquidity will not necessarily have a significant impact on average pricing levels. However, data do indicate that larger aggregations of buyers and sellers tend to lead to more uniform pricing.[15] The losers with increased liquidity thus tend to be sellers whose value proposition is based on information asymmetry, specifically, on the ignorance of certain buyer segments. Buyers, low-cost sellers, and sellers who add value in other ways (beyond discounting) will thus tend to benefit from increased liquidity.

Liquidity benefits tend to be large in asset-intensive businesses where yield management is a key profitability driver due to high fixed costs and perishable inventory. Examples include airlines, trucking, and bandwidth suppliers. It is estimated that 35 percent of airline seats go unsold,[16] $31 billion of trucking capacity is wasted due to dead-heading (returning empty) and sub-optimal scheduling,[17] and 80 percent of telecommunications infrastructure is idle.[18] By aggregating more buyers, online market makers can increase the likelihood of finding a buyer for underutilized assets. For instance, Priceline makes a market in unsold airline seats, the National Transportation Exchange makes a market for trucking services, and Enron, Band-X, and Arbinet-thexchange all make markets for bandwidth.

Beyond these attributes of high fixed costs and perishable inventory, potential gains from increasing liquidity are greatest in businesses with the following attributes:

- *Customers Are Willing to Switch Suppliers.* Customers may be locked into suppliers for many reasons, ranging from personal relationships to long-term contracts to tightly-integrated information systems.
- *There Is Some Basis for Supplier Differentiation.* If suppliers find it difficult to distinguish themselves, there is not much point in expanding liquidity. Opportunities for differentiation are likely to be greatest in businesses with (1) large numbers of stock-keeping units because this increases the odds that some suppliers will be out of stock; (2) substitutable products, which benefit suppliers who can give buyers advice on when buyers can save money by switching to a cheaper product; (3) a rapid rate of new product introduction, so some suppliers have access to new and better items than others and need a channel to communicate new product benefits; and (4) rapid changes in supply and demand, so suppliers will face frequent stock-outs because of the difficulty in managing inventories. Note that some of these advantages are easier than others for a previously unknown supplier to communicate to a prospective buyer through an electronic marketplace.

Transaction-Processing Cost Savings

Processing a purchase order takes, on average, 14 steps.[19] The process is rich with information and—unless it is automated—very labor intensive. For example, customers may demand (1) real-time information on product availability and shipping status, (2) the ability to designate different shipping arrangements for distinct line items to optimize shipping expense, (3) options to expedite orders in exchange for a higher price, (4) coordination of deliveries from different suppliers, and (5) the ability to make substitutions for back-ordered items.[20]

Cost savings in information-retrieval and order-processing activities can follow from the automation of transactions through an electronic marketplace. Specifically, online transaction processing can eliminate manual effort associated with placing/receiving an order (including providing shipping instructions), checking on order status and verifying delivery, and managing accounts payable/receivable. Automating buyer-seller interaction reduces phone tag, misplaced faxes, and the probability of misunderstood instructions. Studies indicate that the cost to manually administer a purchase order ranges from $40 to $200, while the cost to process an electronic purchase order ranges from $1 to $20. British Telecom, for example, has reduced its cost of processing purchasing transactions by 90 percent through use of the Internet.[21]

Transaction-processing cost savings are especially important for orders valued under $1,000, which typically represent more than 70 percent of a corporation's purchasing transactions but less than 5 percent of the dollar value of the total purchases.[22] Hence, indirect purchases of low-cost items like office supplies often realize significant transaction-processing cost savings (as a percentage of total purchase cost) through automation.

Automating transactions not only reduces labor expenses but it may result in savings by giving companies more control over decentralized purchasing decisions. "Maverick" purchases, which typically involve indirect goods and services, are orders that do not comply with a company's directives requiring employees to take full advantage of volume purchase agreements. Studies indicate that 30 percent of corporate purchases are maverick and that maverick buyers pay 18 percent to 27 percent above the price they would have paid had buyers used preferred suppliers.[23] Online market makers can help reduce maverick purchases by providing an easily accessible purchasing platform which monitors adherence to company policies.

In general, transaction-processing cost savings are most significant in businesses with the following attributes:

- *Transaction-Processing Costs Are Large in Relation to the Total Value of Orders.* This attribute tends to follow from (1) the nature of the production process (e.g., batch versus continuous process businesses), (2) the level of industry fragmentation (which tends to lead to many small orders), and (3) the direct versus indirect nature of purchases (see discussion above). Consider, for example, a chemical plant's orders for feedstock versus a small business's orders for office supplies. In the former case, transaction-processing costs will be a much smaller percentage of the total order value than in the latter case.
- *Trading Partners Lack EDI Infrastructure.* As noted above, EDI reduces order-processing costs, but historically, such links have been expensive to build and maintain, so it has only been economical to use EDI for exchanges between large buyers and suppliers. In fragmented businesses, the use of EDI tends to be limited.
- *Buyers Place Frequent Orders, Each with Large Numbers of Items, and Require Close Coordination of Delivery Schedules.* Consider the volume of orders and order-status inquiries generated by an electronics-assembly facility relying on "just-in-time" production processes: Electronic order management can offer large transaction-processing cost savings.
- *Orders Pass through Multiple Approval Layers.* Costs and delays increase substantially when an order is passed manually (by mail or fax) through multiple levels of approval. For example, in the case of construction supplies, this might, at the extreme, include the subcontractor seeking approval from the general contractor, who must check with the architect, who must check with the developer, who must check with the building owner.

Offline distributors often are important intermediaries in markets that meet the criteria listed above. By holding inventory from multiple manufacturers, offline distributors reduce transaction-processing costs related to ordering, delivery, and payment processing, compared to the costs that would be incurred if manufacturers shipped directly to buyers. In many markets, offline distributors are integrating their information systems with those of buyers and manufacturers to further reduce transaction-processing costs. If distributors are successful, they may usurp the value-added services that online market makers aspire to deliver. Online market makers, conversely, are in no position to disintermediate distributors—unless, like distributors, market makers are willing to hold inventory and ship products to customers. For these reasons, many industry observers believe that online market makers should seek alliances with leading offline distributors.

More broadly, it should be clear from the discussion above that transaction-processing cost savings are not unique to the online market maker business model: Companies that Web-enable their purchasing processes can capture such savings without help from an online market maker. In fact, eMarketer, Inc. estimates that in 2000, about 93 percent of all B2B e-commerce was conducted by companies funneling transactions through their own websites, rather than through sites operated by an online market maker.[24]

Integration Benefits

Managing transactions online allows buyers and suppliers to more tightly integrate a number of processes and thereby increase asset liquidity (i.e., the speed at which assets can be monetized) and can even improve product design. The classic example is the inventory management problem for direct purchases. Companies in the middle of a supply chain cannot readily predict the demand of their customers and cannot view the available capacity of their suppliers. To protect against upstream and downstream surprises, companies must build inventory. One study concluded that U.S. companies collectively have $1.4 trillion of inventory on their balance sheets, 40 percent of which is obsolete.[25] Dell Computer's Paul Bell says that inventory is "the physical embodiment of bad information."[26]

The traditional way for a company to reduce inventory is to push it back on suppliers, but this is largely a zero-sum game (or worse, it sometimes forces smaller companies with a higher cost of capital to bear the cost of extra inventory). Tighter integration of buyers and suppliers through electronic networks has the potential to reduce inventory throughout the supply chain by allowing suppliers to peer into their customers' order book and by letting customers view suppliers' inventory levels and work loads. Covisint, the much publicized automotive supply exchange being built by GM, Ford, and DaimlerChrysler, is targeting this problem. Software providers such as i2 Technologies, Ariba, Commerce One, and Oracle also are seeking to address the inventory problem with their software platforms.

In a similar manner, tighter buyer-supplier integration holds the promise of solving the accounts payable paradox. Traditionally, small vendors selling to large companies have waited 30 to 90 days to be paid. This is a remnant of delays inherent in paper-based payment systems, but treasury departments also are motivated to stretch their accounts payable as a source of free financing. Paradoxically, when large buyers have lower costs of capital than their suppliers, stretching accounts payable in this manner ultimately results in higher costs for buyers. Tighter integration between buyers and sellers should result in faster payments from buyers in exchange for deeper discounts from sellers.

Again, as with transaction-processing cost savings, it should be clear that integration benefits are not unique to the online market maker business model: Benefits are available whenever supply-chain partners establish electronic links.

Anonymity and Off-Exchange Trading

In some instances, market makers can create value by facilitating anonymous buying and selling. Market participants typically can employ brokers to achieve the same benefits, but, depending on their rules for market governance, online market makers may automatically provide anonymity—and at a lower cost. Anonymity sometimes allows market participants to realize better prices for the goods they trade and to avoid conflict with channel partners. For instance, a mutual fund does not want other securities traders to know that it is selling a large position in a particular stock, because that news may scare off potential buyers, reducing the value that the mutual fund realizes. This problem is relevant in many other markets. For example, the commercial shipping industry features brokers who specialize in discreetly matching ship sellers with ship buyers. Sellers fear that if other market participants learn that they are selling a ship, it may jeopardize sellers' ability to market shipping services. Manufacturers who wish to liquidate obsolete inventory without engendering conflict with their distributors holding similar inventory also may benefit from anonymity. Priceline's value proposition hinges on a similar motive: When they name their own price for an airline ticket, Priceline's users do not learn the carrier's identity until *after* they have purchased the ticket. Thus, airlines can liquidate inventory without publicly advertising the deeply discounted fares received by Priceline's users—and without facing demands from travel agents and other customers for similar discounts.

Market participants may have other motives for preserving anonymity beyond protecting the integrity of their pricing and channel structures. For example, job seekers who do not want their current employer to learn that they are searching for a new position must protect their anonymity when posting resumes at online job sites like Monster.com. Individuals liquidating art and antiques due to bankruptcy or divorce often request anonymity from an auction house like Sotheby's to avoid personal embarrassment.

In some cases, it may be to the market maker's advantage if prospective buyers and sellers do not learn each other's identity. To the extent that market makers perform only a matching service, they are vulnerable to "off-exchange trading" by parties who rely on the online market maker's pricing information but subsequently conduct offline transactions to avoid transaction fees levied by the market maker. Of course, if the prospective trading partners cannot contact each other, they cannot complete an offline trade. Typically, however, market participants are unwilling to close a transaction unless they know they are dealing with a reliable trading partner. Unless market makers are able to certify that this is the case (perhaps through a user rating system like eBay's), market makers must allow participants to disclose their identities—and necessarily will increase the risk of off-exchange trades.

Online market makers may take several steps to reduce the risk of off-exchange trading. For example, market makers can structure their fees as subscription payments (e.g., a flat rate per month), rather than per-transaction payments, to reduce incentives to circumvent the system. Also, they can draft and enforce rules that penalize participants who engage in off-exchange trades—at the extreme, banning offenders from the marketplace. Ultimately, however, the best defense against off-exchange trading is to broaden the benefits provided to market participants beyond simple matching to encompass transaction-processing cost savings and integration benefits that require electronic links to trading partners' legacy information systems. Online market makers also can reduce the risk of off-exchange trading by offering value-added ancillary services related to logistics, shipping, warehousing, inspection, escrow, and insurance.[27]

ONLINE MARKET MAKER ECONOMICS

This section examines sources of revenue for market makers, the accounting rules that determine whether a market maker should recognize gross revenue (i.e., the total value of goods or services traded by marketplace participants) or net revenue (i.e., only the transaction fees earned by the market maker), market makers' cost categories and the factors that drive costs, and current and prospective profitability for online market makers.

Sources of Revenue

Online market makers have a number of potential sources of revenue, the most important of which are described below.

Transaction Fees. Market makers may levy fees for each transaction completed by market participants; such fees may be structured as flat payments or as a percentage of the transaction value and may be paid by the buyer, seller, or both parties. However, transaction fees are usually hard to maintain unless a market maker is able to erect strong barriers to entry; consequently, transaction fees often represent only a small proportion of market makers' overall revenues. Leading offline and online auctioneers provide notable exceptions: Companies such as Sotheby's and eBay generate nearly 90 percent of their revenue from transaction fees. Auctioneers benefit from strong entry barriers related to network effects in the market for unique, collectible items: Traders in such items tend to congregate in just a few markets.

Markup. Markup, or spread, is earned when a market maker buys a product then resells the product at a higher price. Priceline, for instance, generates most of its revenue from the spread between the prices offered by consumers and airlines. Priceline only purchases a ticket from an airline when it has a binding offer from a consumer.[28]

Membership and Subscription Fees. Some market makers have built their businesses around a subscription-based model, e.g., a recurring monthly payment. Avail's ILS Division, for instance, maintains a database of aircraft parts, used primarily by aircraft-parts brokers. ILS charges users a subscription fee to access its parts database as well as a parts listing fee; ILS reported 1999 earnings of $16.7 million on revenue of $29.8 million.

Data Sold to Third Parties. Data (e.g., aggregated market statistics; company performance data such as delivery, payment, returns, back-orders, etc.; and information on buyer behavior and preferences) are increasingly seen as a revenue source for market makers. For example, data sales contributed 17 percent of the New York Stock Exchange's total 1999 revenue, slightly less than transaction fee revenue.[29] DoubleClick's Abacus Alliance also makes a market in data. Abacus is a cooperative arrangement through which direct-mail marketers and offline retailers contribute their customers' purchasing histories to Abacus' database in exchange for the right to purchase the full range of Abacus' information and market research services.[30] As evidenced by the recent consumer backlash against DoubleClick's perceived privacy violations, data sales are not without risk. In the B2B arena, data ownership has become a contentious issue: All market participants seem to think they own the data generated by their transactions.

Software Sales and System Integration Fees. As of late 2000, several companies in the B2B enterprise software space were blurring the distinction between market maker and software provider. Ariba, Oracle, i2 Technologies, and Commerce One were all licensing market-making software platforms under terms that effectively make them shareholders in the resulting online market makers. These companies' licensing agreements typically included installation and hosting fees plus revenue-sharing agreements. Additionally, each of these firms had plans to create software links between its customers' markets to facilitate inter-market trading.

Ancillary Services. Many market makers generate revenue from ancillary services that they provide to market participants. The range of services depends on the needs of the specific market; typical services include credit verification, transaction clearing, insurance, shipping, custody, and warehousing.

Advertising Fees. In addition to enabling transactions, some online market makers offer directories and charge companies for listings that describe their businesses. By our earlier definitions, publishing directories is a content-provider role, not a market-maker role; some hybrid companies employ both business models. For example, VerticalNet, which has organized online trading communities for dozens of vertical markets (e.g., HydrocarbonOnline.com, PulpandPaperOnline.com, BakeryOnline.com, SolidWaste.com), derived 53 percent of its 1999 income from listings; the balance of their revenue came from transaction fees. Listing fee-based business models are fairly easy to implement as long as the market maker can demonstrate value to advertisers in the form of incremental revenue generated. Because directories tend to list sellers rather than buyers, market makers who heavily depend on listing fees often adopt a sell-side affiliation.

Revenue Recognition

There is some controversy over the revenue-recognition policies of online market makers. At issue is whether market makers should report gross (notional) revenue or net revenue. Of course, the choice of accounting approach has no effect on cash flows, but it is very important to keep the gross versus net distinction in mind when interpreting and comparing market makers' financial statements. The SEC's current policy states that a company should report gross revenue when it[31]

1. Acts as the principal in the transaction,
2. Takes title to the products,
3. Has risks and rewards of ownership, such as the risk of loss for collection, delivery, or returns, and
4. Acts as an agent or broker (including performing services, in substance, as an agent or broker) with compensation on a commission or fee basis.

According to the SEC, "If the company performs as an agent or broker without assuming the risks and rewards of ownership of the goods, sales should be reported on a net basis."

For example, consider eBay's business model. eBay organizes auctions and earns fees based on the value of the items auctioned on its site but does not take title to the products traded. Consequently, eBay reports revenue on a net basis; its 1999 revenue was only $248 million, while goods worth about $4.5 billion were auctioned through eBay.[32]

Priceline, by contrast, reports revenue on a gross basis, arguing that it takes title to the airline tickets it sells. Some analysts have criticized this accounting decision, arguing that while Priceline takes title to the tickets it sells, the company takes no significant ownership risks because it only resells tickets when it has a binding order, backed by a non-refundable charge on the consumer's credit card.

Cost Categories and Cost Drivers

Market making, like other information-intensive businesses, features high fixed costs. The principal cost categories for online market makers include cost of revenue, product development, sales and marketing, and general and administrative. This section describes the factors that drive costs for online market makers, using data for the first three quarters of 2000 for a sample of four companies: eBay, Priceline, Ventro, and VerticalNet (see Exhibit 6-1). In interpreting this data, it is important to note that Priceline and Ventro report revenues on a gross basis, while eBay and VerticalNet report on a net basis.

Exhibit 6-1 INCOME STATEMENTS FOR A SAMPLE OF ONLINE MARKET MAKERS, Q1–Q3 2000

	$ in Millions	% of Revenue		$ in Millions	% of Revenue
eBay			***Priceline***		
Revenue	$297.4		*Revenue*	$1,007.2	
Cost of revenue	71.5	24.0%	*Cost of revenue*	848.6	84.3%
Gross profit	225.9	76.0%	*Gross profit*	158.6	15.7%
Sales and marketing	117.7	39.6%	*Sales and marketing*	113.6	11.3%
Product development	41.7	14.0%	*Product development*	24.0	2.4%
General and administrative	54.1	18.2%	*General and administrative*	39.9	4.0%
Operating income	12.4	4.2%	*Operating income*	(18.9)	−1.9%
Ventro - *Revenue* - Transactions - Other - *Cost of revenue* - Transactions - Other - *Gross profit*	 $77.2 72.3 4.9 72.7 68.7 4.0 4.5	 93.7% 6.3% 94.2% 89.0% 5.2% 5.8%	***VerticalNet*** - *Revenue* - Net exchange revenue - Advertising and other	 $154.7 83.0 71.8	 53.7% 46.4%
			Editorial and operations	28.8	18.6%
Sales and marketing	44.7	57.9%	*Sales and marketing*	93.8	60.6%
Product development	33.8	43.8%	*Product development*	22.1	14.3%
General and administrative	20.5	26.6%	*General and administrative*	61.6	39.8%
Operating income	(94.5)	−122.4%	*Operating income*	(51.6)	−33.4%

Note: Operating Income reported is before amortization, merger-related and stock compensation charges.
Source: Adapted from company 10Q and 10K statements.

Cost of Revenue. Cost of revenue (COR) as a percentage of revenue differs greatly for online market makers, depending on their accounting policies. For example, eBay and VerticalNet, both of whom report revenue on a net basis, had COR equal to 24 percent and 19 percent of revenue, respectively, for the first three quarters of 2000. Expenses related to customer support and site operations (i.e., hosting) are included by eBay in COR, which tends to vary with transaction volume. For VerticalNet, we have defined COR to include editorial-and-operations expenses, which tend to be fixed costs. For Ventro and Priceline, both of whom report revenue on a gross basis, COR (equal to 94 percent and 84 percent of revenue, respectively) includes only the cost of goods and services sold (which varies directly with transaction volume): Site operations and customer service costs were recorded in other cost categories.

Product Development. At first glance, product development—spending by online market makers to build and maintain their websites—varies considerably among market makers, ranging from just 2 percent of revenue for Priceline to 44 percent for Ventro. In absolute dollar terms, however, there is less variance between the companies in the sample: Spending ranges from $22 million for VerticalNet to $42 million for eBay. This suggests that product development is a large and recurring expenditure for market makers. Before they launch, most online market makers must spend heavily to develop proprietary technology and databases for matching buyers and sellers, then incur significant ongoing expenses to upgrade systems and maintain databases. Such costs do not tend to vary with transaction volume. However, market makers that seek to provide buyers with visibility into suppliers' inventories also must undertake system-integration projects, an investment that tends to vary with the number of suppliers added to the marketplace.

Given the information-intensive nature of market making, it is not surprising that established market makers continue to spend heavily on their information systems. Consider, for instance, the experience of two mature market makers: During 1999, Sotheby's spent $121 million (27 percent of net revenue) on computer systems and the NYSE spent $227 million (31 percent of net revenue) on systems.[33]

Sales and Marketing. Sales and marketing expenses for the sample of online market makers also varied widely as a percentage of revenue, ranging from 11 percent for Priceline to 61 percent for VerticalNet. Priceline's figure is actually inflated, because it includes expenses for credit-card–processing fees, "charge backs" (bad debt expenses), and outsourced call center operations. Priceline's actual advertising spending was only 5 percent of revenue.[34]

Sales and marketing efforts to increase liquidity can take many forms. For example, eBay spends heavily on portal distribution deals, e.g., it signed a four-year, $75-million agreement to provide auctions for AOL subscribers. Also, eBay invests in trade promotion: It sets up booths at local fairs to court "power sellers," semi-professional collectors who drive a large share of its volume.[35] While eBay spends heavily on marketing, it also has successfully amassed a huge customer base: eBay spent only about $10 per new customer acquired in 1999.[36]

By contrast, B2B online market makers tend to spend heavily on a direct sales force. For example, VerticalNet spent most of its sales and marketing budget—which totaled $94 million for the first three quarters of 2000—on direct sales personnel who recruit buyers and sellers for VerticalNet's many marketplaces and who sell listings in its online directories. Ventro, likewise, spent most of its sales and marketing budget on direct sales activities, as is typical for newly formed B2B market makers. Ventro's 2000 sales and marketing costs (through the third quarter) were $45 million, 58 percent of revenue. At the end of February 2000, Ventro had 123 sales and marketing professionals serving 95 customers, with the top four customers (3M, Biogen, DuPont, and Eos Biotechnology) representing 63 percent of 1999 revenues. Assuming Ventro acquired all 95 customers in 1999 (the company had 1998 sales of only $28,000), the average cost of customer acquisition was $250,000—expensive by any measure. On the supply side, Ventro entered into a strategic alliance with VWR, a distributor of laboratory products. As part of this alliance, Ventro gave VWR 2.5 million shares of Ventro pre-IPO stock valued at $14 million (at the time of issuance). While the Ventro-VWR relationship may prove to be very valuable, it also has been extremely costly.[37]

Ventro's customer-acquisition cost seems high by B2B market-maker standards. For example, Marshall & Swift, in building a contractor exchange network for the insurance industry, had spent $16 million over four years and had acquired 1,500 contractors and 2,000 claims agents. Counting both the contractors and claims agents as customers, the firm had an acquisition cost per new customer of $4,571. During the four-year period, the firm had gross transaction volume of $136 million, yielding transaction fees of about $8 million—less than half its spending for customer acquisition.[38]

Many new market makers are justifying their heavy early spending on customer acquisition on two premises: (1) Network effects will allow market makers to spend less to acquire additional customers after reaching critical mass and (2) marketing expenditures to *retain* customers will be modest, because those expenses will be locked in by the value realized from marketplace participation. These premises will be examined in detail in the section below entitled, "Get Big Fast: A Strategic Imperative for Online Market Makers?" If the premises turn out to be correct, online market makers may earn outsized gains in the long run.[39]

Prospective Profitability

Among the companies in our sample, only eBay earned a modest operating profit during the first three quarters of 2000: $12 million (4 percent of revenue) before expenses related to employee stock options and the amortization of merger-related intangibles. Measured on the same basis, Priceline, VerticalNet, and Ventro lost $19 million, $52 million, and $95 million, respectively.

Notwithstanding these less-than-inspiring early results, the advent of Internet market makers appears likely to create tremendous value for reasons explained above. However, history suggests that it is difficult to predict who will capture that value: See Exhibit 2 for projections of the share of value that B2B online market makers may capture in different categories and Exhibit 3 for forecasts of B2B e-commerce transaction volume.

Exhibit 6-2 VALUE RETAINED FROM B2B e-COMMERCE

Industry Type	% of Economy	Sample Industries	Buyer	Supplier	Marketplace Owner	Technology Provider
High buyer concentration	35%	Automotive manufacturing	70%	10%	10%	10%
High supplier concentration	15%	Plastics, steel	20%	60%	15%	5%
Fragmented buyers and suppliers	50%	Healthcare, life sciences, agriculture	25%	25%	35%	15%

Source: Adapted from Charles Phillips and Mary Meeker, "The B2B Internet Report," Morgan Stanley Dean Witter Equity Research citing Ventro Research, April 2000, p. 9

Exhibit 6-3 B2B TRADE FORECAST, 2000–2005

$ in billions	2000	2005E
Offline B2B trade	$11,120	$8,758
Online B2B trade through individual company procurement sites	$311	$4,137
Online B2B trade through Internet market makers	$25	$2,206
Total B2B trade	$11,456	$15,101

Source: Adapted from Jean-Gabriel Henry and John Katsaros, "US Business-To-Business Internet Trade Projections," Jupiter Communications, September 2000, p. 12

Just as automobiles transformed the twentieth century, bringing us suburbs, McDonald's, even the word *motel*, many industry observers believe there is a good chance that Internet market makers will transform the twenty-first century. But turning again to the example of the auto industry, it is interesting to note that while 2,000-odd auto manufacturing firms were launched in the United States during the early decades of the twentieth century, only three have survived.[40]

We might consider two other historical examples to gauge the potential for online market makers. First, recall another network-based business, railroads. Like today's online market-maker entrepreneurs, railroad barons pointed to economies of scale and barriers to entry. The fact is, however, few rail companies ever paid a dividend. Of the 5,000 U.S. railroad carriers that have existed during the last 150 years, 99 percent went out of business. The Great Western Railway, the most admired rail carrier in Britain during the nineteenth century, paid an annual return to shareholders of just 5 percent from 1835, when the company was established, through 1913.[41] It turned out that while tremendous value was created by the rail systems, it was difficult for rail companies to capture that value. Instead, farmers, department stores, and packaged goods companies were among the major beneficiaries of the rail infrastructure.

Second, consider the NYSE. With $8.9 trillion in gross notional transactions, the NYSE is by far the world's largest market maker. It enjoys a dominant position, including all of the benefits of network effects, market liquidity, and economies of scale. Given its advantages, the NYSE surely must be an enormously profitable business, right? Not quite—for 1999 the NYSE reported just $735 million in net revenue and $125 million in EBIT, figures that would fail to even place it in *Fortune* magazine's list of the 1,000 largest U.S. companies. While the existence of the NYSE creates untold economic value and is critical to the existence of entire industries (e.g., rating agencies, media and news companies like Bloomberg and Reuters, investment banks) the NYSE captures only a small fraction of the value it creates. Why?

The NYSE faces competition from intermediaries that offer off-exchange trading, including electronic crossing networks (ECNs). This competition prevents the NYSE from sharply increasing its fees: Thus, for every $1 of stock traded on the NYSE, the exchange charges on average only $0.0000155 in transaction fees. While the NYSE provides remarkable liquidity to market participants, its experience demonstrates that liquidity is not necessarily a barrier to entry.[42]

From these examples it should be clear that even market makers who have been wildly successful at promoting liquidity may capture only a modest portion of the value they have created. Consider the risk to eBay, by far the market leader in the

United States for online consumer auctions: eBay has demonstrated the value of liquidity and already earns a modest profit margin as proof. However, eBay is under attack by a group of "meta–market makers" including Bidder's Edge and AuctionWatch. These companies make a market of markets. Users specify an item at the Bidder's Edge website. Bidder's Edge then searches Amazon, Yahoo!, eBay, and a host of other online auctions, returning a composite of the results. Indeed, eBay takes Bidder's Edge seriously and has sued them, claiming that meta-intermediaries trespass on eBay's intellectual property.[43]

So, will online market makers be profitable? It is too soon to say. We *do* believe that online market makers will radically change the business landscape for all the reasons cited above: increased liquidity, reduced transaction-processing costs, and improved integration of supply-chain partners' business processes. Against these goals, there is still much work left to be done. There were 850 Internet market makers in operation as of this writing, but 97 percent of the payments for transactions completed were still made offline.[44] According to Broadview International, an investment bank, there were over 20 Internet market makers in each key vertical market.[45] Surely not all of these startups will succeed—remember the examples of railroads and car makers—and simple-minded models (e.g., "by exploiting network effects, we will take a 1 percent transaction fee of our $100 billion market") are likely to disappoint investors. Among those that do succeed, it would not be surprising if market makers' key to success was finding clever ways to appropriate more of the value they create—possibly through patents or the creation of technical standards.

GET BIG FAST: A STRATEGIC IMPERATIVE FOR ONLINE MARKET MAKERS?

Many Internet companies have pursued Get Big Fast (GBF) strategies, involving massive upfront investment in customer acquisition. The premise of such strategies is that the early days of the Internet are a "land grab": According to this view, companies will find it easier to stake out wide swaths of empty territory now rather than try to capture that territory later, after it has been settled by others. A competing strategy might be labeled "Get It Right First" (GIRF). When following this strategy, companies grow at a more measured pace, expanding only when sure that the value proposition for customers is sound and that the company can deliver against this value proposition in a high quality manner. This section explores the conditions under which GBF and GIRF strategies make sense for online market makers.

Conditions Supporting a GBF Strategy

Farmers say, "make hay while the sun shines." Amazon's founder, Jeff Bezos, reduced this maxim to Get Big Fast. The comparison is more than superficial. If a company plans to grow faster than its retained earnings, it must secure outside financing. Through early 2000, Internet companies that funded GBF strategies were pushed by a powerful supply-side tailwind: the rapid growth of the venture capital market. Consider that in 1996, U.S.-based venture capitalists (VCs) invested a total of $11.2 billion. During the first three quarters of 2000, U.S.-based VCs invested $80 billion, and their total investment in 2000 is predicted to exceed $100 billion—nearly a tenfold increase since 1996.[46] With so much money available, entrepreneurs were pressured to put it to work and VCs often encouraged the adoption of GBF strategies.

Of course, the capital markets tightened significantly after the sharp correction in technology stocks in April 2000. In the wake of that correction, capital providers were only likely to fund GBF strategies when the following conditions applied:

1. *Markets Exhibit Winner-Take-All Structural Characteristics.* The payoff from the GBF strategy tends to be strongest when network effects are strong, scale economies (beyond network effects) are significant, and customer retention rates are intrinsically high. The extent to which online market makers' businesses meet these requirements is explored below.
2. *The Cost of Customer Acquisition Is Less than the Lifetime Value of Customers.* This condition is straightforward, but it is sometimes difficult to estimate the lifetime value of a customer in a new market, because the dynamics of the market are not yet well understood.
3. *Competitive Risks Are Reasonable.* Assessing this risk is a delicate matter: The history of technology businesses is replete with examples of first movers who were not able to hold their market (e.g., Osborne Computer, Prodigy, VisiCalc, Lotus 123, Apple's GUI OS, Japanese and European developers of analog HDTV technologies). On the one hand, it makes sense to accelerate growth strategies when there is a threat that a competitor may preempt the market. On the other hand (1) if too many competitors simultaneously pursue GBF strategies, the result can be an enormously expensive war of attrition and (2) second movers often can learn from pioneers' mistakes.
4. *Executional Risks Are Manageable.* Simply put, only race when you can go fast but still keep the wheels from flying off your car. In practice, however, it is very hard to grow 100 percent per quarter and still deliver high-quality service. This requires the ability to attract, retain, and train employees at a very rapid rate and to continuously scale information systems and business processes. One of the most impressive aspects of Amazon's performance has been its ability, in the executionally-intensive online retailing business, to maintain high service levels while growing to a $2 billion annual run rate in less than four years.

Conditions Supporting a GIRF Strategy

From the launch of Netscape in 1995 through the Nasdaq meltdown of April 2000, Get Big Fast was the mantra for most Internet companies. In fact, online companies that earned profits were often criticized for sacrificing market share for earnings! Market manias aside, as noted above, there often are solid reasons for pursuing a GBF strategy, but following a Get It Right First strategy may be more appropriate under certain circumstances. GIRF works best in markets with the following attributes:

1. *Protecting Quality Is Imperative.* B2B and B2C market participants tend to diverge on the importance of transaction reliability. For example, B2C market-maker eBay's rapid growth has not been without problems. During 1998, eBay's site crashed and was down for several days because its systems were overloaded. In 1999, eBay was the target of a hacker attack that closed the site for several hours. It turns out that while traders were inconvenienced by its outages, eBay's auctions are not really "mission critical." Despite all these problems, eBay recovered and still holds the dominant share of the online consumer auction business. Contrast eBay's experience to the situation facing many B2B

market participants. Large enterprises have a host of integration issues that must be resolved before they turn over mission-critical aspects of the business to online intermediaries. A suppliers' failure to deliver a single order against a "just-in-time" schedule can shut down an assembly facility. While many Old Economy industrial companies have been criticized by Internet enthusiasts for "not getting it," it takes time to retool complex supply chains.

2. *"Learning By Doing" Is Important.* Building an online marketplace requires major changes in buyer and supplier behavior and inevitably involves trial and error as the market maker adapts its business model in response to customers' evolving needs. Under these conditions, following a GBF strategy may be very expensive: Market participants are initially sold (often at great expense in terms of direct sales activities) on one value proposition, only to be resold on a new plan. A shifting business plan is not likely to inspire customers' trust in a new intermediary, and trust is a market maker's most valuable asset.

This focus on learning by doing raises the question: Should online market makers seek *second-mover* advantage? As noted above, Industry Net failed to exploit its first-mover advantage in building an industrial B2B market and filed for bankruptcy in 1997. VerticalNet, as a second mover, has been able to learn from some of Industry Net's mistakes. While the early bird may get the worm, according to Paul Saffo of the Institute for the Future, it is the second mouse who gets the cheese.[47]

Do Online Market Makers Exhibit Winner-Take-All Structural Characteristics?

Three structural characteristics determine whether a business faces winner-take-all dynamics: strong network effects, significant scale economies (beyond network effects), and intrinsically high customer-retention rates. When these characteristics are present, a company that pulls ahead of its competitors will tend to continue to do so at an accelerating pace as users attract additional users through a network effect and these new users are locked in by factors that promote retention. As the company grows, new users are progressively less expensive to serve due to scale economies. Cost advantages can then be plowed back into features that differentiate the service, reinforcing the growth cycle.

Network Effects. Network effects occur when the adoption of a product or service by a new customer increases the value of that product or service for customers already using it because existing customers now can connect with more parties.[48] The concept of connectivity applies for any network which facilitates point-to-point transactions, e.g., a postal system, a telephone network, or a railroad. To use the classic example, the value of each existing fax machine increases very slightly for its owner upon the sale of every new fax machine because the owner can now reach additional users in the network. In fact, according to what has become known as Metcalfe's law (after Bob Metcalfe, inventor of Ethernet), the value of a network is equal to the number of its users squared; hence, there is an exponential benefit from a linear increase in the size of a network.

Almost by definition, online market makers are subject to very strong network effects. For the sake of convenience, buyers and sellers generally will prefer to transact in a single marketplace, so the leading market maker will tend to pull away from the pack. Network effects are likely to be particularly strong when participation in one network precludes participation in others. This is often the case for sellers auctioning one-of-a-kind items. You cannot post the same item simultaneously on both eBay and Yahoo! Auctions, unless you are willing to withdraw that item from one of the auctions upon successfully selling through the other. With some auctions, this behavior would violate marketplace rules. At a minimum, it could tarnish a party's reputation for trustworthiness—a serious issue when trading partners rate your performance, as they do at eBay. Because network effects are stronger when participation in other markets is precluded, market organizers frequently will try to recruit trading partners who will commit to exclusive arrangements. Some online market makers grant equity to strategic partners (i.e., leading industry participants) to accomplish this objective.

Markets also vary in terms of potential participants' sensitivity to aggregate participation rates. This sensitivity can be expressed through adoption curves, which relate the probability that a typical prospect will join an online marketplace to the percentage of that prospect's existing offline trading partners already active in the marketplace (see Exhibit 2). For some businesses, the presence of just a few partners provides sufficient incentive to participate (i.e., the curve is concave as in Scenario 1 in Exhibit 4); this is most likely to be the case when the switching costs entailed in participating in the new market (e.g., system integration efforts, employee training) are modest. By contrast, when switching costs are high, the adoption curve may be "S"-shaped: After a critical mass of the typical prospect's existing offline trading partners have joined the market, the probability that the prospect also will join increases sharply (see Scenario 2, Exhibit 4). This "S"-shaped adoption pattern is called a "tipping" model, because adoption accelerates ("tips") past the threshold point.[49] Network effects are eventually strong in both Scenario 1 and Scenario 2, but they "kick in" much sooner under Scenario 1.

Differential sensitivities to aggregate participation rates may explain the rapid growth of B2C market makers like eBay and Napster versus the slower growth of B2B market makers like Ventro. The entry costs to a consumer (e.g., a hobbyist collecting Civil War memorabilia) associated with participation in eBay's market are minimal: Items can be listed for a few dollars and no special software, hardware, or training is required to participate in auctions. Even if a collector only finds a few items of interest, it is probably worthwhile for him to bookmark the eBay site and check its listings periodically. So, even with low aggregate participation rates, collectors begin to settle on eBay. Once they do, the network effect accelerates the arrival of others.

Contrast this pattern to the experience of pioneer buyers and suppliers considering whether to participate in a B2B marketplace, for example, in construction supplies procurement. In principle, a contractor may be interested in joining an online marketplace that presents its RFQs to additional distributors; with more bidders, the contractor can expect to realize better prices. But in practice, contractors rely heavily on just a few key distributors; if those suppliers avoid online auctions, the contractor is unlikely to post its RFQs in the online marketplace. In that event, the online market maker may stall, because it fails to reach critical mass.

Besides differing sensitivities to aggregate participation rates, there are other reasons why B2B market makers generally have had less success in exploiting latent network effects compared to their B2C counterparts. Specifically there are three principal reasons why a potential B2B market participant might avoid trading through an online market maker: (1) Participants expect their price realization to suffer when they move online, (2) participants are deterred by the costs associated with the move online, or (3) participants are concerned about the quality risks inherent in conducting mission-critical transactions through a new medium.

Exhibit 6-4

MARKETPLACE ADOPTION PATTERNS

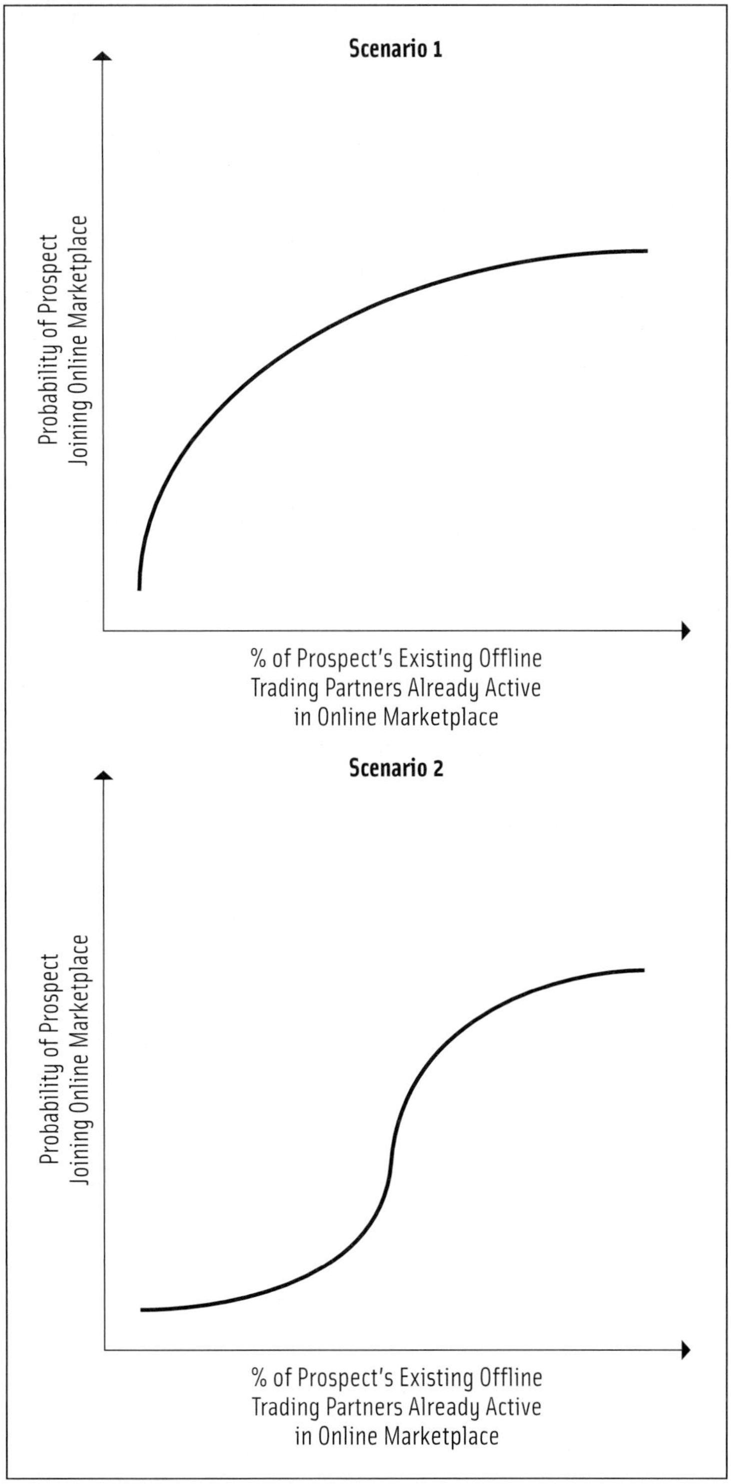

Source: Authors' analysis.

The relative importance of the first two barriers may be explained in part by the manner in which online market makers seek to create value for market participants (i.e., liquidity versus transaction-processing cost savings) and by the transaction types they employ (i.e., auctions versus catalog). B2B market makers that focus on delivering liquidity benefits often employ auctions (or reverse auctions, i.e., RFQ processes). Increased liquidity tends to benefit the party that initiated the auction. Again, with online RFQ processes, one buyer plus more bidders equals lower prices paid by the buyer. Some aggressive suppliers (perhaps those with favorable cost structures or a solid basis for differentiation through superior customer service) may prosper as an online marketplace expands suppliers' reach, but most other suppliers are likely to worry about the impact of increased liquidity on their prices and profitability. Given this concern, unless buyers force their involvement, it may be difficult to secure suppliers' participation in online auctions.

B2B market makers emphasizing transaction-processing cost savings rather than liquidity often offer online catalogs that provide end-to-end visibility into distributors' inventories and provide links into trading partners' accounting systems. This reduces the time required to check on stock availability, place orders, and track order status, and can automate receivables and payables processing. Of course, when an online catalog aggregates multiple suppliers, buyers may realize value through convenient price comparison features, but such value is likely to be of secondary importance. The primary benefit is from cost savings related to the automation of manual transaction processes, and this benefit accrues to *both* buyers and suppliers. When a market maker's principal concern is transaction-processing cost savings, suppliers are *less* likely to be concerned about their price realization and hence are *more* likely to join the market.

When a market maker's principal concern is transaction-processing cost savings, however, both suppliers and buyers may still be deterred by the second barrier to B2B marketplace entry: the costs of moving online. For example, system integration and employee-training costs associated with a move online can be high. Providing the capability to view a distributor's inventory through an online catalog is quite demanding, from a system development perspective. It requires the upfront creation of a database to track products and their specifications. This is important because it allows buyers to undertake parametric searches for equivalent items from different manufacturers. In some industries, a common database is already used by all participants; typically, the online market maker must create a database from scratch. When market makers emphasize liquidity benefits through auction processes, by contrast, market makers do not tend to require such extensive system development efforts: Buyers simply specify their requirements, which market makers forward to the appropriate parties, whose bids are then sent back to the buyer, and so forth. The systems required to manage such a process are not especially complex.

It should be apparent from the analysis above that B2B market makers face very different barriers to adoption whether they emphasize liquidity/auctions or transaction-processing cost savings/catalogs. In each case, however, the barriers to adoption are potentially quite strong. Furthermore, in both cases, these barriers are exacerbated by the personal risks to managers who must make "go/no go" decisions about participation in a marketplace. The customers of B2B online market makers are usually middle-level managers who are buying and selling items critical to their businesses and, on a personal level, their careers: People lose jobs over botched purchasing schemes (remember: "No one ever got fired for buying IBM"). These managers will not jeopardize mission-critical transactions—the third barrier to entry—until they are fully convinced of the benefits of a new online market.

With all of these barriers to adoption, even highly committed companies are finding the going slow. Dell Computer, for example, had planned to register all 1,400 of its suppliers on Ariba's procurement network by April 2000. Twelve months into its project, in November 2000, Dell only had nine of its suppliers fully integrated into its system.[50] In the end, B2B online marketplace adoption is constrained by the understandable risk aversion of managers and the required build-out of the supporting technologies. This leads to fundamentally different adoption patterns for B2B market makers than we see with consumer-focused market-maker rollouts like eBay's or Napster's, where users are already equipped with PCs, Internet access, and Web browsers, and require little else to initiate transactions.[51]

While the constraints related to the need for systems integration and behavioral change are formidable, there is a silver lining: These constraints may eventually lead to favorable economics for market makers who are able to overcome them. In other words, barriers to adoption may become barriers to entry. In the meantime, such challenges make it difficult to execute a GBF strategy in the B2B arena.

Scale Economies. As noted in the previous section, most online market makers exhibit significant scale economies. For a typical B2B market maker recognizing revenue on a net basis, most costs are either purely fixed (e.g., expenses related to site development, trade marketing, and management overhead) or vary with the number of new users signed up (e.g., direct selling expenses, system integration activities)—but not with transaction volume generated by those new users. Furthermore, the cost of acquiring each new user may be expected to decline over time if the market maker successfully harnesses network effects. With the exception of hosting expenses (and, in the case of market makers who recognize revenue on a gross basis, the cost of goods and services sold), few costs incurred by online market makers vary directly with revenues or overall transaction volumes. Thus, in forecasting earnings for SciQuest, a market maker for specialty chemicals, U.S. Bancorp projects that the company will spend a total of $52.2 million on product development, sales and marketing, and general and administrative expenses in 2000, and $65.4 million in 2001—a 25 percent increase. However, SciQuest's revenues are projected to increase four-fold between 2000 and 2001, from $66.4 million to $275.0 million.[52]

Customer Retention. If a site has a high retention rate, then GBF investments in customer acquisition are likely to have a higher payoff. If retention rates are low, then a website becomes a "leaky bucket": Customers are acquired at a high cost, but they leak away and need to be replaced, incurring additional acquisition costs.

Assuming they can attract market participants in the first place, most successful online market makers should experience very high user-retention rates. Network effects tend to lead to lock-in; traders cannot afford to abandon the dominant market maker. Online market makers benefit from other switching costs as well, in particular, users' investments in (1) creating transaction history records (easy accessibility to past orders may expedite the preparation of new orders), (2) training employees to use the market maker's systems, (3) integrating information systems (accounting, inventory management) with the online market maker's systems, and (4) building reliability ratings.

On the last point, eBay's rating system has proved to be a powerful retention tool. Parties to a transaction on eBay rate each other in terms of their performance against expectations (e.g., Were goods shipped on schedule? Was quality consistent with agreed levels? Was payment received on time?). In fragmented markets where transaction partners do not know each other and where brand reputation cannot serve as a proxy for trustworthiness, such rating systems are especially valuable. Once a user accumulates a large number of positive ratings at an online marketplace, the user faces a very large switching barrier: She cannot transfer that strong ranking to a competing marketplace and her lack of a reliability ranking at the new marketplace could reduce prospective partners' willingness to do business.

SUMMARY

As long as the markets reward breadth, exchanges will spend their energies adding new markets, rather than deepening penetration of existing ones. Now, with the stock market's pullback, we will see investors reject more superficial expansion . . . This creates a Darwinian moment during which those firms who can focus fast and hard will gain traction, while those who cling to prior successes will falter. For b-to-b companies, it is time for new metrics—niche market success metrics.

—Geoffrey Moore, The Chasm Group, May 2000[53]

As noted above, online market makers exhibit characteristics that favor pursuit of a Get It Right First strategy. Online market makers have complex business models, which implies an opportunity to "learn by doing," and their customers—especially in the B2B arena—often view reliable execution to be of paramount importance. At the same time, online market makers exhibit structural characteristics that improve the odds of a positive payoff from a Get Big Fast strategy: Online market makers face very strong network effects, very strong scale economies, and intrinsically high customer-retention rates. But companies can only exploit these advantages if they overcome adoption barriers—which are quite strong in many B2B markets—that may discourage market participants from shifting offline trades to online markets. So, how can B2B online market makers rapidly build liquidity (i.e., Get Big Fast) in the face of these adoption barriers? More specifically, what tactics can online market makers employ to attract customers, beyond direct selling and trade advertising?

One obvious tactic is to reduce the cost of marketplace participation by waiving transaction or listing fees or by subsidizing costs associated with system integration. Of course, this is expensive, and it is often hard to raise prices later once introductory prices have been set very low.

A second tactic for building liquidity is to merge with a competitor. With relatively low entry barriers and strong first-mover advantages, most B2B categories have become overcrowded with competitors; in the chemical industry, for example, over 25 online market makers have been launched.[54] Merging is one way to avoid the "racing behavior" and "train wrecks" that can result when several well-funded startups simultaneously pursue the same opportunity. Not surprisingly then, consolidation among Internet market makers is becoming common. Recent examples include[55]

- On October 24, 2000, Cephren and Bidcom, two of the three largest market makers in the construction industry, merged to form Citadon.
- On October 26, 2000, MyAircraft.com and AirNewco announced that they would combine their businesses. MyAircraft.com was formed by United Technologies, Honeywell, BFGoodrich, and i2 Technologies. AirNewco was formed by Air France, American Airlines, British Airways, Continental

Airlines, Delta Air Lines, Iberia Airlines, SAirGroup, United Airlines, United Parcel Service, and Ariba.

- On October 30, 2000, SeafoodAlliance.com and Gofish.com signed a letter of intent to combine their Internet markets.

A third way to rapidly build liquidity is for an online market maker to give a portion of its equity to key market participants in exchange for their commitment to shift transactions to the online market. As mentioned above, Priceline employed this strategy when it granted equity warrants to Delta and other airlines; Ventro did the same through its equity grant to laboratory products distributor VWR.

The transaction volume from new equity partners can serve as a catalyst that can put network effects into motion. On the other hand, a key supplier's or buyer's investment in a marketplace may raise suspicions among other industry participants about the market maker's objectivity: Will the strategic partner have preferential access to information or perhaps a "first crack" at certain transactions? Priceline made such concessions to secure Delta's support as its first major airline partner. At the extreme, the involvement of a major buyer or seller in an online marketplace may encourage its competitors to back another service. One way to avoid this problem is to give equity to several companies simultaneously. Of course, this approach can be highly dilutive.

Fourth, online market makers also can seek to build their user base by skewing their affiliation, without necessarily going as far as giving equity to industry participants. Adopting a strong sell-side affiliation can be an effective way to build liquidity: Suppliers are always interested in selling more products. Internet market makers that adopt a sell-side affiliation need to mitigate the potential for channel conflict (e.g., between manufacturers and their brick-and-mortar distributors) and must find ways to reduce the emphasis on sellers' prices. VerticalNet seeks to accomplish this by providing storefronts (i.e., display ads) where suppliers can explain their points of differentiation beyond price.

Buy-side affiliation can also be a viable model for building liquidity. Ariba, for instance, sells a software platform to corporations to facilitate online procurement. In addition to selling the software and related services, Ariba takes an equity position, whenever it can, if the resulting online unit is established as a stand-alone company. As explained previously, Ariba also offers customers the ability to link with online purchasing units that Ariba has built for other corporations; in this manner, Ariba builds liquidity and will gradually evolve into a buy-side affiliated online market maker.

In some industries, major buyers and suppliers resist the idea of dealing with new intermediaries on principle. By 1999, like their counterparts in brick-and-mortar retailing, many industrial companies had became reluctant to surrender the value created by the Internet to start-ups. As GE executive Jay Pomeroy succinctly put it, "Our policy is not to put anyone between us and our customer."[56] Skewing affiliation to build critical mass is unlikely to be a successful tactic for pure-play online market makers facing such opposition. This "avoid new middlemen" mentality is behind many of the industry consortia that emerged during 2000 to establish jointly-owned online market makers. Covisint and MyAircraft.com are examples of industry consortia for the automotive and commercial aircraft industries, respectively. As noted previously, such consortia are controversial from an antitrust perspective. It may also be difficult for industry competitors to overcome years of rivalry and to learn to work together in order to build an Internet market maker. Finally, industry suppliers may avoid participating in an online marketplace where the rules of engagement are set by buyers, and vice versa. While it is too soon to tell if these industry consortia will get off the ground, the aggregate purchasing power of their combined owners will ensure that these market makers enjoy instant liquidity if they succeed.

ENDNOTES

[1]Carl Shapiro and Hal R. Varian, *Information Rules* (Boston, MA: Harvard Business School Press, 1999), pp. 21–22.

[2]MP3 is a standard for compressing music into digital files, which facilitates their transmission over the Internet.

[3]Nate Sleeper, *The New York Stock Exchange: Taking Stock of a Changing Landscape*, Harvard Business School course project, May 2000, p. 2.

[4]*Encyclopedia Britannica*, Volume 28, p. 767.

[5]There are a number of newly coined terms, some of which are quite colorful, used to describe what we call market makers: fat butterfly markets, paradigm violators, vortex markets, and dynamic pricing infomediaries, just to name a few. Critics of our use of the term *market maker* will note that in the financial services industry, the term is specifically reserved for broker-dealers on a securities exchange who maintain market stability and who, trading for their own accounts, profit from bid/ask spreads. See endnote 28 for a discussion of whether these broker-dealers would be classified as market makers based on the definitions proposed in this chapter.

[6]John Hagel, McKinsey & Company, as quoted in *The Economist,* "The Net Imperative: The Rise of the Infomediary," June 26, 1999, p. 23.

[7]Nate Sleeper, *The New York Stock Exchange: Taking Stock of a Changing Landscape*, Harvard Business School course project, May 2000, p. 2.

[8]According to www.techencylopedia.com, Electronic Data Interchange (EDI) is a system for the electronic exchange of documents between businesses, e.g., orders, confirmations, and invoices. EDI is based on standards developed by the American National Standard Institute (ASC X12) and a United Nations Commission (EDI for Administration and Commerce). Superficially, EDI looks like Internet e-commerce; however, unlike Internet communications, EDI runs across private data networks and is inherently point-to-point. The implications of these two differences are profound. First, because EDI runs across dedicated telecommunications lines, its bandwidth expense is much higher than Internet packet-switched communications, where several users can share the same line. Second, the architecture of EDI is not as flexible as HTML/XML based systems. Third, EDI was designed almost exclusively for point-to-point communication, thus, multi-party online collaboration via EDI is not practical. On the other hand, EDI offers a high level of security and is extremely efficient at communicating high volumes of pre-defined documents between two parties. Based on interviews with Stuart Sawanbini, President, Eventra, the cost to integrate EDI with existing large company enterprise software systems typically falls between $750,000 and $1 million. Small company EDI installations cost about $10,000. These costs are similar to the cost of integrating an XML-based Internet system. As a result of its cost and lack of flexibility, EDI has been primarily used in applications to connect large companies (often retailers and auto companies) with their tier-one suppliers to coordinate direct purchases.

[9]Mohanbir Sawhney and Steven Kaplan, "Let's Get Vertical," *Business 2.0*, September 1999, p. 8.

[10]Internet market makers have the potential to consolidate purchasing power into a single unit called a monopsony. The Federal Trade Commission and the Bundeskartellamt (the German government's antitrust agency) reviewed Covisint to determine its monopsony potential.

[11]Mark Walsh, Chairman, VerticalNet, in a speech delivered to the New York Venture Forum, October 2, 2000.

[12]Das Narayandas, "VerticalNet (www.verticalnet.com)," HBS Case no. 500-041, November 2, 1999, p.4.

[13]Philip Evans and Thomas S. Wurster, *Blown to Bits* (Boston, MA: Harvard Business School Press, 1999).

[14]Scot Ethrens and Peter Zapf, "The Internet Business-to-Business Report," Bear Stearns Equity Research, September 1999, p.130.

[15]Charles Phillips and Mary Meeker, *The Internet B2B Report*, Morgan Stanley Dean Witter Equity Research, April 2000.

[16]Thomas Eisenmann and Jon K. Rust, "Priceline WebHouse Club," section 6, *Internet Business Models: Text and Cases*, or HBS Case no. 800-287, August 1, 2000.

[17]Scott Ethrens and Peter Zapf, "The Internet Business-to-Business Report," Bear Stearns, September 1999, p. 155.

[18]Ibid p. 22.

[19]Bill Cafiero, GEIS, *Electronic Commerce Bootcamp Seminar*, produced by the New England EDI Users' Group, October 21, 1999.

[20]Charles Phillips and Mary Meeker, "The Internet B2B Report," Morgan Stanley Dean Witter Equity Research, April 2000, p. 95.

[21]Pam Woodall, "Untangling e-conomics," *The Economist*, (September 23, 2000): p. 11.

[22]Bill Cafiero, GEIS, "Electronic Commerce Boot-Camp Seminar," produced by the New England EDI Users' Group, October 21, 1999.

[23]Charles Phillips and Mary Meeker, "The Internet B2B Report," Morgan Stanley Dean Witter Equity Research, April 2000, p. 31.

[24]Darnell Little, "Let's Keep This Exchange to Ourselves," *BusinessWeek,* December 4, 2000, p. 48, citing data from eMarketer, Inc.

[25]Charles Phillips and Mary Meeker, "The Internet B2B Report," Morgan Stanley Dean Witter Equity Research, April 2000, p. 95.

[26]Paul Bell, Dell Computer Operations Manager Europe, Middle East and Africa, as quoted in , "E-Management Survey," *The Economist* (November 11, 2000): 9.

[27]Mohanbir Sawhney and Steven Kaplan, "Let's Get Vertical," *Business 2.0*, September 1999, p. 92.

[28]In financial markets, some broker-dealers (who are also referred to as "market makers") trade as principals for their own account, i.e., they hold securities, speculating that they will be able to resell them and earn a positive spread. By our definitions, we would define these broker-dealers as market makers only if their central purpose is to organize a market (with trading for their own account being a byproduct activity). However, this test does not hold for most securities broker-dealers because earning trading profits is their central purpose and because market organization functions (providing a place to trade, rules for exchange, and infrastructure) are provided by established market makers such as NYSE and Nasdaq.

[29]NYSE Annual Report, 1999.

[30]DoubleClick's 10-K, 1999.

[31]Charles Phillips and Mary Meeker, *The Internet B2B Report*, Morgan Stanley Dean Witter Equity Research, April 2000, p. 351.

[32]George Anders, "The Auctioneer," *Wall Street Journal* (November 22, 1999): R69 interviews eBay CEO Meg Whitman, who says that eBay's fees average 5 percent to 6 percent of the value of items auctioned through the site.

[33]Sotheby's SEC filings and NYSE annual report, available on the Exchange's website.

[34]While Priceline's modest spending on advertising as a percentage of revenue may appear impressive, it is worth noting that the company reports revenue on a gross basis. On a net basis, Priceline spent 31 percent of revenue on advertising. Also, Priceline charged $1 billion in 1999 to Other Costs related to the amortization of warrants which were given to airlines in exchange for the airlines participating in their market—more than twice its gross revenue! These expenses might reasonably be considered marketing costs, since they served to build marketplace liquidity.

[35]According to Lisa Guernsey, "The Powers Behind the Auctions," *The New York Times* (August 20, 2000): section 3, p. 11, 10 percent of eBay's sellers account for 80 percent of its sales.

[36]George Anders, "The Auctioneer," *Wall Street Journal* (November 22, 1999): R69 quoting eBay CEO Meg Whitman, who says in addition that roughly one-half of eBay's new customers are acquired through word-of-mouth referrals from existing customers. New eBay users who are also AOL subscribers, for example, tell on average seven friends, co-workers, or family members about their eBay experience.

[37]Ventro 10-K, 1999.

[38]Casewriter interview with Peter Wells, Senior Vice President, Marshall & Swift.

[39]Of course, as the economist John Maynard Keynes observed, in the long run we are all dead.

[40]Pam Woodall, "Untangling e-conomics," *The Economist*, (September 23, 2000): 19.

[41]Pam Woodall, "Untangling e-conomics," *The Economist*, (September 23, 2000): 19.

[42]Nate Sleeper, *The New York Stock Exchange: Taking Stock of a Changing Landscape*, Harvard Business School course project, May 2000.

[43]eBay 10-K, 1999.

[44]David Pecaut, President iFormation Group, in a speech delivered to the conference *Managing and Growing on the Internet*, November 6, 2000.

[45]"eBusiness Perspective," Broadview International LLC, October 2000, p. 21.

[46]*Venture Economics News*, November 3, 2000.

[47]Quoted in "Untangling e-conomics," *The Economist* (September 23, 2000): 34.

[48]See Carl Shapiro and Hal R. Varian, *Information Rules* (Boston, MA: Harvard Business School Press, 1999), pp. 173–225 and Philip Evans and Thomas S. Wurster, *Blown to Bits* (Boston, MA: Harvard Business School Press, 1999) pp. 112–113.

[49]Malcolm Gladwell, *The Tipping Point: How Little Things Can Make A Big Difference* (Little Brown & Company, Feb. 2000).

[50]Alorie Gilbert, "E-Procurement: Problems Behind the Promise," *InformationWeek.com*, (November 20, 2000): 56.

[51]Philip Lay, *Under The Buzz*, November, 2000, Website published by The Chasm Group LLC.

[52]Jon M. Ekoniak, "SciQuest.com, Inc.," U.S. Bancorp: Equity Research Notes, February 14, 2000.

[53]Geoffrey Moore, "Approaching the Chasm," *Industry Standard,* May 15, 2000: p. 88.

[54]Spencer Ante, "Why B2B is a Scary Place to Be," *BusinessWeek,* September 11, 2000: p. 34.

[55]Audrey Manring, "Net Markets Gather B-To-B Momentum," *InformationWeek.com,* (November 20, 2000): 80.

[56]Julia Angwin, "Many Internet Users Find Themselves Stuck At Their Old Addresses" *Wall Street Journal*, April 7, 2000: 1.

PRICELINE WEBHOUSE CLUB

We are a theory-driven business. We think about things first and then execute them, as opposed to most Internet businesses that really just execute, execute, execute. They are all about first-mover advantage. Generally, we couldn't care less about that. We are about best *mover advantage. We actually spent three years in a laboratory talking theory before we started thinking about execution. We believe in getting big fast. But I would argue, get* smart *fast. Get big thereafter.*

—Jay Walker, Founder, Priceline

As Internet brands flooded America's consciousness in 1999, a handful stood out from the crowd, easily recognizable and unique. Priceline was one. Thanks in part to spokesperson William Shatner, who played Captain Kirk in *Star Trek*—one of American popular culture's defining TV programs—Priceline had pierced the Internet hubbub with an idea that took it where no Internet company had gone before. Simply, Priceline empowered consumers to "name their own price" for airline tickets, hotel rooms, and other products and services; then it shopped these offers to marketers.[1] Priceline's founder Jay Walker described the resulting transactions as a new ecosystem, which helped consumers realize lower prices while allowing marketers to turn excess inventory into profit—and, in doing so, price discriminate without damaging their brands or their published prices. Walker explained:

> We address the excess capacity of the entire airline industry. With our help, airlines can fill every plane at a higher profit level than if they hadn't sold every seat—and still maintain the integrity of their pricing systems. That's a big accomplishment since the airlines have an average capacity utilization of only 65%. Now, how many airline industry analysts know that's what Priceline does? None. In fact, some of them think, "Ah well, the airlines will eventually do this themselves." But the airlines *can't* do it themselves. They can't publicly advertise or accept lower prices without affecting their retail fare structure. The airlines need a shield. That's Priceline.

Walker explained that Priceline provided a shield to the airlines in two ways. First, because the buyer could select only a specific city-pair—and could not specify a particular airline or travel time—the seller's brand and product configuration were protected. Only after the guaranteed bid was accepted did the buyer learn the airline's identity and flight times. Second, Priceline protected airlines from having to advertise fares lower than their published prices. This helped them avoid free riders—people who benefit from a discounted price even though they would have been willing to pay a higher price.

On January 1, 2000, less than two years after its April 1998 launch, Priceline accounted for more than 3% of all leisure airline tickets sold in the United States. All eight major full-service U.S. airlines participated in the enterprise, as well as 20 international carriers. It had 3.8 million unique customers, with nearly half registering during the last six months of 1999. According to marketing surveys, 94% of these customers were satisfied with the Priceline experience and said they would use the company again. Revenues for 1999 were $482 million; projected revenues for 2000 were $1 billion. While the company was not yet profitable, gross margins were 14.2% and climbing, and operating margins were trending steadily towards the black. Meanwhile, Jay Walker's 49% share of Priceline—via direct and indirect stock ownership—was worth $4.4 billion and had been valued as high as $9 billion during a September 1999 run-up of Internet stocks.

Dean's Research Fellow Jon K. Rust prepared this case under the supervision of Professor Thomas Eisenmann as the basis for class discussion rather than to illustrate either effective or ineffective handling of an administrative situation.

[1]In other words, Priceline collected demand at an entirely new range of price points, and then presented this new consumer demand to providers who previously had no way of identifying unserved sectors of their markets. "In effect," said Walker, "Priceline makes visible what had been invisible to them."

Priceline's Business Model

In the air travel business, Priceline generated revenue in two ways. First, it retained the spread between a consumer's bid and the lowest fare offered to Priceline by an airline partner. This lowest fare, which constantly changed based on airline computer decisioning, was "unpublished": it was visible to Priceline, but not to the consumer. Likewise, the consumer's bid was unpublished: Priceline did not reveal the bid to its airline partners. Rather, Priceline functioned as a market maker that compared bid and ask prices, determined if a sale was possible, then acquired the product at the seller's ask price and resold it to the consumer at the consumer's bid price. For example, if a consumer was willing to pay $100 for a ticket from Boston to St. Louis, and one of Priceline's partners was willing to sell a ticket (with no more than one stop in between) for $70, Priceline would retain the $30 spread.

Second, Priceline offered consumers the opportunity to increase the value of their bids by participating in "adaptive marketing" and "cross-subsidy" promotional programs. For example, when a consumer bidding for an airline ticket concurrently signed up for a new credit card, Priceline might add $20 to the consumer's $100 bid (at no extra cost to the consumer), increasing the odds that a match would be found with an airline. Meanwhile, credit card companies would pay Priceline roughly $50–$75 for each new credit card customer. If an airline's lowest acceptable fare was below the customer's $100 bid, Priceline not only pocketed the spread, it also kept all of the sponsorship revenue from the credit card company. If the lowest possible fare was between $100 and $120, Priceline used a portion of the credit card sponsorship revenue to subsidize the consumer's bid. If the bid, even after subsidization, was below all participating airlines' unpublished fares, Priceline still retained the adaptive marketing revenue, even though it didn't sell a ticket.[2]

Supporting Priceline's business model were a series of patents that barred the door to direct competitors. While critics described these patents as barbed wire fences on the Internet free range, in fact, most of Priceline's patents were related to specific software and business methods and not to broad business models. For example, the key patents protecting Priceline revolved around a "demand collection system," which took credit card numbers from consumers—thus guaranteeing payment to prospective sellers of goods and services if bids were accepted—and then shopped that demand to interested sellers. Said Walker:

> We spent years thinking about the Internet and about what's going to happen and why. For example, we had recognized that English and Dutch auctions would be large on the Internet.[3] We couldn't own them, because the idea of an auction itself wasn't patentable. But once auctions become large, they can collapse under their own weight. We invented and patented specific solutions for how you fix an auction once it breaks down, which will happen for many reasons, most notably because they are consumer unfriendly.

Licensing such patents would provide one future revenue stream for Priceline's affiliated company, Walker Digital, the intellectual property laboratory that invented Priceline. Jay Walker, chairman of Walker Digital, also saw an opportunity to own or influence huge markets directly. Airline tickets and hotel reservations were only the starting point. Walker believed that his "demand collection system" could eventually cover broad categories across the entire GNP, and by the end of 1999, he had extended Priceline into the mortgage, new car sales, and car rental businesses. In November, he launched Priceline WebHouse Club to bring the "name-your-price" concept to groceries, with plans to eventually scale WebHouse to include almost every type of retailing. Walker said: "If we drive you to a retail store, that's an opportunity for WebHouse. Non-retail sales are the province of Priceline. The central WebHouse idea is to use the Internet to allow consumers to reduce prices in local retail stores *before* they go shopping."

[2]Priceline actually placed a portion of adaptive marketing revenues into a "hidden account" for the customer as part of its customer retention program. For example, if a credit card company paid Priceline $50 for a new credit card registration, Priceline might apply $20 against the customer's immediate bid (which might or might not be used to subsidize the bid, depending on the best price available from airline partners), while placing another $20 into the "hidden account." As the same customer made future bids, funds in this hidden account could be used to bridge any gap between the customer's bid and a partner's lowest acceptable offer. Thus, even Priceline customers who made only lowball bids might periodically score a ticket if they had participated in enough adaptive marketing offers. Also, with new customers, Priceline sometimes directly subsidized bids that fell short within a certain range, thus incurring a negative spread, in order to complete a transaction and thereby strengthen the relationship with a new customer.

[3]In an English auction, a seller places a unique item on sale, and publishes a reserve price below which the item will not be sold. The auction is timed, and the highest bidder at the end of the auction wins the item at their bid price. Dutch auctions may involve multiple identical items, with winners all paying the same amount as the lowest winning bid.

WebHouse

A fixed price is always the wrong *price. Always. It's either too high or too low for everybody. We engage in price discovery based on elasticity in advance of the purchase process.*

—Jay Walker

WebHouse was established as a separate company with Jonathan Otto, former owner of Rockbottom Stores, Inc., as CEO; Jose Suarez as general manager; and its own board of directors. It licensed Priceline's "name-your-price" business method, affiliated trademarks, technologies, and software systems. In exchange, Priceline received royalties from WebHouse, as well as warrants to acquire a majority stake in the company upon certain triggers. Investors such as Vulcan Ventures (the investment organization of Microsoft founder Paul Allen), Wit Capital's Arista Fund, Walker Digital Capital, and Goldman Sachs provided $65 million in first-round financing. Access to the site was through priceline.com's home page.

The idea behind WebHouse was to use the Internet to deliver prices rather than products, leveraging existing consumer shopping patterns and the U.S. retailing and distribution infrastructure already in place. Driving this idea was the theory that cost savings—not convenience, not service, not brand—was the main factor motivating the vast majority of American shopping decisions. The first product category for WebHouse was groceries. Said Walker:

> The problem with these online grocery stores—like Webvan and Streamline—is that they were thinking about execution, not theory. That is an error. The theory says, "Don't deliver." Right off the bat, these online companies are taking costs that are traditionally absorbed by the consumer—fuel, labor and automobile depreciation—and they are converting them into commercial costs. Moreover, there are no real scale economies with fuel, labor or depreciation.
>
> You can say, "Okay, what I am really going to do is sell the customer back his own time because there is a mega-trend that says people have less time than ever before." That ultimately is a niche idea. No marketer believes the notion that a giant company can be built around the proposition of selling time back to a consumer. 7–11 may be the most convenient store in America, but it's not one of the biggest, and for a good reason. *Wal-Mart* is the biggest store and they may be the *least* convenient. They are located on the outside of town, which can be a pain in the neck.
>
> So, the problem with the online grocers is that they are not theory driven. They never step back and say, "Here is the theory: I am going to sell customers their own time back for $10 an hour." Now, you have no evidence anywhere that there is a mass market for buying time back at $10 an hour. There might be a carriage trade of 2% of the market at $10 an hour. But you'll say, "2% of the $450 billion grocery industry—that's $9 billion. Can't that support a giant company?" At first glance, yes. But wait a second. What is the infrastructure cost going to look like to support a $9 billion low margin business? And you'll say, "Oh, it's not low margin, low margin derives from brick and mortar." Well, the last time I checked, fancy automated warehouses were brick and mortar. These businesses don't conceptualize the main issues because most of them were created by engineers who are consumed with re-engineering the wrong problem.

WebHouse launched November 1, 1999 in New York City with more than 600 participating supermarkets and grocery stores. Within a week, it had attracted 15,000 members, who priced more than 188,000 grocery items. By Christmas, more than 100,000 members were pricing an average of 500,000 grocery items a week, making groceries the top selling item on the Internet in New York City. By February, the site exceeded 200,000 members—or 3% of all households in the New York area—and was selling 8,000 grocery items per hour, seven days a week, or 150,000 grocery items each day.

Media reviews were generally glowing; *The New York Times*' On-Line Shopper columnist called it "my best online shopping experience" (see Exhibit 1).[4] And word-of-mouth was rampant. By February 2000, WebHouse had extended its service area to cover more than 1,200 supermarkets and grocery stores in Philadelphia, Washington and Baltimore, as well as parts of New Jersey and Connecticut. Stephen Mott, president of WebHouse and a 1979 MBA graduate of the Harvard Business School, pointed out: "In cities where WebHouse is available, traffic on the priceline.com site is 28% higher and airline ticket offers triple the rate of markets in which WebHouse has not been launched yet." Despite rapid growth, over 80% of all WebHouse sales were already made to repeat customers, and members indicated they planned to use the service, on average, 45 times a year, said Mott.

---

[4]Michelle Slatella, "Online Shopper: To Boldly Go to the Supermarket with Captain Kirk," *The New York Times*, January 6, 2000.

Revenue Model

The revenue model for WebHouse included adaptive marketing opportunities but not spread income. Unlike the airline segment, it did include transaction fees paid by the manufacturer and a monthly $3 transaction processing fee (after the first 90 days) paid by the customer.[5] Walker said:

> Initially, we are charging the manufacturer nothing in order to get things going. But we've told them that we're planning on their support in return for measurable, incremental sales. We believe that ultimately manufacturers will pay us 15 cents a unit or a 5–10% transaction fee if we sell their goods to the customer at the price named by the customer. You can't do spreads for most grocery items, because the manufacturers see WebHouse as an administrator in a system that sells products to a brand-flexible customer. Manufacturers don't mind giving savings to the customer if it leads to a product sale; they're already doing that with newspaper coupons. But they won't allow us to take more money in the transaction than they believe we're worth as an administrator, because in their eyes, it's the discount making the sale, not WebHouse. In the case of airlines, they don't need tight control, because all they care about is filling as much of their fixed capacity as possible. They just want to know what revenue they're getting.
>
> The real money for WebHouse, though, comes from our adaptive marketing sponsors—the AT&Ts, Citibanks and MCIs—who are paying us to persuade our customers to try their products and services.

To use the site, customers registered with a credit card number and received a debit card from WebHouse, which was mailed to them. Members then "named their price" for products in over 175 categories, representing more than 700 product brands, by selecting at least two acceptable brands in whichever product categories they desired (see Exhibit 2). The lower the price they indicated, the lower the chance of having their offer selected. A portion of the adaptive marketing revenues generated by a customer—maintained in a "house account" that was managed at the customer's discretion—could be used to improve the odds.[6] After all selections had been made, the member reviewed her shopping cart, submitted her offers, and learned which products she had "won."[7] Her credit card was immediately billed for these items with savings averaging $13 on a typical shopping trip expenditure of $35. After the customer used her computer to print out a shopping list, which included a bar code, the customer took the printout to her participating grocery store of choice and picked up the items. At checkout, the WebHouse products were separated from any non-WebHouse products and the grocer debited the customer's WebHouse Club membership card for the full amount that the customer otherwise would have paid for the products without using WebHouse. If, by chance, a customer found a product priced cheaper at the grocery store than it had cost on WebHouse, the difference was rebated to the member's "house account" by Priceline.[8] "That virtually never happens," said Jonathan Otto, CEO of WebHouse. "Prices named by the consumer are always the lowest." Meanwhile, WebHouse covered the gap between the lower price paid by the customer and the price it remitted to the grocery store by a combination of revenue streams, including payments from sponsors and manufacturers. (See Exhibit 3 for WebHouse money flow.)

While Walker rejected any comparison to grocery couponing, the pervasiveness of that marketing practice highlighted the opportunity for WebHouse. In 1998, more than 249 billion coupons were distributed to American consumers, primarily through glossy "free-standing inserts" in Sunday newspapers.[9] According to industry surveys, 97% of all households used coupons in a given month with the greatest use being by middle- and high-income groups, those with higher educational levels, and those who were urban, less brand loyal, and less store loyal.[10] Nearly one-half (46%) of consumers used three to seven coupons weekly.[11] The average face value of grocery product coupons distributed in 1998 was 63.5 cents; health and beauty was 82.7 cents.[12] In 1998, consumers redeemed 4.8 billion coupons, saving $3.6 billion.

---

[5]WebHouse charged the $3 fee only in months when the service was used.

[6]As with Priceline, WebHouse also administered a "hidden account" for the customer, and sometimes directly subsidized first-time customers.

[7]The WebHouse site was designed to look like a slot machine. This design, as well as other features of the site's organization, were created with game theory in mind.

[8]To receive payment, the member was responsible for initiating a rebate process with WebHouse. It was not automatic.

[9]According to the Food Market Institute, 0.004 percent were delivered over the Internet.

[10]David Loudon and Albert J. Della Bitta, *Consumer Behavior: Concepts and Applications,* McGraw Hill, pp. 556–557.

[11]"New Survey Details Promotional Practices," *Chain Store Age,* Nov. 1998.

[12]"Worldwide Coupon Distribution and Redemption Trends," NCH NuWorld Marketing Limited, 1999.

There were various ways to structure coupon discounts. The most prevalent method was for manufacturers to advertise directly to consumers, who would use the coupons to attain immediate discounts while buying a particular product. Retailers would collect the coupons at the point of sale and remit to the manufacturer—or a third-party collection agency—for reimbursement. Manufacturers would pay a handling fee to the retailer—and the collection agency if one were used—which often surpassed the face value of the coupon.[13] In addition to marketing directly to consumers, manufacturers also provided "trade allowances" to retailers to encourage them to coupon or temporarily lower prices locally. In 1999, such trade allowances led to retail price discounts of 14.4% in laundry detergent, 13% in paper towels, 12% in bathroom tissue and 9% in diapers.[14] Crain Communications reported that in one three-week period in early 2000, for instance, major retailers such as Target Stores, Kmart Corp., Kroger Co., Eckard Drug Co., CVS Pharmacy and Winn-Dixie Stores advertised Tide laundry detergent as much as 40 percent below the regular price at some of those chains, and 15% lower than the everyday low price at mass merchandisers such as Wal Mart Stores.[15] Because direct manufacturer control of absolute price in a retail establishment was forbidden under the Sherman Act, however, manufacturers could not be guaranteed that trade allowances to retailers would actually be passed onto consumers in price savings.

Strategic Issues Facing WebHouse

The theory of our business is that we are the first pricing system in history that allows the buyer to trade brand flexibility for savings, and allows the seller to price discriminate based on the customer's willingness to trade off brands or sellers.

—Jay Walker

Several pressing issues confronted the WebHouse management team at the end of 1999. First, the company had yet to close a deal with any major brand manufacturer. Thus, to satisfy customers, WebHouse subsidized member savings out of its own coffers, leading to negative margins.[16] Second, this subsidization and the early consumer success led to significant losses and cash burn. To continue its customer acquisition, Walker projected that \$200–\$500 million in additional capital would be necessary. Meanwhile, the company confronted questions about where and how quickly it should expand.

According to Randy Christofferson, President and CEO of Walker Digital Corporation, former CEO of FirstUSA (a leading credit card provider), and a 1983 MBA graduate of the Harvard Business School, Walker was a brilliant innovator and marketer, but he wasn't the strongest process manager. Christofferson said:

> Jay is one of the most creative people I have ever met. He's also probably the best marketer I've ever met. I've been in consumer marketing for twenty years, and we spent a billion and a half dollars in consumer marketing in my previous company, but we didn't have anyone that could come anywhere close to matching his marketing skills. Not only has he created a fundamentally new pricing system—the first one in a thousand years—he also writes the tag lines for Shatner. It's an unbelievable mix of stuff. But managing a company with a lot of processes is not his strength. He's an entrepreneur.

Walker readily agreed, admitting that what he enjoyed was focusing on the next big idea. He said:

> I don't run the business. I don't run Priceline. I don't want to run Priceline. I don't imagine I would be particularly good at it, so that's why I hire the best people out there. I give my point of view, but these are powerful executives. They listen to my point of view and they weigh it and they decide whether or not they want to follow my suggestions. If not, no problem. We're looking for the right answer, not whose answer it is.

The casewriters visited Jay Walker and his management team in December 1999 to learn more about the strategic issues facing WebHouse. We explained to our hosts that a good business school case study posed one or more "trigger issues" that were currently confronting a company, encouraging students to put themselves into management's shoes. Walker paused for just a moment, then said, "Okay, let me give you a half dozen trigger

[13]Fraudulent redemption of coupons by retailers (or their employees) represented a narrow, although expensive, problem for manufacturers.
[14]Crains Communications, April 3, 2000.
[15]Ibid.

[16]The negative margins were anticipated by Priceline management, who understood the costs as part of customer acquisition and the ramping up of a start-up.

issues." He spoke, virtually uninterrupted, for over an hour as our tape recorder rolled.

We recognize that it is unusual to provide students with a long, unfiltered transcript in a case study, but we also believe that Jay Walker is an unusual entrepreneur, and there is much to be learned from hearing him explain his ideas in his own words. Hence, what follows are direct quotes from our conversation with Walker. In bold are the fundamental issues he posed; the rest of each section provides context he offered regarding each issue.

Priorities for Expansion

What are the priorities for WebHouse Club expansion? Should we first expand groceries as fully as possible, rolling out nationally to prove what we already know in New York, and remove any question that the concept is broadly applicable? Or should we diversify as rapidly as possible into other retailing categories, specifically, health and beauty aids, gasoline, and general merchandise? The question is, If you were the CEO, how would you allocate the firm's limited resources?

> Everything else we have done with Priceline was launched nationally except for cars. Air travel is inherently national in scope. And we knew we had to get airline tickets working before we diversified. But with WebHouse there are a lot of pacing issues. There are issues regarding management bandwidth, system development, and promotional budget allocation. There are capital cost implications—which strategy is better for raising money?—because you are going to need a lot of money for any strategy you pursue. Which will return the cost of capital faster?
>
> There are manufacturer issues, as well. By expanding geographically, the manufacturer gains scale fast in one category. But by expanding the product line, you get more leverage over individual manufacturers, and your offer for consumers is more complete.

Cross Subsidies vs. Manufacturers' Support

Another contentious issue is what percentage of the company's revenue should be derived from adaptive marketing programs versus manufacturers' support? Emphasize the adaptive marketing sponsors and WebHouse starts to look like a promotion-driven business. Emphasize the manufacturers and it looks like an efficiency-driven business. Is one better than the other?

> If it's sponsor-oriented, you tell the customer: "The reason we can save you this much money is that you are doing all kinds of neat and fun and interesting things with our sponsors, and you are benefiting by receiving price savings on your groceries." You explain that if they don't care who delivers their fuel oil, tunes their car or does their dry cleaning, they might be able to get $20 more in free grocery money. Basically, you create the type of sub-market that frequent flyer programs have evolved into.
>
> Or do you say to the customer, "Look, sponsors are just one piece of what we do here. Manufacturers contribute a lot, and you don't have to take sponsor offers to make this work." It is a very different positioning.

Level Playing Field vs. Preferential Treatment for Certain Partners

The third question is should the business strive to be a utility, so that all partners play on a level playing field, or should it sell preferences to specific partners in return for faster, deeper commitments and commissions? And if it makes sense to enter into a category-specific preference deal, under what terms should we do so?

> For example, if a packaged goods company came and said, "I will give you $5 million now, but I want you to always fill with my brand of ketchup for the next three years," do you want to do that? Remember, our customers don't care exclusively about the brand, so, the customer isn't badly served by this deal. Customers have already told you they don't mind if you fill with Hefty trash containers every time. They like Hefty Bags. But what if after Hefty came to you and said, "I want to pay you a fee, and I want to be the preferred trash bag provider at WebHouse," Glad Bag told you they were never going to participate? Would you do it then?
>
> In the airline market, preferences were absolutely necessary to launch. But it was also absolutely necessary to remove such preferences if we were to grow. That's why we gave Delta Airlines, our first major airline partner, $1 billion in warrants to remove certain veto rights that we had originally agreed to. But in the grocery market, you don't need the same kind of level

playing field. You can collect a lot of fees by just finding one preferred provider in each category, and your P&L looks much, much better. Then each year, manufacturers can bid to become the preferred provider. It is sort of like the Olympics, where the U.S. Olympic Committee accepts only one sponsor for each advertising category.

In the long term, however, you have to build a business that will survive. One has to think about the integrity of the system. If you implement preferences, what is the excluded partner to do? Imagine that it seeks to enable a competitor. What then? Should you have paid attention to this risk? How does your patent protection start to filter into the game? How about your marketing clout? Your brands? For example, AOL sells preferences. Their business is built on it. One could argue that selling preferences has been a great model for AOL. But one could also argue that this turned out to be pretty good for Yahoo!, too; someone who is not the preferred provider on AOL suddenly says, "I have to find another portal."

Capital Markets

Given that the WebHouse Club will need to raise $200 to $500 million for customer acquisition and ongoing expansion, would priceline.com be better off exercising its warrants and bringing the privately-held WebHouse fully into publicly-traded Priceline? Or would it be better off going to the outside capital markets with a separate initial public offering where Priceline would own a percentage of a new publicly-traded company?

If WebHouse goes public, you get two shareholder bases that share a common customer story; sort of like the Coca-Cola and Coca-Cola Enterprises, which owns local bottling companies. They have different shareholder bases, so their interests are not perfectly aligned. Enterprises wants, of course, to get the lowest costs from Coca-Cola, while Coca-Cola wants to have the highest costs. Yet they both try to build the Coca-Cola brand and achieve success in the market.

To make this decision, you have to understand the overall strategy for priceline.com, and you have to try to gauge how much value might be created through a public offering versus funneling capital into the licensee, Priceline, from the licensor, WebHouse.

Priceline doesn't have enough capital at the moment to finance the customer acquisition program, but it obviously could raise the required amounts. But if you exercise the warrants, how does that affect Priceline's investor story? Currently, we have a company that has been steadily growing toward profitability: we should be profitable in 2001 or sooner. This is a pretty good story; an Internet company that will be profitable, fast, with huge revenues.

Now, if you didn't go public and instead you financed customer acquisition from Priceline, your story changes. It's still a good story, but it's different. You would say, "Look, here are the results of our work. We have spent this much money acquiring WebHouse customers." Basically, you turn into a cable play: "We are going to acquire cable households for $X and it is going to cost us $Y to build out the infrastructure. So, look at our free cash flow projections rather than our P&L."

Global Player Partnership

Supposing a large, global-50 retailer offered to purchase a piece of the WebHouse Club at a fair price. Should the WebHouse Club allow a global-50 retailer or a consumer package goods manufacturer—say, a Wal-Mart or a Procter & Gamble—to purchase equity in the WebHouse Club? And if so, what should the WebHouse Club do to make equity available to other large players that are also partners in the system? Should it simply make a single exception, because a global-50 player is a global-50 player?

It's a little bit akin to what we did with Delta Airlines, only Delta didn't put up any money. With WebHouse, you'd actually have somebody coming and putting up the money.

Many Internet companies have very challenging partner problems because they don't have a value proposition that allows them to scale their business on its own merits. So, they need to come up with barter-like structures to scale their businesses. WebHouse doesn't have that challenge, because it has a sound value proposition, and because priceline.com can drive traffic to the site. However, WebHouse will still confront large players who say, "We will participate in this, but only if we can invest. If we can't invest, we may end up participating some day. But we are not interested now."

WebHouse is a no-brainer for the grocery retailers if they think about it. We let them compete with warehouse clubs while still realizing their full retail price, and we drive a lot of traffic to their stores. Unfortunately, sometimes it takes a lot of effort to get them to think about it. I mean, no one is calling us up and saying, "Hey, come over here." But the manufacturers are tougher to convince. In the end, once a few leaders sign on, they'll all go. But how important is it for you to accelerate that process?

Of course, the big manufacturers recognize that if they can buy in, the company's going to go up in valuation. Let's just say that the current value of WebHouse is $400 million and a global-50 company wants to put up $50 million. Immediately, the value of the business might jump to a billion dollars. The endorsement of a global-50 company would say something to the capital markets, as well as to your potential competitors. It would also say something to the other retailers you wanted in the business or to the other manufacturers. Look at what happened with priceline.com. Once we had one airline as an investor, they all had to be there, and they all wanted warrants.

But what are the benefits? Are you better off having all of the grocery stores in America own a small piece of this company, as a co-op? Or are you better off with none of them owning a piece? It's a hard question because each one that buys in makes the value proposition for all the rest more attractive. It ultimately becomes self-fulfilling, people sort of say, "Hey, this thing must work, look at all the grocery stores that have invested." That's a big deal, because it discourages competition and creates an aura of inevitability in the business, which is powerful. That's one of the reasons why getting big is so important in the Internet space. It creates an aura of inevitability.

The Timing Option

The final question is, Should you allow single companies to offer "name-your-price solutions" where there is no other brand choice, but there is a choice regarding the timing of a transaction? This is contrary to our established model that to get lower prices customers must accept flexibility around brands.

For example, starting soon, priceline.com will let you name your own price for a 21-inch color television. You'll get a yes or no answer, but you've got to take RCA, Panasonic or Toshiba. That's the Priceline model. But here's another version of the model. You go to Best Buy and you name your price for a 21-inch Toshiba, but you tell Best Buy that you're willing to buy it anytime during the next eight weeks at that price. So, Best Buy can say, "Let me see if I ever need this business. I don't need it right now, but if sales are really soft, I might want to grab it." It becomes a kind of clearance solution for retailers.

If you do this, however, are you ultimately creating more consumer confusion than it's worth? One argument says don't try to line extend your concept; it's a classic trap. Another argument says that the more ways people can name their price, the stronger the brand becomes, because ultimately you stand for a set of solutions and not a single solution. And all the solutions equal cost saving for the consumer.

So, it boils down to the question, How far do you allow your core consumer proposition to be broadened? Do you stay pure with the idea that the consumer never chooses the brand? Or do you allow them to choose brand by giving up something else, for example, time? In the end, what we do at Priceline is help the seller get incremental sales and the buyer get savings. It's all about flexibility. The flexibility exists in three dimensions. There's flexibility of brand. There's flexibility of retailer. And there's flexibility of product configuration. The question is how much can we exploit flexibility of configuration without confusing the consumer?

Exhibit 1 "ONLINE SHOPPER" COLUMN IN *THE NEW YORK TIMES*

The New York Times
ON THE WEB

To Boldly Go to the Supermarket With Captain Kirk
by Michelle Slatalla

01/06/2000
The New York Times
Page 4, Column 1

FOR weeks, I avoided using Priceline's new online grocery service because I was sure I would hate it.

Let's leave aside for the moment Priceline's reputation in the name-your-price airline ticket business (too many stopovers, crazy departure times) and the annoying television ads for the new grocery service featuring the "Star Trek" actor William Shatner (as if Captain Kirk ever set foot inside a Waldbaum's, much less knew the first thing about how to keep a low profile with extra items in the express line). More important, Priceline's online grocery service, called the Priceline WebHouse Club, would force me to confront one of life's worst weekly horrors—grocery shopping—not once, but twice.

Here's how it would work: Before I even went to a supermarket (where you know I would have to pilot a cart with one skewed wheel through a crash course of cereal displays, stand in line forever and—since I live in the New York area—await the privilege of bagging my own food), I would have to sit at my computer and pick out every item I wanted on the site, which offers thousands of items, from apples to Ziploc bags. For each item, I would specify quantity, at least two brands I would be willing to accept and a discounted price I thought was reasonable.

Then I would type in a credit card number and would have to agree to pay for items fitting my criteria before the service's software would negotiate with the manufacturers' software and spit out a list of the items I had actually bought.

Then I would print the list (oh, did I forget to say you need a printer?) and take it to one of the hundreds of participating stores in 12 major chains in the New York area. There, I would have to pick out the right sizes and brands. (The service is also available in Philadelphia and just began in Washington and Baltimore; Boston will be next.) The company says 10,000 people are using Priceline each day in the New York area.

Then—are you still with me?—at the checkout, I would have to separate Priceline items from everything else and get them by using a special debit card, which I had to send away for (it took a few days to arrive). After 90 days, Priceline would charge me $3 a month in months when I used the service. Oh, yes—I would still have to bag everything.

All that made me want to scream. But last week, I finally screwed up enough courage (a gin and tonic helped) to go to www. Webhouse. priceline.com. And you know what? I loved it. In fact, it may have been my best online shopping experience.

The Priceline grocery service is the opposite of most Internet conceits, which sound really cool in the abstract but fall far short in the execution. With Priceline, the biggest hurdle was embracing the headache-provoking concept. After that, the service performed beautifully.

It is important to remember, however, that the idea behind Priceline groceries, like the one behind Priceline airline tickets, is not about convenience. It's about saving a lot of money. According to the company, the average Priceline shopping basket totals $32, $12.75 less than the same items would otherwise cost.

I decided on a few items for a test run. Take diapers, for example. I agreed to buy a package (containing 36 to 56 diapers, depending on size) and to accept either Pampers or Huggies. The site said the typical price range was $11.99 to $13.79 (I usually pay $13.49), then suggested that I name a lower price. Five lower amounts, ranging from $6.45 to $10.67, were listed, or I could type in another amount. The higher I went, the greater the chance I would get the item. I chose the lowest specified amount, $6.45, a price that would be subsidized from a stash of coupons called WebHouse dollars I received for being a first-time customer.

After I chose the diapers and eight other items, I clicked on the Buy button. The site quickly announced that I had bought all nine items for $40.76, which was immediately charged to my American Express card. But as I printed the list, I panicked. I had just paid for this stuff, but what if the store didn't have it in stock?

So I called the site's toll-free customer service number—and got a shock. In less than 30 seconds, a knowledgeable person who told me her full name answered my questions in a calm and forthright manner. She was, in fact, the first online customer service representative I had badgered—er, spoken to—in weeks whose voice didn't sound as shifty as a Nixon administration operative trying to explain erased tapes. I could use my prepaid grocery list to pick up any item on it for up to 90 days. After that, Priceline would automatically issue a refund.

But that wasn't necessary. My local store had every item. And a friendly checkout clerk was so familiar with the procedure—she said she rang up at least one Priceline sale a day and planned to register on the site herself—that she reminded me that the debit card's PIN was 5555. I saved nearly $35 on nine items, paying $40.76 instead of the $75 the store would otherwise have charged.

Did that make me happy, like those people in Priceline ads? No, it made me paranoid. Had I had been a patsy in a setup from an old episode of "Mission Impossible"? Now that I thought about it, that clerk had looked suspiciously like Peter Graves in a wig. So I phoned Price line's founder, Jay Walker.

"Who's bankrolling this thing?" I asked. That's the question we always ask in my house when we're not quite sure what's going on.

Exhibit 1 "ONLINE SHOPPER" COLUMN IN *THE NEW YORK TIMES* cont.

"The manufacturers," Mr. Walker said. "And they'll do it forever." The grocers handle Priceline sales as if the shoppers had coupons—purchases are subsidized by manufacturers or Priceline itself.

The reason, Mr. Walker said, is this: By agreeing to accept more than one brand, a Priceline shopper demonstrates a fickle nature. "The manufacturers would rather not give you a discount, of course, but if you prove that you're willing to switch brands, they're willing to pay to keep you," Mr. Walker said.

As for my getting all nine items, that was unusual. Shoppers who want nine things are usually able to get only five or seven, he said. "But for a first-time customer, our software bends over backward," he said. "So if the price you're willing to pay is 10 cents off what the manufacturer is willing to accept, the first time we let you have it."

To see if I could repeat my success without being a first-time customer, on Monday I tried nine other items. Again, I got all nine. I paid $16.12, saving $10.28.

A couple of tips if you plan to try Priceline: Don't buy an item if you cannot accept a brand you usually don't choose. For instance, I would be afraid to play Russian roulette with canned tuna, fearing that I would end up with fish that had bits of scary dark flesh and those little bones. But when it comes to diapers, I'll take either Pampers or Huggies. And if I can get them for half-price, I don't care that Priceline collects information about what I buy or that Priceline shares it with manufacturers or sponsors. In fact, to ensure a continued supply of very cheap diapers, I ratted on four friends. I gave their e-mail addresses to Priceline in return for an extra 10 WebHouse dollars. You can get more WebHouse dollars by filling out marketing surveys on the Priceline site.

If more than one manufacturer will accept the price you offer for a product, you are matched randomly with one of them. Later, you are more likely to be matched with the same brand because your previous purchase indicates that you like it.

So far, I have no complaints with Priceline. Even the William Shatner issue has been resolved. "We've moved to testimonials showing real people," Mr. Walker said. "But we did consumer research, and you'd be surprised at how high William Shatner's credibility was."

"As a grocery shopper?" I asked.

"No," Mr. Walker said. "He was Captain Kirk. Remember?"

Exhibit 2 PRICELINE WEBHOUSE CLUB: HOW IT WORKS

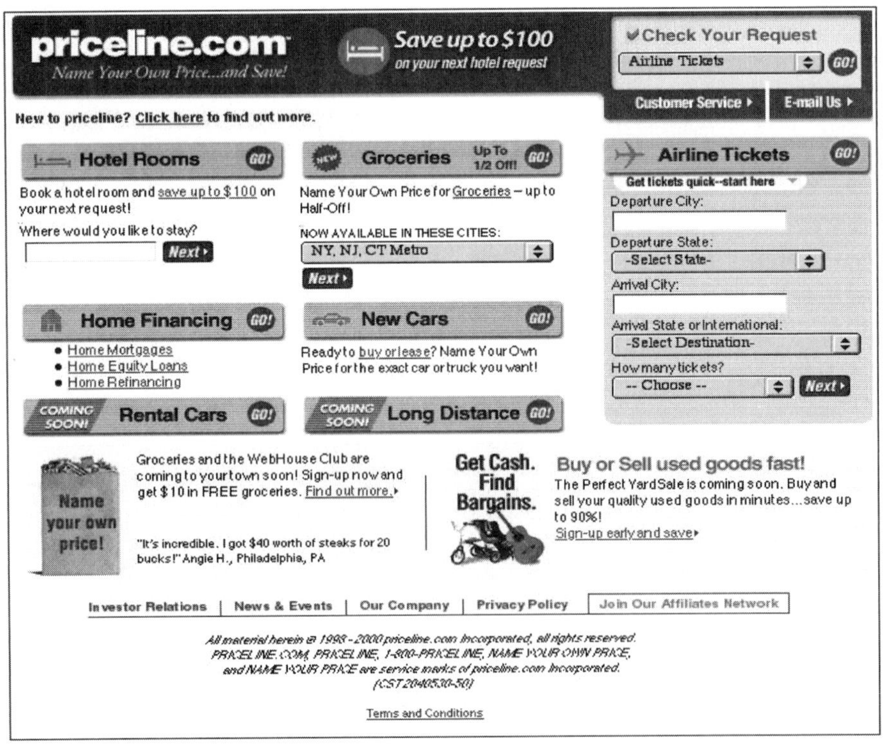

Exhibit 2

PRICELINE WEBHOUSE CLUB: HOW IT WORKS cont.

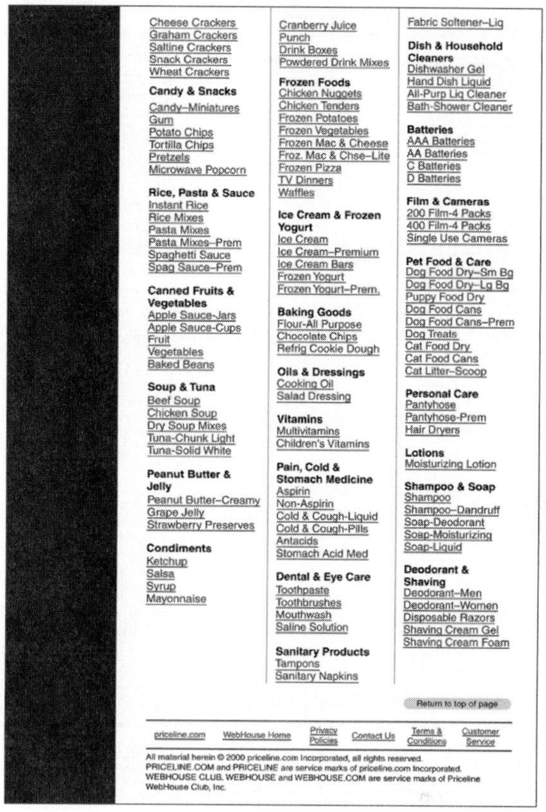

Exhibit 2

PRICELINE WEBHOUSE CLUB: HOW IT WORKS cont.

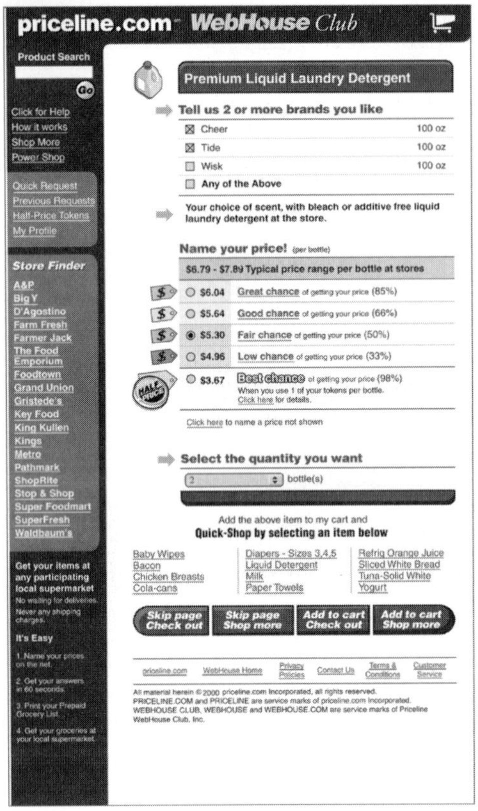

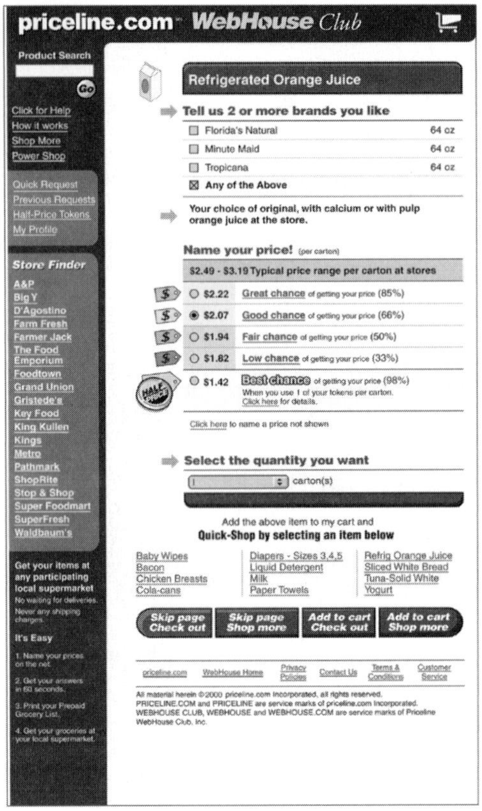

Exhibit 2

PRICELINE WEBHOUSE CLUB: HOW IT WORKS cont.

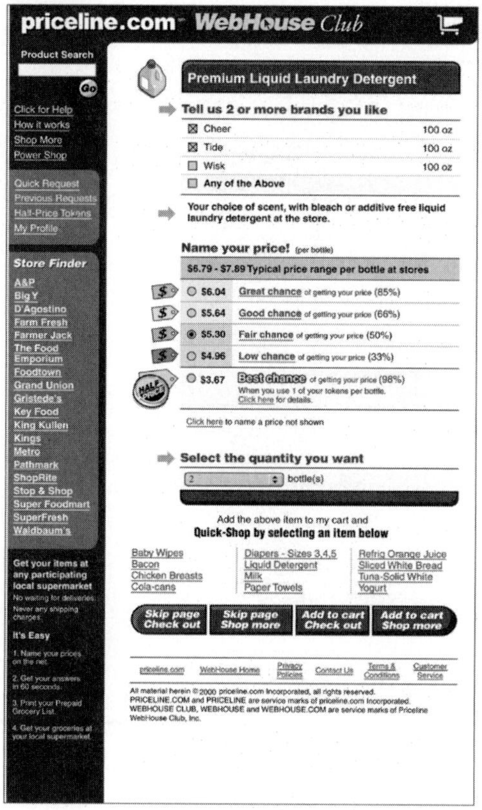

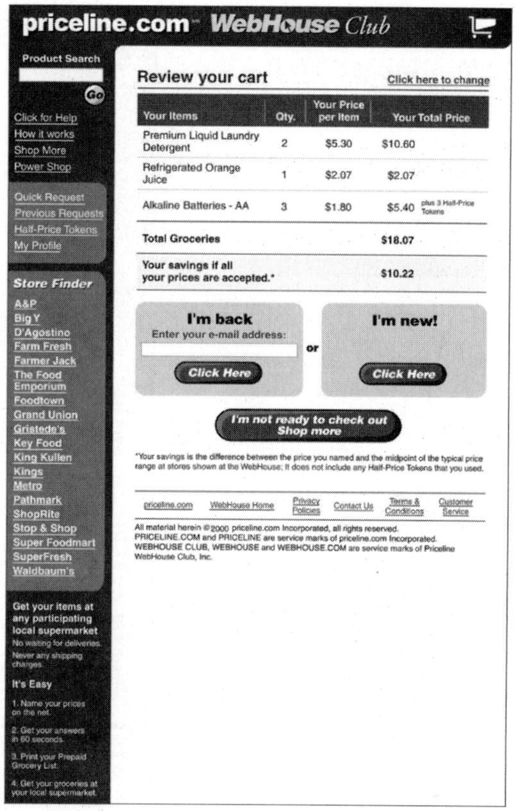

Exhibit 2 PRICELINE WEBHOUSE CLUB: HOW IT WORKS cont.

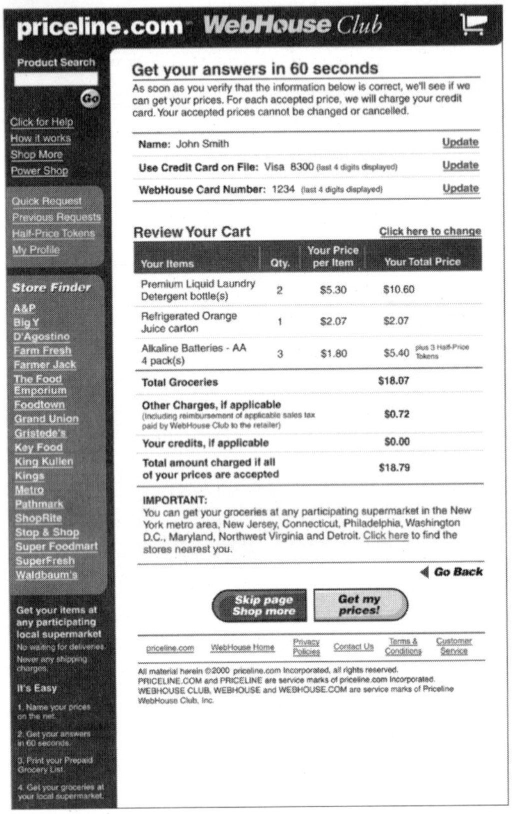

Exhibit 2 PRICELINE WEBHOUSE CLUB: HOW IT WORKS cont.

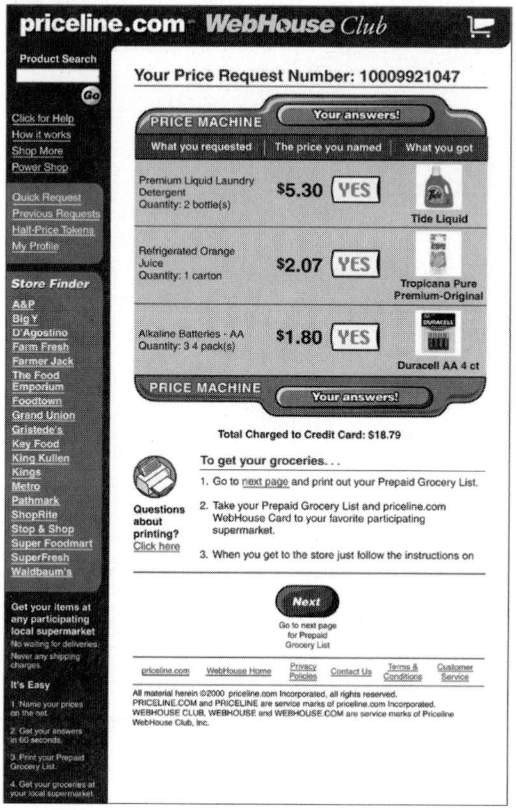

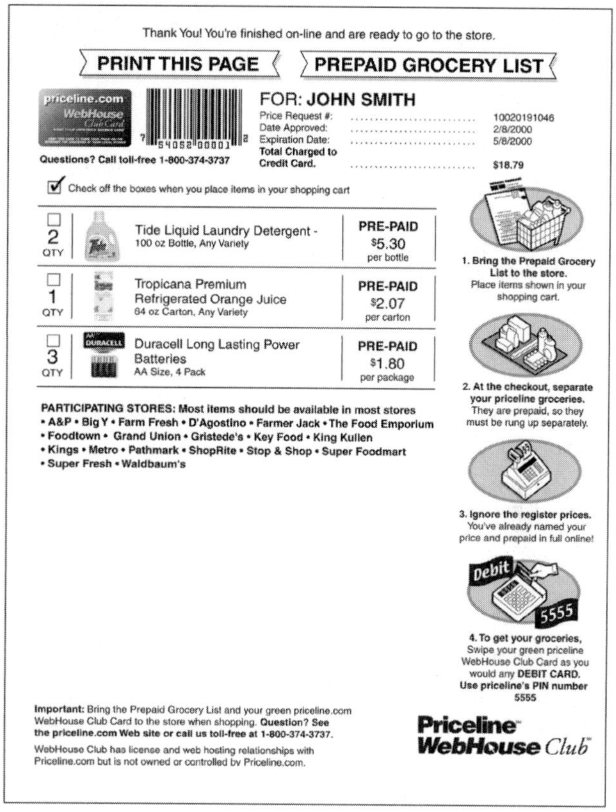

Subject: **Your Priceline WebHouse Club Request Number 10020191046**
Date: Thu, 11 Nov 1999 13:23:31 -0500
From: Priceline WebHouse Club
Organization: Priceline WebHouse Club
To: John Smith

Dear John Smith,

Congratulations! We were able to find all the items you requested
at the prices you named!
Tide
Tropicana Pure Premium-Original
Duracell AA 4 ct

The total amount charged to your credit card was 19.60
The total amount of Money from your House Account used was 5.40

If you haven't already done so, you'll need to return to
www.priceline.com and print out your Prepaid Grocery List.
It will give you a description of the exact brand, size and quantity
of each item you requested. Take it with you to the store to get
your prepaid items. Or, to get your list, simply click on the link
below:

http://webhouse.priceline.com/checkstaus.asp

Thanks for using the Priceline WebHouse Club. We value your
membership and want to help you get products you want
at the price you name.

Sincereley,

The Priceline WebHouse Club Customer Care Team
****
Save by naming your own price - only at priceline.com!
Check out all our name your own price services at
http://www.priceline.com

Groceries - Airline Tickets - Hotel Rooms - New Cars
Home Mortgages - Mortgage Refinancing - Home Equity Loans

NAME YOUR OWN PRICE!
http://www.priceline.com
****

Exhibit 3 WEBHOUSE CLUB MONEY FLOW cont.

Example 1: First-time Customer

Customer receives 10 free WebHouse dollars for joining WebHouse Club. Using the full amount to subsidize her offers, the member's credit card is billed $10 for $20 worth of groceries.[a]

1. WebHouse places $10 credit in new customer's House account as part of its customer acquisition program.
2. The customer chooses several items to purchase while selecting the "1/2 price special" option for each product. This allows the member to use WebHouse Club dollars to subsidize half the price of each product. After review by WebHouse, all of the member's product offers are accepted—at a total value of $20—thus using up all 10 of the member's WebHouse dollars.
3. The customer's credit card is billed $10.
4. Customer picks up the pre-paid items at a local participating grocery store and uses her WebHouse card to "pay" for the items. The actual retail price of the products at check-out is $20.60, which is billed to WebHouse.
5. Manufacturers reimburse a specified amount per particular product purchased via WebHouse, i.e. $0.75 for 30 oz. container of bleach. Total payment to WebHouse: $3.25.[b]
6. Net loss for WebHouse: $7.35
7. Remaining WebHouse dollars in House Account: $0.00.

WebHouse Account	
FUNDS IN	*FUNDS OUT*
	$10 to House account (1)
$10 from House account for "1/2 price specials" (2)	
$10 charged to customer credit card (3)	
	$20.60 is charged on debit card by retailer (4)
$3.25 payment from manufacturers (5)	
$10+10+3.25−10−20.60 = $7.35 loss	

Member House Account	
FUNDS IN	*FUNDS OUT*
$10 new member bonus (1)	
	$10 used in "1/2 price special" offers (2)
$10−10 = $0	

[a]*Value of groceries on the Website is determined as the sum of the average list price of the products at all participating supermarkets in the area. The retail price charged to WebHouse will almost certainly be different.*
[b]*Manufacturer payments are actually paid upfront before individual transactions are made. For example, a manufacturer would pay $200,000 for WebHouse to fulfill demand with X number of its products.*
Source: Company interviews.

Exhibit 3 WEBHOUSE CLUB MONEY FLOW cont.

Example 2: Sponsorship Cross-subsidization

Returning customer signs up for a new credit card. Member is billed $35 for $57.95 worth of groceries.[c]

1. WebHouse Club offers customer an opportunity to earn $25 for signing up for a new credit card. Upon member's participation, WebHouse places 25 WebHouse dollars into the member's House Account, which is controlled by member.
2. WebHouse places a $10 credit into the member's "Hidden Account," which is controlled by WebHouse.
3. The credit card company pays WebHouse $50 for the new customer acquisition.
4. Member makes several product offers, which total $45 for $57.95 worth of groceries (including $20 at the "1/2 price special"). Thus, the member chooses to use $10 of her WebHouse Club dollars (for her portion of the "1/2 price special") and $35 in cash to pay for the items, if they are accepted.
5. With the help of $4 subsidization from the member's Hidden Account, all of the member's offers are accepted.
6. Customer's credit card is billed $35.
7. Customer picks up the pre-paid items at her local, participating grocery store and pays for them at check-out using her WebHouse debit card. The actual retail price of the groceries at check-out is $57.45, which is paid by WebHouse Club.
8. Manufacturers reimburse specified amount per particular product purchased via WebHouse, i.e. $0.45 for liter of soda. Total payment to WebHouse: $9.25.
9. Net gain for WebHouse: $15.80.
10. Remaining WebHouse dollars in House Account: $15.
11. Remaining credit in Hidden Account: $6.

[c]*House and Hidden account balances are earmarked for particular members as a result of these members' participation in sponsorship programs. Hidden account balances can be changed at any time.*
Source: Company interviews.

WebHouse Account	
FUNDS IN	*FUNDS OUT*
	$25 to House account (1)
	$10 to Hidden account (2)
$50 payment from sponsor (3)	
$10 from House account for "1/2 price specials" (4)	
$4 from Hidden account to subsidize offers (5)	
$35 charged to customer credit card (6)	
	$57.45 is charged on debit card by retailer (7)
$9.25 payment from manufacturers (8)	
$50+10+4+35+9.25–25–10–57.45 = $15.80 gain	

Member House Account	
FUNDS IN	*FUNDS OUT*
$25 bonus for signing up for credit card (1)	
	$10 used in "1/2 price special" offers (4)
$25–10 = $15[c]	

Member Hidden Account	
FUNDS IN	*FUNDS OUT*
$10 bonus for signing up for credit card (2)	
	$4 is used to subsidize offers (5)
$10–4 = $6[c]	

The Float

WebHouse makes money on the float in several ways. First, it books revenue from the manufacturers by contracting to fulfill a specified demand of product for an upfront payment. This payment is then used to create the product discount for the WebHouse member at the discretion of WebHouse. Second, the member pays WebHouse automatically by credit card once the member's offers have been accepted. WebHouse does not pay for these products until the member picks them up from the participating supermarket, using the WebHouse debit card. Finally, sponsorship revenue that is earmarked for the member's House or Hidden accounts is available to WebHouse until it is used by the member according to WebHouse rules.

Exhibit 4

PRICELINE.COM—INCOME STATEMENT COMPARISONS, 1998–2000E ($ IN THOUSANDS, EXCEPT EPS)

	Annual					Estimated vs. Actual	
	1998A	1999A	2000E[a]	2001E[a]	2002E[a]	03/00E[a]	03/00A
Revenue	$35,246	$482,410	$1,383,798	$1,775,000	$2,076,750	$220,000	$313,798
Transaction Revenue (Gross Revenue)	31,196	443,729	1,249,725	1,544,250	1,765,238	202,000	287,125
Fee-based Revenue	4,050	38,681	134,073	230,750	311,513	18,000	26,673
Adjusted Cost of Revenue	33,504	423,056	1,163,004	1,461,890	1,694,628	189,200	264,771
Adjusted Gross Profit[b]	1,742	59,354	220,795	313,110	382,122	30,800	49,027
Operating Expense	54,165	121,209	260,428	298,000	332,000	43,800	64,928
Sales & Marketing	25,544	79,522	169,449	200,000	220,000	28,800	40,449
Systems & Business Development	10,873	14,024	27,618	34,000	39,000	5,000	5,868
G&A	17,748	25,851	54,454	64,000	73,000	10,000	12,704
Adjusted Operating Income[c]	(52,423)	(60,043)	(30,727)	15,110	50,122	(12,250)	(9,994)
Revenue Mix							
Travel Services	89%	92%	90%	87%	85%	92%	92%
Other	11%	8%	10%	13%	15%	8%	9%
Headcount	127	300	498	650	800	325	378
Annualized Revenue Run-Rate	–	–	–	–	–	$880,000	$1,255,192
Annualized Revenue/Headcount	–	–	–	–	–	$2,708	$3,321
Annualized Operating Expense/Headcount	–	–	–	–	–	$539	$687
Important Metrics							
Net Unique Offers ('000)[d]	1.175	4.334	9.888	14.545	22.222	1.692	2.350
Q/Q Change	–	–	–	–	–	23%	71%
New Customers ('000)[e]	–	–	6.418	8.000	10.000	1.100	1.518
Q/Q Change	–	–	–	–	–	23%	70%

Exhibit 4 PRICELINE.COM—INCOME STATEMENT COMPARISONS, 1998–2000E ($ IN THOUSANDS, EXCEPT EPS) cont.

	Annual					Estimated vs. Actual	
	1998A	1999A	2000E[a]	2001E[a]	2002E[a]	03/00E[a]	03/00A
Cumulative Number of Customers ('000)[f]	–	3.724	10.160	18.160	28.160	4.842	5.260
Sales & Marketing per New Customer	–	–	–	–	–	$26	$27
% Repeat Use[g]	–	–	35%	45%	55%	35%	35%

Source: Morgan Stanley Dean Witter, Mary Meeker and Mark Mahoney, April 25, 2000.
[a]E = Morgan Stanley Dean Witter estimates.
[b]Adjusted Gross Profit excludes airline warrant charges.
[c]Adjusted Operating Income excludes options/compensation expense and airline warrant charges.
[d]Net Unique Offers excludes all resubmitted offers.
[e]The number of new customers is based upon the number of unique credit card accounts submitted during the quarter.
[f]Cumulative customer base excludes Priceline WebHouse Club customers.
[g]Repeat use is measured by the ratio of new unique customers to new unique offers.

Exhibit 5 LEADING WEB SHOPPING PLATFORMS: GROSS MERCHANDISE SALES

	Gross Merchandise Sales ($MM)	Last Reported Quarter
America Online	$3,900	CQ1:00
Yahoo!	$1,000	CQ1:00
eBay	$1,150	CQ1:00
Amazon.com	$670	CQ1:00
CNET	$574	CQ1:00
priceline.com	$444	CQ1:00

Source: MSDW Internet research.

eBRICKS.COM

No man ever wetted clay and then left it, as if there would be bricks by chance and fortune.

—Plutarch, 46 A.D.

In mid-November 1999, the five co-founders of eBricks.com—Tawfik Hammoud, Jorge Henriquez, Nikitas Koutoupes, Enrique Macotela, and Tim Perini—gathered to celebrate in their downtown Manhattan offices. There was some debate over which milestone had led them to break open a bottle of Champagne: the completion of the first version of their website; hiring their 25th employee; or signing up their 20th beta site customer. The debate was settled when one of the co-founders proposed an anniversary toast. No one could recall the precise date, but it had been almost exactly one year since the eBricks.com team had started work on their business plan as second-year students in Harvard Business School's MBA Program.

eBricks.com was an online market maker facilitating the procurement of construction materials (see Exhibit 1 for excerpts from eBricks.com's business plan, which had been honored in March 1999 as one of four finalists among over eighty entrants in the HBS Business Plan Competition). In July 1999, eBricks.com had secured its first round of venture capital, raising $3 million from Warburg Pincus Ventures, a New York-based venture capital and private equity firm that previously had invested in Chemdex, StarMedia, Covad, and Intuit, among other Internet and technology startups. By November, eBricks.com had twenty-five employees; the Chief Technology Officer's job and senior positions in Engineering and Operations had been filled by executives with extensive construction and IT industry experience (see Exhibit 2 for excerpts from a presentation the company prepared for prospective investors in November 1999). The eBricks.com management team was working closely with a web development firm that had been retained to build the company's website, and was finalizing plans for beta-tests with blue-chip charter customers, aiming to have the first transactions conducted by early January. eBricks.com planned to launch its service during the first quarter of 2000, initially focusing on customers based in the Northeast region and on the electrical and mechanical segments of the construction industry.

As the eBricks.com team prepared for launch, they faced two major strategic issues. First, eBricks.com had received a merger proposal from Blueline Online Inc., an Internet company that provided project management tools for architects and contractors. Blueline's competitors had announced plans to add procurement solutions to their respective suites of project management tools; Blueline saw merger with eBricks.com as the best way to provide similar capabilities. Second, the eBricks.com team faced a fundamental decision about where in the construction industry value chain to compete. Their existing business plan assumed that eBricks.com would develop online markets through which subcontractors specializing in a given line of construction work (e.g., electrical; mechanical; plumbing; heating and ventilation; roofing) would procure materials principally from distributors who were similarly specialized. In addition to this opportunity, however, it had become clear to the eBricks.com team that the industry required a second online market maker positioned between the distributors and the manufacturers of the materials that distributors sold to subcontractors. Was this second opportunity more attractive than the first? Should eBricks.com pursue *both* opportunities?

Blueline Online

Large construction projects generated an enormous volume of blueprints and technical plans as well as a nonstop flow of messages about design and schedule changes between architects, engineering firms, and contractors.

Professor Thomas Eisenmann prepared this case as the basis for class discussion rather than to illustrate either effective or ineffective handling of an administrative situation.

Managing this information was a time consuming and error-prone task: a single design change could require the modification of many different documents required by a dozen independent subcontractors. Many of these documents were too large to send by fax. Failure to accurately send or receive information regarding a design or schedule change could be very expensive: laborers might sit idle waiting for materials to be delivered or waiting for another subcontractor to finish work. Or worse, a job might be completed despite inconsistencies with new specifications, requiring the subcontractor to subsequently scrap the work and start again from scratch.

Online project management tools addressed many of these problems. Geographically dispersed project participants paid a subscription fee for access to secure websites, where they could create, modify, organize, store, and share a range of documents, including blueprints, photographs, requests for information, change orders, and meeting minutes. According to academic studies, when architects, engineering firms and contractors employed web-based tools, projects were completed more quickly and with better quality, and project administration costs could be reduced by 10% or more.[1]

Blueline Online, Inc., founded in 1997 and based in Palo Alto, was one of several firms pursuing the market for web-based construction project management solutions. Engineering giant Bechtel was an equity investor in Blueline, as well as the company's largest customer. Blueline Online had about 100 employees in late 1999. The startup had closed a $10 million venture capital round in May, and was in the midst of raising another $30–40 million—cash that could be used to meet eBricks.com's funding requirements if the companies merged. Blueline's competitors included Bidcom and buzzsaw.com, both of which were based in San Francisco. Bidcom, started in 1997, was closing a $46 million third round financing; it had received venture capital from Oracle and Internet Capital Group (which had invested in over 40 business-to-business Internet startups, including VerticalNet and e-Chemicals). buzzsaw.com, founded in 1999, was a spin off from Autodesk Inc., the leading provider of computer-aided design software. In addition to backing from Autodesk, buzzsaw.com, which had 70 employees in late 1999, had received $15 million in its first round of venture capital financing from Crosspoint Ventures Partners.

[1] *Wall Street Journal*, "Blueprint for Change," November 15, 1999.

By late 1999, Bidcom and buzzsaw.com had both announced in-house development efforts to broaden their services to include materials procurement. This was a natural line extension for both firms that would enhance their respective value propositions for both architects and contractors. Architects frequently specified the materials to be used in a construction project, so they needed access to information about the properties and costs of the different materials they could employ. Such information was aggregated in manufacturer and distributor catalogs and in product directories, which increasingly were available online. If architects used online project management tools to transmit their specifications to contractors, there was an opportunity for contractors to subsequently "explode" those specifications into an online bill of materials which then could be sent as a "request for quotation" (RFQ) to multiple distributors. Finally, contractors could use this web-based bill of materials to facilitate the online procurement of materials.

Integration into materials procurement by online project management companies clearly posed a competitive threat to eBricks.com. It seemed likely that eBricks.com could develop software "hooks" that would allow contractors to electronically transfer specifications from various project management systems into eBricks.com's systems. However, it also was apparent that contractors would only bother to do so if eBricks.com offered superior procurement solutions. So, when Blueline Online approached eBricks.com about a merger, the eBricks.com management team faced several issues. If eBricks.com did not accept the merger proposal, how would it fare in competition against Bidcom, buzzsaw.com, and Blueline? If eBricks.com did merge with Blueline, would it be more difficult to capture procurement transactions from contractors that used project management tools from Bidcom or buzzsaw.com? Blueline's management believed that the company was positioned to complete an IPO as early as the first quarter of 2000, especially if they could present plans to move into procurement. It seemed unlikely that eBricks.com could complete an IPO on this timetable as an independent company. Would eBricks.com's investors realize a greater return as minority shareholders in Blueline, or by selling eBricks.com to the public or to another strategic investor at a later date? Finally, if it merged with Blueline, what share of the equity in the combined entity should eBricks.com's shareholders receive? While the eBricks.com team believed they offered a superior online procurement solution for construction materials, there were a couple of other startups focusing on the same markets that could be alternative candidates for acquisition by Blueline.

Where to Compete?

In researching the requirements of specialty distributors, the eBricks.com team realized there was a need for a second online marker maker positioned between distributors and the manufacturers who supplied them with materials. The same type of "pain" that eBricks.com had encountered in downstream markets (i.e., between subcontractors and distributors) also was present upstream. Specifically, the upstream market was similarly fragmented, with few large companies in any segment. Roughly 250,000 distributors and retailers sold construction materials that were manufactured by about 175,000 different companies. On average, a distributor might deal regularly with 100 to 2,000 manufacturers, and a typical manufacturer might sell to 2,000 or more distributors. But high search costs for distributors and high sales and marketing costs for manufacturers precluded either side from dealing with the full range of prospective partners in their market segment. Hence, there were information gaps: distributors had trouble finding the right products at the right price available for delivery to a subcontractor; price discrepancies existed for otherwise similar products; and manufacturers had difficulty selling new products to distributors and retailers. Furthermore, procurement processes were labor intensive and expensive. A few large distributors and manufacturers had introduced EDI links; more typically, distributors employed paper catalogs to check on product specifications, then called the manufacturer to confirm availability and price.

As they learned more about the upstream market, eBricks.com's managers were intrigued: should they pursue this market in addition to, or perhaps instead of, the downstream market? As yet, none of the players serving the downstream market had signaled intentions to move upstream, and eBricks.com could find no other companies with serious plans to create an upstream marketplace. In evaluating this opportunity, several issues seemed relevant:

- *Would a company realize synergies from participating both upstream and downstream?* It was clear that when architects specified materials requirements, RFQs sometimes traveled all the way upstream to manufacturers, who provided distributors with proposals for custom solutions to their special materials requirements. So, online market makers in the downstream market might have an advantage if they could facilitate the online transfer of specifications to manufacturers.

  Furthermore, one could imagine that the programming work required to create an online catalog for the downstream market might be leveraged in creating an online market upstream. A downstream catalog required a database of all manufacturers' products, as well as "hooks" into distributors' inventory management systems. The database and "hooks" both might be repurposed in creating software to serve the upstream market.
- *Would distributors accept the same company as both a downstream and upstream market maker?* A downstream market maker would have relationships and credibility with distributors, and presumably would be well positioned to recruit distributors for the upstream market. But would distributors balk at a value proposition that allowed them to realize lower prices by broadening their base of manufacturers, but at the same time subjected them to price pressure from contractors, seeking to broaden their base of suppliers?
- *From a practical standpoint, could a startup with twenty-five employees conceivably target both the downstream and upstream opportunities?*

The eBricks.com team approached this decision with mixed emotions. On the one hand, it was somewhat disconcerting at this stage in the company's development to be asking, "Where should we compete?" That was a great question to pose late in a business school class discussion, but it seemed somewhat disruptive to raise such a fundamental issue while the company accelerated its launch plans and prepared to raise its second round of venture capital. On the other hand, successful web-based businesses constantly seemed to create growth options. Perhaps this was simply proof that eBricks.com's co-founders had cause to break out the Champagne . . .

Exhibit 1 EXCERPTS FROM eBRICKS.COM'S MARCH 1999 BUSINESS PLAN

I. Executive Summary

eBricks.com is a business-to-business market maker that will leverage the Internet to provide the construction supplies industry with an outstanding and cost-competitive way to carry out procurement transactions.

The characteristics of the $200 billion construction supplies industry provide an attractive opportunity for an online business-to-business startup. Extreme market fragmentation, large price discrepancies, information asymmetry, and serious inefficiencies in current procurement processes all imply significant value added by an agent that leverages the Internet to facilitate the procurement of construction materials.

eBricks.com will provide an Internet-based procurement service for construction materials and equipment that will include: 1) online bidding capabilities; 2) an extensive and searchable catalog for materials and equipment allowing buyers to complete transactions on a real-time basis; and 3) a market where surplus materials can be liquidated. In addition, the site will offer services that span the entire procurement process, from cost estimation by owners/developers through a "clearinghouse" for payments. eBricks.com will carry no inventory, and will charge customers a modest fee for facilitating procurement transactions. Customers will pay no membership or listing fees.

eBricks.com will add value to *buyers* (owners, developers, architects, general contractors and subcontractors) by streamlining existing estimation and purchasing processes and by increasing market liquidity, i.e., by allowing buyers to negotiate with a larger set of suppliers. Benefits to buyers will include better prices, faster and more reliable processes, wider product selection, and one-stop-shopping. The value proposition for *suppliers* (manufacturers, distributors and retailers) includes increased sales from access to a broader set of buyers, more effective and lower cost marketing, improved service with lower processing cost, and better inventory management.

eBricks.com's management team boasts a diverse group of individuals with construction, sales, and consulting experience combined with an Advisory Board of senior executives that add years of experience, contacts and credibility. Industry heavyweights such as Perini Corporation, Raytheon, Beacon-Skanska, and Techint are represented in the Advisory Board, as are institutions such as the law firm White & Case and the Harvard Business School.

eBricks.com intends to introduce its services on a modular basis to ensure fast entry into the market. The company is currently seeking $5.5 million from investors to fund the launch of its first module of services in January 2000. This includes the development of the company's web site and a marketing effort aimed at acquiring 50 contractors and corresponding suppliers. In accordance with its modular growth strategy, eBricks.com will require additional financing in 2000 to finalize its catalog product. The company is expected to be cash flow positive by 2001. Revenues (the dollar value of procurement transactions completed using the service) are expected to reach $100 million for the year 2000, growing to approximately $2 billion by 2003. The expected cash flows for the company imply an internal rate of return of over 75%. These financial projections do not reflect growth outside the general building materials segment and outside the United States, both of which are expected within two to four years.

II. Market Analysis

A. The Construction Industry[2]

i. Current Industry Structure

Representing approximately 8% of U.S. GDP in 1998, construction is a gigantic $660 billion industry. Construction has been and continues to be a very fragmented and regional industry, both on the contractor side and the materials supply side. The *1997 DOC Census of Construction Industries* reports that there were approximately 2 million construction establishments in the U.S.; however, only 400,000 consisted of 5 or more employees. The top 400 U.S. contractors made up only 17.1% of the entire U.S. construction industry. The top five contractors, including Fluor Daniel, Bechtel Group, Brown & Root, Centex Corporation and Turner Corporation, accounted for a mere 2.6% of U.S. construction.[3]

[2]The main source of information used in this section is the *1999 Construction Outlook Second Report*, FMI Corporation, February 1999.
[3]*The Top 400 Contractors Sourcebook*, Engineering News-Record Supplement, November 1998.

The technology-at-use in the construction industry today is at best archaic. Calling construction one of the "20 industries that must change," *Business2.0* magazine recently estimated that e-commerce in construction would grow from approximately $400 million in 1998 to over $28 billion by 2003, representing over 3% of the market.[4]

ii. Industry Trends and Economics

Most U.S. construction sectors are expected to experience modest but steady growth over the next several years. Building construction, including single-family homes, educational buildings, office buildings, and public safety and administrative buildings, represents 80% of construction industry revenue and is expected to grow annually at 3.2% over the next five years. Low mortgage rates should continue to encourage building construction. The non-building sector is expected to grow at an annual rate of 4.0% between 1999 and 2004, fueled by highway construction activity following the recent passage of the $198 billion TEA-21 highway bill. Also, non-building utility construction growth should be strong as companies invest in telecommunications and natural gas infrastructure.

Other relevant construction industry trends include:

Increasing Competition. Despite the consolidation of some large contractors, specialty subcontractors, and suppliers, the strong economy should ensure that a steady stream of firms will continue to enter the market and thus maintain its fragmented nature.

Rise of Information Technology. Contractors increasingly are using web-based project management applications (such as bluelineonline.com or bidcom.com) to better coordinate their projects, increase productivity, and reduce paperwork. Contractors are also beginning to use hand-held technology to enter time and cost information in the field as well as laptops to track real-time job performance versus estimates. Although the trend is not widespread, contractors are beginning to use the Internet to order materials and supplies.

B. The Construction Supplies Market

i. Market Description and Trends[5]

Like the overall construction market, the construction supplies market (which includes materials and equipment, but excludes construction labor) is extremely fragmented and inefficient. Of the $660 billion in total "put-in-place" construction in 1998, 32% or $214 billion was spent on materials, components, supplies, and rental costs for machinery.

The largest material supplier, Home Depot, generated over $20 billion in revenue in 1998, representing only about 10% of the total material supplies industry. Most material firms are not large, and are primarily devoted to local or regional domestic markets. Other examples of fragmentation in this market are: 1) in 1998, in the $17.2 billion ready-mixed concrete industry, the top three manufacturers accounted for only 6.9% of the market; 2) in the $14.5 billion millwork industry (wood doors, windows, and molding), the top three manufacturers held approximately 21% of the market; and 3) in the $9.2 billion bathroom products industry (toilets, bathtubs, faucets, etc.), the top three manufacturers held approximately 31% of the market.

Because very few materials are sold directly to contractors by their manufacturer, the actual fragmentation of the industry supply chain is much greater than indicated above. The extensive network of intermediaries supplying construction materials includes distributors, small and large hardware stores, and catalog companies.

ii. Products

Materials purchased in the construction industry can be broken down into two categories: *commodity products,* such as lumber, concrete, asphalt, and steel, and *non-commodity products,* such as plumbing supplies, electrical components, roofing, and flooring materials. Non-commodity products represent approximately 70% or $135 billion of the construction supplies industry. In general, the $126.5 billion non-building structure market utilizes mostly commodity products; these are generally large, public-works infrastructure projects that require a lot of earth-moving work and the construction of basic structures using large quantities of concrete, lumber, form-work, and reinforcing steel. Such projects are highly equipment- and labor-intensive, with materials accounting for only 35–40% of total project costs. In a typical building project, by contrast, materials make up 50–60% of total costs and non-commodity products are the norm.[6]

Construction products can be further subdivided based on the amount of time it takes to procure them. In general, longer-lead items are higher priced.

[4] *Business2.0* Magazine, "20 Industries That Must Change." January 1999.

[5] Adapted from Snapshot International U.S. Construction Industry reports, 1998 (www.snapdata.com).

[6] Material percentages in this section and the description of the procurement process in the next section are based on information gathered from over 25 interviews with contractors.

Long-lead items generally take several months to procure and require extensive interaction with suppliers, particularly if the items require special fabrication instructions and an extensive approval process involving the designer/owner. Examples of long-lead items include custom-fabricated steel parts and permanent facing materials such as marble and tiles.

Medium-lead items usually can be purchased within a week to several weeks. These items are not custom-fabricated, but they generally require more time to locate and deliver. Examples of medium-lead items are hard-to-find electrical components, specialty lumber (versus stock lumber), and mechanical parts (e.g., heating, ventilation, and air conditioning—HVAC—products).

Short-lead items are purely "off-the-shelf" supplies such as hand tools, stock lumber, nails, personal protective clothing, etc., that can be purchased within a week to a matter of hours and require little interaction with the supplier.

iii. Current Materials Supply Chain

The fragmentation of the construction materials industry creates a complex and inefficient supply chain where materials often pass through two or three layers of intermediaries. This fragmentation creates opportunities for retailers to demand large volume discounts from manufacturers and to place significant markups on the materials they sell to the end user. Large warehouse retailers such as Home Depot and Lowes typically buy at about 40% below the manufacturer's list price, and then mark up prices to buyers in the range of 10–40%, depending on the product. Acting individually, smaller retailers have substantially less buying power, but can increase their power by teaming with each other through dealer networks and cooperative buying. Most importantly, the current supply chain is inefficient and costly for buyers (general contractors and subcontractors) who are forced to pay substantial premiums for products and to weed through confusing layers of suppliers to find the products they want. Finally, architects, engineers, and designers play a crucial role in the supply chain in that they often specify the materials to be used in a project and thus influence what general contractors and subcontractors ultimately pay for these products.

C. Procurement Processes for Construction Supplies

Procurement of supplies for the construction business is a complicated and outdated process that has undergone little change over time. Across the industry, most buyers of construction materials go through a process that can be divided into 5 stages. The value that eBricks.com adds at each step of the process is explained in detail in Part III.

Step 1: Pre-bid Estimation and Buyout. During this stage, general contractors commit to bid on a project and mobilize their estimating departments to price a job. For most building projects, over 70% of the work is bid out by general contractors to specialty subcontractors, who provide estimates of their cost (including all labor and materials) to perform specific work, for example all plumbing installations, electrical installations, or concrete work. In estimating costs, prices for most materials are simply plugged in based on past experience and historical cost data. However, for large-ticket or long-lead items that are unique to a job or that require extensive interaction with a supplier, subcontractors usually send out "bid-fax" requests-for-quotation (RFQs) to distributors and other suppliers. These bid-faxes specify all the criteria required for a product including quantity, adherence to specifications, delivery conditions, schedule constraints, etc. Since construction is a very local business, subcontractors will usually select only those suppliers whom they know well or who have credible recommendations. The industry norm is to look for three quotations. Subcontractors expend little effort searching for unknown suppliers beyond their immediate region.

The bid-fax process is cumbersome and confusing. Just before a bid is closed, faxes are sent between parties at a frantic pace. One contractor called this faxing process "a curse" because of the confusing paper stream it creates during bidding and because suppliers always consider their latest fax as a binding confirmation in writing. "Buyout" occurs just before the RFQ process closes when subcontractors determine which suppliers are likely to provide them with the lowest prices.

Step 2: Bidding and Negotiation. Just before their bid is finalized, general contractors will try to secure the lowest prices from subcontractors by playing their prices off one another; subcontractors, in turn, may engage in a final round of "bid shopping" with suppliers to realize higher margins for themselves and to be more competitive in their final proposal.

Step 3: Post-bid Procurement and Buyout. After winning a job, subcontractors will generally assign a project manager and/or engineer and an estimator to continue the buyout process. This includes specifying the quantity and types of short lead-time materials to be purchased, and when they should be delivered. Buyers want to receive supplies "just-in-time" because of restricted storage space on most jobs and the likelihood materials will get damaged, lost or stolen.

As a job progresses, materials are either purchased through a central office or from the job site, but the process is the same for both. As with the estimating phase, purchasing agents (often the project managers) rely on inefficient methods to locate suppliers, including their Rolodex of contacts, word-of-mouth, industry supplier listings (e.g. The Blue Book and Thomas Register), and recommendations from other contractors or suppliers. They waste time making multiple phone calls and trading messages with suppliers and then faxing documents such as specifications and copies of contract drawings. When these efforts fail, particularly for hard-to-find specialty items, they rely on a handful of local suppliers from whom they can obtain almost anything. Unfortunately, such last-minute buying invariably translates into higher prices. But if laborers are idle due to a lack of materials, a contractor's profits can evaporate quickly.

Step 4: Delivery and Payment. Having agreed on price and other terms, large subcontractors usually send out purchase orders to suppliers, occasionally through EDI but usually filled out by hand and faxed. This is a cumbersome process, particularly when multiple approval signatures are required. Smaller subcontractors often cannot buy on credit, and must pay in advance with a check or credit card (one small New York contractor estimated that only 3 of his 20 suppliers allow him to buy on credit). One point of frustration for contractors is that products are often not delivered as agreed. Shipments are often late and do not include exactly what was ordered, and delivery arrangements often are inadequate (e.g., suppliers fail to provide a union driver when required or any means to unload material). With little put in writing up front, there is often disagreement over what had been negotiated. Another problem occurs when suppliers bill for materials that were not actually delivered. Some suppliers take advantage of large contractors who purchase many products every day and who have difficulty keeping track of the shipments and invoices.

For suppliers, the biggest risk is not getting paid. Contractors make a point of delaying payments as long as possible, and some fail to pay altogether. In fact, a large form-work supplier from Boston estimated that his bad debt write-offs amounted to almost 20% of his yearly pre-tax profits. Since most payments take 45 to 75 days, suppliers will often agree to lower their prices if contractors guarantee payment within 30 days.

For most large-scale construction projects, contractors are required to submit material certifications as a condition for getting paid by developers. These certifications ensure the owner that a contractor has used the materials specified by the architect for a project (rather than a lower quality substitute) and that they conform to testing criteria. Suppliers are notorious for failing to provide materials certifications, so contractors must spend time chasing them down or face delays in getting paid by developers.

Step 5: Resale. At the end of every project, contractors are burdened with having to dispose of excess materials and equipment or paying to transport them to other project sites. With few avenues to sell these products, contractors face high costs in demobilizing their jobs.

III. Business Opportunity

A. The Rationale for Change

We believe the characteristics of the construction supplies industry as described in Part II provide a significant business opportunity for an on-line business-to-business start-up. eBricks.com has been conceived to capture first mover advantages and capitalize on the following opportunities:

Market Fragmentation. Both buyers and sellers of construction supplies are highly fragmented. If there were only a few dominant companies on either the buyer or seller side, the opportunity for a startup might disappear, since larger players might be able to create online markets on their own.

Information Gaps. Buyers and sellers in this industry suffer from an information gap: with over one million unique SKUs there is a *very* high level of product variety, and many products have complex features. Moreover, there is a high rate of new product introductions in some segments. Information opacity creates burdens for each side: buyers find it hard to locate product information and low-priced suppliers, while sellers have a hard time reaching all potential customers and communicating the merits of their new products.

Process Inefficiency. As noted above, the current procurement and order fulfillment processes are expensive and frustrating for all parties. As has been seen in the case of TPN Register, another business-to-business market maker, a shift from phone/fax procurement to an online system can decrease processing costs by approximately 20%.

Price Discrepancies. Information gaps and high transaction costs contribute to significant price differentials between vendors, even for the commodity products. This warrants the emergence of new online intermediaries that can reduce search and purchasing costs and increase liquidity in the market.

Industry Profit Pressures. The construction industry consistently ranks in the bottom quartile of U.S. industries in terms of return on equity. Many contractors and suppliers barely make money. This represents a major opportunity for new players that offer cost saving and revenue-generating solutions.

Proven Internet Solutions. Similar issues have been addressed in other industries via the Internet. The technologies used in these solutions are increasingly reliable and available "off the shelf".

B. Business Concept

Unlike some online market makers, eBricks.com *initial* goal is not to displace existing players in the value chain. Rather, it aims to reduce the inefficiencies that characterize the industry, creating lasting value for all players and ultimately increasing the industry's overall profit pool. eBricks.com will re-distribute the value as equally as possible between buyers and sellers, while building a profitable and sustainable business on a transaction-fee based revenue model. To unlock the value hidden in the current supply chain, eBricks.com will offer the following services:

Online Catalog. eBricks.com will offer a single, aggregated source for product and equipment information and ordering that doesn't exist in the industry today. We will create a multiple-supplier database with an advanced search engine capability. By integrating with suppliers' internal inventory management systems, the system will provide buyers with up-to-the-minute, online information on product prices, features, inventory availability, substitution options, payment and delivery terms. The technology will allow the buyer to choose one or more purchasing criteria and rapidly compare offers from several suppliers on a single screen. Importantly, the system will allow the buyer to purchase all the products required to complete a field operation, i.e., it will provide "one stop shopping".

Online Bidding. Today, the construction industry's "bid-fax" process (described in Part II) amounts to a "slow motion" auction. eBricks.com proposes to take this approach online and offer an interactive "downward price bid" model involving real-time bidding by multiple suppliers responding to a given buyer's request-for-quotation (RFQ). eBricks.com will give buyers the ability to specify key bidding parameters, e.g., whether suppliers can bid to provide a subset of products versus all the products required for an operation; auction duration; open/closed list of suppliers; delivery date; reserve prices; etc. The buyer will upload an RFQ into our system, which then will analyze the RFQ and make it available to appropriate suppliers. In addition, eBricks.com will allow specifications, shop drawings and other instructions to be sent electronically along with RFQs. Eventually, there will be a seamless connection between the eBricks.com system and web-based project management systems where the specifications will reside.

Online Market for Surplus Materials. eBricks.com will create an efficient secondary market for building materials and equipment. eBricks.com will help contractors liquidate their surplus material at the end of a project, either through auctions or through fixed price sales. Likewise, on the seller side, eBricks.com will make suppliers' excess inventories and one-time promotional offers instantly available.

Payment Aggregation/"Clearinghouse." By aggregating payments by customer and job, each buyer and supplier will receive an account statement monthly instead of having to write or receive countless checks. For buyers, the eBricks account statement will be organized by project and can be linked into accounting systems. eBricks.com's customizable "My Account" feature will be available electronically and will contain all the buyer's transaction records, sorted according to project or specific operation. To facilitate payment processing, eBricks.com will integrate the material certification process into its procurement system. eBricks.com might also serve as a payments "clearinghouse", collecting funds from buyers and disbursing payments to suppliers. Since this clearinghouse function would likely expose eBricks.com to credit risks, if the company decides to pursue this role, it is likely to seek partnerships with financial institutions to hedge these risks.

Other Services. To improve on-time delivery performance—a crucial concern for contractors—eBricks.com will facilitate the delivery of customized electronic "reminders" to suppliers and will allow buyers to track the shipment status of their orders online. To increase the willingness of buyers to deal with unfamiliar suppliers (and vice versa), eBricks.com will develop a rating system akin to eBay's, whereby the parties to a transaction rate each others' performance. Cumulative ratings will be visible to all participants in the eBricks.com marketplace.

C. Competitive Analysis

Due to market fragmentation, few players in the construction supplies industry have enough power to affect the entire supply chain. eBricks.com faces potential competition from a few large suppliers and from emerging Web-based information sources and intermediaries. *However, none of these players currently offer an integrated, one-*

stop-shop, online marketplace for contractors' procurement needs. To secure a first-mover advantage in this realm, eBricks.com will seek alliances with companies having deep industry knowledge and extensive information resources, but who have yet to launch online business-to-business services.

i. Competition from Industry Suppliers

While many supply chain intermediaries are expected to move online, very few are large enough to command a formidable share of the online procurement market. The largest suppliers are retail warehouses such as Home Depot and Lowes, who currently command about 10% and 5% of the building supplies industry, respectively. Both currently have web sites, but neither has yet ventured into listing and selling products online. eBricks.com fully expects these companies to offer e-commerce features, but only in the form of single-source catalog purchasing, not a one-stop-shop, integrated solution. eBricks.com will offer substantially more value by offering the lowest industry prices by tapping into a enormous supplier database and using multiple-source catalog purchasing and auction-style bidding.

Other suppliers who could expand their online selling capabilities include chain hardware stores, large construction supply catalogs, and product manufacturers. Given their relatively small market shares, chain hardware stores such as Ace and True-Value seem likely to have difficulty attracting a critical mass of buyers to their isolated websites. Catalog companies like McMaster-Carr, Grainger, and 3M are already selling their products online, but their systems are still unsophisticated. McMaster-Carr, for example, simply posts links to Adobe Acrobat files of its paper catalog. While online catalogs may be of some value to customers, they do not provide the opportunity to compare products and prices from multiple catalogs. Because buyers will gravitate to a more complete information resource, catalog companies will be compelled to list their products with eBricks.com. Finally, manufacturers of construction products could benefit greatly from directly selling their products online, but the existing industry structure seems likely to make this difficult. Most manufacturers have traditionally sold through layers of manufacturer's reps and specialty distributors, and thus lack experience with selling and lack relationships with buyers.

ii. Other Web-Based Competition

The construction and building materials industries are clearly late entrants into the Internet realm. Nevertheless, a few companies already have announced plans to offer Internet procurement solutions for contractors, and more are expected. These web-based competitors can be subdivided into three categories: directory services, project management sites, and auction sites. While we expect growing competition, as yet there is no evidence of a site that provides an integrated solution and a level of sophistication that rivals eBricks.com's planned capabilities.

Directory Services. Recently, well-established construction industry information providers have launched services that allow buyers to search for construction materials. These services include Sweets.com, a division of McGraw-Hill; thebluebook.com, billed as the "yellow pages" of the construction industry; and Buildnet.com, which calls itself the "world's largest & most active building industry and home improvement search engine." These sites are essentially product directories that provide basic information about suppliers and manufacturers as well as links to the suppliers' web sites, where a buyer then can browse specific product information.

Sweets.com also offers direct access to its product database without having to link through to suppliers' websites, but the content is simply an Internet version of Sweet's printed catalog, and thus provides little added value.

thebluebook.com has a similar catalog feature, but has been more proactive in developing web-based interaction between buyers and sellers. Through a service called "BB-bid", a password-protected bid management system, thebluebook.com allows contractors to maintain a private database of projects and "favorite" suppliers and to send out RFQs by email and fax. Unlike eBricks.com, however, BB-bid does not integrate the procurement process seamlessly within a single website.

Dirtpile.com is the first of potentially many contractor-launched web sites. Developed by a local Boston contractor, dirtpile.com is essentially a portal for construction information of all types but offers limited e-commerce capabilities. Because it sells only limited range of products from a very small group of suppliers, dirtpile.com does not presently pose much threat to eBricks.com.

Project Management Sites. Web-based project management companies, such as bluelineonline.com and bid.com, may also pose a threat to eBricks.com if they venture beyond project management solutions into procurement. Having developed powerful on-line tools for communication between industry players, they seem likely to attempt to do so. However, given the very heavy spending required to establish their core project management services, they may be constrained in their ability to rapidly develop procurement systems.

Auction Sites. Newly developed auction sites, such as metalsite.com, are unlikely to challenge eBricks.com because they are too focused on a particular niche (e.g. steel products at metalsite.com). By contrast, eBricks.com will create an integrated, one-stop-shop.

eBricks.com expects to benefit from several entry barriers that favor an aggressive first mover. Switching costs will follow from users' investments in: 1) creating transaction history records; 2) gaining familiarity with the eBricks.com site; 3) integrating eBricks.com services with their internal operations (e.g., supplier inventory management systems); and 4) building their reliability ratings. Brand recognition will also be a significant entry barrier. Finally, the fixed costs of entering the market and achieving critical mass should not be discounted.

D. Potential Roadblocks

While it is impossible to be aware of all the roadblocks that may lie ahead, we view four issues as the main obstacles to eBricks.com's widespread adoption:

Long-term Relationships. Like any other industry, the construction industry has its fair share of business done between preferred contractors and vendors, based on multi-year relationships and the perception of fair prices and great customer service. We do not discount the benefits from long-term relations, especially in cyclical industries like construction where there is not always ample supply for some materials. However, our customizable bidding capabilities will allow buyers to get "market clearing" prices and real-time information on supply levels so they can test new suppliers while retaining the option to continue doing business with their preferred vendors. For example, eBricks.com customers might split an order between the lowest-price supplier and a trusted vendor they've been doing business with for 25 years.

Customers Bypassing eBricks.com. A buyer satisfied with a new vendor identified through eBricks.com might be tempted to bypass us and deal directly with the newfound supplier, thus avoiding our transaction fees. Several factors should minimize this risk. First, the dynamic nature of the industry with fluctuating prices and product availability makes it impossible for a supplier to provide best offer on every bid. The new vendor might offer a great deal for this transaction, but buyers will still need to use eBricks.com to determine the best supplier for the next transaction. Second, our customers will value a range of services provided by eBricks.com (e.g., automation of order processing, materials certification, and record keeping), not just our ability to get the lowest prices available. If they take transactions offline, they will lose access to these services. Third, our fees will be driven by both total volume of transactions and amount-per-transaction, to avoid creating incentives to circumvent the system. Finally, eBricks.com will draft legal contracts to support its business model, and will make the legal requirements clear and paramount in our sales pitch. As the company becomes more established, if customers circumvent us after using eBricks.com to complete a transaction, they will be penalized, even to the extent of being banned from our marketplace.

Signing up a Large Supplier Base. How will eBricks.com convince suppliers to sign up for our online bidding services and subject themselves to more intense price competition? Three factors should facilitate customer acquisition. First, low-cost suppliers with growth ambitions will immediately see the potential of our concept. As Chemdex's CEO Dave Perry found out: "Vendors that like an efficient market welcomed us". Second, construction, like every industry, has technological innovators and early adopters on both buyer and seller sides. Our approach will provide built-in incentives for tech-savvy suppliers willing to join, such as higher reliability ratings, which will in turn attract more buyers. Finally, contractors themselves should be our best sales representatives by demanding that their suppliers start interacting with them through eBricks.com.

Industry's Lack of Technological Sophistication. While the construction industry may have a significant installed base of computers; it still lags behind most industries in terms of technology usage. We view this as small short-term constraint but also a huge medium-term opportunity. As with any company bringing dramatic change to long-established business practices, eBricks.com will need to educate the market. We believe that an online market maker that makes this investment can build strong, long-lasting relationships with its customers.

Exhibit 2 EXCERPTS FROM EBRICKS.COM PRESENTATION, NOVEMBER 1999

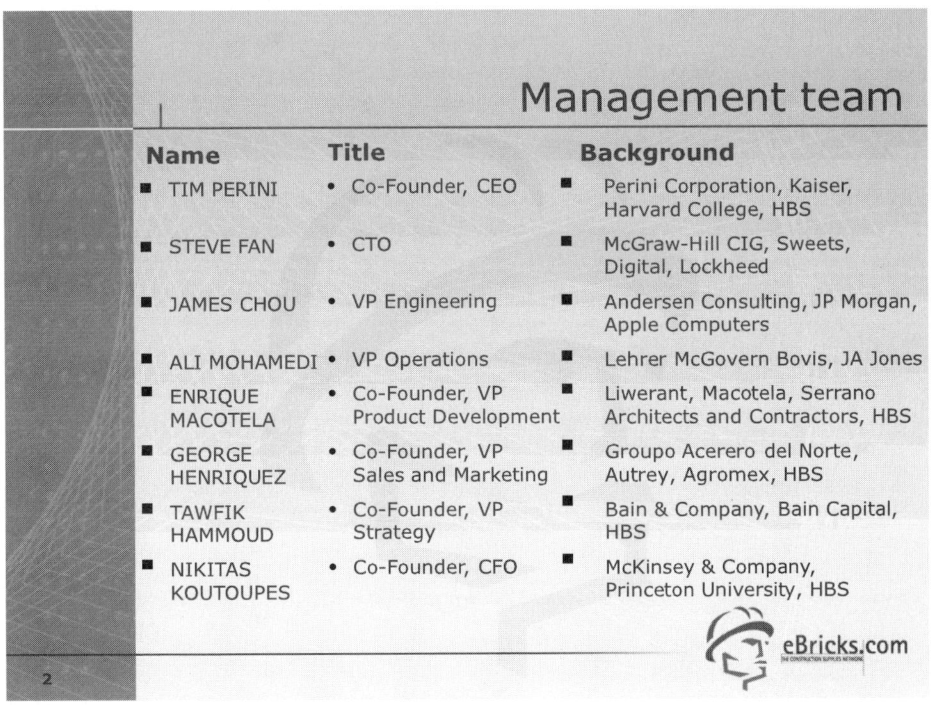

Advisory board

Construction

- DAN P. ARMSTRONG, Director, Worldwide Procurement, Raytheon Engineers and Constructors
- THOMAS E. DAILEY, frm. National President, Association of General Contractors; Vice Chairman, National Construction Employers' Council
- JAMES BECKER, President and CEO, Beacon-Skanska
- LORENZO ENAUDI, Chairman, Techint Foundation
- TONY MON, Chairman, Maywood Investment Company; Co-Founder, Vice Chairman, Pacific Greystone
- DAVID PERINI, Chairman Emeritus, Perini Corporation

Business

- KEVIN CLARK, CEO, ScreamingMedia.net, frm. Chairman and CEO, Poppe Tyson, Chairman, KMC Holdings
- TOM EISENMANN, Professor, Harvard Business School, frm. Partner, McKinsey & Company
- ANANTH RAMAN, Professor, Harvard Business School, supply chain management expert
- DONALD P. MADDEN, Senior Partner, White & Case, LLP

eBricks.com

3

Investors

Warburg Pincus Ventures

- $12 billion assets under management
- 300 investments across diverse industries since 1971
- 66 professionals, 35 partners
- Chemdex, StarMedia, BEA Systems, Cobalt Group, Covad, Intuit, Radnet, TradeCard, Veritas Software, Workspace
- $500 million in fees to Wall Street annually

eBricks.com

4

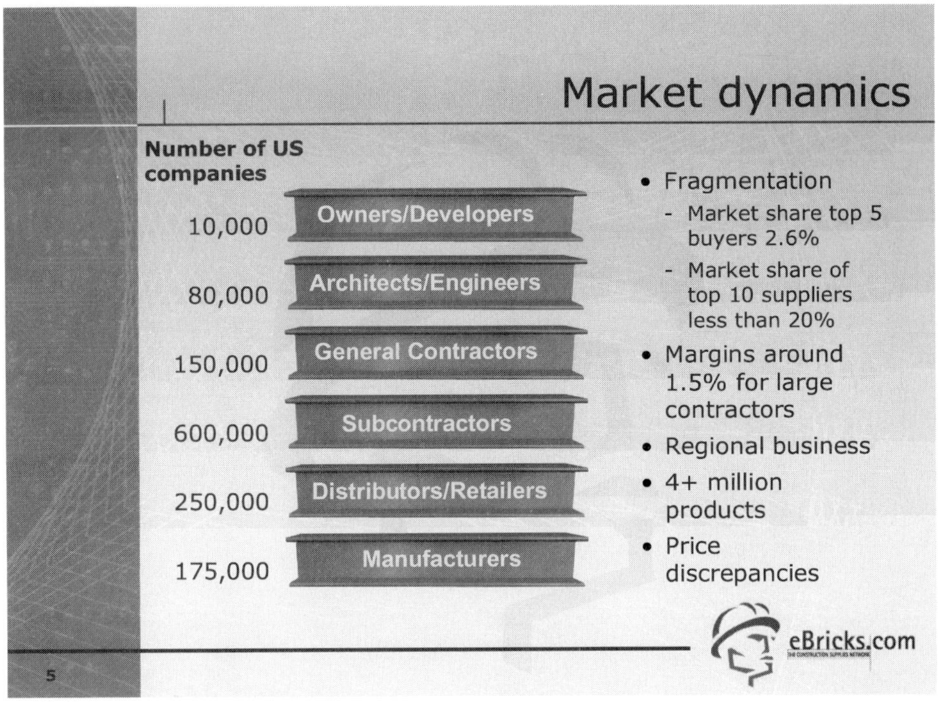
Market dynamics
Number of US companies
10,000
Owners/Developers
80,000
Architects/Engineers
150,000
General Contractors
600,000
Subcontractors
250,000
Distributors/Retailers
175,000
Manufacturers
• Fragmentation
- Market share top 5 buyers 2.6%
- Market share of top 10 suppliers less than 20%
• Margins around 1.5% for large contractors
• Regional business
• 4+ million products
• Price discrepancies
eBricks.com
5

Emergence of online players
• eBricks.com
• BuildNet
• buildingsuppliesweb .com
• PrimeContract.com
• PurchasePro/ AEConnect
eCommerce
Yellow Pages
• The Bluebook
• Sweets.com (McGraw-Hill)
• FirstSource.com (CMDG)
• Invitation to Bid
Project Collaboration
• Blueline-Online
• BidCom
• Buzzsaw.com
• Emerging Solutions
• Framework Technologies
• Meridian Systems (Prolog)
• Primavera
• BricsNet
INDUSTRY PORTAL
Content
Project News
• MacGraw-Hill Construction
• Construction Market Data Group (e.g., R.S. Means)
eBricks.com
6

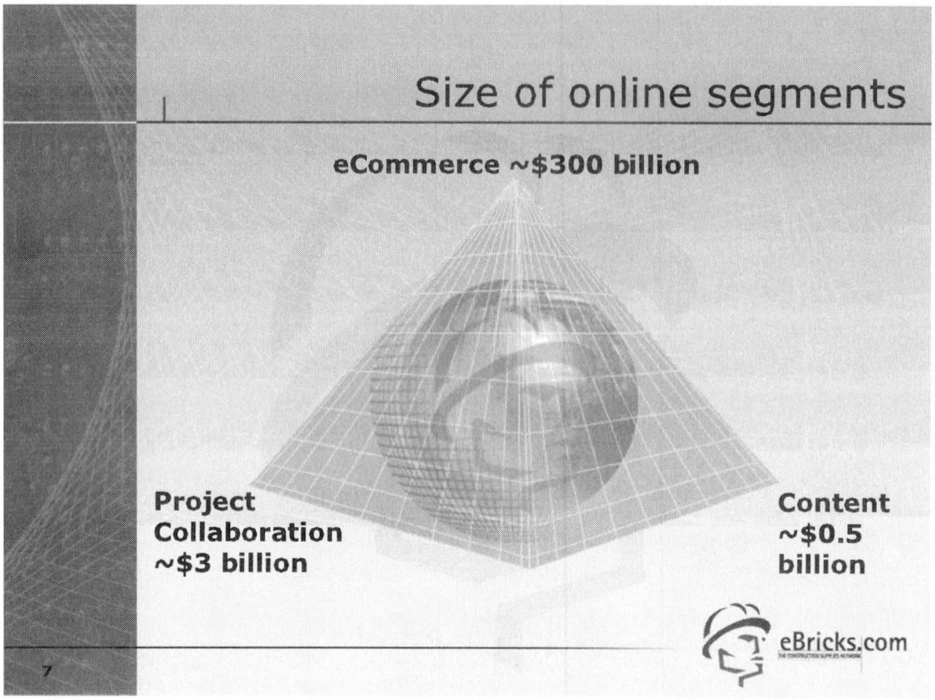
Size of online segments
eCommerce ~$300 billion
Project Collaboration ~$3 billion
Content ~$0.5 billion
eBricks.com
7

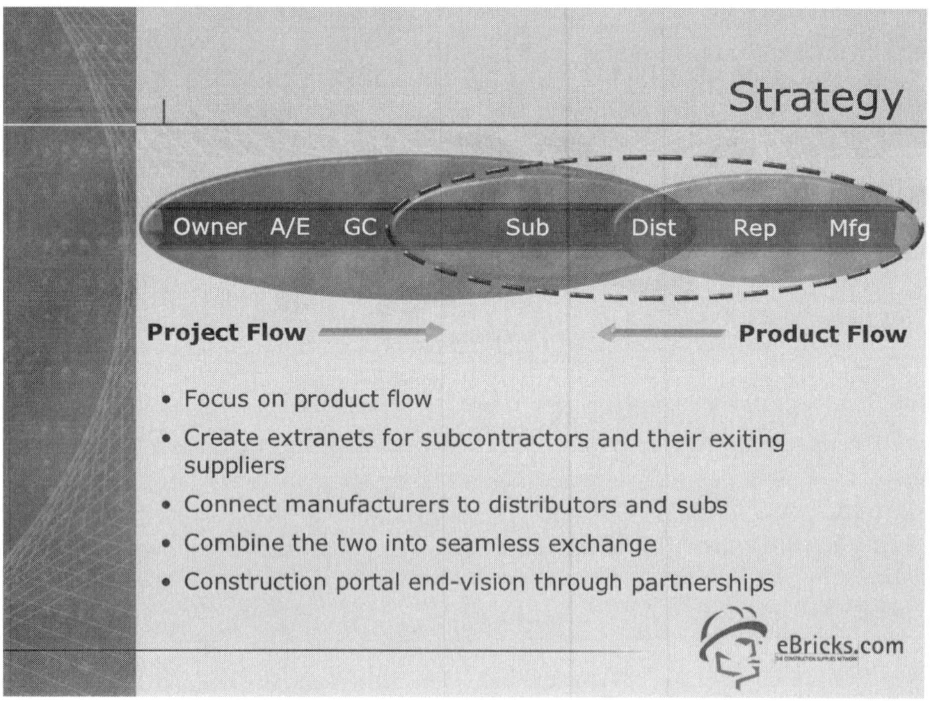
Strategy
Owner A/E GC Sub Dist Rep Mfg
Project Flow
Product Flow
• Focus on product flow
• Create extranets for subcontractors and their exiting suppliers
• Connect manufacturers to distributors and subs
• Combine the two into seamless exchange
• Construction portal end-vision through partnerships
eBricks.com

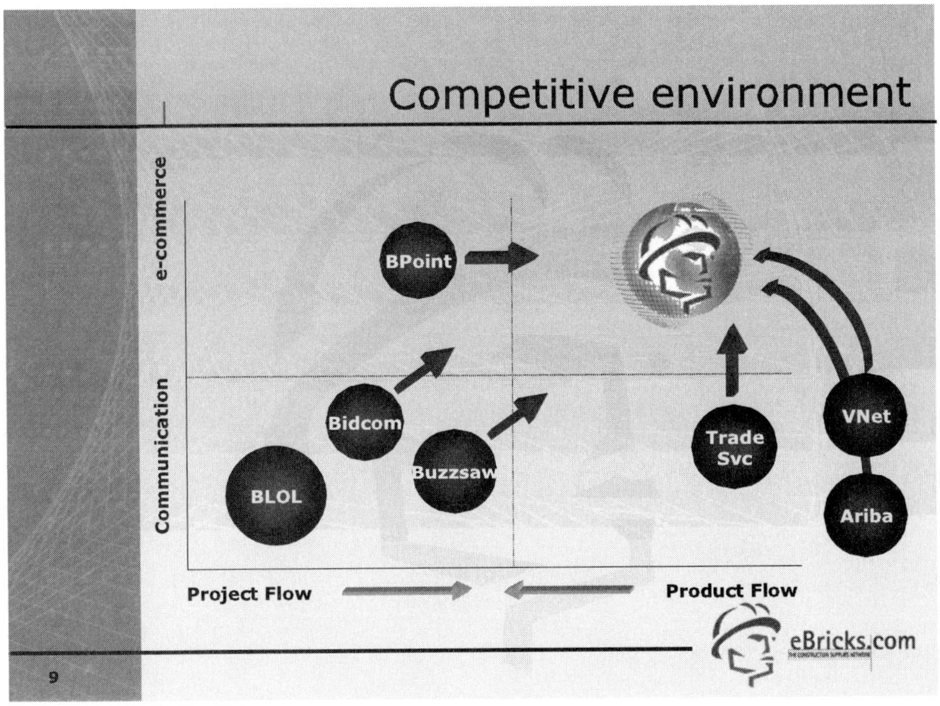
Competitive environment
e-commerce
Communication
BPoint
Bidcom
Buzzsaw
BLOL
Trade Svc
VNet
Ariba
Project Flow
Product Flow
eBricks.com
9

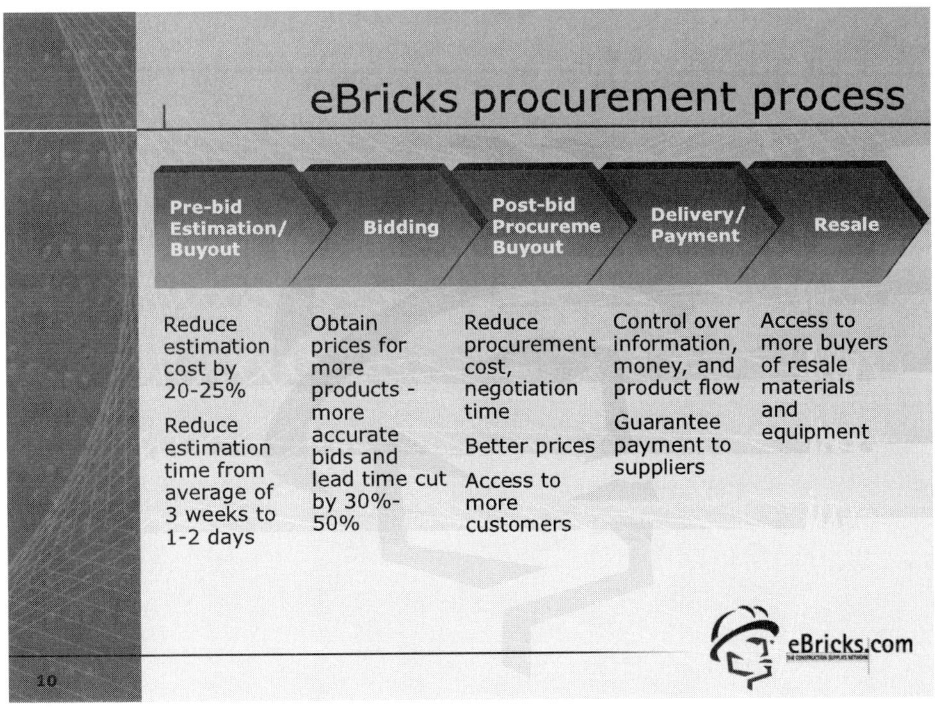
eBricks procurement process
Pre-bid Estimation/ Buyout
Bidding
Post-bid Procureme Buyout
Delivery/ Payment
Resale
Reduce estimation cost by 20-25%
Reduce estimation time from average of 3 weeks to 1-2 days
Obtain prices for more products - more accurate bids and lead time cut by 30%-50%
Reduce procurement cost, negotiation time
Better prices
Access to more customers
Control over information, money, and product flow
Guarantee payment to suppliers
Access to more buyers of resale materials and equipment
eBricks.com
10

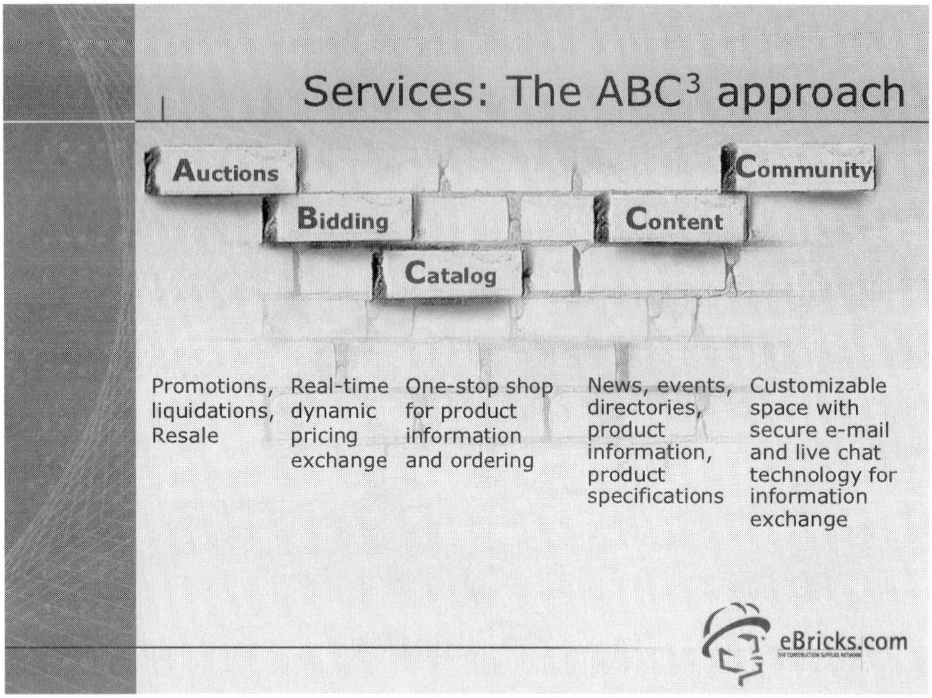
Services: The ABC3 approach
Auctions
Bidding
Catalog
Content
Community
Promotions, liquidations, Resale
Real-time dynamic pricing exchange
One-stop shop for product information and ordering
News, events, directories, product information, product specifications
Customizable space with secure e-mail and live chat technology for information exchange
eBricks.com

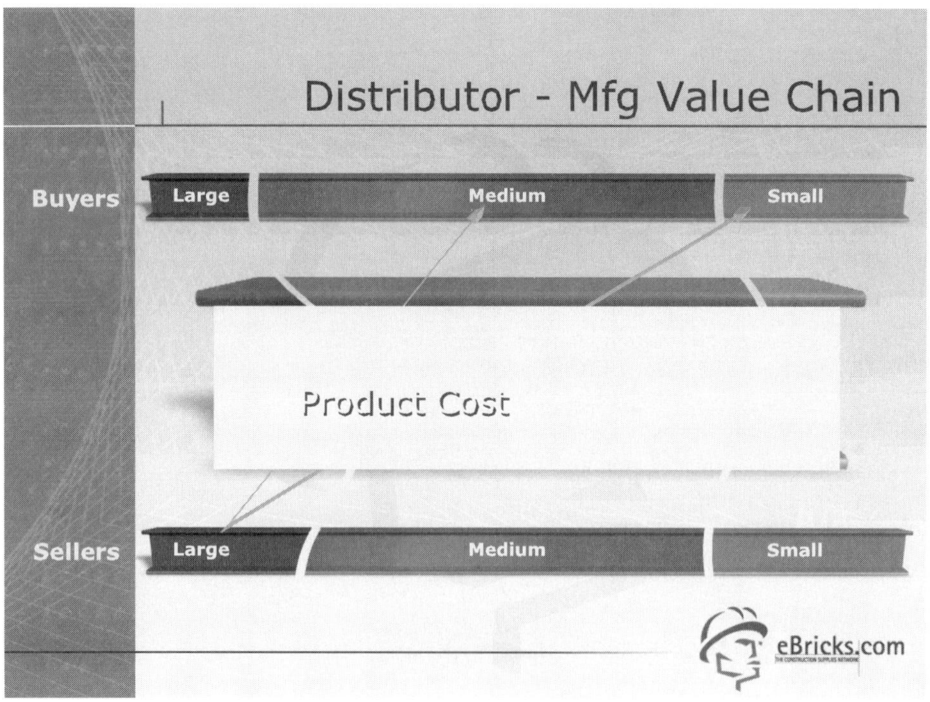
Distributor - Mfg Value Chain
Buyers
Large
Medium
Small
Product Cost
Sellers
Large
Medium
Small
eBricks.com

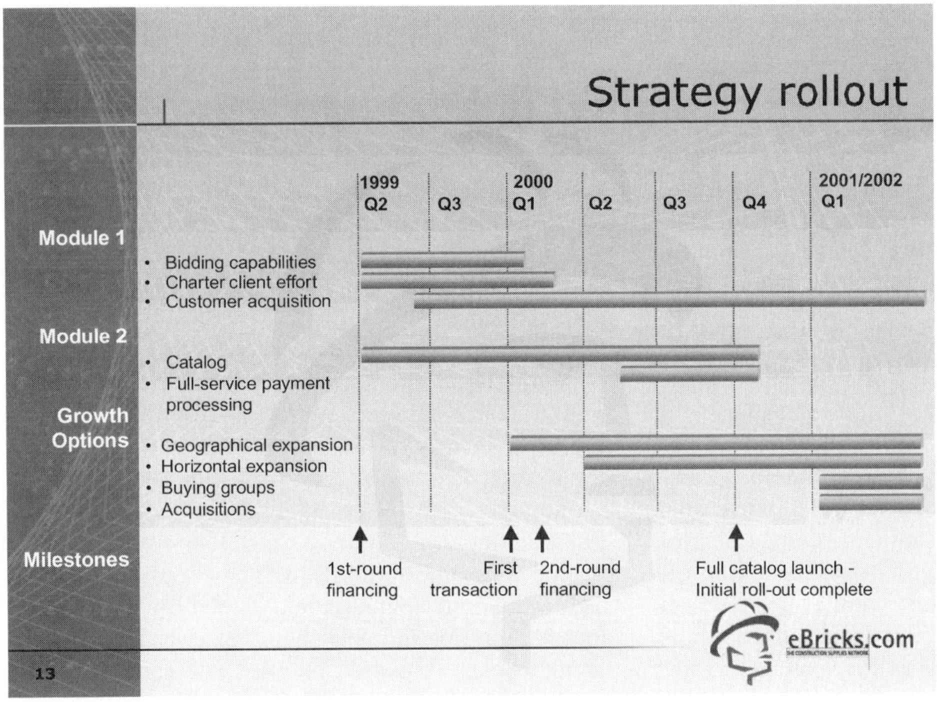

Financial highlights

Projections

- Financing needs of \$15-\$20 million in second round
- Round to be closed by January 30, 2000
- Cash positive by 2001
- Profitable by 2001

Strategy

- Invite investors bringing more than cash
- Option for mezzanine round
- Complete 2nd round concurrently with launch of bidding capabilities

Key Sensitivities

- Pricing strategy
- Time-to-market
- Customer adoption pace
- Sales expenditures
- Technology investment

eBricks.com

14

SOTHEBYS.COM

We are building the world's premier art and antiques auction sites. If you are looking for authenticated high-end items, we're it. The quality of what we sell and our expertise make us unique.

—Craig Moffett, MBA '89
and President, Sothebys.com

After 255 years in the fine arts auction business, the venerable firm Sotheby's (pronounced "SUH-thuh-beez") had decided to take half of its auctions completely online, while continuing its famous live auctions. Its Internet initiative, Sothebys.com, operated two separate sites: one bearing its own name and the other called Sothebys.Amazon.com. The primary question on Moffett's mind was how Sothebys.com should exploit the opportunities for leverage created by the Internet.

History and Mystique of Sotheby's Auctions

Sotheby's, arguably the most famous auction house in the world, enjoyed a reputation for selling important paintings, jewels, and antiques at record-breaking prices to the super-rich and glamorous. In 1985 Sotheby's sold Vincent Van Gogh's "Landscape with Rising Sun" for $9.9 million. Subsequently, Van Goghs began flying off auction blocks at record prices. Sotheby's also held celebrity auctions, such as the sale of the Duchess of Windsor's jewels and keepsakes (including a souvenir slice of her wedding cake). This sale quintupled Sotheby's highest estimates, raising over $50,000,000.[1]

New York-based, but with a major presence in London and offices in 98 other cities, the auction business operated under the umbrella of Sotheby's Holdings. Other divisions included Sotheby's Financial Services, Sotheby's Trusts and Estates Services, Sotheby's International Realty Group, Sotheby's Appraisal Services, Sotheby's Insurance Brokerage Services, and Sotheby's Restoration Services. In 1999 worldwide sales of goods at auction increased 16% to $2.3 billion (see Exhibit 1 for financial statements).

The company traced its origins to Samuel Baker, an eighteenth century English book dealer who bought aristocrats' libraries and sold them to newly affluent Londoners. Baker advertised his sales with catalogues. One from the 1750s announced, "He who bids most is the Buyer." Over the years, Sotheby's added prints, drawings, paintings, furniture, jewelry, and china to its auctions. This began a rivalry between Sotheby's and its primary competitor, Christie's, another auction house founded in the eighteenth century, which had always specialized in fine arts. That rivalry continued into the twenty-first century.

Live Auction Process

Property owners wanting to sell something through Sotheby's "consigned" it (consignment meant legally transferring a property to an agent for sale on the owner's behalf). This made Sotheby's responsible for the property until it was sold. In order to consign, prospective sellers would contact the Sotheby's specialist department most relevant to the best items for sale. Specialist departments covered fields such as "Old Master Paintings," "Nineteenth Century European Painting," and "East Asian Art." These departments were staffed with experts (specialists) considered to be among the best in their fields. According to one manager:

> It takes 20 years to develop a world-class specialist. Their skills can only be found in three places: Academia, top antique/fine arts/collectibles dealers, and the best auction houses. In many ways, our specialists are our rarest resource.

Research Associate Abby Hansen, Ph.D. prepared this case under the supervision of Professor Roger Hallowell as the basis for class discussion rather than to illustrate either effective or ineffective handling of an administrative situation.

[1]Historical data from Robert Lacey, *Bidding for Class* (Boston: Little, Brown, 1998).

If the appropriate Sotheby's specialist deemed the property owner's items likely to be valuable, he or she might arrange a site visit, request photographs, or ask the owner to send the items to Sotheby's in New York or London. After examining the property and determining its authenticity, the specialist would research recent prices fetched by comparable objects and present the owner with an appraisal of potential market value. The owner then decided whether or not to consign the property to Sotheby's for auction.

Property consigned to the auction house was generally taken or shipped to the New York (or London) headquarters. There it was received, given a receipt, and stored, with its shelf location carefully entered in a database. Sotheby's kept the property in its own storage space during this process. The property was then catalogued. This involved writing a description of the item, including its physical condition and the history of its ownership (if available). This description, and often a photograph, were included in the catalogue of lots to be sold at a particular auction. (A "lot" was a single item or several pieces grouped to be sold together for a single price). Photographs could be expensive, as owners were charged $900 for quarter-page color photos (smaller, black-and-white photos cost considerably less). After being catalogued and photographed, items were returned to their designated shelf spaces and stored to await exhibition and sale. Sotheby's specialists mailed catalogues to individuals known to be interested in the type of goods to be sold in a particular auction. Catalogues were also sold by subscription. An executive estimated that the cost of catalogue production (including photographs) and mailing, compared with the associated revenues, amounted to break-even.

Before the auction, specialists familiar with potential bidders phoned to let them know that an interesting item was coming up for sale. Collectors might phone specialists to ask for more details about particular lots. If they wished, prospective buyers could leave bids (the most they were willing to pay for a piece) with Sotheby's Left Bid Department. If bidding during a live auction stalled at a figure lower than the left bid, a Sotheby's employee would bid at the next increment called by the auctioneer, on behalf of the absent customer. Thus a buyer who left a bid could acquire an item for less than the bid he or she had left.

A few days before an auction, Sotheby's removed all items to be sold from storage and displayed them in a room near the auction hall—usually at Sotheby's, but sometimes in a private home. Potential bidders gathered at stipulated viewing times to examine the lots, with Sotheby's staff present to answer questions.

Before each sale, the exhibitions were dismantled and the lots stored behind the stage where the auctioneer would stand. Individuals wanting to bid had their credit approved by Sotheby's before the auction. This was not usually burdensome, as many were long-time Sotheby's clients. Once approved, bidders were issued numbered paddles, which they raised to signify agreement with a bid called by the auctioneer during the sale. At the predetermined time, bidders gathered like an audience, facing the auctioneer's podium. The auctioneer displayed each lot and described it as he or she called for bids, speaking rapidly and varying the pace based on the feeling of the room. Live auctions were glamorous, dramatic events that capitalized on the emotional aspect of competitive bidding.

The auctioneer led the bidding much as a musical conductor leads a performance. He or she determined the bidding increments, which grew larger as prices rose. Some clients bid by phone through a Sotheby's representative, or (as noted) left a maximum bid. When the bids slowed to a trickle, the auctioneer called fair warning and asked for a final bid. If no bidder volunteered, the auctioneer "dropped the hammer" (banged a ceremonial gavel) to signify that the last bid had won the lot. The lot was then removed from the podium and placed backstage.

Consignors (sellers) had the option of specifying a reserve price, below which a lot would not be sold. If the bids did not exceed this price, the lot would be "bought in" by the auction house on behalf of the seller. Estimates varied, but managers believed Sotheby's buy-in rate for live auctions was approximately 30%. Lots bought in might be held over for another auction or returned to the consignor, based on his or her wishes.

After the hammer fell, the high bidder could go to the shipping counter, pay immediately, and take the lot. If the buyer did not physically carry the piece out, he or she could have Sotheby's Purchasing Accounts Department write up an invoice. Once that was settled, Sotheby's Art Transport Department would arrange shipping with an outsourced shipper, at the buyer's risk and cost.

Well-educated, trained receptionists staffed counters placed near the entrance to the exhibit hall or auction room to answer questions before and during auctions. An executive estimated that about six people staffed the counter in New York. Receptionists sometimes directed clients to appropriate specialist departments. A few VIP customers had specific individuals assigned to them to take care of their needs.

Managers noted that auction houses usually accepted whole estates when they contained rare and precious items. Even when Sotheby's suggested that some of the less valuable items be given to a local antique (or semi-antique) dealer to sell, many sellers preferred that everything be sold by the auction house. As a result, items of modest value remained in the consigned estates. This forced Sotheby's, as one executive commented, "to sell off the silver in order to get the Modigliani"— a requirement that sometimes proved costly. The executive explained: "The process of cataloguing any item for sale is essentially the same, so we can end up spending more than we earn to sell, say, a piece of silver worth $1,250." The executive estimated that the majority of the items sold at traditional, live auctions either broke even or lost money for the firm.

Revenues

Sotheby's collected fees (called "premiums") from both consignors (see Exhibit 2) and buyers. The live auction buyer's premium was 20% of the hammer price up to and including $15,000, 15% of the next $85,000, and 10 percent on amounts exceeding $100,000. Executives noted that it was easier to sell lots than to get good lots to sell. They agreed, however, that "you have to be the best place to buy to attract buyers. And you have to be the best place to sell to attract sellers."

Online Auctions

Internet consumer auctions were anticipated to generate $19 billion in gross revenues by 2003.[2] (See Exhibit 3 for demographic data.) Hundreds of sites auctioned anything from fine arts to fossils. eBay, the largest and best known of the online auction businesses, had a stated mission to "help people trade practically anything on earth." Anyone could post items for sale on eBay and anyone else could bid on them. In 2000, eBay described itself as having over 10 million users. On a single day during April 2000, eBay offered 4,344,000 separate items in 4,372 categories with an average price point between $35 and $50 (estimates varied). eBay realized 1999 revenues of $224.7 million and profit of $10.8 million.[3]

[2]www.forrester.com, "Consumers Catch Auction Fever," January 18, 2000.

[3]Source: eBay Web site.

In January 2000, Edward Dolman, Christie's CEO, announced that Christie's would put everything in its auction catalogues on its web site, but not hold online auctions. Instead, the firm would provide live streaming videos, enabling bidders to participate in live auctions from their computer terminals.[4]

Sotheby's Creates Sothebys.com

Craig Moffett noted that 80% of Sotheby's lots sold for less than $5,000. He believed that many of these could be offered for sale on the Internet:

> You don't have to touch a lot of what we're selling to appreciate it. Think about stamps and coins, for example. For other types of things, we can provide much better photos online than we could in catalogues. We'll provide two or three shots of a single painting, and even let you see the frame. Catalogues don't do that, and lots of people buy paintings and jewelry from auction catalogues—in fact, 30% of what we sell in live auctions goes to buyers on the telephone or leaving left bids.

Moffett believed that the potential market of buyers was enormous. For example, he pointed out that there were 8 million millionaires in the country, most of whom had never thought of attending a Sotheby's auction. Now they could do so, just by going to their computers.

Sotheby's Holdings continued to conduct live auctions for very expensive items and for those consignors uncomfortable with the Internet auction medium. As a result, Sotheby's offered two auction formats through three separate vehicles: traditional live auctions, Sothebys.com for fine arts and antique objects typically selling for between $1,000 and $10,000, and Sothebys.Amazon.com for collectibles and general arts that typically sold for between $100 and $1,000 (in practice, price points became somewhat blurred). A Sotheby's executive stated that the combined online sites were expected to offer approximately the same number of lots per year as the live auctions did.

In the new business model, modestly priced property acquired along with large estates—items which the company might previously have urged sellers to consign to local dealers or refused to accept—was likely to be

[4]Source: "Ex-rugby player to tackle Christie's drive at the future," The Financial Times, London, Thursday, January 13, 2000, p. 8.

appropriate for one of the online sites. As a result, the volume of lower-priced lots that the firm handled increased.

Another element of the new business model was the formation of a network of fine arts, antiques, and collectibles dealers authorized to sell on the web sites. These were called Sotheby's Associates. Since Sotheby's guarantee extended to lots sold through all media (see Exhibit 4), its experts selected dealers carefully for reliability and expertise and checked their qualifications. In addition, Sotheby's experts reviewed the web sites daily for dealer-posted items that seemed questionable.

Once accepted as Associates, dealers were required to guarantee their merchandise and to auction goods online only on Sotheby's sites (or their own, if any). Dealers who sold fine arts, antiques, and collectibles were permitted to sell on either of Sotheby's sites. Those who specialized in collectibles and memorabilia were restricted to Sothebys.Amazon.com.

Before the sites launched, the company expected between 500 and 600 dealers to sign up. At launch, there were 3,000. By March 2000, 4,769 had signed, with about 1,000 selling only on the Sothebys.Amazon.com site.

Dealers posting items on the sites provided the same information (catalogue entries, photographs) that Sotheby's did for consigned goods and used the same format. In addition, dealers were required to provide email addresses to enable customers to contact them with questions about their merchandise. Dealers also packed and shipped their own goods. Unlike consignors, however, they paid no seller's premium. One Sotheby's executive said, "It's as if we're giving that antiques dealer on a dirt road in New Hampshire who has an eighteenth century grandfather clock a Madison Avenue address—for free."

Sothebys.Amazon.com

Sotheby's chose Amazon.com as a partner for one of its web sites because of Amazon's 15 million qualified buyers and well-developed technology. Sotheby's and Amazon.com split all profits and expenses from the new auction site (the split percent was undisclosed), and Sotheby's agreed to auction a certain quantity of lots consigned to it on the Amazon.com site every week. Amazon.com maintained the site and provided customer support for questions about registering, passwords, using the site, bidding, and billing. Requests for greater detail about properties on the site were funneled either to Sothebys.com's internal customer service department or to the dealers who had posted the items. In addition, Amazon.com handled all billing and the receipt of payments. (Because Amazon.com was responsible for customer service at the Sothebys.Amazon.com site, this case will focus primarily on the Sothebys.com site, unless otherwise noted.)

The Sothebys.com Site

Sotheby's took the process of bidding in live auctions directly to the web, with few changes. After viewing lots on the web site, a customer could bid by clicking on an icon. (In order to bid, customers had to pre-qualify by entering a credit card number; bidding on lots valued over $20,000 required a credit check or an existing Sotheby's relationship.) Customers could also leave a maximum bid. The buyer's premium was 10% of the hammer price.

Bidding moved in predetermined increments, which increased as the bid passed certain points (see Exhibit 5). Confusion surrounding the amount of the increment at a given point occasionally created disappointments for customers whose maximum bids, although higher than the winning bid, failed to win a lot. For example, it was possible for a bidder to leave a maximum bid of $5,025 and lose an item to a customer who bid $4,950. This situation would occur if bidding began at an amount such as $4,550. For bids between $1,000 and $5,000, the bidding increment was $100. This would mean that the following would be acceptable bids: $4,550, $4,650, $4,750, $4,850, $4,950. Because, for bids between $5,000 and $10,000 the bidding increment was $250, the next acceptable bid would be $5,200. As a result, $5,025 would not be recognized as an acceptable bid, and the highest acceptable bid ($4,950) would win the item. Managers were in the process of resolving this problem by implementing an automated system that would only accept an appropriate bid.

Auctions tended to last for two weeks, with information on time remaining for each lot prominently located on the web page that displayed the lot in question. Customers leaving maximum bids were sent automatic emails to notify them if they were outbid during the auction. Customers placing the winning bid also received an email. This message informed them of their purchase and instructed them to contact Sothebys.com customer service to arrange for shipping (for lots consigned to

Sotheby's) or to contact the dealer who had posted the lot (for Associates' lots).

Physical Lots for Virtual Auctions

The process of getting sellers to consign lots to Sotheby's online auctions was identical to the process used for live auctions. However, once consigned, lots for online auctions were handled differently. All lots (except furniture) consigned to Sotheby's for sale on either web site were handled in warehouse space leased from Sothebys.com's outsourced fine art shipper. Furniture was handled in a separate facility leased from a furniture moving company. After a specialist accepted a lot for consignment to an online auction, it was delivered to the outsourced warehouse. Although Sotheby's leased most of the warehouse's two top floors, only the very top floor space was uninterrupted. The space on the floor beneath included two very large storerooms, but these did not connect with one another.

Once received, each lot was entered into inventory and stored temporarily. (All jewelry was stored in a vault where all further operations were conducted and only one Sotheby's registrar had access.) Each lot was then catalogued (described, including its physical condition). A Sotheby's manager decided if the lot went to Sothebys.com or to Sothebys.Amazon.com. An employee of the outsourced shipper measured and weighed each lot and entered this information into a computer system that calculated approximate packing and shipping costs for the United States and the United Kingdom (this information was later posted online).

Each item was then digitally photographed in one of eight photo areas, each set up to accommodate different sizes of objects. On average, four photos were taken for Sothebys.com lots and three for Sothebys.Amazon.com lots. Photo instructions came from the cataloguing specialists, who stipulated which views they wanted. The photographs were edited using image-management software and uploaded into a database. Lots were then shelved, given bar codes and identification numbers to specify locations, and left to await auction.

Each day, a report came from Sothebys.com and Sothebys.Amazon.com listing lots that had been sold and paid for. (Nothing was shipped until payment was received.) From this report, a daily "pick list" of items was generated, and items on this list were physically removed from their storage locations and electronically removed from inventory.

The lots were then transported to another portion of the warehouse, which was controlled by the outsourced shipper. The outsource shipper's staff scanned the lots into their computer, accepting them into their inventory, and then packed them.

Wrapping and boxing required the time of 8.5 full-time-equivalent warehouse employees, plus a pricing agent. Packing was complex. There were 3 sizes of padded envelopes; 13 standard box sizes; 4 "strong box" sizes (for paintings and certain prints); and 3 flat box sizes for two-dimensional objects like prints. Custom-made crates were required for objects with unique dimensions or paintings worth over $10,000 (these boxes were made of wood strong enough to resist puncture by a forklift). Packing materials included bubble wrap, gray foam, tissue paper, and unprinted newsprint stock. An executive estimated that 50% of the cost of shipping a painting came from packing and materials. The executive commented, "You can't sell a $300 item that costs $500 to ship without creating 'clicker shock'; we've had auction winners try to withdraw their bids when they learn what shipping will cost. The better the information we provide online, the less buyer remorse will result." After packing, items were sent to buyers by mail or independent carrier.

An executive compared shipping in traditional versus online auctions: "In traditional auctions, slightly more stuff was shipped than was taken away by hand. In the dot com auctions, 100 percent of the items are shipped."

Dealer Lots for Virtual Auctions

Associates (dealers) were responsible for uploading all information about their properties into Sotheby's database. This included shipping estimates, catalogue entries, and photographs. Once this information was uploaded, it was checked by a Sotheby's specialist and immediately available on the site.

When an Associate's lot sold at auction, Sotheby's notified him or her by email. The Associate arranged for shipping, finalizing the charges based on the buyer's location. Associates provided shipping costs to Sotheby's, which then charged those costs, the sale price, and the buyer's premium to the buyer's credit card. For buyers of very expensive lots, information was provided on how to transfer the correct amount of money to Sotheby's. When Sotheby's received payment (by bank wire or credit card), it instructed the dealer, by email, to ship the property. The Associate then packed and shipped the item and notified Sotheby's of the shipment. When Sotheby's received this notification, it forwarded the sale price and shipping charges to the Associate.

Sothebys.com Customer Service

Sothebys.com chose to outsource its call center (called "tier one"). Managers called it the company's "first line of defense." The call center's role was to answer questions about the web site and auction process (see Exhibit 6 for typical customer service problems and proposed solutions). Customer service agents at the center funneled more difficult questions—relating to specific lots, or billing—to Sothebys.com in-house customer service staff in New York or London. This was called "tier two." There, questions were either answered or sent to the company's specialists in the appropriate areas. Specialists responded via tier two, which relayed their messages to tier 1, which contacted customers. Questions about shipping were sent to Sothebys.com's outsourced shipping firm, called "tier three," which responded through a process similar to that used by tier 2. Customers with questions about Associate-posted lots (including condition reports and shipping estimates) contacted the Associates directly. Dealers selling on Sothebys.com posted email addresses, and sometimes phone numbers and addresses. Tier one often had to refer customers to Associates.

Sothebys.com chose a call center provider with operations near a major mid-western city with several universities. A manager commented, "We wanted a location where people would have heard of Sotheby's." The center operated 24 hours a day, 7 days a week. Because the outsourcer also ran campaigns for other clients, it could assign employees to Sotheby's on a temporary basis during periods of unusually high volume.

Part of this company's appeal to Sotheby's was its ability to offer online chat in addition to inbound and outbound telephone calls and emails. The company was also able to demonstrate systems to ensure quality service. For example, alarms went off or reports were triggered if calls weren't answered within a specific number of rings or if emails weren't responded to in a certain number of hours.

The call center charged Sotheby's on a cost-plus basis. Typical calls cost Sotheby's approximately $10 and required 4 to 5 minutes of agent time. Emails required only 2 to 3 minutes, sometimes fewer if the agent could use a template to construct the response. Online chats often took 20 to 30 minutes, but left free time between responses. Agents and managers agreed that more than half of the questions they answered involved how to use the web site, including how to find information. Most customers preferred to speak with customer service over the phone.

Reaching Customer Service

Visitors to the Sothebys.com web site who clicked on the "help" icon or the large "instant help" button on the web page were linked to screens that asked if they wanted a call back (an agent to telephone them), to send an email, or to engage in online chat. The outsourced center did not offer a toll-free telephone number in the United States, although callers from Europe incurred only local charges. To find the center's telephone number, viewers clicked through several pages to one that held a drop-down box in which the number appeared.

Managers noted that between January 1 and March 31, 2000, 35,000 interactions (inbound and outbound calls, online chat, and emails) occurred between customers and the outsourced customer service center. During the same period the Sothebys.com site sold 7,000 lots.

Operations

The agents at the center responded to 85% of telephone calls, requests for a call back, and online chats within 30 seconds; 90% of emails received a response within four hours. Inquiries escalated to tier two or three were included in these statistics if customers were informed that their inquiry had been forwarded within the appropriate time frame.

The center operated with three shifts. The morning shift included 12 agents; the afternoon, 19; and the evening, 7. Most requests came in between 10 AM and 1 PM Central Time—lunch time on the East Coast. A manager pointed out that most questions could be answered with information on the site, but people—especially those lacking experience with computers—"wanted their hands held." Most of the inquiries that came during the night shift were from inexperienced computer users in Europe.

In general, customers new to Sotheby's and to auctions in general accounted for a large proportion of the call center's interactions. Customers often contacted the center several times to inquire about issues that had been escalated. Many calls requested clarification of bidding procedures. Web site navigation also presented a challenge to some customers.

A Sotheby's manager noted that, since Sothebys.com had begun posting U.S. and U.K. shipping estimates onsite with each of its consigned items, the volume of calls regarding shipping had fallen dramatically: "Before we put shipping information on the site, half of the bidders would contact us for an estimate. Fortunately, we identified and fixed this problem almost immediately. Now in a busy week when we sell over 1,000 lots with good shipping information posted onsite, we may get 20 calls about shipping." He added that each of the approximately 20 inquiries remaining were very expensive because of the number of steps involved in responding.

Managers believed that volume was predictable. Questions often increased toward the end of auction periods. In addition, following an auction, bidders were sometimes confused about why they had not won.

Much of their confusion stemmed from a peculiarity of Internet technology: during the last hour of an auction (when bidding activity was often intense), bidders needed to refresh their screens in order to see the true high bid and the precise amount of time left in the auction. Many bidders, however, were unaware that they needed to do this. In addition, Sothebys.com had adopted one particular element of the live auction process when it put its auctions online by creating what it called "popcorn time"—an automatic extension of an auction for 10 minutes when a bid came in during the last hour. Agents at the outsourced call center had to master the complexities of these issues in order to explain them to customers.

Processing Emails

When an email came in to the center, a keyword in its text ("shipping," "registration," or "bidding") shunted it to an electronic "box." Agents worked through different boxes during their shifts, in addition to taking calls and conducting chats. When they selected an email to answer, a template often appeared on their screen suggesting a routine answer based on the email's keyword. In addition, scripted phrases would appear for the agent to cut and paste electronically, if appropriate. Even with standardized templates and scripts, each email had to be customized and checked for appropriateness. A manager estimated that templates generally saved between 30 seconds and 2 minutes per email, and 35% of the email requests the center received could be answered with some use of templates (see Exhibit 7).

Customer Service Agents

In contrast to agents at many telephone-only call centers, Sothebys.com agents needed additional expertise. Managers preferred that agents have some college education, typing skills, the ability to use the Internet, good grammar, polite conversational style, and a fundamental inclination to be helpful. A manager noted, "Some people follow up with customers because it's in their personality. You can't train for that. Eventually, those who don't have it will fall out." Agents received a one-third premium in salary (relative to agents at the outsourcer's other call centers). Managers on-site hoped to reduce employee turnover to 25%.

New agents received a week of classroom training. During this period they learned about Sotheby's and simulated interactions with customers. After this, they spent another week "double jacking," or plugging their headsets into the same telephone jack as an experienced agent. During this time, they sat beside that agent, listening. Then they were allowed to take calls while sitting beside the agent with whom they had been double-jacked so that they could ask for help when appropriate. In addition, coaches monitored all new agents' emails and some of their phone calls. Of the 38 agents assigned to the account at the center, 13 were considered competent to send emails without supervision.

Customer Service Challenges

Customer service agents needed to understand many technical complexities, such as the difficulties encountered by users of AOL or the English Internet service provider Freeserve. Because neither of these browsers interacted smoothly with the Sotheby's site, customers who used them contacted the customer service center frequently to ask why they were having difficulty in placing bids online. A less technical issue involved the condition reports posted online for lots being auctioned. A manager commented that inadequate condition reports caused about 50% of customers wanting to bid on a piece to contact the outsourced call center for information (managers identified this problem and had it fixed by early January 2000). Customers also often experienced frustration when they asked to speak with an agent who had helped them previously and that agent was unavailable—either on another call or interaction, or working on a different shift that day.

Managing the Web Site

Jennifer Macdonald, Sothebys.com senior vice president for Interactive Design and Content, stated, "Before starting the online auctions, Sotheby's had a web site that functioned largely like the online equivalent of a flat brochure." She called it an "old club" site, designed for Sotheby's existing customers. Her response to the challenge of taking a large part of Sotheby's business completely to the Internet involved radically rethinking the site, which would continue to advertise live sales and satisfy existing customers' needs, while adding online auctions.

Macdonald commented that having an "800-pound gorilla" (eBay) in the online auction field "had created functional benchmarks against which all auction sites are now gauged—notions which Sothebys.com would have to accept and adapt, without abandoning the core of its own identity, brand, and business purpose."

Macdonald stated that "the first version of the web site that Sotheby's agency provided looked good, but was dysfunctional." (See Exhibit 8) The home page was organized using a grid structure that lacked compatibility with most viewers' browsers. The web pages frequently failed to load. In addition, several of the clickable buttons that linked viewers to information about live auctions and the Amazon.com site were located "below the fold" (not visible in a normal page view without scrolling down). Macdonald commented, "The design of the early sites was not only technologically unworkable, it didn't adequately address the customer's needs."

The agency produced further designs that were more functional. These, however, failed to satisfy Macdonald's desire for a look and feel of "spare elegance" that conveyed a sense of "assurance" expressing Sotheby's trademark style (see Exhibit 9). Macdonald rejected these designs, deciding to develop a more attractive, functional web page in-house.

Macdonald believed most web sites are envisioned three-dimensionally, despite their flat onscreen appearance. She noted, "Linguistically, we refer to clicking through pages, because our metaphors about the web largely reference space." She believed that this functional aspect of web pages implied a need for simplicity, to avoid confusing or frustrating users. Thus, when Macdonald redesigned the outsourced web page, she "uncluttered" it, increasing the amount of "white" space surrounding important images, text, and clickable icons (see Exhibit 10 for redesigned web page).

Navigation, Page Design, Business Purpose

Macdonald believed that navigation comprised both the way one moved among the web pages on a site and the design of individual pages. She commented that navigation had to reflect "the overarching purpose of the whole enterprise." Her goal was to make the typical Sothebys.com web page more "transparent," a term she used referring to users' lack of awareness about devices used to move them seamlessly through a web site (she compared it to the invisibility of well-done special effects in a movie). She also emphasized "page-to-page redundancy" in design (creating web pages that carried the same kind of information and icons in the same places). She believed that redundancy allowed visitors to learn to locate information so quickly that the skill felt like an instinct.

Macdonald summed up the multiple functions of web pages and their relation to the way a site functioned: "The primary goal of a successful e-commerce web site should be to reduce (through good design and a well-honed business model) the distance between a user's desire for an object and the gratification of that desire through successful online acquisition. The paradigm is simple and virtually foolproof: the shorter the distance, the more successful the customer will be acquiring what he or she wants."

In the future, Macdonald looked forward to web site design in which viewers could think of web pages not hierarchically (with some underneath and some on top), but organically and associatively, more akin to the way in which people's minds work. She noted, "Increasingly, database design and its visual counterpart will be able to be responsive to the associative and inductive aspects of the way our minds arrive at what we want, and as such will reduce further the distance between 'want' and 'have.' The customer imagines something, finds it, clicks on it, and has it."

Continuous Improvement

Macdonald's group conducted frequent studies, informally asking colleagues to use the site and carefully observing where they had problems. They also held formal focus groups. The information they gained was analyzed and applied to make incremental improvements to the site (see Exhibit 11 for a page with comments for improvement). An example: The introduction of subtle lines behind topic headings—lines that changed color as the cursor slid over them, indicating that they were clickable and could link the viewer to more information. Metrics were continually collected to analyze where people clicked on the site, and how often. This illustrated where they got stuck, or confused, failing to find the information they sought—all indications of areas in need of clearer design. The endpoint of these studies was to help people get all the information they needed to make an informed decision. Macdonald's group analyzed click metrics daily, and conducted studies to interpret the meaning of unusual numbers of clicks. Each conclusion suggested a possible improvement, but, as Macdonald pointed out, "Change is expensive; people underestimate this."

A future improvement planned for the site was "My Sotheby's." This function would let viewers list items they were looking for (for example, for a 19th century blue Canton vase between 18 and 23 inches high) and enable a search engine to find them anywhere on the site. Most important, this search would occur daily until the request was canceled.

Macdonald noted that people often underestimated the sheer technical complexity of maintaining a functioning web site. For example, Sotheby's online auction search engine could only provide information about online auction items. In addition, the site initially posed problems for people placing bids through AOL or the British Internet service provider Freeserve.

Further complicating the technological aspect of web design was the intricacy of combining existing IT systems with new Internet functions. A manager stated that web designers need "to integrate complicated database structures with off-the-shelf software and 'middleware' solutions to enable 'legacy systems' to be used." Macdonald added, "You wouldn't believe what kinds of problems you see behind a web site. It's a contraption cobbled together from different kinds of software. That's the dirty little secret of *every* web site out there—we all just hope the problems don't sink us."

In practice, Macdonald pointed out that technology posed powerful constraints, not only because of incompatibility with existing databases, search engines, and servers, but because of the limitations of customers' hardware and software. She lamented: "There are beautiful navigational structures I would love to use, but I can't because too many web users just don't have the proper plug-ins and settings to interact with them. All of the new stuff—the fun, innovative stuff—you can't use unless you are willing to lose a huge percentage of your viewing audience (in certain instances, all AOL users). These are bargains that no serious e-commerce web site would make."

Developing the Associates Network

> *For the classic antique dealer it's not about making money—it's about a lifestyle. It's a habit. Despite this, anyone trying to make a living as a dealer needs to buy or sell something just about every day. Buying is what's fun—but in order to buy, you've got to sell.*
>
> —Chris Jussel

Chris Jussel, senior vice president of the Associates Program and original host of the popular Public Broadcasting System television series, *Antiques Roadshow,* was hired by Sotheby's to develop and manage the Associates (dealers) network. Although the majority of Associates who signed up had never placed a lot on either site, Jussel believed that they would realize the benefits of using the network soon. He stated:

> If you ask a trader for a definition of inventory, it's what isn't selling. Because dealers find collecting an obsession, only about 30% of them agree with this definition—more in Europe. Those 30% are the ones we target to be Associates and work with after they join. They use the web sites as an inventory management tool—and to expand their market by cherry picking some of Sotheby's best customers, new and old.

Jussel commented on choosing new Associates:

> We'll get a recommendation from a specialist that a dealer should be considered. First we work with the specialist to establish the dealer's honesty, experience, and level of quality. Then we go out to visit the shop. When I walk in I ask myself, "Could we sell everything in here through the live business?" If the answer is no, the dealer's not right for us.

Changing Associate Behavior

Industry observers noted that just after Sothebys.com started, there was a feeling that "the Associate network would sell itself." Jussel disagreed, saying:

> No prudent manager says a product sells itself. They just don't. In this case, different Associates have different needs. Our job is to find out what the need is and meet it, one by one—it's the only way.

Another manager noted:

> Our biggest challenge is overcoming inertia. Associates are conservative. Besides, there's a history of rivalry between auction houses and dealers—many dealers think we've tried to take over their market. In the past, we used to sell mostly to them. Now a lot of the buyers at an auction are retail, so in a way we are competing. When you add in the emotions that surround art and antiques, you get a complicated situation.

Jussel's group dedicated to recruiting and working with Associates included 17 FTE employees. Many of these individuals were specialists with primary responsibilities in other areas. These individuals were torn between doing whatever it took to get an Associate to post lots on the site and becoming what one manager called "glorified customer service reps." Jussel, however, stressed the need for his people to train and work with Associates:

> What are we supposed to do with an Associate who has questions—send him to customer service? Besides, once they're up and running, some place a lot of items on the sites. We've got an Associate who has hundreds of lots up at any given time. It takes about a month of hand-holding to get someone going. It isn't impossible. Our best person can handle 300 Associates, about a third of whom are in that first-month stage.

Sotheby's offered training for Associates, inviting them to come to week-long sessions held every few months in New York, London, Paris, Los Angeles, or Chicago. There, they learned cataloguing, digital photography, and how to upload information about their auction lots onto the sites. While Associates were responsible for their own expenses, Sotheby's covered all training costs. Sotheby's was experimenting with sending trainers to very large Associates with significant potential. Jussel, however, thought it worked better when Associates came to Sotheby's.

Jussel's group had identified approximately 11,000 potential Associates in the United States and 38,000 in Europe and Asia. Of these, he estimated that perhaps 20% to 30% would not qualify on closer inspection.

Conclusion

The Internet sites had, by all managers' accounts, been a success. By the end of their first month in operation they were already selling more lots than all other fine-art related auction sites combined. After four months in operation, Sothebys.com and Sothebys.Amazon.com predicted 50% buy-in rates. Unlike in live auctions, bought-in lots could be re-offered almost immediately. (The buy-in rate for re-offered lots was similar to that for lots offered the first time.) Several "event" auctions, such as the sale of a major baseball memorabilia collection on Sothebys.Amazon.com, had a buy-in rate below 1%. The hammer price of the average lot selling on Sothebys.com was $2,000. On Sothebys.Amazon.com, it was $600. Managers believed that there was "a virtually inexhaustible supply of art and antiques in our price ranges."

One thousand Associates had listed at least one lot, and 500 Associates were actively selling on the web sites. Several managers agreed that dealers seemed to prefer to sell through Sothebys.com. Dealers actively selling offered an average of 10 lots for auction at any given time. Given the two-week auction cycle, this meant that these active Associates were placing 260 lots per year. In the first three months of operation, the volume of dealer lots on the sites had doubled. According to an executive:

> Aside from the opportunity to reach new retail customers, the sites are a great business-to-business opportunity: A dealer can sell through a shop at a 200% markup and turn inventory twice a year; or, he can sell through us at a 150% markup and turn inventory in four weeks.

Despite the successes, there were challenges. One Sothebys.com executive noted, "The longer I'm here, the more the specialists drive us toward operating like the live business." Another noted, "In the past, a specialist talked up an auction by calling collectors and sending out some catalogues—how do we do that for the web sites?"

Sotheby's expected to accept 100,000 consigned lots during 2000, half of which would be auctioned live and half on-line at its two sites. While some of the lots sold through the Internet represented new volume, many would have been sold through live auctions in the past. Incremental costs from the Internet strategy, net of additional revenues from increased numbers of lots consigned to Sotheby's, were expected to be $40 million in each of the first and second years of the Internet strategy. Almost all of those costs were fixed. According to Moffett, "We're losing money on most of the lots consigned to us."

Moffett took out a pencil, a pad of paper, and his calculator to check the fundamental economics of the new business model one more time. Because he wasn't sure what volume would be moving through each of his web sites, he simplified his math by putting everything through Sothebys.com, at least for his first pass at the numbers.

Exhibit 1 SOTHEBY'S HOLDINGS FINANCIAL STATEMENTS ($ IN THOUSANDS, EXCEPT PER-SHARE DATA)

	1999	1998
Revenues		
Sales of goods at auction	$2,258,752	$1,939,743
Commissions (premiums) and related fees	$390,101	$367,204
Other	52,484	79,848
Total revenue	$442,585	$447,052
Expenses		
Direct costs of services	85,563	76,313
Salaries and related costs	159,686	153,959
General and administrative	125,711	108,240
Depreciation and amortization	17,452	12,562
Non-recurring charges	–	15,200
Total expenses	$388,412	$366,184
Operating income	54,173	80,868
Interest income	$ 4,373	$ 3,560
Interest expense	(5,589)	(10,545)
Other income (expense)	(807)	20
Income before taxes	$ 52,150	$ 73,813
Income taxes	19,296	28,788
Net income	$ 32,854	$ 45,025
Basic earnings per share	$ 0.57	$ 0.79
Diluted earnings per share	$ 0.56	$ 0.79
Dividends per share	$ 0.40	$ 0.40

Exhibit 1 ANNUAL BALANCE SHEET ($ IN THOUSANDS) cont.

	As of December 31	
	December 1999	December 1998
Assets		
Cash and cash equivalents	$ 42,319	$ 71,238
Net receivables	641,345	440,882
Inventories	20,843	16,915
Other current assets	31,740	40,007
Total current assets	$ 736,247	$569,042
Gross plant, property and equipment	305,124	169,068
Accumulated depreciation	72,463	60,154
Net plant, property and equipment	$ 232,661	$108,914
Investments at equity	35,982	36,737
Other investments	42,535	17,115
Intangibles	24,124	32,588
Other assets	1,963	5,614
Total assets	$1,073,512	$770,010
Liabilities		
Notes payable	$ 272	$ 2,098
Accounts payable	126,263	104,251
Taxes payable	20,427	38,944
Accrued expenses	@CF	@CF
Other current liabilities	429,825	296,908
Total current liabilities	$ 576,787	$442,201
Long-term debt	100,000	–
Deferred income taxes	9,126	11,789
Other liabilities	10,555	1,933
Equity		
Common stock	5,885	5,716
Capital surplus	156,125	104,092
Retained earnings	215,034	204,279
Common equity	$ 377,044	$314,087
Total equity	$ 377,044	$314,087
Total liabilities and equity	$1,073,512	$770,010
Common shares outstanding	58,844	57,160

Exhibit 2 SELLERS' (CONSIGNORS') PREMIUM SCHEDULE FOR LIVE AND ONLINE AUCTIONS

Consignors pay a selling commission that is deducted, along with any agreed-upon expenses, from the hammer price. Sotheby's charges a commission based on the total hammer prices of all property sold or purchased by a consignor at Sotheby's auctions (including Sothebys.com and Sothebys.amazon.com) in the calendar year in which the property is sold. The rates on a consignor total sales and purchases are set forth below:

Total Hammer Prices of Sales and Purchases	Commission (percentage of hammer price)
$0–$1,999	20%
$2,000–$7,499	15%
$7,500–$99,999	10%
$100,000–$249,999	8%
$250,000–$499,999	7%
$500,000–$999,999	5%
$1,000,000–$2,499,999	4%
$2,500,000–$4,999,999	2%
$5,000,000 and more	Special terms on a case-by-case basis

If a consignor's property remains unsold, we will ask the consignor for a reduced commission rate of 5% of the reserve price, and a minimum handling charge of $75.
Source: Sothebys.com web site, May 4, 2000.

Exhibit 3 CHARACTERISTICS OF ONLINE AUCTIONS USERS(BY PERCENT)

Married	66%
Incomes below $50,000 per year	53%
Less than a college degree	49%
Less than 40 years old	49%
Expert PC users	33%

Source: *Wall Street Journal Interactive*, March 23, 2000,

Exhibit 4 SOTHEBY'S GUARANTEE

Terms of Live Auction Guarantee

Sotheby's warrants the authenticity of Authorship of each lot . . . on the terms and conditions set forth below.

1. ***Definition of Authorship.*** "Authorship" is defined as the creator, period, culture, source of origin, as the case may be, as set forth in the **BOLD TYPE HEADING** of a lot . . .
2. ***Guarantee Coverage.*** Subject to the exclusions in 5 and 6 below, Sotheby's warrants the Authorship (as defined above) of a lot for a period of five years from the date of sale of such lot and only to the original purchaser of record at the auction. If it is determined to Sotheby's satisfaction that the **BOLD TYPE HEADING** is incorrect, the sale will be rescinded . . . provided the lot is returned to Sotheby's at the original selling location in the same condition in which it was at the time of sale. It is Sotheby's general policy, and Sotheby's shall have the right to have the purchaser obtain, at the purchaser's expense, the opinion of two recognized experts in the field, mutually acceptable to Sotheby's and the purchaser, before Sotheby's determines whether to rescind a sale under the above warranty. . . .
5. ***Exclusions.*** This warranty does not apply to: (i) Authorship of any paintings, drawings or sculpture created prior to 1870, unless the lot is determined to be counterfeit (a modern forgery intended to deceive). . . .

Source: Sale 7359, New York, Sotheby's, October 20 and 21, 19.

Terms of Sothebys.com Guarantee

- . . . Where items of property are offered for sale on this Site by a Seller other than Sotheby's, the Seller of such item is solely responsible for estimates, descriptions, condition, authenticity, title and all other matters relating to the offer and sale of such item, and neither Sotheby's, the site Provider nor any of their affiliated entities have seen the relevant item or are responsible for any errors or omissions with respect to such information.
- **Limitations of Guarantees**
  . . . Other than as set forth in the specific warranty and guarantee set forth in paragraph 3, all Property on the Site is sold AS IS. . . .
- **Certain Guarantees**
  Sellers make certain guarantees with respect to property offered for sale on the Site. Please note that ONLY statements in fields labeled as "Guaranteed" on the lot description page, and which are not otherwise expressly qualified in the applicable field as being "Not Guaranteed," are guaranteed by the Seller . . . In addition, statements relating to the authenticity, creator or originator and culture or source of origin of a lot are further qualified by the specific limitations set forth in the following subparagraph (i), even if the field in which such statement is made is labeled as "Guaranteed" on the lot description page.

  (i) *Authenticity Guarantee.* Subject to the limitations set forth above and below, the Seller guarantees that (i) the lot is not a counterfeit (as defined below), and (ii) the creator or originator of the lot, and/or the date on which or period during which the lot was created, and/or the culture or source of origin with which the item is identified, is as set out in the Guaranteed Property Description of the lot (the "Authenticity Guarantee") . . . The Authenticity Guarantee of each lot sold on the Site is given for a period of three (3) years . . . and is only given to the Site Provider and the person who purchased the lot on the Site and not to any subsequent owner. . . .

Exhibit 4 SOTHEBY'S GUARANTEE cont.

The Authenticity Guarantee does NOT apply to:

The actual authorship of any paintings, drawings or sculpture created prior to 1870, unless the lot is determined to be a counterfeit . . . The authorship of Chinese and Japanese paintings, regardless of the date of creation; The date of execution and type of wood for Chinese furniture. . . .

If it is determined to the Seller's reasonable satisfaction that a sale is subject to rescission under the terms of the Authenticity Guarantee or applicable law, the Seller is obligated to rescind the sale in accordance with paragraphs (iii) and (iv) below, provided that the lot is returned to the Seller at its place of business in the same condition as it was at the time of sale and free from any claims by third parties. The Seller may request, before determining whether to rescind a sale under the Authenticity Guarantee, that the Buyer obtain the written opinion of up to two recognized experts in the relevant field who are mutually acceptable to the Seller and the Buyer.

(ii) *Physical Condition Guarantee*—The Seller also warrants that the description of a lot's physical condition is substantially correct based upon a fair reading of the description of the item taken as a whole. This warranty applies only for a period of two (2) weeks from the date the lot is received by the Buyer . . .

(iii) *Seller is Liable.* As stated in paragraph 1, where items of property are offered for sale on this Site by a Seller other than Sotheby's, the Authenticity Guarantee and the Physical Condition Guarantee are offered solely by the Seller . . .

Source: Sothebys.com web site, January 23, 2000.

Exhibit 5 SOTHEBYS.COM BIDDING INCREMENTS

Amount Bid	Bidding Increment
10–100	10
100–50	25
500–1,000	50
1,000–5,000	100
5,000–10,000	250
10,000–20,000	500
20,000–50,000	1,000
50,000–100,000	2,500
Over 100,000	3,000

Source: Adapted from information from Sothebys.com.

Exhibit 6 TYPICAL OUTSOURCED CUSTOMER CENTER SERVICE PROBLEMS AND RECOMMENDED SOLUTIONS

Service Problem	Recommended Solution
Log In/Password/Registration Issues	[six-step process to address these issues]
Cookies	Offer the following–set cookies to "set to accept all"
AOL problems	Ask if they use a MAC or PC, and which browser. If client is using AOL, will need to minimize AOL and download Internet Explorer or Netscape.
If using Microsoft Internet Explorer or Netscape AND problem still exists	Check which version is being used.
If MAC + Internet Explorer Combination	Launch Netscape instead.
Using Freeserve (U.K. ISP)	Use another ISP.
WebTV	We do not currently support WebTV users.
Search Function not performing	Check browser, modify search page.
Credit Card Validation error when trying to bid	[seven-step process]
Customer Finding Sold/Closed Lots	Remove lot
Problems with Lots Currently being Auctioned	Escalate to supervisor.
Server Error/Timing Out	Have user click "refresh/reload" icon.

Source: Sotheby's.

Exhibit 7 OUTSOURCED CUSTOMER SERVICE CENTER—LIST OF ISSUES FOR WHICH TEMPLATES EXISTED

ArtLink
Valuation Forms
- English
- Italian
- French
- Spanish

Replies to clients whose e-mails have been forwarded to Tier 2
Request for catalogues
Request for auction results
Request to send digital photos
Request for photos
Research Questions (Artist)
"Antiques Roadshow"
"At the Auction"
Sotheby's Institute
"I am a dealer, how can I become a Sotheby's online Associate?"
"I would like to sell in your Internet auctions, how can I do that?"
Shipping
Viewing Property
Private Offers
Responding Too Late to Specialist Inquiry
Bulk Shipping?
"Can I Pick Up My Purchases?"
Delay in Receiving Transaction Statements
Request for Overnight Delivery
"Why was I Charged Tax?" (Non-Dealer)
"It's Broken."

Source: Sotheby's.com

Exhibit 8 OUTSOURCED WEB SITE: PAGE VIEW OF FIRST VERSION

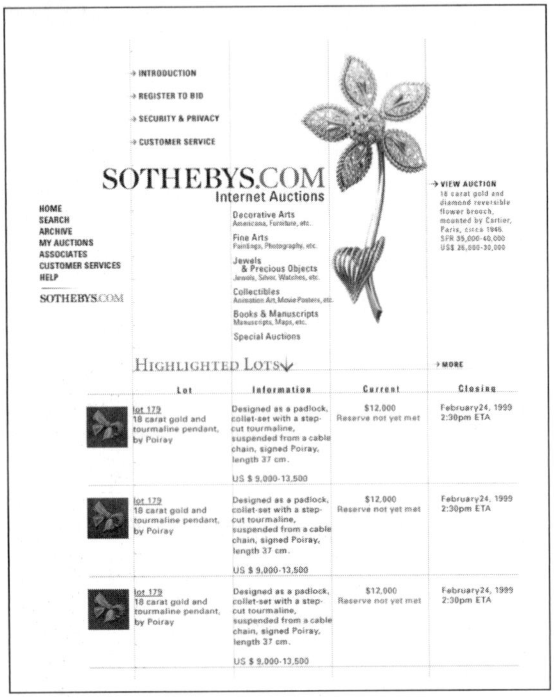

Exhibit 9 OUTSOURCED WEB SITE: SECOND VERSION

Exhibit 10 IN-HOUSE DESIGNED WEB SITE

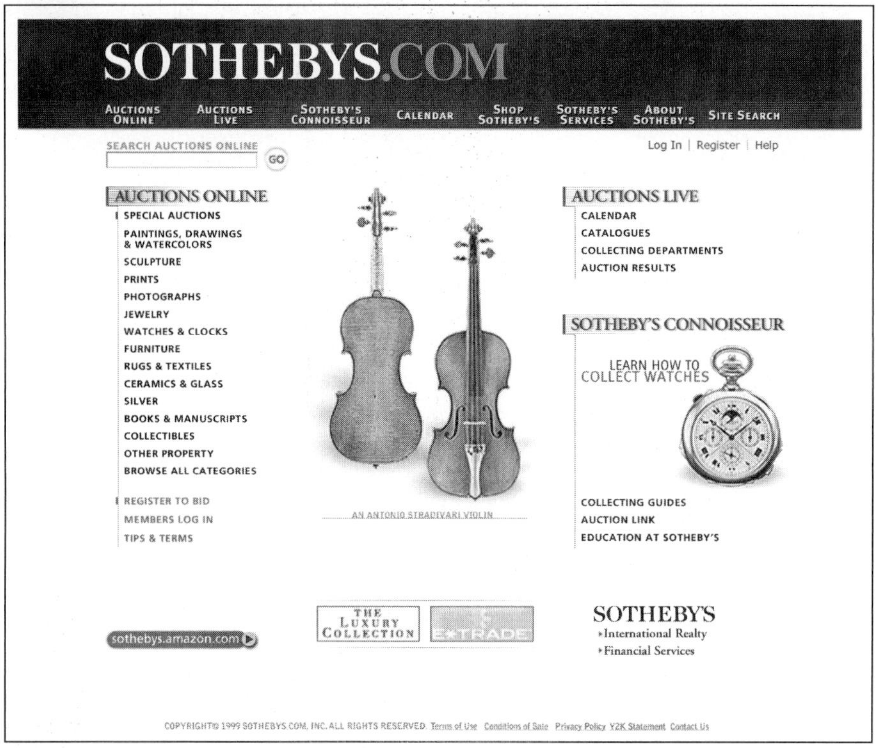

Exhibit 11 ANNOTATED WEB PAGE WITH COMMENTS FOR IMPROVEMENT

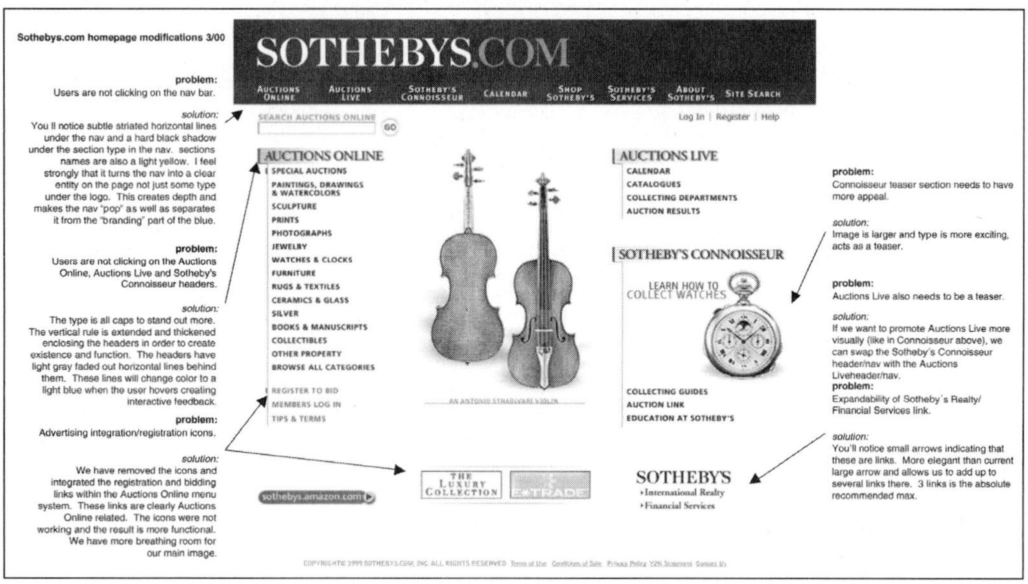

7

Networked Utility Providers

Networked utilities are software programs that connect users with destination websites or with each other, allowing users to complete specialized tasks that are beyond the basic capabilities of Web browsers and e-mail programs, e.g., accessing "rich media" or chatting in real time. Utilities are downloaded—usually free of charge—as browser "plug-ins" ("applets" that extend the functionality of browsers when specific connectivity features are required) or as "thin clients" that run in parallel with browsers.[1] Examples of utilities include Adobe's Acrobat Reader, which allows users to download and read documents; RealNetworks' RealPlayer, through which users can access audio and video content "streamed" over the Internet;[2] and America Online's ICQ service, which allows instant messaging between groups of Internet users.

Assistant Professor Thomas Eisenmann and Research Associate Alastair Brown prepared this note as the basis for class discussion.

Because networked utility providers facilitate specialized tasks that require connectivity (user-to-website or user-to-user), providers typically must develop technical standards.[3] In doing so, the providers face many strategic challenges not encountered with other Internet business models. Online portals, content providers, and retailers, for example, do not need to propagate standards; they can count on the universal acceptance of HTML and TCP/IP and the ubiquitous availability of browsers that leverage these standards. By contrast, networked utility providers frequently battle with each other to establish the dominant standard for a given application. The stakes are high—often winner-take-all. Furthermore, the tactics that networked utility providers use to advance their standards sometimes make it difficult for providers to profit if they do succeed. For example, revenue generation may prove difficult when, to encourage widespread and rapid adoption, a standard is made freely available to any interested party that wishes to exploit it.

The first section of this chapter defines and describes ways to categorize utilities, explaining the differences between the networked-utility-provider business model and the models employed by some other Internet companies, such as content providers and portals. The second section discusses the economic model for networked utilities, focusing on revenue and cost drivers. The third section examines some of the challenges that networked utility providers encounter in establishing a standard and describes tactics that they can employ to improve the odds of success. Building on that analysis, the final section examines the payoff to networked utility providers from pursuing a "Get Big Fast" strategy, i.e., investing heavily in customer acquisition.

DEFINITION, CATEGORIZATION, AND DELINEATION

Definition and Categorization

Networked utilities may be categorized by the types of applications that are provided. Major categories include media players, communications enablers, and e-wallet applications.

- *Media players* such as RealPlayer, Adobe Acrobat, and Shockwave are used to access files that incorporate prerecorded audio, photos, animation, and/or video elements.[4] Such files may be streamed (i.e., viewed immediately) or downloaded to a user's PC for later consumption. In addition to helping users with file access and playback, media players may provide other functions, such as searching for relevant content, "digital rights management" (e.g., matching decryption keys to verify that a user has been authorized to access copyrighted content and processing payments for such content), and management of users' archives of downloaded files.
- *Communications enablers* include applications like ICQ for instant messaging and software that facilitates Internet Protocol (IP) telephony.[5]
- The *e-wallets* are software programs that store credit card and user contact information to facilitate secure and convenient online purchasing.

The application types described above share a common characteristic: The networked utility provider who distributes them must mobilize a network of users, i.e., exploit a network effect.[6] Consumers, for example, will only adopt a given e-wallet if they can use it at a wide range of e-commerce destination sites, and commerce sites will only support the e-wallet if a large number of consumers use it. Some downloadable software otherwise fits the description of a utility (i.e., it augments browser capabilities to complete a specialized task) but is not networked. For example, Atomica's free downloadable reference software allows users to point at a word on a webpage, then simply "alt-click" to instantly receive contextually relevant information, ranging from dictionary definitions to weather forecasts to stock quotes. Atomica's users do not connect with each other, nor does Atomica rely on the participation of large numbers of third-party destination websites. Atomica is a utility, but it is not a *networked* utility.[7]

Hybrid Internet Business Models

Companies that offer networked utilities sometimes do so in combination with other Internet business models. An example is Macromedia's popular Shockwave software, which allows Internet users to interact with rich-media files authored through Macromedia's Director Shockwave Studio (and through other multimedia authoring tools). By mid-2000, Macromedia had distributed 140 million Shockwave players (players had been installed on 51 percent of desktop PCs), many of which were downloaded through a destination website called Shockwave.com. In addition to facilitating downloads, Shockwave.com served as a portal for rich-media content: Users could go to the site to access a wide variety of games (e.g., "Deerhunter," "Centipede," and "Real Pool"), music videos, animated short features (e.g., the very popular and grotesque "Frog in a Blender" and "Stainboy"), and animated greeting cards. Shockwave.com had 20 million registered users and 5.7 million unique visitors in July 2000 and was projected to earn $23 million in ad revenue during 2000. In addition to aggregating third-party content, Shockwave.com had itself commissioned animated shorts, including "webisodes" (episodes featuring the same set of characters) from the creators of the animated television series "South Park." Thus, in developing its Shockwave franchise, Macromedia simultaneously served as a networked utility provider, a portal, and an online content provider. Macromedia earned ad revenue through the latter two business models and profited as a networked utility provider through the sale of authoring tools to website developers.[8]

Just as networked utility providers sometimes develop portals, mass-market portals frequently serve as networked utility providers—especially with respect to communications applications. Yahoo!, for example, offers instant messenger software and IP telephony service through partnerships with delta three and Net2Phone. The synergy between the portal and networked utility provider business models is clear. Portals seek "stickiness": They offer features that encourage users to linger on the site and generate additional advertising page views.[9] Networked communications applications meet this need well. At the same time, in establishing a technical standard, networked applications benefit from access to a large user base. The leading mass-market portals—Yahoo!, AOL, and MSN—each reach 50 to 70 percent of U.S. Internet users in a given month. Thus, any of these services can create a self-contained community for networked communications applications, such as instant messaging.

NETWORKED UTILITY ECONOMICS

The economic model for networked utilities is similar in some respects to that for online content providers: Both types of businesses incur significant fixed costs in creating a product, then incur minimal variable costs in distributing copies of that product.[10] Both types of businesses thus have an incentive to give their product away to end users. By making their content freely available, online content providers can maximize their audience and thus their primary source of revenue, advertising. Similarly, networked utility providers tend to make their software freely available to end users, but for another reason: Quickly increasing a site's installed base improves the odds that it will establish a dominant standard.

Such networked utility providers then may earn revenue by selling server software and authoring tools to companies that want to deliver content to that installed base. Also, like online content providers, many networked utility providers sell ads to marketers that wish to target their users.

The discussion of networked-utility-provider economics that follows will focus on companies that provide media players because media players represent the largest category of networked utilities and because financial data is readily available for three publicly-traded companies that have established dominant standards in their respective segments: RealNetworks, Adobe Systems, and Macromedia.

Sources of Revenue

Networked utility providers earn revenues from three principal sources: (1) server software, authoring tools, and professional services, (2) premium versions of end-user software, and (3) advertising.

Server Software, Authoring Tools, and Professional Services. The largest revenue stream for most networked utility providers is from the sale of server-side software, authoring tools, and professional services such as hosting. By late 2000, RealNetworks had distributed 182 million copies of its RealPlayer software and 50 million copies of RealJukebox (which, in addition to accessing streamed content, enabled users to download and archive MP3 music files and other software). Consequently, about 85 percent of all streaming webpages were powered by RealNetworks server software. RealNetworks earned roughly 70 percent of its 2000 revenues from (1) authoring and encoding tools used by content providers to prepare audio or video for digital streaming, (2) server software (sold for about $2,000 per copy) that monitored available bandwidth, streamed content at an appropriate rate to the RealPlayer software, and inserted ads into the content stream, and (3) fees related to managing content delivery networks on behalf of content providers and ISPs.[11]

As another example, Macromedia was projected to earn $100 million and $50 million in its fiscal year ending March 2001 from the sale of its Flash and Director authoring tools, respectively.[12] Flash (sold for $300 to $400 per copy) was used by over 500,000 website developers to create animated webpages that were streamed to Flash Players, which had been pre-installed (by browser-software providers or PC manufacturers) or freely downloaded by users to 248 million desktop PCs. The Director Shockwave Studio (sold for about $1,000 per copy) was used to integrate several media formats (including animation, photos, audio, and video) into rich-media webpages. The only other source of revenue from Macromedia's Flash and Director franchise was from advertising generated by the Shockwave.com website, projected to be $23 million in fiscal year 2001.

Likewise, Adobe had developed PDF (portable document format) into the dominant standard for transferring documents over the Internet, having freely distributed over 200 million Acrobat Readers worldwide.[13] Adobe exploited the PDF standard by selling Acrobat software (for $249 per copy), which allowed users to create PDF documents. The Acrobat family also included the PDF Merchant software that encrypted PDF documents and integrated with a customer's e-commerce transaction systems to facilitate digital rights management. Adobe charged $5,000 plus 2 percent of transaction revenue for its Merchant software. Finally, for a $10 monthly fee, Adobe provided an outsourced PDF creation service whereby clients could e-mail a document to Adobe, then receive (by e-mail) a PDF-formatted file. In total, Adobe was expected to realize about $200 million in sales from Acrobat software during 2000.[14]

Premium Client Software. Another source of revenue for networked utility providers is from the sale of premium versions of client software, offering features not available with the free basic version. For example, an estimated 11 percent of total revenue in 2nd quarter 2000 for RealNetworks came from sales of RealPlayer Plus and RealJukebox Plus, the advanced versions of its downloadable media players, which were typically priced at $30 per copy. About 1 to 2 percent of users who downloaded RealNetworks' software elected to upgrade to these premium versions.[15]

Adobe also sold a premium version of the Acrobat Reader, called Business Tools, priced at $49 per copy. Business Tools did not allow users to create PDF files but added value by facilitating workgroup collaboration. Users could mark up PDF documents electronically, enable digital signatures, and reuse information in tables from PDF files.[16]

Still, not every networked utility provider was able to command a premium for advanced versions of its client software: In the Fall of 1999, Macromedia had put plans to sell a plus version of its Shockwave player on hold, citing a lack of consumer understanding of the value of an upgrade.[17]

Advertising. Successful networked utility providers frequently generated heavy website traffic when visitors downloaded their software. For example, RealNetworks' Real.com aggregated rich-media content—e.g., movie trailers, music videos, games—thus encouraging repeat visits by users who discovered the site when they visited to download RealPlayer software. Some utilities, including RealPlayer, Shockmachine, ICQ, and Internet telephony provider Net2Phone, also incorporate advertising directly within their client software, targeting a captive audience of registered users. Exploiting these opportunities, RealNetworks earned about 15 to 20 percent of its total revenue from advertising.[18]

Cost Structure

Networked utility providers tend to have very high gross margins: The server and telecommunications costs incurred in facilitating free downloads tend to be modest, as do the production costs for server software and authoring tools (usually distributed on CD-ROMs). RealNetworks, for example, had a projected gross margin of 83 percent for 2000, typical for a successful networked utility provider (see Exhibit 1 for RealNetworks' income statement).

Exhibit 7-1 REALNETWORKS' PROFIT AND LOSS

$ in millions	1999	2000E	2002E
Software license fees	$90.6	$153.1	$230.0
as a % of revenue	69%	60%	52%
Service revenues	$26.5	$55.9	$110.0
as a % of revenue	20%	22%	25%
Advertising	$14.1	$47.2	$100.0
as a % of revenue	11%	18%	23%
Total Revenue	**$131.2**	**$256.2**	**$440.0**
Cost of revenue:			
Software license fees	$13.0	$19.5	$32.0
Service revenues	$6.6	$13.8	$24.0
Advertising	$2.9	$8.9	$14.5
Total cost of revenues	$22.5	$42.3	$70.5
Gross profit	**$108.8**	**$213.9**	**$369.5**
Gross margin	82.9%	83.5%	84.0%

Exhibit 7-1

REALNETWORKS' PROFIT AND LOSS cont.

$ in millions	1999	2000E	2002E
Research and development	$38.4	$57.1	$96.0
as a % of sales	29%	22%	22%
Sales and marketing	$53.5	$101.6	$138.0
as a % of sales	41%	40%	31%
General and administrative	$16.4	$32.2	$52.0
as a % of sales	12.5%	12.6%	11.8%
Total operating expenses	**$108.3**	**$191.0**	**$286.0**
as a % of sales	82%	75%	65%
Operating income	**$0.5**	**$22.9**	**$83.5**
Margin	*0.4%*	*9.0%*	*19.0%*

Source: Adapted from Andrew Marcus, "RealNetworks, Inc.," Deutsche Banc Alex Brown, August 1, 2000

Because networked utility providers must develop and maintain technical standards, they tend to spend heavily on research and development. R&D as a percentage of 2000 revenue was projected to equal 22 percent for RealNetworks, 20 percent for Adobe, and 25 percent for Macromedia. (Note that the latter two firms were not pure networked utility providers: They generated a majority of their sales from traditional software sales.)[19]

Networked utility providers also tend to spend heavily on sales and marketing to promote and protect their standards. Sales and marketing as a percentage of 2000 revenue was projected to equal 40 percent for RealNetworks, 32 percent for Adobe, and 43 percent for Macromedia. Sales and marketing includes the fixed costs related to consumer and trade advertising as well as the cost of direct sales personnel who call on corporate customers (a cost that tends to vary with the number of accounts covered).

Finally, networked utility providers incur general and administrative expenses—largely fixed—related to staff functions such as human resources and finance, outsourced professional services, and so forth (13 percent, 9 percent, and 9 percent of projected 2000 revenue for RealNetworks, Adobe, and Macromedia, respectively).

Profitability

The three companies profiled in this section have all successfully established dominant standards, and as a result, they all earn healthy operating margins: Operating income as a percentage of 2000 revenue was projected to be 9 percent for RealNetworks, 31 percent for Adobe, and 12 percent for Macromedia. Of course, this sample is skewed by survivorship bias: It is difficult to ascertain the number of companies that have attempted to create a standard, but failed. By profiling these successful companies, the authors do not intend to imply that creating a standard is an easy task; on the contrary, it is very difficult.

ESTABLISHING STANDARDS

A de facto standard is created when a critical mass of targeted users adopts a networked utility provider's software. Since utility providers give away their software, one might suppose that it would be easy to achieve widespread adoption. Yet, networked utility providers frequently face competition from other software distributors who may charge lower prices or simply have a better product. How can you charge less than zero? You can simply pay your partners to distribute your software. Netscape, for example, once paid computer manufacturers to incorporate its browser software onto new computers' desktops.[20]

Key Decisions

A networked utility provider involved in a standards war faces a number of important decisions. Readers interested in further analysis of the dynamics of standards wars should consult Chapter 9 of *Information Rules,* by Professors Carl Shapiro and Hal Varian of the University of California at Berkeley. The text expands on several of the points presented below. [21]

Launch and Upgrade Timing. First-mover advantages can be powerful when network effects are strong. At the same time, offering a technically superior product can provide the competitive edge in a standards battle. Thus, speed to market and technical superiority are conflicting goals: It takes extra effort and time to build "a better mousetrap," and the sheer passage of time may allow developers to incorporate technologies newly invented elsewhere. Apple Computer's experience with its Newton personal digital assistant (PDA) demonstrates the dilemma. Apple launched Newton in 1993 with great expectations. However, Newton sales stalled due to its high price, the uneven performance of its handwriting recognition technology (on which almost all functions depended) and a small screen for inputting text.[22] A few years later, 3Com launched its PalmPilot PDAs which solved these problems and achieved strong sales.

Backward Compatibility. Standard setters sometimes launch new formats that are not compatible with the existing base of software acquired by users of the previous format. For example, when consumer electronics companies and record labels introduced CDs, the new equipment could not play existing vinyl LPs or cassettes. Shapiro and Varian call this a standards "revolution," and contrast this approach to "evolutions" (e.g., Microsoft's progression from DOS through its various versions of Windows), which ensure backward compatibility for users who previously purchased software for use with earlier product versions. Shapiro and Varian also cite a guideline proposed by Andy Grove, the Chairman of Intel: To succeed, a standards revolution must provide at least a tenfold improvement in product performance.[23]

New versions of networked utilities, especially media players, tend to involve evolutions. The newest version of the Flash animation player, for example, can play streams from servers with software developed to support earlier versions. The reverse is not true, however: Leading-edge content providers that seek to exploit the performance advantages available in the latest Flash server software deliver streams that cannot be played by users with early versions of Flash Player. Those users will receive a message encouraging them to upgrade to the latest version of Flash Player, so they can experience the rich media.

Thus, like many networked utility providers, Macromedia faces a "chicken-and-egg" problem with its Flash upgrades: Content providers will be reluctant to deploy the company's latest software, because users who lack the latest player may skip over their streams, rather than hassle with another download. Users will only take the time to download the latest version if (1) they encounter particularly compelling content that requires its use, or (2) over time, they have encountered (and skipped over) a critical mass of content that requires the upgrade and eventually recognize the need to upgrade. Faced with this situation, networked utility providers can employ several tactics to engender a network effect. For example, providers can (1) offer price breaks to leading-edge content providers, (2) aggregate compelling content at their own destination website, increasing the incentive for users to upgrade, and (3) design a quick, pain-free download process, to minimize switching costs borne by users.

Compatibility with Rival Standards. Companies with smaller installed user bases often have an incentive to seek compatibility with software and/or hardware offered by the market leader; if they fail to do so, the companies' users may become frustrated by their inability to share files and communicate with the users of the dominant standard and by software developers' reluctance to release versions compatible with the less popular standard. Apple's Macintosh operating system has faced this problem for years. In response, Apple has designed its computers to read floppy disks formatted for Windows (offering Mac users the ability to use files created by Windows users). The reverse, however, is not true: Microsoft has not built the ability to read Mac-formatted disks into Windows. In this case and many others, there is little incentive for the market leader to push for compatibility.

Networked utility providers face similar decisions about whether to provide compatibility with providers of rival standards. For example, in developing its Reader software, which greatly improves the screen resolution of eBooks, Microsoft has not yet provided for compatibility with Adobe's popular PDF file format. Microsoft does offer conversion tools that reformat HTML and Microsoft Word files for use with its Reader and says vaguely on its website, in response to a question about PDF compatibility, "we anticipate that additional conversion tools will be available."[24] It will be interesting to see whether Microsoft provides such conversion tools for PDF files. On the one hand, doing so would encourage the more rapid adoption of its Reader software because users could access a much greater range of content. On the other hand, Microsoft makes no money from its freely downloadable Reader; like most networked utility providers, the company hopes to profit instead from the sale of authoring tools and server software. If Microsoft can establish the dominant standard for eBook display, it is likely to earn substantial profits from such sales—far more than it could earn from licensing PDF conversion tools.

Adobe has pursued a different strategy in attacking Macromedia's successful Flash franchise. Rather than introduce its own animation player, Adobe has developed authoring software (called LiveMotion) which outputs files in Flash format. According to Salomon Smith Barney, "Long term, we expect Adobe to focus more on the SVG format, leaving it less dependent upon its rival's installed base of players and providing an opportunity to become a standard itself down the road."[25] SVG (Scalable Vector Graphics) is a new XML-based file format created through the joint efforts of over 20 companies and the World Wide Web Consortium (W3C), a non-profit standard-setting body. SVG provides a number of advantages to Web designers working with high-resolution graphics and animations, including smaller file sizes (and thus faster downloads), display device and printer independence (ensuring consistency across different types of hardware), and text search functions (e.g., allowing users to search for city names on a map). Since the current versions of Web browsers do not support SVG, a plug-in player will be required to display SVG graphics. This provides an opportunity for Adobe to leapfrog Macromedia's Flash Player by introducing a new player that is compatible with both Flash and SVG—and to profit by selling LiveMotion authoring tools that output both formats.

Interconnection. When applied to user-to-user networks (e.g., communications and transportation networks) compatibility is referred to as interconnection. Again, rival network operators must decide whether to allow their users to interconnect. Doing so will increase the value of the combined networks for all users, because they can connect with additional parties. This should accelerate user adoption rates. At the same time, however, interconnection forfeits the potentially powerful competitive advantages that may accrue to a closed network provider. When a network remains closed, if its users wish to connect with another party, that party must join the network. If a closed network gains enough momentum, it can capture a large share of the market and can enjoy very high user retention rates.

AOL's interconnection strategy for its Instant Messenger (IM) service illustrates this dynamic. AOL has steadfastly refused to allow competing IM providers to interconnect with its service.[26] AOL's closed network has been sustainable, because the company serves a critical mass of users—nearly half of all online U.S. households use its service. Having closed its IM network, AOL has a powerful retention tool and a strong selling point for prospective subscribers: If prospects want to be on a friend's, family member's, or co-worker's "buddy list," they must subscribe to AOL. To neutralize this competitive advantage, AOL's competitors such as Microsoft's MSN have been desperate to interconnect their IM services to AOL's and have on several occasions hacked into AOL IM, interconnecting without AOL's permission. AOL has rebuffed these efforts. As AOL has maneuvered to secure approval for its acquisition of media giant Time Warner in the face of intense antitrust scrutiny; however, competitors have exploited AOL's window of vulnerability. They have lobbied government authorities, asking them to force AOL to interconnect with their IM services as a condition for merger approval.[27]

Segmentation. Networked utility providers facing a standards battle must make difficult customer-targeting decisions. Specifically, should they attempt to serve the broadest possible market with a one-size-fits-all product or tailor their software to the needs of specific customer segments? Adobe faces this issue in deciding how to exploit the emerging market for eBooks.[28] Microsoft has made aggressive moves to establish its Reader software as the de facto standard for eBooks. In doing so, Microsoft has targeted its distribution and marketing efforts against the consumer market (rather than the educational and technical/professional publishing markets). Adobe's Acrobat standard enjoys advantages that are valued in the educational and technical/professional segments to a greater extent than in the consumer market, namely, the ability to print (which Microsoft's Reader does not provide) and superior abilities to display graphics. Should Adobe target only the segments where its capabilities are most highly valued, thereby ceding the consumer market to Microsoft, or seek to serve the entire market for eBooks?

Two scenarios are possible when broadly and narrowly focused companies compete. If a broad-based competitor can exploit a strong network effect, it may capture the market even though a narrowly focused company might offer a better solution for a specific segment. Alternatively, an entrant may capture share in a specific segment by providing a superior product, then use that position as a beachhead to attack the dominant incumbent in additional segments. The payoff from targeting a narrow segment seems to depend on whether users in that segment can be isolated from the broader market. If users require the ability to connect with users in other segments or to access content that is valued by users in other segments, then a narrowly focused competitor may never gain traction.

Pricing. Microsoft's victory over Netscape in the browser wars taught networked utility providers a lesson: Give your client software away to facilitate widespread distribution. Since this tactic will almost certainly be used by all parties involved in a present-day standards battle, it cannot confer competitive advantage. Therefore, the pricing game shifts to the server-side: Should competitors deeply discount their authoring tools and/or server software to encourage adoption of their standards?

Adobe must wrestle with this decision as it develops its strategy for eBooks. Sales of its Acrobat 4.0 software, used to create PDF files, provide the company with significant profits. But if Adobe gave away this software, it might extend its dominance in electronic document distribution to the eBook arena. Microsoft took this approach in challenging RealNetworks' dominant RealPlayer franchise. Microsoft has bundled the software that streams audio and video files to its Media Player into its Windows NT server software. The Media Player server software is available free of charge to any customer who runs NT servers. However, Microsoft does not support Media Player through other operating systems, which limits the potential adoption of its software, since many websites use Unix-based servers.[29]

Distribution Partnerships. Networked utility providers typically seek distribution partnerships with portals and other websites that can encourage downloads of their client software. These distribution agreements may or may not be exclusive; the latter approach, of course, can be much more expensive. For example, in August 2000, Microsoft secured an agreement with Amazon to be the online bookseller's preferred eBook format. Barnes & Noble's website, bn.com, by contrast, has reached nonexclusive agreements with both Microsoft and Adobe, among other eBook providers.

Net2Phone has achieved dominance in the consumer market for IP telephony by distributing its client software on a co-branded basis with every leading mass-market portal, including AOL, Yahoo!, MSN, GO.com, and Excite.[30] Net2Phone's deal with MSN is typical of the agreements it has reached with these portals: MSN makes Net2Phone's software available to users of MSN's instant messenger service, who use it to originate phone calls through a microphone-equipped PC. After Net2Phone recovers its costs, the companies share revenues from banner ads displayed within Net2Phone's client software while a user completes a call.

Software Partnerships. In addition to distribution partnerships, companies engaged in battles to establish dominance for their media players frequently secure high-profile partnerships with content providers to encourage adoption of particular standards. For example, Microsoft secured exclusive rights to serve as the eBook format for new Star Wars books and Michael Crichton's newest novel, *Timeline*. Adobe also has used this tactic: It had previously convinced the IRS to use the PDF format for online tax forms.[31] In these examples, Microsoft and Adobe secured agreements to convert existing content to their electronic formats. As noted above, Shockwave.com has moved beyond agreements that reformat existing content and has actually funded the creation of original content that exploits its software.

Content Aggregation. As noted above, two companies that offer media players—Macromedia and RealNetworks—have taken the premise behind software partnerships a step further and have created destination websites that aggregate a large volume of compelling entertainment content that exploits their respective software standards. In effect, Shockwave.com and Real.com have become entertainment portals, destinations for consumers seeking interactive games, music videos, short films, and animated programs. To fund its website, Macromedia raised $44 million in venture capital, selling a one-third stake in Shockwave.com to Sequoia and Netscape founder Jim Clark. Macromedia seemed somewhat ambivalent about its investment in Shockwave.com, however. Even though Wall Street analysts had valued the investment at over $100 million, the company worried about the impact of Shockwave.com's ongoing losses—which were typical for a successful vertical portal but were, nevertheless, a drain on corporate profitability. Macromedia had announced plans to reduce its equity stake in Shockwave.com below 50 percent, so it could deconsolidate the business for reporting purposes.[32]

In addition to the potential impact on earnings, networked utility providers that hybridize their business models by developing portals face potential channel conflict, because existing mass-market portals often serve as major distributors for their software. Also, when portals operated by networked utility providers give prominent exposure to a particular content provider's titles, that content provider's competitors—who are also likely to be customers of the networked utility provider's server software and authoring tools—may become upset.

The strategic decisions described above are geared to foment aggressive growth. They are predicated on the belief that a standard can be created through this growth; thus, the ends justify the means. Yet, is aggressive growth truly necessary for success, or will companies outstrip their resources in the middle of the battle? Put another way, will a Get Big Fast strategy have an attractive payoff?

GET BIG FAST: A STRATEGIC IMPERATIVE FOR NETWORKED UTILITIES?

Many Internet companies have pursued Get Big Fast (GBF) strategies, involving massive upfront investment in customer acquisition and brand building. The premise of such strategies is that the early days of the Internet are a "land grab": According to this view, companies will find it easier to stake out wide swaths of empty territory now rather than try to capture that territory later, after it has been settled by others. The payoff from the GBF strategy tends to be strongest when the following conditions apply: Network effects are strong, scale economies (beyond network effects) are significant, and customer-retention rates are intrinsically high.

It should be clear from the analysis above that these conditions apply strongly for networked utility providers. First, by definition, *networked* utility providers are subject to network effects—either by providing user-to-user connectivity or by propagating a standard that encourages the creation of additional content that exploits the standard. Second, as explained above, the cost structures for most networked utility providers are heavily skewed toward fixed components, so the providers enjoy significant scale economies. Finally, customer-retention rates tend to be intrinsically high in the presence of strong network effects: Users become locked in through their need to communicate with other users or to access content that is exclusively available through the networked utility provider. Other factors may encourage customer retention as well, e.g., developers' investment in training their staff to use a specific set of authoring tools, end-user familiarity with a utility's interface, registry settings in PC operating systems that instruct the machine to default to specified software when a given file format is encountered.

Hence, the payoff for a successful GBF strategy tends to be high for networked utility providers. When network effects are strong, it often makes sense for a company to invest heavily to gain first-mover advantage. As users beget users, the first mover may develop an unassailable lead. Strong scale economies exacerbate this winner-take-all dynamic: If the market leader has a superior cost structure, that company can reduce its prices or invest in superior features and thereby increase its lead. Finally, if users can be locked in before they sample a competitor's service, a first mover may cement its lead.

Confronting these winner-take-all dynamics, companies that aspire to develop a dominant networked utility frequently engage in what economists call racing behavior: They spend heavily and aggressively pursue partnerships to preempt their competitors. When competitors are closely matched—as Adobe and Microsoft appear to be in the eBook market—the all in winner-take-all can be dissipated by overheated competition. The winner in a standards battle may earn a Pyrrhic victory.[33]

ENDNOTES

[1]According to *www.webopedia.com*, with a "client-server" architecture, a client is an application that runs on a personal computer or workstation and relies on a server computer to perform some operations.

[2]According to *www.webopedia.com*, streaming is "A technique for transferring data such that it can be processed as a steady and continuous stream. Streaming technologies are becoming increasingly important with the growth of the Internet because most users do not have fast enough access to download large multimedia files quickly. With streaming, the client browser or plug-in can start displaying the data before the entire file has been transmitted. For streaming to work, the client side receiving the data must be able to collect the data and send it as a steady stream to the application that is processing the data and converting it to sound or pictures. This means that if the streaming client receives the data more quickly than required, it needs to save the excess data in a buffer. If the data doesn't come quickly enough, however, the presentation of the data will not be smooth."

[3]According to *www.webopedia.com*, a standard is a definition or format that has been approved by a recognized standards organization or is accepted as a de facto standard by the industry. Standards exist for programming languages, operating systems, data formats, communications protocols, and electrical interfaces. From a user's standpoint, standards are extremely important in the computer industry because they allow the combination of products from different manufacturers to create a customized system. Without standards, only hardware and software from the same company could be used together.

[4]Web browsers are, of course, a type of media player: They allow users to access HTML-formatted pages from the World Wide Web. This chapter will not analyze the browser business, however, because the strategic issues confronting the two participants in this somewhat lopsided duopoly have been analyzed in depth elsewhere: See especially Michael A. Cusumano and David B. Yoffie, *Competing on Internet Time: Lessons from Netscape and Its Battle with Microsoft* (New York: FreePress, 2000).

[5]IP telephony breaks voice traffic into data packets that are sent though data routers over the Internet, then reassembled at the receiving end. Pauses in a conversation generate little data (fewer packets) and thus require little bandwidth for transmission. Consequently, packet-switched networks are inherently more efficient in their use of bandwidth than traditional switched-circuit telephony networks, which hold open a dedicated point-to-point circuit of fixed bandwidth through the entire duration of a phone call. This efficiency allows IP telephony providers to price at a significant discount, compared to incumbents offering switched-circuit service.

[6]*Connectivity-related network effects* occur when the adoption of a product or service by a new customer increases the value of the product or service for customers already using it, because existing customers now can connect with more parties. *Software supply-related network effects*, on the other hand, often are present for standards that govern the creation of new hardware and/or software. When software supply-related network effects are strong, the propagation of a standard leads to the creation of more software that employs the standard, which in turn leads to the further propagation of the standard, and so forth. For more background on network effects, see Carl Shapiro and Hal R. Varian, *Information Rules* (Boston, MA: Harvard Business School Press, 1999), pp. 173–225.

[7]Atomica does secure some third-party content through partnerships, but these partnerships do not constitute a network in the same sense that a successful e-wallet provider would need to enlist the support of thousands of online commerce sites.

[8]Data in this paragraph are from Jonathan Rosenzweig, "Macromedia," Salomon Smith Barney Equity Research, October 16, 2000.

[9]See Thomas Eisenmann and Sanjay Pothen, "Online Portals," section 2, *Internet Business Models: Text and Cases*, or HBS Case: 801-305, December 2000.

[10]See Thomas Eisenmann and Alastair Brown, "Online Content Providers," section 3, *Internet Business Models: Text and Cases*, or HBS Case no. 801-261, December 2000 for complete information on the content business model.

[11]All information in the preceding paragraph is from Andrew Marcus, "RealNetworks, Inc.," Deutsche Banc Alex Brown, August 1, 2000.

[12]Jonathan Rosenzweig, "Macromedia," Salomon Smith Barney Equity Research, October 16, 2000, p. 72.

[13]Mary Tripsas, "Adobe Systems Incorporated," section 7, *Internet Business Models: Text and Cases*, or HBS Case no. 801-199, November 27, 2000.

[14]Elizabeth Corcoran, "Go Forth And Publish," *Forbes,* October 2, 2000.

[15]Andrew Marcus, "RealNetworks, Inc.," Deutsche Banc Alex Brown, August 1, 2000.

[16]Mary Tripsas, "Adobe Systems Incorporated," section 7, *Internet Business Models: Text and Cases*, or HBS Case no. 801-199, November 27, 2000.

[17]G. Beato, "Shock Jock," *Business2.0,* May 2000, p. 293.

[18]Andrew Marcus, "RealNetworks, Inc.," Deutsche Banc Alex Brown, August 1, 2000.

[19]For RealNetworks, see Exhibit 1; Jonathan Rosenzweig, "Adobe Systems," Salomon Smith Barney Equity Research, October 20, 2000; Jonathan Rosenzweig, "Macromedia," Salomon Smith Barney Equity Research, October 16, 2000.

[20]David B. Yoffie and Michael A. Cusumano, "Building a Company On Internet Time: Lessons from Netscape," California Management Review: CMR147, April 1, 1999.

[21]Carl Shapiro and Hal R. Varian, *Information Rules* (Boston, MA: Harvard Business School Press, 1999).

[22]Ken Siegmann, "Why the Newton Called Me Rick 5 Jeffries," *The San Francisco Chronicle* (August 4, 1993): B1.

[23]Carl Shapiro and Hal R. Varian, *Information Rules* (Boston, MA: Harvard Business School Press, 1999), Chapter 9, for a discussion of standards wars and p. 196 for a discussion of Andy Grove's guideline.

[24]*http://www.microsoft.com/reader/news/faq.htm#12*

[25]Jonathan Rosenzweig, "Adobe Systems," Salomon Smith Barney Equity Research, October 20, 2000, p. 19.

[26]AOL will license its own branded IM service to other ISPs and websites, but refuses to interconnect with IM services branded and operated by other parties.

[27]D.C. Denison, "The Battle For Instant Messaging: AOL Fending Off Challenges In A Market That Is Growing Into A Global Network," *The Boston Globe* (December 11, 2000).

[28]Mary Tripsas, "Adobe Systems Incorporated," section 7, *Internet Business Models: Text and Cases*, or HBS Case no. 801-199, November 27, 2000.

[29]Andrew Marcus, "RealNetworks, Inc.," Deutsche Banc Alex Brown, August 1, 2000, p. 8.

[30]Brian Boyer, "Net2Phone," First Analysis Securities Corp., August 9, 2000.

[31]Mary Tripsas, "Adobe Systems Incorporated," section 7, *Internet Business Models: Text and Cases*, or HBS Case no. 801-199, November 27, 2000.

[32]Jonathan Rosenzweig, "Macromedia," Salomon Smith Barney Equity Research, October 16, 2000.

[33]Pyrrhus, King of Epirus, earned victories over the Romans but sustained enormous losses.

ADOBE SYSTEMS INCORPORATED

"Are we a dot-com company? No. Do we buy Super Bowl ads? No. Are we . . . getting incredible valuations to spend lots of money on advertising? No. Are we using the Internet in almost every aspect of our business? Yes . . ."

—John Warnock, Chairman of the Board and CEO, Adobe Systems Incorporated

As he sat in his office in the Adobe Systems Incorporated towers in downtown San Jose, John Warnock, Chairman and CEO, pondered the wealth of opportunities facing the company he and his colleague, Chuck Geschke, had founded almost 20 years ago. With annual revenues of about $1 billion, Adobe was the leading supplier of software to the graphic arts and publishing industries. Although the print world had been Adobe's traditional customer base, the firm had successfully transitioned to meet the exploding demand for web authoring tools. Adobe's image editing software, Photoshop®[1] was used by 91% of web sites, and its illustration software, Illustrator® by 74%. In addition, Adobe had made acquisitions in the web animation and web design spaces and was poised to take advantage of growth in that arena. Revenue linked to the web had grown from 50% in 1999 to 61% in the second quarter of 2000, and was expected to continue on a steep trajectory. Adobe's share price had gone from a low of $12.15[2] in August, 1998 to $157.56 in September, 2000, providing evidence that Wall Street was finally beginning to recognize what Warnock had known for some time—Adobe was well positioned to take advantage of the growth of the Internet. The question was which opportunities to pursue and how.

Warnock was particularly intrigued by the recent explosion of interest in the eBook (electronic book) market. On March 15, 2000, best-selling novelist Stephen King had been the first major author to release a title exclusively on the Internet as an eBook. Accompanied by much fanfare, his novella *Riding the Bullet,* was available for electronic download from 150 different web sites, including Amazon.com and BarnesandNoble.com. Over 400,000 copies of the book had been downloaded within 48 hours, demonstrating to the publishing and bookselling industries a surprisingly high level of consumer interest in this emerging technology.

Warnock's interest in eBooks stemmed from Adobe's historical position as a leading provider of technology and standards to the publishing industry. He felt that Adobe could leverage its strong reputation and existing relationships with professional publishers as this new space evolved. In particular, he felt that Adobe was in a strong position to have its electronic document technology become the de facto standard format for eBooks.

Adobe had been a first mover on the Internet in the more broadly defined electronic document or "eDoc" space with its Acrobat® product which first shipped in 1993. Acrobat enabled the creation of documents that could be viewed on a wide variety of computing platforms while retaining their original formatting. These documents were saved in Adobe PDF (portable document format). With the rise of the web, the need for a universal document format had grown significantly, and PDF had taken off, becoming the de facto standard for formatted content on the web. Everything from IRS forms to Harvard Business School cases were posted on the web in PDF format.

Individuals wanting to view or print PDF documents simply needed to download the free Acrobat® Reader™ from the Adobe web site. Almost 200 million copies of the free Acrobat Reader had been downloaded as of July, 2000 (see Exhibit 1). While the Acrobat Reader was given away

Professor Mary Tripsas prepared this case as the basis for class discussion rather than to illustrate either effective or ineffective handling of an administrative situation. Research assistance was provided by Hagar Doitel and Jennifer Zide.

[1]Adobe, the Adobe logo, Acrobat, Acrobat Reader, PDF Merchant, Acrobat Capture, Distiller, Acrobat Messenger, Illustrator, InDesign, Framemaker, PageMaker, PressReady, Acrobat InProduction, After Effects, GoLive, LiveMotion, Adobe Premiere, Photoshop, Adobe PhotoDeluxe, ActiveShare, ePaper, Acrobat Exchange, and PostScript are either registered trademarks or trademarks of Adobe Systems Incorporated in the United Sates and/or other countries.

2Adjusted for stock splits.

for free, Adobe made money on the sale of the full Acrobat product (list price of $249) which individuals needed to buy in order to create PDF documents (see Exhibit 2).

Despite Adobe's early lead, Microsoft was moving aggressively into the eBook space, attempting to establish an alternative standard to PDF. Microsoft was pushing its own format for use with its Microsoft Reader. Microsoft had so far targeted the mainstream consumer market, enlisting over 50 leading publishers to create eBook content in the Microsoft Reader format. Microsoft had also spent significant amounts of money to obtain preferred status for Microsoft's format on the leading online bookstore, Amazon.com.

Given Microsoft's vast resources, Warnock wondered how best to compete. Should Adobe focus on a more narrow, segmented set of eBook users, or should they fight Microsoft head on in the consumer space? What alliances should Adobe be forging in order to drive critical mass around PDF? Should Adobe fight the battle over eBooks, or focus on the broader eDocs market? And assuming Adobe won the standards war and established PDF as the de facto eBook standard, how could they leverage that position in order to make money?

Adobe History: The PostScript Era

Adobe Systems Incorporated was founded in 1982 by two Xerox PARC scientists, John Warnock and Charles Geschke. Both PhDs, Warnock and Geschke had developed leading edge software at Xerox to facilitate the printing of integrated text and graphics. Frustrated by Xerox desire to keep the technology proprietary, they decided to form their own company to commercialize it. Warnock's thesis advisor was on the board of Hambrecht & Quist and introduced the pair to Bill Hambrecht who helped to get the venture funded. They named the firm Adobe after a local creek.

What Is PostScript?

Adobe's first product, PostScript®, was a driving force behind the desktop publishing revolution of the mid-1980's. PostScript provided an interface between a computer program and an output device such as a printer. It comprised three parts, 1) a page description language which was open, documented, and free, 2) an interpreter, which was licensed to output device manufacturers, and 3) fonts, which were sold to end customers such as graphic artists.

PostScript Page Description Language. Software developers used the PostScript page description language to tell an output device what a printed page should look like. The computer application sent instructions written in the PostScript language to the output device. An application that produced PostScript would work with any PostScript printer. In contrast, software developers who did not use Postscript had to write separate software for each printer their application supported. For instance, WordPerfect 4.1 asked the user to choose from 209 different printer models. PostScript also supported multiple resolutions, meaning the same software application could print on a 300 dpi laser printer or a high-end 5000 dpi imagesetter. This feature was particularly important to the graphic arts community since it meant material created with a PostScript application could be proofed on inexpensive laser printers before high quality printing.

In order to encourage software developers to use the PostScript language, Adobe made it open to anyone for free. The language was meticulously documented in what programmers fondly called "The Red Book," and strong technical support was provided to third party developers working with the language. As a result, the number of applications supporting PostScript increased from 180 in 1986 to over 5000 by 1991.

Co-founder, Geschke reflected on the initial choice to make PostScript an open standard:

> We made a decision early on that the standard itself—the documentation for how you describe the page—would be open, freely available and we would publish it. We would retain the copyright and the trademark, but we would make the interface open to anyone, recognizing that over time, that would invite competition. In order to be successful and set a standard, we had to do that, and instinctively we felt that, if we were the best implementers of it, we should continue to make good revenue off it even though eventually competitors would emerge.

PostScript Interpreter. PostScript output devices, such as a laser printer or high end imagesetter, had an embedded, microprocessor-driven PostScript interpreter that translated a PostScript program from an application into dots to be placed on a page. Adobe licensed PostScript interpreter technology to printer and imagesetter manufacturers on a royalty basis: Adobe collected a percentage fee for each PostScript printer or imagesetter sold.

To accelerate the diffusion of PostScript output devices, Adobe developed a boilerplate controller design based on the Motorola 68000 chip. Printer manufacturers interested in licensing PostScript had free access to this design, thus accelerating the development time for PostScript products. In addition, Adobe engineers often worked on joint product development teams with customers in order to help with the design of customized PostScript interpreters. The number of PostScript licensees increased from just one, Apple, in 1985 to 60 by 1994.

PostScript Fonts. PostScript also provided a way for describing high quality professional fonts in a standard format. Historically a font could only be used on the specific output device it was designed for. In contrast, a PostScript font could be used on any PostScript output device. PostScript also significantly increased the ability to manipulate fonts, allowing for scaling and rotating.

Adobe invested a large amount in creating its own library of PostScript fonts. In 1986 Adobe invested 16% of sales in font development, and dollar investments continued to increase from 1985 through 1992. The number of PostScript fonts in the Adobe collection increased from 35 in 1985 to 2000 in 1994. These fonts were valued most highly by graphic artists designing pages for professional publishing.

Making Money from PostScript

The first PostScript products were introduced in 1985 through a strategic alliance among four firms: Adobe, Apple, Aldus and Linotype. The combination of products from these firms sparked the desktop publishing revolution, or democratization of typesetting. For the first time, individual desktop users could create newsletters and other documents that had a professional look and feel; documents could integrate graphics and text, using professional quality fonts.

This result was accomplished through a system of products: Aldus PageMaker® software, which ran on the Apple Macintosh, enabled the creation of documents that integrated text and graphics. PageMaker required a PostScript device for printing. The Apple LaserWriter was the first PostScript printer and incorporated a PostScript interpreter licensed from Adobe. Finally, professional looking documents also required high quality fonts such as Times Roman or Palatino, which typically were only available to professional publishers. Linotype, a firm with over 100 years of experience in the typesetter industry licensed a set of its most popular fonts to Adobe so that Adobe could offer them in PostScript format. The LaserWriter came with 35 PostScript fonts built in. Linotype also introduced a high-end PostScript imagesetter, so that PageMaker documents could be used in professional publishing.

By 1989 PostScript had become the de facto standard for printing in the graphic arts and publishing industries. Almost 100% of high end imagesetters on the market incorporated PostScript. While penetration in the general laser printer market only reached about 25%, penetration of PostScript in laser printers used by graphic artists was closer to 100%.

Adobe also leveraged the underlying graphics technology of PostScript in applications software for the graphic arts community. (see Exhibit 3 for descriptions of Adobe's software product portfolio). The first end-user application, Adobe Illustrator was introduced in March, 1987 and gained wide acceptance among graphic artists. Illustrator created PostScript output and helped to create demand for PostScript printers. Adobe also acquired a number of software products, including Photoshop, for digital image editing in 1989, and Aldus PageMaker in 1993. These products were extremely successful, with Photoshop capturing over 90% of the market for photo-editing software.

Ownership and leveraging of the PostScript standard had reaped huge rewards for Adobe; between 1984 and 1995, revenue had grown from $2.2 million to $762 million—a compound annual growth rate of 70%. Adobe's share price growth had been equally impressive, increasing at an average annual rate of 29% between 1986, when the firm went public, and 1995.

Establishing PDF

Adobe shipped the first version of Acrobat on June 15, 1993. Acrobat enabled users to convert any electronic document into a universal document format called PDF (Portable Document Format). Once in PDF format, a document could be transferred to other users and would display and print exactly as it had in its original application—the receiving user simply needed to have an Acrobat Reader installed on their computer. The PDF format could handle not only text, but also graphics and images. Given the variety of computer platforms and software used in corporations, Adobe felt that Acrobat provided a compelling value proposition. Anyone in a corporation could share documents as long as the Acrobat Reader was widely distributed. Adobe initially charged $50 for each Acrobat Reader. In order to create PDF documents, users had to purchase either Acrobat® Exchange® for $195, or a more sophisticated product, Acrobat® Distiller®, for $695.

As with the PostScript standard, the specification for PDF was open. By using documentation from Adobe, other firms could create files in PDF format.

Sales of Acrobat, however, were originally quite disappointing and reached only about $2.5 million in 1993. As John Warnock commented,

> It's a funny technology. In 1992 I said, 'Gee, there's a way to build a universal document and a way to, without asking permission from anyone, get this done.' We implemented it, and I thought people would instantly appreciate the value proposition there. It's actually taken many years and the explosion of the Internet for people to figure it out.

Given the advent of the Internet, Adobe modified its Acrobat strategy. Instead of focusing exclusively on document exchange among workers within a corporation, Adobe also targeted Internet users. The goal was to make PDF the de facto standard for posting and exchanging documents on the Internet.

Adobe encouraged adoption of the Acrobat Reader by changing its previous policy of charging $50. The Acrobat Reader became widely available for free. In 1994, an alliance with AOL made the Acrobat Reader available to all AOL users. Adobe also established relationships with a number of computer vendors such as Compaq, Dell and Sony to preload the Acrobat Reader on PCs they sold. And in 1995 free downloads of the Acrobat Reader were made available from the Adobe web site. When a user visited a site with PDF content, they were instructed to click on a link to Adobe.com to get the free Acrobat Reader (see Exhibit 4 for the download page). Downloads of the Acrobat Reader exploded starting in 1997 and by July, 2000 over 197 million Acrobat Readers had been downloaded, with ongoing downloads of about 6 million more each month. (see Exhibit 1). Traffic to the Adobe site was also significant, with about 11 million unique visitors a month according to Media Metrix.

Downloads also drove sales of the full Acrobat product, needed for PDF creation (The features of Acrobat Exchange and Acrobat Distiller had been combined into one product: Adobe Acrobat priced at $249.) Adobe market research indicated that 88% of full Acrobat purchasers had used the Acrobat Reader prior to buying the full product.

In order to encourage the posting of PDF documents on the web, Adobe targeted high profile customers. In 1997, the IRS made tax forms available electronically for the first time. The forms were posted on the IRS web site in PDF format. Since PDF files could not be edited after they were downloaded with the Reader, they were ideal for applications that required integrity of the original document. Adobe also incorporated functionality targeted at Web users. For instance Acrobat 2.0 released in 1994 supported hyperlinks to HTML documents. Acrobat 4.0, which shipped in April 1999 added features for forms creation and digital signatures. When Adobe commissioned a "spider" of the web it had found that by mid-1999 over 2.6 million unique URLs contained PDF documents.

In June, 2000 Adobe decided to try and take advantage of the large number of visitors to the Adobe.com site for Reader downloads. Adobe began to offer PDF creation through their web site on a subscription basis. For $9.99 a month, or $99.99 a year, customers could create an unlimited number of PDF documents. The user simply uploaded a document to Adobe, and a PDF document would be emailed back to them. Other than by purchasing the full Acrobat product, this was the only way for individual users to create PDF documents.

In October 1999, Adobe further unbundled the full Acrobat product, introducing Acrobat® Business Tools software, targeted at the office user of Acrobat. While many individuals within an organization share documents, Adobe market research had shown that the majority of office workers do not need to create documents. Acrobat Business Tools was meant for users who simply needed to interact with documents. It enabled users to mark up PDF documents electronically, digitally authorize and sign documents, and reuse information from tables in PDF documents. It did not enable creation of PDF documents (see Exhibit 2 for a comparison of full Acrobat, Acrobat Business Tools, the Acrobat Reader and Adobe.com).

Acrobat Business Tools was just one way of adding value around PDF. Adobe saw ongoing growth opportunities in areas such as managing B2B processes. The Business Forms Management Association estimated that four out of every ten business documents is a form that needs to be acted upon. In many cases, these forms required signatures. With digital signatures gaining legal acceptance, PDF's digital forms and digital signature capabilities provided an ideal solution for electronically managing a number of B2B interactions.

In addition to its success on the web, PDF also began to penetrate Adobe's traditional print publishing customers as a substitute for PostScript. Print publishers had a need for a document format that would smooth out their print workflow—the process of integrating all the pieces that went into a publication. PDF made it easier for text, graphics and images from multiple sources to come together. In order to address this market, Adobe had a number of high end products with increased functionality (see Exhibit 3). The most recent of these was the Acrobat Distiller Server announced in June 2000, which enabled the high-volume conversion of PostScript files to Adobe PDF documents.

Finally, Adobe had entered the Digital Rights Management area, announcing PDF Merchant™ software and Acrobat Reader with Web Buy in August, 1999. PDF Merchant was a server-based technology that enabled web sites to sell documents without fear of illegal copying. It encrypted PDF files which were then unlocked with Web Buy. PDF Merchant was designed to be integrated with a firm's eCommerce and transaction systems. PDF Merchant sold for $5000, plus a per transaction royalty in an amount equal to 2% of the transaction revenue or $.05, whichever was greater.

Over 15 firms had signed up with Adobe to begin testing and integration of PDF Merchant and Web Buy in order to distribute and sell titles over the Internet. Industry players evaluating and/or using PDF Merchant included companies such as Barnes & Noble, Fatbrain.com, RR Donnelley & Sons, Simon & Schuster, Inc. Salon.com, Seybold Publications, and Xerox Corporation. Amazon.com had used Adobe PDF Merchant in order to sell downloads of the well-publicized Stephen King novella, *Riding the Bullet.* By the fall of 2000, almost 100 million copies of the Acrobat Reader with Web Buy had been downloaded.

Given the success of PDF, demand for Acrobat had taken off, with sales of Acrobat products increasing over 100% between 1998 and 1999. By the third quarter of 2000, Acrobat family sales accounted for almost 20% of total Adobe revenues, with Wall Street Analysts projecting significant growth (see Exhibit 5 and Exhibit 6).

The eBook Market

"You could have printed that [Stephen King] novella on a banana and people would have taken the time to read it."

—Jeff Bezos, Founder, Amazon.com

Experimental ventures with electronic books began in the early 1980's with products such as IBM's BookMaster and Electronic Book Technologies' Dynatext. These products primarily targeted the reference manual market. Computer manufacturers such as Silicon Graphics and Novell created electronic reference manuals since they were more convenient for customers to access and utilize, and they saved the manufacturer printing and shipping costs.

The value proposition for consumers of eBooks in 2000 was similarly driven by convenience. Early adopters of eBooks were typically professionals wanting to access reference information. One of the best-selling eBooks on PDAs (Personal Digital Assistants), was the Physicians Reference Manual. eBooks were also becoming popular in the textbook sector, where the ability to customize content and provide keyword searches was particularly valued. Analysts felt that the consumer market for fiction got the least value from eBooks (see Exhibit 7).

Overall projections for the eBook market, were quite uncertain, with a wide variety of estimates. IDG predicted that by 2004 annual eBook sales would be approximately $500 million with 2.8 million dedicated eBook reading devices.[3] Forrester projected that 13% of online book sales would be done via digital download by 2004, resulting in eBook sales of $426 million.[4] Anderson Consulting, in a study for the American Association of Publishers, was the most sanguine, projecting eBook sales of $2.3 billion—almost 10% of the $21.9 billion consumer book market—by 2005. Anderson also projected that by 2005 about 28 million eBook reading devices would have been adopted.[5]

Uncertainty about the market hinged on a number of factors. One of the major impediments to adoption of eBooks was onscreen readability. Anti-aliasing technology had been developed by both Adobe (CoolType) and Microsoft (ClearType), improving text resolution by up to 300%. eBook resolution, however, was still not close to matching the quality of paper. So far the price of eBooks was similar to or higher than that of print books, constraining demand. In addition, dedicated eBook reading devices had been relatively expensive, costing a minimum of $250. Finally, the selection of eBooks was still quite limited, and eBooks formatted for one device could generally not be used on another. Depending upon their assumptions about pricing and standards, analysts had different perspectives on the potential of the market. The Anderson Consulting estimates, for instance, were clearly predicated on adoption of a single open eBook standard.

[3] "E-Book's Brass Band," *Business Week*, 4/3/00

[4] C. Johnson, "Digital Downloads Accelerate," Forrester Report, January 2000.

[5] Anderson Consulting Report, AAP web site.

The eBook Value System

The process of creating and distributing an eBook involved both traditional publishing industry players as well as start-up organizations. The roles of these players were continuing to evolve (see Exhibit 8).

Authors. Authors in the eBook space so far were performing much the same role they had traditionally performed. They created content. The web, however, provided authors with an ability to bypass publishers and traditional books stores and distribute their creative content directly through a web site. After distributing *Riding the Bullet* through his publisher, Stephen King had established his own web site for distribution of a serial novel "The Plant" and posted the comment, "My friends, we have a chance to become Big Publishing's worst nightmare." In addition, some self-publishing sites such as Xlibris and iUniverse had emerged, where unknown authors could publish work online without screening. While this venue for distributing work had yet to take off, some authors had achieved a modicum of notoriety. In fact, an online work, "The Angels of Russia" had been nominated for Britain's prestigious Booker prize.

Publishers. Since the release of the King novella, publishers had become much more sanguine about the eBook market. Kate Tentler, publisher of Simon & Schuster Online commented that the success of the King novella had "galvanized Simon & Schuster's electronic book creating efforts."[6] With printing, warehousing and distribution accounting for more than half of a publisher's revenue (see Exhibit 9), eBooks had the potential to significantly cut publisher's costs. Publishers had yet to realize significant savings however. Random House's digital division was spending $15 million on a digital infrastructure with the division head commenting "We don't have any savings to pass along."[7] The royalty structure was also under pressure since authors expected to benefit from the publisher's eventual cost savings. In contrast to the typical 10% royalty, some eBook publishers, such as Mighty Words, were giving authors up to 50% of list price.

eBooks potentially gave publishers the opportunity to bypass booksellers and go directly to consumers. Time Warner had announced its own online publishing site, iPublish, and had made direct investments in other sites such as bookface.com. Similarly, Random House had taken a 49% stake in Xlibris, an online publisher. A Simon & Schuster executive commented, "Digital publishing provides an opportunity for publishers to have a much closer connection to consumers. I don't believe we will not have retailers, but certainly the middleman component will be a smaller one."[8]

Online Bookstores. Books were available in electronic format from a wide variety of web sites ranging from popular online booksellers such as Amazon.com and Barnesandnoble.com (bn.com) to sites that carried only eBooks such as ibooks.com and books24x7.com. The number of eBooks available varied, although bn.com with over 2700 popular titles available as eBooks had one of the largest inventories. The business models for these sites also varied and were continuing to evolve. Some sites such as eBookMall.com simply charged customers a fee to download the eBook. Others such as books24x7.com operated using a subscription model: for a monthly fee, customers could access a library of eBooks. Finally others such as bookface.com and Bartleby.com operated using an advertising model: users could access eBooks for free, but were required to view ads. Overall sales of eBooks had been extremely slow, with the average eBook selling only a few hundred copies.

Device Manufacturers. EBooks could be read on three general types of devices: 1) PCs with reader software, 2) personal electronic devices such as a Palm Pilot PDA with reader software, and 3) dedicated eBook devices.

PC-based reader software aimed to enhance the online reading experience. These readers provided users with a number of value-added features such as full-text search, on-line dictionary access, highlighting and bookmarking. PC-based readers were offered by both Adobe and Microsoft.

PDAs such as the Palm Pilot had also gained traction in the emerging eBook market. A start-up, Peanut Press, specialized in eBooks for the Palm with over 500 eBook titles available on its web site. It was also developing software to support Win CE devices. Finally, Microsoft had bundled its Reader software with the Pocket PC operating system, enabling Pocket PC devices by firms such as HP to read eBooks.

As of September, 2000 there were only two dedicated eBook reading devices on the market, the Rocket eBook

---

[6] "New Technologies Transform Publishing Industry," Information Week Online, March 27, 2000.

[7] P. Kafka, "Horror Story," *Forbes*, August 21,2000.

[8] "The Struggles Over E-Books Abound," *The New York Times*, November 27, 2000.

and the SoftBook, both offered by Gemstar (see Exhibit 10 for pictures and descriptions of the devices). The Rocket eBook had been available since June, 1998 and with a price of about $250 was targeted at consumers. The Softbook cost $600 and was targeted at the business and education fields. Magazines, textbooks, and documents were available on the SoftBook. It was estimated that about 10,000 of each of these devices had been sold as of January, 2000.[9] Other dedicated eBook devices had been announced, but not shipped.

eBook Standards

After the well-publicized battle between the VHS and Beta formats in the VCR industry, both producers and consumers were wary of a standards war. No consumer wanted to be stuck with the equivalent of a Betamax VCR—an orphan product with no tapes to play on it. Likewise, producers did not want to be on the losing end of a standards war. It was unclear how standards in the eBook market would evolve.

Most of the players in the eBook market were publicly advocating a single, open eBook standard. In the interest of establishing open standards, NIST (National Institute for Standards and Technology), an Agency of the US Commerce Department, had formed an Open eBook (OEB) working group in 1998. The group comprised leading publishers as well as major eBook players including Microsoft, Gemstar, and Adobe. The group had released the final version of its Open eBook Publication Structure 1.0 in September, 1999. The OEB specification was based on XML (Extensible Markup Language) an HTML-based language for describing data. It described what format content should take.

While Adobe employees had been involved in the approval of the OEB specification, Adobe did not adopt it. They felt that OEB was technically inferior to PDF, particularly in the area of graphics. The OEB specification also did not allow for printing, a function that Adobe believed was still important, even in the eBook world. Microsoft, in contrast, adopted the OEB specification as part of its Microsoft Reader format.

Since the OEB specification only covered content, however, it did not ensure compatibility among its users. In other words, OEB eBooks formatted for one vendor's eBook reader did not work on another vendor's reader. This difficulty arose because of the lack of agreement on a standard for the packaging of the content. Each eBook vendor had used its own proprietary packaging to implement the standard. As a result, even though eBooks in Microsoft Reader format complied with the OEB specification, the format was proprietary in that only Microsoft or Microsoft partners could create and read eBooks in Microsoft Reader format. In contrast, the PDF format had publicly described both the eBook content and its packaging. (Exhibit 11 provides a detailed comparison of PDF and Microsoft Reader format.)

An individual at Adobe described the situation as follows:

> To use a grocer analogy, we've agreed on an open standard for vegetables [OEB] but everybody is making their own cans, so you need a different can opener for each. In theory it's all "open vegetables," but being stuck on a desert island without the right kind of proprietary can opener can be pretty frustrating.

To further complicate matters, there was also confusion about digital rights management. Forewarned by the experience of the music industry with Napster and MP3, the publishing industry was extremely concerned about the ability to control the illegal distribution of content. Their fears seemed justified: eBookNet.com, a site devoted to tracking the eBook industry reported that illegal copies of Stephen King's novella were circulating just 3 days after its release, despite encryption. A number of firms were continuing to work on solutions to the digital rights management problem, many of which were incompatible.

Adobe vs. Microsoft in the eBook Space

Adobe had an early lead over Microsoft in terms of both content available in PDF format as well as readers capable of displaying or printing PDF content. A Barnes & Noble executive had commented at a NIST conference in September, 2000, "With Adobe PDF there are over 100,000 eBooks available; with any others there are only dozens." The 200 million Acrobat Readers that had been downloaded also dwarfed the number of Microsoft Readers. Microsoft, however, was moving aggressively into the eBook space. (See Exhibit 12 for a timeline of Adobe and Microsoft eBook announcements, and Exhibit 13 for a summary of eBook format adoption.)

Content: Publishers. Publishers were for the most part agnostic about format. Ideally, they wanted a single, open

[9] Business and Industry Online Reporter, January 24, 2000.

eBook standard, but not wanting to be left behind, most publishers were jumping ahead despite the lack of a ubiquitous standard. Since it was expensive to convert titles to digital form both Adobe and Microsoft were pursuing relationships with publishers, hoping to pre-empt alternative formats. So far, publishers had been willing to accommodate both PDF and Microsoft Reader formats. Lightning Source, a unit of Ingram Industries with over 9000 titles in its library, announced an agreement with Adobe to publish content in PDF format using PDF Merchant in late May, 2000. Just a few weeks earlier the firm had announced a similar agreement with Microsoft. Simon & Schuster had also agreed to make titles available in both PDF and Microsoft Reader format.

Microsoft had, however, secured some exclusive deals. Microsoft had obtained the exclusive rights from Random House to publish Michael Crichton's newest novel, *Timeline,* as an eBook in Microsoft Reader format. Another exclusive deal was struck with Simon & Schuster for a series of 15 popular Star Wars books. For a limited period of time, these eBooks would not be available in any other format.

Despite Microsoft's aggressiveness, Adobe still felt that it had a significant advantage over Microsoft. Adobe had strong historical relationships with publishers and continued to provide them with authoring tools for both print and web publishing (see Exhibit 3). Given that publishers used Adobe software, an estimated 70% of publishers' digital archives of print titles were already saved in PDF format.[10] In addition, in September 1999, Adobe had launched a new product for professional desktop publishing called Adobe InDesign®. InDesign competed directly with QuarkXPress, which had dominated the high-end professional segment. So far InDesign had made significant inroads, capturing about a 30% share of shipments since its introduction.[11]

Content: Online Bookstores. Online bookstores varied in their approach to format standards. In January 2000, Microsoft and Barnesandnoble.com had agreed to establish a Microsoft-branded part of the BarnesandNoble.com eBook store. In August 2000, Adobe and BarnesandNoble.com had announced plans for a similar Adobe-branded eBook store with PDF content to be established on the BarnesandNoble.com site. Adobe and Microsoft were to be given equal placement, with a third format, Rocket eBook, also offered. In contrast, Amazon.com had extracted an undisclosed sum from Microsoft in August, 2000 in return for giving the Microsoft Reader format a dominant, although not exclusive, position in Amazon's eBook store. Adobe had no ongoing formal relationship with Amazon despite Amazon's previous use of Adobe PDF Merchant for the sale of Stephen King's *Riding the Bullet.* While Amazon had been a late mover in eBooks, relative to BarnesandNoble.com, 75% of the downloads of Stephen King's *Riding the Bullet,* had been through Amazon.[12] In addition, Amazon commanded a dominant overall position, with over 75% share of the online book market.[13] The majority of smaller online eBook stores offered content in PDF format, given the ubiquity of the Acrobat Reader. For instance, when Stephen King offered his serial novel, *The Plant,* through his own web site, it was offered in PDF format.

Desktop Readers. With almost 200 million copies downloaded, the Acrobat Reader was by far the most dominant desktop reader. While not designed as an eBook reader specifically, the Acrobat Reader could be used to read books in PDF format on a Windows or Macintosh computer. In addition Adobe had acquired Glassbook, Inc., a maker of PDF eBook reading software, in September, 2000. The Glassbook display looked more like a book and incorporated more user friendly reading features. Penetration of the Glassbook PDF reader, however, was currently much lower with an estimated 700,000 copies downloaded as of October, 2000.[14]

Microsoft had made an eBook reader available as a free download for Windows users in August 2000, but downloads to date had been minimal. It was possible that the Microsoft Reader would be bundled with the next release of Windows. The Microsoft Reader was not available for the Macintosh, although plans to support the Mac had been announced.

Despite the possible ubiquity of a Microsoft Reader bundled with Windows, Adobe felt it had a number of advantages over Microsoft. Foremost, one couldn't print with the Microsoft Reader. A recent survey completed by

[10]B. Darrow, "Adobe, Microsoft Square Off in eBook Arena," TechWeb News, May 31, 2000.

[11]Prudential Securities Adobe Systems analyst report, February 23, 2000 (citing PC Data).

[12]SiliconValley.com, August 28, 2000.

[13]D. Ries and V. Truong, "Amazon.com," C.E. Unterburg analyst report, October 13, 1999.

[14]"EBooks digital future isn't likely to arrive soon," *Wall Street Journal,* October 2, 2000.

Sherwood Research had shown that 80% of respondents would prefer to print a book out using an application like Adobe Acrobat rather than download the book to a handheld device.[15]

PDAs. Adobe had plans to develop Acrobat Readers for devices other than the PC and Mac. As John Lin, Product Manager for eBook readers commented, "We want to deliver on the holy grail of publishing: publish once, view or print anywhere. Content will automatically re-purpose itself to be viewed easily on the desktop or on a PDA." Acrobat Readers for both Palm and Windows CE platforms had been demonstrated at conferences. In addition, since PDF was an open standard, third parties such as BCL Computers and Ansyr had developed PDF readers for the Palm Pilot.

In April, 2000, a version of the Microsoft eBook Reader was shipped with the Pocket PC operating system. All Pocket PC devices, therefore had immediate access to content in Microsoft Reader format. Franklin Electronic had also announced an eBookman PDA device, to be shipped in the fall of 2000, that would display eBooks in Microsoft Reader format.

Digital Rights Management. In addition to the PDF Merchant product described earlier, Adobe had announced its intention to provide digital content server products to provide total solutions to digital rights management for eBook stores. With the acquisition of Glassbook, Adobe had gained access to leading edge digital rights management software called, EBX. In addition, Adobe had announced a relationship with Price Waterhouse Coopers and InterTrust to develop digital rights solutions around PDF and Acrobat. Microsoft had also announced a Digital Asset Server platform and was in beta test with Barnes & Noble and Lightning Source. The initial version of the Microsoft Reader, however, had shipped without digital rights management.

Creating "Buzz." In addition to its many announcements, Microsoft had achieved a great deal of publicity about its eBook initiatives. Much of this publicity revolved around Dick Brass, Microsoft's VP of Technology. Dubbed an "eBook Evangelist" by the press, Brass was a powerful personality known for his outspokenness. Reporters often made him the focal point of their stories, even commenting on his "bushy eyebrows and . . . walrus moustache."[16] Brass had been aggressive in his promotion of both Microsoft and eBooks, predicting that "20 years from now, 90% of everything published will be published electronically."[17]

Adobe was constantly feeling the pressure to keep up with Microsoft. In February 2000, Sarah Rosenbaum, Group Product Manager of Adobe Desktop Solutions commented,

> I was at the gym working out watching CNBC when Steven Riggio of Barnes & Noble and Dick Brass from Microsoft came on. Microsoft was announcing Pocket PC with the built-in eBook reader and ClearType technology. For three minutes of CNBC they were talking about Microsoft and eBooks. I started off doing 140 strides a minute, and when they finished I was doing 190! That's the type of stuff we need to be going out there and pushing and getting ourselves into, but given Microsoft's resources to throw at this sort of thing I'm not sure how we can keep up.

Gemstar. While Adobe was focusing most of its attention on Microsoft, one other firm had its sites on controlling an eBook standard. Henry C. Yuen, Chairman and CEO of Gemstar, had been aggressively pursuing the eBook market, having acquired both eBook device makers, Nuvomedia and Softbook for $400 million in January, 2000. Gemstar had developed the VCR Plus+ System, which allows users to record programs on their VCR by using program codes published in newspapers and television program guides. In addition to the eBook acquisitions, Gemstar had also recently acquired TV Guide.

Yuen had planned a number of moves. Two next generation eBook devices were to be introduced in the fall of 2000 at a price of about $250. They were to be manufactured by Thomson under license from Gemstar, and were to carry the RCA brand. A $100 million marketing campaign was planned for their introduction. While the Rocket eBook and Softbook had had limited distribution through high-end catalogs and a select number of online retailers, the RCA eBook readers were to have broad distribution through bricks and mortar consumer electronics retailers. Yuen was boldly predicting that 500,000 of the new devices would be sold in 6 months.

---

[15]Stephanie Miles, "eBooks gauge budding market," CNET News.com, June 26, 1998.

[16]D. Gates, "E-Book Evangelist," *The Industry Standard,* September 25, 2000, p.129.

[17]D. Gates, "E-Book Evangelist," *The Industry Standard,* September 25, 2000, p.129.

Gemstar/RCA eBooks were in Rocket eBook format which was not compatible with Microsoft Reader format or PDF. There was, however, some content already available in that format, and Gemstar had plans to provide its own eBook store directly accessible from the eBook device. Consumers could bypass the Internet and simply dial up the Gemstar eBook store using the device's built-in modem.

Gemstar had also begun moving into the European eBook market with the acquisition of a French online publisher Les Editions 00h00 (Zero Hour). Les Editions carried 600 titles, and planned to publish online material in many European languages.

Next Steps

While Adobe had an early lead, its eBook strategy was rapidly evolving. Joe Eschbach, VP of the ePaper® Solutions Group had significantly increased the firm's commitment to eBooks, hiring a number of individuals, including Mike Looney, a new Senior Director of eBooks in August, 2000. Looney identified a number of critical choices he faced as he took on his new responsibilities.

Which Target Segments? While Microsoft had charged head on into the consumer market, Looney wondered whether Adobe should instead focus elsewhere. Other segments, such as Professional and Technical users, while smaller than the general consumer market, seemed to place more value on what eBooks had to offer and were leading in their adoption. In addition, Adobe's superior graphics capability was more highly valued by the professional market. If Adobe ceded the consumer market to Microsoft, however, would it ever be able to win it back? If Microsoft got a strong foothold in the consumer market, would they eventually leverage that in other market segments as the Microsoft Reader became more competitive with PDF?

The eBook market was only just beginning, and it was unclear when it would take off, if at all. How important was the eBook market as opposed to other markets for ePaper Solutions? Adobe had always included eBooks as a subset of ePaper Solutions, a category that included business and professional documents as well as books. The print market for documents was estimated at $59 billion, as opposed to $30.5 billion for books (see Exhibit 14). Estimates of the market for online sales of business and professional information were also large, with a forecasted size of about $52 billion by 2003.[18] Should Adobe concentrate on establishing PDF as the dominant standard for those interested in selling electronic documents instead of fighting in the eBook space? What would the long-term implications of this strategy be?

On-demand Printing? New digital printers had changed the economics or print runs enabling "on-demand" printing. Since one of Adobe's huge advantages over Microsoft was the ability of PDF to print, Looney wondered how aggressively the firm should pursue the market for on-demand printing. Bricks and mortar booksellers such as Barnes & Noble had articulated a vision of offering customers the ability to print titles on-demand in their physical stores. Customers would benefit from a larger inventory of books immediately available, and retailers would save the cost of physical inventory. Like eBooks, however, print on demand was an emerging market whose viability had yet to be proven. Could Adobe leverage its ties to the print world in order to dominate this emerging market?

Business Model? So far Adobe had little experience selling products in a form other than shrinkwrap software for desktops. More and more firms were adopting an ASP (Application Service Provider) model whereby they rented software to customers, offering the customer end-to-end solutions. Looney wondered whether Adobe should leverage an ASP model for its PDF Merchant digital rights management software, and charge a much higher price than the current $5000.

Give Away PDF Creation? While there was a lot of PDF content in existence, Microsoft was aggressively building content in their Reader format. Should Adobe respond by making it free to create PDF documents? Currently only 2% of desktops had the full Acrobat product. In contrast, Microsoft Word was present on 75% of editor's desktops.[19] If Microsoft made creation of Microsoft Reader format easier through built-in functions in Microsoft Word, it wouldn't take long for a large amount of Microsoft Reader content to be created. Would the market then tip in favor of Microsoft?

Giving away the ability to create PDF documents, however, seemed like giving away the crown jewels and would hurt Acrobat sales significantly. The number one

[18]Veronis, Suhler & Associates, Simba Information.

[19]Global Industry Analysts, Inc. "Adobe Systems Inc. A Competitive Assessment Report," 7/00.

reason users purchased Acrobat was to create PDF documents. Could Adobe capture enough value through the creation of complementary products such as Acrobat Business Tools or the digital rights content server? And if Adobe didn't give away the ability to create PDF, would competition emerge in that market. Since PDF was an open standard, there was nothing to stop other firms from developing a competitive product. Would Adobe become a victim of its own success, encouraging competition if PDF became a dominant standard?

Looney felt himself in a quandry. If Adobe lost the war, then PDF might be relegated to the status of the Betamax—a footnote in technology history. On the other hand, if Adobe aggressively moved to make PDF a standard, it was unclear how they would make money from owning the standard. In the meantime, reporters were continuing to call looking for an angle on an eBook story. Given the publicity Dick Brass of Microsoft had been attracting, Looney wondered what he could do to gain similar publicity for Adobe.

Exhibit 1 CUMULATIVE NUMBER OF ACROBAT READER DOWNLOADS, JULY 1996—JULY 2000

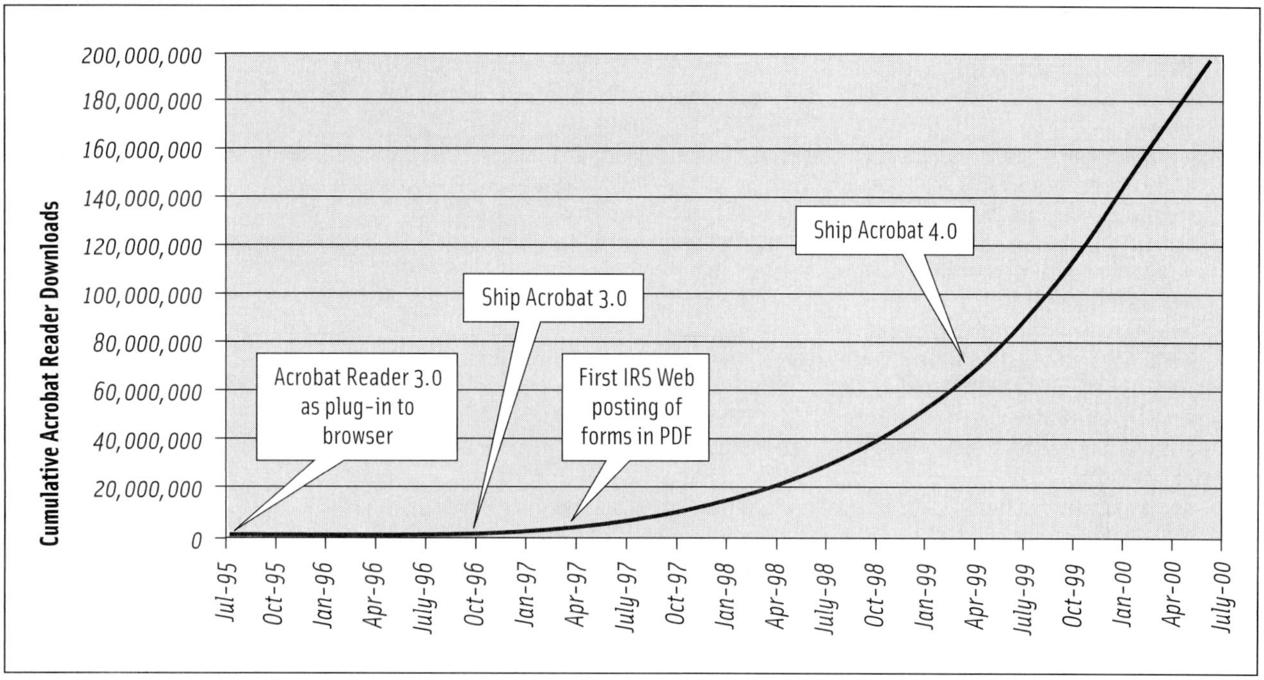

Source: Adobe Systems Incorporated

Exhibit 2 ACROBAT PRODUCT FEATURE OVERVIEW

	Acrobat Reader	Acrobat Business tools	Acrobat 4.0	Adobe.com
View and print PDF files	✓	✓	✓	
Fill in and submit Adobe PDF forms	✓	✓	✓	
Download and read eBooks	✓	✓	✓	
Mark up documents electronically		✓	✓	
Create "snapshots" of Web pages		✓	✓	✓
Digitally sign documents		✓	✓	
Create PDF files			✓	✓
Scan paper into PDF files			✓	✓
Create PDF forms			✓	
Price	free	$49.00	$249.00	$9.99/month $99.99/year

Source: Adobe Systems Incorporated

Exhibit 3

ADOBE PRODUCT LINE OVERVIEW

- EPaper® Solutions
  - **Adobe Acrobat®:** *Complete PDF Solution* ($249). Convert electronic documents into Adobe PDF files that can be viewed, annotated, and printed on any computer, with their original appearance preserved. Incorporates the functionality of Acrobat Reader and Acrobat Business Tools.
  - **Adobe Acrobat® Reader™:** *View and print* (free). Allows users to view and print PDF files, fill out PDF forms, and read PDF eBooks.
  - **Adobe Acrobat® Business Tools:** *Review and mark-up* ($49 special). Collaborate on PDF documents using Acrobat's markup, digital signature, search and Web capture tools.
  - **Adobe PDF Merchant™:** *EBooks.* ($5000 + 2% fee). This server-based software enables eBook and content providers to sell and distribute documents electronically with complete security.
  - **Adobe Acrobat® Capture®:** *Convert to PDF* ($699). Turn printed documents into searchable PDF files for electronic distribution and archiving.
  - **Adobe Acrobat® Distiller® Server:** *Server-based conversion.* ($5000). A server-based solution for the high-volume conversion of PostScript files to Adobe PDF documents.
  - **Adobe Acrobat® Messenger™:** *Workgroup delivery* ($1499). This paper to digital dispatch center that converts paper documents into PDF files and delivers them via e-mail, the Web and more.
- Print Publishing
  - **Adobe Illustrator®:** Drawing, painting and editing artwork for graphic arts professionals.
  - **Adobe InDesign®:** Page layout and design for publishing professionals.
  - **Adobe Framemaker®:** For professional publishers, Framemaker is intended for publishing long, content-rich documents such as books for a variety of media.
  - **Adobe PageMaker®:** Page layout software for business professionals
  - **Adobe PressReady®:** Allows graphic designers to print color proofs from desktop color inkjets
  - **Adobe Type Library:** Collection of over 2500 PostScript fonts.
  - **Adobe Acrobat® InProduction™:** Targeted at print publishing professionals, InProduction extends the functionality of Acrobat to include tools for the management and analysis of PDF files used in a print workflow.
  - **Adobe Design Collection:** Bundle comprising InDesign™, PhotoShop®, Illustrator®, and Acrobat®.
  - **Adobe Publishing Collection:** Bundle comprising PageMaker®, PhotoShop®, Illustrator®, and Acrobat®.
- Web Publishing
  - **Adobe After Effects®:** A graphics and visual effects program, to aid designers and visual effects artists in creating motion graphics and visual effects for film, video, multimedia, and the Web.
  - **Adobe GoLive™:** Visual design and programming for website creation.
  - **Adobe LiveMotion™:** A Web graphics and animation authoring tool designed to compete with Macromedia Flash authoring programs. It supports both Flash and SVG (Scalable Vector Graphics).
  - **Adobe® Premiere®:** Digital video editing software for video professionals in multiple media.
  - **Adobe Photoshop®:** Professional image editing software for all media. Users can modify and retouch digital images, paint, draw, create types, design animation, and prepare images for the web.
  - **Adobe® PhotoDeluxe®:** A simplified consumer version of Photoshop.
  - **Adobe ActiveShare**: Consumer software for organizing, enhancing, and sharing photos on the web.
  - **Dynamic Media™ Collection:** A bundle comprising After Effects®, Premiere®, Photoshop®, and Illustrator®.
  - **Web Collection:** A bundle comprising GoLive™, Photoshop®, Illustrator® and LiveMotion™.
- OEM PostScript and Other
  - **PostScript®:** PostScript interpreters licensed to high end imagesetter and laser printer OEMs

Source: Adobe Systems Incorporated

Exhibit 4 ADOBE READER DOWNLOAD PAGE

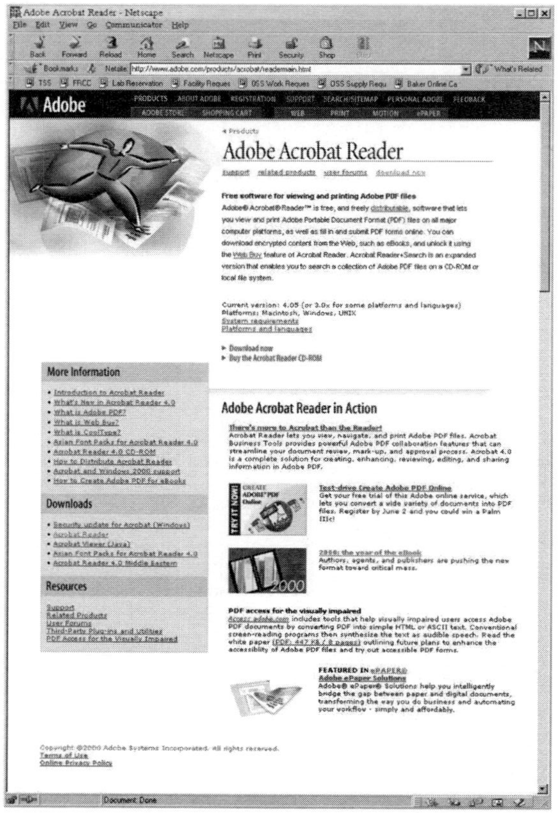

Source: Adobe Systems

Exhibit 5 ADOBE SYSTEMS INCORPORATED SALES BY SEGMENT: 1998–2Q 2000

	Year ending 11/27/98	Year ending 12/3/99	Nine months ended 9/1/00
Revenue by segment			
Web publishing	354.2	394.1	368.9
Print publishing	272.2	353.9	293.7
ePaper® solutions (Acrobat)	58.0	129.3	148.4
OEM PostScript & other	210.4	138.2	100.2
Total revenue	894.8	1015.4	911.2
% of total revenue			
Web publishing	39.6%	38.8%	40.5%
Print publishing	30.4%	34.8%	32.2%
ePaper® solutions (Acrobat)	6.5%	12.7%	16.3%
OEM PostScript & other	23.5%	13.6%	11.0%
% dollar change yr to yr			
Web publishing	13.6%	11.2%	32.3%
Print publishing	-15.2%	30.0%	15.0%
ePaper® solutions (Acrobat)	22.9%	123.2%	61.2%
OEM PostScript & other	-9.3%	-34.3%	-6.6%
Total revenue	-1.9%	13.5%	24.2%

Source: Adobe Systems Incorporated and Paine Webber Estimates

Exhibit 6

ADOBE SYSTEMS INCORPORATED FINANCIAL STATEMENTS ADOBE SYSTEMS INCORPORATED—INCOME STATEMENT (MILLIONS)

	Nine Months Ended 9/1/00	Nine Months Ended 9/3/99	Year Ending 12/3/99	Year Ending 11/27/98
Revenue	911.2	733.7	1,015.4	894.8
Direct Costs	65.0	70.5	94.5	101.0
Gross Profit	846.2	663.2	920.9	793.8
Operating Expenses				
Research and Development	179.9	140.5	197.5	188.3
Sales and Marketing	288.0	242.8	328.5	315.5
General and Administrative	84.6	78.7	103.6	118.6
Other	9.3	23.4	314.5	459.9
Total Operating Expenses	561.8	485.3	661.0	668.4
Operating Income	284.4	177.9	259.9	125.3
Total Nonoperating Income, Net	36.6	43.2	114.6	42.3
Income Before Income Taxes	321.0	221.1	374.4	167.7
Income Tax Provision	112.3	80.7	136.7	62.6
Total Net Income	208.6	140.4	237.8	105.1

ADOBE SYSTEMS INCORPORATED—BALANCE SHEET (000S)

	9/1/00	12/3/99	11/27/98
Assets			
Cash and equivalents	191,015	171,145	110,871
Other assets	852,622	632,714	656,460
Total Assets	$1,043,637	$803,859	$767,331
Liabilities and Stockholders' Equity			
Total Liabilities	369,953	291,650	250,966
Stockholders' Equity			
Paid-In Capital			
Accumulated deficit			
Total Stockholders' Equity	673,684	512,209	516,365
Total Liabilities and Stockholders' Equity	$1,043,637	$803,859	$ 767,331

Source: Adobe Systems Incorporated

Exhibit 7 eBOOK MARKET SEGMENT CHARACTERISTICS

Category	Online Affinity of Audience	Importance of Fast Delivery	Key Word Value	Customizability of Content	Potential for Multimedia Enhancement	Scarcity
Textbooks	◐	◐	●	●	●	◐
Professional and Technical	●	○	●	●	◐	●
Business	●	◐	◐	●	○	◐
Fiction	◐	○	○	○	○	○
Non-Fiction	◐	○	◐	◐	◐	◐
Juvenile	○	○	○	○	◐	○
Reference	●	○	●	◐	◐	◐
Travel	●	●	●	●	●	◐

● High ◐ Medium ○ Low

Source: Jupiter Communications, "eBooks: An Emergent Opportunity, but Stephen King Is Not the Model," August 2000

Exhibit 8 THE eBOOK VALUE SYSTEM

Activity	Create Content	Layout/Typeset Book	Create Digital eBook File	Distribute/Sell Inventory of eBooks	Read eBook	Print eBook
Players	• Author • Illustrator	• Author • Publisher - Graphic artist - Typesetter	• Author • Publisher • Distributor	• Author with website • Online publishers (e.g., iUniverse.com) • Online bookstores (e.g., Amazon.com)	• Customer - Consumer - Professional - Student	• Customer • 'On-demand' professional printer
Tools	• Software - Word processing - Illustration - Digital imaging	• Page layout software (e.g., Adobe InDesign, QuarkXPress)	• eBook formats - PDF - Microsoft Reader (.LIT) - HTML - OEB - Proprietary • Conversion software (e.g., Adobe Acrobat, Overdrive)	• Digital rights management systems (e.g., Adobe PDF Merchant) • Content server service providers (e.g., Lightning Source)	• Dedicated eBook device (e.g., Rocket eBook) • PDA with reader software (e.g., Palm Pilot or Pocket PC device) • Desktop or notebook PC with reader software (e.g., Acrobat Reader, Glassbook Reader, Microsoft Reader)	• Laser printer • 'On-demand' printing system

Exhibit 9 TYPICAL REVENUE DISTRIBUTION FOR A HARDCOVER BOOK

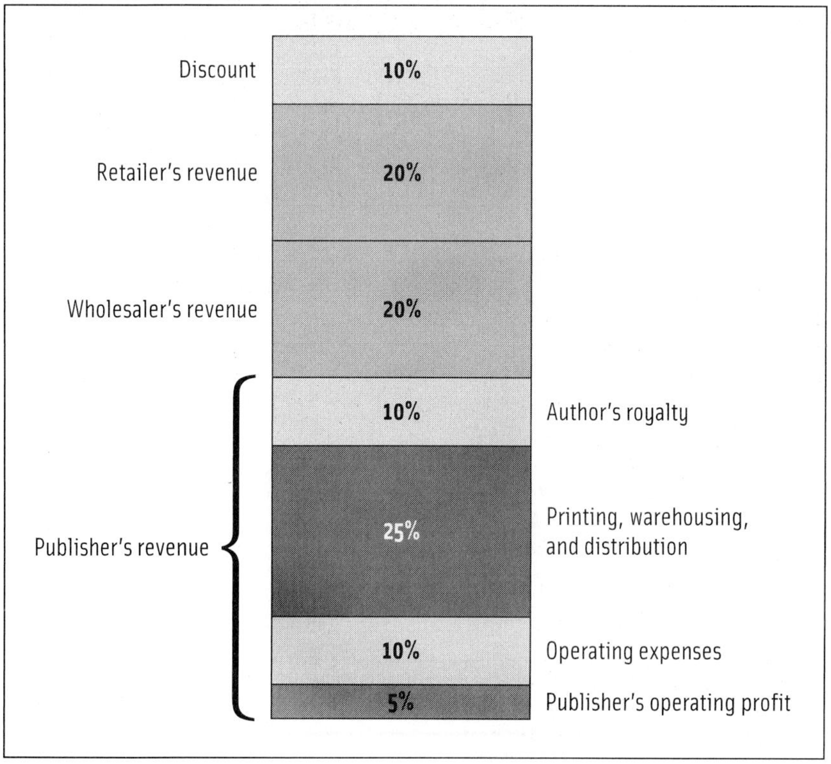

Source: Association of American Publishers; CIBC Oppenheimer; "Horror Story," *Forbes*, 8/21/00

Exhibit 10

DEDICATED EBOOK READING

a. Rocket eBook

The Rocket eBook is 5″x7.5″x1.5″, the size of a standard paperback book, weighs 22 ounces and holds about 3,200 pages of reading material, approximately 10 paperback books. The Pro version of the Rocket eBook holds 15,200 pages — about 40 books or documents.

The Rocket eBook attempts to mimic the use of paper books and is targeted at consumers. Users of the eBook can thus underline passages, insert notes, set bookmarks, find specific texts, look up words from a built-in Random House Dictionary, and display the list of owned eBooks on a virtual bookshelf. The Rocket eBook also features tools for the manipulation of text size and backlight intensity, includes a page navigation bar, and is touch-sensitive. The resolution of the eBook is approximately 106 dots per inch, with a high light contrast, monochrome display which allows a wide viewing angle. Users of the Rocket can download published material from the Internet through their PC, as well as store personal material from their computer.

The Rocket eBook sells online for $250, with the Pro version listed at $270.

b. Softbook

The SoftBook is 6″ x 8″ with a grayscale, backlit, touch-sensitive LCD and a protective leather cover. It weighs 2.9 pounds and can store about 4000 pages with standard memory. The SoftBook has a number of tools including sophisticated search, bookmarking, hyperlinking, text markup and a stylus for marking and highlighting. The battery lasts for 2-5 hours of reading time. Users can download published materials directly from the SoftBook Network without the need for a PC.

The SoftBook costs $599.95 or $299.95 plus a $19.95 per month content package for 24 months.

Source: Gemstar NuvoMedia, Softbook

Exhibit 11 COMPARISON OF ADOBE PDF AND MICROSOFT READER FORMATS

Feature	Adobe PDF	Microsoft Reader Format
Publicly Available Specification	Y	N
Proprietary Viewer	N	Y
Raster Graphics (PNG, JPEG)	Y	Y
Resolution Independent Graphics	Y	N
Display Layout	Y	Y
Publicly Available Packaging Standard	Y	N
Open, Extensible Rights Management	Y	N
Windows	Y	Y
Mac	Y	N
Unix/Linux	Y	N
Windows CE	D	Y
Palm	D	N
Dedicated Devices	D	D
LCD-Enhanced Type	D	Y
XML-Based Content	Y	Y
Scale/Reflow to Fit Screen Size	D	Y
Printing/Print-on-Demand	Y	N
Supports HTML Content	Y	Y
Wide Range of Content Available	Y	D

D = In Development
Source: Adobe Systems Incorporated

Exhibit 12 ADOBE AND MICROSOFT eBOOK ANNOUNCEMENTS

Date	Adobe Systems Incorporated Announcements	Microsoft Announcements
10/98		VP Dick Brass endorses Open eBook Standard.
8/31/99	Pre-release availability of PDF Merchant and Web Buy. Partners for testing and product integration include Barnes & Noble, Everybook, Fatbrain.com, Glassbook, Pearson, R.R. Donnelley and Simon & Schuster. Relationship with Xerox Content Guard to develop digital rights management systems.	
9/6/99		Microsoft Reader, an eBook reader that uses ClearType text technology announced
9/21/99		Open eBook Standard agreement and release reached by Microsoft and its committee on OEB.
10/6/99	Partners CyberTrust, InterTrust, Plug'n'Pay, PublishOne Inc., SheetMusicPlus.com and SoftLock.com begin testing PDF Merchant.	
10/14/99		Partnership with publisher Penguin for the creation and release of eBook CD featuring eBooks in Microsoft Reader format.
10/21/99		Partnership with Havas to transfer the French publisher's material into a French version of Microsoft Reader format.
11/4/99	Collaboration with Reciprocal to distribute and sell secure content online.	Partnership with R.R. Donnelley & Sons Co. to convert thousands of print books to Microsoft Reader format.
1/7/00		Partnership with Barnes & Noble to create an eBook store on bn.com with content in MS Reader format.
2/7/00	Adobe PDF Merchant and Web Buy ship.	
	CoolType, technology to improve the quality and resolution of on-screen text is announced.	
2/11/00		Pocket PC, a PDA operating system that includes Microsoft Reader is announced.
2/22/00	Announces alliances with publishing companies Salon.com, Seybold Publications, Total Training, Planet PDF, and PeachPit Press.	
3/27/00	Partnership with Amazon and publisher Simon and Schuster to extend online availablilty of Stephen King's *Riding the Bullet* to Macintosh users.	
3/28/00		Partnership with Contentville.com.
4/00		Pocket PC with Microsoft Reader ships.
4/11/00	DeepCanyon announces the availability of its research reports for electronic purchase in PDF format, using PDF Merchant.	
4/28/00		Made minority investment in Xerox spin-off Content Guard in the area of digital rights management.
5/15/00		Partnership with Lightning Source, an Ingram Subsidiary, to create eBooks in Microsoft Reader format.

Exhibit 12 ADOBE AND MICROSOFT eBOOK ANNOUNCEMENTS cont.

Date	Adobe Systems Incorporated Announcements	Microsoft Announcements
5/23/00		Time-Warner's iPublish.com to offer eBooks in MS Reader format. Exclusive release of Michael Crichton's *Timeline* in Microsoft Reader format, available for download on bn.com.
5/24/00	Mary Higgins Clark's new book, *Before I Say Goodbye,* is published as PDF, along with eighteen previously print novels and other works.	
5/00		Microsoft-led Open eBook Authoring group releases criticized draft recommendation for Open eBook 1.0 Specifications.
5/29/00		Announces partnership with OverDrive Inc., to develop a set of authoring tools and services for publishers creating eBooks in Microsoft Reader format.
5/31/00	Partnership with Lightening Source, an Ingram Subsidiary, to create eBooks in PDF format using PDF Merchant. Price WaterHouse Coopers and InterTrust agree to develop eBook publication solutions using PDF and Acrobat.	Announces partnership with Quark, Inc. to facilitate creation of Microsoft Reader format eBooks from QuarkXPress files.
6/00		Participation of over 30 publishers in launching program for Microsoft Reader eBooks, potentially making more than 800 eBooks available for readers.
6/2/00		Licensing arrangement with Labyrinten Data AB and isSound to allow text and audio synchronization for eBooks in Microsoft Reader format.
6/15/00		Partnership with Chapters Online to launch a Microsoft Reader eBook store in its digital book section.
6/19/00	Introduces Acrobat Distiller Server, which allows network users to create PDF files on a central server.	
6/27/00		Partnership with Franklin Electronic Publishers to incorporate Microsoft Reader into Franklin's new eBook devices.
7/11/00		Partnership with Toshiba to develop high-resolution LCD for eBook devices.
8/8/00		Microsoft Reader made available to desktop Windows users, not just owners of hand held devices.
8/9/00		Barnes and Noble opens a new section of its Microsoft Reader eBook store, with several hundred eBook titles, making it the largest source of Microsoft Reader-compatible eBooks. Collaboration with Association of American Publishers to create a new eBook anti-piracy initiative.
8/28/00	Acquisition of Glassbook, a maker of PDF-based eBook reader software. Partnerships with Barnes and Noble to create an Adobe-branded eBookstore with content in PDF format. Announces partnerships with iUniverse.com and AvantGo.	Partnership with Amazon.com to make Microsoft Reader its preferred eBook format.
8/29/00		Certifies OverDrive to provide eBook copyright protection to eBook marketplace based on Microsoft's Digital Asset Server (DAS) technologies.

Exhibit 13

ADOPTION OF eBOOK STANDARDS

Online eBook retailers	eBook Formats supported	Notes
Barnesandnoble.com	Microsoft Reader, Rocket eBook, Glassbook Reader	The Glassbook Reader can read PDF files
Amazon.com	Microsoft Reader, Rocket eBook, PDF	
eBookmall.com	Microsoft Reader, HTML, PDF	An Amazon.com zshop partner
Powells.com	Rocket eBook	
iPublish.com	Microsoft Reader, Rocket eBook, Softbook, PeanutPress, PDF	Unit of Time-Warner
Xlibris	PDF	49% owned by Random House; offers "on-demand" printing in addition to eBooks
Books24x7.com	HTML, PDF	Subscription service for IT technical reference books
PeanutPress.com	Proprietary	Content for Palm pilot
Dedicated Reading Devices		
Gemstar Nuvomedia, Rocket eBook	Rocket eBook format	
Gemstar Softbook	Softbook format	
Franklin eBookman PDA	Microsoft Reader	Scheduled to ship fall, 2000; priced at $129.95
Thomson-RCA Brand	Rocket eBook	Scheduled to ship fall, 2000; Licensed technology from Gemstar
N-vision technologies	PDF	No ship date announced. Licensed Everybook technology
Other Devices		
Palm Pilot	PDF	
Pocket PC PDAs	Microsoft Reader	PDF Planned
Windows desktops, Laptops	PDF, Microsoft Reader	
Mac desktops, Laptop	PDF	
Publishers		
Lightning Source (Ingram)	PDF, Microsoft Reader	
Simon and Schuster	PDF, Microsoft Reader, Rocket eBook	
Random House	PDF, Microsoft Reader, Rocket eBook	

Exhibit 14 PRINT PUBLISHING MARKET SIZE ESTIMATES

Document Market Segment	Approximate Number of Publishers	Approximate Number of Publications	Annual Sales (billions)
Newsletters	8,000	24,000	$ 8.0
Journals	12,000	73,000	$22.0
Research and Special Reports	2,000	8,000	$20.0
Directories and Catalogs	5,000	15,900	$ 5.0
Trade Magazines	3,000	20,400	$ 3.0
Total	30,000	141,300	$59.0
Traditional Book Market			$30.5

Source: Adapted from Veronis, Suhler & Associates, Simba Information, AAP, estimates.

Exhibit 15 ADOBE SYSTEMS INCORPORATED ORGANIZATION CHART

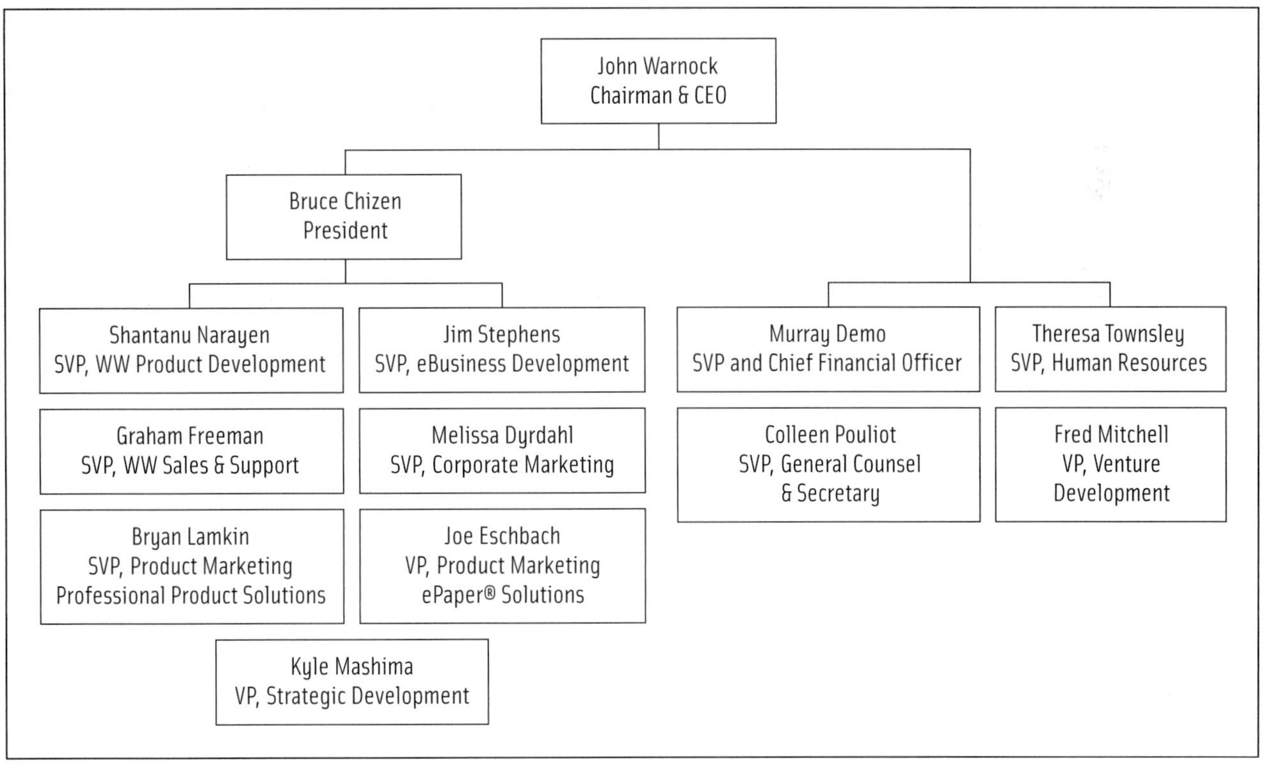

Source: Adobe Systems Incorporated

8

Application Service Providers

Five years from now, if you're a CIO with a head for business, you won't be buying computers anymore. You won't buy software either. You'll rent all your resources from a service provider.

—Scott McNealy, CEO, Sun Microsystems[1]

The new economy is a *networked* economy: It is characterized by unprecedented levels of electronically-mediated communication, collaboration, and commerce among businesses, among consumers, and between businesses and consumers. A new business model, that of application service provider (ASP), promised to accelerate the movement of business processes to electronic networks. ASPs allow companies to access application software on remote servers using the Internet. Through ASPs, application software is "rented," i.e., customers make regular subscription payments to ASPs, rather than buying software and installing it on their own computers. ASPs' customers are relieved of the burden of maintaining software—a large benefit for companies with limited or overtaxed information technology (IT) personnel. Customers also value the fact that employees and external business partners can access applications from any computer with Internet access; there is no need to extend local or wide-area networks to include new users.

For decades, the software industry had evolved in an evolutionary manner using a familiar business model: Users purchased software, then installed it on their own computers or hired a systems integrator to do so. Within this context, software had migrated from proprietary to packaged applications, and the infrastructure on which the software ran had evolved from mainframe to client-server architectures.[2]

By the late 1990s, however, three separate trends had converged to bring into being a new business model for software delivery.[3] The first was IT outsourcing. For years, firms had been selective in outsourcing their IT infrastructure. Initially, firms might only be

---

Professor Thomas Eisenmann and Research Associate Sanjay Pothen prepared this note as the basis for class discussion.

willing to outsource base-level infrastructure such as data networking. Next came the outsourcing of system services such as the maintenance of desktop PCs and generic networked applications such as messaging. Finally, companies became more comfortable outsourcing user applications themselves. A second trend that led to the ASP business model was application hosting. Internet service providers (ISPs) emerged to provide access services (i.e., connectivity for Internet users who wished to access websites and exchange e-mails and files) as well as hosting services (i.e., the outsourced management of websites).[4] Such hosting services naturally complemented a new class of application-software vendors that used the hosting model to provide Internet-based applications. A third important trend was the emergence of "portals." Portals (e.g., Yahoo!, Lycos) aggregated applications in order to create convenient user experiences ("one-stop shopping") and to thereby increase "stickiness," i.e., the amount of time users lingered at the portal.[5] Building on this theme, some ASPs began aggregating complementary suites of applications accessible through a single website.

These trends converged to create the model of delivering a set of applications from an offsite data center to a community of users. Some observers even believed that the aforementioned trends could be extrapolated into a future where companies no longer acquired and maintained any user applications on local computers. According to ASPnews.com, an online newsletter, "Within a few years, users will not want to install applications locally. Instead, they will access the applications they need, on demand, from online providers who will charge them by the second for the precise value of the specific features and resources they choose to use."[6]

Not surprisingly, enthusiasm for the ASP model was great in late 2000: Most analysts predicted rapid growth.[7] Some analysts said ASPs would be the Internet's next killer application and proclaimed that businesses needed to rapidly embrace this transforming phenomenon to survive.[8] Other analysts noted that the ASP business model was still young and evolving and numerous challenges loomed; these analysts warned that ASPs could be another example of New Economy "hype gone haywire." Gartner Group, for example, believed that the ASP model showed promise but observed that there was a glut of aspiring ASPs and predicted that fewer than 40 percent of the 300 or so ASP startups active early in 2000 would survive until the end of 2001.[9]

This chapter examines the Application Service Provider business model. The first section of the chapter defines the ASP model and describes different ways to categorize ASPs. The second section presents a brief summary of the various ways that ASPs create value for their clients. The third section analyzes the economic model for ASPs, focusing on their revenue and cost drivers. Building on that analysis, the final section examines the payoff to ASPs from pursuing a "Get Big Fast" strategy, i.e., investing aggressively in customer acquisition.

WHAT IS AN ASP?

An ASP is defined as an organization that "manages and delivers application capabilities to multiple entities from a data center across a Wide Area Network (WAN)."[10] ASPs typically rented access to software for a recurring fee. As noted by the "serial" entrepreneur, K.B. Chandrasekhar, cofounder first of the Internet hosting firm Exodus and then the ASP Jamcracker, ASPs were similar in many ways to telephone, power, and water utilities: "We learned very well at Exodus that outsourcing works. You don't run your own generator in order to have electricity."[11]

An ASP combined a number of service offerings that typically were not associated with a single company, including application software, system-integration services, data center and connectivity services, and application monitoring and end-user support.[12]

- *Application Software.* Obviously, the primary offering was the software product itself. Some ASPs licensed applications from independent software vendors (ISVs) such as SAP or PeopleSoft. Other ASPs were vertically integrated: They developed their own applications.
- *System Integration Services.* To promote scalability (i.e., the ability to expand rapidly without adding personnel), many ASPs preferred to minimize the degree to which they would customize their software to meet unique user requirements. Sometimes, however, such tailoring was unavoidable, and ASPs had to help their customers with implementation. Such services were traditionally provided by systems integrators such as Andersen Consulting (now Accenture) or by the service arms of ISVs, such as IBM Consulting. ASPs often partnered with such concerns.
- *Data Center and Connectivity Services.* ASPs usually partnered with hosting companies such as Exodus to provide data-center operations and with Internet Service Providers (ISPs) to provide telecommunications services.
- *Application Monitoring, Metering/Billing, and End-User Support.* In addition to systems integrators and ISVs, who usually provided such services, firms specifically dedicated to these tasks were emerging. For example, InteQ was a Boston-based management service provider that provided ASPs and ISPs with network management services.

Thus, an ASP was required to have expertise with network management and systems integration, as well as with the software application itself. To this end, an ASP could choose to develop the necessary portfolio of services in-house, or it could license these services from business partners. At the extreme, an ASP could become a virtual corporation, orchestrating its business partners' efforts and retaining only the crucial sales-and-marketing and account-management functions. At the same time, firms that were well-established providers of one of the component services, e.g., systems integration or hosting, could position themselves as ASPs by wrapping other functions around their core service offering.

As a result of this maneuvering, the structure of the ASP industry was very much in flux. While some ASPs were backward-integrating into data-center operations in an effort to differentiate their service, ISPs and hosting firms were forward-integrating into application services, and ISVs were both backward- and forward-integrating into infrastructure and customer management, respectively. All of this leeway in business-model design also led to some confusion over the definition of an ASP. However, the defining characteristic of an ASP was that it was the sole owner of the customer relationship. It was the ASP that sold the service and was accountable if any service problems occurred.

Taxonomy

In addition to being characterized by the set of functions they performed in-house versus through partnerships, ASPs could be categorized along four other dimensions: solution focus, customer focus, breadth of application solutions, and application-sourcing strategy (see Exhibits 1 and 2 for projections of the size of the market for hosted applications by application type and by customer size, respectively).

Solution Focus. Applications could be classified in two ways: Whether applications were externally- versus internally-focused, and whether they were horizontally-, vertically-, or enterprise-focused.[13] Externally-focused applications connected a company with its suppliers and/or customers; internally-focused applications were used only by company employees. To a greater extent than applications used within a single enterprise, externally-focused applications took advantage of the low-cost connectivity afforded by the Internet, and thus were expected to dominate the hosting market. Key externally-focused applications included procurement facilitation and customer relationship management (CRM). Interestingly, hosting of supply-chain planning software was expected to be more limited due to complex and unique system configurations that made replication of this type of software difficult.

Horizontal applications were used by customers across a wide range of industries. Examples included messaging, work-group collaboration, and office-productivity applications that were provided in prepackaged, relatively inexpensive formats. ASPs that fit in the horizontal application category included Critical Path, a provider of e-mail and messaging services, Works.com, a procurement application provider, and Employease, a human resources application provider. Vertical applications, on the other hand, were tailored to specific industries such as healthcare or high technology. The ASPs that provided these applications often

Exhibit 8-1 PROJECTED U.S. APPLICATION HOSTING MARKET BY APPLICATION TYPE, 2000–2003 ($ IN MILLIONS)

Application Type	2000	2003E
e-Commerce	$630	$4,738
Customer relationship management	$475	$2,453
Manufacturing and logistics	$325	$1,686
Human resources	$182	$911
Finance and accounting	$263	$916
Supply chain	$39	$269
Product development	$32	$224
Industry specific	$17	$115
Total	**$1,964**	**$11,311**

Source: Adapted from Forrester Research, "Sizing Application Hosting," December 1999

Exhibit 8-2 PROJECTED U.S. APPLICATION HOSTING MARKET BY CUSTOMER SIZE, 2000–2003 ($ IN MILLIONS)

Customer Size	2000	2003E
Small: less than 100 employees	$649	$3,850
Medium: 100 to 999 employees	$1,188	$6,623
Large: 1,000 to 4,999 employees	$100	$605
Very Large: more than 5,000 employees	$27	$233
Total	**$1,964**	**$11,311**

Source: Adapted from Forrester Research, "Sizing Application Hosting," December 1999

also provided more customized, and thus more expensive, solutions. Examples of these ASPs included AristaSoft, a provider of enterprise resource planning (ERP) applications to the high-technology industry, CollegeNET, which focused on managing forms used in college administration, and TriZetto, a healthcare ASP that integrated patient, doctor, and insurance company information. Finally, enterprise applications provided customized and expensive solutions tailored to the needs of larger, more complex organizations. These offerings were built around high-end, integrated ISV applications such as ERP, CRM, and e-commerce packages. Examples of ASPs that provided this type of application were Corio and USinternetworking.

Customer Focus. ASPs also could be defined by the characteristics of their customers, including customers' size, age, pace of growth, and business complexity.[14] Small (less than 100 employees) and medium-sized (100–999 employees) businesses were projected to account for $3.9 billion and $6.6 billion, respectively, of application-hosting revenue in 2003—most of the market (Exhibit 2). Small companies were expected to spend heavily on the rental of human resources and finance applications, since many had not yet automated these basic internal business processes. Medium-sized businesses were expected to source more strategic applications such as customer relationship management and procurement. In contrast, large companies (more than 1,000 employees) were not projected to spend as heavily on application rentals, because most already had the IT infrastructure and expertise required to develop and maintain their software in-house.[15]

Many ASPs targeted young customers on a steep growth trajectory, because such firms tended to have (1) acutely strained IT departments, (2) less investment in legacy systems that would be rendered obsolete or would require customization, and (3) greater reluctance to invest in new in-house software and hardware that might soon be outgrown. ASPs also tended to target companies with less complex business processes, because an outsourced application's predefined functionality was less likely to conflict with how they already ran their businesses.

Breadth of Application Solutions. ASPs tended to vary in the breadth of their application solutions. Some ASPs specialized in a single application. For example, eOnline built its offering around SAP's R/3 ERP product, and NetAbacus solely provided an online purchasing solution. Other ASPs aggregated an entire portfolio of applications. For instance, Surebridge offered many applications, often with different vendors' products available for each application. Surebridge sold products from Baan, Epicor, Great Plains, and Solomon, with solutions for accounting, CRM, ERP, human resources, and supply-chain management. ASPs that aggregated multiple applications often did so to earn a greater return on their direct-sales activities: It was expensive to contact small and medium-sized companies, so it often made sense to try to sell a range of software to those businesses. Some ASPs that sold multiple applications also integrated them to facilitate data sharing, so customers could avoid manual re-entry of data.

Application Sourcing Strategy. Increasingly, ISVs were moving away from the "shrink-wrapped" software-delivery model and were eyeing the Internet as a powerful new distribution channel that would enable the delivery of "software as service." ISVs were thus eager to adapt their software for use by third-party ASPs or to operate as ASPs themselves. Examples of such firms were Microsoft, Oracle, PeopleSoft, and SAP. Indeed, Microsoft's decision to begin offering its Office software as an Internet service was widely acknowledged as validation of the ASP model.[16]

Thus, in categorizing ASPs, a crucial distinction was between those that offered Internet-enabled applications and those that provided Web-native applications. Internet-enabled applications that ISVs like PeopleSoft and SAP were producing were originally built for a client-server environment, then subsequently redesigned to run over the Internet. This entailed writing an HTML "front-end" for existing applications. By contrast, Web-native applications were designed from inception to operate only over the Internet. These software applications were usually based on Java, JavaScript, or XML. Examples of ASPs that produce Internet-enabled applications include AristaSoft, Corio, and USinternetworking, while examples of those that produce Web-native applications include Employease and Works.com.

HOW DO ASPS CREATE VALUE FOR CUSTOMERS?

ASPs promised what Bill Gates termed "frictionless commerce."[17] More specifically, ASPs addressed three key points of friction: (1) the high up-front cost of a packaged software license, (2) the difficulty of recruiting and retaining inhouse IT resources to install and maintain software, and (3) the need to build and maintain the IT infrastructure necessary to support the application.

Researchers estimated that less than 5 percent of small businesses had automated basic internal processes like financial reporting and human resources record keeping due to the high cost of packaged solutions.[18] Even if an organization could afford the software in question, the tight employment market of 2000 often prevented it from obtaining the IT personnel needed to install and maintain the application. For example, studies showed that the number one reason firms chose to outsource business applications was a "lack of in-house expertise."[19] Lastly, firms were wary of the maintenance costs of in-house IT infrastructure. For instance, an ASP customer remarked that, "I have 25 people in my company; I have to pay a systems administrator $75,000 a year just to keep all the computers and my e-mail system running."[20]

ASPs solved these problems. By offering turnkey solutions that bundled software, hardware, and systems integration, ASPs reduced the burden of IT management and freed existing IT staff to work on mission-critical systems. Through monthly charges that incorporated the software license, ongoing maintenance, connectivity, and sometimes even up-front implementation fees, ASPs also offered their customers a lower up-front investment and more predictable IT costs. Finally, in some cases, ASPs enabled customers to deploy applications more rapidly. For example, while the average deployment of an ERP system exceeded 12 months, the average deployment time for an ERP system through an ASP (albeit a system with less end-user customization) was 90 days.[21]

Barriers to Adoption. Notwithstanding these benefits, ASPs faced significant barriers to customer adoption of their model. Many prospective customers were concerned about the security of data that traveled over the public Internet; others worried about handing off mission-critical applications to an outsider's data center and relying on a haphazardly-organized public network that was notorious for congestion. ASPs tried to address this last concern about network reliability by offering service-level agreements that guaranteed 99.9 percent uptime and by engineering networks with high levels of redundancy.[22]

ASPs also faced other barriers to adoption. Larger companies sometimes objected to ASPs' reluctance to customize applications. Smaller companies often lacked the basic computing infrastructure to connect employees to Internet-enabled applications. A J.C. Bradford & Co. analyst reported, for example, that 50 percent of customer help calls received by ASPs had nothing to do with the hosted applications themselves; rather, the calls dealt with basic problems such as users not being equipped with the latest version of browser plug-in software needed to run Java-based applications.[23] Finally, prospective customers were concerned about the fact that the ASP model was still untested, and many ASPs were expected to fail. How would a company deliver applications if its bankrupt ASP pulled the plug on its servers?

ASP ECONOMICS

It was difficult to generalize about the economics of ASPs due to (1) the diversity of their activities (in terms of both the breadth of applications they provided and the range of functions they kept in-house), and (2) the fact that only a few ASPs were publicly-traded as of year-end 2000, so little financial data was available on their performance. The information that was available indicated that the ASP business model was not yet a profitable one. For example, during the first nine months of 2000, Corio lost $68 million before amortization charges related to stock compensation and mergers; on the same basis, USinternetworking (henceforth, USi) lost $105 million[24] (see Exhibit 3 for income statements for Corio and USi). Nevertheless, some investors believed the ASP model would be attractive over the longer term due to its promise of predictable, recurring revenue.

Sources of Revenue

An ASP's revenues usually were comprised of (1) rental fees for software services and (2) fees for professional services, mostly earned up front when an ASP set up its data center and network to handle a new customer's applications, and assisted them with any application customization, data transfer, and employee training. In general, as ASPs matured, a larger portion of their revenue was expected to

Exhibit 8-3 INCOME STATEMENTS FOR USINTERNETWORKING AND CORIO, FIRST THREE QUARTERS OF 2000

USinternetworking	$ in millions	% of revenue	Corio	$ in millions	% of revenue
Revenue	$72.3		**Revenue**	$29.5	
			Application management services	$8.2	27.8%
			Professional services	$21.3	72.2%
Costs			**Costs**		
Direct cost of services	$46.8	64.7%	*Direct cost of application management services*	$22.5	76.3%
			Direct cost of professional services	$19.8	67.1%
Network and infrastructure costs	$19.4	26.8%			
General and administrative	$19.9	27.5%	*General and administrative*	$17.6	59.7%
Sales and marketing	$52.7	72.9%	*Sales and marketing*	$28.6	96.9%
Depreciation / amortization of equipment	$36.4	50.3%			
Product development	$2.3	3.2%	*Product development*	$8.8	29.8%
Noncash stock compensation expense	$15.9	22.0%	*Amortization of stock-based compensation*	$12.6	42.7%
			Amortization of intangible assets	$1.7	5.8%
Total operating expenses	$193.2	267.2%	*Total operating expenses*	$111.8	379.0%
Loss from operations	($120.9)	−167.2%	*Loss from operations*	($82.3)	−279.0%

Source: Adapted from company SEC filings

be derived from recurring software rental fees. For example, through the first nine months of 2000, Corio earned 28 percent of its $30 million in revenue from software rental; the balance was from professional fees. On average, each of Corio's 75 customers paid about $20,000 to $25,000 per month for software-rental services.[25] USi, an older and larger firm than Corio, earned a much larger share—84 percent—of its $72 million in revenue from software rental during the first three quarters of 2000.[26]

ASPs were experimenting with a variety of software-rental pricing structures. Some employed flat-fee pricing but often found it difficult to pass along price increases as a customer grew. Other ASPs priced on a "per user per month" basis, i.e., based on the number of the customer's employees who accessed applications. While this approach was attractive for cash-constrained small business customers, it made less sense for many larger enterprises, whose large base of employees implied high fees. Hybrid pricing schemes also were common; such schemes tracked factors such as usage levels and the ASP's performance against network reliability targets.

Cost Categories and Cost Drivers

ASP's expenses were divided into four main categories: cost of services, sales and marketing, product development, and general and administrative (G&A). The first three categories are described below; G&A expense includes typical corporate overhead items such as salaries for legal, human resources, and finance staff, and is not discussed further.

Cost of Services. ASPs accounted for cost of services differently, but in renting software applications all of them incurred costs related to (1) network operations and monitoring, (2) data center operations, and (3) customer support. ASPs like Corio and USi that licensed third-party software (rather than developing their own applications) also paid license fees to ISVs. Costs related to software rental were mostly variable with transaction volume, and, in Corio's case, were quite large in relation to software-rental revenue. In 2000, Corio's cost of software rental was $22.5 million, while its software-rental revenue was only $8.2 million. USi also earned a negative gross margin on software rental: Including direct costs for software rental, plus all charges related to network infrastructure and depreciation (unlike Corio, USi owned its data centers), USi's total cost of software rental was 157 percent of revenue in 2000. Since USi owned much of its network infrastructure, as capacity utilization increased in its data centers, gross margins could be expected to improve.

Direct costs incurred in delivering professional services were mostly related to personnel and the overhead required to support professional staff. Corio earned a modest gross margin of 7 percent on professional services; USi earned 35 percent.

Sales and Marketing. Most ASPs spent heavily to acquire customers and develop their brands. For example, during 2000, Corio and USi spent 97 percent and 73 percent, respectively, of their revenues on sales and marketing. ASPs typically maintained large direct sales forces. At the end of March 2000, for example, 101 of Corio's 456 employees were engaged in sales-and-marketing functions. At that time, USi had 45 sales reps. In addition, ASPs often generated sales through partnerships with ISVs and systems integrators, and ASPs frequently gave their partners equity warrants as an incentive. Corio, for example, had granted Cap Gemini Ernst & Young warrants to acquire 7 million shares at $6.50; this was a large grant in relation to Corio's 38 million shares outstanding as of the end of 3rd quarter 2000, although the company's stock was trading well below the warrant strike price at that time. ASPs' sales-and-marketing expenses also included trade advertising and booths at trade shows, as well as market research and the distribution of promotional materials.

The largest portion of sales-and-marketing expenditures—the cost of direct sales reps—varied with the number of prospects targeted. In theory, after ASPs signed up accounts, less direct-selling time would be required to renew contracts than to sign them in the first place, so sales-and-marketing expenses as a percentage of revenue for ASPs could be expected to decline as the company matured.

Product Development. The magnitude of product-development expenses depended on whether an ASP developed its own applications or licensed them from ISVs. In the later case, as at Corio and USi, product-development expenses were incurred to create a platform that allowed customers to exchange data between multiple applications. Corio spent $8.8 million, or 30 percent of its revenue through the first three quarters of 2000, on such activities. USi spent less heavily: Its product-development expenses for that period were $2.3 million, or 3 percent of revenue. ASPs were expected to incur ongoing product-development expenses—these were mostly fixed compensation costs for engineering staff—as ASPs integrated new applications and upgraded existing applications.

GET BIG FAST: A STRATEGIC IMPERATIVE FOR ASPS?

Many Internet companies have pursued Get Big Fast (GBF) strategies, involving massive upfront investment in customer acquisition. The premise of such strategies is that the early days of the Internet are a "land grab": According to this view, companies will find it easier to stake out wide swaths of empty territory now rather than try to capture that territory later, after it has been settled by others. The payoff from the GBF strategy tends to be the strongest when the following conditions apply: Network effects are strong, scale economies (beyond network effects) are significant, and customer-retention rates are intrinsically high. This section explores the extent to which these conditions apply for application service providers.

Network Effects

Network effects occur when the adoption of a product or service by a new customer increases the value of that product or service for customers already using it, because existing customers can now connect with additional parties. The fax machine is a good example of a product that benefits from network effects: A fax machine is worthless if you are the only one who owns one, but when many people own them the machines are valuable. When network effects are strong, it often makes sense for a company to invest heavily to gain first-mover advantage. As users beget users, the first mover may develop an unassailable lead.

The strength of network effects for ASPs varied significantly, depending on their application-sourcing strategies. While network effects tended to be modest for ASPs that delivered Internet-enabled applications, the effects were often strong for those that provided Web-native software that required data exchange between companies.[27] The user base for many Internet-enabled applications (e.g., sales-force productivity software) was restricted to employees of a single company. For such applications, as ASPs added new customers, the incremental value derived by their existing customers did not increase, because there was no need for different customers using the same sales-force productivity software to connect with each other. Other Internet-enabled applications, such as supply-chain planning software, did require data exchange between companies, but even if Company A rented such software from an ASP, its supply-chain partner, Company B, might license the software directly from the original ISV. Hence, there was a network effect for the *application*, but not necessarily for the *ASP*.

By extension, it should be clear that Web-native applications that required data exchange between companies would benefit from a proprietary network effect. Very simply, the only way for a company to access a given brand of software was to become a customer of the ASP that rented that software.

Scale Economies

Companies benefit from scale economies when they can spread fixed costs over a growing revenue base. Strong scale economies promote a winner-take-all dynamic: If the market leader has a superior cost structure, that company can reduce its prices or invest in superior service or features and thereby increase its lead.

As highlighted in the previous section, a large portion of application service providers' costs—e.g., network management, data-center operations, and customer support—varied fairly directly with transaction volumes. There were some scale economies in such functions, related to capacity utilization when infrastructure was owned outright and related to the purchasing clout that accrued to large customers when such services were outsourced. The magnitude of scale economies in these functions also depended on an ASP's software-sourcing strategy, because Web-native applications typically were engineered to run more efficiently over the public Internet, compared to Internet-enabled applications. In particular, Web-native applications typically could handle multiple customers from a single server, whereas Internet-enabled applications tended to require a separate server for each customer. As explained by Bill Gurley, a venture capitalist with Benchmark, "I think the [Internet-enabled model] is of marginal advantage over the status quo. I'm not convinced that there's an economic advantage to their approach, because none of those applications were written to run multiple users on a single system. That means that, basically, for each customer these guys have, they're running a separate rack of servers. So you could say, well, maybe there's some scale in that one guy gets to sit there and monitor all 40 servers as opposed to having a specialist on site. But it's certainly not evolutionary or revolutionary. It's just kind of incremental."[28]

Sales and marketing was not likely to be a source of significant scale economies for ASPs. Direct-selling costs varied initially with the number of prospects targeted, and as an ASP matured, with the number of existing accounts requiring maintenance contact to secure contract renewal. Finally, scale economies in product development were significant for ASPs that developed their own applications, but were more modest for ASPs that licensed Internet-enabled applications from third-party ISVs. In short, the ASP business model seemed far less subject to scale economies than some other Internet business models, such as portals and online content providers.

Customer Retention

The payoff for GBF strategies improves when customer-retention rates are high. If customers can be locked in before they sample a competitor's service, a first mover may cement its lead. Retention rates tend to be high in the face of strong network effects—for example, once an auction marketplace aggregates a dominant share of the buyers and sellers of a given product, participants are reluctant to do business elsewhere. Other factors can promote customer retention, most notably switching costs, such as the hassles that customers incur when they switch Internet Service Providers and must obtain a new e-mail address, or when they switch online stock brokers and must transfer securities and funds between accounts.

ASPs that provided Web-native applications experienced high customer-retention rates due to the network effects mentioned above. When served by an ASP that developed its own Web-native applications requiring data exchange between customers, these customers were effectively locked in. ASPs that provided both Web-native and Internet-enabled applications benefited from switching costs that typically made their customers reluctant to change service providers, provided users were receiving acceptable service at reasonable rates. Switching costs included the cost of retraining employees, integrating systems into a new ASP's data center, and the risk of compromising data integrity and disrupting mission-critical applications during such a move. Given these factors promoting retention, one equity analyst predicted that annual customer retention rates for Corio would be 90 percent.[29]

Summary: the Payoff for GBF Strategies

The payoff from a Get Big Fast strategy seems dubious for most ASPs. With the exception of ASPs that offer Web-native applications requiring data exchange between a trading community, network effects for ASPs are modest, as are scale economies. While high switching costs suggest that customers acquired through a GBF strategy may be retained, there are two strong arguments against the pursuit of aggressive customer-acquisition efforts. First, as explained above, the barriers for prospects considering whether to shift mission-critical applications to an ASP are quite substantial; to date, the ASP selling cycle has been long, and many companies have adopted a go-slow attitude. Second, rapid growth is likely to strain an ASP's operations and could compromise service quality and reliability—a major concern for prospective customers. However, if ASPs do pursue a "Get It Right First" strategy rather than a Get Big Fast strategy, they must consider the risk of competitive preemption by another ASP offering similar applications and locking in early adopters.

ENDNOTES

[1]Quoted in Paul Davis, "Infrastructure and Application Solutions Overview," Banc of America Securities, May 2000.

[2]According to *www.webopedia.com*, with a "client-server" architecture, a client is an application that runs on a personal computer or workstation and relies on a server computer to perform some operations.

[3]Farleit Limited, "Anatomy of an ASP: Defining the New Genus," May 2000, a white paper available for download through ASPnews.com website.

[4]Thomas Eisenmann and Dan Green, "Internet Access Providers," section 1, *Internet Business Models: Text and Cases*, or HBS Case no. 801-304, December 2000.

[5]Thomas Eisenmann and Sanjay Pothen, "Online Portals," section 2, *Internet Business Models: Text and Cases*, or HBS Case no. 801-305, December 2000.

[6]Farleit Limited, "Anatomy of an ASP: Defining the New Genus," May 2000, a white paper available for download through ASPnews.com website.

[7]See David Lake, "Time to Learn Your ASPs," *Industry Standard*, November 6, 2000 p. 226 for a summary of forecasts from Gartner Group, IDC, and Yankee Group.

[8]For an example Gary Dean, "ASPs: The Net's Next Killer App," J.C. Bradford & Co., 2000, accessed via (*http://aspisland.com/trends/jcbradford/*).

[9]Christopher Koch, "When a Stranger Calls," *Darwin Magazine*, June–July 2000.

[10]ASP Industry Consortium definition (*http://www.allaboutasp.org/faqs.cfm*).

[11]Sarah L. Roberts-Witt, "Jam On It," *Business 2.0*, August 22, 2000.

[12]Gary Dean, "ASPs: The Net's Next Killer App," J.C. Bradford & Co., 2000, accessed via (*http://aspisland.com/trends/jcbradford/*).

[13]Andrea Grosz, "Emerging ASP Models," First Union Securities, May 18, 2000.

[14]Gary Dean, "ASPs: The Net's Next Killer App," J.C. Bradford & Co., 2000, accessed via (*http://aspisland.com/trends/jcbradford/*).

[15]Stacie S. McCullough, "Sizing App Hosting," *The Forrester Report*, December 1999.

[16]Jon Swartz and Patrick McMahon, "Microsoft Unveils 'dot-net' Next-Generation Software Vision," *USA Today*, (June 23, 2000): 6B and World Reporter: "Microsoft Shifts Focus to Internet," *San Jose Mercury News*, (June 23, 2000).

[17]Bill Gates, Nathan Myhrvold, and Peter Rinearson, *The Road Ahead* (New York: Penguin, 1996).

[18]Stacie S. McCullough, "Sizing App Hosting," *The Forrester Report*, December 1999.

[19]Ibid.

[20]Gary Dean, "ASPs: The Net's Next Killer App," J.C. Bradford & Co., 2000, accessed via (*http://aspisland.com/trends/jcbradford/*).

[21]Philip Gill, "ERP: Keep It Simple," *PlanetIT.com,* August 9, 1999.

[22]Jennifer Maselli, "Growing Pains: ASPs and Their Customers Still Face Challenges," *InformationWeek,* July 24, 2000.

[23]Gary Dean, "ASPs: The Net's Next Killer App," J.C. Bradford & Co., 2000, accessed via (*http://aspisland.com/trends/jcbradford/*).

[24]Company SEC filings are the source for all figures cited in this section, unless otherwise noted. Also, unless otherwise noted, all references to year 2000 financial data for Corio and USi in this section reflect data reported to the SEC for the first nine months of the year only.

[25]Terrence Tierney, "Corio," U.S. Bancorp Equity Research, November 2000.

[26]Company SEC filings.

[27]Lee Gomes, "The Providers—Talking Revolution: Bill Gurley Makes the Case for a New Kind of Software," *Wall Street Journal*, November 11, 1999.

[28]Ibid.

[29]Terrence Tierney, "Corio," U.S. Bancorp Equity Research, November 2000.

EVERDREAM

Gary Griffiths was feeling stumped, a feeling he wasn't used to. Griffiths, the CEO of Everdream, had spent most of his career at IBM developing PC products such as the PS2 and the Thinkpad, leaving IBM in 1995 to start SegaSoft Networks with his former boss. After running SegaSoft for several years, he left to explore starting something once again. He met with dozens of people over several months, but felt that "Everdream was the only opportunity I came across that wasn't just an e-commerce way to sell dog food."

Everdream was a pioneer in Internet-based subscription computing for very small businesses (see Exhibit 1), which Everdream defined as those businesses with 20 computers or fewer. Everdream offered small businesses a turnkey package of PCs, software, Internet access, and "one-stop service" for a monthly fee of $150 per computer, with a 30-month commitment after a one-month trial. By Spring 2000, little more than six months after Griffiths joined Everdream, the company had 83 employees and had begun selling its systems.

Everdream offered its customers what it called "hassle-free" computing, customers viewing Everdream as their "virtual computer expert." By controlling the computing environment and providing services such as daily backups (via the Internet) and automatic downloads of software updates and patches, Everdream kept customer problems to a minimum. When problems did occur, Everdream promised customers that they would never be handed off to another vendor; if the company's always readily available Solutions Analysts could not solve the problem, then a new hard drive, complete with the customer's applications and data (from the previous night's backup) would be sent to the customer via Federal Express. Everdream hoped to build a large and loyal customer base on the strength of its core service offering. In addition, the company planned to offer its customers access to a variety of small business-oriented goods and services through the BizCenter on its Internet portal.

This morning, Griffiths was mulling over an issue he felt was central to the company's long-term success: providing Everdream customers with some sort of guarantee. During his tenure at other firms, Griffiths had often felt that management was trying to "make the service part of the business go away," often handing service off to a third party. At Everdream, however, Griffiths—and the entire management team—viewed superior end-to-end service as *the* critical part of the company's value proposition. If a customer experienced a problem with the Everdream-supplied system, the company was prepared to do whatever it took to get the customer up and running again—"no excuses" service, as Griffiths called it. The Everdream team wanted to find a way to convey, simply yet powerfully, the extent of their service commitment, and management had been discussing customer guarantees as a vehicle for accomplishing that. But every time the team thought they had the guarantee concepts and wording down, another idea—or potential hurdle—popped up.

Griffiths headed outside for a walk around the block at Everdream's Mountain View, California, offices. He hoped the fresh air would allow his thoughts to settle and an answer to crystallize before his meetings that afternoon.

Everdream Background

Brothers Russell and Lyndon Rive, ages 27 and 22 respectively, founded Everdream in late 1998, building on Russell's technology background and Lyndon's sales expertise.

Russell Rive was attending engineering school when he received a call from his cousins, asking him to join them at Zip2, a company they had founded to help develop, host, and maintain Web sites for media companies. At Zip2 Russell was in charge of the company's server room, and in that role he focused on developing a system that had "self-healing" properties. In addition he helped set up Zip2's remote offices, each of which was equipped with its own computer equipment. Russell found that he constantly received calls for help when the

---

Director of the Harvard Business School California Research Center Christina Darwell prepared this case under the supervision of Professor Roger Hallowell as the basis for class discussion rather than to illustrate either effective or ineffective handling of an administrative situation.

remote computers went down. This sparked an idea: that people should be able to pay a monthly fee for computers, just like rent, and should receive as part of this fee comprehensive support that would address the needs of customers like the users in Zip2's remote offices.

Russell discussed his idea with his brother Lyndon and asked him to move from South Africa, where both brothers had been born and raised, and join the new business. Lyndon had worked since age eleven, proving himself a gifted salesperson.

Believing Russell had identified a big opportunity, Lyndon moved to California in October of 1998. The two moved to the coastal town of Santa Cruz just south of Silicon Valley and began going door to door offering computers to small businesses, experimenting with a variety of service contracts. In addition to perfecting their surfing techniques, they learned several important lessons while in Santa Cruz: 1) it was difficult to service small businesses' existing computers as they tended to be old systems with several tacked-on upgrades; 2) "99 percent" of most small businesses' computing needs could be satisfied by a new high-end computer loaded with standard software, and 3) what small businesses really wanted was a "24x7 IT staff at reasonable cost."

The brothers quickly found themselves running out of computers and money, and decided to approach venture capitalists for funding. They talked to several venture firms, but found that Draper Fisher Jurvetson (DFJ) seemed to grasp their concept more quickly than others. In fact, DFJ had been conducting research on the subscription computing market and was enthusiastic about its potential.

Andreas Stavropoulos (HBS '97) of DFJ commented on why his firm invested in Everdream:

> We had actually spoken with several competitors in Everdream's space but weren't comfortable with the management teams. Russ and Lyndon were both very talented people and willing to be flexible. They gave us two board seats and agreed to bring in a CEO and a number of new managers.

Building the Management Team

The Rives interviewed twelve potential CEOs, finally finding Griffiths. Lyndon noted, "Gary was perfect. He had lots of experience, and he's the youngest person at heart here." They also hired Andy Efron as director of customer service. Efron, a 1998 graduate of Stanford Business School, had considerable interest in and experience with customer service.

Brian Golson (HBS '97) joined Everdream as CFO in September 1999. He had been working at a private equity investment firm, but had kept in touch with his business school friend, DFJ's Stavropoulos. Stavropoulos told Golson about Everdream; over time, Golson became more and more interested in the opportunity. In addition to finalizing a second round of funding immediately after joining, Golson focused on developing the company's business plan and model. Golson commented that, unlike many Silicon Valley startups, Everdream's model was "highly debt oriented because of the upfront hardware costs associated with each new customer." Golson also commented on the many large fixed costs a startup like Everdream encounters:

> There are a lot of upfront fixed costs in a business like this. We spent $400,000 last month to build a server room. Some companies outsource this function, but we felt it was necessary to do this ourselves in order to guarantee that our many systems were integrated effectively. Also, building a call center is very expensive; for example, we spent $800,000 on the implementation of Siebel CRM[1] software. Approximately $200,000 went to purchase perpetual licenses from Siebel and over $500,000 was spent with Grant Thornton to customize the software to make it scalable for our business. We spent $200,000 building a manufacturing software system that would enable us to communicate highly customized orders correctly to our contract manufacturing site. We've also had to pay several hundred thousand dollars in fees to the companies we're partnering with, such as our Internet service provider, to enable them to customize their products for our customers. In total, we'll spend several million in up-front fixed costs to deliver the quality of service that will differentiate us.

Everdream's Business

Strategy and Business Model

Everdream's mission was to "simplify the computing experience for small businesses." Everdream management intended to provide service superior to its competitors by

[1]CRM stood for customer relationship management. CRM software supported sales, marketing and customer support activities (including call centers), providing employees and managers with quick access to all customer information, such as a customer's service history and past purchases.

1) reducing the number of problems encountered by customers, and 2) resolving remaining customer inquiries and problems more quickly and more responsively than other firms. Everdream's approach to reducing the number of problems encountered consisted of two parts. First, customers were not given dozens of options from which to choose, as was common when ordering a PC from a firm such as Dell or Gateway; hardware was specified by Everdream, and software options were kept to a bare minimum (see Exhibit 2). Second, Everdream had its PCs manufactured with certain safeguards; the hard disk was partitioned with one part holding the Everdream-supplied software, and the other part containing a mirror of that software (for backup), as well as room for users to add their own applications.

Some observers believed that the $150 per month ($1,800 per year) price tag would be a strong selling point given an industry analyst's calculation that the average annual total cost per PC in small businesses of under 100 employees was $7,850.[2] However, Griffiths believed that most small businesses did not keep track of their computer-related costs and that even when they did, owners were often optimistic that "next year would be different." In addition, other subscription-computing vendors leased their product for as little as $25 a month. These other vendors always include what was called "24/7" customer support, but numerous problems such as hand-offs to other vendors were reportedly not uncommon.

Everdream was focused on two target markets: small businesses with 20 or fewer computers and physically small, remote offices of large companies. Although most of Everdream's initial sales and marketing activities were aimed at the small business market, Lyndon Rive—in his role as vice president of partnership development—had been approached by and had discussions with several Fortune 500 companies regarding serving their remote offices. Everdream management had also discussed targeting vertical markets—that is, industry—or application-based markets—such as law firms. If the company were to target such markets, they would have to support some special purpose software, build specialized customer screens, and do additional customer service-related training. To-date, Everdream management excluded the consumer market.

[2]This figure excluded employee time. See Susan Moran, "Beyond the Box: The pair behind Everdream hope to get a piece of the small-business explosion by creating a one-stop IT shop," Business 2.0 (January 2000).

In addition to "hassle-free computing," Everdream wanted to build a small business community. Everdream's BizCenter (a single click from the Everdream desktop) offered a wide variety of products and services for Everdream members. The BizCenter included the "Everdream superstore" which offered books, movies and music; Internet-based travel agencies; office supplies; shipping services and telecommunications services. In addition, the BizCenter helped customers find individual service providers in a variety of fields through Everdream's partnership with eLance. Management planned to expand the BizCenter to feature services local to a particular member, highlighting and promoting members' businesses. A dry cleaning operation in search of a lawyer might learn about a local law office—and fellow Everdream member—at the BizCenter. Thus the benefits of the BizCenter to the member would grow as Everdream grew.

Over the long term, subscription revenues were projected to be approximately 70 percent of total revenues, the other 30 percent coming from sales of add-on products such as printers, as well as advertising and e-commerce revenues from the BizCenter. (See Exhibit 3 for Everdream's financial and customer base projections.) Managers believed that the BizCenter offered upside potential. DFJ's Stavropoulos shared this belief:

> We look for infinite scalability. You can make dollars on the core Everdream business, but that might be squeezed if prices decline. But if you become the trusted advisor for outsourced services and the customer finds value in those services, Everdream—as the holder of the pipe—can take a toll from everything that passes through.

Sales and Marketing Approach

Everdream management believed that it would be too expensive to use a direct sales force to reach the small business market. As a result, they planned to use VARs (value added resellers) as an alternative. Many VARs had excellent relationships with small business owners, but made only slim margins selling PCs; for example, typical PC commissions were 6 percent with the average machine costing $2,000. Because of this, many VARs preferred installing networks, where margins were higher and labor was a larger percentage of the total system cost. Very small businesses were less likely to have networks installed and therefore, less likely to have an ongoing service relationship with a VAR. When these business owners used VARs on an ad hoc basis, VARs typically charged $70 an hour or more for their services.

However, the majority of VARs considered much of this ad hoc work a distraction and preferred not to do it. They were happy to install networks, but much less happy to receive calls about issues such as software problems. As a result, certain services for very small businesses were last on their priority list. Everdream offered VARs a $250 sales fee plus an additional $75 installation fee (if the consumer chose to have the VAR install their machine) for each Everdream machine. When sales came in through other channels, e.g., when a customer called Everdream directly, Everdream put $250 per PC subscription sold into a pool for VARs. At the end of the year, this pool of money would be allocated according to each VAR's total Everdream sales.

Lyndon Rive explained why the Everdream product was attractive to VARs:

> The industry is changing from product-centric to customer-centric, and VARs are beginning to realize it. We asked VARs who they thought would be a perfect partner, and they told us it would be someone who could build the desktop, take care of annoying phone calls, maintain the desktop warranty—and call them when on-site service was needed.

Everdream signed up VARs in Northern California, where the company planned to launch its product. By 2000, Everdream signed up over 100 resellers in the San Francisco Bay Area. Everdream's VARs were varied, as was the VAR market. Small VARs had on average 100 to 160 small business customers, sold on average 16 computers per month, and had one to two storefronts. These VARs were focused on an immediate geographic area and delivered a high level of customer service to some customers, generating high customer loyalty. Large VARs were less geographically focused, tailoring their products and services to particular industry segments. They shipped between 100-500 computers per month and had between 5 and 20 storefronts. VARs were often trusted by small businesses because they were not tied to any one product or service.

Although there were many reasons to sell through VARs, Everdream management and the board recognized some shortcomings as well. Stavropoulos of DFJ commented that "VARs are very conservative and won't sell our systems until it's easier to sell an Everdream machine than what they are used to selling." To address this issue, Everdream had several employees who worked directly with VARs, and the company was developing training programs to help VARs learn to sell the Everdream product. Lyndon Rive commented that "everything VARs sold in the past was tangible, but now they are selling an intangible." Two full-time trainers worked with the VARs, emphasizing such points as the importance of *not* opening the Everdream machines, as VARs were inveterate tinkerers. The company also produced a high quality customer demonstration video that VARs could show to potential customers. Finally, VARs were loaned an Everdream PC for a month, but the company was hesitant to give VARs their own machines outright until they had demonstrated they could sell Everdream systems. In late 1999 the company began an advertising campaign, placing ads in VAR industry magazines and on billboards in the San Francisco area. (See Exhibit 4 for a sample Everdream advertisement.)

The Everdream Product

Hardware

Customers received pre-configured,[3] relatively high-end PCs.[4] Russell Rive described the machines as "8 on a scale of 1 to 10." Customers could get larger monitors or printers for an additional fee. One industry observer noted that it would cost about $60 per month to lease a computer and software similar to Everdream's offering; this of course would not include installation, customer support, or e-services such as those offered by the Biz-Center.

Manufacturing of the Everdream machines was outsourced. Everdream had developed an automated system that, triggered by an order number, specified exactly what programs, email address and account identification (e.g., name, address) were to be burned into the customer's hard drive. No human intervention was necessary. By having all their PCs built to the same specifications, Everdream was able to create a machine that was more cost effective to service and manufacture. Russell Rive commented that "small businesses don't want to specify every component in the computer, they simply

[3]Pre-configured PCs came with all parts assembled and all software loaded. The customer had to follow ten simple steps, one of which was plugging the mouse and keyboard into the computer, to be able to use the machine.

[4]*As of 2000, each Everdream machine included a 500 MHz Intel Pentium III with an Intel motherboard, 128 MB of memory, a 17GB hard drive, a 48X CD-ROM, a 56K modem, an Intel Network card and a 17" monitor.*

want a reliable and powerful enough computer to help them run their business and someone else to worry about keeping it running and up-to-date."

Software

All Everdream machines included applications commonly used by small business owners, including Microsoft Windows 98, Internet Explorer, and Office 2000 Small Business Edition (Word, Excel, PowerPoint, Publisher, and Outlook). Also included were Adobe Acrobat Reader, Norton AntiVirus, and RealPlayer G2. Customers could add QuickBooks Pro, Act, and Access for an additional fee. The company's customer service group supported all of these programs.

All machines included six free online training courses for desktop applications such as Word. Everdream had a partnership with Headlight.com, a company that provided online training for small and medium-sized businesses. Everdream customers had one year from the time of initial sign-up to use the six free programs; they also had access, through the desktop, to six other training modules for which they had to pay the regular fee, which ranged from $25 to $149 per course.

Each machine also contained e-support software from Support.com. This software was loaded onto the hard drives of both users and service providers. The software did three things: kept certain problems from occurring in the first place through use of a "healing agent;" enabled customers to help themselves through the use of self-service tools; and facilitated remote problem diagnosis and resolution by service providers through the Internet. Everdream used the self-service and remote diagnostic tools, but did not use the healing agent tool since it created longer application launch times and restricted the customer's ability to customize application preferences. In addition, Everdream preferred the customer interaction that took place when the company's solutions analysts solved problems—and Everdream believed their customers preferred it as well.

Efron commented on what the e-support software meant to him as head of customer services:

> We really believe that having this kind of software is a necessity. The way the self-service component works is that you tell the software to "protect" a certain application—at a time when that application is running well. It looks at all the application's dependencies, such as printer, email, Windows, etc. In essence, it takes a snapshot so that it knows what is "right." Later, if that application experiences problems, either the user or one of our solutions analysts can use the software to put the application back the way it was "pre-problem." Most of our customers prefer to call or email us when they have a problem; they don't seem to be using the self-service option on their own that often, but we're starting to teach them.
>
> We're developing our own technology to do this, but we're not ready yet. One feature we've developed in-house, based on technology created by Microsoft, is the ability for our customer service personnel to view exactly what is on the customer's desktop, and—with permission from the customer (which they can give us with the click of their mouse)—take control of the customer's desktop for the purpose of resolving any problems.

The Dream Side/Flip Side

Originally, the Everdream computer had two distinct parts, the "dream side"—on which resided the preloaded, fully-supported software—and the "flip side"—on which customers could load other programs, such as games or ancillary software, that they wished to use. Everdream management had purposefully limited and protected the software that Everdream supplied—isolating it from other software that a customer might install—to minimize problems caused by the interaction of standardized, supported software, with games, beta software, and other less reliable applications. Everdream could fix dream side problems quickly, or send a replacement hard drive if necessary. If there were problems with applications on the flip side, customers could contact Everdream, and a Solution Analyst would attempt to solve the problem. However, if the Solution Analyst was unable to solve the problem after a reasonable period of time—one manager defined reasonable as about 45 minutes—the analyst would refer the customer to other (external) sources of help, explaining that Everdream was unable to support software it didn't provide.

The problem the company encountered with the dream side/flip side approach was that it took a minute and a half of reboot time to switch from the dream side to the flip side, and customers complained. The engineering group subsequently reconfigured the computer so that there were two "virtual file systems," allowing core programs to remain protected without making customers reboot to switch between sides. Management was nonetheless considering keeping the "switching" concept, perhaps by having a button on the desktop requiring only a few seconds of switching time, as they felt that switching gave customers an extremely secure feeling about the dream side of their computers.

Russell Rive, who managed the evolution of the Everdream product in his role as CTO, believed that by combining a standard high end PC with 1) controlled software, 2) the virtual file system, and 3) excellent customer support, Everdream delivered a computer service rather than a computer product.

Customer Support

All customers received nightly data back-up with unlimited storage; unlimited ISP connectivity (free DSL[5] service was available to customers with more than 10 PCs and was available to other customers for an additional fee); 24/7 help desk support which covered not only questions about problems encountered, but questions about how to use programs; automatically downloaded upgrades and patches; a personalized email account; and, should customer service not be able to resolve a problem in a timely manner, quick and free replacement of any problem part. When Everdream sent out a replacement (usually just the hard drive), they first loaded the disk with the customer's applications and data (from the most recent data backup).

Customers were encouraged to contact Everdream, as management believed that customers' positive experiences with Everdream's Solution Analysts would translate into loyalty. Solution Analysts ended phone calls by telling customers, "If you have any other problems please call us back again." This approach was in distinct contrast to those software and computer vendors that intentionally left callers on hold for extended periods, reasoning that the callers would give up or perhaps be forced to consult the manual or a local service provider, solving the problem themselves. It was not unusual for callers to Microsoft's non-800-number to wait for 30 minutes before a customer service representative answered the phone, only to be passed on to yet another vendor.[6]

An Everdream customer commented on Everdream's service: "The beauty of Everdream is that their support people can take over your machine and solve the problem. This is especially great for someone running a business on a PC without a computer support department."

An Everdream manager commented: "It is the combination of our product and the service that provides value to our customers. But if you force me to tell you what's going to sustain our success, I think it's the service—assuming we can get it right."

Company Culture

Everdream's culture was part typical Silicon Valley startup and part Everdream-specific. One observer, an out-of-town consultant working for Everdream, commented on how he viewed Silicon Valley culture:

> I've been in Silicon Valley several months now and I see five distinct elements of culture. First, everything—working, playing, eating, sleeping—is on Internet time. Everyone puts in two weeks of work in one week. Second, people take a team approach; instead of "let's hire people and beat them into submission," it's "let's hire bright young people with open minds and give them a piece of our company." Third, decisions are made quickly. Here companies make decisions based on their best judgment and move ahead rather than creating piles of documents to cover their backsides. Fourth, and this ties back to the other points, this is more of a work culture than a social culture. And fifth, networking is *really* big here. Everyone asks "What are you guys developing and how can it help us?"

Everdream was a representative Silicon Valley company in terms of its fast-paced, open, and informal environment. The management team spent a fair amount of time discussing culture and had worked to instill certain values (see Exhibit 5). For example, every new employee had to assemble his or her own Everdream computer from scratch on the first day of work, building the machine in an open and central area. An extensive manual helped the less technologically adept. If employees got stuck, they had to ask one of the senior managers (whose desks were near by) for help. Management believed that in addition to being a bonding experience, this exercise provided early interaction with management and taught employees the physical details of the Everdream system. Everdream management wanted to

---

[5]DSL refers to digital subscriber lines. DSL technologies used sophisticated modulation schemes to pack data onto copper wires. They were sometimes referred to as "last-mile technologies" because they were used only for connections from a telephone switching station to a home or office, not between stations. DSL lines enabled data to be sent at speeds much faster than 56K modems.

[6]Susan Moran, "Beyond the Box: The pair behind Everdream hope to get a piece of the small-business explosion by creating a one-stop IT shop," *Business 2.0* (January 2000).

build a flat organization, with high accessibility to managers; job postings always included the statement: "Our philosophy is simple: we strongly believe that every employee has a key voice in determining the company's direction."

Efron (head of customer service) commented that management wanted to "keep employees surprised" by developing different fun activities, although it wasn't always easy for management to find the time to do this. The customer service management team was particularly aware of high turnover rates in service departments and so strove to create special bonds among their employees. They provided many non-cash benefits such as afternoon or evening breaks at the local Laser Quest[7] and "mini-massages" to relieve sore necks and backs. As one customer service manager noted, "We really want to get to know employees and their families and to make day-to-day work life fun."

Customer Service

Although many companies outsourced all or part of their customer service, Everdream's management team never considered it. Management believed that their "one-stop support" was unique, as was their emphasis on customer service personnel who would go to great lengths to solve a problem. Russell Rive noted that Everdream wanted to provide "on-site style service without on-site presence."

Customer Service and Call Center Operations

Everdream's decision to keep their call center—which they gave the more broad name of solutions center—operations in-house helped ensure high levels of service through control as well as by forging a tight link between customer service and engineering. Everdream hired Pacific Call Center Solutions, Inc. (PCCSI) of Honolulu, Hawaii, to help set up the company's call centers, involving the two PCCSI principals in everything from recruiting employees to advising on the purchase of call center software and telephone equipment. PCCSI was given the opportunity to make a small equity investment in Everdream, which it did.

A PCCSI principal gave an overview of the call center development process:

> There are several major factors one has to consider in developing a new call center. First, you have to know what types of calls are coming in; for example, are they inbound, reactive Solution Analyst calls, outbound survey or Solution Analyst calls, or, in the case of Everdream, inbound reactive product support calls? If inbound product support, do they concern software, hardware or other issues such as networking? Second, you have to know the volume or projected volume of inbound and outbound calls, as well as inbound and outbound emails. Third, you have to think about where you are going to locate your center. Approximately 50 percent of the ongoing cost of a call center is people, and the geographic location affects factors such as education levels and tax rates, so it affects quality as well as cost. Fourth, you have to think about the type of infrastructure you need to build. Do you need computer-telephony integration (CTI)?[8] Do you need a voice response unit (VRU)?[9] You have to consider data—computers; voice—telephones; facilities—furniture and ergonomics, and workflow—how work moves through the system and how you want to automate it. If you don't do the infrastructure right up front, you'll end up doing it over again. Once you've come up with a design, you have to focus on ramping up the operation, which includes continuous training and revision of procedures as needed. A lot of people don't understand that if you are a service company, one of your core competencies *must* be training. You will always have some kind of training going on.

[7]Laser Quest, a few blocks from Everdream's headquarters, was an entertainment center where groups of people could play a game of tag using toy laser guns. Teams competed against one another to see who could make the most "tags" using laser beams.

[8]CTI refers to systems that essentially tie together the telephone caller with his/her customer record. Applications of this technology allow call centers to "pop" the customer's information onto an agent's terminal when they call, route them for special handling (for example, delinquent credit card customers are routed to collections even though they requested customer service as their menu option) or special messaging (gold card customers hear gold card specials on hold but regular callers do not, etc.).

[9]VRUs are a subset of broader IVR (interactive voice response) technology. VRUs are accessed from touch-tone phones and generally consist of a series of pre-recorded messages accessed from a menu. VRUs are used for high-volume routine customer service inquiries or to route incoming calls to the appropriate person or department. IVR technology is used for more complicated inquiries, generally involved accessing a database; for example, if a caller to the IRS wanted to schedule an appointment, an appointment database would be accessed.

The major tradeoff in call centers is the cost of service versus the quality of service. Call centers are like spigots—there are lots of dials to ratchet the service level up or down. You can adjust how quickly you answer calls, how quickly you escalate calls, and so on. Everdream has taken the high touch, high quality approach: the company wants to treat every customer as a god. But the company also wants to pre-empt calls by preventing problems from occurring in the first place, and several things are being done along those lines. However, until we have much more data in the call center database, it will be difficult to do that as effectively as we might.

Call centers, done right, are expensive. A 100-seat call center typically costs about $3 million in capital start-up costs.[10] These costs would include furniture, equipment (computers, networks, telecommunications equipment) and build-out costs. Software capital start-up costs—for everything from the operating system to customer interaction software (CIS)[11]—would run hundreds of thousands of dollars. The biggest chunk of capital start-up costs would be for services; for example, you might pay $200,000 for the CIS software but then pay up to $3 million to customize it. The last chunk of capital start-up costs is for overall project management and that can run around 15 percent of the total cost. Many start-up costs are fixed, so a 33-seat call center might cost 50 percent of a 100-seat call center.

Ongoing costs for a 100-seat center can run around $750,000 a month for a high-end center. The largest cost is labor, which runs around 50 percent. The next largest cost is what we call "operating costs" at about 40 percent, which includes such things as telephone charges and software depreciation. Monthly telephone costs can run up into the high five digits, especially if the company offers an 800 number. The last 10 percent of costs includes depreciation and occupancy. Of course, occupancy can be a higher percent depending on where you locate the call center.

[10]An industry observer noted that this would typically amortize over five years.

[11]CIS refers to software that connects frontline service providers with data on the customer that has contacted them. That data is complex to retrieve as it often exists in systems separate from those being used by the frontline service providers, frequently located outside the call center. Using CIS can result in shorter calls (because the agent knows

Approach to Service

The core customer service/solutions center team consisted of Efron, the two principals of PCCSI, the solutions center manager, Lael Weyenberg, and the solutions center supervisor. The team believed that most help desks focused on solving problems, whereas Everdream wanted its customer service operations focused on "creating satisfied customers." Weyenberg used the example of a customer calling in because her printer wasn't working when she needed a copy of her resume immediately for an important proposal. Weyenberg commented on the approach she taught Everdream's Solution Analysts to take:

> If fixing the printer is going to take more time than the customer has, and the customer's priority is to get a copy of her resume, then the Solution Analyst should find a "workaround." For example, the customer could email the resume to the solutions center, and then the Solution Analyst could print it and fax it back. Once that immediate problem was solved, the Solution Analyst could move on to fixing the printer itself.

The group also believed that it was important to delight the customer by going above and beyond what the customer expected. Weyenberg recalled: "When I joined Everdream, Andy told me that we should 'under-promise and over-deliver.' I was initially unsure about that approach, but now I'm 100 percent behind it because, to a large extent, customer satisfaction is about setting appropriate expectations."

The Mountain View Solutions Center

Everdream's first solutions center was built in the company's headquarters, even though it was generally acknowledged by the service team that Silicon Valley—with its high labor costs, expensive real estate, and tight labor market—was one of the worst places to locate a call center from a cost perspective. The center was small relative to the projected size of future centers—30 seats, which implied 45–55 employees for a 24x7 operation—but would ensure that top management, engineering and product development would always receive immediate feedback on how Everdream was doing in the field.

Because the company was not yet receiving calls in volume, it was difficult to project the average cost per call or even the average number of calls a customer might make over the life of a 30-month contract. According to

PCCSI, the average white-box[12] reseller received 7.5 calls during the first 90 days after a sale was made. Then the number became quite variable by customer, but dropped on average to one per month. The great majority of calls were expected to come in to the call center between the hours of 8AM and 6PM; given that Everdream would eventually be operating in all four mainland U.S. time zones, call centers would have to handle calls in volume for 13 hours a day.

PCCSI anticipated that the average call would take about 20 minutes, including call documentation and escalation to more knowledgeable associates if necessary. PCCSI noted that in the financial services industry, the average inbound call to a live agent lasted two minutes and cost approximately $2.75, although the calls generally concerned information gathering, e.g., customers checking on their account balance, rather than problem resolution. For those companies that outsourced their call center operations, the typical charge per call for software support desks was $10. Outsourcers charged either a flat fee per call or a fee per minute, and in either case, usually charged on a sliding scale based on volume.

The company had instituted a specific call escalation policy (see Exhibit 6). Solution Analysts were the first to interact with the customer and were expected to be able to handle the vast majority of calls. The customer could choose from a wide variety of ways to contact Everdream customer service: telephone, online chat, e-mail, fax, or mail. Once the Solution Analyst was aware of a problem, he or she reviewed the customer's history and following that, might ask the customer to give more details about the problem. If the Solution Analysts couldn't solve the problem in a reasonable time period, the problem was escalated to a level 2 technician. If the level 2 technician couldn't solve the problem after a reasonable time, the problem was escalated further, to engineering. If the engineer was unable to solve the problem, the customer would be sent a replacement hard drive. Before sending out the hard drive, all of the customer's applications and data were downloaded onto the drive, a process that could take several hours. (The data were available from the previous night's back up, assuming that the customer had left the machine "on" so that the back up could take place.) The hard drive was sent *via* overnight mail, along with a special key; upon receipt, the customer unlocked and removed the old hard drive and replaced it with the new one. Finally, the customer mailed the key and the old hard drive back to Everdream.

The Everdream solutions center had not yet been faced with large volumes of calls, but had dealt with calls covering a wide variety of subjects such as forgotten email passwords, networking problems, file transfer questions (e.g., moving files from Word Perfect to Word), and operating system issues. Everdream was already planning its next solutions center, which was to be located in the eastern time zone and have a capacity of 100 seats. Exhibit 7 provides estimated length of queue ("hold time") information for such a center.

Recruiting and Training Customer Service Employees

One of Everdream's biggest challenges in ramping up customer service operations was recruiting and training employees. Efron explained Everdream's unusual approach to hiring and its effect on training:

> Most technical people don't relate well to customers. We have focused on hiring people who enjoy working with people and solving their problems—who have empathy; we then teach them about the technology. We ask all job applicants to write a paragraph on their approach to customer service, and this has proven very helpful to us. When we interview applicants we look for enthusiasm, creativity, and people who want to better themselves and do something with their lives. The people we have hired to date have a mix of high school and college degrees. We pay a salary, not an hourly wage since we consider this a professional position. Compensation is $32,000–$35,000 plus options. Employees can choose their salary level—they receive more options at the lower levels. Our people are mostly in their twenties and come from diverse backgrounds; one came to us via the West Virginia coal mines and the Air Force, another was a caregiver for the elderly.
>
> We do about eight weeks of classroom-based training, going through five modules: soft skills (for example, using the proper tone of voice, having patience, eliminating jargon); using the phone system; using the Siebel software;[13] using the Everdream

[12] White-boxes were non-name brand desktop PCs, generally built by and sold through systems integrators and VARs.

[13] Everdream used Siebel customer-relationship-management software for both sales and service.

intranet; and finally, understanding Word, Excel, PowerPoint, etc. Because of the type of person we hire, we have higher training costs than other customer support operations.

Our goal is to keep employee turnover low. Ideally, we'd like to have no turnover, but at a minimum we would like to be at half or less than the typical customer service/call center operation in this area, which we've heard is 30 percent. To do that, we have to create a very cohesive group. We want this to be like a family.

Promises, Promises

Griffiths came back from his walk full of ideas, but still not certain which route to take. He felt that the guarantees the team was considering were good, but wondered if they were guaranteeing the right things—and whether they were promising too much or too little. He wanted to be sure a guarantee would help customers and employees understand the value Everdream could deliver. Exhibit 8 provides selected competitor data; as of Spring 2000, none of the competitors listed offered a service guarantee.

The management team planned to discuss the following types of guarantees in the afternoon meeting:

- guarantees about data, e.g., "Everdream guarantees you will never lose your data," a guarantee that Griffiths felt would be incredibly powerful—and unlikely to be matched by others—but which might be dangerous to offer;
- guarantees about phone response times, e.g., "Everdream guarantees that *all* calls will be answered within 1 minute;"
- guarantees about fixing problems, e.g., "Everdream guarantees to fix your problems," a guarantee that could be applied to 1) all the customer's computer problems (which also would be powerful, but again, perhaps, dangerous) or 2) just those aspects of the hardware and software that were supplied by Everdream;
- guarantees about "up time," e.g., "Everdream guarantees to keep your computer up and running 100 percent of the time."

Griffiths knew that the power of a guarantee was inversely related to the number of conditions attached to it. Still, he wondered what he should promise, under what conditions, and what he should offer if Everdream failed to meet its obligation. He looked forward to another spirited management team discussion and resolving the hot topic of guarantees.

Exhibit 1 THE SMALL BUSINESS AND SUBSCRIPTION COMPUTING MARKETS

The small business market was defined by some analysts as companies with 100 or fewer employees and by others analysts as companies with up to 500 employees. Everdream considered its target market to be very small businesses with 20 or fewer desktop PCs. The best analogy for this market was the small office/home office (SOHO) market, which included firms with 10 or fewer employees, and home-based businesses. In 1998, there were 5.7 million very small businesses and 22.2 million home-based businesses.[a] The SOHO information technology market was $51 billion in 1998 and projected to grow to $71 billion by 2002. The average SOHO business spent roughly $7,200 on information technology annually, up from $2,000 in 1996.[b]

The subscription computing market was a relatively new one. Subscription computing loosely referred to paying for a computer on a monthly basis.

Some subscription computing vendors offered a variety of small business-focused online goods and services to their customers. Vendors had noticed that small business online orders were growing rapidly, from $11.4 billion in 1998 to $19 billion in 1999. Some of the most popular and rapidly growing small business services included travel services, education and training, shipping, real estate, and a wide variety of employee-related offerings.[c]

Most subscription computing vendors provided name-brand computers; Everdream was the primary vendor providing white-boxes (white-boxes were non-name brand desktop PCs). The white-box market represented approximately 20 percent of all 1999 PC shipments.[d]

Subscription computing vendors targeted either the small business or consumer market. The two types of vendors targeting small businesses were PC manufacturers (e.g., Dell, IBM, Gateway) and startups such as Everdream and Centerbeam. Santa Clara, CA-based Centerbeam focused on small businesses with networks. San Francisco-based PeoplePC, a startup, was the main vendor providing subscription computing to the consumer market. The price per month per PC ranged from $25 for PeoplePC to $165 for Centerbeams' "basic service." In the case of PeoplePC, the buyer was actually paying off a loan over a thirty-six month period of time; the buyer had the alternative of paying the entire amount of the loan, $789, up front.[e]

[a] "SOHO Market for Technology Tops $51 billion in 1998," an excerpt from International Data Corporation's report, SOHO Market Overview: Small Businesses with Fewer than 10 Employees and Home-based Businesses, *http://www/idc.com/dat/consumer/content/csb040899pr.htm;* viewed on 2-15-2000.

[b] "Internet Drives SOHO Technology Spending," excerpt from Cahners In-Stat Group's report Opportunities Abound: SOHO Market Forecasts 1998-2002, *http://www.instat.com/rh/mm/sh9802ms_summary.htm;* viewed on 2-15-2000.

[c] Stuart Gibbell, "Online Orders from Small Businesses Up More than 95 percent," Cyber Dialogue, *www.cyberdialogue.com/press/releases/small_biz3.html;* viewed 2-4-2000.

[d] George Hulme, "Small Business Sector–White-Box Remains Strong," VAR Business (November 22, 1999), p. 77.

[e] Ibid.

Exhibit 2 THE EVERDREAM SERVICE

- 24/7 live and unlimited customer support
- Daily remote file back-up with unlimited storage
- Unlimited Internet Connectivity (Dial-up or optional DSL)
- Web-based Application Training
- Top of the Line Hardware
  - Pentium III, 500 Mhz
  - 128 MB RAM
  - 17" monitor
  - 18 GB hard drive
- Windows 98, 2nd Edition
- Pre-loaded/Fully Supported Applications
- MS Office 2000 Small Business Edition
  - Word
  - Excel
  - Outlook
  - Publisher
  - Small Business Tools
- Web Plug-ins
- Optional Software
- PowerPoint and Access
- QuickBooks/Quicken
- Act!2000

Exhibit 3

EVERDREAM FINANCIAL PROJECTIONS—BALANCE SHEET ($000S)

	2000	2001	2002	2003	2004
Cash and equivalents	$ 3,434	$ 5,535	$ 5,407	$ 8,879	$ 3,905
Other current assets	4,907	19,390	41,741	65,497	89,260
Unbilled hardware and software	36,580	130,059	252,490	387,534	533,623
Property and equipment	2,841	5,820	9,234	12,430	15,084
Other assets	37	37	37	37	37
Total Assets	$47,799	$110,841	$308,909	$474,377	$641,909
Current Liabilities	$ 9,995	$ 33,990	$ 70,034	$109,089	$148,143
Long-term debt	15,747	54,617	101,512	140,601	156,075
Equity invested	42,500	92,500	117,500	132,500	132,500
Retained earnings	-20,443	-20,266	19,863	92,187	205,191
Total liabilities and equity	$47,799	$160,841	$308,909	$474,377	$641,909

EVERDREAM FINANCIAL PROJECTIONS—INCOME STATEMENT ($000S)

	2000	2001	2002	2003	2004
End users (number)	23,335	91,082	196,684	306,181	419,707
Revenue	$20,033	$134,149	$353,930	$627,366	$904,470
Cost of sales	12,195	78,433	204,771	357,918	512,485
Gross margin	7,838	55,716	149,159	269,448	391,985
Sales and marketing	16,036	37,724	63,757	101,569	142,485
Other operating expense	7,666	14,429	24,226	35,103	46,066
Operating income	-15,864	3,563	61,176	132,776	203,434
Interest expense	557	3,386	7,805	12,236	15,094
Income taxes			13,242	48,216	75,336
Net income	-16,421	177	40,129	72,324	113,004

Exhibit 4 EVERDREAM ADVERTISEMENT

Exhibit 5 EVERDREAM BELIEFS, MISSION AND VALUES STATEMENT

Everdream Belief Statement

We believe the unlimited potential of computing and the Internet will be realized through the transforming power of service.

Everdream Mission Statement

Everdream provides unprecedented service, to build trusted customer relationships, turning information technology and the Internet into simple tools through cool, reliable technology.

Everdream Statement of Values

The customer is central to all we do.

Customers are the top priority of every job at Everdream. We treat customers with the highest professional courtesy and surprise them with service above and beyond their expectations.

We stand behind our products and services. We meet our commitments and do whatever it takes to ensure that our customers are delighted with Everdream. Any problem, any time–no excuses.

We are a team of professionals who are committed to excellence and dedicated to creating a premier service organization. We treat one another fairly, with respect and dignity. We value diversity in our team. We help our employees to realize their full potential, providing a work environment with trust, open communication, encouragement, recognition and opportunity for personal and professional growth.

We realize that the quality of what we do is more critical than the scope. That is, we would rather do one task exceptionally than ten with mediocrity. We continuously seek to innovate and reach for perfection.

As owners, we treat Everdream's resources at least as preciously as our own. We take pride in frugality and economy, actively exploring ways to provide our services more efficiently and competitively.

Our honesty and integrity will not be compromised. We are relentless in maintaining high ethical standards in all of our interactions. We are socially responsible, making positive contributions to the communities in which we work and live.

We like to have fun in our work and we want our customers to share our enthusiasm. We take customer service very seriously, but never ourselves.

Source: Everdream

Exhibit 6 EVERDREAM CALL ESCALATION PROCESS

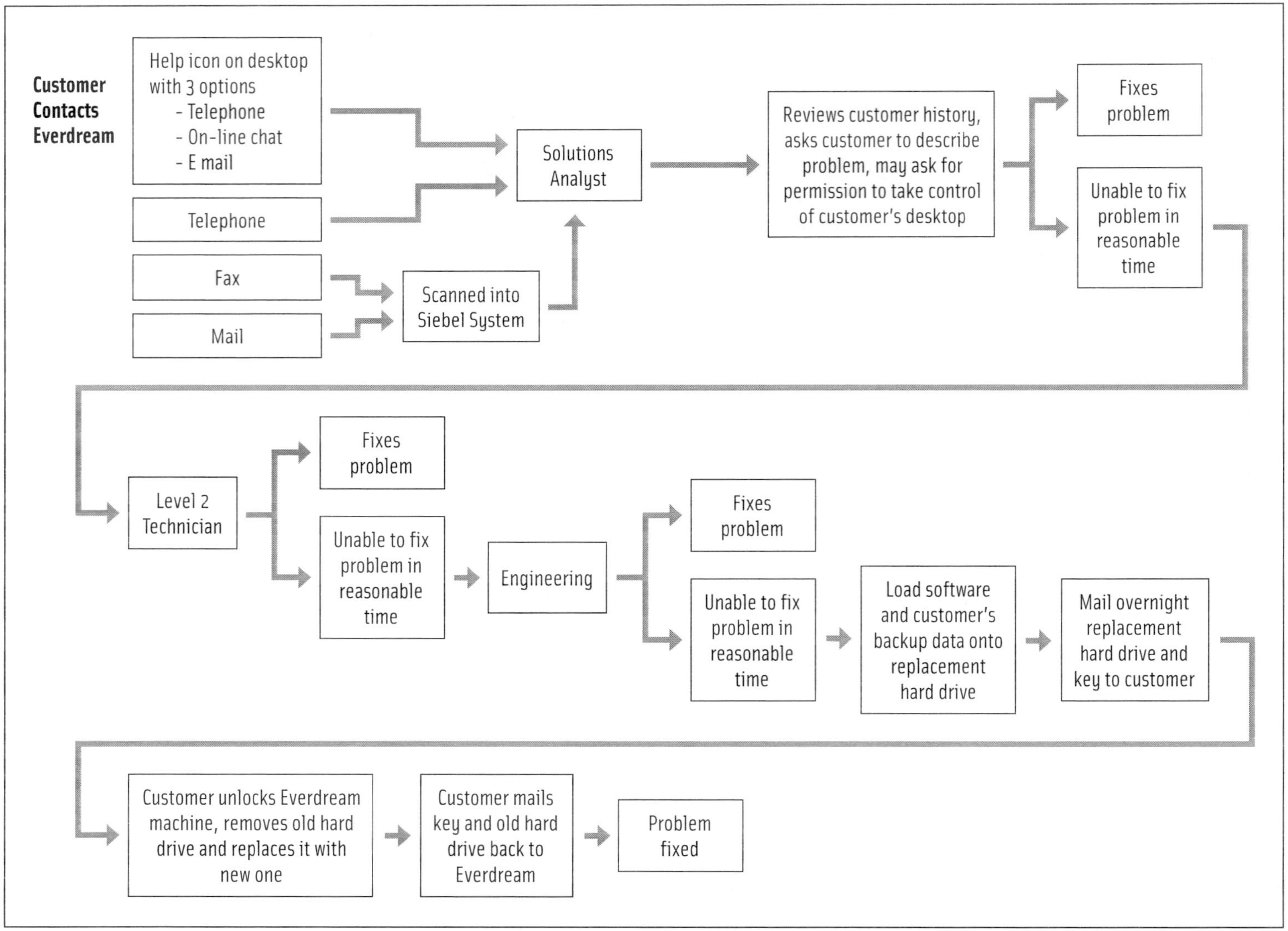

Source: Everdream interviews.

Exhibit 7

EXPECTED LENGTH OF QUEUE FOR A 100-SEAT CALL CENTER

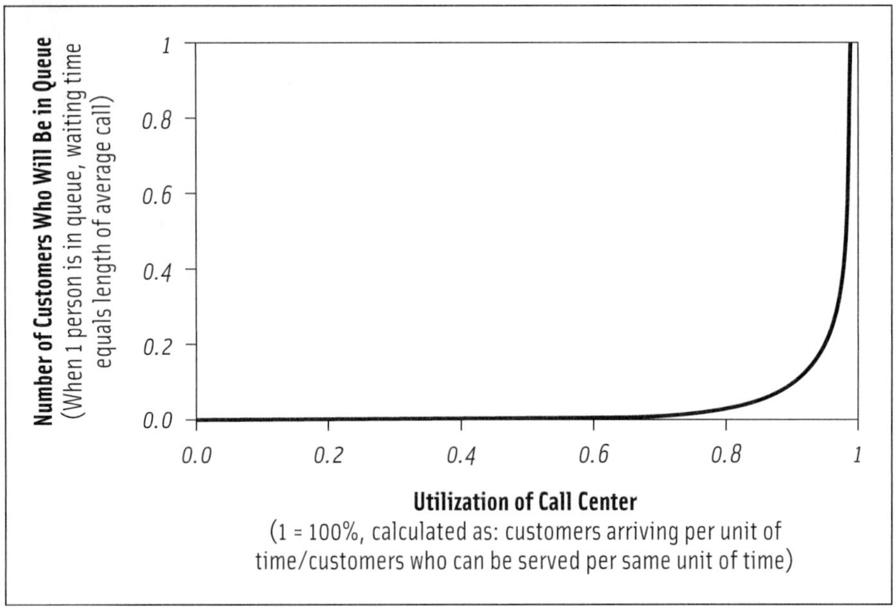

Exhibit 8 SELECTED SUBSCRIPTION COMPUTING VENDORS

Company	Target Market	Hardware Provided	Software Provided	Communication Services and Other	Business Goods and Services Offered	Customer Support	Term of Contract	Price per User per Month
Everdream	Small businesses with 20 or fewer computers	• Everdream-branded PC with Pentium III 500 MHz processor • 128 MB RAM • 17 GB hard drive • 48X CD-ROM drive • 17 inch color monitor • optional: laser printer	• MS Windows 98 • MS Outlook 2000 • Internet Explorer 5.0 • Small Business Edition MS Office 2000 (Word, Excel, etc.) • Norton Anti-Virus • Adobe Acrobat 4.0 • RealPlayer • optional: many options such as MS PowerPoint, Intuit QuickBooks	• dial-up ISP • DSL access included for customers with more than ten PCs • optional: DSL for customers with fewer than 10 PCs • personalized email • 6 web-based training courses	• The BizCenter offers goods and services such as travel services, shipping services, music and books, and access to freelancers	• 24/7 "one-stop" support daily data backup can run diagnostics and fix problems online; reps can take control of customers' desktops replacement hard drive available overnight if necessary support covers Everdream PCs, and other hardware and software from Everdream	30 months	$150
Centerbeam	Small businesses with networks	• exact hardware specifications dependent on on-site survey • Dell and Compaq PCs • server(s), firewall, printers	• MS Windows 2000 • MS Office 2000 (Word, Excel, etc.) • MS Exchange (collaboration tools) • "productivity software" • Website templates • optional: many options such as financial and accounting software	• DSL internet access • on-site survey • company intranet • tools to create company website • personalized email	• The Marketplace™ offers goods and services such as office supplies, online training, and online recruiters	• 2 levels of support –6 a.m. –6 p.m., 5 days a week, or –24/7 for higher fee • 800# or contact online • daily data backup • can run diagnostics and fix problems online • "if a computer fails, you'll have a replacement PC in the morning" • support covers Centerbeam-supplied printers, PCs, laptops, networking equipment and services, and software	36 months	$165 for basic package

Exhibit 8

SELECTED SUBSCRIPTION COMPUTING VENDORS cont.

Company	Target Market	Hardware Provided	Software Provided	Communication Services and Other	Business Goods and Services Offered	Customer Support	Term of Contract	Price per User per Month
People PC	Consumers	• "name brand computer" (currently Compaq) • 380 MHz Intel Celeron processor • 64 MB RAM • 6 GB hard drive • 32X CD-ROM drive • 15-inch monitor • optional: 17-inch color monitor	• MS Windows 98 • Internet Explorer • MS Money • Microsoft Works (word processing, spreadsheets, etc.) • Quicken Basic 99 • McAfee Anti-Virus • Trellix Web (website creation software)	• dial-up ISP (UUNET) • no DSL option • 10 MB online storage for website • personalized email	• Online shopping discounts with partner vendors such as more.com, office.com, and 1-800-flowers	• 3-year hardware with on-site service • 24/7 help desk (email or phone in) • if problem can't be fixed, PeoplePC pays for shipping to and from their service center (no replacement computer) • support covers queries about People PC-provided PC, ISP, and membership offers	36 months	$24.95
Dell	Small businesses	• Dell 466 MHz Intel Celeron processor • 64 MB RAM • 6.4 GB hard drive • 17-inch color monitor	• MS Windows 2000	None	None	• 3-year next-business day, on-site response • "if you have a problem, 70% of the time, the problem is solved within 15 minutes" • support covers computer hardware	36 months	$37

Sources: Company websites viewed on 2-7-2000: *www.centerbeam.com, www.peoplepc.com, www.dell.com;* everdream website (*www.everdream.com*) and Everdream interviews.
Note: Subscription computing vendors charge an additional fee for all optional features.

DOUBLETWIST, INC.

John Couch, chief executive officer of DoubleTwist, Inc. (DoubleTwist), looked out his window at the brilliant blue of Lake Merritt, marvelling at the serenity of the scene 11 floors below. His meditation did not last long; he got up quickly and walked down the the halls of DoubleTwist—the genomics portal company he had headed up for three years—stopping to talk to various executives. Oakland, California-based DoubleTwist, originally an enterprise software company, had become the biotechnology industry's first application service provider, or ASP, in late 1999.[1] The DoubleTwist portal, *www.doubletwist.com,* provided easy access to research agents, databases, and powerful tools that enabled life scientists to process and analyze genomic data in a way previously available only to the largest companies. (See Exhibit 1 for graphic depicting the DoubleTwist portal.)

Couch had a hard time hiding his exuberance that morning in early May. Other biotechnology (biotech) companies, such as Celera Genomics Group (Celera) and Incyte Genomics, Inc. (Incyte), had received enormous amounts of publicity during the prior three months, as the end of the race to map the human genome was finally within sight. Lengthy articles had appeared in many major publications, such as the New York Times and Wall Street Journal, predicting a rosy future for biotech once basic genomic data became widely available. In 1990 the U.S. government funded what was estimated to be a fifteen-year project to identify all of the 80,000 to 100,000 genes in human DNA. The Human Genome Project (HGP), as it became known, also had goals to determine the sequences of the approximately 3.2 billion chemical bases that made up human DNA and to store all the newly discovered information in databases, developing tools for data analysis and visualization. The HGP estimated that it would complete its work in 2003.[2] Celera had begun a similar project more than seven years later in early 1998, building on the HGP's publicly available results, but using a different approach to decoding. (The publicly funded HGP routinely made its results available to researchers for free through public databases.) Celera announced in early April 2000 that it had completed sequencing the genome although it had not yet assembled the sequence in proper order; the HGP then announced that it would complete a "rough draft" of the human genome—covering about 90% of all human genes—by June 2000.[3] (See Exhibit 2 for a glossary of life sciences terms referred to in this case.)

During this time, DoubleTwist kept a relatively low profile, focusing on adding intelligence to the endless raw data and discoveries being generated by others. One of the company's major goals was annotating the human genome. Only about 3% of the total genome was actually made up of genes; the rest was evolutionary and its purpose unknown. The genes themselves were special sequences of hundreds or thousands of base pairs that provide the templates for all the proteins which the body needs to produce. Couch likened the raw genomic data—unannotated—to the letters of the alphabet, with DoubleTwist's annotations and research agents enabling life scientists to, in essence, write sentences.

Annotating the human genome had proven an enormous resource hog; DoubleTwist had more than 300 advanced Sun Microsystems, Inc. (Sun) workstations devoted to the task. During the prior week, Couch had called an ex-colleague—now head of Sun's server business—to argue that Sun's donation of additional high-end processing power in exchange for the positive publicity that would accrue from being associated with DoubleTwist's exciting genomics work was a win-win

Christina Darwall of the HBS California Research Center prepared this case under the supervision of Professor Joseph Bower with the assistance of Sonja Ellingson Hout as the basis for class discussion rather than to illustrate either effective or ineffective handling of an administrative situation.

[1]Application service providers charged customers a fee for "renting" software programs which customers accessed via the Internet using a standard browser. The advent of the Internet allowed software programs to be sold as a service rather than a product.

[2]"About the Human Genome Project," http://www.ornl.gov/hgmis/about.html, viewed 5-8-00.

[3]Nicholas Wade, "Firm Boasts of Milestone in DNA Race," *The San Jose Mercury News,* April 7, 2000, p. A2.

proposition. Sun agreed, and just days earlier, had given DoubleTwist access to three new Sun supercomputers at Sun's Beaverton, Oregon facility. The new computers would allow the three-month project to be completed in three weeks or less.[4#5]

Over the weekend, the processing team told Couch they had reached the 40% mark in annotating the genome. Today, on Monday May 2, Couch was informed that the percentage had climbed to 72%. He knew the company would complete the annotation soon, and that this would present DoubleTwist with a unique opportunity to catapult the company into the public eye. But already he was thinking ahead, something he felt compelled to do. He could envision how the next few months would play out; he knew that, although the path was not without risks, DoubleTwist would be in an enviable position, able to lure new customers once the annotation was complete. Couch felt confident in his strategy to create a company and an infrastructure that would empower the individual scientist by democratizing genomics; however, he knew that the "jury was still out" and that the next year would be a critical one for DoubleTwist.

The Genomics and Bioinformatics Market

During the late 1990's, as the HGP grew closer to the end of its work—and private companies such as DoubleTwist began entering the fray—interest in genomics heated up. As more and more genetic information became available, the promise of exciting new drug discoveries or cures for diseases prompted the media to provide increasing coverage of the genomics field. Scientists were quick to point out that making sense of the data was not an easy task. Bioinformatics—also called biological computing—was a new and rapidly growing field that combined biology, computer science and mathematics. Bioinformaticians analyzed DNA sequences in hopes of finding genes and other interesting patterns in the strings of chemical letters. That process, called annotation, was considered the most difficult part of a sequencing project,[6] and was akin to tryingtodecipherthissentencewithoutknowingwhereone-wordendsandthenextonebegins.[7]

Bioinformaticians developed mathematical and statistical formulas, or algorithms, for processing massive[8] amounts of raw data to find genes. Certain algorithms worked better than others did; often researchers would run several algorithms against one set of data to raise the odds of identifying genes correctly. In large pharmaceutical companies, research scientists would turn to in-house bioinformaticians for help in analyzing raw genomic data. The bioinformaticians knew how to use the necessary algorithms and other software programs, and had access to the computing power needed to run the resource-intensive analyses. Scientists in smaller firms or academic settings were at a distinct disadvantage. DoubleTwist estimated that there were more than 200,000 life scientists, bench chemists, professors and others worldwide who did not have access to the algorithms, genetic data or high-throughput processing necessary for their research; the company projected four year growth of such potential users to be greater than 10% annually. (See Exhibit 3 for more detail on number of potential users.)

DoubleTwist management believed that total available revenue for their market was approximately $1.4 billion, given approximate spending of $10,000 per commercial scientist and $1,000 per academic scientist for current bioinformatics products plus some minor additional e-commerce revenues. An industry observer commented that most industry statistics pointed to an overall market size of $1.5 to $2.0 billion for traditional bioinformatics solutions, out of $20 billion spent on target identification and validation research, which itself was part of the $50 billion spent on total drug research and discovery.

The Evolution of DoubleTwist

Background on Pangea Systems, Inc. and John Couch

Two Stanford graduate students originally founded DoubleTwist in 1993 as Pangea Systems, Inc. (Pangea). Co-founder Joel Bellenson ran the Stanford Sequencing Lab at the time. The other co-founder, Dexster Smith, was a computer scientist in the industrial engineering

[4]Tom Abate, "New Player in Race to Track Genome: DoubleTwist.com Says It Has Partial Draft," The San Francisco Chronicle, May 8, 2000, p. A1.

[5]Pound (#) sign indicates a hotlink in the online version of the case.

[6]Tina Hesman, "The Meaning of Life," *Science News*, vol. 157, April 29, 2000, pp. 284–286.

[7]Todd Woody, "DNA Detectives," *The Industry Standard*, May 29, 2000, pp. 166–188.

[8]DoubleTwist estimated that there were 2–4 terabytes of publicly available genetic data in early 2000.

department. The two realized that with the advent of sequencing technology, they were witnessing a second "industrial revolution," this time in biology. Realizing that they could write relational databases and query against them—thus adding much efficiency for biotech researchers—they began developing specialized databases for Stanford on a consulting basis. They went on to develop several other software programs, including the initial version of Incyte's LifeSeq® database and Oxford GlycoScience's ROSETTA™ proteome system. After three years of developing software for others—and witnessing those others build substantial businesses—the pair decided to leverage their efforts and write enterprise software that could be bought and used by many organizations. In February 1997, they raised $7.5 million in their first venture capital round. Mayfield Fund (Mayfield), Institutional Venture Partners (IVP)[9], and Kleiner Perkins Caufield & Byers—all well respected in the biotech arena—provided the first round funds.

In the spring of 1997, John Couch became an executive-in-residence at Mayfield. Previously Couch had held several pivotal roles at Apple Corporation (Apple). Joining Apple when it had only $7 million in revenue, Couch held a series of positions—from director of new products to vice president and general manager of the personal office systems division where he pioneered Apple's initial graphical user interface (GUI) computer—helping the company grow to over $1 billion in sales. He then took 10 years off to create an educational foundation to fund technology in schools; he also took over a failed private school during the same time. Couch used the school, a preschool through 12th grade school with 150 students, to prototype some of his ideas regarding the use of technology in education. He consulted to several corporations during this time, receiving goods for the school—from satellite dishes to computers—in exchange. The school thrived, and quickly gained a reputation for its digital curriculum and unique facilities, which included such attractions as one of the earliest digital editing studios. The advent of the Internet caused Couch to consider returning to the business world. With the school having grown to 900 students and turned profitable, Couch once again moved to Northern California.

Shortly after joining Mayfield in May 1997, Couch began consulting to Pangea Systems, one of Mayfield's portfolio companies. Reflecting back on that time, Couch recalled a company where the "burn rate was high, and there were few execution capabilities in place."

Focus on Enterprise Software

In September 1997, the Pangea board asked Couch to become the company's CEO. Couch agreed, but stipulated that the venture investors exercise $2.5 million in warrants, giving the company a much-needed window of time in which to put together a new business plan. Couch reflected on his decision to become CEO:

> At first, I didn't even know what bioinformatics meant. When I learned that it was the application of IT to life science research, I realized that it was a market that had yet to be created. And in the two previous companies I had worked for—Hewlett Packard and Apple—I was fortunate enough to be part of two markets that were created from scratch, the hand-held calculator and then the PC. So I was intrigued by the opportunity to help create yet another new market.
>
> When I agreed to join, I indicated to the board members that we ought to slow down our burn rate, which was then $1 million a month, and re-evaluate our direction. Bill Hewlett once told me that more companies die from indigestion than starvation, and I think the company definitely had a mild case of indigestion. So we slowed down the burn rate to $600,000 a month and began to revise the strategy.

When Couch joined the company, there were approximately 60 employees—most either life scientists or computer scientists—plus additional contract personnel, mostly programmers. The company had released an early version of its first product, GeneWorld®, an automated, high throughput sequence processing application. Pangea's two founders left the company two years later, with one founder remaining on the board of directors and both becoming members of the company's scientific advisory board.

After trimming the number of consultants, Couch focused the company on its enterprise software business. The other parts of Pangea's business, the consulting projects and research partnerships, were slowly phased out. During this time, Pangea developed a variety of products including GeneThesaurus® (a database of integrated public data) and CAT (cluster and alignment tools software).

In April 1998, Ward Wolff, a 1973 graduate of Harvard Business School, joined the company as chief finan-

[9]In 1999, part of IVP merged with part of Brentwood Partners to form a new venture firm, Versant Ventures, focused solely on biotech and healthcare. Some of the remaining partners and associates of the two firms also merged to form yet another firm, Redpoint, focused on Internet and new economy investments.

cial officer. (See Exhibit 4 for bios of DoubleTwist's management team.) Wolff had previously served as chief financial officer of an e-commerce company, taking it public in 1995 and later merging it with a company based in Atlanta. Not wanting to move to Atlanta after the merger, Wolff researched several opportunities. He explained his reasons for joining Pangea:

> One thing that attracted me to the company from the beginning was the high quality of the venture investors—not just the firms but the individuals involved. Brook Byers, Grant Heidrich and Sam Collela are all outstanding venture capitalists and are well known in the biotech area. Also I really enjoyed John and his approach to the business. Finally, I was drawn to the blend of software and life sciences—something different from traditional e-commerce businesses.

During most of 1998, Couch and Wolff focused on raising a second venture round. The biotech industry experienced a dramatic crash in the middle of a major fundraising road trip, causing the comparables used in the company's slides to suddenly become irrelevant. Couch recalled a biotech conference sponsored by Kleiner Perkins that year where "many of the companies had more cash in the bank than valuation."

By the end of the year, Couch and Wolff put together a $19.7 million second round of funding, led by MDS Capital Corporation, a Canadian firm. All of Pangea's earlier investors participated in the second round, and newcomers included Boston Millennia Partners and Mitsui & Company, Inc. Once the round finally closed, Couch went on another road trip, this time to visit Pangea's customers. At the end of the trip, he realized that Pangea's tools were used solely by bioinformaticians, not life scientists, thereby forcing life scientists to rely on intermediaries to process their data. He also learned that many of the bioinformaticians did not fully understand the scope of the product, often questioning him about what the product could and couldn't do. Finally, it worried Couch that Pangea customers not only had to pay hundreds of thousands of dollars for the software, but also had to purchase mainframe-equivalent hardware and pay specialized personnel to operate the system once it was in place. Couch saw interesting analogies to earlier situations in his career:

> When I was at HP in the seventies, we were selling half-million dollar computers to organizations. Those computers were centralized, difficult to use and required dedicated personnel. One evening Steve Jobs came to my home, put an Apple II on the table, looked at my three year old son, and said "You can keep this if your dad comes to work for me." What I realized that weekend was that the microprocessor now allowed us to deliver computational processing to the individual—and subsequently the industry shifted from centralized computers to decentralized; from expensive computers to affordable; and from difficult-to-use computers to easy-to-use computers with the cut-and-paste paradigm that we created.
>
> I realized that if we could create and host a new bioinformatics research environment, we could drop the costs for users and empower the individual scientist. The missing ingredient was the equivalent of the cut-and-paste paradigm.

Of all the customer interviews Couch conducted, one stood out in his mind: the interview with Yannick Pouliot, the bioinformatician at Progenitor. Pouliot had been the most successful of Pangea's enterprise software users, and had even written some specialized code on top of GeneWorld®. Pouliot had several ideas, including that of developing an agent that would continuously monitor all relevant public data. Couch hired Pouliot as a consultant during this time, as Progenitor was going out of business, and later hired him as Pangea's head bioinformatician.

DoubleTwist: Building a Life Sciences Portal

On April 24, 1999, Couch and Pouliot made a presentation to the Pangea board at a meeting held in Boston. Couch had some trepidation about the message he was bringing to his new investors—as he summarized it, "this dog won't hunt." Given the interviews he conducted, Couch believed strongly that the size of Pangea's target market would not support the board's goals for the company. He also believed strongly that the new direction he was proposing was the right one. Couch told the board that the company needed to gain mindshare among life scientists and asked the board to approve a $100,000 experiment. The company would build a prototype research agent that would demonstrate how a molecular biologist could do computational work at his desk without using intermediaries such as bioinformaticians and expensive computers.[10] The idea was to create a "point and click research environment" that would use the agent, an automated program that would run multiple

[10] A research agent is a computational tool programmed to perform a variety of genetic analyses given a DNA or protein sequence.

algorithms against multiple databases, thereby reducing the complexity of genomic research. Couch also told the board of his belief that Pangea needed to host the software on its own computers in order to make the product affordable for everyone in the biotech and academic communities.

The prototype agent was shown at the June board meeting. The board was impressed, and said in essence, "Let's go for it, but write a business plan first." Couch replied that there was "no time to do a business plan" and that instead, the company should focus all its efforts on preparing for the TIGR (The Institute for Genomic Research) conference to be held in Miami that September. He proposed "letting the product speak for itself."

Couch recalled the challenges he faced:

> We had to totally revamp the company and completely change the culture. I inherited an organization of scientists and programming teams whose focus was on yearly product releases and production schedules. If I had been starting from scratch, building the kind of culture we needed would not have been difficult, but changing the one in place was. We needed to add new types of people, and we needed to change attitudes and processes.

Couch added several high level executives during the summer of 1999. He hired Rob Williamson, a partner at the Boston Consulting Group (BCG), as the vice president in charge of product marketing, business development and e-commerce; Williamson later commented that the e-commerce part of his title was initially intended primarily as a signal to competitors. Williamson, who had an MBA from Stanford, focused on life sciences and e-commerce while at BCG. Couch originally called Williamson to get a reference on another BCG consultant eventually hired as director of Pangea's e-commerce efforts. At the conclusion of the reference conversation, Couch felt that Williamson himself would make an excellent candidate to help with the company's transition. Williamson elaborated on his thought process in deciding to join Pangea and on how his role in the company differed from his role at BCG:

> I joined the company to get general management experience and to pursue two passions of mine, life sciences and the Internet. At BCG, I had seen the need for a web portal for genomic research, and because a colleague of mine was already at the company, I had an insider's knowledge of both the opportunities and the challenges. I didn't know if the company could execute on the challenges, but I wanted to see if I could help. I had actually had conversations with another genomics company, but found that they moved terribly slowly. I knew that there was an incredible opportunity for someone, and that the company that was going to succeed had to move incredibly quickly. Whoever was going to win would have to change drastically, and I wanted to go where I thought there was the best chance of that happening.
>
> My role here is different from when I advised Fortune 500 CEOs. Here I err on the side of not thinking too hard about how something should work. Elegance is not important. As a consultant I wrote presentations that described what the company *should do.* Here I write presentations about what we *have already done.* There is no time to write before you take action. You have to communicate in person, get people in a room and hash things out. After the fact, I make presentations to share the results—here's what you've told me and here's what we've done.

A third BCG employee, Colin Freund—a Stanford MBA who had focused on the pharmaceutical and biotech market—later joined as vice president of business development, and in August 1999, Stephen Sanders joined as vice president of sales. Sanders' background combined sales experience in both software and life sciences.

Change continued at lower levels as well. Williamson described the extent of the transition:

> In the groups under me, there is only one employee that is still in his or her original position. Some groups, such as business development and e-commerce, are all new. Half of the people in product marketing are new and the other half have moved in from other groups. We took some of the best people from sales and put them in product marketing because they really knew what the customers wanted.

Eventually Williamson was promoted to chief operating officer, at which time the engineering group was added to his responsibilities. (See Exhibit 5 for DoubleTwist organization chart.)

The company's new genomics portal was named DoubleTwist—referring to the double helix configuration of DNA—and launched at the TIGR conference in September 1999; on the first day of the conference the New York Times ran a lengthy feature article on the company.[11] At the same time, DoubleTwist was installed at Stanford, as Stanford became the company's first beta site. The new portal included services, content, e-commerce, and community building. The "Daily Twist" featured fresh content such as daily genomics news; the editor-in-chief had previously worked at Biospace, a popular information-oriented biological sciences Web site. In December 1999, the company changed its name from Pangea to DoubleTwist to signal its focus on the Internet and its new strategy. Williamson commented:

> Traditional companies don't dramatically change their strategies—or throw them out—but that's why many of them are going out of business.

An updraft of interest in the highly visible and much-touted genomics market helped create a standing-room-only crowd at Couch's presentation to the January 2000 Chase/Hambrecht & Quist industry conference. The presentation was successful in deepening investor interest in DoubleTwist, and in the words of Wolff, served as a "watershed" for the company at a time when the company was seeking to raise a $20 million third round of venture funding. DoubleTwist received offers for $90 million. Cutting back on some investors and eliminating others, the company finalized a $37 million round in February 2000. DoubleTwist management also spoke with several investment bankers interested in taking DoubleTwist public; in fact, the company prepared most of the materials necessary to go public, working with Lehman Brothers, whom the company had chosen as lead banker, Dain Rauscher Wessels and Thomas Weisel Partners LLC, as co-managers. However, in May of 2000, plans for an IPO were put on hold because of uncertainty in the public markets and because the company did not have to raise cash at that time.

Competition in the Bioinformatics Market

Most life scientists worked on research and development activities aimed at identifying specific genes and their functions in hopes of treating and curing a range of diseases and other medical disorders. There were four phases in the drug development process: research leading to discovery, pre-clinical analysis, clinical testing, and marketing and distribution. DoubleTwist and most of its competitors operated at the early end of the first phase.

[11]Lawrence Fisher, "Surfing the Human Genome," *The New York Times*, September 20, 1999, p. B1.

In mid 2000, there were more than 50 private and public companies that offered bioinformatics products and services.[12] These companies did one or more of the following: collecting and storing data, searching databases, and interpreting data. Many sold access to their information to pharmaceutical and biotech companies for subscription prices that went as high as several million dollars per year. All bioinformatics competitors had to deal with the overwhelming amount of genomics data, constantly refining their technologies, research approaches and business models.

DoubleTwist managers often referred to the bioinformatics market as a pyramid, with the "top of the pyramid" referring to the largest of the approximately 2,000 pharmaceutical and biotech companies and the "bottom of the pyramid" referring to the 200-300,000 individual life scientists who were potential subscribers to DoubleTwist. The first category of bioinformatics competitors focused on the biggest users, selling enterprise-wide systems and consulting services to the firms at the top of the pyramid. Privately held LION Bioscience, headquartered in Germany, had been particularly successful at selling large enterprise-wide systems, inking a precedent setting $100 million deal with Bayer.[13] LION and Bayer agreed to cooperate in identifying new targets and markers for Bayer, with LION retaining the rights to any new software developed by the collaboration.[14] Companies that sold enterprise-wide systems emphasized that the large systems could be tailored to individual clients, and that their software—and customers' data—resided behind corporate firewalls, providing high security.

A second group of competitors sold shrink-wrapped bioinformatics software targeted at departments and/or individuals. The desktop products generally featured Internet access to a limited number of databases. This category of competitors included Informax, Inc. (Informax) of Rockville, MD, and Oxford Molecular Group (Oxford) located in England. Privately held Informax had grown from within, whereas Oxford had made many acquisitions, of both small companies and analytical software packages. Oxford, a public company, had US$30 million in revenues in 1999, with a net loss of US$39.7 million. Both Informax and Oxford had migrated to offering enterprise-wide systems as well as desktop solutions.[15]

[12]Ken Howard, "The Bioinformatics Gold Rush," *Scientific American*, July, 2000, p. 58.

[13]Ibid., p. 62.

[14]Anonymous, "LION Bioscience Company Profile," *http://www.lionbioscience.com,* viewed 5-2-2000.

Yet another group of competitors had one foot solidly in the drug discovery market and one just as solidly in the bioinformatics market. These companies did much of the wet lab experiments that produced original data. DoubleTwist management viewed Celera and Incyte as the two best examples of firms that played in the pharmaceutical market—themselves working towards patenting gene or drug discoveries—and the data mining market at the same time. These competitors often sold only their own data (rather than providing a mix of proprietary and public data) and were in direct competition with their customers researching new drugs; however, their proprietary offerings were generally highly valued. Customers paid up to several million dollars a year to receive their data.[16] Couch viewed these competitors as providing content—information analogous to "crude oil"—that the large pharmaceutical and biotech customers then had to "refine" in-house. Although these companies had the option to move "upstream" to provide more refined data to the marketplace, DoubleTwist management believed that such a move would be at odds with their core competence.

Celera's revenues for the fiscal year ended June 1999 were $12.5 million with a net loss of $44.9 million; 20% of the company's revenues came from subscriptions to Celera's genomics data.[17] Incyte's calendar 1999 revenues were $157 million with a $26.8 million net loss; 78% of Incyte's revenues came from subscriptions to database and partnership programs.[18] Celera worked primarily on its own, while Incyte, like other smaller, genomics-knowledgeable firms, had paired up with a pharmaceutical giant—Pfizer of New York City—to participate in pharmacogenomics, the field of developing drugs tailored to specific genes.[19] These competitors had been moving to the Internet slowly but surely. Incyte, for example, announced that it was developing a suite of Internet-enabled database products and that by 2001, it would be "primarily an online company."[20] Being on the Internet provided these companies with an easy way to provide their data "by the slice," allowing customers to use less and pay less, getting around the high price tag issue. This also made it possible for DoubleTwist to pursue partnerships with them.

The large pharmaceutical companies' internal bioinformatics departments also provided competition for standalone bioinformatics companies. Many firms set up comprehensive departments to integrate and service computer software and to facilitate database access across multiple groups. Most also developed strategic alliances, entered licensing agreements, and acquired smaller biotech companies.

The final category of competitors included Internet-focused firms that targeted smaller firms and even individuals, such as academics or students, in addition to larger companies. These Web-based firms—which included DoubleTwist, eBioinformatics, Inc. (eBioinformatics) and LabOnWeb.com (operated by Compugen)—offered what some referred to as "one-stop Internet shopping." Privately held eBioinformatics was an ASP focused on providing bioinformatics tools to scientists. Founded in Australia in 1998, it moved to and was incorporated in northern California in 1999. The company priced on a subscription basis, but switched to a pay per use pricing structure in early 2000, charging according to the volume of work performed.[21] Founded in Israel in 1993, privately-held Compugen, Inc. (Compugen) initially focused on hardware and software based accelerators for genomic searches; the company later developed sets of algorithms and analytical tools that it sold to major pharmaceutical firms. Compugen also commercialized genes and proteins that the company discovered using its own tools. In late 1999, the company—which had opened an office in New Jersey—launched a Website aimed at individual life scientists, LabOnWeb.com. LabOnWeb.com provided access to public and proprietary databases and allowed scientists to automate processes such as sequence elongation, which could take months when done manually in the lab, but could—according to the company—be finished in minutes on the Web.[22] These companies, more than any other category of competitors, had to focus on interoperability—among research agents, databases, etc. These companies were often thought of as content providers,

[15]Anonymous, "About Informax," *http://www.informaxinc.com/news/corp_view.html;* Anonymous, "Corporate Profile," *http://www.oxfordmolecular.com/corp/profile.shtml,* viewed 5-2-2000.

[16]Yali Friedman, "Celera: Here Today, Genome Tomorrow," About.com, *wysiwyg://14http://biotech.about.com/industry/biotech/library/weekly/aa022110e.htm,* viewed 4-6-2000.

[17]Anonymous, "Corporate Profile: Celera Genomics," *www.bull-market.com/tdbi/Biotechp.htm,* viewed 4-6-2000.

[18]Anonymous, "Incyte Reports Record Fourth Quarter Revenues," Incyte Press Release, *http://biz.yahoo.com/prnenws/000126/ca_incyte_l.html,* viewed 4-6-2000.

[19]Ken Howard, "The Bioinformatics Gold Rush," *Scientific American,* July, 2000, p. 52.

[20]Todd Woody, "DNA Detectives," *The Industry Standard,* May 29, 2000, pp. 166–188.

[21]Anonymous, "eBioinformatics Corporate Profile" and "Press Releases," *http://www.ebioinformatics.com,* viewed 5-2-2000.

[22]Anonymous, "About LabOnWeb.com," *http://www.labonweb.com/sitehtml/about_labonweb.html,* viewed 5-2-2000.

a label that some DoubleTwist managers disliked, preferring instead to be viewed primarily as a "research site." This category of competitors emphasized their comprehensive offerings, their ease-of-use and their accessibility.

Because no single company came close to providing all the data and algorithms that life scientists needed, partnerships among all types of competitors were exceedingly common. For many companies, partnerships were critical to maintaining a competitive edge. Every time a new partnership was formed, the participating companies would issue a press release—"marketing by press release" as Couch referred to it. The number and frequency of press releases had increased steadily as the race to map the human genome headed towards the finish line, yet the decision regarding with whom to partner was not always an easy one. Software programs had to be integrated with other software programs; databases had to be easily accessible; and all components offered to the customer had to work together seamlessly. Often, an announced partnership failed to take hold as one or both of the partners stumbled during execution.

DoubleTwist's Business Model

DoubleTwist's strategy was to provide life scientists with a secure and comprehensive research environment and community via the Internet. As an ASP, DoubleTwist enabled any life scientist to perform sophisticated genomic analysis regardless of his or her level of bioinformatic expertise or access to robust computing power. DoubleTwist's research agents retrieved and interpreted data by applying multiple algorithms across multiple databases based on the specific type of analysis. The research agents also monitored for changes in data, notifying users of updates by email. The agents helped scientists perform tasks such as discovering new members of a gene family, analyzing the gene structure of human genomic DNA, and monitoring patent status. DoubleTwist's research agents used approximately 20 algorithms, including some developed internally and others developed externally. These algorithms enabled rapid, intelligent searching of the more than two dozen databases—some proprietary and others public—available to DoubleTwist users (see Exhibit 6 for list of databases provided). As a portal, DoubleTwist provided life scientists a way to keep up-to-date on developments in their field, make purchases of supplies related to their research, and exchange ideas with colleagues.

Management believed that DoubleTwist's strategy gave the company several key advantages relative to its major competitors. The research agents provided the advantage on the front end, bringing intelligence and efficiency to biotech research; DoubleTwist's robust processing infrastructure provided the advantage on the back end. A leading provider of Internet hosting for complex mission-critical Internet operations hosted the company's servers. DoubleTwist management believed that the DoubleTwist portal provided yet another competitive advantage; by bringing valuable information to life scientists on a daily basis, features such as the "Daily Twist" added to the "stickiness"[23] of the site. Finally, unlike several of the company's primary competitors, DoubleTwist did not engage in biotech research or the patenting of genes. Management believed that because the company was truly neutral, life scientists would feel comfortable doing their research on the DoubleTwist site and potentially storing their results there as well.

Couch reflected on the challenge of winning customers over to DoubleTwist's new business model:

> Just as we had to work to change the culture of the organization inside, we have to work on re-educating our customers. We know there will be a transition to a new way of doing drug and gene research and we want to help accelerate that change. We have the same challenge that Apple had when it first began selling its computers—and I want to create evangelists in the same way Apple did.
>
> The barrier to adoption is not so much intellectual content as vocabulary. Kids can do this work, but they have to get past the vocabulary. One thing we've done to help with that is that when you view the human genome on our site, it's zoomable, clickable and graphical—very intuitive.

Products and Pricing

Pangea Systems made money by selling large enterprise software systems with prices ranging from $150,000 to $500,000. The new DoubleTwist business model called for revenues from multiple sources. First and most important, the company charged fees for subscribing to its services: access to databases, algorithms, research agents and DoubleTwist's computing power. Anyone could log onto the site and access some of what DoubleTwist had to offer free

[23]Stickiness—a recycled marketing expression—referred to a site's ability to retain customers.

of charge, but as the number of sequences analyzed and databases accessed increased, the price of the subscription increased. Academic scientists paid $40 to $400 a month for subscriptions that allowed them to run between 100 and 500 sequences a month. Commercial subscribers paid $50 to $1,250 a month. The company also generated revenues via e-commerce. A scientist running a certain sequence might be alerted to a particular article, lab supply or reagent—relevant to his or her research—and then told how it might be purchased online; or, a scientist doing searches on a certain gene might be given the opportunity to purchase that gene from a company like AlphaGene, one of DoubleTwist's partners. The third component of revenues was the sale of software components, expected to decline over time; as outright software sales diminished, so would revenues from maintenance and consulting services.

Large pharmaceutical companies generally had invested heavily in their own integrated enterprise systems. Couch shared his thoughts about this segment of the market:

> One of the things that Bill Hewlett and Dave Packard taught me was that you don't attack a well-built fortress. For us to go into those companies and say that we think our way is better and that they should throw out everything they've invested in would probably not be a wise strategy. So what we've done is allowed pharmaceutical companies to buy components of DoubleTwist.com so that over time, more and more DoubleTwist functionality will be embedded in their internal systems. And each of those components links back to the DoubleTwist.com portal.

Components were priced like enterprise software; the new annotated database being assembled, named Prophecy, was priced at $650,000—much more expensive than an individual subscription to DoubleTwist.com but much less expensive than competitor's similar products. Prophecy would be installed behind a customer's firewall and updated every two weeks. Another important DoubleTwist component was GeneForest, the company's annotated human gene index, also for use behind a customer's firewall. (See Exhibits 7a and 7b for DoubleTwist's historical and projected financials.)

Wolff commented on the importance of proving the new business and revenue models in 2000:

> This is an industry that has not delivered on its revenue promises. Our goal this year is to get to a revenue model that has some traction. We believe we've created a model that allows for multiple steady streams of revenue rather than large "lumps" of revenue—and that is critical to creating long-term value.

Sales Approach

Management believed that hosted subscriptions would ultimately provide 80% of DoubleTwist's revenues. The original financial model assumed that the portal would "pull" in over half of DoubleTwist's subscribers; in May 2000, management believed that paying subscribers would come primarily from companies and institutions sold by the sales force—more of a "push" approach. To increase the number of scientists and others using the DoubleTwist portal, the company offered bundled packages; if, for example, a pharmaceutical company subscribed to the Prophecy database, the company would automatically receive subscriptions for a certain number of portal users bundled in with the database sale. Couch kept a chart outside his office that showed how the number of portal users at each of the company's beta sites kept increasing over time; he theorized that one user led to another as scientists shared with one another the efficiencies possible with DoubleTwist.

Stephen Sanders, DoubleTwist's vice president of sales, believed that DoubleTwist had to sell its vision at the chief executive level. Sanders, who had started and sold several technology companies before joining DoubleTwist, commented on the company's approach to sales:

> When I first arrived here, we were still selling enterprise software and it was clear that our market was limited. We had a long sales cycle and few potential buyers. When we moved to the ASP model, we were able to shorten the sales cycle and increase the number of potential users. We think that high level relationship selling is the best approach; we must sell our vision to the senior executives of each company. We talk to the CEO and other senior managers about the mission for their company and then show them how DoubleTwist can help accomplish that mission.
>
> Selling the DoubleTwist portal is currently a "push" activity, which is not an efficient way to sell it. The ASP needs to be a "pull" sell, using marketing and PR. At an average price of $900 per month per seat, we can't afford to have a salesman and an application scientist calling on people to close the sale. As our PR increases, we are increasingly receiving inbound calls. In the meantime, we bundle seats of DoubleTwist.com with sales of Prophecy, since we believe that no company in

the biotech or pharmaceutical industries can afford to search for new and novel drug targets without it. There will be a lot of peer pressure on companies to purchase the best databases and tools, and everyone knows that time is of the essence. The window for identifying novel genes will shrink greatly.

We have e-sales and telesales teams that I believe will become more effective over time. Our e-sales people focus on two activities—capturing PR-generated leads and converting users of our free bronze level service to our higher value added silver level service. With e-sales, we can give someone a demo on their computer, taking control of their desktop while a telesales person talks with them on the phone.

The key to long term sales of subscriptions is realizing value on the bottom part of the pyramid. We want to help the bench scientist—who is often not a Ph.D.—understand that the PC and the DoubleTwist portal can make a difference in his daily work. Currently, after we meet with a CEO, we also have meetings with the scientists and bench chemists to explain DoubleTwist. If the senior executives have already bought into the vision, then we don't have to worry about addressing every minor detail raised by the scientists.

Challenges in Implementing the New Business Model

Implementing the new business model brought with it many challenges. One challenge faced by Couch was how to set goals and manage a company that was doing something that hadn't been done before. He shared his thoughts:

> How do you plan on accomplishing something that's never been accomplished before? It's like going to the moon. You don't get to the moon in a straight line. There's a midcourse correction every 24 hours. The physics need to be recalculated. That's what it's like when you're involved in leading a company into a market that has yet to be created. There are no well-worn footsteps to follow. There is no textbook to read.
>
> I employ a specific model I call leadership by vision, which was originally developed from my Apple experience. The model entails first developing a shared vision, unique strategic directions, and creative tactical steps; next, empowering the partners that take the journey; and finally, developing guidelines that focus on relationships rather than rules. Our vision is to empower all life scientists and scientists-in-training to conduct genomic research. The direction we've decided to take is using the Internet as a computational engine to reach the scientist. Given our vision and direction, we can be very creative about the specific steps we take towards our goal—empowering scientists to find the cause and hopefully the cure for many diseases.

Transforming the Engineering Function

One of the functional groups most affected by the shift in business models was engineering. Edward Kiruluta, vice president of engineering, commented on the sweeping changes in his group:

> We changed from an enterprise software company to a Web-based company in less than three months. It was wrenching.
>
> When we were an enterprise application software company we had a linear way of developing products. First we did market research and validation, then we wrote a detailed product definition, then we spent 6-12 months building the product, then we did QA, then beta testing, and finally we shipped. With the Web, there is an expectation that things will be different every day, so it collapses the time lines and forces you to change your development process. What has changed most is that we have to do much more integration of the marketing and development functions. Now we do discovery—market testing and validation—*while we develop.* We also have many more projects at one time. Managing that many projects has taken some reorganization and new skills. Developers are often working on two to three projects at the same time.
>
> The time line crunch also forces changes in culture. Now there is more urgency. You see more late night work and more meetings because schedules change so quickly and you have to keep up with the new ideas. We're very flexible on when people come in to work—some come in the early afternoon and stay quite late—but everybody has to be aware of what is going on. All our people walk around with phones attached to their backs. We use a lot of email, and we archive what we've done on several Websites, so that when people come back from vacation they can catch up quickly.
>
> I also have to hire very differently now. Before, we could hire someone with a fairly narrow background,

say, C++ programming. Now, you still have to have a skill, but you also have to be familiar with a systems approach and not just an application approach. You have to understand the entire network, how things are put together, and how your piece interacts with the Web server and the application server and the database.

Our understanding of systems design has had to increase quite a bit to handle these complexities. Also, load has become much more important. Before, 20 to 30 people in a company might use our product. Now, the system could potentially get up to 20,000 to 30,000 hits—and the variation in users is much greater. We have to think a lot more about the user interface since not everyone will have read a manual or gone through training; all they have to do to use the product is type in the URL. This forces product development to be a much more multidisciplinary exercise.

Setting Priorities in a Complex Environment

Williamson had also seen enormous changes since his arrival approximately one year prior. He reflected on the experience and the importance of priority setting:

> When I arrived here, we had three products and 70 employees. Now we have twice as many people, and depending on how you look at it, 50 products or one really complex product. Our site is one of the most complicated I've ever seen, and as a consultant I saw many. This exponential increase in complexity—which took place in a very short period of time—has greatly increased our need for speed and communication. We have to quickly develop products and react to market conditions.
>
> This is like flying a plane and parts are falling off and you're adding parts, all at the same time. When we were Pangea Systems, we had long lead times and long product development and testing cycles. Now we have business partners who expect partnerships to come to fruition on the Website within months, if not weeks. Also, customers use the site, and say "this feature is horrible, take it away or fix it." You have other customers who suggest other new features, and say "if only you did this, we would spend ten times as much money on your product." You have a daily, immediate feedback loop, and you need to respond to it—for competitive, customer and partner reasons. The key in this situation becomes keeping your priorities straight. You have input from many sources and you have to prioritize across all those inputs and try to keep the ship steady within certain parameters, so that you aren't running from one fire to the next, but are instead migrating in the right direction and being responsive.
>
> Managing the priority setting process is extremely important. Historically there was a disconnect between what was seen as a priority by the sales force, the development people, the marketing people and the actual projects the development people were working on. Now we have a master product plan, based on customer input, and we have a prioritization process where the constituencies within the organization sit down every week and discuss their priorities, both long and short term. We delete from the list and add to the list and that's fed back into the master plan.

A weekly prioritization meeting was held every Monday to go over the development activities underway. Management might have a list of 50 product ideas under consideration; 15 might be in the pipeline. The purpose of the weekly meeting was to allocate resources among the 15 projects according to the week's priorities.

Customer input for the master product plan was gleaned from three different sources. First, market validation was done using classic focus groups. Second, DoubleTwist's beta sites provided additional input. Academic institutions such as Stanford and commercial beta sites at companies like Chiron had provided intense, detailed feedback for three to four months. Finally, various mechanisms allowed the broader base of DoubleTwist users to give feedback to the customer support group. Every week the sales force produced a top ten list and the customer support group developed its own top ten list of the significant issues mentioned repeatedly during the prior week. These lists were then used in developing and updating the master product plan.

Developing New Processes and Coordinating Functions

Both Williamson and Colin Freund, the vice president of business development, championed re-crafting processes whenever necessary, although in many cases, they were simply adding *some* process where previously there had been none. Freund commented:

> We have grown very rapidly in the last six months and we need to change our processes as we grow. I head up

the process re-engineering group. We try to ensure that we grow our processes at the same time that we're growing our people and our products.

Williamson expanded on the importance of creating smoothly functioning processes and ensuring that DoubleTwist's various groups were coordinated in their efforts:

> At some of our competitors, there are lots of 'silos'—30 or more vice presidents and individual empires that never talk to one another. Here, we're constantly trying to 'de-silo' the company.
>
> One of the needs we identified when we did the recent process re-engineering exercise was for cross-functional teams to develop and implement new products—and we had just developed a new product development system for traditional products that we had to scrap. Interestingly, the process re-engineering itself solved half our problems because we got everyone in one room to discuss what they did and how.

Recruiting

Another challenge was hiring and keeping good people. Couch believed it was critical to hire people who "weren't afraid of change." Freund spoke about the people he had hired in the business development group:

> My team is young, bright and enthusiastic. I don't worry very much about their lack of experience. They're very energetic and feel they have something to prove. I review deals at the end of the process and give them the latitude to develop the deal themselves. Because we're an Internet company, we haven't encountered problems with this approach. Even gray-haired managers at large companies think it's fine that our people are so young; they say, "Well, they're an Internet company."

Williamson believed that recruiting and retaining good people was the company's biggest challenge. He elaborated:

> We just can't recruit fast enough. If we don't meet our plans, it will be because we can't hire fast enough. We've done several things to speed up hiring, including assigning everyone to a recruiting team; the teams will receive bonuses as a team based on the number of people they refer to the company and that are subsequently hired. At the same time, we can't hire just anyone; we turn away a lot of people. Everyone we hire has to pass the passion test and the teamwork test or we won't hire him or her.

Negotiating and Implementing Partnerships

There were several issues associated with negotiating and implementing partnerships. One of the major challenges for business development was choosing from among a very broad range of partners. Also, even though DoubleTwist management prioritized potential partners up front, once discussions began, it often became clear that the potential partner viewed the Internet with some mistrust. Many partner companies were relatively uninvolved with the Internet, staffed by scientists, and worried about potential channel conflict.

There were three types of partners the company pursued: research content companies (which divided into two sub-categories—data and tools), e-commerce companies that sold supplies for life scientists' wet lab experiments, and companies relevant to community building, e.g., those supplying scientific news and literature.

DoubleTwist management evolved its approach to implementing partnerships over time. Originally, marketing was involved at the beginning stage of talks with potential partners, while engineering was not, largely due to the tremendous demands on engineering's time. Business development then negotiated the deal, a press release was issued, and engineering began integrating the new partner's functionality. The initial approach created occasional problems. Because marketing was not involved with the final terms of the contract, certain issues—e.g. pricing—could arise. Because engineering was not involved up front, occasionally estimates for time to completion were inaccurate. Lastly, salespeople—often spurred on by excited current and potential customers that had read the press release—pre-sold the new feature without complete knowledge of the new functionality or the timing of the product release.

DoubleTwist management made several changes intended to improve the business development process. First, they created a master product plan (see also "Setting Priorities in a Complex Environment") showing all the planned changes and additions to the product with accompanying timelines. This change helped several groups, in particular international sales. Next, business development began bringing engineering into partnership planning meetings at an early stage; this change grew out of some of the early strategy planning meetings. Also, marketing began to review final partnership contracts in addition to providing front-end input. Finally, the company undertook an experiment with the project management function, which engineering had historically performed. In May 2000, DoubleTwist experimented with a small, separate project management group that would "own" the function—getting input from marketing, engineering and business development—and clarify roles, set management expectations, and develop plan timelines. If the experiment were successful, the approach would be implemented throughout the company.

Perhaps the most common issue with partners was developing mutually agreeable pricing. Sophie Yazdi, vice president of marketing, gave her perspective:

> When we developed our pricing we tried to keep it simple for our customers. We fine-tuned our pricing over the last year based on feedback from both customers and partners. Since we are building a new marketplace for our partners, we have to educate them about pricing on the Internet. Some partners want users to pay an annual subscription fee and receive functionality for a year; others want users to get access to certain pages for, say, 3 months at a time, and then to have to pay again.
>
> We use annual subscription pricing for our own products to keep it simple, but we generally implement what we call "pay per view" pricing—that is, "pay per run" pricing—for our partners. This means that users pay per unit of work processed, for example, a sequence run. We do this because if users were to purchase all the software functionality for themselves and pay the partner as the partner is usually paid—on an annual subscription or one-time purchase basis—the users would be paying $10,000 to $30,000 on average. By implementing pay per view, we can charge much less for, say, just ten runs or so. In the case of our partner, "Alpha," users would normally have to pay about $200,000 for the hardware and software, and this doesn't even include maintenance or support. But on the DoubleTwist portal, we can charge around $1,000 for ten runs and the user can suddenly have access to this very powerful software for a reasonable fee.
>
> We have gotten feedback from users that, although they really like the pay per view approach, it is often difficult for them to obtain many small purchase orders. Also, they want to know up front what their *total* charges will be. So we decided to implement a program that will let users buy a fixed amount of pay per view functionality—say $10,000 worth. We are going to develop the system so that every time they use pay per view, they will be notified about how much they've spent and how much they have left in their accounts.

Occasionally the company encountered other implementation issues with partners. An example of the problems posed for DoubleTwist management arose with a partner code-named "Alpha." Alpha was a large public biological tools and analysis company that had entered into a partnership with DoubleTwist to provide an Internet channel for their tools. In the process of implementing the partnership, the DoubleTwist team had encountered several issues, including integration of the new tools onto the DoubleTwist site, porting the Alpha software from one hardware platform to another, and coordinating Alpha's and DoubleTwist's technical teams. Yazdie, Freund and Kiruluta met regularly to review progress and resolve issues such as these.

Mapping Plans for the Future

The final major challenge facing the company was mapping a strategic path for the future. Freund headed up a strategic review process meant to develop a framework for assessing new opportunities. He commented on the importance of the process:

> We're faced with a strategic nightmare because we have so many options. I think one of the critical decisions we need to make is whether to remain a database and content player as well as an aggregator. We also need to decide whether to go into data services, which would allow us to provide even more support to companies in terms of processing their genomic data. In essence, do we continue to do some sideline products or do we focus purely on the dotcom?
>
> At this moment DoubleTwist is very focused on life science research. There are many new areas we could get into within research that would complement what we are doing now. They are all interesting ideas, and because people here are very motivated by the emerging science, you tend to want to dip your toe into lots of different things. But my concern is that we will get so caught up in the computational and data generation activities that we will lose our focus on the dot com, and therefore become less effective at both. I think we need to focus on the low hanging 'non dot com' fruit, but we are constantly being tested on this dimension. The situation is made more problematic by the tension between resources and win-

dows of opportunity. For example, a company came to see us last week with a potential mass-market opportunity. They have a good technology. We shouldn't do this right now, but if we *don't* do it, we may have no opportunity to do it in the future.

The View from the Top

After making the rounds on the eleventh floor and stopping briefly for a quick game of foosball, Couch returned to his office. His assistant told him that three reporters had called in the previous half-hour. Once again Couch looked down at the lake below. He believed he had carved out a clear and compelling mission for DoubleTwist. The next twelve months would reveal much about the direction in which the nascent genomics market would move. Couch felt confident in the company's strategy to sell components to the large pharmaceutical companies, not yet ready to go directly to the Internet, while focusing primarily on establishing a robust environment for empowering the individual scientist. But specifics would depend critically on how the burgeoning market played out. For DoubleTwist to succeed in implementing its compelling vision, its team of managers and engineers would have to maintain their breakneck pace of development, reacting positively as options played out.

Exhibit 1 THE DOUBLETWIST PORTAL AND ASP

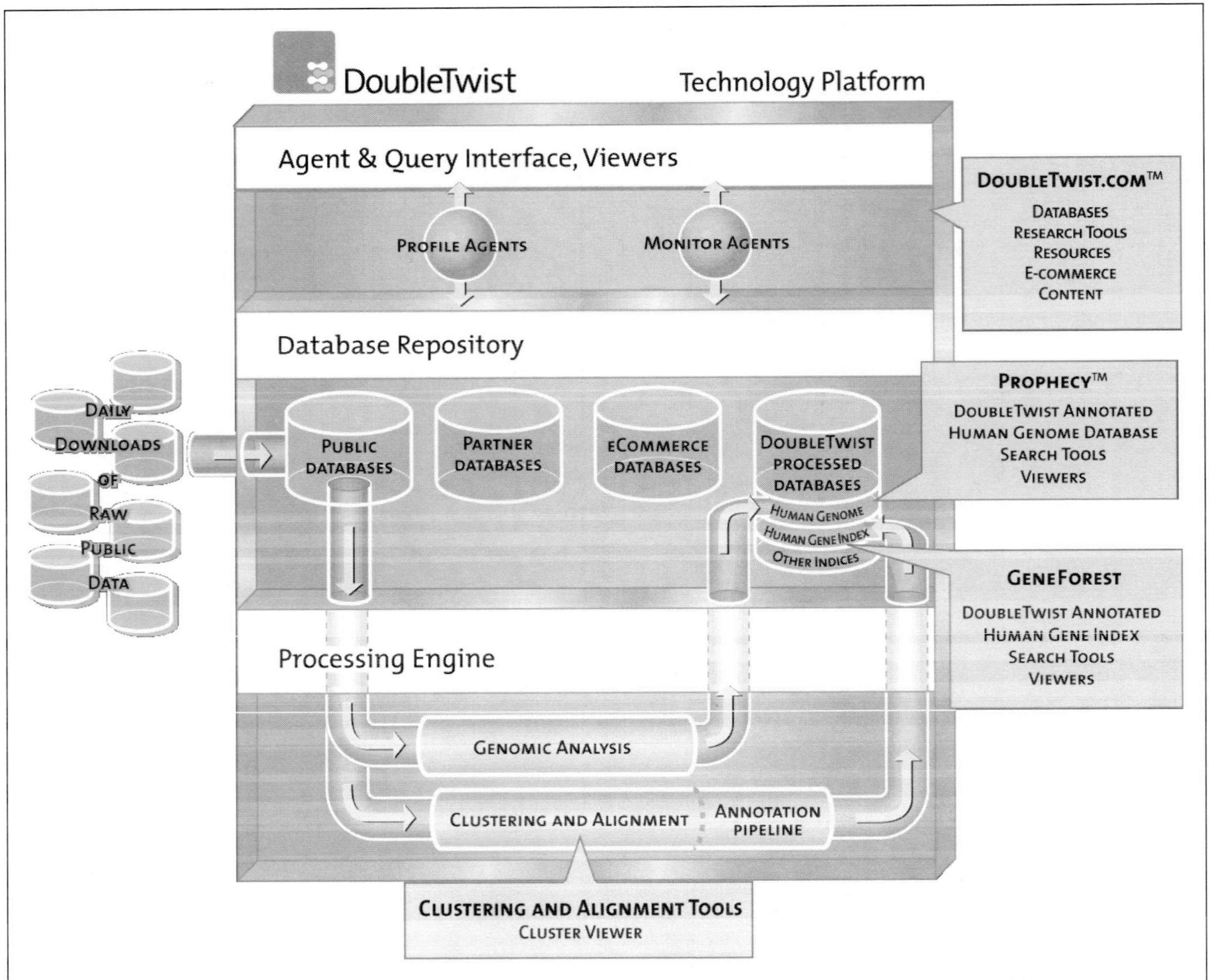

Source: DoubleTwist, May 2000.

Exhibit 2

LIFE SCIENCES TERMS

Base	One of the molecules which form part of the structure of DNA and RNA molecules. The order of bases in a DNA molecule determines the structure of proteins encoded by that DNA.
Base Pair (bp)	Two complementary nucleotide bases joined together by chemical bonds. The two strands of the DNA molecule are held together in the shape of a double helix by the bonds between base pairs.
Bioinformatics	The science of informatics as applied to biological research. Informatics is the management and analysis of data using advanced computing techniques. Bioinformatics is particularly important as an adjunct to genomics research because of the large amount of complex data this research generates.
cDNA	mRNA templates are synthesized in the lab into cDNA, which stands for "complementary DNA".
DNA	The molecule that encodes genetic information. DNA is a double-stranded helix held together by bonds between pairs of nucleotides.
Expressed Sequence Tag (EST)	A short strand of DNA (approximately 200 base pairs long) which is part of a cDNA. Because an EST is usually unique to a particular cDNA, and because cDNAs correspond to a particular gene in the genome, ESTs can be used to help identify unknown genes and to map their position in the genome.
Full Gene Sequence	The complete order of bases in a gene. This order determines which protein a gene will produce.
Gene Expression	The process by which the information in a gene is used to create proteins.
Genome	All the genetic material in the chromosomes of a particular organism; its size is generally given as its total number of base pairs.
Genomics	The study of genes and their function.
mRNA	The DNA of a gene is transcribed into mRNA (for "messenger RNA") molecules, which then serve as a template for the synthesis of proteins.
Nucleotide	The "building block" of nucleic acids such as the DNA molecule.
Proteome	All the proteins being made by a cell according to the instructions in the mRNAs.
RNA	A molecule similar to DNA, which helps in the process of decoding the genetic information carried by DNA.
Sequence	The order of nucleotides in a DNA or RNA molecule, or the order of amino acids in a protein.
Sequence Tagged Site (STS)	Short (200 to 500 base pairs) DNA sequence that has a single occurrence in the human genome and whose location and base sequence are known. STSs are useful for localizing and orienting the mapping and sequence data reported from many different laboratories and serve as landmarks on the developing physical map of the human genome. Expressed sequence tags (ESTs) are STSs derived from cDNAs.

Source: The Genomics Lexicon, a database of terms and definitions, jointly developed by the Pharmaceutical Research and Manufacturers of America and the Foundation for Genetic Medicine, Inc.: *http://209.52.56.28/lexicon* (viewed on 4-13-2000).

Exhibit 3

PROJECTED GLOBAL GENOMIC MARKET

	2000	2001	2002	2003	2004
– *Global Market Size* – (Total Industry Employees)					
– Biotech	230,965	251,752	274,410	299,107	326,026
– Pharmaceutical	296,402	303,859	311,455	319,242	327,223
– Academic	457,740	480,774	504,299	529,514	555,990
– Total	985,107	1,036,385	1,090,164	1,147,863	1,209,239
– *Global Market Size*					
– (Potential DoubleTwist Users)					
– Biotech	63,932	69,686	90,205	98,323	107,172
– Pharmaceutical	15,328	15,711	25,257	25,888	26,536
– Academic	126,377	132,696	176,349	185,166	194,424
– Total	205,637	218,093	291,810	309,378	328,132

Source: DoubleTwist estimates, May 2000.

Exhibit 4

DOUBLETWIST MANAGEMENT BIOGRAPHIES

John O. Couch, Chairman and CEO

From 1995 to 1997, Couch was a management consultant, providing strategic planning, management and technology advice to various companies. Prior to that, Couch held several positions at Apple Computer, Inc., including vice president and general manager of personal office systems and vice president of software. Prior to Apple, Couch served as section manager in the general systems division of Hewlett-Packard Company. Couch received a BA in computer science and an MS in electrical engineering and computer science, both from the University of California at Berkeley.

Robert F. Williamson, Chief Operating Officer

From 1991 to 1999, Williamson was with the Boston Consulting Group; he was elected a partner in May 1998. During his tenure at BCG he led the firm's West Coast healthcare practice, co-led the West Coast e-commerce practice, and was a senior member of the global high tech practice. Prior to that, Williamson founded and ran several small businesses and worked as a research assistant for the Federal Reserve Board of Governors. He received a BA in Economics from Pomona College and an MBA from Stanford Graduate School of Business.

H. Ward Wolff, Vice President and Chief Financial Officer

From 1992 to 1998, Wolff served as head of finance and administration and was chief financial officer for Premenos Technology Corporation, a provider of e-commerce software and services. In 1996 he was promoted from vice president to senior vice president. Prior to that, he served as an executive director of Russell Reynolds Associates, an international management recruiting firm, and held a number of positions with Price Waterhouse as a certified public accountant. Wolff received a BA in economics from the University of California at Berkeley and an MBA from Harvard Business School.

Stephen H. Sanders, Vice President of Sales

Sanders served as executive vice president with the Mega Systems division of SafeGuard Scientifics, Inc. from 1998 to 1999. From 1996 to 1998, Sanders served as vice president of sales with Azron, Inc., a company that provides health care information solutions. From 1993 to 1996, Sanders was the regional sales manager for Molecular Simulations, Inc. (Biosym). He has also held senior sales and marketing positions with Enviro Track, Inc. and Chevron Chemical Company. Mr. Sanders holds a BA in political economics from the University of Washington.

Colin Freund, Vice President of Business Development

From 1992 to 1999 Freund was with the Boston Consulting Group in London and San Francisco, where he was a project leader. During his tenure, he was a member of the firm's healthcare, IT and high-tech practice areas. Freund also worked at IBM in Stuttgart and Alza Pharmaceuticals in Palo Alto. He received a BA in economics from Cambridge University in England and an MBA from the Stanford Graduate School of Business.

Edward Kiruluta, Vice President of Engineering

Kiruluta has over 15 years of experience in the software industry with extensive software design, systems architecture, relational database design, high-throughput parallel computing, team building, and leadership skills. He has led the integration of complex data types into a traditional relational database management system. Kiruluta has also held senior technical positions at MacSys, Inc., a Canadian systems integrator and Transport Canada, Telecommunications. Kiruluta's educational background is in electrical engineering.

Sophie Yazdi, Vice President of Marketing

Yazdi has over ten years of sales and marketing experience in the field of pharmaceutical and biotech software products. Prior to becoming vice president of marketing, she was vice president of sales and customer service at DoubleTwist. She previously worked for Oxford Molecular and Chemical Design, Ltd., two innovators in the field of cheminformatics and bioinformatics. Her other experience includes working at a number of systems integrators and Novartis Pharmaceuticals. Yazdi received her PhD and BSc in medicinal chemistry from University College London.

Exhibit 5 DOUBLETWIST ORGANIZATION CHART, MAY 2000 (TOTAL EMPLOYEES = 147)

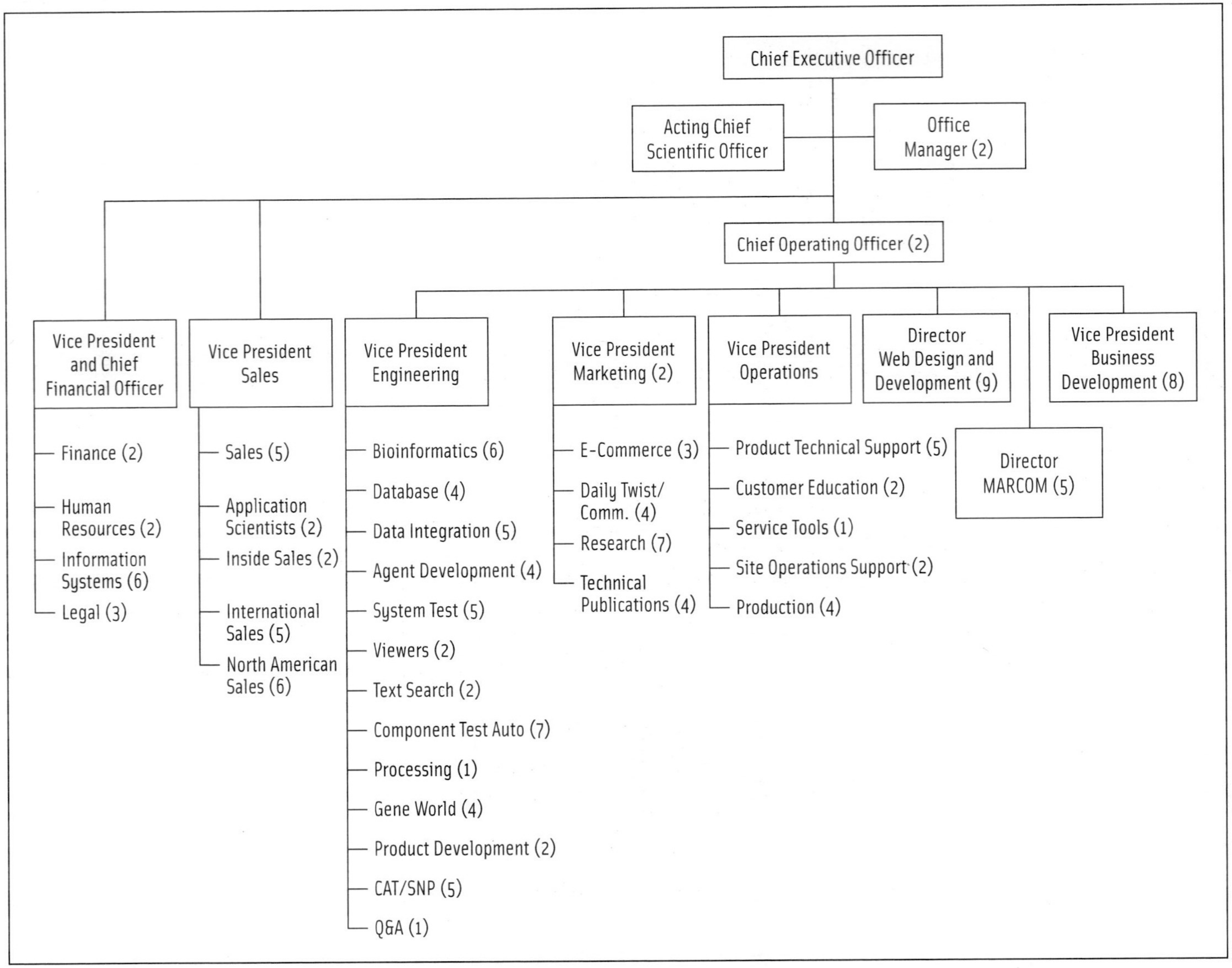

Source: DoubleTwist Management, May 2000.

Exhibit 6 DATABASES AVAILABLE THROUGH THE DOUBLETWIST PORTAL

Sequence/Motif Databases	DoubleTwist Partner Databases
SwissPort	Myriad Genetics ProNet On-Line
TREMBL	AlphaGene clones database
DbEST	Clontech clones and reagents
PDB	HighWire Press literature database
PIR	Derwent Genseq patent database[a]
BLOCKS+	Invitrogen cDNA database[b]
PRODOM	EraGen Master Catalog[c]
PRINTS	
PFAM	**DoubleTwist's Proprietary Databases**
OMIM	Annotated Human Genome Database
Patent Database	Human Gene Index Database
GenBank non-redundant nucleotide	Mouse Gene Index Database
GenBank non-redundant protein	Arabidopsis Gene Index Database
GenBank daily DNA updates	Drosophila Gene Index Database
GenBank daily protein updates	Comprehensive Vector Database
	Microbial Metabolic Databases

Source: DoubleTwist.com Fact Sheet, May 2000.
[a]Available as of September 2000.
[b]Available as of July 2000.
[c]Estimated availability as of November 2000.

Exhibit 7a DOUBLETWIST HISTORICAL AND PROJECTED FINANCIALS ($000S)

	Year Ended December 31–Actual				
	1995	1996	1997	1998	1999
Revenues					
License Fees	N/A	N/A	$ 506	$2,779	$2,289
Services and Other	$755	$1,474	770	1,473	1,295
Total Revenues	755	1,474	1,276	4,252	3,584
Cost of Revenues	208	687	370	1,463	1,046
Gross Profit	547	787	906	2,789	2,538
Operating Expenses					
Sales and Marketing	68	314	2,153	4,037	4,708
Product Development	282	555	4,999	5,282	6,826
G & A	184	514	1,993	1,723	2,286
Total Operating Expenses	534	1,383	9,145	11,042	14,816
Income (Loss) from Operations	13	–596	–8,239	–8,253	–11,191

Source: DoubleTwist

Exhibit 7b SAMPLE DISGUISED NUMBERS FOR PROJECTIONS

	Disguised Financial Projections: Year Ended December 31					
	2000	2001	2002	2003	2004	2005
Revenues						
Hosted Subscriptions	930	7,870	19,307	36,360	59,814	84,935
Data Subscriptions	771	5,308	8,896	11,001	12,400	13,640
Software	2,312	750	500	250	0	0
eCommerce	12	123	343	639	1,026	1,529
Advertising	0	182	413	530	612	805
Maintenance	532	416	254	78	0	0
Services	30	18	12	8	0	0
Total Revenues	4,587	14,667	29,725	48,869	73,852	100,909
Cost of Revenues	3,440	5,280	10,106	13,305	18,463	22,198
Gross Profit	1,147	9,387	19,619	35,564	55,389	78,711
Operating Expenses						
Sales and Marketing[a]	9,283	14,502	19,608	22,486	26,723	30,422
Product Development	8,826	10,334	11,509	12,030	13,130	14,890
G&A	3,230	3,310	3,720	3,966	5,233	6,275
Total Operating Expenses	19,339	28,136	34,837	38,482	45,086	51,587
Income (Loss) from Operations	–20,192	–18,749	–15,218	–2,918	10,303	27,124

Source: DoubleTwist
[a]Includes commissions.